Why Do You Need This New Edition?

If you're wondering why you should buy this new edition of *Human Sexuality Today,* here are 5 good reasons!

1. Engaging online resources will help you succeed! MyDevelopmentLab for Human Sexuality provides you with the online study resources to help make your study time even more effective. Includes the Pearson eText—just like the printed text, you can highlight and add your own notes. Students save time and improve results by having access to an interactive text online, where they can click to relevant MyLab material right from the book!

2. A revised study guide at the end of each chapter contains helpful quizzes and tips that will help you succeed in your course.

3. Every chapter of the seventh edition has been updated with current and relevant research that informs the field of human sexuality; instructors will include this new information on your exams.

4. New and compelling topics for many of the book's feature essays will enrich your understanding of how the study of human sexuality impacts our lives today.

5. A brand-new, full-color design and revised photos and diagrams richly illustrate the fascinating topic of human sexuality.

PEARSON

Human Sexuality Today

Seventh Edition

Human Sexuality Today

Bruce M. King

Clemson University

Prentice Hall

Boston   Columbus   Indianapolis   New York   San Francisco   Upper Saddle River
Amsterdam   Cape Town   Dubai   London   Madrid   Milan   Munich   Paris   Montréal   Toronto
Delhi   Mexico City   Sao Paulo   Sydney   Hong Kong   Seoul   Singapore   Taipei   Tokyo

Editor in Chief: Jessica Mosher
Editorial Assistant: Jacqueline Moya
Executive Marketing Manager: Jeanette Koskinas
Marketing Assistant: Craig Deming
Media Editor: Paul DeLuca
Senior Production Project Editor: Pat Torelli
Manufacturing Buyer: Debbie Rossi
Editorial Production, Composition, and Interior Design: Integra
  Software Services, Inc.
Photo Researcher: Naomi Kornhauser
Cover Designer: Kristina Mose-Libon

Library of Congress Cataloging-in-Publication Data

King, Bruce M.
  Human sexuality today / Bruce M. King.—7th ed.
    p. cm.
  ISBN-13: 978-0-205-01567-2
  ISBN-10: 0-205-01567-0
  1. Sex instruction for youth—United States. 2. Sex. 3. Sex (Biology) 4. Sex (Psychology)
  5. Sexual health—United States. I. Title.
  HQ35.2.K56 2012
  306.7—dc22

                                                        2010046146

Prentice Hall
is an imprint of

10 9 8 7 6 5 4 3 2 CKV 15 14 13 12

www.pearsonhighered.com

ISBN 10:   0-205-01567-0
ISBN 13: 978-0-205-01567-2

BRIEF CONTENTS

CONTENTS

In the last year and a half before I submitted the manuscript for the present edition, only 18% of the over 1,500 students enrolled in my course said that they had ever had a meaningful discussion about sex with their parents. The large majority had been taught abstinence-only sex education in high school.

There has never been a greater need for comprehensive human sexuality education than at the beginning of the 21st century. Unfortunately, with the AIDS crisis and high teenage pregnancy rate, a lot of important information has been presented in a negative way. Although one of my goals in writing this book is for students to understand the relevant facts in order to make responsible decisions in their daily lives, an equally important goal has been to present the information in a warm, non-threatening way that leaves students with positive feelings about sex and their own sexuality.

When I began to write this text, I recalled my students' complaints about the dryness, sterility, and length of books I had used previously. So with them in mind, I tried to create a book that was factual and thorough, yet readable and interesting. Thus, I have included numerous case studies (most contributed by my own students!) to supplement and make more personal the substantial coverage of scientific studies. Although my writing style is purposely conversational, I have worked hard to maintain the scientific foundation of my presentation. This seventh edition has over 2,000 references for students who wish to use the book as a resource. This includes over 600 new references. In addition, the section on HIV/AIDS is as thorough and up-to-date as can be found in any human sexuality textbook.

The cost of textbooks to students has become an increasing concern to many. Besides the cost of the primary textbook, already prohibitive for some, there is the added cost of a student's study guide. However, because it has been the goal of Prentice Hall and myself to publish a high-quality textbook at the lowest possible expense to the students, the Student Study Guide is included at the end of each chapter at no additional cost to the student.

The final test for any textbook is whether students will read it, learn from it, and enjoy it. As a result of feedback from students and reviewers, the book has continually evolved in an attempt to create an ever-better product. Prentice Hall and I have also worked hard to improve the illustration program.

PEDAGOGY

Human Sexuality Today, Seventh Edition includes the following features:

- **Special sections on "Cross-Cultural Perspectives" and "Sexuality and Health"** are presented throughout the book to provide students with a global perspective and to familiarize them with the impact of cultural and ethnic factors.

- **End-of-chapter study guides featuring interactive reviews and true/false, matching, and fill-in-the-blank questions** provide students with self-contained, self-assessment tools (answers are provided at the end of the book).

- **Learning objectives at the beginning of each chapter, boldfaced key terms, and marginal and end-of-text glossaries** provide students with tools to help them focus and build their understanding of the material.

- **Numerous case histories provided by students** draw students into the content and make the material more relevant.

- **The Instructor's Manual contains numerous multiple-choice, true/false, and essay questions** for instructor-assigned tests or homework activities.

THE SUPPLEMENTS PACKAGE

For the Instructor

For access to all instructor supplements for *Human Sexuality Today,* Seventh Edition and any other Pearson text simply go to www.pearsonhighered.com/irc and follow the directions to register (or log in if you already have a user name and password). Once you have registered and your status as an instructor is verified, you will be e-mailed a login name and password. Use your login name and password to access the catalog. Enter the author name "King" and the title *Human Sexuality Today* and/or the text ISBN (0205015670). Click on the title. Under the Resources tab, the supplements are listed with links that allow you to download and save each to your desktop.

If you have any questions, please contact your local Pearson sales representative. If you do not know your representative, go to www.pearsonhighered.com/replocator/ and follow the directions for locating your sales representative.

INSTRUCTOR'S MANUAL WITH TESTS (ISBN: 0205015727) Prepared by the author, Bruce M. King. Thoroughly updated to reflect the new research included in this edition. Contains over 75 test questions per chapter.

MYTEST (ISBN: 0205015719) The NEW Pearson MyTest is a powerful assessment generation program that helps instructors easily create and print quizzes and exams. Questions and tests can be authored online, allowing instructors ultimate flexibility and the ability to efficiently manage assessments anytime, anywhere. For more information, go to www.PearsonMyTest.com.

POWERPOINT PRESENTATION (ISBN: 0205015700) This completely revised PowerPoint presentation has been created specifically for the seventh edition and incorporates text art and outlines key points for each text chapter. The presentation is available from the Pearson Instructor's Resource Center www.pearsonhighered.com/irc.

VIDEOS Qualifying adopters (based on adoption size) can choose their video selections from the Films for Humanities and Sciences catalog. Please contact your local Pearson representative for more details.

Student Supplements

MY DEVELOPMENTLAB FOR HUMAN SEXUALITY With this exciting new tool students are able to self-assess using embedded diagnostic tests and instantly view results along with a customized study plan.

The customized study plan will focus on the student's strengths and weaknesses, based on the results of the diagnostic testing, and present a list of activities and resources for review and remediation, organized by chapter section. Some study resources intended for use with portable electronic devices are made available exclusively through the MyDevelopmentLab, such as key term flashcards. Students will be able to quickly and easily analyze their own comprehension level of the course material and study more efficiently, leading to exceptional exam results! An access code is required and can be purchased at www.pearsonhighered.com or at www.mydevelopmentlab.com.

Supplementary Textbooks Available for Course Packaging

SEX MATTERS FOR COLLEGE STUDENTS: SEX FAQS IN HUMAN SEXUALITY, SECOND EDITION, WRITTEN BY SANDRA CARON, UNIVERSITY OF MAINE, ORONO (0131734261) Looking for the answers to questions you may be too shy to ask in class? Find the answers in this supplemental text designed to tell you everything you need to know about sexuality and more. Please contact your Pearson representative for more details.

ACKNOWLEDGMENTS

I offer my deepest gratitude to those who helped with the early development of the book. These people include Dr. Cameron Camp, Dr. Anne Downey, Vic Hughes, Cheryl Stout, Desiree Comeaux, Chantelle Boudreaux, Corbie Johnson, Teresa Weysham, Jim Pipitone, Cynthia Hingle, and Kathryn King. My greatest thanks go to my wife Gail, without whose support this book would never have been possible.

Thanks to everyone at Pearson who worked on this edition. Special thanks to editor in chief Jessica Mosher, and also to Laura Barry, Jeanette Koskinas, Paul DeLuca, Pat Torelli, Naomi Kornhauser, and Kristin Jobe of Integra-Chicago.

My sincere appreciation and thanks to the following colleagues for their valuable input and constructive feedback in reviewing the seventh edition of this book:

Scott Arcement, Canyon College of Idaho
Helen Benn, Webster University
Sheryl Buotte, Tri-Country Technical College
Christopher Ferguson, Texas A&M International University
Tony Foster, Lone Star College–Kingwood
Jennifer Myers, University of North Carolina, Wilmington
Kendra Ogletree, University of South Carolina
Staci Simmelink-Johnson, Walla Walla Community College
Kevin Sumrall, Lone Star College–Montgomery

Thanks to everyone who reviewed previous editions. For the first edition, Susan Graham-Kresge, University of Southern Mississippi; Kendra Jeffcoat, Palomar College; Deborah R. McDonald, New Mexico State University; Ken Murdoff, Lane Community College; Janet A. Simons, University of Iowa; and Janice D. Yoder, University of Wisconsin-Milwaukee. For the second edition, Kendra Jeffcoat, Palomar College; Deborah R. McDonald, New Mexico State University; Ken Murdoff, Lane Community College; and Janet A. Simons, University of Iowa. For the third edition, Donna Ashcraft, Clarion University of Pennsylvania; Robert Clark/Labeff, Midwestern State University; Betty Dorr, Fort Lewis College; and Priscilla Hernandez, Washington State University. For the fourth edition, Nanette Davis, Western Washington University; Xiaolin Xie, Cameron University; Betty Dorr, Fort Lewis College; Carrie Yang Costello, University of

Wisconsin–Milwaukee; Lillian Rosado, New Jersey City University; and Judith A. Reitan, University of California–Davis. For the fifth edition, Bob Hensley, Iowa State University; Sonia Ruiz, California State University–San Marcos; Patricia A. Tackett, San Diego State University; and Mary Ann Watson, Metropolitan State College of Denver. For the sixth edition: Elizabeth Amaya-Fernandez, Montclair State University; Tony Foster, Kingwood College; Debra L. Golden, Grossmont College; Dawn Graff-Haight, Linfield College; Katherine Helm, Lewis University; Suzy Horton, Mesa Community College; Judith Stone, SUNY Suffolk; Mary Ann Watson, Metropolitan State College of Denver; and Edward Zalisko, Blackburn College.

Finally, I cannot thank enough the thousands of students who provided me with chapter reviews and/or case histories. This book was written with students in mind. I hope it helps them to lead healthier, happier, and more fulfilling lives.

Bruce M. King

Bruce M. King received a B.A. in psychology from UCLA in 1969 and a Ph.D. in biopsychology from the University of Chicago in 1978. He taught for 29 years at the University of New Orleans and is presently in the Department of Psychology at Clemson University. He has taught human sexuality to over 50,000 students. In addition to conducting research in the field of human sexuality, Dr. King has co-authored a textbook on statistics and has published over 70 papers in peer-reviewed journals on the biological basis of feeding behavior and obesity. He is a Fellow in the Association for Psychological Science, the American Psychological Association, and the International Behavioral Neuroscience Society. Dr. King taught HIV/AIDS education to high school teachers in New Orleans and he is presently on the Board of Directors for Planned Parenthood Health Systems (South Carolina, North Carolina, Virginia, and West Virginia).

Human Sexuality Today

Why a Course in Human Sexuality?

Amoebas at the start
Were not complex;
They tore themselves apart
And started sex.

—Arthur Guiterman

Sexuality is an important part of our lives. We need only to look at the world population of nearly 7 billion people to see that sexual motivation is very strong. Although sex is necessary for procreation, it is doubtful that many people think of this on more than just an occasional basis when having sexual intercourse. Sex can be a source of great physical and emotional pleasure, enhancing our sense of health and well-being. It can relieve tensions and anxieties. It can boost self-esteem and make us feel more masculine or feminine. It is also the vehicle through which couples can express their affection for one another. In fact, there are a couple hundred reasons people give for having sex (Meston & Buss, 2007).

So why are you taking a course in human sexuality? Surely someone in your life took the time and responsibility to educate you about this important topic. Surveys in my course have consistently revealed that fewer than one third of the students each semester have ever had a serious and meaningful discussion with their parents about sex. For many teens whose parents did talk to them about sex, it was just a single discussion—one "birds and bees" talk that was supposed to prepare them for life. Here are a few comments that I have received

When you have finished studying this chapter, you should be able to:

- Describe cultural perspectives other than our own with regard to sexual behaviors and attitudes.
- Explain the historical influence of Judaism and Christianity on contemporary attitudes about sexuality.
- Summarize the Victorian era's sexual views and its influence on our sexual values and behaviors today.
- Explain the contributions of Sigmund Freud, Henry Havelock Ellis, Alfred Kinsey, and Masters and Johnson to the field of sexuality.
- Understand the uses and limitations of surveys, correlational studies, direct observations, case studies, and experimental research.
- Explain the process of socialization and define a socializing agent.
- Understand how the media have become omnipresent agents for sexual socialization.
- Explain the role of sexuality education as a socializing agent.

Sexuality ■ All of the sexual attitudes, feelings, and behaviors associated with being human. The term does not refer specifically to a person's capacity for erotic response or to sexual acts, but rather to a dimension of one's personality.

from students regarding their prior sex education. They are typical of the many comments I have gotten on end-of-semester course evaluations.

> "My father thinks this class is a waste because he feels people instinctively know how to deal with their sexuality. Maybe I'm just a freak of nature, but I've never had any instincts explaining any of this to me."

> "My boyfriend doesn't like me taking the course. He says, 'You don't need a classroom to teach you about sex. I'll teach you everything you need to know.'"

> "Until now my parents never spoke to me about sex. I'm from a very strict family. They made me feel as though it was a sinful subject to talk about."

> "I remember my mother finding a book my sister was reading and screaming at her, so everyone in the house could hear about what an awful, dirty book it was. It wasn't pornography. It was a book on sex education. She just wanted to learn something correctly."

> "When I was young the word sex was never brought up. My mother had one short talk with me, and that was to explain what a period is."

> (All examples are from the author's files.)

Students also provided the following comments regarding the usefulness of a human sexuality course. Apparently, it is never too late to learn.

> "I'm glad I registered in the class. I sure thought I knew it all and found I knew very little. I've been married 6 years and knew little about my own body, much less about my husband's."

> "I am a 46-year-old student with four children from 13 to 38. I knew nothing about sex before this course. I will now make sure my kids do."

> "When selecting this course, the thought came to me that it would be a very easy class because I knew everything about sex because Mother told me. After all, there are 18 of us in the family. Boy, was I wrong. I've learned more in one semester than Mother could teach me in 20 years."

> "I was very surprised at the amount of material I learned. I thought it was going to be just about sex. There is a lot more to sex than just sex."

> (All examples are from the author's files.)

Where, then, did most of us learn about sex? Today's teens and college students say that they received most of their sex education from friends and the media rather than parents (Nonoyama et al., 2005; Sprecher et al., 2008). The media as sex educators? Nearly three fourths of television shows contain talk about sex or show sexual behavior (Eyal et al., 2007). The number of sexual scenes on television is almost twice as great as it was in the late 1990s (Kaiser Family Foundation, 2005). Over two thirds of television shows include sexual content, averaging 5.9 scenes per hour. The typical viewer sees only one instance of preventive behavior for every 10 instances of sexual behavior. Many R-rated movies have sexually explicit scenes. The large majority of teens now have Internet access and at least half have visited a sexually explicit website (Braun-Courville & Rojas, 2009). Many stores have erotic magazines on open display. Advertisements frequently use sex (e.g., seductively dressed models) to sell products (Reichert, 2003). Sex is everywhere, and children are exposed to it all day long.

In the presence of all this, many parents continue to be silent with their children on the subject of sex. However, this, too, is a source of sex education. Making something mysterious only makes adolescent children want to know more about it—yet much of the information they receive from their friends is incorrect, and as a result a majority of Americans are amazingly ignorant about sexual behaviors and sexual health (Reinisch, 1990). Many believe, for example, that people over 60 do not have sex, that masturbation is physically harmful, or that you cannot get AIDS if you are heterosexual.

What all this adds up to is that many people do not fully understand or appreciate the consequences of engaging in sexual relations. Nationally, about 46% of all high school students have had sexual intercourse (over 62% of 12th graders), and 5.9% started before the age of 13 (Eaton et al., 2010). Three fourths of Americans have had sex by age 20 (Finer, 2007). Each year, over 750,000 pregnancies occur among girls aged 15 to 19, and 19 million Americans (of all ages) contract a sexually transmitted infection (Centers for Disease Control and Prevention [CDC], 2010; Eaton et al., 2010). Most young people do not know the symptoms of sexually transmitted infections and do not know where to turn if they think they have one (Clark et al., 2002).

So, once again, why are you taking a course in human sexuality? Probably because you desire to have factual information about a subject that plays, or will play, an important role in your life. If parents are not going to assume the responsibility, the next best alternative is the schools. Surveys consistently show that over 85% of Americans support the teaching of comprehensive sexuality education in public schools (see Constantine, 2008, for a review). This includes a large majority of all religious, age, ethnic, educational, and income groups. Canada and most northern European countries have extensive sexuality education programs that usually begin in grade school, and the teenage pregnancy rates are much lower in these countries than in the United States (Darroch et al., 2001; Lottes, 2002; Singh & Darroch, 2000).

The purpose of taking human sexuality courses is much more than just learning about reproduction and sexually transmitted infections. People want to feel comfortable with their own sexuality

©Tribune Media Services, Inc. All Rights Reserved. Reprinted with permission.

of our bodies should be shrouded in mystery. Understanding our partners' bodies will help in communication and prevent unnecessary problems. Appreciating that all people are sexual beings can give us a greater understanding of our children, parents, grandparents, and friends. Studies show that sexuality education courses in schools also result in a more tolerant attitude toward others (SIECUS, 1992). Understanding that people are different from ourselves, without condemning them, is an important part of getting along with others.

PERSONAL REFLECTIONS

From whom (or from where) did you acquire most of your information about sex (e.g., parents, friends, the media, teachers, the Internet)? Did your parents discuss sexuality with you? If not, why do you suppose they did not? From whom do you hope your children will learn about sexuality?

and to feel good about themselves. Knowing about their bodies and understanding their feelings and emotions can help people achieve this. No part

A Sexual Knowledge Quiz

Many of you may already be sexually experienced, and as a result, you may think that you do not need a course in human sexuality. There is more to sexuality, however, than engaging in sexual intercourse. See how well you do on the following 50-question quiz. Do not be afraid to admit that you do not know the correct answer (don't guess)—no one but you will see the results. The answers are at the end of the quiz.

	True	False	Don't Know
1. Erections in men result, in part, from a bone that protrudes into the penis.	——	——	——
2. Sperm can be produced only in an environment several degrees lower than normal body temperature.	——	——	——
3. The hymen is a reliable indicator of whether a woman is a virgin.	——	——	——
4. The inner two thirds of the vagina is highly sensitive to touch.	——	——	——
5. Many men experience nipple erection when they become sexually aroused.	——	——	——
6. Most men and women are capable of multiple orgasms.	——	——	——
7. Breast size in women is related to the number of mammary glands.	——	——	——
8. Before puberty, boys can reach orgasm, but they do not ejaculate.	——	——	——
9. During sexual intercourse, orgasm in women results from direct stimulation of the clitoris by the penis.	——	——	——
10. Menstrual discharge consists of sloughed-off uterine tissue, blood, and cervical mucus.	——	——	——
11. For hygiene reasons, you should avoid sex during menstruation.	——	——	——
12. Ovulation generally occurs just before menstruation.	——	——	——
13. After a vasectomy, a man can reach orgasm but does not ejaculate.	——	——	——
14. AIDS is the diagnosis for people who have human immunodeficiency virus (HIV).	——	——	——
15. A girl can get pregnant as soon as she starts having menstrual periods.	——	——	——
16. The combination birth control pill works primarily by preventing implantation of a fertilized egg.	——	——	——
17. Taking the oral contraceptive pill results in fewer serious health problems than do pregnancy and childbirth.	——	——	——
18. Women show a dramatically higher level of sexual desire than usual at the time of ovulation.	——	——	——
19. There are about 19 million new cases of sexually transmitted infections in the United States each year.	——	——	——
20. The major cause of AIDS is homosexuality.	——	——	——

	True	False	Don't Know
21. If gonorrhea is not treated, it can sometimes turn into syphilis.	____	____	____
22. Most women do not show symptoms in the early stages of gonorrhea or chlamydia.	____	____	____
23. Gonorrhea, syphilis, and herpes can be successfully treated with antibiotics.	____	____	____
24. In vitro fertilization involves a process where part of fetal development occurs in a test tube.	____	____	____
25. It is usually safe to have sexual intercourse during the 7th and 8th months of pregnancy.	____	____	____
26. "Prepared childbirth" (e.g., Lamaze) refers to delivering a baby without the use of drugs.	____	____	____
27. Most healthy people in their 60s or older continue to engage in sexual behavior.	____	____	____
28. Men's descriptions of orgasm are different from women's descriptions of orgasm.	____	____	____
29. Excessive masturbation can cause serious medical problems.	____	____	____
30. The birth control pill gives women some protection against sexually transmitted infections.	____	____	____
31. Women who masturbated to orgasm during adolescence generally have less difficulty reaching orgasm during intercourse than women who never masturbated.	____	____	____
32. The frequency of sexual relations is highest for married couples aged 25 to 35.	____	____	____
33. Adult male homosexuals have lower-than-normal levels of male hormones.	____	____	____
34. Douching is an effective method of birth control.	____	____	____
35. Recent evidence indicates that environmental factors are the most important in determining one's sexual orientation.	____	____	____
36. Prostitutes are generally hypersexual and have pathological sexual needs.	____	____	____
37. Most convicted rapists committed their crimes because of an uncontrollable sex drive.	____	____	____
38. There is a demonstrated link between the availability of pornography and sex crimes.	____	____	____
39. Until recently, it was against the law in many states for a married couple to engage in sexual behaviors other than penile–vaginal intercourse.	____	____	____
40. Most cases of child molestation involve an acquaintance or relative of the child.	____	____	____
41. A pregnant woman can transmit syphilis to the unborn baby.	____	____	____
42. Exhibitionists and voyeurs often attempt to rape their victims.	____	____	____
43. Nocturnal emissions ("wet dreams") are often an indication of a sexual problem.	____	____	____
44. Alcohol is a central nervous system excitant that enhances sexual performance.	____	____	____
45. Humans can crossbreed with animals with the use of artificial insemination techniques.	____	____	____
46. Women's sexual desire decreases sharply after menopause.	____	____	____
47. Vaginal infections can be prevented by regular use of feminine hygiene products.	____	____	____
48. A woman's ability to have vaginal orgasms is related to penis size.	____	____	____
49. Oral herpes can be transmitted to another person's genitals by oral-genital sexual relations.	____	____	____
50. Unless testosterone is present during embryonic development, nature has programmed everyone to be born a girl.	____	____	____

Answers

1. false
2. true
3. false
4. false
5. true
6. false
7. false
8. true
9. false
10. true
11. false
12. false
13. false
14. false (only in the final stages)
15. true
16. false
17. true
18. false
19. true
20. false
21. false
22. true
23. false
24. false
25. true
26. false
27. true (homosexuality) does not cause AIDS)
28. false
29. false
30. false
31. true
32. true
33. false
34. false
35. false
36. false
37. false
38. false
39. true
40. true
41. true
42. false
43. false
44. false
45. false
46. false
47. false
48. false
49. true
50. true

These questions were not intended to be tricky or difficult. They are representative of the type of material that is covered in this book. How did you do? Fewer than one fourth of the students in my classes are able to answer 40 or more questions correctly at the beginning of the semester. Fewer than half get 30 or more correct. Did you really know all the ones that you got right, or did you just make a good guess on some of them? If you were not certain of the answers to some of the questions, then that is sufficient reason to read this book.

CROSS-CULTURAL COMPARISONS

It should come as no surprise that people are different. Some people like short hair, while others like it long. Some people like to dress up; some like to dress down. People's sexual attitudes and behaviors differ as well. Some people, for example, have sexual intercourse only in the **missionary position** (i.e., the woman lying on her back with the man on top—so called because Christian missionaries instructed people that other positions were unnatural). Others prefer a variety of positions. Some people are most aroused by looking at breasts or a hairy chest. Other people become highly aroused by looking at legs or buttocks.

We learn to accept that other people in our own culture are different from ourselves, and we do not regard them as abnormal when their behavior falls within what we consider the "normal" range of responses. What is normal, however, is defined by the community in which we live. An outsider, such as a person from a different country, is often regarded as very strange by many people. Unfortunately, Americans have a reputation around the world of being **ethnocentric**—that is, viewing our own culture's behaviors and customs as correct or as the way things ought to be (a perception leading to the image of the "ugly American"). We must not lose sight of the fact that if we traveled to another country *we* would probably be regarded as strange. One country's customs and beliefs should not be regarded as correct or normal and another's as incorrect or abnormal.

The topics covered in some chapters of this book are the same for all peoples of the world (e.g., anatomy, physiology). When you read about behaviors and attitudes, it will be primarily from the perspective of people in the United States. Behaviors of people in other cultures will be presented in special boxes. However, before going on, here is a brief introduction to sexual attitudes and behaviors in a few other cultures around the world. Some of them may seem strange, but remember, *we seem just as strange to them as they seem strange to us.*

Sexual Attractiveness

Cultures differ with regard to which parts of the body they find to be erotic. In the United States, most people have negative thoughts about armpits, but Abkhazian men are highly aroused at seeing women's armpits. The sight of a navel is considered highly arousing in Samoa, while a knee is considered to be erotic in New Guinea and the Celebes Islands. When anthropologist Martha Ward visited New Guinea in the early 1970s, she deboarded the plane wearing a miniskirt, blouse, and brassiere, customary clothing for American women at that time. She caused quite a ruckus. She wrote the following letter to one of her colleagues in the United States:

> Dear Len,
> I have had to change my manner of dressing.... The minidresses and short skirts you all are wearing in the States cause quite a stir here. It seems that breasts are regarded as normal female equipment and useful only for feeding babies. Clothing for many women consists of a large towel or three-yard length of brightly colored cloth. This is worn around the waist inside the house or in the yard.... [In public] if you have on a bra, you don't need a blouse. Bras are considered proper dress for women.... When Americans are not around, it is sufficient to cover oneself only from the waist down....
> Breasts are not really erogenous, but legs are. Particularly that sexy area on the inside of the knee! No more miniskirts for me. Fitting in and observing local customs means that I have lengthened my skirts to below the knee....
> The American men watch women with nothing on above the waist. The Pohnpeian men comment on American women with short skirts. I am now dressed to please the standards of two cultures....
>
> (Excerpt from *Nest in the Wind: Adventures in Anthropology on a Tropical Island*, by Martha C. Ward. Copyright © 1989 by Waveland Press, Inc. Reprinted by permission.)

Just as in New Guinea, there are many areas of the world where women's naked breasts have no erotic significance at all (see Figure 1–2). They are important only to hungry babies. On the other hand, American men find female breasts so sexually arousing that women cannot even breast-feed in public. Here is an experience of one of my students,

---

Missionary position ■ A face-to-face position of sexual intercourse in which the woman lies on her back and the man lies on top with his legs between hers. It was called this because Christian missionaries instructed people that other positions were unnatural.

Ethnocentric ■ The attitude that the behaviors and customs of one's own ethnic group or culture are superior to others.

an African woman from Chad, shortly after she arrived in New Orleans:

> "One day my husband was driving and I was sitting in the back nursing my baby. The police stopped us and arrested me...."

Polynesian men are as fascinated with the size, shape, and consistency of women's genitals as American men are with breasts (Marshall, 1971). In some African cultures, a woman's labia minora are considered to be the most erotic part of her body.

Many groups of people find body weight to be an important determinant of sexual attractiveness. There is a great deal of pressure in our culture, for example, for men and women to remain thin. It is no coincidence that fashion models are very thin and that movie stars who are considered to be "sexy" have small waistlines. In many other countries, however, these people would not be considered attractive. For example, women who would be considered obese by most American men are found highly attractive in some other cultures. Adolescent girls are sometimes kept in huts and fed high-calorie diets in order to become more attractive (Gregersen, 1982).

What is considered to be sexually attractive can also change over time. Plump women, for example, were also considered to be very attractive in Western cultures a few centuries ago. If you do not believe this, just look at some famous paintings of naked women that were done 300 years ago (see Figure 1–1).

Although walking around naked in public would be considered highly deviant by most people in the United States, there are some cultures in New Guinea and Australia where people go about completely naked. They do, however, have firm rules about staring at other people's genitals. The Zulus of South Africa also have public rituals that call for people to be naked. They believe that a flabby body results from immoral behavior, and thus if someone refuses to undress for these rituals, it is taken as a sign that the person is trying to hide his or her immorality (Gregersen, 1982). These attitudes about the human body are in marked contrast to those that prevail in Islamic societies, where female sexuality is suppressed and women must cover their entire body and most of their face when they leave the privacy of their homes.

In some cultures people carve holes in their lips, while in others they stretch their lips or necks, or wear needles through their noses. In parts of Indonesia, the Philippines, and Malaysia, it is common for men to insert objects (e.g., ball bearings, precious stones, rings) in their penises (Hull & Budiharsana, 2001). In Borneo, for example, it is common for men to wear a rod through the end of their pierced penis. The rod, called a penis pin, has protuberances (e.g., gemstones, feathers, pig's

FIGURE 1–1 Rubens' *The Three Graces*, painted in 1630, is a good example of how cultural ideals change over time. Thinness is considered to be physically attractive today, but a thin woman in Rubens' time would have been considered unattractive.

bristles) at each end, which the men believe enhances women's pleasure during intercourse (Brown, 1990). Elaborate abdominal scars are considered to be very sexually attractive on women of the Kau culture in Sudan. It is obvious from the lack of universal standards that attitudes about the human body, and what is considered to be sexually attractive, are culturally learned responses.

Sexual Behaviors and Attitudes

Kissing is a highly erotic and romanticized part of sexual relations in Western cultures. You will probably be surprised to learn, therefore, that this practice is not shared by many cultures, including the Japanese, Hindus of India, and many groups in Africa and South America (Ford & Beach, 1951; Gregor, 1985). "When the Thonga first saw Europeans kissing they laughed, expressing this sentiment: 'Look at them—they eat each other's saliva and dirt'" (Ford & Beach, 1951). Foreplay before intercourse is entirely unheard of in some cultures.

Anthropologists believe that the most sexually permissive group of people in the world are the Mangaians, who live on the Cook Islands in the

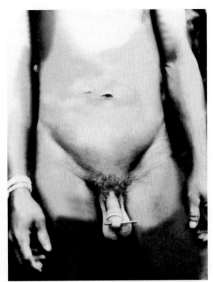

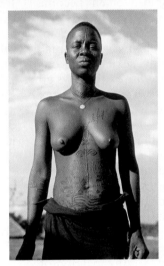

FIGURE 1–2 Cultures differ widely with regards to what they find to be attractive. In New Guinea, many men wear only a bamboo penis sheath (top L), while in Borneo men have penis pins (top R). Body scarification is common among Kuba (now Zaire) women (center). In contrast to these customs of nearly complete nudity, Islamic women must keep their faces covered while in public (middle L). In Samoa, men regard heavy women to be most attractive (top center). Along the Ono River in Ethiopia, women use cans as lip ornaments (middle R), whereas among the Karen in Thailand an elongated neck is considered beautiful (bottom R). Elaborate headdress and ear piercing is attractive among men in Tanganyika (bottom L).

South Pacific (Marshall, 1971). Mangaian boys and girls play together until the age of 3 or 4, but after that they separate into age groups according to sex during the day. When the boys approach adolescence, the arrival of manhood is recognized by superincision of the penis (cutting the skin of the penis lengthwise on top). As the wound heals, the boy is instructed in all aspects of sex, including how to bring a girl to orgasm, which is considered important. Girls receive similar instructions from older women. The boy is then given to an experienced woman, who removes the superincision scab during intercourse and teaches the boy an array of sexual techniques. After that, the boy actively seeks out girls at night, having sex an average of 18 to 20 times a week. Mangaian adolescents are encouraged to have sex with many partners and engage in all types of sexual activities. Once they reach adulthood, Mangaian men and women become monogamous.

Many other societies in the South Pacific, including Samoa and Pohnpei, similarly encourage their teenage children to enjoy sexual relations (Ward, 1989). In some of these cultures, the boys go into the huts where teenage girls live and have sex with them while the girls' parents are present. The parents ignore them and act as if the children are invisible. In all of these societies, the physical pleasure of both sexes is emphasized and emotional attachments come later. They regard our custom of emphasizing love before sex as very strange.

The most sexually repressed society in the world is believed to be the Inis Baeg, a fictitious name (coined by anthropologists to preserve anonymity) for a group of people who live on an island off the coast of Ireland (Messenger, 1971). Any mention of sex is taboo, so that children are never told about things like menstruation and pregnancy, which are greatly feared. Nudity is strictly forbidden. Even married adults do not see each other completely naked—they do not bathe together and they wear smocks during sexual intercourse. Sexual relations are not regarded as something positive by either sex. Foreplay is unheard of, and intercourse, which is always done in the missionary position, is completed as quickly as possible because men consider it to be dangerous to their health (and, unlike Mangaian women, Inis Baeg women almost never achieve orgasm).

Between the two extremes of the Mangaians and the Inis Baeg is a large range of sexual attitudes and behaviors. You will find that many cultures are more restrictive (or repressed) than our own. For example, until very recently it was taboo to openly discuss sex in China, Japan, Russia, and many African cultures (Ecker, 1994; Kitazawa, 1994; Rivkin-Fish, 1999). Oral-genital sex is common in Western cultures, but most African cultures consider it to be disgusting. In many Islamic parts of the world, women's sexuality is suppressed by mutilation of the genitals during childhood (see Box 4–A).

On the other hand, many cultures are more permissive (or tolerant) than our own. In Chapter 9, for example, you will read about the Sambian culture where homosexual relations are expected among young boys and teenaged boys (Box 9–A). Sex with minors is a crime in Western culture, but in the Tiwi culture (Melville Island) girls are married to an adult man at age 7 and begin having sexual intercourse shortly afterwards (Goodall, 1971). Incest is also a taboo in Western culture, but marriage between cousins or between uncles and nieces is often expected in other cultures (Box 15–C). Similarly, monogamy is the standard in Western cultures, while in many others polygamy is practiced (Box 12–A).

Even the overall approach to sex can differ among cultures. For example, sex in Western cultures tends to focus on genital stimulation, orgasm, and physical gratification, whereas Eastern Tantric cultures emphasize spiritual union during sex (Box 13–A). On the other hand, in New Guinea there is a tribe called the Dugum Dani that expresses little interest in sex (Heider, 1979). Although they appear to be normal physically, husbands and wives sometimes go as long as 5 years without having sex. Unlike the Inis Baeg, they do not have a negative attitude about sex; they just do not regard sex as important.

Cultural Diversity Within the United States

To this point, I have referred to Western culture as if it were composed of a homogenous group of people. North America may originally have been settled primarily by caucasian Christians of European descent, but the population today is much more diverse. A sizable proportion of the U.S. population is made up of African Americans, Latinos, and Asian Americans. However, even within these ethnic groups there are often distinct subgroups. Among Asian Americans, for example, there are people whose ancestors came from Japan, China, Vietnam, Thailand, Korea, the Philippines, and South Pacific islands. Within each subculture there are several factors that can influence sexual attitudes and behaviors. These include religion, level of education, and socioeconomic status (see Hodes, 1999). In short, it is sometimes difficult to make generalizations even about cultural subgroups. With these cautions in mind, what generalizations can we make?

One example of cultural differences in sexual behavior in the United States is found when we examine oral-genital sexual relations. This has been a very common behavior among white middle-class (especially college-educated) Americans for at least 60 years (Kinsey et al., 1948, 1953). Today, it is also common among Latinos, but is practiced by only a minority of African Americans, with Asian Americans in between (Laumann et al., 1994). The small proportion of African Americans engaging in this behavior is explained in part by their African ancestry and also by the socioeconomic status of many black Americans. Oral-genital sex is less common among all low-educated, low-income groups, regardless of ethnic background. The sexual behavior of middle-class African Americans more closely resembles that of middle-class whites (Laumann et al., 1994).

On the other hand, African Americans tend to begin sexual intercourse earlier than Caucasians (Cavazos-Rehg et al., 2009). Asian Americans are generally the least permissive in their sexual attitudes and behaviors (Ahrold & Meston, 2010; Okazaki, 2002). This is partly a reflection of restrictive attitudes about sex in Asian countries, but also results from the strong emphasis that people from many Asian countries place on family and social conformity. Asian Americans tend to have very low rates for both premarital intercourse and multiple sexual partners. On the other hand, they have the highest rate (among the subcultures discussed) for abortions. This is a reflection not only of non-Western religious beliefs (that do not question the morality of abortion) but, often, also a result of having immigrated from overpopulated countries where the prevailing attitude is that it is best for the general good to limit the number of children one has.

Another factor that can influence sexual attitudes and behaviors is the number of generations that have passed since one's ancestors immigrated to the United States. As people from other countries become more acculturated to American culture, their attitudes and behavior come to resemble those of mainstream Americans (e.g., Ahrold & Meston, 2010; Okazaki, 2002). Much of what you will read in the chapters ahead is true for nearly all subcultures in the United States. However, when there are major differences, you will read about them also.

PERSONAL REFLECTIONS

Has your own cultural heritage affected your attitudes about sex? If so, how?

HISTORICAL PERSPECTIVES

If the Mangaians and Inis Baeg represent the two extremes, where does American culture fall on this continuum? In many ways our behavior is permissive—we live during the so-called sexual revolution—but our attitudes about sex are often less than positive (evidenced, for example, by the fact that parents and children rarely talk about it together). The constant emphasis on sex on TV, in movies, in magazines, and on the radio gives children one type of message—sex is fun, sex is exciting, sex is great. At the same time, these same children get another type of message from their parents, school, and church—sex is not for you! Is it any wonder that many Americans are confused about sex? Sex is something good on the one hand, yet bad on the other. We fall somewhere between the Mangaians and Inis Baeg. We are permissive, yet repressed. To see how we arrived at this point in the 21st century, we must examine the history of sexual attitudes in our own culture.

Judaism

Life for the biblical Jews was harsh and they considered it a great advantage to have many children. The Jews were directed to do so in the first chapter of the first book of the Old Testament:

> And God blessed them, and God said to them, "Be fruitful and multiply, and fill the earth and subdue it." *(Genesis 1:28, Revised Standard Version)*

Having many children assured the survival of the Jewish people and was viewed as an obligation. Thus, the Hebrews recognized that the primary purpose of sex was for *procreation* (to have children). Celibacy was looked upon as neglect of one's obligations and was regarded as sinful.

Sons were especially valued because of their dual roles as providers and defenders. In the strongly patriarchal Hebrew society, daughters and wives were regarded as property (of fathers or husbands), and there were many rules to guarantee that material property was passed on to legitimate offspring. Thus the Hebrews were very concerned with the social consequences of sex. Sex outside of marriage, for example, was severely condemned and punished. A Jewish woman caught committing adultery was stoned to death, but a man who committed adultery was considered only to have violated another man's property rights. Rape, too, was considered to be a violation of property rights. The punishment for homosexuality and bestiality was death (Leviticus 18:22–29).

In contrast to those harsh views, the Old Testament presents a positive view of sex within a marriage. A good example of this can be found in the Song of Solomon (Song of Songs):

> How graceful are your feet in sandals,
>   O queenly maiden!
> Your rounded thighs are like jewels,
>   the work of a master hand.
> Your navel is a rounded bowl
>   that never lacks mixed wine....
> Your two breasts are like two fawns,
>   twins of a gazelle....
> You are stately as a palm tree,
>   and your breasts are like its clusters.
> I say I will climb the palm tree
>   and lay hold of its branches.
> *(Song of Solomon 7:1–8, Revised Standard Version)*

The human body, including the genitals, was not considered to be obscene, for God had created Adam and Eve in his own image. Mutual sexual pleasure was very important to Hebrew couples. In fact, sex between husband and wife was cause for rejoicing, a gift from God. A married couple could engage in any sexual activity, with only one restriction—the husband had to ejaculate within his wife's vagina (not doing so was considered "spilling of seed" because it could not lead to having children).

PERSONAL REFLECTIONS

The Hebrews of biblical times believed that humans were created in the image of God, and therefore they were not ashamed of any part of their bodies, including their genitals. What do you think about this? How do you feel about your own body? (Do not just respond "good" or "bad," but explain in some detail.)

The Greeks and Romans

The ancient Greeks and Romans, like the Jews, placed a strong emphasis on marriage and the family. Although procreation was viewed as the primary purpose of marital sex, a couple had children for the state, not God. Unlike the biblical Jews, Greek and Roman men were allowed considerable sexual freedom outside marriage. In Greece, sexual relations between men and adolescent boys in a teacher–student relationship were not only tolerated, but were encouraged as part of the boy's intellectual, emotional, and moral development.

The Greeks idealized the human body and physical beauty (as is evident in their art), but in the latter part of the Greek era there was a strong emphasis on spiritual development and a denial of physical pleasures. The basis for this change was **dualism,** the belief that body and soul are separate (and antagonistic). Dualism gave rise to an *ascetic philosophy,* which taught that from wisdom came virtue, and that these could only be achieved by avoiding strong passions. Plato, for example, believed that a person could achieve immortality by avoiding sexual desire and striving for intellectual and spiritual love (thus the term *platonic* for sexless love). As you will see next, dualism was a major influence on early Christian leaders.

Christianity

Like the theology of the latter-period Greeks, Christian theology separated physical love from spiritual love. The period of decline of the Roman empire,

which coincided with the rise of Christianity, was marked by sexual excess and debauchery. The views of the early Christians regarding sex were partly the result of an attempt to keep order.

It is written in the Gospel of Matthew that Jesus said, "Everyone who looks at a woman lustfully has already committed adultery with her in his heart" (Matthew 5:27, Revised Standard Version). Thus, it was not enough for a Christian to conform behaviorally; there was to be purity of inner thoughts as well.

The teachings of the early Christian writers reflect their own personal struggles with sexual temptation. One of the most influential of the early writers was **Saint Paul** (about A.D. 5–67), who regarded the body as evil and struggled to control it:

> **For I know that nothing good dwells within me, that is, in my flesh. I can will what is right, but I cannot do it. For I do not do the good I want, but the evil I do not want is what I do....** *(Romans 7:18, 7:22–23, Revised Standard Version)*

Saint Paul blamed Eve for the expulsion from the Garden of Eden and viewed women as temptresses. He strongly believed, as did many others, that the second coming of Christ (signifying the end of the world) would occur in his lifetime and preached that a celibate lifestyle was the way to heaven. Marriage was only for the weak willed:

> **It is well for a man not to touch a woman.... To the unmarried and the widows I say that it is well for them to remain single as I do. But if they cannot exercise self-control, they should marry. For it is better to marry than to be aflame with passion...if you marry, you do not sin.... From now on, let those who have wives live as though they had none.** *(Corinthians 7:1, 7:8–9, 7:28, 29, Revised Standard Version)*

Some have interpreted these ambiguous passages to mean that Paul believed that sex within marriage was sinful. Scholars now say that Paul did not believe that marital sex was a sin, but that he was concerned that married couples who sexually desired one another would become too involved in worldly (physical) concerns (Deming, 1995; Poirier & Frankovic, 1996). Paul's argument was that celibacy was spiritually superior to marriage. Thus, Paul regarded marriage as a compromise (and a rather poor one at that) for dealing with the problems of the flesh. His followers believed that women should be subordinate to men, and therefore should assume the bottom position during sexual intercourse.

Saint Jerome (about A.D. 340–420) said that a man who loved his wife too passionately was guilty of adultery:

> **A wise man ought to love his wife with judgment not with passion.... He who too ardently loves his own wife is an adulterer.** *(Hunt, 1959, p. 115)*

Dualism ■ The belief that body and soul are separate and antagonistic.

Pope John Paul II created some controversy within the Catholic Church when he appeared to echo the beliefs of Saint Jerome:

> **Adultery in the heart is committed not only because a man looks in a certain way at a woman who is not his wife...but precisely because he is looking at a woman that way. Even if he were to look that way at his wife, he would be committing adultery.** (New York Times, *October 10, 1980*)

The major influence on Christian beliefs was **Saint Augustine** (A.D. 354–430) (Figure 1–3). As a teenager and young adult he led a promiscuous lifestyle, which included a mistress and son born out of wedlock (Boswell, 1980), and which some (but not all) scholars believe included a same-sex affair (e.g., Martindale, 1957; West, 1982). He is reported to have prayed, "Give me chastity and continence, but do not give it yet" (*The Confessions*, Book VIII, chap. 7). After reading the works of Saint Paul, he converted to Christianity and thereafter led an ascetic life.

It was Augustine, more than anyone else, who solidified the Church's antisexual attitude. Augustine believed that all sexual intercourse was sinful, and thus all children were born from the sin of their parents. As a result of the downfall of Adam and Eve, he argued, sex was shameful and equated with guilt. Augustine recognized that married couples had to engage in sexual intercourse for procreation, but denounced sex between a husband and wife for the purpose of pleasure (see Soble, 2009). He even considered marital sex for the purpose of procreation to be an unpleasant necessity:

> **They who marry...if the means could be given them of having children without intercourse with their wives, would they not with joy unspeakable embrace so great a blessing? Would they not with great delight accept it?** (Cited in Goergen, 1975)

Augustine not only departed from the Hebrews in denying the pleasures of (marital) sex, but in the process also differed from them by showing complete disgust for the human body: "Between feces and urine we are born."

Augustine's views on sexual intercourse were shared by nearly all early Christian leaders:

> **Arnobius called it filthy and degrading, Methodius unseemly, Jerome unclean, Tertullian shameful, Ambrose a defilement. In fact there was an unstated consensus that God ought to have invented a better way of dealing with the problem of procreation.** (Tannahill, 1980, p. 141)

The Catholic Church's view that the only reason married couples should engage in sex is for procreation was confirmed by Pope John Paul II as recently as 1993 ("Veritatis Splendor") and 1995 ("Evangelium Vitae"). Although not all Christians today are of the same denomination, they all share the same early history, and thus they all have been influenced by the beliefs of Saint Paul and Saint Augustine.

> "I grew up being told my body was a filthy thing, sex was a sin, and I would burn in hell if I paid any attention to it. Everybody shoved the word 'sin' down my throat and showed disgust at the slightest infraction, real or imagined, of 'God's rules.' The result is that I had an extremely low self-esteem during adolescence, as well as an inner struggle between Mother Nature and the expectations of 'God,' which about drove me nuts."
>
> (from the author's files)

PERSONAL REFLECTIONS

Christian views about sex were strongly influenced by Saint Augustine, who believed that the only legitimate reason to engage in sex was to have children. How do you feel about engaging in sex for pleasure? How do you feel about masturbation? With regard to sexual behavior, how has your religious upbringing affected your opinions about what is right or wrong?

FIGURE 1–3 Saint Augustine (A.D. 354–430). Augustine was the major influence on Christian attitudes about sex. He believed that all sexual acts were driven by lust and were therefore evil, including sex within marriage.

Victorianism

The 19th century is often referred to as the **Victorian era,** after Queen Victoria (1819–1901), who reigned in England for most of the century. It was an era of public prudery and purity. All pleasurable aspects of sex were denied. Influenced by conservative reform ideals of the British Evangelicals in the late 1700s and early 1800s, the Victorians came to view women (who just a few centuries before had been considered sexual temptresses) as asexual (i.e., having no interest in sex) and as innocent as children (Cott, 2002). Men were the ones who were viewed as responsible for lust. According to Victorian moralists, a woman's place was in the home, and wives engaged in sex only to perform their "wifely duties." Women's dresses covered the neck, back, and ankles, and the prudery was carried to such an extreme that even piano legs were covered. At the dinner table, it was considered improper to ask for a "breast" of chicken.

The medical views of the 19th century generally supported the antisexuality of the era. A prominent Swiss physician named Tissot had published a book in 1741 in which he claimed that masturbation could lead to blindness, consumption, other physical disorders, and insanity. As early as 1727 Daniel Defoe had written that excess sex leads to "Palsies and Epilepsies, Falling-Sickness, trembling of the Joints, pale dejected Aspects, Leanness, and at last Rottenness, and other Filthy and loathsome Distempers...." (p. 91). Victorian physicians believed that loss of semen was as detrimental to a man's health as loss of blood, a belief that had originated with the Greek physician Hippocrates (Haller & Haller, 1977). Even the thought of sex was believed to be harmful to a man's health:

> If the thought is permitted to center upon the sexual relation the blood will be diverted from the brain and the muscles and the entire man will suffer because of the depletion.... *(Dr. Sylvannus Stall, 1897)*

As a result of these beliefs, parents often went to ridiculous lengths to prevent masturbation (Hall, 1992) and nocturnal emissions ("wet dreams," or spermatorrhea, as it was called then), including having their boys circumcised or making them wear antimasturbation devices to bed at night (see Stephens, 2009). Between 1856 and 1932, the U.S. government awarded at least 33 patents for sexual restraint devices (Schwartz, 1973); even more were awarded in England. Two such inventions are shown in Figure 1–4.

Adults were supposed to show restraint in their desires for sexual intercourse as well, even within marriage. Here is an example of the attitudes that prevailed during that time:

> At this point, dear reader, let me concede one shocking truth. Some young women actually anticipate the wedding night ordeal with curiosity and pleasure! Beware such an attitude! One cardinal rule of marriage should never be forgotten: give little, give seldom, and above all give grudgingly. *(Ruth Smythers,* Instruction and Advice for the Young Bride, *1894)*

The amount of misinformation that was distributed by the medical community during the Victorian era is really quite appalling. For example, a group of British doctors claimed to have evidence that touching a menstruating woman could spoil hams (*British Medical Journal*, 1878). Consider also a book titled *Perfect Womanhood* by "Mary Melendy, M.D., Ph.D.," published in 1903. It was a book of advice for women, and in addition to the usual warnings about masturbation and excessive sex, it contained the following advice about when it was safest to have intercourse (to avoid pregnancy):

> It is a law of nature—to which there may be some exceptions—that conception must take place at about the time of the menstrual flow.... It may be said with certainty, however, that from ten days after the cessation of the menstrual flow until three days preceding its return, there is little chance of conception, while the converse is equally true....

As you will learn in Chapter 3, this is not true.

The private lives of most Victorians may not have been as repressed and prudish as the image conveyed by the moralists of that era. A questionnaire given to 45 married women in a study conducted by Dr. Clelia Mosher in 1892 reveals that most of the women desired and enjoyed sex (Jacob, 1981). There

"If sex is dirty and disgusting, why should I save it for someone I love?"

Reproduced by special permission of *Playboy* magazine. Copyright © 1993 by Playboy.

Victorian era ■ The period during the reign of Queen Victoria of England (1819–1901). With regard to sexuality, it was a time of great public prudery (the pleasurable aspects of sex were denied) and many incorrect medical beliefs.

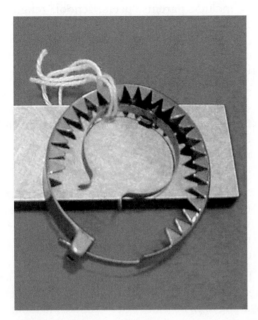

FIGURE 1–4 Two antisex devices invented and patented during the Victorian era: (left) a spermatorrhea ring to prevent nocturnal emission; (right) a "surgical appliance" made of leather straps and metal pockets to prevent masturbation.

was also a great deal of hypocrisy during this era. Prostitution and pornography flourished, and extramarital affairs were common (Trudgill, 1976).

Although Queen Victoria died in 1901, the Victorian era of repressed sexuality continued well into the 20th century. For example, some television shows in the 1950s would show Elvis Presley only from the waist up. During this same time period, television hosts and actors were not even allowed to use the word "pregnant" ("with child" was considered to be the proper term). When Lucy of the *I Love Lucy* show first said "pregnant" on television, it caused a public outrage. With this degree of negativity and repressiveness regarding sex, how did Western culture enter into the sexual revolution?

The Sexual Revolution

It was not unusual for our great-great-grandfathers, whether they worked on the farm or in the city, to put in 12- to 16-hour days, often 6 days a week. Child labor was common, so that many children were also working these hours. In addition to puritanical Victorian ideals, the lack of leisure time limited opportunities for sexual relations.

The industrial revolution slowly changed all this. Mechanization and more efficient means of production eventually led to shorter workweeks, freeing people to engage in leisure activities. The invention of the automobile allowed young people to get away from the watchful eyes of their parents and neighbors. The Great Depression of the 1930s and then World War II in the 1940s again prevented most people from having

much leisure time. The 1950s saw the first peacetime generation of American teens whose families were affluent enough to provide them with an automobile. For the first time, Americans had two things necessary to engage in leisure sex: time and mobility.

The growing women's rights movement eventually resulted in more equality for women, and they began to take an active role in sexual matters (they were not the passive, asexual creatures portrayed by Victorian moralists). With the introduction of penicillin in 1940, people worried less about sexually transmitted infections such as syphilis and gonorrhea. If they got these diseases, they could now be cured.

In 1960, the birth control pill and the IUD became available, so that having sexual intercourse could be spontaneous and people did not have to worry about unwanted pregnancies. The major impact of this was that the pleasurable aspects of sex could be completely separated from the reproductive aspects. It did not take long before people began to think that one had nothing to do with the other.

As a result of these several factors, we entered the so-called **sexual revolution,** a time when more people than ever in the past were supposedly engaging in premarital sex, beginning at an earlier age, and with more partners. The newest generation of Americans to come of age was under pressure, not to abstain from premarital sex, but to engage in it.

The sexual revolution continued unabated in the 1960s and 1970s, but the 1980s saw the emergence

Sexual revolution ■ A period in U.S. history, beginning about 1960, of increased sexual permissiveness.

of HIV (human immunodeficiency virus) and AIDS (acquired immunodeficiency syndrome) as a worldwide life-threatening infection. However, when the large majority of new cases in the United States were diagnosed in gay men and intravenous drug users, Americans were slow to respond. The percentage of college students who had engaged in sexual intercourse did not decline during the 1980s, and may have even increased. By the mid-1990s more and more people were becoming aware that the virus leading to AIDS could be spread during heterosexual intercourse, and researchers began to see evidence of what may be a more conservative attitude about sex. Between 1991 and 2005, there was a decline in the number of teenagers who had had sexual intercourse (Gavin et al., 2009). As a result, there was also a decline in teenage pregnancies, births, and abortions (National Center for Health Statistics, 2006). However, the teen birth rate increased again in 2006 and 2007, but decreased slightly in 2008 (National Center for Health Statistics, 2010). The U. S. teenage pregnancy rate is still higher than for any other developed country (United Nations, 2007).

We do not yet know whether these recent trends signal an end to, or a change in, the sexual revolution. Compared to past generations, behaviorally our society is still permissive, but many people still do not have a positive attitude about their own sexuality. Many of the negative attitudes of the early Christian church and the Victorian era are still with us. Even at the height of the sexual revolution, most parents could not bring themselves to have meaningful discussions with their children about sex. It is no wonder that so many people still have so many questions, doubts, and anxieties about sex.

PERSONAL REFLECTIONS

Did Saint Augustine's and the Victorians' views about sex seem strange or silly to you? Do you think people 100 years from now will think what we presently consider as "normal" to be strange?

WHAT INFLUENCES OUR ATTITUDES ABOUT SEX TODAY?

Socialization refers to the manner in which a society shapes individual behaviors and expectations of behaviors (norms). The social influences that shape behaviors are often referred to as **socializing agents.**

Socialization ■ The process of internalizing society's beliefs; the manner in which a society shapes individual behaviors and expectations of behaviors.

Socializing agent ■ The social influences (e.g., parents, peers, the media) that shape behaviors.

These include parents, peers, school, religion, and the media. You have just learned that for centuries religion was the primary socializing agent for sexual attitudes in Western culture. For some teens, this is still true.

"The media has always shown that everyone is having sex, no matter what type or what age. I have never followed the example of the media and that is mainly because of my religious beliefs. I don't believe that sex is wrong. I have just been taught that you wait until marriage."

"I was raised in a Catholic home and I have been taught to wait until marriage, etc. Just because I see something on TV or in a magazine does not want to make me go out and try something."
(All examples are from the author's files.)

Teens who identify themselves as religious tend to have conservative attitudes about sex, often resulting in waiting until an older age to initiate intercourse, and often with a fiancé or new spouse (Brewster et al., 1998; Simons, 2009). Nevertheless, about 40% of fundamentalist teenage girls and over half of Catholic teen girls are sexually active (Brewster, et al., 1998).

Although learning about sex from parents and one's church leaders tends to delay initiation of sex, learning from friends and the media increases the likelihood of engaging in sexual intercourse (Bleakley et al., 2009). In the beginning of the chapter you learned that the major sources of sexual information for most teens today are friends and the media, and your friends probably got most of their information from the media (Nonoyama et al., 2005; Sprecher et al., 2008).

Would it surprise you to learn that the average American child spends 6 to 8 hours a day watching, listening to, or reading some form of the media (Roberts, 2000)? Not surprisingly, probably no other socializing agent has as much of an impact on young children's and teenagers' sexual attitudes and behaviors as the media. When considered together, the sexually related messages received by young people from different branches of the media—television, movies, radio, music, magazines, and tabloids—are omnipresent and pervasive, and generally overwhelm the input received from all other sources combined (Huston et al., 1998).

"I would see on television and movies that everyone had sex. That's when I would say I used television to overcome my fear of sleeping with other people."

"To me it's never a question of when to become sexually active. It's always how to become sexually active. What I really mean is that when you are watching television you see some love scenes and they make you want to try the same thing."

"I was raised in a very religious household, which made me kind of sexually repressed. My parents and my church made me think my innermost thoughts were dirty. However, when I got to about 16 and saw that the same things I discussed with my parents were on television, I realized I wasn't strange. It was normal to have fantasies and occasional dirty thoughts. The songs on the radio echoed my feelings."

"From a young age seeing sexual references and acts on TV clued me in on sex being a lot of fun and highly enjoyable. So sex was something I greatly anticipated. I watched women on shows or movies who were considered sexy and I wanted to be like them."

"I had a very negative attitude towards sex and my body. I was raised with everything being a taboo. Now since I am so into television and movies and magazines, my whole sexual attitude has changed. I have dropped all of the negative attitudes that I was taught and I try a lot of the things that I see in the media."
(All examples are from the author's files.)

Let's look now at different media sources.

Magazines and Tabloids

You do not have to go to XXX bookstores to find magazines that use sex to make sales. *Playboy, Penthouse, Hustler*, and other magazines for men are openly sold in drugstores and newsstands. And sell they do, with (double-digit) millions sold every month. Even if you do not read (look at?) these magazines yourself, you are very aware of them simply because they are sold openly everywhere and you cannot avoid seeing the covers. Although not as explicit, magazines such as *Maxim*, which emphasizes cleavage and large breasts, are becoming increasingly popular with young men. Recent issues included articles with titles such as "The Sex Olympics (…a List of Sex Acts in Public Places That'll Score You and Your Girl Points)" and "Cook Her Pants Off (Do It Right and You'll Be Dessert)."

FIGURE 1–5 Publishers of popular magazines frequently use sex appeal on the covers in order to sell their products.

Even more mainstream magazines sometimes increase their sexual content to boost sales. *Sports Illustrated* normally sells over 2 million copies a week, but its annual swimsuit issue sells over 5 million. News magazines such as *Newsweek* and *Time* have more than tripled their references to sex since the start of the sexual revolution.

Many magazines for women also emphasize sex. Nearly all the articles in *Cosmopolitan* are about sex. As an example, the cover of a recent issue emphasized articles on multiple orgasms ("Yes! Yes! Yes! Cosmo's Come-Again Guide to Help You Climax Over and Over. Read This, Grab Him, and Head to Bed"), men's attitudes on swimsuits ("Is Your Thong Wrong? Is Your Itsy Too Bitsy? Does Your Tank Turn Him On?"), and sex skin secrets ("Fake Perfect Post–'O' Glow"). *Redbook* and *Mademoiselle* also have a heavy dose of articles related to sex.

About 75% of girls aged 12 to 14 years old read at least one magazine a month (Klein et al., 1993), and magazines that target teenaged girls frequently have articles and ads about boys and relationships (Walsh-Childers et al., 2002). Even magazines that target young teen and preteen girls, such as *YM*, often have sexually related articles ("Look Summer Sexy"). The girls and models in magazines for teenaged girls are always thin, and teenaged girls say that these magazines have a strong influence on their attitudes about weight, beauty, and the perfect body shape (Field et al., 1999).

Tabloids, of course, are full of sexually related and sexually stimulating material. Romance novels, sexual advice books, and novels with sexual plots occupy much of the space on store bookshelves.

PERSONAL REFLECTIONS

What effect has the sexual content in magazines and magazine advertisements had on your attitudes about physical attractiveness? Masculinity? Femininity? Sex, and what is sexually normal?

Music

A survey of undergraduates on a college campus found that students spent an average of 36 hours a month watching music videos (Ward, 2002). In today's music world, it is common for groups and performers to release CDs with sexually explicit lyrics. Much of this is not even played on the radio because it is so explicit, but it is readily available to teens at stores, their iPods, and YouTube. Two thirds of music videos contain sexual imagery (Pardun & McKee, 1995). What effect do you suppose it has on teens when they watch their favorite rock and pop stars accompanied by sexual imagery? Teens who watch music videos a lot are generally more sexually

FIGURE 1–6   Rock and pop stars such as Lady Gaga (left), Adam Lambert (top right), and Janet Jackson and Justin Timberlake (bottom right) commonly use sex in music videos and on stage to promote themselves.

permissive than teens who do not. They also tend to view women as sexual objects and believe in stereotypical gender roles (Kistler & Lee, 2010; Zhang et al., 2008).

Radio

As a means of mass communication, radio serves more than just music. Howard Stern became a national celebrity as a radio talk-show "shock jock." We do not hear that term much anymore because almost every large urban area has a local disc jockey who focuses on sexual jokes, stories, and innuendoes. It is no longer shocking. Nor is it regulated; children of any age can turn on the radio in the morning and listen to adults make constant references about sex.

PERSONAL REFLECTIONS

What effect have references to sex in music and disc-jockey talk about sex had on your attitudes about sex? Have you ever wanted to be a rock star? Are rock stars sexier than other people? Why?

Movies

Most Hollywood movies have an R rating, usually for sexual explicitness, and although teens are not supposed to see these movies until they are 17, most teens have seen an R-rated movie by the time they are 13 years old (Greenberg et al., 1993). Most teens not only have access to TV, but also to cable and CD players (Roberts, 2000), which allows them to watch almost any movie. The movie industry continues to push the limits of what is considered acceptable. Hollywood did not show women's breasts until the mid-1960s, but by the 1990s films showing women in full frontal nudity were commonplace. Sharon Stone's leg-crossing scene in 1992's *Basic Instinct* caused quite a stir, but since then films with male genitals (e.g., *Boogie Nights*, 1997; *The Full Monty*, 1997) have become common as well. *Eyes Wide Shut* (1999), starring Nicole Kidman and Tom Cruise, was full of steamy sex scenes, including group sex. In 2000, Hilary Swank won an Academy Award for her performance in *Boys Don't Cry*, which featured several explicit lesbian scenes. Hollywood has also released movies that focus on autoeroticism

(*American Pie*, 1999), mother-son incest (*Spanking the Monkey*, 1994), and necrophilia (*Kissed*, 1997). Heavy sexual content is now commonplace in today's main-stream movies (e.g., *Knocked Up*, 2007; *The Ugly Truth*, 2009; *Zack and Miri Make a Porno*, 2008; *The Hangover*, 2009; *Good Luck Chuck*, 2007). Are the sex scenes always an integral part of the story, or are they included for gratuitous reasons, to arouse and titillate? Well, according to people who were present when *Basic Instinct* was being filmed, director Paul Verhoeven arrived on the set one day and loudly asked, "How can we put more tits and p— into this movie?" (Zevin, 1992).

Television

Life does not imitate art; it only imitates bad television. *(from Woody Allen's 1992 movie* Husbands and Wives*)*

Gossip Girl, Entourage, The Real World, Hung, True Blood—just a few examples of the many television shows today with heavy sexual content. The average American child watches Television for several hours a day. In fact, about one fourth of preschoolers and two thirds of children 8 to 16 years old have a television in their bedroom (Roberts, 2000). One expert on communication has described television as "the most powerful storyteller in American culture, one that continually repeats the myths and ideologies, the facts and patterns of relationships that define and legitimize the social order" (J. D. Brown, 2002, p. 44). And what is the primary message that television presents about sex? Two other prominent

researchers have stated: "TV presents sex as a distorted, realistic oriented, exploitive, casual activity without dealing with the consequences" (Strouse & Fabes, 1985, p. 255).

Are these researchers exaggerating? Over three fourths of the programs shown at evening prime time have sexual content (70% of the shows that teens rate as their top-20 favorites and almost half of these involve sexual behaviors), with an average of 5.9 scenes per hour (Collins et al., 2004; Eyal et al., 2007; Kaiser Family Foundation, 2005). Mostly it is talk about sex, but about 10% of prime-time shows have scenes in which sexual intercourse is depicted or strongly implied. About 16% of the characters on TV having sexual intercourse are teens or young adults (Eyal & Finnerty, 2009). Scenes about unmarried intercourse outnumber those about married intercourse by a 5 to 1 ratio (see Greenberg & Hofschire, 2000).

Only about 11% of television shows with sexually related content make any reference to sexual health or responsibility (e.g., unintended pregnancies, birth control, sexually transmitted infections) or risks (Kaiser Family Foundation, 2005). It is obvious that television studios find it easier to show pleasure and passion than responsibility and problems. As stated by researcher Jane Brown, "Content analyses suggest that media audiences are most likely to learn that sex is consequence-free, rarely planned, and more a matter of lust than love" (2002, p. 45).

Parents may attempt to regulate which programs their children watch, but parents are not always home. Many teens and preadolescents do not watch the same programs when they are alone that they do when their parents are around.

FIGURE 1–7 Many radio and TV personalities appeal to young people's interest in sex. Howard Stern (left) emphasizes the crude and vulgar aspects of sex, whereas Dr. Drew Pinsky (right) teaches sexual responsibility.

Advertisements

Did you know that the average American child sees about 40,000 commercials each year (Robinson et al., 2001)? And that is just on television alone. Many of these advertisements use sexual appeals to sell their products.

Sex certainly sells, or at least manufacturers of perfumes and colognes, liquor and beer, cigarettes, and clothing think so. People find ads that use sexual appeals to be more attention-getting, more likable, and more persuasive than ads that do not use sexual appeals (Reichert, 2003). As a result, sexual explicitness in ads has risen sharply since 1990 (Reichert, 2003). In my own metropolitan area there is a weekly magazine with hundreds of photographs of used cars for sale that always has a cover photo of a young woman in a bikini sitting on or standing next to a car. There has also been a big increase in recent years in sexualized images of men in advertisements for men's magazines such as *Sports Illustrated, Popular Mechanics,* and *GQ* (Rohlinger, 2002). These images of the "erotic male" work to establish male consumers' (as well as women's) ideas about masculinity and what a "real" man is.

Parents, churches, and others attempt to tell young adolescents that they are not ready for sex, but advertisements direct the attitudes and beliefs of young people in a different direction. As one researcher put it, coming of age has become a "process to be worked out in the market place rather than at home" (Brumberg, 1997, p. 41).

The aim of sexy or romantic themes in advertisements is **identification,** not product information. The message of using young attractive models in sexy or romantic poses is that if you use this product, you too can be sexy and have exciting and romantic interactions. Advertisers argue that the use of models in ads merely reflects the present cultural attitudes.

The Internet

Most children now have access to the Internet within their own home. Already today the most

FIGURE 1–8 Many advertisers use sex (in a process called identification) rather than product information to sell their product.

commonly used search term is *sex*. Although there are sites providing information about healthy sexual behavior (e.g., Planned Parenthood's www.teenwire.org, American Social Health Association's www.iwannaknow.org), over half of American teens have visited a sexually explicit website (Braun-Courville & Rojas, 2009; Brown, 2009; Tsitsike et al., 2009). Even many who do not seek it out are exposed to it anyway (Wolak et al., 2007). Many teens are now naming it as one of their primary sources of sexual information (Zillmann, 2000). This material is readily available, and try as they might, many parents have difficulties preventing their children from obtaining it. However, in this chapter we focus on mainstream magazines, movies, and television programs. You will learn about the effects of pornographic material in Chapter 16.

Sexual Socialization: Cause and Effect?

What specific evidence is there to support the idea that the media play a major role in sexual socialization? For one, children who watch television

---

Identification ■ Two meanings: (1) the adoption of the sex roles of the same-sex parent by a child, and (2) in advertising, to identify or relate to a product.

shows with a lot of sexual content are more likely to begin having sexual intercourse earlier than other children (Brown & Newcomer, 1991; Hyde & Price, 2007; Peterson et al., 1991). This is true even when other characteristics of individuals are controlled for (Collins et al., 2004). A national survey of teens conducted over 3 years found that the teens who watched the most sexual content on TV were twice as likely (12% to 5%) as others to get pregnant or get someone pregnant (again, the experimenters controlled for other known variables) (Chandra et al., 2008). The problem with correlational studies is that we do not know which came first—maybe teens who have a greater interest in sex are drawn to TV shows with sexual content. However, in controlled experiments, teenagers who had just watched television shows with a lot of sexual content gave more positive ratings to casual sex than teenagers who had not been shown the programs (Bryant & Rockwell, 1994) and showed a greater acceptance of sexual stereotypes as well (Ward & Friedman, 2006). As for the question of cause or effect, it probably works in both directions. One study of 14- to 16-year-old teens (that again controlled for other variables) found that sexually active teens were more likely to access sexual content in the media, and that this exposure made it more likely that their sexual activity would increase (Bleakley et al., 2008).

In a review of many studies, Greenberg and Hofschire (2000) concluded that frequent sexual content on television has four major effects on viewers: (1) overestimation of the prevalence of certain sexual activities in the general public; (2) disinhibition—a more liberal attitude about sex;

(3) increased interest in sexual issues; and (4) learning about sexual topics.

It is not uncommon for a publisher of a magazine, or a producer of a particular television show, to deny that his or her product could possibly, by itself, influence the attitudes and behaviors of large numbers of people. They are probably correct, yet at the same time they are missing the point. Kunkel et al. (1999) have summed up the process of socialization very nicely:

> **As with most aspects of media influence, the effect of viewing sexual content.... is not thought to be direct and powerful, with a single exposure to a particular program [movie, or magazine] leading a viewer to think or act in any given way. Rather, the effects of messages about sex are conceptualized more as the product of a slow and cumulative process. Because such influence tends to be gradual in nature, it is the overall pattern of messages across the [media] landscape that is of primary interest for explaining the effects of long-term exposure. (p. 235)**

What is the *long-term cumulative* message? By watching television and movies, looking at magazines, and listening to the radio, children eventually develop attitudes and answers to questions such as "When is it okay for me to start having sex?"; "With whom is it okay for me to have sex?"; "What sexual behaviors are okay to engage in?"; and "Why is it okay?" In other words, the *cumulative effect* is that children take what they see and hear in the media to learn social norms (Brown et al., 1990). One group of communication experts described the mass media as "a kind of sexual super peer" (Brown et al., 2005).

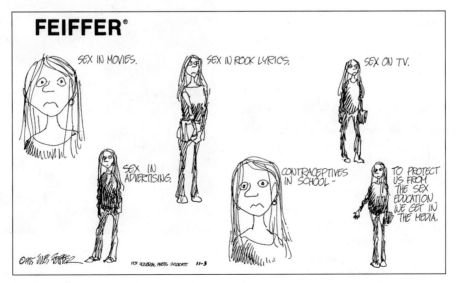

© Jules Feiffer

One of the biggest problems is that the input to children from the media begins much earlier than input from schools and churches, and often years before parents start to talk to their children about sex. The early exposure to media, and the huge quantity of information that children receive from the media, simply overwhelm the input from other socializing agents. In order to have any chance of balancing the media's sexual messages, parents and school-based sex education programs need to find ways to incorporate what is shown on television and in movies and heard on the radio and CDs into their discussions (Kyman, 1998).

There can be little doubt that the avalanche of sexual content in the media contributes to the sexual socialization of children and adolescents. But can heavy sexual content in the media explain all the sexual attitudes and behaviors of American teenagers? The answer may not be that simple. European television, magazines, and advertisements contain a great deal more nudity than their American counterparts, yet European teens do not begin sex at a younger age than American teens, and the teenage pregnancy rate in most European countries is much lower than it is in the United States (Singh & Darroch, 2000). Obviously, it is not just the amount of sexual content that is important. Perhaps the nature of the sexual content (e.g., types of behaviors shown) in the media is equally important. European media may show more nudity, but the sexual behaviors portrayed tend to be less exploitative and birth control techniques are advertised openly. Keep in mind, too, that the media do not work in splendid isolation. Recent studies have found that the messages and practices shown or talked about in the media intersect with the influences of school, family, and friends (Steele, 1999). Europeans generally receive a more balanced approach from all the various agents of sexual socialization. Parents are more open about sex, and school-based sex education begins early in life for most European children. What do you suppose accounts for the difference?

PERSONAL REFLECTIONS

In the three previous Personal Reflections, you were asked about the effects of specific branches of the media on your sexual attitudes and behaviors. You may have denied or minimized the effect of any one branch. Now consider them all together, and the fact that you have been bombarded with messages about sex since early childhood. Do you suppose your attitudes about sex would be any different if you had been raised in a culture with no radio, movies, or television, or if the media presented a negative portrayal of sex?

SEX AS A SCIENCE

Until the last few centuries, religion was the primary influence in intellectual endeavors. The rise of science was slow and was met with much resistance. Galileo (1564–1642), for example, was forced to publicly recant his support for Copernicus' theory that the earth moved around the sun—and not vice versa, as stated in church doctrine—or face excommunication. People's desire for facts and knowledge could not be stifled, however, and the following centuries saw great advances in the biological and physical sciences. Science slowly replaced religion as the authority on most subjects.

Unfortunately, sexual behavior as a subject for scientific investigation met with more resistance than most others. It was not until the mid-1900s that researchers interested in studying sexual behavior were able to apply the two tools necessary for scientific inquiry: observation and measurement. Let us take a brief look at a few individuals who were responsible for making sexual behavior a serious, objective field of study. Further details of their work will be discussed in later chapters.

Sigmund Freud (1856–1939)

Sigmund Freud, perhaps more than anyone else, is responsible for demonstrating the influence of sexuality in human life (Figure 1–9). It is all the more remarkable that he did so during the antisexual atmosphere of the Victorian era. In actuality, Freud was not a sex researcher. Rather, he merely discussed sexuality as a primary motivation for behavior. Sexual energy—or *libido,* as Freud called it—was

FIGURE 1–9 Sigmund Freud. Freud lived during the Victorian era, a period often described as being indiscriminately antisexual. He is given the major credit for showing the importance of sexuality in human behavior and motivations.

said to be channeled into particular areas of the body at different ages. Freud developed psychoanalysis as a means for evaluating and treating unconscious sexual motivations.

Although many people disagree with Freud's theory today (see, for example, Gray, 1993b), he remains important for his ideas on sexual motivation and sexuality in infants and children. However, like other Victorian doctors, Freud had many incorrect beliefs about sex, including the belief that loss of semen was as detrimental to a man's health as was loss of blood.

Henry Havelock Ellis (1859–1939)

When he was a young man in the 1800s, **Henry Havelock Ellis** (Figure 1–10) had frequent nocturnal emissions (wet dreams), which at the time was called spermatorrhea because Victorian physicians believed it was caused by the same thing that caused gonorrhea. The end result, Ellis was told, would be blindness, insanity, and eventual death. He wanted to commit suicide but was too fearful, so instead he kept a diary to document his death by this dreaded "disease." When his eyesight and reasoning did not deteriorate over the passing months, Ellis concluded that loss of semen did not really lead to death, and he became angry about the misconceptions held by the medical profession. He devoted the remainder of his life to sexual research (although he reputedly remained a virgin himself).

As a physician practicing in Victorian England, Ellis collected a large amount of information about people's sexual behaviors from case histories and cross-cultural studies. He eventually published six volumes of a series titled *Studies in the Psychology of Sex* between 1896 and 1910, and a seventh in 1928. He argued that women were not asexual and that men's and women's orgasms were very similar. Ellis was particularly important for his emphasis on the wide range of human sexual behaviors and for his belief that behaviors such as masturbation and homosexuality should be considered normal. His tolerant view of sexuality was in marked contrast to that of the Victorian moralists and was a major influence on researchers for several generations.

Alfred C. Kinsey (1894–1956)

The modern era of sex research did not begin until the publication of Alfred Kinsey's studies (1948, 1953) 20 years after Ellis' last volume. Similar to Ellis' boyhood fears of nocturnal emissions, as a boy Kinsey was greatly afraid he would go insane because he masturbated. Later in life he told a friend, "I decided I didn't want any young people going through the nonsense I went through" (Ericksen, 2000). When asked to teach a course on marriage at Indiana University in 1938, **Alfred C. Kinsey** was amazed to find how little objective data there were on sexual behavior. He started collecting his own data by giving questionnaires to his students, but he soon decided that personal interviews resulted in a greater amount of more detailed data. He was joined by Wardell Pomeroy, Clyde Martin, and Paul Gebhard (see Figure 1–11). Their final samples had a total of 5,300 men and 5,940 women.

Kinsey's work opened the door to a whole new field of research, but this did not come without a price. His findings that most people masturbated,

FIGURE 1–10 Henry Havelock Ellis. Between 1896 and 1928, this English researcher published seven volumes about the psychology of sex. His views were remarkably tolerant compared with those of most Victorian physicians and scientists.

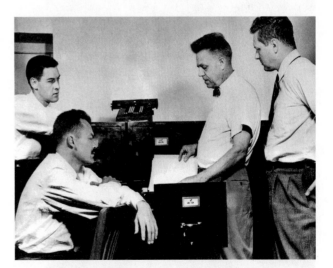

FIGURE 1–11 Alfred C. Kinsey and colleagues. This college professor's surveys in 1948 of male sexual behaviors and in 1953 of female sexual behaviors marked the beginning of the modern era of sexuality research. From left to right: Clyde Martin, Paul Gebhard, Kinsey, Wardell Pomeroy.

that many people engaged in oral-genital sex, that women could have multiple orgasms, and that many men had had a homosexual experience shocked many people. He was accused of being antifamily and amoral. One Columbia University professor stated that "there should be a law against doing research dealing exclusively with sex" (*New York Times*, April 1, 1948). Some researchers believe that Kinsey was the major influence in changing 20th-century attitudes about sex (Bullough, 1998). The Kinsey Institute for Research in Sex, Gender, and Reproduction at Indiana University continues to be a major center for the study of human sexuality.

Masters and Johnson

Kinsey paved the way for scientific studies of sexual behavior, but the study of functional anatomy and physiological studies of sex were still limited to experiments with laboratory animals. William Masters (1915–2001), a physician, and Virginia Johnson (1925–), a behavioral scientist (Figure 1–12), did not believe that experiments with rats could tell us a great deal about sexual behavior in people. Therefore, in 1954, **Masters and Johnson** started to directly observe and record the physiological responses in humans engaged in sexual activity under laboratory conditions. Their results, which were based on over 10,000 episodes of sexual activity of 312 men and 382 women, were not published until 1966 (*Human Sexual Response*). Although some people were shocked at Masters and Johnson's observational approach, calling them "scientific

FIGURE 1–12 William Masters and Virginia Johnson. Their laboratory studies of the physiological responses that normally occur during sexual arousal led to the development of modern-day sexual therapy techniques.

peeping Toms," most people in the medical community appreciated the importance of their findings.

As in all other areas of medical science, the understanding of anatomy and physiology led to methods for treating clinical problems and abnormalities. Masters and Johnson developed the first methods for treating sexual problems and opened a sexual therapy clinic in 1965. Their techniques were described in their 1970 book *Human Sexual Inadequacy*. The behavioral approach to treating sexual disorders, based on Masters and Johnson's work, has helped thousands of people to overcome sexual problems.

Edward O. Laumann and the National Health and Social Life Surveys

In 1989, a panel of the National Academy of Science's National Research Council asked federal agencies to fund new surveys of sexual behavior in order to help with AIDS prevention. In the same year, the U.S. Department of Health and Human Services initially approved $15 million for a large survey of 20,000 Americans that would be led by sociologist Edward Laumann. However, U.S. Senator Jesse Helms of North Carolina introduced an amendment in the Senate to eliminate funding for surveys of sexual behavior, and the White House Office of Management and Budget eventually blocked attempts to fund the survey.

Despite the new political obstacles, Laumann and his colleagues Robert Michael, John Gagnon, and Stuart Michaels (see Figure 1–13) eventually received $1.7 million from private foundations, and after scaling down their project, in 1992 they interviewed 3,432 adults (Laumann et al., 1994). Their random sample had a 79% participation rate (very high for this type of survey) and was a good representation of all English-speaking adults aged 18 to 59 living in the United States. In short, the National Health and Social Life Survey was the most comprehensive nationally representative survey to date, as in-depth as the Kinsey surveys, but with scientifically sound sampling techniques. Since their initial work, Laumann's group has continued to publish results of their surveys (e.g., Laumann et al., 1997, 1999, 2006, 2009).

The 2010 National Survey of Sexual Health and Behavior

In 2010, the first nationally representative sample of sexual behavior since the 1994 Laumann et al. study was published. The study was conducted by the Center for Sexual Health Promotion, led by Michael Reece, at Indiana University's School of Health, Physical Education, and Recreation. It was a comprehensive study of 5,865 people aged 14 to 94.

FIGURE 1–13 Robert T. Michael, John H. Gagnon, Stuart Michaels, and Edward O. Laumann. They headed the first sexual survey for which the sample was representative of the United States population.

Unlike previous surveys, much of the data were collected via the Internet. The participation rate was a respectable 52.6% for adults, but only 38.2% for adolescents. One of the most important findings was that Americans engage in a wide variety of sexual behaviors. You will see many references to this study in the chapters ahead (see Reece et al., 2010a).

PERSONAL REFLECTIONS

How do you feel about sex as a subject for scientific study? Do you think researchers should ask people about their sexual behaviors? What about physiological studies in which researchers measure bodily responses while people actually engage in various sexual acts?

SCIENTIFIC METHODOLOGY

Surveys and Samples

Throughout this book you will see statistics about sexual behaviors (e.g., percentages of people, frequencies of behavior). In order to know such things, it was necessary for someone like Kinsey, for example, to ask people about their sexual attitudes and behaviors. This involves taking a survey. A **survey** is a study of people's attitudes, opinions, or behaviors. The researcher generally asks a standard set of questions, either in a face-to-face interview or on a paper-and-pencil questionnaire.

The researcher begins by specifying the **population**—the complete set of observations about which he or she wishes to draw conclusions. The population of interest may be quite large (e.g., all adults living in the United States), or it can be small (e.g., all adults living in a town). If the population of interest is large, it may not be possible to obtain responses from everyone. In this case, the researcher must take a **sample** (subset) from the population. There have been many surveys of sexual behavior, including surveys done by *Redbook, Cosmopolitan*, and other magazines. Sometimes the results of these surveys agree, but in other cases they disagree, sometimes considerably. Which ones should we trust to be true? Are any of them accurate?

It might seem to make sense to some of you that the accuracy of a survey would depend on the size of the sample (i.e., the number of people surveyed). Although sample size is important, there are other factors that, if not considered, can negate any advantage obtained by using a large sample. One of the most important questions is whether the sample is representative of the entire population. For this to occur, the sample must be taken randomly.

What is random sampling? Does it mean blindly picking names from a phone book or stopping people on the street? No, because these types of samples might have a built-in bias. A **random sample** is one in which observations are drawn so that all possible samples of the same size have an equal chance of being selected (see King et al., 2011). A special type of random sample is a **stratified random sample**, sometimes called a *representative sample* because it

Survey ■ A study of people's attitudes, opinions, or behaviors. Responses are usually obtained either in a face-to-face interview or on a paper-and-pencil questionnaire.

Population ■ The complete set of observations about which a researcher wishes to draw conclusions.

Sample ■ A subset of a population of subjects.

Random sample ■ A sample in which observations are drawn so that all other possible samples of the same size have an equal chance of being selected.

Stratified random sample ■ A sample in which subgroups are randomly selected in the same proportion as they exist in the population. Thus the sample is representative of the target population.

quite accurately represents the target population. This is the type used by the Gallup and Harris polls to predict the outcome of presidential elections. Before they take their surveys, these polls break the entire country down by sex, race, education, income, geographic location, and many other factors. They know, for example, exactly what percentage of the population is white, Protestant, college educated, and living in the Northeast. Their sample survey includes this percentage of people with these characteristics. As a result, the Gallup and Harris surveys are rarely off by more than a few percentage points. Yet both polls survey only about 2,500 people out of an estimated 100 million voters.

Kinsey's two studies were quite large, but his samples were not randomly drawn from the U.S. population. They were what is known as *convenience samples*—samples made up of whatever group is available (such as students in a course). Kinsey's samples overrepresented midwestern, white, college-educated people, and also included a disproportionately large number of inmates from local prisons. Surveys conducted by magazines are also generally quite large, sometimes with over 100,000 respondents, but are they representative of the country as a whole? One third of the respondents to a 1982 *Playboy* magazine questionnaire said that they had engaged in group sex. Do you really believe this is true for the entire country?

There are more problems in taking a survey of people's sexual behavior than making sure it is representative of the population. Ask yourself the following questions:

1. How often do you masturbate?
2. How many sexual partners have you had in your lifetime?
3. Do you have sexual intercourse in different positions?
4. Do you engage in oral-genital sex?
5. Have you ever had a homosexual experience?
6. Have you ever had an extramarital affair?

Answering some of these questions may have made you feel uncomfortable, for these are very personal questions. How would we know that the people we are surveying are telling the truth? Some people might try to make themselves look good by lying when answering questions about their personal life, so some questionnaires contain "truth items," that is, questions such as "Have you ever told a lie?" It is assumed that everyone has told a lie in his or her life (maybe just a little one), so someone responding negatively to this item would be assumed to be not telling the truth.

Incorrect answers are not necessarily the result of intentional deceit, but can also be due to faulty recall. How well do you remember all the events of your childhood, for example? If couples are surveyed, what does the interviewer do if there are discrepancies in the answers given by the two people? How can the interviewer decide who is telling the truth, or is it the case that they both recall events differently?

Some people may exaggerate their sexual experiences. Surveys often find, for example, that the number of female sexual partners reported by men is greater than the number of male partners reported by women (see Wiederman, 1997b). Problems like these can sometimes be minimized if the survey is done by questionnaire rather than by interview and the questions can be answered anonymously; that is, the respondent is assured that no one (including the person doing the survey) will ever know who he or she is (Durant & Carey, 2000).

Okay, so now you know enough to design a good sex survey. First you stratify the population of people in which you are interested, and then you randomly sample a specified number of people from each of the subgroups. The questionnaires will be filled out anonymously and contain a few items to check for truthfulness. After all this, however, there is another major problem that plagues sex survey research. What do we do when people refuse to participate? In a survey by Morton Hunt (1974), which was an attempt to update Kinsey's data (1948, 1953), only 20% of the people contacted agreed to participate. From a scientific point of view, it is necessary that everyone randomly selected to be in a survey participate in it, but it probably would not surprise you to learn that many people refuse to answer questions like those you just read. We cannot force people to do so. This is the problem of **volunteer bias.**

Are there differences between people who agree to participate in a sex survey and those who do not? In fact, studies have found several differences between people who volunteer to participate in sexual studies and those who refuse. Volunteers had more sexual experiences, were more interested in variety, had a more positive attitude about sex, and had less sexual guilt (Bogaert, 1996; Strassberg & Lowe, 1995). What this means is that the greater the number of people in a survey who refuse to participate, the more cautious we should be in making generalizations about the entire population.

An Example of Problems in Survey Studies: What Do "Sex," "Had Sex," and "Sexual Relations" Mean?

In 1998, when President Clinton appeared on national television to address accusations that he had had sexual relations with Monica Lewinsky, a White House

---

Volunteer bias ■ A bias in research results that is caused by differences between people who agree to participate and others who refuse.

intern, he claimed, "I did not have sexual relations with that woman." Many people assumed that he had lied when it was later discovered that the president and Ms. Lewinsky had engaged in oral-genital relations. But did he really lie?

In a study conducted by the Kinsey Institute, researchers asked students at a midwestern state university, "Would you say you 'had sex' with someone if the most intimate behavior you engaged in was...a person had oral (mouth) contact with your genitals?" or "...you had oral (mouth) contact with a person's genitals?" (Sanders & Reinisch, 1999). Only 40% of the college students responded that they would say that they had "had sex." Interestingly, 20% of the respondents did not regard penile-anal intercourse as having "had sex."

It should be noted that the Kinsey Institute's data were collected in 1991 (before the Clinton-Lewinsky episode). In 1998 (after the episode became public knowledge), five news organizations conducted telephone surveys (see Smith, 1999, for a review) in which they asked people if "sexual relations" included (a) more than sexual intercourse or (b) "oral sex." When phrased this way, 73% to 87% of respondents said yes, but this still means that 18% to 27% disagreed or were not sure. Today, many college students still do not regard oral sex as having sex (Byers et al., 2009; Hans et al., 2010), although they are more likely to regard it as having sex if they are considering the behavior of people other than themselves (Gute et al., 2008).

> "...about a year into the relationship, after engaging in oral sex, we came very close to actually having sexual intercourse. I stopped because I didn't want to have sex until marriage..."
> (from the author's files)

The Kinsey Institute's study makes it very clear that sex researchers must be specific when they use terms such as "sex" or "had sex." Unless otherwise specified (e.g., vaginal intercourse, anal intercourse, oral-genital sex), in this book I will use the terms "*sex*" and "*had sex*" in the way defined by the National Health and Social Life Survey (Laumann et al., 1994):

> ...By "sex" or "sexual activity," we mean any mutually voluntary activity with another person that involves genital contact and sexual excitement or arousal, that is, feeling really turned on, even if intercourse or orgasm did not occur.

PERSONAL REFLECTIONS

Would you tell the truth on a survey about sexual behavior? What if you could answer anonymously? Why or why not?

Correlation

You are probably aware that there is a relationship between performance on certain standardized tests (the SAT or ACT, for example) and freshman-year grades. **Correlation** is a mathematical measure of the degree of relationship between two variables. Correlations can be either *positive* (increases in one variable are associated with increases in the other) or *negative* (increases in one variable are associated with decreases in the other).

The relationship between two variables is rarely perfect. We all know students who had mediocre scores on their SAT or ACT test but who did very well in college (perhaps because they were exceptionally motivated and worked hard). On the other hand, a few students who do very well on their entrance tests do rather poorly in college (perhaps because they were not motivated). Generally, however, the association is good enough so that colleges and universities can use the test scores to predict performance in school. The greater the correlation between two variables, the more accurately we can predict the standing in one from the standing in another.

Correlations are also found in studies of human sexuality. For example, in their nationally representative survey, Laumann and his colleagues (1994) found that the more sex a married person has, the more likely he or she is to masturbate (a positive correlation). This may be interesting, but there is a major limitation to the correlational method—correlation never proves causation. In the case of the relationship between sex and masturbation, we cannot tell whether frequent intercourse leads to (causes) frequent masturbation or frequent masturbation leads to frequent intercourse. Or maybe there is a third variable that similarly affects both frequency of intercourse and frequency of masturbation. Laumann's group, for example, believed that frequency of intercourse and masturbation was a reflection of a person's overall sex drive. Although we must use caution in drawing conclusions from correlations, they are often very useful in pointing the way to more systematic research.

Direct Observation

You have just learned that one of the main problems with conducting a survey is ascertaining the truthfulness of responses. One way around this problem is to make **direct observations** of people's behavior. Anthropologists do this when they study the behavior of people of other cultures in their natural settings. This is the type of study that Marshall (1971) did of

Correlation ■ A mathematical measure of the degree of relationship between two variables.

Direct observation ■ Observing and recording the activity of subjects as they conduct their activities.

the Mangaians and Messenger (1971) did of the Inis Baeg. Of course, people may not behave normally if they know that they are being observed (the *observer effect*), so it is necessary for the observer to take great care to interfere as little as possible.

Direct observation studies can also be done in the lab. The classic example is the work of Masters and Johnson, who, you recall, observed over 10,000 episodes of sexual activity in their laboratory in St. Louis (Masters & Johnson, 1966). For Masters and Johnson, the advantage of observing behavior in the lab was that they could make close observations and also take measures with electrophysiological recording equipment. However, the same limitations apply here as with the previous methods. Were the people Masters and Johnson studied affected by the fact that they knew they were being observed (observer effect)? Are people who would volunteer to have sex under these conditions different from the general population (volunteer bias)? Masters and Johnson were interested in physiological responses, which are probably the same for most people, but we still must be cautious when making generalizations about the entire population.

Case Studies

Clinical psychologists and psychiatrists commonly do in-depth studies of individuals, called **case studies.** They may gather information from questionnaires, interviews with other persons, and even public records, but most of what they learn usually comes from face-to-face interviews conducted over a long period of time. The goal of a case study is to understand a person's behavior and motivations as much as possible. Some of Freud's case studies—such as the case of Little Hans, a 5-year-old boy who had a great fear of horses—are still read today. Freud eventually concluded that Hans' fear of powerful animals grew out of his masturbatory behavior and was actually a disguise for his fear that his father might cut his penis off.

One potential problem with case studies is that the therapist's observations and conclusions might be biased by his or her own beliefs and values (**observer bias**). During the Victorian era, for example, Freud and other physicians believed that masturbation was dangerous and would eventually lead to neurosis (Groenendijk, 1997). In today's world, self-exploration is regarded as normal for young children. Do you suppose that a therapist today would attach great importance to Hans' masturbation?

Case study ■ An in-depth study of an individual.

Observer bias ■ The prejudicing of observations and conclusions by the observer's own belief system.

Experimental method ■ A study in which an investigator attempts to establish a cause-and-effect relationship by manipulating a variable of interest (the independent variable) while keeping all other factors the same.

Experimental Research

The biggest limitation of the research methods you have just read about is that none of them can be used to demonstrate cause-and-effect relationships between two variables. To do so, we must use the **experimental method.** With this approach, the researcher systematically manipulates some variable, called an *independent variable*, while keeping all other variables the same. The variable that is measured is called the *dependent variable*. Typically, the researcher compares two groups (sometimes more). One group receives the experimental treatment and the other (called a control group) does not. If there is any difference between groups in the dependent variable, we can conclude that it was caused by manipulating the independent variable.

While experimental research has advantages over the other methods, it, too, often has limitations. Often, the two groups studied are convenience samples, so we must be cautious about generalizing the results. Moreover, researchers simply cannot use experimental designs to address some questions. We may believe, for example, that an infant's hormone levels shortly after birth strongly influence future sexual orientation, but we cannot purposely manipulate hormones in children in order to prove our hypothesis.

In the chapters ahead you will see references to hundreds of studies. Although each study has its limitations, it is often the case that a particular topic has been studied in numerous investigations using a variety of methods. The more agreement there is among the results of different studies, the safer we can feel about making general conclusions.

SEXUALITY EDUCATION

According to historian Phillippe Ariès (1962), "in medieval society the idea of childhood did not exist." Young children were treated as miniature adults and expected to start working in the fields shortly after they learned to walk. The idea of a separate category called childhood, different from adults, did not arise until the mid-1700s. Although other scholars disagree with Ariès, they agree that the concept of childhood was different than the way we view it in Western culture today. In England during the 1600s, for example, children were believed to be carriers of original sin, prone to evil impulses, and thus childhood was the time of life in which parents and society had to instill control. During the 1700s, this view gave way to the modern view of children as vulnerable and needing protection (Hockey & James, 1993). However, at that time children were considered asexual. Just a century later Freud argued that even young children between the ages of 3 and 5 were sexual. Children now had to be protected from their own sexuality.

The biological immaturity of children is an irrefutable fact, but "childhood is a concept, and it is determined by how a society interprets that biological fact, and by the meanings it attaches to it" (Parsons, 2000). Children of the 1600s, 1700s, and 1800s were understood differently because the concept of childhood was different for each of those time periods. We can see verification of this by examining how other cultures interpret childhood. In the section on cross-cultural comparisons you read about both the Sambian culture in the South Pacific where young boys (starting at age 7) are expected to perform oral-genital sex on adolescent boys (Herdt, 1993) and the Tiwi culture (Melville Island, north of Australia), where girls are married and begin having intercourse at age 7 (Goodall, 1971). Boys of the Batek tribe in northern Sumatra are introduced into sex by masturbating with an older man (Geertz, 1960). Among the Azande of Sudan, boys perform the role of wives to adult warriors (Ford & Beach, 1951). In the Hausa culture of Nigeria, childhood for girls ends abruptly at age 10 when they are married (James et al., 1998). In other cultures (e.g., Chewoy in Malaysia) girls are not regarded as women until they give birth. In our own culture, a person is generally not recognized as an adult until he or she turns 18. Obviously, different cultures attach different meanings to childhood and being a child.

Most of us assume that sex educators teach factual information. But as you have just learned, what is believed to be factual about children's sexuality depends on the culture and the era. What do you suppose sex educators (parents, others) in Mangaia, the most sexually permissive culture in the world, teach children about sexuality? How do you suppose this would differ from what the sex educators among the Inis Baeg, the most sexually repressed culture in the world, teach children?

In the United States, sex education in schools originated as part of a social hygiene movement to prevent rising levels of sexually transmitted infections (Imber, 1994). The first printed matter for sex education appeared in the early 1900s (see Fitz-Gerald & Fitz-Gerald, 1998). The "education" (lectures and printed matter) was in actuality moralistic and anti-sex, designed to repress sexual behavior (Kyman, 1998). Why? In addition to sexually transmitted infections, recall that the medical profession of that era also believed that loss of semen was harmful to men's health (Stephens, 2009). Masturbation, for example, was called "self-abuse," and physicians believed it to be the cause of insanity. Thus, for sex educators the prevailing philosophy of the day was prophylactics—protection from "distorted knowledge" by teaching restraint (Penland, 1981). Girls, in particular, were to be protected because of their delicate and asexual (pure) nature. The teaching of sexual physiology and hygiene was reserved for boys.

By 1940, the focus of sex education in the United States was changing from prophylactics to personal relationships and long-term adjustment. The curriculum now included a biological component, but the basic approach was still moralistic, focusing on sex within marriage and family life (Penland, 1981). Normal, healthy sexuality was supposed to be expressed only in marriage. As was the case earlier in the century, the basic message was still "Just Say No" (Moran, 2000). Girls were now allowed to take sex education, but classes were almost always segregated by sex (Fine, 1988).

Another generation later the sexual revolution was in full swing. By the mid-1960s, numerous scientific surveys and studies had been conducted (e.g., Kinsey and colleagues and Masters and Johnson). The philosophy that emerged among sex educators was a comprehensive sex education presented in a nonjudgmental, impartial manner with open discussion (Kyman, 1998). Girls were now included in the same classes as boys. In addition to sexual anatomy and sexual health, a variety of behaviors were presented as normal (e.g., masturbation, oral-genital sex), so that people could now engage in them without guilt or shame.

It should be obvious from this brief history that what is taught in sex education reflects the prevailing concept of child sexuality of the time. However, sex education is also a powerful socializing agent for

DUNAGIN'S PEOPLE

"DON'T WORRY. WHEN SEX EDUCATION IS PRESENTED IN A CLASSROOM SETTING, IT WILL BECOME AS FOREIGN TO THE STUDENTS AS MATH AND SCIENCE."

children and adolescents; thus, today sexuality education has become a battleground among groups with different moral and political ideologies. Even if sex educators do not openly talk about values, sex education cannot be value-free (Reiss, 1995), and conflict about values is probably inevitable in democratic societies in which there is a diversity of ethnic, religious, and sexual groups.

On one side of the debate are those who wish to guide their children toward their own view of the world and who regard sexuality education as the exclusive right of the family (thus protecting the children from other points of view). This group is guided by the belief that there has been a decline in morals within our society and that only a narrow set of sexual behaviors is normal and moral. They tend to view sexual diversity as part of the problem of moral decline, and their ideology with regard to sex education is to restrict the curriculum.

On the other side are those who favor what is called comprehensive sexuality education. They believe that children should be exposed to a wide variety of beliefs so that they can make their own choices as to what is best for them. Furthermore, they generally believe that it is the duty of the state to impose this education for the "public good."

Nowhere is the battle over curriculum more heated than with regard to the subject of how to prevent teenage pregnancy and sexually transmitted infections. At the heart of this debate is the central issue of the purpose or goal of sexuality education. Those favoring comprehensive education argue that students should be taught about birth control methods and the use of condoms in the interest of public health. Those favoring a restrictive curriculum, on the other hand, see schools as agents of socialization that shape the moral and sexual norms of future generations, and they want sexuality education to promote family values and abstinence.

Nationally, only a small minority of Americans favor abstinence-only education, but politically they have a strong voice (see Constantine, 2008). Abstinence-only programs often have children make a formal virginity pledge. Some studies claim that it works (e.g., Bersamin et al., 2005; Martino et al., 2008), but many well-conducted studies have found that any behavioral changes made by abstinence-only programs are only short term, and that those who take abstinence-only education and/or virginity pledges are more likely to engage in oral-genital sex (Brückner & Bearman, 2005), less likely to use protection (Rosenbaum, 2009), more likely to get pregnant (Kohler et al., 2008), and to later deny having made such a pledge when they begin having sexual intercourse (Rosenbaum, 2009). In 2007, a national study authorized by Congress reported that abstinence-only programs had no effect on whether or not teenagers engaged in sex (Mathematica Policy Research, 2007).

The National Institutes of Health's (NIH) Consensus Panel on AIDS concluded that "abstinence-plus" programs (programs that teach abstinence, contraception, and the prevention of sexually transmitted infections) are more effective than "abstinence-only" programs (NIH Consensus, 1997). A review of sexuality education programs done for the World Health Organization concluded that the programs did not increase sexual experimentation or activity, and that they often resulted in teens postponing sexual intercourse and/or initiating safer sex practices (Grunseit et al., 1997; see also Shears, 2002a). The American Medical Association, the American Academy of Pediatrics, the American College of Obstetricians and Gynecologists, the American Nurses Association, and the American Public Health Association have all endorsed comprehensive sex education.

The battle is now being fought in the political arena. Between 1998 and 2009, the federal government spent over $1.3 billion on abstinence-only sex education programs (Jayson, 2009). In most states, this effectively ended teaching about other types of birth control. However, because of the many studies showing that abstinence-only education does not work, by 2008 several states had declined to accept federal abstinence money. President Obama's administration has pledged to quit funding abstinence-only in favor of more comprehensive programs.

Recall that many northern European countries introduce sexuality education to school children as early as elementary school, and that these countries have much lower rates of teenage pregnancies and sexually transmitted infections than in the United States (Lottes, 2002; Singh & Darroch, 2000). In these countries teenage sexuality is not regarded as a political or religious issue, but instead as a health issue (Kelly & McGee, 1999).

Adolescent sexual health in these countries is based on values of rights, responsibility, and respect. Government and the general society consider it not only a duty to provide accurate information and confidential contraceptive services to the young, but also that provision of such services and information to adolescents is part of their rights. There is no attempt to motivate behavior of teenagers through a collective effort to demand abstinence. Thus, the goal is not to prevent adolescents from having sex but to educate and thereby empower them to make responsible decisions. By respecting the independence and privacy of adolescents the expectation is that, in return, the majority will act responsibly to try to avoid pregnancy and sexually transmitted infections. *(Lottes, 2002, pp. 80–81)*

Studies in the United States also find that the earlier children learn about sexuality, and the more they learn from schools about birth control and teenage pregnancy, the less likely they are to engage in sexual behavior (Somers & Surmann, 2005).

Often left out of the debate are the opinions of young people themselves. Most teens want to receive sexual health education in school. Here are some opinions of students in my own course:

> "I believe human sexuality should be taught in public schools. The media exposes young people to every imaginable kind of sexual topics already."

> "I think that sex education should be included in public high schools.... I knew girls that actually thought urinating after sex or bathing after sex prevented pregnancy. I think it is vital that teens know the real truth about a very important issue."

> "Yes, because it gives students, especially at that age, the ability to learn about sex without feeling stupid because their friends know more than they do."

> "Ignoring the fact that teens have sex will never help them to be responsible. By giving them knowledge of the consequences and responsibilities that go along with having sex, they are more inclined to make a better decision."

How should we resolve these differences in ideology and construct a sexuality education curriculum? In a thoughtful essay, Alexander McKay (1997) argues for a democratic philosophy of sexuality education that is committed to freedom of belief:

In sum, a democratic sexuality education does not insist that students consider the moral dimensions of sexuality from the perspective of a particular sexual ideology. Rather, a democratic sexuality education encourages students to exercise their liberty of thought to deliberate critically between competing ideological perspectives in clarifying their own beliefs and at arriving at new ones. *(p. 295)*

A good compromise has been suggested (Shtarkshall et al., 2007): "Parents are, and should be, the primary socializing agents for most children" (e.g., teach them values), but schools are the best providers of factual information, and both parents and schools should work together.

As a student at a college or university, you were probably not required to take this course. When you enrolled, you exercised your freedom of choice. In this text, I will provide accurate information and attempt to make you aware of the diversity in sexual behavior and values. I do not advocate one lifestyle over another or one set of values over another. My goal for you is that, upon completion of this course, you will feel more comfortable with your own sexuality, and at the same time find a tolerance and respect for the beliefs of others.

PERSONAL REFLECTIONS

Do you believe that sexuality education should be taught in school? If not, why not? If so, beginning at what level? Why?

STUDY GUIDE

KEY TERMS

case study 26
correlation 25
direct observation 25
dualism 10
Henry Havelock
  Ellis 21
ethnocentric 5
experimental method 26
Sigmund Freud 20
identification 18

Alfred C. Kinsey 21
Masters and Johnson 22
missionary position 5
observer bias 26
population 23
procreation 9
random sample 23
Saint Augustine 11
Saint Paul 10
sample 23

sex ("had sex") 25
sexuality 1
sexual revolution 13
socialization 14
socializing agent 14
stratified random
  sample 23
survey 23
Victorian era 12
volunteer bias 24

INTERACTIVE REVIEW

Some people feel that sexuality education should be the responsibility of parents, yet only about one third of all college students report ever having a meaningful discussion with their parents about sex. Most young people turn to (1) _____ and (2) _____ for information about sex, but much of what they learn is incorrect. The best alternative would be for children to receive factual information in school. Surveys indicate that more than (3) _____ %

of Americans favor sexuality education in school.

Sex is only a part of (4) _____, which encompasses all of the sexual attitudes, feelings, and behaviors associated with being human. Sexual behaviors and attitudes (such as what is considered to be sexually attractive) vary from culture to culture, and can even change within a culture over time. American sexual attitudes are both permissive and repressed, and as a result many people in the United States have ambivalent feelings about sex.

The idea that the primary purpose of sex is for procreation (to have children) originally came from (5) _____, but they also had a very positive attitude about their bodies and sexual pleasure between husbands and wives. The early (6) _____ affirmed the procreational purpose of sex, but completely denied its pleasurable aspects. Sexual desire, even within marriage, was now associated with guilt. The biggest proponent of this view within Christianity was (7) _____. In Western culture, negative attitudes about sex reached their zenith during the reign of (8) _____ of England. During this time, the medical profession contributed many incorrect negative beliefs about engaging in sex, including the belief that excess sex, particularly masturbation, could lead to serious medical problems and eventually to insanity.

The industrial revolution slowly changed Americans' lives, including their sex lives. With shorter workdays and workweeks and greater mobility (e.g., automobiles) than in past generations, people now had more free time to spend together. With the availability of (9) _____ during World War II and the marketing of

(10) _____ in 1960, the United States entered the sexual revolution.

The manner in which society shapes behaviors and attitudes is called (11) _____. There is probably no other socializing agent with as much of an impact on young people's sexual attitudes and behaviors as (12) _____, especially television. Many advertisements, whether on television or in magazines, provide little product information, but instead use sex to sell their products in aprocess called (13) _____. Sexual socialization does not occur as a result of a single exposure, but instead is a slow and cumulative process. The sexual content in the media is omnipresent, but the manner in which sex is portrayed may be just as important as the quantity. The media in (14) _____ show more nudity than in the United States, but the teenage pregnancy rate is much lower.

Because of the antisexual attitudes of the Victorian era, scientific study of human sexuality was slow to develop. (15) _____, who emphasized the sexuality of all people, including children, and (16) _____ , who published seven volumes about the psychology of sex, were two researchers of the Victorian era who attempted to counter antisexual attitudes. However, it has only been within the last 40 years that the scientific and medical communities have accepted sex as a subject for serious discussion and research. The first large-scale surveys were done by (17) _____ in the 1940s and early 1950s. (18) _____ published their physiological investigations of human sexual behavior in 1966. Even today, however, there is some resistance on the part of governmental agencies to fund research on human sexual behavior.

SELF-TEST

A. TRUE OR FALSE

T   F   19. The Old Testament presents a positive view of sex within marriage.

T   F   20. American sexual behaviors are considered to be the norm by the rest of the world.

T   F   21. Because of AIDS, all states now require that public schools offer education about sexually transmitted infections.

T   F   22. The larger the number of people in a survey, the more accurate it always is.

T   F   23. All cultures consider women's breasts to be highly erotic.

T   F   24. Kissing is one sexual behavior that is done worldwide.

T   F   25. One good method of obtaining a random sample is to randomly pick names from a phone book.

T   F   26. Half of all Americans will get at least one sexually transmitted infection in their lifetime.

T   F   27. Over half of all American teenagers have had sexual intercourse by the time they graduate from high school.

T   F   28. The era of permissiveness known as the "sexual revolution" started during the Victorian era.

T   F   29. Kinsey's surveys are a good example of the use of random sampling techniques.

T   F   30. A strong positive correlation between two variables is evidence of a cause-and-effect relationship.

T F 31. Starting in the late 1990s, there has been a decline in the percentage of teenagers engaging in sexual intercourse and in teenage pregnancies.

T F 32. According to historian Phillippe Ariès, the idea of childhood did not exist in medieval society.

T F 33. The biological immaturity of children is an irrefutable fact, but childhood is a social concept.

T F 34. In some cultures girls are expected to marry and begin having intercourse before puberty.

T F 35. School-based sex education is a socializing agent.

T F 36. Children who watch a lot of television shows with sexual content are no more likely than others to have begun sexual intercourse.

T F 37. In a controlled experiment, teenagers who had just watched television shows with a lot of sexual content gave more negative ratings to casual sex than teens who had not watched the programs.

B. MATCHING, PART 1

_____ 38. A Victorian-era physician who emphasized the sexuality of children and adults

_____ 39. He viewed sex for procreation as an unpleasant necessity and equated guilt with sexual desire

_____ 40. Conducted the first large-scale physiological study of human sexual behavior

_____ 41. They believed that the purpose of sex was for procreation, but had a very positive attitude about sexual relations between a husband and wife

_____ 42. They believed in an ascetic philosophy: Wisdom and virtue come from denying physical pleasures

_____ 43. He conducted the first large-scale survey of American sexual attitudes and behaviors

_____ 44. The first major influence on Christian sexual values, he regarded bodily pleasures as evil and thought it "well for a man not to touch a woman"

_____ 45. A Victorian-era sex researcher with a tolerant attitude about sexuality

_____ 46. They held antisexual attitudes that were reinforced by the mistaken medical beliefs of that time

_____ 47. He headed a recent survey of a nationally representative sample of adults living in households

a. Henry Havelock Ellis
b. Edwardians
c. Saint Paul
d. ancient Greeks
e. Jesus
f. Sigmund Freud
g. Masters and Johnson
h. biblical Hebrews
i. Puritans
j. Victorians
k. Saint John
l. Saint Thomas Aquinas
m. Alfred Kinsey
n. Saint Augustine
o. Edward Laumann

C. FILL IN THE BLANKS

48. Anthropologists believe the most sexually repressed society in the world to be the _____.

49. Four important influences that led to the sexual revolution were (a)_____, (b)_____, (c)_____, and (d)_____.

50. A random sample is properly defined as a sample drawn from a population in a manner so that has an equal chance of being selected.

51. _____ believed that intellectual love could lead to immortality.

52. A major influence on early Christian thought was the Greek philosophy of dualism, which separated _____ and _____.

53. Victorian physicians called nocturnal emissions _____ because they believed they were caused by the same thing that causes gonorrhea.

54. In the National Health and Social Life Survey (Laumann et al., 1994), "sex" or "had sex" was defined as _____.

55. _____ has been called "the most powerful storyteller in American culture, one that continually repeats the myths and ideologies, the facts and patterns of relationships that define our world and legitimize the social order" (Brown & Steele, 1996).

SUGGESTED READINGS AND RESOURCES

Bullough, V. L. (1998). Alfred Kinsey and the Kinsey report: Historical overview and lasting contributions. *Journal of Sex Research, 35,* 127–131. Puts Kinsey's contribution in proper perspective.

D'Emilio, J., & Freedman, E. (1988). *Intimate matters: A history of sexuality in America.* New York: Harper & Row. A very scholarly history.

Journal of Moral Education, 26(3), 1997. This issue is devoted exclusively to articles about the debate over sexuality education and how to arrive at a curriculum in a culture with a diversity of religious, ethnic, and sexual groups.

Journal of Sexual Medicine, 7 (Supp15), 2010. This issue was devoted to the results of the 2010 National Survey of Sexual Health and Behavior.

Maier, T. (2009). *Masters of sex. The life and times of William Masters and Virginia Johnson, the couple who taught America how to love.* New York: Basic Books.

Marshall, D. S. (1971, February). Too much in Mangaia. *Psychology Today.*

Messenger, J. L. (1971, February). Sex and repression in an Irish folk community: The lack of the Irish. *Psychology Today.*

Michael, R. T., Gagnon, J. H., Laumann, E. O., & Kolata, G. (1994). *Sex in America: A definitive survey.* Boston: Little, Brown. The condensed, popularized version of the landmark survey conducted by the National Opinion Research Center.

Reichert, T. (2003). Sex in advertising research: A review of content, effects, and functions of sexual information in consumer advertising. In J. R. Heiman & C. M. Davis (Eds.), *Annual review of sex research* (Vol. VIII). Allentown, PA: Society for Scientific Study of Sexuality.

Suggs, D. N., & Miracle, A. W. (1993). *Culture and human sexuality.* Pacific Grove, CA: Brooks/Cole. Cross-cultural essays about human sexuality.

Wiederman, M. W. (2001). *Understanding sexuality research.* Belmont, CA: Wadsworth Thomson Learning. A short, but excellent book on methodology problems in sex research with many real-world examples.

Kinsey Institute for Research in Sex, Gender, and Reproduction Indiana University
Morrison Hall 302
1165 E. Third Street
Bloomington, IN 47405
www.indiana.edu/~kinsey
Kinsey Library (E-mail):
    kinsey@indiana.edu

SIECUS (Sex Information and Education Council of the U.S.)
130 West 42nd Street, Suite 350
New York, NY 10036-7802
(212) 819-9770
www.siecus.org

Society for the Scientific Study of Sex
P.O. Box 416
Allentown, PA 18105-0416
(610) 530-2483
www.sexscience.org

Our Sexual and Reproductive Anatomy

So God created man in his own image, in the image of
God he created him; male and female he created them.

—Genesis 1:27, Revised Standard Version

Many of the first words that we learn are anatomical
terms. Parents often spend hours teaching their young
children to point to and name different parts of the
body, such as the mouth, eyes, ears, and nose.
Unfortunately, when naming body parts, many parents
simply skip from arms, chest, and "tummy" to legs,
knees, and feet, completely omitting any mention of
the genitals and anus. Other parents teach their children the correct anatomical words for all other parts of
the body, but substitute such "cute" words as
"weeney," "booty," "peanut," and "talleywacker" for
the genitals. As for the functions of this mysterious
body area, many of us are simply taught during toilet
training to make "pee-pees" and "poo-poos." Although
some adults became sexually experienced without
ever knowing the correct anatomical terms, many others who know better nevertheless feel very uncomfortable about teaching their children to say the words
"penis" and "vagina."

As we grow older, we learn new words from our
peers that describe our sexual anatomy and behavior, but quite often these are slang terms. Men are
more likely than women to use slang terms when referring to the **genitalia** (and generally use a greater
number of terms) (Braun & Kitzinger, 2001; Fischer,
1989). Many of the slang terms have negative connotations. Interestingly, both men and women are
likely to have a negative opinion of those who use
sexually degrading terms for female genitals
(Murnen, 2000).

Slang terms can also result in misinformation
about sexual anatomy and behavior. In response to
an item on a questionnaire given on the first day
of my class, many students indicated that they believed that an erection in men occurs when a bone

*When you have finished studying this chapter,
you should be able to:*

- Describe each part of the external female
  anatomy—mons veneris, labia majora, labia
  minora, clitoris, and vaginal and urethral
  openings—and explain its function(s).

- Discuss attitudes about an intact hymen and their
  implications for women of different cultures.

- Understand why early detection of breast cancer
  can save lives and explain how to perform a breast
  self-examination.

- Explain the risks associated with breast augmentation
  operations.

- Describe each of the female internal anatomical
  structures—vagina, uterus, Fallopian tubes, and
  ovaries—and explain its function(s).

- Explain the importance of pelvic examinations and
  Pap smears for women's health.

- Describe each of the structures of the external and
  internal male anatomy—penis, scrotum, testicles,
  epididymis, vas deferens, ejaculatory ducts, urethra,
  prostate gland, seminal vesicles, and Cowper's
  glands—and explain its function(s).

- Discuss the advantages and disadvantages of
  circumcision of the penis.

- Explain how to perform a testicular self-examination.

- Identify the early signs of prostate problems and
  understand the importance of regular prostate
  examinations for men's health.

- Describe how other parts of the body (lips, mouth,
  hair, buttocks, etc.) may also be considered part of
  our sexual anatomy.

Genitalia ■ The external reproductive organs of the man or
woman.

33

protrudes from the base of the penis. This belief should not be surprising, for after all, why else would an erection be called a "boner"? Slang terms such as "cherry," "nuts," and "pussy" can be misleading.

There is perhaps no better example of the distorted negative attitudes that some people have toward sex than the common use of the word "fuck" instead of intercourse. It is frequently used to express displeasure ("What the fuck is going on here?"), trouble ("I got fucked over at work"), or aggression ("Fuck you!"). At many other times we think of sexual intercourse as a pleasurable experience. The word "fuck" probably originated from the Middle English word "fucken." At one time its use was not considered improper, but the word acquired negative connotations in the mid-1600s.

It is not my intent to teach "dirty" words or slang terminology. In fact, people who take courses in human sexuality often end up using the proper terms more frequently (Fischer, 1989). We must acknowledge the fact, however, that many of us come to class with a sexual vocabulary that consists almost entirely of slang words. The question that many students have, of course, is, "What good will it do to learn the correct anatomical terms, which are almost always Latin or Greek?" The lack of such knowledge obviously does not hinder most people from becoming sexually experienced. Learning correct anatomical terms may result in our becoming less inhibited about our own bodies and those of our partners. Many people are so ashamed of their genitals that they do not consider their genitals to be a positive part of their anatomy. This is more often true of women than men (Reinholtz & Muehlenhard, 1995). Here are a few comments that I have received from students.

> "As for the illustrations in Chapter 2, I thought they were good and very well illustrated, but they were rather embarrassing to look at."

> "Figure 2–3 made me feel uncomfortable. I felt as if everyone could see me."

> "The pictures in this chapter were quite graphic. I wish they were on another separate page so that we wouldn't have to look at them the entire time we read a particular page. Even just reading this by myself was a little embarrassing."

> "I had difficulties looking at the pictures without embarrassment and shame. I should be able to look without any bad feelings."

No one should feel embarrassed or ashamed about any part of his or her own body, including the genitals. If you have never done so, I encourage you to examine yourself during this part of the course.

Vulva ■ A term for the external female genitalia, including the mons veneris, labia majora, labia minora, clitoris, vaginal opening, and urethral opening.

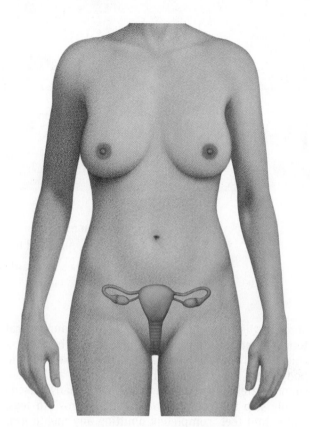

FIGURE 2–1 Anatomical location of the female reproductive system.

PERSONAL REFLECTIONS

Do you use sexual slang terms (a) to refer to your genitalia or (b) when you are upset? Why? If you do, list the terms you use, then write down the correct word next to each. Say each correct term out loud a few times. Are you comfortable or uncomfortable doing this? Could you use these terms in normal conversation without being embarrassed or uncomfortable? If you cannot, why not? After all, you probably use the slang terms.

EXTERNAL FEMALE ANATOMY

You can see the location of the female reproductive system in Figure 2–1. A picture of the external female genitalia, collectively known as the **vulva** (Latin for "covering"), is shown in Figure 2–2. The vulva consists of the mons veneris, the labia majora, the labia minora, the clitoris, and the vaginal and urethral openings. When examining herself (which requires use of a hand mirror), a woman should not consider herself to be abnormal if she does not look identical to the drawing in Figure 2–2. As with all other parts of the body, women's genitalia vary in appearance from person to person, differing in size, shape, and color (see Figure 2–3). The positive or negative feelings that a woman has toward her genitalia are directly related to her participation in and enjoyment of sexual activity (Reinholtz & Muehlenhard, 1995).

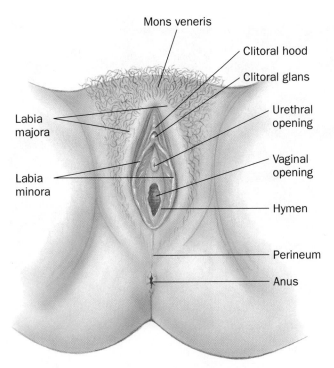

Mons veneris

Clitoral hood

Clitoral glans

Urethral opening

Labia majora

Vaginal opening

Labia minora

Hymen

Perineum

Anus

FIGURE 2–2 The female genitalia (vulva), with the labia parted to show the vaginal and urethral openings.

Source: *Hock, Human Sexuality,* © 2007 Prentice Hall, Inc. Reproduced by permission of Pearson Education, Inc.

The Mons Veneris

Translated from Latin, **mons veneris** means "mount of Venus." The term refers to the soft layer of fatty tissue overlaying the area where the pubic bones come together. Venus, of course, was the Roman goddess of love, and the mons area is considered to be very erotic after puberty, when it becomes covered with hair.

Our sensitivity to touch is dependent on the density of nerve endings in a particular area of skin. Areas such as the lips and fingertips have a high density of nerve endings and thus are very sensitive to touch, while areas such as the back have a much lower density of nerve endings and are much less sensitive to touch. Because of numerous nerve endings in the mons area, many women find gentle stimulation of the mons pleasurable.

The soft layer of fatty tissue cushions the pubic region during intercourse, but one can only speculate as to what purpose nature intended *pubic hair* to serve. Some researchers believe that this pocket of hair on an otherwise mostly hairless body is meant to be sexually attractive.

Until the 1970s, it was uncommon for women to shave their pubic area. This changed as bikini bottoms and panties became smaller. At first, women just trimmed their pubic hair or got bikini waxes, but today it is very common for women to shave or wax most or all of their hair (Ursus, 2004). Unfortunately,

this has led many people to have negative attitudes about women who do not shave and many women now feel pressured to do so. Here are some representative attitudes from students in my course.

Men:

"I don't have any preference when it comes to women's pubic hair. Sometimes shaved can be more attractive, but both are equally acceptable."

"Personally, I like hair. To me it looks more appealing with hair on the vagina. But too much hair is a turn off. I like hair to be trimmed."

"I do not like women's pubic hair at all. It is much more attractive to see a girl with none. Pubic hair can sometimes be a turn off."

"I think that women's pubes are kind of a turn off depending on how much they have. If they've got a jungle down there I don't want to mess with it."

"I feel that female pubic hair is gross. I can't imagine playing in a jungle, so I feel that it's common courtesy for a woman to at least trim."

"I think pubic hair on a woman is disgusting. Women should never have hair on their bodies unless it is their heads. Men, however, can have pubic hair. It is manly."

Women:

"I am a very neat person when it comes to my appearance. Since women shave their underarms and legs, why not shave other body parts too? Being smooth and hairless makes me feel sexy."

"I shave pubic hair because it is gross and annoying. I do not see why it is any different than shaving your legs. Plus pubic hair gets in the way during menstruation."

"I started shaving my pubic hair early on. I felt personally that it was just bad hygiene not to, when boys would hook up with girls that had not shaved they would talk like it was disgusting. I didn't want to be that girl."

"I prefer being fully shaved, and my boyfriend likes it too. It started in early high school. A lot of guys made fun of girls who weren't shaved. So I guess it started as a peer pressure thing, but now I like it. I feel sexier."

"I shave my pubic hair because one time a guy I liked said he wouldn't have sex with me unless I shaved it. Just hearing him say that made me wish I never had pubic hair."

"I shave my bikini area, but not completely. If a man doesn't like it, he can get over it."

Mons veneris ■ The soft layer of fatty tissue that overlays the pubic bone in women. It becomes covered with pubic hair during puberty.

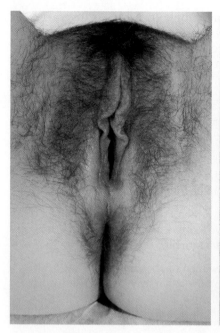
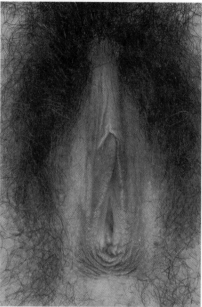
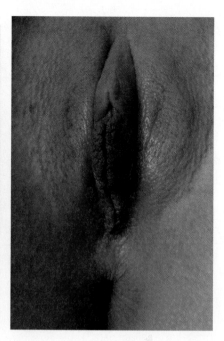

FIGURE 2–3 Some variations in the appearance of female genitalia.

"Anytime a girl becomes sexually active, they become very insecure about what their partner will think of their body, especially pubic hair. Shaving is painful, time consuming, and just a nuisance. Most girls assume guys like shaven because that's how most women in the media are portrayed. Models wearing next to nothing; it's obvious they shave, but most women aren't models and don't need to be hairless for a photo shoot. Pubic hair is part of a woman's body and should be embraced, not something to be ashamed of."

PERSONAL REFLECTIONS

What do you think have been the major socializing agents leading to the change in attitude about women's pubic hair during the last 3–4 decades? Is this change in attitude good? Should women be made to feel self-conscious or ashamed about yet another part of their bodies?

Labia majora ■ Two elongated folds of skin extending from the mons to the perineum in women. Its outer surfaces become covered with pubic hair during puberty.

Labia minora ■ Two hairless elongated folds of skin located between the labia majora in women. They meet above the clitoris to form the clitoral hood.

Perineum ■ Technically, the entire pelvic floor, but more commonly used to refer to the hairless bit of skin between the anus and either the vaginal opening (in women) or the scrotum (in men).

Clitoral hood ■ The part of the labia minora that covers the clitoris in women.

Bartholin's glands ■ Glands located at the base of the labia minora in women that contribute a small amount of an alkaline fluid to their inner surfaces during sexual arousal.

The Labia

The labia consist of two outer (**labia majora,** or major lips) and two inner (**labia minora,** or minor lips) elongated folds of skin, which, in the sexually unstimulated state, cover (and thus protect) the vaginal and urethral openings. The labia majora extend from the mons to the hairless bit of skin between the vaginal opening and the anus, called the **perineum.** The outer surfaces of the labia majora become covered with hair at the time of puberty. After childbirth it is not uncommon for the labia majora to remain separated to some extent in the unstimulated state.

The pinkish and hairless labia minora are located between, and sometimes protrude beyond, the labia majora. Among some African groups, particularly the Hottentots, elongation of the labia minora is considered to be highly erotic, and girls are taught to pull on them from early childhood. Some "Hottentot Aprons," as they are called, can protrude as much as 7 inches.

The labia minora, which meet at the top to form the **clitoral hood** (or *prepuce*), are very sensitive to touch. They have numerous blood vessels that become engorged with blood during sexual stimulation, causing them to swell and turn bright red or wine colored.

Located at the base of the labia minora are the **Bartholin's glands,** which, during prolonged stimulation, contribute a few drops of an alkaline fluid to the inner surfaces via ducts. The small amount of fluid does not make a significant contribution to vaginal lubrication during sexual intercourse, but it does help to counteract the normal acidity of the outer vagina (sperm cannot live in an acidic environment).

Piercing of the labia and clitoral hood has become increasingly popular in recent years. However, the practice is associated with a significant number of problems (Meltzer, 2005).

The Clitoris

The **clitoris** (from a Greek word meaning "hill" or "slope") develops from the same embryonic tissue as the penis, but has twice as many nerve endings as the much larger penis, making it extremely sensitive to touch. In fact, it is the only structure in either men or women with no known function other than to focus sexual sensations (Masters & Johnson, 1970). The only visible portion is the *glans*, which in a sexually unaroused woman looks like a small, shiny button located just below the hood of skin formed where the two labia minora meet.

The body, or *shaft*, of the clitoris is located beneath the clitoral hood. It is about 1 inch long and one-quarter inch in diameter. The clitoris contains two parallel cylinders of spongy tissue called *corpora cavernosa*, which toward the rear form much larger structures called *crura* (Latin for "legs") that fan out and attach to the pubic bone (O'Connell & DeLancey, 2005). The spongy tissues of the clitoris become engorged with blood during sexual arousal. This causes the clitoris to increase in size; but because of the way it is attached to the pubic bone, the clitoris does not actually become erect like the penis. If sexual stimulation continues, the clitoris pulls back against the pubic bone and disappears from view beneath the clitoral hood.

Contrary to what some people may believe, the sexual pleasure of women is not related to the size of the clitoris (Money, 1970). Another popular myth is that women are more sexually responsive the shorter the distance between the vaginal opening and clitoral glans (so that the penis can more easily stimulate the clitoris); but this, too, is untrue. The penis, in fact, usually does not come into direct contact with the clitoris during sexual intercourse. The thrusting of the penis only indirectly stimulates the clitoris, by causing the clitoral hood to rub back and forth over the glans.

Surgical removal of the clitoris was sometimes performed in the United States and Europe during Victorian times in order to prevent girls from masturbating and growing up "oversexed." *Clitoridectomy* is no longer legally performed in America, but it is very common in Northern African countries and parts of the Middle East, Malaysia, and Indonesia (see Box 4–A).

Thick secretions called *smegma* can accumulate beneath the clitoral hood and result in discomfort during sexual intercourse by causing the glans to stick to the clitoral hood. The secretions can generally be washed off, however, by bathing thoroughly.

The Vaginal Opening

The vaginal and urethral openings are visible only if the labia minora are parted. The area between the two labia minora is sometimes referred to as the **vestibular area** (Latin for "entrance hall") and the vaginal opening as the *introitus* (Latin for "entrance"). The vaginal opening has lots of nerve endings and thus is very sensitive to stimulation. It is surrounded by the **bulbocavernosus muscle,** a ring of sphincter muscles similar to the sphincter muscles surrounding the anus. Sexually experienced women can learn to voluntarily contract or relax these muscles during intercourse. In sexually inexperienced women, on the other hand, these muscles may involuntarily contract as a result of extreme nervousness, making penetration very difficult. The **vestibular bulbs,** which are located underneath the sphincter muscles on both sides of the vaginal opening, also help the vagina grip the penis by swelling with blood during sexual arousal.

In sexually inexperienced women, a thin membrane called the **hymen** (named after the Greek god of marriage) may partially cover the opening to the vagina. This membrane is found only in human females. Until shortly before birth, the hymen separates the vagina from the urinary system. It ruptures after birth, but in humans remains as a fold of membrane around the vaginal opening. It is found in all normal newborn girls (Berenson, 1993). The hymen may have one or more openings that allow for passage of menstrual flow. In the rare instance that the hymen has no opening, a simple surgical incision can be made at the time of first menstruation.

The hymen has no known physiological function, but the presence of the hymen has been used by men throughout history as proof of virginity (Blank, 2007). In the time of the biblical Hebrews, a newly wed woman who did not bleed during first intercourse was sometimes stoned to death:

But if the thing is true, that the tokens of virginity were not found in the young woman, then they shall bring out the young woman to the door of her

Clitoris ■ A small, elongated erectile structure in women that develops from the same embryonic tissue as the penis. It has no known function other than to focus sexual sensations.

Vestibular area ■ A term used to refer to the area between the two labia minora.

Bulbocavernosus muscle ■ A ring of sphincter muscles that surrounds the vaginal opening in women or the root of the penis in men.

Vestibular bulbs ■ Structures surrounding the vaginal opening that fill with blood during sexual arousal, resulting in swelling of the tissues and a narrowing of the vaginal opening.

Hymen ■ The thin membrane that partially covers the vaginal opening in many sexually inexperienced women. Its presence or absence, however, is really a very poor indicator of prior sexual experience.

father's house, and the men of her city shall stone her to death with stones, because she has wrought folly in Israel by playing the harlot in her father's house.... *(Deuteronomy 22:20–21, Revised Standard Version)*

Even today, in many parts of the world a newly wed wife can be divorced or exiled if her husband believes her to be unchaste. Many Muslims, Chinese, and Moroccans display a bloodstained sheet on the wedding night as proof of a new bride's chastity. In other cultures, girls are ritually "deflowered" with stone phalluses or horns. Although these extreme customs are not found in Western culture, many American men nevertheless expect their female partners to bleed during first intercourse.

> "When my girlfriend and I first had intercourse it was just understood by listening to my peers that she was supposed to bleed and I should see some kind of skin hanging (hymen). This didn't happen and for years it bothered me because I thought she lied to me when she told me that I was her first. It wasn't until after taking this course that I realized how ignorant my friends and I were."

> "Being very athletic came natural for me and by the time I was 12, I had won four athletic trophies and many certificates. My mother took me to a doctor right after I turned 14 and he told her that I was not a virgin because my hymen was not in place. I cried for 2 weeks. It was not true. My life was very traumatic for the next 6 months. Now at 40 years old, I am still angry."

(All examples are from the author's files.)

In actuality, there is often very little bleeding or discomfort during first sexual intercourse. The hymen sometimes ruptures during insertion of a tampon, and in some women the opening in the hymen only stretches rather than tears during first intercourse (thus there would be no bleeding). Untold millions of women throughout history have probably suffered much grief (and even death) for failing to display what many men wrongly believe is the appropriate response to first intercourse.

The Urethral Opening

Urine passes from the bladder through a small tube called the **urethra** and out the urethral opening, which is located below the clitoris and above the

Urethra ■ The passageway from the bladder to the exterior of the body. In men, it also serves as a passageway for semen during ejaculation.

Breasts ■ In women, glands that provide milk for infants; located at the front of the chest.

Mammary glands ■ Milk-producing glands of the breast.

vaginal opening. A man's urethra serves for the passage of sperm as well as urine, but a woman's urinary system is not related to her reproductive system. Women are more susceptible to urinary tract infections than men. Many factors increase the risk, including recent sexual intercourse and rectal bacteria (see Chapter 5).

The Breasts

Although **breasts** are not part of a woman's reproductive system, they are considered to be highly erotic by most men in Western societies, and therefore we must consider them part of a woman's sexual anatomy. Recall from Chapter 1, however, that women's breasts have no erotic significance in many cultures around the world.

Breasts develop at puberty as a result of increasing levels of the hormone *estrogen*, which is produced by the ovaries. Thus, the breasts are really a secondary sex characteristic, just as pubic hair is. Interestingly, it is common for one breast (usually the left) to be slightly larger than the other.

Each adult breast consists of 15 to 20 **mammary (milk-producing) glands** (see Figure 2–4). A separate duct connects each gland to the *nipple*, which is made up of smooth muscle fibers and also has lots of nerve fibers (making the nipples sensitive to touch). When a woman becomes sexually aroused, the smooth muscle fibers contract and the nipples become erect. The darkened area around the nipple, called the *areola*, becomes even darker during pregnancy. The small bumps on the areola are glands that secrete oil to keep the nipples lubricated during breast-feeding. For those who are interested, nipple piercing apparently does not interfere with breast-feeding in the future (Martin, 1999).

In the late stage of pregnancy, a hormone called *prolactin* from the pituitary gland (at the base of the brain) causes the mammary glands to start producing milk (called *lactation*). A baby's sucking on the nipple causes the pituitary to produce the hormone *oxytocin*, which results in the ejection of milk. There can also be secretions from the breasts at other times (a condition known as *galactorrhea*) as a result of certain drugs, birth control pills, stress, or rough fabrics rubbing against the breasts. Some people, including men, have inverted nipples or an extra nipple, but this generally does not pose a health problem.

Breasts vary in size from woman to woman (see Figure 2–5). Breast size is not determined by the number of mammary glands, which is about the same for all women, but by the amount of fatty (adipose) tissue packed between the glands. This is determined primarily by heredity. There is no relation between breast size and sensitivity to touch (Masters & Johnson, 1966). Large breasts do not

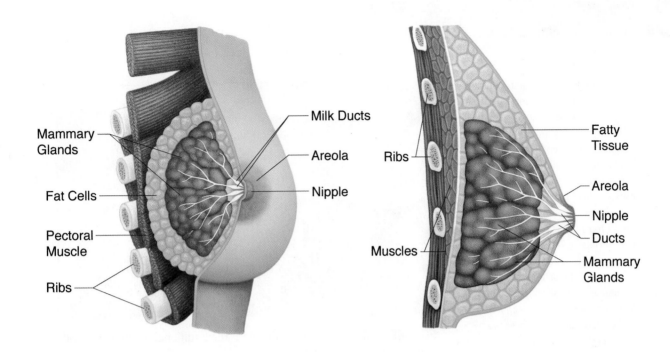

FIGURE 2–4 Anatomy of the female breast.

have a greater number of nerve endings than small breasts. Nevertheless, because of the attention that many men give to breast size, some women attempt to enlarge their breasts.

Breast augmentation exercises and the lotions and mechanical devices advertised in women's magazines do not work (remember, breast size is determined by the amount of fatty tissue). In the 1960s, plastic surgeons began implanting soft pouches filled with silicone to increase the size of breasts. About 200,000 American women have their breasts enlarged in this manner each year, 80% of them for cosmetic purposes (Springen, 2003). However, complications are common. Sooner or later, most implants begin to leak. This initially raised concerns about the possibility of cancer and autoimmune disease. As a result, manufacturers began making saline-filled implants.

However, the Institute of Medicine concluded that there was no evidence that silicone implants caused cancer or connective tissue disease (see S. L. Brown, 2002), and after temporarily removing them from the market the Food and Drug Administration approved their use again in 2005.

One study found that nearly 15% of women who receive breast implants (silicone or saline) a painful fibrous capsule forms around the implant (called capsular contracture), making the breast hard, tight, unnatural in appearance, and often requiring additional surgery (Hvilsom et al., 2009). Another study found that the number of these complications was 25% (S. L. Brown, 2002). Talk-show host Jenny Jones has had six operations because of the damage her implants did to her breasts. She was quoted in *People* magazine as saying, "I hate my

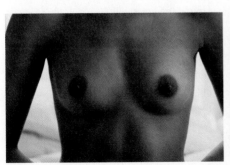
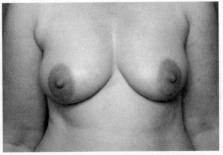
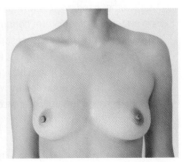

FIGURE 2–5 Some variations in the appearance of female breasts.

Box 2–A Sexuality and Health

Breast Cancer and Examination

Apart from skin cancer, cancer of the breast is the most common type of cancer (and the second leading cause of cancer death) in women, with 192,000 new cases and over 40,000 deaths per year (American Cancer Society, 2010). One in 8 American women will develop breast cancer in her lifetime. A fact that is less well known is that men can get breast cancer too and the number of cases has been increasing (about 1,900 men will be diagnosed this year) (Onami et al., 2010).

Some of the factors that put a woman at high risk include a family history of breast cancer (about 5% to 10% of new cases are caused by an inherited gene mutation), extensive dense breast tissue, being older than 50 years (most women with breast cancer are postmenopausal), never having given birth or having the first child after age 30, starting menstruation before age 12, or undergoing menopause after age 55 (see Armstrong et al., 2000; Li et al., 2008; Lichtenstein et al., 2000; Smith & Saslow, 2002). Other risk factors include obesity, alcohol consumption, and smoking (Smith & Saslow, 2002).

A majority of breast cancers (especially in postmenopausal women) are fueled by the female hormone estrogen (Rosenfeld, 2005). Most birth control pills contain estrogen, but the current consensus is that if the birth control pill does increase the risk, the increase is only very slight, and only with long-term use or in women with the inherited gene mutation (Collaborative Group on Hormonal, 1996; Narod et al., 2002; Romieu et al., 1990). On the other hand, there is now conclusive evidence that long-term hormone replacement therapy for postmenopausal women increases the risk of breast cancer (Manson et al., 2003; see Chapter 10 in this text). There is hope that we will eventually have a breast-cancer vaccine (Jaini et al., 2010).

Mammogram ■ Low-radiation X-rays used to detect breast tumors.

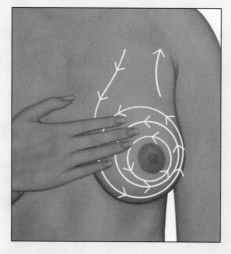 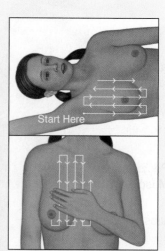

FIGURE 2–6 Breast self-examination: the traditional method (left) and new alternative method (right).

About half of all cases of breast cancer have spread beyond the breast before they are discovered. However, with early detection, there is a 96% survival rate (American Cancer Society, 2010). Unfortunately, there is currently a big controversy about what women should do to detect breast cancer early. The American Cancer Society (2010) recommends that women should examine their breasts on a monthly basis starting at age 20 and have a **mammogram** (breast X-ray) every 1 to 2 years between the ages of 40 and 49 and an annual mammogram after the age of 50. On the other hand, an independent panel of experts recommended against self-exams and routine mammograms before the age of 50, claiming that the procedures resulted in too many false positives, unnecessary biopsies, and saved very few lives (U.S. Preventive Services Task Force, 2009). So, what should you do? Consult with your doctor and decide with him or her what is best for you. If you wish to conduct self-exams, the best time is immediately after menstruation ends, when estrogen levels are low and the breasts are not tender or swollen. First look at yourself in front of a mirror. Do this with your hands at your sides, then with your hands on your hips, and finally with your hands raised above your head. Look for any bulging, flattening, dimpling, or redness. The symptoms are usually painless. In each position, examine one breast with the opposite hand. With fingers flat, press gently in small circular motions, starting at the top, and check the outermost part of the entire breast in clockwise fashion (see Figure 2–6). It is normal to have a ridge of firm tissue in the lower curve of each breast. After you have completed the circle, move your fingers an inch closer to the nipple and make another complete check around the breast. At least three to four complete circles around the breast will be required. Be sure to examine under your arms as well, because this is one of the most common areas for cancer to occur. In addition, examine the nipple by squeezing it and noting any discharge. Repeat the same procedure on the other breast. An alternative method of examining the breasts in which you examine yourself with vertical strips has been gaining in popularity (Barton et al., 1999).

Whichever method you use, report any suspected abnormality to your doctor immediately.

"I am a 33-year-old nurse that has instructed many other women about self-examination, but unfortunately, did not practice what I preached. After one of your lectures I did examine my breasts and was horrified to find a small lump."
(from the author's files)

Eight out of 10 lumps that are discovered are benign (noncancerous) cysts (fluid-filled sacs) or fibroadenomas (solid tumors). They are known as *fibrocystic disease* and (because they are rare after menopause) are believed to be caused by hormones. Therefore, do not panic if you find a lump in your breast, as the chances are good that it is not malignant.

Should you have a lump and it is diagnosed as cancerous, a number of surgical procedures might be performed: (1) radical *mastectomy*, in which the entire breast, underlying muscle, and lymph nodes are removed; (2) simple mastectomy, in which only the breast is removed; and (3) *lumpectomy*, in which only the lump and a small bit of surrounding tissue are removed, followed by radiation therapy. Studies show that *with early detection*, lumpectomy and radiation treatment are as effective as radical mastectomy (Fisher et al., 1995). If one or both breasts have to be removed, breast reconstruction through plastic surgery is often possible (over 50,000 breast cancer patients choose to do this every year).

Whatever the therapy, it is not uncommon for women with breast cancer to experience sexual problems and the need to make adjustments (Meyerowitz et al., 1999; Moyer, 1997). The reaction of a woman's partner is important. For example, a woman who has had a breast removed needs to be reassured that she is not going to be desired or loved less than before. Would you expect your partner to love you less if you lost a toe, foot, leg, finger, hand, or arm? Of course not. So why should it be any different if she loses a breast? This may seem obvious to you, but your partner will probably want to hear you say it.

"I came from a family consisting of five daughters and no one had ever been diagnosed with breast cancer. I had never given it a thought that I would be the one to have a lump in my breast.... I had a modified radical mastectomy of my left breast.... When my doctor told my husband and me my husband was wonderful about it. All you need to get over the shock is an understanding and supportive husband and family. Emotionally I was able to get over the surgery because he never made me feel like 'half' a woman."
(from the author's files)

For more information and for help in finding the most appropriate tests and therapies, call the National Cancer Institute hotline: 1-800-4-CANCER.

PERSONAL REFLECTIONS (women)

Do you regularly examine your breasts for abnormal lumps? If the answer is no, why not? The Centers for Disease Control and Prevention report that nearly 85% of women aged 40 or older have had a mammogram (Blackman et al., 1999). If you are in this age group and have not had one, why not?

body a thousand times more now than I ever did before.... I would sell everything I own to be able to have the body back that I gave up." Students in my class have relayed similar experiences:

"My mom had a breast augmentation job done about 2 years ago and has had nothing but problems. She started growing too much scar tissue and lumps in her breasts, and now, after all the pain and money and aggravation she went through, she's having them removed this summer. I know she did it for my dad, but she can never tell me enough times how sorry she is she ever did it."

Many naturally large-breasted women would like to be smaller. One common reason is that nearly all very large-breasted women suffer from bad back pain (Kerrigan, 1999):

"I currently wear a DD cup.... My chest has become a large nuisance. It is hard for me to dance, jog, or do any kind of activity that involves moving around a lot. Finding clothes is very hard.... I just recently talked to a friend of mine who had a breast reduction. I really want to have this operation. It would make me feel better about myself."

PERSONAL REFLECTIONS (women)

Do you wish you had different-sized or different-shaped breasts? How would you like to be different? Why? Should a woman's breast size be an important factor in sexually pleasing a partner?

INTERNAL FEMALE ANATOMY

The vagina, uterus, Fallopian tubes, and ovaries are often referred to as a woman's reproductive system (see Figure 2–7). The vagina serves as a depository for the man's sperm. Eggs are produced by the ovaries. During a woman's reproductive years, one or more eggs will mature on a monthly basis and will be released from an ovary and picked up by one of the Fallopian tubes. It is in the Fallopian tube that an egg and a sperm unite to start a new living being. The fertilized egg then travels through the tube and implants itself within the uterus (see Chapter 7).

The Vagina

We have already discussed the vaginal opening as part of the genitalia or external anatomy, but the **vagina** (Latin for "sheath") is really an internal structure located behind the bladder and in front of the rectum. It serves not only as a depository for sperm during sexual intercourse but also as the birth canal, and thus is capable of expanding to about 4 inches in diameter. Many of the derogatory slang terms that men use to describe female genitals imply that it is "simply a hole to be filled" (Braun & Kitzinger, 2001). However, the vagina is not an open orifice always ready to accommodate the insertion of a penis. In the unstimulated state, it is about 3 to 5 inches long and its walls are collapsed. It is not until a woman becomes sexually aroused that the walls of the inner two thirds of the vagina begin to expand to accommodate a penis. The vaginal opening actually narrows during sexual arousal (see Chapter 4).

The vaginal walls have three layers. The inner layer has a soft mucosal surface similar to that of the inside of the mouth. Before puberty, the walls of the vagina are thin and relatively inelastic. The rising levels of female hormones at puberty cause the vaginal walls to thicken and become more elastic and highly vascularized (i.e., having lots of blood vessels). Vaginal lubrication during sexual arousal results from the walls of the vagina becoming filled with blood, with the resulting pressure causing fluid (super-filtered blood plasma) to be secreted from the mucosal lining. At menopause (the time in life when a woman's reproductive capacity ends) the ovaries atrophy, and the consequent loss of hormones causes the walls of the vagina to again become thin and inelastic, similar to their condition before puberty. There is also a decrease in the blood supply to the vaginal walls after menopause, resulting in decreased vaginal lubrication, and thus many

older women may require a lubricant during sexual intercourse.

The vagina is a self-cleansing organ. Many potentially harmful bacteria from the outside environment are destroyed by other bacteria that are found naturally within the vagina. In addition, the walls of the vagina continually secrete fluids that help to maintain an acidic environment. A healthy vagina has a musky odor. Vaginal odors act as a sexual stimulant to the males in most mammalian species and in laboratory studies most men do not find musky vaginal odors offensive (Hassett, 1978). However, if a person hears enough dirty jokes and stories about vaginal odors before becoming sexually experienced, he or she will come to believe this, even though it is not true. How did these stories get started? Probably because most women will occasionally get a vaginal infection that can be accompanied by a foul odor (you will read about vaginal infections in Chapter 5). These infections can be easily and quickly cured. In order to sell their products, however, advertisers of feminine hygiene sprays and douches imply that vaginal odors are always offensive and must be masked with a perfumed substance. The fact is that these products do not cure vaginal infections; in fact, they often make them worse by further changing the chemical environment of the vagina.

> "A year ago I started using a feminine hygiene deodorant spray. I had used this spray for an average of 5 months before I realized that my discharge was abnormal. After talking with my doctor I found that I had a yeast infection. All of this could have been avoided if I had only stayed away from feminine deodorant sprays."
> (from the author's files)

Studies have found that regular douching increases the risk of sexually transmitted infections, bacterial vaginosis, pelvic inflammatory disease (a serious infection of a woman's reproductive system; see Chapter 5), and ectopic pregnancy (Klebanoff et al., 2010; Tsai et al., 2009; Zhang et al., 1997). Women should avoid using douches unless told to do so by a physician.

PERSONAL REFLECTIONS

Women, do you have any anxieties or insecurities about whether your vaginal odors may be offensive? Do you use feminine hygiene products or douche regularly? If so, why? If you answered "yes," how did you acquire these negative feelings about the female body? Men, have you ever told a joke, or laughed at a joke, about offensive vaginal odors? If so, how would you feel (and how would it affect feelings about your own sexuality) if women commonly told jokes about offensive penis odors?

Vagina ■ The sheathlike canal in a woman that extends from the vulva to the cervix and that receives the penis during intercourse.

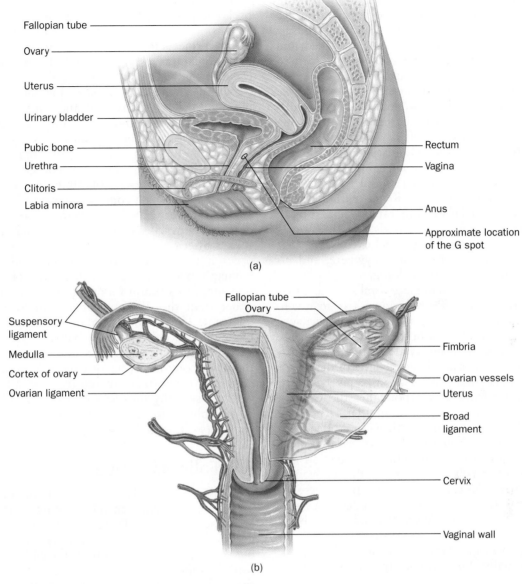

Fallopian tube

Ovary

Uterus

Urinary bladder

Pubic bone

Urethra

Clitoris

Labia minora

Rectum

Vagina

Anus

Approximate location of the G spot

(a)

Suspensory ligament

Medulla

Cortex of ovary

Ovarian ligament

Fallopian tube

Ovary

Fimbria

Ovarian vessels

Uterus

Broad ligament

Cervix

Vaginal wall

(b)

FIGURE 2–7 (a) The internal female reproductive system, viewed from the side. (b) A frontal view of the internal female reproductive system.

Source: Hock, *Human Sexuality,* © 2007 Prentice Hall, Inc. Reproduced by permission of Pearson Education, Inc.

Although the vaginal opening is very sensitive to touch, the walls of the inner two thirds of the vagina are relatively insensitive to touch as a result of having few nerve endings. It has been demonstrated that some women cannot even tell when their inner vaginal walls are being touched by a probe (Kinsey et al., 1953). Does this mean that the presence of a penis in the vagina does not contribute to a woman's subjective feelings of pleasure during sexual intercourse? Not necessarily. Although the vaginal walls are sparse in nerve endings, the vagina is surrounded by a large muscle, the **pubococcygeus (PC) muscle,** which is more richly innervated with nerves. It has been found that women who have little vaginal sensation during intercourse (some report that they cannot even feel the penis) have a weak pubococcygeus muscle (Kegel, 1952). As a result, some sex therapists have advocated daily exercises to strengthen this muscle in order to enhance pleasure during sexual intercourse (Barbach, 1976; Graber, 1982; Perry &

Pubococcygeus muscle ■ The major muscle in the pelvic region. In women, voluntary control over this muscle (to help prevent urinary incontinence or to enhance physical sensations during intercourse) is gained through Kegel exercises.

Whipple, 1981). These exercises, called **Kegel exercises,** are the same ones that many physicians instruct women to do after having a baby, in order to regain urinary control. The pubococcygeus muscle controls urine flow, but it becomes stretched and weak during pregnancy, causing many women to suffer from urinary incontinence.

Here are the steps for doing Kegel exercises: (1) Learn what it feels like to contract the PC muscle by stopping yourself in the middle of urinating with your legs apart; (2) after you know what it feels like to contract the PC muscle, insert a finger into your vagina and bear down until you can feel the muscle squeeze your finger; and (3) once you can do this, start doing daily Kegels without a finger inserted. Physicians and therapists suggest practicing 10 contractions of 3 seconds each three times a day. The best thing about Kegel exercises is that they can be done anytime and anywhere, and no one else knows what you are doing.

There is an exception to the general statement that the vaginal walls are relatively insensitive to touch. The second one fifth of the front wall has a richer supply of nerves than the rest of the vagina (Song et al., 2009). In fact, some women have a small very sensitive spot in this area (at about the level of the top of the pubic bone) (see Figure 2–7a). This has been named the **Grafenberg (G) spot,** after the German doctor who first reported it in 1950 (Perry & Whipple, 1981). Stimulation of the G spot often leads to an orgasm that some women say feels different from an orgasm caused by clitoral stimulation (see Chapter 4). Originally it was claimed that all women had a G spot (Ladas et al., 1982), but later studies suggested that only 10% or fewer women have this area of heightened sensitivity (Alzate & Londono, 1984).

One in every 4,000 to 5,000 girls is born without a vagina (Harnish, 1988). When this occurs, physicians are usually able to surgically construct one.

The Uterus

It is within the **uterus,** or womb, that a fertilized egg will attach itself and become an embryo and then a fetus. Resembling a small inverted pear, the uterus

in women who have not had children measures only about 3 inches long and 3 inches across at its broadest portion, but it is capable of tremendous expansion. The *cervix,* the narrow end of the uterus, projects into the back of the vagina and can be easily felt (as a slippery bump) by inserting a finger into the back of the vagina. The broad part of the uterus is called the *fundus.* Ligaments hold the uterus in the pelvic cavity at about a 90-degree angle to the vagina, although in some women it may tilt slightly forward or backward.

The uterus has three layers: the innermost **endometrium,** where the fertilized egg implants; a strong middle layer of muscles called the *myometrium,* which contracts during labor; and an external cover called the *perimetrium.* The endometrium thickens and becomes rich in blood vessels after ovulation, but if fertilization does not occur it is sloughed off and discharged from the woman's body during menstruation. The cervical opening, or *os* (Latin for "mouth"), is normally no wider than the diameter of a matchstick, but it dilates to 10 centimeters (about 4 inches) at childbirth to allow delivery of the baby.

Unfortunately, the cervix is the site of one of the most common types of cancer in women. It is extremely important, therefore, that all women, whether sexually inexperienced or sexually active, go to a physician for regular examinations and Pap smears (see Box 2–B).

The Fallopian Tubes

Extending 4 inches laterally from both sides of the uterus are the **Fallopian tubes,** or oviducts, as they are sometimes called. There is no direct physical connection between the Fallopian tubes and the ovaries, but the fingerlike projections at the end of the tubes (called *fimbria*) brush against the ovaries. After an egg is expelled from an ovary into the abdominal cavity at ovulation, it is picked up by one of the fimbria. If a sperm fertilizes the egg, it will usually do so within the tube. The fertilized egg then continues its 3- to 4-day trip through the tube and normally implants itself in the endometrium of the uterus.

The Ovaries

The **ovaries** are the female gonads and develop from the same embryonic tissue as the male gonads, the testicles. They are suspended by ligaments on both sides of the uterus. The ovaries have two functions: to produce eggs, or *ova* (sing. *ovum*), and to produce female hormones (*estrogen* and *progesterone*). At birth, a girl has all the immature eggs that she will ever have, about 300,000 to 400,000 in each ovary. Each egg is surrounded by some other cells and contained within a thin capsule to form what is called a **primary follicle.**

Kegel exercises ■ Exercises that are designed to strengthen the pubococcygeus muscle that surrounds the bladder and vagina.

Grafenberg (G) spot ■ A small, sensitive area on the front wall of the vagina found in about 10% of all women.

Uterus ■ The womb. The hollow, muscular organ in women where the fertilized egg normally implants.

Endometrium ■ The inner mucous membrane of the uterus where a fertilized egg implants. Its thickness varies with the phase of the menstrual cycle.

Fallopian tubes ■ The passageways that eggs follow on their way to the uterus.

Ovary ■ The female gonad in which ova are produced.

Primary follicle ■ An immature ovum enclosed by a single layer of cells.

Box 2–B **Sexuality and Health**

Cancer of the Female Reproductive System

Cancer of the Cervix

The cervix is a common site for cancer in women. Each year up to 2 million American women are diagnosed with precancerous conditions of the cervix called cervical dysplasia (Fey & Beal, 2004). About 11,300 American women are diagnosed with invasive cervical cancer (spread beyond the surface of the cervix) (American Cancer Society, 2010). It results in about 4,100 deaths a year. Women can have this cancer at almost any age. Women at high risk include those who began having sexual intercourse at an early age or who have had numerous sexual partners and those whose partners have had numerous sexual partners. Cancer of the cervix is rare among celibate women. *It is not sex itself that is the cause of cervical cancer but certain types of human papillomaviruses (HPV), a virus that is spread during sexual activity* (see Chapter 5) (van der Graaf et al., 2002; Walboomers et al., 1999). Regular use of barrier methods of contraception (such as condoms and diaphragms) reduces the risk of getting cervical cancer.

A *pelvic exam* and **Pap smear** test (named after Dr. George Papanicolaou, who developed the test) are a necessary part of female health care. Regular Pap smears prevent over 70% of cancers of the cervix (Policar, 2008). Today, there are variations of the Pap smear test such as Thinprep, but the conventional Pap smear is just as effective (Siebers et al., 2009). Most cervical cancer–related deaths occur in women who do not get regular Pap tests (Policar, 2008). Dr. Patricia Braley, who headed a National Institutes of Health panel on cervical cancer in 1996, said, "In theory, cervical cancer is a cancer we can completely prevent. If we could reach all the women in this country who are not getting regular Pap tests we could eradicate this type of cancer." Since then, a vaccine (called Gardasil) has been developed that is very effective for the major types of HPV that cause cervical dysplasia (see Chapter 5).

Many women are nevertheless reluctant to get a Pap smear because of embarrassment. The first step, therefore, is to find a doctor with whom you are comfortable and who shows concern for his or her patients (as by warming instruments to body temperature before using them). In the examination room, the woman lies flat on her back with her legs apart and her feet in footrests called stirrups (Figure 2–8). An instrument called a speculum, which is shaped like a duck's bill, is inserted into the vagina and gently opened so that the vaginal walls and cervix may be inspected. A cotton swab or thin wooden stick is used to gently skim the surface of the cervix in order to collect cells, which are then examined under a microscope for abnormalities. During the exam, the doctor will also check the vaginal walls and vulva for possible infections. Some doctors may include a rectal exam at this time. The entire process generally takes only a few minutes, and although some women

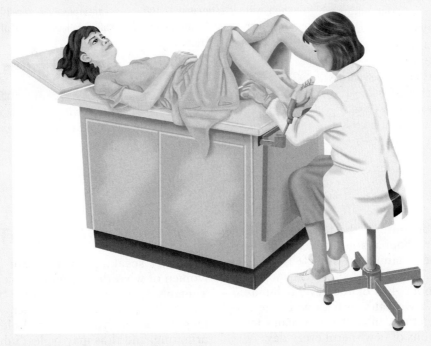

FIGURE 2–8 The pelvic examination.

(*Continued*)

may experience discomfort, it is generally not painful.

> "Human sexuality class has made me more educated about my body, and I became more aware. Before I entered this class I was very scared of going to the gynecologist for a visit (age 20). Recently I went for my first visit and found my fears were ridiculous. It was not bad at all and I even felt better to find out I was OK."

> "At the beginning of the semester you mentioned UNO's Health Services and I decided to check them out. When the results of my Pap smear came in, I had tested positive. I had stage II dysplasia. I had cryotherapy.... If it had not been for this class, I don't know how long I would have waited to get a Pap smear or what the results would have been."

(All examples are from the author's files.)

Any detected abnormalities of cells are treated according to severity. In the precancerous stage, the localized abnormal cells are often destroyed by extreme cold (cryotherapy) or intense heat (electrocoagulation). Precancerous abnormalities in cells often take as long as 8 years before they start to invade other tissues. If cancer of the cervix is found, a woman may have to have a *hysterectomy* (surgical removal of the uterus).

The American Cancer Society advises women that annual checkups should begin when they start having sexual intercourse. Because cervical cancer is "slow growing," the American College of Obstetricians and Gynecologists (2009) recently recommended that women in their 20s get Pap smears every other year, and every third year after that. Check with your doctor about what is best for you.

Recent studies have found that testing directly for the presence of human papillomavirus is superior for detecting precancerous cells than is the Pap test (Mayrand et al., 2007). Some experts believe that this test will eventually replace the Pap test (see Rubin, 2007). Talk to your doctor about what tests are currently available.

Pelvic exams are also done to fit a diaphragm or IUD, to check for vaginal infections, and to examine the uterus during pregnancy. Many women assume that their doctor routinely checks for sexually transmitted infections when taking a Pap smear, but most do not unless specifically asked to do so. If you have had multiple sexual partners (and are thus at high risk to get a sexually transmitted infection), you should consider these additional tests at this time.

Cancer of the Endometrium and Ovaries

Cancer of the endometrium is also very common, with an estimated 42,100 new cases and 7,800 deaths per year in the United States (American Cancer Society, 2010). Typically, the first symptom is abnormal vaginal bleeding, so if you should experience this, go to a physician immediately. He or she will make a diagnosis by dilation and curettage (D & C). Should cancer be found, your doctor will probably recommend a hysterectomy.

Ovarian cancer is a rare disease (lifetime risk of less than 1.5%), but a deadly one. It causes the death of more American women each year (approximately 14,600) than either cervical or endometrial cancer (American Cancer Society, 2010). Most cases are found in postmenopausal women or women approaching menopause (between 50 and 59 years old). It is more common in women who have never been pregnant, and less so in women who use oral contraceptives. However, the highest risk factor is a family history of ovarian cancer (Lynch & Lynch, 1992).

Cancer of the ovaries is usually painless in the early stages. Thus the tumors are often quite large by the time they are discovered, making effective treatment difficult. Today there is a blood test for women at high risk (it tests for CA-125, a protein produced by cancerous ovarian cells). Treatment usually involves removal of the ovaries and radiation.

PERSONAL REFLECTIONS (women)

About 90% of women aged 25 to 64 have had a Pap smear (or equivalent) test in the last 3 years (Nelson et al., 2009). Have you? Have you had one within the last year? If not, why not?

At puberty, one or more of the follicles is stimulated to mature on about a monthly basis (the menstrual cycle). When mature, the follicle is called a *Graafian follicle*. This process ends at menopause, and thus only about 400 of the several hundred thousand ova in a woman's ovaries will ever mature during her lifetime. In contrast, a man's testicles produce millions of new sperm every day.

Pap smear ■ A test for cancer of the cervix in women; named for Dr. Papanicolaou, who developed it.

EXTERNAL MALE ANATOMY

Generally speaking, men have a better idea than women of what their genitals look like. Not only is a man's genitalia more visible to him than a woman's genitalia is to her, but boys are taught at a very young age to hold the penis while urinating, and thus may be less inhibited than girls about touching and examining themselves. Although they differ in appearance, many of the male structures develop from the same embryonic

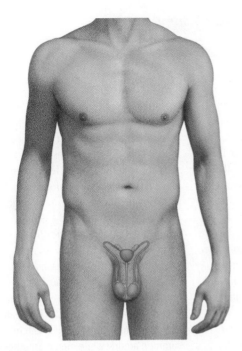

FIGURE 2–9 Anatomical location of the male reproductive system.

tissue as female structures (the penis and clitoris, for example). The male reproductive system and genitalia are shown in Figure 2–9 and Figure 2–10. Penises differ in appearance just like any other part of the body, and men should not consider themselves abnormal if they do not look identical to Figure 2–10.

PERSONAL REFLECTIONS

What were your feelings when you first looked at Figures 2–3 and 2–10? If you experienced any discomfort or anxiety, why? As part of this chapter, I have suggested that you examine your own genitals. Were you able to do this without feelings of guilt or anxiety? If not, why do you think you have negative feelings about looking at this part of your body?

The Penis: Outer Appearance

The **penis** (Latin for "tail") has both a reproductive and a urinary function. It serves to deposit sperm in a woman's vagina and also to eliminate urine from the bladder. When a man is unaroused, the penis is soft and hangs between the legs. It hardens and becomes erect during sexual stimulation, thus enabling penetration of the vagina. The average size of the penis in the unstimulated (flaccid) condition is 3.75 inches in length and 1.2 inches in diameter; it is about 4.5 to 6.0 inches in

length and 1.5 inches in diameter when erect (see Chapter 4). Some penises are curved to the left or right, and others are curved up or down. In a rare condition called micropenis, the penis never develops to more than 1 inch in length (usually due to low levels of the male hormone testosterone; see Aaronson, 1994). In Chapter 4, we will consider whether penis size relates to sexual satisfaction in women.

The skin of the penis is very loose to allow for expansion during erection. At birth the *foreskin* folds over the glans, the smooth rounded end of the penis, but many men have had their foreskin cut off in a surgical procedure known as **circumcision** (see Figure 2–10). If you should have an uncircumcised son, be sure to teach him that good hygiene includes cleaning under the foreskin (see Box 2–C). However, when bathing a newborn, do not pull back forcibly on the foreskin for the first several months, because it is often partially adhered to the penis during this time. In some boys it is still adhered at 3 years of age (Williams et al., 1993).

The Penis: Internal Structure

The penis has three parts: the body or shaft; the glans; and the root. Only the first two parts are visible (see Figure 2–11). In cross section, the *shaft* of the penis can be seen to consist of three parallel cylinders of spongy tissue, two *corpora cavernosa* (or "cavernous bodies") on top and a *corpus spongiosum* (or "spongy body") on the bottom. Each is contained in its own fibrous sheath. The corpora cavernosa do not extend the full length of the penis. Instead, the spongy body expands greatly in front to form the round, smooth *glans*. The raised rim at the border of the shaft and glans is called the *corona* (and is the most sensitive to touch of any part of the penis). The *urethra*, which serves as the passageway for urine and sperm, runs through the corpus spongiosum, and thus the urethral opening (or *meatus*) is normally located at the tip of the glans. Occasionally it is located to one side of the glans, and although this usually poses no major problem, it can cause a man to have a negative perception of his own genitals. For reasons not yet determined, this condition (called *hypospadias*) has nearly doubled in frequency of occurrence since 1970, but it can be corrected by surgery (Paulozzi et al., 1997).

Penis ■ The male organ for sexual intercourse and the passageway for sperm and urine.

Circumcision ■ In men, the removal of all or part of the foreskin of the penis. In women, the removal of the clitoral hood.

Box 2–C Cross-Cultural Perspectives/Sexuality and Health

Male Circumcision

Circumcision has been performed on boys since at least 4000 B.C. Egyptian mummies dating from this period give evidence of it, and the Greek historians and geographers Herodotus and Strabo later wrote about observing it in their travels (Glick, 2005). The ancient Egyptians and Ethiopians performed circumcisions for cleanliness (Herodotus), and the practice was borrowed by the Hebrews at about the time of Abraham (the custom later fell into disuse but was revived by Moses). Today, Jewish boys are circumcised on the 8th day of life to symbolize the covenant with God made by Abraham (Genesis 17:9–14). Muslim boys are also circumcised as part of a religious ceremony, often at 13 years of age.

In many cultures today, the operation is performed as a puberty rite, and sometimes it involves more than the cutting away of the foreskin. The Mangaians

and other South Pacific islanders cut lengthwise along the top of the penis (superincision) all the way to the abdomen (Marshall, 1971). Primitive tribes in central Australia make a slit to the depth of the urethra along the entire length of the lower side of the penis (subincision) so that men urinate at the base of the penis, requiring that they sit like women (Gregersen, 1982). Still other cultures insert rods with gemstones, feathers, or bristles attached to the end (D. Brown, 1990; see Figure 1–2 in this text). Many anthropologists believe that these customs are performed as symbolic pledges of loyalty to the group.

In the United States and England, circumcision became popular during the 19th century because Victorian physicians believed that circumcised penises were less sensitive and that the operation would therefore prevent

masturbation and hypersexuality. Circumcision reached its height in popularity between World Wars I and II, but then fell out of favor in most English-speaking countries. Today, fewer than one quarter of boys are routinely circumcised in countries such as England, Canada, New Zealand, and Australia, leaving the United States the only country in which circumcision is still performed for nonreligious reasons on a majority of boys. About 79% of all newborn boys are circumcised yearly in the United States (National Center for Health Statistics), but the practice is much more common among white men than other ethnic groups (Xu et al., 2007).

Circumcising boys' penises, of course, does not stop them from masturbating. In fact, a study found that circumcised men had greater sexual satisfaction and fewer sexual problems than uncircumcised men,

 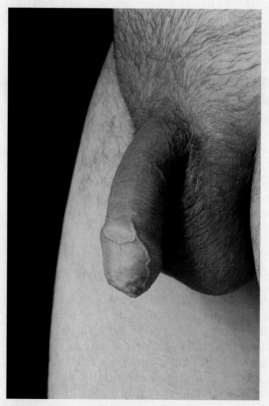

FIGURE 2–10 A circumcised (left) and uncircumcised (right) penis.

and more of them masturbated (Laumann et al., 1997). Today, the reason for circumcision most commonly given by American physicians is to ensure proper hygiene, but there is considerable debate about this, even within the medical community. Glands located beneath the foreskin secrete an oily substance that gets mixed with dead cells to form a cheesy substance called **smegma.** Without proper hygiene, the smegma serves as a possible breeding ground for bacteria. People who favor circumcision point out that the rate of urinary tract infections in uncircumcised infants is at least 4 times greater than in circumcised infants, but the overall rate of these infections is less than 1% in the United States and is usually easy to treat. Several studies have also found that circumcised men have a much lower chance of getting HIV (the virus that causes AIDS) and some other sexually transmitted infections (herpes, human papillomavirus) if they have unprotected

vaginal intercourse with infected partners (see Gray et al., 2009, 2010; Londish & Murray, 2008; Tobian et al., 2009). As a result, in 2007 United Nations health agencies urged that heterosexual men be circumcised (Hargreaves, 2007). However, rates of HIV are relatively low in the United States.

On the other side of the argument are the health risks associated with circumcision, including infection (Poland, 1990). In addition, circumcision is often done on infant boys without the use of anesthesia or analgesia. Thus, for many infants circumcision is a painful operation that causes them to cry for hours (see Boyle et al., 2002).

After a review of 40 years of research about the benefits and risks, in 1999 the American Academy of Pediatrics opposed the *routine* circumcision of newborns (American Academy of Pediatrics, 1999). The academy also advised doctors to use a topical cream anesthetic when circumcision is performed. (One potential downside of the Academy's decision is that Medicaid coverage for circumcision was ended, which affects the poor.)

All of these medical arguments are no doubt very confusing to most parents. My advice to parents is that you should educate yourself about both sides of the argument and then make a decision that feels right for you.

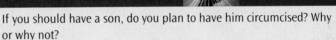
PERSONAL REFLECTIONS

If you should have a son, do you plan to have him circumcised? Why or why not?

Note: You will read about circumcision of the clitoris in Box 4–A.

The *root* of the penis consists of the expanded ends of the cavernous bodies, which fan out to form *crura* and attach to the pubic bone (note the similarity in structure to the clitoris), and the expanded end of the spongy body (called the *bulb*). The root is surrounded by two muscles (the *bulbocavernosus* and the *ischiocavernosus*) that aid in urination and ejaculation.

In men, an erection does not result from a bone protruding into the penis, as in some mammalian species (e.g., dogs), nor does it result from voluntary contraction of a muscle. When a man becomes sexually aroused, the arteries going to the penis dilate and the many cavities of the cavernous and spongy bodies fill with blood. Valves in the veins that drain the penis simultaneously close. Expansion of the sinuses (cavities) and contraction of the muscles at the base of the penis may further aid this process by pressing against the veins and partially cutting off the drainage. In brief, an erection results from the spongy tissues of the penis becoming engorged (filled) with blood. *Detumescence*, or loss of erection, is not as well understood, but probably occurs as a result of the arteries beginning to constrict, thus removing pressure from the veins and allowing drainage.

Some men have a severe curvature of the penis. This is sometimes due to developmental abnormalities, but it is often due to injury to the fibrous sheath (elastic tissue) that holds the three parallel cylinders

of spongy tissue, and is called *Peyronie's disease* (Deveci et al., 2007). If the fibrous sheath is injured at any spot, the elastic tissue is replaced by scar tissue that does not expand during erection, thus causing curvature of the penis. If the curvature is too extreme, it can cause pain during intercourse. In some positions of sexual intercourse, men can place too much pressure or weight on their penis, and this can result in a "fracture" (rupturing of the cavernous bodies), which may require surgery (Adducci & Ross, 1991).

The Scrotum

The sac located beneath the penis is called the **scrotum.** It holds the testicles outside of the body cavity. Sperm are produced in the testicles, but they can only be produced in an environment several degrees lower than the normal body temperature of 98.6 degrees Fahrenheit. Scrotal temperature is typically about 93 degrees Fahrenheit. The skin of the scrotum is sparsely covered with hair and has many sweat glands that aid in temperature regulation. The scrotum also has small muscle fibers that contract

Smegma ■ The cheesy secretion of sebaceous glands that can cause the clitoris to stick to the clitoral hood or the foreskin of the penis to stick to the glans.

Scrotum ■ The pouch beneath the penis that contains the testicles.

when it is cold to help draw the testicles closer to the body cavity for warmth. When it is hot, the muscle fibers relax and the testicles are suspended farther away from the body cavity.

In tropical areas of the world, it is not uncommon for men to suffer from elephantiasis of the scrotum (caused by a parasite), a condition in which the scrotum can get as large as a basketball.

INTERNAL MALE ANATOMY

The male internal reproductive system consists of the testicles, a duct system to transport sperm out of the body, the prostate gland and seminal vesicles that produce the fluid in which the sperm are mixed, and the Cowper's glands (see Figure 2–11).

The Testicles

The **testicles** (the male gonads, or *testes*) develop from the same embryonic tissue as the ovaries (the female gonads). Like the ovaries, the testicles have two functions: to produce *sperm* and to produce male hormones. Millions of new sperm start to be produced each day in several hundred *seminiferous tubules* (the entire process takes about 70 days). Each tubule is 1 to 3 feet in length, and if they were laid together end to end they would measure over one-quarter mile in length. In between the seminiferous tubules are cells called *interstitial cells of Leydig*, which produce male hormones. Male (or masculinizing) hormones are called *androgens*. The most important is *testosterone* (you will find many references to this hormone in later chapters). Another hormone produced in the testicles (by Sertoli cells) is called *inhibin*, discussed in Chapter 3.

The testicles are in the abdominal cavity for most of fetal development, but about 2 months before birth they descend through the inguinal canal into the scrotum. They fail to descend in about 2% to 5% of male births, a condition known as cryptorchidism (Kollin et al., 2006). This usually corrects itself (only 1% to 2% have failed to descend by 3 months), but if it persists, it can result in sterility and increased risk of hernia and cancer of the testicles.

Testicles ■ The male gonads that produce sperm and male hormones.

Epididymis ■ The elongated cordlike structure on the back of a testicle. It is the first part of the duct system that transports sperm out of a man's body.

Vas deferens ■ The second part of the duct system that transports sperm out of a man's body.

Ejaculatory ducts ■ One-inch-long paired tubes that pass through the prostate gland. The third part of the duct system that transports sperm out of a man's body.

Urethra ■ The passageway from the bladder to the exterior of the body. In men, it also serves as a passageway for semen during ejaculation.

Each testicle is suspended in the scrotum by the *spermatic cord,* a tubelike structure that contains blood vessels, nerves, the vas deferens, and a muscle that helps to raise and lower the testicles in response to changes in environmental temperature and level of sexual arousal (the testicles are drawn closer to the body during sexual arousal). Each testicle is enclosed in a tight fibrous sheath.

In right-handed men it is normal for the left testicle to hang lower than the right one, and vice versa in left-handed men (the reason is unknown). Both testicles, however, should be about the same size. The testicles are very sensitive to pressure, and men differ as to whether they like to have them touched during sexual relations.

Men should be aware of health problems associated with the testicles. The virus that is responsible for mumps, for example, causes the testicles to swell painfully, and the pressure against the fibrous sheath can crush the seminiferous tubules, resulting in sterility if mumps occurs after puberty. The testicles are also the site of a form of cancer (see Box 2–D).

The word *testes*, by the way, is derived from a Latin word for *witness* ("to testify"). People shake hands when completing a deal or sealing a promise today, but in biblical times a man held the testicles of the man to whom he gave an oath. The idea was that if he broke his oath, the children of the other man had the right to take revenge.

The Duct System

After sperm are produced in the seminiferous tubules, they pass through a four-part duct system before being expelled from the penis during an ejaculation. The seminiferous tubules converge to form the **epididymis,** coiled tubes (about 20 feet long if uncoiled) that can be felt on the top and back of each testicle. Sperm mature (become more fertile and achieve greater motility) as they travel through the epididymis, which takes up to 6 weeks (Orgebin-Crist, 1998). From here the sperm pass into the paired 14- to 16-inch **vas deferens.** The vas begin in the scrotum, then travel through the spermatic cord and enter the abdominal cavity through the inguinal canal. From there, they go up and over the bladder toward the prostate gland. Many sperm are stored in the expanded end of the vas, called the *ampulla*, prior to ejaculation.

During orgasm, rhythmic muscular contractions force the sperm into the **ejaculatory ducts,** short (about 1-inch-long) paired tubes that run through the prostate gland, where they are mixed with fluids from the prostate and seminal vesicles to form *semen.* The two ejaculatory ducts open into the **urethra,** which passes through the spongy body of the penis. Sphincter muscles surround the part of the urethra coming from the bladder. These involuntarily contract during an erection so that urine does not get mixed with semen.

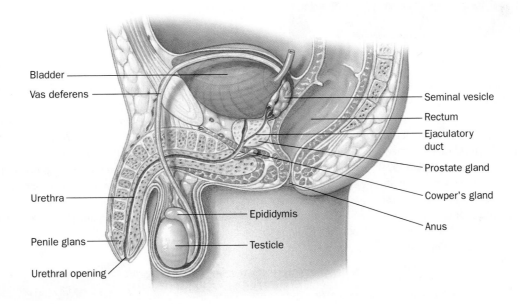

Bladder

Vas deferens

Urethra

Penile glans

Urethral opening

Seminal vesicle

Rectum

Ejaculatory duct

Prostate gland

Cowper's gland

Anus

Epididymis

Testicle

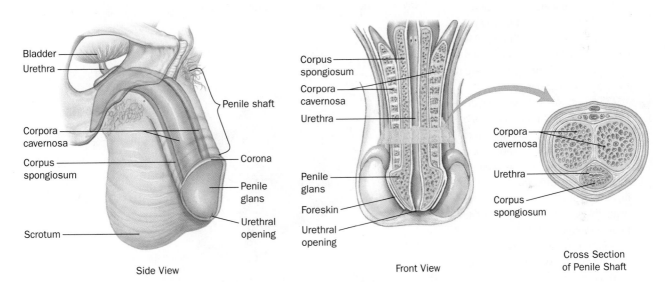

Bladder
Urethra

Corpora cavernosa

Corpus spongiosum

Scrotum

Penile shaft

Corona

Penile glans

Urethral opening

Side View

Corpus spongiosum

Corpora cavernosa

Urethra

Penile glans

Foreskin

Urethral opening

Front View

Corpora cavernosa

Urethra

Corpus spongiosum

Cross Section of Penile Shaft

FIGURE 2–11 The internal male reproductive system: (top) from a side view; (bottom) from a frontal view and cross section of the penis.

The Prostate Gland and Seminal Vesicles

Although an average ejaculation contains about 200 million to 300 million sperm, they make up very little of the total volume. Most of the volume is seminal fluid from the **seminal vesicles** (accounting for about 70% of the fluid) and the prostate gland (about 30%). Among other substances, the seminal vesicles (misnamed because anatomists once thought that was where sperm were stored prior to ejaculation) secrete fructose, prostaglandins, and bases. Fructose (a sugar) activates the sperm and makes them mobile, while prostaglandins cause contractions of the uterus, aiding movement through that structure. Bases neutralize the normal acidity of the vagina so that sperm will not be destroyed on their way to the more favorable alkaline environment of the uterus. The **prostate gland**

Seminal vesicles ■ Two structures in a man that contribute many substances to the seminal fluid.

Prostate gland ■ A gland in men that surrounds the origins of the urethra and neck of the bladder and contributes many substances to the seminal fluid.

Box 2–D Sexuality and Health

Testicular Cancer and Self-Examination

Cancer of the testicles is not very common. About 8,400 new cases occur in the United States each year (American Cancer Society, 2010). However, it is the most common type of cancer in men aged 20 to 35 (Forman & Moller, 1994). This type of cancer received much attention when bicyclist Lance Armstrong (seven-time winner of the Tour de France), comedian Tom Green, and Olympic Gold Medal–winning skater Scott Hamilton were diagnosed with it. Men at highest risk are those whose testicles did not descend into the scrotum before the age of 10, those who had an early puberty, and those with inguinal hernias (United Kingdom Testicular Cancer Study Group, 1994). Cancer of the testicles is not related to masturbation, frequent sex, or sexually transmitted infections.

The most common symptom of testicular cancer is a small lump or a testicle that is slightly enlarged. In the first stages of testicular cancer, the tumors are painless; thus it is important that all men (particularly those in a high-risk group) examine themselves regularly—once a month is advised. Examine yourself after a warm bath or shower. This causes the testicles to descend and the skin of the scrotum to relax. Examine your testicles one at a time by placing both thumbs on top and the middle and index fingers on bottom (see Figure 2–12). Gently roll your testicle between the thumbs and fingers. When doing so, you will also feel your epididymis, which feels like a spongy rope on the top and back of each testicle.

Not all abnormal lumps are cancerous, but if a lump should be, treatment usually involves surgical removal of the affected testicle and chemotherapy. The cancer rarely spreads to the other testicle. Sexual functioning is usually normal (Jonker-Pool et al., 2001). The unaffected testicle can produce enough sperm to father a child. Synthetic implants can be inserted into the scrotum to give the man's genitals a normal appearance.

PERSONAL REFLECTIONS (men)

Do you regularly examine your testicles for abnormal lumps? If not, why not? The self-exam takes only about 3 minutes.

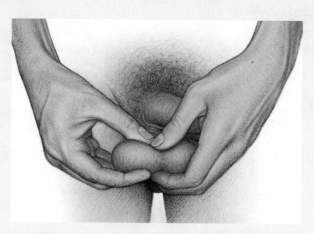

FIGURE 2–12 Testicular self-examination.

secretes all of these substances and another substance (fibrinogenase) that causes semen to temporarily coagulate after ejaculation, thus helping to prevent spillage from the vagina. The prostate also secretes an antibiotic, possibly to protect the male and female reproductive systems from infection. The prostate is the site of the second most common type of cancer found in men and should be checked annually when men reach middle age (see Box 2–E).

Cowper's glands ■ Two pea-shaped structures located beneath the prostate gland in men that secrete a few drops of an alkaline fluid prior to orgasm.

The Cowper's Glands

The **Cowper's,** or *bulbourethral,* **glands** are two pea-sized structures located beneath the prostate. They secrete a few drops of an alkaline fluid (a base) that may appear at the tip of the penis prior to orgasm. The fluid neutralizes the normal acidity of the urethra, and thus sperm are not destroyed when passing through the penis during ejaculation. Many couples use withdrawal as a contraceptive technique (i.e., the man withdraws his penis from his partner's vagina just prior to orgasm), but the fluid from the Cowper's glands often contains sperm, making this an unreliable method of birth control (see Chapter 6).

Box 2–E **Sexuality and Health**

Prostate Problems and Examination

Cancer of the prostate is the most common nonskin cancer among men in the United States, with approximately 192,300 new cases and 27,360 deaths each year (American Cancer Society, 2010). An average of 1 in every 6 men will be diagnosed with prostate cancer by age 85. The rates are considerably higher among African-American men than among white men. Although the cause of prostate cancer is still unclear, two suspected risk factors are high testosterone levels and dietary fat. The good news is that cancer of the prostate is usually a very slow-growing type of cancer. If it is detected and treated early, before the tumor spreads outside the prostate, there is about a 90% chance that a man will live at least 15 years. However, many men show no symptoms in the early stages. As the cancer advances, symptoms may include difficulty in urination or a frequent need to urinate (especially at night), blood in the urine, and continuing pain in the lower back or pelvic region. By the time symptoms appear, there is only a 30% chance that the tumor is confined to the prostate and is curable.

The traditional method for diagnosing prostate cancer has been the rectal examination, in which a physician feels the prostate for any abnormalities. However, nearly 70% of the cancers detected by it are already in an advanced stage. There is now a blood test for detecting prostate cancer. The test measures levels of prostate-specific antigen (PSA), a substance produced by prostate cells. PSA levels are usually higher in men with prostate cancer. However, a combination of diagnostic techniques is better than any single technique. *The American Cancer Society recommends that all men have a yearly exam starting at age 50, or 45 if you are African American or have a family history of prostate cancer.*

Prostate cancer was traditionally treated by either radical prostatectomy (surgical removal of the prostate, seminal vesicles, and other tissues), laparoscopic surgery, and/or radiation. However, side effects of these treatments frequently included impotence and urinary incontinence (inability to control the bladder), and many men felt that the cures were worse than the disease (Sanda et al., 2008). Today, computer-aided surgery can often target the prostate tissue without damaging vital nerves. Because localized early-stage prostate cancer is often slow to develop, many doctors have advised that the best treatment is "watchful waiting"—doing nothing except regular monitoring until there is a threat that the cancer will spread to surrounding tissue (Lu-Yao et al., 2009). Men aged 65 and older who are diagnosed with early-stage prostate cancer generally die of other causes before the cancer spreads (Ketchandji et al., 2008). However, studies have found that for both young and older men early intensive treatment results in longer survival (Johansson et al., 2004).

Cancer is not the only problem a man can have with his prostate. Inflammatory infections (e.g., prostatitis), sometimes resulting from untreated sexually transmitted infections, can occur. In addition, as men grow older it is common for the prostate to enlarge as a result of overgrowth of normal prostate tissue. This condition, called *benign prostatic hyperplasia* (often called BPH), affects about 50% of men over the age of 60 (Davidson & Chutka, 2008). The overgrowth pinches off the urethra, causing increase in frequency of or difficulty in urination. The traditional treatment has been transurethral prostatectomy, in which the prostate tissue is removed by an instrument inserted through the urethra. However, about 10% to 15% of men who have had this operation suffer complications, including impotence (although some cases of impotence may be psychological in origin). Drugs are available to shrink the prostate, but the most promising new treatments are devices that use microwaves or radio waves to kill the excess tissue. Many physicians believe that unless the urethra is completely blocked or there are other bothersome symptoms (such as urinary difficulties), the best approach, again, is watchful waiting (Wasson et al., 1995).

PERSONAL REFLECTIONS (men)

If you are over 50 years old (or 45 if you are African American), have you been to a doctor for a prostate examination? If not, why?

OUR SEXUAL BODIES

In the United States, cultural standards continue to emphasize extreme stereotypes as the most admired physiques. Over the years, *Playboy* magazine centerfolds have become thinner (Garner et al., 1980), while *Playgirl* magazine's male centerfolds have become heavier and more muscular (Leit et al., 2001). We are taught to desire these extreme physiques beginning in childhood. Girls are told that the nearly physically impossible, busty, thin-waisted Barbie doll is the feminine ideal, while over the years the GI Joe action figures have become more and more muscular to the point of human impossibility

(Pope et al., 1999). It is not surprising, therefore, that adult men desire a hypermuscular 6-pack-abs body for themselves (see Frederick et al., 2007; Hatoum & Belle, 2004)—as well as a smaller waist-to-hip ratio (e.g., Furnham et al., 2006; Singh, 1993) and longer leg-to-body ratio (Swami et al., 2006) in their female partners. Consequently, it is also not surprising that many men and women are dissatisfied with their bodies and have low self-esteem because they cannot achieve these stereotypical ideals (Blond, 2008; Hatoum & Belle, 2004).

A positive body image is strongly associated with better sexual functioning (Weaver & Byers, 2006), whereas body shame is related to greater sexual problems (Sanchez & Kiefer, 2007). Unfortunately, most Americans are unhappy with their bodies (Garner, 1997). Many Americans have become obsessed about their bodies and have become so image conscious that they pay thousands of dollars for face-lifts, breast or penis enlargements, hair transplants, and even padding for their buttocks and legs. But is sex only for the very beautiful? Of course not. Physical appearance might make us sexually appealing to others at first, but a good healthy sexual life involves having *sensuality*, which encompasses all of our senses and who we are as a total person. A person's voice, feel, taste, smell, and personality can all be sensual and contribute to his or her sexuality. For example, an overweight person who appreciates the importance of touching and taking his or her time may be a much better sexual partner than one who physically may be a perfect "10."

Think how boring the world would be if we all looked the same, even if all our bodies were perfect. We each have different ideas and standards as to what we find sexually arousing. Some men are preoccupied with becoming bald, but many women find bald men sexy, so much that many young men shave their heads. We are all unique, and if we can appreciate that uniqueness and love ourselves, then we also have the capacity to truly care for others. Chances are that our partners have (or will have as they grow older) as many unique physical features as we do. So, find a partner who appreciates you for who you are and how you look, and vice versa, and learn to feel good about yourself. In the excitement of sexual relations with someone we truly enjoy and care for, a paunchy midline, a bald spot, or a small penis or small breasts are not important. We all have the capacity to be sensual beings, and we all have bodies that are sexual.

PERSONAL REFLECTIONS

What body parts of others do you find to be most sexually arousing? Why? Do you think this is a learned response, or is it biologically determined? If the latter, how do you account for the fact that people in other cultures may not be aroused by parts of the body that you find to be arousing (see Chapter 1)?

STUDY GUIDE

KEY TERMS

androgens 50
areola 38
Bartholin's glands 36
breasts 38
bulb (of penis) 49
bulbocavernosus
    muscle 37
cervix 44
circumcision 47
clitoral hood 36
clitoris 37
corona 47
corpora cavernosa 37, 47
corpus spongiosum 47
Cowper's glands 52
crura 37, 49
ejaculatory ducts 50
endometrium 44

epididymis 50
Fallopian tubes 44
fimbria 44
foreskin 47
fundus 44
genitalia 33
glans 37, 47
Graafian follicle 46
Grafenberg (G) spot 44
hymen 37
introitus 37
Kegel exercises 44
labia majora 36
labia minora 36
Leydig, interstitial cells of 50
mammary glands 38
mammogram 40
mons veneris 35

nipple 38
os 44
ova (ovum) 44
ovary 44
oxytocin 38
Pap smear 45
pelvic exam 45
penis 47
perineum 36
primary follicle 44
prolactin 38
prostate gland 51
pubic hair 35
pubococcygeus (PC)
    muscle 43
root (of penis) 49
scrotum 49
semen 50

INTERACTIVE REVIEW

When referring to their genitals or breasts, many people feel more comfortable using slang terms than the correct anatomical names. The use of sexual slang often reflects ambivalent feelings about sex and may lead to misinformation.

Women's genitalia are collectively known as the (1) _____. This includes the (2) _____, (3) _____, (4) _____, (5) _____, (6) _____, and (7) _____. The (8) _____ and (9) _____ become covered with hair at puberty. The (10) _____ has no known function other than to focus pleasurable sensations. It is most similar in structure to a man's (11) _____. The (12) _____ meet at the top to form the clitoral hood. The area between the labia minora is called the (13) _____. Sexually inexperienced women have a thin membrane, called the (14) _____, that partially covers the vaginal opening. A woman's breasts are not part of her reproductive anatomy, but in cultures where men consider them to be erotic, they are part of her sexual anatomy. One in (15) _____ women will get breast cancer sometime in their lifetimes.

A woman's internal reproductive system includes the (16) _____, (17) _____, (18) _____, and (19) _____. The (20) _____ is the depository for sperm, the birth canal, and the exit route for menstrual fluids. It is a self-cleansing organ, and its odor is generally not offensive. The walls of the inner two thirds of the (21) _____ are relatively insensitive to touch, but about 10% of all women have an area of heightened sensitivity on the front wall called the

(22) _____. When a mature ovum (egg) is released from an (23) _____, it is picked up by a (24) _____, which then transports it to the (25) _____. If fertilized by a sperm, the egg usually implants in the (26) _____ of the uterus. Women should have regular pelvic exams and Pap smears to test for (27) _____.

Men's external anatomy consists of the penis and the (28) _____, which contains the (29) _____. Erection of the penis occurs when the two (30) _____ and the (31) _____ become engorged with blood. The rounded end of the penis, called the (32) _____, is covered by the (33) _____ unless this excess skin has been surgically removed in an operation called (34 _____. The American Academy of Pediatrics opposes routine circumcision of newborns.

Men's internal reproductive system includes the (35) _____, which produce sperm and the male hormone (36) _____, and a four-part duct system (starting from the testicles) consisting of the (37) _____, (38) _____, (39) _____, and (40) _____, which transports sperm out of the body. During an ejaculation, sperm are mixed with fluids from the (41) _____ and (42) _____ to form (43) _____. A small amount of fluid is released by the (44) _____ before a man reaches orgasm. Cancer of the (45) _____ is the most common type of cancer in men aged 20 to 35. The most common cancer (other than skin cancer) among all men in the United States is cancer of the (46) _____.

SELF-TEST

A. TRUE OR FALSE

- ☐ T ☐ F 47. The testicles in adult men normally produce millions of new sperm every day.
- ☐ T ☐ F 48. It is normal for one testicle to hang lower in the scrotum than the other.
- ☐ T ☐ F 49. Sperm can only be produced in an environment that is several degrees lower than normal body temperature.
- ☐ T ☐ F 50. Most doctors routinely check for sexually transmitted infections when they perform pelvic exams.
- ☐ T ☐ F 51. Most women have a G spot.

[T] [F]   52. The American Cancer Society advises that women should have mammograms starting at age 40.

[T] [F]   53. The ovaries produce hundreds of new eggs every month during a woman's reproductive years.

[T] [F]   54. The American Academy of Pediatrics presently favors the routine circumcision of boys for health reasons.

[T] [F]   55. The use of feminine hygiene sprays and douches is a recommended part of normal feminine hygiene.

[T] [F]   56. There is no direct physical pathway between the ovaries and the Fallopian tubes.

[T] [F]   57. The labia majora are hairless and meet at the top to form the clitoral hood.

[T] [F]   58. Deep, pleasurable vaginal sensations during intercourse are due to sensitive vaginal walls.

[T] [F]   59. Erections in men are due in part to a bone that protrudes into the penis.

[T] [F]   60. The hymen is a good indicator of whether or not a woman has had sexual intercourse.

[T] [F]   61. A woman's sexual responsiveness is related to breast size.

B. MATCHING

_____ 62. areola
_____ 63. mons veneris
_____ 64. perineum
_____ 65. introitus
_____ 66. corpora cavernosa
_____ 67. bulbocavernosus muscle
_____ 68. corona
_____ 69. fimbria
_____ 70. glans
_____ 71. Bartholin's glands
_____ 72. smegma
_____ 73. pubococcygeus muscle
_____ 74. vestibular bulbs
_____ 75. spermatic cord

a. term used to refer to the vaginal opening
b. darkened area around the nipple
c. hairless area of skin between the vaginal opening and the anus
d. cheesy substance secreted by glands in the foreskin and clitoral hood
e. soft layer of fatty tissue overlaying the pubic bone
f. two spongy cylinders in the penis
g. large muscle that surrounds the vagina and the bladder
h. raised ridge where the glans and shaft of the penis meet
i. tiny fingerlike endings of the Fallopian tubes
j. smooth rounded end of the penis
k. two glands located at the base of the labia minora
l. ring of sphincter muscles that surround the vaginal opening and root of the penis
m. structures located on both sides of the vaginal opening that become engorged with blood during sexual arousal
n. tubelike structure that suspends the testicles in the scrotum

C. FILL IN THE BLANKS

76. All men over the age of 50 (or 45 for African-American men) should have an annual examination to check for cancer of the _____.

77. In women, the two outer elongated folds of skin that extend from the mons to the perineum are called the _____.

78. The innermost layer of the uterus, which is sloughed off and discharged from the woman's body during menstruation, is called the _____.

79. In men, an erection results from the spongy tissues of the penis becoming engorged with _____.

80. When a man becomes sexually aroused, a few drops of a clear fluid produced by the _____ may appear at the tip of the penis.

81. Breast size in women is determined by the _____.

82. The best time for most women to examine their breasts for abnormal lumps is _____.

83. After sperm travel through the vas deferens, they enter the paired _____.

84. Most of the fluid in an ejaculation comes from the _____.

85. The best time for a man to examine his testicles for abnormal lumps is _____.

86. Two glands that secrete small amounts of alkaline fluid into ducts at the base of the labia minora are called _____.

87. Sperm are produced in the _____ of the testicles.

88. Both the penis and the _____ have corpora cavernosa.

89. The muscle surrounding the vagina and bladder is called the _____ muscle.

90. In women who have a G spot, it is located on the _____ wall of the vagina.

91. The pituitary hormone that causes production of milk is _____.

SUGGESTED READINGS AND RESOURCES

Boston Women's Health Book Collective (2005). *Our bodies, ourselves: A new edition for a new era.* New York: Simon & Schuster. For women, with an emphasis on health care.

Love, S. (2005). *Dr. Susan Love's breast book.* New York: De Capo Lifelong Books. All about breast care, with many illustrations.

Morgentaler, A. (1993). *The male body: A physician's guide to what every man should know about his sexual health.* New York: Simon & Schuster. The title says it all.

Schover, L. R. (1997). *Sexuality and fertility after cancer.* New York: John Wiley & Sons. Many survivors of cancer suffer sexual problems. This book will help.

Zilbergeld, B. (1999). *The new male sexuality.* New York: Bantam Books. An excellent source of information about male sexuality and health, this book also provides information about female sexual anatomy.

American College Health Association
891 Elkridge Landing Road, Suite 100
Linthicum, MD 21090
(410) 859-1500
www.acha.org

CANCER
American Cancer Society
Information Center:
1(800) ACS-2345
Local units can be found in your telephone directory.
www.cancer.org

National Cancer Institute Cancer Information Service
1(800) 4-CANCER
www.cancer.gov

3 | Hormones and Sexuality

We live in a greeting card culture where, for [$2.50], we purchase socially approved statements about childbirth, marriage, or death. But Hallmark manufactures no cards that say, "Best wishes on becoming a woman." Rather than celebrate the coming-of-age in America, we hide the fact of the menarche, just as we are advised to deodorize, sanitize, and remove the evidence.

—Excerpt from *The Curse: A Cultural History of Menstruation* by Janice Delaney, Mary Jane Lupton, & Emily Toth, 1988, University of Illinois Press.

When you have finished studying this chapter, you should be able to:

- Identify and describe the hormones of the endocrine system that are involved in reproduction.
- Describe the four phases of the menstrual cycle.
- Explain the difference between menstrual and estrous cycles.
- Understand the history behind negative attitudes about menstruation and realize their lack of factual basis.
- Define and explain menstrual problems such as amenorrhea, premenstrual syndrome (PMS), dysmenorrhea, endometriosis, and toxic shock syndrome (TSS).
- Explain the regulation of testosterone and sperm production in men.
- Understand the dangerous effects of anabolic steroids.
- Understand the relationship between hormones and sexual desire.

What are hormones? Do you know what they do? Although most people have heard of hormones, very few are certain of their function. Here are some typical responses by students enrolled in my course. Many had no idea what hormones do:

"Before I was enrolled in this course I did not know what hormones were. All I knew was that they were part of our body and were there for some reason." (woman)

"I knew hormones made you grow and sweat. But I didn't know they had anything to do with menstruation. I didn't even know they had any purpose besides just being there." (woman)

"I thought hormones were the building blocks of our body, like DNA, except hormones were related to attitudes of an individual." (man)

Many thought that hormones controlled our moods:

"I thought that hormones controlled my moods. Whenever I'm happy, sad, mad, angry, or even 'in the mood' it was all hormones. Any unusual behavior was because of hormones." (woman)

"I believed that hormones were really only in women and they were only in use when a female was on her period. When women had cramps, I've always heard people say, 'She's on her period. Her hormones are acting up!'" (woman)

Others thought that hormones had only to do with sexual behavior:

"I thought hormones made guys horny and go after girls. The girls would always tell us 'The hormones must be flowing' whenever we would do anything to try to impress them. So I figured only guys had them." (man)

"I always thought hormones made a person horny. I always heard people say that when a person was interested in sex 'their hormones were going crazy.'" (woman)

"I always thought that hormones determined how feminine or masculine someone can be. I thought it was what made people gay or straight or in-between." (man)

Let us now see what role hormones really play in human sexuality.

THE ENDOCRINE SYSTEM

Hormones play a crucial role in both men and women. They are important for growth (growth hormone), metabolism (thyroid hormone), water retention (antidiuretic hormone), reaction to stress (cortisol), and many other functions. They are also important for the development and maintenance of our reproductive system, and they influence our sexual behavior.

Hormones are chemical substances that are released into our bloodstream by ductless glands. They are carried in the blood to other parts of the body, where they exert their effects. Hormones released by one gland often cause another gland to release its own hormones. This network of ductless glands is called the **endocrine system.**

Not all glands in the body are endocrine glands. Salivary glands and sweat glands, for example, are not endocrine glands. They secrete their products (saliva and sweat) through ducts to the surface. The testicles and ovaries, on the other hand, are part of the endocrine gland system. The *testicles* manufacture and release **testosterone,** which is often referred to as the "male hormone"; the *ovaries* produce the "female hormones" **estrogen** and **progesterone.** However, testosterone is also produced in small amounts by the ovaries, and estrogen in small amounts by the testicles. The *adrenal glands* (located near the kidneys) also produce small amounts of these hormones; thus, all three hormones are found in both men and women.

What causes the testicles and ovaries to secrete their hormones? The immediate answer is that it is the *pituitary gland,* which is located at the base of the brain (see Figure 3–1). The pituitary gland releases eight different hormones into the bloodstream. Two of these have their effect on the ovaries and testicles, and are thus called *gonadotropins* ("gonad-seeking"). In women, **follicle-stimulating hormone (FSH)** stimulates the maturation of a *follicle* (an immature egg) in one of the ovaries. This was its first known function, and thus how it received its name. However, FSH is also released by a man's pituitary to stimulate the production of sperm in the testicles.

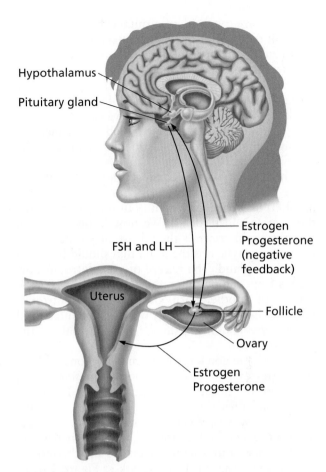

FIGURE 3–1 The brain–pituitary–gonad feedback loop in women.

A second pituitary gonadotropin hormone is called **luteinizing hormone (LH).** In women, LH triggers *ovulation* (release of an egg). In men, it stimulates the testicles to produce male hormones.

Hormones ■ Chemical substances that are secreted by ductless glands into the bloodstream. They are carried in the blood to other parts of the body, where they exert their effects on other glands or target organs.

Endocrine system ■ A network of ductless glands that secrete their chemical substances, called *hormones,* directly into the bloodstream, where they are carried to other parts of the body to exert their effects.

Testosterone ■ A hormone that is produced by the testicles (and in very small amounts by the ovaries and adrenal glands).

Estrogen ■ A hormone that is produced by the ovaries (and in very small amounts by the testicles and adrenal glands).

Progesterone ■ A hormone that is produced in large amounts by the ovaries after ovulation. It prepares the endometrium of the uterus to nourish a fertilized egg.

Follicle-stimulating hormone (FSH) ■ A gonadotropin hormone released by the pituitary gland that stimulates the development of a follicle in a woman's ovary and the production of sperm in a man's testicles.

Luteinizing hormone (LH) ■ A gonadotropin hormone released by the pituitary gland that triggers ovulation in women and stimulates the production of male hormones in men.

There are two other pituitary hormones that you will read about in later chapters. **Prolactin** and **oxytocin** are important for milk production and release during breast-feeding (Chapter 7). Oxytocin has also been implicated in contractions of the uterus during both labor and orgasm (Mah & Binik, 2001). Some researchers have called oxytocin the "love hormone" because blood levels increase during romantic attraction, touching, and cuddling (see Chapter 12).

The pituitary was once called the "master gland" of the body because many of its hormones (like FSH and LH) influence the activities of other glands (like the ovaries and testicles). We now know, however, that the brain controls the release of pituitary hormones, so maybe it is the brain that should be called the master gland. The release of gonadotropin hormones from the pituitary, for example, is under the control of another hormone, called **gonadotropin-releasing hormone (GnRH)**, which is manufactured in the *hypothalamus,* a small area at the base of the brain (see Figure 3–1).

GnRH, the gonadotropins, and the gonadal hormones (testosterone, estrogen, and progesterone) are regulated by negative feedback loops. To better understand a negative feedback loop, think of how a thermostat works. When the room is cold, the thermostat triggers the furnace to go on. An increase in room temperature eventually causes the thermostat to turn the furnace off. Now look at Figure 3–1. In women, increases in blood levels of GnRH from the hypothalamus cause an increase in the release of FSH from the pituitary gland, which in turn results in increased blood levels of estrogen from the ovary. The increased estrogen levels then work to decrease the production of GnRH. There is a similar feedback loop among GnRH, LH, and progesterone.

These are just the basics. The complete story, of course, is more complicated. For example, another ovarian hormone, called **inhibin,** helps to regulate

FSH production, and input from the brain affects release of GnRH. The feedback-loop model of hormonal regulation is made even more complicated by the fact that a woman's pituitary and gonadal hormones vary cyclically on about a monthly basis. This is known as the **menstrual cycle,** which will now be described in more detail. We will consider the regulation of male hormones later in the chapter.

THE MENSTRUAL CYCLE

An ovum (egg), you recall, is surrounded by other cells within a thin capsule of tissue to form what is called a **follicle.** At birth, each ovary has about 300,000 to 400,000 immature (called primordial) follicles, and the ovaries do not produce any new follicles during a woman's lifetime. Instead, after birth about 1,000 follicles begin to mature every month. The entire growth phase of a follicle proceeds through several stages (primordial, primary, secondary, antral, and Graafian) and takes at least 220 days (McGee & Hsueh, 2000). However, during the first several years of life the follicles never complete their development beyond the antral stage, and only about 200,000 primordial follicles remain in each ovary at the time of puberty. When a girl reaches puberty, follicle-stimulating hormone from her pituitary gland allows one or more antral follicles to enter the final stage of growth, which takes a little less than a month. During this phase of growth, called the menstrual cycle, the endometrium of the uterus thickens and becomes highly vascularized (supplied with lots of blood vessels) in preparation for implantation of a fertilized egg. If the egg is not fertilized by a sperm, endometrial tissues are discharged from the body, accompanied by bleeding (**menstruation**), and a new follicle then begins the final stage of maturation. This process will end at *menopause,* when the ovaries shrivel up to the point that no follicles can mature (usually around the age of 50), and thus an average woman will have about 400 menstrual cycles in her lifetime.

The average length of an adult human menstrual cycle is about 28 days. I will describe the hormonal events that occur in a 28-day cycle as consisting of four phases (Hatcher & Namnoum, 2008). *In numbering the days, it is customary to refer to the start of menstruation as day 1.* This is because menstruation is the only event of the cycle that all women can recognize. *In actuality, however, menstruation is really the last of the four phases of the cycle,* so we will begin with the events that occur after menstruation, on about day 5 (see Figure 3–2). Try not to be confused by the system used for numbering days. As you will soon learn, consistent 28-day cycles are not very common, so the numbers of the days in parentheses will be different for shorter and longer cycles.

Prolactin ■ A hormone released from the pituitary gland that stimulates milk production in the breasts.

Oxytocin ■ A pituitary hormone associated with milk release, labor and orgasmic contractions, and erotic attraction and touch.

Gonadotropin-releasing hormone (GnRH) ■ A hormone released by the hypothalamus in the brain that causes the pituitary gland to release the hormones FSH and LH.

Inhibin ■ A hormone produced by the testicles and ovaries that inhibits release of follicle-stimulating hormone from the pituitary gland.

Menstrual cycle ■ The monthly cycle of hormonal events in a woman that leads to ovulation and menstruation.

Follicle ■ A sac in the ovary containing an ovum and surrounding follicular cells.

Menstruation ■ The monthly discharge of endometrial tissue, blood, and other secretions from the uterus that occurs when an egg is not fertilized.

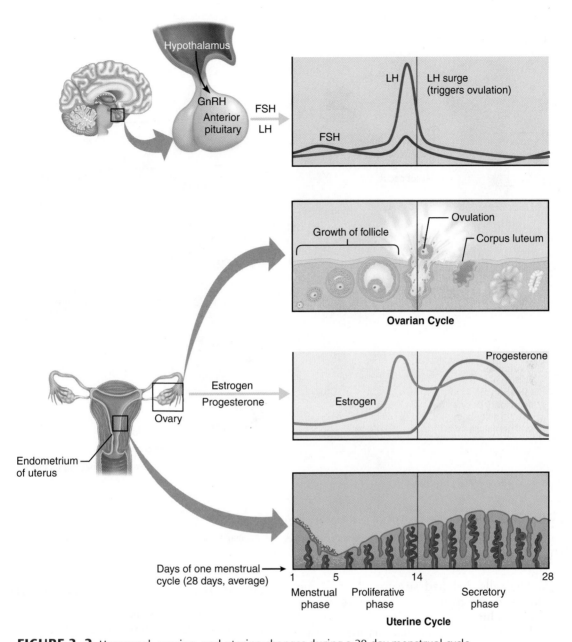

FIGURE 3–2 Hormonal, ovarian, and uterine changes during a 28-day menstrual cycle.

Source: Johnson, Michael, *Human Biology: Concepts and Current Issues,* 3rd, © 2006. Printed and Electronically reproduced by permission of Pearson Education, Inc., Upper Saddle River, New Jersey.

Preovulatory Phase (Days 5 to 13)

This phase is also referred to as the *follicular* or *proliferative phase*. The pituitary secretes relatively high levels of follicle-stimulating hormone (FSH), which, as the name indicates, stimulates the development of a follicle in the ovary. The growing follicle, in turn, becomes a temporary endocrine gland and secretes increasingly higher levels of estrogen. Estrogen is carried in the bloodstream back to the brain and pituitary, where it inhibits further release of FSH (see Figure 3–1). Estrogen also stimulates release of luteinizing hormone (LH) from the pituitary and promotes proliferation (growth) of the endometrium of the uterus. Near the end of this phase, estrogen levels reach their peak, which triggers a release of LH from the pituitary (called the LH surge).

Ovulation (Day 14)

The LH surge (along with a sharp increase in FSH) signals the onset of ovulation within 12 to 24 hours. By this time, the mature follicle (now called a *Graafian follicle*) has moved to the surface of the ovary (see Figure 3–3). At **ovulation,** the follicle ruptures and the ripe ovum is expelled into the abdominal cavity, where it will soon be picked up by a Fallopian tube. Only the ovum is expelled during

Ovulation ■ The expulsion of an egg from one of the ovaries.

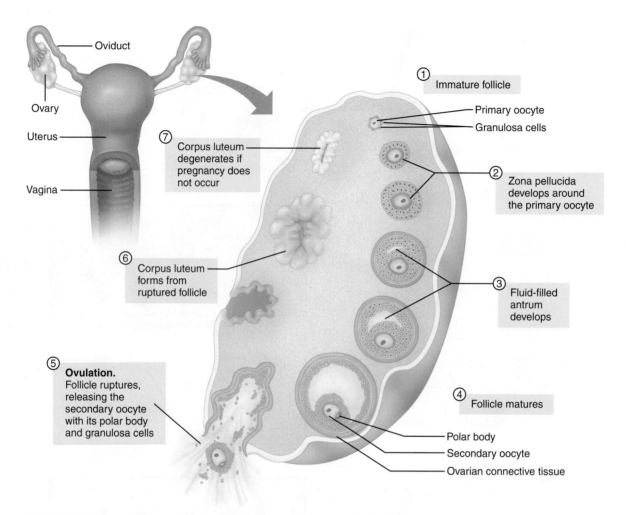

FIGURE 3–3 Changes that take place in the ovary during a menstrual cycle.

Source: Johnson, Michael, *Human Biology: Concepts and Current Issues,* 3rd, © 2006. Printed and Electronically reproduced by permission of Pearson Education, Inc., Upper Saddle River, New Jersey.

ovulation. The cells that had surrounded it in the follicle remain in the ovary and now have a new name, the **corpus luteum.** In addition, the hormonal changes induce a change in the quantity and consistency of cervical mucus—from white and sticky to clear and slippery like an egg white—to provide a more hospitable environment for sperm.

Some women experience lower abdominal cramps for about a day during ovulation. This is sometimes referred to as *Mittelschmerz* (German for "middle pain"). It is more common among young women than older women.

For a woman to get pregnant, both an egg and sperm must be present. An egg remains ripe for only about 24 hours, but sperm can live in a Fallopian tube for up to 5 days (Wilcox et al, 1995). Thus, the fertile period for women is 5 days before ovulation to 1 day afterwards. You will read more about this in Chapter 6.

Corpus luteum ■ The follicular cells that remain in the ovary after the follicle expels the ovum during ovulation. They begin to secrete progesterone in large quantities in the postovulatory stage.

Postovulatory Phase (Days 15 to 28)

The postovulatory phase is also referred to as the *luteal* or *secretory phase*. The cells of the corpus luteum, which are already secreting estrogen, also begin to secrete large levels of progesterone after ovulation. Progesterone inhibits further release of LH from the pituitary and further prepares the thickened endometrium in case the egg is fertilized. The endometrium develops small blood vessels, and its glands secrete nourishing substances. If the egg is fertilized by a sperm, it continues its trip through the Fallopian tube and implants itself in the endometrium. The developing placenta produces the hormone *human chorionic gonadotropin (HCG)*, which ensures that the corpus luteum will continue to secrete estrogen and progesterone to maintain the endometrium (thus HCG serves the same role as the pituitary hormones).

But how often in a woman's reproductive lifetime will one of her eggs be fertilized and result in pregnancy? Not too often. Most of the time fertilization does not occur, and in the absence of implantation,

Gm Gm

the corpus luteum degenerates. When this happens, there is a sharp decline in estrogen and progesterone.

Menstruation (Days 1 to 4)

With the decline in levels of estrogen and progesterone, there is loss of the hormones that were responsible for the development and maintenance of the endometrium. The endometrium is sloughed off and shed over a 3- to 6-day period. Menstruation is the discharge of sloughed off endometrial tissue, cervical mucus, and blood (about 4 to 6 tablespoons over the entire menstrual period). The loss of estrogen (which was inhibiting the release of FSH, you recall) also results in the pituitary gland once again secreting FSH, and a new cycle begins.

PERSONAL REFLECTIONS

Do you regard menstruation as a normal bodily process that is experienced by all women in good health (between puberty and menopause)? If your answer is "yes," but you answer "no" to either one of the next two Personal Reflections, examine your feelings more carefully.

LENGTH OF THE MENSTRUAL CYCLE

In the previous section, you learned that the average length of a woman's menstrual cycle is 28 days. Actually, this is not true until women are full adults, often not until they are in their 30s (see Treloar et al., 1967). During adolescence, most girls' cycles average longer than 28 days. Even for adult women most cycles do not last exactly 28 days. There is considerable variability from woman to woman and from cycle to cycle in the same woman. Most women have cycles that vary in length by 8 days or more (Harlow & Ephross, 1995). The variability in cycle length is greatest during the 2 to 5 years after a girl's first menstruation and before a woman's menopause. There is more variability in the preovulatory (follicular) phase than in the postovulatory (luteal) phase. Interestingly, a recent study found that pregnancy rates were highest for women who had regular menstrual cycles of 30 to 31 days (Small et al., 2006).

Many things can affect the length of the menstrual cycle, including stress, nutrition, illness, drugs, and—as you will see next—other women's cycles.

MENSTRUAL SYNCHRONY AND PHEROMONES

The sexual behavior of animals is greatly influenced by their sense of smell. If you have ever owned a female cat or dog, you know about this. When your pet was "in heat," male animals from all over the neighborhood started showing up in your yard. They were attracted by natural body scents called **pheromones.** In the scientific literature, pheromones are defined as "a substance secreted by an animal to the outside of that individual which is then received by another individual...of the same species, which then elicits some behavioral or developmental response in the latter" (Karlson & Luscher, 1959). The excretion of pheromones has been well established for many nonhuman species (Rodriguez, 2004), and it has also been found that the receptor site is a structure called the vomeronasal organ, part of the olfactory (smell) system. In humans, pheromones are odorless. Many people use perfumes and colognes to enhance their sexual attractiveness, but is there any evidence that human sexuality is influenced by natural, odorless body secretions?

The answer might be yes. In a study of 135 college coeds, Martha McClintock (1971) found that roommates came to have similar menstrual cycles while living together over the course of a year. At the beginning of the year, their cycles were an average of 8.5 days apart, but by the end of the year their cycles were an average of only 4.9 days apart. Mothers and daughters who live together, as well as women who work together, also display menstrual synchrony (Weller & Weller, 1993, 1997; Weller et al., 1999). McClintock suggested that some undetermined natural body odor synchronized women's cycles. Results of later studies support her hypothesis (see McClintock, 1999, for a review). Women who were regularly smeared under the nose with sweat collected from the underarms of other women began to have menstrual cycles that coincided with those of the sweat donors (Preti et al., 1986).

Do pheromones affect attraction? It has been found that men are more attentive toward their female partners during ovulation (see Haselton et al., 2007). How would men know? A recent study found that when men smelled T-shirts that had been worn by women, the scent of T-shirts that had been worn during ovulation caused an increase in testosterone levels. This response was not observed for T-shirts worn at other times of the menstrual cycle (Miller & Maner, 2010).

Studies also suggest that male pheromones may affect women's menstrual cycles. Several studies, for example, found that women who had regular sexual experiences with a man had more regular menstrual cycles (e.g., Cutler et al., 1985). Women with abnormal menstrual cycles who were regularly smeared under the nose with underarm secretions

Pheromones ■ Chemical substances secreted externally by animals that convey information to, and produce specific responses in, members of the same species.

collected from men began to show more normal cycles (Cutler et al., 1986).

Several studies have tested the effects of synthetic "human sex attractant" hormones (derived from underarm secretions) on actual sexual behavior. Compared with people given a placebo, a greater number of both men (Cutler et al., 1998) and women (McCoy & Pitino, 2002) showed increases in sexual behavior and the desire to sleep next to a romantic partner. The same was found for postmenopausal women (Rako & Friebely, 2004). The substances did not increase the frequency of masturbation, indicating that the effects were on sexual attraction and not sexual motivation. Now, before you run out to purchase these products, you should be aware that the effects were far less than 100% and that it is still not understood under just what circumstances these substances actually work (and some researchers doubt that they actually do). You will probably be better off improving your social skills and increasing your displays of affection toward your partner.

MENSTRUAL VERSUS ESTROUS CYCLE

Does a woman's interest in sexual relations differ, depending on the phase of her menstrual cycle? Well, apparently some people think so:

Dear Abby:

You advised "Mismatched," the woman whose sexual appetite didn't match her husband's, to seek therapy. Bad advice, Abby. It's just another example of the guilt trip that has been laid on women ever since Freud and Kinsey came along with their crackpot theories about sex.

It is a biological truth that female mammals, which includes human beings, have a brief period of sexual desire when the ovum is ready for impregnation by the male.

This period is easily observed in wild mammals and is familiar to owners of female dogs and cats. We humans have chosen to ignore its existence, and try to make our females feel guilty because they desire sex far less frequently than males, whom nature created to be always ready for action....

Happily Married

Dear Married: The female of the human species need not be in her fertile phase to desire sex. The biological "truth" you cited is a misconception. (No pun intended.)

(*Dear Abby* by Abigail Van Buren a.k.a Jeanne Phillips and founded by her mother Pauline Phillips. © 1984 Universal Press Syndicate. Reprinted with permission. All rights reserved.)

Estrous cycle ■ The cycle of hormonal events that occurs in most nonhuman mammals. The females are sexually receptive ("in heat," or in estrus) to males only during ovulation.

That is correct, Abby! There are some obvious differences between women and cats and dogs. Women, for example, do not walk on all fours or bark or meow. So why is it so difficult for some people to believe that sexual desire in women may be determined differently than in nonhuman species? Only women and females of a few other primate species (mostly apes) have menstrual cycles. The females of other species, including cats and dogs, have **estrous cycles.** Although owners of female cats and dogs may have noticed some periodic vaginal discharge, these animals do not have a menstrual period. The slight discharge (called spotting) occurs during ovulation, and it is only at this time that the female is sexually receptive ("in heat," or in estrus) to the male.

Numerous studies have investigated whether women's sexual interest changes with different stages of the menstrual cycle. The results of early studies were contradictory. One problem is that results are influenced by which aspect of sexual activity is measured (e.g., interest, fantasy, dreams, physiological arousal, masturbation, or intercourse). More recent studies have found that there is, indeed, an increase in women's sexual activity in the days leading up to, and including, ovulation (Bullivant et al., 2004; Hedricks, 1995; Wilcox et al., 2004). Not only do women report feeling more attractive and desirable near ovulation (Röder et al., 2009), but olfactory and visual perceptions also change around mid-cycle in a direction that might indicate increased sexual motivation—they become more attentive to "maleness" features (Macrae et al., 2002; Tarin & Gomez-Piquer, 2002; see Röder et al., 2009). For example, in one study researchers showed photos of men's faces to women during different times of their cycles. They found that women preferred men with stereotypic rugged masculine features (hunks?) around the time of ovulation (Penton-Voak et al., 1999). However, all of these increases were modest and what is important to remember is that women, unlike the females of most other mammalian species, can become sexually aroused at any time of the cycle. In most other species fertility and sexual behavior are physiologically linked (by hormones and pheromones), but in women nonphysiological influences (such as the social context and happiness within the relationship) become much more important for linking sexual behavior with the fertile period. The importance of this will become more obvious when you read about women's sexual desire in Chapter 4 and Chapter 13.

By the way, what is the purpose of menstruation? It is more speculation than fact at this point, but some researchers have suggested that menstruation serves as a defense against sperm-borne pathogens (Howes, 2010; Profet, 1993).

ATTITUDES ABOUT MENSTRUATION: HISTORICAL PERSPECTIVES

The biblical Hebrews regarded a menstruating woman (*Niddah* in Hebrew) as "unclean" or "impure," and believed that she could transfer her condition of uncleanliness to a man during sexual intercourse:

> When a woman has a discharge of blood which is her regular discharge from her body, she shall be in her impurity for seven days, and whoever touches her shall be unclean until the evening. And everything upon which she lies during her impurity shall be unclean; everything also upon which she sits shall be unclean. And whoever touches her bed shall wash his clothes, and bathe himself in water, and be unclean until the evening.... And if any man lies with her, and her impurity is on him, he shall be unclean seven days; and every bed on which he lies shall be unclean. *(Leviticus 15:19–21, 24, Revised Standard Version)*

Sexual intercourse was strictly forbidden for 7 days from the time a woman first noticed menstrual blood. If no blood was noticed on the 8th day, she immersed herself in a *mikvah* (ritual bath) and was again considered "pure." The menstrual taboo later was extended to all physical contact, and a *Niddah* was required to leave her home and stay in a special house called a house for uncleanliness. Orthodox Jews still adhere to a literal interpretation of the passages in Leviticus. (See also Box 3–A.)

Attitudes about menstruation were even more negative during the time of the Roman Empire. Consider, for example, this passage from the Roman historian Pliny (a.d. 77) describing the possible effects of menstrual blood (Delaney et al., 1988):

> Contact with it turns new wine sour, crops touched by it become barren, grafts die, seeds in gardens are dried up, the fruit of trees falls off.... the edge of steel and the gleam of ivory are dulled, hives of bees die, even bronze and iron are at once seized by rust, and a horrible smell fills the air, to taste it drives dogs mad and infects their bites with an incurable poison.

As you will see in the next section, many people in the United States still have very negative attitudes about menstruation today.

PERSONAL REFLECTIONS

How was menstruation first described to you: as something positive (e.g., "becoming a woman"), as just a fact of life, or as something negative? What effect do you think these early experiences have had on your present attitudes about menstruation? Are you able to talk about menstruation in your family today? If not, why not?

ATTITUDES ABOUT MENSTRUATION TODAY

Although our country no longer has formal menstrual taboos, there are still many people who have negative attitudes about menstruation (see Johnston-Robledo et al., 2003, for a review). Both men and women tend to have negative feelings toward women when they are menstruating (e.g., less likable, less agreeable, less clean, more irritable) (Forbes et al., 2003; Roberts et al., 2002). Not surprisingly, in its 1997 Body Image Survey, *Psychology Today* magazine found that three fourths of women said that menstruation made them have negative feelings about themselves (Garner, 1997). Among women, those who view menstruation as shameful tend also to have higher levels of shameful attitudes about breast-feeding (Johnston-Robledo et al., 2007).

Many people believe menstrual myths—that is, incorrect beliefs, such as women should avoid bathing, swimming, and exercise during menstruation (see Cumming et al., 1991). Here are a few more provided by students in my class:

> "When I was about 10, I was told that if a woman was on her menstrual cycle, she shouldn't visit friends who had infant boys because the baby would get a strain."

> "My mother told me to tie a piece of black thread around my baby's foot when I went out in public. She claimed that women menstruating would give the baby colic."

> "When you had your period not to cook or go around the stove while cooking red gravy because it would curdle."

> "All my mother said was, 'Never wash your hair when you are on your period. It will give you cramps.' Not being able to wash my hair for almost a week was pure torture."

The majority of American men and women seldom initiate sex during menstruation (Barnhart et al., 1995; Hensel et al., 2004; see Hedricks, 1995, for a review). Sex during menstruation is more common among better-educated young women, people in committed relationships (Allen & Goldberg, 2009), and especially among women who are comfortable with their sexuality (Rempel & Baumgartner, 2003). When people can be persuaded to try sexual intercourse during menstruation, they are often surprised by their reaction:

> "My girlfriend sometimes wanted to have sex while she was menstruating. However, I was always reluctant. After taking this course I decided to give it a shot. Much to my surprise, I didn't mind it at all. In fact, she enjoys herself more than normal."

Box 3–A Cross-Cultural Perspectives

Menstrual Taboos Versus Menstrual Celebrations

A taboo is defined as "forbidden and excluded persons, acts, words, thoughts, and things that supposedly threaten a group's welfare and survival and are, therefore, used to that group's advantage" (Voight, 1984). In many cultures, menstruation is a taboo in that menstruating women are portrayed as sick, impure, or filthy.

In our own culture, we have a long history of negative attitudes about menstruation. The Bible instructed that no one touch a woman while she was in her "impurity," and as recently as the Victorian era physicians advised that menstruating women be kept away from the kitchen or pantry so that they would not spoil hams (*British Medical Journal*, 1878).

Today, **menstrual taboos** persist in many cultures around the world, including such geographically diverse places as central Africa, Alaska, and the South Pacific. For example, the Havik Brahmins of southern India believe that if a woman touches her husband while she is menstruating, it will shorten his life (Ullrich, 1992). This is similar to the belief held by Sambian (Melanesian) men that menstrual blood endangers their health (Herdt, 1993).

> "I am from the Sara-Kaba tribe in Chad. When a woman is menstruating, she is not supposed to go in the kitchen and cook. She has a special dish to drink from because the men believe if they drink from it, it could cause an accident and even death."
> (from the author's files)

The Lele of the Congo believe that if a menstruating woman enters the forest, it will ruin hunting for the men (Douglas, 1966), while the Thonga of South Africa believe that sex with a menstruating woman will cause the

Menstrual taboos ■ Incorrect negative attitudes about menstruating women.

FIGURE 3–4 Menstrual huts in New Guinea where menstruating women are isolated for 7 days.

man to be weak in battle (Ford & Beach, 1951).

In order to ensure that a menstruating woman has no contact with men, many cultures require that she remain in a small menstrual hut for an entire week. Figure 3–4 shows a group of such huts in New Guinea (Ward, 1989). This practice is carried to an extreme among the Kolish Indians of Alaska, who lock young girls in a small hut for as long as a year after their first menstruation (Delaney et al., 1988). Women of the Dyak tribe (Southeast Asia) must live for a year in a white cabin while wearing white clothes and eating nothing but white foods. Other cultures do not use special huts, but do require that a woman sleep outside of the house while she is menstruating (Ullrich, 1992).

It is a common practice in these cultures to introduce menstrual taboos to young girls during initiation ceremonies held about the time of their first menstruation (Schlegel & Barry, 1980). These ceremonies are rites of passage into adulthood, signifying that the girls are ready for sexual activity or marriage.

Anthropologists believe that the taboos serve to emphasize the low status and inferiority of women in these cultures, where the social organization (including division of labor) is based on sex (see Forbes et al., 2003). Formal menstrual taboos are most frequently observed in small food-gathering or horticultural societies (Schlegel & Barry, 1980).

Larger societies generally do not have formal adolescent initiation ceremonies, and there are some cultures in which people do not have negative attitudes about menstruation. In Japan, for example, parents celebrate a daughter's first menstruation in a positive manner (Delaney et al., 1988).

> "Growing up, I was not told much about sex by my parents. As a result, I felt uncomfortable about beginning menstruation. My best friend's mom, on the other hand, who was from Japan, told her about menstruation early and openly. When she began menstruation, she felt comfortable telling her mom, and according to the custom of her native country, a celebration dinner

was planned to celebrate her entrance into womanhood." (from the author's files)

Which girl do you suppose felt better about herself as a blossoming woman during adolescence?

Many Native American cultures also held celebrations at the time of a girl's first menstruation (and some still do) (Owen, 1993). The Mescalero Apaches, for example, had annual celebrations for all the girls who had passed from childhood to womanhood. During menstrual periods, the women of some Native American cultures were segregated together in "moon lodges." This was regarded as a positive experience, a time of bonding without any chores (Angier, 1999). However, cultures that view menstruation (or first menstruation) in positive terms are clearly in the minority. For most, it remains an event viewed with great negativity.

"The first time my girlfriend and I had sex during menstruation I told her that she was going to have to remove the condom afterwards without me looking. The thought of it disgusted me. But as we started, we found that we enjoyed it much more because we did not have to worry about getting her pregnant, it relaxed her afterwards, and because of the added fluids, she was much more lubricated. Now we look forward to sex during menstruation."

"I enjoy making love to my boyfriend while I'm having my periods. It might be messy, but it gives me pleasure, and most important it makes my period light the next day. Anyone who hasn't tried making love this way is crazy. If their only excuse is that it's messy, haven't they ever heard of a shower?" (All examples are from the author's files.)

Most American men have such negative attitudes about menstruation that they are too embarrassed to buy tampons or sanitary napkins for their partners:

"One class session you asked how many men would buy tampons for their girlfriend. I don't think that is a fair question, because I wouldn't ask my girlfriend to buy condoms for me." (from the author's files)

When a person buys condoms, it is with the intent of having sex. Tampons, sanitary napkins, and new products such as Instead are not used for sexual relations. In fact, menstruation has nothing to do with whether or not a woman is sexually experienced. Sexually inexperienced women menstruate. However, even many women are embarrassed about purchasing menstrual products:

"Before taking this class I didn't realize what effect attitudes in the U.S. had on me. When I went to the store to buy sanitary napkins I would try to hide them until I was getting ready to pay for them. I would not want a man to see me pay for them. I felt that they would think or say she's on her period." (from the author's files)

If you would be uncomfortable about buying tampons or sanitary napkins, ask yourself why. No one feels uncomfortable about buying toilet paper at the store. The reason for this, of course, is that we all know that everyone has bowel movements. It is a normal physiological event for both men and women. Menstruation is a normal physiological occurrence for women.

In her book *Outrageous Acts and Everyday Rebellions* (1983), feminist Gloria Steinem asked what our attitudes about this subject would be if men were the ones who menstruated:

Clearly, menstruation would become an enviable, boastworthy, masculine event: Men would brag about how long and how much. Young boys would talk about it as the envied beginning of manhood. Gifts, religious ceremonies, family dinners, and stag parties would mark the day.... Sanitary supplies would be federally funded and free. Of course, some men would still pay for the prestige of such commercial brands as Paul Newman Tampons, Muhammad Ali's Rope-a-Dope Pads, John Wayne Maxi-Pads—"For those Light Bachelor Days!" (*Gloria Steinem,* Outrageous Acts and Everyday Rebellions, *1983*)

"Oh, don't be such a wimp, Edwards. Surely you can pick me up a package of tampons on your lunch hour."

Reproduced by special permission of *Playboy* magazine. Copyright 1985 by Playboy.

There is nothing dirty or nasty about menstruation, and with a little knowledge, it is not even mysterious, but rather a basic, important biological function. The discharge, you recall, consists of nothing more than some sloughed off endometrial tissue, mucus, and a small amount of blood. From a contraceptive perspective, menstruation is the safest phase of the cycle in which to have unprotected intercourse (although pregnancy is not impossible if a woman were to have a very short cycle).

PERSONAL REFLECTIONS

What are your attitudes about menstruation? Do you regard it as a normal physiological event, or is it something about which you or your sexual partner feel ashamed or embarrassed? Test your attitude by answering one of the following two questions: (1) Women, would you feel comfortable asking your boyfriend or husband to buy you some tampons or sanitary napkins at the store? (2) Men, if your girlfriend or wife asked you to do so, would you feel comfortable buying her some tampons or sanitary napkins at the store? If not, why not?

MENSTRUAL PROBLEMS

Many women experience problems that are associated in some manner with the menstrual cycle.

Amenorrhea

Amenorrhea refers to the *absence of menstruation for 3 months* or longer in women who previously had regular menstrual cycles (or, in younger girls, no menstrual periods by the age of 15) (Nelson & Baldwin, 2008). *Oligomenorrhea* is the absence of menstruation for shorter intervals, or unevenly spaced menstrual periods. Amenorrhea is normal, of course, when a woman is pregnant, and it is not unusual during breast-feeding or in the first few months after a woman discontinues use of birth control pills. It is also common for menstrual cycles to be irregular during the first few years after **menarche** (a girl's first menstrual period). With the exception of these reasons, women should be having menstrual periods on about a monthly basis from their late teens until they approach menopause, at which time their cycles will again become irregular. However, about 3% of women in their reproductive years have

Amenorrhea ■ The absence of menstruation for 6 months or longer.

Menarche ■ The term for a girl's first menstrual period.

Premenstrual syndrome (PMS) ■ A group of physical and/or emotional changes that many women experience in the last 3 to 14 days before the start of a menstrual period.

amenorrhea, and oligo even more common (Harlow & Ephross, 1995; Schachter & Shoham, 1994).

As you will learn in Chapter 7, a failure to ovulate (and menstruate) may be due to pituitary or ovarian problems (Crosignani et al., 1999). However, a woman's health can also affect her hormone levels. There is a relationship between body fat levels and age of menarche. Girls with high body fat levels generally start menstruating at a younger age than girls with low levels of body fat. Amenorrhea is common among female athletes (Odden & Fick, 1998). Women with the eating disorder anorexia nervosa are often considerably underweight, and as a result rarely menstruate (Katz & Vollenhoven, 2000). On the other hand, extreme obesity can also result in amenorrhea (Friedman & Kim, 1985). Adult women who are not menstruating regularly should not assume, however, that this is due to diet or abnormal body-fat levels.

While poor health can result in amenorrhea, amenorrhea can also affect a woman's health. For example, the low levels of estrogen usually associated with amenorrhea often result in long-term problems such as osteoporosis and cardiovascular disease (Schachter & Shoham, 1994). Thus, a premenopausal woman who is not menstruating regularly should consult a physician.

Premenstrual Syndrome (PMS)

In recent years, **premenstrual syndrome (PMS)** has received more attention than any other menstrual problem. PMS refers to a group of physical and/or emotional changes that many women experience in the *last 3 to 14 days before the start of their menstrual period* (i.e., during the postovulatory, or luteal, phase of the cycle). Physical symptoms may include bloating, breast tenderness, abdominal swelling, swollen hands and feet, weight gain, constipation, and headaches. Emotional changes may include depression, anxiety, tension, irritability, and an inability to concentrate. Women with PMS usually do not have all of these symptoms, but about 75% of women with regular menstrual cycles have some symptoms (Steiner & Pearlstein, 2000).

Numerous articles have claimed that marital conflicts, job absenteeism, accidents, suicide attempts, and criminal acts are more common in the last several days before the start of menstruation than at other times of the menstrual cycle (e.g., Dalton, 1960, 1964, 1980; Hylan et al., 1999). This has led to the commonly portrayed stereotype of the premenstrual woman as "a frenzied, raging beast...prone to rapid mood swings and crying spells,...out of control, and likely at any moment to turn violent" (Chrisler et al., 2006). However, research in this area is plagued with methodological flaws and inconsistencies, so some researchers believe that no conclusion can yet be

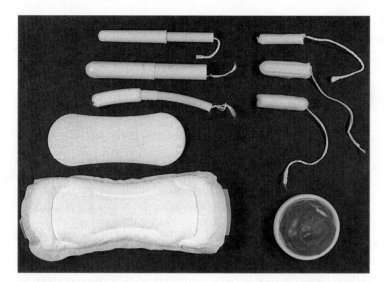

FIGURE 3–5 Menstrual products. Top: examples of three types of tampons—with applicators (left) and without applicators (right). Bottom: examples of two types of menstrual pads—underpant liner for light flow and larger one for heavier flow (left) and a newer product (Instead), a soft disposable plastic cup that fits under the cervix, molds to a woman's body, and collects menstrual flow for up to 12 hours (right). Instead is left in during sexual intercourse (but it is not a contraceptive). Some companies now make reusable cotton menstrual pads (e.g., GladRags).

reached (e.g., Chrisler & Caplan, 2003). In fact, for the large majority of women the symptoms of PMS are mild (Chrisler et al., 2006).

In addition, some researchers say that the term PMS is widely overused—and misused (Chrisler & Caplan, 2003; Hardie, 1997). They claim that most women who perceive themselves as having PMS do not really have a recurrent pattern of premenstrual mood changes and mistakenly attribute high stress, poor health, and work problems to PMS. When asked to complete surveys about these problems, men score just as high as most women who perceive themselves as having PMS (Hardie, 1997). So what distinguishes PMS from other conditions with similar symptoms? In order to be classified as true PMS, the symptoms must regularly occur in a cyclic fashion before menstruation and *must end within a few days after the start of menstruation.*

For some women, premenstrual mood changes are severe. In fact, the American Psychiatric Association recently decided to classify some of the more severe symptoms of PMS as **premenstrual dysphoric disorder, or PMDD** (2000 edition of the *Diagnostic and Statistical Manual of Mental Disorders*). To be diagnosed with PMDD, a woman's symptoms must "markedly interfere" with social relations, work, or education, and include at least one of the following symptoms: markedly depressed mood, marked anxiety or tension, persistent and marked irritability or anger, or "marked affective lability" (extreme changes

in mood, such as sudden sadness) (see Endicott, 2000; Steiner, 2000). It is estimated that 3% to 9% of all women in their reproductive years have PMDD (Nelson & Baldwin, 2008; Halbreich et al., 2003; Potter et al., 2009).

> "I am a 29-year-old female who is suffering with PMS. It starts exactly 2 weeks before my menstrual period. I can tell when my PMS starts because I start to get very frustrated for no reason at all. Little things that I can normally handle seem impossible at this time. I start to regret that I have children and I desire a divorce from my husband. It seems like the walls are closing in on me and I suddenly get the urge to run away. I can't make any sense out of myself at this time and a lot of times I think of suicide. I know that I am going through PMS but I have no control of my emotions and actions, and thinking. I hate myself at this time. As soon as a drop of blood is released from my body (menstruation) I feel like all my stress and anxieties are released with that blood. All of a sudden I feel like myself again."
> (from the author's files)

Women with PMS or PMDD generally have normal hormone levels and normal estrogen/progesterone ratios (Steiner, 2000). The current consensus of opinion is that the ovarian hormones act in combination with a brain chemical called serotonin to produce the symptoms (Rapkin & Winer, 2008). Several studies have found that the antidepressant drug Prozac (fluoxetine) substantially reduces the tension and irritability in many women with PMDD (e.g., Clayton, 2008). Prozac blocks the reuptake of serotonin into brain cells. Selective serotonin reuptake–inhibiting drugs such as sertraline have proven to be very effective in reducing PMDD symptoms.

Is there anything that women with mild symptoms of PMS (i.e., the majority of women) can do? Some of the symptoms can often be relieved by medication and changes in diet. Diuretics ("water pills"), for example, can be prescribed to eliminate excess body fluid, which causes bloating and swelling; cutting down on salt intake can also achieve this. Caffeine (found in coffee, tea, many soft drinks, and chocolate) should be avoided because its stimulating effect will worsen problems like nervousness, irritability, and anxiety.

Although a hormonal basis for PMS is suspected, social and cultural factors can also play a role (see Chrisler & Caplan, 2003). PMS is not even known in many non-Western cultures. Several researchers have noted that PMS is greatest in women who have a very negative attitude about menstruation. With so

Premenstrual dysphoric disorder (PMDD) ■ A severe form of PMS that markedly interferes with social relations, work, or education.

many people still treating menstruation as taboo, is it any wonder that some women are depressed during the few days before it begins?

Dysmenorrhea

Many women experience *painful abdominal cramps during menstruation,* called **dysmenorrhea.** Symptoms can also include backaches, headaches, a feeling of being bloated, and nausea. Up to 72% of women of reproductive age have experienced menstrual pain, and in 10% to 15% it is severe enough to disrupt normal activities (Nelson & Baldwin, 2008). It is most common in young adult women 17 to 24 years old.

There are two types of dysmenorrhea—primary and secondary. In *primary dysmenorrhea,* the symptoms are not associated with any pelvic abnormalities; whereas in *secondary dysmenorrhea* there are pelvic abnormalities. Secondary dysmenorrhea is often caused by endometriosis (see next section), pelvic inflammatory disease (see Chapter 5), or ovarian cysts.

Primary dysmenorrhea is not a psychological condition, as was once believed. It is the result of an overproduction of *prostaglandins,* substances that cause contractions of the uterus. The symptoms may be severe enough to cause many women to occasionally miss work or school.

> "My periods used to ruin 5 days out of the month. I could barely get out of bed with extreme cramps to the point of nausea. Nothing helped, not even over-the-counter medicine. I have been on birth control pills for almost a year. It is the best thing that ever happened. I haven't experienced any pain."

> "The cramps kept me doubled over for days at a time, feeling like I was going to die. Only recently did I find out about drugs like Advil."

> "Sex actually seems to relieve the severity of the cramps for a while."
> (All examples are from the author's files.)

All three of these personal experiences reflect common (and usually successful) ways of alleviating primary dysmenorrhea. Drugs like ibuprofen

Dysmenorrhea ■ Painful menstruation.

Menorrhagia ■ Heavy vaginal bleeding.

Endometriosis ■ The growth of endometrial tissue outside of the uterus.

(trade names Motrin, Advil, and others) inhibit the production of prostaglandins. Many physicians prescribe birth control pills for women who suffer from dysmenorrhea. Finally, Masters and Johnson (1966) reported that orgasms relieve the symptoms, at least temporarily.

Heavy Bleeding (Menorrhagia)

Some women bleed heavily for days or even weeks with every cycle (Nelson & Baldwin, 2008; Painter, 2009). This is called **menorrhagia** and is most common in women approaching menopause, but it can occur at any age. Not only can this severely interfere with one's personal life, but medically it can cause anemia. Treatments include birth control pills, an intrauterine device containing progestin, and in women who do not want more children, endometrial ablation or hysterectomy.

Endometriosis

The endometrium of the uterus grows and thickens during each menstrual cycle and is then sloughed off and discharged during menstruation. **Endometriosis** refers to a condition in which the *endometrial tissue also grows outside the uterus.* It occurs in 5% to 10% of women of reproductive age (Bulun, 2009). Endometriosis may involve the Fallopian tubes, ovaries, external surface of the uterus, vagina, pelvic cavity, and other areas. Like endometrial tissue in the uterus, the out-of-place tissue grows and then breaks apart and bleeds during the menstrual cycle, but the blood cannot drain normally like the inner uterine lining. The abnormal bleeding becomes surrounded by inflammation, and scar tissue forms, in many cases causing adhesions (abnormal growth that binds organs together).

It is not fully understood how endometriosis develops, but those who have it suffer severe cramps and abdominal soreness, especially at menstruation, and often there is excessive menstrual bleeding. Some women experience deep pelvic pain during sexual intercourse as well:

> "I have had problems with severe menstrual cramps since I was a junior in high school. The pain got worse and worse over the years. I would have to wear a tampon and two sanitary napkins just to catch the blood. It was awful. I remember missing many days of school because the pain was so severe I could not walk. Then it was discovered that I had endometriosis."
> (from the author's files)

For women who have painful symptoms, relief can often be achieved with hormone therapy that reduces estrogen levels (Bulun, 2009). The birth control pill is often helpful. In some cases, surgical removal of the abnormal abdominal tissue is required (Özkan & Arici; 2009).

Toxic Shock Syndrome (TSS)

"I work at a local hospital.... One evening a patient came in with flu-like symptoms. The woman got progressively sicker as time went by and her color was actually turning purple in tint. The doctor looked her over from head to toe and then stated that he had found an old tampon in the back of her vagina. He diagnosed her with TSS. The patient's symptoms were getting worse so we went ahead with an emergency transfer by helicopter. After she left, the clerk answered the phone and told us it was the helicopter. Our patient had died."

(from the author's files)

Toxic shock syndrome (TSS) is caused by toxins produced by a bacterium *(Staphylococcus aureus)*. The symptoms, which are often mistaken for the flu, include a sudden high fever, vomiting, diarrhea, fainting or dizziness, low blood pressure, and a red rash that resembles a bad sunburn (Hanrahan, 1994). It sometimes results in death. Although children and men can get TSS, over 85% of all TSS cases are related to menstruation (Bryner, 1989).

There were over 300 cases of TSS in 1980, when the Centers for Disease Control released the first published report of the disease. Most of the cases were in women who had used extra-absorbent tampons. The number of cases of TSS fell dramatically after highly absorbent tampons were removed from the market, but there are still close to 200 cases reported nationwide each year.

The *Staphylococcus* bacteria need oxygen to multiply, and the air pockets in tampons contain oxygen. If the *Staphylococcus* bacteria are in the vagina and the person does not have antibodies to them (most people do by the time they are adults), the conditions are right for the development of toxic shock. Tampons do not cause toxic shock, but women who use tampons should change them three or four times a day and switch to sanitary napkins at night before going to bed. If any of the previously described symptoms should develop during menstruation, be sure to see a doctor immediately.

MENSTRUAL SUPPRESSION: A CURE OR MORE NEGATIVITY?

In 2003, the Food and Drug Administration approved *Seasonale®*, a birth control pill that could be taken for 84 days in order to suppress menstruation during that time. This was followed by a similar pill, *Seasonique*, and in 2007, the FDA approved *Lybrel®*, a birth control pill that allowed women to suppress their periods for a year or longer. This medical technology followed the publication of a book titled *Is Menstruation Obsolete?* (Coutinho & Segal, 1999) in which the authors argued that menstruation is unhealthy.

Menstrual suppression was touted as a cure for menstrual disorders (endometriosis, dysmenorrhea). It was also recommended for female athletes and military personnel. More recently, it has been advertised as a lifestyle choice. Women in my course give a variety of reasons why they take menstrual suppression pills:

"...because I have always had long, heavy periods with a great deal of cramping and bloating."

"...because I have endometriosis and the pills allow me to avoid painful cramps."

"...I don't have to deal with tampons and a mess. It is easier, so why not?"

"It is a hassle to deal with periods. This is especially true when I have a lot of college work. It is just easier to skip the whole process altogether."

"I can count several occasions when women don't want to be on their period: formals, spring break, exams. I don't want to have to worry about scheduling my activities around my period."

PERSONAL REFLECTIONS

Menstrual suppression is viewed more positively by women who consider menstruation to be shameful or bothersome (Johnston-Robledo et al., 2003). Many experts believe that advertisements for menstrual suppression products contribute to our culture's negativity about menstruation. "It perpetuates a lot of negative attitudes and taboos about menstruation, that it's something that's bothersome and dirty and debilitating and shameful" (Ingrid Johnston-Robledo, quoted by Stein, 2007). What do you think?

REGULATION OF MALE HORMONES

In men, the hypothalamus, pituitary gland, and testicles operate in a feedback loop (see Figure 3–6) much like the feedback loop in women. Let us first consider sperm production. Release of gonadotropin-releasing hormone (GnRH) from the hypothalamus causes release of follicle-stimulating hormone (FSH) from the pituitary. Increases in blood levels of FSH stimulate production of sperm in the seminiferous tubules of the testicles. FSH production is inhibited by increases in blood levels of inhibin, produced in men by Sertoli cells in the testicles (Plant et al., 1993).

Testosterone production increases when GnRH from the hypothalamus stimulates release of luteinizing hormone (LH) from the pituitary gland. Higher blood levels of testosterone (produced by the Leydig's

Toxic shock syndrome (TSS) ■ A syndrome with symptoms of high fever, vomiting, diarrhea, and dizziness; caused by toxins produced by the *Staphylococcus aureus* bacterium.

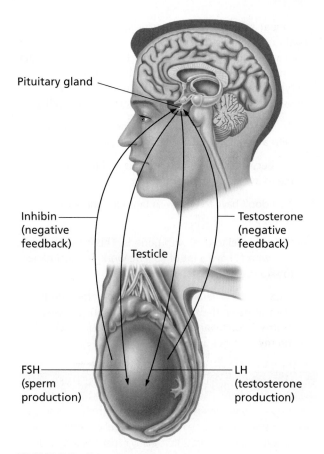

Pituitary gland

Inhibin (negative feedback)

Testosterone (negative feedback)

Testicle

FSH (sperm production)

LH (testosterone production)

FIGURE 3–6 The brain–pituitary–gonad feedback loop in men.

cells in the testicles, you recall) then inhibit the production of GnRH.

You have to just read how women's pituitary and gonadal hormones fluctuate (go through cycles) on about a monthly basis during their reproductive years. However, the levels of FSH, LH, and testosterone in men are relatively stable. There is a diurnal rhythm of testosterone production (higher levels during the day than at night), but testosterone levels do not change dramatically in a monthly cycle.

What accounts for the fact that women of reproductive age have monthly cycles of fluctuating hormone levels while men do not? Are women's pituitary glands different from men's pituitary glands? Research with animals has shown that when male pituitary glands are transplanted into females, these glands also begin to secrete FSH and LH cyclically. Thus, the difference is in the hypothalamus of the brain, not in the pituitaries. A woman's hypothalamus is, in fact, different in both structure and connections from a man's hypothalamus, and it is for this reason that women show cycles in FSH and LH (and consequently, the gonadal hormones) and men do not (Whalen, 1977). I will have more to say about this later in the book.

TESTOSTERONE AND SEXUAL DESIRE

Is the degree of our sexual desire related to our hormone levels? Do people with high sex drives have high levels of hormones while people with low sex drives have low levels? Do some hormones influence sexual desire more than others?

Research on sex and hormones relies heavily on two types of studies: those investigating the effects of administering hormones and those investigating the effects of a loss of hormones (usually after surgical removal of the ovaries or testicles). We will restrict our discussion to human studies, because as you have already learned in reading about menstrual versus estrous cycles, the differences between human sexual behavior and the sexual behavior of most nonhuman mammalian species is so great as to make generalizations from studies with laboratory animals very questionable.

In humans, there is considerable evidence for testosterone playing a role in sexual desire. After puberty in boys, 6 to 8 milligrams of testosterone are produced every day (95% of it by the testicles and 5% by the adrenal glands), and among very young (12 to 14 years old) adolescent boys, sexual activity increases as testosterone levels increase (Halpern et al., 1998). There is a gradual decline in testosterone production as a man grows older, but men who are sexually active often have high testosterone levels. However, we do not know which came first (the old chicken-and-egg question). Men exposed to sexually explicit pictures show a short-term increase in testosterone levels (Rowland et al., 1987).

Hypogonadal men (zmen who have abnormally low levels of testosterone) show very little interest in sex. Hormone replacement therapy generally restores sexual desire (Shah & Montoya, 2007). It was once believed that elevating testosterone levels beyond a minimum threshold had no further effect on sexual desire, but more recent studies have found that administration of testosterone enhances sexual desire and activity, even in men with normal hormone levels (Alexander et al., 1997; R.A. Anderson et al., 1992; Bagatell et al., 1994).

In some parts of the world, men who were once used as harem attendants were forced to have their testicles removed (castration, or *orchiectomy*) so that they would not be interested in the women they were supposed to protect. In many cases this worked, especially if the men were not yet sexually experienced at the time of castration. However, there were also stories of some eunuchs (as they are called) having the time of their lives, like roosters guarding a henhouse. Modern studies of castrated men show, however, that sex drive and behavior are drastically or completely suppressed in a high percentage of cases. In most men, the decline is rapid,

Box 3–B **Sexuality and Health**

Anabolic Steroids

In their pursuit to be the best, athletes are always looking for an edge over their competitors. Megavitamins, painkillers, stimulants—all have been used in the desire to win. The most commonly used substances today are **anabolic steroids** (the more correct name is anabolic-androgenic steroids). These steroid hormones are derivatives of testosterone. They have masculinizing (androgenic) effects and also promote growth by enhancing protein uptake by the muscle cell (the anabolic effect).

In recent years, there have been numerous scandals involving the misuse of steroids by athletes. In 2007 alone, Floyd Landis was stripped of his 2006 Tour de France title, Marion Jones admitted to having used steroids when she won five Olympic medals, World Wrestling Entertainment (WWE) wrestler Chris Benoit killed his family and himself while using heavy dosages of steroids, and the (Senator George) Mitchell Report accused dozens of professional baseball players (including Barry Bonds and Roger Clemens) of using performance-enhancing drugs.

When administered in proper dosages by a physician, anabolic steroids often have therapeutic value for people recovering from illness or surgery. However, in an attempt to gain weight and build muscle mass and strength, many athletes started taking many times (often 100 times) the normal dose. Unfortunately, steroid use is not restricted to athletes. Steroid use among high school students doubled between 1991 and 2003 (Centers for Disease Control and Prevention [CDC], 2005). Today, about 4% to 6% of teenage boys have used illegal steroids (Eaton et al., 2010; Harmer, 2010).

The misuse of anabolic steroids can have serious harmful effects (Bonetti et al., 2007). These include high blood

FIGURE 3–7 In recent years, many athletes have been accused of using steroids, including baseball stars Mark McGwire (above), Barry Bonds, Roger Clemens, and Alex Rodriguez.

pressure and other serious cardiovascular diseases; tumors of the liver and prostate gland; decrease in size of the testicles and impaired reproductive function in men; and lumps in the breast tissue. Steroids can also stunt growth in boys who have not yet reached their full height. Taking anabolic steroids will not make a man's penis bigger, and steroids are likely to cause acne.

Men are not the only ones who take anabolic steroids. About 1.5% to 3.2% of teenage girls have used them at least once (Eaton et al., 2010; Harmer, 2010). Women who take steroids risk sterilization, masculinization of the fetus should pregnancy occur, and a much greater-than-normal chance of breast cancer. Anabolic steroids also have a marked masculinizing effect in women

(e.g., causing facial hair growth, male pattern baldness, and deepening of the voice), which is not reversed by discontinuing use of the drugs.

Although anabolic steroids often boost energy and self-esteem, at least temporarily, other behavior changes may include anxiety, irritability, depression, impaired judgment, and paranoid delusions. One study found that one third of steroid abusers suffered mild to severe mental disorders as a result of using the synthetic hormones (Pope & Katz, 1988). Steroid use also

Anabolic steroids ■ Synthetic steroid hormones that combine the growth (anabolic) effects of adrenal steroids with the masculinizing effects of androgenic steroids.

(Continued)

increases aggressiveness and violent behavior (Beaver et al., 2008; Lumia & McGinnis, 2010).

Here are some personal experiences related by students taking my course:

> "My friends and I worked out in high school. It was a goal of mine to be bigger and stronger than the others. I decided to take anabolic steroids. Not sure how to do it, I had another inexperienced friend help me inject it into my buttocks. About 2 weeks later I noticed my testicles were getting smaller. In another week I started to get severe abdominal pains."

> "I am 19 years old and started using steroids last summer. I wanted to bench press 500 pounds. I gained about 40 pounds. These steroids tended to make me irritable and edgy. I occasionally got bad acne on my back and my testicles shrunk."

Many high school athletes and some college athletes probably take anabolic steroids without knowing much about their side effects, but many world-class athletes who know better continue to do so. Why? For most users, self-fulfillment is most important and they deny any harmful effects (Monaghan, 2002). Would they stop even if they accepted that steroids were harmful? In two independent surveys, world-class athletes were asked if they would take a drug that would make them Olympic champions but kill them within 1 to 5 years. A majority responded that they would (Goldman et al., 1987; Mirkin & Hoffman, 1978). This may be a sad commentary on our attitude about winning.

but castrated men may continue to show some interest in sex for years (Bancroft, 1984).

What about women? The loss of estrogen and progesterone at menopause (or after surgical removal of the ovaries) does not reduce sexual desire in most women. In those postmenopausal women who do show a decrease, estrogen replacement therapy alone generally has no effect (Levin, 2002). Administration of testosterone, on the other hand, enhances sexual desire (Davis et al., 2008). It appears, therefore, that testosterone is also the most important hormone for sexual desire in women (Davis et al., 2008). Small amounts of testosterone (0.5 milligram) are normally produced daily by a woman's ovaries and adrenal glands. Several studies have found that testosterone levels in women are directly related to measures of sexual behavior and desire (Alexander & Sherwin, 1993; Guay, 2001; Persky et al., 1982; Sherwin, 1988). Administration of testosterone in sexually normal women produces an increase in genital arousal and sensations (Tuiten et al., 2000). A deficiency in testosterone produces a marked decrease in sexual desire and responsiveness in women but is restored with testosterone replacement therapy (Davis et al., 2008; Shah & Montoya, 2007). In conclusion, a stronger case can be made for the influence of testosterone on sexual desire in women than for estrogen and progesterone. However, as you will learn in the next chapter, women's sexual desire is highly correlated with relationship and intimacy needs.

STUDY GUIDE

KEY TERMS

adrenal glands 59
amenorrhea 68
anabolic steroids 73
corpus luteum 62
dysmenorrhea 70
endocrine system 59
endometriosis 70
estrogen 59
estrous cycle 64
follicle 60
follicle-stimulating hormone (FSH) 59
follicular (proliferative) phase 61
gonadotropin-releasing hormone (GnRH) 60

gonadotropins 59
hormones 59
human chorionic gonadotropin (HCG) 62
inhibin 60
luteal (secretory) phase 62
luteinizing hormone (LH) 59
menarche 68
menopause 60
menorrhagia 70
menstrual cycle 60
menstrual taboos 66
menstruation 60
Mittelschmerz 62
orchiectomy 72

ovaries 59
ovulation 61
oxytocin 60
pheromones 63
pituitary gland 59
premenstrual dysphoric disorder (PMDD) 69
premenstrual syndrome (PMS) 68
progesterone 59
prolactin 60
prostaglandins 70
testicles 59
testosterone 59
toxic shock syndrome (TSS) 71

INTERACTIVE REVIEW

Hormones are chemical substances that are released into the bloodstream by ductless (1) _____ glands. The ovaries and testicles are part of this system. The testicles produce the "male hormone" (2) _____, and the ovaries produce the "female hormones" (3) _____ and (4) _____. Hormones from the (5) _____ cause the ovaries and testicles to produce their hormones.

In adult women, an egg matures on an average of every (6) _____ days. The pituitary hormone that starts the menstrual cycle is called (7) _____. This hormone stimulates the development of a (8) _____ in the ovary. During the preovulatory phase of the menstrual cycle (also called the (9) _____ phase), estrogen from the follicle promotes growth of the (10) _____, inhibits release of (11) _____, and stimulates release of (12) _____. The (13) _____ surge signals the onset of (14) _____, at which time the ovum is expelled into the (15) _____ and is picked up by a (16) _____. During the postovulatory phase of the cycle, also called the (17) _____ phase, the (18) _____ secretes progesterone in large amounts. If the egg is fertilized by a sperm, it normally implants in the (19) _____. If the egg is not fertilized, the corpus luteum degenerates and the (20) _____ is sloughed off and discharged in a normal physiological process called (21) _____. Although the average length of the menstrual cycle is 28 days, the large majority of women have cycles that vary in length by (22) _____. In most nonhuman mammalian species, this cycle of hormonal events is called the (23) _____ cycle. Unlike human women, females of species with this type of cycle are sexually receptive to males only during (24) _____. Some cultures have menstrual (25) _____ that prohibit contact with a menstruating woman. Even in our own culture many women and their partners avoid sexual intercourse during menstruation, but this generally reflects inaccurate information and/or negative culturally learned responses. Menstrual discharge consists simply of (26) _____, (27) _____, and (28) _____.

In men, FSH stimulates (29) _____, while (30) _____ stimulates the production of (31) _____ in the Leydig's cells of the testicles. Misuse of anabolic steroids, derivatives of testosterone, can cause serious harmful effects such as (32) _____ (name three effects).

Some women experience menstrual-related problems. The absence of menstruation is called (33) _____. Emotional and/or physical changes taking place (34) _____ days before the start of menstruation are referred to as (35) _____. What distinguishes this condition from other emotional states is that it ends (36) _____. The major cause of (37) _____, painful menstruation, is an overproduction of (38) _____. Endometriosis refers to a condition in which (39) _____. Women who use tampons but do not change them frequently risk getting a serious bacterial infection called (40) _____.

In men, sexual desire appears to be related to circulating levels of (41) _____. Studies of women after menopause, or after surgical removal of the ovaries, suggest that women's sexual desire is not strongly affected by the hormones (42) _____ or (43) _____. Other studies indicate that the hormone (44) _____ does influence sexual desire in women.

SELF-TEST

A. TRUE OR FALSE

[T] [F] 45. Hormones are important for women's sexual desire, but not for men's.

[T] [F] 46. Testosterone is found only in men, and estrogen is found only in women.

[T] [F] 47. All female mammals have menstrual cycles.

[T] [F] 48. Most women's menstrual cycles are 28 days in length.

[T] [F] 49. It is medically safe for a man to have sexual intercourse with a menstruating woman.

[T] [F] 50. Women who use tampons should change them three or four times a day, even if the tampons are advertised as long lasting.

T	F	51. Women show a dramatic increase in sexual desire around the time of ovulation.
T	F	52. Women's ovaries produce new eggs throughout their lifetimes.
T	F	53. Near the end of the postovulatory phase of the menstrual cycle, there is an LH surge.
T	F	54. There is some evidence suggesting that women's menstrual cycles can be altered by odorless body secretions.
T	F	55. Only women can get toxic shock syndrome.
T	F	56. Estrogen, according to most research, is the primary hormone responsible for sexual desire in women.

B. MATCHING

_____ 57. endocrine system

_____ 58. testosterone

_____ 56. luteinizing hormone

_____ 60. estrogen

_____ 61. FSH

_____ 62. follicular phase

_____ 63. corpus luteum

_____ 64. amenorrhea

_____ 65. luteal phase

_____ 66. dysmenorrhea

_____ 67. *Mittelschmerz*

_____ 68. inhibin

_____ 69. ovulation

_____ 70. prostaglandins

_____ 71. premenstrual syndrome

_____ 72. endometriosis

a. substances that cause contractions of the uterus

b. cells surrounding the ovum that are left behind at ovulation

c. emotional and/or physical changes that precede menstruation

d. "male" hormone produced in testicles, ovaries, and adrenal glands

e. cramps experienced for about a day during ovulation

f. postovulatory phase when the corpus luteum begins to secrete large amounts of progesterone

g. endometrial tissue growing outside the uterus

h. network of ductless glands

i. rupture of the mature ovum into the abdominal cavity

j. "female" hormone produced in ovaries, testicles, and adrenal glands

k. preovulatory phase when the pituitary secretes FSH and the follicle secretes estrogen

l. pituitary hormone that stimulates production of sperm and maturation of ova

m. absence of menstruation

n. pituitary hormone that triggers ovulation in women and the production of testosterone in men

o. painful cramps during menstruation

p. substance produced in the ovaries and testicles that inhibits production of FSH

C. FILL IN THE BLANKS

73. The gland located at the base of the brain that secretes follicle-stimulating hormone and luteinizing hormone is the _____ gland.

74. Natural body scents that can affect the behavior of other members of the same species are called _____.

75. Each immature ovum is surrounded by other cells within a thin capsule of tissue to form what is called a _____.

76. During ovulation, the cells that surround the ovum in the follicle remain in the ovary and are then referred to as the _____.

77. If an egg is fertilized by a sperm and implantation occurs, the corpus luteum is maintained by a hormone from the developing placenta called _____.

78. The hypothalamic hormone that causes release of FSH and LH from the pituitary is called _____.

79. In the female hormone feedback loop, LH production is suppressed primarily by _____.

80. In the male hormone feedback loop, LH production is suppressed primarily by _____.

81. In the male hormone feedback loop, FSH production is suppressed by _____.

82. The pituitary hormone associated with milk release, labor and orgasmic contractions, and romantic attraction is called _____.

83. In a woman's menstrual cycle, the fertile period is _____ day(s) before and _____ day(s) after _____.

SUGGESTED READINGS

Adler, J. (2004, December 20). Toxic strength. *Newsweek*, 45–52. An excellent article on the use and dangers of anabolic steroids among teenagers.

Boston Women's Health Book Collective. (2005). *Our bodies, ourselves: A new edition for a new era*. New York: Simon & Schuster.

Delaney, J., Lupton, M. J., & Toth, E. (1988). *The curse: A cultural history of menstruation*. Urbana and Chicago: University of Illinois Press.

McClintock, M. K. (1999). Whither menstrual synchrony? In R. C. Rosen, C. M. Davis, and H. J. Ruppel Jr. (Eds.), *Annual Review of Sex Research* (vol. 9, pp. 77–95). Allentown, PA: Society For Scientific Study of Sexuality. By the person whose paper started it all in 1971. Examines all the complexities of menstrual synchronization.

Small, M. F. (1999, January/February). A woman's curse. *The Sciences*. Discusses why women historically have been isolated during menstruation.

Steinem, G. (1978, October). If men could menstruate. *Ms.* A humorous and political view of menstruation.

Svoboda, E. (2008, January/February). Scents and sensibility. *Psychology Today*. Is sexual attraction based, at least in part, on smell?

4 Similarities and Differences in Our Sexual Responses

How can biologists, behaviorists, theologians, and educators insist in good conscience upon the continued existence of a massive state of ignorance of human sexual response, to the detriment of the well-being of millions of individuals?.... Can that one facet of our lives, affecting more people in more ways than any other physiologic response other than those necessary to our very existence, be allowed to continue without benefit of objective, scientific analysis?

—Excerpt from *Human Sexual Response* by William Masters & Virgina Johnson, 1966, Lippincott, Williams & Wilkins.

When you have finished studying this chapter, you should be able to:

- List and describe the four phases of Masters and Johnson's model of the sexual response cycle in order of their occurrence.

- Explain why researchers after Masters and Johnson chose to add a desire phase.

- Explain why the Masters and Johnson model is not appropriate for understanding women's responses.

- Understand the process of vaginal lubrication and penile erection.

- Understand why many women's subjective arousal is correlated poorly with their physiological arousal.

- Explain and discuss several controversies about orgasm.

- Understand the role of penis size in sexual pleasuring.

- Discuss the validity of reputed aphrodisiacs.

- Explain and discuss the practice of female genital cutting in other cultures.

- Appreciate that people with disabilities, like everyone else, are sexual human beings.

The primary tools of behavioral scientists are observation and measurement. The mechanisms involved in most human behaviors have been under investigation since the 19th century, but because of the negative attitudes that have prevailed since the Victorian era, human sexual behavior was considered off-limits as a subject for scientific inquiry. The first major surveys of human sexual behavior were not published until the mid-1900s (Kinsey et al., 1948, 1953). Then, in 1966, William Masters and Virginia Johnson published their book, *Human Sexual Response,* based on direct laboratory observation of hundreds of men and women engaged in sexual activity on thousands of occasions. Human sexuality as a topic for research was thereafter no longer taboo. In this chapter, you will learn about the physiological responses that occur during sexual arousal.

MEASUREMENT OF SEXUAL RESPONSES

You were introduced to the work of **Masters and Johnson** in Chapter 1. How did they actually make their observations and do their recording?

Masters and Johnson recruited their sample of 312 men and 382 women from the local community. The ages of their volunteers ranged from 18 to 89. The laboratory was a plain room that had a bed

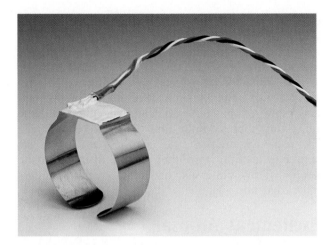
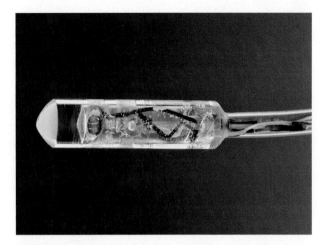

FIGURE 4–1 An early model penile strain gauge (left, the Geer gauge) and vaginal photoplethysmograph (right, the Barlow gauge) used by Masters and Johnson to measure vasocongestion in the genitals.

and recording equipment. The subjects were first allowed to have sex with no one else present so that they would feel comfortable, but after that there was always one or more investigators present. Masters and Johnson recorded over 10,000 sexual episodes leading to orgasm. This included people engaged in masturbation, intercourse, and oral-genital sex. Many subjects were observed dozens of times in order to determine the amount of variability in their responses.

The subjects were hooked up to equipment that measured physiological responses such as heart rate, blood pressure, muscle tension, respiration, and brain waves. Rather than rely on subjects' self-reports of degree of sexual arousal, Masters and Johnson had special equipment made to record the volume of blood in the genitals. Two of these devices are shown in Figure 4–1. The *penile strain gauge* is a thin rubber tube filled with mercury that fits over the base of the penis and transmits a small electric current that can record even a slight change in the circumference of the penis. The *vaginal photoplethysmograph* fits like a tampon into the vagina and has a light and photocell to record blood volume in the vaginal walls (by measuring changes in the reflection of light).

The main criticism of studies like those of Masters and Johnson is the unnatural setting of the laboratory. Were the subjects affected by the presence of observers or by the recording equipment? Furthermore, how normal were the subjects themselves? Would you volunteer to participate in a study like this? However, it is generally assumed in medical research that studies of normal physiological processes (digestion, for example) do not require a random sample of subjects because these processes will be more or less the same from person to person.

PERSONAL REFLECTIONS

Do you think it is important that we know the physiological responses that normally occur during sexual arousal? Is it important that physicians and therapists have this information? What do you think about studies, such as those by Masters and Johnson, that require observing and recording individuals engaged in sex? If your opinion is negative, how else could we learn about the normal physiological responses during sexual arousal?

MODELS OF SEXUAL RESPONSE

Masters and Johnson described the physiological responses that take place in men and women as occurring in four phases: (1) excitement, (2) plateau, (3) orgasm, and (4) resolution. They referred to this response pattern as the **sexual response cycle**. It must be emphasized that the phases are only a convenient model. Even Masters and Johnson admitted that the phases are arbitrarily defined, and rather than indicating a noticeable shift, they often flow together. Hardly anyone, for example, would be aware of the precise moment of leaving the excitement phase and entering the plateau phase.

Others have proposed models that divide the sexual responses into fewer or more phases than the model used by Masters and Johnson. **Helen Kaplan** (1979), for example, proposed a model for sexual responses that has only three phases: desire, excitement, and orgasm. From a subjective point of view,

Sexual response cycle ■ The physiological responses that occur during sexual arousal, which many therapists and researchers have arbitrarily divided into different phases.

her model is appealing because most people would be able to distinguish the change in these phases.

More recently, feminist scholars have questioned the adequacy of both Masters and Johnson's model and Helen Kaplan's model in describing women's sexual responses (e.g., Basson, 2000, 2001a, b; 2002a, b, c; Basson et al., 2003; Tiefer, 2001). The focus of the older models was on genital responses, whereas the newer models emphasize the greater complexity of women's responses. We will begin with a description of men's sexual responses and then compare and contrast those with women's responses.

MEN'S SEXUAL RESPONSE CYCLE

Two models of the male sexual response cycle are presented in Figure 4–2. The following description combines the two models into a five-phase model: desire, excitement, plateau, orgasm, and resolution.

Desire

Desire, according to Helen Kaplan (1979),

> is experienced as specific sensations which move the individual to seek out, or become receptive to, sexual experiences. These sensations are produced by the physical activation of a specific neural system in the brain. When this system is active, a person is "horny"; he may feel genital sensations or he may feel vaguely sexy, interested in sex, open to sex, or even just restless.

Others define desire more simply as "an intrinsic motivation to pursue sex" (Peplau, 2003).

The addition of a desire phase has been very popular with many sex therapists, particularly those who feel that the subjective aspects of sexual responsiveness (how one thinks and feels emotionally) are as important as the physiological responses. A man can have the physiological response (e.g., erection) without feeling aroused. This separation will take on even greater importance when we consider women's sexual desire.

Regardless of what specifically motivates an individual, once a man has sexual desire, the physiological responses that occur during excitement and the remaining phases do not differ with different stimuli. The responses are the same regardless of whether the source of arousal is another person, of the opposite sex or of the same sex, or oneself (fantasy and/or masturbation).

Excitement (Arousal)

Sexual arousal in men can follow a wide variety of physical and/or cognitive/emotional cues (Janssen et al., 2008). The first physical sign of arousal in men, of course, is *erection of the penis* resulting from the spongy tissues of the corpora cavernosa and the corpus spongiosum becoming engorged with blood (see Figure 4–4). This **vasocongestive response** starts within 3 to 8 seconds after stimulation begins but usually does not result in a full erection right away. Many men, however, worry if they do not have a "steel-hard" erection immediately upon stimulation. Remember, the **excitement phase** is just the initial phase of the response cycle, and it is not unusual for men to be easily distracted at first by either mental or external stimuli, resulting in fluctuation in the firmness of the erection.

Desire ■ A state that "is experienced as specific sensations which move the individual to seek out, or become receptive to, sexual experiences" (Kaplan, 1979).

Vasocongestive response (vasocongestion) ■ The engorgement (filling) of tissues with blood.

Excitement phase (men) ■ The first phase of the sexual response cycle as proposed by Masters and Johnson. The first sign is vasocongestion of the penis, leading to erection.

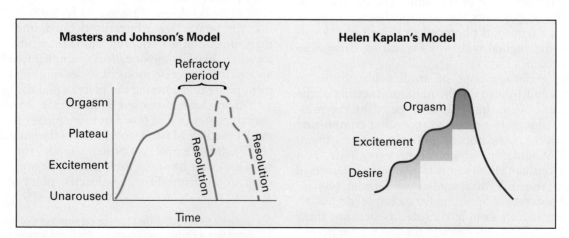

FIGURE 4–2 Two models of the male sexual response cycle. This book combines Kaplan's desire phase with Masters and Johnson's four-phase model (excitement, plateau, orgasm, and resolution).

Vasocongestion of the penis results from nerve impulses causing dilation of the arteries that carry blood to the penis (Giuliano & Rampin, 2004). To better understand this, look at Figure 4–3. There are two centers in the spinal cord responsible for erection. The more important of the two is located in the lowest (sacral) part of the spinal cord. Nerve impulses caused by stimulation of the penis travel to this center, which then sends nerve impulses back to the penis in a reflex action. The nerve impulses release a chemical in the penis (cyclic GMP) that causes the smooth muscles in the spongy tissue to relax, allowing dilation of the arteries (and vasocongestion). Many men with spinal cords cut above the sacral erection center can still get erections in this reflexive manner, although they cannot feel stimulation of the penis. This is true for quadriplegics as well as paraplegics (C. J. Alexander et al., 1993). In men with intact spinal cords, nerve impulses from the brain (generated by such things as sights, sounds, and fantasies) are carried to the erection center and result in vasocongestion. A second erection center, located higher in the spinal cord (thoracolumbar), also receives impulses originating in the brain, and

thus it too contributes to psychologically caused erections. Although vasocongestion of the penis sounds like a mechanically easy process, a number of things can interfere with it, including physical or emotional stress and/or fatigue (see Chapter 13).

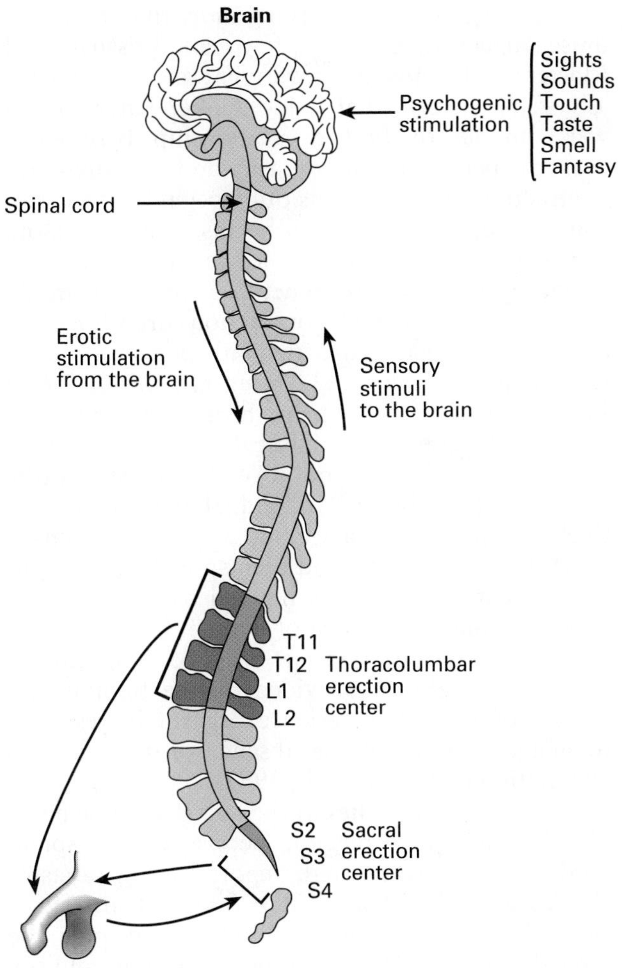

Vasocongestion of the penis is not the only response that happens in men during the excitement phase. Any time we become excited there is an increase in heart rate and blood pressure. During sexual excitement, the scrotum thickens (th muscle layer contracts) and the spermatic cord shortens, thus elevating the testicles toward the body. Late in the excitement phase, the testicles also start to become engorged with blood and enlarge (see Figure 4–4). In addition, nipple erection occurs in some men, a reaction that is not related to a man's masculinity or femininity.

Plateau

The **plateau** phase is a period of high sexual arousal that potentially sets the stage for orgasm. In some men this phase may be quite short; in others it may last a long time. In this phase, the diameter of the penis further increases, especially near the corona. In addition, the testicles become fully engorged with blood (increasing in size by 50% to 100%) and continue to elevate and rotate until their back surfaces touch the perineum, an indication that orgasm is near (see Figure 4–4). The Cowper's glands secrete a few drops of clear fluid that may appear at the tip of the penis. About 25% of men experience a *sex-tension flush* on various areas of the skin (resembling a measleslike rash) due to the skin undergoing a vasocongestive response.

Orgasm

The Essence of Orgasm

With continued and effective stimulation, men experience intense physical sensations lasting a few seconds that are referred to collectively as **orgasm** (climax, or "coming"). Masters and Johnson define orgasm as a sudden discharge of the body's accumulated sexual tension. But does this definition describe the real essence of orgasm? If a Martian were to land on earth and ask you what an orgasm is, how would you describe it? Here are some responses male students in

FIGURE 4–3 Neural mechanisms involved in an erection.

Plateau ■ The second phase of the sexual response cycle proposed by Masters and Johnson. Physiologically, it represents a high state of arousal.

Orgasm ■ The brief but intense sensations (focused largely in the genitals but really a whole body response) experienced during sexual arousal. During orgasm, rhythmic muscular contractions occur in certain tissues in both the man and woman. The third phase of the sexual response cycle proposed by Masters and Johnson.

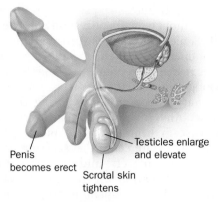

Penis
becomes erect

Testicles enlarge
and elevate

Scrotal skin
tightens

Excitement

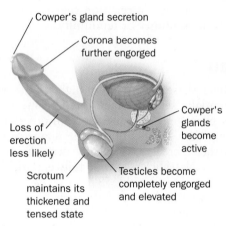

Cowper's gland secretion

Corona becomes
further engorged

Loss of
erection
less likely

Cowper's
glands
become
active

Scrotum
maintains its
thickened and
tensed state

Testicles become
completely engorged
and elevated

Plateau

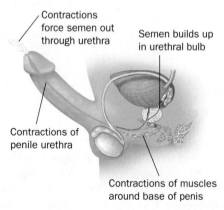

Contractions
force semen out
through urethra

Semen builds up
in urethral bulb

Contractions of
penile urethra

Contractions of muscles
around base of penis

Orgasm and Ejaculation

FIGURE 4–4 Men's physiological sexual responses: excitement, plateau, and orgasm and ejaculation.

Source: Hock, *Human Sexuality*, © 2007 PrenticeHall, Inc. Reproduced by permission of Pearson Education, Inc.

my class gave me when I asked them to describe their orgasms for someone who had never had one:

"...like a bomb but feels great. When you reach your max, you feel like you are going to burst open. Then you feel like you are floating in the sky."

"...like a roller coaster. At first you feel excited, your whole body feels tingly. My heart feels like it's falling in my chest. Then my stomach and leg muscles tighten up, and all tension is then released in a moment."

"Like a bolt of lightning strikes you in the back of your spine. You get stiff, curling your toes and making ludicrous faces."

"...like you have been drinking 10–15 beers on a road trip and the person driving won't pull over for you to relieve yourself. The feeling is like when they finally do pull over, and the first few seconds of relief."

Obviously, it is difficult to adequately describe orgasm in words. I guess that you have to have had one to really know what it is.

Using electrophysiological recording equipment, Masters and Johnson (1966) found that orgasm consisted of rhythmic muscular contractions in specific parts of the body that initially occurred every 0.8 second, but then diminished in intensity and regularity. Others have reported that the first contractions are only 0.6 second apart (Bohlen et al., 1980), but the really important thing is that for the first time definite physiological responses could be identified in specific tissues.

Is an orgasm really nothing more than rhythmic muscular contractions in a few genital tissues? Did Masters and Johnson record what an orgasm actually is, or merely what it looks like? Later studies were unable to find a relationship between a person's perception of orgasm and the muscular contractions. Contractions often begin before a person's perception of orgasm begins, and end before the person reports orgasm to be over. Moreover, strong contractions are sometimes seen with "mild" orgasms, whereas weak contractions are sometimes associated with orgasms that are perceived as intensely pleasurable (Bohlen et al., 1980, 1982; Levin & Wagner, 1985). In short, researchers can measure the contractions, but they cannot measure the pleasure. The perception of the orgasm can be measured only by the individual person. Subjectively, people report a feeling of pleasure focused initially in the genitals and then spreading throughout the entire body. This has led some experts to conclude that the essence of orgasm lies not in the genitals but in the brain (see Mah & Binik, 2005). Evidence for this is provided by the finding that some women can experience orgasm in response to imagery alone, in the absence of any physical stimulation (Whipple et al., 1992).

Additional proof lies in the fact that some paraplegics and quadriplegics, people whose spinal cord has been transected, report having orgasms (C. J. Alexander et al., 1993; Sipski et al., 1999; Whipple & Komisaruk, 1999). They display the typical heart rate changes, muscle tensions, and sex flushes that people with undamaged spines show.

In summary, it appears that orgasm is a perceptual experience (generated in the brain, thus not always requiring genital stimulation) and that its occurrence is subjective.

Men's Orgasms

In men, orgasm occurs in two stages. In the first stage, called *emission,* rhythmic muscular contractions in the vas deferens, prostate gland, and seminal vesicles force the sperm and the prostate and seminal fluids into the ejaculatory ducts, thus forming *semen.* Sphincter muscles (circular bands of muscle fibers) contract and close off the part of the urethra that goes through the prostate, and the semen causes it to swell to two to three times its normal size (called the urethral bulb). These initial contractions give men a feeling of ejaculatory inevitability (the famous "I'm coming")—the feeling that orgasm is about to happen and cannot be put off.

In the second stage, called *expulsion,* these contractions are joined by contractions in the urethra and muscles at the base of the penis to force the semen from the penis—**ejaculation.** During this stage, the sphincter muscles surrounding the part of the urethra coming from the bladder are tightly contracted so that urine is not mixed with semen. A few men have a medical problem known as *retrograde ejaculation* in which the sphincter muscle that allows passage of semen through the penile urethra closes (instead of opening) and the sphincter muscle surrounding the part of the urethra from the bladder opens (instead of closing), thus forcing semen into the bladder instead of out of the body.

Although ejaculation occurs at about the same time as orgasm in men, *they are really two different events.* Orgasm refers to the subjective pleasurable sensations, while ejaculation refers to the release of semen from the body. The passage of semen through the penis has nothing to do with the sensation of orgasm or the intensity of orgasm. Think about it: If the passage of fluid through the urethra were the cause of the pleasurable sensations, at which other times during the day would men have a very intense orgasm (but do not)? Orgasm and ejaculation, in fact, do not always occur together. Before puberty, for example, boys can have orgasm, but do not ejaculate (the prostate and seminal vesicles do not enlarge until puberty). Ejaculation in the absence of orgasm has also been reported with some types of illness and medications.

Resolution

Resolution is defined as a return to the unaroused state. In men, this involves a loss of erection, a decrease in testicle size, movement of the testicles away from the body cavity, and disappearance of the sex flush in those who have it. Loss of erection (detumescence) is due to the return of normal blood flow to the penis. Some of the excess blood is pumped out by the orgasmic contractions, and normal blood flow then returns as the arteries begin to constrict and the veins open. The testicles had become swollen with blood during the plateau phase, and if orgasm is delayed or not achieved, men may now experience testicular aching (what is sometimes known as "blue balls"). The discomfort is only temporary and is not dangerous—and the testicles and scrotum do not turn blue.

Many men, of course, are capable of reaching orgasm two or more times while having sex. If emotional and/or physical stimulation continues after an orgasm, a man's physiological responses may not fall all the way to preexcitement-phase levels, but they will drop below plateau level for some period of time. Partial or full erection may be possible, but the man will be unable to have another orgasm until his responses build up to plateau level again. (Remember, it is not possible to have an orgasm until one's responses have built up to the high-intensity level that Masters and Johnson called plateau.) The period of time after an orgasm in which it is physiologically impossible for a man to achieve another orgasm is called the **refractory period** (see Figure 4–2). It is not a fixed amount of time; the refractory period differs from individual to individual. It tends to grow longer as men age, and also after each successive orgasm (should he have two or more orgasms). Of course, the most important factor is the amount of stimulation. For example, the refractory period may be very short if a man is having sex with a new partner. This is known as the "Coolidge effect," named after American President Calvin Coolidge. President and Mrs. Coolidge were being conducted on separate tours of a farm. When Mrs. Coolidge reached the henhouse, she asked the farmer whether the continuous and vigorous sexual activity of the hens was really the work of just one rooster. After the farmer acknowledged that it was, Mrs. Coolidge responded, "You might point that out to Mr. Coolidge." Her statement was relayed to the president, who then asked the farmer whether the rooster had sex with a new hen each time. When the farmer responded "Yes," Mr. Coolidge replied, "You might point that out to Mrs. Coolidge."

Ejaculation ■ The expulsion of semen from the body.

Resolution ■ The fourth and final phase of the sexual response cycle proposed by Masters and Johnson. It refers to a return to the unaroused state.

Refractory period ■ In men, the period of time after an orgasm in which their physiological responses fall below the plateau level, thus making it impossible for them to have another orgasm (until the responses build back up to plateau).

WOMEN'S SEXUAL RESPONSE CYCLE

There is greater variation in women's sexual responses than is observed in men. Masters and Johnson's model for men was a linear model that focused on physiology and genital arousal. They attempted to explain women's responses by the same model. More recently, feminist scholars have emphasized the role of intimacy needs, the relational context of arousal, and cognitive interpretation of sexual stimuli in women's sexual responsiveness. **Rosemary Basson** (2000; 2001a, b; 2002b, c; Basson et al., 2003) has proposed a model that incorporates these features (see Figure 4–5). Similar to Masters and Johnson's model, her model has its critics (e.g., Both & Everaerd, 2002), but it is important for its distinction between physiological arousal and subjective arousal—and particularly for its ability to explain some sexual problems (see Chapter 13).

Desire/Interest

There are some important differences between men's and women's sexual desire. First, several researchers have concluded that men have a higher level of sexual desire, as evidenced by how frequently they think

---

> Desire (women) ■ For many women, sexual desire is motivated less by biological urges than it is by relationship and intimacy needs.
>
> Excitement (arousal) phase (women) ■ Arousability has been defined as "the capacity to become sexually aroused in response to situational cues" (Peplau, 2003). For many women, relationship and intimacy needs provide the situational cues.

---

about sex, their preferred frequency of sex, frequency of masturbation, and so forth (Baumeister, 2000; Baumeister et al., 2001; Basson, 2000; Levine, 2002; Oliver & Hyde, 1993; Peplau, 2003; Regan & Atkins, 2006). In Masters and Johnson's and Kaplan's models of sexual response, sexual desire is considered to be an innate motivation, that is, they depict "sexual desire as a spontaneous force that itself triggers sexual arousal" (Basson, 2001c, p. 397). For men, sexual desire is determined largely by biological factors such as levels of testosterone (see Chapter 3).

Second, for most women sexual **desire** is motivated less by biological urges than it is by relationship and intimacy needs (Basson, 2000; 2002a, c; Byers, 2001; Haning et al., 2007; Peplau, 2003; Regan & Berscheid, 1999; Tiefer, 2000). Look at Rosemary Basson's model in Figure 4–5. In her words, "The crucial factor [for sexual desire] is the measure of willingness and ability to find and respond to sexual stimuli. The motivation to move from a state of sexual neutrality to one of sexual arousal and potential sexual desire to continue the experience often stems from wanting to enhance emotional closeness to the partner" (Basson, 2002c, p. 293). "Sexual desire then is a responsive rather than a spontaneous event" (Basson, 2000, p. 53).

Excitement (Arousal)

As with men, sexual arousal can follow a wide variety of physical and nonphysical stimuli (Graham et al., 2004). Let us first review Masters and Johnson's description of what occurs during the **excitement phase**. Similar to men, the first sign of sexual arousal in women is a vasocongestive response, and

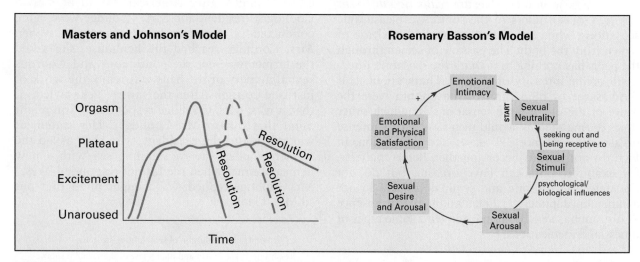

FIGURE 4–5 Two models of the female sexual response cycle. Masters and Johnson's model for women resembles their model for men in its emphasis on physiological (largely genital) responses. Rosemary Basson's model places a greater emphasis on emotional intimacy and cognitive interpretation of stimuli.

Source: Reprinted with permission from Rosemary Basson, "Are our definitions of women's desire, arousal, and sexual pain disorders too broad and our definitions of orgasmic disorder too narrow?" *Journal of Sex & Marital Therapy*, Vol. 28, pp. 293. Copyright © 2002 Routledge. Reprinted by permission of the publisher (Taylor & Francis Group, http://www.informaworld.com).

just as in men, it begins within seconds after the start of stimulation. The vaginal walls become engorged with blood, and the pressure soon causes the walls to secrete drops of fluid (superfiltered blood plasma) on the inner surfaces. This is called *vaginal lubrication.* However, while it is difficult for a man not to notice that his penis is getting firm, many women may not be aware that their vagina is lubricating until several minutes have passed.

Many men mistake the presence of vaginal lubrication as a sign that their female partner is ready to begin intercourse. Although lubrication makes vaginal penetration easier and prevents irritation during thrusting, remember that this is just the first physiological response experienced by a woman and does not mean that she is emotionally, or even physically, ready to begin sexual intercourse (discussion follows).

In addition to vaginal lubrication, the labia majora, which normally cover and protect the vaginal opening, flatten and begin to move apart. The walls of the vagina, which are collapsed in the unstimulated state, begin to balloon out, and the cervix and uterus pull up, thus getting the vagina ready to accommodate a penis (see Figure 4–7). The clitoris, which is made up of two corpora cavernosa, becomes engorged with blood, resulting in an increase in diameter of the shaft (and length in 10% of women) and a slight increase in diameter of the glans. As a result, the clitoris is more prominent during the excitement phase than at any other time (see Figure 4–6).

The nipples also become erect during the excitement phase—a result of contraction of small muscle fibers, not vasocongestion. Vasocongestion of breast tissues is responsible, however, for a slight increase in breast size late in the excitement phase.

Did you notice the focus on genital vasocongestive responses in Masters and Johnson's description of the excitement phase? For men, genital vasocongestion (leading to erection) confirms or amplifies their arousal. But is this true for women? Arousability (excitement) can be defined as "the capacity to become sexually aroused in response to situational cues" (Peplau, 2003). Unlike men, *for many women subjective arousal is very poorly correlated with genital measures of physiological arousal* (vasocongestion) (Chivers et al., 2010). In many cases, women's autonomic nervous systems respond to "sexual" stimuli with genital vasocongestion, but the women do not interpret it as sexual arousal, and some may even find it to be unpleasant (see Basson et al., 2003).

So, what are the situational cues that result in many women's arousal? Most women are concerned more with subjective arousal than physical arousal (Ellison, 2000; Tiefer, 2001). According to Basson (2002a, p. 2), "the contextual cues surrounding the sexual stimuli simultaneously are cognitively appraised [and viewed as positive or negative] and contain the potential to trigger subjective arousal." For many women, it is the relational context that is important—"emotional closeness, bonding, commitment,... and desire to share physical sexual pleasure—for the sake of sharing more than for satisfying sexual hunger. In this manner, [women] move from a state of sexual neutrality—however, with a willingness for this to change as [women] allow stimuli to arouse [them]—and access sexual desire to continue for sexual as well as intimacy reasons" (Basson, 2001a, p. 34). Thus, in this model (see Figure 4–5), *women's sexual arousal commonly precedes sexual desire,* "having arisen from a deliberate finding or acceptance of sexual stimuli: that are necessary to move her from neutrality to arousal" (Basson, 2001b, p. 106). An interesting conclusion of this model is that, in contrast to men, *many women do not separate desire from arousal*—it is all one process (Basson, 2002c; Tiefer, 2001).

PERSONAL REFLECTIONS

Do you know what factors influence your continued arousal as you go through the excitement, plateau, and orgasm phases of the sexual response cycle? Do you know which kinds of stimulation will give you the most pleasure? Do you know what pleases your partner most? Is it assumption or fact? Have you talked with your partner about how best to please each other? If not, why not?

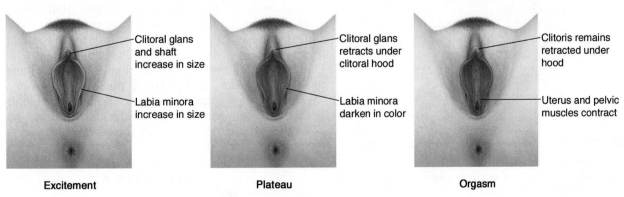

Excitement — Clitoral glans and shaft increase in size / Labia minora increase in size

Plateau — Clitoral glans retracts under clitoral hood / Labia minora darken in color

Orgasm — Clitoris remains retracted under hood / Uterus and pelvic muscles contract

FIGURE 4–6 Changes in the clitoris and labia during sexual arousal.

Plateau

To describe plateau, we will return to Masters and Johnson's model. Many events occur during this period that make the plateau phase distinct from the excitement phase (see Figure 4–7). While the

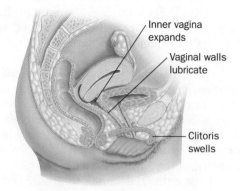

Excitement

Inner vagina expands
Vaginal walls lubricate
Clitoris swells

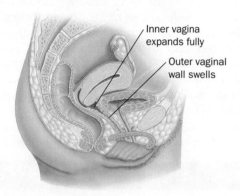

Plateau

Inner vagina expands fully
Outer vaginal wall swells

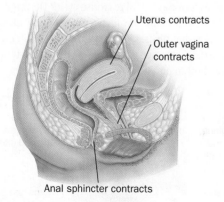

Uterus contracts
Outer vagina contracts
Anal sphincter contracts

Orgasm

FIGURE 4–7 Women's physiological sexual responses: excitement, plateau, and orgasm.

Source: Hock, *Human Sexuality,* © 2007 PrenticeHall, Inc. Reproduced by permission of Pearson Education, Inc.

inner two thirds of the vagina continue to expand like an inflated balloon and the uterus continues to elevate (creating a "tenting effect" in the vaginal walls), something quite different happens in the tissues of the outer third of the vagina. These tissues become greatly engorged with blood and swell, a reaction that Masters and Johnson call the *orgasmic platform*. The swelling of tissues results in a narrowing of the vaginal opening by 30% to 50%. Thus, the tissues of the outer third of the vagina grip the penis during this stage (negating the importance of penis size, according to Masters and Johnson).

Changes in blood flow cause a measleslike rash to appear on areas of the skin early in the plateau stage (or late in the excitement stage). This *sex-tension flush*, as it is called, occurs in 50% to 75% of all women and generally appears on the breasts, upper abdomen, and buttocks, although it can appear on any part of the body.

There are three additional responses occurring in women during the plateau phase that are sometimes misinterpreted by men to mean that the woman is no longer aroused, when in fact she is at a very heightened stage. First, the clitoris pulls back against the pubic bone and disappears beneath the clitoral hood (see Figure 4–6). Second, the breasts, and particularly the areola, become engorged with blood and swell, increasing in size by 20% to 25% in women who have not breast-fed a baby and to a lesser extent in those who have. This obscures the nipple erection that was so prominent in the excitement phase. Third, the secretion of fluids from the vaginal walls may slow down if the plateau phase is prolonged (the Bartholin's glands secrete a few drops of fluid during this stage, but not enough to contribute to lubrication). Some men may worry about the disappearance of some responses that were so prominent during the initial excitement phase, but once again, these are the normal physiological responses when women become highly aroused. The glans of the clitoris, for example, is extremely sensitive to touch at this stage, and indirect stimulation is generally sufficient to maintain arousal. In fact, some women find direct stimulation of the clitoris during this phase to be too intense and less pleasurable than indirect stimulation.

The labia minora also become greatly engorged with blood during the plateau phase, resulting in a doubling or tripling in thickness and a vivid color change (from pink to wine color). The thickening of the labia minora helps to further push the labia majora apart and expose the vaginal opening. Masters and Johnson claim that the color change in the labia minora means that a woman is very close to orgasm.

Orgasm

Incredible as it may seem, until just a few decades ago many people (including many physicians and therapists) did not believe that women had orgasms. This mistaken belief was due in part to attitudes left over from the Victorian era. Women at that time were not supposed to enjoy sex and were thought to participate only to "do their wifely duties."

It was not until Masters and Johnson recorded electrophysiological responses from women that the debate was finally ended. Like men, women also had rhythmic muscular contractions in specific tissues that were initially 0.8 second apart. These tissues included the outer third of the vagina (the orgasmic platform), the uterus, and the anal sphincter muscles. Unlike men's orgasms, women's orgasms occur in a single stage, without the sense of inevitability (the sense of "coming") that men have.

In addition to the nearly identical recordings, men and women also describe orgasms similarly. Compare the following responses provided by my female students with those provided earlier in the section on men:

> "It feels like all the tension that has been building and building is released with an explosion. It is the most pleasurable thing in the whole world."

> "It is at first a force that feels as if you're on a roller coaster ride and are about to be propelled off. Then come the contractions that feel as if the roller coaster ride is hitting every bump on the track."

> "A feeling that kind of feels like waves of electricity rushing through your whole entire body. It kind of ripples through and makes your toes and fingers curl."

> "…like when you have to urinate extremely bad and when you finally relieve yourself, you sometimes shake. Compare this at 100 times greater and it feels like an orgasm."

When physicians and psychologists were presented with descriptions of orgasm such as those just cited, they were unable to distinguish those that had been written by men from those written by women (Vance & Wagner, 1976; Wiest, 1977). Men's and women's ratings of adjectives describing their subjective experience of orgasm are also nearly identical (Mah & Binik, 2002).

Resolution

A woman's physiological responses, like those of men, generally drop below the plateau level after orgasm and return to the unaroused state (see the first solid line in Masters and Johnson's model in Figure 4–5). Some women, however, are capable of having true **multiple orgasms**—two, three, four, or numerous full orgasms in quick succession without dropping below the plateau level (see the dotted line in Figure 4–5). They must be capable, of course, of having the first orgasm, and additional orgasms are possible only with continued sexual desire and effective stimulation. As many as 10% of sexually experienced women have never had an orgasm (see the wavy line in Figure 4–5). Only about 14% to 16% of women regularly have multiple orgasms (Kinsey et al., 1953), but perhaps as many as 40% have experienced them occasionally (Darling et al., 1991). Thus, the female sexual response cycle is highly variable. It differs from person to person and from occasion to occasion (Basson, 2000; Tiefer, 1991).

Many women report that multiple orgasms are most easily experienced during masturbation, when they are not distracted by the partner and when sexual fantasy is maximal.

> "Sometimes [I get] two or three orgasms right after each other. I can have multiple orgasms as much as eight times in a row, but this is only during masturbation."
> (from the author's files)

Multiple orgasms have become the one and only goal in sex for some men and women. This can be self-defeating, as these people feel like failures when the goal is not achieved. Many individuals are completely satisfied by a single orgasm, and they should not put additional pressure on themselves by treating sex like an Olympic event. This sexual Olympics mentality can only detract from having a good, healthy, and sexually satisfying experience and can lead to sexual problems as well (see Chapter 13).

At some point after a single orgasm or multiple orgasms, a woman's responses will start to fall below plateau level and return to normal. The blood drains from the breasts and the tissues of the outer third of the vagina, the sex flush disappears, the uterus comes down, and the vagina shortens in width and length. The clitoris returns to its normal position within seconds, but the glans may be extremely sensitive to touch for several minutes.

PERSONAL REFLECTIONS

Do you judge your sexual experiences by your ability to reach orgasms or your frequency of orgasm? Your partner's orgasm? Why? Many women do not experience orgasm during sexual intercourse. How do you think they feel about it? How would you feel if it were you? Is it necessary to have an orgasm to enjoy sex?

Multiple orgasms ■ Having two or more successive orgasms without falling below the plateau level of physiological arousal.

CONTROVERSIES ABOUT ORGASMS

Are All Women Capable of Orgasm During Sexual Intercourse?

"I have had sex but never actually had an orgasm. If I have I did not know it. Sex feels good, but I think I never had one because of the way people say an orgasm feels."

"Unfortunately, I have yet to learn how to have an orgasm with a partner during intercourse, but I have no problem reaching orgasm during oral sex."
(All examples are from the author's files.)

About 5% to 10% of American women have never had an orgasm under any circumstances (Spector & Carey, 1990). Kinsey's group found that only 40% to 50% of adult women experienced orgasm regularly during intercourse. However, in their nationally representative study, Laumann and colleagues (1994) found that 75% of married women and 62% of single women usually had an orgasm during sexual intercourse. Even so, this still leaves a sizable minority of women who do not.

Both psychosocial and biological factors appear to play a role in women's ability to reach orgasm (Basson, 2000; Mah & Binik, 2005; Raboch & Raboch, 1992). From years of experience in her own clinical practice, sex therapist Helen Kaplan (1974) concluded; "There are millions of women who are sexually responsive, and often multiply orgasmic, but who cannot have an orgasm during [vaginal] intercourse unless they receive simultaneous clitoral stimulation." On the other hand, Masters and Johnson (1966) and others (e.g., Barbach, 1980) claimed to have successfully treated similar women and believe that all women in good health are capable of orgasm during intercourse without additional stimulation. We will return to this issue in Chapter 13.

How Many Types of Female Orgasm Are There?

Sigmund Freud, unlike many of his Victorian colleagues, not only believed that women had orgasms, but started another controversy when he said that there were two types of female orgasms, one due to clitoral stimulation and one resulting from vaginal sensations. Unfortunately, he claimed that *clitoral orgasms* were infantile and a sign of immaturity (because they were caused by noncoital acts), whereas *vaginal orgasms* were "authentic" and "mature" and a sign of normal psychosexual development (the result of stimulation by the penis). "The elimination of clitoral sexuality," he wrote, "is a necessary precondition for the development of femininity."

The inner two thirds of the vagina has few nerve endings. Kinsey and colleagues (1953), who doubted the authenticity of vaginal orgasms, had five gynecologists touch the vaginal walls of 879 women with a probe. Most women could not tell when their vagina was being stimulated, but were very much aware when their clitoris was touched.

Masters and Johnson (1966) later reported that all women's orgasms were physiologically the same. No matter whether the source of stimulation was clitoral or vaginal, identical rhythmic muscular contractions were recorded in the same structures, and the focus of subjective sensation was the clitoris. The same contractions were recorded in women who had reached orgasm from breast stimulation alone. Masters and Johnson concluded that an orgasm is an orgasm, regardless of the source of stimulation, and that they are all clitoral.

On the other hand, several studies found that some women subjectively distinguished between orgasms caused by clitoral stimulation during masturbation and orgasms during intercourse (which were described as "fuller, but not stronger," "more internal," and "deeper" [e.g., Bentler & Peeler, 1979; Butler, 1976]). Some women say that they have never had an orgasm from clitoral stimulation—that their orgasms always result from vaginal stimulation:

"I am a 30-year-old woman who has been sexually active since my late teens. I've always been very responsive sexually, resulting in multiple, intense orgasms during intercourse. The significant point is, I have orgasms during intercourse, but never during oral sex or direct clitoral stimulation. My orgasms are strictly vaginal, they are never clitoral. I'd always felt fine about this until I had a relationship with a man who said there was something wrong with me because I did not reach orgasm during oral sex. He made me feel so bad that I literally lost all of my self-esteem and self-confidence. I truly believed I was abnormal."
(from the author's files)

If the walls of the inner two thirds of the vagina are so sparse in nerve endings, what could be the anatomical basis for vaginal orgasms? Recall from Chapter 2 that the muscle surrounding the vagina, the pubococcygeus (PC) muscle, has a richer supply of nerve endings than the vaginal walls, and that women who report vaginal sensations during intercourse tend to have strong PC muscles (Kinsey et al., 1953). In 1982, Ladas, Whipple, and Perry suggested in their book, *The G Spot*, another possible basis for a vaginal orgasm. The **Grafenberg (G) spot** was first described by the German gynecologist Ernst Grafenberg (1950) in the 1940s. It was described as being a very sensitive area about the size

Grafenberg (G) spot ■ A small, sensitive area on the front wall of the vagina found in about 10% of all women.

of a dime located on the front wall of the vagina, about halfway between the back of the pubic bone and the front of the cervix (just under the bladder) (Song et al., 2009; see Figure 2–7). It swells when stimulated, and a woman's first reaction (lasting a few seconds) may be an urge to urinate. Some studies suggest that only 10% or less of women have a distinct G spot (Alzate & Londono, 1984).

Ladas, Whipple, and Perry described three types of orgasm. In the *tenting type*, described by Masters and Johnson (1966) and Helen Kaplan (1974), orgasm results from clitoral stimulation (which travels via the pudendal nerve). In the *A-frame type*, orgasm results from stimulation of the Grafenberg spot (which travels via the pelvic nerve). A third type was described as *blended*.

> "I believe I've had clitoral orgasms, vaginal orgasms, and the blended type. All of these feel different.... For me the best type of orgasm is the blended type because I feel it all over and when it is over my body trembles as if I had just stopped running."
> (from the author's files)

More recently, Whipple and Komisaruk (1999) found that stimulation of the cervix can result in orgasm, even in many women with spinal cord injury, and that sensations were carried by the vagus nerve.

Women's experiences of orgasm can also differ with regard to the duration of the orgasm. For example, Rosemary Basson (2000) found that for some women orgasm is not a short, intense release of sexual tension (as occurs in men, and as shown by a little blip on a curve like Figure 4–5), but can last for well over a minute.

Is all this just a question of semantics, that is, of people confusing the stimulus with the response? The most effective stimulus for erection in men is touching the glans of the penis (light pressure stimulates the pudendal nerve), but the orgasmic contractions come from the base of the penis and perineum (deep pressure stimulates the pelvic nerve). Yet no one argues whether there are glans or perineal orgasms in men. Instead, men are viewed as having a total-body orgasm, with different ranges of the same experience (some mild and others intense).

So do women have different types of orgasm, or do they experience different ranges of one orgasm that has both clitoral and vaginal components? Circumstances and emotional climate (e.g., masturbation versus having sex with a partner) can certainly affect the experience. As psychiatrist and sex therapist Helen Kaplan said: "You use the same muscles to eat a hamburger that you use to eat a dinner at Lutèce, but the experiences are very different" (Lutèce is a fancy, expensive New York restaurant) (quoted by Gallagher, 1986). As for the opinion of the author of this text, a man, I prefer the view of William Masters, who said: "Physiologically, an orgasm is an orgasm, though there are degrees of intensity. But psychologically—don't ask me about women. I'm a man, and I know that I don't know" (Gallagher, 1986).

There is one thing that all sex therapists agree on today—that one type should not be viewed as infantile, immature, or less important and another type as mature, authentic, or more important. In short, a woman should not worry about what kind of orgasm she has. As Barbara Seaman (1972) writes, "The liberated orgasm is any orgasm a woman likes."

Do Women Ejaculate During Orgasm?

Adult men ejaculate during orgasm, but do women also ejaculate? The emission of a fluid by some women during orgasm was noted as early as 300 years ago by the Dutch embryologist Regnier de Graff, who described the fluid as coming from the small glands surrounding the urethral opening. This was confirmed in the modern scientific literature by Ernst Grafenberg (after whom the G spot was named) in 1950. The emission of fluid in some women was described as a dribble and in others as a gushing stream.

> "I have always achieved vaginal orgasms with fluid. The fluid is clear and white. It has no odor and is not unpleasant. I thought all women have this type of orgasm."

> "The first time I emitted a fluid, I thought I had urinated on myself and my boyfriend. I mean it was all over. My boyfriend kept looking at me real strange and I couldn't explain it. After the first time I kept making sure that I went to the bathroom before we had intercourse. When it happened after I knew I couldn't have that much fluid in my bladder. I got a little worried, but my boyfriend enjoyed watching me 'let loose' and got very excited."
> (All examples are from the author's files)

Prior to the 1980s, women who emitted a fluid during orgasm were almost always told by physicians that they suffered from urinary incontinence, which is the inability to control urination during stress. In 1981, however, three articles on female ejaculation appeared in *The Journal of Sex Research*, followed in 1982 by a book about the Grafenberg spot and ejaculation (Ladas, Whipple, & Perry, 1982). They confirmed that the fluid was emitted not from the vagina but from the **Skene's glands** located in the urethra (Belzer, 1981; Perry & Whipple, 1981). These glands were thought to

Skene's glands ■ Glands located in the urethras of some women that are thought to develop from the same embryonic tissue as the man's prostate, and that may be the source of a fluid emitted by some women during orgasm.

Box 4–A Cross-Cultural Perspectives

Female Genital Cutting

Cutting of girls' genitals has been a common practice in many cultures since antiquity. The first record we have of it was reported by the Greek historian Herodotus in 450 B.C. in ancient Egypt (Joseph, 1996).

Today, cutting of girls' genitals is still performed in many parts of the world. Some cultures practice *sunna circumcision*—removal of the clitoral hood and cutting or pricking part of the clitoris, while many others subject girls to *excision* (removal of the clitoris and upper labia minora). These two forms of cutting account for about 80% of all the cases worldwide (WHO, 2008). However, in its most extreme form, called *infibulation* (or *pharaonic circumcision*), it involves cutting away the entire clitoris, labia minora, and labia majora, and then sewing together the raw sides of the vulva except for a small opening for urine and menstrual flow.

Female genital cutting is usually performed by an older village woman ("midwife") with a knife or razor and without anesthesia, requiring that the girl be tied or held down. It is usually done during early childhood, but in some cases, as in Nigeria, it is carried out just prior to marriage. With infibulation, many of the girls suffer hemorrhage or shock, and long-term effects include chronic vaginal and pelvic infections and difficult, painful childbirth (Adam et al., 2010; Utz-Billing & Kentenich, 2008).

> Once I was inside the hut, the women began to sing my praises, to which I turned a deaf ear, as I was overcome with terror. "Lie down there," the excisor suddenly said to me, pointing to a mat stretched out on the ground. No sooner had I laid down than I felt my thin frail legs tightly grasped by heavy hands and pulled wide apart. I lifted my head. Two women on each side of me pinned me to the ground. My arms were also immobilized. Suddenly, I felt

FIGURE 4–8 Seita Lengila, a 16-year-old Kenyan girl, is held down by village women as her clitoris is cut away with a razor. The wound was then cleaned with cow urine and smeared with goat fat to stop the bleeding.

> some strange substance being spread over my genital organs. I would have given anything at that moment to be a thousand miles away: then a shooting pain brought me back to reality from my thoughts of flight. First I underwent the ablation of the labia minor and then of the clitoris. The operation seemed to go on forever.... I was in the throes of endless agony.... I felt wet. I was bleeding. The blood flowed in torrents. Then they applied a mixture of butter and medicinal herbs which stopped the bleeding. Never had I felt such excruciating pain!
>
> (Joseph, 1996, pp. 3–4)

The World Health Organization estimates that 100 million to 140 million women have had their genitals cut in this manner. This includes the large majority of women in Egypt (95.8%), Somalia (97.9%), Gambia (78.3%), Ethiopia (74.3%), with smaller numbers in other African countries (World Health Organization, 2008). Most of the cultures in which genital cutting is performed are Muslim, but it is not an official Muslim practice (it is not mentioned in the Koran). Instead, it is a cultural custom that is also practiced by Christians and Jews that live in these areas.

Why are girls subjected to this? Many reasons have been given, including myths that the clitoris is evil, poisonous, or will grow like a penis. However, these are not the major reasons. In the words of Raqiya Dualeh Abdalla, a Somali woman who denounced the practice in her 1982 book *Sisters in Affliction*:

The various explanations and mystifications offered to justify the practice...all emanate from men's motive to control women economically and sexually and as personal objects.

Most genitally cut women do not enjoy sex, and sexual intercourse is often painful for those with excisions or infibulations (Utz-Billing & Kentenich, 2008). The men in these cultures believe that the elimination of sexual desire in women "frees them to fulfill their real destiny as mothers." Proponents of genital cutting often argue that the practice helps cultural cohesion and identity. Marriage and motherhood are generally the only roles allowed for women in cultures where genital cutting is performed, and for a girl to refuse to submit is to give up her place in society (see Gruenbaum, 2006).

A second, but related, reason is economic. The countries where genital cutting is practiced are strongly patriarchal, and thus there is great concern about guaranteeing the inheritance of property from fathers to legitimate sons. The sewing together of the vulva guarantees that a new wife is a virgin on the wedding night and the elimination of sexual desire reduces infidelity, so that any offspring are almost assuredly the husband's.

The World Health Organization and all African governments have approved tougher action to end the practice of female genital cutting. However, attempts by outsiders to put an end to genital cuttings have resulted in a clash of cultural values. Westerners generally cite humanitarian and feminist values, but many in Western cultures ritually follow the practice of cutting away the foreskins of boys, usually without the use of anesthesia (see Box 2–C). There is legitimate concern that Western people's negative reaction to the practice will generalize to the cultures where it is practiced (see Bell, 2005; Silverman, 2004). In the words of Nahid Toubia, a Sudanese author:

> Over the last decade the...West has acted as though they have suddenly discovered a dangerous epidemic which they then sensationalized in international women's forums creating a backlash of over-sensitivity in the concerned communities. They have portrayed it as irrefutable evidence of the barbarism and vulgarity of underdeveloped countries...[and the] primitiveness of Arabs, Muslims, and Africans all in one blow. (1988, p. 101)

The practice of female genital cutting has declined in some areas (Caldwell et al., 2000), but the practice will probably continue unabated in many areas. A survey conducted in the Sudan, for example, found that 90% of the women wanted their daughters' genitals cut, and half of them favored the extreme infibulation (Williams & Sobieszczyk, 1997). The usual justification is that it is the tradition.

PERSONAL REFLECTIONS

What was your reaction to reading about genital cutting in some African and Islamic cultures? What is your view about male genital circumcision in the United States? We do not cut women's genitals in this country to deny them their sexuality. Do we deny women's sexuality in other ways? How?

develop from the same embryonic tissue as men's prostate (Heath, 1984), and the fluid, which was said to differ in color (clear to milky white) and odor from urine, was found to contain prostatic acid phosphatase, an enzyme found in prostate secretions (Addiego et al., 1981; Zaviacic & Ablin, 2000; Zaviacic et al., 1988b). As a result of this, the Federative International Committee of Anatomical Terminology, which has the responsibility of naming body parts, has proposed that the G spot be renamed the "female prostate." However, not all female ejaculators emit a fluid that is chemically different from urine (Whipple & Komisaruk, 1999).

How many women emit a fluid (ejaculate) during orgasm? Perry and Whipple (1981) claimed in their initial article that "perhaps 10% of females" did so, but later claimed in their book that perhaps as many as 40% of women had experienced this on occasion. More recent studies agree with this (Darling et al., 1990; Zaviacic et al., 1988a). It would appear, therefore, that while it can no longer be doubted that some women emit a fluid from the urethra during orgasm, there is some question as to the nature of the fluid. No doubt some women do suffer from stress-induced incontinence, but in others it may actually be a true ejaculation.

Can Men Have Multiple Orgasms?

Masters and Johnson originally took the position that only women could have true multiple orgasms—two or more orgasms within a short time without dropping below plateau. Whenever they recorded orgasm with ejaculation from men, it was always followed by a refractory period. Only when a man's level of arousal built back up to the plateau level could he have another orgasm. However, two survey studies questioned whether there is a true sex difference in the ability to have multiple orgasms. The first study reported 13 men who said that they had multiple dry "mini-orgasms" by withholding ejaculation before having a full wet orgasm (i.e., with ejaculation). The wet orgasm was always followed by a refractory period (Robbins & Jensen, 1978). In the second study, 21 men reported experiencing a variety of multiple orgasms (Dunn & Trost, 1989). Some had one or more dry orgasms before ejaculating, while others had an orgasm with ejaculation followed by one or more dry orgasms.

> "In the 50 questions you had us answer, one of them said that most men cannot have multiple orgasms. I am a male that has this ability..."

> "My boyfriend keeps his erection for hours and can continue to copulate continuously without stopping, even after ejaculating, and can ejaculate multiple times."

As you have learned, scientists have always been the last ones to believe people's claims about experiencing different types of orgasm. Until someone records rhythmic muscular contractions during multiple dry orgasms, that will probably be the case here as well.

PENIS SIZE: DOES IT MATTER?

In an article written for *Cosmopolitan* (1984), Michael Barson stated that "for a man, the one emotion more disquieting than his own sense of not being big enough is the terror of finding himself in bed with a woman who shares his opinion." It should not be surprising that many men have anxieties about the size of their penis, for penis size has been a focus of attention throughout history. Priapus, the Greco-Roman god of procreation, was always displayed as having an enormous penis. Many writers have also described the penis in exaggerated terms. More recently, penis size has been emphasized in X-rated movies. Bernie Zilbergeld (1978), a noted sex therapist, has said that "it is not much of an exaggeration to say that penises in fantasyland come in only three sizes—large, gigantic, and so big you can barely get through the front door." All of this tends to leave the impression that penis size is related to the ability of a man to sexually please a woman, so that even men with normal-sized penises may wish they were larger.

> In the many hours we have spent talking to men in and out of therapy, we have heard every conceivable complaint about penises. They are too small (the most common complaint)...
> (Zilbergeld, 1978)

> "I have an inferiority complex about my penis size. Even though my penis is larger than normal (about 7 inches)...no matter how many women tell me that my penis is large, I still have that complex."
> (from the author's files)

For most heterosexual men the only opportunity to compare themselves with others is in the locker room, where they may get a false impression. The average size of a flaccid penis is about 2.8 to 4.3 inches in length and 1.0 to 1.2 inches in diameter (Masters & Johnson, 1966). Researchers at the Kinsey Institute have found, however, that there is considerably more variation in penis size in the flaccid condition than in the erect state. Penises that

appear small when flaccid display a proportionately greater increase in size upon erection than penises that appear large in the unaroused state (Jamison & Gebhard, 1988). Frequent intercourse does not cause a penis to get larger. Also, contrary to some popular stories, penis size is not related to height, weight, build, shoe size, or the like.

The human penis is, in fact, larger than that for any of the other great apes (Bowman, 2010). This is not to say that all penises are the same size when erect. Several studies that used self-measurement have found that the average size of an erect penis (measured along the top) was about 6.2 inches in length and about 1.5 inches in diameter (Bogaert & Hershberger, 1999; Jamison & Gebhard, 1988; Richters et al., 1995; A. M. A. Smith et al., 1998). However, some men probably exaggerated and the technique has proven unreliable (Harding & Golombok, 2002). Studies that did not rely on self-reports (penis length was measured by health professionals) found the length of an erect penis to be smaller, with most men in the 4.5- to 5.75-inch range (da Ros et al., 1994; Sparling, 1997; Wessells et al., 1996), with an average length close to 5 inches.

Are there ethnic differences? No study has found a substantial difference between white and black men. See former Black Panther Eldridge Cleaver's book, *Soul on Ice,* for a discussion of how the story that black men have larger penises got started.

There is no evidence that the penis-enlarging pills advertised on television and the Internet work (Nugteren et al., 2010b). Today, some men are paying thousands of dollars to have their penises made larger (by cutting ligaments that hold part of the penis inside the body and injecting fat from other parts of the body). However, the American Society of Plastic and Reconstructive Surgeons has issued a warning about the safety of this procedure (CNN Health Library, 2008), and many men are unhappy with the results (see Nugteren et al., 2010a). Before any man considers having this operation, let us examine whether the size of a man's penis really is important in pleasing a woman during sexual intercourse.

In order to answer this question, we must first re-examine some basic facts about female anatomy. In the unaroused state, the vagina measures 3 to 5 inches in length and its walls are collapsed. When a woman becomes sexually aroused, the walls of the inner two thirds of the vagina expand and its depth averages 6 inches, which perhaps, not coincidentally, is about the same length as the average penis (isn't nature wonderful?). In its capacity to physically stimulate the vagina, therefore, there is no real advantage to having a penis any longer than about 6 inches, for there is no place for it to go. And do not forget that the walls of the inner two thirds of the vagina are relatively sparse in nerve endings anyway. Most important, remember that the focus of

FIGURE 4–9 The fertility gods of the Greeks and Romans were always sculptured to have an enormous penis.

physical sensations in most women is not the vagina, but the clitoris, which usually does not come into direct physical contact with the penis during intercourse. Thrusting of the penis stimulates the clitoris only indirectly by causing the clitoral hood to rub back and forth over the clitoral glans.

Do women consider the size of a penis important? One study found that over half of women said that it was at least somewhat important (Stulhofer, 2006). However, another study found that depictions of large penises produced no more arousal in women than depictions of smaller ones (Fisher et al., 1983). In another study several hundred women were asked what was most important to them during sexual intercourse. Not one mentioned penis size (Zilbergeld, 1978). In surveys conducted in my class, only once has a woman expressed a preference for large penises. For the large majority of women, penis size was not important. Here are some typical responses:

"Penis size—of course it doesn't matter!"

"And about penis size, we don't care!"

"Also, penis size doesn't mean anything, especially to women."

"It's not what you have that's so important, but how you use it."

"It is not the size of the ship that matters, but the motion of the ocean."

Why is penis size unimportant to most women? Read again the sections on desire and excitement in women's sexual response cycle. Desire and excitement in most women are related to relationship and intimacy needs. The women in the above surveys were more concerned with their male partner taking his time and his total response to her during sexual intercourse.

PERSONAL REFLECTIONS (MEN)

Do you wish you had a different-sized or different-shaped penis? How would you like to be different? Why? Should the size of a man's penis be an important factor in sexually pleasing a partner?

APHRODISIACS: DO THEY HELP?

"Many of my older friends believe that if you eat raw oysters before you have sex you can last for hours."

"… As one of my friends ordered oysters, he commented on how it was such a good aphrodisiac… He explained that every time he goes to a seafood restaurant and eats oysters he is 10 times better in bed."
(All examples are from the author's files.)

People have searched for **aphrodisiacs**—substances that enhance sexual desire or prolong sexual performance (named after the Greek goddess of love, Aphrodite)—for centuries. At one time or another, over 500 substances have been believed to be aphrodisiacs, including bull's testicles, powdered rhinoceros horn, elephant sperm, turtle eggs, ginseng roots, and vitamin E, as well as such common foods as bananas, potatoes, tomatoes, asparagus, garlic, and radishes (Castleman, 1997). Some people like to believe that oysters are an aphrodisiac. Many of these foods gained their reputation as aphrodisiacs during the Middle Ages when it was commonly thought that plants and foods announced their usefulness by the way they looked. Thus, phallic-looking things such as carrots, bananas, and the horns of animals, or soft moist foods that resembled women's genitals (such as oysters) became popular. However, the fact is that none of these substances has any physiological effect on sexual responsivity. Any temporary improvement

Aphrodisiacs ■ Substances that enhance sexual desire or performance.

in sexual functioning is purely a psychological effect (believing that something will work can be arousing), and the effect will wear off shortly.

Spanish fly (*cantharides*), made from powdered beetles that are found in Spain, is perhaps the most famous reputed aphrodisiac. Taken orally, the active substance causes inflammation and irritation of the urinary and genital tracts, which some may interpret as lust. Spanish fly can also cause a painful, persistent erection (priapism), even when there is no desire for sex—as well as ulcers of the digestive and urinary tracts, diarrhea, and severe pain.

Alcohol is commonly believed to enhance sexual desire and responsivity. One of its initial effects is dilation of blood vessels in the skin, which gives a feeling of warmth and well-being. A drink or two depresses certain areas of your brain, making you less inhibited about engaging in sex or other behaviors that you might not ordinarily do. However, anything more than a single drink can impair the nervous system responses needed for engaging in sex. As Shakespeare says of drink in *Macbeth*, "It provokes the desire, but it takes away from the performance." Alcohol, in fact, is an **anaphrodisiac**, a suppressant of sexual functioning in both men and women (McKay, 2005).

Some illegal drugs also have reputations as sexual stimulants. Cocaine is a central nervous system stimulant, and thus may give the user a temporary burst of energy and a feeling of self-confidence, but the drug's effects are often equally due to heightened expectations and the social situation in which it is used (i.e., like alcohol, drugs give people an excuse that they can use afterwards to justify their having had sex). The use of cocaine, however, can often result in erectile failures and difficulties reaching orgasm for both men and women (Cocores et al., 1986; Henderson et al., 1995).

Amphetamines ("speed" or "uppers") in low doses can also give the user a burst of energy (sometimes used for marathon sexual encounters), but will decrease sexual functioning in higher doses (Buffum et al., 1981) and can result in severe paranoia if used chronically.

Most marijuana users report that the drug improves sexual pleasure (Kolodny et al., 1979). It does not increase desire or arousal, nor does it intensify orgasm, but it enhances relaxation, thus allowing increased awareness of touch. Men who use marijuana chronically, however, may experience erectile problems, lowered testosterone levels, and decreased sperm production (Kolodny et al., 1974).

Among young people, Ecstasy (3, 4-methylenedioxymethamphetamine, or MDMA) has become popular as an aphrodisiac. The drug causes release of the brain chemical serotonin and is related to hallucinogens and stimulants. It gives users a feeling of euphoria and blissfulness. Recently, it has become popular to take it with Viagra—the combination is often called "sextasy" (Breslau, 2002). However, the combination often causes pounding headaches and prolonged painful erections. Research has shown that even a single dose of Ecstasy can cause permanent brain damage in animals and that moderate use in humans leads to memory loss (Walters et al., 2002).

Several studies have focused on pharmacological agents that affect central nervous system neurotransmitters—the chemical substances that allow brain cells to "talk" to one another. Yohimbine hydrochloride, a substance derived from the sap of an African tree, has a positive effect on sexual desire and performance in men with psychologically caused impotence (Ernst & Pittler, 1998; Rowland et al., 1997). However, it appears to have little or no effect on men who do not have erectile problems. Some Ayurvedic herbs (popularly known as SaFed Musli and Shatavari) have a reputation for both treating impotence and as aphrodisiacs, and recent research has shown that they enhance the sexual performance of male rats (Thakur et al., 2009). Keep in mind, there is a big difference between rat sexual behavior and human sexual desire.

Some of you may have heard of a commercially sold product called Libido (also sold as Ardorare, Erosom, Libid, and Libbido). You have also probably seen advertisements for pheromones or perfumes and colognes with pheromones added (e.g., Realm, Jovan) that promise increased sexual attention from others. Researchers from one company that markets pheromones reported that men who added a synthesized nonodorous pheromone to their aftershave lotion showed increased levels of sexual intercourse and "sleeping" with a romantic partner compared to men in a control group with no pheromones (Cutler et al., 1998; see also Berliner et al., 1996). Similar results have been reported for women who used a synthesized female hormone (McCoy & Pitino, 2002). These results are very interesting, but do not get too excited yet. Much more work needs to be done, including independent replication, before we can assume that all we need to do to attract others sexually is to slap on some pheromone-added perfume or cologne. The products are not magic elixirs that can guarantee you a sexual experience.

"When I was 18 years old, I read about this pheromone spray which allegedly would attract women and make them desire sex with me. The pamphlet I got in the mail had several alleged true stories of the success of this stuff. I thought it was a fantastic breakthrough and immediately sent off my $65.00. In return I received a very small (2 fluid oz.) bottle of this spray which I excitedly sprayed on before I hit the town. Did I get laid? Hell no. I didn't even get a nice conversation."
(from the author's files)

Anaphrodisiacs ■ Substances that suppress sexual functioning.

Despite the lack of scientific evidence that most of the chemicals tried as aphrodisiacs really work, some people will probably continue to search for a problem-free drug that enhances sexual performance. Their efforts would probably be better rewarded if they instead took the time to learn how to communicate and be intimate with their partners. We will discuss how to do this in later chapters.

SEXUALITY AND PEOPLE WITH DISABILITIES

Is sexual pleasure reserved only for the young and beautiful? Judging by the number of jokes about the sexual behavior of the elderly and obese, and of other people whom our society often labels as "unattractive," many people apparently think so. These negative attitudes are often extreme in the case of people with disabilities. What about people who are blind, deaf, or spinal cord–damaged, or suffer from other physical disabilities? What about the mentally impaired? Do these groups of people have sexual desires and feelings? If so, should they be allowed to express those desires?

In this chapter we focused on the physiological events that occur during sexual arousal. Masters and Johnson's model places emphasis on sex as a physical act. But is sexuality just physical? Look again at the definition of **sexuality** at the beginning of Chapter 1. Here is another definition, one that was given by a group of women with complete spinal cord injury:

> "It is a tremendous core of who I am. Everything else comes out of that. How I think and feel about my body, my physical body. How I would define myself as a woman. How I am in all my relationships, whether they are sexual or otherwise. How I decorate my house. It's everything that I am. I may not have another way… another component that is so strong that I could say sums up everything that I am. So it's the physical, it's spiritual, it's emotional, everything."
> (from Richards et al., 1997)

Earlier in the chapter you learned about the effects of one kind of physical disability on sexual functioning: the effects of spinal cord damage on the ability to achieve erection and/or orgasm (C. J. Alexander et al., 1993; Sipski et al., 1999; Whipple & Komisaruk, 1999). However, as difficult as a person's physical disabilities may make it to engage in sex, a greater barrier to most people with disabilities having a sexual relationship is society's attitude about them (Sakellariou, 2006). For example, I recently received the following note from a spinal cord–damaged student:

> "Recently my boyfriend's mother wanted him to explain to me that she wants grandchildren. I guess

she assumed that because I'm in a wheelchair that I'm incapable of having children. Her ignorance amazed me. People who are in wheelchairs, whether they be paraplegics or quadriplegics, are no less sexually able. Sexuality is basically psychological, in terms of its influence upon a person's overall behavior. Thus, the fact that one is paralyzed from the neck down or from the hips down doesn't discount from one's sexual drive or fertility."

Many people treat adults with physical or mental disabilities as if they were asexual or childlike and think it ridiculous that these groups should even have any interest in sex (see Milligan & Neufeldt, 2001, for a review). Parents of children with disabilities sometimes try to "protect" them by withholding sexual information, and friends and acquaintances of handicapped adults often try to protect them by never discussing the subject in their presence. As a result, persons with disabilities often have low sexual esteem and seriously limit how they express themselves sexually (McCabe et al., 2003).

> "I know the feeling well—anxious to form relationships, but no one approaches you for a date; raised to expect that you will never marry; given little information on reproduction except that it should be avoided at all costs."
> (from Nosek et al., 1997)

Even the medical profession has only recently begun to realize the importance of a holistic approach in treating people with disabilities. People with recent disabilities want to learn (or relearn) more than just how to be capable. They also want to know how to love and be loved. Current rehabilitation approaches now include sexual counseling in helping patients and staff deal with the emotional, self-esteem, and social issues that may impair sexual functioning (C. J. Alexander et al., 1993).

The well-intended but incorrect assumption of those who would protect people with disabilities by denying their sexuality is that they have more important things to worry about. For example, in the case of spinal cord–damaged people, it is often assumed that they would (or should) not be interested in sex but instead be most concerned about physically rehabilitating the functional parts of their bodies. In fact, women with physical disabilities generally have as much sexual desire as other women (Nosek et al., 1997).

Are sexual relations really so unimportant that they should be given such a low priority? To answer this question, we must first ask why it is that people engage in sex. Sexual relations are important to many people for the shared intimacy. Equally important to the physical intimacy is the opportunity for

Sexuality ■ All of the sexual attitudes, feelings, and behaviors associated with being human. The term does not refer specifically to a person's capacity for erotic response or to sexual acts, but rather to a dimension of one's personality.

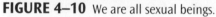
FIGURE 4–10 We are all sexual beings.

emotional intimacy provided by the closeness of sexual relations. Hugging, holding, kissing, and shared affection are as important in sexual relations as is intercourse for many people. Physical closeness can be very psychologically exciting (see Figure 4–10). Here is part of a letter from the husband of a woman who had undergone three years of surgeries and rehabilitation for severe spinal cord damage suffered in an automobile accident:

> "In July 'Susan' felt well enough to try once more. Sex was very good that day...we took it slow and easy.... We compensated with lots of holding and touching, something that often had been lacking in our pre-accident relationship. Incredibly, just holding each other in bed became very satisfying, and it actually seemed to bring us closer together emotionally."

People with spinal cord damage usually show an initial "shutting down" and "shutting out" of sexuality after the injury, followed by relationship disconnection (avoidance of sex with a partner) (Richards et al., 1997). The sexual desire of the partner can help overcome this. With proper support, spinal cord–damaged people eventually go through a phase of sexual exploration (both giving and receiving sexual pleasure) and sexual reaffirmation (becoming comfortable with their own sexuality). Spinal cord–injured individuals often have the same sexual needs and desires as others (Moin et al., 2009). They may show a decrease in sexual intercourse but often compensate for this with other sexual activities that are both satisfying and mutually pleasurable for the partner (Ostrander, 2009). There are, in fact, many ways to enjoy sexual relations besides intercourse.

What about people with traumatic brain injury or severe mental impairments? They display sexual behavior, including touching, kissing, and masturbation, but are often unable to differentiate between appropriate times and places. This "inappropriate" (by normal standards) behavior results in many people, even special education teachers and administrators, having negative views of sexual behaviors in developmentally handicapped or brain-injured persons (e.g., Scotti et al., 1996; Wolfe, 1997). However, denial of sexuality in (and for) the mentally impaired is not a realistic solution. "Regardless of their specific disabilities, persons with mental retardation are individuals with sexual feelings who develop physically at a rate comparable to that of normal young adults and respond to many of the same sexual stimuli and situations as do persons without mental retardation" (Scotti et al., 1996). A more realistic approach is to provide sexuality education to both persons with mental disabilities and to their service providers (Ames, 1991; Medlar, 1998).

People with hearing or vision impairments also have sexual desires and needs that should not be ignored by family, educators, and healthcare providers (Gannon, 1998). Different handicaps present different problems in one's ability to have sexual relations, but none of the physical problems is as great an obstacle to healthy sexuality as society's attitude about handicapped people (Sakellariou, 2006). Remember, regardless of what we look like or our physical or mental capabilities, we are all sexual beings.

PERSONAL REFLECTIONS

If you were to have an accident and become physically disabled, do you think you would still want to hug, hold, kiss, and share affection (and have sex, if possible) with your partner? How do you presently react when you see a person with disabilities engaging in these behaviors?

STUDY GUIDE

anaphrodisiacs 94
aphrodisiacs 93
Rosemary Basson 84
desire 80, 84
ejaculation 83
erection of the penis 80
excitement phase 80, 84
Grafenberg (G) spot 88

Helen Kaplan 79
Masters and Johnson 78
multiple orgasms 87
orgasm 81
orgasmic platform 86
plateau 81
refractory period 83
resolution 83

retrograde ejaculation 83
semen 83
sex-tension flush 81
sexuality 95
sexual response cycle 79
Skene's glands 89
vaginal lubrication 84
vasocongestive response 80

INTERACTIVE REVIEW

(1) _____ observed and recorded physiological responses from hundreds of people engaged in sexual activity. They divided the physiological responses during sex into four phases: (2) _____, (3) _____, (4) _____, and (5) _____. This pattern of responses is often referred to as the (6) _____. Other researchers have organized the responses into fewer or more phases, and this chapter follows the model of sex therapist (7) _____ and includes (8) _____ as the first phase.

The first physiological response in the excitement phase for both men and women is a (9) _____ response, which results in (10) _____ in men and (11) _____ in women. However, in women, physiological arousal does not correlate well with (12) _____, which depends more on relationship and intimacy needs. During the (13) _____ phase in women, the tissues of the outer third of the vagina become swollen with blood, causing the vaginal opening to narrow. This response is referred to as the (14) _____. Also during this phase, the clitoris (15) _____. Early in the plateau phase, (16) _____% of all women and about 25% of all men experience a rash on the skin called the (17) _____.

At the time of orgasm, both men and women have (18) _____ in specific tissues that initially occur every 0.8 second. However, recent studies indicate that the real essence of orgasm is not in the genitals, but in (19) _____. Men's and women's descriptions of orgasm are (20) _____. Men's orgasms occur in two stages, (21) _____ and (22) _____. The expulsion of semen from the penis is called (23) _____. After men have an orgasm, their physiological responses generally dip below plateau, during which time they cannot have another orgasm. This period of time is called the

(24) _____. Unlike most men, some women can have (25) _____, defined as two or more orgasms in quick succession without dropping below the plateau level. The return to the unaroused state is called (26) _____.

By most estimates, only (27) _____ % of adult women experience orgasm regularly during sexual intercourse. Masters and Johnson claimed that all women in good health are capable of reaching orgasm during intercourse, but Helen Kaplan and others believe that many women are incapable of reaching orgasm during intercourse without simultaneous (28) _____ stimulation.

Freud believed that there were two types of female orgasm, one caused by (29) _____ stimulation and another by (30) _____ sensations. Masters and Johnson originally claimed that all female orgasms were identical and were focused in the (31) _____. However, some women report having experienced different types of orgasms, and work conducted in the 1980s revealed that many of these women had a sensitive area on the (32) _____ wall of the vagina called the (33) _____. Stimulation of this area sometimes resulted in (34) _____ during orgasm. In some women the fluid was identified as urine, but in others it contained an enzyme found in secretions from men's (35) _____. Most women say that the size of a partner's penis is (36) _____ for their pleasure during intercourse. Many people have tried to enhance their sexual desire or performance by taking substances called (37) _____, but there is little evidence that they have any real effect.

People with disabilities may have special problems communicating or engaging in the physical act of sex, but sexuality is more than just the physical responses described by Masters and Johnson. It includes emotional and spiritual feelings and how we relate to others. We are all sexual human beings.

SELF-TEST

A. TRUE OR FALSE

38. The first physiological signs of arousal in men occur within seconds, but take several minutes to begin in women.
39. Many women do not separate desire from excitement (arousal).
40. Vaginal lubrication is actually superfiltered blood plasma.
41. The presence of vaginal lubrication means that a woman is ready to begin sexual intercourse.
42. Both men and women can experience nipple erection during the excitement phase.
43. When the clitoris pulls back and disappears beneath the clitoral hood, it means that a woman is less sexually aroused than before.
44. The secretion of fluids from the vaginal walls may slow down if the plateau phase is prolonged.
45. Generally speaking, descriptions of orgasm written by women can be easily distinguished from those written by men.
46. Orgasm and ejaculation occur at the same time in men and are actually the same event.
47. The rhythmic muscular contractions during orgasm recorded by Masters and Johnson are not strongly related to a person's subjective sensations of pleasure.
48. A full orgasm for men, with ejaculation, is almost always followed by a refractory period.
49. Some people who have suffered severe spinal cord injuries can experience orgasm.
50. The walls of the inner two thirds of the vagina are very sensitive to touch, thus making penis length an important factor during intercourse.
51. There is more variation in penis length in the unaroused condition than in the erect state.
52. Alcohol excites the central nervous system and enhances sexual performance.
53. Regular long-term use of marijuana can lower testosterone levels and decrease sperm production.
54. A man's penis size is related to his height, weight, and race.
55. Regular use of cocaine often leads to erectile problems and difficulties reaching orgasm.
56. There is a strong relationship between vaginal vasocongestion and a woman's subjective sense of sexual arousal.

B. MATCHING

(some questions have multiple answers)

_____ 57. desire
_____ 58. excitement phase
_____ 59. plateau phase
_____ 60. orgasm phase
_____ 61. resolution phase
_____ 62. vasocongestive response

a. Cowper's glands secrete a few drops of clear fluid
b. penis starts to become erect
c. labia minora become engorged with blood
d. specific sensations cause the individual to seek out, or become receptive to, sexual experiences
e. rhythmic muscular contractions occur in outer vagina, uterus, and anal sphincter muscles
f. clitoris pulls back against the pubic bone
g. vaginal lubrication begins
h. blood drains from breasts, outer third of the vagina, labia minora, and clitoris
i. sex-tension flush appears
j. nipples become erect
k. clitoris is most prominent at this time
l. scrotum thickens and helps pull the testicles toward the body
m. blood drains from penis and testicles
n. walls of the inner two thirds of the vagina begin to balloon out
o. return to the unaroused state
p. rhythmic muscular contractions in vas deferens, prostate gland, urethra, and anal sphincter muscles
q. outer third of the vagina becomes engorged with blood
r. nipples appear to be less erect
s. labia majora flatten and spread apart
t. testicles increase in size by 50% to 100%
u. in men, a fluid is emitted from the urethra

C. FILL IN THE BLANKS

63. Tissues becoming filled with blood during sexual arousal is called _____.

64. Some women emit a fluid during orgasm that comes from the _____.

65. Most women and many men get a skin rash called the _____ when they become highly sexually aroused.

66. The engorgement and swelling of the outer third of the vagina was named the _____ by Masters and Johnson.

67. A sensitive area that is found on the front wall of the vagina in about 10% of all women is called the _____.

68. After ejaculating, most men have a period of time called the _____ during which it is impossible for them to have another orgasm.

SUGGESTED READINGS

Basson, R. (2001). Human sex-response cycles. *Journal of Sex & Marital Therapy*, 27, 33–43. Offers an alternative sexual-response cycle for women that stresses relationship and intimacy needs.

Bell, K. (2005). Genital cutting and Western discourses on sexuality. *Medical Anthropology Quarterly*, 19, 125–148. An even-handed look at genital cutting in Africa.

Kaufman, M. (1995). *Easy for you to say: Q & A's for teens living with chronic illness or disability*. Toronto: Key Porter Books. A lengthy, excellent chapter on sexuality.

Masters, W., & Johnson, V. (1966) *Human sexual response*. Boston: Little, Brown. The classic work.

Rowland, D. L. (1999). Issues in the laboratory study of human sexual response: A synthesis for the nontechnical sexologist. *Journal of Sex Research*, 36, 3–15. An excellent review of the advantages and disadvantages of laboratory studies of human sexual responses.

Toubia, N. (1993). *Warrior marks: Female sexual mutilation and the sexual blinding of women*. New York: Harcourt Brace.

Wood, J. M. et al. (2006). Women's sexual desire: A feminist critique. *Journal of Sex Research*, 43. Challenges Masters and Johnson's biomedical model.

5 | Sexually Transmitted Infections and Sexually Related Diseases

When a person has sex, they're not having it just with that partner. They're having it with everybody that partner has had it with for the past 10 years.

—Otis Bowen, former U.S. Secretary of Health and Human Services

When you have finished studying this chapter, you should be able to:

- Explain what causes sexually transmitted infections, how they are spread, and who can get them.

- Describe the symptoms of gonorrhea, chlamydia, syphilis, chancroid, herpes, hepatitis, genital warts, HIV/AIDS, trichomoniasis, pubic lice, and scabies.

- Understand that with many STIs it is possible to be infected and have no symptoms (for particular STIs, name whether men or women are more likely to be asymptomatic, and at what stage).

- Describe the method of diagnosis and treatment for each STI.

- Summarize the complications that can occur if STIs are not treated early.

- Discuss the possible effects on the fetus and newborn if a pregnant woman has various STIs.

- Describe the different types of vaginal infections and discuss vaginal health care.

- Discuss safer sex practices.

Sexually transmitted infections (STIs) are at epidemic proportions. The United States has the highest rate of sexually transmitted infections of any industrialized country (Aral & Gorbach, 2002). Every year approximately 19 million Americans contract an STI (Centers for Disease Control and Prevention [CDC], 2010; see Table 5–1). One in 4 teenage girls has an STI (including 50% of African-American teenage girls)(CDC, 2010), and 1 in 2 Americans will contract at least one sexually transmitted infection in their lifetime (Guttmacher Institute, 2010a). The actual number of sexually transmitted infections occurring annually in the United States may be much higher than 19 million, because many cases go undiagnosed and therefore are not reported. A study in Baltimore, for example, found that 7.9% of a large sample of people aged 18 to 35 had undiagnosed gonorrhea, chlamydia, or both (Turner et al., 2002). It is to everyone's advantage, therefore, that we educate ourselves about the causes, symptoms, modes of transmission, and treatments for these infections. If left untreated, some of these infections can cause sterility, blindness, and even death, not to mention ruined relationships.

WHAT ARE THEY, AND WHO GETS THEM?

Some people believe that sexually transmitted infections are punishment for having sinful or immoral sex and that only promiscuous persons get STIs. These beliefs are not only incorrect, they are also

TABLE 5–1	*STIs in the United States*
Type of Sexually Transmitted Infection	Estimated New Cases per Year
Trichomoniasis	7,400,000
Human papillomavirus infection	6,200,000
Chlamydia	2,300,000+
Genital herpes	1,000,000
Gonorrhea	700,000+
Hepatitis B (sexually transmitted)	30,000
Syphilis	36,000
HIV/AIDS	56,000+

Source: Centers for Disease Control and Prevention (2010)

cruel, for hundreds of thousands of loyal and faithful men and women have caught these infections from unfaithful partners. A similar number of innocent newborns have contracted them from infected mothers.

> "I got gonorrhea from my boyfriend. I, myself, thought that I was engaged in a monogamous relationship. However, it was not monogamous for him."

> "Over the past 2 years, I have had one steady boyfriend. I have never slept around and I thought he was faithful to me. I would have put my life on the line to prove this. During these 2 years I have contracted chlamydia three times, PID, and trichomoniasis."

> "My first time having sex was at 16. My only fear was getting pregnant. My boyfriend said he was infertile so I couldn't get pregnant. We had sex. Approximately 1 month later I found out I had gonorrhea. I had no idea I could be a victim of an STI."

> "I am a 48-year-old woman who contracted a sexually transmitted infection from my husband. As a result, I had to have a total hysterectomy."

> (All examples are from the author's files.)

These people were not promiscuous, yet they still contracted sexually transmitted infections. What causes STIs? It is not sexual behavior itself; the behavior is merely the mode of transmission for bacteria, viruses, or parasites that must be present for the infections to be transmitted. *Sexually transmitted infections (STIs) are spread, for the most part, by sexual contact* (including vaginal and anal intercourse and oral-genital contact) *with someone who has the bacteria, viruses, or parasites that cause the infections.*

Bacteria are very small single-celled organisms. They lack a nuclear membrane but have all the genetic material (RNA and DNA) and metabolic machinery

to reproduce themselves. **Viruses** are just a protein shell around a nucleic acid core and cannot reproduce themselves. They invade host cells that provide the material to manufacture new virus particles. The bacteria and viruses responsible for STIs live outside the body for only a short period of time. The common belief that you can catch these infections from a toilet seat is greatly exaggerated, although it might be possible to expose yourself to the bacteria or viruses by using a damp towel soon after someone with an infection uses it (and in this case, you are more likely to spread it to your eyes than to your genitals).

Some people believe (or at least would like to believe) that sexually transmitted infections occur only in, or primarily in, the poor, the uneducated, and minority groups. Sexually transmitted infections, however, are nondiscriminating. The bacteria or viruses that cause these infections do not care whether you are white, black, yellow, or brown; whether you are on welfare or a millionaire; whether you bathe every day or only once a week; or whether you are a grade school dropout or college-educated. In fact, at least one of these infections (chlamydia) is at epidemic proportions among college students today. The point, here and in the previous case histories, is that anyone having sex is at some risk for contracting a sexually transmitted infection.

Some of these infections were once called *venereal diseases* (after the Roman goddess of love, Venus), but this term generally referred to infections that are spread almost exclusively by sexual contact (gonorrhea, syphilis, and three other lesser known diseases). Most of you have heard these and other infections referred to as *sexually transmitted diseases (STDs)*. Today, however, health professionals prefer the term **sexually transmitted infections (STIs)** to emphasize that they are *infectious* diseases (other diseases, such as heart disease, are not). The term refers to the original venereal diseases plus other infectious diseases that can be, but are not always, transmitted by sexual contact.

There are still other diseases of the sexual organs that are caused by overgrowths of yeast or fungal organisms found naturally in the body, and these too can sometimes be passed on during sex. I will refer to these as **sexually related diseases**. A few other

Bacteria ■ Small, single-celled organisms that lack a nuclear membrane, but have all the genetic material (RNA and DNA) to reproduce themselves.

Virus ■ A protein shell around a nucleic acid core. Viruses have either RNA or DNA, but not both, and thus cannot reproduce themselves. They invade host cells that provide the material to manufacture new virus particles.

Sexually transmitted infections (STIs) ■ Infections that can be, but are not necessarily always, transmitted by sexual contact.

Sexually related diseases ■ Diseases of the reproductive system or genitals that are not contracted through sexual activity. Often involve overgrowths of bacteria, yeasts, viruses, or fungal organisms that are found naturally in sexual and reproductive organs.

sexually transmitted infections are not really infections at all, but rather infestations of parasites (pubic lice and scabies) that are transmitted from person to person during sexual contact.

PERSONAL REFLECTIONS

How would you feel if you found out you had a sexually transmitted infection (or, if you have been infected, how did you feel)? Would you feel differently than you would if you had contracted the flu? Why? How would you tell your partners of their possible infection?

WHERE DID THEY COME FROM?

Some people argue that humans first contracted sexually transmitted infections by having sex with animals, but no animal species is known to have gonorrhea. Later you will learn that the virus that causes AIDS originated in nonhuman primates, but it was probably first transmitted to humans by contact with blood, not by sex. It is more likely that previously harmless bacteria or viruses mutated (they are highly susceptible to change) into strains causing infection.

Although where and how STIs originated remain unknown, some of these sexually transmitted infections have been around for at least a few thousand years, as many famous Greeks, Romans, and Egyptians (including Cleopatra) were described as having the symptoms. In fact, public kissing was banned by emperor Tiberius in Roman times because of an epidemic of a disease that was described as being identical to what we now know as herpes. An epidemic of syphilis also swept through Europe in the early 1500s, and it is still hotly debated whether Columbus and his sailors brought it back from the New World, or vice versa (e.g., Catterall, 1974; Luger, 1993). In fact, Columbus died of advanced syphilis.

The fact is that it does not really matter where or how STIs originated; they are here to stay and we must deal with them. Surveys of teenagers indicate that most know very little about sexually transmitted infections, although they believe themselves to be well informed (Clark et al., 2002). Many people are unaware, for example, that they can have an STI but show no symptoms and still be contagious. As a result, they do not seek treatment as early as they should. I will discuss some precautionary measures that can help you avoid

---

Gonorrhea ■ A sexually transmitted infection caused by the *Neisseria gonorrhoeae* bacterium (often referred to as "the gonococcus"), which lives on mucous membranes.

---

contracting sexually transmitted infections and will outline what to do in case you should get one. First, let us examine the symptoms and treatment for some of the most widely known infections.

GONORRHEA

Gonorrhea (from the Greek *gonos*, "seed," and *rhoia*, "flow"; also known as "the clap" or "the drip") is probably the oldest of the STIs. Its symptoms are described in Leviticus in the Old Testament, which dates back to about 1500 B.C., and were also described in detail by Greek physicians. The Centers for Disease Control and Prevention (2010) estimates that there will be over 700,000 new cases in the United States this year. However, about half go undiagnosed (and unreported). The rate of infection is considerably higher among African Americans than it is among Latinos or whites and is most commonly found in people under the age of 25 (Kuehn, 2005). The rates for gonorrhea in the United States are dramatically higher than in all other developed countries except Russia (Aral & Gorbach, 2002; Panchaud et al., 2000).

Symptoms and Complications

Gonorrhea is caused by a bacterium (*Neisseria gonorrhoeae*, often referred to as gonococcus) named after Albert Neisser, who discovered it in 1879. It lives on warm, moist mucous membranes in the urethra, vagina, rectum, mouth and throat, and eyes. A person gets gonorrhea by having his or her mucous membranes come into contact with another person's infected membranes. Because of the location of these membranes in the body, this normally occurs only during intimate contact. This includes, of course, vaginal intercourse, but the gonococcus can also infect the anus and rectum (during anal intercourse) and the throat (during oral-genital sex, particularly fellatio). The bacteria have been found to survive for a short time outside the body, but your chances of picking them up from nonsexual contact, particularly a dry toilet seat, are extremely remote.

In men who become infected during sexual intercourse, the gonococcus bacteria invade and cause inflammation of the urethra (*gonococcal urethritis*). This usually results in a thick, puslike white or yellowish discharge from the urethra ("the drip"), starting 2 to 10 days after infection (see Figure 5–1). There is generally an irritation or a burning sensation at the urethral opening, and urination is often frequent and painful. Because the symptoms are painful and obvious, most men seek treatment immediately. However, *about 20% to 25% of men show no symptoms* (are *asymptomatic*), while in

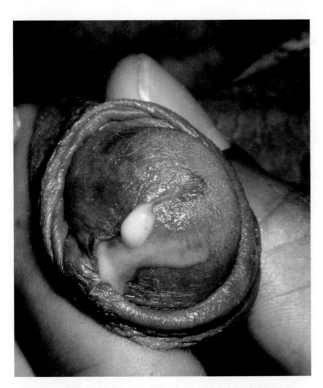

FIGURE 5–1 Urethral puslike discharge of gonorrhea.

others the early symptoms disappear (Cates, 2004). These asymptomatic men are still infected and can pass the gonococcus to new partners. If left untreated, gonorrhea spreads up the man's reproductive system and causes inflammation of the prostate, seminal vesicles, bladder, and epididymis. By this time, he usually experiences severe pain and fever. In 1% to 2% of cases, the disease gets into the bloodstream and causes inflammation of the joints (*gonococcal arthritis*), heart, or brain covering, as well as skin lesions (Brown et al., 1999). However, gonorrhea rarely results in death.

In women, the gonococcus initially invades the cervix, but unlike men, *most women show no symptoms during the early stages*. They are often unaware of their infection unless told about it by an infected male partner, and thus can unknowingly pass gonorrhea on to new partners. In the 20% to 40% of women who show symptoms, there may be an abnormal vaginal discharge and irritation of the vulva and urethra, causing burning during urination. Because so many women are asymptomatic, they often go untreated, and the gonococcus spreads through the uterus into the Fallopian tubes. In up to 40% of untreated women, the tubes become swollen and inflamed, a condition known as **pelvic inflammatory disease (PID)**, with symptoms of severe abdominal pain and fever (Marrazzo et al., 2008; see page 105). Hospitalization may be necessary at this stage. PID can cause scarring of the Fallopian tubes, which blocks passage of the sperm

and egg—a common cause of sterility and tubal pregnancies in women (see Chapter 7).

If a pregnant woman contracts gonorrhea, the fetus will usually not be infected because the gonococcus normally is not carried in the bloodstream (although joint and blood infections are possible). However, a baby's eyes can become infected at delivery as it passes through the infected cervix and vagina (a condition called *gonococcal opthalmia neonatorum*; see Figure 5–2). This can rapidly lead to blindness (Meyers, 2005). In some developing countries, 3% to 15% of babies are at risk, but the rate for gonorrhea in pregnant women in the United States is less than 1%, and most states require that an antibiotic or silver nitrate drops be put into all babies' eyes at birth to prevent possible infections. Adults can also transmit the gonococcus to their eyes by a contaminated hand (see Guerrero et al., 2010).

Diagnosis and Treatment

Most individuals with symptoms of gonorrhea will seek treatment immediately. Remember, however, that many people—particularly women—have no early symptoms. Therefore, if you suspect that you have had sex with someone who has gonorrhea, see a doctor as soon as possible. Until recently, a culture test was always used to test for gonorrhea. A cotton swab was inserted into the area of suspected infection, and the cells were grown in culture for a couple of days and then tested. Today, an accurate urine test is routinely used to test for gonorrhea in the urethra (technically called a nucleic acid amplification assay).

Little could be done for people with gonorrhea prior to the discovery of antibiotics. Fortunately, penicillin was discovered around the time of World War II and proved to be highly effective. Unfortunately, the bacterium developed resistance to penicillin over time. Physicians switched to tetracycline, but the bacterium became resistant to it as well. Today, most physicians treat gonorrhea with ceftriaxone or cefixime (CDC, 2007a). However, gonorrhea is also becoming resistant to many currently used drugs (Marrazzo et al., 2008). This means that we are quickly running out of inexpensive antibiotics to treat gonorrhea, and that soon we may have to turn to expensive injectable antibiotics to fight the disease. About 25% to 40% of people diagnosed with gonorrhea are also found to have chlamydia at the same time, so a drug that works with both infections is advised (Marrazzo et al., 2008).

Pelvic inflammatory disease (PID) ■ A bacterially caused inflammation of a woman's reproductive tract, particularly the Fallopian tubes, that can result in sterility. The most common (though not the only) cause is untreated gonorrhea and/or chlamydia.

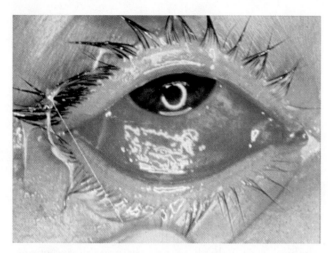

FIGURE 5–2 Eye infection caused by gonorrhea.

Should you ever be diagnosed with gonorrhea, be sure to tell all your recent partners that they may have gonorrhea so that they, too, can be treated. Gonorrhea is not like chicken pox, where you become immune after having had the infection. You can catch gonorrhea again if you again have sex with someone infected with the gonococcus. In fact, well over 10% of people with gonorrhea become infected again (Hosenfeld et al., 2009).

CHLAMYDIA AND NONGONOCOCCAL URETHRITIS

Any inflammation of the urethra not caused by the gonococcus is called **nongonococcal** (or **nonspecific**) **urethritis (NGU)**. This term is often reserved for men with an inflamed urethra, but the organisms that cause it cause infection in women (*cervicitis*) as well. Several organisms can cause infection (including *Ureaplasma urealyticum* and *Trichomonas vaginalis*), but the one that is most frequently responsible today is *Chlamydia trachomatis* (Bradshaw et al., 2006). The infection caused by this sexually transmitted bacterium is called **chlamydia.**

Chlamydia is much more common than gonorrhea, with at least 2.3 million new cases in the United States this year (CDC, 2010). It is especially prevalent in teenagers and young adults. Similar to gonorrhea, the rates for chlamydia are much higher in the United States than in all other developed countries except Russia (Aral & Gorbach, 2002; Panchaud et al., 2000).

Nongonococcal (nonspecific) urethritis (NGU) ■ Any inflammation of the urethra that is not caused by the *Neisseria gonorrhoeae* (gonococcus) bacterium.

Chlamydia ■ A sexually transmitted infection caused by the *Chlamydia trachomatis* bacterium, which lives on mucous membranes.

Because many students have never heard of chlamydia, they think that it cannot be all that bad. In fact, although its initial symptoms are usually milder than those of gonorrhea, if left untreated it is more likely than gonorrhea to cause damage to the reproductive organs.

Symptoms and Complications

Like the gonococcus, *Chlamydia trachomatis* lives only on mucous membranes. Chlamydia is spread when the infected membranes of one person come into contact with the membranes of another person.

If a person with chlamydia shows early symptoms, he or she will start doing so within 1 to 3 weeks after infection. The early symptoms are milder than, but similar to and sometimes mistaken for, those of gonorrhea: irritation and burning of the urethra (although usually not painful) and a discharge (usually thin and clear rather than puslike). However, about 80% of women and a large proportion of men have no symptoms at all in the initial stage (Einwalter et al., 2005; Geisler, 2010).

> "When I was attending LSU, I went to see the doctor for a regular gynecological exam. The nurse suggested that I consider some other tests for STIs because some of them had few or no symptoms. At first I declined, thinking that I had not slept with many people and, also, that if I had anything I would surely know from symptoms. But I changed my mind and was tested. When I called for results, I was shocked to find out that I was positive for chlamydia."

> "After dating a guy for about a month, we broke it off. We had been sexually active throughout our relationship and had unprotected sex (without condoms) only one time. Right after breaking it off, I went in for my annual exam and, just by chance, opted to get an STI check. I even joked about it with my roommates saying 'better safe than sorry.' Two days later I got a call from Redfern saying I had tested positive for chlamydia."
> (from the author's files)

The Centers for Disease Control and Prevention recommends that *all sexually active women aged 25 and younger get routine annual screenings for chlamydia.* Why? Although about half of chlamydia cases resolve on their own within 1 year (Geisler, 2010), if left untreated, chlamydia spreads through the reproductive system, which in men can cause infection of the prostate and epididymis and possibly sterility (Bradshaw et al., 2006). In up to 40% of women the spread of chlamydia causes pelvic inflammatory disease, which can leave the Fallopian tubes scarred and result in sterility or increased risk of tubal pregnancy (see next section). At this stage the infection can be quite painful and may require hospitalization. Research has shown that *a single attack of chlamydia is about 3 times more likely than* gonorrhea to cause sterility in women. Babies born to women who have chlamydia at the time of delivery can get eye infections (*chlamydia conjunctivitis*) and/or nose-throat infections (Einwalter et al., 2005). In underdeveloped countries, the chlamydia bacterium often causes an eye infection called *trachoma*, which is spread to other people's eyes by flies. It is the leading cause of blindness in those areas. In tropical countries, certain subtypes of chlamydia are also responsible for a serious sexually transmitted infection called **lymphogranuloma venereum (LGV)** (fewer than 150 cases annually in the United States).

If left untreated, LGV causes the inguinal lymph nodes to swell, followed by swelling of the penis, labia, or clitoris (sometimes enormously so, resulting in elephantiasis of the external genitalia) (Brown et al., 1999).

Recall that many people with chlamydia also have gonorrhea (Marrazzo et al., 2008). About 14% of people who are diagnosed with chlamydia eventually are infected again (Hosenfeld et al., 2009).

Diagnosis and Treatment

As with gonorrhea, the culture test for chlamydia infections *of the urethra* has been replaced with a noninvasive urine test. For other mucous membranes, it is a culture test. If chlamydia is confirmed, it is usually treated with doxycycline or azithromycin (Marrazzo et al., 2008). Remember, many people have no symptoms in the early stages, so if you think someone you have had sex with has chlamydia, seek treatment immediately.

Pelvic Inflammatory Disease (PID) in Women: A Likely Consequence of Untreated Chlamydia or Gonorrhea

In the discussion of gonorrhea and chlamydia, I referred to pelvic inflammatory disease in women as a possible consequence if the infections went untreated. In fact, about 20% to 40% of women who are not treated early will eventually develop pelvic inflammatory disease (Cook et al., 2001). PID is a general term for an infection that travels from the lower genital tract (vagina and cervix) to the Fallopian tubes and sometimes to surrounding structures such as the ovaries and pelvic cavity. It results from infection with a variety of organisms, but 50% to 75% of cases are caused by *Chlamydia trachomatis* or *Neisseria gonorrhoeae* (Brunham et al., 1988; Rice & Schachter, 1991).

About 8% of American women have had PID (Haggerty et al., 2010), with over 1 million cases each year, requiring about 180,000 hospitalizations (Marrazzo et al., 2008). Symptoms may include tenderness or pain in the lower abdomen (sometimes to

the extent that standing up straight is impossible), high fever, and chills. However, 3 times as many women experience a persistent low-grade infection, either with no symptoms or with intermittent abdominal cramps. In these "silent" infections (i.e., the women do not go to a physician for diagnosis), the long-term inflammation can result in pelvic adhesions and abscesses. The inside diameter of a Fallopian tube is only about that of a human hair; thus, even a small amount of scar tissue can result in an ectopic (tubal) pregnancy or in permanent sterility (Weinstock et al., 1994).

SYPHILIS

The consequences of untreated gonorrhea or chlamydia can be serious, but untreated **syphilis** is far worse, being responsible for the deaths of over 100 million people worldwide in the 20th century (Chiappa & Forish, 1976). Syphilis is caused by *Treponema pallidum*, a spiral-shaped bacterium (spirochete).

Worldwide, there are about 12 million cases of syphilis per year. Most cases are in Southeast Asia and Africa (Singh & McCloskey, 2001). In the United States, the disease last peaked in 1990, when 50,578 cases were reported. Over 36,000 cases were reported in 2008 (CDC, 2010), of which nearly two thirds were among men who have sex with men. In the United States, the disease is found mainly in southern states and large urban areas and is much more common among African Americans than whites.

Symptoms and Complications

Almost all cases of syphilis are transmitted by sexual contact. This includes oral sex (Ciesielski et al., 2004). However, unlike the bacteria that cause gonorrhea and chlamydia, which require contact of mucous membranes for transmission, the spirochete that causes syphilis can also pass directly through any little cut or scrape of the skin into the bloodstream. This means that one could potentially get syphilis by merely touching the sores of another person, as has happened to some dentists and physicians. If a person has been infected by the spirochete, the first symptoms generally appear 2 to 4 weeks later. If many bacteria are transmitted, the incubation period can be as short as 10 days; but if only a few are transmitted, the sores can take as long as 90 days to appear.

Lymphogranuloma venereum (LGV) ■ A sexually transmitted infection common in tropical countries that is caused by chlamydia. If left untreated, it causes swelling of the inguinal lymph nodes, penis, labia, or clitoris.

Syphilis ■ A sexually transmitted infection caused by the *Treponema pallidum* bacterium (spirochete), which can also pass directly through any cut or scrape into the bloodstream.

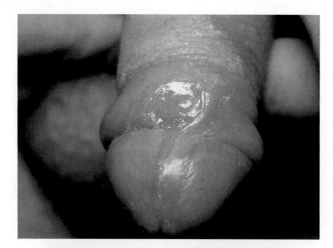

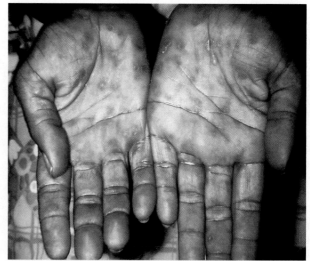

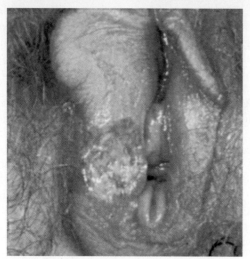

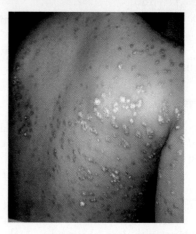

FIGURE 5–3 A primary-stage syphilis chancre on the penis (top) and labia (bottom).

FIGURE 5–4 Secondary-stage syphilis rash on the palms and body.

The symptoms of syphilis generally occur in four stages (Brown et al., 1999). The *primary stage* begins with the appearance of a very ugly ulcerlike (raised edges with a crater) sore called a *chancre* (see Figure 5–3) at the site where the spirochete entered the body (usually the penis, cervix, lips, tongue, or anus). The chancre is full of bacteria and highly infectious, but even though the chancre looks awful, it is usually painless, and thus some people do not seek treatment. Because the painless chancre generally appears on the cervix in women, they usually are unaware that they are infected during the initial stage unless they get a pelvic exam. Even if a person is not treated, the sore will usually disappear in 10 to 14 days. However, the spirochete continues to be carried in the person's bloodstream, and thus individuals remain infected *and* infectious even after the chancre disappears.

Symptoms of the *secondary stage* of syphilis usually appear within 4 to 6 weeks after the chancre heals, but sometimes symptoms do not appear for several months. The main symptom is an *itchless,*

painless rash that appears all over the body, including the palms of the hands and the soles of the feet (see Figure 5–4). In the moist areas around the genitals, the rash appears as large sores called *condylomata lata*, which break and ooze a highly infectious fluid full of bacteria. Other symptoms can include a sore throat, a persistent low-grade fever, nausea, loss of appetite, aches and pains, and sometimes even hair loss. These symptoms are bothersome enough that many infected people will seek treatment, but many people mistake the symptoms for the measles, an allergic reaction, or some other disease. Syphilis is sometimes called "the great imitator." If treatment is not obtained, these symptoms, like the chancre of the primary stage, will also disappear (within several weeks to 1 year) and not return.

An infected person now enters the symptomless *latent stage*, and after about a year is generally not contagious because the spirochete is no longer found on the mucous membrane surfaces. This stage may last for years with no noticeable signs,

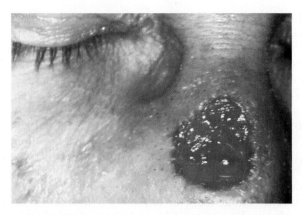

FIGURE 5–5 Late-stage gumma on the nose.

but all the while the bacteria are attacking the internal organs of the body, particularly the heart and blood vessels and the brain and spinal cord.

About two thirds of the people with untreated syphilis will not experience any more problems with the disease, but one third will develop serious complications as a result of the accumulated organ damage. They are now in the *late* (or *tertiary*) *stage*. Large ulcers called *gummas* often appear on the skin and bones. Damage to the heart and blood vessels frequently results in death, while damage to the central nervous system can lead to paralysis, insanity, and/or deafness.

Particularly heartbreaking is the fact that *an unborn baby can catch syphilis from an infected mother*. This happens because the spirochete travels from the pregnant woman's blood into the placental blood system. If it is not diagnosed and treated, the fetus will be aborted, stillborn, or born with a rather advanced stage of the infection called *congenital syphilis* (see Singh & McCloskey, 2001). The number of reported cases rose to 349 in 2006 (CDC, 2010). Complications of congenital syphilis can include deformation of the bones and teeth, blindness, deafness, and other abnormalities that can result in an early death. Blood tests for syphilis are done routinely during pregnancy tests, and if detected the infection can be treated.

Diagnosis and Treatment

The spirochete taken from a chancre or sore can be identified under a microscope, but blood tests are almost always done as well. The saddest thing about any suffering or death that occur from syphilis is that the spirochetes are so easily eradicated with antibiotics. Penicillin G is very effective, with the amount and duration of treatment depending on the stage of infection (Marrazzo et al., 2008). Although antibiotics can eradicate the bacteria at any stage, they cannot reverse any organ damage that may have already occurred if the disease was left untreated until the late stage. It is important, therefore, that people seek treatment as early as possible.

MYCOPLASMA GENITALIUM

Mycoplasma genitalium is a bacterium that was first discovered in the 1980s. We still do not know much about it, but it is frequently found in men with urethritis and women with cervicitis who do not have gonorrhea or chlamydia. In a nationally representative sample of young adults, *Mycoplasma genitalium* was more prevalent than gonorrhea and was 22 times more common in people who were having sexual intercourse than in poeple who were not (see Manhart et al., 2007).

LESS COMMON BACTERIAL STIs

There are other types of bacterially caused STIs that are common in tropical climates but rare in the United States. I have already mentioned lymphogranuloma venereum (see the section on chlamydia); two additional examples are chancroid and granuloma inguinale. **Chancroid** is caused by *Hemophilus ducreyi* and is characterized by small bumps on the genitals or other sites that rupture into soft, craterlike sores (see Figure 5–6). The incubation period from the time of infection to the appearance of the first sores is only 3 to 14 days. Unlike the syphilis chancre, chancroid is painful. The lymph nodes in the groin area often become inflamed and swollen. There are about 7 million cases of chancroid in the world annually (Spinola et al., 2002), but fewer than 50 new cases are reported in the United States each year (CDC, 2010). However,

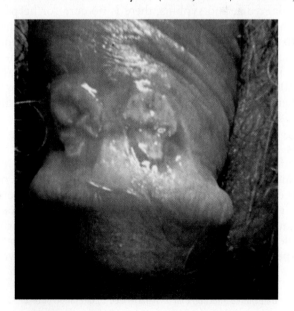

FIGURE 5–6 Two adjacent chancroid lesions on the penis.

Chancroid ■ A sexually transmitted infection, caused by the *Hemophilus ducreyi* bacterium, which is characterized by small, painful bumps.

the number of unreported cases is certainly higher. Chancroid can be treated with several different antibiotics (Marrazzo et al., 2008).

Granuloma inguinale is rare in the United States, with fewer than 50 cases per year, but is much more common in tropical areas of the world. The main symptom is a painless pimple that ulcerates and spreads to surrounding areas, permanently destroying the tissue and causing death if not treated. It is treated with doxycycline or trimethroprim-sulfamethoxazole (Marrazzo et al., 2008).

Shigellosis is another uncommon sexually transmitted infection. It is contracted from exposure to feces infected with the *Shigella* bacterium (a result of behavior such as oral stimulation of the anus). Symptoms include acute diarrhea, fever, and pain. Thirty percent of the cases in the United States occur in male homosexuals. Shigellosis is treated with tetracycline or ampicillin.

PERSONAL REFLECTIONS

How would you feel if your best friend told you that he or she had an STI? Your teenage son told you that he had an STI? Your teenage daughter told you that she had an STI? Your partner told you that he or she had an STI acquired from a previous relationship?

HERPES

Every year, about 1 million Americans become infected with genital herpes. Unlike gonorrhea, chlamydia, and syphilis, there is no cure for herpes. The men and women infected this year will be added to those who already have it, making the total number of genital herpes sufferers at least 45 million—1 in 5 Americans age 12 or older (Marrazzo et al., 2008). Another 100 million Americans have oral herpes. This includes almost 60% of 14- to 49-year-old people (Xu et al., 2006).

Herpes (from a Greek word meaning "to creep") is *spread by direct skin-to-skin contact* (from the infected site on one person to the site of contact on another person). Two different types (1 and 2) of the virus were identified in the mid-1960s. The type 1 virus is much more common than type 2. Both types cause painful blisters (which often rupture to form ulcers), but in the mid-1960s there was a 95% site specificity: Ninety-five percent of people with fever

blisters or a cold sore around the mouth had *herpes simplex virus type 1* (and thus this type was called "oral herpes"), and 95% of people with blisters around the genitals had herpes *simplex virus type 2* (which thus came to be called "genital herpes"). Thus, it was mistakenly believed that HSV type 1 was acquired only by kissing and HSV type 2 only by sexual intercourse.

Today, there is no longer a strong site specificity, particularly in young people. Among sexually active adults, the type 1 herpes virus causes almost as many genital infections as it does infections of the mouth (Langenberg et al., 1999). *Both the type 1 and type 2 viruses can be transferred from mouth to genitals, and vice versa.* Nevertheless, many people persist in their mistaken belief that oral herpes can only be caught by kissing and genital herpes only through intercourse. Perhaps this letter to Ann Landers will be more persuasive:

> Dear Ann Landers:
>
> I got genital herpes from my boyfriend of two years from an innocent fever blister on his lip. I could not believe a woman could get a venereal disease from indulging in oral sex with someone who had a simple cold sore. My doctor cultured it and sure enough it came back Herpes Simplex Type I (the oral kind). But now I have genital herpes.
>
> I developed a high fever after being exposed to the virus on his lip. That virus caused two fever blisters on my genitals. They reappear every two months and are quite painful.
>
> My boyfriend dumped me when he learned I was infected. He remains "pure" and does not come down with a sexually transmitted infection, while I am alone and scared. There is no justice! Please, Ann Landers, inform the public at once. Tell them what can happen if a person has contact with those innocent-looking sores near the mouth.
>
> Sign Me Dumb and Angry
>
> Dear Angry: I have printed this information in my column more than once. Several readers wrote to say I was ill-informed, stupid, and just plain nuts. Thanks for your testimony.
>
> (*Dear Ann Landers* and Reply Sign Me Dumb and Angry.
> By permission of Esther P. Lederer Trust and
> Creators Syndicate, Inc.)

I will refer to herpes blisters or ulcerations on the mouth as **oral herpes** and blisters or ulcerations on the genitals as **genital herpes,** without worrying whether the blisters were caused by the type 1 or type 2 virus (see Figure 5–7). Genital herpes is almost always contracted by intimate sexual contact (genital-to-genital, mouth-to-genital, genital-to-anal). More women have genital herpes than do men, evidence that it is easier to spread from an infected man to a woman than vice versa. Consistent use of condoms greatly reduces the risk of spreading the infection (London, 2006).

Granuloma inguinale ■ A rare (in the United States) sexually transmitted infection that is characterized by ulceration of tissue.

Shigellosis ■ An infection that can be contracted during sexual activity by exposure to feces containing the *Shigella* bacterium.

Oral herpes ■ A herpes infection in or around the mouth. It can be caused by herpes simplex virus types 1 or 2.

Genital herpes ■ Herpes infection in the genital region. It can be caused by herpes simplex virus types 1 or 2.

Most cases of oral herpes are not contracted by intimate sexual contact (Xu et al., 2006). Experts believe most cases in adults to be reactivations of latent infections acquired during childhood. The virus can be easily spread by even a quick, casual kiss, and thus *it should not be assumed that a person suffering an attack of oral herpes was recently involved in sexual activity*. By the way, not all mouth ulcers are caused by the herpes virus; they can also be caused by bacteria, allergic reactions, or autoimmune responses. Canker sores, for example, are not caused by herpes virus. However, "fever blisters" and most cold sores are herpes.

There are actually eight human herpes viruses, but only types 1, 2, and 8 are sexually spread. The herpes simplex virus types 1 and 2 are very closely related to the viruses that cause chicken pox in children and shingles in adults (varicella zoster virus), infectious mononucleosis (Epstein–Barr virus), cytomegalic ("large-cell") inclusion disease in infants (cytomegalovirus), and Kaposi's sarcoma. Kaposi's sarcoma is a cancer of the capillary system that is common in AIDS patients. It is caused by herpes virus 8, which is sexually transmitted (Grulich et al., 2001).

Symptoms—Primary Attack

Symptoms of the initial herpes attack normally appear about 2 to 20 days after contact with an infected person, with an average of 6 days. The symptoms occur in three stages. In stage one, the *prodromal stage,* the person feels a tingling, burning, itching, or anesthetic-like sensation on the skin surface where he or she came into contact with the virus. Sometimes the symptoms are more diffuse; in the case of genital herpes, for example, the infected person may feel pain running down the buttocks and thighs. These initial signs indicate the beginning of viral *replication and shedding* (i.e., viruses traveling from the source, free to incorporate themselves into other cells). Therefore, the individual should immediately cease all intimate contact involving the infected area.

Within a few hours the skin surface will break into fluid-filled *blisters* called *vesicles* (see Figure 5–7). These can be excruciatingly painful. After a while, the vesicles break open, resembling pustules and then ulcerated running sores. Although herpes lesions generally resemble blisters, many people have sores that are more ulcerative in appearance (see Figure 5–7). These symptoms mark the second, or *vesicle stage*, which can last from 2 to 3 weeks. The first, or primary, herpes attack includes more than just painful blisters, however. The person often has flulike symptoms, suffering muscle aches and pains, headache, fever, and swollen lymph glands. Urination can be quite painful for those with genital herpes (catheterization is sometimes required), and even walking or sitting can be extremely painful sometimes.

The sores begin to develop scales and form scabs, and the lesions eventually heal without leaving scars. This is the third, or *crusting-over stage*. Viruses are still being shed during the crusting-over stage; thus, intimate contact with the infected area should be avoided until all the sores are fully healed. The average duration of a primary attack is about 16 days.

The primary attack is severe because the person has not yet built up antibodies to the virus. A person can have more than one primary attack of herpes, however. An individual could have a primary attack after exposure to the type 1 virus, for example, and later be exposed to the type 2 virus and have another primary attack. Primary attacks to different strains of the same virus are also possible. A person with genital herpes, therefore, should not assume that it is safe to have intercourse with someone who also has herpes.

Recurrent Attacks

During the primary herpes attack, some of the virus migrates up sensory nerves from the infected site to the nerve's ganglion (the nerve cell center). The virus becomes dormant (inactive) when it reaches the ganglion. A recurrent attack occurs as a result of

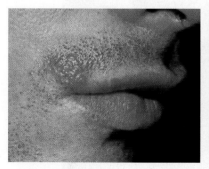 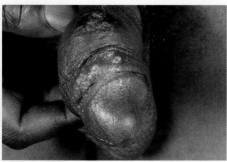 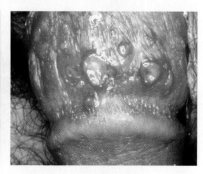

FIGURE 5–7 Herpes blisters on the mouth (left) and penis (center). Photo (right) shows ulcerated herpes lesions on the penis.

the virus reactivating and traveling down the sensory nerve to or near the same area as the initial sores, where it again starts multiplying. In the genital region, people with type 2 herpes suffer an average of four recurrent attacks a year, compared with one a year for those with type 1 herpes (Brown et al., 1999). Recurrent attacks are usually less severe than the primary attack (because the individual now produces antibodies) and generally last only from 5 to 10 days.

What causes recurrent attacks? Stress to the immune system, either of a physical or emotional nature, seems to be the major cause. A recurrent attack can be brought on by illness, fatigue, menstruation, too much sunlight, and/or anxiety.

Asymptomatic and Unrecognized Infections

The herpes viruses are easily spread when sores (blisters or ulcerations) are present. The sores are an obvious sign of viral shedding, and infected persons should take measures to prevent the spread of the virus to other persons at this time. However, in many people the symptoms are mild, while still other individuals are asymptomatic shedders of the virus. In fact, as many as 75% to 90% of people infected with herpes simplex type 2 in the genital region are unaware that they are infected (Marrazzo et al., 2008). Half or more of these individuals have clinically recognizable symptoms, but the symptoms are so mild that the individuals do not recognize them as herpes. Experts now believe that most transmission of genital herpes occurs during periods when there are no recognizable symptoms (Brown et al., 1999).

> "The guy I had been dating for two years told me that he had 'jock itch' and showed me a sore at the base of his penis. I didn't know what jock itch even looked like, much less herpes, so I believed him. His sore went away. About a month later another sore

came up, so he went to the doctor ... [who] told him he had herpes. Two days later I had a sore on my labia.... The doctor diagnosed the sore as herpes."
(from the author's files)

Serious Complications

We generally think of herpes blisters as occurring only on the mouth and the genitals or anal area, but *the blisters may appear on any part of the body.* The virus can be spread to the eyes (by touching blisters that appear elsewhere on the body and then rubbing the eyes, or by using saliva to insert contact lenses), resulting in *herpes keratitis,* or ocular herpes. This is *the leading cause of blindness resulting from infection in the United States today* (see Figure 5–8). Lesions on the eyeball result in scarring as they heal. It is the scars that eventually cause blindness. So if you have herpes, be sure to wash your hands if you touch the sores.

Cervical cancer is caused by human papillomavirus infections (see later section). However, if a woman also has genital herpes, it increases the chance that HPV infections will develop into cancer by two to three times (Smith et al., 2002).

Occasionally, dormant oral or facial herpes migrates to the brain rather than to the face, resulting in *herpes encephalitis,* a rare but often fatal condition. Primary attacks of herpes sometimes include inflammation of the membranes covering the brain and spinal cord (*herpes meningitis*), but full recovery usually follows.

Herpes can result in serious complications during pregnancy. There is a higher-than-normal rate of premature births, spontaneous abortions, and congenital malformations (e.g., brain damage or mental retardation).

The greatest risk is to the baby, particularly for women who have a primary attack near the time of labor. *Neonatal herpes* is devastating. If a woman has an active case of genital herpes during delivery, there is at least a 50% chance that the baby will

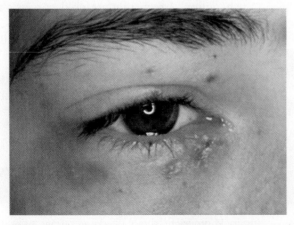 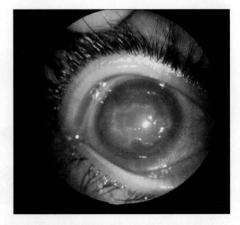

FIGURE 5–8 Herpes infection on the eye lid (left) and on the eye itself (right).

catch it. Many babies who get herpes at birth (at least several hundred cases each year) suffer permanent and severe heart or neurological problems or die (Ambroggio et al., 2009; Donoval et al., 2006). The disease is so virulent in newborns because they have no defenses to fight off the infection. Unfortunately, it is not possible to assess the risk of spreading infection to the baby by looking for symptoms in the mother prior to birth. Most babies who become infected are born to mothers who do not display genital blisters at the time of delivery (Stone et al., 1989). It is for these reasons that most doctors prefer to deliver babies by cesarean section to women with genital herpes. An active case of oral herpes is not a risk factor at the time of delivery, but parents (or anyone else) with an active case of oral herpes should avoid kissing or fondling a baby.

Diagnosis and Treatment

First, the bad news: As yet, there is no cure for herpes. Nothing you can do or take will rid your body of the herpes virus. The virus lies dormant in the ganglion cells between active outbreaks, and the potential for another attack is always there. Herpes sufferers nevertheless remain persistent in their attempts to find a home cure. None of these has proven effective in scientific tests, and some of these home remedies (e.g., ether) have proven to make matters even worse in some cases. Creams and ointments should also be avoided because they help to spread the virus to adjacent areas and prevent the skin from drying. Many people attempt to control herpes through diet, but the Centers for Disease Control and Prevention indicates that there is no merit to these specific diet claims.

Now the good news. Although there is no known cure for herpes, antiviral drugs are available that relieve symptoms and speed up the healing process during the primary attack (Marrazzo et al., 2008). One drug is called *acyclovir* (marketed under the name Zovirax) and is available both as an ointment and as a tablet. Two newer, equally effective, antiviral drugs are *valacyclovir* (Valtrex) and *famciclovir* (Famvir). These drugs decrease viral shedding and herpes outbreaks by 85% to 95% and greatly reduce the risk of transmission to an uninfected partner (Corey et al., 2004). Another antiviral cream, *penciclovir*, helps heal cold sores (oral herpes) (Spruance et al., 1997). Still another antiviral drug is available to help treat ocular herpes. These drugs are not a cure, however, and recurrent attacks will return once they are discontinued.

There has been considerable research to find a herpes vaccine, but none have proven to be highly effective. The best vaccine produced so far protects 75% of women who had not previously been exposed to the virus, but it is not effective in men (Stanberry et al., 2002).

The Personal Side of Herpes

Besides the physical symptoms, individuals suffering with genital herpes almost always have some psychological difficulties adjusting to their infection. They often pass through several stages: shock, emotional numbing, isolation and loneliness, and sometimes severe depression. The reactions of others may make them feel like "social lepers." A survey of readers of *the helper* (a magazine for people with herpes) found that in the previous 12 months, 52% had suffered depression and fear of rejection, 36% had feelings of isolation, and 10% had self-destructive feelings (Catotti et al., 1993).

So how should you deal with personal relationships if you have herpes? Accept the fact that although there is no cure, you do not have the plague. *The use of condoms will reduce the chances of infecting a partner* (in case there is viral shedding without symptoms). If you have frequent or long-lasting attacks, talk to your doctor about taking one of the antiviral drugs. Contact the American Social Health Association. They will provide you with current up-to-date information on herpes research, therapy, and care.

PERSONAL REFLECTIONS

Many babies are born with sexually transmitted infections as a result of their mothers being infected during pregnancy. Is having an STI an indication of immorality, irresponsibility, both, or neither? Explain (you may wish to reconsider your answers to the first two personal reflections at this point).

HEPATITIS

Hepatitis is an inflammation of the liver that can have many causes. We will address three types caused by viruses. The incubation period (time period before symptoms appear) is 2 to 6 weeks for hepatitis A and 6 weeks to 6 months for hepatitis B. The symptoms can range from mild (poor appetite, diarrhea) to severe (fever; vomiting; pain; fatigue; jaundiced, or yellow-tinged, skin and eyes; dark urine). See Figure 5–9.

Hepatitis A (infectious hepatitis) is caused by a small virus (HAV) that is spread by direct or indirect oral contact with contaminated feces. From the mid-1970s to the mid-1990s, there were 150,000 to

Hepatitis A, B, and C ■ Liver infections caused by viruses. Type A is spread by direct or indirect contact with contaminated feces. Type B is transmitted by infected blood or body fluids, with about 50% of the cases contracted during sex. Type C is spread mainly by contaminated blood, but may possibly be spread during sexual intercourse in some cases.

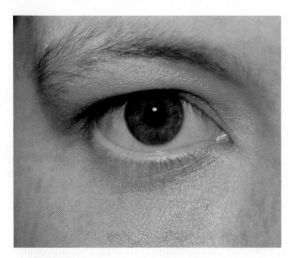

FIGURE 5–9 A typical symptom of hepatitis is jaundice: yellow-tinged eyes and skin.

450,000 new cases in the United States each year, but rates have fallen to about 32,000 new cases a year with more widespread use of a vaccine (CDC, 2007a). The infection can be spread sexually (by contact with the anus of an infected person during sex) and has a higher incidence in male homosexuals than in other groups. However, it is most often contracted through nonsexual means, such as eating food handled by infected individuals, or shellfish taken from contaminated waters. To reduce the prevalence of this disease, the Centers for Disease Control and Prevention *recommends routine vaccination of children, men who have sex with men, and people who use drugs intravenously.*

Hepatitis B (serum hepatitis) is caused by a different, larger virus (HBV) and is transmitted by infected blood or body fluids such as saliva, semen, and vaginal secretions. It can cause a number of liver diseases, including cancer and cirrhosis. As many as 400 million people worldwide are infected with this virus, which causes 1 million deaths a year (Kane, 1995). About 5% of Americans have been infected with hepatitis B at some time in their lives. However, because of a widespread vaccination program, the number of new cases in the United States has declined to 60,000 a year (CDC, 2007a). Over 50% of the new cases are spread during heterosexual intercourse (Marrazzo et al., 2008). Over two thirds of all pregnant women infected with hepatitis B pass the infection to their babies. Four drugs are now available to treat patients with hepatitis B: interferon, lamivudine, entecavir (Baraclude), and adefoir dipivoxil (Hepsera). About 90% of those with hepatitis recover, but up to 10% remain chronically infected and thus become carriers of the disease.

Human papillomaviruses (HPV) ■ Viruses that cause abnormal growths in epithelial cells. There are over 100 types. A few (types 6 and 11) cause genital warts, while others (types 16, 18, 31, 33, and 45) can lead to cancer of the cervix.

The Centers for Disease Control and Prevention has *recommended that all children (babies as well as adolescents) be vaccinated* against the hepatitis B virus.

Hepatitis C, which is caused by still another virus (HCV), was not identified as a specific virus until 1988. At least 300 million people are infected worldwide. This includes 3% to 4% of people in many Asian countries, 10% of people in central Africa, and 2% of Americans (Edlin & Carden, 2006; Thompson, 2009). About 75% of them remain chronically infected, although many go 10 to 20 years or longer before they show any symptoms (Flamm, 2003). About one fifth will develop cirrhosis of the liver and/or liver cancer, resulting in about 8,000 to 12,000 deaths a year (Zule et al., 2009). The number of deaths is expected to double or triple over the next 10 to 20 years. The hepatitis C virus is most commonly spread through contact with contaminated blood (blood-to-blood contact), and thus it is frequently found in people who inject illicit drugs and share needles. About 50% to 90% of injection drug users have hepatitis C (Aceijas & Rhodes, 2007). The virus is only rarely spread during sex (Marrazzo et al., 2008), but in many areas as many as 90% of people infected with HIV also have hepatitis (many people also get HIV by injecting drugs) (Aceijas & Rhodes, 2007). There is no vaccine available for protection against hepatitis C. The disease is treated with long-acting interferon in combination with ribavirin, but this is effective in only about 50% of cases.

GENITAL HUMAN PAPILLOMAVIRUS INFECTION

Have you ever heard of genital human papillomavirus (HPV) infection? Many college students have not, yet this is the most common sexually transmitted infection caused by bacteria or viruses in the United States and worldwide (Marrazzo et al., 2008). It is estimated that 20 million Americans are already infected with HPV and that there are at least 6.2 million new cases every year (CDC, 2010a; Liddon et al., 2010). As many as 80% of sexually active teenaged girls eventually are infected with HPV and 60% to 90% of their male partners are infected (Marrazzo et al., 2008). The large majority of infections (at least 80%) disappear on their own within several months. However, there are very serious consequences in cases that persist.

Human papillomaviruses (HPV) infect epithelial cells (the covering of internal and external surfaces of the body). Over 100 different types have been identified, of which about 40 can be transmitted during sex (CDC, 2007a). HPV infections are called *clinical infections* if there are symptoms visible to the naked eye, and *subclinical infections* if there are

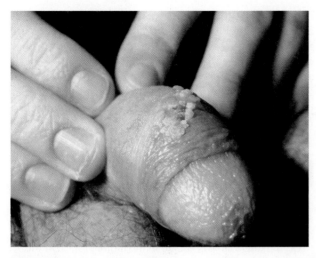 

FIGURE 5–10 Early-stage (left) and late-stage (right) genital warts on the penis caused by human papillomavirus.

no visible symptoms. Subclinical HPV infections are at least 10 times more common than clinical infections (Rudlinger & Norval, 1996).

We can separate clinical HPV cases into three broad categories: (1) those that cause a rare skin condition (epidermodysplasia verruciformis) that appears as reddish plaques, (2) those that cause nongenital warts (including common, plantar, and flat warts), and (3) those that cause warts in the genital and anal area (although these can also cause problems in the mouth, pharynx, and larynx). There are about 25 different human papillomaviruses that can cause anogenital warts, but 90% of genital warts are caused by HPV types 6 and 11 (Kahn, 2005). It was once thought that the only type of genital wart was *condyloma acuminata*, the type shown in Figure 5–10, but recent studies have shown that HPV can result in a wide variety of anogenital lesions and that a single individual can have many different-appearing warts (e.g., papular, macular) (Brown et al., 1999).

In the United States, about 1 million people visit a doctor every year for genital warts (Marrazzo et al., 2008). For those people who develop **genital (venereal) warts,** the first symptoms generally appear anywhere from 3 weeks to 8 months after contact with an infected person. The warts can cause itching, irritation, or bleeding. In men, the warts generally appear on the penis, scrotum, and/or anus, but they can also grow within the urethra. In women, the warts can appear on the cervix and walls of the vagina as well as the vulva and anus, and thus the virus can be transmitted to a baby during vaginal delivery. Women are much more likely than men to develop visible warts (and serious complications—as will be discussed) because the cervix has a zone of cells that are continually undergoing cell division (which makes it easier for the viruses to exploit them). The skin of the penis, on the other hand, resists transformation by the virus. Genital warts can substantially decrease one's quality of life (Marra et al., 2009).

"I contracted venereal warts from a married woman I frequently slept with. I then gave them to my girlfriend. I did not know I had the affliction until she was diagnosed during a semi-annual exam with her gynecologist. The removal procedure for me as a man was rather simple as opposed to her treatment. Her first treatment involved cryogenically freezing her cervix. After that unsuccessful attempt they resorted to laser surgery. She is still not cured."

"When I was 17 years old I went to the doctor for a Pap smear. He found warts on my cervix. My doctor performed laser surgery to get rid of the warts. A year and a half later I had another outbreak, had surgery, and within seven weeks after the surgery they came back. These last two times they weren't just on the cervix, they spread all the way to the vulva. . . . I have abstained from sex since the beginning of the second outbreak."

(All examples are from the author's files.)

Women with HPV infections have a greatly increased risk of developing cervical and/or vulvar cancer. In fact, nearly all women with cervical cancer are found to have HPV infections (Fey & Beal, 2004; Kahn, 2005). The latency period between infection with HPV and detection of cancer is 5 to 25 years. About 15 kinds of human papillomaviruses are found in cervical cancers, most commonly HPV 16 and 18 (70% of cases), 31, 33, and 45 (Kahn, 2005). Types 16 and 18 also cause 25% to 35% of oral cancers, 40% of penile cancers, and 90% of anal cancers (Liddou et al., 2010; see also Kreimel et al., 2010;

Genital (venereal) warts ■ Warts in the genital and anal regions caused by human papillomaviruses (mainly types 6 and 11). The warts are cauliflowerlike growths.

Nyitray et al., 2010). Note that these types of HPV are different from the two types that cause most genital warts (types 6 and 11). What this means, of course, is that *most women with HPV infections who are at risk of developing cervical cancer will have no visible symptoms.* Each year, nearly 2 million American women are diagnosed with mild cervical dysplasia (Fey & Beal, 2004). Remember, most infections disappear on their own. Only women with persistent infections will develop cervical cancer—about 11,000 a year in the United States, resulting in over 4,000 deaths. Worldwide, over 250,000 women die each year of cervical cancer (World Health Organization, 2009). Because of this, a regular pelvic exam and Pap smear are an essential part of female health care. Women who test positive for HPV should have Pap smears at least every 6 months. There is now an HPV DNA test that can be done to identify the highest-risk types of HPV for cervical cancer (Mayrand et al., 2007). Many experts believe that this test is superior to the standard Pap smear test for screening for the risk of developing cervical cancer (Rubin, 2007). Although HPV has been associated with cancer of the penis, it is much less likely that the viruses will lead to cancer in men (as is the case for visible warts, you recall).

Recall that most HPV infections are subclinical (no visible symptoms) and that most disappear on their own—i.e., the individuals eventually test HPV negative (e.g., Carter et al., 1996). For individuals who have anogenital warts, various treatments are available, but none is ideal for all patients (Marrazzo et al., 2008). Small external warts can be treated by applying a solution of podophyllin (sold in stores as Condylox) or imiquimod (Aldara), which causes them to dry up. Larger warts can be removed by cauterization or minor surgery. Internal warts are often removed by laser surgery. For HPV infections of the cervix, cryotherapy (freezing) is the preferred therapy. However, none of these methods attacks the virus directly, so recurrences of the warts are common (see previous case histories). Injection with antiviral or immunomodulatory drugs has shown some promise.

Because millions of Americans infected with HPV have no symptoms, they are unaware that they can infect others. The best way to eliminate the disease would be to vaccinate people before they are exposed to the virus. In 2006, a highly effective vaccine (called *Gardasil*) for HPV types 16 and 18 (accounting for 70% of cervical cancers), and 6 and 11 (accounting for 90% of genital warts) became available. A second vaccine (*Cervarix*) is now available that protects against HPV types 16 and 18. The vaccines provide partial protection against other HPV types (Herrero, 2009). A government advisory panel has *recommended that all girls be vaccinated at ages 11 or 12.* Because a large number of men also get HPV infections (warts and oral, anal, and penile cancers) (see Palefsky, 2010), in 2009 the U.S. Food and Drug Administration *recommended that boys and men aged 9–26 years also be vaccinated.*

PERSONAL REFLECTIONS

Have you ever engaged in sex with a new partner while under the influence of alcohol? If your answer is "yes," did your use of alcohol result in your engaging in unprotected sex? If it did, what will you do in the future to prevent this?

Widespread HPV vaccination of girls in Australia has led to a dramatic decrease in the number of cases of genital warts (Fairley et al., 2009). Unfortunately, in the United States HPV vaccination of young teens has become a political issue more so than a public health issue. Despite the fact that about 80% of sexually active teens will get HPV (Marrazzo et al., 2008), many state legislatures have voted against the vaccine because of concerns that it would promote promiscuity.

MOLLUSCUM CONTAGIOSUM

Molluscum contagiosum is a painless growth that is caused by a pox virus. The virus is easily spread by direct skin-to-skin contact, but the large majority of cases are not spread during sex (Marrazzo et al., 2008). Infected individuals can easily spread it to other parts of their bodies. The virus incubates for 2 weeks to 6 months and then erupts into dome-shaped growths that are usually 1 to 5 mm in diameter and look like small pimples filled with kernels of corn. Molluscum contagiosum is easily diagnosed by the appearance of the growths, and is usually treated by removing the growths. However, they usually disappear on their own within 6 to 9 months.

HIV INFECTION AND AIDS

In the early 1980s, doctors in California were puzzled when five men were diagnosed with *Pneumocystis carinii pneumonia,* a rare respiratory infection usually seen only in people with depressed immune systems. Several young men in Miami were simultaneously diagnosed as having *Kaposi's sarcoma,* a rare cancer of the capillary system that appears as purple blotches on the skin (see Figure 5–11). It, too, is a sign of a depressed immune system. More and more cases of depressed immune systems began to appear, but it

Molluscum contagiosum ■ A sexually transmitted virus with symptoms that look like small pimples filled with kernels of corn.

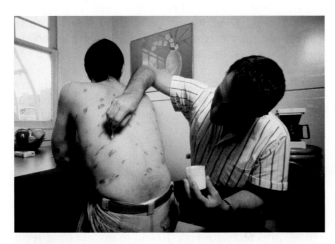

FIGURE 5–11 Kaposi's sarcoma lesions on a patient with AIDS.

was not until 1982 that the new infection was given a name: **acquired immunodeficiency syndrome,** or **AIDS.** It was not until 1984 that the cause of AIDS was identified as a virus, named **human immunodeficiency virus,** or **HIV.**

In technical terms, HIV is a Lentivirus, a subfamily of retroviruses. Retroviruses reverse the normal pattern of reproduction in cells. There are two major types of HIV: HIV-1, which is the most common type worldwide, and HIV-2, found mainly in West Africa. HIV-2 was not observed in the United States until 1987. HIV displays considerable genetic variability (Robertson et al., 2000). To date, researchers have identified 11 major HIV-1 subtypes (classified as group M subtypes A, B, C, D, F, G, H, J, K and at least 11 recombinant forms) and two very aberrant subtypes (groups N and O). The most common subtypes found in Africa are A, C, and D; the most common subtype found in the United States is B. However, different subtypes can be found in different people living in the same area, and HIV "superinfections" (an individual infected with multiple subtypes) are becoming more common (Blackard et al., 2002). HIV has obviously undergone extensive mutation, but examination of the genetic makeup of various subtypes suggests that all the subtypes evolved from a single virus.

HIV and the Body's Immune System

The **immune system** is that part of your body that defends against bacteria, viruses, fungi, and cancerous cells. White blood cells, or *lymphocytes*, are the main line of defense in this system. There are several types. One type, called *CD4+ lymphocytes* (also called *helper T cells* and *T4 lymphocytes*), has the job of recognizing the disease-causing agents and then signaling another type of white blood cell (*B cells*) to produce antibodies. The antibodies bind to the recognized agents so that they can be identified by yet another type of white blood cell, the *killer T cells* (T is for the thymus gland, where the

cells develop). The CD4+ cells then signal the killer T cells to destroy the identified disease-causing agents. In addition to CD4+ cells, there are also *suppressor T cells* that suppress the activity of the B cells and killer T cells. A person normally has twice as many CD4+ (helper) cells as suppressor T cells.

Recall now that viruses must invade and live in normal body cells (called host cells) in order to replicate themselves. The human immunodeficiency virus infects CD4+ cells and reproduces itself, causing death of the cell in about 112 days and the release of more of the virus. The replicated virus then invades other CD4+ cells. As many as 2 billion CD4+ cells are killed each day (Perelson et al., 1996). Thus, HIV destroys the cells that ordinarily would work to fight it off. The body tries to replace the dead cells, but the number of CD4+ cells begins to decline early in the course of HIV infection. The victim eventually has fewer helper (CD4+) T cells than suppressor T cells, leaving the body defenseless against viruses, bacteria, and other infection-causing agents.

CD4+ white blood cells are not the only body cells invaded by HIV. The virus has also been found in cells of the brain, gastrointestinal tract, kidney, lungs, cerebrospinal fluid, and other blood and plasma cells. However, it is the destruction of CD4+ cells that leads to the condition we call AIDS.

Progression of HIV Infection

After invading the body, HIV reproduces unchecked at first, reaching enormous levels in the bloodstream. The amount of HIV in early infection depends, in part, on the amount of HIV that was in the donor (Hecht et al., 2010). Between 50% and 75% of newly infected persons experience flulike symptoms (e.g., fever, headache, diarrhea, tiredness, skin rash) starting 13 to 15 days after infection (Lindbäck et al., 2000b). This is called **primary HIV infection** and can last for several weeks (Lindbäck et al., 2000a). The body's immune system then launches a huge counterattack that kills the virus by the billions, reducing it to very low levels. In time, however, the virus regains the upper hand by slowly killing off the CD4+ cells.

Acquired immunodeficiency syndrome (AIDS) ■ An often fatal infection caused by a virus (HIV) that destroys the immune system. It is spread by intimate sexual activity (the exchange of bodily fluids) or contaminated blood.

Human immunodeficiency virus (HIV) ■ A virus that kills CD4+ cells, eventually resulting in AIDS.

Immune system ■ The bodily mechanisms involved in the production of antibodies in response to bacteria, viruses, and cancerous cells.

Primary HIV infection ■ The first few weeks of HIV infection, during which HIV reaches enormous levels in the blood and 50% to 75% of infected individuals experience flulike symptoms.

A normal, healthy person has between 1,000 and 1,200 CD4+ cells per cubic millimeter of blood. Although CD4+ cell counts decline with time, people with HIV show no visible symptoms in the first stage of the chronic infection, called **asymptomatic HIV infection.** This stage often lasts for years.

Infected persons generally start to show symptoms of a weakened immune system when their CD4+ cell count falls below 500 per cubic millimeter of blood. Symptoms may include fatigue, persistent headaches, loss of appetite, recurrent diarrhea, loss of body weight, low-grade fever (often accompanied by "night sweats"), swollen lymph nodes, and "colds," "flus," and yeast infections that linger on and on. At this point, the infection is called **symptomatic HIV infection.**

HIV infection is not called AIDS until it has become life-threatening. As the CD4+ cell count approaches 200 per cubic millimeter of blood, infected persons' immune systems have become so weakened that they fall prey to what are referred to as *opportunistic infections*—diseases such as lymphomas, Kaposi's sarcoma (see Figure 5–11), *Pneumocystis carinii* pneumonia, recurrent bacterial pneumonia, pulmonary tuberculosis, cryptococcal meningitis, wasting syndrome, and invasive cervical cancer (Katlama & Dickinson, 1993). These are often accompanied by a severe decline in mental ability, referred to as HIV-associated dementia (Clifford, 2000). In 1993, the Centers for Disease Control and Prevention expanded the definition of AIDS to include a *CD4+ cell count below 200,* regardless of whether the person had yet fallen victim to an opportunistic disease. Some people whose CD4+ cell counts have dropped below 200 have gone 3 years or longer without developing AIDS-related illnesses (see Hunt, 2009). In the end, however, AIDS patients die as a result of the opportunistic infections (not as a direct result of HIV). AIDS patients die as a result of the opportunistic infections (not as a direct result of HIV).

Once an individual is infected with HIV, how long does it take to develop a full-blown case of AIDS? Without medication, about 40% to 45% of HIV-infected individuals will have reached the symptomatic stage within 2 years (Morgan et al., 2002). About 5% will develop AIDS within the first 3 years after infection with HIV-1; about 20% within 5 years; and 50% in 10 years. Only 12% of infected persons will not yet have been diagnosed with AIDS after 20 years (Buchbinder et al., 1994; Munoz & Xu, 1996; Rutherford et al., 1990). Fewer than 0.5% of HIV-infected individuals are

called *long-term nonprogressors.* Despite their infection, they maintain high CD4+ levels and do not develop symptoms (Hunt, 2009; Migueles & Connors, 2010).

Today, it is still the case that many people are not diagnosed as HIV-positive until they are late in the symptomatic stage. Over one third of people diagnosed with HIV develop AIDS within 1 year (Johnston & Collins, 2010).

What accounts for the fact that some HIV-infected people progress to AIDS in just a few years while others take many years? The type of HIV may be one factor. For example, persons infected with HIV-2 take much longer to develop AIDS than those infected with HIV-1 (and many are long-term nonprogressors) (van der Loeff & Aaby, 1999). People who already have a weakened immune system (as a result of age or illness, for example) have a more rapid progression to AIDS. Individuals who experience acute primary HIV infection (flulike symptoms or worse upon initial exposure) are more likely to develop AIDS earlier than people who are asymptomatic upon initial infection (Sinicco et al., 1993).

Several studies have shown that the best single predictor for progression to AIDS is not an individual's CD4+ cell count but his or her plasma HIV RNA levels, which show the amount of virus in the blood (Mellors et al., 1996; O'Brien et al., 1996). This is called the *viral load.* The higher the viral load, the sooner the person will develop AIDS. HIV-infected persons can have the same CD4+ cell count but very different levels of the virus; and if the viral load is high, infected persons can have AIDS symptoms even if their CD4+ count is well above 200 (Hennessey et al., 2000). The combination of HIV RNA levels and CD4+ cell count is an even better predictor of the progression to AIDS (Lima et al., 2009).

How long can an HIV-infected person expect to live after being diagnosed with AIDS? Without medication, the survival time is only about 1 year. However, new drug therapies have allowed many HIV and AIDS patients to live longer, productive lives (see section on treatment). Of Americans diagnosed with AIDS in 1997, two thirds were still living in 2005 (CDC, 2007b).

Where and When Did Human Immunodeficiency Virus Originate?

There is no question that HIV-1 and HIV-2 are new to the human species, but where did they come from? "Conspiracy" theories are popular. At one time, the Soviets blamed it on U.S. biological experiments gone awry. Many African Americans continue to believe that AIDS is man-made (DeBerry, 2005). Filmmaker Spike Lee publicly said that AIDS was "a government-engineered disease targeted at gays, African

Asymptomatic ■ Showing no symptoms.

Asymptomatic HIV infection ■ A stage of HIV infection in which infected individuals show no visible symptoms.

Symptomatic HIV infection ■ The early symptoms of HIV infection, which eventually lead to AIDS.

Americans, and Hispanics" (November 1992). Another person circulated a booklet claiming that WHO, the World Health Organization, "murdered Africa with the AIDS virus" (Douglass, 1988). He, as well as others, said that the virus was injected into people with various vaccines.

Scientific studies of the origins of HIV do not support conspiracy theories. There is a diverse genetic pool of nonhuman *simian* (primate) *immunodeficiency viruses (SIV)*. The viruses are found in rhesus monkeys, sooty mangabeys, African green monkeys, and chimpanzees. SIV normally does not cause illness in these nonhuman hosts, but a new strain is now causing AIDS-like illness in chimpanzees (Weiss & Heeney, 2008). The SIV in sooty mangabeys has been clearly identified as the origin of HIV-2 (Chen et al., 1997; Gao et al., 1992). In other words, humans acquired HIV-2 through cross-species transmission, i.e., the virus is a "simian immunodeficiency virus residing in and adapting to a human host" (Myers et al., 1992).

What about HIV-1? Studies have now definitely established that this virus was transmitted to humans from chimpanzees (Gao et al., 1999; Hahn et al., 2000; Keele et al., 2006). Considerable evidence indicates that this first occurred in colonial French Equatorial Africa around 1931 (Hahn et al., 2000; Korber et al., 2000), and may have originated as early as 1902 to 1921 (Sharp & Hahn, 2008).

The chimp-to-human transmission probably occurred by exposure of humans to primate blood during food preparation (Hahn et al., 2000). The virus was probably isolated for some time, but with big increases in the population more and more people came to rely on bushmeat (including chimpanzee meat). Tests of stored blood samples show that HIV-1 was definitely starting to spread by 1959 (Zhu et al., 1998), and by the 1970s high rates of Kaposi's sarcoma were being reported in central Africa. The rest is history.

Unfortunately, there are still some people (including leaders of some governments) who argue that HIV does not cause AIDS and even argue against the use of antiretroviral drugs to fight it (Chigwedere & Essex, 2010). This probably has cost several hundreds of thousands of lives.

How Is HIV Spread?

Can you get AIDS by casual contact with an HIV-infected person? The answer is NO! If HIV could be contracted from casual contact, you would expect that family members living with AIDS patients would be at great risk. However, no family member of an AIDS patient has ever become infected by sharing household facilities and items, and no child has ever become infected by just playing with or living with an AIDS-infected brother or sister. HIV has sometimes been found in body fluids such as

tears and saliva, but not in high enough concentrations to pose a threat. A protein found in saliva helps block HIV from infecting human cells (Shugars et al., 1999). In fact, the concentrations in saliva are so low that your chance of acquiring the virus by being bitten by an HIV-infected individual is extremely slim (Richman & Rickman, 1993).

In the final stages of AIDS, patients cannot hold food down, often have uncontrollable diarrhea, and generally sweat profusely. Yet except for a few people who accidentally stuck themselves with a contaminated needle and a few others whose skin was exposed to a large amount of contaminated blood (which may have entered the body through a small cut), none of the doctors, nurses, or other medical personnel who have cared for the most seriously ill AIDS patients on a daily basis has ever developed an HIV infection (Ippolito et al., 1999).

Malaria and some other diseases are spread by mosquitoes, but it is certain that HIV is not spread in this manner (Castro et al., 1988). If it were, we would be seeing a much larger number of children and elderly people with AIDS.

So, how is HIV transmitted? There are three main ways: (1) sexual contact with an *infected* person; (2) exposure to infected blood (mainly needle sharing among intravenous drug users); and (3) mother-to-infant transmission. Thus, HIV is transmitted almost exclusively by intimate sexual

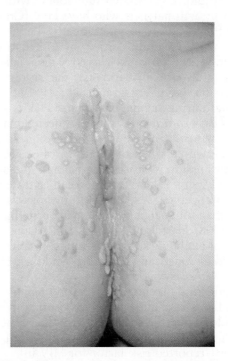

FIGURE 5–12 All of the STIs covered in this chapter can be transmitted during anal intercourse. This individual has genital warts (caused by human papillomavirus) heavily in the anal region and also on the labia.

contact and contaminated blood. Let us examine each of these means of transmission.

Many people continue to believe that a person can get HIV by having sex with an uninfected partner, particularly if the partner is a homosexual or bisexual man (Herek et al., 2005). Again, the answer is NO! To have any chance of getting HIV during sex, the sexual partner must be infected with HIV. HIV is found in the semen and vaginal fluids of HIV-infected individuals (see Mostad & Kreiss, 1996). The risk of transmission of HIV during sex is directly related to the infected person's viral load (Attia et al., 2009; Quinn et al., 2000). Remember, the concentrations of HIV are greatest at the very beginning of the infection, then decrease dramatically, and then increase again as the disease progresses toward the AIDS stage. This means that the risk of transmission of HIV is greatest in the first 60 days and then later in the symptomatic HIV and AIDS stages. (Recall from Box 2–C that circumcision of the penis reduces the chance of contracting HIV.)

A major factor is whether HIV is transmitted onto an uninfected person's mucous membranes or directly into his or her blood. Any sexual activity in which bleeding occurs would greatly increase the risk. Because of this, anal intercourse is one of the easiest ways to spread HIV from an infected person to another. Many male homosexuals engage in anal intercourse, but it is also common among heterosexual couples (see Chapter 11). About 30% of men who have unprotected anal intercourse with other men do so with partners who have HIV (Crepaz et al., 2009). Some do so intentionally (Berg, 2009). Sores on the genitals caused by other sexually transmitted infections such as syphilis, chancroid, or herpes also greatly increase the risk of HIV transmission (see Vernazza et al., 1999). Studies show that during vaginal intercourse HIV is at least twice as easy to transmit from an infected man to a female partner than vice versa (see Vernazza et al., 1999). However, when there are sores on the genitals, transmission is easier from woman to man.

Most experts believe that HIV can be transmitted during oral-genital sex, but that the risk is much smaller than for anal or vaginal intercourse (Baggaley et al., 2008; Hasselrot et al., 2010). Again, this is because of inhibiting substances found in saliva. Over one third of Americans think they could get HIV by kissing (*Newsweek*, 2006).

As previously mentioned, a second major way in which HIV is transmitted is by exposure to contaminated blood. Needle-sharing drug users are at especially high risk. It is presently "the third most frequently reported risk factor for HIV infection in the United States, after male-to-male sexual contact and high-risk heterosexual contact" (CDC, 2009). But what about our chances of getting HIV from a blood transfusion? At one time this was a major

concern. Several thousand people contracted HIV from blood transfusions before screening tests were begun in 1985. Today, because all blood is tested, only 1 of every 677,000 units is likely to be infected with HIV (Glynn et al., 2000). A few units of infected blood still get through because the test cannot detect HIV if the blood donor has just been infected (see page 121). In the United States, you will not get HIV from donating blood!

The third major way that HIV is transmitted is from an infected mother to her infant (see John & Kreiss, 1996). Worldwide, about 1,500 children are infected with HIV every day, during either childbirth or breast-feeding (Kozinetz, 2001). Without antiviral drug therapy, the transmission rate is about 20% to 25% (Lindegren et al., 1999). The infections can occur either very late in pregnancy, during delivery, or by breast-feeding (Chasela et al., 2010; European Collaborative Study, 1992, 1994). The risk is greatest in women who have high levels of the virus in their blood (Landesman et al., 1996; Mofenson et al., 1999). The frequency of transmission of HIV-1 by breast-feeding is about 35% (Liang et al., 2009). This is so high that in 1998 the United Nations recommended that women with HIV not breast-feed their babies.

Who Has HIV/AIDS?

HIV infection is a true pandemic infection. Currently, worldwide there are about 11,780 new infections a day (4.3 million a year) and about 33.4 million people currently living with HIV. This includes about 2.3 million children. About 2.9 million people die of AIDS every year, including 380,000 children (UNAIDS, 2010). Over 35 million people worldwide have already died of AIDS. The U.S. Census Bureau's World Population Profile estimated that 121 million people could be infected by the year 2020.

At present, 90% of persons infected with HIV live in developing countries (UNAIDS, 2010). Close to two thirds of the world's cases are in sub-Saharan Africa, where HIV originated; countries such as Botswana, Lesotho, Swaziland, and South Africa have been devastated (see Figure 5–13). In some places, more than 1 out of every 4 people are infected with HIV, resulting in an average reduction Box 5–A).

HIV may have originated in Africa, but the World Health Organization says that "the most alarming trends of HIV infection are in Southeast Asia where the disease is spreading in some areas as fast as it was a decade ago in sub-Saharan Africa." Until recently, HIV in China was restricted to a few high-risk groups (e.g. intravenous drug users, female sex workers), but well over one third of new cases are now via heterosexual contact (Lu et al., 2008). The same is true in Vietnam, and the epidemic is even much worse in Papua New Guinea (Piot et al.,

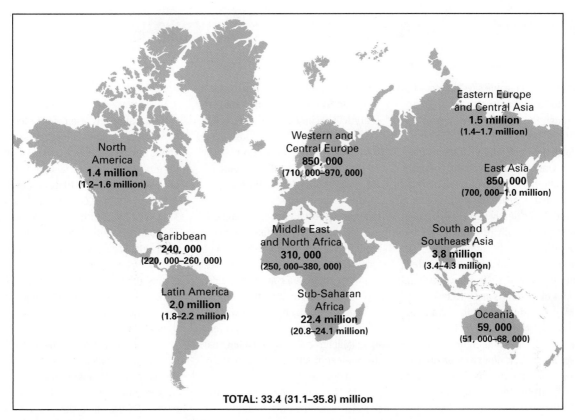

FIGURE 5–13 Adults and children estimated to be living with HIV in 2008.
Source: From UNAIDS 2007. *AIDS Epidemic Update: December 2007*, p. 39. © UNAIDS and WHO 2007. Reproduced by kind permission of UNAIDS.

2009). India is another country where HIV has reached epidemic proportions.

What about the United States? The Centers for Disease Control and Prevention reported that there were over 1.1 million Americans living with HIV/AIDS in 2008 (CDC, 2010). Over one fifth of these were undiagnosed (see Campsmith et al., 2010). Over 56,000 new cases were undiagnosed in 2008. To date, well over 1 million Americans have been diagnosed with AIDS and nearly 56% of them have already died. In some places in the United States, the prevalence of HIV is approaching that seen in many African countries—at least 3% (including 6.5% of black men) in Washington, D.C., for example (Tanne, 2009). By the mid-1990s, AIDS had become the *leading cause of death among Americans aged 25 to 44*, ahead of accidents, cancer, and heart disease.

Of the new HIV/AIDS cases reported to the CDC in 2008, 74% were in men and 26% were in women (CDC, 2010). Among men, 71% got HIV during male-to-male sexual contact, 10% during injection drug use, 4% during both, and 14% during heterosexual sex. In some places in the United States, as many as 25% of men who have sex with men are infected with HIV (Schwarcz et al., 2007). Among women, 16% got HIV during injection drug use and 83% during heterosexual sex. About

half of new HIV infections are in young people aged 15 to 24 (Wilson et al., 2010). However, you might be surprised to learn that nearly 25% of Americans with HIV are 50 years old or older (Schmid et al., 2009). Recall that HIV progresses to AIDS much faster in older individuals.

A disproportionate number of the new AIDS cases in 2008 occurred among African Americans (51%) and Latinos (about 18%), particularly those in low-income groups. AIDS is the leading cause of death in African–American women (Piot et al., 2009). Former U.S. Surgeon General David Satcher said, "I don't think there is any question that the epidemic in this country is becoming increasingly an epidemic of color" (Kalb & Murr, 2006).

Worldwide, the largest proportion of new HIV infections is acquired by heterosexual transmission. In sub-Saharan Africa, for example, 59% of the millions of people infected with HIV are women (UN-AIDS, 2006), but many heterosexuals in the United States still do not believe that they can get HIV. However, the most dramatic change in new HIV and AIDS cases has been among heterosexuals. In 1985, only 2% of men and 27% of women diagnosed with AIDS got HIV during heterosexual sex. In 2008, *nearly one third of all new cases were contracted during heterosexual sex* (see Figure 5–14).

Box 5–A Cross-Cultural Perspectives/Sexuality and Health

AIDS in Africa: A Look into the Future?

Newsweek magazine says that to take a trip to sub-Saharan Africa is to "peer through the portals of hell and glimpse the holocaust to come" (Bartholet et al., 2000). In the United States, about 1.1 million people have HIV, about 0.33% of the population. Sub-Saharan Africa, on the other hand, accounts for nearly two thirds of all HIV cases globally (UNAIDS, 2010). In some parts of sub-Saharan Africa, more than 20% of adults are infected with HIV (UNAIDS, 2010). In Swaziland, 25.9% of all adults are infected; nearly 17% of all adults in South Africa are infected (UNAIDS, 2010). The result is devastating: 2.3 million deaths and over 5.3 million new cases of HIV each year, and the numbers keep increasing yearly. AIDS is the leading cause of death in Africa (Piot et al., 2009). In the United States, life expectancy increased by 30 years during the 1900s. In many parts of Africa, it has dropped from 59 years of age in 1990 to 34 to 37 (UNAIDS, 2010). The devastation caused by HIV in Africa rivals that caused by the Black Death in Europe during the Middle Ages, when one fourth of the population was lost.

In actuality, the situation is even worse because the previous statistics are for all adults. The percentage of infected persons is even higher for adults in the 15- to 40-year-old age group. Two thirds of Botswanans aged 15 today are expected to die of AIDS before they are 50. In most of sub-Saharan Africa, there are more elderly people than young adults.

What about the children? Have you ever read *Lord of the Flies*? At the end of 2010, there were 18.4 million AIDS orphans in sub-Saharan Africa, over 1.4 million in South Africa alone (Andrews et al., 2006; Skinner, 2010). Over half of the children in Zambia have lost one or both parents. With income normally very low even before AIDS, the elderly are unable to care for the orphaned children, and there are not enough funds to support all the orphanages. As a result, an undeterminable number roam the streets, malnourished and often infected themselves. To make matters worse, there is a commonly held myth among African men that you can be cured of AIDS by having sex with a virgin, so many young girls are preyed upon (Millner, 2002). Within a few years, the number of African AIDS orphans is likely to double.

The HIV epidemic has affected the prevalence of other infectious diseases as well. People with HIV have an increased susceptibility to tuberculosis and malaria, which results in increased transmission rates for these diseases (Corbett et al., 2002).

It takes more than introduction of a new virus to result in an epidemic of this magnitude. Certain demographic and social conditions also have to be present (Fauci, 1999). Massive migration from rural areas to large cities, the resulting breakups of traditional family units, sexual promiscuity (including frequent use of prostitutes)—all have contributed to the epidemic. A potent strain of HIV (type C) is common in Africa, and transmission of the virus is helped by: (a) high numbers of cases of other sexually transmitted infections that cause genital ulcerations (Corbett et al., 2002); and (b) the preference by many African men for "dry" sex (no vaginal lubrication), which also causes vaginal abrasions.

Ignorance has also contributed. Most African leaders refuse to talk about the problem. None showed up for the 11th International Conference on AIDS in Zambia in 1998, and at the 13th International Conference in South Africa in 2000, South African President Thabo Mbeki denied that HIV causes AIDS (Chigwedere & Essex, 2010). Many Africans continue to believe that AIDS is caused by spirits and supernatural forces (Kalichman, 2004). Among the African people, AIDS victims are stigmatized.

Economies are collapsing under the weight of the epidemic. There is widespread famine because so many farm workers have died of AIDS. Use of antiretroviral drugs might slow the infection, but African nations have little money to pay for health services. Each year, a greater proportion of children go uneducated (and uncared for), giving little hope for the future.

In the 2 minutes it took you to read this box, 20 more people in Africa became infected with HIV. Since the time you woke up yesterday morning, more than 6,000 African men and women have died of AIDS. HIV spread through Africa many years before it appeared in the United States. If we do not take the necessary precautions, could the same fate that has befallen Africa happen here? Perhaps Dr. Ward Cates of the Centers for Disease Control and Prevention put it best: "Anyone who has the least ability to look into the future can already see the potential for this disease being much worse than anything mankind has seen before."

The Human Side of AIDS

With each passing year, more and more of us do not have to read a newspaper to get a firsthand experience with AIDS. AIDS is more than a disease; it is a personal tragedy, not only for the patient but for the patient's family and loved ones as well. Some students in my course have asked me to share their experiences. Here are a few:

"My reaction to a low T-cell test was devastating. It was like a bomb exploding inside or a knife through

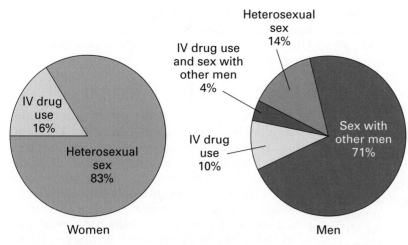

FIGURE 5–14 Sources of HIV infection among American men and women first diagnosed with AIDS in 2007 (CDC, 2010).

the heart. My time is near and each day is a gift to cherish.... Finding out I was HIV positive was not as shocking as finding out that what I have changed to improve the quality of my life makes little difference in my life expectancy."

"My father has AIDS. You really don't know the severity of a problem until you're faced with it. Watching my father die has been extremely painful and stressful."

"I still believe that most students don't think that AIDS can happen to them. I have seen AIDS happen firsthand. I learned in one of the most painful ways I can imagine. Two years ago my older brother died of AIDS. I was only 19, he was 24. It had been said that everyone's lives would be touched by AIDS, and when I was younger I didn't believe it. Now I do."

Many people have led productive lives for years after being diagnosed with AIDS. There is increasing evidence that stressful life events can speed up the progression of HIV infection (Leserman et al., 2000). It is important, therefore, that HIV-infected individuals not give up hope and that they receive as much positive support as possible.

Testing for HIV

There are tests that can detect a single HIV-infected white blood cell among 100,000 healthy ones. However, the tests are very expensive. The standard tests for HIV do not test for the virus directly, but instead detect antibodies to the virus that are produced by an infected person's immune system. Blood is first checked with the EIA (enzyme immunoassay) test. However, the test can result in "false positives" (i.e., uninfected blood testing positive). To ensure against false positives, the EIA test is repeated if the results are positive. If there is a second positive indication, the blood is tested again with either the Western Blot or IFA (immunofluorescent assay)

tests. These are more expensive and demanding tests that give information about particular antibodies. A negative test result means only that a person *probably* has not been infected with HIV. Remember, it often takes several months for an infected person's body to start producing antibodies to the virus; a person who has just recently been infected will not test positive.

Until recently, HIV tests were invasive (blood had to be drawn). New tests are now available that measure the presence of antibodies to HIV in saliva or urine, or with a finger stick (a single drop of blood). The sample is checked with the EIA test and positive results are then confirmed with the Western Blot blood test. These tests are less accurate than the blood test, but may be more appealing to some people than blood tests.

In 2006, the Centers for Disease Control and Prevention recommended that *testing for HIV should be a routine part of medical care for all Americans between 13 and 64 years of age.*

Treatment for HIV/AIDS: Hope and Limitations

Many drugs have been approved for treating patients with HIV. One group of antiretroviral drugs is technically called *nucleoside reverse transcriptase inhibitors* (e.g., zidovudine). They slow the progression of HIV infection by blocking an essential enzyme (called reverse transcriptase) needed for the virus to replicate itself. A second group is called *non-nucleoside reverse transcriptase inhibitors* (e.g., nevirapine). These drugs block the same enzymes as the nucleoside drugs, but in a different manner. *Protease inhibitors* block an enzyme called protease that is critical to the last stages of HIV replication. In 2002 the first of a new group of drugs called *fusion inhibitors* was added. They are the first to directly block the entry of HIV into cells. By early 2010, there were over 25 antiretroviral drugs (from six different groups) being used to fight the progression of HIV infection.

The first antiviral drug used was zidovudine (AZT). Zidovudine has proven to be most successful in treating HIV-infected pregnant women. Treatment of HIV-infected pregnant women with zidovudine reduced the transmission of the virus to babies from 1,650 cases in 1991 (about 24%) to less than 240 cases in 2006. Another drug, nevirapine, reduces the transmission rate even further, and a transmission rate of less than 2% can be achieved if the mother uses the HIV drugs and has a cesarean delivery (International Perinatal HIV Group, 1999). Because of these successes, the Centers for Disease Control and Prevention has recommended that all pregnant women be tested for HIV.

Among adults with HIV, the virus quickly becomes resistant to any antiviral drugs used alone. Thus, in the 1990s health professionals began using several drugs (three or more from at least two different groups of drugs) in combination. This is commonly called *highly active antiretroviral therapy* (HAART). Administration of nucleoside inhibitors and/or nonnucleoside inhibitors, in combination with protease inhibitors, simultaneously attacks the replication of HIV at two different places. In many patients, this approach initially knocks blood HIV levels down to undetectable levels, raises CD4+ cell counts, and partially restores immune responses (Wainberg & Clotet, 2007). Until recently, HAART was not used until people were in the late symptomatic or AIDS stage of HIV infection, but studies have shown that HAART works best when it is started early in the infection when CD4+ cell counts are about 500 (Thompson et al., 2010). As a result, the National Institutes of Health is considering a new "test and treat" policy, for which anyone who tests positive for HIV will be started on HAART (Johnston & Collins, 2010).

The initial optimism that HAART might be a cure for HIV infection was followed quickly by some sobering reality (see Fauci, 1999; Hirschel & Opravil, 1999, for reviews). Many patients cannot tolerate the side effects (Sax & Gathe, 2005). For example, long-term use often results in giant accumulations of body fat and insulin resistance, or conversely, extreme loss of body fat (resulting in caved-in faces) (Cabrero et al., 2010), and neurologic and psychiatric complications (Treisman & Kaplin, 2002). The real Achilles heel of HAART has been adherence to the medication schedule, which in some cases involves taking many pills every day (e.g., Atkinson & Petrozzino, 2009). People may not adhere to a drug schedule for a variety of reasons, but if they do not, it can result in HIV becoming resistant to the drugs (see Pham, 2009).

Now the worst news. For almost all HIV/AIDS patients, *the new antiretroviral drug therapy is not a cure!* (Trono et al., 2010). There are a growing number of HIV-infected people who have strains of HIV that are multidrug resistant (e.g., Kaplan & Mounzer, 2008). Others receiving HAART are known as "immunological nonresponders"—their viral load decreases dramatically but their immune system (CD4+ count) does not improve, leaving the possibility of opportunistic diseases (Gazzola et al., 2009). Most importantly, although HAART generally lowers HIV levels to extremely low levels, HIV can still exist in places where the drugs do not affect it (e.g., Dornadula et al., 1999; Furtado et al., 1999). One of these places is resting memory T cells (another part of

the immune system), and these cells survive for a very long time. If patients decide to stop the drug therapy, HIV levels increase dramatically within days (e.g., Chun et al., 1999; Davey et al., 1999).

Prevention of HIV Infection

Health experts agree that the use of antiretroviral drugs alone will not bring an end to the HIV pandemic. Even if the problems could be overcome, people in developing countries simply cannot afford the drugs. The cost of the new once-a-day pill is about $1,000 a month (Bridges, 2006). In developing countries (e.g., sub-Saharan Africa), circumcision of all young men could potentially reduce the number of people with HIV by half (Londish & Murray, 2008). Development of an anti-AIDS microbicide gel (to be used during sex) would help, and recent clinical trials have been promising (*Time*, 2010).

An ideal way to combat HIV would be to develop a vaccine. About 30 vaccines are presently being tested with humans. Unfortunately, there are some major problems with developing an HIV vaccine (see Barouch & Korber, 2010; Virgin & Walker, 2010). First, it will be difficult to develop a vaccine that is effective against all the different genetic subtypes of HIV. The genetic subtype amino acids differ by as much as 30% (Gaschen et al., 2002). The best vaccine developed to date was announced in late 2009, but it only reduced the rate of infection by about 30% (Sternberg, 2009). Individuals with HIV "superinfections" (infected with multiple subtypes of the virus) who continue to engage in risky sexual behavior are also making the job more difficult (Blackard et al., 2002). Second, because the virus continues to mutate, a vaccine developed today may become ineffective over time. In the words of one notable researcher, "The virus is a moving target. It is constantly changing its genetic makeup through mutations" (Dr. Gary Nabel, quoted by Park, 2010). Some researchers hope that by studying long-term nonprogressors (rare individuals who have HIV, but who maintain stable CD4+ cell counts and never develop symptoms), an effective vaccine might eventually be developed (Migueles & Connors, 2010).

In the meantime, the best way to minimize your own chance of ever contracting HIV is by your own behavior. That means not having multiple sexual partners (both yourself and your partner), and/or always using condoms, and not using injecting drugs (both yourself and your partner). See the section on "Practicing Safer Sex."

Public Reactions to AIDS

Despite the laws of the land, discrimination continues to play a brutal and important role in the lives of those infected with HIV. The extent and the cruelty of such discrimination have been brought forth in heartrending testimony to the National Commission at each of

its many hearings. As a colleague and I wrote recently, "The pain, suffering and despair of the disease alone are dreadful enough. The added stigma makes it virtually unbearable. You lose not only your life, but also your pride, your job, your insurance, your friends and your family. Posterity remembers you for dying of AIDS, not for having lived."

(Dr. David Rogers [1992], vice chair of the National Commission on AIDS)

HIV-positive individuals have to deal with more than the fact that they have a deadly infection. They must also deal with the stigma of having HIV/AIDS (Piot et al., 2009). The American public's attitudes toward people with AIDS became more tolerant during the 1990s, but still about one third of Americans have negative feelings (e.g., anger, disgust, fear) toward infected individuals (Herek et al., 2002; see also Bruce & Walker, 2001). The public's fear of AIDS has been fueled by well-publicized cases of individuals who knowingly put others at risk. In fact, a sizable minority of people who discover that they are infected with HIV continue to engage in unsafe sexual activity (Diamond & Buskin, 1999). Even worse, 63% to 75% of HIV-infected individuals do not reveal their infection status when having sex with casual partners (O'Brien et al., 2003; Serovich & Mosack, 2003).

But the negativity directed at people with AIDS is not limited to the few who would knowingly spread the infection. Some young children who contracted AIDS have been temporarily barred from attending school. In Florida, the home of three hemophiliac children with AIDS was burned to the ground when they attempted to go to public school.

How should we as a society deal with the HIV epidemic? First of all, it is important to educate the public that the virus is not spread by any type of casual contact, and thus there is no medical basis for avoiding nonsexual interactions with infected individuals. Most states now have laws that protect HIV-infected persons against discrimination in the workplace and in housing. Ensuring the privacy and equal treatment of persons with HIV infection is essential to the success of testing, treatment, and outreach programs. Public health officials will not gain the confidence and cooperation of infected individuals if these persons are not legally protected from stigma and irrational prejudice. As former President Ronald Reagan said, "It is the disease that is frightening, not the people who have it."

PERSONAL REFLECTIONS

What do you do to protect yourself from sexually transmitted infections? Now that you have learned more about STIs, what changes in your sexual lifestyle do you plan to make to better protect yourself?

PARASITIC INFESTATIONS

Viral and bacterial infections are not the only things that can be transmitted from one person to another during sex. It is also possible to pick up parasites from an infested person. Condoms will do little good in preventing these types of infestations.

Pubic lice (*Phthirus pubis*, the crab louse, or "crabs") are 1 to 2 mm long, grayish (or dusky red after a meal of blood), six-legged parasites that attach themselves to pubic hair and feed on human blood (see Figure 5–15). *They are not the same as head lice.* Infestation with pubic lice is technically called *pediculosis pubis*. The lice travel very slowly, so they are almost always transmitted by skin-to-skin contact. Your chance of getting them during sex with an infested partner is about 95% (Brown et al., 1999). The lice cause intense itching.

FIGURE 5–15 Top: *Phthirus pubis* (crab lice). Bottom: gravid female *Sarcoptes scabiei* mite.

Pubic lice ■ An infestation of the parasite *Phthirus pubis*, which attach themselves to pubic hair and feed on blood. Also known as "crabs."

"I was a senior in high school and I was sleeping with a guy who I had been involved with for a year. For about 2 weeks I had been itching in the pubic area. The longer it went on, the more irritating it got. Finally, I examined my pubic hair and found little crab-looking things. I was shocked and disgusted."

"I noticed an itching down in my pubic area. It got extensively annoying so I took a look to see what was happening down there. I almost started to scream when I noticed little flat insects crawling around that area."

(All examples are from the author's files)

The lice typically do not live for more than 24 hours away from the human body, but any eggs that fall off can survive and hatch up to 10 days later (Meinking & Taplin, 1996). You could, therefore, pick them up from the sheets, towels, or clothing of an infested person. Normal bathing will not wash the lice off, but you can eliminate them by applying pyrethrin products (e.g., 1% permethrin cream rinse) or 1% lindane (Kwell) lotion, cream, or shampoo to the infested area *and all other hairy body areas*. Repeat the treatment in 7 to 10 days. To avoid reinfestation, be sure to use very hot water to clean all clothing, sheets, and towels that might be infested.

Scabies is a contagious infestation of 0.3 to 0.4 mm long, pearly white, parasitic itch mites (*Sarcoptes scabiei*; see Figure 5–15). The eight-legged mites burrow under the skin to lay their eggs, resulting at first in extremely itchy, red, pimple-like bumps when the eggs hatch. Large patches of scaling skin result if the mites are not immediately destroyed. Secondary bacterial infection is common.

"In between my junior and senior year of high school I got scabies. It itched so horribly that I would claw my skin off in my sleep and even while I was awake. It was absolutely awful."

(From the author's files)

The itch mite is acquired by close contact with infested persons (the mites survive 24 to 36 hours off the body), and thus is most common in people living and sleeping in crowded conditions. Sexual contact is not necessary, but sexual transmission is common among adults (Brown et al., 1999). The mite "is notorious for its lack of respect for person,

age, sex or race, whether it be in the epidermis of an emperor or a slave, a centurion or a nursling, it makes itself perfectly at home with undiscriminating impudence and equal obnoxiousness" (Friedman, 1947). Scabies has traditionally been treated with 1% lindane lotion or permethrin 5% cream, but a single oral dose of ivermectin is also highly effective (Meinking et al., 1995). Should you ever get scabies, be sure that you also wash all your sheets, towels, and clothing to avoid reinfestation.

Pinworms (*Enterobius vermicularis*) live in the large intestine and are generally gotten through non-sexual contact with the eggs. The female pinworms leave the rectum at night and lay their eggs around the anus, which causes intense itching (see Weber, 1993). Pinworms are common in children, who pass them from one to another by hand-to-mouth contact while playing. Pinworms can also be transmitted sexually in adults by manual or oral contact with the anus of an infected person. This mode of transmission occurs most commonly among homosexual men. Such sexual practices can also result in the transmission of a one-celled animal (*Entamoeba histolytica*) that causes intestinal **amebiasis,** or amebic dysentery (Petri & Singh, 1999).

VAGINAL INFECTIONS

It is rare that a woman does not experience a vaginal infection at least once in her lifetime. Symptoms generally include discomfort or pain during urination, along with a vaginal discharge that often has a disagreeable odor. Here are some common causes.

Trichomoniasis (Trichomonal Vaginitis)

Only one type of vaginitis, trichomoniasis, is usually contracted by sexual contact. In the United States, there will be about 7.4 million new cases of "trich" this year, which is more than gonorrhea, chlamydia, syphilis, and genital herpes combined (CDC, 2010a). A recent study found 3.2% of American women aged 14 to 49 had trichomoniasis (Allsworth et al., 2009).

Trichomoniasis is caused by a one-cell protozoan named *Trichomonas vaginalis* that lives in the vagina and urethra. Symptoms in women generally appear from 4 days to 1 month after exposure and include a copious, foamy, yellowish-green discharge with a foul odor accompanied by severe vaginal itching (see Figure 5–16). However, as many as 80% of infected women show no symptoms (Allsworth et al., 2009).

"About 2 weeks after becoming sexually involved with my boyfriend, I began to have severe pain during intercourse. Soon I noticed a discharge,

Scabies ■ A contagious infestation of parasitic mites *(Sarcoptes scabiei)* that burrow under the skin to lay their eggs.

Pinworms ■ Small worms *(Enterobius vermicularis)* that live in the large intestine and are generally transmitted through nonsexual contact with the worms' eggs, but which can be transmitted sexually by manual or oral contact with the anus of an infected person.

Amebiasis ■ Dysentery caused by infestation of amoebae, one-celled organisms.

Trichomoniasis ■ A type of vaginitis caused by a one-celled protozoan that is usually transmitted during sexual intercourse.

Box 5–B **Sexuality and Health**

Vaginal Health Care

For women, vaginal infections are probably second in frequency only to the common cold. Here are some hygiene tips to help minimize your chances of getting vaginitis:

- Bathe regularly, avoiding deodorant soaps and bubble baths, and do not share washcloths and towels.

- Dry the vulva thoroughly and wear cotton panties (synthetic fabrics retain heat and moisture, conditions in which bacteria thrive).

  "I used to get yeast infections several times a year. Every time I would visit or call my doctor.... I finally figured it out on my own with a little help from one of the hottest days in June. I would always wear silk or polyester blend underpants and nylon hosiery. Do any

of these materials allow absorption? Of course not. I ran out and bought cotton underpants and hosiery with garter belts. Five years have passed and not one yeast infection yet."
(from the author's files)

- Never wear synthetic underpants to bed.

- Avoid feminine hygiene products.

- After a bowel movement, wipe the anus from front to back, not back to front, as this can spread rectal bacteria to the vagina.

- Allow time for adequate vaginal lubrication during intercourse, and if you use a lubricant, use a water-soluble one such as K-Y jelly (petroleum-based lubricants not only harbor bacteria, but disintegrate condoms as well).

- If you and your partner engage in any type of anal stimulation during sex, be sure to wash the hands or penis before touching the vaginal area again.

- If your partner has sexual relationships with people other than yourself, make sure he uses a condom during intercourse.

- If you have frequent yeast infections, ask your doctor about douching with a mild acidic solution.

- Keep stress to a minimum, eat well, and get adequate sleep.

- See a doctor as soon as you notice any of the previously mentioned symptoms. Remember, vaginal infections are very common and nothing to be ashamed of. They can be treated very easily.

---

itching, and an extremely foul odor. After many weeks of shame I finally went to the infirmary with my roommate, who was having urinary problems. Imagine how surprised we were to find out that we both had trichomoniasis. How could we catch such a thing? The only person she had sex with was her boyfriend and the only person I had sex with was my boyfriend! In the end we found out that our boyfriends went out together one night and had unprotected sex with a girl that they had known less than 6 hours!"
(from the author's files)

T. vaginalis can survive in urine or tap water for hours or sometimes days, so it is possible to pick it up by using a wet toilet seat or by sharing towels. Nonetheless, the vast majority of cases are transmitted by sexual intercourse. At least half of men infected with trich show mild to moderately severe urethral irritation and discharge (thus making it a type of nongonococcal urethritis) (Bowden & Garnett, 2000; Krieger, 2000). Still, *many men act as asymptomatic carriers*, spreading it to new female partners—just the opposite of what we often see in the early stages of gonorrhea, chlamydia, and syphilis.

Trichomoniasis can be very irritating (due to itching and burning), but until recently most authorities did not believe that there were any serious long-term consequences if it was left untreated, and thus

regarded trich as a "minor" STI. However, studies have found that trichomoniasis can lead to infertility, premature labor in pregnant women, and facilitates transmission of HIV from an infected partner (Bowden & Garnett, 2000; Hupport, 2006).

The diagnosis of trich is made by examining any discharge and growing the parasite in culture. However, the tests have not been totally reliable. If trichomoniasis is suspected, both the infected woman and her partner should be treated. Otherwise, he will just reinfect her when intercourse resumes. Trich is easily eradicated by a drug called metronidazole (its trade name is Flagyl), but it should not be taken during pregnancy (Marrazzo et al., 2008).

Moniliasis (or Candidiasis)

Moniliasis is caused by an overgrowth of a microorganism that is normally found in the vagina (*Candida albicans* in 80% of cases and other *Candida* species in 20%) (Hudson & Kochan, 2005). It is a fungus or yeast infection that is very common in women. Three fourths of all women will experience it at least once in their lifetimes, and 40% to 45% will experience it at

Moniliasis ■ Sometimes called *candidiasis*. A type of vaginitis caused by the overgrowth of a microorganism (*Candida albicans*) that is normally found in the vagina. Moniliasis is a fungus or yeast infection and usually is a sexually related, rather than a sexually transmitted infection.

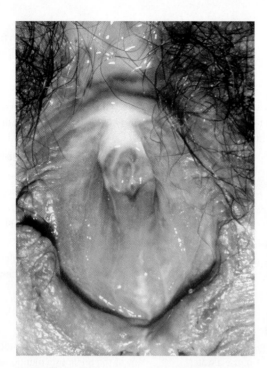 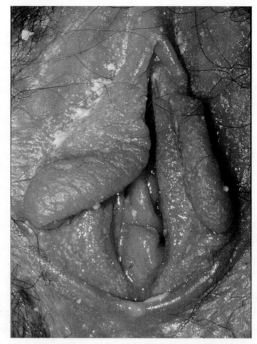

FIGURE 5–16 (a) The whitish-green discharge in trichomoniasis is usually copious and frothy; (b) Vaginal discharge in a patient with monilial (yeast) infection showing a white cheesy appearance.

least twice (Wilson, 2005). About 10% to 20% of women have what is called *recurrent candidiasis*—four or more episodes a year.

Symptoms include a thick, white, cheesy discharge accompanied by intense itching (see Figure 5–16). Unfortunately, many women do not realize how common normal yeast infections are and feel alone or dirty when it happens to them.

> "The first time I got a yeast infection I was terrified. I didn't know what it was. All I knew was that the itching was intolerable and I had this discharge that wasn't normal."

> "The first time I had it was when I was 16. I started to have an uneasy itchy feeling. I took a shower and thought it would go away. It not only continued, but it became worse. I felt very dirty."

> (All examples are from the author's files.)

Yeast infections are sometimes transmitted sexually, but the vast majority of cases are *not* contracted in this manner. *Children, even babies, can get this, too* (Robinson & Ridgway, 1994). Thus, monilial infections are not really considered a sexually transmitted infection, such as trichomoniasis, but are a sexually related disease. The microbe can also invade the mouth (where it is called thrush), anus, and skin, as well as internal organs. Thrush is often caused by high blood sugar, a weakened immune system, or use of steroids.

Anything that changes the normal chemical environment of the vagina can result in an overgrowth. This includes hormone changes, diabetes,

heavy use of antibiotics (which kill off the "friendly" bacteria in the vagina that keep the yeast in check), and even overly zealous hygiene (e.g., the use of perfumed feminine hygiene products). Many women first experience a monilial infection during pregnancy, for example, or when they first start taking oral contraceptives.

> "Once when I had an infected tooth, my dentist prescribed an antibiotic. About the third day I developed a yeast infection. No one had ever told me I could get a yeast infection from an antibiotic. When I told some of my friends, they told me this had happened to at least two of them before."

> "I had my first yeast infection when I was pregnant with my first child. I was so embarrassed about having this terrible itch in the genital area that I couldn't tell anyone. Finally it was time for my regular prenatal checkup, and when the doctor examined me and saw that I had scratched myself raw he wanted to know why I had not called him. I was just too embarrassed to say I had an itch in the genital area."

> (All examples are from the author's files.)

Women with immune deficiencies (e.g., HIV infection and AIDS) are particularly susceptible to yeast infections.

Yeast infections are often treated with antifungal creams or suppositories. There are over-the-counter drugs that you can purchase in the drugstore (e.g., Monistat and Gyne-Lotrimin). Drugs that you can take by mouth (Fluconazole, Itraconazole) are also available (Marrazzo et al.,

2008). However, if the symptoms do not go away within a few days, see your doctor immediately, for you might have one of the other types of vaginitis.

Bacterial Vaginosis

Bacterial vaginosis is the most common of the three types of vaginitis (CDC, 2010). It is caused by several vaginal bacteria (particularly *Gardnerella vaginalis*) replacing other H_2O-producing vaginal bacteria (Marrazzo et al., 2008). Until recently, bacterial vaginosis has not been considered a sexually transmitted infection, but recent research suggests that it is (see Schwebke, 2009). In one recent study, there were no cases of bacterial vaginosis among sexually inexperienced women, but 6% of sexually experienced women had the infection (Fethers et al., 2009). The use of condoms decreases the prevalence (see Schwebke, 2009). Vaginal douching increases the likelihood of getting bacterial vaginosis (Klebanoff et al., 2010) suggesting that the infection can also be acquired by nonsexual means.

The main complaint of patients is a vaginal odor (sometimes described as fishy), but there is also an abnormal discharge (grayish and nonclumpy). We now know that this type of infection can lead to serious upper reproductive tract infection (Eschenbach, 1993). The antibiotics of choice are metronidazole or clindamycin, but the recurrence rate is very high (Marrazzo et al., 2008).

CYSTITIS AND PROSTATITIS

Cystitis refers to a bacterial infection of the bladder, often called a urinary tract infection. As many as 20% of women will experience this sometime in their lifetime (Hooton, 2003). Because a woman's urethra is considerably shorter than a man's, and thus bacteria have a shorter distance to travel, cystitis is much more common in women than men. It is especially common in sexually active young women and is strongly associated with recent intercourse. However, many cases are unrelated to sexual activity. The bacterium *Escherichia coli*, for example, is often transmitted from the rectum to the urethral opening by wiping forward from the anus after a bowel movement. Women should always wipe themselves from front to back.

Symptoms may include a frequent urge to urinate, painful urination, and lower abdominal pains. Cystitis is treated with either sulfa drugs or antibiotics. Vigorous intercourse, especially in women first becoming sexually active, can also result in urinary tract infection (hence the term *honeymoon cystitis*) by causing inward friction on the urethra, allowing nonsexually transmitted bacteria to ascend.

For those women who experience postcoital urinary tract infection, trimethoprim and sulfamethoxazole taken together within 2 hours of intercourse prevents infections (Stapleton et al., 1990).

Some women suffer from chronic inflammation of the bladder, a condition called *interstitial cystitis* (see Robb-Nicholson & Schatz, 2004). Researchers are not sure what causes it, but it is not caused by the bacteria that cause other types of cystitis. Many experts believe it is caused by small holes in the mucus lining of the bladder, allowing substances in urine to irritate the walls of the bladder.

The *E. coli* bacteria can also be transmitted to a man's prostate during sexual activity, resulting in **prostatitis.** Symptoms may include lower back and/or groin pain, fever, and burning during ejaculation. This, too, is treated with antibiotics.

PRACTICING SAFER SEX

Add them up: 2.3 million new cases of chlamydia per year, 7.4 million new cases of trichomoniasis, nearly 1 million new cases of gonorrhea, 6.2 million new cases of human papillomavirus infection, 1 million new cases of genital herpes, an unknown number of new HIV infections—plus syphilis, sexually transmitted cases of hepatitis, chancroid, and others. There will be at least 19 million new cases of sexually transmitted infections this year—over 52,000 new cases every day—with most cases occurring within your age group (late teens through 40). Of course, some people who are sexually active will be infected with the same STI two or more times in a single year, or even get two or more different STIs at once. Yes, having one does not prevent you from getting others, so it is possible to hit the jackpot and have more than one at once.

What are you doing to avoid sexually transmitted infections? It appears that many college students are doing little or nothing. In fact, many continue to engage in high-risk behaviors. There is a strong association between number of sexual partners and having, or having already had, a sexually transmitted infection (Joffe et al., 1992); yet, according to surveys, many young people have had multiple lifetime sexual partners. (Eaton et al., 2010).

Why do so many people continue to engage in high-risk sexual behaviors (see Box 5–C)? Many young men and women who have had multiple sexual partners believe "it won't happen to me" (Kusseling et al., 1996). Recall, however, that it *will*

Bacterial vaginosis ■ A type of vaginitis caused by the interaction of several vaginal bacteria (particularly *Gardnerella vaginalis*).

Cystitis ■ A bacterial infection of the bladder (often caused by the bacterium *Escherichia coli*).

Prostatitis ■ Inflammation of the prostate gland.

Box 5–C Sexuality and Health

Impediments to Practicing Safer Sex

During the 1980s, it was hoped that educating people about AIDS and the transmission of HIV would lead them to practice safer sex. Most young people today are, in fact, knowledgeable about HIV and AIDS. However, researchers find that there is no relationship at all between people's knowledge of AIDS and their sexual behavior (DiClemente et al., 1990; Klepinger et al., 1993; Lou & Chen, 2009). This has led many researchers to conclude that, by itself, knowledge is "not sufficient for compliance to safer-sex guidelines" (Ahia, 1991; Helwig-Larsen & Collins, 1997; Sheeran et al., 1999; Tate et al., 2002).

If it is not lack of knowledge that prevents many people from practicing safer sex, what is it? Actually, there are many reasons. We will consider a few of the most important.

One of the most common reasons that men give for not using condoms is that one was not available when they were in the mood to have sex (Carter et al., 1999). Many men are embarrassed about buying condoms (Murphy & Boggess, 1998). Young people are also less likely to use condoms if they use alcohol or drugs prior to sex (Coleman & Cater, 2005; George et al., 2009).

People are more likely to have a condom available if they have used them in the past, especially if they are with a partner with whom they have agreed to use condoms. The major problem here is that to have come to an agreement, a couple has to have talked about using condoms, and most people, including those who are college educated, do not know how to initiate and engage in conversation about condoms (Sheeran et al., 1999). "The ability to negotiate condom use is a skill...." (Noar et al., 2002). Practicing safer sex means that you must be able to talk with partners about using condoms, as well as about

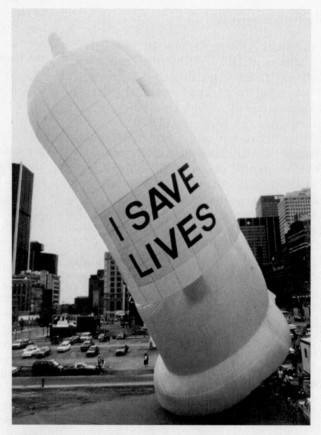

FIGURE 5–17 A giant condom displayed at the Fifth International AIDS Conference in Montreal.

their sexual history, and that you must be able to put a stop to sexual activity if your partner will not use one. This requires some degree of assertiveness. Young people who have these behavioral skills are much more likely to practice safer sex (Fisher & Fisher, 1992; Noar et al., 2006; Widman et al., 2006; Wingood & DiClemente, 1998; Zamboni et al., 2000).

One factor that prevents some women from acting in their own best interest is the perceived power difference between men and women. Many women do not believe that they even have the right to make decisions about contraception (Rickert et al., 2002). If a woman's predominant experience of relations between men and women is of men exerting power over women

and always getting their way, they are not likely to insist that a man use a condom if he does not want to (Browne & Minichiello, 1996; Seal, 1996). This may be common in cultures that emphasize the ideal that men are virile and macho.

Even when there is little or no power difference, communication between a man and a woman about safer sex is often hindered by cultural double standards and sexual "scripts" (Ehrhardt, 1992; Metts & Fitzpatrick, 1992). In American culture, men are given more sexual freedom than are women. Thus, a woman may be viewed negatively by a partner and by others if she openly expresses a desire for sex or if she carries condoms (Hillier et al., 1998), and she may be considered respectable only if she refuses a partner's sexual advances. Women who believe that their partners endorse this standard are not likely to provide a condom or suggest that their partner use one. On the other hand, women often underestimate how often men want to use condoms (Edwards & Barber, 2010).

Another problem is that sexual scripts often work against the use of condoms when one starts dating a "respectable" and "safe" partner where the goal is the formation of a relationship (Afifi, 1999; Browne & Minichiello, 1996; Fortenberry et al., 2002; Hynie et al., 1998). There is a negative relational

significance associated with condoms: if they are not being used for birth control, their only other use is for the prevention of STIs with an "unsafe" partner. When the focus of "getting to know you" is on the other person's suitability as a relational partner, the subject of condoms may be viewed negatively, suggesting promiscuity and possible infection (by oneself or the other) and increasing the likelihood of rejection (see Choi et al., 1994). In fact, some people purposely do not use condoms "as a strategy to find and maintain a primary relationship, establish trust and increase intimacy" (Corbett et al., 2009).

People (incorrectly) take a partner's willingness to talk about AIDS as a sign that he or she is safe. Even when condoms are used during early sexual episodes, they are likely to be abandoned once the two individuals perceive themselves as starting a relationship (Crosby et al., 2000; Manning et al., 2009). But without previous explicit, honest discussion about prior sexual experiences, you cannot be certain. Or, put another way, "You know if you're using a condom or you're not. You don't know if you're picking the right partner" (Heterosexual AIDS, 1988).

happen to 1 in 2 Americans in their lifetimes (Guttmacher Institute, 2007a). So let's get serious and consider how you can minimize the chances of it ever happening to you.

The only way to completely avoid any chance of ever getting an STI is never to have sex, but few of us wish to live the life of a Tibetan monk. There is no such thing as safe sex with another person; anyone having sex is at some risk. We can, however, practice "**safer sex**"—behaviors that minimize the chances of contracting an STI.

One safer sex solution is to *restrict your sexual activity to a mutually faithful, long-term monogamous relationship*. If neither you nor your partner has an STI at the start of the relationship and neither of you has other partners, you do not have to worry about STIs. However, there are problems with this approach. First, while many of us limit our sexual behavior to monogamous relationships, most monogamous relationships do not last forever. Many of us have lifestyles of what is commonly called *serial monogamy*. We break up and eventually enter into another monogamous relationship. You may have been having sex with only one person for a certain period of your life, but how many monogamous relationships have you had in your lifetime? If just one of those partners had an STI, he or she could have transmitted it to you. When we have new sexual partners, we can rarely be sure of their sexual history. Many people are unaware of their partners' current high-risk behaviors (other sexual partners, past injection drug use) (Witte et al., 2010). In additon, a great many people have lied to new partners about their past sexual experiences (Cochran & Mays, 1990).

"A friend of mine was going out with a guy from ____. They had a sexual relationship and

used condoms most of the time. He only recently mentioned that he had tested positive for the AIDS virus in the past. My friend is under tremendous psychological distress."
(from the author's files)

A second problem is that few of us can be 100% certain that our partner will remain monogamous. Read again the personal case histories at the beginning of the chapter.

A second solution is to *always use condoms*. A study of 256 heterosexual couples in which one partner was infected with HIV found that for those couples who used condoms consistently, none of the noninfected partners became infected during a total of 15,000 episodes of intercourse (De Vincenzi et al., 1994). It is certainly best to use condoms if you are going to engage in "casual" sex. For women whose partners refuse to wear condoms, there are some birth control techniques that reduce the risk of HIV (or other STI) infection (see Box 6–A in Chapter 6).

There are problems with condoms (as STI prevention) as well. Even if you and your partner or partners use them consistently and properly, they sometimes tear (see Chapter 6). Even microscopic tears are large enough to allow the passage of viruses. In other words, as is the case with practicing monogamy, condoms cannot guarantee that you will never get a sexually transmitted infection.

Which method is better? In a study that used probability modeling to test the amount of risk reduction, the authors concluded that "consistent and

Safer sex ■ Sexual behaviors involving a low risk of contracting a sexually transmitted infection. These include consistent use of condoms and/or abstaining from sex until one enters a long-term monogamous relationship.

careful condom use is a far more effective method of reducing HIV infection than is reducing the number of sexual partners" (Reiss & Leik, 1989). Whichever behavioral strategy you use—condoms or the practice of monogamy (in a *long-term* relationship)—you will greatly reduce your chances of ever getting a sexually transmitted infection.

PERSONAL REFLECTIONS

Do you and your new partner(s) discuss safer sex? Why or why not? Be sure to read Box 5–C.

WHAT TO DO AND WHERE TO GO IF YOU HAVE AN STI

You would think it would be obvious to people what to do if they thought they might have, or thought they were at risk for, a sexually transmitted infection—go to a doctor! However, many people hesitate to do this out of fear, shame, guilt, or just plain denial. Now that you know the consequences of untreated STIs, I hope that this will not include you. If you think you have an STI (or if you have put yourself at high risk of getting one):

1. See a physician immediately. Many primary care physicians lack the knowledge and experience to diagnose and treat sexually transmitted infections (Wiesenfeld et al., 2005). So, if possible, see a doctor who specializes in treating infectious diseases.

2. If he or she diagnoses you as having an STI, abstain from having sex until you are cured (or use condoms if there is no cure).

3. If you have an STI, tell your partner or partners so that they, too, can be treated and not infect others or yourself again.

There are two other reasons that someone might not go to a doctor immediately. Some (e.g., poor college students) may not be able to afford the doctor's charges and lab test costs, and others might not know where to go even if they had the money (they might not have a doctor, or they may wish to avoid the family doctor). Fortunately, the U.S. Public Health Service provides clinics for the diagnosis and treatment of sexually transmitted infections—often free of charge. The government is committed to eradicating STIs. So there is no excuse not to be treated. Contact the Public Health Service clinic in your area.

The Centers for Disease Control and Prevention also has an STI informational National Hotline toll-free number: 1-800-227-8922.

POSITIVE SEXUALITY IN THE ERA OF AIDS

AIDS, human papillomavirus infections, herpes—the attention being given to these and other sexually transmitted infections is making many people afraid of sex. My intent in this chapter has been to educate you about some of the *possible* consequences of sexual behavior, not to scare you so badly that you will want to avoid ever having sexual relations.

"It's not that I don't trust you, Kevin, I just don't trust the women who've been with the men who've been with the women who've been with the men who've been with the <u>women</u> you've <u>been</u> with."

Reproduced by Special Permission of *Playboy* magazine: Copyright 1990 by Playboy.

There are many activities human beings engage in that involve risk. Take skiing, for example. No one has to tell us that going down a snow-and-ice-covered mountain on a pair of skis is a dangerous activity. If trees, boulders, and other skiers are not avoided, the result can be terrible injury, yet this does not detract from the tremendous enjoyment many people derive from this winter sport. Those who ski learn that there are limitations to how they seek that pleasure. Skiing out of control has its consequences.

The same is true of driving an automobile. Many people own sports cars, and many others would like to. They get a certain thrill by accelerating quickly and driving fast. But, again, there are limitations. Taking a corner at too high a speed can be fatal. At high speeds, we must be able to react to unanticipated events (e.g., another car cutting in front of us) in a fraction of a second. Driving while having impaired judgment and motor coordination due to alcohol consumption is certainly an often fatal high-risk behavior. The fact that each year thousands of people are injured or killed because they foolishly took that risk does not detract from the pleasure that the rest of us often get from driving our cars.

AIDS is not the first sexually transmitted infection, only the most recent. Syphilis and gonorrhea were greatly feared before the discovery of antibiotics. Many millions more have died of syphilis than of AIDS, yet this has not stopped people from enjoying sex. Why? *Because sex, by itself, does not cause any of these infections.* Like driving an automobile, if we avoid foolish, high-risk behaviors, we can still enjoy the pleasures of sexual relations. The few seconds it takes to put on a seat belt does not detract from you enjoying your automobile. Similarly, the few seconds it would take you or your partner to put on a condom will not detract from the enjoyment of sex. Like drinking and driving, making sexual decisions while under the influence of alcohol is also foolish.

AIDS does not strike randomly—it only affects those who are exposed to the virus. If you make just a few adjustments to reduce the risk of exposure, sex can be as pleasurable and exciting as always.

STUDY GUIDE

KEY TERMS

acquired immunodeficiency syndrome (AIDS) 115
amebiasis 124
asymptomatic 116
asymptomatic HIV infection 116
bacteria 101
bacterial vaginosis 127
chancre 106
chancroid 107
chlamydia 104
cystitis 127
genital herpes 108
genital (venereal) warts 113
gonorrhea 102
granuloma inguinale 108
hepatitis A 111

hepatitis B 112
hepatitis C 112
human immunodeficiency virus (HIV) 115
human papillomaviruses (HPV) 112
immune system 115
lymphogranuloma venereum (LGV) 105
molluscum contagiosum 114
moniliasis 125
mycoplasma genitalium 107
nongonococcal (nonspecific) urethritis (NGU) 104
opportunistic infections 116
oral herpes 108

pelvic inflammatory disease (PID) 103
pinworms 124
primary HIV infection 115
prostatitis 127
pubic lice 123
safer sex 129
scabies 124
sexually related diseases 101
sexually transmitted infections (STIs) 101
shigellosis 108
symptomatic HIV infection 116
syphilis 105
trichomoniasis 124
virus 101

INTERACTIVE REVIEW

There are about 19 million new cases of sexually transmitted infections in the United States every year. One in (1) _____ Americans will have at least one STI sometime in their life.

Sexual behavior does not cause STIs. The behavior is merely the mode of transmission

for (2) _____, (3) _____, and/or (4) _____, that must be present for the infections to be transmitted. These causative agents are nondiscriminating—anyone having sex with an infected partner can get a sexually transmitted infection.

The three most common STIs (in the United States) caused by bacteria are (5) _____, (6) _____, and (7) _____. In the early stages of (8) _____ and (9) _____, most women and many men show no symptoms. If they are not treated, the bacteria that cause these two STIs can invade the upper reproductive tract and cause prostatitis and epididymitis in men and (10) _____ in women. (11) _____ passes through several stages, and if left untreated can cause organ damage and death. These types of STIs can be cured with (12) _____.

Sexually transmitted infections caused by viruses are generally incurable because the viruses live inside normal body cells. Herpes has been around since biblical times and is spread by direct (13) _____-to-_____ contact. Genital herpes is almost always transmitted by genital-to-genital or mouth-to-genital contact; oral herpes is often spread by more casual contact. After the primary attack, many herpes sufferers experience (14) _____ attacks when the virus replicates and sheds. The virus is most easily transmitted during active attacks, but can be transmitted at other times.

Hepatitis is an inflammation of the (15) _____ that can be caused by contact with contaminated (16) _____ (hepatitis A) or infected (17) _____ (hepatitis B). One fourth to one half of all cases of hepatitis B are sexually transmitted. Five million Americans are infected with hepatitis C.

Warts in the genital and anal areas are caused by a few types of the (18) _____ virus. Other types of the virus are associated with cancer of the cervix and penis. Physicians can attempt to remove the warts or abnormal cervical cells, but they cannot attack the viruses directly; thus, in many cases, the condition reappears.

AIDS is caused by the (19) _____. HIV invades and destroys (20) _____ (also called helper T) cells, white blood cells that are a critical part of the body's (21) _____ system. Most people infected with HIV remain asymptomatic for several years. HIV infection is not called AIDS until the immune system is so weakened that the individual's life is threatened. People with AIDS eventually die from a variety of (22) _____ infections. Without medication, about half of all individuals who become infected with HIV will develop AIDS within (23) _____ years. HIV originated in Africa from simian (nonhuman primate) immunodeficiency viruses. It is transmitted by (24) _____ and exposure to infected (25) _____. It is not spread by (26) _____. HIV infection is a true pandemic, with at least 120 million cases expected worldwide by the year 2020. Worldwide, most cases are spread by sexual activity between (27) _____. Presently, there is no cure, but there are several antiretroviral drugs that slow the progression of the infection.

Pubic lice and scabies are not really infections, but (28) _____. Pubic lice attach themselves to pubic hair and feed on blood. Scabies is caused by a mite that burrows under the skin to lay its eggs.

There are three general types of vaginal infections. (29) _____ is caused by a one-celled protozoan that is transmitted during sexual intercourse. (30) _____ vaginitis is a fungus or yeast infection that is very common in women. Anything that changes the chemical environment of the vagina can cause a yeast infection. Probably the most common type of vaginal infection is (31) _____, caused by several vaginal bacteria that replace H_2O-producing bacteria. Vaginal infections are very common and are nothing to be ashamed of.

STIs do not strike randomly—they only affect those who are exposed to the bacteria or viruses. You can greatly reduce your chances of ever contracting a sexually transmitted infection by practicing safer sex. This means making one of two choices: (1) using condoms properly and consistently, or (2) abstaining from sexual relations until you are reasonably confident that you are in a long-term monogamous relationship.

SELF-TEST

A. TRUE OR FALSE

| T | F | 32. People who have had a sexually transmitted infection in the past are immune to getting that type of STI again. |

| T | F | 33. Cold sores and fever blisters are symptoms of herpes. |

| T | F | 34. Homosexuality is one of the causes of AIDS. |

| T | F | 35. If left untreated, gonorrhea can turn into syphilis. |

| T | F | 36. Yeast infections (monilial vaginitis) can usually be prevented by using feminine hygiene products. |

[T] [F] 37. A person with a cold sore on the mouth can give his or her partner genital herpes during oral-genital sex.

[T] [F] 38. Gonorrhea, chlamydia, and syphilis are often contracted by people who use toilet seats previously used by infected individuals.

[T] [F] 39. Chlamydia is more common than gonorrhea.

[T] [F] 40. It is possible to contract HIV by hugging, touching, or being close to an infected person.

[T] [F] 41. The large majority of women do not show any symptoms in the early stages of gonorrhea or chlamydia.

[T] [F] 42. Herpes can sometimes be cured with antibiotics.

[T] [F] 43. A person can have only one type of sexually transmitted infection at a time.

[T] [F] 44. HIV, the virus that causes AIDS, is sometimes spread by mosquitoes.

[T] [F] 45. Pelvic inflammatory disease can be caused by infections that were not contracted during sex.

[T] [F] 46. Condoms are generally ineffective against the human immunodeficiency virus.

[T] [F] 47. The eggs of pubic lice can survive for days on towels or sheets.

[T] [F] 48. A person who has no symptoms does not have to worry about having gonorrhea, chlamydia, or syphilis.

[T] [F] 49. Only women can contract trichomoniasis and monilial infections.

[T] [F] 50. Herpes can be cured with a drug called acyclovir.

[T] [F] 51. The human papillomaviruses that cause cervical cancer are the same as those that cause genital warts.

[T] [F] 52. Regular douching decreases the risk of pelvic inflammatory disease.

[T] [F] 53. Recurrent herpes attacks are generally more painful, and last longer, than the first (primary) attack.

[T] [F] 54. Herpes is the leading infectious cause of blindness in the United States.

[T] [F] 55. Hepatitis A is most often spread by nonsexual means.

[T] [F] 56. Worldwide, most cases of HIV infection (infection with the virus that causes AIDS) are contracted by sex between heterosexuals.

[T] [F] 57. Generally speaking, people who get AIDS this year are those who became infected with HIV 5 to 15 years ago.

[T] [F] 58. To minimize their chance of a vaginal infection, women should wear panties made of synthetic fabrics.

[T] [F] 59. People who get HIV are extremely contagious in the first 60 days after exposure.

[T] [F] 60. HIV/AIDS can be considered cured when drug therapy reduces HIV to nondetectable levels.

B. MATCHING

Symptoms

_____ 61. painful, craterlike sores

_____ 62. itchless, painless rash all over the body

_____ 63. puslike discharge and/or burning during urination

_____ 64. intense itching caused by grayish, six-legged parasites

_____ 65. thick, white, cheesy vaginal discharge and intense itching

_____ 66. loss of appetite, fatigue, slow recovery from colds and flus, continual yeast infections, purple blotches on skin, pneumonia

_____ 67. cauliflowerlike growths

_____ 68. severe abdominal pain and fever

_____ 69. scaling skin caused by pearly mites

_____ 70. large, ulcerlike, painless sore

_____ 71. fluid-filled blisters

_____ 72. copious, foamy, yellowish-green vaginal discharge and odor

_____ 73. wartlike growths that look like small pimples filled with kernels of corn

_____ 74. thin, clear discharge and irritation of the urethra

_____ 75. jaundiced or yellow tinge of skin and eyes

_____ 76. large ulcers (gummas) on the skin and bones; damage to the heart and nervous system

_____ 77. inflammation of the bladder

Infection (or Infestation)

a. chancroid

b. chlamydia

c. gonorrhea

d. hepatitis

e. herpes

f. HIV infection (AIDS)

g. molluscum contagiosum

h. moniliasis (yeast infection)

i. PID

j. primary-stage syphilis

k. cystitis

l. secondary-stage syphilis

m. scabies

n. trichomoniasis

o. venereal warts (human papillomavirus infection)

p. late-stage syphilis

q. pubic lice

C. FILL IN THE BLANKS

78. Trichomoniasis, pubic lice, and scabies are all caused by _____.

79. In women, untreated gonorrhea or chlamydia can lead to _____.

80. A woman who has had _____ is at high risk of getting cancer of the cervix.

81. The sexually transmitted infection that impairs the immune system is called _____.

82. Trichomoniasis, moniliasis, and bacterial vaginosis are all _____.

83. A viral liver infection that can be sexually transmitted is _____.

84. Two serious possible consequences of PID are _____ and _____.

85. Three sexually transmitted infections that can be passed from an infected pregnant female to the fetus are _____, _____, and _____.

86. _____ is the most common thing that brings on recurrent herpes attacks.

87. The bacteria that cause gonorrhea and chlamydia live on _____.

88. Any inflammation of the urethra not caused by the gonococcus is called _____.

89. Antibiotics commonly lead to _____ infections.

90. _____ live in the large intestine and can be transmitted during sex, but are generally acquired by children through nonsexual means.

91. Many people diagnosed with gonorrhea are also found to have _____.

92. HIV attacks immune system cells called _____.

93. People with HIV are most contagious (when) _____.

94. The most common AIDS test tests for _____.

95. Gonorrhea, chlamydia, syphilis, herpes, HPV infection, HIV infection, trichomoniasis—for which of these infections do women usually not have visible symptoms in the initial stage? _____

96. For which of the infections listed in the previous question do men usually not show symptoms in the initial stage? _____

97. The best ways to avoid sexually transmitted infections are _____ and _____.

98. The most common sexually transmitted infection/infestation in the United States is _____.

99. The most common STI in the United States caused by a bacterium or virus is _____.

SUGGESTED READINGS AND RESOURCES

American Social Health Organization. (2003). *HPV in perspective: A patient guide* (2nd ed.). Research Triangle Park, NC.

Boston Women's Health Book Collective. (2005). *Our bodies, ourselves: A new edition for a new era.* New York: Simon & Schuster. The landmark book on women's sexuality and health.

Cates, J. R., et al. (2004). *Our voices, our lives, our futures: Youth and sexually transmitted diseases.* Chapel Hill, NC: School of Journalism and Mass Communication.

Ebel, C., and Wald, A. (2002). *Managing herpes: How to live and love with a chronic STD.* Research Triangle Park, NC. The best book ever written about herpes.

Jefferson, D. (2006). How AIDS changed America. *Newsweek*, May 15.

Newsweek. (2006, May 15). AIDS at 25. Several articles about how HIV/AIDS affects Americans today.

Planned Parenthood. *Vaginitis: Questions and answers.* 16 pages.

United Nations Programme on HIV/AIDS (December, 2008). *Report on the global HIV/AIDS epidemic.* Geneva, Switzerland: United Nations.

American College Health Association
P.O. Box 28937
Baltimore, MD 21240-8937
(410) 859-1500
www.acha.org

American Social Health Association
P.O. Box 13827
Research Triangle Park, NC 27709
1(800)277-8922
www.ashastd.org

National AIDS and STD Information Clearinghouse
1(800) 458-5231
Service provided by the Centers for Disease Control and Prevention.

STD Hotline (919) 361-8488
Service provided by the American Social Health Association.
www.ashastd.org

Birth Control

We should not delude ourselves: The population explosion will come to an end before very long. The only remaining question is whether it will be halted through the humane method of birth control, or by nature wiping out the surplus.

—Excerpt from *The Population Explosion*, by Paul & Anne Ehrlich, 1990, Simon & Schuster.

Over 75% of American married women use contraception (Seager, 2003), and as a result, the average age at which American women have their first baby is 25 (National Center for Health Statistics, 2010). Unfortunately, consistent use of contraception is apparently not as common among teens. While over 85% of teens say that they want to avoid pregnancy (see Gibbs, 2010), the teenage pregnancy rate in the United States is the highest of any developed country in the world (see Table 6–1). It is eight times higher than in Japan, seven times higher than in Sweden and Denmark, over five times greater than in France, and three times greater than in Canada (United Nations, 2007).

As a result, the teenage birth rate in the United States is also higher than in other developed countries. This is not a recent phenomenon. Births to teenagers in the United States reached a peak in 1957. What is new is the proportion of births to unwed teens. Only 15% of teenage births were out of wedlock in 1960, but this figure rose to 49% by 1980, and reached 76% in 1991. The percentage of children born to unwed mothers (of all ages) reached a peak of 40.6% in 2008 (the last year recorded as of this edition) (National Center for Health Statistics, 2010). The greatest increase in pregnancy rates has been among young teens aged 14 to 17 without a high school education. About 78% of pregnancies to teens are unintended, and nearly half of these are terminated by abortion (Henshaw, 1998a). Over one third of woman who have had an unintended pregnancy have another unintended pregnancy (Wildsmith et al., 2010), and repeat unintended pregnancies may be increasing (Collier, 2009).

When you have finished studying this chapter, you should be able to:

- Discuss the teenage pregnancy problem in the United States and understand the worldwide need for effective contraceptive techniques.
- Explain the lactational amenorrhea method as a temporary method of birth control after childbirth.
- Explain how the various fertility awareness methods of contraception are supposed to work.
- Compare and contrast the various barrier methods of birth control and their effectiveness.
- Discuss the latest developments in intrauterine devices.
- Describe the various hormonal methods of contraception, how they work, and their potential side effects.
- Understand how emergency contraception works.
- Describe the various sterilization procedures and explain their advantages and disadvantages.
- Discuss the various methods of abortion.
- Discuss the contraceptive methods that also help to prevent sexually transmitted infections.
- Determine which contraceptive technique is right for you.

TABLE 6–1	*Yearly Teenage (15–19 Years Old) Pregnancy Rate (per 1,000 Women) in Developed Nations*
United States	41.2
Russian Federation	28.5
England and Wales	26.7
Australia	16.3
Canada	13.3
Spain	11.5
Germany	10.1
Finland	9.4
Norway	8.7
France	7.8
Italy	7.0
Sweden	5.9
Denmark	5.9
Japan	5.1
Netherlands	3.8

Source: Adapted from the *United Nations Demographic Yearbook 2006,* Dept. of Economic and Social Affairs. Copyright © 2006 United Nations. Reprinted by permission.

The high teenage pregnancy rate in the United States comes in spite of significant improvements since the early 1990s. The percentage of high school students (all grades) who had ever engaged in sexual intercourse decreased from 54.1% in 1991 to 46.0% in 2009 (Eaton et al., 2010). The U.S. teenage pregnancy and birth rates also began to decline after 1991, and by 2005 had reached their lowest levels since 1976 (Gavin et al., 2009). The teen birth rate increased slightly in 2006 and 2007, but dropped again in 2008 (National Center for Health Statistics, 2010).

The birth rate is much higher for African-American and Latino teenagers than it is for white or Asian-American teens (Eaton et al., 2010). However, the birth rate for African-American teens has also decreased substantially since 1991, and the rate for unmarried black teens is the lowest it has been in 40 years. On the other hand, the rate for Latino teens is increasing. White teens are much more likely than black or Latino teens to "hide" an unintended pregnancy by getting married. Because the divorce rate for couples married as teenagers is much higher than average, many of these prematurely married white teens end up as young single parents anyway (see Coley & Chase-Lansdale, 1998).

What is responsible for the decline in teenage pregnancies in the last decade? According to Sarah

Brown, director of the National Campaign to Prevent Teen Pregnancy: "There are only two ways these rates could have gone down. Kids are having less sex and they're using contraceptives better" (quote by Pitts, 2001). In fact, among sexually active teens, about 60% (girls) to 80% (boys) reported that condoms were used during their last sexual intercourse, and 19.8% reported that birth control pills were used (Eaton et al., 2010; Fortenberry et al., 2010; Reece et al., 2010a). Condom use was highest among black and Hispanic teens (Dodge et al., 2010; Reece et al., 2010a; Sanders et al., 2010). Nevertheless, the high pregnancy rate among U.S. teens compared with that of other developed countries reflects that there is still widespread nonuse or inconsistent use of **contraception.**

Why do some people have sex without using contraception? Some of the most common reasons are method-related difficulties and side effects, infrequent sex and leaving it to chance, or just plain not really caring (Frost et al., 2007; Richters et al., 2003b). Teens with repeat pregnancies generally have a history of behavior problems (school problems, drug and alcohol use, etc.) (Gillmore et al., 1997).

Among young teens, ignorance about reproduction and contraception is common.

"As a paramedic I've delivered more babies than I can count. Once I responded to a person with 'rectal bleeding.' To my surprise, a young girl greeted me saying that 'she has something coming out her rectum and she is bleeding all over.' The 15-year-old was scared to death, still clothed in underwear, bleeding, with a large mass between her legs, inside the underwear. I gained information from the family that no one had any inclination that this 15-year-old was even pregnant. What an education for a 15-year-old. Is this really what we want for our children, or do we want to provide the availability of more classes such as Human Sexuality? I vote for the latter."
(from the author's files)

However, most teens know about contraception, and also know that if they have sex without contraception they are taking a chance. But if they have already taken that chance without having it result in pregnancy, they are likely to take the chance again. Eventually, they begin to feel that they cannot get pregnant—that it will not happen to them.

"I have been having sex since I was 16. I have had different partners and unprotected sex with all of them. I always believed that I couldn't get pregnant. It only happens to bad girls and people who wanted it to happen. There were a couple of late periods and worrying, but it never made me want to try birth control.... I found out I was 2 months pregnant. I was completely shocked."
(from the author's files)

Contraception ■ The prevention of conception.

The teenage pregnancy rate in the United States is related to social and economic status (B.C. Miller, 2002; Singh et al., 2001). Teenage pregnancies are much more likely to occur among those with low income or low levels of education, and/or who live with a single parent. Thus, the teenage girls most likely to have babies are generally the ones least prepared to take care of them—teens who are already living in poverty and with low educational aspirations (Coley & Chase-Lansdale, 1998; Harden et al., 2009; Letourneau et al., 2004). Teenage mothers are much more likely to have high-risk babies with health problems, problems often made worse because many pregnant teens never seek prenatal care (Hein et al., 1990). As a result, the United States has one of the highest infant mortality rates among developed countries (Singh & Yu, 1995).

Being an unwed teenage mother does not guarantee that she will be locked into poverty with no job skills and little education, but most will experience long periods of hardship because of early childbearing (see Coley & Chase-Lansdale, 1998, for a review). Teens who become mothers complete about two fewer years of schooling than women who delay giving birth (Hofferth et al., 2001).

In addition to not being economically or physically ready to have children, teenagers are generally not emotionally ready to have children either. Studies of children who grew up unwanted reveal that most suffered from long-term psychological and physical health problems (David et al., 2003; Sigal et al., 2003). Children of teenage parents are also much more likely than other children to be victims of child abuse and neglect (Goerge & Lee, 1997). The children of teen parents who later become young teen parents themselves often report that they experienced emotional deprivation at an early age, have had significant depressive symptoms, and "seek emotional closeness through sexual activity and early parenthood" (Horwitz et al., 1991).

© Jimmy Margulies

Who are the male partners responsible for these teenage pregnancies? Half of the fathers of babies born to girls aged 14 to 17 are at least 20 years old, and 27% are at least 5 years older (Lindberg et al., 1997; Taylor et al., 1997). Nevertheless, many male teenagers also become fathers. Only about half of these fathers spend any time with their children and only one fifth contribute money (Rangarajan & Gleason, 1998). Men who do poorly in school, lack long-term goals, come from impoverished backgrounds, and engage in other socially deviant behaviors (e.g., drugs) have the most irresponsible attitudes about reproduction. In fact, many of these men consider getting a woman pregnant a sign of masculinity.

> "I am an admitted 'serial monogomist.' One of these types of relationships led to pregnancy right after high school.... My ex and I no longer speak to each other and he has never been a part of his own child's life (by choice)."
> (from the author's files)

Perhaps the most unfortunate part of all this is that the high rate of births to teens continues to occur in a day and age when highly effective means of birth control are available. This was not always the case. The prevailing attitude toward sex during Victorian times and throughout the history of the Christian church, as you recall, was that it was for procreation only, and thus birth control was opposed. In many states it was against the law to sell or distribute contraceptive devices. As a result, women generally had several children, and many poor women who worried that they could not feed another child died during crude and often self-attempted abortions. It was as a result of watching one of these poor tenement women die from a self-induced abortion attempt in 1912 that Margaret Sanger gave up a nursing career and founded the Birth Control League (later changed to Planned Parenthood). The work of reformers and the changing attitude about the role of women in general gradually had their effect.

The last of the state laws prohibiting the sale of contraceptive devices to married couples was finally repealed in 1965 (by a U.S. Supreme Court decision in the case of *Griswold v. Connecticut*), and laws preventing the sale to unmarried persons were struck down in 1972 (*Eisenstadt v. Baird*). By then, 81% of the public approved of the availability of birth control information. The birth control pill was introduced in 1960, but until recently condoms and other birth control devices that did not require a visit to the doctor were kept behind the counter in drugstores, which inhibited many people from purchasing them.

Today, worldwide (each year), "Family planning programs prevent an estimated 187 million unintended pregnancies, including 60 million unplanned births and 105 million abortions, and avert an estimated 2.7 million infant deaths and 215,000 pregnancy related deaths" (Amy & Tripathi, 2009).

FIGURE 6–1 Margaret Sanger, a founder of the birth control movement, was forbidden to talk about birth control, so in 1929 she voluntarily had her mouth taped and wrote about the subject on a blackboard.

Unfortunately, in the United States there has been a major decline since the mid-1990s in government funding for family planning programs (Bongaarts & Sinding, 2008). In the private sector, health insurance covers Viagra so that men can get erections, but doesn't cover birth control for women.

PERSONAL REFLECTIONS

Are you prepared at the present time to assume the responsibilities of being a parent? Why or why not? How would your life change if you or your partner were pregnant (consider your relationship, finances, career goals, etc.)?

WORLD POPULATION

In addition to personal reasons, there are other reasons why a society as a whole should practice birth control. Imagine two shipwrecked couples on a small South Pacific island in the year 1700. The island has a small supply of fresh water, some animal life but no predators, edible vegetation, and a small amount of land suitable for farming. For these four people, the island is Utopia—it has more than they will ever need. Each couple is fertile and has four children (probably an underestimate without birth

control), and the children in turn pair off in their late teens to form four couples, each of which has four more children. Thus, in each generation there would be twice as many people as in the previous generation. If there were no accidental deaths and the people lived until age 65, there would be at least 224 people living on the island by the year 1800. For those people, the island is no longer Utopia. The animals have all been killed, the edible plant life is consumed within days of becoming ripe, and there is not nearly enough farmland to support a population of this size. What is worse, even the water supply must be rationed, and the population continues to increase. Soon there will be large-scale death from starvation and dehydration.

Wildlife experts are used to seeing this happen to populations of deer in areas where there are no predators, but is this scenario too far-fetched for humans? Consider that the world is really just an island. We have a limited amount of natural resources, including water. Should these resources become exhausted, we would find ourselves in the same situation as the inhabitants of our hypothetical island. The world population has been increasing at an alarming rate (see Figure 6–2), and it is now more than 25 times greater than in the year a.d. 1. It was about 800 million in 1760, reached 5 billion in 1987, and reached 6 billion at the end of 1999. By July 2010 it was 6.83 billion, and was projected to reach 7 billion in 2012. The United Nations estimates that the world population will be 9.1 billion in 2050. The Population Reference Bureau predicts 9.4 billion (*Energy Bulletin*, 2009). In that year, the three most populated countries are expected to be India (1.529 billion), China (1.478 billion), and the United States (349 million).

Many experts predict that unless this world population explosion is substantially slowed, the end result will be widespread starvation, poverty, and political instability. Already, half the children born today are at poverty levels. Robert Repetto of the World Resources Institute estimates that if the present population doubles, all of the current cropland in the world would have to produce 2.8 tons of grain per acre per year, equivalent to the most productive American farms. Read again the warning by Paul and Anne Ehrlich, authors of *The Population Explosion* (1990), at the beginning of the chapter. They add:

> We realize that religious and cultural opposition to birth control exists throughout the world; but we believe that people simply do not understand the choice that such opposition implies. Today, anyone opposing birth control is unknowingly voting to have the human population size controlled by a massive increase in early deaths.

David Pimentel (1998) of Cornell University adds that unless something is done soon, by 2100

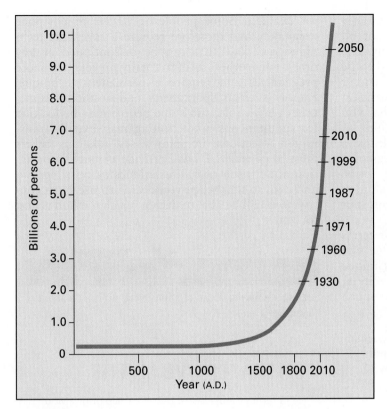

FIGURE 6–2 World population growth. Notice how rapidly the world population has increased since the beginning of the 20th century.

"12 billion miserable humans will suffer a difficult life on Earth."

In some parts of the world, mass starvation is no longer hypothetical, but already a reality. It is happening in Ethiopia, Somalia, and in many other parts of Africa and in Asia. In India, infanticide (the killing of children, especially newborn girls) is not uncommon (Cohen, 2000). China, presently the world's most populated country with about 1 billion people, has much less farmland than the United States. There is only one fifth of an acre of land per person, which is just enough to provide food for one person. Any additional increase in the population will mean starvation for millions. As a result, the Chinese government was forced in 1982 to order mandatory birth control. For the next 100 years, couples will be told not to have more than one child. As a result of this policy, China's fertility rate has fallen dramatically from about 6 children per woman in 1970 to about 1.8 to 2.1 children in 1997 (Attané, 2000).

During the "baby boom" years (following the end of World War II through 1960, there was an average of 3.5 babies born to each American couple (Gibbs, 2010). If that rate had continued, the population of the United States today would be around 500 million, nearly twice what it actually is. Just imagine what the congestion and pollution would be like. Would our natural resources have been strained? I do not know, but our average lifestyle could not possibly be as good as it is today.

What prevented the United States from having this population explosion? Quite simply, it was the use of birth control, which has made it possible for people to limit the number of children they have. The birth rate started to fall in the early 1960s, and by 1970 the average American woman had 2.0 births in her lifetime. In 2006, the U.S. birth rate increased to 2.1 births in a lifetime, the figure that the government says is necessary for the population to replace itself (National Center for Health Statistics, 2007). The fertility rate is now below the replacement level in 20 developed countries, and as low as 1.3 in southern and central Europe (see Longman, 2009). In eastern and western Africa, on the other hand, the fertility rate is 6.2, and 3.8 to 4.2 in western and south-central Asia (Potts, 2000). Accessible birth control in developing countries could avoid 76 million pregnancies every year, which according to some experts, could help the environment by slowing climate change (*The Lancet*, 2009).

Stop and think about it for a minute: Would you really like to see us in a situation where our population doubles every generation? We might be able to continue to live comfortably during our lifetime, but what would life be like for our grandchildren?

EVALUATING DIFFERENT BIRTH CONTROL METHODS

If all fertile couples practiced unprotected sexual intercourse (no pills, condoms, diaphragms, etc.) and did not abstain from having sex at any time of the month (no fertility awareness methods), about 85% of them would conceive within a year. In judging the effectiveness of the various birth control techniques, we need to know how many couples using a particular contraceptive method would conceive in a year's time. There are actually two figures here that are important: the perfect-use pregnancy rate and the typical-use pregnancy rate.

For a particular contraceptive technique, the **perfect-use pregnancy rate** is the percentage of couples who would conceive if all couples who were using the technique used it consistently and

Perfect-use pregnancy rate ■ For a particular birth control technique, the percentage of pregnancies during the first year of use by couples who use the technique properly and consistently.

properly. The **typical-use pregnancy rate** is usually higher than the perfect-use rate because not all people use a method consistently or properly. The birth control pill, for example, was designed to be taken every day, but not all women remember to do so, and this results in some pregnancies. Although all the birth control techniques that you will learn about are better than using nothing at all, some are more effective than others. Ideally, a couple wishing to postpone or prevent pregnancy would like their birth control technique to be 100% effective (zero pregnancies in a year's time). Some contraceptive methods approach this, but others do not.

Pregnancy rates are almost always stated in terms of the number of pregnancies that occur *in the first year of use* for every 100 couples using the technique (see Table 6–2). Although I will follow that tradition, most people want to use birth control for a much longer period. In fact:

> To achieve the family size she desires, a fertile woman today must practice birth control throughout most of her potential reproductive years—as many as 30 of the roughly 36 years between menarche and menopause. *(Schwartz & Gabelnick, 2002, p. 310)*

If a couple's chosen contraceptive technique has a pregnancy rate of 5% in the first year of use, what are the chances of an unplanned pregnancy if they continue to use the technique over a much longer time period? The 10-year pregnancy rate is between 23% (this assumes that the risk will have declined to zero by the end of that time span) and 40% (this assumes that the risk remains constant) (Ross, 1989). For a contraceptive technique with a first-year pregnancy rate of 10%, the 10-year pregnancy rate is between 40% and 66%. Some of the contraceptive techniques that we will consider have a first-year pregnancy rate of 20%. Over a 10-year time period, the chance of having an unplanned pregnancy while using these techniques is between 67% and 90%. Thus, while contraceptive methods reduce the number of unplanned pregnancies, most are far from being 100% effective over a long period of time.

In evaluating birth control techniques, we must look at more than just their effectiveness. Some techniques are more suitable for certain subgroups of the population than others. The birth control pill is highly effective, but it is not recommended for women with diabetes or cardiovascular problems,

for example. Some people only wish to postpone pregnancy and therefore require a reversible technique (i.e., one that can be discontinued at any time), while others wish to totally prevent any more pregnancies and require a permanent technique. Factors such as spontaneity and aesthetics sometimes play a role, and some people may be looking for simultaneous protection against sexually transmitted infections. In many cases, religious beliefs must be considered. I will provide as much information about each of the techniques as possible, pro and con, so that when you decide to use birth control, you will be able to decide which method is best for you.

PERSONAL REFLECTIONS

If you are having sexual relations, what do you do about contraception?

CONTRACEPTIVE MYTHS

> "In high school I heard that if a male drinks Mountain Dew or Surge cold drinks they would have a low sperm count and could have sex and not get the girl pregnant."

> "I heard a while back that the soft drink Surge made men sterile, so if he drank one before sex, his sperm count would be near zero."

> (All examples are from the author's files.)

Teens are often given a great deal of misinformation about contraception by friends and potential partners. Some of the information is so incorrect that it can be considered myth. For example, some of you may have heard that if a man drinks Mountain Dew before sex it reduces his sperm count, or that if a woman douches with Coca-Cola or ice water afterwards she cannot get pregnant. How many of you were told, "You can't get pregnant the first time you have sex" or "You can't get pregnant if you don't kiss"? Well, these stories are just not true. A girl is capable of reproduction as soon as she starts having menstrual cycles (recall that in the United States, the first menstrual period occurs at an average age of 12½). This is evidence that she is ovulating, i.e., producing eggs. Some of you may have been told that a woman cannot get pregnant if she is on top or if she has sex while standing up (because of gravity), but these statements are also untrue. It is also not true that a woman must have an orgasm during sex in order to get pregnant. No doubt there are other stories that you have heard, but unless they are included in the remainder of the chapter (i.e., they have a basis in fact), chances are they just are not true.

Typical-use pregnancy rate ■ For a particular birth control technique, the percentage of pregnancies during the first year of use by all couples who use the technique, regardless of whether or not they use it properly or consistently.

TABLE 6–2	*Number of Pregnancies per 100 Women During the First Year of Continuous Use*	
Method	Perfect Use	Typical Use
Male sterilization	0.1	0.15
Female sterilization	0.5	0.5
Implanon	0.05	0.05
Depo-Provera (3-month shot)	0.3	3
Combination birth control pill	0.3	8
Progestin only (mini) pill	0.3	8
OrthoEvra ("patch")	0.3	8
NuvaRing (vaginal ring)	0.3	8
IUD (Paragard)	0.6	0.8
IUD (Mirena)	0.2	0.2
Male condom (without spermicide)	2	15
Lactational Amenorrhea Method (6 months)	2	—
Female condom	5	21
Diaphragm (with spermicide)	6	16
Cervical cap (for women who have not given birth)	9	16
Contraceptive sponge (for women who have not given birth)	9	16
Spermicides alone	18.0	29.0
Withdrawal	4.0	27.0
Fertility awareness:		
Calendar	9	25
BBT	3	25
Billings	3	22–25
Standard Days	5	25
Sympto-thermal	1	20
Emergency contraception (Plan B)	11	11
No method	85	85

Source: From Trussell J. "Contraceptive Efficacy." In Hatcher, R. A., J. Trussell, A. L. Nelson, W. Cates, F. H. Stewart, and D. Kowal. *Contraceptive Technology,* 19th Revised Edition. Copyright © 2007 Ardent Media. Also online at http://www .contraceptive-technology.org/table.html; retrieved May 14, 2010. Reprinted with permission.

RELATIVELY INEFFECTIVE METHODS

One of the most popular ways in which young people try to prevent pregnancy is **withdrawal (coitus interruptus)**, where the man withdraws his penis just before reaching orgasm and ejaculates outside his partner's vagina. Well over half of sexually active teens have used withdrawal on at least one occasion (Kowal, 2008). It sounds logical, for if the man does not ejaculate in the woman's vagina, there should be no sperm there. The Cowper's glands, you recall, secrete a few drops of fluid before a man reaches orgasm. The fluid contains very little, if any, sperm (see Wynn et al., 2009) and, in fact, the perfect-use pregnancy rate is 4% in the first year. The real problem is that many men do not always withdraw before ejaculating. Thus, studies find that about 27 out of

Withdrawal (coitus interruptus) ■ Withdrawal of the man's penis from his partner's vagina before ejaculation in order to avoid conception. It is sometimes ineffective because fluids from the Cowper's glands may contain sperm.

every 100 women using the withdrawal method conceive within the first year of use (Kowal, 2008).

> "An ex-boyfriend of mine thought if he pulled out before 'he came,' then a girl wouldn't get pregnant. He was shocked when he found out his current girlfriend was pregnant. He claimed he couldn't be the father because he didn't 'come.'"
>
> (from the author's files)

Withdrawal is better than nothing, but it is ineffective compared with most types of contraception.

Some women believe that **douching** is an effective method of birth control.

> "I was told that douching and/or using the bathroom right after sex would get rid of the sperm and you would not get pregnant."
>
> (from the author's files)

Again, it sounds logical. If you wash out the contents of the vagina, there should be no sperm. The problem is that no matter how quickly a woman douches after intercourse, some sperm will have already made it into the cervix. In fact, the pressure caused by douching can actually force sperm into the cervical opening (Cates & Raymond 2004). Over 40 out of every 100 couples who use douching as their only means of birth control will conceive in a year's time. Frequent douching can also increase the likelihood of pelvic inflammatory disease and ectopic pregnancy (Zhang et al., 1997).

ABSTAINING FROM SEX

The most effective way to avoid an unwanted pregnancy is to abstain from sexual intercourse. Abstinence does not mean that you have to avoid other types of sexual activity. Individuals who make this decision can be 100% worry free about getting pregnant or getting someone pregnant. However, 95% of Americans have had sex before marriage, and this is true for women as well as men (Finer, 2007).

What about sex education programs that teach abstinence-only as birth control? From 1998 to 2009, the U.S. government provided over $1.3 billion to the states to teach abstinence-only programs (Jayson, 2009). This approach is popular with those who believe that unplanned pregnancies are a big problem and that a decline in moral standards has contributed to the problem (Mauldon & Delbanco,

1997). But how effective are these programs? Studies find that any behavioral changes are usually just short term (Brückner & Bearman, 2005). A study authorized by Congress found that abstinence-only programs had no long-term effect (Mathematica Policy Research, 2007; see Chapter 1). In fact, teens who take abstinence-only courses are less likely to use condoms when they do have sex and are more likely to get (or get someone) pregnant (Kohler et al., 2008; Rosenbaum, 2009; Yang & Gaydos, 2010).

"Abstinence-plus" programs that teach abstinence *and* contraception, on the other hand, have often proved to be very effective in reducing teenage pregnancy rates (e.g., NIH Consensus, 1997; Tiezzi et al., 1997). Some comparisons with other countries might be helpful here. Denmark, for example, has comprehensive sexuality education in its schools. Danish teenagers become sexually active at as young an age as American teens (half by age 17), but the vast majority use contraception, and the teenage birth rate in Denmark is among the lowest in the world (see Table 6–1). Switzerland promoted condoms for teens to combat AIDS. Condom use increased dramatically and did not lead to any major changes in number of sexual partners or frequency of sex (Dubois-Arber et al., 1997).

Although abstinence-only programs have not proven to be very successful, it remains true that individuals who choose to abstain will avoid unwanted pregnancies. Apparently, more teens are, in fact, making that choice. Results of recent national surveys show that (beginning in the 1990s) there has been a decline in the number of teenagers engaging in sexual intercourse (Gavin et al., 2009; National Center for Health Statistics, 2010).

LACTATIONAL AMENORRHEA METHOD

Breast-feeding has been called "nature's contraceptive." There is some truth to this. In fact, breast-feeding as a temporary method of birth control after childbirth has come to be known as the **lactational amenorrhea method**. The sucking response of the baby on the mother's nipple inhibits the release of FSH and LH from the pituitary, thus preventing normal menstrual cycles and ovulation. Before modern contraceptive techniques were introduced, breast-feeding was the major factor that determined the length of the interval between pregnancies and still is in many countries. If a mother is fully breast-feeding *and is not menstruating*, the chance of pregnancy during the first 6 months is less than 2% (Amy & Tripathi, 2009; Kennedy & Trussell, 2008). This must include regular feedings at night (King, 2007). *The risk of ovulation rises quickly if a woman continues breast-feeding beyond 6 months.*

Douching ■ A feminine hygiene practice of rinsing out the vagina, usually with specifically prepared solutions.

Lactational amenorrhea method (breast-feeding) ■ In reference to contraception, the sucking response by a baby on the mother's nipple inhibits release of follicle-stimulating hormone, thus preventing ovulation.

FERTILITY AWARENESS: ABSTAINING FROM SEX DURING OVULATION

The **fertility awareness method** (also called the *rhythm method* or *natural family planning*) may be the only method acceptable to many of you because of your religious beliefs. For example, these are the only birth control methods that are not opposed by the Catholic Church and some evangelical Protestant denominations. There are four variations to this method, but *all are based on predicting when ovulation occurs.* A woman can only get pregnant when sperm are present during the first 24 hours or so after ovulation. After that, the egg is overly ripe and a sperm cannot fertilize it. Fertility awareness methods involve the identification of "safe days" in a woman's menstrual cycle and the abstinence of sex during the "unsafe period." Which days are "safe"?

Sperm can live in a Fallopian tube for several days. Although most do not live for more than 3 days, some can live for as long as 5 days. Wilcox, Weinberg, and Baird (1995) calculated the following probabilities of conception (in relation to the day of ovulation):

Day	Probability
−5	0.10
−4	0.16
−3	0.14
−2	0.27
−1	0.31
0 (ovulation)	0.33

In a woman with perfect 28-day cycles, ovulation would be at midcycle. The problem is that few women have cycles of the same length month after month. It is normal for a woman's cycle to differ in length over time by several days, typically by about 8 days (Harlow & Ephross, 1995). While only about 1.5% of woman have cycles shorter than 21 days or longer than 35 days (Hatcher & Namnoum, 2008), only about one third of women ovulate regularly between days 10 and 17 of their cycle (Wilcox et al., 2000). All of the fertility awareness methods must take this variability into account. Many young women have 10 or fewer menstrual cycles a year. *It would be almost impossible for a woman who is not having regular menstrual cycles to use the following techniques.*

Calendar Method and Standard Days Method

The first thing a woman must do to use this method is to keep track of the length of her menstrual cycles

for a minimum of eight cycles (more would be better). Let us take a hypothetical example of a woman who has kept track of 10 cycles and found that although her average cycle length was 28 days, she had one that was only 24 days and another that lasted 32 days. The **calendar method** uses a formula to calculate the unsafe period. Subtract 18 from the length of the shortest cycle (24 − 18 = 6) and 11 from the length of the longest cycle (32 − 11 = 21). The unsafe period would thus be from days 6 through 21 (by the numbering system explained in Chapter 3; day 1 is the start of menstruation). This is a period of over 2 weeks that the woman and her partner must abstain from having sexual intercourse. If the woman had had a cycle shorter than 24 days or longer than 32 days, the period of abstinence would have been even longer.

The calendar method has proven to be very unreliable, with most studies reporting a typical-use failure rate of about 25% per year (Trussell, 2008). However, the perfect-use pregnancy rate can be much lower for women who *typically* have menstrual cycles of 26 to 32 days. If your cycles are almost always within these limits, then avoiding unprotected intercourse during days 8 through 19 reduces the pregnancy rate to 5% (although the typical-use pregnancy rate is 12% to 25%) (Jennings & Arevalo, 2008; Trussell, 2008). This is called the **Standard Days Method.** *Cyclebeads,* a string of 32 color-coded beads, help women using the Standard Days Method to keep track of their fertile days (see Figure 6–3). Women move a black rubber ring over one bead a day. Dark beads indicate a low risk of pregnancy and the 12 white beads a high risk. However, all it takes for the method to fail is just one cycle that is shorter or longer than previously observed.

There are two variations of the fertility awareness method that use biological markers to identify the time of ovulation.

Basal Body Temperature Method

A woman's basal (resting) body temperature rises by at least 0.4 degrees Fahrenheit about the time of ovulation and stays there for at least 10 days (Jennings & Arevalo, 2008). In the **basal body temperature**

Fertility awareness methods ■ Methods of birth control that attempt to prevent conception by having a couple abstain from sexual intercourse during the woman's ovulation.

Calendar method ■ A fertility awareness method of birth control that attempts to determine a woman's fertile period by use of a mathematical formula.

Standard Days Method ■ A fertility awareness method of birth control for women who typically have menstrual cycles of 26 to 32 days.

Basal body temperature ■ The temperature of the body while resting. It rises slightly after ovulation.

FIGURE 6–3 Cyclebeads are used by women who typically have menstrual cycles of 26 to 32 days. The white beads indicate high-risk days.

method, couples abstain from having sexual intercourse from the end of menstruation until about 4 days after a temperature rise is noted. The basal body temperature should be taken at the same time every day (with a special thermometer), preferably first thing in the morning (before going to the bathroom, eating, drinking, or smoking). Note that this method still involves a long period of abstinence. Even those women who attempt to use it properly often get pregnant, for its success depends on being able to detect a very small temperature increase (and, more importantly, is based on the assumption that the increase in body temperature is due to ovulation). The typical-use pregnancy rate is about 25 pregnancies per 100 couples per year (Trussell, 2008).

Billings Method (Cervical Mucus or Ovulation Method)

The fertility awareness method that is most widely used today is the **Billings method,** which attempts to pinpoint the time of ovulation by noting changes in the consistency of a woman's **cervical mucus.** It is named after two Australian doctors who developed

---

Billings method ■ A fertility awareness method of birth control in which changes in the consistency and quantity of cervical mucus are used to tell when ovulation has occurred.

Cervical mucus ■ The slimy secretion of mucous membranes located inside the cervix.

Sympto-thermal method ■ A combination of the basal body temperature and Billings fertility awareness met

Spermicides ■ Chemicals that kill sperm. In most products, the chemical is nonoxynol-9.

---

it (Billings et al., 1974). Mucus is discharged from the cervix throughout a woman's menstrual cycle, and its appearance changes from white (or cloudy) and sticky to clear, slippery, and stretchy (like that of an egg white) a day or two before ovulation. Typically, a woman notes this change with a finger test, that is, placing a finger in the vagina and then examining the mucus. A couple is instructed to abstain from sexual intercourse from the end of menstruation until 4 days after the mucus has changed consistency.

Theoretically, the Billings method has only a 3% pregnancy rate, but the typical-use pregnancy rate is much higher. Most studies have found about 22 to 25 pregnancies per year for every 100 couples using this method (Jennings & Arevalo, 2008; Trussell, 2008). Some couples combine the basal body temperature and Billings methods (along with other signs of ovulation, such as ovulatory pain) to enhance the effectiveness of these fertility awareness methods. This is often referred to as the **sympto-thermal method.** With perfect use, the pregnancy rate is 2% to 3% (Jennings & Arevalo, 2008).

Why are the typical-use pregnancy rates for the various fertility awareness methods so high when the perfect-use rates are much lower? Probably because the techniques require a great deal of training and a high level of motivation to abstain during the fertile period (the average period of abstinence for all of the fertility awareness methods is 10 to 17 days per cycle). Most of the pregnancies do, in fact, result from conscious deviations from the rules. However, another problem with any method based on changes in cervical mucus is that perhaps as many as one third of young women and women approaching menopause do not have the typical mucus pattern. Home test kits that can predict ovulation at least 5 days in advance are being developed, but as of 2010 none have proven reliable enough to be marketed (Jennings & Arevalo, 2008). Not surprisingly, only about 2% of all American women use fertility awareness for birth control.

SPERMICIDES: SUBSTANCES THAT KILL SPERM

Spermicides contain chemicals that kill sperm (*nonoxynol-9*). They are sold in a variety of forms. Spermicidal foams, jellies, creams, and film (VCF, or *vaginal contraceptive film,* is a square of film that is placed over the cervix) help hold the sperm-killing chemicals in the vagina against the cervix and simultaneously act as a barrier to sperm. Suppositories and tablets are also available. Specific instructions differ for each type of spermicide, but all of them must be placed in the back of the vagina shortly before sexual intercourse begins. They lose their effectiveness over time, so new spermicide must be inserted shortly before each time a woman has intercourse.

Surveys have found the typical-use rate to be about 29 pregnancies per 100 couples per year (Cates & Raymond, 2008; Trussell, 2008). In fact, when used alone, the perfect-use pregnancy rate is only 18%. One recent review concluded that spermicides "are not reliable if used alone" (Amy & Tripathi, 2009). Thus, spermicides are generally viewed as a method to be used in combination with barrier methods of contraception.

Initial studies suggested that in addition to their contraceptive benefit, spermicides reduced the risk of contracting sexually transmitted infections, including HIV. However, recent studies have found that spermicides *do not protect women* against gonorrhea, chlamydia, or HIV, and frequent use may even increase the risk of HIV sexual transmission (by irritating the vaginal lining) (see Boonstra, 2005; Cates & Raymond, 2008).

Most college women rate spermicides as one of their least preferred types of contraception. The most common complaint is that, like the condom and the diaphragm, inserting the spermicidal material just before intercourse interferes with the spontaneity of sexual relations and detracts from the mood. Others complain that spermicides are messy or detract from oral-genital sex. However, as a backup to barrier techniques, spermicides have advantages that for many women may outweigh the disadvantages.

BARRIER METHODS: PREVENTING SPERM FROM MEETING EGG

Barrier (blockade) methods of birth control are designed to prevent pregnancy by placing a blockade between the penis and cervix so that sperm cannot reach the egg if ovulation has occurred. Thus, these methods do not require you to abstain from sexual intercourse, but they may interfere with the spontaneity of sexual relations by requiring you to stop and put something on or put something in.

Male Condoms

Condoms ("rubbers," "safes," or prophylactics) are thin sheaths made of latex rubber, lamb intestine, polyurethane, or synthetic elastomers that fit over the penis and thus trap the sperm. About 97% of the condoms sold in the United States are made of rubber. Because they also serve as a barrier between the man's membranes and his partner's membranes, rubber condoms *are also highly effective in*

preventing the spread of many sexually transmitted infections, including HIV and HPV (National Institutes of Health Consensus Report and Centers for Disease Control and Prevention Fact Sheet—see Cates, 2003; Warner & Steiner, 2008; Winer et al., 2006). (Lamb intestine condoms do not prevent the spread of viruses.) In fact, condoms were originally invented for this purpose in the 1500s. A French writer in 1761 described condoms as "armor against love, gossamer against infection."

Today's condoms come rolled up, dry or lubricated, and in a variety of sizes, shapes, and colors. They present no major health hazards and are available without a prescription. There are only a few simple rules to remember:

1. Put the condom on before you start having intercourse. This is important to protect yourself from sexually transmitted infections, but many teens start sex without a condom and put one on later (Paz-Bailey et al., 2005). *Unroll it on the penis; do not try to yank it on like a sock* (see Figure 6–4). If the condom does not have a nipple tip, leave a little extra space at the tip of the penis to catch the ejaculate. If you are uncircumcised, pull back the foreskin while putting on the condom.

2. Hold on to the base of the condom when you are finished and withdraw. Otherwise, you might leave it and its contents in the woman's vagina.

3. Use a condom only once. If you have intercourse more than one time while having sex, use a new condom each time. If you try to reuse a condom it will eventually tear.

4. Check the expiration date. Do not store rubber condoms for long periods of time in a warm place (such as your wallet) or where they are exposed to light. This will eventually deteriorate them. Store them someplace cool, dark, and dry. Also, *do not use rubber condoms in combination with mineral oil, baby oil, vegetable oil, hand lotions, Vaseline, or other petroleum jellies*, for these, too, can damage them.

> "During a recent sexual experience, my partner and I used oil from one of those fancy 'bath and body stores' for lubrication in conjunction with a condom. During intercourse, the condom disintegrated."
> (from the author's files)

Barrier (blockade) method ■ General term for contraceptive methods that block the passage of sperm.

Condom ■ For men, a thin sheath made of latex rubber, lamb intestine, or polyurethane that fits over the penis. For women, a polyurethane intravaginal pouch held in place by two flexible rings. Condoms are effective as contraception and for prevention of sexually transmitted infections.

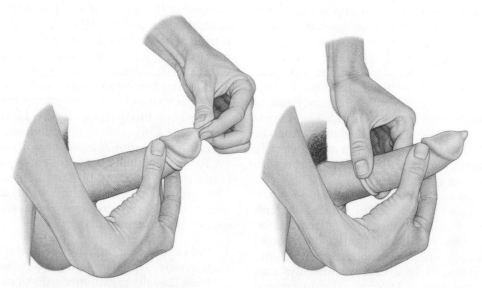

FIGURE 6–4 Use of the condom.

If a lubricant is needed, use a water-based one like K-Y Jelly or Today Personal Lubricant. Do not confuse "water-based" with "water-soluble." (The polyurethane condoms can be used with oil-based lubricants.) Some condoms are sold with spermicide, but the amount of spermicide is so small that they are no more effective (but more expensive) than other lubricated condoms (Warner & Steiner, 2008).

If these very simple instructions are followed, the perfect-use pregnancy rate is only about 2%. However, the typical-use rate is about 15 pregnancies per 100 couples per year (Warner & Steiner, 2008). Make sure that you use condoms that fit; otherwise, it can cause breakage or slippage (Crosby et al., 2010). Several studies have found that during human use, the breakage rate is about 3% during vaginal intercourse, but may be higher during anal intercourse. Condom failure due to breakage is most common among men who do not use condoms regularly (Messiah et al., 1997), and/or who do not use them properly (Crosby et al., 2002). Slippage of condoms occurs in about 2% of cases, often due to penetration beyond the end ring or improper withdrawal (see rule 2).

Condom use has increased dramatically since 1990, and it is now the third most popular method of contraception (Warner & Steiner, 2008). Nevertheless, recent studies have found that many unmarried men do not use condoms (Fortenberry, 2010; Martinez et al., 2006; Reece et al., 2010a). If condoms are so effective, why aren't all sexually active men using them? Here are some lines that women in my class have told me that men commonly use to keep from using a condom (Oncale & King, 2001):

"I promise I will not come in you."

"I will pull out before I nut."

"It doesn't feel the same."

"I can't feel anything with it on."

"I don't have a disease."

"If you're not having sex with anybody else, why should I use it? If you trust me, you wouldn't make me use it."

Before they have ever tried one, most men have heard many times that condoms will reduce sensitivity and sexual pleasure. The more that a man believes this, the less likely he will use condoms (Randolph et al., 2007). Many man actually lose their arousal because of their negative attitudes about condoms (and other safer-sex products) (Higgins et al., 2009). Their preconceived notions probably exaggerate the problem. Condoms will reduce a man's sensitivity, but only slightly. In fact, a nationally representative survey found that men who use condoms rate their sexual experience just as positively as men who do not use them (Sanders et al., 2010). *Consumer Reports* (1989) found that many men find the reduced sensitivity to be something positive because it makes sex last longer. Polyurethane condoms are only half as thick as rubber condoms and transmit heat better than rubber. Men generally prefer these to rubber condoms in regard to comfort, sensitivity, lack of smell, and natural feel.

Others complain that they are allergic to rubber. About 1% to 3% of men and women are allergic, but again, some condoms are made of natural animal membranes or polyurethane. Still others complain about the loss of spontaneity, that it is a nuisance to stop and put a condom on in the middle of having sex. How long does it take to put on a condom? The answer is, only a few seconds. These reasons for not wearing condoms are in many cases simply excuses. The real reason many men will not use condoms is that they are too embarrassed to go into a store and purchase them (Bell, 2009).

> "During high school, I was actually embarrassed to buy condoms. I only would get them in those bathroom machines. Perhaps if they were discreetly available, then more teens would buy them."
>
> (from the author's files)

A few women in my classes have said that they have talked a partner out of using a condom, but the large majority have to talk partners into using them. Here are some lines that women say they have used successfully to get a male partner to use a condom (Oncale & King, 2001):

> "No condom, no sex."
>
> "If you choose not to use a condom, you're choosing not to have sex with me."
>
> "If you don't use one, you won't get none."
>
> "It's not that I don't trust you; I don't trust who you've been with."
>
> "There will be no action in the ballpark until the player with the bat puts his glove on."

Remember, condoms are used for reasons other than to prevent pregnancy. If you are sexually active and have multiple partners over time, or if your partner has had multiple partners or is an intravenous drug user, you are in a high-risk category for contracting a sexually transmitted infection and should be using rubber condoms (see Box 6–A for additional information).

PERSONAL REFLECTIONS

Whose responsibility is it for birth control—your responsibility or your partner's? Why? If you answered that it is your partner's responsibility, do you think that you share any of the responsibility for the consequences of engaging in sexual intercourse?

The Female Condom

It was not until 1993 that we saw the introduction of the first woman-controlled barrier method of contraception designed to give simultaneous protection against sexually transmitted infections. The **female condom** (trade name: Reality), as it is called, is actually an intravaginal pouch—a 7-inch-long polyurethane bag that is held in place in the vagina by two flexible rings (see Figure 6–5). A woman inserts it with her fingers by pushing the closed-ended ring against the cervix, as she would a diaphragm. It

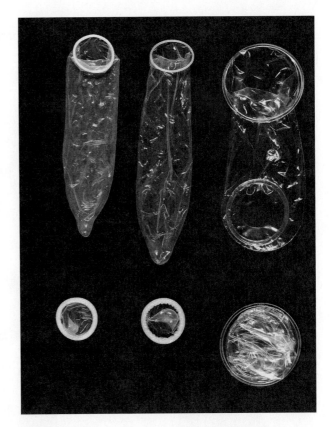

FIGURE 6–5 Male condoms (left and middle) are sold rolled and in two sizes. Female condoms (right) are intravaginal pouches that are held in place by two flexible rings.

is held in place by the outer ring, which fits on the outside of the vagina, partially covering the labia (see Figure 6–6). A new female condom (FC2) is softer and more flexible than the original. The female condoms raise no major health concerns and do not have adverse effects on the vaginal wall. Moreover, they offer protection against the bacteria and viruses that cause sexually transmitted infections (Cates & Raymond, 2008). Thus, for those women whose partners refuse to wear a male condom, the female condom provides them with the opportunity to protect their own health.

Many people are put off by the appearance of the female condom, but it is thinner than male condoms, feels softer than rubber, and transfers heat. Thus many of those who try it say that it feels more like unprotected intercourse than sex with male condoms.

> "I have never liked male condoms. Even when I would use extra lubricant the friction was very irritative. Then one day a friend suggested that I try using female condoms. I haven't used anything else since. Even my man says it feels like we aren't using anything at all."
>
> (from the author's files)

Diaphragm

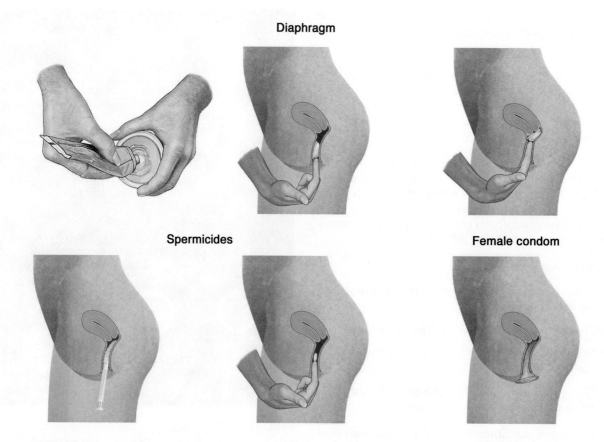

Spermicides   Female condom

FIGURE 6–6 Use of the diaphragm (with spermicide), spermicides (foam and suppository), and female condom.

The main complaint that women have about female condoms is the noise it makes during intercourse, but this can be eliminated by using additional lubricant.

Studies have found that the pregnancy rate during typical use is about 21% (Cates & Raymond, 2008; Trussell, 2008). Some of the failures are due to slippage, often the result of women failing to learn how to insert them properly. For those who use the female condom correctly, the first-year pregnancy rate is about 5% or less.

The Diaphragm

A **diaphragm** is a large, dome-shaped rubber cup with a flexible rim that fits over the cervix. It works by preventing the passage of sperm into the uterus. The ancient Greeks used empty pomegranate halves to block sperm from getting into the uterus, and in biblical times, women sometimes inserted camel or crocodile dung into the back of the vagina to prevent the sperms' passage. Fortunately for today's women, the rubber cup was invented in 1882 in Germany. By the 1930s, the diaphragm was being

used by one third of all couples who practiced birth control. With the introduction of the birth control pill in 1960, the use of the diaphragm became almost nonexistent.

A woman has to be fitted for a diaphragm by a physician or healthcare worker (the distance between her cervix and pubic bone is measured). She will then be given a prescription for a diaphragm that fits her. You may have to be refitted if your body undergoes any major changes (e.g., pregnancy or weight changes of 10 pounds or more). A woman getting her first diaphragm is also going to need instructions and coaching on how to insert it properly and quickly (see Figure 6–6).

After you have learned to insert your diaphragm properly, there are only a few simple rules to remember:

1. Most doctors still recommend that diaphragms be used with a spermicidal jelly because it improves the pregnancy rate a bit (Cates & Raymond, 2008). Spread spermicidal jelly on the inside part of the diaphragm (the part in contact with the cervix) and rim before insertion.

2. Insert the diaphragm no more than 3 hours in advance of starting intercourse. Otherwise, the spermicide dissipates and adds little additional protection. For maximal effectiveness, the

Diaphragm ■ A dome-shaped rubber cup with a flexible rim that fits over the cervix and thus acts as a contraceptive device by serving as a barrier to the passage of sperm into the uterus.

diaphragm should be put in immediately prior to intercourse, although this may interfere with spontaneity.

3. Leave the diaphragm in for 6 to 8 hours after intercourse to make sure that there are no more live sperm. If you have intercourse more than once while having sex, place more spermicide in the vagina before each time. Do not remove the diaphragm to do this (sperm may get into the cervix while the diaphragm is removed), but instead use a plunger or some other means of application. Do not leave a diaphragm in for more than 12 hours.

When used in combination with a spermicide, the perfect-use pregnancy rate for the diaphragm is usually stated as about 6% per year (Cates & Raymond, 2008; Trussell, 2008). The typical-use pregnancy rate is about 16% per year. About half of these pregnancies, particularly among young women, are due either to inconsistent or improper use.

Women with a history of urinary tract infections should not use a diaphragm, especially with a spermicide. On the other hand, the diaphragm may offer women some protection against cervical cancer and some sexually transmitted infections (Moench et al., 2001).

The most common complaint about the diaphragm is aesthetics. Some complain that insertion is a nuisance, interfering with spontaneity, and that spermicides can be messy and detract from such sexual behaviors as oral-genital sexual relations. These complaints are not heard as often, however, in women who are sexually experienced and in a monogamous relationship.

> "For years I used a diaphragm. My partners always said that they could not feel it in me and that it did not take away from their pleasure."
> (from the author's files)

FIGURE 6–7 The diaphragm.

The most important thing to consider is that the diaphragm offers an inexpensive, safe, and relatively effective means of birth control when used consistently and properly.

The Cervical Cap and FemCap

Like the diaphragm, the two contraceptive devices discussed here are barrier devices that are designed to prevent passage of sperm from the vagina into the uterus. Made of latex rubber, the **cervical cap** is smaller and more compact than a diaphragm and resembles a large rubber thimble (see Figure 6–8). *It is used with a small amount of spermicide* (for added effectiveness) and fits over the cervix by suction. Like with the diaphragm, women must be fitted by a doctor or healthcare worker. Insertion and removal of the cap are more difficult than for the diaphragm, but once in place it is more comfortable than the diaphragm and can be left in for 24 hours. Women should check each time after having sexual intercourse to make sure that the cap has not been dislodged.

Although the cervical cap is popular in parts of Europe, you may have trouble finding it in the United States. However, there is a new version of the cap called **FemCap** that is more readily available. Made of silicone (which is more comfortable than latex rubber), it has a concave side that fits over the cervix. Spermicide can be applied to both the inside and outside surfaces. Once inserted it can be left in place for as long as 48 hours (Cates & Raymond, 2008). *FemCap* comes in three sizes, and a woman must be fitted to find the one that best suits her.

Both of these cervical barrier devices require a prescription. One major advantage is that they can

FIGURE 6–8 The cervical cap (left) and FemCap.

Cervical cap ■ A contraceptive device that fits over the cervix by suction, thus blocking the passage of sperm into the uterus.

be placed in the vagina 6 to 8 hours before having intercourse. *FemCap* must be replaced with a new one after a year; diaphragms are good for several years. The first-year typical-use failure rate in women who have not had children is about 16%, but is only about 6% when used correctly. The pregnancy rate is higher for women who have given birth (Cates & Raymond, 2008).

The Contraceptive Sponge

The polyurethane Today **contraceptive sponge** is 2 inches in diameter and 1 inch thick, and contains spermicide (nonoxynol-9). It works by blocking the cervical opening and killing sperm (see Figure 6–9). In addition to the Today sponge, there is also a Canadian sponge called Protectaid that is available online.

The sponge has several advantages over the diaphragm. First, it does not require a pelvic exam. It is sold in one size without a prescription. Second, users report that it is very easy to insert. A woman simply moistens it with tap water and inserts it deep in the vagina. One side has a concave dimple that fits over the cervix to decrease the chance of it being dislodged. Last, but not least, it can be left in for 24 hours, during which period the woman may have intercourse as many times as she wishes without having to add more spermicide. The sponge has

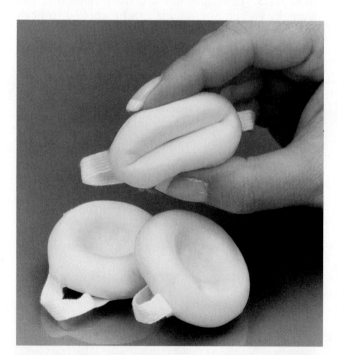

FIGURE 6–9 The contraceptive sponge.

Contraceptive sponge ■ A contraceptive device made of polyurethane sponge that contains enough spermicide to be effective for 24 hours after being inserted into the vagina.

Intrauterine device (IUD) ■ A birth control device, usually made of plastic with either a copper or progesterone coating, that is placed in the uterus to prevent conception and implantation.

a small loop on one side for removal, and is thrown away when the woman is done.

Studies of the effectiveness of the sponge show a typical-use pregnancy rate of about 16% for woman who have not had children, but only 9% with perfect use. However, the pregnancy rates are much higher (32% and 20%, respectively) for women who have given birth (Cates & Raymond, 2008).

Barrier Methods and Spontaneity

All of us, I suppose, would like our sexual relations to be passionate and spontaneous, with no interruptions. Putting on a condom or inserting a diaphragm, contraceptive sponge, or spermicide does not take very long for many sexually experienced people. Some individuals even integrate the use of barrier methods (e.g., putting on a condom) as part of foreplay. But some couples occasionally take chances and have unprotected intercourse because they do not want to stop and possibly ruin the mood. This is one of the most common cause of failure for barrier methods. The contraceptive techniques that we will cover next get around this problem by not requiring anything be done at the time when you want to have sex (except getting your partner in the mood, of course).

THE IUD

Can you guess what the most commonly used reversible contraceptive in the world is? No; it is not the birth control pill. It is the **IUD** (**intrauterine device**), used by over 100 million women worldwide (Rivera & Best, 2002; Salem, 2006). However, fewer than 2% of contraceptive users in the United States use an IUD. Why? The reputation of the IUD in the United States still suffers from the story of the Dalkon Shield, a very bad IUD that was removed from the market long ago (see Hubacher, 2002, for a full history). But let's look at today's IUDs.

The IUD is a small plastic or polyethylene device (of various shapes) that is placed into the uterus by a physician (see Figure 6–10). This is actually a very old idea—camel drivers used to insert a stone into a female camel's uterus to prevent pregnancy (don't ask me how they came up with this idea). IUDs work primarily by preventing fertilization, mostly by their effect on sperm transit through the uterus (Amy & Tripathi, 2009; Grimes, 2008). Contrary to what you may have heard, they do not work by causing an abortion. There are two IUDs sold in the United States today. The Copper-TCu 380A (Paragard) is made of polyethylene and has a fine copper wire wrapped around the vertical stem and both horizontal arms (see Figure 6–10). It remains effective for 10 to 12 years. The Mirena IUD is also made of polyethylene and slowly releases the hormone progesterone. It remains effective for 5 to 7 years. It is the copper and progesterone that impair the passage of sperm.

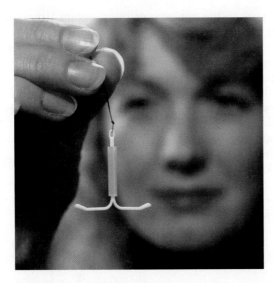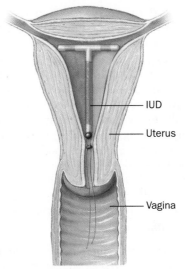

FIGURE 6–10 An IUD (intrauterine device), inserted (right).
Source: (right) Hock, *Human Sexuality,* © 2007 PrenticeHall, Inc. Reproduced by permission of Pearson Education, Inc.

These IUDs are highly effective, with typical-use pregnancy rates of much less than 1% per year (Grimes, 2008). Compared to long-term use of other contraceptives, they are also relatively inexpensive.

Once the IUD is inserted, the woman's uterus sometimes attempts to expel the foreign object (2% to 10% of first-year users) (Grimes, 2008). Because some women do not notice that their IUD has been expelled, manufacturers have added a polyethylene string to the IUD that protrudes from the cervix into the vagina so that women can check to see if their IUD is still in place. The copper IUD increases vaginal bleeding (which can be countered with drugs), whereas the Mirena IUD greatly reduces bleeding (a real advantage for women who normally have heavy menstruations).

Today's IUDs are not associated with an increased risk of pelvic inflammatory disease, ectopic pregnancy, or endometrial cancer. A woman becomes fertile again as soon as the IUD is removed (Amy & Tripathi, 2009).

Of those women who use an IUD, the large majority have a favorable opinion about it. The continuation rate, for example, is higher than for the birth control pill (Grimes, 2008). In many parts of the world, IUDs are inserted immediately after a woman has a baby.

> "After the birth of my second child, my doctor strongly advised no more children for a while. I was only 24 years old, so my doctor suggested an IUD. It was very easily done in the doctor's office and my doctor advised me it was safe to have sex right away. It was a wonderful method of birth control."
>
> (from the author's files)

Until recently, doctors have been cautious about prescribing IUDs to teenagers and young adults (because of the Dalkon Shield story). However, today's IUDs are regarded as perfectly safe for young women who are at low risk of contracting a sexually transmitted infection. In fact, both the American College of Obstetricians and Gynecologists and the World Health Organization now support use of the IUD by teens (Deans & Grimes, 2009; see also *Contraception,* 2010). In the words of two experts:

> **The contemporary copper intrauterine device (IUD) is one of the safest, most effective, and least expensive contraceptives available. It is a spectacularly effective, reversible contraceptive, rivaling female sterilization, injectables, and implants for pregnancy prevention. The IUD is convenient. Once inserted, it is nearly maintenance-free (except for monthly self-checks to locate the IUD string) for up to a decade. Only one follow-up visit to a healthcare provider after 1 month of use is suggested.** *(Rivera & Best, 2002, p. 385)*

HORMONAL METHODS OF CONTRACEPTION

Oral Contraception (The Birth Control Pill)

The birth control pill is one of the two most popular reversible methods of contraception. Worldwide, it is used by more than 100 million women (United Nations, 2001) and by over 10 million American women. In fact, 4 out of 5 American women who were born after 1945 have used birth control pills (Nelson, 2008).

The perfect-use pregnancy rate is close to zero (only 3 in 1000 during the first year of use). If a woman consistently follows just one simple rule, she really does not need to worry about getting pregnant. What is the rule? Take the pill every day, at the same time. However, the typical-use pregnancy rate is eight pregnancies per year for every 100 couples using the pill (Nelson, 2008). Most of the pregnancies that do occur are due to user, not method, failures. Studies show that 20% to 50% of pill users do not take their pills every day (see Smith & Oakley, 2005). If you forget to take the pill for even a couple of days, you should use a backup method of birth control until you have taken daily an entire package of pills. Women, as well as their doctors, should also be aware that *the pill is rendered less effective by simultaneous use of many types of antibiotics, barbiturates, analgesics, and tranquilizers.*

> "During our senior year in high school, my cousin came to me because she was afraid that she was pregnant. She was on the pill, and she was taking them correctly. We could not figure out what went wrong.... About a month before she became pregnant, she went to the doctor for a bad cold. It turned out that the medicine which was prescribed for the cold made the birth control less effective."
> (from the author's files)

There is really not just one pill, but several different types. In fact, there are over 70 types marketed in the United States. The most widely used and most effective are the **combination pills,** which contain synthetic *estrogen* and synthetic progesterone (*progestins*). Most contain a fixed amount of the two hormones in each capsule, but there are also combination pills (called *multiphasic* pills) that adjust the levels of progestins weekly in an attempt to mimic the natural hormonal phases of the menstrual cycle. Regardless of the type, most brands of the pill are taken for 21 days and then discontinued for 7 days to permit menstrual bleeding (and for a shorter, lighter period, some brands offer a pill with 24 days of hormones and 4 days off). Most companies package the 21 pills containing hormones with 7 additional pills that contain no hormones (placebos), so that women will not get out of the habit of taking a pill every day. New "extended cycle" pills are designed to reduce the number of menstrual periods. *Seasonale* is taken for 84 days in a row followed by 7 placebos, and thus women will have only four periods a year. Another pill (named *Lybrel*) suppresses monthly periods for an entire year. These extended cycle pills are just as safe as other combination birth control pills (Nelson, 2008; Teichmann et al., 2009).

The combination pill works primarily by (a) thickening cervical mucus, which prevents sperm from traveling, and (b) preventing ovulation. The hormones in

Combination pill ■ An oral contraceptive that contains both synthetic estrogen and synthetic progesterone.

Progestin-only pill ■ An oral contraceptive that contains only progestins.

the pill prevent the pituitary from releasing FSH and LH (see Figure 6–11). Without an egg present, it is impossible to get pregnant. When woman decide to stop using the pill, their menstrual cycles typically return to normal in about 2 weeks (Nelson, 2008).

There is also a **progestin-only pill** (also called the *minipill*) that contains only progestins. It works

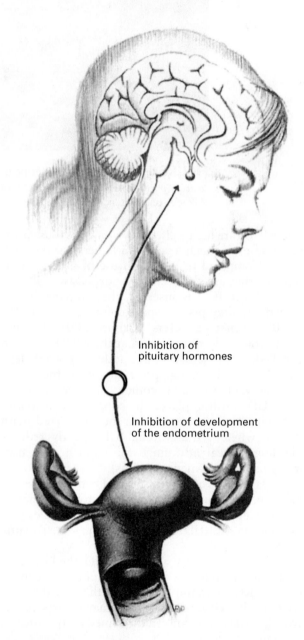

Inhibition of pituitary hormones

Inhibition of development of the endometrium

FIGURE 6–11 How oral contraceptives work.

Source: From Robert Demarest, *Contraception, Birth, and Contraception: A Visual Presentation,* 2e © 1976 The McGrawHill Companies, Inc. Reprinted by permission of The McGrawHill Companies. McGrawHill makes no representations or warranties as to the accuracy of any information contained in the McGrawHill Material, including any warranties of merchantability or fitness for a particular purpose. In no event shall McGrawHill have any liability to any party for special, incidental, tort, or consequential damages arising out of or in connection with the McGrawHill Material, even if McGrawHill has been advised of the possibility of such damages.

primarily by keeping cervical mucus thick, impairing the passage of sperm. Ovulation is often inhibited as well (Raymond, 2008). This pill is for women who are breast-feeding (estrogen inhibits milk production), or who cannot tolerate the side effects of the estrogen-containing pill. It is only slightly less effective than the combination pill, but just as safe, if not safer. However, in some women these pills may cause menstrual bleeding irregularities.

There was a decline in the use of the combination pill during the 1970s and early 1980s when discoveries of serious health risks were reported. However, these studies were conducted with the first-generation, high-dosage pill. Today's pills contain only a small fraction of the estrogen and progestins that the first-generation pills had. The combination pill also has some significant health benefits. Nevertheless, there are specific subgroups of women who should not use the combination pill. Let us examine the risks and benefits in detail.

Negative Side Effects and Health Risks: Facts and Myths

An early study claimed that some women showed a decreased sex drive after they begin to take the combination pill, and this was repeated in many women's magazines. However, a review of many studies found no evidence that this is true (Schaffir, 2006) and, in fact, most women on the pill show an increase in sexual interest and satisfaction (Nelson, 2008; Ott et al., 2008). And while a small percentage of women experience negative mood changes when they take oral contraceptives, most experience "less variability in [mood] across the entire menstrual cycle, and less negative affect during menstruation" (Oinonen & Mazmanian, 2002).

Some women do not use the birth control pill because they have heard that they might gain weight, but numerous clinical trials have demonstrated that this, too, is not true (Nelson, 2008).

It is not uncommon for women who are first starting to take the pill to experience some symptoms that mimic those of early pregnancy. These may include nausea, cramping, breast tenderness, and a bloated feeling. These responses usually occur during the days that women are not taking the hormone pills (i.e., they are taking the placebo pills). About half of women who choose to go off the pill do so because of these side effects (Amy & Tripathi, 2009). If these symptoms do not diminish within a few months, one good alternative is the "extended cycle" pills. Also, some of the newest oral contraceptives contain new types of progestins that do not result in as many of these side effects. Check with your doctor. As a result of the lowered dose of hormones in today's pill, breakthrough bleeding (i.e., bleeding during the 21 days of hormone use) sometimes occurs, but it usually

disappears during the first 4 months of use. Despite these problems, the large majority of women who use the pill have a very favorable opinion of it as a contraceptive technique.

A (very) few women experience hypertension as a result of the combination pill. They can switch to the progestin-only pill. They new low-dose combination pills do not cause diabetes. The incidence of headaches is no greater for women on the pill than it is for other women. However, the pill is not recommended for women who have migraine headaches with aura. Birth control pills also do not increase the risks of birth defects (in those women who take the pill when they do not know that they are pregnant) (see Nelson, 2008).

The first-generation, high-dosage oral contraceptives were associated with serious cardiovascular problems (blood clots, heart attacks, and strokes). What about today's low-dose pills? Pill users who are younger than 35, *do not smoke*, and do not have high blood pressure or diabetes have very little risk of stroke or heart attack (Nelson, 2008). The newest pills slightly increase the risk of a blood clot, but overall this is a rare event. Oral contraceptive users over the age of 30 who smoke still have an unacceptably high risk of heart attack and stroke and should not use the combination pill.

There were also concerns for many years that use of birth control pills containing estrogen would increase the risk of breast cancer. Although some studies claimed to have found a link between the pill and breast cancer, some 20 other studies, including one by the Centers for Disease Control and Prevention, have found that pill users are at little or no greater risk than nonusers. A review of 54 studies found that women currently taking the combination pill have only a slightly increased risk of breast cancer and that there was no increase in risk 10 years after stopping the pill (Collaborative Group on Hormonal Factors, 1996). More recent large studies also found little or no increased risk of breast cancer, including women with a family history of breast cancer (see Nelson, 2008).

Health Benefits

It must be emphasized that birth control pills *do not protect against* sexually transmitted infections. However, women who take the birth control pill are at less risk for some health problems than nonusers. The major benefits include a decreased risk of cancer of the endometrium and cancer of the ovaries, a substantial decrease in the number of benign breast tumors (one-fourth as likely), and reduced rates of ovarian cysts (one-fourth as likely), endometriosis, and pelvic inflammatory disease (one-half as likely) (Amy & Tripathi, 2009; Nelson, 2008). The birth control pill is also known to reduce premenstrual syndrome, reduce menstrual pain and bleeding (anemia is only two thirds as likely), and improve acne. In fact, some doctors prescribe the pill to women primarily to reduce menstrual problems, and only secondarily as a contraceptive technique.

> "I am now on the birth control pill.... My cramps were minimized a great deal and so was the length and heaviness of my period."
> (from the author's files)

For older women who do not smoke, are not obese, and do not have hypertension or cardiovascular problems, today's low-dosage pills are also being prescribed to regulate menstrual cycle disturbances that are common before menopause (Nelson, 2008).

Conclusions About Safety of the Pill

When considering the health risks associated with use of the pill, you should put things into proper perspective and compare the risks to what would happen if nobody used the pill. For women who do not smoke, *the health risks (including deaths) are significantly less than those caused by pregnancy and childbirth* (Nelson, 2008). In fact, a large study that followed over 46,000 women for 39 years recently concluded that women who have taken the birth control pill *"had a significantly lower rate of death from any cause,"* including cancer and heart disease (Hannaford et al., 2010).

Injectable Contraception ("The Shot")

If you are one of the 20% to 50% of women who cannot remember to take your oral contraceptive regularly, you might consider "the shot." **Depo-Provera** (or its new form called *Depo-subQ provera 104*) is an injectable drug containing a progestin (medroxyprogesterone acetate, or DMPA, a synthetic form of progesterone). All you have to remember is to return to the doctor every 3 months to get another shot. It works by preventing ovulation, thickening cervical mucus, and preventing buildup of the endometrium. After a woman stops injections, it often takes 9 to 10 months for fertility to return. The perfect-use pregnancy rate is only 0.3%, but the typical-use rate is 3% (because some women do not remember to get their shots on time) (Goldberg & Grimes, 2008). The shot *does not protect against sexually transmitted infections.*

Depo-Provera ■ Market name for medroxyprogesterone acetate, a chemical that when injected suppresses ovulation for 3 months.

Implanon ■ A hormone implant with a single progestin-releasing rod that is effective for 3 years.

Depo-Provera is a safe alternative for women who should not take estrogen (because of a history of stroke, for example) (Spencer et al., 2009). However, there are some possible side effects that might cause some women to discontinue this method. These include irregularities in menstrual bleeding and weight gain. Most women experience prolonged bleeding at first, but eventually little or no bleeding (although some women regard this as a positive effect). The shot also reduces bone density, but this is not permanent, (i.e., bone mineral density returns when a woman stops injections (Goldberg & Grimes, 2008; Spencer et al., 2009).

Hormone Implants

Norplant, the first hormonal implant, was designed to offer contraceptive protection for 5 years. It consisted of six flexible silicone tubes, each about the size of a match, that were inserted under the skin on the inside of a woman's upper arm. However, because of concerns that the hormone was not being released in adequate amounts and difficulties removing it, the manufacturer stopped making Norplant in 2002.

A new hormone implant that has been used in other countries for several years is now available in the United States (see Raymond, 2008). **Implanon** was approved for use in the United States in 2006. It is a single rod that contains progestin and remains active for 3 years. It works by thickening cervical mucus and preventing ovulation. The pregnancy rate is no greater than 1 in 1,000 women (Raymond, 2008). (Figure 6–12). As with all progestin-only techniques, the major side effect is irregular vaginal bleeding, often prolonged at first, followed by little or no bleeding. The changes are not as great as observed in women using Depo-Provera (Hubacher et al., 2009), and many teens prefer Implanon over the birth control pill (Lewis et al.,

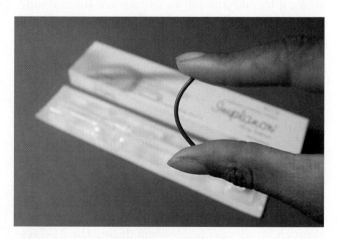

FIGURE 6–12 Implanon.

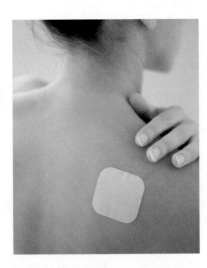

FIGURE 6–13 Two new alternatives to oral contraceptives are the contraceptive patch OrthoEvra (right; worn for 1 week; three weekly patches are followed by a patch-free week) and NuvaRing (left; a vaginal ring worn for 3 weeks, followed by a ring-free week).

2010). There is also an implant called **Jadelle** with two progestin-releasing rods that is effective for 5 years. The Food and Drug Administration approved Jadelle in 1996, but it is not yet marketed in the United States. It is being used in several European countries.

The Patch and the Ring

For women who want a highly effective hormonal contraceptive, but do not want to worry about remembering to take a pill every day, there are now two new alternatives. **OrthoEvra** is *a 20-square-cm patch* that you apply to the skin (on the abdomen, buttocks, upper torso, or upper arm) like a Band-Aid (see Figure 6–13). It stays in place for 1 week, even during exercise and bathing, and slowly releases estrogen and progestin (the same hormones as in the combination pill) into the bloodstream. Three patches (3 weeks) are followed by a patch-free week (menstruation). Studies show that more women remember to change their patches regularly than take their pills. The side effects are the same as low-dosage oral contraceptives (some women also experience skin reactions at the patch site). The patch also exposes women to higher levels of estrogen than the pill, thus the chance of a stroke is higher for the patch (but rare in both cases, less common than caused by pregnancy) (Jensen et al., 2008). Talk to your doctor first to make sure you are at low risk.

NuvaRing is a clear, flexible ring that is inserted into the vagina and worn for 3 weeks (see Figure 6–13). It, too, slowly releases estrogen and progestin, and after 3 weeks is removed for a

ring-free week (menstruation) before inserting another one. It may also be removed for a short time during sexual intercourse. The ring actually releases fewer hormones than the pill and thus is regarded as very safe (Nanda, 2008). The side effects are similar to the pill (some women may experience vaginal irritation and discharge), but like the patch, compliance rates are higher than for the pill.

The perfect-use pregnancy rate is about 0.3% for both the patch and the ring (Amy & Tripathi, 2009). *Neither one protects against sexually transmitted infections.*

EMERGENCY CONTRACEPTION

What options does a woman have if she has unprotected intercourse (resulting, for example, from unplanned intercourse, a condom tearing, forgetting to take her birth control pills, or rape)? If she acts within a few days, there is **emergency contraception.** If taken in a high enough dosage, many commonly used birth control pills can be used as emergency contraception within 5 days of intercourse (Stewart et al., 2008). However, the World Health Organization recommends *Plan B*.

Plan B is a progestin-only (0.75 mg levonorgestrel) emergency contraception product. Two pills are taken together or 12 hours apart. Plan B is 89% effective if taken within 3 days. It is now available in most drugstores without a prescription for women age 17 and older (some pharmacists refuse to carry it). Plan B may cause nonserious side effects such as nausea, headache, and breast tenderness. In 2010, the Food and Drug Administration approved a second emergency contraception pill—ulipristal acetate, marketed as *Ella*. It is effective for up to 5 days after unprotected intercourse (Thomas, 2010). Probably the most effective method of emergency contraception is implantation

---

Jadelle ■ A hormone implant with two progestin-releasing rods that is effective for 5 years.

OrthoEvra ■ A contraceptive patch (containing the same hormones as the combination birth control pill) that applies to the skin and is effective for 1 week.

NuvaRing ■ A flexible ring containing the same hormones as the combination birth control pill that is inserted into the vagina and is effective for 3 weeks.

Emergency contraception ■ Methods that prevent contraception when used in the first few days after sexual intercourse.

of a copper IUD (within 7 days after intercourse) (Stewart et al., 2008).

Emergency contraception is not an abortion! It is not the same as the abortion pill (RU 486). Emergency contraception works by preventing ovulation, fertilization, or implantation of a fertilized egg (the American Academy of Obstetrics and Gynecology defines pregnancy as implantation). If implantation of a fertilized egg has already occurred, emergency contraception is not effective—and will not harm the embryo. Now that emergency contraception is easily available, it could prevent as many as 1 million to 2 million unintended pregnancies each year and greatly reduce the number of abortions (Stewart et al., 2008). The availability of emergency contraception has not led to an increase in teenage sexual behavior (Harper et al., 2008).

VOLUNTARY STERILIZATION

The most commonly used method of contraception worldwide is sterilization; 220 million couples rely on it. Would you be surprised to learn that more Americans (about 15 million) also rely on **sterilization** for birth control than on any other birth control technique (Pollack et al., 2008)? For a couple to rely on this method, it is not necessary that they both be sterilized, so this figure is derived by adding male and female sterilizations (27% of contraceptive users rely on female sterilization and 9.2% on male sterilization). In fact, more than half of all married couples eventually use sterilization after the birth of their last planned child. Sterilization has recently become very popular among unmarried (especially African-American) women as well (Bumpass et al., 2000).

In men, the sterilization procedure is called **vasectomy.** In Western cultures, it has traditionally been done by making a small incision or two in the scrotum (under local anesthesia), then tying off, cutting, or cauterizing the vas deferens. The entire procedure takes only about 20 minutes. As an alternative, a "no-scalpel" vasectomy has been introduced from China. With this technique, the skin of the scrotum is simply pierced with a sharp instrument. It takes less than 10 minutes, produces less bleeding, and results in fewer infections (Pollack et al., 2008). Another technique is called *Vasclip,* a plastic clamp no larger than a grain of rice that

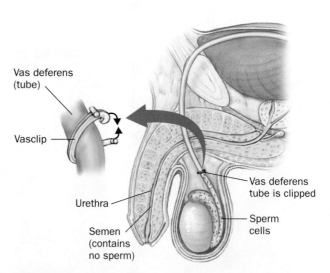

FIGURE 6–14 A vasectomy can be performed by cutting the vas deferens or, as shown above, by using a plastic clamp (Vasclip) to block the flow of sperm.

Source: Hock, *Human Sexuality* © 2007 PrenticeHall, Inc. Reproduced by permission of Pearson Education, Inc.

snaps onto the vas deferens to block sperm flow (see Figure 6–14). It causes less pain and fewer complications than traditional vasectomy.

A vasectomy does not interfere with the production of hormones or sperm in the testicles. New sperm simply cannot get past the point where the vas have been tied and cut, and eventually they are destroyed by other cells called phagocytes. Sperm that are already past this point at the time of operation, however, must be eliminated before a man is "safe." Other means of contraception should be used until the man has had 12 to 16 ejaculations. Some men are reluctant to get a vasectomy because they think that they will no longer be able to ejaculate (obviously confusing ejaculation with orgasm), but recall from Chapter 2 that nearly all of the fluid (about 98%) in a man's ejaculation comes from the prostate gland and seminal vesicles, which are unaffected by the procedure. A man with a vasectomy will still ejaculate during orgasm, but his ejaculation will contain no sperm.

In women, the term *tubal ligation* is often used for a variety of techniques, but the more descriptive term is **tubal sterilization.** There are three basic techniques. In all three, the Fallopian tubes are tied, cut, or clamped, to prevent passage of the egg and sperm (see Figure 6–15). The egg is absorbed by the woman's body. Unlike the male technique, a woman may safely engage in sexual intercourse as soon as she feels the desire to do so.

In a *minilaparotomy,* 1-inch incisions are made in the abdomen, and the Fallopian tubes are pulled to the opening and cut, tied, or blocked with clips.

Sterilization ■ A general term for surgical techniques that render an individual infertile.

Vasectomy ■ The male sterilization technique in which the vas deferens is tied off and cut, thus preventing passage of sperm through the reproductive tract.

Tubal sterilization ■ A female sterilization technique that originally referred only to the tying of the Fallopian tubes, but which is now often used as a general term for a variety of female sterilization techniques.

Box 6–A **Sexuality and Health**

Contraceptive Methods That Help Prevent Sexually Transmitted Infections

Sexually active individuals who are not in monogamous relationships must (and should) worry about sexually transmitted infections in addition to pregnancy. Unfortunately, contraceptive development has concentrated almost entirely on preventing pregnancy and has ignored STIs. What do we know about the effectiveness of currently available contraceptive devices in preventing STIs?

The contraceptive methods that are the most effective in preventing pregnancy (e.g., sterilization, implants, Depo-Provera, the IUD, and the birth control pill) offer no protection against STIs (see Hatcher et al., 2008). The same is true for fertility awareness methods. In fact, use of hormonal contraceptive techniques reduces the likelihood that teens will use condoms during sexual intercourse (Ott et al., 2002).

Until recently, it was believed that the active ingredient in most spermicides, nonoxynol-9, not only killed sperm but also was effective against most of the bacteria and viruses that cause STIs, including HIV. However, studies have shown that nonoxynol-9 does not protect against gonorrhea and chlamydia, and frequent use may actually increase an individual's risk of catching HIV from an infected partner by irritating the vaginal or rectal walls

and making transmission of HIV easier (Cates & Raymond, 2008).

What about the barrier methods of contraception? For men, of course, use of rubber condoms will reduce their risk of getting STIs that are spread by exchange of body fluids. "Skins" (condoms made of sheep intestine) have pores that are large enough for the passage of HIV and other viruses. Condoms also offer some protection against syphilis (Koss et al., 2009). Condoms break about 2% of the time during vaginal intercourse, and more often during anal intercourse (Warner & Steiner, 2008).

Of course, if condoms were always used correctly and consistently, their effectiveness at STI prevention would be much greater. In one study of 124 serodiscordant couples (only one member was HIV positive) who used condoms consistently, none of the HIV-negative partners became infected during a total of 15,000 acts of intercourse (De Vincenzi et al., 1994). Some groups have questioned the effectiveness of condoms, but both a National Institutes of Health Consensus Report and a Centers for Disease Control and Prevention Fact Sheet reached the same conclusion—condoms are effective in protecting against sexually transmitted infections (see Cates, 2003).

What about women and barrier methods? At first glance, an obvious choice might be to have their partners always wear condoms, but this "may be unrealistic because traditional sex roles in most cultures do not encourage a woman to talk about sex or to initiate sexual practices or otherwise control an intimate heterosexual encounter" (Rosenberg & Gollub, 1992). Among women at high risk for getting an STI, the female condom would appear to be a good alternative (Cates & Raymond, 2008). However, while most women at high risk are willing to try it, only a minority like it well enough to use it consistently. Diaphragms offer some protection against STIs, but are far from being highly reliable (Cates & Raymond, 2008).

The real hope for the future lies in development of a **microbicide,** a bacteria-and-virus-killing cream or gel that a person can apply vaginally or rectally before intercourse. Many types are now undergoing testing, and at least one (with the antiretroviral drug tenofovir) has proven very promising in clinical trials (*Time,* 2010). When these become available, women will indeed be able to take measures to protect themselves. However, do not expect them to reach the market for several years (Gabelnick et al., 2008).

A *laparoscopy* is a procedure in which a laparoscope, a long, tubelike instrument that transmits TV pictures, is inserted through a small incision in the navel. Once the tubes are located, surgical instruments are inserted through the laparoscope (or other tiny incisions) and the tubes are cut or cauterized. Both procedures are usually done with general anesthesia, but do not require lengthy hospitalization. Most women go home the same day.

In 2002, the Food and Drug Administration approved Essure, a nonsurgical (no incisions or punctures) technique (called *transcervical sterilization*) that does not require general anesthesia and takes only about half an hour to complete. With this technique, the Fallopian tubes are

reached via the cervix and a micro-insert is placed in each tube. The device looks like a little spring and is anchored inside the tubes by flexible coils. Dacron-like mesh in the coils then irritates the lining of the tubes, which results in scar tissue that plugs up the tubes. Most women are able to

Microbicide ■ A cream or gel that is applied intravaginally or intrarectally before sex in order to kill, block, or inactivate bacteria and viruses that cause sexually transmitted infections.

Laparoscopy ■ A technique that involves inserting a slender, tubelike instrument (laparoscope) into a woman's abdomen to examine (via fiberoptics) her reproductive organs or a fetus. The procedure is often used to perform female sterilizations.

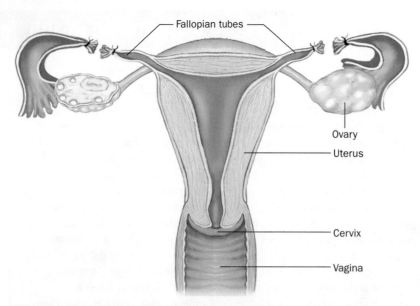

Fallopian tubes

Ovary
Uterus

Cervix

Vagina

FIGURE 6–15 With a tubal sterilization, the Fallopian tubes are cut or blocked so that a sperm and egg cannot meet.

Source: Hock, *Human Sexuality,* © 2007 PrenticeHall, Inc. Reproduced by permission of Pearson Education, Inc.

return to normal activities (including work) within 24 hours afterwards.

Complications

Surgical complications resulting from vasectomy are uncommon (less than 5%) and generally minor. Some sperm leak into the bloodstream, and as a result, at least half of the men who have had a vasectomy produce antibodies to their own sperm. However, several large studies have concluded that this has not resulted in any health problems (Pollack et al., 2008). A few studies raised concerns that vasectomy might increase men's risk of prostate cancer. However, after a scientific panel at the National Institutes of Health met to discuss these findings, they concluded that there was no evidence that vasectomy increased the risk of prostate cancer (see Cox et al., 2002).

Sterilization in women has a definite health benefit: It substantially decreases their risk of getting cancer of the ovaries (Pollack et al., 2008). However, some physicians have suggested that there is a "post–tubal ligation syndrome" characterized by heavier-than-normal menstrual bleeding and more severe menstrual cramps. Studies conducted by the World Health Organization found no increase in menstrual bleeding associated with sterilization (World Health Organization, 1984, 1985), and a later large-scale study found that most women experienced no change or a decrease in menstrual and other uterine bleeding (Peterson et al., 2000). On the other hand, for reasons that

are not yet known, women who have had tubal sterilization are more likely than other women to eventually have a hysterectomy (Pollack et al., 2008).

Can Sterilizations Be Reversed?

Sterilization procedures are highly effective, with failure rates of 0.15% for male sterilization and 0.5% for female sterilization (Trussell, 2008). Today, they should also be considered permanent. Few people who decide to be sterilized ever wish to have the procedure reversed. About 5% of men eventually regret the decision, as do 5% of women over the age of 30. About 20% of women under 30 regret the decision (Amy & Tripathi, 2009). For those who want a reversal, there is no guarantee of success. The problem is that the sewing together of the vas deferens or Fallopian tubes requires very skilled microsurgery techniques (the inside diameter of a Fallopian tube, for example, is no greater than a human hair). The pregnancy rate after vasectomy reversal is between 38% and 89% (Pollack et al., 2008). Success depends on the length of time since the vasectomy. This is probably due to the increased levels of the man's antibodies to his own sperm. Successful reconstruction of the Fallopian tubes is very difficult because the slightest scarring can impair passage of the egg (and result in tubal pregnancy even if fertilization occurs). Success rates range from 43% to 88%, depending largely on the original type of sterilization. So, while there have been successful reversals in both men and women, the success rates are still far less than 100%. Therefore, only people who are quite sure that they do not want any more children should opt for these procedures.

If a couple decides that they do not want any more children, which person should agree to be sterilized? Perhaps this will help: A recent review concluded that "Vasectomy is simpler, safer, less expensive, and as effective as female sterilization" (Pollack et al., 2008, p. 381).

PERSONAL REFLECTIONS

Considering all factors (including your sexual lifestyle), which birth control technique is best for you? If you are not presently using it, how can you obtain it?

FUTURE TECHNOLOGY

In more and more societies, rich with technological diversity and replete with seemingly endless permutations of consumer goods, it is odd indeed that [the present array of contraceptive technologies], central to the lives of so many individuals, families and societies, is so limited. *(Harrison & Rosenfield, 1996)*

There has been considerable research and development of female-controlled barrier methods of contraception that will be easier to use and more comfortable than the diaphragm and female condom (Gabelnick et al., 2008). Two silicone devices (more comfortable than rubber) are in the final stages of testing. The *SILCS intravaginal barrier* resembles a diaphragm, but does not require fitting by a doctor (one size fits all) and is easier to insert and remove. The *Ove's contraceptive cap* resembles a cervical cap in that it fits over the cervix and can be left in place for 3 days. It is currently used in England and France.

In addition to vaginal microbicides (see Box 6–A), researchers are working on a medication that would block movement in the tail of the sperm, thus preventing them from swimming (Carlson et al., 2003). If perfected, woman would take a pill shortly before or just after having sexual intercourse. A similar drug has been found that prevents the heads of sperm from penetrating the membrane of an ovum, but in this case the drug would be taken by the man (Travis, 2001).

Research into a *male pill* continues, but do not expect it on the market any time soon. The problem is trying to find a pill that inhibits sperm production without simultaneously lowering sexual desire or a man's ability to get and maintain an erection. There was some success with *gossypol*, a Chinese derivative of cottonseed oil that disables sperm-producing testicular cells, but acceptance is unlikely because as many as 20% of men who take it remain permanently sterile (Coutinho et al., 2000). Present research is focusing on the administration of hormones to block the pituitary hormones responsible for sperm production (see Chapter 3), while simultaneously delivering other hormones to assure that there will be no loss of sex drive. The most likely choice appears to be a combination of progestin and androgens (Liu et al., 2008). This may be available as a male hormonal contraceptive within a few years in some Asian countries.

One promising future means of birth control is *vaccination* (Stewart & Gabelnick, 2004). It might be possible to prevent pregnancy the same way you can the flu. Researchers are trying to develop vaccines that will cause the body to produce antibodies to proteins in either sperm or eggs (e.g., O'Rand et al., 2004). Scientists in India are already clinically testing a vaccine that stimulates the production of antibodies to HCG (human chorionic gonadotropin), a hormone necessary to maintain pregnancy. With this vaccine, a fertilized egg could not implant and would be discharged during menstruation. In another variation, if women could be inoculated with a vaccine that triggered production of antibodies to a protein found only in sperm, this would prevent fertilization. However, the pharmaceutical industry has greatly slowed research in this area because of concerns about being sued should a vaccine result in any healthcare problems (Schwartz & Gabelnick, 2008).

Development of drugs for contraception is a long, expensive process—up to 14 years for approval and an investment of $400 million to $800 million. Government funding for contraceptive research is less than it takes to develop one new product (Gabelnick et al., 2008). However, the biggest deterrent to new contraceptive methods is not technology or lack of research, but an insurance–product liability problem. American consumers are accepting of the fact that contraceptive methods sometimes fail to prevent pregnancy, but they are less forgiving about side effects. When a legal case involves an individual versus a large corporation, juries often award large settlements to the individual in the belief that the corporation can afford it. A jury awarded $5 million, for example, to a couple who claimed that their child's birth defects were caused by spermicides, even though the authors of the study that claimed to link spermicides with birth defects had repudiated their own results. A few more cases like this and we may see the end of spermicides, the contraceptive sponge, and all hormonal methods of contraception. In just the last few years we have seen Norplant and Lunelle taken off the market.

Financial factors, political pressures and legal concerns are among the obstacles that have impeded the research and development of new contraceptive products in the United States.... Insofar as contraception is bound up with sexuality, it is subject to the same cultural, moral and religious influences, and therefore has political as well as personal dimensions. The growing threat of lawsuits, even those resulting in favorable outcomes, has imposed substantial costs on the pharmaceutical industry and chilled its involvement in contraceptive research. *(Baill et al., 2003)*

There has never been a contraceptive device that was not associated with some risk, but unless consumers change their attitudes and stop unrealistically expecting perfection, we may retreat to the days when there was nothing available except the condom.

RIGHT, THE PRICE OF AN IUD *IS* PRETTY STEEP. HERE'S THE INSTALLMENT PLAN: WE HAVE 21 YEARS TO PAY $230,000, PLUS TUITION.

© Nick Galifianakis

TERMINATING PREGNANCIES: ABORTION

There is no reversible method of contraception that is 100% effective (although implants, Depo-Provera, and the IUD come close); thus, unwanted pregnancies sometime occur even for couples who are using the most reliable forms of contraception. If an unwanted pregnancy should occur, a woman (or a couple) really has only three options: to continue with the pregnancy and keep the baby; to continue with the pregnancy and put the baby up for *adoption;* or to terminate the pregnancy (**abortion**). Of these three options, only abortion can be considered a method of birth control.

Over 40 million abortions are performed annually throughout the world, of which only about 60% are performed under safe conditions by

---

Abortion ■ Termination of pregnancy. Depending on how far the pregnancy has advanced, this can be done by taking a pill (RU 486); scraping the uterine lining (dilation and curettage); removing the uterine lining by suction (dilation and evacuation); or inducing labor (by injecting hypertonic saline or prostaglandins).

---

trained providers (Sedge, et al., 2007). Worldwide, about 80,000 deaths during pregnancy are the result of unsafe abortions (Shears, 2002a). In the United States, about one fourth of pregnancies end in abortion (Paul & Stewart, 2008), about 1.2 million per year. After declining for about a decade, the teen pregnancy and abortion rates increased in 2006 (Guttmacher Institute, 2010). Abortion rates are highest for women who are unmarried and economically disadvantaged (Jones et al., 2002a). While the abortion rate is high among teens who get pregnant, about one third of women over 40 who get pregnant choose to have an abortion (Nelson & Stewart, 2008).

Nearly 90% of all women who obtain abortions do so within 12 weeks of conception (Guttmacher Institute, 2007b). One of the most widely used arguments today by abortion opponents is that "abortion harms women." Well-conducted scientific studies do not support this (see Jordon & Wells, 2009). Death resulting from a legal abortion is very uncommon—less than 1 per 100,000 abortions—and, in fact, is much less common than deaths resulting from childbirth. Modern first-trimester abortions do not increase a woman's subsequent risk of infertility, miscarriage, ectopic pregnancy, or having a low-birthweight baby (see Paul & Stewart, 2008). They also do not increase the risk of developing breast cancer (Henderson et al., 2008; Paul & Stewart, 2008).

What are some of the possible consequences of legalizing abortion? Of abolishing abortion? If abortion were made illegal in the United States, it would result in an increase of 440,000 births per year (Levine et al., 1999). In Romania, the abolishment of legalized abortion led to the highest maternal mortality rate in Europe and the abandonment of tens of thousands of children in institutions (Stephenson et al., 1992).

There are several methods used to terminate a pregnancy (see Paul & Stewart, 2008):

1. *Medical (nonsurgical) abortion:* RU 486, or mifepristone, is a pill that can be used to chemically induce an abortion up to 8 weeks after a woman's last menstrual period. It is distributed under the name Mifeprex. It is about 92% effective when taken in combination with oral prostaglandins (misoprostol, which causes contractions of the uterus that expel the embryo) within the first 7 weeks after implantation. RU 486 works by blocking the body's use of progesterone, the hormone necessary for maintaining the endometrium of the uterus, thus causing shedding of the uterine lining. Another drug combination (methotrexate and misoprostol) has proven to be equally effective in terminating early pregnancies. In both cases, a woman

takes the first drug at a doctor's office and the second drug at home 6 hours to 3 days later. The main side effects are nausea, cramping, and prolonged uterine bleeding. For these reasons, many women may prefer the surgical abortion (D & E), which is completed in 1 day. Of course, the advantage of chemical abortion is greater privacy; a woman does not have to go to an abortion clinic.

2. *Dilation and curettage (D & C):* Once the standard procedure for unwanted pregnancies of 15 weeks or less, D & C procedures are now used less and less for purposes of abortion. Under general anesthesia, a woman's cervix is dilated, and the lining of the uterus is then scraped with a metal instrument called a curette. In addition to the risks associated with general anesthesia, this procedure results in more bleeding and discomfort than D & E procedures (next).

3. *Dilation and evacuation (D & E):* In this procedure, which does not require general anesthesia, a tube is inserted through the cervix and the fetal material is removed by suction. About 88% of all legal abortions in the United States are now performed by this method. Today, with use of a hand-held vacuum syringe, the procedure can be done 8 days after conception, and it takes only 5 minutes. For early abortions, most women prefer D & E over medical abortions because of the ease, quickness, and less bleeding and discomfort. D & E can be done without anesthesia in the first 4 to 6 weeks of pregnancy, but requires local anesthesia and dilation of the cervix for pregnancies terminated during weeks 7 through 12. Later-stage abortions may require gentle scraping of the uterine walls in addition to suction.

4. *Induced labor:* This method is used exclusively for termination of pregnancies that have proceeded beyond 16 weeks (which accounts for less than 5% of all abortions). A solution of hypertonic saline or prostaglandins (hormones that cause smooth muscle contractions) is injected into the amniotic sac and induces labor within 12 to 36 hours. The fetus is born dead.

Emotional Reactions to Having an Abortion

Most women have abortions because of limited resources (e.g., interference with work, being financially unable to provide for a child) and lack of partner or family support (Finer et al., 2005). Nevertheless, for some women abortion is very difficult:

"At the age of 18 I became pregnant. My boyfriend of 4 years and I had recently broken up, so I was alone. I suppose I could have told my parents, but I was too scared of their reactions. At three months I terminated my pregnancy. It hurt very badly

emotionally. Occasionally I think of how old my baby, boy or girl, would be today."
(from the author's files)

Large, well-conducted studies have found that women who have first-trimester abortions do not experience emotional or psychological problems afterwards at a rate any greater than women who give birth to unwanted babies (Charles et al., 2008; Major et al., 2009). In fact, most feel a sense of relief because of compelling health or economic considerations (Westhoff et al., 2003). Women who became pregnant before age 21 and chose abortion later achieve a higher level of education than do those who did not have an abortion (Fergusson et al., 2007).

The Present Status and Future of Abortion in the United States

Abortion is a subject that has polarized people throughout the nation. Those opposed to abortion ("right-to-lifers") express concerns about protecting human life. "Pro-choicers," on the other hand, wish to retain the right of individuals to make decisions about something that will have a major impact on their own lives. In national surveys conducted in 2010, 45% of people identified themselves as pro-choice and 47% as pro-life (Gallup Poll); 38% believed that abortion was morally acceptable, 50% said morally wrong, and 9% said it depended on the situation (Gallup Poll); yet 59% wanted the U.S. Supreme Court to uphold *Roe v. Wade*, while only 38% wanted it overturned (ABC News/*Washington Post* Poll).

The laws regarding abortion have been in a state of transition for over 3 decades. Prior to 1973, each state could allow or prohibit abortion as it wished, but in that year a 7 to 2 Supreme Court decision (*Roe v. Wade*) prohibited the states from interfering with decisions made between a woman and her doctor during the first 3 months of pregnancy. The ruling also prevented states from prohibiting abortion in the second trimester of pregnancy, but did allow for more regulations designed to protect a woman's health (hospitalization, e.g.). Antiabortion forces won a victory in 1977 when the Supreme Court upheld the Hyde Amendment, which disallowed the use of federal Medicaid money to pay for abortions. Without public funding, obtaining a legal abortion became difficult for women with limited incomes. The number of abortion providers also decreased substantially during the 1990s, falling from 2,400 in 1992 to 1,800 in 2000 (Guttmacher Institute, 2007b).

Although the decision in *Roe v. Wade* giving a woman the right to choose is still the law, subsequent court decisions have given states greater leeway in regulating abortion. In 1989, a sharply divided Supreme Court upheld by a 5-to-4 vote (*Webster v.*

Reproductive Health Services) a Missouri law that further restricted public funds and facilities for abortions and that also required physicians to test for fetal viability (the potential for the fetus to survive) at 20 weeks. The earliest point of fetal viability is 24 weeks (the law allowed for a 4-week margin of error in determining the time of conception), and the vast majority of abortions have already been performed before the 20th week. Today, in many states, opponents of abortion are attempting to pass laws banning abortion at the 20th week of pregnancy with the argument that at that point a fetus can feel pain (Young, 2010). In 1990, the Court voted 6-to-3 to uphold state laws that ban abortions for girls under the age of 18 unless a parent is notified. In a 1992 case (*Planned Parenthood v. Casey*), the Court, in another 5-to-4 vote, upheld a Pennsylvania law that imposed a 24-hour waiting period, required doctors to tell women about other options, and also required parental notification in the case of minors. In 2003, President Bush signed a bill passed by the United States Congress that banned "partial birth" abortions and this was upheld by a 5-to-4 decision by the Supreme Court in 2007 (*Gonzales v. Carhart*).

Religious beliefs regarding abortion have often changed as well. Within the Catholic Church, for example, the first pope to declare that abortion was murder was Sixtus V in 1588, but that was reversed just 3 years later by Pope Gregory XIV. For the next 300 years, abortion was allowed up to the time of what was termed "animation by a rational soul" (up to 40 days after conception in the case of a male embryo and for the first 80 days in the case of a female fetus; Connery, 1977; Grisez, 1970). In 1869, however, Pope Pius IX again declared that abortion was murder, and this has remained the belief of every pope since.

With the diversity of opinion regarding this subject, religious and legal beliefs about abortion will probably continue to change for many decades to come. In the meantime, both sides would probably benefit by supporting an increase in family planning services. Many studies have shown that "increasing the use of effective contraception leads to declines in induced abortion rates" (Shears, 2002b; see also Marston & Cleland, 2003). For example, in Russia and Eastern Europe, where until recently contraception was not readily available, abortion rates fell dramatically in the 1990s as effective contraceptive techniques became more available (Henshaw et al., 1999).

CHOOSING A CONTRACEPTIVE METHOD

It is important that men and women choose a method of birth control with which they and their partner are comfortable. A woman may like the diaphragm, but it will not be good if her partner resents her stopping in the middle of having sex to put it in. A man may prefer that his female partner take the pill, but it will not be good for the couple's relationship if she resents having to suffer possible side effects. A couple can work these kinds of problems out only by talking about the matter and communicating with each other on a regular basis.

Choosing a particular birth control method does not mean that you have to stick with it if you are unhappy about it for any reason. As you know by now, there are many alternatives. For example, about 40% of married women and 61% of unmarried women using contraception switch their contraceptive method within 2 years (Grady et al., 2002). Unfortunately, many of these women use no type of contraception at all for at least a month after stopping use of their first choice (Grady et al., 2002). If you do not presently wish to have children and are unhappy with the birth control method you use, decide on an alternative method *before* you stop using your present one.

When deciding which type of birth control to use, ask yourself the following questions; they were developed to help you decide whether the method you are considering is a good choice or a poor choice *for you* (adapted from Robert Hatcher et al., 2004. Reprinted with permission of the publishers.)

Method of birth control you are considering using: _____

Length of time you used this method in the past: _____

Answer "yes" or "no" to the following questions:	**Yes**	**No**
1. Have I had problems using this method before?	____	____
2. Have I ever become pregnant while using this method?	____	____
3. Am I afraid of using this method?	____	____
4. Would I really rather not use this method?	____	____
5. Will I have trouble remembering to use this method?	____	____
6. Will I have trouble using this method correctly?	____	____
7. Do I still have unanswered questions about this method?	____	____
8. Does this method make menstrual periods longer or more painful?	____	____

9. Does this method cost more than I can afford? _____ _____
10. Could this method cause me to have serious complications? _____ _____
11. Am I opposed to this method because of any religious or moral beliefs? _____ _____
12. Is my partner opposed to this method? _____ _____
13. Am I using this method without my partner's knowledge? _____ _____
14. Will using this method embarrass my partner? _____ _____
15. Will using this method embarrass me? _____ _____
16. Will I enjoy intercourse less because of this method? _____ _____
17. If this method interrupts lovemaking, will I avoid using it? _____ _____
18. Has a nurse or doctor ever told me not to use this method? _____ _____
19. Is there anything about my personality that could lead me to use this method incorrectly? _____ _____
20. Am I at any risk of being exposed to HIV (the AIDS virus) or other sexually transmitted infections if I use this method? _____ _____

Total Number of "Yes" Answers: _____ _____

(Adaptation from *Contraceptive Technology*, 18th ed. (p. 6-54), R.A. Hatcher et al., 2004, New York: Ardent Media. Adapted with permission.)

Most individuals will have a few "yes" answers. "Yes" answers mean that potential problems may lie in store. If you have more than four "yes" responses, you may want to talk to your physician, counselor, partner, or friend. Talking it over can help you to decide whether to use this method, or how to use it so it will really be effective for you. In general, the more "yes" answers you have, the less likely you are to use this method consistently and correctly.

This chapter has only introduced the various contraceptive methods. If additional information is desired, you are urged to contact your local Planned Parenthood organization or your state family planning clinic. The people who work there will be glad to help you.

Sex is for people who are ready and willing to take a lifetime responsibility for the outcome of sex. *(Sue Finn, as quoted by L. Smith, 1993)*

STUDY GUIDE

KEY TERMS

abortion 160
adoption 160
barrier (blockade) method 145
basal body temperature 143
Billings method 144
calendar method 143
cervical cap 149
cervical mucus 144
combination pill 152
condom 145
contraception 136
contraceptive sponge 150
Depo-Provera 154
diaphragm 148
dilation and curettage (D & C) 161

dilation and evacuation (D & E) 161
douching 142
emergency contraception 155
female condom 147
FemCap 149
fertility awareness methods 143
Implanon 154
IUD (intrauterine device) 150
Jadelle 155
lactational amenorrhea method (breast-feeding) 142
laparoscopy 157
microbicide 157
nonoxynol-9 144

NuvaRing 155
OrthoEvra 155
perfect-use pregnancy rate 139
progestin-only pill 153
progestins 152
RU 486 160
spermicides 144
Standard Days Method 143
sterilization 156
sympto-thermal method 144
tubal sterilization 156
typical-use pregnancy rate 140
vasectomy 156
withdrawal (coitus interruptus) 141

INTERACTIVE REVIEW

The teen pregnancy rate in the United States is (1) _____ as high as in most other developed countries. About 78% of pregnancies to teenagers in the United States are unintended, and (2) _____ are terminated by abortion. Unfortunately, the teens most likely to have babies are those least prepared to take care of them.

Worldwide, there is need for effective contraceptive technology. World population is expected to increase to over 9 billion by the middle of this century, yet already there are many parts of the world experiencing food shortages and mass starvation.

While all the methods of birth control discussed in this chapter are better than using nothing, some are more effective than others. The best way to avoid unintended pregnancy is (3) _____. Relatively ineffective methods include withdrawal and douching. Methods that require fertility awareness are called the (4) _____, (5) _____, and (6) _____ methods. They rely on calculating when (7) _____ will occur and abstaining from intercourse during that period. The typical-use pregnancy rates for these methods are higher than for most others. The (8) _____ method works by breast-feeding inhibiting pituitary hormones. (9) _____ work by killing sperm and are generally used in combination with a barrier method of contraception— (10) _____, (11) _____, (12) _____, or (13) _____. Barrier methods block sperm from getting into the (14) _____. Barrier methods often interfere with spontaneity, but for people who are not in a monogamous relationship, a major advantage of these methods (not offered by other methods) is that they (15) _____.

Intrauterine devices (IUDs) have had a reputation for causing serious problems, but today's IUDs are safe as well as highly effective. However, they are recommended only for women who are at low risk of contracting sexually transmitted infections. The combination birth control pill contains synthetic (16) _____ and (17) _____ and works by preventing ovulation. The pills used today contain low dosages of estrogen and are safer than the high-dosage pills used in the past. Nevertheless, there are certain groups of women who, for medical reasons, should not take the pill. The (18) _____ and (19) _____ contain the same hormones as the combination pill, but do not require that a woman remember to use contraception every day. (20) _____ (the shot good for 3 months) and (21) _____ (the single-rod implant good for 3 years) contain only progestin and are believed to be safer than the pill. All three hormonal methods of contraception have theoretical failure rates of less than 1%. For women who have had unprotected intercourse, emergency contraception pills are effective when taken within (22) _____ hours of intercourse, or an IUD may be implanted within 7 days.

If you consider male and female sterilization techniques together, more Americans rely on sterilization for birth control than any other method. In a vasectomy, the (23) _____ is tied off and cut. Afterwards, the man still ejaculates during orgasm, but his ejaculation contains no sperm. For a (24) _____ or (25) _____, a woman's Fallopian tubes are cut, cauterized, or blocked by clips. In a new nonsurgical technique (Essure), the tubes are blocked by a micro-insert. The failure rate is close to zero.

For women who have an unplanned or unwanted pregnancy, one option is abortion. Various techniques can be used to terminate pregnancy, including chemicals, scraping or suctioning away of the endometrium, and induced labor.

It is important for you to choose an effective contraceptive technique before you have sexual intercourse. A questionnaire is provided at the end of the chapter that is designed to help you decide which method is best for you.

SELF-TEST

A. TRUE OR FALSE

- [T] [F] 26. The contraceptive sponge is effective for 24 hours.

- [T] [F] 27. Sweden and Denmark have substantially lower teenage birth rates than the United States.

- [T] [F] 28. The world population is expected to stabilize by the year 2010 because of increased use of birth control.

- [T] [F] 29. The U.S. fertility rate is presently about 2.1 births per woman.

- [T] [F] 30. If the perfect-use pregnancy rate for a contraceptive method is 20%, then for 100 couples who start using the method, about 20 of them will have conceived after 3 years.

- [T] [F] 31. In order for a woman to get pregnant, she must have an orgasm.

T F 32. More couples rely on sterilization than on the birth control pill.

T F 33. It is possible for a girl to get pregnant as soon as she starts having menstrual periods.

T F 34. A relatively effective method of birth control for women is to wash out the contents of the vagina immediately after sexual intercourse.

T F 35. The birth control pill reduces the risk of getting a sexually transmitted infection.

T F 36. A vasectomy works as birth control by preventing ejaculation.

T F 37. If carefully washed and dried, male condoms can be used safely on more than one occasion.

T F 38. Most women gain weight when they start taking the birth control pill.

T F 39. The contraceptive sponge is more effective than the diaphragm.

T F 40. Taking antibiotics makes the birth control pill less effective.

T F 41. Legal abortions do not increase a woman's later risk of infertility, miscarriage, or a low-birth-weight baby.

T F 42. Today's IUDs are effective and considered to be safe products.

T F 43. The major difference between the cervical cap and the diaphragm is that the cervical cap does not need to be used with spermicide.

T F 44. Emergency contraceptive techniques work by causing abortion.

T F 45. Breast-feeding a baby inhibits the release of follicle-stimulating hormone from a woman's pituitary gland.

T F 46. The patch and vaginal ring are just as effective as the combination birth control pill.

T F 47. Pregnancy and childbirth result in more maternal deaths than does the use of the birth control pill.

T F 48. In the future, it will probably be possible to be vaccinated to prevent pregnancy (as is done for the flu).

T F 49. Rubber condoms are more effective than "skin" condoms for prevention of STIs.

T F 50. The female condom is actually an intravaginal pouch.

T F 51. In high dosages, combination birth control pills can be used as emergency birth control.

T F 52. Most women who are over the age of 40 and do not smoke can continue to take the combination birth control pill.

T F 53. The diaphragm offers women some protection against gonorrhea and chlamydia.

B. MATCHING

(Some answers can be used more than once)

Contraceptive Method

_____ 54. breast-feeding
_____ 55. calendar method
_____ 56. basal body temperature method
_____ 57. Billings method
_____ 58. spermicides
_____ 59. male condom
_____ 60. female condom
_____ 61. diaphragm
_____ 62. cervical cap
_____ 63. contraceptive sponge
_____ 64. emergency contraception
_____ 65. the patch (OrthoEvra)
_____ 66. IUD
_____ 67. combination pill
_____ 68. Depo-Provera
_____ 69. vasectomy
_____ 70. tubal ligation
_____ 71. laparoscopy
_____ 72. vaginal ring (NuvaRing)
_____ 73. Implanon

a. once believed to work by preventing implantation, but now known also to work by preventing fertilization
b. active ingredient kills sperm
c. prevents release of FSH
d. involves noting changes in cervical mucus in order to determine when to abstain from intercourse
e. prevents sperm deposited in the vagina from getting into the uterus
f. involves tying, cutting, or cauterizing Fallopian tubes, or blocking them by clips
g. contains enough spermicide to be effective for 24 hours
h. blocks sperm from getting into the vagina
i. uses a simple mathematical formula to determine when to abstain from intercourse
j. progestins prevent ovulation
k. uses changes in resting temperature to determine when to abstain from intercourse
l. involves tying or cutting off vas deferens
m. synthetic estrogen helps to prevent ovulation
n. prevents implantation

C. FILL IN THE BLANKS

74. Withdrawal is not a highly effective method of birth control because of secretions from _____.
75. After a vasectomy, a man is not sterile until _____.
76. If a woman's shortest recorded menstrual cycle is 25 days and her longest is 31 days, by the calendar method she should abstain from intercourse from day _____ to day _____.
77. Women's basal body temperature _____ 24 to 72 hours after ovulation.
78. Women's cervical mucus becomes _____ at the time of ovulation.
79. Rubber condoms should not be used in combination with _____ lubricants.
80. The IUD is regarded as a safe contraceptive method for women _____.
81. Three nonprescription barrier types of contraception are the _____, _____, and the _____.
82. Three birth control techniques that offer women some protection against STIs are _____, _____, and _____.
83. In cases of unprotected intercourse, pregnancy may be avoided within the first few days by _____.
84. Sperm can live in a Fallopian tube for as long as _____.
85. The best way to avoid an unwanted pregnancy is _____.

SUGGESTED READINGS AND RESOURCES

Collier, A., (2007). *The humble little condom—A history*. Amherst, MA: Promethetheus Books. An entertaining and educational history of the condom.

Gibbs, N. (2010). Love, sex, freedom and the paradox of the pill. *Time*, May 3, 2010, 40–47. 50th anniversary of the pill—how it has helped change American society.

Hatcher, R., et al. (2008). *Contraceptive technology* (19th ed.). New York: Ardent Media. This is the most comprehensive and technical review of contraceptive methods.

Institute of Medicine (2004). *New frontiers in contraceptive research: A blueprint for action*. The National Academies Press (www.nap.edu).

Potts, M. (2000, January). The unmet need for family planning. *Scientific American*, 88–93. Looks at the high fertility rate in many parts of the world.

Advocates for Youth
2000 M Street, N.W.
Suite 750
Washington, DC 20036
(202) 419-3420
www.advocatesforyouth.org

Guttmacher Institute
125 Maiden Lane, 7th Floor
New York, NY 10038
1-800-355-0244
www.guttmacher.org

NARAL Pro-Choice America
1156 15th street, N.W., Suite 700
Washington, DC 20005
(202) 973-3000
www.naral.org
The leading pro-choice abortion group.

Planned Parenthood Federation of America
434 West 33rd Street
New York, NY 10001
(212) 541-7800 1-800-230-7526
www.plannedparenthood.org
You can contact the national headquarters to get the address and phone number of the clinic closest to you.

Pregnancy and Childbirth

7

Sex is separateness: a division of reproductive labor into specialized cells, organs, and organisms. The sexes of a species are the classes of reproductively incomplete individuals. In order for a sex member to contribute to the physical foundations of its species, to reproduce part of itself into the next generation, it must remedy its incompleteness. The remedy is found in the union of incomplete parts from complementary complete organisms: eggs and sperm cells unite.

—Gordon Bermant & Julian Davidson, 1974

Pregnancy and childbirth are intense experiences, remembered for a lifetime. The most potent human emotions—hope, fear, love, loneliness, depression, and joy—are often felt at their maximum levels. The first time that a woman feels a fetus move inside her, her first labor contractions, the first time that a child is viewed by its parents after birth—these are often the things that make life worth experiencing. Giving birth means assuming a great responsibility, for the newborn is totally dependent upon his or her parents. Relationships change with the addition of a new life and new responsibilities within a family. This requires that many adjustments in living be made. As you will see, it is important to begin making these adjustments before the baby is born—sometimes even before the baby is conceived.

CONCEPTION AND IMPLANTATION

As you learned in Chapters 2 and 3, the ovaries store eggs (**ova**). Each egg is surrounded by a small sac, forming what is called a **primary follicle.** As a result of the release of follicle-stimulating hormone (FSH) from the pituitary gland, one (or more) of these primary follicles matures to become a **Graafian follicle.** About midway through a 28-day menstrual cycle,

When you have finished studying this chapter, you should be able to:

- Explain the process of conception, including the terms primary follicle, Graafian follicle, capacitation, and zygote.

- Trace the process of development from the zygote through implantation, and discuss some problems that sometimes occur with implantation.

- Describe what occurs in each trimester of pregnancy for both mother and embryo/fetus.

- Summarize the possible effects of smoking, alcohol, drug use, and environmental hazards in the embryo and fetus.

- Discuss traditional and alternative birthing practices, including Lamaze, Bradley, home births, and the use of midwives.

- Explain the three stages of labor and the events that occur in each.

- Identify and explain the problems that can occur during breech deliveries, cesareans, and preterm deliveries.

- Discuss the benefits of breast-feeding.

- Discuss recommendations concerning sexual intercourse during and following pregnancy.

- Compare and contrast the various methods for dealing with infertility.

Primary follicle ■ An immature ovum enclosed by a single layer of cells.

Graafian follicle ■ A mature follicle.

167

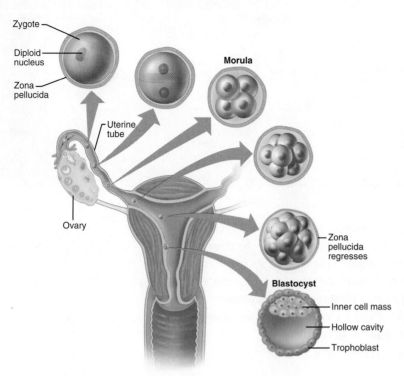

FIGURE 7–1 Ovulation, fertilization, and implantation.

Source: Hock, *Human Sexuality,* © 2007 PrenticeHall, Inc. Reproduced by permission of Pearson Education, Inc.

the Graafian follicle breaks open and the **ovum** is released into the abdominal cavity, where it is picked up by one of the Fallopian tubes. The ovum moves through the Fallopian tube to the uterus. It will take 3 to 7 days to reach the uterus, but *the ovum can only be fertilized during the first 24 hours after it leaves an ovary* (Moore, 1993). If a sperm does not penetrate the ovum during this time, the ovum becomes overly "ripe" and eventually disintegrates in the uterus, leaving the woman's body during her menstrual flow.

Sperm begin their development in the outer wall of a seminiferous tubule and migrate to the center of the tubule as they mature. A developing sperm

Ovum (ova, pl.) ■ An egg; the female reproductive cell.

Sperm ■ The germ cell of a man.

Capacitation ■ A process that sperm undergo while traveling through the woman's reproductive tract in which their membranes become thin enough so that an enzyme necessary for softening the ovum's membrane can be released.

Conception ■ The union of an egg and a sperm.

Zygote ■ The one-celled organism created from the fusion of a sperm and egg.

Morula ■ The collection of cells formed when the zygote begins rapid cell division.

Blastocyst ■ The fluid-filled sphere that reaches the uterus after fertilization and which was created by the transformation of the morula through continued, rapid cell division.

goes through several stages: from spermatogonium, to spermatocyte, to spermatid, to a mature spermatozoon (which has a head and a "tail" called a flagellum). The entire process takes about 70 days.

At orgasm during sexual intercourse, a man will ejaculate an average of 200 to 400 million **sperm** into the vagina. The sperm then attempt to pass through the cervix and uterus to the Fallopian tubes. This is not an easy journey. Some sperm are stopped by the force of gravity, some by the acidity of the woman's reproductive tract, some by clumping, and some simply by taking wrong turns (because usually only one egg is released, only one Fallopian tube will be the right path for the sperm to follow). Only a few thousand will live long enough to reach the Fallopian tubes, and fewer than 50 will reach the egg within the Fallopian tube (Moore, 1993). Most sperm live for only 3 days inside a woman's reproductive tract, but a few may live for as long as 5 days (Wilcox et al., 1995). Thus, intercourse can result in conception only 6 days out of every 28-day menstrual cycle (*5 days before ovulation and the day of ovulation*). If you want to know the probability of conception on any one of these 6 days, go back to the section on fertility awareness methods in Chapter 6.

While the sperm are in the woman's reproductive tract, they undergo a process called **capacitation** in which their membranes become thin enough so that an enzyme (called hyaluronidase) can be released to soften the egg's outer layers. The egg sends out tiny projections and pulls one sperm to its surface, the *zona pellucida*. That sperm secretes the enzyme and penetrates the egg's surface, and **conception** takes place. An almost instantaneous chemical reaction within the ovum then prevents other sperm from penetrating the ovum. Within 24 to 30 hours, the nuclei of the sperm and the ovum fuse to form a one-celled organism called a **zygote**. This single cell contains the complete genetic code, or blueprint, for a new human being.

Shortly afterward, the zygote splits into two separate cells, then four, then eight, and so on (see Figure 7–1). As cell division occurs, each individual cell gets smaller. This collection of cells is called a **morula**. While cell division is rapidly taking place, the morula is slowly continuing its trip toward the uterus. When the conceptus has about 100 cells, it has developed a fluid-filled center and is then called a **blastocyst.** After the blastocyst reaches the uterus, it may float there for several days. At this point it is still smaller than the head of a pin.

At about 8 to 11 days after ovulation, the blastocyst attaches itself to the endometrium via hairlike roots called *villi* (Wilcox et al., 1999). This is called **implantation.** By this time the endometrium has a large supply of blood that can serve as a source of nutrients and oxygen. The blastocyst is now called an embryo; it is called a fetus at about 8 weeks (see following section on pregnancy).

PERSONAL REFLECTIONS

What qualities do you possess that will make you a good parent? Do you have any qualities that might not make you a good parent? What things can you do to prepare yourself to be a good parent? How well-suited is your partner to be the mother or father of your child?

The outer cell layers of the embryo are called the **trophoblast** (from the Greek *trophe,* meaning "to nourish"). The trophoblast begins to grow rapidly and forms four protective layers or membranes, each with a special function. One produces blood cells for the embryo until it can produce its own. Another cell layer forms the **umbilical cord**—the major link between the developing embryo and its mother. The third membrane is called the **amnion.** It is a thick-skinned sac filled with water that surrounds the embryo. By surrounding the developing embryo with liquid, the amnion protects against bumps, sudden movements by the mother, and changes in temperature. The fourth membrane, called the **chorion,** will develop into the lining of the placenta. The **placenta** is an organ that serves as a connection or interface between the embryo's systems and those of the mother. The embryo is connected to the placenta by the umbilical cord. Through it, the embryo receives nourishment from its mother. It also receives antibodies for protection against infection. Wastes from the embryo's system travel from the umbilical cord to the placenta, and from there are taken up by the mother's excretory system.

Over 98% of term pregnancies result in the birth of a single baby. What causes twins (or other multiple births)? If two different ova are fertilized by two different sperm, the result is *dizygotic* (fraternal or nonidentical) twins. *Monozygotic* (identical) twins result when a fertilized ovum subdivides before it implants in the uterus. Interestingly, the chance of having multiple births increases with the age of the mother (Lazar, 1996).

Problems with Implantation

It has been estimated that about three fourths of conceptions either fail to implant or are spontaneously aborted within the first 6 weeks (Wilcox et al., 1999).

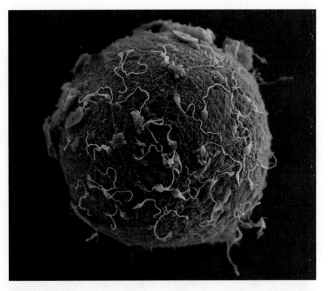

FIGURE 7–2 Many sperm attempting to penetrate the membrane of an ovum. Only one will be successful.

Over 20% of implanted embryos that fail before pregnancy can be detected by chemical tests (Wilcox et al., 1988), and one in seven confirmed pregnancies end in miscarriage (Springen, 2005). Failure to implant may be a means of "weeding out" or preventing the further development of blastocysts that are not completely healthy or normal.

One type of problem with implantation is called **ectopic pregnancy** (from the Greek *ektopos,* meaning "out of place"). In this case, conception is successful, but implantation takes place outside the uterus. In about 96% of these cases, implantation occurs in a Fallopian tube. In rarer cases, implantation can occur on an ovary, on the cervix, or in the abdomen. When implantation occurs in a Fallopian tube (often called a *tubal pregnancy*), there is simply not enough room for the embryo to grow. Unlike the uterus, the Fallopian tubes are not capable of much expansion. The embryo usually aborts on its own, but if it continues to grow after the 8th week, it may burst the tube. This is a serious complication of pregnancy, and it can be fatal. Although

Implantation ■ The process by which the blastocyst attaches itself to the wall of the uterus.

Trophoblast ■ The outer four cell layers of the embryo.

Umbilical cord ■ The cord that connects an embryo or fetus to the mother's placenta.

Amnion ■ A thick-skinned sac filled with water that surrounds the fetus.

Chorion ■ The fourth membrane of the trophoblast; it develops into the lining of the placenta.

Placenta ■ An organ that serves as a connection or interface between the fetus' systems and those of the mother.

Ectopic pregnancy ■ The implantation of a fertilized egg outside of the endometrium of the uterus.

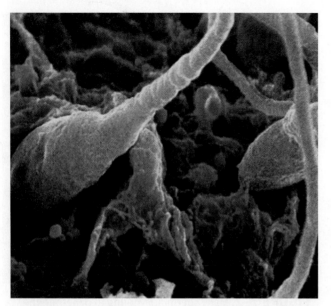

FIGURE 7–3 A close-up photo of sperm on the surface of an ovum.

the mortality rate has been dropping due to earlier detection, ectopic pregnancies still account for about 6% of all pregnancy-related deaths.

Ectopic pregnancies account for about 1.5% to 2.0% of all pregnancies (Barnhart, 2009). They are caused by conditions that block or slow passage of the conceptus to the uterus. The most common cause is scarring of the Fallopian tubes due to pelvic inflammatory disease (often resulting from untreated chlamydia or gonorrhea) (Barnhart, 2009). Other factors include anatomical malformations, increasing age at time of conception, smoking, and douching. If a woman has an ectopic pregnancy, she has an increased risk of having more ectopic pregnancies in the future, because many of the causes of the original problem, such as scarring, will still be present in later pregnancies.

> "I got pregnant only to learn it was tubular.... One year later I got pregnant again, and again it was tubular. The specialist told me I needed surgery to remove scar tissue that was choking my Fallopian tube."
> (from the author's files)

In the past, women diagnosed with tubal pregnancy always had part of the affected tube surgically removed, which greatly reduced the chances of preg-

Trimesters ■ Three-month periods of pregnancy (months 1–3, 4–6, and 7–9), so labeled for descriptive purposes.

Human chorionic gonadotropin (HCG) ■ A hormone secreted by the chorion that stimulates the ovaries during pregnancy.

"Morning sickness" ■ A symptom of early pregnancy involving nausea.

Couvade syndrome ■ The experiencing of pregnancy symptoms by male partners; sometimes called "sympathy pains."

nancy in the future. Today, ectopic pregnancy is treated either by administering a drug (methotrexate) or by laparoscopic surgery (Hoover et al., 2010).

PREGNANCY

Pregnancy lasts an average of 260 to 270 days. "Due dates," the dates that physicians set as the "expected time of arrival" for babies, are rarely the dates of actual birth. This is because the exact date of conception is hard to measure with complete accuracy and because there is great variability among births, even with the same parents. Because pregnancy lasts about 9 months, this time is divided into 3-month periods, called **trimesters,** for descriptive purposes.

The First Trimester—The Mother

When a menstrual period is late, women often want quick and accurate information about whether they are actually pregnant. To get this information, they take a "pregnancy test." The test works by determining if a hormone secreted by the placenta (**human chorionic gonadotropin, or HCG**) is present in a woman's urine. This test is most accurate (95% to 98%) 2 weeks or more after a missed period. Tests that measure HCG in blood can detect if a woman is pregnant even sooner than this.

The most common symptom of early pregnancy is nausea. It is called **"morning sickness"** (medically referred to as *nausea and vomiting of pregnancy*), though it can occur at any time of the day. Fifty percent to 80% of pregnant women experience mild or moderate morning sickness (Atanackovic et al., 2001). It generally begins 4 to 6 weeks after conception, reaches its peak by 8 to 12 weeks, and then usually (although not always) spontaneously disappears by the 20th week (Zhou et al., 1999). Although there are a number of speculations as to its cause (particularly rising estrogen levels), nothing has been proven conclusively (Deuchar, 1995). Some women eat crackers, drink soda water, and try a variety of other home remedies to cope with morning sickness, but there is no known safe yet effective way of treating it. Many men experience some of the same symptoms of pregnancy as their partners. In the United States this is sometimes called "sympathy pains," but the medical term for it is **couvade syndrome** (from a French term for the birthing process).

Other symptoms that women may exhibit during the first trimester include enlarged and tender breasts, prominent veins on the breasts, darkened areolas, enlarged nipples, increased frequency of urination, and irregular bowel movements. In addition, many women feel tired and run-down.

The First Trimester—The Embryo/Fetus

In the first trimester of pregnancy, a substantial amount of development takes place (see Figure 7–4). When the blastocyst implants, it is less than one third of an inch in diameter. After implantation, it is known as an **embryo.** Cell differentiation begins to take place now, and development occurs in orderly ways. Growth in the embryo occurs from the head downward and from the center (spine) outward. As mentioned earlier, the outer layers of the blastocyst form structures designed to nourish and protect it. In the embryo, three inner cell layers will form specific parts of the body: The *ectoderm* forms the nervous system, skin, and teeth. The *mesoderm* forms the muscles, skeleton, and blood vessels. The *endoderm* forms the internal organs (lungs, liver, digestive system, etc.).

In the 3rd week of pregnancy, a central structure called a neural tube becomes a dominant feature. The neural tube will become the central nervous system.

Embryo ■ The term given to the blastocyst after it has implanted.

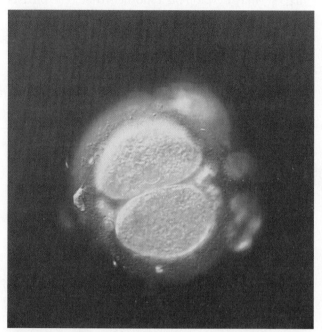

(a) 1 day (two cells)

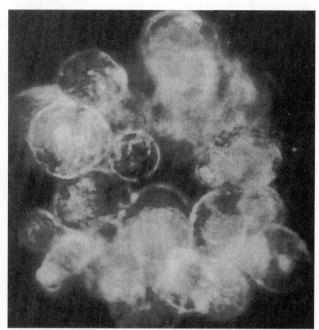

(b) 3½ days

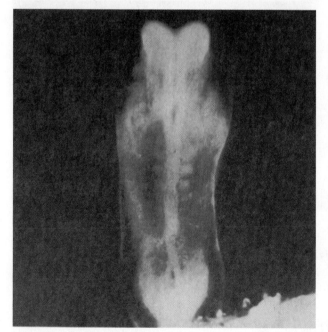

(c) 21 days (note the primitive spinal cord)

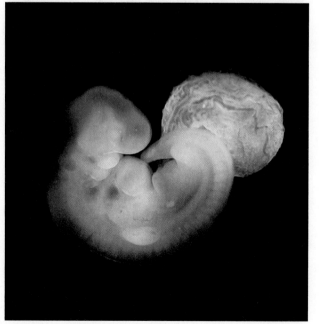

(d) 4 weeks

FIGURE 7–4 Stages of prenatal development. The heart and nervous system begin to function by the end of 4 weeks.

By the end of the 4th week, the umbilical cord, heart, and digestive system begin to form. At 6 weeks, the embryo has a "tail," which will become the tip of the spine. It also has structures that look like gills but are actually parts of the neck and face that have not yet fully developed. At 8 weeks, the embryo is about 1⅛ inches long. All organs have begun to develop. The heart is pumping, and the stomach has begun to produce some digestive juices. The embryo, although small, is well on its way toward developing into a unique human being. After 8 weeks and until birth, the developing organism is called a **fetus.**

The Second Trimester—The Mother

In the 4th or 5th month of pregnancy, the movements of the fetus can be felt by its mother. This first experience of movement is called **quickening.** Although a woman generally knows by this time that she is pregnant, this knowledge is usually an abstract or "intellectual" thing. Once a woman begins to feel a new life moving inside her, the fetus begins to be viewed as a person, and an emotional attachment to her unborn baby generally begins to form.

> "During my 5th month of pregnancy, I felt the baby move for the first time. It almost felt like the rumbling

Fetus ■ The term given to the embryo after the 8th week of pregnancy.

Quickening ■ The first time a pregnant woman experiences movement of the fetus, usually in the 5th month.

a stomach makes when you're hungry. It could be described as a 'fluttering,' and it is very exciting. Unfortunately, it doesn't happen that often at first, so you have to 'catch it' if you want your partner to share in the experience."
(from the author's files)

Women generally begin to get over their morning sickness in the second trimester. They also notice that their figures are changing, and they may worry about no longer being attractive to their partners. As her abdomen expands, red lines, or "stretch marks," may develop on a mother-to-be. The breasts begin to swell and may start to leak *colostrum,* a thick, sticky liquid that is produced before milk starts to flow. Water retention may cause edema (swelling) in the ankles, feet, and hands. Women may begin to develop varicose veins and/or hemorrhoids. The cessation of morning sickness often brings an increase in appetite.

The Second Trimester—The Fetus

At this time, the fetus begins to make sucking motions with its mouth. In the 5th month, the fetus has a detectable heartbeat. It will respond to sound, and it begins to show definite periods of sleep and wakefulness. If born at this time, the fetus has only a 1-in-10,000 chance of survival. In the 6th month, the fetus can open its eyes. It will suck its thumb and respond to light. At the end of the second trimester, the fetus is about 1 foot long and weighs about 1 pound.

(a) 8 weeks

(b) 12 weeks

FIGURE 7–5 Stages of prenatal development. Note the umbilical cord connection with the placenta in the photo taken at 8 weeks.

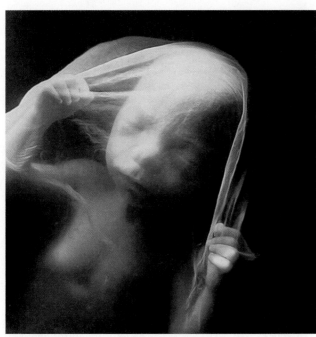

16 weeks

FIGURE 7–6 The fetus is recognizably human by 16 weeks.

The Third Trimester—The Mother

For the expectant mother, walking, sitting, and rising become more difficult. Pregnant women often have to learn new ways to sit down and to get up out of a chair. Expectant mothers often experience back pain from carrying a new weight load in front of them, which shifts their center of gravity. The uterus, enlarging with the rapidly growing fetus, puts pressure on the bladder and stomach. As a result, urination becomes more frequent—a woman may have to urinate four or five times a night. Indigestion, heartburn, gas, and constipation are also common complaints. Leg cramps may occur, a condition sometimes treated by taking extra calcium. The woman's navel may push out. Often she experiences a low energy level.

The Third Trimester—The Fetus

By the end of the 7th month of pregnancy, the fetus is about 15 inches long and weighs about 1½ pounds. Fatty tissues bexgin to develop under the skin. A lack of these tissues is what causes premature infants to look so skinny. In the 8th month, the fetus' weight begins to increase dramatically. At the end of the 8th month, it will weigh about 4 pounds and will be 16 to 17 inches long. From this point on, the fetus will gain about ½ pound per week. In the 9th month, the fetus will grow to about 20 inches in length and weigh an average of 7 to 7½ pounds. There is considerable variation in these measurements, however.

The fetus is covered with light hair (**lanugo**) and a waxy bluish substance (**vernix caseosa**). These will make the newborn look very interesting, but they serve as protective devices. Today, the vernix is

often allowed to be absorbed into the skin after birth rather than being immediately washed off.

Sexual Intercourse During Pregnancy

Two patterns of sexual activity have been observed during pregnancy. For the majority of women, there is a steady decline in sexual activity throughout pregnancy (Call et al., 1995; Regan et al., 2003). However, a large-scale study found that 90% of couples were still having intercourse in the 5th month of pregnancy (Hyde et al., 1996).

> "The fact that it's impossible to get any more pregnant, it makes sex during pregnancy very exciting. My senses seemed much more heightened and both my husband and I found it to be extremely pleasurable."
> (from the author's files)

For a few women, there is an increase in sexual activity from the first to the second trimester (Masters & Johnson, 1966; Regan et al., 2003). Freed of the worry about getting pregnant, some women begin to express their sexuality fully for the first time. This is followed by a decreased interest in sex during the third trimester (von Sydow, 1999). As you might expect, attitudes about sex during pregnancy are related to attitudes about sex before pregnancy (Fisher & Gray, 1988). The declining interest in sexual desire during pregnancy is also associated with changes in hormone levels (Regan et al., 2003).

Women (and men) list three general reasons for a declining interest in sexual intercourse during pregnancy. One reason is physical discomfort. The traditional man-on-top position can be increasingly uncomfortable for the woman as pregnancy progresses. This discomfort can be alleviated through the use of alternate positions that lessen pressure on the woman's abdomen during intercourse. The woman-on-top position is probably most comfortable.

A second reason for decreased interest in sex is that women may feel that they no longer appear attractive.

> "We never had sexual intercourse after the first 5 months. I felt disgusted, embarrassed and upset with the way my body had changed."
> (from the author's files)

Interestingly, men generally do not list this as a cause of decreased sexual activity. One of the best predictors of a woman's sexual satisfaction during pregnancy is her relationship satisfaction (De Judicibus & McCabe, 2002).

The third reason is fear about the pregnancy or about the possibility of harming the fetus (Bogren, 1991).

Lanugo ■ Light hair that covers a newborn baby.

Vernix caseosa ■ A waxy bluish substance that covers a newborn baby.

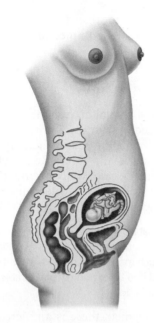

FIGURE 7–7 THIRD MONTH.   The fetus is now about 3 inches long and weighs about 1 ounce. It may continue to develop in the position shown or may turn or rotate frequently. The uterus begins to enlarge with the growing fetus and can now be felt extending about halfway up to the umbilicus.

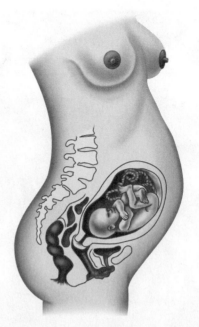

FIGURE 7–8 FIFTH MONTH.   The fetus measures about 10 to 12 inches long and weighs from ½ to 1 pound. It is still bright red. Its increased size now brings the dome of the uterus to the level of the umbilicus. The internal organs are maturing at astonishing speed, but the lungs are insufficiently developed to cope with conditions outside of the uterus.

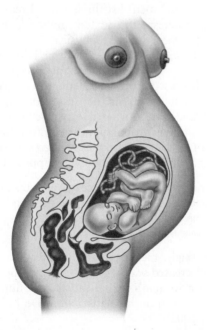

FIGURE 7–9 SEVENTH MONTH.   The fetus' weight has about doubled since last month, and it is about 3 inches longer. However, it still looks quite red and is covered with wrinkles that will eventually be erased by fat. At 7 months the premature baby has a fair chance for survival in nurseries cared for by skilled physicians and nurses.

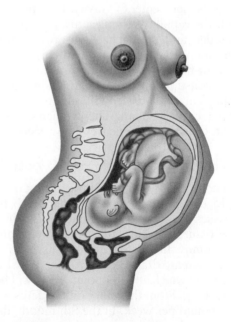

FIGURE 7–10 NINTH MONTH.   At birth or full term the baby weighs on average about 7¼ pounds if a girl and 7½ if a boy. Its length is about 20 inches. Its skin is coated with a creamy coating. The fine downy hair has largely disappeared. Fingernails may protrude beyond the ends of the fingers.

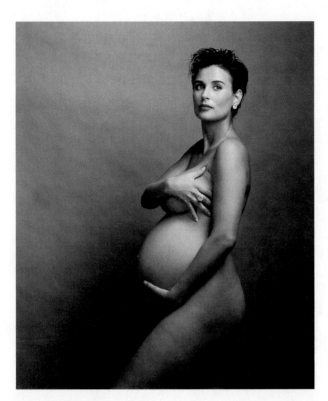

FIGURE 7–11 In a pose for *Vanity Fair* magazine (August 1991), actress Demi Moore shows that pregnancy is a time when a woman can still be proud of her body.

"At about the middle of my pregnancy, my husband had a decrease of interest in sex while my interest had increased. I was already feeling fat and ugly, and this just made things worse. Many nights I stayed up crying because not only did I think I was fat and ugly, but I thought my husband did too. Then I realized his problem was that he was scared he was going to hurt me or the baby. I tried to convince him that he wouldn't, but I guess he just couldn't stop thinking about it while we were having sex."

(from the author's files)

This leads to an important question: How far into pregnancy is it safe to engage in sexual intercourse? A review of 59 studies found that if there are no other risk factors, sexual intercourse during pregnancy does not harm the fetus (von Sydow, 1999). The consensus of opinion is summed up in the highly regarded *Williams Obstetrics*: "It has been generally accepted that in healthy pregnant women, sexual intercourse usually does no harm before the last four weeks or so of pregnancy" (Cunningham et al., 1997). What about the last 4 weeks? Here, there is some debate and you should consult with your doctor.

In any case, sexual behavior is not limited to intercourse, and in the latter stages of pregnancy alternative forms of sexual stimulation may be preferred. Hugging, touching, and other displays of affection are important ways of communicating attraction. It is important to speak to a pregnant woman about love and devotion and to express pride in her and hope for the future. Telling her that she is beautiful may be a far more effective way for her partner to show that he cares than having sexual intercourse.

COMPLICATIONS OF PREGNANCY

About 97% of all births result in a healthy, normal infant. However, complications of pregnancy can occur. Many of these can be prevented if parents-to-be are aware of them.

Substances that can harm an embryo or fetus are called **teratogens** (from the Greek word *tera*, meaning "monster"). Until recently, the placenta was thought to be a perfect filter that kept out all harmful substances. Now we know of hundreds of teratogens that can cross the placental barrier. Three things determine the harm caused by teratogens—the amount of the teratogen, the duration (amount of time) of exposure to the teratogen, and the age of the embryo or fetus. Each part of the developing body has a time, called a **critical period**, when it is most susceptible to damage. These are the times when it is undergoing most of its formation. During critical periods, body parts are sensitive to "signals" or "messages" about how to develop. This sensitivity means that the developing embryo or fetus can be easily influenced by teratogens. Although teratogens should be avoided at all times, most body parts are maximally susceptible to damage during the first 8 weeks of development (see Figure 7–12).

Remember that in the first 8 weeks of pregnancy, many women will not be sure if they are pregnant. There is an important lesson to be learned from this. If a woman wants to change her behavior to improve the chances of having a healthy baby (e.g, stop drinking alcohol), it is better for her to do this when she is trying to become pregnant rather than after she finds out that she is pregnant. The woman's partner can encourage healthier habits by also changing his habits at the same time.

Smoking

About 13% of all pregnant women smoke (Martin et al., 2009). Cigarette smoking during pregnancy is a concern because it is associated with a substantial increase in the risk of having a low-birth-weight baby (Nordentoft et al., 1996) and increases the

---

Teratogens ■ Substances that can harm an embryo or fetus.

Critical period ■ In relation to teratogens, the time during embryonic or fetal development during which a particular part of the body is most susceptible to damage.

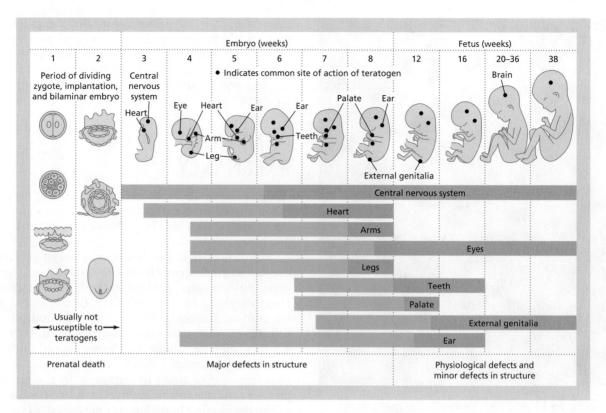

FIGURE 7–12 Critical periods in prenatal development. The ▬▬ areas represent highly sensitive periods; the ▬▬ areas represent less sensitive periods.

Source: Ciccarelli, *Psychology,* Figure 7.4, p. 351, © 2006 Pearson Education, Inc.
Reproduced by permission of Pearson Education, Inc.

risk of miscarriages, ectopic pregnancies, preterm births, and infant mortality (see DiFranza & Lew, 1995, for a review). Mothers who smoke during pregnancy at least double the risk that their baby will die of sudden infant death syndrome ("crib death") (Haglund et al., 1990).

Alcohol

About 12% of pregnant women report having had a drink in the previous month (Grant et al., 2009). Drinking during pregnancy can have dire consequences, and binge drinking (five or more drinks) is especially bad for the fetus (Walling, 2005). Approximately 2 out of every 1,000 children born in the United States have physical deformities and/or mental retardation because of damage caused by the mother's use of alcohol during pregnancy (*Newsweek*, 1989). The condition is known as **fetal alcohol syndrome** (**FAS**). Children born with FAS are underdeveloped and have facial deformities, abnormally spaced eyes, and small heads.

Research with animals indicates that alcohol probably has its maximum effect on the developing fetus in the 3rd week of pregnancy (Sulik et al., 1981), but it can have negative effects throughout pregnancy. Even moderate alcohol consumption can result in children with emotional problems, learning disabilities, and inability to cope in school (Willford et al., 2006). These data indicate that *it is probably best to avoid alcohol entirely during pregnancy.* If you wouldn't give your newborn baby an alcoholic drink, why would you give it one before it is even born?

Many women who drink also smoke. The combined effect during pregnancy greatly increases the chances of having preterm labor and a low-birth-weight baby (Odendaal et al., 2009).

Cocaine

Ten percent to 15% of babies born in large urban areas are affected by their mothers' use of cocaine—over 100,000 babies a year (U.S. General Accounting Office, 1990). The most widely reported effects of cocaine exposure during pregnancy are diminished growth and preterm birth (both resulting in low birth weight) and decreased head circumference and brain weight (see Jones & Johnson, 2001). "Crack babies" have a variety of sensory-motor and behavioral deficits, including irritability and disorientation.

Fetal alcohol syndrome (FAS) ▪ A condition common to infants born to alcoholic mothers, involving physical and nervous system abnormalities.

There is also a real potential of later learning problems and behavioral disorders (see Singer et al., 2002, for a review).

Other Drugs

Many drugs can cross the placental barrier. These include illegal drugs, prescription drugs, and over-the-counter drugs. About 5,000 to 10,000 babies are born each year to opiate-dependent (e.g., heroin-dependent) mothers (see Jones & Johnson, 2001). These infants must go through withdrawal after being born, showing symptoms such as fever, tremors, convulsions, and difficulty in breathing. Also, use of marijuana during pregnancy can result in both brain and behavioral problems (Jones & Johnson, 2001).

Numerous prescription drugs, such as antibiotics and tranquilizers, are clearly harmful to the fetus. In addition, commonly used drugs such as antihistamines (in allergy medication and cough medicine) and megadoses of certain vitamins have proven to have harmful effects. Even aspirin can be harmful. The Food and Drug Administration has issued a warning against taking over-the-counter aspirin products during the last 3 months of pregnancy because they can affect fetal circulation and cause complications during delivery. Caffeine (found in coffee, tea, many soft drinks, and chocolate) has been found to result in reduced birth weights (Vlajinac et al., 1997). Even too much vitamin A during pregnancy can cause birth defects (Rothman et al., 1995). The best advice, which is being given by increasingly large numbers of physicians, is not to take any drugs during pregnancy if at all possible.

PERSONAL REFLECTIONS

Do you or your partner smoke, drink alcohol, or take drugs? Do you and your partner eat a well-balanced diet and get ample sleep? What decisions about health can you and your partner make to ensure the health of your baby during pregnancy and afterwards?

Preeclampsia

A pregnant woman can have a disease called *toxemia of pregnancy*. In its early stages, this disease is called **preeclampsia,** and about 3% to 5% of pregnant women will experience it (Wang et al., 2009). Its symptoms include protein in the urine (which allows it to be detected by physicians), high blood pressure, weight gain, and swollen joints due to excessive water retention. In some cases, the disease advances to *eclampsia*, characterized by convulsions and coma. Worldwide, preeclampsia and eclampsia cause over 60,000 deaths each year.

"During my first pregnancy, they discovered that I had toxemia. I was immediately put on a low-sodium diet and had to stay in bed for the rest of my pregnancy. When she was born, my baby weighed only 4 lbs. 10 oz. and her weight then fell to 4 lbs. 1 oz. She had respiratory problems and severe jaundice. They kept her in an incubator for about 4 weeks. She was a very pretty baby, but took a long time to start crawling, walking, and talking. I didn't get toxemia in my second or third pregnancies."
(from the author's files)

Toxemia occurs after the 20th week of pregnancy. It begins in the placenta and quickly results in widespread maternal endothelial disorders (Wang et al., 2009). It is most likely to occur in younger women, especially if it is the first birth. Women who develop toxemia in their first pregnancy often do not have it in later pregnancies. Also, women who used barrier contraceptives (e.g., condoms, diaphragms) prior to pregnancy have a much higher risk of preeclampsia. These results suggest that the disease is due to altered immune responses as a result of being exposed to semen (see Pipkin, 2001). Contrary to popular belief, large doses of vitamins do not prevent preeclampsia (Roberts et al., 2010). The only way to treat preeclampsia is to delivery the baby prematurely (Wang et al., 2009), but of course this causes health risks for the baby.

Rh Incompatibility

There is a protein in the blood of a majority of people called the **Rh factor.** It got its name from the rhesus monkey, the species in which this blood protein was first discovered. If a person has the protein, he or she is "Rh positive." If not, the person is "Rh negative." Each person has two genes (one gene is received from each parent) that determine whether he or she has the protein. The Rh positive gene is dominant, which means that if a person has one Rh positive and one Rh negative gene, the blood will have this protein. A person can have Rh negative blood only when both genes are Rh negative.

In about 8% of all pregnancies in the United States, the mother will be Rh negative and the fetus will be Rh positive. When this occurs, there is an Rh compatibility problem. For the first birth, this situation usually is not dangerous. But during labor and delivery, blood of the fetus and the mother, kept separate in the placenta during pregnancy, may mix together. If this happens, the mother's blood treats

Preeclampsia ■ A disease of pregnancy characterized by high blood pressure, weight gain, swollen joints, and protein in the urine. Unless it is corrected, it can lead to convulsions and coma.

Rh factor ■ A protein in the blood of most individuals. If a mother does not have it and the fetus she carries does, she can develop antibodies against the Rh factor. This is called an Rh incompatibility problem.

the Rh factor in the baby's blood as if it were a dangerous foreign substance, forming antibodies that will attack and destroy the "invader" in the future. If the mother then has another Rh positive fetus, these antibodies can cross the placental barrier and attack the fetus' blood supply, causing a miscarriage, possible brain defects in the fetus, or even death.

Fortunately, there is an injection that can be given to the mother to prevent these antibodies from forming. The drug used for this is called *Rhogam*. It consists of Rh negative blood that already has these antibodies in it. Because Rhogam already has antibodies, the mother's system does not produce very many of its own. The antibodies in Rhogam eventually die off, leaving the mother capable of carrying another Rh positive fetus.

Detection of Problems in Pregnancy

There are several techniques for detecting problems in the fetus while it is inside the uterus. One is called **chorionic villus sampling** (see Brambati & Tulvi, 2005). As you learned earlier, the chorion surrounds the embryo and develops early in pregnancy. In chorionic sampling, a small tube is inserted through the vagina and cervix. Guided by ultrasound, the tube will remove some hairlike cells (villi) from the chorion by gentle vacuum suction. These cells can be examined to detect chromosomal problems (such as Down syndrome) or abnormalities in the fetus, or to look for evidence of certain diseases. One of the major advantages of chorionic sampling is that it can be used to detect problems early in pregnancy (from the 10th to 12th week of pregnancy), but after 12 weeks of pregnancy all of the villi of the chorion are gone.

Another technique that provides similar information is **amniocentesis** (Brambati & Tulvi, 2005). In amniocentesis, a hollow needle is inserted through the abdomen and uterus of the mother, through the membrane of the amniotic sac, and into the amniotic fluid surrounding the fetus. Some of the amniotic fluid is then extracted, and fetal cells that have dropped off and have been floating in the fluid are examined for evidence of abnormalities. This procedure can only be used between the 14th and 18th weeks of pregnancy. For both chorionic villus sampling and amniocentesis, the chance of a miscarriage is only about 1 in 200 (Evans & Wapner, 2005).

Chorionic sampling and amniocentesis are called "invasive" techniques, meaning that they invade, or get inside of, the uterus and/or the fetus. A balance must be found between detecting potential problems and creating new problems when these procedures are used. **Ultrasound** is considered a "noninvasive" technique because it only bounces sound waves off the uterus and fetus. Ultrasound can be used to diagnose problems such as a malformation of the skeletal system. It cannot detect genetic defects as amniocentesis can. An ultrasound is recommended *only if the expectant mother has an increased risk factor for a problem with a pregnancy or delivery.*

Alpha-fetoprotein (AFP) screening involves testing a pregnant woman's blood between the 16th and 18th week of pregnancy. This test is used to detect abnormalities in neural development, including spina bifida.

Fetal Surgery

One of the newest methods in treating a problem pregnancy is **fetal surgery**—performing an operation on the fetus while it is still in the uterus of the mother. The technological advances in this field have been rapid. In 1989, physicians performed the first successful major surgery on a fetus, repairing a hernia of the diaphragm that if left untreated probably would have resulted in death shortly after birth (Harrison et al., 1990). Doctors have also corrected spina bifida on 23-week-old fetuses (Adzick et al., 1998).

In the future, doctors will be able to use *in utero gene therapy* (Zanjani & Anderson, 1999). Here, doctors inject healthy genes into the cells of an organ of a patient with a genetic disease (e.g., neurologic or immunologic genetic diseases). The injected genes kill off the bad cells. This is already done in children and adults, but the advantage of doing it to the fetus while still in the uterus is that a disease can be eliminated before the appearance of any clinical symptoms. Scientists say that by injecting the genes into a fertilized egg, genetic diseases could also be avoided in later generations (see Designer Babies, 1998).

Miscarriages (Spontaneous Abortions)

Earlier in this chapter you learned that about three fourths of all conceptions fail to survive beyond 6 weeks. Of the remaining quarter, about one in seven fail to survive to term (Springen, 2005). There are many possible causes for **miscarriage**, including

Chorionic villus sampling ■ A technique used for detecting problems in a fetus during the 10th to 12th weeks of pregnancy. Hairlike projections (villi) of the chorion are collected and examined.

Amniocentesis ■ A technique for detecting fetal problems, involving collection of amniotic fluid between the 14th and 18th weeks of pregnancy.

Ultrasound ■ A noninvasive technique for examining the internal organs of a fetus; it uses sound waves like a radar or sonar scan to create a picture.

Fetal surgery ■ A surgical operation on the fetus while it is still in the uterus.

Miscarriage ■ A spontaneous abortion.

genetic, anatomic, and hormonal causes; infections; maternal autoimmune responses; and the smoking of cigarettes or use of cocaine (e.g., Speroff & Fritz, 2005). Usually, physicians will not attempt to diagnose causes of miscarriage until the woman has had three of them. *Recurrent miscarriages*, as these are called, occur in 0.5% to 1.0% of women (Alberman, 1988).

For many couples, a miscarriage can be a heavy emotional disappointment:

> "I have been married for 14 years. I conceived seven times, and every time I had a miscarriage at about 4½ months. My doctor diagnosed that my uterus was too weak to carry the baby after 4 months and no matter what and how I tried I couldn't have a baby of my own. I get very depressed sometimes and cry. Lately I feel very uncomfortable around other people's babies."

> "Some people may think only women are upset because of losing a baby due to miscarriage...but this hurt me in ways unimaginable.... First of all, I felt as if it was my fault for not being there. It hurt the most because a part of us had not yet had a chance to grow and mature into our baby. Our relationship is just now returning to normal."
> (All examples are from the author's files)

It is important to allow people who experience miscarriage to express their emotions and grieve (Price, 2008). It often takes several months to recover.

At this point I would like to emphasize that hundreds of millions of babies are born without serious problems. A fetus is incredibly resistant to harm. It is important that you eat well, avoid toxic substances, get early and regular care from a physician, and prepare for the birth of your child through study and training (which I will describe shortly). These all go a long way toward making pregnancy, labor, and birth an enriching, happy experience.

NUTRITION AND EXERCISE DURING PREGNANCY

One of the best ways to increase the chances of having a healthy baby is to eat well during pregnancy. A poor diet can increase the risk of complications such as toxemia, anemia, and low birth weight.

Remember, if you are pregnant, you are now eating for two. You will need to eat more *good-quality* foods than you usually do (see Boston Women's Health Book Collective, 2005). The U.S. Public Health Service recommends that pregnant women also *supplement their intake of folic acid* by taking a multivitamin. Your physician may make additional recommendations if you have certain conditions (such as adjusting salt intake to ease toxemia).

Some women have negative feelings about gaining weight during pregnancy, but remember, this is not only normal but necessary. Never put yourself on a low-calorie diet during pregnancy. It is also not good to gain too much weight because it can result in a high-birth-weight baby (Ludwig & Currie, 2010). In 2009, the Institute of Medicine made the following recommendations for weight gain during pregnancy: 28–40 pounds for underweight women, 25–35 pounds for normal-weight women, 15–25 pounds for overweight women and 11–20 pounds for obese women.

There has been some concern that vigorous exercise during pregnancy might cause premature labor and delivery. A large-scale study found not only no evidence to support this, but also that regular exercisers who were in good condition had timely deliveries (reduced the chance of a preterm birth) (Hatch et al., 1998).

PREPARING FOR CHILDBIRTH

In the United States, nearly 20% of pregnant women never bother to have a **prenatal examination** (Rosenberg et al., 1996). Prenatal exams are an essential part of healthcare during pregnancy (Walker & Humphries, 2007). However, there is more to giving birth than ensuring the safety of the mother and baby. What about a woman's psychological well-being and emotional adjustment? Modern maternity care in developed countries is aided by many technological advances, but, as Ulla Waldenström (1996) asks, "Does safety have to take the meaning out of birth?" In this section you will learn about several alternatives to the traditional medical model of birthing—methods that are concerned with safety, but also try to make childbirth a meaningful experience.

The use of general anesthesia, labor rooms where women waited for hours, and delivery rooms were all instituted to make it easier for health professionals to deliver their services. Women were usually given very little education about what was to come, with only the expectation that it would be painful. For some of these women, labor and delivery are not positive experiences (Waldenström et al., 2004).

> "At age 20 I prepared to give birth to my first child. 'Induced labor' was a convenient form of delivery for the physician, and widely practiced in the 70s. At my last visit to his office, he 'broke the water bag,' handed me five Kotex pads, and told me to walk across the street to _____ hospital and admit myself. He said he would check on me later that evening. The delivery room nurse started a 'drip' to begin contractions. I now know why the old _____ hospital had bars on the labor room

Prenatal examination ■ A health checkup by a physician during pregnancy.

windows. I cannot describe that intense pain, especially not having been prepared for natural childbirth. To jump would have been a blessing."

"My experience with childbirth was very traumatic. The pain I had to endure.... I remember reaching out to punch the nurse because the prepping solution she used on me was so cold. The next thing I knew, the gas mask covered my face and I was out cold."

(All examples are from the author's files)

Fathers were generally the forgotten person when a baby was born. They seldom were allowed to be with their wives during any part of labor or delivery.

"I went out of the room to get a candy bar while the nurse gave my wife an exam (neither I nor my wife had ever heard of Lamaze then). When I returned to her room, I saw my wife being taken away. The nurse explained that my wife was giving birth. I'd been awake for several nights with my wife, so I laid down on her bed to rest and fell asleep. Shortly after 6 P.M., the phone next to the bed rang and the nurse told me I was the father of a baby girl."

(from the author's files)

In 1932, a British physician named Grantly Dick-Read wrote a book in which he advocated the practice of *natural childbirth* (Dick-Read, 1972). He became the founder of a movement away from "modern" techniques. Dick-Read concluded that modern birthing techniques, in which pregnant women were regarded as "patients," led to a **fear–tension–pain cycle.** He reasoned that women were being put into strange environments, not knowing what was going to happen next, and surrounded by strangers—and that this created fear. He believed that fear could cause physiological changes associated with tension, such as tightened muscles. These things were believed to increase substantially the sensation of pain felt by mothers during labor and delivery. Instead, he advocated educating mothers-to-be about pregnancy, labor, birth, and birth procedures to relieve fear of the unknown (see Larimore, 1995, for a history). He also advocated training in relaxation techniques to relieve the physiological effects of tension. Drugs were permissible if thought necessary, but were to be avoided if possible. Today, people more properly refer to these techniques as **prepared childbirth** rather than natural childbirth.

Fear–tension–pain cycle ■ According to prepared childbirth advocates, the cycle of events that women experience during labor when they are not properly educated about labor and childbirth.

Prepared childbirth ■ Courses or techniques that prepare women for labor and childbirth, with the goal of making it a positive experience.

The Lamaze Method

A French physician, Fernand Lamaze, traveled to the Soviet Union in 1951 to study birthing techniques in that country. Throughout the Soviet Union, Lamaze saw that women were giving birth without using anesthetics or experiencing great pain. The Soviets had extended the conditioning techniques of Ivan Pavlov into the area of labor and delivery. Women were conditioned to learn pleasant new associations for the sensations of labor and birth. They were also taught relaxation and breathing techniques to aid in making labor easier. Lamaze returned to France, modified the Soviet techniques slightly, and began using this new approach to childbirth in his practice (Lamaze, 1970). An American woman, Marjorie Karmel, used this approach under Lamaze's guidance and wrote about her experience in a best-selling 1959 book titled *Thank You, Dr. Lamaze.* Since then, the *Lamaze method* has become the most popular form of prepared childbirth in the United States. Compare the following childbirth experiences from two individuals who went through Lamaze training with the two case histories that were presented at the beginning of this section. Which persons do you think remember giving birth as a positive experience?

"I have gone through three different ways of giving birth—the first being totally drugged out. I didn't get to see my baby until the next morning. The next two deliveries were natural childbirth using a birthing room and I didn't have any restraints on me. You are given the freedom and dignity of childbirth. I used a birthing chair with my last baby. It was a more natural way of delivery and I found pushing to be less of an effort. The relaxation and breathing techniques taught with Lamaze training really kept me focused and prepared. You know what you want—this is the way you have chosen to give birth.... My husband was there the whole time encouraging me. It was such a joy to see what love had produced. The smile on my husband's face. We could hold the baby after its birth—there bonding begins."

"We had our children using Lamaze. The thing I remember most is how in control my wife was, even at the very end. She had drawn her own focal point a few weeks before and concentrated on it every contraction while doing her breathing and effleurage. The absolutely best thing about the births was both of us being there to see our children the moment they were born. It was important to be there when my wife was giving birth, to be part of the experience. I cannot remember any other moment when I felt so connected to her and so alive."

(All examples are from the author's files)

The Lamaze approach tries to determine the specific causes of pain and provides methods for dealing with each cause. What are the causes of perceived pain in childbirth? Basically, these break down into (1) anxiety and fear; (2) muscle tension; (3) stretching of muscles; (4) too little oxygen getting to muscles; and (5) pressure on nerves. Here are some ways that Lamaze training deals with each of these (see Lothian & DeVries, 2005).

1. **Anxiety and fear.** Pain is a subjective experience. A football player may break an arm or leg and yet be unaware of it and continue to play until after the game is over (when the pain may suddenly become unbearable). Some people, on the other hand, wince and scream when they get a blood test before the needle even touches them. These examples illustrate two things that influence the experience of pain. The first is the anxiety and fear associated with the experience, and the second is the attention paid to the source of pain.

    In Lamaze training, fear and anxiety are first dealt with through education. The unknown is always frightening, and if a woman in labor does not know what to expect, her anxiety will increase her experience of pain. This is counteracted by teaching expectant mothers about pregnancy and childbirth. They learn about the different stages of labor and medical procedures associated with childbirth and take a tour of the maternity ward and birthing facilities. In this way, the expectant mother knows what to expect and is more familiar with the environment where labor and birth will take place.

    Another way that the subjective experience of pain is reduced is through learning to focus attention or concentration. During labor, the mother-to-be picks out something outside her body, such as a favorite doll or a piece of furniture, and learns to focus all her attention on that thing, or "focal point." By concentrating on the focal point, she is not concentrating on her pain, and so the perception or subjective experience of pain is reduced. Throughout their training, labor, and delivery expectant mothers are accompanied by a "*coach.*" The coach is often the father of the baby, but can also be a friend. The coach helps the mother utilize her training, providing support, encouragement, and instruction. It is the coach's responsibility to keep the mother-to-be as comfortable as possible, while at the same time keeping her concentration focused and her spirits up.

2. **Muscle tension.** When people are anxious or fearful, muscles tighten up. This is a natural reaction and can be adaptive, because it allows quick movement in a "fight-or-flight" situation. However, keeping muscles tense over long time periods can cause them to ache and be used inefficiently. Labor is just such a situation. One of the first exercises in Lamaze training involves learning to know when muscles are tense and how to relax them.

3. **Stretching of muscles.** Like any set of muscles, the muscles used in labor will get tired and begin to ache if they are overworked, especially if they are out of condition. In Lamaze training, women are taught exercises so that these muscles can be toned up and strong when the baby decides to arrive.

4. **Too little oxygen getting to muscles.** Muscles use so much energy during vigorous exercise that they often cannot get enough oxygen, and so they begin to ache. The same is true in labor. In order to help deal with this, expectant mothers and coaches learn a variety of breathing techniques. These different types of breathing are generally used during contractions, while the woman's attention is fixed on her focal point.

5. **Pressure on nerves.** Pressure on nerves caused by the fetus moving through the birth canal is dealt with through the use of *effleurage*, or massage. One type of effleurage involves having the expectant mother lightly touch her abdomen with her fingertips, tracing large ovals on her skin during contractions. This light massage generally is a pleasant sensation, and by continually pairing the discomforts of contractions with a pleasant sensation, the subjective experience of pain is reduced. As labor progresses, deep muscle massage of the small of the back by the coach may also reduce the discomfort.

Today, there are several other birthing techniques that couples can use in place of the traditional hospital–general anesthesia approach. Here are a few of them.

The Bradley Method

The second most popular type of prepared childbirth in the United States is based on the work of Robert Bradley in the 1940s. He, too, was inspired by Dick-Read and believed that pain during childbirth resulted from culturally learned fear. He argued against the "meddlesome interference with nature's instinctual conduct and plans" (Bradley, 1981). He emphasized childbirth without medication and had husbands play an even greater role than in Lamaze.

The Leboyer Method

Another French physician, Frederick Leboyer, wrote an influential book in 1975 called *Birth without Violence.* He felt that traditional techniques of delivery were traumatic for babies, and instead advocated "gentle birth." In the *Leboyer method,* the baby is delivered and immediately placed on the mother's abdomen. The room is dimly lit to simulate the lighting inside the mother's body. The umbilical cord is not cut for several minutes, until it stops pulsating. The baby is then put in a warm bath (to simulate the amniotic fluid). The idea is to allow the transition of the baby from life inside the mother's body to life in the outside world to be as smooth as possible.

Home Birth, Birthing Rooms and Centers, and Modern Midwifery

In 1870, fewer than 1% of women gave birth in hospitals (Tew, 1990). In the late 1990s, only about 1% of women gave birth outside of a hospital (Curtin, 1999). Today, in Europe and the United States, there is a growing movement back to having births in the home. This movement has been driven, in part, by economic considerations. Home births are much less expensive. There are also personal considerations. Many couples feel that having a baby in familiar surroundings is more natural than a hospital birth. It also provides an opportunity for the entire family to be present and participate. The American College of Obstetricians and Gynecologists oppose home births for safety reasons, but for pregnant women who are at low risk for complications, home birth is a safe alternative to hospital delivery (Janssen, 2009b). Women who have delivered at home almost always say that it was a very positive experience (Janssen et al., 2009a).

To compete with this movement, many hospitals have "birthing rooms," which are designed to look like bedrooms rather than hospital rooms. Labor and delivery take place in the same bed, and often a crib is present so that the baby can sleep in the room with the mother after birth. In some areas, a closely related option is *birthing centers*, institutions that offer delivery in a homelike atmosphere with the assistance of skilled individuals such as midwives or physicians. They have proved to be just as safe for women as traditional hospital care (Waldenström & Nilsson, 1997), but this may be partly because *birthing centers* are really an option only to women with no foreseeable complications.

Whether the choice is to deliver at home, in a birthing center, or in a hospital, there is also a growing trend to use **nurse-midwives** rather than physicians. In many European countries, over two thirds of all babies are delivered by midwives, but only about 10% of vaginal births in the United States are attended by nurse-midwives (and most of these are in hospitals) (Barger, 2005). Nurse-midwives are generally registered nurses trained in obstetrical techniques who are well qualified for normal deliveries and minor emergencies. (It should be noted

that other types of midwives may not have this type of formal education.) They are less expensive than physicians, and they provide personal care during the latter parts of pregnancy, labor, and delivery. Studies indicate that the outcome for babies (and mothers) is just as good when they are attended by nurse-midwives as when they are attended by physicians (Walsh & Downe, 2004).

ANESTHETICS OR "NATURAL" CHILDBIRTH?

In the Book of Genesis, God punishes women for Eve's transgression (eating the forbidden fruit) by making childbirth painful:

> **I will greatly multiply your pain in childbearing; In pain you shall bring forth children.** *(Genesis 3:16, Revised Standard Version)*

When painkillers were first used for childbirth in the 1800s, the British clergy opposed it, arguing that it was against God's will. It was Queen Victoria who decisively argued in favor of painkillers.

Many people reading this book came into the world in a drugged state. This is because anesthetics were used during their mother's labor to relieve pain. Under general anesthesia, a woman is unable to push during contractions. As a result, the infant has to be pulled into the world with forceps, which resemble tongs. Anesthetics cross the placental barrier and enter the fetus. This is one reason why some infants have to be slapped in order to get them to cry and begin breathing. Babies born without the use of anesthetics generally come into the world with eyes open and ready to breathe without having to be slapped into consciousness.

Today, most births in which anesthetics are used do not involve general anesthetics. The mother-to-be can be given an *epidural*, a spinal anesthetic that deadens sensations from the waist down. Thus, it is possible to be anesthetized and still be conscious. However, epidurals are associated with some complications. Labor tends to last longer, the chance of fever is 5 times as great, and there is a much greater risk of hypotension (Leighton & Halpern, 2002).

The number of women choosing prepared childbirth courses in recent years has dropped dramatically, from 70% (first-time mothers) in 2000 to 56% in 2005 (Childbirth Connection, 2007). More than half of American women who give birth receive an epidural (Hawkins et al., 1999). A little less than half are given opioids for labor pain relief. In fact, some women who do not have to are choosing to have a cesarean section (see later section).

So, which method should you choose? Women who have some form of prepared childbirth and/or who are assisted during labor and delivery by a midwife generally require less medication for pain,

---

Nurse-midwife ■ A registered nurse, trained in obstetrical techniques, who delivers babies, often at the expectant mother's home.

need fewer cesarean sections, and have more positive feelings about the experience (Butler et al., 1993; Turnbull et al., 1996). However, a word of caution: Do not start thinking of childbirth as a contest to see if you can get through with the least amount of medical help. This attitude can make the use of anesthetics or a C-section seem like a "failure." That should not be the case. Any birth that results in a healthy mother and baby is a good one, regardless of the technique used. That is always the goal of childbirth, and should not be forgotten.

PERSONAL REFLECTIONS

Make a list of all the words that come to your mind when you think of childbirth, labor, and delivery. Examine your list for negative stereotypical concepts. Are there alternatives?

CHILDBIRTH

Before birth, the fetus will generally rotate its position so that its head is downward. This can happen weeks or hours before birth and is what is meant when people say "the baby dropped." It is also called **"lightening"** because once the fetus' head (its

largest part) has lowered in the uterus, pressure on the mother's abdomen and diaphragm is greatly reduced. Being able to breathe more easily makes a mother feel like the load that she has been carrying (the fetus) weighs less (is "lighter").

Shortly before a woman begins to give birth ("goes into labor"), she may experience a burst of energy. A woman may feel better than she has in months, and may start to clean house or do some other type of work as a means of "burning off" this energy. It is probably a good idea to save some of this energy for later, when it certainly will be needed.

True Versus False Labor

Throughout the latter stages of pregnancy, the uterus will undergo contractions—tightenings and relaxations of the muscles. These are involuntary, and for most of the pregnancy will go unnoticed. These contractions, called **Braxton-Hicks contractions,** are a type of natural "exercise program" for

Lightening ■ Rotation of the fetus prior to childbirth so that its head is downward, resulting in decreased pressure on the mother's abdomen.

Braxton-Hicks contractions ■ Uterine contractions experienced during the last trimester of pregnancy that are often incorrectly interpreted as the beginning of labor; also called false labor.

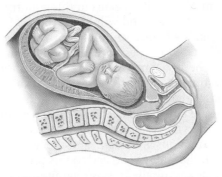

(a) Fully Developed Fetus Before Labor Begins

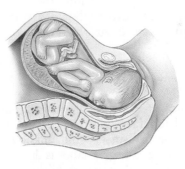

(b) Stage One Labor

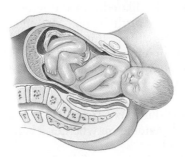

(c) Stage Two Labor

(d) Stage Three Labor

FIGURE 7–13 The stages of childbirth.

Source: Hock, *Human Sexuality,* © 2007 PrenticeHall, Inc. Reproduced by permission of Pearson Education, Inc.

the uterus. Sometimes these contractions become so strong that they are noticed and mistaken for true labor. Parents-to-be sometimes worry and go to a hospital, only to be told that they have had a **false labor** and should return when the woman is in "real" labor. Here are some guidelines that help distinguish false labor from true labor.

One important sign of labor is the time between contractions. The uterus is basically a muscle in the shape of a bag. Its job is to push the fetus into the world. Like most muscles engaged in prolonged, heavy labor, it must repeatedly contract, or tighten. If contractions are coming 10 minutes apart on a regular basis, this is a good sign that labor has begun. False labor contractions are usually less regular. The duration of each contraction also should be measured. If contractions are 30 seconds long on a regular basis, this is a good sign that labor has begun. False labor contractions are usually shorter than contractions marking true labor.

Two important signs of the beginning of labor involve the cervix. The first sign is **dilation.** In the last month of pregnancy, the cervix will dilate to about 1 centimeter in diameter. When a woman goes into labor, the uterine contractions help cause the cervix to dilate more. It must eventually dilate to 10 centimeters (about 4 inches) in diameter before the baby can be born. In the first stage of labor, the cervix will dilate to about 2 or 3 centimeters. The second sign is **effacement.** The cervix must stretch until it is "thinned out," or "effaced," so that it won't block the baby's passage into the birth canal (vagina). A good sign of true labor is that the cervix is 70% or more effaced. At birth, it will be 100% effaced.

Stages of Labor

There is an abundance of evidence suggesting that it is the fetus that determines when labor begins, although the exact mechanism is still unknown (Norwitz et al., 1999). Once it begins, labor is divided into three stages. The initial stage of labor is a

start-up stage and involves the woman's body making preparations to expel the fetus from the uterus into the outside world. This stage usually lasts from 6 to 13 hours. At this time, uterine contractions begin to push the fetus downward toward the cervix. The cervix begins to dilate and efface. At first, contractions are far apart (one every 10 to 20 minutes) and do not last long (15 to 20 seconds), but eventually they begin to come closer together (1 to 2 minutes) and last longer (45 to 60 seconds or longer).

During pregnancy, the cervix becomes plugged up with a thick layer of mucus. This prevents the amniotic sac (bag of water) and the fetus from having direct contact with the outside environment (through the vagina). During labor, this mucous plug will come out. A discharge of mucus and blood (known as a "bloody show") is a sign of labor. However, for some women the mucus comes out a little at a time, so that this sign is not clearly seen. In other women, the plug literally pops out like the cork in a bottle of champagne.

For about 10% of pregnancies, the amniotic sac will break before labor begins. In some women, the break is a small tear and the fluid seeps out. In other women, the water gushes out. This is what happens when a woman's *"water breaks."* Labor usually begins within a day after the amniotic sac breaks. If not, most physicians will induce labor with drugs. Physicians sometimes break the amniotic sac on purpose in order to speed up labor. It is even possible to give birth with the fetus enclosed in an unbroken amniotic sac. Physicians in this country do not allow this to happen and will break the sac first. However, in parts of Asia, children born in this manner are believed to be blessed with good fortune.

The last part of the first stage of labor is called the **transition phase,** so called because it marks the end of the initial stage of labor and the beginning of the next (birth) stage. This phase takes place when the cervix is almost fully dilated (8 to 10 cm). Contractions are severe, and the woman may start to think that there is no end to this process. Fortunately, transition usually lasts 40 minutes or less.

The **second stage of labor** begins when the cervix is fully dilated and the fetus begins moving through the birth canal. It ends with birth. Contractions during this stage of labor are accompanied by an intense desire to push or "bear down." The contractions cause the opening of the vagina to expand, and expectant mothers often get a "second wind" because they now can see an end to their work. This stage lasts from 30 to 80 minutes on the average, depending on whether it is the first child or a later child.

The first sign of the fetus is usually the sight of its head at the opening of the vagina. This is called **crowning,** because ideally the crown of the head is leading the way. The person delivering the baby will tell the expectant mother when and how hard to

---

False labor ■ A set of temporary contractions of the uterus that resemble the start of labor.

Dilation ■ Becoming wider or larger.

Effacement ■ The thinning of the cervix during labor.

Start-up stage of labor ■ The stage of labor that begins with uterine contractions pushing the fetus downward toward the cervix and ends when the cervix is fully dilated.

Transition phase ■ The last part of the start-up stage of labor, during which the cervix dilates to 10 cm in order for the baby to be able to enter the birth canal.

Second stage of labor ■ The stage of labor that begins when the cervix is fully dilated and the fetus begins moving through the birth canal. It ends with birth.

Crowning ■ The appearance of the fetus' head at the vaginal opening during childbirth.

push during contractions in order to get the baby into the world. The head is delivered first, with the physician reaching beneath the infant's chin to be sure that the umbilical cord is not wrapped around the baby's neck before the head is brought out. Once the head is delivered, suction is applied to the mouth and nose with a small rubber bulb so that the baby can breathe more easily. The head then turns, and the shoulders and rest of the body come out rather quickly. The mouth and nose are suctioned again.

The umbilical cord will be cut about 1½ inches from the baby's body. This stub will fall off in a few days, leaving the navel. (The navel is either an "inny" or an "outty," but the type of navel you have seems to depend on heredity, not on how the umbilical cord was cut.)

In the **third stage of labor,** the placenta detaches from the uterus and leaves the mother's body. This is what is called the **afterbirth.** This stage usually lasts only 10 to 12 minutes. The physician examines the afterbirth to make sure that it is in one piece; then it is discarded. If even small pieces of the placenta stay in the uterus, infection and bleeding can occur. When this takes place, physicians use a procedure called D & C (dilation and curettage), in which the cervix is dilated to allow access to the uterus, which is then scraped clean.

Episiotomy

In the United States, about 40% of women who deliver vaginally in hospitals are given an **episiotomy** just before they give birth (Weeks & Kozak, 2001). An episiotomy is an incision made from the bottom of the vagina (through the perineum) toward the anus, thus enlarging the vaginal opening. An episiotomy is a useful procedure if the baby is in distress. Although the number of episiotomies has dropped substantially since 1980 (64% then), many authorities still believe that most episiotomies are unnecessary and are done routinely only for the benefit of the physician (see Graham & Davies, 2005). In fact, several studies have found that women having vaginal deliveries who did not have episiotomies had fewer problems, including less damage to the perineum and less likelihood of urinary incontinence, than women who did have them. When sewing up the incision, a few physicians add a "honeymoon stitch" (or "husband's stitch") in the lower part of the vaginal opening in order to make it tighter during intercourse. Both of these procedures should be abandoned as routine birthing practices. (Graham & Davies, 2005).

PROBLEMS WITH CHILDBIRTH

Pregnancy and childbirth do not always go as planned. Worldwide, nearly 350,000 women die each year as a result of childbirth (Hogan et al., 2010).

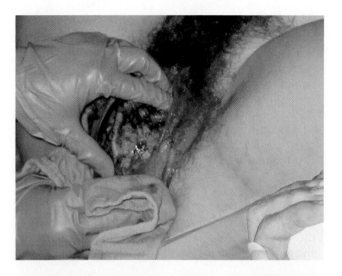

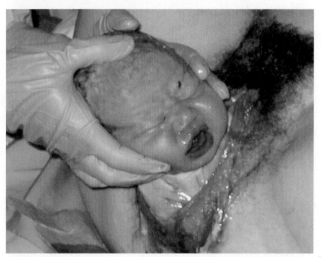

FIGURE 7–14 Childbirth.

This is down from 526,000 in 1980, but the maternal mortality rate is still high in a lot of developing countries. The maternal mortality rate in the United States is 8.4 per 100,000 live births (Hoyert et al., 2000), but this is still higher than at least 25 other countries. The major causes of death are blood clots, hypertension, and hemorrhage. Deaths may be uncommon, but there are other complications that occur much more frequently. Let us examine a few of the most common ones.

Breech Births

Babies, you recall, are generally born head first. This occurs in about 96% of all births, and ideally

Third stage of labor ■ Detachment and expulsion of the placenta from the uterus after childbirth.

Afterbirth ■ The expulsion of the placenta from the uterus after a baby is born.

Episiotomy ■ A surgical procedure performed on women just before giving birth to reduce the risk of tearing the perineum.

the back of the head, or crown, leads the way. Sometimes, a fetus will try to come through the birth canal feet or buttocks first. This is called a **breech birth** and occurs in 2% to 4% of all births. Sometimes during labor a woman will be asked to try lying in different positions, such as on her side, in the hope that this will cause the fetus to change to a head-first position. A physician can sometimes turn the fetus by grasping the mother's abdomen and manually changing the fetus' position.

Today, some physicians may try to perform a vaginal ("normal") delivery even if a breech birth is unpreventable. This will depend on the circumstances and the physician. If the physician feels that the risks of a vaginal delivery are too great, he or she may perform a cesarean section.

Placenta Previa

The blastocyst normally implants in the upper part of the uterus. However, for about 1 out of every 200 pregnant women, implantation occurs in the lower uterus (Iyasu et al., 1993). As the placenta grows, it often blocks the cervical opening, a condition called **placenta previa**. This does not affect the fetus, but it may prevent a vaginal delivery.

Cesarean Sections and Induced Labor

A **cesarean section** (also spelled *caesarean*), or **C-section,** is an incision through the abdominal and uterine walls to deliver a baby. Although the name is often attributed to the way in which Julius Caesar was born, in actuality it is derived from *lex cesarea*, a Roman law (715 B.C.) that allowed a fetus to be saved in the case of its mother's death.

There are many legitimate reasons for performing a cesarean section. These include some cases of breech birth or placenta previa; the baby's head being too big for the mother's pelvis; maternal illness or stress; and fetal stress. However, compared with vaginal births, cesarean sections are associated with a higher rate of postdelivery complications (Declerq et al., 2007; Liu et al., 2007). Cesarean sections accounted for 5% of live births in the United States in 1970, but had increased to over 32.3% by 2008 (National Center for Health Statistics, 2010). Many individuals, including many

health professionals, have begun to call for changes in the way physicians decide when to use this procedure (Flamm et al., 1998; Resnik, 2006).

It used to be that once a woman had a C-section, all later pregnancies would have to end with C-section deliveries (because the cuts were made vertically through the horizontal abdominal muscles and through the contracting part of the uterus). Today, however, incisions are made horizontally through the abdomen and then through the noncontracting part of the uterus. In most cases, it is generally safe for a woman who has had a cesarean section to deliver vaginally (Crawford & Kaufman, 2006). The surgical technique to perform cesareans has been modified to follow WHO/UNICEF guidelines and be more "woman-centered" (Smith et al., 2008), and interestingly, many women today say they would prefer a C-section over a vaginal delivery because they can choose when to deliver (e.g., Pope, 2004). The president of the American College of Obstetricians and Gynecologists was quoted as saying, "The time is coming; if not already here, for the maternal choice cesarean" (Torassa, 2000). Because C-sections are so common, it is advisable for a pregnant woman to talk with her physician about his or her attitudes regarding their use before she goes into labor.

About 22% of births in the U.S. follow induced labor (Caughey et al., 2009). This is sometimes necessary because of complications to the mother or fetus, but today is often chosen by women (called "elective" induction of labor) for nonmedical reasons. Interestingly, this choice decreases the need for a cesarean delivery (Caughey et al., 2009).

Preterm Infants

Nine out of every 1,000 births in the United States result in the death of the baby after it is delivered. Over 70% of infant mortalities are from preterm births (Williamson et al., 2008). An infant is considered preterm if it weighs less than 5½ pounds and the mother was pregnant for less than 37 weeks. Sometimes people use the term "premature infants" to describe such children, but others prefer an alternative term, such as "low-birth-weight infants." I will compromise and use the phrase **preterm infants.** Preterm births account for about 12.3% of all U.S. births (about 540,000 a year), up from 9.4% in 1981 (National Center for Health Statistics, 2010). Conditions such as malnutrition and preeclampsia increase the risk of having a preterm birth; other risk factors include a previous preterm birth and age (the risk increases as women age) (Khoshnood et al., 2005). Taking a multivitamin that includes folic acid can greatly reduce the chance of a preterm birth (Bucowski et al., 2009).

Advances in neonatology (the care of newborn babies) have reduced the limit of viability to about 23 to 24 weeks after conception. One of the biggest

---

Breech birth ■ A birth in which the baby is born feet or buttocks first.

Placenta previa ■ A condition in which the placenta blocks the cervical opening.

Cesarean section (C-section) ■ The surgical removal of a fetus through the mother's abdomen.

Preterm infant ■ An infant born weighing less than 5½ pounds and before week 37 of pregnancy.

problems facing a fetus born at this time is that it has great trouble breathing. Before the age of 23 weeks (around 5 ½ months), the fetus cannot produce a liquid called *surfactin*. Surfactin lets the lungs transmit oxygen from the atmosphere to the blood. After 4 months of age, the fetus can produce some surfactin, but it cannot maintain the liquid at the necessary levels until about 8 or 9 months of age. Newborns who cannot maintain proper levels of surfactin develop **respiratory distress syndrome** and die.

> "When I was exactly 8 months pregnant my amniotic sac broke and labor was induced. When I saw my baby in the nursery, she was under oxygen, had all kinds of wires connected to her, an IV in her foot, and she had a lot of trouble breathing. I wasn't ready for this. However, I feel that if I was more informed about premature births I would have understood better."
> (from the author's files)

Most preterm births happen at 34 to 36 weeks, but over 1.6% occur at 33 weeks or earlier (March of Dimes, 2010). Before 1980, there was little hope of survival for babies born weighing less than 2 pounds. Today, about 17,000 infants per year born weighing less than 2 pounds are placed in *intensive care nurseries* (ICNs), where new techniques and equipment allow these infants a good chance of survival. Infants weighing just over 1 pound have about a 20% to 30% chance of survival, while those weighing about 2½ pounds have about an 80% chance of survival (Draper et al., 1999). In addition, premature infants run a high risk of having disabilities that can require treatment for many years. Babies born weighing 3 pounds or less are much more likely than others to have poor psychomotor skills, low IQ scores, and poor performance in school (Shenkin et al., 2004; Swamy et al., 2008).

AFTERWARDS

In 1980, the average stay in a hospital room was 3.2 days for a vaginal delivery. This dropped to 1.7 days in the early 1990s, when most insurance companies refused to pay for more than one day. In a revolt against these "drive-by deliveries," many states passed laws in 1995–1996 requiring insurance companies to pay for at least 2 days. As a result, the average woman giving birth vaginally now stays 2.1 days (Raube & Merrell, 1999; see Weiss et al., 2004).

Breast-Feeding the Baby

Milk production (lactation) begins about 3 days after a woman gives birth. Recall from Chapter 2 that two hormones produced by the pituitary gland are responsible for milk production. **Prolactin** stimulates the breasts to produce milk, while **oxytocin**

FIGURE 7–15 Mother's milk contains many infection-fighting proteins and is easier for a baby to digest than cow's milk.

causes the breasts to eject milk. When the baby sucks on the breasts, a milk-flow reflex is created. In fact, over time mothers merely hearing the baby cry can cause the breasts to begin ejecting milk. At first, the breasts give out **colostrum**, which is high in protein and also helps immunize the infant against diseases. After about 3 days, milk begins to flow. The average amount of milk produced is 2½ to 3 cups per day, but there is a lot of variation among individuals.

The World Health Organization recommends that babies be exclusively breast-fed for 6 months (WHO, 2001). Both the American Academy of Pediatrics and the Institute of Medicine (1991) also endorse breast-feeding. Why? Mother's milk contains many infection-fighting proteins that protect the infant from gastrointestinal illnesses (e.g., diarrhea), respiratory infections, meningitis, skin diseases, and other problems (e.g., Raisler et al., 1999). Breast-fed babies also have higher IQs as adults (Mortensen et al., 2002). Breast-feeding has benefits to mothers as well. When a mother begins nursing, a hormone is released that helps the uterus to contract and helps stop internal bleeding. Breast-feeding also reduces the mother's chance of developing breast cancer (Collaborative Group, 2002). In 2008, 77% of new mothers were breast-feeding their babies during the first few weeks (Centers for Disease Control and Prevention). Keep in mind, however, that drugs and pollutants can be transmitted to the infant through mother's milk. Before taking any medication (including birth control pills),

Respiratory distress syndrome ■ An illness common in premature infants; caused by insufficient levels of surfactin.

Prolactin ■ A hormone released from the pituitary gland that stimulates milk production in the breasts.

Oxytocin ■ A hormone released from the pituitary gland that causes the breasts to eject milk.

Colostrum ■ A thick, sticky liquid produced by a mother's breasts before milk starts to flow.

therefore, it is important for nursing mothers to consult their physicians or pharmacists.

Postpartum Depression

The first 3 months after childbirth are called the *postpartum period*. Although most women look forward to having a baby, many experience a period of negative emotions during this time. In some cases their distress can be extreme:

> "After I had my son I spent weeks and weeks sitting alone on the kitchen floor with him on my lap and crying and crying uncontrollably."

> "I was so depressed after giving birth to a little girl. If somebody touched her, I screamed. When my baby was 3 days old I had a fight with my mother-in-law and husband. Actually, they tried to help me out, but I was so depressed that I always fought with them. Things got worse and I thought I was going to get divorced.... "

> "I can remember being depressed for a couple of months.... I felt so helpless.... Sometimes I resented my baby because I felt so bad and was so exhausted. I hated myself for having these feelings."
> (All examples are from the author's files.)

There is a range of negative emotions that women can experience after childbirth, and it is customary to distinguish three types of depression on the basis of severity (Miller, 2002). About half of women experience a letdown in the first week or two after delivery, called **postpartum blues.** Symptoms may include a depressed mood, confusion, anxiety, and crying, but the condition is mild and does not last long. However, up to 15% of women experience **postpartum depression,** characterized by a deeper depression and anxiety, guilt, fatigue, and often obsessive-compulsiveness (Pearlstein et al., 2009). The stricken mother may feel that she cannot face daily events, is overwhelmed by childcare, and feels ashamed and guilty about her inadequacy as a mother. One in 10 men also experience postpartum depression (Paulson & Bazemore, 2010). About 1 in 1,000 women experience **postpartum psychosis,** characterized by affective (mood) symptoms and hallucinations in what often resembles a manic depressive state. I will focus here on postpartum depression.

Biological factors, particularly hormone changes, may contribute to postpartum depression (Miller, 2002). The placenta secretes high levels of estrogen and progesterone during pregnancy, and there is a sudden drop in the levels of these hormones after birth. But social and psychological factors certainly play a major role. Stress factors include low socio-economic status, unemployment and financial problems, and lack of social support. Marital unhappiness and lack of support by the spouse and family, for example, can contribute to the depression (Knudson-Martin et al., 2009; Miller, 2002).

Many studies indicate that if postpartum depression lasts several weeks, it can affect the infant's emotional, behavioral, and cognitive development (Almond, 2009). It is probably a mother's style of interacting with her child (brought on by the depression) that results in these negative consequences. Women with postpartum depression generally are treated in the same manner as other depressed patients (Miller, 2002).

Sexual Intercourse After Birth

> "We tried to make love again when our first baby was about 3½ weeks old. The pain from the episiotomy made this impossible and we both wound up very frustrated and wondering if our sex life would ever be back to normal. We finally did succeed at about 6 weeks but still it wasn't very comfortable."
> (from the author's files)

Labor often leaves a woman tired and sore for some time, and stitches from an episiotomy may leave her uncomfortable. Vaginal bleeding continues for 2 to 6 weeks in most women and the loss of estrogen results in vaginal dryness and irritation during intercourse for some time (Marchant et al., 1999; von Sydow, 1999). Most physicians advise that sexual intercourse not be resumed until 4 to 6 weeks after the birth.

Postpartum depression often results in reduced sexual relations after childbirth (Ahlborg et al., 2005; De Judicibus & McCabe, 2002). Women also may worry about their sexuality because of stretch marks, extra weight left over from pregnancy, and "flabby" stomach muscles. The stretch marks soon become paler, and problems with weight and stomach muscles can be helped through exercise. Some women also worry that their vagina has become too large after birth, but the vaginal muscles generally become firm and tight again, especially if the woman continues to practice Kegel exercises (see Chapter 2).

The best time to resume sexual relations depends on many factors. In all cases, however, a man and a woman must learn to relate to each other both as sexual partners *and* as parents. The stress of being a new parent (with all of the new responsibilities) often negatively affects a couple's sexual relations (Botros et al., 2006). For women, relationship satisfaction and fatigue are good predictors of a woman's sexual desire after childbirth (Ahlborg et al., 2005; De Judicibus & McCabe, 2002). Making this adjustment to new roles and

---

Postpartum blues ■ A mild, transient emotional letdown experienced by a majority of women after giving birth.

Postpartum depression ■ A deep depression experienced by about 10% of women in the first few months after giving birth.

Postpartum psychosis ■ A psychotic state experienced by about 1 in 1,000 women after giving birth.

feelings requires time and patience. Differences in sleep patterns with an infant that must be fed at night, demands on time and energy made on parents by children, and difficulty finding periods of privacy all force couples to make adjustments in their sexual behaviors.

Despite these concerns, couples do resume sexual intercourse an average of 7 weeks after childbirth (Hyde et al., 1996). However, sexual activity tends to be lower than before pregnancy for several months, and sexual problems (e.g., painful intercourse, decreased desire, vaginal dryness) during the first few months are common (von Sydow, 1999). Women who are breast-feeding show less sexual activity than others (Visness & Kennedy, 1997), and women who had a cesarean delivery tend to start earlier than those who delivered vaginally. As you might expect, sexual attitudes in general play a role. Couples who had a positive attitude about sex before pregnancy tend to resume sexual relations earlier than couples with a less than totally positive attitude (Fisher & Gray, 1988).

New Responsibilities

Becoming a parent is like being asked to start a new job with little or no training. Just because someone has given birth or fathered a child does not mean that she or he has natural parenting ability. Learning how to deal with children effectively and to provide the right balance of discipline and love is not easy. Although 97% of women (and 98% of men) say that "the rewards of being a parent are worth it" (Martinez et al., 2006), most find the demands of new (and multiple) roles in their lives to be stressful (Doss et al., 2009). Studies find that after the transition to parenthood, happiness within the marriage is directly related to the sharing of childcare and housekeeping responsibilities (Hackel & Ruble, 1992). Many new fathers, for example, complain

"Pretend you're carrying your golf clubs, and you won't mind it."

Reprinted courtesy of Bunny Hoest and *Parade* magazine. Copyright © 1998.

about a diminished sex life and their wives' mood swings, yet do little to relieve their partners in their new responsibilities. Men, do you value your relationship enough to share these responsibilities?

PERSONAL REFLECTIONS

Will pregnancy affect your sexual relationship with your partner? How? Why? Will being parents affect your sexual relationship? How? Why? What steps can you and your partner take to ensure that as parents your sexual relationship will continue to be fulfilling?

SPACING PREGNANCIES

How much time in between pregnancies is best for producing a healthy, full-term baby? A large-scale study found that a woman should wait at least 11 months after giving birth before getting pregnant again (Grisaru-Granovsky et al., 2009). Getting pregnant sooner than this greatly increases the chance of a premature (and undersized) baby. Another study recommended waiting 18 to 23 months (Zhu et al., 1999). Waiting 18 to 23 months has an added advantage for mom and dad as well—you won't have two babies in diapers at the same time.

INFERTILITY AND IMPAIRED FECUNDITY

Infertility is defined as the inability of a couple to conceive. The ability of a couple to conceive within a certain period of time is called **fecundity**. For most studies, fecundity is measured over a year's time. Notice that these two terms have different meanings. A person can be fertile, but not very fecund. For example, as people age from their early 20s to their late 30s, most are still fertile, but they become less fecund. Infertility increased from about 8% of couples in the 1980s to 12% now, but much of the increase is due to many people delaying childbearing (problems with fecundity due to an increase in age) (Oliwenstein, 2005).

Most people think of an infertile couple as a couple who have never been able to conceive, called *primary infertility*. However, the inability to conceive after having had one child, called *secondary infertility*, is about as common (Mosher & Pratt, 1991).

The causes of infertility are many and varied because so many organs of both sexes must function properly for conception to take place. About 40%

Infertility ■ The inability of a couple to conceive.

Fecundity ■ The ability of a couple to conceive within a certain period of time.

of the problems involved with infertility are due to the man, with another 40% due to the woman. About 20% of the cases result from problems in both partners (Hudson et al., 1987; Moore, 1993).

Infertility in Men

It has been known for a long time that fecundity in women decreases with age (Maheshwari et al., 2008). This is true for men as well (Ford et al., 2000). The probability that it would take longer than a year to conceive is only 8% for men under 25 years of age, but nearly doubles to 15% for men over 35. This is due to declining numbers and quality of sperm (American Society for Reproductive Medicine, 2008).

As you may remember, only a very few of the millions of sperm cells released during ejaculation survive the trip to the egg. If a man's reproductive system cannot produce enough sperm, and/or if the sperm he produces are too slow or too weak, the probability that fertilization can occur is substantially reduced. Low numbers of sperm are caused by a variety of factors, including endocrine problems (low levels of pituitary or gonadal hormones), drugs (including alcohol and many antibiotics), marijuana, radiation, and infections. If a man gets mumps after puberty, for example, it often spreads to the testicles and causes severe swelling that destroys the seminiferous tubules where sperm are produced. Other infections, including some sexually transmitted infections, can result in blockage of a man's duct system (just as some STIs can lead to blockage of the Fallopian tubes in women). Varicosity of the veins in the spermatic cord (*varicocele*) can also lead to a low sperm count. Because sperm can only be produced at a temperature several degrees lower than normal body temperature, sperm count is sensitive to temperature variations. See Kamischke and Nieschlag (1999) for a review of the many possible causes.

A review of 61 studies conducted worldwide in the 1990s concluded that the average sperm count per ejaculation had dropped by more than half in the previous 50 years (Carlsen et al., 1992). What could cause such a dramatic change? Neils Skakkeback, one of the authors of the paper, said, "It would have to be something in the environment or lifestyle. Changes that occur within a generation could hardly be due to a change in genetic background" (quoted by Epstein in AP release, September 1992). Further evidence is found in the fact that the rates for testicular cancer tripled during the same time period. Could industrial chemical pollutants have such effects? Boys born to (and breast-fed by) mothers exposed to high levels of pollutants can have testicular malformations and dramatically undersized penises, and the same is true for many species in the wild (see Begley & Glick, 1994). Many of the suspected pollutants resemble the female sex hormone estrogen in structure (see Joensen et al., 2009).

Infertility is not just a physical problem; it also affects men emotionally:

> "Several months ago we began trying to have kids unsuccessfully. When I was younger I had an...operation and my doctor said that because of this I would not be able to have children. My wife and I wanted children, and this situation has really put a strain on our marriage."

> "Being sterile is not an easy thing to discuss. On top of diminishing dreams and goals, it has made finding the right girl to begin a lifelong relationship with very difficult.... My future wife and I will never be able to have children of our own.... I've always wanted to teach my son to play sports or take my daughter to dancing lessons.... Hopefully someday I will find the right woman and we can adopt."
> (All examples are from the author's files.)

What are the medical treatments for male infertility? Infertility due to varicose veins in the spermatic cord (8% to 23% of cases) can often be corrected with surgery (Mishail et al., 2009). If the cause is hormonal, treatment with pituitary hormones (or brain hormones that cause release of pituitary hormones) or gonadal hormones (androgens) is often successful. A blocked duct system in men is much easier to correct through surgery than are blocked tubes in women.

When a man is found to have a low sperm count, a procedure called **artificial insemination** is often used. In this procedure, sperm are collected via masturbation and inserted into the female partner's uterus immediately after ovulation. Several ejaculations are usually collected and stored by freezing (frozen semen is just as effective as fresh). For example, if a man's average ejaculation were found to contain 50 million sperm, six to eight ejaculations (totaling 300 million to 400 million sperm) might be collected and frozen. When enough sperm have been collected, they are gathered together for a single insertion. The success rate is close to 20%, but this can be improved to about 33% if fertility drugs are also given to the woman to induce "super-ovulation" (Guzick et al., 1999). Sperm can be safely preserved for more than 10 years, and some men make deposits in sperm banks before having a vasectomy, undergoing chemotherapy, working a hazardous job, or going off to war.

If a man's sperm count is so low that combining several ejaculations will not help, a couple can choose to use sperm from another, usually anonymous, man. In these cases, artificial insemination is often called

Artificial insemination ■ A method of treating infertility caused by a low sperm count in men. Sperm are collected during several ejaculations and then inserted into the partner's vagina at the time of ovulation.

donor insemination. About 70,000 babies are conceived in this manner every year in the United States.

The newest and most successful technique involves injecting a single sperm directly into an egg, called **intracytoplasmic sperm injection (ICSI)**, and then the egg is placed in the uterus by in vitro fertilization (see next section). Nearly two thirds of all assisted reproductive procedures include ICSI (see Figure 7–16) (Centers for Disease Control and Prevention, 2007).

Infertility in Women

The discovery that she is infertile can be emotionally devastating to a woman and her partner (Clay, 2006):

> "My husband and I have been unsuccessful in our attempts to have children. My doctor gave me some fertility drugs and after about 4 months I got pregnant and miscarried. We tried the same drugs again with no success and finally threw in the towel. All of this took about 5 years.
>
> "The experience is terribly isolating. People don't understand what you're upset about—after all, you didn't lose anything that they can see. All of our friends have had their kids. When we got together with our friends the main topics were breast-feeding and details about their pregnancy and delivery. It was heartbreaking not to be able to be happy for them because at the time we just happened to be in a lot of pain."
>
> (from the author's files)

For women of reproductive age, problems with fertilization generally come from two sources—structural problems in the Fallopian tubes or uterus and failure to release eggs (ova). Blockage of the Fallopian tubes accounts for about 25% to 35% of all cases (Honoré et al., 1999; Rebar, 2004). Blockage can be due to anatomical malformations, growths (e.g., polyps), endometriosis (discussion

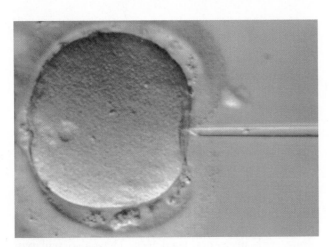

FIGURE 7–16 Intracytoplasmic sperm injection: injecting a sperm into an egg.

follows), infections, and scar tissue. Cigarette smoking and douching also increase the risk of infertility by increasing the risk of pelvic inflammatory disease and blocked tubes (Baird et al., 1996; Buck et al., 1997). Scar tissue from sexually transmitted infections, especially chlamydia and gonorrhea (resulting in pelvic inflammatory disease), accounts for at least half the cases of infertility from blocked tubes. Given the epidemic levels of these infections, this will continue to be a primary cause for both ectopic pregnancies and infertility in the near future (see Chapter 5).

The diameter of the passageway that an egg takes through the Fallopian tube is only about half that of a human hair. Sometimes surgeons are able to reopen these tiny structures, but the success rate for microsurgery is only about 50% (Honoré et al., 1999).

About 25% to 40% of infertile women have endometriosis to some degree (see Lessey, 2000, for a review). Endometriosis can cause infertility by the growth of endometrial tissue in the Fallopian tubes and/or around the ovaries. Many women today are postponing pregnancy, and endometriosis is known as the "career women's disease" because it is most common in women in their mid-20s and over, especially if they have postponed childbirth. Hormone treatment to control the growth of endometrial tissue or surgery to remove it has commonly been used. Today, laparoscopic surgery (with cauterization) is being used with greater frequency for endometriosis-related infertility.

One of the major causes of infertility in women (accounting for about 20% of cases) is a failure to ovulate (Urman & Yakin, 2006). This becomes more common as women age (Maheshwari et al., 2008). Some infertile women have too much of a hormone called prolactin, while others have too little or too much of what are called gonadotrophic hormones (hormones that stimulate the ovaries). Perhaps the most common cause of failure to ovulate is polycystic ovarian syndrome, in which eggs only partially develop within the ovary and there is an excess of male hormones. For women with ovulatory problems, a good diet (e.g., slowly digested carbohydrates, no trans fats) can sometimes improve ovulation and chances of pregnancy (see Chavarro et al., 2008).

If a woman is having problems becoming pregnant because she is not having regular menstrual cycles, and thus eggs are not being released, her physician will try **fertility drugs** (see Crosignani et al., 1999). There are two major types. One type stimulates the pituitary gland to secrete FSH and LH, the hormones necessary to start the cycle (see Chapter 3).

Intracytoplasmic sperm injection (ICSI) ■ A procedure used to treat men who have a low sperm count; injection of a single sperm directly into an egg.

Fertility drugs ■ Drugs that improve the chance of conception in women who are infertile owing to hormone deficiencies. The drugs either stimulate the pituitary gland to secrete FSH and LH or stimulate the ovaries directly.

Clomiphene is an example of this type of drug. A second type stimulates the ovaries directly (HMG, or human menopausal gonadotropin, is an example). The success rate for fertility drugs is about 50% to 70% in cases where the problem is entirely hormonal.

Fertility drugs increase the chance of multiple births from 1% or 2% to 10% to 20% (Luke et al., 1994; Ventura et al., 1997). There was some concern that fertility drugs may increase the risk of ovarian cancer, but large studies have found no evidence for this (Jensen et al., 2009).

Assisted Reproductive Technology

The techniques for overcoming infertility entered a new era with the development of **in vitro ("in glass") fertilization (IVF)** in England in the 1970s. Here, eggs and sperm are combined in a Petri dish, and after fertilization takes place, one or more fertilized eggs (usually at about the four-cell stage) are placed into the woman's uterus. Each year in the United States, close to 50,000 have babies as a result of IVF (Hammond et al., 2009). Children conceived with in vitro fertilization are often called "test-tube babies" by the press and others, but as you can see, the procedure does not even use test tubes.

The success rate is 65% to 83% for women under 35 years of age over an entire course of treatment of IVF/ICSI (several IVF cycles) (Malizia et al., 2009). The success can be improved by transferring two fertilized eggs (rather than one) to a woman's uterus (Baruffi et al., 2009), but this increases the chances of a multiple birth to 20% to 23%. (When "Octomom" Nadya Svleman gave birth to eight babies in 2009 after IVF, it caused a lot of criticism, but the fault was due to a doctor who ignored guidelines and implanted numerous eggs.)

In the mid-1980s researchers modified the IVF procedure (Asch et al., 1984). They bypassed the Petri dish by putting eggs and sperm into a pipette and inserting them directly into a Fallopian tube. They called the technique **gamete intrafallopian transfer**

In vitro fertilization (IVF) ■ A process in which a mature ovum is surgically removed from a woman's ovary, placed in a medium with sperm until fertilization occurs, and then placed in the woman's uterus. This is usually done in women who cannot conceive because of blocked Fallopian tubes.

Gamete intrafallopian transfer (GIFT) ■ A procedure for treating female infertility in which sperm and eggs are gathered and placed directly into a Fallopian tube.

Zygote intrafallopian transfer (ZIFT) ■ A method of treating infertility caused by blocked Fallopian tubes. An ovum taken from the infertile woman is fertilized by sperm from her partner and then transferred to the unblocked portion of a Fallopian tube.

Surrogate mother ■ A woman who carries a fetus to full term for another couple, agreeing to give the infant to the other couple after it is born. The infant generally represents a union of the sperm from the man and either his partner's ovum or the ovum of the surrogate mother.

(GIFT). But that is not the end of the story. In order to ensure fertilization, Asch's group had fertilization take place in a Petri dish (as with IVF) and then placed the fertilized eggs directly into a Fallopian tube, a procedure called **zygote intrafallopian transfer (ZIFT)**. However, after several years, the pregnancy rates for GIFT and ZIFT have not proved to be much better than for in vitro fertilization. Because GIFT and ZIFT require major surgery, most physicians have returned to the simpler, less invasive IVF procedure.

These techniques can also be used to screen potential embryos (preembryos) for genetic defects, and also to select the sex of the child (see Kalb, 2004).

The biggest obstacles to advancement in this field are social, political, and legal. Many people oppose these procedures to treat infertility. The Roman Catholic Church, for example, rejects both artificial insemination and in vitro fertilization, proclaiming that procreation must be "a physically embodied love act." The U.S. government has refused to fund research on IVF. Joseph Schulman, a former section director at the National Institutes of Health, said, "I can think of no other examples where for a decade and a half a whole area of investigation that has in fact proven itself to be of massive value to thousands and thousands of couples has been pigeonholed" (quoted in Baker, 1990). Studies indicate that most people have favorable opinions of infertility treatments that produce a child that is biologically related to both members of the couple (they have less favorable opinions of interventions that use donor eggs, donor sperm, or surrogacy; Halman et al., 1992). How do you feel about this?

PERSONAL REFLECTIONS

Imagine that you and your partner have tried to conceive for five years. How do you feel? What would you do next? What options would you consider? What options would you never consider? Why or why not?

Surrogate Mothers

One of the most controversial fertility solutions is **surrogate motherhood**, sometimes resorted to when a woman cannot conceive or carry a fetus during pregnancy (see Ali & Kelley, 2008). In such a case, a couple may create a zygote through in vitro fertilization and then have the fertilized egg implanted in the uterus of another woman. In a second method, the surrogate mother is impregnated with the male partner's sperm, usually through artificial insemination. The surrogate mother gives birth, and the infant is raised by the infertile couple. The couple will generally pay for the surrogate mother's medical expenses, along with necessary legal fees. They also will pay the surrogate mother a fee for providing this "service" (usually $20,000 to $25,000).

Surrogate mothers have been used since biblical times (see Genesis, chapter 16). Today, some states have passed laws that allow surrogacy, while others have attempted to outlaw it. In cases where the surrogate mother has attempted to keep the baby, the courts have ruled in favor of the intended parents.

Delayed Childbearing and Assisted Reproductive Technology

You have just learned that as women grow older, their fecundity declines (Maheshwari et al., 2008). After age 30, the chances of having a healthy baby decrease by more than 3% each year. The problem is not with the uterus but with the decreased number and quality of eggs as women age. At menopause, you recall, the ovaries stop working entirely and women are no longer capable of reproduction—or at least that was what was thought until recently.

As more and more women have entered careers and chosen to delay pregnancy, they have often been faced with fertility problems when they do decide they are ready for motherhood. Today, however, in vitro fertilization and the related procedures have allowed even some postmenopausal women to become pregnant and have children. Eggs are donated by a young woman (and thus are usually of high quality), and then in vitro fertilization is attempted to achieve fertilization and implantation. The uterus is kept functional with injections of estrogen and progesterone.

More recently, postmenopausal women over the age of 50 have elected to have children by egg donation and in vitro fertilization. In 1994, a 62-year-old Italian woman gave birth after receiving donated eggs. In 2008, a 56-year-old Ohio woman gave birth to triplets. To date, the "record" is 70 years old. In the words of Marcia Angell, executive editor of the *New England Journal of Medicine*, "The limits on the childbearing years are now anyone's guess."

Many people, including many physicians, are debating the ethics and health-related issues of assisted delayed childbearing. The older a woman is during pregnancy, the greater the risk of a low-birth-weight baby. There are also risks to the woman herself— diabetes, high blood pressure, and increased likelihood of having to have a cesarean section (Gilbert et al., 1999). These problems might be minimized by careful screening, but what about the ethical considerations? For those who oppose assisted reproductive technology, proponents offer two arguments. First, there is often a double standard, with many people admiring older men who father children. Why shouldn't women have the same opportunity? Second, qualities like love, experience, and responsibility are more important than age in determining who will be a good mother. As the chairperson of the Council of the British Medical Association said, it is better to have "a fit, healthy 59-year-old than an unfit, unhealthy 19-year-old" mother. What qualities do you think make a good mother?

SUPERFERTILITY

For some women, having children is, apparently, very easy. According to the *Guinness Book of World Records*, the most prolific mother alive is Leontina Albina of Chile, who gave birth to 59 children— always triplets or twins. She was one of three triplets sent to an orphanage, but while her two brothers were adopted, she was not. She promised herself that if she ever had children, she would never give them away. Leontina married at age 12 and continued to have children into her 50s.

A word of caution: Studies show that women who have had six or more pregnancies are at higher risk for coronary heart disease and cardiovascular disease (Ness et al., 1993). Please take this into consideration if you are planning a large family.

STUDY GUIDE

KEY TERMS

afterbirth 185
alpha-fetoprotein (AFP) screening 178
amniocentesis 178
amnion 169
artificial insemination 190
blastocyst 168
Bradley method 181
Braxton-Hicks contractions 183

breech birth 186
capacitation 168
cesarean section (C-section) 186
chorion 169
chorionic villus sampling 178
colostrum 187
conception 168
couvade syndrome 170
critical period 175

crowning 184
dilation (cervix) 184
eclampsia 177
ectopic pregnancy 169
effacement (cervix) 184
embryo 171
episiotomy 185
false labor 184
fear–tension–pain cycle 180

INTERACTIVE REVIEW

Sexual intercourse can result in conception on only about 6 days of the menstrual cycle (from about (1) _____ days before (2) _____ to about (3) _____ days afterwards). Fertilization usually occurs within a (4) _____, and implantation normally occurs in the (5) _____ of the uterus. Implantation of a fertilized egg at any other location is called an (6) _____ pregnancy, and the most common cause is scarring of the Fallopian tubes due to (7) _____. Pregnancy tests are positive if a woman's urine or blood contains a hormone secreted by the developing placenta called (8) _____.

Pregnancy is divided into three 3-month intervals called (9) _____. After implantation, the conceptus is called an (10) _____ for the first (11) _____ months and then a (12) _____ for the last (13) _____ months of pregnancy. An expectant mother can first feel her unborn baby moving, an experience called (14) _____, during the (15) _____ month of pregnancy. Sexual intercourse during pregnancy is generally thought not to be harmful to the fetus, although some health professionals recommend that a pregnant woman not engage in intercourse during the 9th month of pregnancy.

There are many possible causes of complications of pregnancy. Substances that can cross the placental barrier and harm the unborn baby are called (16) _____. Examples include viruses, smoking, alcohol, cocaine, and other drugs. Fetal abnormalities can often be detected by ultrasound or by a variety of invasive techniques such as chorionic sampling, and (17) _____. Today, it is sometimes possible to perform surgery on a fetus while it is still in the uterus.

Prepared childbirth courses attempt to break the (18) _____ cycle through education and preparation. Lamaze and other techniques generally include a "coach" (usually the woman's partner) to help the expectant mother through labor and delivery. These methods hold to a philosophy that the mother-to-be and the coach should be in control of the birthing process and that anesthetics should not be used unless absolutely necessary. Today, there is a growing movement advocating going back to giving birth in the home (or in a homelike environment), usually with the aid of a nurse-(19) _____ rather than a physician.

The actual birthing experience is known as labor. Before giving birth, many women experience false labor. True labor is distinguished from false labor by the timing and length of (20) _____ and by the (21) _____ of the cervix. Labor proceeds in three stages. The initial or (22) _____ stage usually lasts from 6 to 13 hours, although each stage of labor varies a great deal from woman to woman and even from birth to birth in the same woman. The (23) _____ breaks (or is broken by the physician) just prior to or during this stage. The last part of the first stage of labor is called the (24) _____. It marks the beginning of the birth process. In the second stage of labor, the cervix is (25) _____ and the fetus begins moving through the birth canal. The baby usually enters the world (26) _____ first, and after delivery the (27) _____ is cut. In the third stage of labor the (28) _____ detaches from the uterus and leaves the mother's body. If complications develop during childbirth, the baby can be delivered surgically through the mother's abdomen by a (29) _____. Today, in most cases, it is considered safe for women who have previously had a C-section to deliver vaginally during subsequent deliveries.

An increasing number of U.S. women are breast-feeding their babies. Mother's milk contains many infection-fighting (30) _____ and is easier to digest than cow's milk. After giving birth, many women experience negative emotions, called (31) _____. Hormone changes, lack of sleep, and new demands can all contribute to this. Most physicians advise that women not resume sexual intercourse for (32) _____ weeks after delivery. Studies find that after the transition to parenthood, happiness within a relationship is related to (33) _____.

Infertility or impaired fecundity affects about one in (34) _____ couples in the United States. About (35) _____ percent of these cases are due to problems with the man, (36) _____ percent to problems with the woman, and about (37) _____ percent to problems with both partners. In men, infertility is usually caused by either blockage of the duct system or (38) _____. For the latter, a procedure called (39) _____ is often used. In women, infertility is usually the result of blocked (40) _____ or a failure to (41) _____. Today, infertile couples can be helped by a variety of assisted reproductive procedures in which an egg is fertilized outside of a woman's body and then placed into her uterus (called (42) _____).

SELF-TEST

A. TRUE OR FALSE

[T] [F] 43. At implantation, the one-celled organism is called a fetus.

[T] [F] 44. About 75% of all conceptions either fail to implant or are spontaneously aborted within the first 6 weeks.

[T] [F] 45. "Morning sickness" is most common during the last trimester of pregnancy.

[T] [F] 46. An expectant mother cannot feel her unborn baby moving inside her ("quickening") until the second trimester.

[T] [F] 47. Sexual intercourse during the 7th and 8th months of pregnancy is often harmful to the mother and/or fetus.

[T] [F] 48. Drugs can adversely affect the fetus, but smoking, while hazardous to the mother, has little effect.

[T] [F] 49. If a woman is Rh positive and her fetus is Rh negative, the condition is called Rh incompatibility.

[T] [F] 50. One beer or one glass of wine a day is thought to be acceptable when a woman is pregnant.

[T] [F] 51. One of the most common causes of scarring of the Fallopian tubes is untreated gonorrhea and chlamydia.

[T] [F] 52. "Prepared childbirth" means having a baby without the use of anesthetics.

[T] [F] 53. A baby is born during the third stage of labor.

[T] [F] 54. If a woman has an ectopic pregnancy, there is an increased risk that her future pregnancies will also be ectopic.

[T] [F] 55. The expression "test-tube babies" refers to the process whereby conception and embryonic development (i.e., the first 2 months) occur outside the mother's body.

[T] [F] 56. Artificial insemination refers to the fertilization of an egg by synthetically manufactured sperm.

[T] [F] 57. "Morning sickness" can be effectively treated with hormones.

[T] [F] 58. True labor is marked by the onset of Braxton-Hicks contractions.

B. MATCHING

(Match the problem with the treatment or solution)

Treatment or solution

_____ 59. artificial insemination

_____ 60. cesarean section

_____ 61. chorionic villus sampling (or amniocentesis)

Problem

a. Susan has a tubal (ectopic) pregnancy.

b. Sherry and John cannot conceive because she is not having regular menstrual cycles.

_____ 62. fertility drugs
_____ 63. fetal surgery
_____ 64. in vitro fertilization
_____ 65. laparoscopic surgery
_____ 66. surrogate mother
_____ 67. intracytoplasmic sperm injection

c. Carol and David cannot conceive because he has a low sperm count.
d. Phyllis is not yet fully dilated and her baby is in distress.
e. Diane cannot carry a fetus during pregnancy, but she and Frank want to have a baby that is biologically theirs.
f. Shelly and Mark cannot conceive. Eggs taken from Shelly are fertilized by sperm from Mark and then placed into Shelly's uterus.
g. Linda and Walter's unborn baby has a life-threatening urinary tract infection.
h. Joan and Tom are worried that their unborn baby may have an abnormality.

C. FILL IN THE BLANKS

68. Zygote, _____, _____, embryo, fetus.
69. The major link between the developing baby and the mother is the _____.
70. A pregnant woman who has gained excessive weight and has high blood pressure and swollen joints may have _____.
71. Before birth, the fetus' head drops lower in the uterus. This is called _____.
72. Three guidelines to determine if labor has begun are _____, _____, and _____.
73. The _____ trimester is when a developing fetus is generally most susceptible to harmful substances.
74. The vast majority of ectopic pregnancies are _____ pregnancies.
75. In 2009, the Institute of Medicine recommended that normal-weight women gain _____ pounds during pregnancy.
76. By the time a fertilized egg has reached the uterus, it is a fluid-filled sphere called a _____.
77. The part of a baby that normally comes into the birth canal first is _____.
78. An egg remains ripe only for about _____ after ovulation.
79. The fetus is protected in a thick-skinned sac called the _____.
80. _____ and _____ are two procedures used by physicians during labor and childbirth that many experts feel are done far too routinely (and unnecessarily).
81. For a baby to have any chance of surviving, it must develop in the uterus for at least _____ weeks.
82. The World Health Organization recommends that babies be exclusively breast-fed for the first _____.
83. To best ensure the chances of a healthy baby, a woman should wait _____ months after giving birth before getting pregnant again.

SUGGESTED READINGS AND RESOURCES

American College of Obstetricians and Gynecologists. (2005). *Planning your pregnancy and birth* (4th ed.). Washington, DC: Author.

Douglas, A. (2002). *The mother of all pregnancy books: The ultimate guide to conception, birth, and everything in between.* New York: John Wiley & Sons. Humorous and very educational.

Jones, S., & Jones, M. (2004). *Great expectations: Your all-in-one resource for pregnancy and childbirth.* New York: Sterling. The title says it all.

Lothian, J., & DeVries, C. (2005). *The official Lamaze guide: Giving birth with confidence.* Seattle: Amazon.

Sher, G., Davis, V., & Stoess, J. (2005). *In vitro fertilization: The A.R.T. of making babies.* New York: Checkmark books.

Walker, W. A., & Humphries, C. (2007, September 17). Starting the good life in the womb. *Newsweek.* About mothers making good choices while pregnant.

Lamaze International
2025 M Street, N.W.
Washington, DC 20036-3309
1(800) 368-4404
www.lamaze.org
Contact them for the name and address of a certified Lamaze instructor in your area.

Resolve: The National Infertility Association
8405 Greensboro Drive, Suite 800
Mclean, VA 22102-5120
(703) 556-7172
www.resolve.org
Provides advice and help about infertility.

Becoming a Woman/ Becoming a Man
Gender Identity and Gender Roles

8

> Our theoretical position is that gender is a social construction, that a world of "two sexes" is a result of the socially shared, taken-for-granted methods which members use to construct reality.
>
> —From Suzanne Kessler & Wendy McKenna, *Gender – An Ethnomethodological Approach*. Copyright © 1978. This material is used by permission of John Wiley & Sons, Inc.

What determines whether we are born with male or female anatomy? How do we learn that we are a boy or a girl? What does it mean to be "masculine" or "feminine"? If a father sees his son playing with a doll, what should the father do? Where do our ideas about "acting like a woman" or "acting like a man" come from? These are the types of questions that we will be addressing in this chapter. However, before we begin, let's look at the definitions of gender, gender identity, and gender roles.

When people hear the word *sex*, most think of biological features (genitalia, reproductive organs, chromosomes, etc.) or an act (lovemaking, having sex).

But what is *gender*? **Gender** (from the Latin *genus* and the Old French *gendre*, meaning "kind" or "sort"), according to Joan Scott (1986),

is a constitutive element of social relationships based on perceived differences between the sexes. (p. 1067)

One text (Doyle, 1985) states that we may use the term *gender*

only **when discussing social, cultural, and psychological aspects that pertain to the traits, norms, stereotypes and roles considered typical and desirable for those whom society has designated as male or female. (p. 9)**

When you have finished studying this chapter, you should be able to:

- Understand the difference between one's gender and one's sex.
- Define gender identity and gender role.
- Explain various biological influences on sexual anatomy and gender identity.
- Describe the various types of intersexed individuals.
- Explain the Freudian, social learning, and cognitive-developmental theories of gender identity development.
- Discuss the concept of androgyny.
- Explain the evolutionary and sociocultural theories of gender role differences between men and women and the evidence for each.
- Summarize the development of gender roles in childhood and adulthood.
- Describe how gender roles have evolved in the United States.

Gender ■ The social construction of femininity and masculinity.

Sandra Harding (1986) adds:

> **In virtually every culture, gender difference is a pivotal way in which humans identify themselves as persons, organize social relations, and symbolize meaningful natural and social events and processes. (p. 18)**

In short, *gender is the social construction of femininity and masculinity* (Kessler & McKenna, 1978) and is used "to distinguish culturally specific characteristics associated with masculinity and femininity from biological features" (Hawkesworth, 1997). Both the American Psychological Association and the Institute of Medicine have endorsed this distinction (see King, 2010).

Gender identity is your sense of self as a man (or boy) or a woman (or girl), while **gender role** includes everything you feel, think, say, and do that shows to yourself and others that you are, in fact, a man or a woman. In other words, gender role is the way you express your gender identity. Gender identity and gender role are not two different things, but rather two different aspects of the same thing. Gender identity is the inward experience of your gender role, and gender role is the outward expression of your gender identity.

In this chapter, you will learn about the forces that shape both gender identity and gender roles. These forces are biological and social, involving both genetics and learning. Most theorists agree that it is the interaction of such forces that ultimately determines gender identity and gender role. I will begin the chapter with a discussion of how gender identity is formed, focusing first on biological aspects of this process.

BIOLOGICAL INFLUENCES ON GENDER IDENTITY

How do we end up as a boy or girl at birth? Genetics certainly plays an important role, but hormones are equally important.

The Role of Chromosomes

A human cell normally has 23 pairs of **chromosomes,** rod-shaped structures that determine a person's inherited characteristics. Eggs and sperm have only half the normal genetic material (one chromosome from each of the 23 pairs). Thus, when an egg and sperm unite (called *conception*), the resultant single cell will again have the normal 23 pairs. One of these pairs determines whether at birth the baby will be genetically a boy or a girl. *Girls usually have two X chromosomes (XX), while boys usually have one X and one Y chromosome (XY).* Thus, it is the sperm from the father that determines the genetic sex of the child, and this is determined at the moment of conception. However, sometimes individuals with an XX combination have male anatomy and other individuals with an XY combination have female anatomy. How is this possible? Researchers have determined that a smidgen of the Y chromosome—a gene called SRY (sex-determining region of the Y chromosome)—determines maleness (Wilhelm et al., 2007). This piece is missing from XY girls' Y, and it is present on XX boys' X. In addition, it has been found that one or more genes on the X chromosome may help determine femaleness (Bardoni et al., 1994; Vilain, 2001).

The Role of Hormones

As two researchers put it, "Nature's rule is, it would appear, that to masculinize, something must be added" (Money & Ehrhardt, 1972). This something is *testosterone*, which must be produced at a critical stage of embryonic development (i.e., during the first 2 months after conception) in order for an XY combination to result in a baby with male anatomy.

Embryos cannot be distinguished anatomically as either male or female for the first few weeks of development. A pair of primitive gonads develops during the 5th and 6th weeks that have the potential for developing into either ovaries or testes. At this stage, the embryo also has two duct systems: (1) the **Wolffian duct system,** which if allowed to develop will become male structures; and (2) the **Mullerian duct system,** which if allowed to develop will become female structures (see Figure 8–1). If the primitive gonads were removed at this stage of development, the baby would always be born anatomically a girl, even if it were genetically XY. Why?

Normally, the SRY gene on the Y chromosome triggers the transformation of the primitive gonads into testicles during the 7th week of gestation (Hiort & Holterhus, 2000). The newly developed testicles begin to secrete testosterone, which promotes the development of the Wolffian duct system into the male internal reproductive system. The masculinizing hormone is also responsible for the development of the external genitalia a few weeks later. What happens to the Mullerian duct system in these male embryos? The SRY gene activates the

---

Gender identity ■ One's subjective sense of being a man (or boy) or a woman (or girl). This sense is usually acquired by the age of 3.

Gender role ■ A set of culturally specific norms concerning the expected behaviors and attitudes of men and women.

Chromosomes ■ Rod-shaped structures containing the genetic material that determines a person's inherited characteristics.

Wolffian duct system ■ A primitive duct system found in embryos that, if allowed to develop, becomes the male reproductive system.

Mullerian duct system ■ A primitive duct system found in embryos, which, if allowed to develop, becomes the female reproductive system.

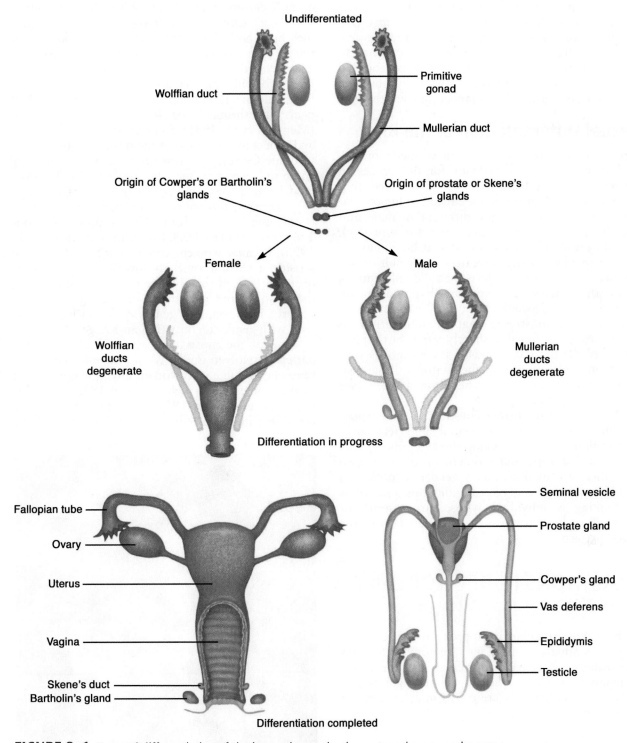

FIGURE 8–1 Prenatal differentiation of the internal reproductive systems in men and women.

testicles to secrete an additional substance called **Mullerian duct–inhibiting substance,** which causes these ducts to shrink.

What happens to embryos with an XX combination (genetically female)? If there is no Y chromosome (and thus no chemical substance to convert the primitive gonads into testicles), the primitive gonads will eventually develop into ovaries. The absence of large levels of testosterone results in the shrinkage of the Wolffian duct system and the development of the Mullerian duct system into the female reproductive system.

> **Mullerian duct–inhibiting substance** ■ A chemical secreted by the testicles during embryonic development that causes the Mullerian ducts to shrink and disappear.

In summary, it would appear that *unless there is a high level of testosterone at a critical stage (the 7th week) of prenatal development, nature has programmed everyone for female development.* In the vast majority of births, the baby's genetic and anatomical sex are matched. Occasionally, however, a different pattern of development may be seen.

Sexual Differentiation of the Brain

Are men's brains different from women's brains, and if so, could this account for differences in behavior? In the 1970s, it was discovered that parts of an area of the brain called the hypothalamus (see Chapter 3) were different in male and female rats (see Kelly et al., 1999, for a review). The difference was not noticeable at birth, but became apparent shortly thereafter as a result of differences in testosterone levels. Studies of humans show that men's and women's hypothalamuses also differ (e.g., Swaab et al., 1992). Experiments with rats demonstrated that administration of testosterone to females shortly after birth masculinized the brain. Obviously, sex hormones very early in life affect not only the anatomy of the genitals but the anatomy of the brain as well (see Becker et al., 2008).

Now for an important question. Is the purpose of chromosomes and embryonic and fetal hormones limited to determining the anatomical characteristics of men and women, or do they also contribute to an individual's gender identity and gender role? One way of examining this question is by looking at individuals whose chromosomes or embryonic/fetal hormone levels differed from the usual pattern.

VARIATIONS IN DEVELOPMENT: INTERSEXED INDIVIDUALS

Due to some irregularities in prenatal development, some individuals are born with anatomical features not usually associated with being a boy or a girl. Often, but not always, this includes ambiguous genitals. These individuals are called **intersexuals**. Let us look at some of the causes.

Chromosome Variations

There are over 70 known irregularities involving the sex chromosomes, and approximately 1 in every 426 people is born with unusual sex chromosome combinations (Nielson & Wohlert, 1991). For example, in 1 out of every 500 live male births, there is one or more

extra X chromosomes (XXY or XXXY), a condition known as *Klinefelter's syndrome*. These biological men have both masculine characteristics, because of the Y chromosome, and feminine characteristics, because of the XX chromosome combination. They tend to be tall with long arms and have poor muscular development, enlarged breasts and hips, a small penis with shrunken testicles, and low sexual desire (Mandoki et al., 1991). Some choose to live as boys, and others as girls. One of the most famous cases is Caroline Cossey, who was raised as a boy, but later chose to live as a woman and became a well-known model and "James Bond girl" (Cossey, 1991).

Turner's syndrome is a condition in which there is only one X chromosome (XO). It occurs in about 1 in every 2,000 to 3,000 live births (Gravholt et al., 1996). Because women with Turner's syndrome are missing a chromosome, the ovaries never develop properly; and in the absence of ovarian hormones, they also do not menstruate or develop breasts at puberty. However, they generally do not have problems with gender identity (Kagan-Krieger, 1998).

One of the most interesting sex chromosome patterns involved Stella Walsh, an internationally renowned athlete who won an Olympic gold medal in the women's 100-meter dash in 1932 and a national pentathlon in 1954 (see Figure 8–2). After her death in 1980, it was found that some of the

FIGURE 8–2 Stella Walsh won an Olympic gold medal in the women's 100-meter dash in 1932. After her death, it was discovered that she had both XX and XY cells.

Intersexuals ■ Individuals with a combination of male and female anatomical features, or in which chromosomal sex is inconsistent with anatomical sex.

cells in her body were XX and others were XY. She had been raised and lived as a woman, but had nonfunctional male sex organs.

The vast majority of us are born with the correct combination of sex chromosomes. However, as you have learned, having an XY chromosome combination does not guarantee that a baby will be anatomically a boy at birth. Hormones are also critically important in the determination of one's sex.

Hormonal Variations

Hermaphroditism is a condition in which a person is born with both male and female reproductive systems as a result of the primitive gonads failing to differentiate properly during the embryonic stage (see Blyth & Duckett, 1991). The term *hermaphrodite* is derived from the Greek mythological figure Hermaphroditus, who merged with the nymph Salmacis to form a single body with male and female genitals. Hermaphrodites are usually genetic females, and even though a uterus is almost always present, they often have an ovary and Fallopian tube on one side and a testicle and a vas deferens and/or epididymis on the other (see Figure 8–3). The external genitalia are usually ambiguous in appearance, but because the phallus is often enlarged, nearly two thirds of these individuals are raised as boys, with complications arising at puberty when they begin to develop breasts and to menstruate. This is a rare condition, occurring in about only 1 in every 65,000 births (Intersexual Society of North America, 2010).

In a variation of hermaphroditism, a South African athlete won the women's 800-meter race at the world championships in 2009, but later was allegedly found to have no uterus and ovaries, but internal testicles. She had been raised as a girl and had the gender identity of a woman.

More common is a condition known as **pseudohermaphroditism**, in which a person with an XX or XY chromosome pattern is born with the proper set of gonads (ovaries or testicles, respectively), but whose external genitalia are either ambiguous or that of the other sex. In women, the most common cause is known as **adrenogenital syndrome (AGS)**, also known as *congenital adrenal hyperplasia*, in which the adrenal glands secrete too much masculinizing hormone during fetal development (Clarnette et al., 1997). The internal organs are normal, but the genitals are masculinized (i.e., the clitoris and labia are enlarged), so that even physicians sometimes mistake these individuals for boys at birth (see Figure 8–4). This condition occurs in about 1 in 20,000 births.

The large majority of AGS babies that are raised as girls show increased male-typical gender roles (Pasterski et al., 2007), but a female gender identity. Although there is an increased likelihood of bisexual or homosexual interests, most have a heterosexual orientation (Dessens et al., 2005; Hines, 2004).

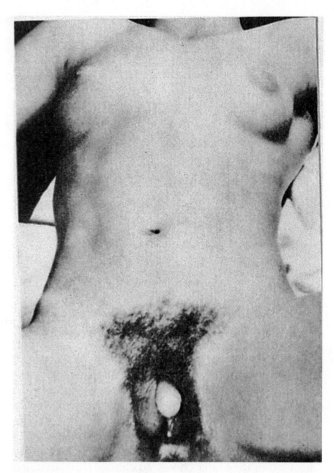

FIGURE 8–3 Hermaphroditism. This individual is genetically a woman (XX chromosomes), has one ovary and one testicle, and has always lived as a man.

The most common cause of pseudohermaphroditism in men is known as **androgen insensitivity syndrome** (sometimes called *testicular feminization syndrome*), in which the testicles secrete normal amounts of testosterone, but the body tissues do not

Hermaphrodite ■ A person with both male and female reproductive systems as a result of failure of the primitive gonads to differentiate properly during embryonic development.

Pseudohermaphroditism ■ A condition in which a person is born with ambiguous genitalia as a result of a hormonal abnormality. See also **adrenogenital syndrome** and **androgen insensitivity syndrome**.

Adrenogenital syndrome (AGS) ■ A condition in girls in which the adrenal glands excrete too much testosterone during fetal development, causing masculinization. This includes enlargement of the clitoris and labia, so that at birth the genitals are sometimes mistaken for those of a boy. Also called **congenital adrenal hyperplasia**.

Androgen insensitivity syndrome ■ A condition in which the testicles secrete normal amounts of testosterone during male embryonic development, but the tissues do not respond to it. As a result, a clitoris, labia, and a short vagina develop, but the internal female structures do not develop because the testicles still secrete Mullerian duct–inhibitory substances.

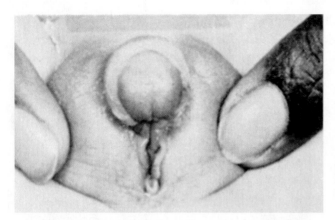

FIGURE 8–4 Adrenogenital syndrome in an infant girl.

respond to it (Kaplan & Owett, 1993). As a result, a clitoris, a short vagina, and labia develop, but the internal female structures fail to develop because the testicles still secrete Mullerian duct–inhibiting substance (see Figure 8–5). This happens in about 1 in 20,000 births. These individuals are generally raised as girls, and because of their insensitivity to testosterone, their estrogen causes them to develop breasts and hips at puberty. They can be very feminine in appearance. Individuals with androgen insensitivity generally have a female gender identity and gender roles, although there is some disagreement about how often they later choose to change their assigned gender (Hines et al., 2003; Mazur, 2005; Meyer-Bahlburg, 2005).

In 1974, 38 boys in the Dominican Republic were discovered who suffered from a type of androgen insensitivity syndrome. They had an XY chromosome combination and prenatally their testicles had produced testosterone and Mullerian duct–inhibiting substance, so that their internal structures were male. However, because of an inherited enzyme deficiency, the testosterone was not converted into dihydrotestosterone, which is necessary for proper formation of the external genitals (the condition is therefore called **DHT deficiency syndrome**). As a result, they had a very small penis that looked like a clitoris, an incomplete scrotum that looked like labia, undescended testicles, and a short, closed vaginal cavity.

Eighteen of these children were reared as girls, but at puberty, when their testicles started secreting large amounts of testosterone, their voices deepened, muscles developed, the testicles descended, and their "clitoris" grew to become a penis. Although the urethral opening was located on the

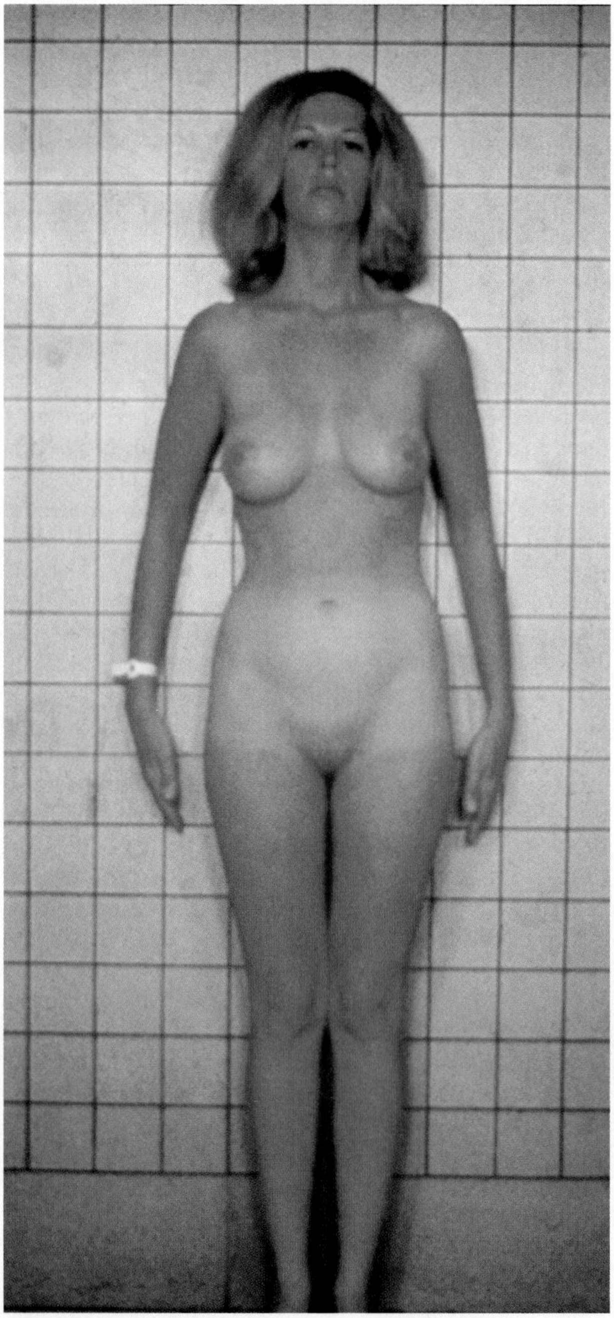

FIGURE 8–5 Androgen insensitivity syndrome in an individual who is genetically a man (XY chromosomes).

perineum and not the tip of the penis, they were capable of ejaculating sperm.

How do you think you would feel if you were being raised as a girl, but suddenly started growing a penis at puberty? The culture in these remote villages has a strong patriarchal "macho" bias. Girls are forced to stay home and do chores, while boys are given considerable freedom, including sexual freedom as adults. Parents of these children generally rejoiced when they discovered that they had an unexpected son. The villagers called them *quevote* ("penis at twelve"). Under these circumstances, it is probably not

DHT deficiency syndrome ■ A type of androgen insensitivity syndrome in which, because testosterone is not converted into dihydrotestosterone, boys' external genitals do not develop properly. Development occurs at puberty with the rise in testosterone.

surprising that 16 of these 18 children decided to become boys and subsequently developed a strong sexual interest in girls (Imperato-McGinley et al., 1979).

It should be noted that anthropologist Gilbert Herdt (1990) believes that this interpretation of the adjustment by the DHT-deficient children is an example of observer bias (see Chapter 1). Western culture categorizes people by two sexes, but the culture in which the children were raised believes in three sexes. In this case, adjustment is easier. Do you suppose that the transition would have been as easy in a country like the United States?

How Many Sexes Are There?

Now that you have been introduced to intersexual individuals, consider the following scenario and question:

> **A person who does not start menstruating as expected during adolescence goes to a physician to find out why. The physician discovers that this person—whose outward appearance [including no penis] and sense of self are both female—has no uterus or ovaries, but instead has male (XY) chromosomes. Is this person female or male?** *(McKain, 1996. Reprinted with permission of the publisher.)*

Did you hesitate to answer? Most people do. Why? Probably because being a boy or a girl is more complicated than having a single characteristic. More importantly, "Hesitation in answering the above question suggests how committed people are to the notion that everyone is *either* female *or* male, period. If people were not so wedded to this notion, they would simply respond that the person described above is female in some ways and male in others" (McKain, 1996).

The important lesson from the first part of this chapter is that there is no direct relationship between sex and gender. You have been introduced to individuals with ambiguous genitalia. Some other cultures recognize three sexes (Herdt, 1990), and at least one scholar has argued that we should recognize at least five different sexes and that human sexuality is not a dichotomy, but a continuum (Fausto-Sterling, 1993; 2000). Today, use of the term *intersexed individuals* recognizes that sex is not dichotomous. Depending on how one defines intersex, 0.02% to 1.7% of all births are intersexed (Fausto-Sterling, 2000; Sax, 2002). In fact, Judith Butler (1990) has convinced many that sex, like gender, is also a social construct. She argues that both concepts can be challenged and changed in any manner.

Attempts to Reassign Sex in Infancy

Is gender identity determined mostly by biology or mostly by teaching the values of society (socialization) through child-rearing practices? Much debate has taken place over this question, but recent studies suggest that biology plays a much stronger role than previously believed. Consider, for example, the following case history.

Identical twin brothers were circumcised at 8 months of age, but due to a surgical mistake, one of the twins lost his penis. After considerable deliberation, and upon the recommendation of doctors, the boy's parents decided to raise the child as a girl. They were encouraged to do so because at that time it was believed that at birth people are psychosexually neutral and that normal psychosexual development depends on the appearance of one's genitals.

When the child was 1 ½ years old, his name was changed from Bruce to Brenda and surgical procedures were done to reconstruct the genitals in order to make them female. The child was dressed in girls' clothing and was encouraged to play with girls' toys and engage in girls' activities.

The published reports during this person's childhood concluded that the sex reassignment had been a success. According to Money (1975), Brenda readily achieved a female gender identity and gender role. The twin brother developed traditional masculine traits. Largely as a result of the "success" of this often cited case, thousands of children born with ambiguous genitals were given sex reassignment surgery (Colapinto, 2000).

Notice that up to this point the underlying assumption in the medical treatment for children with ambiguous genitals (whatever the cause) was that sex was dichotomous—an individual was either a boy or a girl. Furthermore, the standard practice was to define a person's sex on the appearance of his or her genitals. It was believed that in the case of babies with ambiguous genitals, all doctors had to do was surgically change them to be more male or female in appearance. The child could then be raised successfully as a boy or girl, and would have a gender identity that corresponded to the surgically altered anatomy.

In the case of Brenda, later interviews revealed many problems. The psychiatrist following "her" development found that "she" had great difficulty in her attempt to become a woman. Brenda rejected girls' clothes and toys, preferring boys' clothes and toys. She imitated her father and was regarded as a tomboy. She frequently urinated (or tried to) while standing up. As Brenda entered adolescence, she became depressed and suicidal, which finally resulted in her parents telling her the truth—"she" was a boy. Brenda was happy and said, "for the first time, everything made sense and I understood who and what I was." Brenda changed his name to David (after the biblical figure who fought Goliath), chose to have a mastectomy, receive male hormone shots, and undergo surgery to partially restore his penis. Afterwards, he married and adopted his wife's children. When asked

FIGURE 8–6 David Reimer, whose penis was cut off at 8 months of age and who became the subject of an unsuccessful sex reassignment study.

why he had rejected all the attempts to raise him as a girl, he said that being a girl "did not feel right" (see Figure 8–6) (Colapinto, 2000; Diamond, 1997). Unfortunately, David suffered from depression and later committed suicide.

Here is another example (Dittman, 1998). A baby boy was born with an extremely rare condition called *penile agenesis*, in which the testicles develop but the penis does not. He was castrated at age 3 and thereafter was raised as a girl, and began hormone treatment to develop breasts at age 14. In his late teens, he rejected these attempts at sex reassignment and had surgery to reconstruct a penis. He fully regarded himself as a man and later married.

These are not isolated cases (Rosenberg, 2007). Many individuals who underwent sex reassignment as infants because of ambiguous or injured genitals have rejected the socialization process (M. Diamond, 2004).

Gender dysphoria ■ The feeling of being trapped in a body of the opposite sex.

Pediatric endocrinologist Bruce Wilson expressed what is becoming the prevailing view in medicine: "We have had to listen to what our former patients are saying. For a lot of us, it has become clear that current practices were causing problems, that we were doing more harm than good, and that we couldn't predict the outcome with any sort of accuracy" (cited in Palmer, 1999).

What can be concluded from these cases? According to M. Diamond (2004), they show that nature sets a predisposition for gender identity and that "one's sexual identity is not fixed by the gender of rearing." In other words, we cannot always define a person's sex (or make assumptions about his or her gender identity) simply on the basis of the appearance of the genitals. Obviously, biology (genetics and hormones) plays a major role. For example, in the cases of children with surgically altered genitals or children with DHT-deficiency syndrome, it may very well be that although their genitals did not develop properly, fetal hormones altered the brain in the manner appropriate for their chromosomal pattern.

Today, there are some organizations that actively work on helping intersexed individuals accept themselves (e.g., Intersexual Society of North America). In fact, more and more intersexed individuals are choosing not to have genital-altering surgery. Most now agree that (unless there are clear reasons for doing so) children born with ambiguous genitals should also be allowed to grow to an age when they can choose for themselves rather than have doctors assign them at birth (see Bostwick & Martin, 2007). Why? Because, as Diamond (1998) puts it, "One's sexual identity is prenatally organized as a function of the genetic-endocrine forces," regardless of the appearance of the genitals. Perhaps Carla Golden (2000) sums it up best: "The natural attitude would certainly be…knowing that there are women with penises, and men with vulvas" (p. 33).

GENDER IDENTITY "DISORDER"

You have just read about a few individuals who had sex reassignment surgery in infancy because of ambiguous-looking or injured genitals. Attempts to raise many of them as persons of the opposite sex were not successful. Are there ever cases in which individuals with normal genitals are not happy with their sex? The answer is yes.

Some people's gender identity does not match their biological sex. These individuals have normal anatomy, both internally and externally, and yet feel that they are actually a member of the opposite sex. They feel intense distress with their anatomy, a condition known as **gender dysphoria** (American Psychiatric Association, DSM-IV-TR, 2000). People with gender dysphoria feel that they are "trapped in the wrong anatomic body" (Pauly, 1985). This feeling of a mismatch between gender identity and anatomy often begins at a very early age, although in some cases it does not arise until adulthood.

> "Ever since I can remember anything at all I could never think of myself as a girl and I was in perpetual trouble, with this as the real reason. When I was 5 or 6 years old I began to say to myself that, whatever, anyone said, if I was not a boy at any rate I was not a girl. This has been my unchanged conviction all through my life." ("Miss D," from Henry Havelock Ellis, 1918)

> "My friend Kelly believes himself to be a male, when in fact he is really a female. Kelly has everyone call him a he. He's a girl, I know, but I call him a he and always have. He gets a lot of torment, so we try not to tell anyone the truth. He wants a sex change, but he doesn't have the money. He lives life as a guy. He has an auto mechanic job and a girlfriend, but I don't think he's gay. It was really weird at first, but I don't even notice it any more."

> (from the author's files)

Adults with this condition have traditionally been referred to as **transsexuals,** and children with the condition are diagnosed as having gender identity disorder of childhood. However, in the American Psychiatric Association's diagnostic manual, DSM-IV-TR (2000), all conditions have been collapsed into a single diagnosis—**gender identity disorder (GID)** (Bradley & Zucker, 1997). The criteria for gender identity disorder are (a) behaviors that indicate identification with the opposite gender and (b) behaviors that indicate discomfort with one's own anatomy and gender roles. On tests of gender role, male-to-female transsexuals identify closely with nontranssexual women, and female-to-male transsexuals identify closely with nontranssexual men (Herman-Jeglinska et al., 2002; Lippa, 2001). Thus, people with gender identity disorder have an intense desire to belong to the opposite sex, prefer to cross-dress, and want to participate in the games and pastimes of the opposite sex. Persistent discomfort with their bodies and bodily functions is almost always the case (e.g., boys are disgusted with their penises and testicles and distressed about facial and body hair; girls do not want to grow breasts, menstruate, or urinate in a sitting position).

A recent study found that about 3% of 7-year-old boys and about 5% of girls showed cross-gender behavior (van Beijsterveldt et al., 2006). However, in a 10-year follow-up study, most were no longer displaying cross-gender behavior; this was true only in the most extreme cases (Wallien & Cohen-Kettenis, 2008). Thus, the percentages are smaller in adolescence. Among adults, male-to-female transsexuals are twice as common as female-to-male transsexuals

(Olsson & Möller, 2003). Among genetic males, transsexualism is found in both heterosexual individuals (most commonly) and homosexual individuals. Among women, it is rare for a heterosexual individual (someone attracted to men) to be transsexual (Dickey & Stephens, 1995). Most female-to-male transsexuals attracted to men have a gay or bisexual sexual orientation (Bockting et al., 2009).

It is important to understand that transsexualism has to do with gender identity, not sexual orientation—it is not the same as homosexuality. Homosexuals have gender identities that agree with their anatomical sex just as often as heterosexuals. Most male-to-female transsexuals, for example, are attracted to men because they wish to be desired and loved as a woman by a heterosexual man.

Transsexuality is also not the same as transvestism. A transvestite, as you will learn in Chapter 14, dresses in the clothing of the opposite sex in order to achieve sexual arousal. However, a transvestite does not want to change his or her biological sex and does not experience gender dysphoria. In contrast, transsexuals cross-dress as a means of attempting to be more comfortable psychologically with their appearance, not for sexual arousal.

The cause(s) of gender identity disorder has not been determined. One researcher claimed that male-to-female transsexualism was caused by erotic interests and not gender identity problems (Bailey, 2003), but there is little evidence to support this (see Dreger, 2008). Studies have found that while adult transsexuals are dysphoric, they do not show signs of other psychopathology and are "normal" in the desired gender (Cohen-Kettenis & Gooren, 1999). A recent large-scale study of twins concluded that extreme cross-gender behavior in children was mostly (but not totally) due to genetic factors (van Beijsterveldt et al., 2006). Autopsy studies have revealed that the brains (more specifically, the hypothalamus) of male-to-female transsexuals are similar to brains of women (Zhou et al., 1995). Thus, it is likely (though unproven) that hormones before birth or shortly afterwards may have had effects on later behavior and gender identity (see previous sections; see also Collaer & Hines, 1995). Psychosexual factors, particularly the parents' preference for a boy or a girl and parent–child interactions (e.g., regardless of whether parents discourage cross-sex behavior), may sometimes play an additional, albeit smaller, role (Bradley & Zucker, 1997; Cohen-Kettenis & Gooren, 1999).

Transsexual ■ An adult whose gender identity does not match his or her biological sex.

Gender identity disorder (GID) ■ A disorder with the criteria: (a) behaviors that indicate identification with the opposite gender, and (b) behaviors that indicate discomfort with one's own anatomy and gender roles.

Until very recently, the medical profession viewed transsexualism as a problem that needed to be corrected. The medical model assumed that there were only two sexes and that sex was defined by the anatomy of the genitals. Even the official medical term, gender identity "disorder," implies a mistake that must be corrected to conform with the dichotomous model and the expectations of society (including doctors)—the expectation of sexual stereotypes (see Denny, 1998). To correct this, medicine offers sex "reassignment" surgery, so that an individual's anatomy and gender identity are in accord with society's expectations. However, Kessler and McKenna (1978) raise an interesting question: Is one's sex primary and gender secondary, or is it the other way around? Most people would probably agree with the former, but Kessler and McKenna point out that when transsexuals choose to "correct" their condition they change their body (their sex), not their gender (also see Diamond, 1998). Many of these individuals prefer to be described as **transgendered** because they believe it better describes themselves (i.e., someone having a gender identity and gender roles in a body opposite to society's expectations) (Denny, 1997; Rosenberg, 2007).

Because it is still common, for the moment let us examine the medical model. Many transsexuals have turned to surgery to deal with the problem (Cohen-Kettenis & Gooren, 1999). The male-to-female transformation can be done in one surgery (Bouman, 1988). The penis and testicles are removed first. Next, a vagina is created using pelvic tissue. Sensory nerves in the skin of the penis are relocated to the inside of the new vagina. Sexual intercourse is possible after the operation, though lubricants may have to be used. Male-to-female surgery is a much simpler procedure than female-to-male surgery.

In female-to-male surgery, the uterus, ovaries, and breasts are removed. Some individuals have no further changes made, while others decide to have an artificial penis created. The new penis is made using flaps of skin and muscle (from the groin, forearm, or other places) or by clitoral enlargement (Hage et al., 1993). It is incapable of normal erection, although artificial means of creating erections are possible, such as those used in treating erectile disorders.

One of the most famous cases of sexual reassignment was that of an ophthalmologist named Richard Raskind (Richards & Ames, 1983). Raskind had attended college and medical school, become a highly ranked tennis player, and married. He hated his maleness and genitalia. "As a child...

FIGURE 8–7 Tennis player Renee Richards as she appeared after a sex reassignment operation.

I would pray every night that I could be a girl. I knew then that I wanted Renee as my name. It means reborn" (*People* magazine, 1976). He eventually decided to have sex reassignment surgery and become Renee Richards (Figure 8–7). After the operation, Renee felt more comfortable with her gender identity, but found that female tennis players did not want to let her compete in the top professional tournaments. However, a judge ruled that Renee could compete on the professional women's circuit. The legal rights of transsexuals (including employment protection and civil status) are still uncertain in the United States (Green, 2010).

It is important to remember that *sex reassignment surgery is used to help confirm an individual's previously established gender identity*. The purpose is to lessen the feeling of gender dysphoria in the transsexual and to contribute to his or her emotional health and well-being. Most studies have found that the vast majority of transsexuals achieve satisfactory results with the procedure, with only about 5% expressing feelings of regret (Cohen-Kettenis & Gooren, 1999; Friess, 2009; Green & Fleming, 1990).

PSYCHOLOGICAL THEORIES OF GENDER IDENTITY DEVELOPMENT

In the previous sections, you learned that biology plays the major role in establishing one's gender identity. This is not to say that the environment has no effect. The two interact. It is likely that "nature sets a predisposition for these sexual developments and within such limits the environment works" (Diamond, 1997). Parents are obviously an important

---

Transgendered ■ An individual whose gender roles are opposite of those that society expects based on his or her anatomy.

part of a child's environment. Three major psychological theories of development claim that the parent is an important role model who influences the development of gender identity (see Gallahan, 2000, for an extensive review).

Freudian Theory

Sigmund Freud believed that psychological development was influenced primarily by sexual development. He called sexual energy *libido* and thought that the location of the libido (the area of the body responsible for sexual pleasure) changed over time. The part of the body where the libido is focused is called an "erogenous zone." The primary erogenous zone, according to Freud, depends on which *stage of psychosexual development* the individual has reached. In the first year of life, the mouth is the primary erogenous zone, so Freud called this the *oral stage*. Pleasure is derived from sucking and from exploring things with the mouth. The second stage is called the *anal stage*, which lasts from age 1½ to about age 3. According to Freud, the primary source of pleasure in this stage comes from holding in and expelling feces.

The third stage, called the *phallic stage*, lasts from about age 3 to 5. Freud believed that gender identity is learned at this time. It is during this stage, according to Freud, that boys begin to derive pleasure through masturbation, and as they do so, they begin to sexually desire their mothers and come to view their fathers as powerful rivals who might punish them for these desires by taking away their penises. This fear is called "castration anxiety" and is based on the fact that previous sources of pleasure have already been taken away through weaning and toilet training. Gender identity formation for boys takes place by resolving these conflicts, known as the *male Oedipus complex* (named after the principal character in the Greek play *Oedipus Rex*, in which a man kills the king of Thebes and then marries his queen, who turns out to be his own mother). Boys try to become like their fathers and adopt their fathers' gender identity. This process occurs unconsciously and is called **identification.** In this way, boys try to ensure that for the future, they, too, will be able to fulfill their sexual desires, just like their fathers.

Freud has a more complicated explanation for how gender identity is learned in girls. In the *female Oedipus complex*, according to Freud, when a girl realizes that she has no penis, she feels envious and angry, a state that he referred to as "penis envy." The girl blames her mother for this and wants to possess her father in order to replace the mother. Once she realizes that this cannot happen, she unconsciously identifies with her mother as a means of ensuring that she, too, will be able to fulfill her sexual desires in the future.

Most psychologists do not believe that Freud's theories are accurate descriptions of development. Many feel that his ideas are blatantly sexist and were the result of thinking founded on Victorian ideas of morality and sex roles (e.g., Lerman, 1986). Nevertheless, Freud was one of the first modern thinkers to discuss the possibility that children were sexual and to relate this to gender identity development.

Social Learning Theory

Social learning theory emphasizes the acquisition of new associations. An important type of learning that may be involved in acquiring gender roles is that of **operant conditioning,** which is based on the principle that an individual's behavior is modified by the consequences of the behavior. For example, a boy may be praised by a parent for "acting like a man" and not crying after he falls down; he may be yelled at or punished for putting on his mother's lipstick; or he may be allowed to stop doing his homework in order to help his father fix the car. In each of these three examples, the boy is being reinforced to behave in a "masculine manner." He is learning a gender identity and a gender role, and he will associate good things with "masculine behavior" and negative things (even punishment) with "feminine behavior." For a girl, encouragement and praise may follow the display of "feminine behavior," while "boyish behavior" may result in being ignored or being shown disapproval by parents. Thus, behaviors that are reinforced will continue, and behaviors that are not reinforced will eventually stop.

According to social learning theorists, children often learn gender stereotyped behavior by **imitating** people of their own sex (Figure 8–8). For example, children love to imitate their parents and learn what "daddy" and "mommy" do simply by watching their parents. It is always interesting to ask children, "What kinds of things are daddies supposed to do?" and "What kinds of things do mommies do?" "Do daddies wash dishes?" "Do mommies use a saw and hammer nails?" Answers to these questions will tell a lot about the gender roles that children learn from their parents. (How did you answer these questions?)

Identification ■ Two meanings: (1) the adoption of the sex roles of the same-sex parent by a child, and (2) in advertising, to identify or relate to a product.

Operant conditioning ■ A type of learning in which an individual's behavior is modified by the consequences of the behavior.

Imitation ■ Following the behaviors of someone taken as one's model.

FIGURE 8–8 Children often learn gender roles and a gender identity by observing and imitating their same-sex parents.

Cognitive-Developmental Theory

Cognitive theory views infants as "information seekers." Rather than talking about an "oral stage of psychosexual development" to explain why crawling infants put things into their mouths, cognitive theory claims that this is done because infants can "know" things and acquire information about the world this way. To a crawling infant without language, the world can be divided into things that can and cannot be put in the mouth. It can also be known in terms of things that taste good, bad, or have no taste. Gender is another category into which children can sort themselves.

This theory (Kohlberg, 1966) states that the concept of "male" is first learned by observing others. For example, a boy's father is a man, and because a boy is more like his father than his mother, he begins to think of himself and his father as males. Boys become motivated to seek out information about what boys and men should do and how he should behave, imitating a ready source of information about male conduct from their fathers. The mother becomes the prime source of information about what is appropriate "female behavior" for girls.

At this early age, children's idea of gender is "concrete," based on physical cues like hairstyle and dress. Cognitive theorists say that while most children have learned that they are a "boy" or a "girl" by the age of 3, they do not yet have an understanding of gender constancy. **Gender constancy** is the

knowledge that one's gender is constant and will not change. For example, a 4-year-old boy may think that because girls have long hair, if he lets his hair grow long he will change into a girl. A 4-year-old girl may believe that when she wears jeans and a football helmet, she is a boy, but when she takes them off, she changes back into a girl again. Because they do not yet have an understanding of gender constancy, young boys may say that they will become mommies when they grow up and girls may say they will be daddies. This is a natural thing to believe until gender constancy has been acquired, which *usually happens by age 6 or 7*. According to cognitive developmentalists, once a child has acquired the concept of gender constancy, he or she actively seeks information about his or her own gender. "Gender identity develops as children realize that they belong to one gender group, and the consequences include increased motivation to be similar to other members of their group...." (Martin & Ruble, 2004, p. 67).

GENDER ROLES

Theories of Gender Role

There are two opposing theories about gender differences in human behavior. According to **evolutionary (or sociobiological) theory** (Buss, 1999; Geary, 1998), behavioral differences between men and women are due to the different reproductive pressures each faced over thousands of generations—*and thus these differences are stable in today's world*. Evolutionary psychologists argue that psychological sex differences are inherent and result from sexual selection pressures. The theory, as described by Wood and Eagly (2002) claims that:

> Women, as the sex that invested more in offspring (e.g., through gestation and nursing), became choosier about potential mates than men, the sex that invested less in offspring. As a result, ancestral men competed with other men for sexual access to women, and men's evolved dispositions came to favor aggression, competition, and risk taking. Ancestral women developed a proclivity to choose mates who could provide resources to support them and their children. Sexual selection in humans also emerged from women's competition with other women to attract marriage partners and men's selection of long-term mates for fecundity and faithfulness. Furthermore, because of females' internal fertilization, ancestral males could not be certain about the paternity of their offspring. To increase paternity certainty and gain fitness benefits from investing resources in their biological descendants, ancestral males developed a disposition to control women's sexuality and to experience sexual jealousy.

Evolutionary psychology is *not* biological (genetic) determinism (see Confer et al., 2010). It does not take

---

Gender constancy ■ The knowledge that one's gender is constant and will not change. This knowledge is usually acquired by age 6 or 7.

Evolutionary (sociobiological) theory ■ In reference to sex differences in human behavior, states that the behavioral differences are due to the different reproductive pressures men and women faced over thousands of generations.

the position that genes determine behavior or psychology without influence from the environment. It does recognize environmental factors, particularly "the selection pressures that give rise to psychological adaptations" (p. 120).

In sharp contrast to the evolutionary model, **sociocultural theory** (also called *social constructionism* or *microstructural theory*) says that the psychological differences between men and women are a social construction. The theory "begin(s) with the postulate that in humans, males and females are born neutral with respect to sex-dimorphic behavior predispositions" (Udry, 2000, p. 445). It is based on the notion that it is society's expectations of male and female behavior (the social structure) that predict how people will behave. The basis of this theory was stated as early as 1903 by psychologist Helen Bradford Thompson:

> The psychological differences of sex seem to be largely due, not to difference of average capacity, nor to difference in type of mental activity, but to differences in the social influences brought to bear on the developing individual from early infancy to adult years (p. 102).

Thus, rather than believing that masculinity or femininity is expressed because of inherent personality traits, sociocultural theory assumes that men and women would behave identically if society had identical expectations of them. Gender-role differences are therefore constructed by the way men and women interact within their environment and with each other.

Before we examine the evidence for these two theories of gender roles, let's look at the range of gender differences in behavior.

Prior to the 1970s, masculinity and femininity were viewed as opposite ends of a unidimensional continuum (Hathaway & McKinley, 1943; Strong, 1936; Terman & Miles, 1936). In this bipolar model, a person who was high in masculinity would have to be low in femininity, and vice versa (see Spence & Helmreich, 1978).

This conceptualization of masculinity and femininity was revolutionized in 1973 by Anne Constantinople, who proposed that masculinity and femininity were independent constructs. According to Sandra Bem (1974), "Both historically and cross-culturally, masculinity and femininity seem to have represented two complementary domains of positive traits and behaviors, a cognitive focus on 'getting the job done' (a masculine or *instrumental* orientation) and 'an affective concern for the welfare of others' (a feminine or *expressive* orientation)."

Bem (1974) developed the Bem Sex-Role Inventory to measure the amount of masculinity and femininity within an individual's gender role. Individuals could be characterized as masculine or feminine if they scored high on one dimension and low on the other. For some individuals, this is

extreme. **Gender-role stereotypes** are oversimplified, rigid beliefs that all members of a particular sex have distinct behavioral, psychological, and emotional characteristics. A person is considered stereotyped if he or she exhibits a relatively high number of characteristics associated with one gender and claims not to have or not to value the other type of characteristics.

A person having high scores on both dimensions of the Bem Sex-Role Inventory would be classified as *androgynous*. The term **androgyny** comes from the Greek words *andro*, for "male," and *gyn*, for "female." An androgynous person is capable of integrating both traditionally masculine characteristics and traditionally feminine characteristics into his or her gender role. He or she can be both assertive and compassionate, logical and emotional, depending on what is most appropriate for a particular situation.

Bem claimed that some people scored low on both dimensions. Such individuals would be labeled *undifferentiated*. These combinations of femininity and masculinity are summarized in Table 8–1.

Androgynous individuals are viewed by these researchers as being socially desirable and healthy because of their flexibility, demonstrating instrumental or expressive orientations as the situation demands (Spence et al., 1975). They are described as being

> behaviorally flexible with respect to all manner of gender related phenomena. As such, they are willing and able to exhibit masculine behaviors, feminine behaviors, or both as situationally appropriate. Individuals with sex-typed personalities, on the other hand, will tend to avoid or exhibit lower levels of cross-sex-typed behaviors. *(Helmreich et al., 1979)*

A more recent study found that while the items on the Bem Sex-Role Inventory did, in fact, measure two different personality characteristics, the two

TABLE 8–1	*Bem's Sex-Role Classifications*	
	High Femininity	**Low Femininity**
High Masculinity	Androgynous	Masculine
Low Masculinity	Feminine	Undifferentiated

Sociocultural (microstructural) theory ■ States that the psychological differences between men and women are a social construction.

Gender-role stereotypes ■ Oversimplified, preconceived beliefs about the gender roles of men and women.

Androgyny ■ The ability of an individual to display a variety of personality characteristics, both masculine and feminine, depending on whether a trait or behavior is appropriate in a given situation. It is often viewed as a positive characteristic that gives an individual greater adaptability.

characteristics no longer had anything to do with masculinity and femininity—the authors of the study suggested the terms **instrumental** and **expressive** (Ballard-Reisch & Elton, 1992). One possibility is that people's perceptions of gender roles have changed over the last 40 years. We will examine this in the following sections.

PERSONAL REFLECTIONS

In your opinion, what traits (other than physical character-istics) make a man masculine? What traits make a woman feminine? Why? Were there any traits shared by both men and women? Why or why not? Can a man be gentle, caring, affectionate, emotional, and nurturing to his children, and still be masculine? Why or why not? Can a woman be assertive, independent, and ambitious in a career, and still be feminine? Why or why not? Do you consider yourself to be stereotyped or androgynous? Why?

Gender-Role Development During Childhood

Evolutionary psychologists point out that the young of many mammalian species display sex differences in their play. One researcher found that young male vervet monkeys preferred "masculine" human toys (e.g., trucks) over "feminine" human toys (e.g., Barbie dolls) (Hines, 2004). Eye-tracking studies in humans have shown that boys aged 3 to 8 months show a preference for toy trucks, while girls show a preference for dolls (Alexander et al., 2009).

Recall that girls with adrenogenital syndrome (exposed to high levels of androgens prenatally) display male-typical play behaviors. Treating very young nonhuman female mammals with testosterone also increases male-typical play (Hines, 2004), and recently it was found that male-typical play in boys and girls was related to their fetal testosterone levels (Auyeung et al., 2009).

What about sociocultural theory? Does society's expectations become a part of the individual's own set of attitudes and behaviors? The process of internalizing society's beliefs is called **socialization.** Cognitive theory, described earlier, shows that young children have difficulty understanding complex

---

Instrumental ■ A personality characteristic; a cognitive focus on "getting the job done."

Expressive ■ A personality characteristic; a cognitive focus on "an affective concern for the welfare of others."

Socialization ■ The process of internalizing society's beliefs; the manner in which a society shapes individual behaviors and expectations of behaviors.

Gender schemas ■ Ideas about gender roles that children create from their interactions with their environment.

---

concepts. Their early learning often consists of dual categories, such as "good and bad" or "big and small." It is not surprising, then, that young children's ideas about gender roles reflect concrete, simple ideas, dividing behaviors or traits into either "masculine" or "feminine."

Sandra Bem (1981, 1983) has proposed that children cognitively organize the world according to gender. She calls this a **gender schema**—a set of ideas about gender roles that children create from their interactions with their environment. Objects in the environment are often treated as masculine or feminine. Why, for example, do we often regard dogs as masculine and cats as feminine? Languages such as French or Spanish classify all nouns as either masculine or feminine. Gender schemas can influence decisions about what activities to take part in or learn about.

Until recently, it was believed that children organize their world according to gender starting at age 2 or 3 (Hort et al., 1991). More recent studies indicate that children have gained this ability by 18 to 24 months of age (see Martin & Ruble, 2010). Young infants can distinguish between male and female faces and voices and young children can distinguish gender groups. In fact, gender may be the first social category used by children (Kohlberg & Ullian, 1974). Bem (1983) concludes that "gender has come to have cognitive primacy over many other social categories because the culture has made it so."

The stereotype for the female gender role is that of a person who nurtures and cares for others; is passive, dependent, and cooperative; seeks social approval; and is expressive in showing her emotions. The male gender-role stereotype emphasizes independence, dominance, competition, aggression, success, achievement, and emotional repression. Most people believe that men and women differ in these ways (Doyle & Paludi, 1991).

Harvard psychologist Jerome Kagan has said, "If I showed you a hundred kids aged 2, and you couldn't tell the sex by the haircuts, you couldn't tell if they were boys or girls" (quoted in Shapiro, 1990). If this is true, when do gender roles start developing, and what (or who) is responsible?

Parents who assume "traditional" (stereotypic) gender roles behave differently toward their children (Ex & Janssens, 1998). In these families, mothers act as the caregivers, while the fathers act as playmates to their infants. Fathers, however, are much more likely than mothers to motivate their children, especially sons, to conform to stereotyped gender roles (Kane, 2006; Leve & Fagot, 1997). In one study, preschoolers were presented with stereotypic gender-role toys. In one condition, children were given toys that matched stereotypic toys for their own gender. However, in another condition boys were asked to play with dolls or kitchen sets the way girls would, while girls were asked to play with army war toys or cowboy outfits the way boys would. This was done while parents were out of the room. The experimenters were interested in studying how the parents would react when they entered the room and saw the types of toys the children were playing with. Mothers reacted similarly, regardless of whether the toys fit gender-role stereotypes, but fathers showed markedly more negative reactions when they found their children playing with toys that did not fit gender roles. This was especially true when boys were playing with "girls'" toys: the fathers often interfered with their sons' play and showed other signs of negative emotions in those situations (Langlois & Downs, 1980) (see Figure 8–9).

> "My godson, Mikey, will definitely grow up with the idea that men are the head of the households and that women are 'under' them. My uncle encourages Mikey to play football and run around in the house, yet when he and his sister dance around it is not

FIGURE 8–9 How would you react if you found your young son playing with a doll? Do you think that playing with dolls can teach boys behaviors that will be useful when they become adults?

acceptable. Mikey is only allowed to play 'boy' games. He is not allowed to cook, because that is what a girl does."

> "For as far back as I can remember my father only allowed us to do 'masculine' type things. Sports, cars, outdoor activities, etc. He never allowed us to play with girls. On one occasion I distinctly remember playing with two girl neighbors. My father came looking for me and found his son playing with dolls. For quite a while after that I was known as his 'faggot son.' I couldn't have been more than 10. I never became the 'faggot' son, but I did leave that day with a low self-esteem that I carried with me for quite some time."

(All examples are from the author's files.)

PERSONAL REFLECTIONS

How would you react if you found your young son playing with Barbie dolls? Why? How would you react if you found your young daughter playing with toy soldiers and footballs? Why?

Other adults treat boys and girls in different ways as well. In another study, individuals were shown an infant and asked to make observations about its appearance and behavior. The types of comments made were very different, depending on whether they were told the infant was a boy or a girl (Condry & Condry, 1977). The socialization process in gender-role development is seen everywhere in the child's environment. Children's toy catalogs often use pink pages to show toys for girls and blue pages for boys' toys (Haffner & Casselman, 1996). The toys available for boys are generally action-oriented (and often violent and competitive), while girls are given toys that emphasize physical attractiveness, nurturance, and domestic skills (Blakemore & Centers, 2005). Take a walk through a toy store and look at the toys being offered. It is interesting to see how toys are packaged. Many have pictures of children playing with the product on the front of the box. How many toys have pictures of both boys and girls playing with the same toy? (Very few.)

The socialization process begins at an early age. As early as 14 months of age, infants play with toys that are gender stereotyped more often than with other toys (O'Brien & Huston, 1985). In one study, it was found that boys aged 1 ½; believed that girls do not fight and that they like to clean house. Girls of the same age believed that boys do not cry and that they like to fight. Boys and girls aged 2 and 3 believed that boys like to help their dads, like to hit, and like to break the rules. They thought that girls liked to help their moms and did not hit (Kuhn et al., 1978). Thus, children show gender-stereotyped behavior even before they have a firm grasp of gender identity or gender constancy, and they begin developing gender-role stereotypes by the age of 3 (see Martin & Ruble, 2010).

In nearly all cultures, the large majority emphasize nurturant behavior in women and achievement and self-reliance in men. In a study of 24 culturally diverse countries, Williams and Best (1990) found that 5-year-old children from all countries believed that men were strong and aggressive and women were weak and softhearted. By the time they were 8, their beliefs were even more stereotyped. The conclusion: Belief in gender stereotypes not only increases with age in all countries, but the same stereotypes can be found in nearly all countries (though to different degrees) (see Gibbons, 2000, for a review).

Gender roles are usually learned first in the home, but when children reach school age peers and teachers become powerful reinforcers of the process of socialization and gender-role development (Fagot, 1995; Moller et al., 1992). The activities and chores that teachers assign to children in the classroom are often determined by stereotypic gender roles (Sadker & Sadker, 1994). Children quickly identify individuals who act "different." Boys or girls who do not display behaviors similar to the gender roles adopted by most of their peers may be singled out for teasing or ridicule. Interestingly, "tomboy" behavior in girls is usually far more tolerated by peers, teachers, and parents than "effeminate" behavior in boys. It is much easier to carry the label of a "tomboy" than that of a "sissy." Peers will apply great social pressure against boys who show "girlish" behavior

(Birns & Sternglanz, 1983). Children generally prefer playmates of the same sex (Powlishta et al., 1993), but if they have to choose, boys prefer girls with masculine play styles to boys with feminine play styles (Alexander & Hines, 1994). As boys and girls approach junior high school age, they tend to participate less in girl-dominated activities and more in male-dominated activities (Sandberg & Meyer-Bahlburg, 1994).

Textbooks and history books in particular have emphasized the central, dominant role of men and the supporting role of women, but there has been some change in recent years. An analysis of third-grade basal readers found that male characters are still portrayed as having mostly masculine traits, but that female characters have evolved from having mostly feminine traits to having a balance of masculine and feminine traits (Witt, 1996). Organized religion also acts as a socializing agent about gender roles (Eitzen & Zinn, 2000). In almost all religions there is an underlying philosophy of male superiority, and church leadership is almost always dominated by men.

PERSONAL REFLECTIONS

How would you react if your teenage son wanted to take home economics instead of machine shop or auto mechanics? Why? How would you react if your teenage daughter wanted to take machine shop or auto mechanics instead of home economics? Why?

"How is it gendered?"

Here is a summary of what we know about the development of gender roles in childhood. There may be little noticeable difference between boys and girls before the age of 2, but there is no question that most children have embraced gender stereotypes by the age of 4. By the age of 3 or 4, children know sex stereotypes about clothing, toys, games, and work, and by the age of 4 or 5 most have stereotyped occupational goals (Huston, 1983). According to Yale psychiatrist Kyle Pruett, "There are rules about being feminine and there are rules about being masculine. You can argue until the cows come home about whether those are good or bad societal influences, but when you look at the children, they love to know the differences. It solidifies who they are" (quoted in Shapiro, 1990).

However, Pruett's own work shows that children do not necessarily have to develop strongly stereotyped views (see Shapiro, 1990, for a review). He followed the development of children in 16 families where the mothers worked full-time and the fathers were mostly responsible for caring for the children. The children had strong gender identities of being a boy or a girl, but more relaxed views of gender roles than their friends. Pruett commented, "I saw the boys really enjoy their nurturing skills. They knew what to do with a baby, they didn't see that as a girl's job, they saw it as a human job. I saw the girls have very active images of the outside world and what their mothers were doing in the workplace" (quoted in Shapiro, 1990). Children raised in single-parent households also tend to be less stereotyped in their attitudes and behaviors (Russell & Ellis, 1991).

Pruett also feels that fathers benefit by assuming more responsibility in raising their children. He says, "The more involved father tends to feel differently about his own life. A lot of men, if they're on the fast track, know a lot about competitive relationships, but they don't know much about intimate relationships. Children are experts at intimacy. After a while the wives in my study would say, 'He's just a nicer guy'" (Shapiro, 1990).

Role of the Media

All television is educational; the only question is: What is it teaching? *(Federal Communications Commissioner Nicholas Johnson)*

Do the media contribute to gender-role stereotypes? Exposure to stereotypes on television begins in early childhood. For several decades television cartoons have portrayed boy characters as active, noisy, and aggressive, and girl characters as concerned about their appearance, domestic, attracted to boys, and often in need of rescue (Barcus, 1983; Streicher, 1974). What's more, young children are aware of these differences and perceive the characters in stereotypical ways (Thompson & Zerbinos, 1997).

These same stereotypes are common in prime-time television shows targeted for teenagers and adult audiences. Female roles on television typically emphasize romance more than work, and beauty more than intelligence, as the main thing by which women are valued.

Television advertisements frequently use stereotyped characters (Aronovsky & Furnham, 2008; Ganahl et al., 2003). Men are much more likely to be shown as the authoritative central figure (except for ads focusing on health or beauty), while women generally assume dependent, supportive roles. Advertisements featuring children generally portray them in stereotypical settings as well (Larson, 2001).

So, does television's portrayal of characters in stereotyped roles affect viewers? You might not be surprised to learn that people who watch a lot of TV generally believe in more stereotyped gender roles (Lips, 1992).

PERSONAL REFLECTIONS

Watch several television shows. Notice the gender roles that are presented for men and women. What do you feel should be changed, if anything?

What Causes Developmental Gender Differences?

Let us now return to the theories about gender role development. There is little question that boys and girls differ and that these developmental gender differences appear early in childhood. What causes these differences?

Recall that sociobiologists and evolutionary psychologists believe that behavioral differences have evolutionary value. Geary (1999) has proposed that gender differences in childhood also have adaptive value from an evolutionary perspective. He says, for example, that rough and tumble (and competitive) play among boys prepares them for male–male competition for women as adults. Girls, on the other hand, engage in play parenting and developing social skills, attributes that will aid them as adults. In other words, according to Geary the function of childhood is to develop competencies that will aid them in reproduction and survival as adults.

Sociocultural theorists, on the other hand, argue that it is the social structure that leads to psychological sex differences, beginning in childhood. Eagly and Wood (1999) have proposed a "biosocial" theory that combines both explanations. They conclude that behavioral differences between boys and girls result from physical differences, which are then influenced by social factors (social structure, cultural beliefs, etc.) (see Wood & Eagly, 2002). There can be no denying that there are basic physical differences between men and women. This includes not only bone structure and muscle mass but hormonal differences as well. For example, men have much higher levels of testosterone than women, which is related to aggression and dominance (Mazur & Booth, 1998), and as you have just learned, to gender-typical play during childhood as well (Auyeung et al., 2009).

Adult Gender Roles in the United States: Historic Overview

Cancian (1989) and Kimmel (1989) examined the way in which adult gender roles have evolved in America. Cancian (1989) claims that love became feminized during the 1800s, when the United States was becoming industrialized. Early American society did not have different gender roles for the expression of love, nurturance, or dependency. According to Cancian (1989), this was because the home was the center of the educational, economic, and social activities of the family, where both men and women shared in all aspects of family life.

With increased industrialization, men began to earn their livings away from home, and the economic activities of men and women began to split. Men were viewed as breadwinners who left the home to compete in a harsh outside world filled

FIGURE 8–10 Gender roles for American women have undergone a dramatic change in recent decades. The illustration on the left is from a 1955 magazine and the advice in the "good wife's guide" included such things as "Have dinner ready…on time for his return," "Prepare yourself and touch up your make-up," "Be happy to see him," "Listen to him," and "Make the evening his." Today, the majority of women contribute to their family's income, often in nontraditional roles such as electrical repair worker and fighter pilot.

with competition and danger. Women continued to stay at home, and the home began to be viewed as a retreat for the husband after finishing his day's labors. Because the woman maintained the home, the qualities of nurturance, love, and devotion became associated with being feminine. The work that a wife did at home was not considered to be as important or meaningful as work done outside the home. Perhaps this was due to the fact that women failed to receive monetary compensation for their labors within the household. Independence, success, achievement, competition, and self-control came to be valued as masculine characteristics as the man pursued work outside the home. It should also be noted that the 1800s saw the opening of the American frontier, and this was seen as a man's job, calling for independence, self-reliance, and the ability to do without female influence.

Kimmel (1989) points out that the end of the 1800s saw a great deal of challenge to traditional masculine and feminine gender roles. Kimmel argues that social changes in the late 1800s gave rise to the "New Woman," who was single, economically independent, and highly educated, and who did not believe that a woman should have to become dependent

on a man in order to be feminine. The New Woman was part of a growing women's movement that attempted to challenge traditional gender roles and create a more equal distribution of power within American society. Kimmel notes that past definitions of masculinity and femininity helped produce power relationships between the sexes, and when those power relationships were challenged, gender roles were questioned as well and began to change. We have similar forces at work in our society today. Women are seeking more control over job opportunities, the same amount of pay as men receive for comparable work, more freedom in the conduct of their personal affairs, and, in general, more equality between the sexes.

Pleck (1976), a leading authority on the male gender role, notes that men in our society have begun to reexamine their own gender roles. This can cause a conflict within a man between what he was taught was appropriate for his gender role when he was a boy and society's current expectations for the "New Man." In order for men to move away from traditional gender-role behavior, they not only need to feel such change is desirable and beneficial as far as improving the quality of their lives, but they also need to make changes in their relationships to women, other men, their children, and to their work environment.

Adult Gender Roles Today

As you have just learned, gender roles among U.S. adults have been in transition for over 2 centuries. In the last few decades, women have not only entered the work force in larger numbers, but have gained entry into careers and attained access to higher-level positions previously dominated by men. In 1960, fewer than 20% of all women with children under the age of 6 were employed outside the home. In the typical American family today, both adults are employed. Women make up nearly half of the U.S. labor force, including "high-paying executive, administrative, and managerial occupations" (Tyre & McGinn, 2003). There are more women than men going to college and earning degrees, including MBAs (Tyre & McGinn, 2003). As a result, attitudes about men and women and jobs/careers have become much more egalitarian, especially among younger generations (Brewster & Padavic, 2000; Spence & Hahn, 1997; Twenge, 1997a). Thus, the idea that being a mother means not having a career is no longer true and is not influencing women to the extent it did in the past.

Nonetheless, gender stereotypes still persist (as judged by ratings of the typical woman by both men and women) (Lueptow et al., 2001; Vonk & Ashmore, 2003). Even if a woman works outside the home, she generally assumes much more responsibility for housecleaning, meals, and child care than does her male partner (Bianchi & Casper, 2000; Wall, 2007). In a national survey conducted by *Newsweek* in 2003, 41% still agreed that "it is much better for everyone involved if the man is the achiever outside the home and the woman takes care of the home and the family" (Tyre & McGinn, 2003). Note that 59% did not agree, perhaps because earning status is also a predictor of time spent with children (Lueptow et al., 2001), and thus more men today are taking a role in childcare than in the past (see Barnett & Hyde, 2001; Tyre & McGinn, 2003). Younger and more educated women are especially likely to find little satisfaction in housework (Baxter & Western, 1998). When husbands do participate in domestic chores, women are happier with them (Baxter & Western, 1998), but men with traditional stereotyped attitudes are likely to evaluate their marriages negatively if "forced" into egalitarian roles (McHale & Crouter, 1992).

PERSONAL REFLECTIONS

Men: Your wife has decided to resume postgraduate studies leading to a career. This will require that she be away from home more than before and that you assume more responsibilities for care of the house and children. Your reaction?

Women: Your husband has decided to pass up a career opportunity (leading to higher rank and salary) to spend more time at home with the children. Your reaction?

Some researchers have noted that as individuals age and develop as adults, they acquire more complex sets of gender roles. For example, the fact of fatherhood may force men to acquire more experience in being nurturing, while working outside the home may force women to become more assertive and independent. The more complexity there is in gender-role patterns of behavior, the greater the chance for integration of gender roles (Labouvie-Vief, 1990). Although men and women arrive at developmental complexity by different routes, the adaptive end point for both genders is an integration of gender roles; that is, gender roles tend to converge in adulthood (see Blanchard-Fields & Suhrer-Roussel, 1992). Thus, gender-role development extends well into adulthood with cross-gender-role characteristics (i.e., behavior of the opposite sex) often emerging among both older men and women.

So, has there been a trend towards androgyny in the United States? In a now classic study, Spence and Helmreich (1972) found that people liked women best who were competent and doing "masculine" things. In a review of numerous studies, it was found that the difference between men and women on measurements of masculinity and femininity had, in fact, decreased since the early 1970s (Twenge, 1997b). Another review concluded that "overall results from systematic studies have failed to support the claims of large, consistent gender differences"

FIGURE 8–11 Husbands devote more time to domestic duties today than in the past, but they still do less than their wives (even when the wives are employed outside the home).

Box 8–A Cross-Cultural Perspectives

The Native American Two-Spirit and Samoan Fa'afafine

Before the influence of Western culture led to their disappearance, there existed among many North American Indian tribes individuals, known until recently as berdaches, who had special gender status. According to Callender and Kochems (1987), a *berdache* was "a person, usually male, who was anatomically normal but assumed the dress, occupations, and behavior of the other sex to effect a change in gender status." Accounts of berdaches date back to the 1500s (Katz, 1976), and they existed in at least 113 groups that extended from California to the Mississippi Valley and upper Great Lakes (list compiled by Callender and Kochems, 1987).

Early observations were heavily influenced by Western values and perceptions and focused primarily on the homosexuality or bisexuality of many of the berdaches. In fact, the word *berdache* is not an Indian term, but

rather a medieval French term meaning "male homosexual." According to Callender and Kochems, homosexuality did not bestow the status of berdache on an individual, but many berdaches became homosexual. Translations of the Indian terms give "halfman-halfwoman" or "man-woman," with no insinuation about sexuality. Native Americans, as well as anthropologists, are presently urging that scholars use the term **two-spirit** or terms within native languages when referring to these individuals (see Jacobs & Thomas, 1994).

The two-spirits were held in awe and highly revered, but were not chiefs or religious leaders (they were not shamans). Individuals became two-spirits by showing a strong interest in the work of the opposite sex during childhood and/or (and more commonly) by having a supernatural vision during adolescence that confirmed the change

in gender status. In almost all groups, a male two-spirit dressed and fixed his hair like a woman and assumed a woman's occupations, at which he excelled—part of the reason he was admired. On certain occasions, he dressed like and assumed the role of a man. He was generally responsible for burial rituals, but because he could cross back and forth between genders, he was especially valued as a go-between for men and women. It was these exceptional gender-mixing abilities that led to his being greatly admired. But, as noted, Western values intervened. Lurie (1953), who studied the Winnebago Indians, reported, for example, that "most informants felt that the two-spirit was at one time a highly honored and respected person, but that the Winnebago had become ashamed of the custom because the white people thought it was amusing or evil."

FIGURE 8–12 We'wha (left), a 19th-century two-spirit from the Zuni tribe, and (right) Samoan Fa'afafine.

Similar to the Native American berdache, in Samoa there is a group of cross-dressing men known as **fa'afafine** ("in the way of a woman") who play the same role in Samoan society as women (e.g., entertainers, teachers, caretakers) and who are well accepted by heterosexuals. They have sex with straight men, but are not considered to be homosexual (homosexuality in Samoa is a strong taboo). In fact, sex between a Samoan man and a fa'afafine is regarded as a heterosexual interaction and the first sexual experience of many young Samoan men is with a fa'afafine. In short, "a person's gender is based more on his or her role in the society than on actual anatomy" (Fraser, 2002). According to Dr. Vena Sele, Dean of Students at American Samoa Community College (and also a fa'afafine), "As long as you're playing the female role socially, and in sex, then you are as good as a woman" (Fraser, 2002, p. 74).

(Barnett & Hyde, 2001, p. 784). However, the change has not been due to men becoming more androgynous (having more feminine traits), but has resulted from women displaying more masculine-stereotyped traits than in the past. A very recent study concluded that the egalitarian trend in gender-role attitudes in the United States reached a plateau during the last decade (Braun & Scott, 2009).

Today, women must contend with conflicting sets of expectations from parents, friends, bosses, and other people about what is appropriate feminine behavior. Is this good? Evolutionary theory would argue no—that mental health is likely to suffer the further one gets away from their "natural" role (e.g., reproduction and child-rearing for women). However, the evidence is in just the opposite direction. In a review, Barnett and Hyde (2001) concluded that multiple roles for women (and men) are beneficial for mental, physical, and relationship health. How? As evidence, they provided several factors, including: (a) a buffering effect—"the negative effects of stress or failure in one role can be buffered by successes and satisfactions in another role"; (b) added income; (c) increased opportunities for social support; (d) "multiple opportunities to experience successes and develop a sense of self-confidence"; (e) "a broader frame of reference... to get perspective on their ups and downs"; (f) increased self-complexity (resulting in less extreme swings in mood and self-appraisal); and (g) similarities of experiences between men and women (resulting in increased communication and relationship quality).

PERSONAL REFLECTIONS

Have you ever considered marriage? If so, what traits do you want in a husband or wife? Are these the same traits you will want in your partner after you become parents? Is your answer consistent with your answers to the previous questions?

An Example of Evolving Gender Roles: The Sexuality of Women

In Western culture, it was the early Christians that first viewed sex as sinful. Saint Augustine, the major influence on early Christian beliefs about sex, believed that lust was the original sin of Adam and Eve and, consequently, that sex was sinful (Saint Augustine, *City of God*, 4). He blamed Eve for the fall from grace, and in the two centuries that followed it was women who came to be viewed as temptresses.

> ...she took of its fruit and ate; and she also gave some to her husband, and he ate. Then the eyes of both were opened, and they knew that they were naked; *(Genesis 3:6–7, Revised Standard Version)*

Thus, in Christianity, women were viewed as seducing men. Augustine believed that if Eve had not tempted Adam, there would have been no lust.

> The husband, exempt from all seductive goading of passion, could have come to rest on his wife's bosom with peace of mind undisturbed and pristine state of body intact. *(Saint Augustine, City of God)*

The prevailing view of women's sexuality began to change at the time of the Crusades and the elevation of Mary in the Roman Catholic Church. The Virgin Mary was perceived as compassionate and pure, and thus a dichotomous view of women evolved: virgins as asexual and pure, and sexually experienced women who expressed sexual desire as evil temptresses.

The general view during the Middle Ages was still that men were ruled by reason and had more control of their sexual impulses, while women were ruled by animal appetites (Murray, 1995, 1998). When men had anxieties about their bodies and sexual impulses, women were blamed for causing (often passively) their lust. Negative attitudes about women reached a fever pitch in the 1500s and 1600s, when tens of thousands of women were executed (generally burned at the stake to "purify" them) as witches.

FIGURE 8–13 In Western culture, women's sexuality has been viewed differently at different times. Women were viewed as temptresses in early Christianity, but during the Victorian era marriageable women were regarded as asexual. Today, women in Western culture have achieved egalitarian roles.

With the rise of courtly love, which reached its peak in the 1600s, women (at least upper-class women) came to be admired and romanticized, but in a nonsexual way (Tannahill, 1980). During the Victorian era, we saw a complete turnabout in the way women were viewed (see Chapter 1). Rather than temptresses, the majority of Victorian moralists considered women to be asexual, and it was men who were now viewed as sexual aggressors who could not control their desires.

> Ordinarily the normal young girl has no undue sexual propensities, amorous thoughts or feelings....Girls... should be aware of giving way to advances on the part of young men which have only one object in view: the gratification of their animal passion.
> *(Henry Stanton, 1922)*

Women's gender roles were very stereotyped at this time, and they were expected to be subservient to men and fulfill their roles as wives and mothers. The noted psychologist G. Stanley Hall was of this opinion (Hall, 1904).

The sexual dichotomy of women was not completely abandoned in the Victorian era. With the rise of modern medicine, psychiatrists simply replaced the concept of whore with nymphomania (see Studd & Schwenkhagen, 2009). Women who did not restrict their sexual behavior to marriage could now be labeled with a medical diagnosis.

> Nymphomania may be defined as excessive venereal impulse in the female.... It is found in the most cultured, in the most modest, and in the most religious, almost to the same degree as in those less carefully

> educated...many of the nymphomaniacs are given to masturbation and...many of these cases end up as prostitutes. *(Max Huhner, M.D., 1916)*

The 1900s witnessed the advancement of the feminist movement, greater autonomy for women, and finally, with the start of the sexual revolution (about 1960, see Chapter 1), sexual freedom and equality. In the time span from Saint Augustine to the present, the prevailing view of women had gone from temptresses, to asexual, to sexual equals.

Gender Differences in Sexuality

In a review of many studies in 1993, Oliver and Hyde concluded that men had a higher level of sexual desire than women. This was evidenced by how frequently men thought about sex, frequency of masturbation, attitudes about casual sex, and sexual experience. Have things changed in the past 2 decades?

In a recent study, men were found to experience sexual desire an average of 37 times per week, compared to 9 times for women (Regan & Atkins, 2006). For those woman who do have high sexual desire and display it by having multiple sexual partners, double standards still exist. A greater number of partners is viewed positively by most boys' peers and negatively by most girls' peers (Kreager & Staff, 2009).

In a study of sexual desire, sociosexuality ("restricted versus unrestricted sexual attitudes and behaviors"), and height (a physical trait) across 53 nations (and 200,000 people), Lippa (2009) found sex differences for all three variables. The differences were greatest for height, but were still substantial for the other two traits. For sexual desire, the variability in results was much greater for women than for men. Nevertheless, differences in sexual desire and height were rather consistent across nations, which supports a biological explanation for the differences. On the other hand, differences in sociosexuality across nations varied according to gender equality and economic development, in support of sociocultural explanations.

In a follow-up to the 1993 Oliver and Hyde review, Petersen and Hyde (2010) looked at hundreds of studies conducted in several nations. As before, large differences between men and women were found for frequency of masturbation, use of pornography,

and attitudes about casual sex, and small differences were found for most other sexual behaviors and attitudes. The differences in behaviors and attitudes related to sexual desire support evolutionary theory. However, across nations and ethnic groups, the magnitude of some of the other differences depended on the degree of gender equity, in support of sociocultural theory. Many of the differences also decreased with age.

In summary, when it comes to differences in sexual behaviors and attitudes between men and women, there is evidence to support both the evolutionary and sociocultural theorists. In addition, life experiences tend to lead to more androgynous attitudes for those traits affected by society and culture.

STUDY GUIDE

KEY TERMS

adrenogenital syndrome (AGS) 201
androgen insensitivity syndrome 201
androgyny 209
chromosomes 198
DHT deficiency syndrome 202
evolutionary (sociobiological) theory 208
expressive 210
fa'afafine 217
gender 197
gender constancy 208
gender dysphoria 204

gender identity 198
gender identity disorder (GID) 205
gender role 198
gender-role stereotypes 209
gender schemas 210
hermaphrodite 201
identification 207
imitation 207
instrumental 210
intersexual 200
Klinefelter's syndrome 200
Mullerian duct–inhibiting substance 199

Mullerian duct system 198
Oedipus complex 207
operant conditioning 207
phallic stage 207
pseudohermaphroditism 201
socialization 210
sociocultural (microstructural) theory 209
transgendered 206
transsexual 205
Turner's syndrome 200
two-spirit 216
undifferentiated 209
Wolffian duct system 198

INTERACTIVE REVIEW

(1) _____ is your subjective sense of being a man or a woman. It is influenced by both biological and social factors. (2) _____ are norms (what is considered appropriate) about the behaviors and attitudes of men and women. They vary from culture to culture and can change over time within the same culture.

A person's genetic sex is determined at conception by the combination of an egg, which has an X chromosome for sex, and a sperm, which can have either an X or a Y chromosome. (3) _____ combinations usually result in girls, while (4) _____ combinations usually produce boys. There are over 70 known irregularities in chromosome combinations. These include men

with one or more extra X chromosomes, (5) _____ syndrome, and women with only one X chromosome, (6) _____ syndrome.

Hormones determine whether an embryo will develop anatomically to be a boy or girl. Unless there are high levels of (7) _____ at this critical stage of prenatal development, nature has programmed the body to develop into a (8) _____. Hormone abnormalities before birth can result in a mismatch between genetic and anatomical sex, or a baby whose external genitalia are ambiguous in appearance. These individuals are called (9) _____. Some individuals feel that they are trapped inside a body of the wrong sex, a feeling called (10) _____. Persons whose gender identity does not match their biological sex are said to have (11) _____. They often elect to undergo sex reassignment surgery.

Studies with intersexed individuals suggest that gender identity is determined, in large part, by biology. That is not to say that the environment does not play a role. (12) _____ theory emphasizes unconscious identification with the parent of the same sex, while (13) _____ theory emphasizes the role of reinforcement and imitation. Cognitive-developmental theory states that children do not acquire the concept of (14) _____ until the age of (15) _____.

(16) _____ theory says that psychological sex differences between men and women are inherent and the result of different reproductive pressures each faced over thousands of generations. (17) _____ theory emphasizes the role of the environment or social context in influencing the way gender roles develop over the life span. In either case, the development of gender roles begins before a child develops gender identity or gender constancy.

Masculinity and femininity were once viewed as opposite ends of a unidimensional continuum, but today they are generally viewed as (18) _____ constructs. This has led to the theory of

(19) _____, which says that a person can be both masculine and feminine and that this is the healthiest of all gender roles because of the flexibility it gives individuals in different situations.

Parents, teachers, the media, and peers are all powerful influences on the process of socialization and gender-role development. Gender is possibly the first social category learned by children. When children cognitively organize the world according to gender, they create gender (20) _____. As individuals become adults, they generally acquire more complex sets of gender roles, and for both sexes there is an integration of gender roles. Continued belief in stereotypic gender roles can adversely affect one's personal and sexual relations with a partner.

Traditional gender roles in our culture evolved over time in response to social forces. Those forces have been changing (an example has been the increased presence of women in the work force), and as a result, gender roles are in a state of transition. Recent studies have shown that some differences between men and women in sexual attitudes and behaviors are better explained by evolutionary theory (such as (21) _____) while others are better explained by sociocultural theory (such as (22) _____).

SELF-TEST

A. TRUE OR FALSE

[T] [F]   23. Transgendered and transsexual mean the same thing.

[T] [F]   24. Hormone levels around the time of birth alter brain anatomy to be either "male" or "female."

[T] [F]   25. By the age of 3, children know whether they are a boy or a girl, but do not understand that this cannot change.

[T] [F]   26. In the absence of testosterone during embryonic development, we would all be born anatomically a girl.

[T] [F]   27. Fathers tend to treat their children in more gender-stereotypic ways than do mothers.

[T] [F]   28. Transsexual is a term for a type of homosexual.

[T] [F]   29. According to social learning theory, imitation is a process by which children may learn gender identity and gender roles.

[T] [F]   30. The rise of industrialization helped create the male gender role of being independent and unemotional.

[T] [F]   31. Gender role is the way you express your gender identity.

[T] [F]   32. The most common cause of pseudohermaphroditism in men is androgen insensitivity syndrome.

[T] [F]   33. Men's and women's hypothalamuses are different.

[T] [F]   34. A transsexual is someone who cross-dresses for sexual arousal.

[T] [F]   35. Children do not show gender-stereotyped behavior until they have developed gender constancy.

[T] [F]   36. In girls, male sex-play behavior is related to fetal testosterone levels.

[T] [F]   37. There is little noticeable difference between the behavior of boys and the behavior of girls before the age of 2.

B. MATCHING

(Some questions have more than one answer)

_____ 38. Tom believes he is a woman, but is anatomically a man and does not want sex reassignment surgery.

_____ 39. Bob is low in instrumental orientation ("getting the job done") and has great affective concern for the welfare of others.

_____ 40. Frank prefers men as sexual partners.

_____ 41. Susan cannot reproduce; she is short and infertile and has one X chromosome.

_____ 42. Joe is neither instrumental nor expressive, neither assertive nor emotional.

_____ 43. David's body did not respond to testosterone during prenatal development; he has female genitalia and undescended testes.

_____ 44. Sam was born with a very small penis that looked like a clitoris, an incomplete scrotum, and a short, closed vaginal cavity. At puberty his voice deepened, his testicles descended, and his "clitoris" grew to become a penis.

_____ 45. Wayne is both instrumental and expressive, assertive and emotional.

_____ 46. Phillip believes he is a woman trapped in a male body and wishes to have sex reassignment surgery.

_____ 47. Carol has an enlarged clitoris and labia because of too much masculinizing hormone during her fetal development.

_____ 48. Mike believes that men should be assertive, aggressive, success-oriented, and unemotional, and play little role in housekeeping and childcare responsibilities.

_____ 49. Harold is tall, with long arms; he has a small penis, shrunken testicles, low sexual desire, and an extra X chromosome.

_____ 50. Barbara is genetically a woman, but has both male and female reproductive systems as a result of the failure of her primitive gonads to differentiate during the embryonic stage.

a. adrenogenital syndrome
b. androgen insensitivity syndrome
c. androgynous individual
d. DHT-deficient individual
e. "feminine" on Bem Sex-Role Inventory
f. gender dysphoric
g. gender identity disorder
h. hermaphrodite
i. homosexual
j. intersexual
k. Klinefelter's syndrome
l. pseudohermaphrodite
m. stereotyped individual
n. transgendered person
o. transsexual
p. Turner's syndrome
q. undifferentiated individual

C. FILL IN THE BLANKS

51. A child's knowledge that his or her sex does not change is called _____ in cognitive-developmental theory.

52. According to Cancian, gender roles for men and women did not start to differ until the _____.

53. According to _____ theory, an individual's gender role results from society's expectations of male and female behavior.

54. According to Freud, children acquire the gender identity of the same-sex parent through the process of _____.

55. The process of internalizing society's beliefs is called _____.

56. Oversimplified, rigid beliefs that all members of a particular sex have distinct behavioral and emotional characteristics are called _____.

57. On Bem's Sex-Role Inventory, a person who scores low on both dimensions is called _____.

58. According to Freud, children acquire their gender identity in the _____ stage of psychosexual development.

59. If an individual scores high on both the femininity dimension and the masculine dimension of the Bem Sex-Role Inventory, he or she would be called _____.

60. Money and Ehrhardt (1972) stated, "Nature's rule is, it would appear, that to masculinize, something must be added." That something is _____.

61. _____ cross-dress for sexual arousal and gratification, whereas _____ cross-dress because they truly believe they are members of the opposite sex.

62. In social learning explanations of gender identity development, when children watch their mothers and fathers and copy them, it is called _____.

63. Gender refers to _____.

64. According to Bem, masculine is to instrumental as feminine is to _____.

65. According to Kagan, boys' and girls' behaviors do not differ at the age of _____.

66. Some languages classify all nouns as either masculine or feminine. This is an example of _____.

67. The presence of _____ shortly before and after birth changes the brain to male anatomy.

68. Among early North American Indian tribes, a _____ was a highly respected man who cross-dressed and assumed the behaviors of a woman.

SUGGESTED READINGS AND RESOURCES

Becker, J., et al. (Eds.) (2008). *Sex differences in the brain: From genes to behavior.* The latest on biological causes of gender differences. Oxford University Press.

Cowley, G., Gideonse, T., & Underwood, A. (1997, May 19). Gender limbo. *Newsweek.* Good article on the lack of success of sex reassignment surgery at birth.

Hyde, J. S. (1996). *Half the human experience: The psychology of women* (5th ed.). Boston: Houghton Mifflin. Comprehensive and well-written review of women and gender roles.

Kessler, S. J. (1998). *Lessons from the intersexed.* New Brunswick, NJ: Rutgers University Press.

Martin, C. L., & Ruble, D. N. (2010). Patterns of gender development. *Annual Review of Psychology, 61,* 353–381. Excellent for those who are academically minded.

Peterson, J. L., & Hyde, J. S. (2010). A meta-analytic review of research on gender differences in sexuality, 1993–2007. *Psychological Bulletin, 136,* 21–38. Finds support for evolutionary differences for some differences, and sociocultural theory for other differences.

Rosenberg, D., et al. (2007, May 21). (Rethinking) gender. *Newsweek,* pp. 50–57. Great article on transgendered individuals.

Schwartz, P., & Rutter, V. (1998). *The gender of sexuality.* Thousand Oaks, CA: Pine Forge Press.

Tyre, P., & McGinn, D. (2003, May 12). She works, he doesn't. The latest twist in jobs and family. *Newsweek.*

Intersex Society of North America
979 Golf Course Drive #282
Rohnert Park, CA 94928
www.info@isna.org

Kinsey Institute for Research in Sex, Gender, and Reproduction
Indiana University
Morrison Hall 302
1165 E. Third Street
Bloomington, IN 47405
www.indiana.edu/~kinsey
Kinsey Library (E-mail): kinsey@indiana.edu

Our Bodies Ourselves
34 Plympton Street
Boston, MA 02118
Phone: 617-451-3666
Fax: 617-451-3664
www.ourbodiesourselves.org

Sexual Orientation

9

It doesn't really matter why people are gay or not gay. That's not the important question. What's really important is how they're treated. I haven't spent that much time thinking about where my sexuality comes from. I've spent a lot more time thinking about how I fit into this world I have to live in.

—David Barr, quoted by Angier, 1991

Are you sexually attracted to men? To women? To both men and women? These are questions about **sexual orientation**—one's sexual attraction to members of the opposite sex, the same sex, or both sexes. Attraction to members of the opposite sex is called **heterosexuality**, while attraction to same-sex individuals is called **homosexuality**. **Bisexuality** refers to sexual attraction to people of either sex.

At one time it was believed that people were either one or the other: heterosexual or homosexual (Gordon & Snyder, 1989). Today, sexual orientation is viewed as a continuum (American Psychological Association, 2010). Kinsey and his colleagues (1948), for example, devised a 7-point rating scale to measure sexual orientation, with 0 representing people who are exclusively heterosexual and 6 representing people who are exclusively homosexual (see Table 9–1). Kinsey's group regarded anyone as bisexual who had a rating of 2, 3, or 4.

When you have finished studying this chapter, you should be able to:

- Define the terms *sexual orientation*, *heterosexual*, *homosexual*, and *bisexual*.
- Summarize what we know about the prevalence of homosexuality and bisexuality in the United States.
- Understand the difference between sexual orientation, gender identity, and gender roles.
- Discuss the origins of sexual orientation, including psychoanalytic, social learning, and biological explanations.
- Trace the history of attitudes about homosexuality in Western culture as well as the prevalence of sexual prejudice today.
- Compare our attitudes about homosexuality with those in other cultures.
- Understand what it involves for an individual to "come out."
- Understand homosexual lifestyles and the ability of homosexuals to parent.

Sexual orientation ■ A distinct preference for sexual partners of a particular sex in the presence of clear alternatives.

Heterosexual ■ An individual with a sexual orientation primarily to members of the opposite sex.

Homosexual ■ An individual with a sexual orientation primarily to members of the same sex.

Bisexual ■ An individual with a sexual orientation toward both men and women.

TABLE 9–1	*Kinsey and Colleagues' (1948) Rating Scale for Sexual Orientation*					
0	1	2	3	4	5	6
Exclusively heterosexual	Predominantly heterosexual; only incidentally homosexual	Predominantly heterosexual; more than incidentally homosexual	Equally heterosexual and homosexual	Predominantly homosexual; more than incidentally heterosexual	Predominantly homosexual; only incidentally heterosexual	Exclusively homosexual

Source: From *Sexual Behavior in the Human Male* (p. 147), by Kinsey et al., 1948, Philadelphia: Saunders. Copyright The Kinsey Institute. Reprinted by permission of The Kinsey Institute for Research in Sex, Gender, and Reproduction, Inc.

PREVALENCE OF HOMOSEXUALITY AND BISEXUALITY

The large-scale surveys by Kinsey and his associates discussed in Chapter 1 (Kinsey et al., 1948, 1953) were the first source of information about the prevalence of homosexuality in the United States. They found that 10% of their sample of white men had been exclusively homosexual for at least a 3-year period in their lives, and that 1% to 3% of women were predominantly or exclusively homosexual.

Kinsey's survey used a convenience sample (see Chapter 1) that was not representative of the U.S. population. What do more nationally representative recent surveys indicate? Laumann and colleagues (1994) found that 2.8% of the men and 1.4% of the women they surveyed identified themselves as homosexual or bisexual. This was consistent with behavior: 9.0% of men and 3.3% of women reported both male and female sex partners since puberty, and only 2.7% of the men and 1.3% of the women in the survey said that they had had sex with someone of their own sex in the past year. Very similar results were found with national surveys in Australia (Smith et al., 2003) and England (Mercer et al., 2007).

In the 2010 National Survey of Sexual Health and Behavior, 4.2% of adult men and 0.9% of adult women identified themselves as homosexual, with another 2.6% of men and 3.6% of women self-identifying as bisexual (Herbenick et al., 2010a, b; Reece et al., 2010b). The percentages for blacks and Hispanics were similar (Dodge et al., 2010). In the past year, about 6% of men aged 18–50 had received oral sex from another man, 2.3% to 6.7% (depending on age group) had performed oral sex with another man, and 4% to 5% had engaged in receptive anal intercourse. For adult women, fewer than 4% had given or received oral sex with another woman in the past year (percentages were higher in the 20–24 age group).

Thus, *about 3% to 7% of American men and about 1.5% to 4.5% of American women are homo-sexual or bisexual.* However, as many as 10% of men and women have had same-sex sexual experiences or attraction on occasion (Herbenick, 2010a). Some surveys have reported higher numbers, but like Kinsey's surveys, they usually have serious methodology flaws (see Hewitt, 1998).

DEFINING SEXUAL ORIENTATION: ANOTHER LOOK

We must look at more than behavior when characterizing people as heterosexual, homosexual, or bisexual. For example, what about sexual fantasies? Many heterosexuals have had fantasies of homosexual experiences (Bell & Weinberg, 1978; Ellis et al., 2005). In Laumann et al.'s (1994) survey, 5.5% of women and 6% of men found the idea of having sex with someone of their own sex appealing. This was twice as many as had actually engaged in same-sex sexual behavior in the past year or who identified themselves as homosexual or bisexual.

How, then, shall we define **sexual orientation**? I will use a modification of the definition by Ellis and Ames (1987): *distinct preferences consistently made after adolescence in the presence of clear alternatives.* Preferences can be reflected in desire and/or behavior, and, as noted by Ellis and Ames, "isolated instances of sexual behavior may or may not reflect one's sexual orientation." In this chapter, I shall attempt to distinguish between *same-sex sexual behavior* and *same-sex sexual orientation.* Only the latter will be referred to as homosexuality.

Perhaps the biggest confusion is with the term *bisexual.* Several studies have found that sexual self-identification as gay, lesbian, or bisexual can change over time (Diamond, 2005; Kinnish et al., 2005; Savin-Williams & Ream, 2007). This is especially true for women, and at least 25% of lesbians have had a long period of heterosexual relations before identifying as lesbian (Kitzinger & Wilkinson, 1995; Larson, 2006). Among women, bisexual behavior is much more common than being exclusively homosexual (Bauer & Jairam, 2008; Rust, 2000, 2003). In

FIGURE 9–1 Millions of American men and women are either homosexual or bisexual.

Laumann's survey, only 0.3% of women were attracted only to women. In a 10-year longitudinal study of bisexuality in women, it was found that bisexuality was a stable identity and not just a transitional phase (Diamond, 2008).

Is bisexuality a behavior, a feeling, or an identity? In a study of nearly 7,000 men who acknowledged sexual experiences with both men and women, it was found that 2% described themselves as homosexual, 69% as heterosexual, and only 29% as bisexual (Lever et al., 1992). Those men who identified themselves as bisexual said that they were predominantly or sometimes homosexual, whereas those who identified themselves as heterosexual were predominantly heterosexual in behavior. Thus, most people who have had sexual experiences with both opposite- and same-sex individuals do not regard themselves as bisexual. This points out the shortcomings of relying exclusively on either behavior or self-identity as a definition. Recent work has emphasized that sexual orientation has at least three distinct components: affective (sexual attraction, feelings of desire and love), behavioral, and self-identity (e.g., Garnets & Peplau, 2001) and that these are not always consistent, particularly for women (see Diamond, 2003).

A commonly used definition of bisexuality was suggested by MacDonald (1981, 1982):

> To be bisexual means that a person can enjoy and engage in sexual activity with members of both sexes, or recognizes a desire to do so. Also, although the strength and direction of preference may be constant for some bisexuals, it may vary considerably for others with respect to time of life and specific partners.

In conclusion, most researchers today agree that bisexuality is a legitimate classification of sexual orientation, distinct from both heterosexuality and homosexuality.

SEXUAL ORIENTATION, GENDER IDENTITY, AND GENDER ROLES

It has been my experience that many students are uncertain (or mistaken) about the relationship between a person's sexual orientation and his or her gender identity and gender roles. The *gender identity* of the vast majority of homosexuals and bisexuals is just as strong and consistent with their anatomical sex as is found among heterosexuals. Homosexuality and bisexuality are not the result of gender dysphoria.

The real misunderstanding concerns *sexual orientation* and *gender roles*. Early sexologists like Freud and Henry Havelock Ellis thought that homosexuality resulted from reversed gender roles. While many male homosexuals are more effeminate than heterosexual men, and many lesbians are more masculine than heterosexual women (Lippa, 2008), whether a person conforms or does not conform to gender stereotypes does not always predict sexual orientation.

Many people are quick to label others who do not appear to be "typical." Many people assume that if a man is masculine he must be heterosexual, and that if a man is feminine he must be homosexual (G. Smith et al., 1998). For example, people are much more likely to assume that a man is homosexual if he works as a nurse or secretary, or if his face has some "feminine" features (Deaux & Lewis, 1983; Dunkle & Francis, 1990). Conversely, many people are quick to attribute feminine characteristics to a man they are told is homosexual (Madon, 1997).

Probably the major reason for beliefs like these is that for many people, masculinity and femininity are basic assumptions of heterosexuality: Men are masculine and attracted to women, women are feminine and attracted to men. If you believe this, then it follows that the less "masculine" a man is, the more likely that he will be perceived as homosexual; and if a man is homosexual, it is more likely that he will be perceived as "feminine." However, as you learned in the previous chapter, gender roles change over time, and this is true within the homosexual community as well as the heterosexual community. Before the 1970s, for example, effeminate qualities were emphasized in the male homosexual community, but more recently masculinity has been emphasized (Sandfort, 2005). Consider, too, the butch and femme roles assumed by many female homosexuals (behavior most prevalent prior to 1960)—their behaviors were quite different, but their sexual orientation was the same. Again, there is no strong evidence that a homosexual or bisexual orientation must be associated with atypical gender roles. A great many homosexuals and bisexuals do not walk, talk, dress, or act any differently than anyone else (Kirk & Madsen, 1989).

> "I was born and raised in the south. During my early years I had not been exposed to anyone that was gay, or at least to my knowledge I hadn't. It was not a subject that was talked about. It was not until I got to college that I ever came into contact with someone who was openly gay. This lifestyle was all new for me and surprisingly I was okay with it.
>
> For pretty much my whole life I was considered the "All-American" type of girl. I had a loving family and I didn't drink or party like most kids do. I graduated with honors from high school. As for sports, I always made the region teams and time after time I won the MVP awards for all three sports. My senior year I received the miss congeniality award and to top it off I was voted prom queen. I was always someone who surrounded themselves with close friends and enjoyed being around others.

FIGURE 9–2 Socrates. This Greek philosopher and teacher believed that any evil committed by human beings is done out of ignorance. He devoted his life completely to seeking truth and goodness.

> In the last 2 years I have come to grips with the fact that I am a girl attracted to other females. It's scary to think that even with all of my accomplishments and being considered such a wonderful person that it will possibly all come to an end. Nowadays, it seems that all that gets trumped by the fact that you have a different sexual orientation. I wonder how people can say that this lifestyle is a choice. Why would anyone chose to live a harder life than they have to?"
> (from the author's files)

THE ORIGINS OF SEXUAL ORIENTATION

Why are some people heterosexual, others homosexual, and still others bisexual? Is sexual orientation biologically determined? Is it the result of the environment (family background, peers, etc.) shaping individuals? There are probably few topics in the study of human characteristics in which the nature-versus-nurture question has been so strongly debated. Let's examine the evidence.

Psychoanalytic Explanations: Do Parents Play a Role?

Sigmund Freud (1905) believed that male homosexuality resulted when a boy had a domineering, rejecting mother and turned to his father for love, and later to men in general. Female homosexuality develops when a girl loves her mother and identifies with her father and becomes fixated at this stage. Two early studies done with a small number of people who were in therapy claimed, in support of Freud, that homosexuals' parents differed from heterosexuals' parents in their social and parenting skills (Bieber et al., 1962; Wolff, 1971). A much larger study of better-adjusted persons failed to support their findings (Bell, Weinberg, & Hammersmith, 1981). Good parenting skills are found just as frequently in same-sex parents as in opposite-sex parents (Biblarz & Stacey, 2010). There is also no evidence that sexual orientation results from children identifying with a particular parent (Bell, Weinberg, & Hammersmith, 1981). In summary, psychoanalytic explanations have not proven very useful in explaining the orgins of sexual orientation (Downey & Friedman, 1998). Furthermore, in a later section, you will learn that children raised by same-sex parents are just as likely to grow up with a heterosexual orientation as are children raised by opposite-sex parents.

The Effects of Environment

If sexual orientation were a learned behavior (a choice), homosexuals would be expected to have had good or rewarding experiences with same-sex

Box 9–A Cross-Cultural Perspectives

Homosexuality in Other Cultures

Homosexuality is viewed very differently in different cultures. In a review of anthropological studies of 294 societies, Gregersen (1982) found that of 59 societies that had a clear opinion of homosexuality, 69% approved of it and only 31% condemned it. In an earlier study that included 76 societies in which homosexuality was noted, Ford and Beach (1951) found that 64% approved and 36% did not. In a more recent survey of 24 developed countries, in 18 of them more than 50% of people regarded adult homosexual relations to be "always wrong" (Widmer et al., 1998). Among major Western industrialized countries, only the United States and Britain bar known homosexuals from the military. Canada, Australia, Germany, France, and the Netherlands are all more tolerant. On the other hand, the psychiatric organizations in China, India, Brazil, Poland, and Belarus still consider homosexuality to be a mental illness (Sleek, 1998).

Recall that in ancient Greece sexual relations between men and adolescent boys (called pederasty) was highly idealized (Plato's *Symposium*). It was believed that a boy could acquire knowledge by swallowing semen from an intellectual tutor. Pederasty is common in many cultures throughout the world. This includes at least 50 Melanesian (part of the South Pacific islands) societies and societies around the Mediterranean, the Middle East, Africa, Asia, and South America (Dykes, 2000; Gebhard, 1985; Herdt, 1993; Rind, 1998). In perhaps the most studied group, the Sambians (Herdt, 1993), boys are separated from their mothers at about the age of 7 and live only with other boys and men. They regularly perform oral sex on older (but not yet adult) boys; swallowing semen is a practice that the Sambians believe assures maleness (makes them strong, virile, and good warriors and hunters). The boys continue this for 6 to 8 years and then reverse roles, becoming semen donors to younger boys. At 16 years of age, a Sambian boy marries, and for the next year or two is given oral sex by his new bride as well as by younger boys. Once his wife gives birth, however, the same-sex behavior stops, and the new Sambian adult is exclusively heterosexual (in desire as well as behavior) thereafter.

In another example of pederasty, male warriors of the Azande in Sudan take boys as "wives" because there is a shortage of women (S. Murray, 1992). The boys perform all the usual tasks of women and are passive partners in intercourse (performed between the thighs). When they grow older, the boys are free to marry women, but may marry a boy if a woman is not available. In the Siwan culture in Africa, all boys are expected to be passive partners in anal intercourse with adult men. Married men loan their sons to one another and openly talk of their same-sex sexual relations with boys (Ford & Beach, 1951).

What about women? Female same-sex practices have not been studied as extensively as men's, but one study found examples of such behaviors in 95 native cultures (Blackwood, 2000). The types of behavior ranged from adolescent sex play to intimate friendships to erotic ritual practices.

Several important points can be learned from these cross-cultural studies. First, we must distinguish between same-sex sexual behaviors and a homosexual orientation. For example, although all Sambian men engage in same-sex practices during a specified time of their lives, Herdt (1987) estimates that fewer than 5% have a homosexual orientation as adults. In Mexico, Brazil, Turkey, Greece, and Morocco and other northern African countries, it is not uncommon for men to engage in oral-genital sex or anal intercourse, but only the passive partner is regarded as homosexual (Carrier, 1980). Thus, what is considered homosexuality is, in part, culturally defined.

The fact that fewer than 5% of Sambian men develop a homosexual orientation as adults also says much about the role of the environment and biology. If environment were more important than biological factors, you would certainly expect to see a larger proportion of homosexual adults. The percentage of homosexuals across cultures that have been extensively studied is about the same: from 1% to 7%, regardless of whether the culture has a negative or positive attitude about homosexuality (Diamond, 1993; Whitam, 1983). Homosexuals in different cultures greatly resemble one another in lifestyle as well, further evidence for a biological basis (Whitam & Mathy, 1986). What does vary from culture to culture are attitudes about homosexuality. That is a learned response, and what is learned depends on the time and the place in which a person is raised.

---

individuals and bad experiences with members of the opposite sex in their early social experiences.

What is the evidence in support of this explanation? Many people assume that homosexuals are people who are not attractive (or masculine or feminine) enough to "make it" with the opposite sex. However, the data do not support this. In Laumann et al.'s study (1994), only 0.3% of women were attracted only to women. In fact, most lesbians have had pleasurable sexual relations with men (Bell et al., 1981; Diamant et al., 1999). They simply prefer sexual relations with women. In Box 9–A you will learn about some cultures in which it is the custom for boys to have sexual relations with men, but the percentage of adult men in these cultures who are homosexual is not greater than in cultures with a very negative attitude about homosexuality. Studies that have looked at childhood sexual abuse and sexual orientation have found either no relationship (Bell et al., 1981) or only a modest association (and only in the case of men) (Wilson & Widom, 2010).

Relation to Gender Roles

Bell et al. (1981) found that a man's sexual orientation was usually well established by adolescence (often years before overt sexual behavior) and that gender (role) nonconformity during childhood was often, but not always, associated later with a homosexual orientation. For example, several studies have found that for boys who persistently play with girls' dolls and display other stereotypically feminine traits, there is a much greater chance of their being homosexual as adults (Bailey & Zucker, 1995; Ellis et al., 2005; Phillips & Over, 1995; Strong et al., 2000).

Richard Green (1987) studied a small sample of extremely effeminate boys (whom he called "sissy boys") over a 15-year period. Most of the boys engaged in homosexual fantasizing and behavior as adolescents, but some developed a clear heterosexual orientation. Thus, even in cases of extreme childhood gender-role nonconformity, one cannot absolutely predict future sexual orientation. Also, keep in mind that homosexual men who were "sissies" as boys are only a portion of homosexuals; many showed typical gender-role behavior as children (Bell et al., 1981; see previous section on gender roles).

Did you notice that the last two paragraphs focused on men? That is because the relation between childhood gender nonconformity and later homosexuality is greater for boys than it is for girls (see Garnets & Peplau, 2000). Many women report being tomboys as children, but only about 1% to 2% of adult women are homosexual or bisexual. Thus, "childhood gender nonconformity does not provide an adequate explanation for the development of sexual orientation in most women" (Garnets & Peplau, 2000). In fact, the developmental pathway to homosexuality and bisexuality is much more diverse for women than for men (see Diamond, 2007; Diamond & Savin-Williams, 2000; Garnets & Peplau, 2001; Rust, 2000). Women are more likely to move back and forth between heterosexual and homosexual relationships, to be bisexual rather than exclusively homosexual, and to have "late-onset" (age) same-sex relations (Diamond, 2003, 2005). Women "are more likely than men to identify themselves in ways that are inconsistent with their sexual behavior or feelings" (Rust, 2000, p. 213). For example, it would not be unusual for a woman who becomes sexually intimate with a best female friend to not be sexually attracted to other women and not to identify as a lesbian (example from Rust, 2000).

Biological Explanations

Genetic Factors

In 1952, Kallman found nearly 100% concordance for homosexual orientation in identical twins (here, concordance means matching, i.e., if one twin was homosexual, the other was too). The concordance for fraternal (nonidentical) twins was only about 10%. Similar results were found by a German researcher (Schlegel, 1962), and together these findings challenged the prevailing view that homosexuality was determined by social influences.

Several more recent studies have also established a possible genetic basis for sexual orientation. Bailey and Pillard (1991) studied 167 pairs of brothers and found that 52% of the identical twin brothers of homosexual men in the study were also homosexual, compared with 22% of nonidentical twins and 11% of adoptive brothers. In another study of 143 pairs of sisters, they found that 48% of identical twins of homosexual women were also homosexual, compared to 16% of nonidentical twins and 6% of adoptive sisters (Bailey et al., 1993). Subsequent studies found similar results (Bailey et al., 2000; Kendler et al., 2000; Whitam et al., 1993). Researchers have also found that gay men are much more likely than heterosexual men to

FIGURE 9–3 Leonardo da Vinci. This Italian Renaissance painter *(Mona Lisa, The Last Supper)*, anatomist, astronomer, and engineer was one of the most versatile geniuses in history.

have a close relative (e.g., brother, first cousin) who is gay (e.g., Schwartz et al., 2010). The same is true for lesbians, but less so than for men (see Mustanski et al., 2003).

These studies leave little doubt of a biological contribution to sexual orientation. But how much? Remember, not all of the identical twins were homosexual. A review concluded that 50% to 60% of sexual orientation is due to genetics (Rahman & Wilson, 2003). Even if the upper estimate is correct, that still leaves a lot of room for the influence of social and environmental factors. Social interactions might well mediate aspects of any genetic role in sexual orientation (Byne & Parsons, 1993).

Brain Anatomy

It has been known for quite some time that the brains of males and females differ anatomically (Gorski et al., 1978). Is there a difference between the brains of heterosexuals and homosexuals? In one study, autopsies were performed on the brains of 19 homosexual men and 16 heterosexual men. It was found that a part of the hypothalamus (at the base of the brain) known to influence sexual behavior was more than twice as large in heterosexuals (LeVay, 1991). Others found that another part of the hypothalamus, the suprachiasmatic nucleus, had twice as many cells in homosexual men as in heterosexual men (Swaab & Hofman, 1990) and that a major fiber bundle that connects the two halves of the brain (the anterior commissure) was 34% larger in homosexual men than in heterosexual men (Allen & Gorski, 1992). Recent studies have found additional differences in cerebral asymmetry (e.g., Rahman et al., 2008), the size of the corpus callosum (the major fiber bundle that connects the two cerebral hemispheres) (e.g., Witelson et al., 2008), and even inner ears (see McFadden, 2008).

What do the anatomical findings mean, and how are they related to the genetic research? Dean Heimer of the National Institutes of Health concluded, "The simplest interpretation would be that there is a gene, or genes, that control the growth of [brain structures]. Both point to the same idea, that there is a biological component of sexual orientation" (cited by Maugh in the *Los Angeles Times*, 1991).

Birth Order (and the Prenatal Environment)

Many studies have found that, on average, homosexual men have more older brothers than heterosexual men (see Bogaert, 2005, for a review). Each additional older biological brother (but not older sister) increases the probability that the younger brother will be homosexual by about 33% (Blanchard, 2001; Cantor et al., 2002). (That does *not* mean that if you are male and have two older brothers that you will be homosexual; the probability is small to start with.) No birth order effect is

observed in homosexual women (Bogaert, 2000). Birth order effects are observed for many personality characteristics, but not in families where children are adopted (Beer & Horn, 1999). There is also no evidence to suggest that the birth order effect for men is due to the sexual activity or influence of older brothers (Bogaert, 2000). This suggests that birth order effects are the result of biological influences. Blanchard and Bogaert (1996) have suggested that the birth order effect for sexual orientation in men may be due to a reaction of the mother's immune system (to the Y chromosome chemicals) triggered by the previous male fetuses. This, they say, affects sexual differentiation of the brain (see Blanchard, 2001). What percentage of homosexual men owe their sexual orientation to this birth order effect? It has been calculated that it is about 1 in 7 (Cantor et al., 2002), and pertains only to extremely feminine homosexual men (Bogaert, 2005b). The important implication of this research is that it points to prenatal factors in influencing sexual orientation.

Hormones (and the Prenatal Environment)

What could account for the differences in brain anatomy between heterosexual and homosexual men? It is likely that the answer is hormones. Let's first look at research with nonhuman animals.

Same-sex sexual behavior is observed in almost all species (Bailey & Zuk, 2009). In rams, this behavior is found to be associated with differences in testosterone (Roselli et al., 2002). Several studies with nonhuman species have shown that treatment with hormones prenatally (before birth) can result in same-sex sexual behaviors as adults (see Kelly et al., 1999, for a review).

In humans, the level of circulating male sex hormones (testosterone) in adult heterosexual and homosexual men does not differ (see Gladue, 1988). Furthermore, giving sex hormones to adult homosexuals (e.g., testosterone to homosexual men, for example) does not change their sexual orientation. So, how and when do hormones exert their effect? Recall from Chapter 8 that women who were exposed to high levels of masculinizing hormones before birth (adrenogenital syndrome) are much more likely than others to prefer boys' toys and activities as children and develop a homosexual or bisexual orientation as adults (Hines, 2004; Pasterski et al., 2007).

Here is what we know about testosterone during prenatal and early development. Levels increase dramatically when the testicles develop in week 7 after conception (see Chapter 8), reach a peak between weeks 10–22, and then decline to the same levels as are found in baby girls (McFadden, 2008). In boys, testosterone levels then dramatically increase after birth for about 20 weeks and then decline again to the level of girls until puberty. Therefore, any early differences in anatomy due to testosterone would

FIGURE 9–4 While there is considerable evidence for a biological cause of sexual orientation, especially in men, recent research "recognizes the great diversity of women's erotic experiences and the many sociocultural factors that shape women's sexuality and sexual orientation across the life span" (Garnets & Peplau, 2000, p. 181).

have to occur during one of these two early testosterone surges (one prenatally and one shortly after birth) (McFadden, 2008).

For obvious reasons, it would be unethical to manipulate hormones in humans prenatally or shortly after birth. However, we now know that testosterone during these time periods affects the development of other anatomical structures, and researchers use these as measures when comparing adult heterosexuals and homosexuals. One such measure is the (index finger length)/(ring finger length) ratio. The ratio tends to be lower than 1.0 in men and about 1.0 in women and is more pronounced in the right hand and in right-handed people. Homosexuals tend to be left-handed more often than heterosexuals (Lippa, 2003) and have finger-length ratios that are different from heterosexuals (see Mustanski et al., 2003). They also tend to have an earlier onset of puberty.

Conclusions

Although there is a growing body of evidence for a biological contribution to sexual orientation, this does not mean that one's sexual orientation is destined by biology (Byne & Parsons, 1993; Gladue, 1994). The studies with identical twins point strongly to a biological factor, but the fact that about half the twins were discordant (in spite of the fact that they had identical genes) shows that environment also plays a role.

Most researchers today agree that biological and social influences *both* contribute to the development of sexual orientation. The question is no longer nature versus nurture, but to what extent each influences orientation. Several groups of

researchers have recently re-examined large groups of identical twins (often thousands) to address this question. The results: genetic influences and the environment both contribute. In a population study of twins in Sweden, genetics accounted for .34–.39 of the variance in men and .18–.19 in women, shared environmental influences accounted for .00 in men and .16–.17 in women, whereas nonshared environmental effects accounted for .61–.66 in men and .64–.66 in women (Långström et al., 2010). A population study of Finnish twins found that when gender-role nonconformity in childhood and a homosexual orientation in adulthood occurred together, the genetic contribution was the strongest, with only a modest role for nonshared environmental effects (Alanko et al., 2010). A modest-to-strong contribution of both genetic influences and environmental influences to childhood gender-role nonconformity were similarly found for twins in England (Knafo et al., 2005), the Netherlands (van Beijsterveld et al., 2006), and Australia (Bailey et al., 2000). Psychologist Daryl Bem (1996) presented an intriguing hypothesis. He proposed that biology (genes, anatomy, hormones) "[does] not code for sexual orientation per se but for childhood temperaments that influence a child's preferences for sex-typical or sex-atypical activities and peers." This then steers an individual in the direction of a particular orientation.

To date, there is much stronger evidence for a biological contribution to homosexuality in men than in women (see Mustanski et al., 2003; Rahman & Wilson, 2003; Veniegas & Conley, 2000). Although there is some evidence for a biological factor in lesbians (see previous sections), the number of women who are exclusively homosexual is quite small, and the sexual fluidity of bisexual women emphasizes the importance of the social context in women's relationships (Diamond, 2003; Diamond & Savin-Williams, 2000; Garnets & Peplau, 2001; Rust, 2000; see also Baumeister, 2000).

BEING HOMOSEXUAL

Homosexuality is a word derived from the Greek *homo*, meaning "same" (do not confuse this with the Latin *homo*, meaning "man"). The term was first used by a Hungarian physician in a pamphlet published in Germany in 1869 (Gregersen, 1982) and was popularized in the English language two decades later by Henry Havelock Ellis. The prefix *hetero*, by the way, is also derived from a Greek word and means "different." Homosexual behavior has been reported in nearly all cultures throughout the world (see Box 9–A). Same-sex sexual behavior (male–male or female–female mounting) has also been observed and studied in a large variety of nonhuman species (Bailey & Zuk, 2009).

Over the years there have been many derogatory terms used to describe homosexuals (e.g., "faggot," "fairy," "dyke"). Most homosexuals prefer the term **gay** for a male homosexual (although in some places the term is used for homosexuals of either sex) and **lesbian** for a female homosexual (derived from the name of the Greek island Lesbos, where, in about 600 b.c., the poet Sappho led a circle of young female disciples). Heterosexuals are often referred to as **"straights."** The word "queer" was once regarded as derogatory, but in the past 10 years it has been increasingly used in the homosexual community as an umbrella term to refer to gays, lesbians, bisexuals, and transgendered individuals. Its use "attempts to negate the notion of sexual identity" (which "are created by society in order to repress individuals wishing to engage in behaviors that deviate from the heterosexual model") (Avila-Saavedra, 2009).

History of Attitudes About Homosexuality

Western attitudes about homosexuality have varied considerably throughout history. In ancient Greece, same-sex sexual behavior between adult men and boys (called **pederasty**) was widely accepted as an alternative to heterosexuality (Scanlon, 2005). Cantarella (1992) wrote that in ancient Greece pederasty had "become in practice an absolutely normal relationship, socially accepted, engaged in with total freedom, and celebrated by the poets." Plato praised homosexual relations in his *Symposium*. Homosexual relations between Greek scholars (e.g., Socrates, Plato) and their students were considered to be a natural part of the young boys' education. Marriage between individuals of the same sex was legal among the upper class during the time of the Roman Empire, but the most common type of same-sex behavior engaged in was also pederasty (see Rind, 1998).

Same-sex sexual activities were practiced—often as part of religious rituals—by many groups of Hebrews prior to the 7th century b.c. As part of a reformation movement designed to unify the many Hebrew groups, male homosexuality was thereafter condemned (along with other acts that had been part of older rituals) and was made punishable by death:

> **If a man lies with a male as with a woman, both of them have committed an abomination; they shall be put to death, their blood is upon them.**
> *(Leviticus 20:13, Revised Standard Version)*

Female homosexuality was dealt with less harshly by the Jews because it did not involve "spillage of seed" or violation of male property rights (Locke, 2004).

European Christians, following the Roman tradition, initially were tolerant of same-sex sexual behaviors, especially pederasty (Boswell, 1980; Rind, 1998). It was not until the time of Saint Thomas Aquinas (a.d. 1225–1274), who emphasized the view of Saint Augustine, that the only purpose of sex was procreation, that homosexuality came to be viewed as unnatural or "against the laws of nature." However, Boswell (1980) notes that while same-sex sexual behavior was considered a sin in the Middle Ages, people who committed the sin were not then viewed as a type of person who was different from others. This remained true during the 1600s and 1700s, when homosexual acts became a crime as well as a sin.

It was not until the late 1800s and the rise of modern medicine (particularly psychiatry) that people who engaged in homosexual acts came to be viewed as a particular class of people—people with a mental illness. Freud (1924) referred to homosexuals as "perverts" in his academic teaching. As a result, there has never been a period in Western culture with as much intolerance of homosexuality as there was in the 20th century. Because they were viewed as mentally ill, the medical profession subjected homosexuals to frontal lobotomies, forced castrations or hysterectomies, electric shock treatments, hormone injections, and endless hours of psychotherapy (Katz, 1976).

Until the 1960s, homosexuals had never been studied outside of a medical or prison setting. Then, in 1957, Evelyn Hooker published a paper showing that nonclinical heterosexual and homosexual men could not be distinguished by the best psychological tests (i.e., the homosexual men were as well adjusted as the heterosexual men). Even Freud had recognized this to be true:

> **Often, though not always, they are men and women who otherwise have reached an irreproachably high standard of mental growth and development, intellectually and ethically, and are only afflicted with this one fateful peculiarity.** *(Freud, 1924, p. 313)*

Finally, in 1973, the American Psychiatric Association decided to discontinue classifying homosexuality as a mental illness (see Hooker, 1993, for a review of some of the events leading to this decision). The decision was not unanimously applauded; 37% of APA members were opposed to the change. Homosexuality remained as a mental disorder in the World Health Organization's *International Classification of Diseases* until 1992.

Gay ■ A term generally used to refer to male homosexuals, although in some places it is used to refer to homosexuals of either sex.

Lesbian ■ A female homosexual.

Straight ■ A term used by homosexuals for a heterosexual.

Pederasty ■ A same-sex sexual behavior between adult men and boys.

Reprinted with special permission of King Features Syndicate.

The APA decision has had far-reaching implications. If homosexuality is no longer considered an illness, there is no need to cure it. However, attitudes often change slowly. Until the Supreme Court ruled against them in 2003, many states still had laws on the books that prohibited the sexual expression of homosexuality (see section on Sodomy Laws in Chapter 11).

Most Christian churches continue to have a rejecting or punitive attitude toward homosexuality. The U.S. military has always banned and discharged homosexuals. At the urging of President Clinton, a "compromise" was enacted in 1993. Under the "don't ask, don't tell" policy, new recruits could no longer be asked if they were homosexual, but they could still be discharged for disclosing their orientation or for engaging in homosexual acts. The military opposed the policy, and since 1993 over 13,000 soldiers have been discharged for their sexual orientation. In 1999, President Clinton called the "don't ask, don't tell" policy a failure. President Obama has promised to repeal the policy and allow homosexuals to openly serve in the military. A 2010 CBS News/*New York Times* survey found that 58% of Americans were in favor of homosexuals serving in the military, while only 28% opposed it.

Sexual Prejudice Today

Views by students in my class about homosexuality and homosexuals are greatly mixed:

> "During my junior year in high school I made a new male friend. The more I got to know him, the more I began to suspect that he was gay. This scared me. As a result of my growing fears I discontinued our friendship."

> "My feeling is that homosexuality is disgusting.... Just thinking about it gives me the creeps."

> "A few of my closest friends are homosexuals. At first, I admit, it was a shock when they told me, but that never stopped me from being their friend. My boyfriend is definitely homophobic and it aggravates me every time he says something negative."

> "To be really honest, if anyone is a homosexual, I don't care, as long as they are good people.... I believe that homosexuals should be legally accepted."

> "I believe that homosexuality is morally wrong. While I try hard not to judge the feelings of others, I do not agree with acting out these feelings."

> "When I was in high school I worked at a flower shop. I didn't realize the owner's son was gay until my junior year. He acted totally normal.... One afternoon I saw him driving somewhere with his boyfriend. Ever since that day I am kind of afraid and don't like to even have conversation with him. I don't know why I fear him so much because he has never done any harm to me."

Many people are prejudiced against others whom they perceive to be different. People discriminate on the basis of skin color, gender, and religion, but hostility toward homosexuals is probably far more accepted among Americans than any other type of bias (Goleman, 1990). For example, in 1966 the editors of the highly respected *Time* magazine wrote a two-page editorial on homosexuals, which concluded with the following statement:

> **[Homosexuality is] a pathetic little second-rate substitute for reality, a pitiable flight from life. As such it deserves fairness, compassion, understanding and, when possible, treatment. But it deserves no encouragement, no glamorization, no rationalization, no fake status as minority martyrdom, no sophistry about simple differences in taste—and, above all, no pretense that it is anything but a pernicious sickness.** *(Time, 1966, p. 41)*

Has there been any improvement in attitudes since then? A *New York Times*/CBS News poll conducted in late 2003 found that 50% of Americans felt that homosexual relations were morally wrong and only 41% believed that they should be legal (Seelye & Elder, 2003).

Homosexuals are often victims of hate crimes. Hate crimes are defined by the FBI as "crime motivated by preformed, negative bias against persons, property, or organizations based solely on race, religion, ethnicity/national origin, sexual orientation, or disability" (U.S. Department of Justice, 1996). Over 90% of gay men have been verbally abused or threatened (Herek, 1989). Two horrific hate crimes occurred in 1998. Matthew Shephard, a college student, was tortured and killed because he was gay, and another gay man, James Byrd, Jr., was dragged to death behind a pickup truck. In 2009, President Obama signed the Matthew Shephard and James Byrd, Jr., Hate Crimes Prevention Act, which made it a federal crime to assault anyone because of his or her sexual orientation, gender, or gender identity.

In such a harsh world, is it any wonder that homosexual and bisexual men and women have a higher prevalence of depression, mood, and/or stress disorders than heterosexuals (e.g., Koh & Ross, 2006)? This is particularly the case for gay men (who are more apt to be the target of sexual prejudice) (Sandfort et al., 2003). Homosexuals, particularly adolescents, are at a much higher risk of committing suicide than are others (Plöderl et al., 2010; Teasdale & Bradley-Engen, 2010). Most of these mental health problems can be attributed to what has been called *minority stress*—the "stigma, prejudice, and discrimination [that] create a hostile and stressful social environment" (Meyer, 2003; see Hatzchbuehler, 2009).

The most widely used term to describe negative attitudes toward homosexuals is **homophobia** a term first used in the 1960s. However, homophobia generally implies that negative attitudes are the result of irrational fears that reflect individual psychopathology. Psychologist Gregory Herek (2000a) has proposed that a better term is sexual prejudice. **Sexual prejudice** is socially reinforced and includes negative attitudes toward individuals, communities, and homosexual behaviors. Sexual prejudice is greater among men than it is among women, and prejudiced men generally have a much greater negative attitude about gay men than they do lesbians (Herek, 2000b, 2002a; Kite & Whitley, 1996). Attitudes toward bisexual individuals is equally or more negative (Herek, 2002b). The use of derogatory terms among boys often begins as early as grade school (Plummer, 2001). Interestingly, many studies have found that sexual prejudice lessens the more interactions one has with homosexuals (see Smith et al., 2009).

Why do some people have such hostility toward homosexuals? Studies find that among men, homophobic views are greatest in those with stereotypic male gender-role attitudes (i.e., men who strongly believe in a masculinist ideology), a religious fundamentalist attitude, and little education, and who score high on measures of authoritarianism (Herek, 2000a; Marsiglio, 1993). Among women, authoritarian attitudes are strongly associated with sexual prejudice (Basow & Johnson, 2000). However, this tells us nothing of the psychological basis of sexual prejudice.

Many antigay heterosexuals view themselves as enforcers of social norms and gender roles (Parrott, 2009). Gregory Herek, the leading authority on homophobia, believes that antigay prejudice is an attempt to suppress any attraction to the same sex (see Herek, 1988), a way to "maintain a positive gender-related identity" (Falomir-Pichastor & Mugny, 2009). Herek says, "The teens and early 20s [are] a time of identity consolidation, struggling with issues of manhood and masculinity, how one becomes a man. By attacking a gay man or a lesbian, these guys are trying symbolically to affirm their manhood"

FIGURE 9–5 Sexual prejudice can be extreme and involve hatred of homosexuals.

(Associated Press, July 1993). (Interestingly, prejudice against very effeminate men is not uncommon even among gay men [Taywaditep, 2001]). Acts of sexual prejudice are most common among men whose peer group has very negative attitudes about homosexuality (Franklin, 2000; Herek, 2000a).

Some of you may be rejecting this explanation of homophobia by men, and attributing it instead to morality issues. If the basis of sexual prejudice by men were morality only, there would be no difference in heterosexual attitudes toward gays and lesbians. However, many sexually explicit male-oriented magazines regularly devote several pages to women-on-women sexual activity, and female-on-female sex scenes are often shown in porn films made for male heterosexual audiences. Why? Publishers and producers of this material would not include it if they were not certain that a great many heterosexual men are aroused by it. In fact, research has shown that many heterosexual men find lesbianism highly erotic and that this improves their attitudes toward lesbians (Louderback & Whitley, 1997).

PERSONAL REFLECTIONS

Sexual prejudice affects relations among heterosexuals as well. It prevents many same-sex family members (most commonly, fathers and sons) and friends from being affectionate with one another. Are you able to hug your same-sex parent? Good friends of the same sex? If not, examine which fears prevent you from doing so. Sexual prejudice hurts everyone, including those who display it.

Homophobia ■ An irrational fear of homosexual individuals and homosexuality.

Sexual prejudice ■ Socially reinforced negative attitudes toward homosexuals, homosexual communities, and homosexual behaviors.

Sexual Identity Development (The "Coming Out" Process)

With so many people in our society having negative attitudes about homosexuality, it should come as no surprise that acknowledging to oneself that one is homosexual, and then publicly declaring it, is often very difficult. The process of disclosing one's homosexuality or bisexuality is called **sexual identity development**, or more commonly, **coming out.** Several models have been offered to describe this process. I will follow the stages outlined by the Boston Women's Health Book Collective (1984).

The first stage is *admitting to oneself that one has a homosexual or bisexual orientation.* Many gays and lesbians knew that they were "different" at a very young age. You will learn in Chapter 10 that sexual attraction (not to be confused with a desire to have sex) begins around the age of 10 for almost everyone (Herdt & McClintock, 2000; Pattatucci & Hamer, 1995). Attraction to individuals of the same sex generally occurs well before sexual activity begins (Bell et al., 1981).

> "I discovered my sexuality at a surprising 6 years old. Naturally I didn't know at that young age that I was a lesbian, but I can remember having 'crushes' on my teachers and female upperclassmen."

> "I think that the most important thing you lectured on was the predisposition of sexual orientation before birth. I, too, felt different as a child as early as by 10."
>
> (All examples are from the author's files.)

Although early recognition is common for many homosexuals (particularly gays), many others (particularly women) do not recognize their sexual orientation until well into adolescence, or even later (Diamond, 2003; Diamond & Savin-Williams, 2000; Garnets & Peplau, 2001; Kitzinger & Wilkinson, 1995). Because so many people have a negative opinion of it, recognizing that one is gay or lesbian is often a lonely and painful experience.

> "As a young gay person, you feel all of the things every other young person feels. You feel all of the normal doubts, uncertainties, questions and frustrations common to that time of life. And you also begin to have feelings and thoughts as precious and deep as any can be: of self, and worth, and love, and life, and purpose. But when you are young and gay, you also face a world of pain and isolation few people have to face.
>
> "We all know how vulnerable and fragile a life can be in those early years. And yet few people

seem ready or willing to consider how it must feel to be young and gay. In a time when nurturing and affirmation are so important, the young gay person is told by his church that he is evil. The law says that she is a criminal. Society says that they are misfits. The media displays freaks. And the world seems to say they are less than a whole person. And so, when you are young and gay, you can feel so much hatred, so much rejection, so unwanted, so unwelcome, so worthless, so unaccepted and so misunderstood.

> "Other people throughout time have known the kind of pain and persecution which reaches deep into a person's heart. There have always been people who were made to feel hated and demeaned because of their color, their religion, their heritage, or their gender. But as much pain and suffering as these people have known, they also knew they were not alone. They always had someone else they could see who was just like them; someone to identify with. And most important of all, they had someone to talk to; someone to share the pain with.

> "When you are young and gay, you feel the same terrible depth of pain. But you look around and there is no one to talk to; no one to share the pain with. There is no one who has feelings like yours or who understands how deeply you hurt. You feel so isolated and so alone. And at times, that vulnerability and pain and isolation can be so terribly overwhelming."
>
> (Steve L., personal communication, New Orleans)

In the next stage, the individual *gets to know other homosexuals*, thus ending the sense of isolation. It is easier to come out if the individual finds acceptance in others, and those most likely to be accepting are other homosexuals. Most gays and lesbians were raised in the same anti-homosexual environment as others, and by coming into contact with other homosexuals, they can replace these negative stereotypes with a more positive attitude about homosexuality—and about themselves.

> "As I was growing up, I heard all of the jokes and stories about the lives gays lived. I saw all of the negative images that the media could dish up for public consumption.... I wanted to find someone I could share the rest of my life with.
>
> "And then I looked for that life and tried to find it.... The only place society had allowed gays to meet was in one small bar-filled pocket of the city. And so I turned to where I was accepted and where I could breathe. But then I heard society condemn me because of the lifestyle I 'chose' to lead.
>
> "In time, I grew to learn that there was more of a life to be had than just the narrow world which society tries to impose upon gays. I met many happy and healthy gay people who helped me to understand and learn and grow."
>
> (Steve L., personal communication, New Orleans)

Sexual identity development ■ A term for disclosing one's homosexuality or bisexuality to others.

Coming out ■ Disclosing to others one's homosexual orientation, from the expression "coming out of the closet."

Once contact is made with other gays and lesbians, a new way of expressing sexuality has to be developed. In many ways, what happens next is quite similar to what happens when heterosexuals begin to date.

In the third, very difficult, stage, the individual *tells family and friends of his or her sexual orientation.* Many hide their sexual orientation from others for long periods.

"But as bad as you hurt, you keep the pain to yourself. You fear being discovered by the people you love and need the most; for everything your world has taught you makes you afraid you will lose their love and friendship if they find out you are gay. The world gives you the pain, and then makes it impossible for you to talk about it because of fear.

"So not only does the world isolate you from learning about your feelings and others who are like you, but you begin to isolate a part of yourself from family and friends. You begin to develop techniques of telling half-truths and skirting around questions. You learn how to hide inside of yourself and smother feelings. You learn how to be around other people without letting them get too close. You learn how to survive.

"And then, you grow tired of hiding. You grow tired of not being able to share the beauty as well as the pain that fills your life. You grow tired of not being as close as you want to be to the people you care most about.

"But the fear is still very strong. You find it is easier to avoid the questions by just staying away more often. And you don't have to find as much strength to hide and be silent. So you drift further and further from the people you love the most and you feel the pain and isolation building up inside."
(Steve L., personal communication, New Orleans)

When an individual does finally disclose his or her homosexuality or bisexuality to the family, it often creates a crisis. Parents have raised their children with the expectations that they will be heterosexual. Thus, verbal and physical abuse by parents (especially by fathers) and other family members is common (D'Augelli et al., 1998). Many gay, lesbian, and bisexual young people end up homeless and on the streets (Prendergast et al., 2002).

"My parents became aware of my sexual preference when I was 18. Since that time, I have endured numerous nasty conflicts with them. My mother told me that she would rather me be a prostitute, and my father told me I would never be anyone as long I was a 'faggot.' They threw me out immediately after graduation from high school and forbade me to enter their house. They took me back on their terms—that I would go straight and live what is in their opinion a good, decent, moral lifestyle.

I agreed and abided for a few months, but found myself extremely unhappy. I ended up moving out after a fight with my father."
(from the author's files)

For those of you who are homosexual and have not yet revealed your orientation to your family, contact PFLAG for help as to how best to go about it. Usually, after the family has been told, the next step is to tell friends, but this too is often met with different reactions.

"I am a 25-year-old female. I've been close friends with 'Darla' since 7th grade. 'Darla' and I used to talk about girl things all the time (boys, dating, sex). I felt there was nothing we couldn't discuss.

"Two years after high school graduation, 'Darla' and I along with another mutual friend got together for pizza and to catch up on old times. 'Darla' then said she had something very important to tell us. She told us she was gay. She said she had those feelings since she was a child and only recently acted on them. I handled her news supportively, but our other friend told 'Darla' that she was 'disgusting' and 'gross.' I'm sure without a doubt that was the hardest day in 'Darla's' life."
(from the author's files)

FIGURE 9–6 Walt Whitman. Many scholars consider his *Leaves of Grass* to be the greatest collection of poems ever written by an American.

The final stage is *complete openness about one's homosexuality or bisexuality*. This includes telling people at work; it completes the process, making one's homosexuality or bisexuality a total lifestyle. Among women who have sex with women, "butch" women generally identify as lesbians, whereas "femme" women frequently self-identify as bisexual (Rosario et al., 2009). The important task for all adults, regardless of their sexual orientation, is to develop an acceptance of their sexuality (i.e., of themselves), to find acceptable ways to express it, and to learn to incorporate their sexuality into their total lifestyle and personality.

PERSONAL REFLECTIONS

Gays, lesbians, and bisexuals: Have you told your family and friends of your sexual orientation? Why or why not?

Lifestyles and Relations

Finding companions and sexual partners can be difficult for many gays and lesbians, especially in rural areas and small towns where there may be little tolerance of homosexuals meeting together in public. In large urban areas there is usually a much larger number of people who are homosexual, as well as a much greater acceptance of their lifestyle. In fact, 60% of gay men with partners live in one of 20 cities (San Francisco, Washington, DC, Los Angeles, Atlanta, and New York are the most popular) (Black et al., 2000). Lesbian couples are less likely to be concentrated in large cities.

The typical member of the gay community today is well educated and in a professional career position (Black et al., 2000). This description, however, fits only those who are openly homosexual. For gay and lesbian individuals who have not yet come out, homosexual relations are still dominated by secret meetings in bars and bathrooms, often with strangers. Bisexuals, in particular, are unlikely to participate openly in the homosexual community (McKirnan et al., 1995).

Many heterosexuals believe that homosexuals are unhappy and lonely. However, the 2000 U.S. census revealed that there were more than 600,000 same-sex couples living together. Studies have found no differences between cohabiting heterosexuals and cohabiting homosexuals in the relationship quality and satisfaction (and often fewer relationship problems) (Balsam et al., 2008; Gottman et al., 2004; Peplau & Fingerhut, 2007; Roisman et al., 2008). In fact, gay and lesbian couples may be better at being "best friends" than heterosexual couples (Peplau, 1988). Contrary to what many heterosexuals believe, most same-sex couples do not create "husband" and "wife" roles,

but instead assume financial and household responsibilities equally (Peplau & Fingerhut, 2007).

Women, whether straight or lesbian, tend to value commitment and romantic love (Leigh, 1989). Even when relationships end, lesbians are more likely to remain friends with ex-partners than are heterosexuals (Harkless & Flowers, 2005). However, there is a difference between the sexual lifestyles of most straight and gay men: Gay men are much less likely to regard monogamy as important (see Peplau & Fingerhut, 2007) and thus have a greater number of lifetime sexual partners. A nationally representative sample of Australians found that the mean number of sexual partners for gay men was 32 (Grulich et al., 2003). A 1970s study conducted in San Francisco (before we knew of HIV/AIDS) found that many gay men had had hundreds of sexual partners (Bell & Weinberg, 1978).

Most homosexuals within a relationship do not take on one sexual role (Hooker, 1965). Lesbian couples generally take a great deal more time touching and caressing one another than heterosexual couples, for whom sexual relations are often dominated by the goal-oriented man (Hite, 1976; Masters & Johnson, 1979). Manual stimulation of the genitals and oral-genital sex are the preferred ways of reaching orgasm for lesbians (Bell & Weinberg, 1978; Masters & Johnson, 1979). Many lesbians engage in tribadism, the rubbing of genitals against another's genitals or other body parts, but very few use dildos (objects shaped like a penis). About 70% to 80% of gay men engage in anal intercourse (Smith, 2001). Most men who engage in anal intercourse do so only once or twice a month, but there are a few who do it much more often (Coxon & McManus, 2000). Overall, heterosexuals and homosexuals are very similar in their sexual repertoires and in their sexual satisfaction (Holmberg & Blair, 2009).

Homosexuals, Marriage, and Parenting

Studies estimate that at least one fourth of gay men and 40% of lesbians are married or have been married (Black et al., 2000; Hewitt, 1998). Millions of homosexual or bisexual men and women are partners in heterosexual marriages (Binder, 1998). While some of these men and women were not aware of their sexual orientations when they married, many others were aware. Of those married people who are consciously aware of their homosexuality or bisexuality, very few admit it to their partners (Stokes et al., 1996). Why would someone who knows he or she is homosexual or bisexual choose to marry a heterosexual? There are many possible reasons, including societal or family pressures, affection for

FIGURE 9–7 Hillary and Julie Goodridge leave church after getting married in Boston in 2004. Their lawsuit resulted in gay marriage becoming legal in Massachusetts.

USA Today/Gallup Poll in 2008 found that 63% of adults felt that same-sex marriages were a "private decision between two people" (Grossman, 2008). However, a 2009 survey conducted by the Pew Research Center found that 53% of Americans opposed same-sex marriages (but 57% favored civil unions). Interestingly, when California voters overturned their state's Supreme Court decision 52% to 48%, a large majority of African Americans, a historically oppressed group, voted against same-sex marriages (Kirchick, 2008). Negative attitudes about same-sex marriage are greater the more homophobic people are (Moskowitz et al., 2010).

The 2000 U.S. census revealed that 250,000 children live in households with same-sex parents (Doyle, 2005). Should an openly gay or lesbian couple be allowed to raise a child? Before we continue, read the following real-life story of Kerry and Val, a lesbian couple:

"Val and I have been together for 6 years. We have two children, a daughter, 5, Nicole, and a son, 2, Nicholas. We both wanted a family but were a little afraid of the effects that our lifestyle would have on the children. We finally decided that in spite of our sexual orientation, we would still be loving, caring parents with much to offer our children.

"Next arose the problem of how to go about it. We ended up choosing a mutual friend of ours to father the children. Val took care of me while I was pregnant. We experienced all of the changes together: hearing the unborn baby's heartbeat, feeling it move, staying up with me when it was too uncomfortable to sleep. Val was with me all through labor and delivery. She got to see the babies being born and was the first to hold them. She was there from beginning to end.

"We both believe that a lot of love and a lot of time spent with our children is the key. We try to never be too busy to listen to them. We both are involved with Nicole's school (Val especially, she is a room parent for Nicole's class), friends, and activities. We also spend a lot of time involved in family activities such as going to the park or zoo, bike riding, camping, etc. We almost always include the kids in everything we do.

"We are very happy together and can't imagine life without one another. We both wish that legally we could be recognized as a couple. If anything ever happens to me, what will happen to the kids? Val loves them as if they were her own and they love her and are very attached to her. I would want them to stay with her, but there is nothing I can do legally.

the partner, desire to have children, and even negative feelings about leading a homosexual lifestyle or internalized homophobia (Higgins, 2002; Isay, 1998).

What about openly gay or lesbian couples? Many gays and lesbians establish long-lasting relationships. Should they be allowed to legally marry? The Netherlands, Belgium, Canada, and Spain (and other nations) recognize same-sex marriages, and in 2004 the Canadian Supreme Court ruled that they are legal. As of August 2010, only five states legally recognized same-sex marriages (Connecticut, Iowa, Massachusetts, New Hampshire, and Vermont). In 2008, the California Supreme Court ruled that same-sex marriages must be legally recognized, and in 2009 Maine's Legislature approved it, but voters in both states subsequently overturned the decisions. Same-sex civil unions are recognized in two states. The U.S. Constitution requires that states honor each other's laws, but in 1996 President Clinton signed the Defense of Marriage Act that defines marriage (in federal law) as the union of a man and a woman and allows states to refuse to honor same-sex marriages performed elsewhere.

Attitudes about same-sex marriages are diverse and often highly emotional. A survey conducted by

"Val and I believe that as far as the children are concerned, we will never lie or hide any information about our lifestyle or their pasts. Along with their everyday education, we will also include the information about our lifestyle as they are able to understand it. We are honest with everyone about our lifestyle. Our friends, families, and employers and coworkers all know we are gay. To us, honesty is the best policy. For the most part we have gotten nothing but respect from our straight friends. Sometimes they are curious, but that is natural. Mostly they respect our privacy and admire our honesty. Once people really get to know us they realize that we are no different from anyone else."
(from the author's files)

The topic of gays and lesbians as parents is viewed very negatively by many heterosexuals. As of 2009, only Florida bars adoption by homosexual parents (although three other states bar adoption by unmarried adults). Even many people who profess to be understanding and tolerant of homosexuality are opposed to gay and lesbian couples raising children:

"My feelings on homosexuals are the same as my feelings on heterosexuals. I have no problems with it.... I do have doubts about them having children."

"I think that homosexuality is the business of that person. Society should let them do their own thing.... I don't know if they should have children."
(All examples are from the author's files.)

This negativity has been reflected in court custody cases as well. In a highly publicized case (*Bottoms v. Bottoms*), a Virginia judge denied a woman custody of her 2-year-old son because her lesbian relationship was "immoral" and illegal. According to child psychiatrist Betty Ann June Muller, who debated on the subject at a meeting of the American Bar Association, "Judges often have cited long-held stereotypes in justifying awarding custody to the heterosexual parent. Those myths include the view that gays and lesbians are mentally ill, have weak parental instincts or are more likely to raise children who will be homosexual or be sexually abused" (Theim, 1994). Several studies have found that very few cases of parental sexual abuse are committed by homosexuals; most are committed by heterosexuals.

If one wanted to, one could find cases where gay or lesbian couples were bad parents and their children suffered serious problems. The same is true of heterosexual couples. But overall, what does the scientific literature show? There is now an abundance of research that shows that children raised by openly homosexual parents are not different from children raised by heterosexual parents (e.g., see Bos & van Balen, 2008, and Patterson, 2006, 2009, for reviews). Their gender identities, gender roles, personal development, and psychological adjustment are the same

as other children, and they grow up with a heterosexual orientation just as frequently as others.

The conclusion? The governing body of the American Psychological Association unanimously approved the following statement: "Research has shown that the adjustment, development, and psychological well-being of children is unrelated to parental sexual orientation and that children of lesbian and gay parents are as likely as those of heterosexual parents to flourish" (*American Psychologist*, 2005).

Media Portrayal of Homosexuals

The top male box office star in Hollywood in the 1950s was Rock Hudson, who was generally cast in leading romantic roles, but who in his personal life was exclusively homosexual. But to admit that one was homosexual in those days was the kiss of death for one's career, so Hudson's studio arranged a marriage (on paper only) so he could keep his orientation secret. Montgomery Clift, another 1950s actor in many romantic roles, was also homosexual. Other leading actors of that day, including Cary Grant and James Dean, were also known to have had sex with men, but they were always portrayed (on screen and off screen) as straight (Leland, 1995).

When Hollywood movies did star a person as being homosexual, he or she was almost always portrayed as a stereotype (e.g., 1996's *The Birdcage*). However, Hollywood and the arts have slowly begun to deal with the subject more honestly. For example, the 1993 movie *Philadelphia* starred Tom Hanks as an AIDS victim. In the 1997 hit movie *In and Out*, actors Tom Selleck and Kevin Kline were shown engaging in a passionate kiss, and greater sexual and romantic content was portrayed in the 2005 movie *Brokeback Mountain* starring Heath Ledger and Jake Gyllenhaal. Lesbianism as a subject for movies has met greater resistance, but in 2000, Hilary Swank won an Academy Award for her role in *Boys Don't Cry*.

FIGURE 9–8 Ellen DeGeneres starred in the first television show built around an openly homosexual individual.

Television has been slower to portray homosexuals in serious roles, but even that is changing. When actress Ellen DeGeneres' character declared her homosexuality on the April 30, 1997, episode of *Ellen*, the TV show became the first to be built around (and star) a lesbian. Today, there are many TV shows that portray openly homosexual individuals in a matter-of-fact manner (without extreme stereotypes). These include *Brothers and Sisters*, *Modern Family*, *Grey's Anatomy*, *House*, and *Glee*, to name a few.

CAN (SHOULD) SEXUAL ORIENTATION BE CHANGED?

Recall that in the not-too-distant past, homosexuality was viewed by the psychiatric profession as a form of psychopathology and that homosexuals could (or should) be "cured." Today, most attempts to "cure" homosexuals are conducted by religious fundamentalist groups (Leland & Miller, 1998). However, when homosexuals were asked if they would choose to take a "magic heterosexual pill" to change their sexual orientation, only 14% of gays and 5% of lesbians said that they would do so (Bell & Weinberg, 1978). Note that these results indicate that the large majority of homosexuals feel comfortable with their sexual orientation and do not wish to change. It is questionable whether those gays and lesbians who seek reorientation truly do so "voluntarily" (Murphy, 1992). Most probably do so because of years of dealing with family pressure, job discrimination, legal hassles, and other negative experiences (Allen & Oleson, 1999).

Today, most experts agree that changing an individual's sexual orientation is not possible. In 1994, the American Medical Association finally reversed a long-standing policy of recommending that psychiatrists make efforts to turn unhappy homosexuals into heterosexuals. The new policy states that most of the emotional problems of homosexuals are "due more to a sense of alienation in an unaccepting

FIGURE 9–9 Homosexuality is not just sexual attraction. It often includes companionship, affection, and love, often for a lifetime.

environment" and that "through psychotherapy, gay men and lesbians can become comfortable with their sexual orientation and understand the social responses to it" (AMA, 1994). Here is the current position of the American Psychological Association (2010):

> **Is Sexual Orientation a Choice?** No, human beings cannot choose to be either gay or straight. **Can Therapy Change Sexual Orientation?** No; even though most homosexuals live successful, happy lives, some homosexual or bisexual people may seek to change their sexual orientation through therapy, often coerced by family members or religious groups to try and do so. The reality is that homosexuality is not an illness. It does not require treatment. Gay, lesbian, and bisexual people may seek psychological help with the coming out process or for strategies to deal with prejudice, but most go into therapy for the same reasons and life issues that bring straight people to mental health professionals.
>
> "To be yourself in a world that is constantly trying to make you something else is the greatest accomplishment." *(Ralph Waldo Emerson)*

STUDY GUIDE

KEY TERMS

bisexual 223
coming out 234
gay 231
gender identity 225
gender roles 225

heterosexual 223
homophobia 233
homosexual 223
lesbian 231
pederasty 231

sexual identity
   development 234
sexual orientation 223
sexual prejudice 233
straight 231

INTERACTIVE REVIEW

In this chapter, sexual orientation is defined as (1) _____ consistently made after adolescence in the presence of clear alternatives. Isolated instances of sexual behavior may or may not reflect one's sexual orientation. Recent surveys indicate that (2) _____% of the adult male population and about (3) _____% of the adult female population have a homosexual orientation. A true bisexual would have a rating of (4) _____ on Kinsey's 7-point rating scale.

The (5) _____ of the vast majority of homosexuals and bisexuals are just as strong and consistent with their anatomical sex as among heterosexuals. Conformity or nonconformity with gender (6) _____ does not always predict one's sexual orientation. A great many homosexuals and bisexuals do not walk, talk, dress, or act any differently than anyone else.

There are three major explanations for the origins of sexual orientation. Psychoanalytic explanations state that heterosexuality is the "normal" outcome and that homosexuality results from problems in resolving the (7) _____ complex. However, later research does not generally support these claims. Homosexuals, as well as heterosexuals, have all kinds of parents, both good and bad, caring and cold. (8) _____ regards homosexuality and heterosexuality as learned behaviors; good or rewarding experiences with individuals of one sex and/or bad experiences with individuals of the other sex (particularly during adolescence) would lead to a particular orientation. However, social and cultural studies show that environment alone cannot explain sexual orientation. In the (9) _____ society in Melanesia, all boys engage in same-sex sexual behaviors for many years, yet the large majority grow up to have a heterosexual orientation.

Recent studies suggest that biology plays a major role in the origin of sexual orientation. Studies with twins indicate a (10) _____ factor, while anatomical studies have found differences in the (11) _____ of heterosexuals and homosexuals. Many researchers believe that differences in (12) _____ before or shortly after we are born predispose us to a particular sexual orientation. Nearly all agree that biological

and social/cultural influences (13) _____ to produce sexual orientation.

Anthropologists find that most societies are (14) _____ tolerant of homosexuality than prevailing attitudes in the United States. Attitudes about homosexuality have varied considerably in Western culture. The (15) _____ and (16) _____ accepted homosexuality, as did the early Christians. It was not until Saint (17) _____ that homosexuality came to be viewed as unnatural or "against the laws of nature," and not until the 1600s and 1700s that it was regarded as criminal. In the 1800s, the medical (psychiatric) model regarded homosexuality as an illness, and homosexual individuals were regarded as having pathological conditions in need of being "cured." In 1973 the American Psychiatric Association removed homosexuality as an official mental illness. Nevertheless, most people in the United States continue to have a harsh and negative attitude.

The process of (18) _____, or identifying oneself as homosexual, involves several often painful stages. The first stage is (19) _____. In the final stages, the individual attempts to gain the acceptance and understanding of friends, family, and coworkers. This is difficult in a society filled with (20) _____, socially reinforced negative attitudes toward individuals, communities, and homosexual behaviors. Today, most metropolitan areas have well-established homosexual communities where individuals can openly associate.

At the time this book was written, homosexual marriages were illegal in 45 states. Most Americans oppose the idea of openly homosexual individuals raising children (even their own), yet research shows that children raised by homosexual parents are emotionally and mentally healthy, grow up to have normal gender identities and gender roles, and almost always have a heterosexual orientation. This last finding again suggests a greater role for biology than environment in the origin of sexual orientation, and it is the hope of the researchers conducting biological studies that their findings will promote greater understanding and tolerance.

SELF-TEST

A. TRUE OR FALSE

[T] [F]   21. In some cultures, same-sex sexual behavior is considered normal for boys during adolescence.

[T] [F]   22. Homosexuals usually act and/or dress differently from heterosexuals.

[T] [F]   23. Bisexuals are people who are afraid to admit to themselves their real homosexuality.

[T] [F]   24. Most homosexuals are unhappy with their sexual orientation and would like to become heterosexual.

[T] [F]   25. A homosexual orientation indicates a gender identity problem.

[T] [F]   26. A male homosexual can be made heterosexual by administering large doses of testosterone.

[T] [F]   27. People who have had same-sex sexual experiences are by definition homosexual in orientation.

[T] [F]   28. Women who have had same-sex sexual relations are more likely to be bisexual than homosexual.

[T] [F]   29. Freud believed that all people were capable of becoming either heterosexual or homosexual, depending on their early childhood experiences.

[T] [F]   30. Researchers have found a higher rate of concordance for homosexuality between identical twins than between nonidentical twins.

[T] [F]   31. A bisexual is anyone who has had sex with both men and women.

[T] [F]   32. Recent studies support Kinsey's findings that 10% of American men are homosexual.

[T] [F]   33. Same-sex sexual experiences before age 15 are a good predictor of adult sexual orientation.

[T] [F]   34. Many homosexuals and bisexuals have gender dysphoria.

[T] [F]   35. Most lesbians have not had pleasurable sexual relations with men.

[T] [F]   36. Extremely effeminate ("sissy") boys always develop a homosexual orientation.

[T] [F]   37. If one identical twin is homosexual, the other twin always is too.

[T] [F]   38. Studies have found that areas of the hypothalamus (in the brain) are different in male heterosexuals and homosexuals.

[T] [F]   39. Most homosexuals adopt a single role ("masculine" or "feminine") in their relationships.

[T] [F]   40. Children raised by openly homosexual parents are more likely to develop a homosexual orientation than children raised by heterosexual parents.

B. MATCHING

_____ 41. Henry has had a few same-sex sexual experiences, but has had sex only with women since he turned 15 ten years ago.

_____ 42. Joyce has been married and enjoyed sexual relations with her husband, but now prefers sexual relations with women.

_____ 43. Frank has had sex with both men and women.

_____ 44. Michael believes he is a woman and has sex only with men.

_____ 45. Carl sometimes enjoys sex with women, but prefers sexual relations with men.

_____ 46. Tom is 12 years old and his few sexual experiences have been exclusively with boys his age.

_____ 47. Alice enjoys sex with men most of the time, but she often enjoys sex with women as well.

_____ 48. Diane has had sex only with men, but occasionally has homosexual fantasies.

_____ 49. Matthew occasionally goes to bathhouses and lets other men give him oral-genital sex.

_____ 50. Mary's gender identity is not consistent with her anatomical sex.

_____ 51. Steve is 19 years old and his only sexual experiences have been with women, but all his sexual fantasies are about men.

a. probably heterosexual
b. probably homosexual
c. probably bisexual
d. probably transsexual
e. not enough information to make a guess

C. FILL IN THE BLANKS

52. In this book, sexual orientation is defined as distinct preferences consistently made after _____ in the presence of clear alternatives.

53. Researchers believe that hormones may affect sexual orientation during which time of life?_____

54. According to this chapter, biological factors probably _____ individuals to a particular sexual orientation.

55. The four stages of the coming-out process are (a) _____, (b) _____, (c) _____, and (d) _____.

56. Name four nonliving homosexuals who made significant contributions to humankind: (a) _____, (b) _____, (c) _____, and (d) _____.

SUGGESTED READINGS AND RESOURCES

American Psychological Association http://www
.apahelpcenter.org/articles/article.php?id=31
Click on "Family and Relationships" and
then click "Sexuality."

De Cecco, J. (Ed.). (1990). *Gay relationships*. New York:
Haworth Press. Essays on many aspects of gay relations.

Herek, G. M. (Ed.). (1998). *Stigma and sexual orientation:
Understanding prejudice against lesbians, gay men, and
bisexuals*. Newsbury Park, CA: Sage.

Kunzig, R. (2008, May/June). Finding the switch.
Psychology Today. Concludes that there are multiple
pathways to a homosexual orientation.

Leland, J., & Miller, M. (1998, August 17). Can gays
"convert"? *Newsweek*, 45–52. Cover story about the
controversy in attempts to convert homosexuals.

Patterson, C. J. (2006). Children of lesbian and gay parents. *Current Directions in Psychological Science*.

Rahman, Q., & Wilson, G. D. (2003). Born gay? The psychobiology of human sexual orientation. *Personality
and Individual Differences*, 34, 1337–1382.

Rust, P. C. R. (2003). Bisexuality: The state of the union.
In J. R. Heiman & C. M. Davis (Eds.), *Annual review
of sex research* (vol. VIII). Allentown, PA: The Society
for the Scientific Study of Sexuality. An excellent
review of bisexuality from the leading researcher
in the field.

Savin-Williams, R. C. (2001). *Mom, Dad, I'm gay.
How families negotiate coming out*. Washington,
DC: American Psychological Association.
Excellent resource book for the coming-out
process.

Federation of Parents and Friends of Lesbians
and Gays (PFLAG)
1726 M Street, Suite 400
Washington, DC 20036
(202) 467-8180
Fax: (202) 467-8194
www.pflag.org

National Gay and Lesbian Task Force
1325 Massachusetts Avenue, N.W.
Suite 600
Washington, DC 20005
(202) 393-5177
Fax: (202) 393-2241
www.ngltf.org

Life-Span Sexual Development

The first debate I won was when, at 11, I persuaded a group of school friends that there was no truth in the exciting idea that penises could be put into girls to create babies. Their use as water pistols was accepted, but this new use had a strange attraction. The argument was decided when we realized that if it were true, our parents must have done this—which we all realized was inconceivable. After all, our parents were "old people."

—John M. Kellett, in *Psycological Perspectives on Human Sexuality*, pp. 355–379. L. T. Szuchman and F. Muscarella, Eds., 2000, John Wiley & Sons.

People are sexual beings. To deny our sexuality is to deny our humanity. It should come as no surprise, therefore, that our sexuality begins from the moment of birth and lasts until our death, even if we live a very long life.

EARLY INFANCY (AGES 0–1)

Ultrasound recordings have discovered that male fetuses have erections months before they are born (Calderone, 1983b). After birth, baby boys often have erections before the umbilical cord is cut. Similarly, baby girls can have vaginal lubrication in the first 24 hours after birth (Langfeldt, 1981).

An important part of emotional development involves the amount of hugging and cuddling that an infant has with its caregivers. Many physicians and psychologists strongly encourage parents to hold their babies soon after birth and to continue to give large amounts of hugging and cuddling throughout childhood. Monkeys raised in isolation and deprived of the opportunity of close physical comfort have difficulty forming relationships later (Harlow, 1959). The same seems to be true for children. Many years ago, a physician reported that 1 in 3 human infants in foundling homes died during the first year of life, even though they were well fed and provided with adequate medical care. What these babies were not receiving was cuddling and hugging—they apparently died from emotional neglect (Spitz, 1945, 1946).

When you have finished studying this chapter, you should be able to:

- Explain infants' exploration of their bodies and their need for close physical comfort.
- Discuss genital exploration and sex play in young children.
- Summarize the changes that occur in boys' and girls' bodies at puberty and identify the hormones that are responsible.
- Discuss sexual behavior among adolescents and the effects of peer pressure.
- Explain how the sexual behavior of emerging adults often differs from that of younger and older age groups.
- Discuss the sexual lifestyles of adults, including marriage, cohabitation, and extramarital sex.
- Describe the characteristics that men and women look for when choosing a short-term or long-term mate.
- Describe the sexual behavior of middle-aged individuals and the physical changes that come with aging.
- Explain the realities of aging that can directly affect sexuality in the elderly, and discuss the prevalence of sexual relations among healthy elderly couples.
- Initiate talks with your own children about sex.

As soon as infants gain sufficient control over their movements, they begin to touch all parts of their bodies. As part of this exploration, infants also touch their genitals. When this happens, infant boys and girls may continue to stimulate themselves. This happens because the nerve endings in the genitals are already developed at birth and transmit sensations of pleasure when stimulated. However, it is important to remember that infants do not comprehend adult sexual behavior. Their behavior is aimed at finding pleasurable physical sensations, not expressing sexual desire.

Although the initial sexual self-stimulation of children may be random, once they discover its pleasurable component, such stimulation quickly becomes purposeful (Lidster & Horsburgh, 1994). Taking a child's hand away from his or her genitals may cause the child to make a face or noises (indicating irritation), and the child may quickly try to resume self-stimulation.

EARLY CHILDHOOD (AGES 2–6)

Bodily exploration before the age of 2 is confined mainly to self-exploration (Figure 10–1). After the age of 2, however, children increasingly play together, and their natural curiosity now extends not only to their own bodies but to those of others. Studies have shown that sexualized behaviors increase dramatically in children after age 2 and reach a peak period from 3 to 5, and then decrease until puberty (Friedrich et al., 1991). Interest in the genitals is very common for boys and girls in this age group, as evidenced by undressing in front of others, sexual exploration games that involve showing one's body and genitals to others, trying to touch other children's genitals, and masturbation (see Heiman et al., 1998; Larsson & Svedin, 2002a; Ryan, 2000; Sandnabba et al., 2003). Let us examine some of the common, normal behaviors frequently observed in young children.

As just mentioned, by the age of 2, children are very interested in their bodies. The fact that boys stand and girls sit while urinating is fascinating to children, and they will try to watch their siblings and parents bathing and urinating.

> "When I was a very young girl, my parents brought me with them to visit some friends of theirs who had two young boys. One boy was my age and one was a couple of years older. I went to the bathroom with them and watched them urinate. My mother got very, very angry. This totally surprised, shocked, and confused me."
>
> (from the author's files)

Young children are interested in the physical differences between boys and girls and will play games that allow for sexual exploration, such as "playing doctor"

FIGURE 10–1 It is normal for young children to explore their own bodies.

and "playing house" (Sandnabba et al., 2003). Most of the time, these games are limited to viewing and touching genitals. More aggressive sexual behaviors like oral-genital contact and inserting objects into the vagina or anus are uncommon and may be an indication of sexual abuse (Friedrich et al., 1991; Heiman et al., 1998; Ryan, 2000). Sexual exploration games will not harm a child's development. What may be harmful is parents reacting too strongly when they "catch" their children engaging in sex play.

> "I can still remember the day my mother caught me playing 'doctor' with my neighbor. I was 5 years old. She got so mad at me that she locked me up in the bathroom. I don't remember how long I was in there. I didn't understand what I had done wrong. I ended up crying myself to sleep on the bathroom floor."
>
> "When I was 4, my cousin (age 5) and sister (age 3) had a slumber party. When we were all lying down we started asking questions and being curious. We then started 'playing doctor.' Well, my parents caught us and I was spanked and punished for a long time. I have very vivid memories of this event and now I do not have very positive feelings about sex or my sexuality."
>
> (All examples are from the author's files.)

Sexual exploration games are often played with playmates of the same sex (Heiman et al., 1998; Larsson & Svedin, 2002b). This is probably more common than sexual contact between sexes, because even at this age children usually play more with playmates of the same sex. Engaging in same-sex contact at this age does not mean that a child will become homosexual as an adult. Adult homosexuals may or may not have been involved in same-sex play in early childhood. The same is true of heterosexual adults.

Recall that Freud said the genitals were the focus of children's pleasure during the *phallic stage* (approximately ages 3 to 7) of psychosexual development (see Chapter 8). It is true that nearly all young children touch and explore their genitals, although young boys engage in genital touching more often than young girls (Friedrich et al., 1991; Sandnabba et al., 2003). Here, too, the way parents respond is very important.

> "My sister has a 5-year-old little boy.... She was all worried that something was wrong with him. He would constantly play with his penis. She scolded him one day and told him that if little boys play with themselves like that it would fall off.... I am afraid that this could scar him for life."

> "I remember distinctly how my initially unhealthy attitude towards my sexuality began. As a small child, I used to masturbate. My mother would hit the ceiling when she would catch me because my favorite time to do this was at nap time. She would yell and scream and slap my hands and tell me that it was nasty. Her contempt for my actions was so obvious that I could not help but develop a negative attitude towards my sexuality. I worried for a long time that I was the only person who did this and felt very guilty about it."

> (All examples are from the author's files.)

Most parents respond negatively to finding their young child exploring and touching his or her genitals (Gagnon, 1985). However, when you become a parent, try not to overreact. Allowing children to explore and satisfy their curiosity enables them to become comfortable with their bodies, both as a child and as an adult. Punishment or negative messages may lead to a poor body image and later sexual problems. It is okay to teach your children that it is not appropriate (as opposed to "bad") to touch their genitals in certain situations; in public, for example. According to one child expert, "The attitude of the parent should be to socialize for privacy rather than to punish or forbid" (Calderone, 1983a). If your child touches herself or himself at home, the best thing to do is ignore it. If you feel that you have to stop the behavior because it bothers you, do not scold; simply distract your child by getting her (or him) involved in another activity.

By now, you should understand that parents' responses to normal behaviors have very important consequences for children's later sexual development and their attitudes about their bodies. According to one group of researchers, "From the earliest period in life, the child's family will reciprocally influence the sexual characteristics of the child. The family establishes a 'psychosexual equilibrium' that is a function of the parents' sexual adjustment, the child's developing sexuality, and the impact of the child's sexual development on parental sexual development" (Friedrich et al., 1991). The way parents react to the sexuality of their children is often an indication of the way they feel about their own sexuality.

PERSONAL REFLECTIONS

Does the thought of young children examining and touching their own genitals make you uncomfortable? If so, why? How would you feel if you found your 5-year-old boy with his pants down playing "doctor"? Why? Would your reaction be any different if you found your 5-year-old girl with her pants down playing "doctor"? Why?

THE INITIAL SCHOOL-AGE YEARS (AGES 7–11)

Freud believed that this time of life was a period of "latency," when children were not concerned with sexuality. Studies have found that American children in fact do engage in less overt sexual behavior at this time (Friedrich et al., 1991) and most parents and teachers believe that sexual interest at this age is unusual or a problem (Ryan, 2000). By the time they begin kindergarten or first grade, children generally have developed a sense of modesty and inhibition about undressing in front of others and for the first time may start demanding privacy in the bathroom (Sandnabba et al., 2003).

Some researchers believe that the amount of sex play by American children does not slow down at this stage, but is simply hidden more from parents. Several recent studies of recollections by adults found that the large majority of adults recalled sexual interactions with other children prior to puberty (see Heiman et al., 1998; Larsson & Svedin, 2002b; Ryan, 2000). This included exposing oneself for others, looking at others, touching, fondling, and various sexual games. A majority could even recall being aroused. Activities involving any kind of penetration are still uncommon at this age, and may be an indicator of sexual abuse (Elkovitch et al., 2009).

Children tend to segregate by sex by age 9. Thus, again, much of their sexual play is with same-sex children (Heiman et al., 1998). Because almost all parents react negatively when they catch their children engaging in sexual exploration games, it is not surprising that sexual activity becomes less overt. Most adults remember feeling "guilty," "curious," or "confused" during their childhood experiences (Ryan, 2000). Girls are often treated more harshly than boys. This establishes a double standard—as a general rule, boys are allowed more freedom to explore their sexuality than girls.

Although the amount of overtly sexual play may decrease during the initial school-age years, curiosity about sex does not, and children will ask their parents questions such as "Where do babies come from?" Again, how parents respond will affect their children's responses (and willingness to ask questions of their parents about sex) in the future. Unfortunately, many parents are evasive or even negative (Ryan, 2000).

FIGURE 10–2 Children will attempt to satisfy their natural curiosity about the human body whenever they get a chance.

> "My mother damaged my attitude about sexuality by responding to my question about the origins of babies by telling me that when a man and a woman kiss, it's called making love and this is where babies come from. Even today, she still refuses to discuss sex or sexuality."
>
> (from the author's files)

In summary, contrary to our culture's expectations, there is an abundance of evidence that sexuality develops steadily throughout childhood. One researcher concluded that we live in "a culture at odds with the bulk of evolutionary, developmental, and cross-cultural evidence demonstrating that children are sexual beings, whose exploration of sexual knowledge and play, is an integral part of their development as fully functioning human beings" (Frayser, 1994, p. 210).

PUBERTY (AGES 7–15)

Puberty (from the Latin *puber*, meaning "of ripe age, adult") is the time of life when we first show sexual attraction and become capable of reproduction. It does not happen overnight, but instead is a *process lasting several years*.

Puberty ■ The time in life when an individual first shows sexual attraction and becomes capable of reproduction.

Secondary sex characteristics ■ Bodily changes that occur during puberty and differentiate men and women.

Puberty is at least a two-part maturational process (Grumbach, 2002). In the first part, the adrenal glands start to mature (called *adrenarche*) when children are between the ages of 6 and 8. The adrenal glands secrete the androgen hormone DHEA (dehydroepiandrosterone), which is then converted to testosterone and estrogen. Notice that at this stage girls as well as boys experience an increase in androgens ("male" hormones).

In the second stage, the testicles and ovaries mature (called *gonadarche*), usually several years after adrenarche. In this stage, the pituitary gland begins to secrete FSH in high doses, stimulating the production of sperm in seminiferous tubules in boys and the maturation of ova in girls (see Chapter 3). Prior to this time, boys do not ejaculate (although they can have orgasms) and girls do not have menstrual cycles (although they, too, can have orgasms) (Janssen, 2007). In girls, the maturing ovary produces estrogen and progesterone, while increased levels of luteinizing hormone from a boy's pituitary stimulates production of testosterone in the testicles. The increased levels of hormones lead to a variety of body changes in girls and boys called **secondary sex characteristics** (e.g., breast development, facial hair). The changes in physical appearance create psychological changes in the way children think about themselves and others. Let us examine these changes in more detail and discuss how they affect adolescents' behavior.

Changes in Girls

Usually, the first sign that puberty is beginning in girls is the development of breast buds (at an average age of 11.2 years) (see Biro & Dorn, 2005). Soon afterwards, a growth spurt starts (at about the age of 12). Many sixth- and seventh-grade boys suddenly realize one day that a lot of the girls in their classroom are taller than they are (a fact they may not discover until those first school dances). The reason for this is that the growth spurt in boys does not start, on average, until about age 14. Most of the boys eventually catch up with and pass the girls, because girls generally stop growing by age 16 and boys keep growing until about 18, but those first couple of years can be awkward.

The development of breasts in girls during puberty (a result of increased levels of estrogen) is viewed with great attention by both girls and boys. Not all girls develop at the same rate, so insecurities may develop early. Some decide to speed things up on their own, as 11-year-old Margaret did in Judy Blume's novel *Are You There God? It's Me, Margaret*:

> I tiptoed back to my room and closed the door. I stepped into my closet and stood in one corner. I shoved three cotton balls into each side of my bra. Well, so what if it was cheating! Probably other girls did it too. I'd look a lot better, wouldn't I? So why not!
>
> I came out of the closet and got back up on my chair. This time when I turned sideways I looked like I'd grown. I liked it! *(Judy Blume, Are You There God? It's Me, Margaret, 1970)*

The increase in estrogen levels also causes an increase in fatty deposits in the hips and buttocks.

Pubic hair generally starts to appear shortly after breast development begins, followed in a couple of years by the appearance of underarm hair (see Biro & Dorn, 2005). The growth of hair on new parts of the body results from increased levels of "male" hormones (mainly from the adrenal gland). These hormones also cause the sweat glands and sebaceous glands to develop, so that body odor and acne often become new sources of concern.

The first menstrual period (called **menarche**) occurs at an average age of between 12 and 13 (Brooks-Gunn & Paikoff, 1997; Herman-Giddens et al., 1997); 80% of girls start menstruating between 11 and 13.7 years of age (Chumlea et al., 2003). There is considerable variability, however, and it is normal for the cycles to be very irregular during the first few years after menarche. The rise in estrogen levels causes the vaginal walls to become thicker and more elastic and also results in lubrication during sexual arousal.

The average age for menarche has been dropping over the last few centuries (Patton & Viner, 2007). A study of New York City girls in 1934 found that the average age was 13.5 years, while the average age in Western Europe in the early 1800s was at least 14.5 years (Bullough, 1981). Some researchers believe that the age of puberty in girls has continued to occur earlier in the last few decades (e.g., Herman-Giddens et al., 1997), but other studies have not found strong evidence for

this (e.g., Sun et al., 2005). The reason for the decline in the last couple of centuries is believed to be better nutrition resulting in an earlier acquisition of some minimally required amount of body fat (the putative signal that tells the brain to start releasing FSH).

The reaction of a young woman to her first menstrual cycle will be influenced primarily by what she has been told. Menarche can be viewed as something very positive (a sign of "becoming a woman"), "a simple fact of nature," or "a curse" and something disgusting. Mothers generally pass on their own attitudes and beliefs about it (Uskul, 2004).

> "My mother told me that menstruation was a 'nasty' experience. As a result, I always did my utmost to totally hide the fact that I was menstruating. I didn't even want other women to know that I was having my period. I would refuse to purchase sanitary products out of the machines in restrooms if anyone else was in the restroom."

> "Then, when my big moment came, instead of treating me as though something natural and exciting were happening, my mother reacted with embarrassment. I was very hurt when she told me to get my sister to show me how to wear a sanitary napkin. We never again talked about any of these things."

> "My mother told me when I was very young that I would have a period around age 13 or so.... Finally, one month before my 15th birthday, I started my period. I remember being so excited 'it' finally came. I called my mom in the bathroom and told her. Well, she was so excited she started calling my grandmothers and her friends. When my dad came home he got all excited too. They were so proud I'd finally 'become a woman.'"

(All examples are from the author's files.)

Which of these girls do you suppose began adolescence with good self-esteem about her body? Fortunately, today, more girls are viewing menarche as a positive experience than in past generations (e.g., Lee, 2009). Girls who are comfortable with menstruation also tend to make better decisions about taking sexual risks (Schooler et al., 2005).

Changes in Boys

As mentioned earlier, pubertal development in boys lags about 2 years behind development in girls. The first noticeable change in boys is usually growth of the testicles and scrotum, the result of increased levels of testosterone (see Biro & Dorn, 2005). Testosterone then stimulates growth of the penis, prostate gland, and seminal vesicles. The growth of the genitals

Menarche ■ The term for a girl's first menstrual period.

begins, on average, about the age of 11 to 12 and is completed, on average, by about the age of 15. Boys generally become capable of ejaculation about a year after the penis begins to grow.

When we sleep, about every 90 minutes we enter a phase called REM sleep. REM stands for "rapid eye movements" (our eyes move around under the eyelids during this phase). Many physiological events normally occur during this stage of sleep, including penile erection and vaginal lubrication. As a result of the erect penis during REM, the first experience many boys have with ejaculation is a **nocturnal emission**, or "wet dream" (and about 40% of girls also experience nocturnal orgasms). Some boys have nocturnal emissions frequently, while others have only a few experiences. Fewer fathers prepare their sons for nocturnal emissions than mothers prepare girls for menstruation, and as a result many boys are ashamed, or even frightened, by these experiences.

> "When I was 13 years old, I had a 'wet dream' for the first time. I was shocked to later find out that I did not have a disease. I honestly thought I had one."
>
> "I was 15 years old, and one morning I woke up finding my sheets wet. I thought I urinated in bed at first until I realized it wasn't urine. I was ashamed and didn't want anyone to know what happened. I quickly changed my sheets..."
>
> (from the author's files)

Because nocturnal emissions are not under voluntary control, there is no reason for shame. It is normal! It is therefore important to educate boys about nocturnal emissions before they begin to occur.

Many boys may also be initially frightened by the emission of a strange fluid from the penis that now occurs during masturbation. A case cited by sex therapist Bernie Zilbergeld (1978) is probably not unusual:

> "I kept stroking, my penis got hard, and the sensations felt better and better. Then I was overcome with feelings I had never before felt and, God help me, white stuff came spurting out the end of my cock. I wasn't sure if I had sprung a leak or what. I was afraid but calmed down when I thought that since it wasn't red it couldn't be blood. I kept on stroking and it hurt. I didn't know if the hurt was connected with the white stuff (had I really injured myself?) or if the event was over and my penis needed a rest. But I decided to stop for the moment. Of course, I returned the next day and did it again."

Nocturnal emission ■ An ejaculation that occurs during sleep in teenaged boys and men; a "wet dream."

Gynecomastia ■ Excessive development of the male breasts.

Precocious puberty ■ A condition in which puberty begins before the age of 8 in girls and 9 in boys.

Many boys also develop temporarily enlarged breasts during puberty, called **gynecomastia**. This results from increased levels of estrogen (Mathur & Braunstein, 1997). Gynecomastia usually disappears by the mid-teens, but unless boys are told why this is happening and that it is a normal, temporary condition, they may feel confused, embarrassed, or ashamed.

> "When I was about 13 years old something started to happen to my chest. It seemed as though I was beginning to grow breasts. I went to my mother and showed her so she brought me to the doctor. I was a wrestler in middle school and all I could think about was how could I avoid taking off my shirt in public for one to two years."
>
> (from the author's files)

Pubic hair starts to grow about the same time as the genitals start to develop, the result of increasing testosterone levels, but underarm and facial hair generally do not appear for another 2 years. The amount of body hair, however, is also determined by heredity. As in girls, testosterone also causes development of the sebaceous and sweat glands with their accompanying problems (acne, body odor).

The appearance of facial hair is often as important to boys as the development of breasts is to young girls, for it is one of the few outward signs that they are becoming men. Another change that is obvious to others is a deepening of the voice, a result of testosterone stimulating the growth of the larynx (voice box). This occurs today at an average age of about 12 to 13, but it may have occurred at a later age in past centuries. It was not uncommon in Europe at one time for boys who sang in the great church choirs to be castrated before puberty (with parental approval) in order to preserve their soprano voices. (If castration is done after puberty, by the way, it does not substantially raise a male's voice because the larynx has already undergone its change.)

Precocious and Delayed Puberty

Although the changes that occur during puberty generally begin about the age of 11 or 12, they have been known to occur much earlier. When secondary sex characteristics appear before the age of 8 in girls and 9 in boys, it is called **precocious puberty** (Cesario & Hughes, 2007). This is due to premature activation of adrenal or pituitary hormones and is 10 times more common in girls than in boys. The youngest girl known to have given birth was only 5 years old: a Peruvian Indian girl who delivered a baby by cesarean section in 1939 (Figure 10–3). This means, of course, that she was ovulating and having menstrual periods by the age of 4 or 5.

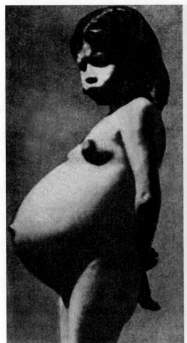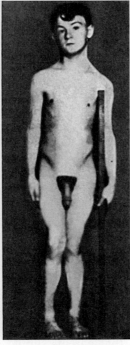

FIGURE 10–3 Two examples of precocious puberty. Linda Medina (left) gave birth when she was 5½ years old. The boy on the right is also only 5 years old.

There have been isolated outbreaks around the world of very young children developing breasts. This has happened to boys and girls as young as 6 months old. A study of thousands of children found that nearly half of the black girls and 15% of the white girls studied had begun to develop breasts, pubic hair, or both by age 8 (Herman-Giddens et al., 1997; see Szabo, 2010). First menstruation still occurred after they had turned 12. It is speculated that the early development of secondary sex characteristics is due to early weight gain, hormones in meat and milk, or what are called environmental estrogens, chemical pollutants that resemble the female hormone estrogen (Cesario & Hughes, 2007). Some skin and hair care products also contain estrogen.

In some children, the appearance of secondary sex characteristics and physical growth do not begin at the same age as in most children. This is called **delayed puberty**. Most clinical referrals are boys who have failed to grow (Kulin, 1996). The usual treatment is to administer gonadotropin-releasing hormone or androgens (male hormones).

PERSONAL REFLECTIONS

Try to recall the feelings you experienced during puberty as your body changed. Would better understanding of these events (via parents or sex education classes) have made it a more positive experience?

Sexual Behavior

Major changes are also occurring in the brain. These changes occur in many mammalian species and happen in areas of the brain that make it more likely that adolescents will engage in risk-taking behaviors (Spear, 2000). This could have evolutionary value by resulting in adolescents exploring new territories and moving toward independence. Sexual behavior is certainly a part of this.

Several studies have found that children's first sexual attraction occurs at age 10, about the fourth or fifth grade (Herdt & McClintock, 2000; Pattatucci & Hamer, 1995). Children of this age may have no understanding yet of sex, but they find themselves attracted to boys or girls. This occurs well before gonadarche and is true for both heterosexual and homosexual attraction. It coincides with rising androgen levels due to the maturation of the adrenal glands (Herdt & McClintock, 2000). This is further evidence that Freud's conception of a latency period between the ages of 6 and 11 is incorrect.

In the developmental process, sexual attraction is followed in order by sexual fantasy and sexual behavior. At age 11, about 25% have held hands and about 16% have kissed. At age 12, the numbers are 41% and 33%, respectively (Waylen et al., 2010). By age 13, the sexual exploration games commonly played by young teens (such as "spin the bottle" and "post office") have a greater erotic content than the games of early childhood.

Adolescence (Ages 13–17)

Adolescence (from the Latin *adolescens*) refers to the time of life between puberty and adulthood. The term was first used in the English academic literature in 1904 by psychologist G. Stanley Hall. In many nonindustrial cultures individuals are considered to be adults when they reach puberty. In our culture, adolescence is a transition period before adulthood, and a rather extended one at that.

For most adolescent boys and girls, the most important issue in their lives is self-identity (Erikson, 1968). Because of their rapidly changing bodies, the search for self-identity first focuses on body image and physical characteristics. According to Maddock et al. (1983), "There is an intensification of body awareness...based upon the fact that the body is a primary 'symbol of self' in which feelings of personal worth, security, and competence are rooted." "An important aspect of the developmental experiences of adolescents is the formation of a sexual identity and sense of self as a sexual being" (Graber & Brooks-Gunn, 2002).

Delayed puberty ■ A condition in which the appearance of secondary sex characteristics and physical growth do not begin until well after they have begun in most children.

Adolescence ■ The time of life between puberty and adulthood.

An adolescent's self-esteem is generally based on his or her subjective views of physical attractiveness. This is also true of teens' sexual esteem (Wiederman & Hurst, 1998). Broad-based self-esteem derived from one's accomplishments develops later. Thus, in the adolescent world there is usually a strong relationship between one's body image and one's overall quality of life (McCabe & Cummins, 1998). This may be especially true of girls, as men greatly prefer partners who are physically attractive (Regan & Berscheid, 1997; see Box 10–A). Unfortunately, many boys come to view girls as sexual objects rather than as persons. An American Psychological Association Task Force (2007)

FIGURE 10–4 Early adolescence is a time of great curiosity about sex. Most boys, and many girls, have begun masturbating by age 15.

concluded that the sexualization of girls in the United States was pervasive, and that this often had a negative effect on their cognitive functioning and mental health.

Masturbation

For many people, the first experience with orgasm occurs during masturbation. The 2010 National Survey of Sexual Health and Behavior (NSSHB) found that for teens aged 15, 72.7% of boys and 43.3% of girls had masturbated (Fortenberry, et al., 2010). Another study found that three fourths of adult men and women recollected having masturbated by age 18, and for most of them it was sporadic or continuous throughout adolescence (Ryan, 2000). However, there may be cultural differences. Studies indicate, for example, that masturbation is more common among white adolescents than among African-American teens (Laumann et al., 1994; see Chapter 11). Although many teens masturbate, nearly half feel that it is "harmful," "sinful," or "wrong," and feel guilty about it (Laumann et al., 1994; Ryan, 2000).

Masturbation may be the single most powerful predictor of adult sexuality (Gagnon, 1977). People who masturbate during adolescence generally engage in sexual activity more frequently and have more positive attitudes about sex (and better sexual self-esteem) than people who do not (see Smith et al., 1996). However, there are few programs, or parents, attempting to communicate anything positive about masturbation. One researcher advises

that parents should at least stop attaching guilt to the practice of masturbation in their children. If nothing else, it is surely the "safest" sexual outlet available (Gagnon, 1977).

Noncoital Sexual Activities

Many sex researchers today define **petting** as noncoital sexual contact below the waist. Any other physical contact is called **necking.** Sexual activity in early adolescence is usually necking. About three fourths of teens have engaged in "deep kissing" by the time they graduate from high school (SIECUS, 1994). The behavior usually progresses to petting during mid-adolescence (ages 15 to 17) (Graber & Brooks-Gunn, 2002).

Because of their lack of sexuality education, many teenaged girls and boys are confused when girls first experience vaginal lubrication:

> "When I first began to feel lubrication I was initially confused. I had no idea that I was supposed to get so slippery and dirty feeling and it almost freaked me out."

> "The first time I felt wetness from lubrication I thought I had just peed on myself."

> "I thought when I was first lubricating vaginally that my period started early. Once I realized it was a clear liquid I was kind of confused and disgusted. I would always feel embarrassed and it was hard for me to relax during any kind of sexual activity."

> "When I first experienced my partner was wet, I thought what is going on here? Is this urine or something else? I then thought it was cum, but when I saw it was clear I didn't know what it was." (man)

(All examples are from the author's files.)

Petting ■ Noncoital sexual contact below the waist.

Necking ■ Erotic physical contact above the waist (kissing, touching breasts).

Box 10–A Cross-Cultural Perspectives

How Do People Select a Mate? An Evolutionary Explanation

The boxes on cross-cultural perspectives presented throughout this book generally show that cultures differ widely in their attitudes and behaviors regarding sexuality. However, David Buss and David Schmitt (1993) surveyed people throughout the world, from Zambia to China, and found that people's mating preferences and attitudes were very much alike. The only major differences were between men's and women's desires and whether people were interested in a short-term relationship (casual sex) or a long-term mate.

Short-term relationships dominate human mating patterns, but men and women engage in short-term liaisons for different reasons, according to the authors of the study. Men tend to engage in casual sex to test their virility, whereas a woman's short-term relationships are largely experimental in nature, either to test her "market value" (to see how desirable she is) or to determine what her desires are. On average, men wanted about 18 women as sexual partners in their lifetime, while the average woman wanted 4 men.

Other studies confirm that, as a general rule, men are much more likely than women to engage in casual sex with someone they hardly know, or do not know at all (see Oliver & Hyde, 1993). In one study, for example, researchers had an attractive man or an attractive woman approach college students and ask them if they would have sex with him or her (Clark & Hatfield, 1989). Three fourths of the men said yes, but none of the women agreed to have sex with an attractive stranger. In a huge cross-cultural study of 52 nations, Schmitt et al. (2003) confirmed that men need far less time to consent to sex than women do and that far more men than women sought short-term partners.

Buss and Schmitt found that in all cultures the idealistic goal was a lasting relationship. This is true for men as well as women (Miller et al., 2002). Across all cultures, over 90% of people eventually marry (Buss, 1985; Epstein & Guttman, 1984). However, this does not mean that people spend their lives with one partner. Many cultures allow people to have more than one mate, a practice called **polygamy.** In fact, about 80% of all societies allow **polygyny**—men to have multiple wives or mistresses (although only about 10% to 20% of men actually do so at any one time) (Buss, 1999; Fisher, 1989). About 2% allow **polyandry**—women to have more than one mate (Frayser, 1985). According to Buss and Schmitt, Western cultures may have outlawed polygamy, but people get around this by having serial marriages (divorce and remarriage) and by having extramarital affairs. In the United States, the divorce rate for first marriages is 43% (Kalb, 2006), and from 25% to 50% of people are estimated to have engaged in adultery (Laumann et al., 1994; Wiederman, 1997a).

Buss and Schmitt believe that, for men, promiscuity is a primal instinct that maximizes reproduction potential. How do men balance their short- and long-term desires? Buss says, "If a man could have his fantasy, he would sequester and monopolize all the attractive women in the country. Indeed, men who are in a position to get what they want—kings, tycoons, celebrities—often do things like that" (quoted by Gura, 1994). Men may enjoy female promiscuity in a short-term relationship, but when looking for a long-term mate they seek a chaste woman, someone who has not yet had sex. Of 37 countries studied by Buss and Schmitt, in more than two thirds of them the men valued chastity in choosing a mate more than the women did.

"I am of Mexican descent. In our culture, it is 'okay' for boys to engage in sex before marriage. In fact, it is encouraged. Girls, however, are not to have sex until after marriage. We are made to believe that a man will not want to marry a girl who is not a virgin. In most cases, it turns out to be true."
(from the author's files)

However, regardless of culture, men placed a high value on physical attractiveness in choosing a long-term mate (Buss & Barnes, 1987; Furnham, 2009; Regan & Berscheid, 1997) and preferred mates who were younger than they were (Buss, 1989; Kendrick & Keefe, 1992). Why this strong preference for physical attractiveness? Evolutionary scientists have found evidence that women's facial and bodily attractiveness signals hormonal and developmental (i.e., reproductive) health (Braun & Bryan, 2006; Thornhill & Grammer, 1999).

Women's mating strategies are different from men's, according to Buss and Schmitt. Because a woman has a limited number of reproductive years and must invest time and energy in childbearing, women prefer mates who can offer them economic and physical protection. Women, more so than men, prefer men who are good financial prospects (Buss, 1989). Factors like a promising career, ambition, and education are important in women's decisions across all cultures (Furnham, 2009).

Polygamy ■ The practice of allowing men or women to have more than one mate at the same time.

Polygyny ■ The practice of allowing men to have two or more wives at the same time.

Polyandry ■ The practice of allowing women to have more than one husband at the same time.

(Continued)

Women prefer older mates, and are not as concerned about physical attractiveness as are men.

In line with their mating strategies, men and women use different strategies to keep a mate interested (Buss & Shackelford, 1997). Women are more likely to make themselves more attractive, while men are more likely to spend money on a mate and give gifts.

Buss and Schmitt believe that there is evolutionary value for what men and women seek in a relationship. Geary et al. (2004) studied mate choices in humans and in nonhuman species and concluded that "the preferred mate choices...of both women and men, and those of other species, have evolved to focus on and exploit the reproductive potential and reproductive investment of members of the opposite sex" (p. 27). Regardless of whether you agree with this, one thing is clear from this large cross-cultural study—love is not really blind.

Sexual Intercourse

The 2010 NSSHB study found that only about one fourth of 16-year-olds have engaged in oral-genital sex, but that about 60% had done so by ages 18 to 19, the same percent as had engaged in vaginal intercourse (Fortenberry et al., 2010; Herbenick et al., 2010a; see also Halpern-Felsher et al., 2005). Many teens believe that oral sex is more acceptable and less risky. Oral sex and vaginal intercourse almost always begin within 6 months of one another (Lindberg et al., 2008; Fortenberry et al., 2010; Herbenick et al., 2010a).

About 46% of American high school students have engaged in sexual intercourse, 5.9% before the age of 13 (Eaton et al., 2010). Over 62% of high school seniors have had sexual intercourse (Eaton et al., 2010), and by age 20, 75% of Americans have engaged in premarital sex (Finer, 2007). The average age at which Americans first have vaginal intercourse is 17.7 years (Else-Quest et al., 2005). About 5% to 6% of 17-year-olds have engaged in anal intercourse (Fortenberry et al., 2010). Nearly 14% of high school students have had four or more sexual partners (Eaton et al., 2010). About 7% to 10% of teenage girls have their first voluntary intercourse with male partners who are at least 5 years older (Leitenberg & Saltzman, 2000).

Overall, the percentage of American teens having intercourse is smaller than for teenagers in some countries, but greater than for most. There are also major gender and ethnic differences (Cavazos-Rehg et al., 2009). Among boys, the average age of first intercourse is much younger for African Americans and much older for Asian Americans. Among girls, Hispanic and Asian-American teens are less likely to have had intercourse than white or African-American teens.

The preceding statistics may have given you a false impression of how sexually active American teens really are. Surveys show that the number of sexually active teens decreased during the 1990s and through 2009 (Eaton et al., 2010; Gavin et al., 2009). The 2010 NSSHB study found that at any one point in time, only about 27% of 17-year-olds are having partnered sexual relations (Fortenberry et al., 2010). In addition, fewer young people now believe that it is okay to have premarital intercourse than was true in the 1980s (Ku et al., 1998). As a result of this change in attitudes, and an increased use of condoms by those teens who are having intercourse, the teenage pregnancy and birth rates also declined during the 1990s through 2005 (Gavin et al., 2009). The teen birth rate climbed slightly in 2006 and 2007, but dropped by 2%, in 2008 (National Center for Health Statistics, 2010). Thus, we may still be in a downword trend (see Figure 10–5).

Teenagers give multiple reasons for engaging in sex. Besides sexual pleasure, these include a desire for intimacy and an increase in social status (Ott et al., 2006). First

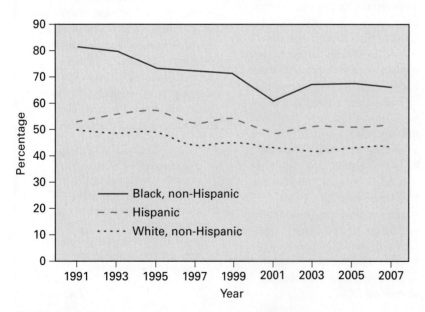

FIGURE 10–5 Percentage of high school students who have engaged in sexual intercourse (from Gavin et al., 2009).

intercourse usually occurs within a romantic relationship (Manning et al., 2000). For teenage girls, love and a committed relationship that is supposed to last are important before engaging in sex. Many girls view the loss of virginity as a gift to their partner (Frieze, 2005). These things are not as important for most teenage boys, for whom it is more important that they "never miss an opportunity" (Taris & Semin, 1997a). Many teenaged boys view their virginity as a stigma and are embarrassed about it (Frieze, 2005).

How do teenagers feel about their first experiences of sexual intercourse? Weis (1983) found that women experience a range of emotions during their first sexual intercourse. About one third have strongly negative emotional reactions (e.g., guilt, anxiety, shame, fear, regret), while another third have highly positive emotional experiences. For the final third, their experience is neither positive nor negative, but a "Is that all there is?" response (e.g., disappointment, boredom). Men generally have more pleasure and less guilt than women during first intercourse (Sprecher et al., 1995).

Another study found that about one third of the women surveyed suffered severe physical pain at first intercourse, while 28% said they had experienced no pain (Weis, 1985). Women with positive experiences and minimal pain generally had an extensive childhood and adolescent history of sex play (kissing, petting, masturbation, and often oral sex), had positive attitudes about their sex play, and had their first intercourse in a safe environment (no

fear of discovery) with a caring partner. Those who had negative reactions and pain had little previous experience with sex play, had not planned it, and "gave in" to the man's pressure (see also Thompson, 1990).

Most teens have experienced sexual regret and wish they had waited until they were older to start having intercourse (Martino et al., 2009; Oswalt et al., 2005). Women who have feelings of guilt after first intercourse are more likely than others to be sexually dissatisfied (e.g., have less enjoyment) as adults (Moore & Davidson, 1997). In contrast, individuals who had positive feelings about their early sexual experiences have greater enjoyment of sex as adults (Bauserman & Davis, 1996).

What about those teens who choose not to engage in premarital intercourse? What differentiates them from teens who do engage in sexual intercourse? Many teens who postpone sexual intercourse do so because they want to wait until marriage (Forste & Haas, 2002). The more religious a teen is, the more likely that he or she will postpone engaging in intercourse (Rostosky et al., 2003). Teens who abstain are less likely to engage in other risky behaviors as well (e.g., drinking, drugs, etc.) (Forste & Haas, 2002; Kandel, 1990; McLeod & Knight, 2010; Whitbeck et al., 1993). Parental involvement also plays an important role (Browning et al., 2005). The quality of the communication between parents and teenage children is positively related to the teenagers' values about sexual abstinence (see Addendum on page 268).

FIGURE 10–6 The biological changes that occur in adolescence lead to an interest in, and the development of, sexual behavior and sexual identity. Many teens engage in sex because of peer pressure.

Peer Pressure

Although many teens engage in sex because they have positive feelings about it, many others who are sexually active are motivated by a desire for acceptance and social status (Ott et al., 2006). One of the major factors that indicate whether a teen will engage in intercourse is his or her perceptions of the social norms (Gillmore et al., 2002). For most teens there is enormous peer pressure to engage in sex. What is **peer pressure**? It is your peer group's expectations of how you are supposed to behave. The more friends a teen has who are sexually experienced, the more likely it is that he or she will engage in sexual intercourse (Sieving et al., 2006). Most young people believe that the average person engages in sexual intercourse after several dates (Cohen & Shotland, 1996), and many overestimate how many of their peers are actually having sex (Whitley, 1998). About one third of teenaged boys have lied about "how far they have gone" (Jayson, 2010). What about those young men who do not wish to become sexually active yet?

> "You were right about the fact that there is great pressure to engage in sex. I didn't have sex until I got married at the age of 22. My friends thought it was dumb for me to want to wait so I lied to them and told them that I had sex and made up a bunch of lies about it. I realize now it was dumb of me. If they were really my friends they would have understood my decision to wait."

> "I am a 19-year-old sophomore and I have not yet had sexual relations. I made a promise to myself long ago that I would not have sex until I am married. I made this promise because of my own moral convictions and I am content with it. I have been the target of a great deal of laughter and ridicule because of this decision."
> (All examples are from the author's files.)

Many teenage girls also feel pressured to engage in sex:

> "I had sex at 17 in my senior year.... So many of my girlfriends would talk about doing it with and for their boyfriends, and would ask me about my experience.

> I was so ashamed for never having done anything throughout my entire life...."

> "My first sexual experience was when I was 15. Everyone else was 'doing it' so I figured I should too. When it was over I cried. I wish I would have waited. Maybe not till I was married, but until I was more mature."

> "I had my first sexual relationships at 14.... I realize now that my reason for these relationships was to be accepted, wanted, have a boyfriend and pleasing him to keep him."
> (All examples are from the author's files.)

For many girls, the need for emotional intimacy is an important part of finding their self-identity (see Shaughnessy & Shakesby, 1992). Unfortunately, many mistake sexual intimacy for emotional intimacy. In many peer groups there is a double standard that also results in a negative sexual experience for many girls.

> "I would let some of the guys from school touch my breasts because of the attention I got from them. I only got a bad reputation instead."

> "Please talk about labelling women. When I was 15, I had some experiences with some older guys around 17. Well, I did some things that I regret. Word got around at my all-girl Catholic high school that I was a slut. You don't know what it is like to walk down a hall and have girls call you a slut. Guys wanted to go out with me for just one thing."
> (All examples are from the author's files.)

To this point, you may have concluded that the only peer pressure among teens is to engage in sex. However, you have also just learned that the number of teens engaging in sexual intercourse has declined since the early 1990s (Eaton et al., 2010). Some experts are giving the credit to positive peer pressure (Alan Guttmacher Institute, 1999). "Many groups want to take credit for the drop in teenage pregnancy, but the credit truly goes to teenagers," said Jacqueline Darroch of the Guttmacher Institute. The reasoning is that when fewer teens engage in sexual intercourse, they set examples for close friends.

Peer pressure ■ Expectations by one's peer group about how one is supposed to behave.

EMERGING ADULTHOOD (AGES 18–25)

The average age at marriage has increased dramatically in recent decades. The median age at which people first get married today is almost 26 for women and almost 28 for men (U.S. Census Bureau, 2008). This is an increase of more than 2 years of age since 1980 and more than 4 years since 1960. As a result, psychologist Jeffrey Arnett (2000) proposed that a new developmental stage of life has emerged in today's society—**emerging adulthood**. This is an extended period of being a single adult that occurs between adolescence and young adulthood. Both parents and their 18- to 25-year-old children agree that at this age people are not yet "grown up" adults (Nelson et al., 2007).

Emerging adults have more freedom from parental restraints and more opportunity for privacy than in the past. This age period generally includes frequent change as individuals explore for their own identities in love, work, and worldviews. There is often an increase in risk behavior as well. This developmental stage is not found in all cultures, but is common in advanced cultures where young people are allowed an extended period of independence and role exploration.

The sexual activity of emerging adults is generally different from that of younger and older age groups (Seidman & Rieder, 1994). By the age of 20, about 75% of emerging adults are sexually experienced and having sex regularly, and most emerging adults have had multiple serial sexual partners during their short lifetimes. Recent nationally representative surveys have found that among unmarried persons aged 18 to 26, about 80% of the men and women had engaged in both vaginal intercourse and oral-genital sex, and at least 25% have engaged in anal sex (Herbenick et al., 2010a; Kaestle & Halpern, 2007). Oral and anal sex were most common in mutually loving relationships. Nearly three fourths of college students have had one or more sexual partners in the last year (American College Health Association, 2004). Studies have found that the earlier a woman becomes sexually experienced, the more likely it is that she will have had multiple sexual partners. Also, the more experienced she becomes, the less time she spends between sexual relationships (Seidman et al., 1992; Tanfer & Schoorl, 1992). In summary, for young adults, the number of sexual partners steadily increases the longer the individual has been sexually experienced.

Several sexual patterns are found during this age period. For some young adults, this is a period of sexual experimentation:

> "This past year I have become very sexually active. I have a steady boyfriend. We love one another to death, but are involved in threesomes and sometimes foursomes. We enjoy sex and have tried everything imaginable. The persons involved in our 'parties' are his roommates. We consider ourselves 'one big happy family.'"
> (from the author's files)

Emerging adulthood ■ A developmental stage of life; an extended period of being a single adult that occurs between adolescence and young adulthood.

FIGURE 10–7 Emerging adulthood is an extended period of being a single adult. The large majority of emerging adults are sexually experienced and have sex regularly.

An increasingly popular sexual lifestyle in recent years is **hooking up**—nonrelationship sex, usually with a friend (also called "friends with benefits"). Many recent studies have found that at least half of emerging adults have had sex with someone they were not dating (e.g., Bisson & Levine, 2009; Fielder & Carey, 2010; Grello et al., 2003; Manning et al., 2005; McGinty et al., 2007; Owen et al., 2010; Puentes et al., 2008). The reason most emerging adults engage in this type of sexual relationship is to avoid romantic commitment (Bisson & Levine 2009). "While it's impossible to say exactly why students would rather hook up than seek traditional boyfriends or girlfriends, students say that greater competitive pressures—to build a résumé, position themselves for grad school, and chart a career trajectory—leaves them little time for romance" (McGinn, 2004).

Many emerging adults engage in a sexual lifestyle called **serial monogamy**—a series of relationships in which sex is reserved for just one person. However, many adolescents and young adults probably begin a sexual relationship with the hope and expectation that it will last. This is true even for one third of individuals who hook up (Manning et al., 2006). About 1 in 10 college students who have initiated sexual intercourse later choose to engage in secondary abstinence (Rasberry & Goodsen, 2009). The type of sexual lifestyle emerging adults choose to follow is strongly influenced by their level of religiosity (Lefkowitz et al., 2004).

The period of emerging adulthood is also a time in which most people gradually become less influenced by peer pressure and gain a better understanding of their own sexual motivations.

> "I now make my own choices and give my opinions without being intimidated about what someone else might think. But most of all I have stopped confusing sex for the attention I was striving for. For example, I used to think that if I give him sex then that means he must like me or is my friend."
>
> (from the author's files)

YOUNG ADULTHOOD (AGES 26–39)

A national survey found that by age 44, 95% of Americans have engaged in premarital sex (Finer, 2007). However, in their review of sexual surveys, Seidman and Rieder (1994) concluded that relatively long-lasting monogamy was the norm for

---

Hooking up ■ Sexual relations with a nonromantic partner (usually a friend).

Serial monogamy ■ The practice of having a series of monogamous sexual relationships.

FIGURE 10–8 Relatively long-lasting monogamy is the norm for most adults aged 25 and older.

most adults aged 25 and older. For people in this age group, about 80% of sexually active heterosexual men and 90% of sexually active heterosexual women report having had only one sex partner within the last year. Nearly identical findings were reported by Laumann's group (1994). However, there is a range of sexual and relational lifestyles even in this age group.

Marriage

People today may be postponing marriage, but the likelihood of a man marrying by age 40 is 81%, and 86% for women (National Center for Health Statistics, 2009).

The frequency of sexual intercourse in the first year of marriage is usually high, an average of about 15 times a month in the first year (Greenblatt, 1983). In fact, for the entire population, the frequency of sexual relations is highest for married couples in their mid-20s to mid-30s (Clements, 1994; Janus & Janus, 1993; Laumann et al., 1994; Herbenick et al., 2010a).

The frequency of sexual relations generally declines after the first year or two of marriage. Why? Sex has to compete with other time demands, such as career advancement. Parenthood means less privacy and more demands and often results in exhaustion at the end of the day (see Ahlborg et al., 2008). It is also normal for sexual relations to decrease somewhat as the novelty wears off and individuals within a relationship become accustomed to one another (Klusmann, 2002).

Studies find that married couples today are more likely to use a variety of sexual techniques than in the past. This is true for positions of sexual intercourse and for oral-genital sex. People with sexual partners are also much more likely to masturbate than people who do not have a partner. This is because sex with a partner and masturbation are both reflections of one's overall sex drive (DeLamater, 2007; Laumann et al., 1994). A majority of both men and women report marital sex to be very satisfying, more so than do singles (Clements, 1994; Laumann et al., 1994). Moreover, numerous studies have found that adults who get and stay married have higher levels of psychological well-being (and, in the case of men, less depression) and even better physical health than individuals who stay single (e.g., Horwitz et al., 1996; National Center for Health Statistics, 2005).

Living Together (Cohabitation)

Today, nearly two thirds of couples who marry live together outside of marriage first (National Center for Health Statistics, 2010) (see Figure 10–9). This represents an increase in *cohabitation* of over 700% since the 1970 census. Forty percent of children live for some period of time in a cohabitating family. The increase in the number of couples living together may be one reason for the older age of couples today who marry for the first time.

People give a variety of reasons for cohabitating (Rhodes et al., 2009). About half hope to eventually marry their partner (Guzzo, 2009). Living together can be a test or trial period before marriage (there is much more to living together happily and successfully than simply enjoying sex), but it can also be an alternative to marriage (King & Scott, 2005). As cohabitation has become more acceptable, a greater number of couples who cohabitate are doing so for temporary convenience (Bumpass & Lu, 2000).

Does living together before marriage improve your chance of a later successful marriage? Interestingly, older studies found that couples who lived together before getting married were more likely than others to experience marital instability

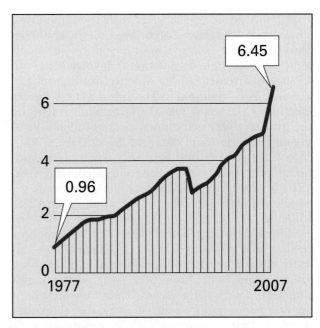

FIGURE 10–9 Number of unmarried cohabitating partners (U.S. Census Bureau). The dip in 1996 occurred because after that year surveys did not include same-sex partners.

and get divorced (Axinn & Thornton, 1992; Bumpass & Lu, 2000; Dush et al., 2003). However, these data were collected at a time when cohabitation was considered to be unusual. Today, with nearly 10% of all heterosexual couples living together being unmarried, cohabitation before marriage is commonplace. So what do recent studies find? For women who had cohabitated only with their eventual husband, the divorce rate is not higher than for those who did not cohabitate first (Jayson, 2008; Teachuau, 2003; Tach & Halpern-Meekin, 2009). It is higher for people who have cohabitated with more than one person, and for couples who had children while cohabitating.

Extramarital Sex—In Supposedly Monogamous Marriages

A recent study found that 1 in 10 people currently in a relationship had had sex with someone other than their partner (Paik, 2010). Is this true for married people as well? In their nationally representative sample, Laumann's group (1994) found that for people in their 50s, 37% of men and 12.4% of women had been unfaithful. For people in their 30s, 27.6% of men and 26.2% of women admitted to having had an affair. This agrees with another nationally representative sample (Wiederman, 1997a). Janus and Janus (1993) found that 35% of married men (and 56% of divorced men) and 26% of married women (and 59% of divorced women) in their survey admitted to extramarital affairs.

These statistics on adultery refer to extramarital *sexual* relations. But, according to psychologist Shirley Glass, "That's a male definition [of adultery]. If you look at emotional involvement and sexual involvement short of intercourse, you add another 20%" (quoted in Mehren, 1991). Whereas men may have solely sexual affairs, women's affairs are almost always emotional or a combination of sexual and emotional (Banfield & McCabe, 2001). Many married persons, especially wives, have emotional affairs over the telephone or the Internet. "The Internet has exploded with sites specifically for people who want to cheat on their spouses" (Ali & Miller, 2004).

Throughout the world, nearly 90% of people believe that extramarital sex is "always" or "almost always" wrong (Widmer et al., 1998). Men are more upset at the idea of their partner's getting sexual with someone else than they are about an emotional attachment. Women, on the other hand, are more concerned about emotional infidelity on the part of their mates and are much more likely than men to forgive a partner for sexual infidelity (Buss et al., 1992; Wiederman & Kendall, 1999).

Why do so many people engage in extramarital sex (or sex outside of any supposedly monogamous relationship)? Some are simply curious to see what sex with another person would be like, while some want more variety in their lives. Some may seek out other partners in order to prove that they are still desirable or young, while others may be looking for the companionship no longer found in their marriages. Of course, there is also the excitement factor. As John Gagnon (1977), points out.

> Most people find their extramarital relationships highly exciting, especially in the early stages. This is a result of psychological compression: the couple gets together; they are both very aroused (desire, guilt, expectation); they have only three hours to be together.... Another source of attraction is that the other person is always seen when he or she looks good and is on best behavior, never when feeling tired or grubby, or when taking care of children, or when cooking dinner.... Each time, all the minutes that the couple has together are special because they have been stolen from all these other relationships. The resulting combination of guilt and excitement has a heightening effect. *(John Gagnon, 1977)*

There is very little association between social background—including political leaning (ultracon-

servative versus ultraliberal) and religion or lack of it—and whether one engages in extramarital affairs (Janus & Janus, 1993). Whitehurst (1972) indicates that two things contribute to having "outside sex." One is simply opportunity. Women who work have more opportunity to meet other men and to have affairs than women who stay at home all day (see Ali & Miller, 2004). As psychotherapist Marcella Weiner puts it, "Women are in the work force to stay now, and they have many more opportunities [to meet men]. It has always been okay with men, but it is becoming more and more a phenomenon with women" (quoted in Mehren, 1991). The second contributor mentioned by Whitehurst is alienation. People can grow apart and develop different interests over time. Thus, if you meet someone else who shares your interests, seems attractive, and seems attracted to you, this can lead to sharing other parts of your life as well.

A behavior that has received a lot of recent attention is older women having affairs with younger men (see Cloud, 2010). These women are popularly referred to as "cougars." A recent study found that women aged 27 to 45 are significantly more sexual than women in younger or older age groups (see Cloud, 2010). Evolutionary psychologist David Buss believes that evolution has resulted in women becoming more sexual as their fertility declines. Obviously, much more research is going to be needed in this area.

Extramarital Sex—Consensual Arrangements

Some couples agree to have sex outside of the marital relationship. One such arrangement is **open marriage**, where both partners agree that it is okay to have sex with others. Even here, however, there are usually some agreed-upon restrictions, such as not having sex with a mutual friend or not having sex with the same person twice (Blumstein & Schwartz, 1983). Couples make these restrictions so that their primary commitment is to the marriage and thus the nonmarital partner will not be viewed as competition. Blumstein and Schwartz (1983) found that perhaps as many as 15% of married couples had some sort of "understanding" that allowed for extramarital sexual relations under some conditions. Although this type of extramarital arrangement is supposed to add role equality and flexibility to a marriage, the divorce rate among open-marriage couples is just as high as for sexually monogamous couples (Rubin & Adams, 1986).

Another arrangement that allows consensual extramarital sex is **swinging** (often called "wife swapping" or the "lifestyle"), where a married

Swinging ■ A type of open marriage relationship in which a couple has extramarital relations together with other couples.

Open marriage ■ A marital relationship in which the couple agrees that it is permissible to have sexual relations outside of the marriage.

couple has extramarital relations together (de Visser & McDonald, 2007). Couples get together by answering ads in newspapers or swingers' magazines, or by going to commercial clubs that encourage recreational sex. The sexual activity often includes sex between the women while the husbands watch, but male homosexual activity is much less common, and in many cases forbidden.

Here are some experiences of couples at a swingers club in New Orleans:

> "I knew that I might be interested in women, so we started out by exploring that. Once we started doing that, he wanted to get some action too... having sex with the women I brought home... rather than cheating on each other because we are sexually bored, we have fun together... and, you get to have no strings sex." (man 35, woman 26, married 3 years)

> "The freedom to experiment and do it without deception. It is probably THE only time you will experience a relationship where both partners openly communicate about sex. No hiding, no wishing, no jerking off to your fantasy, no cheating, no guilt. Everything is 'out on the table' so to speak. It's wonderful." (man 37, woman 32, married 12 years)

> (All examples are from the author's files.)

Swinging reached its peak in popularity in the 1970s and declined during the 1980s, but has since rebounded. Although there has been an increase in the number of swing clubs nationally, no recent research has been done to establish the overall prevalence (Jenks, 1998). Except for the fact that they tend to be white, to be less religious than others, and to have had more premarital sexual experience, swingers are no different from other couples, and many are middle class and conservative (Jenks, 1998).

MIDDLE AGE (AGES 40–59)

Christian and Victorian views of sex emphasized that sex within a marriage was for procreation only and excluded sexual activities for pleasure. Thus, Western culture came to view older individuals who were no longer able to conceive as asexual. For example, many students believe that their own parents and grandparents love each other, but how many students think of their parents and grandparents as being sexually active? Studies have found that many college students have difficulty accepting their parents' sexuality and underestimate how often their parents have sex by about half (Allgeier & Murnen, 1985; Pocs & Godow, 1977). Here are a variety of responses from students in my course:

> "I was about 14 when my mom told me she and my dad have sex. I was shocked and thought it was disgusting. I didn't want to hear it any more."

> "My parents don't have sex. They have other things to do."

> "The thought of my parents actually possessing sexuality or having sex mortified me."

> "And plus they are in their late 40s and early 50s—I just can't imagine them having sex."

> "When I was a teenager, it would make me uncomfortable when they would go in their room and shut and lock the door because I knew what they were going to be doing and I just felt it was weird because

FIGURE 10–10 The addition of children may change the pattern of sexual relations, but not necessarily the frequency. Married couples in their mid-20s to mid-30s have sex more often than any other group.

to me, they were 'old.' Now that I'm in my 20s, it makes me feel good to know that my parents still love and care about each other, and it helps me to believe that I will have a positive sexual attitude well into my 40s and 50s."

"Sometimes I tease them a little when I catch my dad home late in the morning because I know he stayed home so they could have sex. I think it's great that they still love each other and express themselves sexually after being married for 25 years."

Pocs and Godow (1977) concluded that "many parents may appear to be nonsexual because they hesitate to discuss the topic of sexuality in any way with their children or because they are not inclined to exhibit loving, affectionate responses, let alone sexual behavior, in the presence of their children." Allgeier and Murnen (1985) later found that children whose parents had discussed sex with them gave more accurate estimates of their parents' sexual frequency.

Ask yourself these questions: "Do my parents enjoy sexual intercourse? How often? Do they enjoy using different positions? Do my grandparents enjoy sex? How often? Do they enjoy using different positions?"

Think about how you answered these questions, and then ask yourself: "What are my attitudes about sex?" For those of you who are sexually experienced, also ask yourself, "Do I like sex? How often do I enjoy it?" If you enjoy sex, why wouldn't your parents or grandparents? Sex therapists have found that the way that you feel about sex now is the best estimate of how you will feel about it in the future (Bretschneider & McCoy, 1988; Masters & Johnson, 1966). If you enjoy sex now, why should you stop enjoying sex later in life? From the previous case histories, which students do you think will enter parenthood with more positive attitudes about sexuality? Believing that parents and grandparents are (or should be) asexual can have negative consequences when you

become a parent yourself. How will you then regard your partner, and vice versa?

"My husband and I were in what seemed an ideal marriage. Not only was our coupling wonderful, but we also shared an extremely intense sexual relationship as well. Two years into our marriage we were informed that we were going to be parents. My husband was great; he was so attentive and supportive during the time I carried our child. . . .

"He was a proud father. However, things were never the same between us after the birth of our daughter. There had been little sex between us since the baby, but I attributed it to his long hours. . . .

"I started sensing that my husband was distant. I told him he was growing away from us instead of with us. I asked him what was wrong . . . He said that ever since I became a mother that he no longer could see me as a sexual partner. I was a mom and that was something sacred that should be put on a pedestal. He said it was impossible to think of me in a sexual way anymore."
(from the author's files)

Older people are aware that young people have unfavorable attitudes about them having sexual relations. This negative attitude is called *ageism*. Barring a tragedy, we will all grow old someday. These negative attitudes must change if today's young people want to be treated decently when they are older.

PERSONAL REFLECTIONS

Does the thought of your parents enjoying sexual relations make you comfortable or uncomfortable? Why? If you have difficulty viewing your parents as sexual human beings, what effect do you think that will have on your own sexual relationship when you and your partner become parents (and view one another as parents)? When you become a parent, will you be embarrassed if your children know that you and your partner enjoy sexual relations? Why?

Frequency of Sex

It is a common belief that sexual activity is highest for young people and that by middle age sexual relations have become stale as people cease to be sexual. The scientific evidence does not support this. The baby-boomer generation is now in their 50s and 60s, and having been raised during the sexual revolution, they do not accept the old stereotypes of aging and sexuality. Many people in their 50s and older are now regarded as sexy: Madonna, Richard Gere, Tom Selleck, Denzel Washington, Pierce Brosnan, Kim Basinger, Bruce Willis, Michelle Pfeiffer,

"Actually, Dad knows quite a bit about sex for a man his age."

Rex May

Sharon Stone, and the list goes on and on. How sexually active are the baby boomers?

As mentioned earlier, national cross-sectional surveys have found that sexual activity is highest for people in their mid-20s to mid-30s (Clements, 1994; Janus & Janus, 1993; Laumann et al., 1994; Herbenick et al., 2010a). Is there a sharp drop-off after that? Not really, at least not until the 60s. Although most surveys do show a decline in sexual activity for people in their 40s and a further decline in the 50s, the drop-off is very gradual, about only one or two times a month less than when they were younger (Clements, 1994; Herbenick et al., 2010a; Schick et al., 2010; Segraves & Segraves, 1995; Seidman & Rieder, 1994). A recent nationally representative survey found that about 56% of men and 70% of women aged 50–70 years had engaged in sexual intercourse in the previous year (Schick et al., 2010). A survey by the American Association of Retired Persons (AARP) found that half of people aged 50 and older *with partners* were having sexual intercourse at least once a week (Jacoby, 2005).

Surveys indicate that married people not only have sex more often than singles (never married or divorced), but are also happier with their sex lives than are singles (Clements, 1994; Laumann et al., 1994; National Opinion Research Center, 2002, cited by Deveny, 2003). When asked if sex is important to them, more people in their 30s, 40s, and early 50s say yes than do people in their late teens or early 20s (Clements, 1994).

Not everyone in their 50s is having sex regularly. For people in their 50s and older, two of the major factors determing whether they are having sex are health and availability of a partner (Lindau & Gavrilova, 2010; Schick et al., 2010). However, the major factors that affect sexual desire in middle age are an individual's cognitions about sex (beliefs/values about the sexuality of people in one's group) and his or her motivation. One important predictor of both men's and women's sexual activity in midlife is the level of sexual activity they had when they were younger (Dennerstein & Lehert, 2004; Haavio-Mannila & Kontula, 1997). Within a relationship, sexual motivation and the quality of sex are highly associated with the overall quality of the relationship (Jacoby, 1999; Kingsberg, 2000). In a recent national survey, Laumann et al. (2006) found that the sexual well-being of men and women aged 40–80 years was strongly associated with both physical and emotional satisfaction with the partner and a good companionate relationship.

Ageism and Sexism

According to the 2000 census, 40% (over 36 million) of Americans aged 45 or older are single. Among divorced or widowed men and women, there are more opportunities for men. By the time people reach their

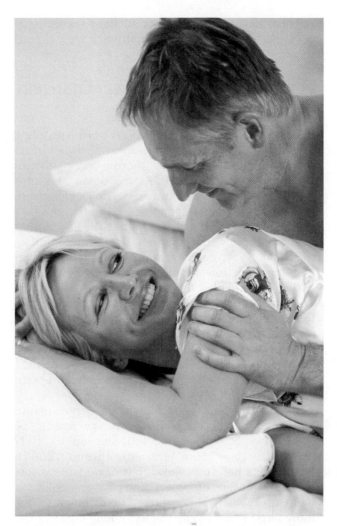

FIGURE 10–11 Over half of 45- to 54-year-old people with partners have sexual intercourse at least once a week. Do you believe that your parents still enjoy sex? When you become a parent, will you be embarrassed if your children know that you and your partner enjoy sexual relations?

early 40s, there are over 200 single women for every 100 single men (Blumstein & Schwartz, 1983). A survey by the AARP found that among people aged 55 to 59, about 90% of men have sexual partners, but only about 70% of women do (Jacoby, 1999).

There is also a double standard in our society. While many people frown upon women having sexual relationships with men much younger than themselves, most feel that it is okay for men to have relationships with younger women. Have you noticed that whenever Hollywood puts a middle-aged leading man in a romantic role it is almost always with a woman 10 to 20 years younger (or even more) than he is? Because of the combination of ageism and sexism, women over age 40 generally have a more difficult time finding new partners than do older men (Carpenter et al., 2006). In other words, if everyone aged 40 or older (especially women) had the opportunity to have sexual partners, the statistical numbers that you have just read would probably be even higher.

Female Sexuality: Physical Changes with Age

Recall from Chapter 3 that girls are born with a few hundred thousand ova (follicles) at birth, and that several hundred begin to mature every month (McGee & Hsueh, 2000). As a woman ages into her 40s, her supply of ova is nearing exhaustion. Her ovaries do not respond as well to the pituitary hormones FSH and LH (see Figure 10–12), so that menstrual cycle irregularities are common after the age of 35. Cycles generally become less frequent and menstruation heavier than before (MacKey, 2009). Eventually, her ovaries atrophy (wither) and she quits having menstrual cycles entirely, thus ending her ability to have children. The last menstruation is referred to as **menopause**. The changes that occur in the few years that precede and the first year that follows menopause are called the **climacteric** (also called the perimenopause) (see Sowers, 2000).

Four fifths of women experience menopause between 44 and 55, with an average age of 51 (Al-Azzawi & Palacios, 2009), but up to 10% experience it before age 40 (Bruno, 2005). Researchers have concluded that menopause is just a natural result of aging, and that the older a woman is when she experiences menopause the more likely it is that she will live a long life (Sowers, 2000). It is well-established that cigarette smoking can cause earlier menopause (Avis et al., 2002).

As the ovaries atrophy, they produce less and less gonadal hormones, and eventually produce no progesterone and only minute amounts of estrogen. Testosterone levels often decrease as well. Most women will experience some symptoms as a result of these hormonal changes. How a woman and her partner react to these changes can affect other aspects of a relationship, so it is important for everyone to understand their physical basis (see Avis et al., 2002, for a review).

Estrogen and progesterone, you recall, inhibit release of FSH and LH from the pituitary. At menopause, the pituitary hormones are no longer inhibited and are released in large amounts. In addition to their reproductive role, these hormones affect the diameter of blood vessels, causing them to dilate. Subjectively, this physiological change is perceived as a *hot flash*, a sudden sensation of warmth or intense heat that spreads over

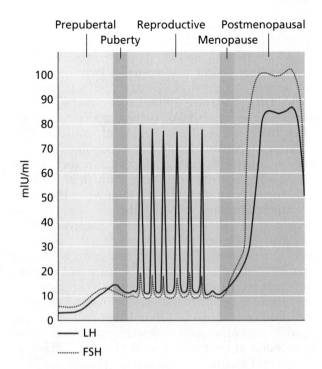

FIGURE 10–12 The pattern of secretion of pituitary hormones during a woman's lifetime. The large increases in FSH and LH after menopause are due to the loss of estrogen and progesterone from the ovaries.

the upper body, face, and head (see Kronenberg, 1994). The sensations last from a few seconds to 15 minutes or more and are very common at night, thus interfering with sleep. This can lead to fatigue, irritability, and depression. Hot flashes generally disappear within a few years, but 20% of affected women may experience hot flashes for 5 years or longer.

The loss of estrogen also causes the vagina to become thinner and less elastic, with a marked *decrease in the amount of vaginal lubrication* during sexual arousal. If the vagina is not properly lubricated, sexual intercourse will be painful, so that some postmenopausal women may start avoiding sexual relations. This is unnecessary, however, if a woman and her partner accept vaginal dryness after menopause as a normal physiological response and not as an indication of lack of desire. The dryness can be countered with vaginal estrogen preparations (tablets, creams, rings; see Crandall, 2002), or a lubricant, such as K-Y Jelly.

A lot of attention has been given to the role of decreased estrogen levels in *osteoporosis*, a condition in which the bones become more brittle with age (see Rozenberg et al., 1994). There are over 250,000 hip fractures a year due to osteoporosis, resulting in up to 50,000 premature deaths in women.

As women grow older, a few will experience severe weakening of the ligaments that hold the

---

Menopause ■ The term for a woman's last menstrual period.

Climacteric ■ The changes that occur in women in the few years that precede and the first year that follows menopause.

vagina and uterus in place, a condition called *prolapse*. Prolapse can usually be corrected, most commonly by reconstructive surgery.

Does a woman's sexual desire end with menopause? I have found that many students believe that women no longer have any interest in sex after menopause. This is generally untrue.

> "I was surprised to find out that a woman still had a sexual desire after menopause. I always believed it to be a time of depression and no sex. Well, you learn something new every day."
>
> "I was totally surprised by the fact that older people still have sex. I often wondered what I was going to do at that age because I enjoy sex tremendously."
>
> (All examples are from the author's files.)

For many women, menopause causes no change in interest in sex (Hallstrom & Samuelsson, 1990; Segraves & Segraves, 1995), and some women actually show an increased interest in sex after menopause (Dillaway, 2005), possibly because they no longer have to worry about getting pregnant. While many women do experience sexual problems during the climacteric and at menopause (including lower desire and lower arousal), these problems are common in younger women as well (see Chapter 13), and there is not enough evidence to attribute this to decreasing estrogen levels (da Silva Lara et al., 2009; Nappi & Lachowsky, 2009).

The Rise and Fall (and Resurrection?) of the Medicalization of Menopause

In 2000, there were approximately 19 million American women in their menopause years, with another 30 million in their postmenopausal years. Thus, postmenopausal women have become a large segment of society that seeks health care, or, depending on your perspective, that is targeted by health care professionals.

Dried ovaries from cows were promoted as preserving youth and vitality in women as early as the late 1800s. Estrogen was synthesized in 1928 and the U.S. Food and Drug Administration approved Premarin (estrogen from pregnant mares' urine) in 1942. In 1962, Dr. Robert Wilson published results of a study in a leading medical journal that claimed that estrogen and progesterone given together prevent breast and endometrial cancer. In a 1966 book entitled *Feminine Forever*, Wilson claimed that estrogen "aside from keeping a woman sexually attractive and potent…preserves the strength of her bones, the glow of her skin, the gloss of her hair… Estrogen makes women adaptable, even-tempered, and generally easy to live with." The medicalization of menopause had begun.

Medicalization refers to "the process whereby the normal processes of pregnancy, childbirth,

menstruation and menopause have been claimed and redefined by medicine" (Kaufert & Lock, 1997). Opponents of the medicalization of menopause claim that the negative expectations of deteriorating health are the result of culturally determined attitudes, promotions by drug companies, and media pressure, and point out (correctly) that older women in our country are already healthier than older men and outlive men by many years (van Hall, 1997).

Many physicians and feminists argue that menopause is a natural part of being a woman that should be allowed to run its course (see van Hall, 1997). While most women experience a decline in well-being in the first 2 years after menopause, feelings improve spontaneously after that (Dennerstein et al., 1997). Women in some other cultures or ethnic groups report few problems during menopause (see Box 10–B).

Let us examine the evidence. There is no question that *hormone (estrogen) replacement therapy* (HRT) can help alleviate some symptoms of menopause such as vasomotor symptoms (hot flashes, night sweats), vaginal atrophy symptoms (vaginal dryness), and osteoporosis (Avis et al., 2002; Nelson et al., 2002). Sleep disorders and depressive symptoms are not directly related to the change in hormone levels (but may be secondary to the other problems).

The medical approach to treating menopause really escalated when some studies conducted in the 1990s indicated that estrogen replacement therapy also offered protection against heart disease, colon cancer, and Alzheimer's disease. Pharmaceutical companies began pushing hormone replacement therapy not only as a cure for troublesome symptoms, but also as a prevention of heart disease. As a result, in 2001 there were 45 million prescriptions for Premarin and 22 million for Prempro (Premarin plus progesterone).

Troubles began when several studies reported an increased risk for breast cancer with long-term use and that the addition of progestin further increased the risk. Several studies also failed to find any beneficial prevention of heart disease associated with hormone replacement therapy. So, in 1997, a large-scale study (called The Women's Health Initiative) began to compare the long-term effects of Prempro versus a placebo. The study was supposed to run for 8 years, but was halted after 5. Why? The women given Prempro had fewer hip fractures and colon cancers, but experienced more heart attacks, strokes, blood clots, and breast cancers (Manson et al., 2003). The bad outcomes far outnumbered the good ones. Later studies found increased risks for both ovarian cancer (Mørch et al., 2009) and breast cancer (Chlebowski et al., 2009; Heiss et al., 2008; Million Women Study, 2003). Results of studies

Box 10–B Cross-Cultural Perspectives

Menopause in Different Cultures

Menopause as a biological event is universal—all women worldwide will eventually stop having menstrual cycles and experience a decrease in estrogen levels. But what about the experience of menopause? Western health practitioners have medicalized menopause and portray the postmenopausal years negatively, as a time in which the body breaks down (but can be repaired by hormone replacement therapy). Western feminists, on the other hand, portray menopause not as a disease but as a normal part of aging that can bring liberation and joy. Which of these views is more realistic?

Richters (1997) reviewed cross-cultural studies of menopause and found many differences. For example, while a majority of American and European women experience hot flashes after menopause, hot flashes are uncommon among postmenopausal women in Japan (and many other areas of Asia) or the Mayans of Mexico (Avis et al., 2001; Beyne & Martin, 2001; Chim et al., 2002; Lock, 1994). The Mayans do not even have a word for it. In some areas of Greece, women experience hot flashes,

but do not think of them as medical symptoms that require going to a physician (Beyne, 1989).

Some, but not all, of these differences can be explained by the social position of women in different cultures (Avis et al., 2001; Richters, 1997). In cultures where women gain prestige and power in middle age, menopause may likely be viewed positively, in contrast to the United States, where older persons are often viewed as a burden. For example, in northwest Cameroon, women are believed to gain wisdom after menopause and thus rise in social status, while in parts of Nigeria postmenopausal women are granted more power (Best, 2002). Traditional Navajo women view menopause as a positive change of life status (e.g., being free of menstrual taboos) and (probably as a consequence) do not experience the same symptoms as Western women (Wright, 1983). Migration from one country to another can rapidly change the perception of menopause. Women in Italy generally have positive roles and positive attitudes about menopause (Donati et al., 2009), but

Italian women who migrated to Australia came to view menopause negatively when those roles were no longer valid (Gifford, 1994).

There are ethnic variations in the experience of menopause within our own country. African-American women are much more likely to experience hot flashes than white or Hispanic women (see Painter, 2010), and Asian-American women generally experience fewer symptoms (see De Angelis, 1997). This may reflect ethnic differences in the social status of aging women, but may also be due to diet (Adlercreutz et al., 1992). Smokers in all ethnic groups experienced greater symptoms (see Avis et al., 2002).

Richters (1997) concluded that many factors might result in the differences in menopausal symptoms. However, one thing can be concluded— the experience of menopause is not the same for all women, either across or within cultures. Attitudes about menopause (and menstruation), the role of women, and health issues (e.g., diet and smoking) all contribute to culturally specific experiences of menopause.

regarding prevention of dementia were mixed (see Rapp et al., 2003; Sherwin, 2002).

In 2007, the same group that authored the first Women's Health Initiative study (Manson et al., 2003) published another paper in the same journal in which group members concluded that they may have raised a false alarm (Manson et al., 2007). A further analysis of their data showed that hormone replacement therapy did not raise the risk of heart disease if women started to take the hormones shortly after menopause. The risk is also reduced by using estrogen patches or vaginal gels rather than pills (Løkkegaard et al., 2008). Nevertheless, among women who normally received hormone replacement therapy (white, over 50 years old), the rates for breast cancer have decreased 10% since the results of the Women's Health Initiative were released and fewer doctors were prescribing hormone replacement therapy (Krieger et al., 2010).

The final conclusion? Most experts today say that if short-term hormone replacement therapy is begun within a few years after menopause, the benefits are greater than the risks (e.g., Wren, 2009). Women should consult with their doctors.

Another controversial medical topic is testosterone replacement therapy for women with low sexual desire. Procter & Gamble has marketed a testosterone patch (Intrinsa) for women who have had ovariectomies and wanted it approved for all postmenopausal women, but the Food and Drug Administration refused. The patch has been shown to increase desire in some postmenopausal women (Davis et al., 2008), but there are concerns about its safety. However, many experts believe that the majority of cases of low sexual desire in women are due to relational and psychological factors (Basson, 2009; see Chapters 4 and 12).

FIGURE 10–13 For middle-aged couples, sexual motivation is highly associated with the quality of the relationship.

Male Sexuality: Physical Changes with Age

Men normally do not experience a *sudden* loss of hormones as experienced by women. Although the term *male menopause* is commonly used, this generally refers to the midlife psychological and emotional reactions that some men have as a response to changing family relationships (e.g., children growing up) and/or an inability to achieve earlier career goals.

Men do show a gradual decline in testosterone levels that begins in their late teens (Sternbach, 1998). By age 55, 20% to 50% of men have testosterone levels that are below the normal range for young adult men. This decrease in testosterone will result in some physiological changes as men age. This is sometimes referred to as *andropause*. The changes include decreased sensitivity of the penis, a longer time to become erect and a less firm erection, shrinkage of the testicles, less forceful ejaculation (often resembling a dribble), and a longer refractory period after orgasm (the length of time before a man is able to have another orgasm), a decline in muscle mass and a reduction in bone density (leading to frailty), sparse beards, and slightly higher voices (Sternbach, 1998). If the drop in testosterone is large enough, it will also affect a man's interest in sex. The production of sperm continues into old age, but it, too, declines after age 40.

If a man is not aware that the previously mentioned changes are normal, he may overreact to them and start to doubt his sexuality, and this performance anxiety can lead to serious problems. Paul Costa, Jr., of the National Institute on Aging, said, "Some older men may say their erections aren't as big as they recall them once being. But then their partners say, 'Well, dear, you overestimated them back then, too'" (quoted in Angier, 1992). For men who develop erectile problems with age, today there are erection-enhancing drugs (Viagra, Cialis, and Levitra).

Today, some doctors are advocating testosterone replacement therapy for the male andropause (e.g., Morley, 2001). However, there are concerns that testosterone might cause prostate cancer and increase the risk of blood clots (leading to heart attacks and strokes) (Kolata, 2002). Thus, while testosterone replacement therapy can increase muscle mass and restore sexual desire, it should be reserved only for men with a definite deficiency in testosterone (Sternbach, 1998). Nevertheless, it is probably the case that other men will begin asking for it as well. We may be on the verge of a medicalization of the male "climacterium" similar to what happened with women. Are we going to repeat the mistake the medical community made with hormone replacement therapy for women (rushing into it before we know all of the long-term side effects)? Dr. Richard Hodis, director of the National Institute on Aging, warns: "In understanding the role of testosterone replacement, we are in many ways where we were decades ago with estrogen replacement with women. It is clear that we do not know enough to inform men and their doctors on the potential advantages or risks of hormone replacement" (quoted by Kolata, 2002).

PERSONAL REFLECTIONS

Does the thought of elderly people enjoying sexual relations make you comfortable or uncomfortable? Why? Do you hope to still enjoy sexual relations when you are in your 50s and older? If not, at what age do you think that you will stop enjoying sex? Why?

THE ELDERLY YEARS (AGE 60+)

> "I didn't think that elderly people thought about sex. I thought when you got older you just lost all interest."
> (from the author's files)

In our culture elderly people are regarded as asexual human beings—neuters. Sex is something enjoyed only by the young and healthy (Gochros et al., 1986). According to Rose and Soares (1993), "Evidence of sexuality among the aged is often joked about, dismissed, or defined as troublesome behavior. A sexually active older man is seen as a 'dirty old man' and a sexually active older woman is considered preposterous or embarrassing. This culturally embedded denial may be rooted in people's difficulty accepting the sexuality of their own parents."

What is the truth? Is it really unusual for elderly people to have an interest in sex? In recent years, there have been several national surveys (Dunn & Cutler, 2000; Jacoby, 2005; Lindau et al., 2007; Laumann et al., 2009; Schick et al., 2010; Waite et al., 2009). Let's see what they found.

Among people in their early 60s, over 70% are having sex regularly. Over 50% of them have sexual intercourse at least once a week. In their late 60s and early 70s, about 50% of Americans are sexually active. In their late 70s and early 80s, only about 25% of people are still sexually active. Notice that there is a decline in the prevalence of sexual activity with age. It is also true that elderly women are less likely to report being sexually active than elderly men (e.g., Kontula & Haavio-Mannila, 2009; Lindau et al., 2007).

Notice that even in the most elderly group there was still a sizable minority who were having sexual relations regularly. A new partner in later life can often reignite the sex drive:

> "There was an incredible chemical reaction with my second husband, for both of us. Quite different from the first marriage which evolves... this was an absolute click. Absolutely incredible! I mean, at that age. It was like a couple of teenagers. I can't tell you. Um, oh, we had a lot of fun. We really did. And, Ah, very romantic.... It's died down now, of course it has, but in the beginning it was, it was quite amazing. It really was. It was amazing...the instantaneous attraction. The ping. You know? The ease. It was enormously easy. That's the great aspect of sex—it should be easy." (Married 78-year-old woman, remarried at age 72)

> "I told the doctor one time and she said, 'Ohmigod! You have more sex than I do in a week!' We had a good sex life. I was really amazed...it was very, very good." (Widowed 81-year-old woman, remarried at age 63)
> (From Clarke, 2006)

Is there any age at which sexual activity stops? Although it was not a representative sample, a study of 202 *healthy* men and women aged 80 to 102 found that three fourths of them still fantasized about sexual relations and enjoyed touching and caressing their partners. Nearly half were having sexual intercourse and a third were engaging in oral-genital sex (Bretschneider & McCoy, 1988). Sexual activity was limited by living arrangements and the availability of partners, not by a lack of interest.

Now you know about frequency of sexual relations among the elderly, but what about quality? About two thirds say their sexual relations are extremely or very satisfactory, as good as or better than when they were younger (Dunn & Cutler, 2000; Jacoby, 1999, 2005). Women describe their male partners as more "romantic" than when they were younger, and perhaps as a result a greater percentage of women were reaching orgasm regularly. Recall from Chapter 4 that sexuality for many women is directly related to how happy they are in a relationship. This is still true in the elderly years (Trudel, 2002).

We must not ignore that there are several factors that can negatively affect sexuality in the elderly years, particularly health and availability of a partner (Lindau & Gavrilova, 2010; Schick et al., 2010). For example, the ratio of single women to single men that we discussed in the section on middle age becomes even more unfavorable to women over the age of 60. In the United States, women outlive men by an average of 7 years (78.9 years versus 72 years) (Gelfand, 2000). For people aged 65 to 74, there are 123 women for every 100 men, and 100 single women for every 27 single men. At ages 75 to 84, there are 151 women for every 100 men, and at ages

Reprinted with special permission of King Features Syndicate.

85 and older, there are 241 women per 100 men (Guralnik et al., 2000; Weg, 1996). About 26% of women aged 57–64, 39% aged 65–74, and 60% aged 75–85 do not have a sexual partner (Waite et al., 2009). Thus, for women, there is a real "partner gap." Many women may be interested in sex, but there is no opportunity (Lutfey et al., 2009).

In the survey of people aged 80 to 102, the people were in good health (Bretschneider & McCoy, 1988). However, many older people experience medical problems and disabilities that substantially shorten their years of being sexually active (Lindau & Gavrilova, 2010). Heart disease, stroke, arthritis, diabetes, prostate problems, and problems due to alcohol, smoking, and overeating are common (Laumann et al., 2007; Lindau et al., 2007). In one survey, women listed "better health for their partner" as the number-one item that would most improve their sex lives (Jacoby, 1999). In another (Dunn & Cutler, 2000), 47% of elderly men said, "I have a medical condition that prevents us from having sex," and 43% of the women said, "My partner has a medical condition that prevents us from having sex."

Sexual problems among the elderly are also common (and are often associated with the medical problems). Laumann et al.'s (1999) nationally representative survey found that 11% of men aged 40 to 49 and 18% aged 50 to 59 have erectile disorders. The percentage of men with erectile problems increases to 30.7% for ages 57–64, and about 44% for ages 65–85 (Waite et al., 2009). About 20% of men aged 57–74 years were unable to reach orgasm and 28% had little or no interest in sex. Among women aged 57–74 years, about 40% had little or no interest in sex, and one third experienced pain during intercourse and/or were unable to reach orgasm. About one third of women and one fourth of men aged 57–74 said that they avoided sex because of these sexual problems.

About 14%–17% of elderly men have tried Viagra, testosterone patches, or other sex-enhancement medications (Lindau et al., 2007; Schick et al., 2010). But what about these men's partners? Over half of them say that their partner's treatment has resulted in increased pleasure for them as well (Jacoby, 2005). However, medical treatment for impotency can also suddenly change the sexual equilibrium in a relationship (Kingsberg, 2000). A few women report that their male partners' treatment had decreased their pleasure. Remember, for most women, their sexual pleasure is directly related to the quality of the overall relationship and relationship unhappiness is the cause of many older women's lack of interest in sex (Jacoby, 1999; Kingsberg, 2000; Laumann & Waite, 2008; see Chapter 4).

The third major factor preventing some elderly people from enjoying sexual relations is the oppor-

FIGURE 10–14 From the moment of birth to the day we die, we are all sexual beings.

tunity for privacy when one is dependent on others for care. This particularly affects the very elderly. Nowhere is our culture's negative attitude about sexuality and the elderly more apparent than in nursing homes (Nay & Gorman, 1999). Administrators and staff in most nursing homes are interested in institutional efficiency and tend to have negative or patronizing attitudes about elderly patients expressing an interest in sex (Kaplan, 1996; Walker & Harrington, 2002; Weg, 1996). Many nursing homes deny elderly couples privacy when the healthy partner of an institutionalized spouse comes to visit (Kaplan, 1996).

So what can we conclude about sexuality in the elderly years? Laumann and Waite (2008) concluded that:

> **Sexual problems among the elderly are not an inevitable consequence of aging, but instead are responses to the presence of stressors in multiple life domains (poor physical or mental health, relationship problems).**

Sexual opportunities are limited for single women, but for healthy men and women with healthy partners, sexual activity will probably continue throughout life if they had a positive attitude about sex when they were younger. In fact, the best predictor of sexual desire in later life is not biomedical factors, but instead a positive attitude about sex (Delamater & Sill, 2005).

Sex surveys tend to measure sexual behavior in terms of physical acts such as sexual intercourse and masturbation, but there is more to sexuality than this. Elderly people often report great sexual satisfaction with emotionally erotic experiences (Shaw, 1994). Sexual pleasure, for example, includes touching, caressing, physical closeness, and intimacy. These can often be achieved even in the most extreme cases:

> Mr. N was deaf, blind, and unable to talk due to a recent laryngotomy. He was quite dependent on Mrs. N who had severe arthritis and had a mastectomy years ago. They typically sat close together, in part to aid communication due to Mr. N's impairments. But the way they held hands revealed great tenderness and affection. They slept in twin beds and indicated they no longer engaged in intercourse. Yet, they had a nightly ritual in which Mr. N helped his wife bathe and then gave her a massage in bed, which they described with some embarrassment and blushing. Interestingly, through this sensual routine, Mr. N, usually the more dependent of the two, was able to offer something of value to his wife.
>
> (Rose & Soares, 1993)

Perhaps the biggest problem for elderly people interested in physical relations in our culture is ageism—the negative stereotypes of the aged as sexless (Barrow & Smith, 1992). Many people poke fun at, or discriminate against, other people who are different from themselves, and this often includes the elderly. Again, unless there is a tragedy, all of us will be elderly some day. Do you enjoy sexual relations now? Do you ever want to give it up? If not, how do you think you will feel if one day younger people think you are silly, preposterous, or even lecherous or perverted for wanting the pleasure of someone else's touch? The time to address these attitudes is now, not later. We are all sexual human beings, from birth to death.

ADDENDUM

Talking with Your Children About Sex

When asked where he received his education, Mark Twain answered, "Throughout my life, except for the years I attended school." This is generally true for most people when it comes to learning about sexually related matters. **Sexual learning** begins in infancy and continues throughout childhood and adolescence. It is informal and is received from family, friends, the media, and the rest of the general environment.

During the preadolescent years, a child's parents are the most powerful influence on his or her beliefs and behavior. Even if parents never discuss sex with their children—and most do not—by their behavior and their attitudes, they still serve as role models from which their children learn.

As children approach their teenage years, their peer groups and the media (primarily television) become their primary sources of sexual information (Stodghill, 1998; see also Nonoyama et al., 2005). The average child watches several hours of TV every day and is exposed to hundreds of references to sex in a year (Eyal et al., 2007; Kaiser Family Foundation, 2005). Between the amount of time that their children spend with peers and watching TV, it is obvious that parents have a difficult time competing as a source of sexual knowledge and values. Yet, despite all the public debate about AIDS and other sexually related matters, most parents continue to remain silent (Beckett et al., 2010; Sprecher et al., 2008):

> "Sex was never a topic in my home when I was growing up. It led to embarrassment when I finally had to ask questions, but I could only ask my friends, never my parents. It shouldn't be like that, it shouldn't be embarrassing and I should have been able to talk to my parents."
>
> (from the author's files)

Surveys show that the vast majority of Americans favor sex education in schools (see Constantine, 2008). So why is there reluctance to teach it at home? Probably because most parents never received sex education themselves and thus are uncomfortable with their own sexual knowledge and feelings (Wilson et al., 2010).

> "I always hoped I would be able to handle such topics with my children, but I guess I was unable because it was never really discussed with me."

> "If I had been educated earlier, beginning at age 9 or 10, I would have been able to help myself and my children with facts of life much better and much earlier."
>
> (All examples are from King & LoRusso, 1997.)

When you complete this book, you should be ready to put an end to the cycle of noncommunication that has existed between parents and each new generation of children. This part of the chapter is intended to help you initiate discussions of sexuality with your children so that they too may acquire factual information. I will try to answer some of the questions that often concern parents.

Which Parent Should Talk with the Children?

Most children would like to turn to their parents for information about sex. Unfortunately, only a few list their parents as their major source of information (Nonoyama et al., 2005; Sprecher

---

Sexual learning ■ Knowledge about sex that is received (usually informally) from family, friends, the media, and society in general.

Planned Parenthood of Hawaii

et al., 2008). When a parent does make the attempt to open communications about sexuality, it is almost always the mother (e.g., K. Miller et al., 1998a; Ogle et al., 2008). This is true for sons as well as daughters. Fathers are notoriously silent! Not surprisingly, teenagers have more positive attitudes about their mothers as sex educators than they do their fathers (Feldman & Rosenthal, 2000).

One thing that prevents discussions between parents and children about sexuality is a defensive climate in the household (Rozema, 1986). When one or both parents have reacted negatively to the subject of sex in the past, children are less likely to open up or approach them with questions. Family communication about sexuality is most likely to occur in households that have an openness in the communication process and when parents have talked to their children about other personal topics as well (K. Miller et al., 1998a; Raffaelli et al., 1998). Children may be more likely to discuss sex with their mothers than their fathers because mothers are often viewed as more emotionally expressive, more likely to answer questions about intimacy, and, as a result, more approachable.

Fathers are doing a disservice to their children by remaining emotionally distant and appearing (to their children) to be unapproachable on the subject. Both parents should make the attempt to open lines of communication, and as you will soon learn, the earlier the better.

Does Telling Children About Sex Lead Them to Do It?

Some of you may worry that if you talk to your children about sex, it will increase the likelihood they will have sex (Jaccard et al., 2000). Studies have shown that children who have had sexuality education are no more likely (and perhaps are less likely) to have sexual relations, to get pregnant, or to contract a sexually transmitted infection than those who have not had sexuality education (Grunseit et al., 1997). In families that have developed strong loving relationships in which parents give their children much positive attention

(including the quality of communication), children are less likely to begin sexual intercourse at a young age or engage in sexually risky behaviors (B. Miller et al., 1998; Mueller & Powers, 1990; Resnick et al., 1997). This is especially true when parents have these talks *before* their teens begin having sexual intercourse (Clawson & Reese-Weber, 2003; K. Miller et al., 1998b; Whitaker et al., 1999). Do you need better reasons to talk to your children about sex?

Why Should I Talk to My Child About Sex?

Unless you are willing to keep your children locked up in a closet until they reach adulthood, *there is no avoiding their learning about sex.* Even if they stay home all the time and do nothing but watch TV and listen to the radio, your children will still see and hear thousands of references to sex every year. Do you really want to leave it to the soap operas and "shock jocks" to educate your children about this important subject? What kind of values do you suppose they will learn? Also, do not fool yourself. Children (in all likelihood your own as well) do talk about sex with their friends. Not only may your child's friends be misinformed, but do you want to leave it to your child's peer group to teach sexual values? Even formal sex education courses are generally value-free. By assuming the primary responsibility for your children's sex education, you not only can make certain that they are getting factual information, but at the same time you can stress the social and emotional aspects of sex and teach them values that you consider important. When parents teach their children about sexual activity and birth control, the children are much more likely to delay engaging in sexual intercourse, and to use birth control when they do begin (Aspy et al., 2007). June Reinisch, former director of the Kinsey Institute, said, "If parents are comfortable and have good information, they can be wonderful sex educators. They can contextualize the sexual information into the fabric of family values, ethics, morals and religious beliefs. Sex is embedded in all of these" (quoted by Henderson, 1990).

PERSONAL REFLECTIONS

Some day you will probably be a parent (if you are not one already). Do you plan to educate your children about sexuality? If so, how? When will you begin?

Will a Single "Birds and Bees" Talk Suffice?

Do you really believe that one talk will prepare your child for a lifetime of sexual relations and problems? The answer is no! Experts say that it is a mistake to think that talking about sex means sitting down for one long, serious conversation (see Roan, 1993). Even if you could fit all the necessary information and values into one talk, that one talk can hardly compete with the hundreds of hours of exposure to sexually related matters your child will receive while growing up. As Mark Twain said, education is a lifelong process. Communication between parents and children about sex and anything else should also be lifelong. Do not wait until your child has reached a certain age to have "the big talk." As researcher Carol Ford says, "Waiting until [age] 10 or 11 for 'the big talk' is less effective than incorporating the topic of sexuality into the course of everyday conversation....Talk about what's on TV, and indicate whether you think it's acceptable or unacceptable behavior.... Discussions won't come easy, but if it doesn't go the way you wish, you can revisit the conversation a few days later" (quoted in Critchell, 2006).

FIGURE 10–15 When a pet gives birth, parents have a great opportunity to teach their children about sexuality.

When Should I Start Talking with My Child About Sexuality?

When asked why she had not yet begun talking to her 13-year-old daughter about sex, a mother said, "I kept waiting for the right time. But I'm just too afraid to bring it up. I'm not sure what to say" (Roan, 1993). Many parents wait too long, and by the time they initiate a talk their children have already begun sexual activities (Beckett et al., 2010).

As I hope you have learned by now, sex education is more than just explaining sexual intercourse. Children should be properly educated about their bodies. For example, you should teach them the correct anatomical terms for their genitals at the same time you teach them the names of the other parts of their bodies. "Penis" and "vagina" are not too difficult for young children to pronounce. American parents are notoriously silent about this. Teaching boys that they have a penis and girls that they have a vagina is honest and helps them attain a healthy attitude about sexuality.

> "My mom never spoke with me about sex. This ignorance caused many misconceptions in my teenage years. So as a young, married adult I changed my attitude. No longer would I follow in the steps of my mother. I have 4- and 5-year-old boys now. They know the proper names for every part of their bodies. They know about exploring their bodies and when it is not appropriate for anyone to touch them. My mom says those words like 'wee wee' and 'petie.' That to me is just as disgusting as saying 'dick.' She becomes angry when I correct her, but she understands."
> (from the author's files)

It is also important to discuss with your children the physiological changes that start at puberty before they actually begin puberty. Some parents do not talk to their daughters about the menstrual cycle or to their sons about "wet dreams" until after they occur. These changes can be frightening to children, who may think that they are sick or dying.

> "There is one thing I would personally put more emphasis on [in the book]. That is the importance of explaining men-

struation in advance. From personal experience, I feel this is critical. I had no idea what was happening to me when I started menstruating for the first time. I can remember that I couldn't stop the bleeding and was scared to death and was afraid and embarrassed to tell anyone. I finally told a friend who was in the dark just as I was. She then told her mother. Her mother gave me a pad and said this would happen every month. That was the extent of communication on the subject."
> (from the author's files)

Be sure to explain the changes associated with puberty in girls to boys and the changes in boys to girls. Men should be able to relate to women with empathy and understanding, and vice versa. Ignorance about the physiological and emotional changes being experienced by the opposite sex is not a good basis on which to build relationships.

Children themselves are often the best guides as to when to initiate talks about a particular topic. It is common, for example, for young children to ask where babies come from. If they are curious enough to ask questions about some sexually related matter, do not avoid discussing it. Never brush them off. If you do, they may avoid coming to you in the future and may rely instead on getting their information from somewhere else.

What Should I Tell My Children About AIDS and Other STIs?

With all the attention devoted to AIDS by the media today, children are naturally going to be curious about it. The first question about sexuality that my son asked me was about AIDS. If you hear your child mention AIDS, be sure to take the opportunity to ask what he or she knows about it. Clear up any myths or misunderstandings. If your child never mentions AIDS, do not ignore the subject, for this is a very serious infection that everyone needs to be educated about. Initiate the discussion yourself. Remember, however, that you must teach your child about sexuality on a level that he or she can understand.

Most parents fear that in order to explain about AIDS, they must explain behaviors like anal and oral sex. This is really not necessary for preschool and elementary school children. Most preadolescent children are not going to understand anal or oral sex. Young children can be taught to be in charge of their own bodies—sexual responsibility—without being told what anal sex is.

What kind of questions is your child likely to ask? Valentich and Gripton (1989) listed many questions about AIDS that are frequently asked by children. Early elementary school–age children may want to know answers to questions like: What is AIDS? Can I get AIDS? Can I get it by playing with friends or by touching someone at school? Will it make me sick? Is there medicine I can take to make it go away?

Children aged 9 to 12 will want to know more about how AIDS is transmitted (e.g., whether they can get AIDS by holding hands, hugging, kissing, having sexual intercourse, or being in the same classroom with someone who has AIDS) and how they can tell if someone has it. Children at this age can also be taught about STIs such as gonorrhea, chlamydia, syphilis, and herpes (and told that they are caused by bacteria and viruses) (SIECUS, 1996). Teenagers will probably want answers to more explicit questions about transmission (e.g., whether they can get AIDS by French kissing, masturbation, genital touching, or sexual intercourse) and prevention (including the use and reliability of condoms). Be sure to include further discussion of other sexually transmitted infections at this time as well.

You should prepare yourself for questions like these so that you can give your child factual information about means of transmission, prevention, and treatment appropriate for his or her age. When answering questions, you can also discuss values with your child. No matter what your child's age, *you should not deny the pleasures of sex or resort to scare tactics*. Teaching children that sex is something good and pleasurable is as important as teaching that it must be handled responsibly.

How Detailed Should Sex Discussions Be?

Your discussions should be frank and explicit. Children do not want "birds and bees" analogies; they want factual information using real terms. In fact, euphemisms and analogies will only confuse them. At the same time, do not make things too detailed for your child's age level. Many parents tend to over-answer. *Keep your answers simple and age-appropriate*. Always check to see if your child understands what you have said. You may have to rephrase your answer to make it clear. Sometimes we give great answers, but not to the question the child asked. Remember, a child may not know what to ask or how to ask it correctly. When a 6-year-old asks where babies come from, for example, many parents worry that they must explain sexual intercourse in detail. Most questions about "sex" asked by children younger than 10 are really about biology (Snegroff, 2000). Keep your answer uncomplicated and tell the child only what he or she wants to know. In this case, you could explain that the baby is in a special part of the mother called a uterus (do not avoid explicitness by saying "tummy"—this is incorrect anyway) and that when it is ready to be born it comes out through an opening called the vagina.

Discussions with your teenage children should definitely be frank and explicit. Parent-to-teen talks about sex tend to focus on values and beliefs rather than facts. In one study, I asked students and their parents if they had ever had a "meaningful" discussion about sex with one another (King & LoRusso, 1997). Over half of the students responded "no," yet for 60% of them one or both parents said that there had been meaningful discussions. Here are some responses by parents who believed that they had had meaningful discussions (but whose children disagreed):

> "I believe children should be taught that total abstinence is the best way.... This is so because of God's law and the design for total inner peace and joy."

"THAT WAS VERY INTERESTING, DAD, BUT MY BIOLOGY TEACHER WANTS A REPORT ON BIRDS AND BEES."

© Wm. Hoest Enterprises, Inc. All Rights Reserved.

> "My discussion with _____ dealt with one's soul. A soul is not to be fragmented—not to be given away in bits and pieces. A soul is sacred—sex is sacred."

> "They [the children] knew what was expected, and they behaved accordingly.... If you asked about teaching morality to my children, the answer is yes, and if you teach and live a good, healthy, moral life, it usually works."

There is nothing wrong with teaching your children values. However, do not substitute morality for factual information.

What if I Feel Embarrassed?

Many parents avoid talking to their children about sex because they are embarrassed (Jaccard et al., 2000). Chances are, your children will also be embarrassed Ogle et al., 2008. Parents' talks with their children about sexuality are most effective when the parents are open, skilled, and comfortable (Mueller & Powers, 1990; Whitaker et al., 1999). Many of you will not be able to avoid embarrassment at times, but the result—your child's education—is worth the initial discomfort of using real terms and direct language. Be honest. Let your children know that you are a bit embarrassed, but that you are glad they asked to talk with you, that you will be happy to answer all of their questions, and that it is okay to talk to you about the subject. What you say to your children is important, but *how you say it is just as important*. Let them know that you are willing to (and want to) listen to their questions.

How Should I Talk with My Child?

Most important, *discuss—never lecture*. Also, be sure not to grill your child about his or her behavior or attitudes. Parents who try to dominate and assert themselves will probably be met with passivity (e.g., Lefkowitz et al., 2000), while those who take an open, collaborative approach will probably find that their children actively engage in discussions (K. Miller et al., 1998a; Whitaker et al., 1999). In other words, allow your child to have his or her input. Two keys are that your children view you to be **"askable"** and **"accepting"** (Snegroff, 2000). "An accepting parent does not convey a negative attitude or exhibit negative behavior when a child's natural curiosity leads to a question or comment. They convey the impression that all questions are good ones and all comments can be discussed" (Snegroff, 2000). Your tone of voice is particularly important, for your child learns attitudes from your tone. Try to sound calm and relaxed at all times. Sol Gordon, author of *Raising Your Child Conservatively in a Sexually Permissive World* (1989), says, "The most important message is that nothing a child does will be made worse by talking to the parent about it. There is no way of dealing with sexuality unless the parent has created the atmosphere of love and caring. Unless that atmosphere is there, nothing works. The child will lie" (quoted by Roan, 1993).

Remember, it is not necessary always to have formal talks; this may create tension. You can break the ice by briefly explaining and discussing sexually related matters that your child sees on TV or hears on the radio. Recall, too, that parent–child talks about sexuality are easier when the parents have a history of talking with their children about other personal topics (Raffaelli et al., 1998).

Askable ■ Being perceived as receptive, a good listener, and accepting.

Accepting ■ Letting your child know that all questions are okay and will not be met with a negative attitude.

Avoid scare tactics. You must teach sexual responsibility without making your child afraid of sex—children should learn that sex is something good and positive, and not something to feel ashamed or guilty about. Scare tactics probably will not work anyway, and they may cause emotional and psychological problems.

PERSONAL REFLECTIONS

How do you suppose you would react if...

1. Your 5-year-old child asked you where babies come from?

2. Your 9-year-old child asked you what sex is?

3. Your 10-year-old child asked you what "French kissing" is?

4. Your 12-year-old son came home from school saying that he had to watch a "gross" movie about girls having their period?

5. Your 15-year-old son asked you about birth control?

6. Your 15-year-old daughter asked you about birth control?

Would your reactions to any of these situations discourage your child from coming to you in the future and talking to you about sex?

What About Morals? Aren't They Important Too?

Sex is more than a biological function. If you want your children to share your beliefs and values about sex, you must talk about them. Children who know that their parents disapprove of teenage sex are more likely to postpone having sex (Ford et al., 2005). However, your success in imposing your values upon your children will depend, in large part, on your overall relationship with them. Parents who generally have good loving interactions with their children are more successful in transmitting values than are parents who generally have poor interactions with their children (Resnick et al., 1997; Taris & Semin, 1997b; Wilson et al., 2010).

When you discuss moral values with your child, there are some important guidelines you should follow. Most importantly, *you can emphasize your values, but do not preach or try to dominate*. It is not wrong for you to say how you feel, but if your child has developed some values that are different from yours, you must learn to discuss your differences rather than dictate. Remember, you want to create an atmosphere that allows your child to be comfortable so that he or she will come to you with any questions. If you always preach and pass judgment, your child may be reluctant to discuss sexuality with you at all, and then you will have no input.

One of the biggest dilemmas facing parents when discussing sexuality with their children is whether to emphasize global moralities or situational ethics. **Global moralities** are values that are supposed to apply to all people under all circumstances. An example is when parents tell their children that sexual relations

FIGURE 10–16 When talking to your children about sex, discuss—never lecture. Let them have their input. Remember, be "askable" and "accepting."

should be reserved for marriage. As you recall, however, surveys show that well over half of all adolescents engage in premarital intercourse. Can you safely assume that your children will never have premarital sexual relations and that you can thus avoid the topic of birth control? Many parents are reluctant to talk about birth control with their children because they think that it promotes promiscuity. The consequences of not talking about it, however, can be devastating (e.g., unwanted pregnancies and/or sexually transmitted infections).

Situational ethics emphasize the proper thing to do in particular situations (i.e., "We prefer that you not do it, but if you're going to do it anyway, then..."). In this case, for example, it could be explained to an adolescent child that condoms substantially reduce the risk of both unwanted pregnancy and sexually transmitted infections. I cannot tell you which of these two approaches to use. Only you can make that choice.

Can My Behavior Affect My Child's Attitudes and Behavior?

You should also be aware that *your own behavior can play a role* in your child's sexuality and moral values. It is important for children to learn that their parents share affection for each other. Hugging between parents and between parents and children

---

Global moralities ■ Values that are supposed to apply to all people under all circumstances.

Situational ethics ■ Values or ethics that emphasize the proper thing to do in particular situations.

teaches youngsters that the open display of affection is appropriate and appreciated.

> "My husband and I have always tended to be very private about showing affection. I guess that's because our parents were that way. However, as a result of what I've learned in this class we've been hugging and kissing in front of our kids—who are both teenagers. They've noticed the changes and have even asked us about it, which has given us wonderful opportunities for open and frank discussions with them. Hopefully, it's not too late."
> (from the author's files)

At the same time, we live in a day when many parents are divorced and have boyfriends and girlfriends of their own. You must avoid appearing to be hypocritical. If you want your child to abstain from premarital sexual relations, for example, you must avoid premarital sexual relations or be very discreet yourself. What message do you suppose you are sending your children if you tell them it is wrong to engage in sex and they know that you are having premarital sexual relations?

Even if you never discuss sexuality with your children, your behavior will still serve as a role model. Unfortunately, many children acquire negative attitudes about sexuality by watching and listening to their parents. Many adults, for example, enjoy "dirty" jokes. What attitude do you suppose is conveyed when children overhear their parents laughing and snickering at jokes involving sex or body parts? Learning that there are "clean" and "dirty" jokes can lead to beliefs that sex is dirty, especially if other sources of

information about sex are unavailable. Also, laughing at a child's use of obscenity or joking about it will only reinforce the behavior, making it increase in frequency (remember, you are a role model). If your child uses an obscenity, don't go overboard. Calmly explain what the word means. Often the child will not know. Reacting calmly tells children that they can discuss anything with you.

How Do I Know if I Have Succeeded?

You can judge the success of your attempts to educate your children about sexuality only by their willingness to come to you when they have questions and problems.

> "I am a nontraditional student with three kids. I didn't know that I should start talking with them about sex at such a young age. My boys are 7 and 9 and my daughter is 5 years old. They are very receptive to our talks. And now they always want to talk to me about anything. 'Open lines of communications.' Thanks."
> (from the author's files)

All normal adolescents will have an interest in sex and will continue to need information about their sexuality as long as they live. They will want to know about dating, courtship, marriage, living together, starting a family, and many different things at different times in their lives. They will seek information about these and other matters from a variety of sources, and you will want to be one of them. This will only happen, however, if communication between children and parents is open and continuous.

STUDY GUIDE

KEY TERMS

accepting 271
adolescence 249
ageism 260
askable 271
climacteric 262
cohabitation 257
delayed puberty 249
emerging adulthood 255
global moralities 272
gynecomastia 248

hooking up 256
hot flashes 262
menarche 247
menopause 262
necking 250
nocturnal emission 248
open marriage 258
peer pressure 254
petting 250
phallic stage 245

polyandry 251
polygamy 251
polygyny 251
precocious puberty 248
puberty 246
secondary sex characteristics 246
serial monogamy 256
sexual learning 268
situational ethics 272
swinging 258

INTERACTIVE REVIEW

People are sexual beings from the moment of birth. In infancy, self-stimulation of the genitals is motivated by a general attempt to explore the body and seek pleasure. As children grow, their curiosity about their bodies continues and, during early childhood, reaches

a peak in the age period from (1) _____ years old. Early childhood games such as "house" or "doctor" allow exploration of same-sex and opposite-sex individuals. In the initial school-age years, children develop a sense of (2) _____. Although overt sexual play may decrease, curiosity about the human body and sexuality does not.

(3) _____ is the time in life in which an individual first shows sexual attraction and becomes capable of (4) _____. Many bodily changes occur, the result of changing (5) _____ levels, and these physical changes require many adjustments for young adolescents. Interest in sex increases dramatically at puberty, and earlier childhood games evolve into more erotic and consciously sexual games such as "spin the bottle." The most important issue in the lives of most adolescents is (6) _____, and during these years there is a focus on body image and physical characteristics. Almost all teenage boys and a majority of girls masturbate, which is usually accompanied by sexual fantasies. Sex therapists feel that masturbation is a safe and healthy sexual outlet for teenagers. Surveys find that (7) _____ of American high school students have engaged in sexual intercourse. For some teens, however, having sexual relations is not a positive experience, yet many engage in it because of (8) _____. The teenage pregnancy rate in the United States has decreased in recent years, but still is one of the highest among industrialized countries.

By the time people are in their mid-20s, most people's sexual lifestyle is characterized by (9) _____, either in marriage or by cohabitation. In all cultures, the idealistic goal is a (10) _____. Throughout the world, men value female promiscuity when pursuing short-term relationships, but when choosing a long-term mate, men in most cultures value (11) _____. When choosing a long-term mate, women generally prefer men who can offer them (12) _____. Despite the ideal, about a third of all married men and about a fourth of all married women eventually engage in extramarital relations. Some do so with the consent of their mate.

Most young adults underestimate the frequency of sex practiced by older adults. Sexual activity is highest for people in their (13) _____, and only gradually declines up through the late 50s. Surveys indicate that married people have sex more often than singles and are happier with their sex lives than are singles. As women grow older, their menstrual cycles become irregular and eventually stop entirely, which is called (14) _____. This usually occurs in a woman's late 40s or early 50s, and the change in hormones can result in hot flashes, a decrease in (15) _____, and osteoporosis. Men show a gradual decline in (16) _____ beginning in their late teens. This also results in some physical changes, such as a decline in muscle mass and strength, less firm erections, less forceful ejaculations, and longer (17) _____ periods. However, most elderly people continue to enjoy sexual relations as long as they remain otherwise healthy and have a partner. For healthy couples, the best predictor of whether they will enjoy sex in old age is (18) _____.

It is important for parents to learn to communicate with their children about sexuality in a positive manner. Your children will learn about sex whether you ever talk to them about it. (19) _____ begins in infancy, and children receive it from their peers, the media, and your own behaviors. Avoid that one long "birds and bees talk" approach; communication between parents and their children about sexuality should begin (20) _____ and be ongoing. Discussions with your children about sexuality should be frank and explicit. When talking to your children about sex, (21) _____ is just as important as what you say. You should strive to create an atmosphere of love and caring, so avoid (22) _____ and do not lecture to them. It is also important that your children view you to be accepting and (23) _____. You can emphasize your own sexual values, but do not preach, and remember that your own behavior will affect your child's attitudes and moral values. The only way you will be able to know whether your attempts to educate your children about sexuality have been successful is by their (24) _____.

SELF-TEST

A. TRUE OR FALSE

[T] [F] 25. Ultrasound recordings have found that male fetuses have erections while still inside the uterus.

[T] [F] 26. Children cannot masturbate to orgasm until they reach puberty.

[T] [F] 27. The growth of pubic hair on girls is the result of increased levels of testosterone.

[T] [F] 28. If a child is found engaging in sexual exploration games with another child of the same sex before age 7, it means the child is probably gay.

[T] [F] 29. Couples who lived together before marriage are less likely than other couples to get divorced.

[T] [F] 30. In a study of 202 men and women aged 80 to 102, it was found that nearly half still engaged in sexual intercourse.

T F   31. The lack of vaginal lubrication in women who have undergone menopause is an indicator that their sex life is coming to an end.

T F   32. The average married couple in their 20s or 30s have sex more often than young singles.

T F   33. Adults almost always quit masturbating after they are married.

T F   34. The average age at which girls have their first menstrual cycle has been decreasing over the last two centuries.

T F   35. "Hot flashes" are due, in part, to increasing levels of pituitary hormones.

T F   36. The best predictor of sexual activity for older women is the amount of vaginal lubrication they had when they were younger.

T F   37. Boys often develop enlarged breasts during puberty.

T F   38. In early childhood it is normal for children to engage in sexual behaviors that imitate adults.

T F   39. The way parents react to the sexuality of their children is generally an indication of the way they feel about their own sexuality.

T F   40. In terms of hormone changes with aging, men and women are very much alike.

T F   41. In men, the production of sperm generally stops by the early 50s.

T F   42. Most women show a decreased interest in sex after menopause.

T F   43. In some cultures, hot flashes are uncommon among postmenopausal women.

T F   44. Pubertal development in boys lags about 2 years behind development in girls.

T F   45. If an adult man is castrated, it substantially raises his voice.

T F   46. Girls as young as 6 or 7 have given birth.

T F   47. Most teenage girls experience severe pain during their first sexual intercourse.

T F   48. The sexual activity of emerging adults is generally different from the activity of younger and older age groups.

T F   49. Men and women are more likely to be upset by their partner's having a sexual relationship with someone else than they are about their having an emotional attachment.

T F   50. There is a strong relationship between social background (religious and political views) and whether or not one engages in extramarital affairs.

T F   51. Children's first sexual attractions occur around age 10.

B. MATCHING

Which hormone changes are most likely to be associated with the following physical or behavioral changes?

_____ 52. breast development in girls
_____ 53. vaginal dryness at menopause
_____ 54. hot flashes in women
_____ 55. development of sweat glands (body odor, acne)
_____ 56. gynecomastia
_____ 57. pubic hair and body hair
_____ 58. menarche
_____ 59. less firm erection and longer refractory period
_____ 60. reversal of effects of menopause
_____ 61. decreased sexual desire in women (review from Chapter 3)
_____ 62. decreased sexual desire in men (review from Chapter 3)
_____ 63. children's first sexual attractions

a. increase in estrogen
b. decrease in estrogen
c. increase in testosterone
d. decrease in testosterone
e. increase in FSH and LH
f. increase in DHEA from adrenal glands

C. FILL IN THE BLANKS

64. The decline in sexual activity among older single women is most often due to _____.

65. The changes that occur in women in the few years that precede and follow menopause are called _____.

66. Before age 2, bodily exploration is usually confined to _____.

67. Freud referred to what this chapter calls the initial school-age years as the _____ stage of psychosexual development.

68. Development of breasts and growth of facial hair are examples of _____.
69. For many teenage girls, the need for _____ is an important part of finding their self-identity.
70. Throughout the world, men tend to engage in casual sex to _____.
71. About 80% of all societies allow men to _____.
72. Women are most concerned about _____ infidelity by their mates.
73. Whitehurst believes that the two things most likely to lead to extramarital sex are _____ and _____.
74. Puberty is at least a two-part maturational process. The two parts are called _____ and _____.

SUGGESTED SEX EDUCATION REFERENCES TO HELP PARENTS

All About Sex: A Family Resource on Sex and Sexuality by Planned Parenthood Federation of America. New York: Three Rivers Press, 1997. Written at an intermediate level and intended for the whole family.

Ask Me Anything by Marty Klein. New York: Simon & Schuster, 1992. Prepares parents to give straightforward answers to anything their children might ask.

Dr. Ruth Talks to Kids by Dr. Ruth Westheimer. New York: Aladdin Paperbacks, 1998. Aimed at children aged 8 through 14. *Time* magazine (May 24, 1993) says that Dr. Ruth's book provides an excellent middle ground between books that teach abstinence only and those that favor a more comprehensive approach.

From Diapers to Dating: A Parent's Guide to Raising Sexually Healthy Children from Infancy to middle school (2nd ed.) by Debra Haffner and Alyssa Haffner Tartaglione. New York: Newmarket Press, 2004.

It's Perfectly Normal: Changing Bodies, Growing Up, Sex and Sexual Health by Robbie Harris. Cambridge, MA: Candlewick Press, 1996. For children approaching puberty.

Talking with Your Child About Sex: Questions and Answers for Children from Birth to Puberty by Mary Calderone and James Ramey. New York: Ballantine Books, 1984.

Ten Talks Parents Must Have with Their Children About Sex and Character by Pepper Schwartz. Boston: Time Warner Trade Publishing, 2000. Includes talks about values and ethics.

What's Happening to Me? by Peter Mayle and Arthur Robins. New York: Carol Publishing, 1992. For children approaching puberty.

The What's Happening to My Body? Book for Boys: The New Growing-Up Guide for Parents and Sons by Lynda and Area Madaras. New York: Newmarket Press, 2000. For children approaching puberty.

The What's Happening to My Body? Book for Girls: The New Growing-Up Guide for Parents and Daughters by Lynda and Area Madaras. New York: Newmarket Press, 2000. For children approaching puberty.

What's Love Got to Do with It: Talking with Your Kids About Sex by John Chirban. Nashville, TN: Thomas Nelson Pubs, 2007.

Where Did I Come From? by P. Mayle and A. Robins. Secaucus, NJ: Carol Publishing, 1999. For young children.

Where Did I Come From? by Peter Mayle. New World, 1986. A 27-minute animated videocassette version of the book. Many video rental stores carry it.

SUGGESTED READINGS

Barbach, L. (1994). *The pause*. New York: Signet Books. All about menopause.

Graber, J. A., & Brooks-Gunn, J. (2002). Adolescent girls' sexual development. In G. M. Wingood & R. J. DiClemente (Eds.), *Handbook of women's sexual and reproductive health*, pp. 21–42, New York: Kluwer Academic/ Plenum Pub. An excellent review of the hormonal, behavioral, and psychological changes.

Jacoby, S. (2005, July/August). Sex in America. *AARP The Magazine*. Sexual behavior of middle-aged and elderly Americans.

Janus, S., & Janus, C. (1993). *The Janus report*. New York: John Wiley & Sons. Results of a nationwide survey of sexual behavior.

Michael, R., et al. (1994). *Sex in America*. Boston: Little, Brown. Results of the Laumann et al. survey, the most scientifically conducted survey ever done. Written for the general public.

Moore, S., & Rosenthal, D. (Eds.) (2006). *Sexuality in adolescence: Current trends*. New York: Routledge, A scholarly book by two experts in the field.

Segraves, R. T., & Segraves, K. B. (1995). Human sexuality and aging. *Journal of Sex Education and Therapy*, 21. A very thorough review of sexuality and health in aging persons.

Wingart, P., et al. (2007, January 15). Understanding menopause: The new prime time. *Newsweek*, 38–63. Almost everything you may want to know about menopause.

Adult Sexual Behaviors and Attitudes

... never before in history has there been such a huge disparity between the open display of eroticism in a society and that society's great reluctance to speak about private sexual practices.

—Robert Michael, John Gagnon, Edward Laumann, & Gina Kolata, 1994

For the human species to survive, men and women must have sexual intercourse. We need only look at the large number of people in the world to know that this is not an uncommon sexual practice. But what about other sexual behaviors—that is, behaviors that are not necessary for procreation? How many people engage in oral-genital sex? Is your partner unusual for wanting to try different positions? Is it normal to have sexual fantasies? Is masturbation unnatural and bad for your health? Many people are unsure about the answers to these questions, and thus may have anxieties about whether the sexual behaviors they or their partners wish to engage in are "normal."

WHAT IS NORMAL?

Just what is "normal" sexual behavior? The answer is, it depends. Many factors are involved, including the period in history in which the person lives. Victorian-era moralists, for example, believed that the only normal sexual behavior was heterosexual vaginal intercourse in the male-on-top "missionary" position. Today, people in Western culture regard a much greater variety of behaviors to be normal. In fact, most American men and women engage in more than one sexual behavior when having sex. The 2010 NSSHB study found 41 combinations (Herbenick et al., 2010a, c). However, we must guard against being ethnocentric (see page 6).

> *When you have finished studying this chapter, you should be able to:*

- Explain what is meant by "normal" sexual behaviors.

- Identify the major historical sources of negative attitudes toward masturbation, and discuss recent findings about this sexual activity.

- Summarize the research findings about the frequency, quality, and role of sexual fantasies in enhancing sexual expression.

- Explain why different cultures, as well as individuals within a culture, use different positions of sexual intercourse.

- Define fellatio and cunnilingus and describe the current research findings on these activities.

- Appreciate that the incidence of some of the sexual behaviors covered in this chapter often differs among Caucasians, African Americans, Latinos, and Asian Americans.

- Define a sexually healthy person.

- Explain sodomy laws and their implications for heterosexual and homosexual individuals.

What is considered to be normal sexual behaviors in our culture may not be considered normal in other cultures, and vice versa. Take a peak ahead to Box 11–A and you will see that even in the United States there are major differences among ethnic groups in the prevalence of some sexual behaviors. What is considered normal also changes over the life span of an individual. We will return to a discussion of "normal" in the beginning of Chapter 14.

In this chapter you will read about several sexual behaviors that can be considered normal (in Western culture) from a statistical point of view. If a behavior is *statistically normal*, it means that a large number of people engage in it. Notice that for a behavior to be called "normal" it does not require that everybody engage in (or even approve of) it. Therefore, you should not consider yourself to be "abnormal" if you have not engaged in all of the behaviors discussed here. It is best to think of normal behavior as a *range of behaviors*.

For any particular behavior, there is also the question of how frequently people engage in it. How often is normal? Averages can be (and are) computed, but you should not interpret "normal" as meaning only the average value. Again, normal involves a *range of values*. For example, what is the normal number of times per month that married women masturbate? The answer is a range (from zero to some higher number).

The incidence and frequency of the various sexual behaviors you will read about in this chapter were obtained by taking sex surveys. Be sure to review the section on surveys and sampling procedures in Chapter 1.

PERSONAL REFLECTIONS

What was your emotional reaction, if any, when you first saw the drawings for this chapter? If your reaction was anxiety or disgust, why? Do you regard the behaviors shown as normal?

MASTURBATION

"Until I became sexually active with a partner, I masturbated every day. Even after marriage, I continue to masturbate." (man)

"The guilt I feel right after masturbating is so painful that I cry at times." (man)

"I have a steady girlfriend who satisfies my sexual needs. But sometimes I am not able to satisfy hers. This is the primary reason why I enjoy masturbating—because I don't have to worry about trying to satisfy anyone but me." (man)

"I didn't masturbate until after I was sexually active, which was in college. In between sex with my boyfriends, I didn't know there were ways I could 'pleasure' myself with sex—and without a partner. Now, after finding it, I truly enjoy it." (woman)

"I had masturbated long before I became sexually active and, as long as I kept it to myself, I never seemed to have a problem with it. Now, when my boyfriend asks me if I ever masturbated, I can't help but feel guilty." (woman)

"I've masturbated since about the age of 14. I still do, with and without my husband present. I have no guilty feelings about it, not even when I was younger. There are times when I would rather masturbate than make love. Not that I would give up intercourse. It's just nicer sometimes." (woman)

"All through my childhood I thought that masturbation was something only guys could do. But *Cosmo* started printing all kinds of articles telling women to masturbate so they can show their partner what to do, and I got confused. I know I shouldn't be ashamed of my body, but I still can't bring myself to do it." (woman)

"I am 36 years old and never in my wildest dreams would I have thought I would be masturbating, but I did and I think it's great because I can stimulate parts that a male partner would not have the slightest idea about." (woman)

(All examples are from the author's files.)

Attitudes About Masturbation

As you can see from these examples, there is a wide range of attitudes and emotions regarding masturbation (see Hogarth & Ingham, 2009). Does it surprise you that many people have a negative attitude? When you were growing up, what kinds of things did you hear might happen to you if you masturbated? Many of us were told (by friends, acquaintances, and sometimes parents) that **masturbation** could cause us to go blind or deaf; have nosebleeds, heart murmurs, acne, or painful menstruation; cause hair to grow on the palms of our hands; and finally, if we did not stop, result in insanity. Others of us were simply told that we had better not do it to excess. The consequences of doing it to excess were never quite spelled out, but the possibilities that it was bad for our health were always implied. And scarier yet, what was considered excessive? Whatever it was, most of us convinced ourselves that it was more than we did it.

It is obvious that masturbation is considered bad by some people, but where did these stories come from? Negative attitudes about masturbation have, in fact, been handed down from generation to generation for centuries. The Greek physician Hippocrates believed that overindulging in sex was harmful to one's health. Ancient Chinese cultures

Masturbation ■ Self-stimulation of one's genitals.

condemned male masturbation as a waste of *yang* (male essence), while the biblical Hebrews considered it "spillage of seed," punishable by death. The early Roman Catholic Church considered the only legitimate purpose of sex to be for procreation and sexual behaviors that did not have this as a goal were considered immoral. The Church's negative view of masturbation was formalized in the 1200s by Thomas Aquinas, who included it as one of the four categories of unnatural acts (Aquinas, 1968). Many scholars believe that the word *masturbation* is derived from the Latin words *manus* ("hand") and *sturpore* ("to defile") or *tubare* ("to disturb").

In 1741, a Swiss physician named S. Tissot published a book entitled *Onania, or a Treatise upon the Disorders Produced by Masturbation*, in which he expanded upon the negative medical views of Hippocrates. In his book, Tissot claimed that excessive sex (especially masturbation) was dangerous because it deprived vital tissues of blood and led to insanity. As proof of this, he said, one only had to look at the many men in insane asylums who sat around openly masturbating. Tissot's views were accepted by many physicians. In Victorian times (the 1800s and early 1900s), many physicians also believed that loss of semen was as detrimental to a man's health as loss of blood. In the "seminal theory," as it came to be called, semen was believed to contain the essence of life, and that during ejaculation these "seeds" were lost (Fitz-Gerald & Fitz-Gerald, 1998; Stephens, 2009). Freud, for example, believed that the loss of 1 ounce of semen produced the same degree of fatigue as the loss of 40 ounces of blood. He also believed that people who masturbated had "poisoned" themselves and that masturbation caused nervous disorders or neurosis ("neurasthenia") (Groenendijk, 1997).

The Victorians, you recall, vehemently denied any pleasurable component of sex and were particularly concerned about masturbation (see Stephens, 2009). Not only were many Victorian era children forced to wear chastity belts and metal gloves to bed (see Figure 1–4), but circumcision and clitoridectomy became popular during this time as means by which parents tried to prevent their children from masturbating. For an example of extreme Victorian beliefs, read the following passages from a book titled *Perfect Womanhood* written in 1903 by Mary Melendy, M.D., Ph.D., which contains the following advice to mothers about what to tell their boys about masturbation:

> Impress upon him that if these organs are abused, or if they are put to any use besides that for which God made them ... they will bring disease and ruin upon those who abuse [them].... He will not grow up happy, healthy and strong.
>
> Teach him that when he handles or excites the sexual organs, all parts of the body suffer, because they are connected by nerves that run throughout the system, this is why it is called "self-abuse." ... The sin is terrible, and is, in fact, worse than lying or stealing!
>
> If the sexual organs are handled it brings too much blood to these parts, and this produces a diseased condition, it also causes disease in other organs of the body, because they are left with a less amount of blood than they ought to have....
>
> It lays the foundation for consumption, paralysis and heart disease. It weakens the memory, makes a boy careless, negligent and listless.
>
> It even makes many lose their minds; others when grown, commit suicide.

Similarly, Dr. J. H. Kellogg (1887) wrote the following about the effects of masturbation in girls:

> Wide observations have convinced us that a great many of the backaches, sideaches, and other aches and pains of which girls complain, are attributable to this injurious habit. Much of the nervousness, hysteria, neuralgia, and general worthlessness of girls originates in this cause alone.
>
> The period of puberty is one at which thousands of girls break down in health. The constitution, already weakened by a debilitating, debasing vice, is not prepared for the strain, and the poor victim drops into a premature grave.

He wrote the following about masturbation in boys:

> In solitude he pollutes himself, and with his own hand blights all his prospects for both this world and the next. Even after being solemnly warned, he will often continue this worse than beastly practice, deliberately forfeiting his right to health and happiness for a moment's mad sensuality. *(J. H. Kellogg, Plain Facts for Old and Young)*

This is the same J. H. Kellogg associated with the breakfast cereals. He invented cornflakes to be used as a breakfast food that would curb youthful lust. Graham crackers were invented by Dr. Sylvester Graham for much the same purpose. In his 1834 book, Graham wrote that if a boy masturbated, he would turn into "a confirmed and degraded idiot."

Although not all cultures have had negative attitudes about masturbation (e.g., the ancient Egyptians believed that the world was created when the God Atum ejaculated), negative attitudes are still widely found in Western societies. For example, the Catholic Church called it an "intrinsically and seriously disturbed act" in 1975 (Patton, 1986), and this view was repeated by Pope John Paul II in 1993. Orthodox Jews still regard it as one of the worst sins mentioned in the Torah.

When former U.S. Surgeon General Joycelyn Elders was fired in 1994 for talking about masturbation at a conference on AIDS, sociologist John Gagnon was quoted as saying, "It remains a puzzle for

"Now they tell us masturbation is harmless!"

Reproduced by special permission of *Playboy* magazine. Copyright 1971 by Playboy.

me why a relatively innocuous behavior evokes tides of anxiety and fear in otherwise well adjusted people."

Incidence of Masturbation

With this long history of scare tactics, you would expect, then, that very few people masturbate. In fact, the large majority of human beings masturbate. This was true when your great-grandparents were young. Kinsey and colleagues (1948, 1953) found that 92% of the men they surveyed had masturbated by age 20. It was generally the first sexual experience to orgasm for adolescent boys. Only a third of the women in Kinsey's study reported that they had masturbated by age 20, but another third had done so by age 40 (a total of 62%). In other words, men were more likely to start masturbating before they experienced sexual intercourse, whereas many women did not start masturbating until after they started engaging in sexual intercourse.

Masturbation remains a significant component of most people's sexual behaviors throughout most of their lifetime. Laumann and colleagues (1994) found that for Americans under the age of 60, 63% of men and 42% of women had masturbated in the past year (the percentages were higher in the 25- to 39-year-old group). The 2010 NSSHB study found that over 60% of men through age 59 had masturbated within the past 90 days, 50% through age 69, and over half of women through age 49 had done so (Herbenick et al., 2010b, c; Reece et al., 2010b; Schick et al., 2010). Recent nationally representative samples of Australians (Richters et al., 2003a) and British people (Gerressu et al., 2008) have found similar (and perhaps slightly higher) results. Several of these surveys found that the better educated a

person was, the more likely it was that he or she masturbated (see Box 11–A). On the average, men who masturbate do so two or three times more frequently than women who masturbate. Interestingly, in a review of many studies, it was found that although women report a much lower incidence of masturbation than do men, their attitudes toward masturbation do not differ from those of men (Oliver & Hyde, 1993).

Are all of these people risking their health or sanity? No. Masturbation, whether done once a month or three times a day, does not cause any of the problems mentioned previously, and few doctors today, if any, would make such claims. (A discussion of choking oneself during masturbation is in Chapter 14.) *It is a perfectly normal human behavior.* How can I be so confident as to call it normal when historically it has been so condemned? Just look at the statistics—when a large majority of people have engaged in a particular behavior, it has to be considered normal. Still, there are some who continue to feel guilty or wrong about it—nearly half of all people who masturbate, according to Laumann et al. (1994).

Methods of Masturbation

People differ in the way they masturbate, but men display less variation than do women. Almost all men masturbate by rhythmically stroking up and down the body and glans of the penis with one hand. They may differ in how much of the penis they stimulate, and in the rhythm and pressure applied, but it is generally still a stroking motion. In order to enhance arousal, many men fantasize and/or look at sexually explicit pictures while masturbating.

Most women who masturbate do so by stimulating the clitoris, labia minora, and/or the entire vulva. Kinsey's group (1953) found that about 11% of women also stimulate their breasts during masturbation. Most women do not insert a finger into their vaginas while masturbating (Hite, 1976; Kinsey et al., 1953), but as many as 30% have tried a dildo on at least one occasion (Herbenick et al., 2010). Today, close to half of adult women have used a vibrator during masturbation (Herbenick et al., 2010).

"In the masturbation section I believe you should emphasize the importance of a vibrator for women. Methods of masturbation seem apparent to males, but I think women need more guidance in this area. In my experience a vibrator is the most intensely pleasurable way to masturbate."
(from the author's files)

Functions of Masturbation

Why do people masturbate? Quite simply, because it feels good. Although masturbation allows for sexual release when a partner is not available, it does not

Box 11–A Cross-Cultural Perspectives

Ethnic Differences in Sexual Behavior

In this chapter you will read about several behaviors that are considered normal in American culture today. However, the statistics given for each behavior generally do not take ethnicity into account. Are the behaviors discussed normal for all ethnic groups?

As an example, let us consider masturbation. In their nationally representative sample, Laumann and colleagues (1994) found that two thirds of white and Latino men and a slightly smaller proportion of Asian-American men had masturbated within the past year. Only

40% of African-American men had masturbated in the last year. As for women, whites were more likely to have masturbated than African Americans or Latinas (see Table 11–1).

Ethnic differences have frequently been found for oral-genital sex as well. African Americans, especially women, are much less likely than others to have engaged in this type of sexual behavior (Belcastro, 1985; Laumann et al., 1994; Quadagno et al., 1998; Weinberg & Williams, 1988). White men and women show the highest percentage of people

engaging in this behavior, while Latinos and Asian Americans are intermediate between these two groups.

On the other hand, Latino men and women are more likely than people of other ethnic groups to have engaged in anal intercourse (Laumann et al., 1994; Van Oss Marin & Gomez, 1994). This is especially true for non-Mexican Latino men (Jeffries, 2009). Anal intercourse is highly prevalent among heterosexuals in Latin America, where the percentage may be as high as 50% to 60% in some countries (Halperin, 1998).

TABLE 11–1	*Incidence in Sexual Behaviors Among Ethnic Groups in the United States*			
	Whites	African Americans	Latinos	Asian Americans
Masturbation (in past year)				
Men	67%	40%	67%	61
Women	44	32	35	no data
Oral-genital sex				
Men	81	50	71	64
Women	75	34	60	no data
Anal intercourse				
Men	26	23	34	15
Women	23	10	17	no data
	Less Than High School	High School Graduates	Some College	College Graduates	Graduate Degree
---	---	---	---	---	---
Masturbation (in past year)					
Men	45%	55%	67%	76%	81%
Women	25	32	49	52	59
Oral-genital sex					
Men	59	75	80	84	80
Women	41	60	78	79	79
Anal intercourse					
Men	21	23	26	30	29
Women	13	17	25	22	29

Source: From *The Social Organization of Sexuality,* by Edward O. Laumann. Copyright © 1994 University of Chicago Press. Reprinted by permission of the University of Chicago Press.

(Continued)

These ethnic differences in sexual behaviors can be partly attributed to differences in power between men and women in relationships and the resulting differences in communication patterns (see Quadagno et al., 1998). The gender dichotomy in power is most notable for traditional Latinos. In some studies of anal intercourse, for example, only 16% of experienced Latina women found it pleasurable, but 80% said that the decision to engage in anal intercourse was always or almost always made by the man (Halperin, 1999).

There are factors other than ethnicity that may account for differences in sexual behavior. In addition to communication patterns, these include age, education, marital status, economic status, and degree of acculturation. For example, while the lowest rates for oral-genital sex are found among African-American women, it is especially low for older African-American women (Quadagno et al., 1998). Ethnic differences become less apparent as people become more acculturated (Meston & Ahrold, 2010; Okazaki, 2002). Look at the bottom half of Table 11–1. As you can see, masturbation and oral-genital sex are more common among higher-educated groups. Within each ethnic group, one's level of religiosity is also a factor (Ahrold & Meston, 2010).

Do ethnic differences still appear when researchers control for these other factors (i.e., looking at white, African-American, Latino, and Asian-American people of the same age, marital status, education, income levels, etc.)? Here, there is some difference of opinion. Some studies find ethnic differences regardless of other factors (Laumann et al., 1994), but others do not (Quadagno et al., 1998). While more research is needed, it is probably safe to conclude that ethnic differences are not as great when we compare people of the same socioeconomic status. Things may also have changed since Laumann et al.'s study (early 1990s). In the 2010 NSSHB study, the incidence of masturbation among African Americans was higher than reported by Laumann et al. (1994), although the incidence of oral-genital sex was still generally lower than for whites (Dodge et al., 2010).

necessarily stop when one forms a sexual relationship with someone. Janus and Janus (1993) reported that 66% of the men and 67% of the women they surveyed agreed or strongly agreed that "masturbation is a natural part of life and continues on in marriage." In fact, Laumann et al. (1994) found high rates of masturbation among young people with sexual partners, and that the more sex a person has, the more likely he or she is to masturbate. In other words, masturbation is not just an outlet for lack of sex, but is also often a reflection of a sexually active lifestyle (Das, 2007), especially among women (Gerressu et al., 2008).

Why do people with sexual partners masturbate? *Variety*—it is a sexual experience that is different (not necessarily better) than sex with their partner.

> "I masturbated a lot when I was without a partner, and now I still do. The orgasm is so different than those I get during intercourse.... My boyfriend doesn't understand...but I love making love with him."
>
> (from the author's files)

Some people argue that it may be habit-forming and prevent development of "normal" adult sexual relations. However, Kinsey's group (1953) found that women who were able to masturbate to orgasm without guilt or shame during adolescence generally had the least difficulty in making the transition to enjoying sex with a partner. Other studies have found that not only is masturbation during adolescence not harmful to sexual adjustment in young adulthood, but also that masturbation during marriage is often associated with a greater degree of marital and sexual satisfaction (Hurlbert & Whittaker, 1991; Leitenberg et al., 1993). So if you suspect your partner of masturbating occasionally, do not assume that he or she is unhappy with your sex life. There would only be a problem if your partner was masturbating (indicating a need for a sexual outlet) but showing little or no interest or sexual desire for you.

Today, some therapists prescribe masturbation as part of their treatment for orgasm problems in women and for greater ejaculatory control in men (LoPiccolo & Stock, 1986; Meston et al., 2004). Thus, what was once a taboo is now often used as part of sexual therapy. This is not to imply, however, that all people should masturbate, particularly if they are comfortable with their sexuality. Just as it was once wrong to make people feel bad because they masturbated, it would be equally wrong to make people feel abnormal if they did not. The important point is that those who have a desire to masturbate should be able to do so without feelings of guilt or worries about their health.

PERSONAL REFLECTIONS

What are your feelings about masturbation? If they are negative, why? Do you have negative feelings when you pleasure yourself by touching (e.g., rubbing, massaging, scratching) other parts of your body? Consider masturbation in context of a larger question: Are genitals reserved only for procreation (to have children), or are they also a source of pleasure?

SEXUAL FANTASIES

"My sister, who was much older than I, would always have friends over and I would fantasize about making love to them while masturbating." (man)

"They [fantasies] almost always include my wife. It may also include another female." (man)

"I enjoy being male, but have occasionally fantasized about what it is like to be female during lovemaking." (man)

"During sex I have sexual fantasies about making love to a woman.... I would view my husband as a woman." (woman)

"My sexual fantasy has been the same since age 16. The man uses me, sometimes beats me, and brings his other female partners around me. This fantasy bothers me." (woman)

"I have sexual fantasies while making love to my husband, usually about men I'm attracted to from work. I think about how it would be and when I come, it's stronger and harder than it usually is." (woman)

(All examples are from the author's files.)

Recall from Chapter 1 that within Christianity there is a long history of condemnation of sexual thoughts, even if the thoughts are not accompanied by sexual behaviors (and even if the thoughts are of one's husband or wife). In the Victorian era it was thought that only men had sexual fantasies (because women were believed to be asexual), but this is not true. Nearly everyone has sexual fantasies from time to time. Sometimes the fantasy may be a warm thought of a romantic interaction with a special person, but often the fantasies are very sexually explicit. Although most men think about sex much more often than women (Laumann et al., 1994; Regan & Atkins, 2006), the large majority of women do have sexual fantasies. In fact, more than 90% of women have had sexual fantasies (Leitenberg & Henning, 1995; Pelletier & Harold, 1988). Women's sexual fantasies tend to be more romantic and emotional, while men's fantasies tend to have more explicit and visual imagery. The frequency, length, and explicitness of an individual's sexual fantasies are related to the person's level of sexual experience (Leitenberg & Henning, 1995).

Sexual fantasies can occur at any time. One of the most common fantasies during intercourse is the replacement fantasy, where one imagines oneself having sex with someone other than one's sexual partner (Hicks & Leitenberg, 2001). If you have ever felt guilty about having these fantasies, as some people do (believing them to be immoral or socially unacceptable), you should be aware that they are so common that chances are that your partner has had them too. One study found that nearly all men and 80% of women in heterosexual relationships have had this type of fantasy within the last 2 months (Hicks & Leitenberg, 2001). The fantasized partner can be a friend, a neighbor, a former partner, a celebrity, or anyone else.

The specific content of sexual fantasies is almost limitless, but we can group fantasies into four general categories: (1) exploratory (experimentation with never-before-tried behaviors such as group sex or same-sex activities), (2) intimacy (sexual activities with a known partner), (3) impersonal sex (sex with strangers or watching others have sex; fetishes), and (4) dominance–submission themes (Leitenberg & Henning, 1995; Meuwissen & Over, 1991). For both men and women, fantasies of intimacy with a present, former, or imaginary partner are most common. Dominance fantasies are more common for men, but submission fantasies of being overpowered or forced into having sex are not at all uncommon for women as well (Binova & Critelli, 2009; Critelli & Binova, 2008).

About one fourth of all people who fantasize feel guilty about it (Leitenberg & Henning, 1995). It should also be noted that a large majority of men and women experience *sexual intrusive thoughts*— sudden, involuntary, unwanted sexual thoughts (Byers et al., 1998). However, while many of us have negative sexual fantasies, the frequency and content of sexual fantasies and intrusive thoughts does not indicate sexual unhappiness, nor does it signify personality or psychological problems (Leitenberg & Henning, 1995; Renaud & Byers, 2001). In fact, sexual fantasies are most common in those individuals who have the fewest number of sexual problems. Most sex therapists view sexual fantasies as something positive to be enjoyed rather than as something bad for one's sexual health. Having a sexual fantasy does not mean that a person actually wants to experience it in real life. Fantasies also provide a safe and private outlet for thoughts that, if actually engaged in, might be considered improper and/or illegal. In fact, in most cases where people have acted out their fantasies, the result has been disappointment. One reason for this is that we are totally in control of the sequence of events in our fantasies, so that they proceed just to our liking; but this is seldom true in real life, where partners can cause distractions and have desires and demands of their own.

PERSONAL REFLECTIONS

Do you have sexual fantasies? (Most people do.) Are you comfortable or uncomfortable with your fantasies—that is, do they cause anxiety or guilt? If your partner told you that he or she had sexual fantasies, what would your feelings be? Analyze the nature of your fantasies (e.g., their content, when they occur). What purpose do you think your fantasies serve?

SEXUAL INTERCOURSE

Frequency and Duration

Among those Americans who are having sex, about 95% say that their sexual activity always or usually includes vaginal intercourse (Laumann et al., 1994). You learned in Chapter 10 (see Middle Age) that the frequency of intercourse declines with age, but how frequently do people aged 25 to 40 have sex? The average is about 110 times a year, but there is a wide range (Michael et al., 1994). About one third of American adults have sex a few times a month, another one third two or three times a week, about 8.5% four or more times a week, and 15% a few times a year.

How long does sexual intercourse usually last? The total shared event (which includes touching and other forms of intimacy before and after intercourse)

Missionary position ■ A face-to-face position of sexual intercourse in which the woman lies on her back and the man lies on top with his legs between hers. It was called this because Christian missionaries instructed people that other positions were unnatural.

Coitus ■ Sexual intercourse.

---

lasts 15 to 60 minutes for 70% of couples (Laumann et al., 1994), but intercourse itself usually lasts 3 to 13 minutes (Corty & Guardiani, 2008). You will read more about frequency and duration in Chapter 13.

Coital Positions and Locations

"Before I became sexually active, I believed that everyone who engaged in sexual intercourse did so in the missionary position in the privacy of their own bedroom. Now I look forward to new positions." (woman)

"[Our sex] was boring me. We always used the same position—his favorite one." (woman)

"My boyfriend has the concept that men should be in control of sex. Well, I say 'What about my pleasure?' My favorite position is 'me on top' because I'm guaranteed to receive an orgasm." (woman)

"… And also I like having sex standing up with my legs wrapped around the male's waist and walking around at the same time." (woman)

"I am a mature, responsible, middle-aged female. I am also an experienced diver with a mate who is equally comfortable under water. In my opinion, the most stimulating, exciting, and extraordinary sex on earth happens beneath the surface of the water. Complete sex beyond the grasp of gravity in a quiet, sensuous, foreign world is beyond our limited language to describe." (woman)

(All examples are from the author's files.)

According to two popular sex manuals, there are 113–116 different positions in which couples can have sexual intercourse. For most Americans, the first experience with sexual intercourse is in the **missionary position,** that is, a face-to-face position in which the woman lies on her back and the man lies on top with his legs between hers. It is called the missionary position because Christian missionaries in foreign countries used to instruct natives that this was the only "proper" way to have sexual intercourse. Saint Paul believed that women should be subordinate to men during intercourse (i.e., on the bottom), and Saint Augustine said that any other position was unnatural and a sin against nature (see Chapter 1). In the 1200s, this attitude was formalized by Thomas Aquinas in his *Summa theologiae* (1968) and became the standard within Christianity (Brundage, 1984).

For many couples, man-on-top may be the only position in which they ever have sexual intercourse (**coitus**). This was true when your great-grandparents were young (Kinsey et al., 1948), but what about today? In a survey of college students, it was found that 45% of men preferred the woman-on-top position (25% preferred man on top and 25% preferred man from behind), while a third of women

Box 11–B Cross-Cultural Perspectives

Sexual Intercourse

Do Americans have sex more or less often than people in other cultures? It depends on the other culture. People in Greece and Croatia, for example, report having sex 134 to 138 times a year, compared to 113 for Americans. People in China, on the other hand, report having sex only 96 times a year, people in India only 75 times, and Japanese people only 45 times (data from the Pfizer Global Study of Sexual Attitudes and Behaviors, see Laumann et al., 2006).

What about positions of sexual intercourse? Face-to-face is the preferred manner of sexual intercourse in all known cultures, but not necessarily man-on-top. In many African cultures, the most common position is with the partners lying side by side, while in Polynesian and many Asian cultures the most common position is with the woman lying on her back and the man squatting or kneeling between her legs (Gregersen, 1982). (By the way, it was the Polynesians who originally called the man-on-top position taught to them by European missionaries the "missionary position.") Actually, in most cultures there is more than one preferred position. Mangaians, for example, practice a variety of positions while preferring some variety of man-on-top, but use the man-from-behind position more often when their partner is pregnant (Marshall, 1971).

Some researchers believe that a culture's preferred position of intercourse is a reflection of women's social status (Goldstein, 1976). In cultures where a woman's sexual satisfaction is consid-ered to be as important as the man's, woman-on-top is usually preferred. The ancient Romans preferred this position. In male-dominated cultures, however, the reverse is true (Langmyhr, 1976). There may be no better reflection of the relation between women's social status and coital position than in our own culture. Here, women's gender roles have changed dramatically since World War II. In the 1940s, Kinsey et al. (1948) found that over two thirds of the couples studied had never attempted any position other than man-on-top. More and more women began to enter the work force after that, and women's rights evolved rapidly in all areas. Today, the majority of couples in the United States have tried the woman-on-top position (e.g., Elliott & Brantley, 1997).

---

preferred woman on top (48% preferred man on top and 15% preferred man from behind) (Elliott & Brantley, 1997). About one third of heterosexual couples have used vibrators together during sex (Herbenick et al., 2010).

The preference for the man-on-top position by many American couples appears to be culturally rather than biologically determined. The woman-on-top position is most popular in some other cultures, especially those in which women enjoy high status (see Box 11–B).

Why do many couples experiment with different positions? After all, the missionary position is perfectly adequate for procreational purposes. Well, to answer this, let's first examine the advantages and disadvantages of the missionary position. Perhaps the nicest thing about this position is that it allows for emotional intimacy while having sex. A couple is face-to-face. But for most women, the benefits stop right there. In most couples, the man is considerably heavier than the woman, which means that she has to support a great deal of weight in the man-on-top position (and more and more so as the man gets tired). Some women may even have trouble breathing in this position. Women in my class have additionally pointed out that they receive very little touching or fondling in this position because their male partners are too busy supporting them-selves. With a woman's hips "pinned to the mat," the man is in total control (probably the major reason that American men like this position), and it is often difficult to fully enjoy sex when you have little or no control over the movement or tempo.

There are other positions that still involve eye-to-eye contact but allow greater freedom and involvement for the woman. As you will see in a later chapter, woman-on-top is a position that is recommended by many therapists for optimal sexual arousal in both people. It is generally a lot easier for the man to support the woman, and it is also a position in which it is easy for the man or the woman herself to manually stimulate the clitoris (and most other parts of a partner's body) during intercourse.

Although these considerations are important, probably the main reason that most couples have sexual intercourse in different positions is to bring variety to their sex lives. Many a sexual relationship has become stale and boring by allowing it to become *ritualized*, that is, by having sex only at the same time of day, in the same place, in the same position.

Couples try different positions to keep their sex lives exciting, fresh, and fun—the way it was at the beginning of the relationship. Sex manuals show drawings of couples in what appears to be hundreds of different positions, but there are really just a few

FIGURE 11–1 Man-on-top, face-to-face ("missionary") position

major variations that a couple can try: They can face each other or one partner can turn around, and they can lie down, sit, or stand up. However, couples should try different positions only because they want to, and not because they feel pressured to do so.

Regardless of whether a couple ever try different sexual positions while having intercourse, it is important that they not allow their sex life to become a

standardized ritual. The secret to that is to allow your sexual relations to be spontaneous, creative, and fun whenever possible. Some people get locked into a habit of never having sex until right before they go to sleep at night. If you and your partner are in the mood in the morning or afternoon, have sex then. Do not postpone it until later, when you might be tired. It is also normal for couples to have sex in a

FIGURE 11–2 Woman-on-top position

FIGURE 11–3 Man-from-behind position

FIGURE 11–4 A variation of the sitting position

variety of places, for example, on the couch, on the rug, in different rooms, or in any other place. There is no rule that states you can have sex only in bed.

Dear Ann Landers:

My wife and I have been married 20 years. We have two sweet children and consider ourselves very fortunate. The problem is one we cannot discuss with our minister.

My wife believes that sex anywhere but in the bedroom is sinful according to the Bible. I say a change of setting can add extra pleasure, and so long as there is complete privacy, it is perfectly moral.

The place I have in mind is the car. We have a garage with a sturdy lock on the door. No one could possibly get in.

We are good Christians and want to know what the Bible says about this. Can you contact a religious scholar?

(Strictly Confidential in Kentucky)

Dear Strictly: Since the Bible predates the automobile by a couple of thousand years, there is no point in bothering a Christian scholar.

If you will settle for my opinion, here it is: It is perfectly all right for a married couple to make love anywhere they choose, providing it is private, safe, and reasonably comfortable.

(*Ann Landers* column. Esther P. Lederer Trust and Creators Syndicate, Inc. Reprinted by permission.)

If you and your partner are on the couch and get in the mood to have sex, there is nothing immoral, sinful, or indecent in spontaneously doing so right there. One of Ann Landers' readers felt compelled to respond to the letter by "Strictly Confidential":

Dear Ann Landers:

I was interested in the letter from the man who enjoyed making love in the car. His wife felt guilty and wanted to know if it was the "Christian" thing to do. You said so long as it was private, not dangerous, and reasonably comfortable, it was nobody's business.

I married one in a million. She was totally uninhibited, willing, and eager to make love any place at any time. I must say, we dreamed up some mighty unusual situations. We traveled quite a bit, and it was not unusual for us to pull off the road in the middle of the day if we ran into a wooded area, a vacant house, a sandy beach, a calm lake, or an inviting motel. On occasion, when the mood came upon us and none of the above was available, we just used the car.

This kept up until we were in our 60s, when my beloved wife passed away. I always felt as if we had the healthiest sex life of anyone I knew because we never stopped turning each other on. Sex was

always unpredictable, imaginative, and fun. Our sexual compatibility spilled over into all areas of our life and we were divinely happy.

You can print this letter if you want to but no name or city, please. Just call me...

(Beautiful Memories)

Dear Beautiful: How lucky you were to find each other. It was a perfect match. Lots of readers will be envious.

(*Ann Landers* column. Esther P. Lederer Trust and Creators Syndicate, Inc. Reprinted by permission.)

PERSONAL REFLECTIONS

How do you expect to keep your sexual relationship from becoming ritualized after 6 months, 6 years, 20 years, 60 years? The brain is your largest sex organ. Make sure you continue to use it to your advantage.

ORAL-GENITAL SEX

"I was highly against oral sex because I thought it was so nasty and demeaning. But when I experienced it, my attitude changed. I didn't realize what I was against could feel so damn good." (woman)

"...What did surprise me was the fact that I enjoyed giving more than receiving. I think it is a great way for two people to share very intimate moments." (man)

"It is a great way to relax, feel unpressured and not worry about pregnancy or how good you perform." (man)

"I do engage in oral-genital sex, but really prefer it as foreplay. I don't like the idea of a guy coming in my mouth—it gags me!" (woman)

"Oral sex is by far the most pleasurable sexual experience I have ever engaged in. It has produced some of the most intense orgasms that I have ever experienced, especially in the 69 position. I also very much enjoy orally stimulating my partner individually as much as being stimulated myself." (woman)

(All examples are from the author's files.)

Sexual relations generally include a great deal of oral stimulation. One of the first sexual behaviors that most people engage in is kissing, which, of course, involves mouth-to-mouth stimulation. This usually progresses from "dry" kissing (lip to lip) to "wet" kissing (also known as "French" or "soul" kissing, involving the tongue) within a short time. It is also normal while having sex for people to kiss and lick other parts of their partner's body (the neck, for example). For many people, this includes their partner's genitals.

FIGURE 11–5 Cunnilingus

Oral stimulation of the penis is called **fellatio** (from the Latin *fellare*, meaning "to suck"), and oral stimulation of the vulva (clitoris, labia, vaginal opening) is called **cunnilingus** (from the Latin words for "vulva" and "licking"). These can be done either as part of foreplay or as the preferred sexual behavior, either by one partner at a time or by both at the same time (the latter is sometimes referred to as "69"). Many women report oral stimulation of the area around the clitoris to be more pleasurable than intercourse (the vaginal walls, you recall, have few nerve endings) and an easier way to achieve orgasm compared to intercourse (Richters et al., 2006). Many men also find fellatio (particularly orgasm during fellatio) to be more intense than intercourse (Janus & Janus, 1993). The pleasure, however, is not always reserved entirely for the recipient. While it is true that

Fellatio ■ Oral stimulation of a man's genitals.
Cunnilingus ■ Oral stimulation of a woman's genitals.

FIGURE 11–6 Fellatio

most people prefer receiving oral sex to giving it (Brewster & Tillman, 2008; Laumann et al., 1994), many others enjoy orally stimulating their partner (and observing their partner's reaction) nearly or equally as much as being stimulated themselves. For many people, giving oral sex represents a moment of extreme intimacy.

How common are these behaviors? Believe it or not, it was very common when your great-grandparents were young (at least among Caucasians). Kinsey's group (1948, 1953) found that about 50% to 60% of the married people they studied had engaged in oral-genital sex. Today, about 70% to 90% of sexually active teens and young adults engage in oral-genital relations (e.g., Gates & Sonenstein, 2000; Kaestle & Halpern, 2007; Herbenick et al., 2010a), and it remains a major component of many peoples' sexual behaviour into their elderly years (Schick et al., 2010). However, there are some notable differences among ethnic groups (see Box 11–A). The appeal of this behavior is positively associated with level of education and negatively associated with how religious one is.

Some individuals consider oral-genital sex disgusting, and no one should feel pressured to engage in a behavior just because a lot of other people do it. On the other hand, if you expect your partner to do it for you, then you should not have a double standard about doing it for him or her. Double standards in sexual relations can lead to serious problems in other aspects of the relationship.

> "My girlfriend refuses to have oral sex with me, but thinks that it is just fine for me to do it to her! Even though I enjoy doing this to her, I don't think it is fair that she would not even try it." (man)

> "My boyfriend and I are compatible emotionally, physically, and intellectually. But there is one flaw that tortures me daily: our oral-genital sex relations to this point have been very one-sided, and I am bewildered. My personal hygiene is wonderful but when I finally got the courage to ask him to give me cunnilingus he was mortified. Yet from the beginning I have not hesitated to give him fellatio when he requests. I felt like his pleasure was my reward. When he refused me I felt insulted and I cried for an hour. I just can't lose the feeling of very deep, very personal humiliation." (woman)

> (All examples are from the author's files.)

Some people may have reservations about engaging in oral-genital sex because of cleanliness. Certainly, people ought to bathe regularly if they expect their partners to give them oral-genital stimulation. Even if a couple has good hygiene habits, however, there may be reservations about the cleanliness of genital secretions. In fact, mouth-genital contact is no less hygienic than mouth-to-mouth contact—the mouth harbors as many germs as the genital orifices. This assumes, of course, that neither person has a sexually transmitted infection, for these can be transmitted during oral-genital stimulation as well as during intercourse. On the other hand, there are no health benefits to swallowing genital secretions (such as curing acne or prolonging youthfulness), as some individuals mistakenly believe.

PERSONAL REFLECTIONS

Try to recall your reactions when someone first told you about French kissing (also called "wet kissing" and "soul kissing"). Was your reaction somewhat negative? Could you really imagine allowing someone else to put his or her tongue in your mouth? How did your attitude change as you began to realize that most people engage in this behavior? Might this same process eventually change your attitude about any of the behaviors discussed in this chapter to which you presently have negative reactions?

ANAL STIMULATION

> "The first time I had ever heard of anal sex was in 1987. A girl I worked with told me that she and her boyfriend had used this. I knew that male homosexuals had intercourse in that manner, but it never once occurred to me that heterosexuals did also!" (woman)

> "Last summer my boyfriend decided he wanted to try some of the different types of things....I will never try sex again in the anus because it was so painful." (woman)

> "I do very much enjoy anal stimulation, if done properly. For me, anal stimulation during oral sex has produced the 'ultimate' orgasm ... if it is done gently and not forcefully." (woman)

> "I like anal sex, probably a lot more than most females. When I first had anal sex, I didn't like it.... The difference is in how fast or slow the guy is in penetrating and also how turned on I am before he goes in." (woman)

> "My boyfriend and I sometimes use a mini-vibrator while making love. While we're in the missionary position, I insert the vibrator through the anus. At the same time, he continues to penetrate. I receive the ultimate feeling in sexual pleasure." (woman)

> (All examples are from the author's files.)

Anal sex refers to a variety of behaviors, including anal intercourse (penis in anus sex), the use of fingers, the use of dildos, fisting, and rimming (oral-anal sex). The anus has numerous nerve endings and is very sensitive to touch. The anal sphincter muscle undergoes rhythmic muscular contractions during orgasm in both men and women, and thus anal stimulation can further enhance the pleasure. Although there is a physical basis for this pleasure, many people feel very negatively about anal sex and consider it abnormal, perverted, or kinky (Janus & Janus, 1993).

Anal intercourse is common among male homosexuals. About 75% of gays in Western cultures have engaged in anal intercourse within the last year (Smith, 2001). But how common is it among heterosexual couples? A review of many studies concluded that the prevalence of anal intercourse has increased dramatically among young people in recent years (McBride & Fortenberry, 2010). For example, the 2010 NSSHB study found a significant increase in this behavior since the Laumann et al. (1994) study of the early 1990s. By this study, 23.7% of men and 39.9% of women aged 20–24 had ever engaged in anal intercourse, and about 40%–45% of people aged 25–50 had done so (Herbenick et al., 2010a). Results of another nationally representative survey indicated that about 22% of 18- to 26-year-olds have tried anal intercourse (Kaestle & Halpern, 2007). Other surveys have found similar results or even higher percentages (Flannery et al., 2003; McBride & Fortenberry et al., 2010).

Among many heterosexuals, anal intercourse is a highly stigmatized behavior, and some people may deny having engaged in it. In one study, many women denied having engaged in anal intercourse at first, but by the third interview 72% said they had tried it at least once (Bolling, 1988; see Voeller, 1991). This was not a nationally representative survey, but the point is that among heterosexuals, anal intercourse may be more common than reported in many surveys.

Interestingly, Laumann's group (1994) reported that only 5% of women found anal intercourse "very" or "somewhat" appealing. When asked why they participate, many women say that it is their least favorite sexual behavior, although they occasionally engage in it for variety or to please their partners. A more recent study found the four most common reasons were "to experience physical pleasure, enhance emotional intimacy, please their male partners, or avoid violence" (Maynard et al., 2009). Women who have engaged in anal intercourse are more likely than others to have begun vaginal intercourse when young and also to have had a greater number of sexual partners—in other words, overall they are more likely to experiment sexually (Flannery et al., 2003).

Why do heterosexual men engage in anal intercourse? Fourteen percent of American men say that anal intercourse is "very" or "somewhat" appealing (Laumann et al., 1994). Some prefer it because it gives them a "tighter" sensation (Halperin, 1998).

However, for others it is an opportunity to display dominance or power (Billy et al., 2009):

> "It (anal sex) is a conquest because women never want to give there.... When you do it there [people say], 'he did her over again,' like a virgin again. I got something that is difficult to get. When friends talk and say, 'I got to do EVERYTHING with that woman,' EVERYTHING doesn't mean normal sex because normal sex isn't everything.... Anal sex is the ultimate, the final barrier."
> (Goldstein, 1994)

For those who engage in this behavior, some words of caution are necessary. First, the anal sphincter muscle contracts in response to attempted penetration, and attempts to force the penis into the anus can result in injury. A water-soluble lubricant (like K-Y Jelly) should be used if you engage in this behavior. The muscle spasms do not relax until 30 to 60 seconds after penetration, so the passive partner often experiences some initial discomfort, even if the male partner proceeds slowly and gently. Even so, this behavior will almost certainly result in rupturing of small capillaries (unlike the vagina, the rectum does not readily accommodate this kind of stimulation) (Agnew, 1986). Anal intercourse itself does not cause AIDS, but the ruptured capillaries maximize the chances of contracting HIV (the virus that causes AIDS) *from an HIV-infected partner*. If you are not in a monogamous relationship, use condoms. It is probably the case, however, that condoms tear more often during anal intercourse than during vaginal intercourse (Silverman & Gross, 1997). In addition, bacteria that are normally found in the 1anus can easily cause infection if introduced into the vagina. Couples who engage in anal stimulation, therefore, should never put anything (finger, penis, objects) into the vagina that has been in contact with the anus unless it has been washed first.

PREFERRED SEXUAL BEHAVIORS

What are the preferred behaviors for most Americans? In their nationally representative study, Laumann and colleagues (1994) found that most Americans aged 18 to 44 were rather traditional. All but 5% of the people in their survey had engaged in vaginal intercourse the last time they had sex. It was by far the most preferred behavior. Among white men and women, receiving oral sex was the second most preferred behavior, followed very closely by watching their partner undress, and giving oral sex was fourth (though twice as many men as women found it "very appealing"). Among African Americans, watching their partner undress was the second most appealing behavior, and receiving oral sex was a distant third. Giving oral sex was a very distant fourth (see Box 11–A). Latino men ranked watching their partner undress as their second most preferred behavior, followed by receiving and giving oral sex. Latina women much preferred receiving oral sex to watching a partner undress. Asian Americans also ranked receiving oral sex higher than watching a partner undress. In terms of it being "very appealing," anal sex was ranked very low by all groups.

Did you notice that watching a partner undress was a "very appealing" behavior among all groups? In fact, overall it ranked second. So, the next time you want to get your partner highly aroused, try undressing a little more slowly and seductively.

PERSONAL REFLECTIONS

What sexual behaviors do you enjoy the most? The least? Why?

THE SEXUALLY HEALTHY PERSON

You have now read about several sexual behaviors that a large number of people engage in. They are normal from a statistical perspective. Does this mean that you should try all these behaviors just because a large number of other people practice them? Do we judge sexual normality by the variety of sexual experiences or number of partners a person has had? No, not at all. Sexual health should not be judged like a decathlon event in the Olympics. Sexual health has been defined in many ways (see Edwards & Coleman, 2004). Here, I define a **sexually healthy person** as someone who (a) feels positively about his or her sexuality (i.e., does not view sex as something naughty, bad, improper, or sinful, and can engage in it without feeling guilty or anxious), and (b) feels free to choose whether he or she wishes to try a variety of sexual behaviors. "Feels free" means free of peer pressure, partner pressure, and social pressure. In today's world of epidemic sexually transmitted infections, sexual health also means freedom from life-threatening infections. Individuals should not engage in sex simply because they are being pressured by peers or a partner. A person can be sexually healthy and still say "no." Always saying "yes" does not prove that one is sexually healthy.

By this definition, someone who has engaged in a wide variety of behaviors with numerous partners, but who gets little fulfillment from his or her sexual relations or who regards sex as dirty, would not be considered sexually healthy. Sometimes we can tell someone's real attitude about sex by how that person regards his or her partner or partners. For example, some people claim to have a positive attitude about sex, but they view their partners as dirty or bad for engaging in sex with them. On the other hand, a person could be sexually inexperienced and still be considered sexually healthy if he or she regarded sex as something good and positive and was choosing not to engage in it for other reasons (e.g., saving sexual relations for someone he or she loved or cared for).

There are many behaviors that a couple can engage in. This chapter covered only the most common ones. (I am reminded of the couple who told Dr. Ruth Westheimer [*Playboy*, 1986] that among their favorite practices was having the woman toss onion rings over her partner's erect penis from various distances.) If a couple view their sexual relationship as something good and satisfying and want to experiment with different techniques, should they or anyone else have any concerns? Most therapists take the view that any behavior between consenting adults done in private that does not cause physical, emotional, or psychological harm to anyone involved is okay.

LAWS AGAINST CONSENSUAL SEX

What do you do behind closed and locked doors in your own home or apartment? You are right, it is none of my business. Is it anyone else's business? Well, you might be surprised to find out that many states have laws prohibiting certain sexual acts, even if done by consenting adults (including married couples) in private.

Seventeen states and the District of Columbia have laws that make *fornication* and/or *cohabitation* a crime. The maximum penalty is generally

---

Sexually healthy person ■ Someone who feels positively about his or her sexuality and who feels free to choose whether or not to try a variety of sexual behaviors.

WAIT...I THINK WE'D BETTER HAVE OUR LAWYER PRESENT.

Reprinted with special permission of King Features Syndicate.

Box 11–C Cross-Cultural Perspectives

Illegal Sex Around the World

In the last part of this chapter you learned that many states prohibit and punish sexual behaviors such as fornication, cohabitation, adultery, and oral or anal sex. However, we are not the only country in which this is true. In fact, most countries make it illegal for consenting adults to engage in some forms of sex. The United States is more restrictive than some countries and more permissive than others. Here is a list of some of the countries around the world and the sexual activities that they consider illegal.

	Fornication	Cohabitation	Adultery	All Anal Sex	All Oral Sex	Homosexual Oral or Anal Sex
Mexico	—	—	✓	—	—	✓
Brazil	—	—	✓	—	—	—
Argentina	—	—	✓	—	—	—
Chile	—	—	✓	—	—	✓
England	—	—	—	—	—	—
France	—	—	—	—	—	—
Germany	—	—	—	—	—	—
Sweden	—	—	—	—	—	—
Italy	—	—	—	—	—	—
Russia	—	—	✓	—	—	—
China	✓	✓	✓	✓	✓	—
Japan	—	—	—	—	—	—
India	—	—	✓	✓	—	✓
Australia	—	—	✓	—	—	✓
Saudi Arabia	✓	✓	✓	✓	✓	—
Iran	✓	✓	✓	✓	✓	—
Egypt	✓	✓	✓	✓	✓	—
Zaire	—	—	—	✓	✓	—
Kenya	—	—	✓	✓	✓	—
South Africa	—	—	✓	✓	✓	—

3 to 6 months in jail and/or a fine. *Adultery*, which is a crime in 24 states and the military, has historically been considered a more serious offense because it violates the sanctity of the family. It is considered to be a very serious crime in many other countries (see Box 11–C).

Are people in the United States ever prosecuted under these laws? Yes; and, in fact, in several states conservatives are attempting to toughen the laws against adultery (Turley, 2010). In states that have laws forbidding adultery, for example, it is not uncommon for one member of a quarreling married couple to press charges against the other to gain an advantage during the settlement, or perhaps just for revenge. Some states have begun prosecuting teenagers for fornication in order to prevent teen pregnancy. Five states (Alabama, Georgia, Mississippi, Tennessee, and Texas) have laws that prohibit the sale of vibrators and other "adult sexual aids."

Sodomy laws ban specific behaviors between consenting adults. At one time, nearly all the states had laws that forbade oral or anal sex, which were often referred to as "crimes against nature" (see Eskridge, 1999). In 2003, 13 states still had sodomy laws. These laws reflected the early Judeo-Christian attitude that the only natural sexual act is heterosexual intercourse because it is the only sexual behavior that can result in reproduction (see Eskridge, 1999, for a history of these laws).

Sodomy laws ■ Laws that prohibit oral and/or anal sex.

In four states (Kansas, Missouri, Oklahoma, and Texas), the sodomy laws were aimed specifically at homosexuals, but in nine others the laws did not distinguish between heterosexual and homosexual couples (Alabama, Florida, Idaho, Louisiana, Mississippi, North Carolina, South Carolina, Utah, and Virginia). The existence of sodomy laws meant, of course, that millions of married American couples were committing crimes for which they could potentially have been put in jail (up to 5 years or more in seven states). In the words of New Orleans lawyer John Rawls, who filed a lawsuit against Louisiana's law, "If oral sex were enforced as a 5-year felony, everyone from the president to the speaker of the house to your next-door neighbor would have to go to prison" (Bell, 1998). However, when the laws were enforced, they were generally enforced only against homosexuals.

Does the U.S. Constitution guarantee us the right to privacy? Let's review the recent legal history on this issue. The U.S. Supreme Court originally upheld sodomy laws in 1986 in a famous case involving a Georgia man who had been arrested for having oral sex with another man in the privacy of his own bedroom (*Bowers v. Hardwick*). However, in 1992, Kentucky's supreme court struck down that state's sodomy law, which was aimed specifically at homosexuals, and courts in Maryland, Tennessee, and Montana later struck down those states' same-sex sodomy laws.

In 1998, two Texas men were arrested when sheriff's deputies, who were responding to a false report of a burglary, caught them having sex in the apartment of one of the men. They were convicted under Texas' sodomy law and their appeals were rejected by the state courts. The U.S. Supreme Court ruled on the case in 2003 (*Lawrence v. Texas*). In a 6 to 3 vote that overturned the Court's 1986 decision, the Supreme Court issued a broad-scoped decision that essentially invalidated all sodomy laws. Speaking for the majority, Justice Anthony Kennedy said that gays and lesbians (and all others) are "entitled to respect for their privacy.... The state cannot demean their existence or control their destiny by making their private sexual conduct a crime.... Adults may choose to enter upon this relationship in the confines of their homes and their own private lives and still retain their dignity as free persons."

PERSONAL REFLECTIONS

Do you believe that a couple should have the right to decide for themselves which sexual behaviors they engage in (assuming, of course, that it is done with mutual consent and does not cause physical or emotional harm to either person)? Or should a state serve as a higher moral authority and regulate the private consensual sexual activities of its citizens?

If you answered "no" to the second question, do you think that you or any other individual should pass judgment on others for their private consensual sexual behaviors?

STUDY GUIDE

KEY TERMS

anal intercourse 291
coitus 284
cunnilingus 289
fellatio 289

masturbation 278
missionary position 284
range of behaviors
   or values 278

sexually healthy
   person 292
sodomy laws 293
statistically normal 278

INTERACTIVE REVIEW

This chapter presents several normal adult sexual behaviors. "Normal" is defined from a statistical point of view, and is best thought of as a (1) _____ of behaviors or values. Thus, you should not regard yourself as abnormal if you have not engaged in all the behaviors discussed here.

Historically, masturbation has been presented as unnatural, immoral, and bad for one's physical and mental health. In his landmark surveys of 1948 and 1953, (2) _____ found that (3) _____% of the men and (4) _____% of the women surveyed had masturbated, thus demonstrating that masturbation is, in fact, a very normal human sexual behavior. Modern medicine has also shown that masturbation has no negative medical consequences. Most men and women masturbate even when they are in sexual relationships.

Compared with those of men, sexual fantasies of women tend to be more (5) _____.
Although at times a fantasy can be very sexually explicit, that does not mean that a person would actually want to do what he or she has fantasized. Fantasies are usually not an indication of sexual un-happiness or personality or psychological disorders.

The most common position for sexual intercourse in the United States is (6) _____-on-top, also called the (7) _____ position. However, there is no "correct" way of having sexual intercourse except what is right for you and your partner. Making your sexual encounters spontaneous, excit-ing, fulfilling, and not ritualized may mean exploring a variety of times, places, and positions.

Oral-genital sex, properly referred to as (8) _____ and (9) _____, is common among many groups in the population. In addition, a considerable number of heterosexual couples have tried anal intercourse on at least one occasion. However, the popularity of these behaviors differs among ethnic groups in the United States. (10) _____ Americans are more likely than other groups to engage in masturbation and oral-genital sex, while (11) _____ are most likely to engage in anal intercourse. Masturbation and oral-genital sex are the least popular among (12) _____.

A healthy and satisfying sexual relationship can contribute to one's overall physical and emotional well-being. (13) _____ individuals consider sex to be a positive and good thing, and feel free to choose when, where, and with whom to engage in a particular sexual activity. Just because many people may be exploring a particular form of expression does not mean it fits into everyone's value system.

Until recently, several states had sodomy laws that prohibited (14) _____ and/or (15) _____ sex between consenting adults. Most people believe that they should have the right to decide for themselves what to do in privacy, and in 2003 the U.S. Supreme Court agreed.

SELF-TEST

A. TRUE OR FALSE

[T] [F]   16. Substantially more men have sexual fantasies than women.

[T] [F]   17. A person can be sexually healthy and choose not to have oral-genital sex, or even sexual intercourse.

[T] [F]   18. Man-on-top is the preferred position of intercourse in all cultures.

[T] [F]   19. Masturbation is normal for men, but not for women.

[T] [F]   20. Assuming that neither person has a sexually transmitted infection, oral-genital sex is no less hygienic than kissing.

[T] [F]   21. Most married people who masturbate do so because they are unhappy in their sexual relationships.

[T] [F]   22. The content of sexual fantasies usually does not indicate sexual unhappiness or personality or psychological problems.

[T] [F]   23. Fantasizing about another person while having sex with your partner is usually an indication of a serious relationship problem.

[T] [F]   24. Surveys have found that most couples have had sexual intercourse in more than one position.

[T] [F]   25. Women's sexual fantasies are just as explicit as men's.

[T] [F]   26. Generally speaking, men have sexual fantasies more often than women.

[T] [F]   27. More people with sexual partners masturbate than people who do not have a sexual partner.

[T] [F]   28. At least 20% to 26% of young adults have attempted anal intercourse.

[T] [F]   29. Until recently, in many states a married couple caught having oral sex in the privacy of their own home could be sent to prison.

B. FILL IN THE BLANKS

30. Couples should not engage in anal and vaginal intercourse without washing in between because of _____.
31. Perhaps the most common type of fantasy during sexual intercourse is _____.
32. The main reason that many people continue to masturbate after forming a sexual relationship is _____.
33. Couples who always have sex in the same place and in the same manner risk letting their sex lives become _____.

34. Laumann and his colleagues (1994) found that the two sexual behaviors most preferred by Americans are _____ and _____.
35. Laumann and his colleagues also found that masturbation is mostly a reflection of _____.
36. The preferred manner of sexual intercourse in all known cultures is _____.
37. _____ is the position of intercourse usually preferred in cultures where a woman's sexual satisfaction is considered to be as important as the man's.
38. A sexually healthy person is someone who (a) _____ and (b) _____.
39. Oral-genital sex is most common among _____ Americans (ethnic group) and _____-educated people.

SUGGESTED READINGS

Comfort, A. (1991). *The new joy of sex*. New York: Crown. A revised edition of a nicely illustrated, well-written sex manual. A best seller since it was first published in 1972.

Friday, N. (1980). *Men in love*. New York: Delacorte Press. All about male sexual fantasies.

Halperin, D. T. (1999). Heterosexual anal intercourse: Prevalence, cultural factors, and HIV infection and other health risks, Part I. *AIDS Patient Care and STDs*, 13, 717–730. A thorough review of results of survey studies about anal intercourse.

Janus, S., & Janus, C. (1993). *The Janus report*. New York: John Wiley & Sons. Results of a nationwide survey of sexual behavior.

Kerner, I. (2004). *She comes first*. New York: HarperCollins. A clinical sexologist tells men how to please a woman.

Kerner, I. (2006). *He comes next*. New York: HarperCollins. A clinical sexologist tells women how to please a man.

Maltz, W., & Boss, S. (1997). *In the garden of desire: The intimate world of women's sexual fantasies*. New York: Broadway Books. All about female sexual fantasies.

Michael, R., et al. (1994). *Sex in America: A definitive survey*. Boston: Little, Brown. A thinner version of the Laumann et al. (1994) study, adapted for the general public. Probably the most scientifically conducted sex survey ever.

Love and Relationships

> ... the apparent paradox that love is both riven with illusions and rooted in reality.
>
> —Garth Fletcher & Patrick Kerr, 2010

Poets write words to rhyme with it. Novelists glorify it in prose. Lyricists praise it in song. Philosophers wonder about its meaning, and politicians all support it.

What is this ubiquitous subject? Why, it is love, of course. Have I exaggerated? Think about it for a moment. How many popular songs that you hear are about love (first love, new love, broken hearts)? In fact, you may have to listen for quite a while before you find one that is not about love. When was the last time that you read a novel that did not include at least one romantic subplot?

Love is obviously an emotion that most humans consider to be extremely important to their lives. But what is *love*? There have probably been as many definitions and thoughts about love as there have been philosophers, behavioral scientists, theologians, and biologists (Reis & Aron, 2008). Freud (1933/1953) believed that love was an emotional feeling that resulted from "aim-inhibited sexual desire." It originates with sexual desire, and when that desire cannot be expressed, the person idealizes the desired one and falls in love. Others have viewed love as a social instinct that satisfies a need for companionship with others. In *The Origins of Love and Hate* (1952), Ian Suttie expressed the belief that "The specific origin of love, in time, was at the moment the infant recognizes the existence of others." In contrast, others have expressed the belief that love results from conditioning (i.e., that it is a learned response). By this account, people come to be desired or loved when others have positive experiences in their presence. Love has also been viewed as a mania (Plato, in *Phaedrus*), a neurosis (Askew, 1965), an addiction (Peele, 1988), a disease (Burton, 1651/1963), and the enshrinement of suffering and death (de Rougement, 1969).

When you have finished studying this chapter, you should be able to:

- Discuss the history of romantic love and the role of sexual desire in romantic love.
- Describe the characteristics that distinguish romantic love from friendship.
- Describe companionate love and its relation to romantic (and passionate) love.
- Discuss the prerequisites for love.
- Explain how attachment styles might affect romantic relationships.
- Discuss Sternberg's triangular theory of love and how different combinations of three components lead to different kinds of liking and loving.
- Describe Lee's different styles of love and his advice on how to find a compatible love relationship.
- Explain what causes jealousy and how best to deal with it.
- Discuss love in other cultures.
- Explain how a couple can maintain a loving relationship and achieve greater intimacy.

297

Christian ideals of love are found in Saint Augustine's definition: "Love means: I want you to be." Viewing love simply as a desire for another person "to be" honors his or her existence. It transcends sexual desire and acknowledges that this emotion can be felt for a lover, a parent, a child, or a friend of the opposite or the same sex. Noted psychoanalyst Erich Fromm echoed similar beliefs about love:

> I want the loved person to grow and unfold for his own sake, and in his own ways, and not for the purpose of serving me. *(Erich Fromm, 1956, pp. 23–24)*

Is this true? As you will soon learn, these definitions may encompass only part (or none at all) of what people mean when they think of love or being "in love."

HISTORY OF ROMANTIC LOVE

A history of love? You probably believe that love has always been a part of the human experience, so why do you need to read about its history? You may be surprised, then, to learn that many scholars believe that romantic love is a relatively recent phenomenon, or that it exists only in Western culture. You will also learn that love is, in part, a social concept whose meaning has changed over time. Let us take a look.

The first thing we must do is identify the nature of romantic love. We do not experience romantic love for a calculated reason (e.g., because the other is a good provider or mate). From culture to culture, and in different time periods, the concept of **romantic love** has one thing in common—*idealization of another*. In the words of anthropologist Charles Lindholm (1998), romantic love is

> experienced as spontaneous, total and boundless in its actual devotion to…the other—to love 'for a reason' is not to love at all. We love because we love, and not because of anything that the beloved other has to offer us beyond themselves. (p. 248)

Lindholm adds, "…falling in love is an act of imagination in which the other is invested with absolute value; the beloved can even be loved for their very faults…. As such, it is…akin to the experience of religious ecstasy" (p. 258).

Early, very influential anthropologists not only dismissed love as a subject for study but even doubted its very existence. Ralph Linton (1936) wrote:

> The hero of the modern American movie is always a romantic lover…. A cynic may suspect that in any ordinary population the percentage of individuals with capacity for romantic love of the Hollywood

type was about as large as that of persons able to throw genuine epileptic fits. However, given a little social encouragement, either one can be adequately imitated without the performer admitting even to himself that the performance is not genuine. (p. 175)

Similarly, anthropologist Robert Lowie (1931) wrote:

> Love exists for the savage as it does for ourselves—in adolescence, in fiction, among the poetically minded. (p. 146)

When anthropologists finally acknowledged the existence of romantic love among ordinary people, many believed that it existed solely in Western culture (e.g., Hsu, 1983; Endelman, 1989). Their argument was that romantic love is unnecessary, and not valued, in primitive clans where there is shared intimacy. As Hunt (1959, p. 10) put it, "… by and large the clanship structure and social life of most primitive societies provide a wholesale intimacy and broad distribution of affection; Western love…is neither possible nor needed." Individuals achieve their identity through the group and close family and religious ties. The same has been said of modern societies that emphasize collectivism over individualism. An example would be China:

> To an American in love, his/her emotions tend to overshadow everything else…. To a Chinese in love, his/her love occupies a place among other considerations. *(Hsu, 1983, p. 50)*

According to these scholars, romantic love, with its idealization of another, was possible only in a fluid society that emphasized individualism (e.g., in modern Western culture). Romantic love was considered to be a way for isolated individuals to achieve identity and meaning in a society that no longer provided meaning through a fixed social structure, religion, or family relations (Beck, 1995).

Several scholars have successfully challenged the belief that romantic love is limited to modern Western culture. There are many accounts of homoerotic romantic love in classical Greece (Evans, 1998). Lindholm (1998) has pointed out that idealization of another occurred among the literate elite in Japan's Tokugawa period (as evidenced in love-suicide plays) and also in the myths and legends of ancient India. In clanships and modern collective societies, marriages are arranged and romantic love is generally prohibited (see Box 12–A). However, even in these societies romantic love is found (see Lindholm, 1998). It is never with one's spouse; it is secret and conducted at great risk, and it is generally not sexual in nature but always involves idealization of another. Lindholm adds that in these cultures "romantic love may offer a way of imagining a different and more fulfilling life" (p. 254). In the most comprehensive cross-cultural study to date, Jankowiak and Fischer (1992) studied 166 cultures

Romantic love ■ The idealization of another; the combination of passion and liking (intimacy).

Box 12–A Cross-Cultural Perspectives

Love and Marriage

Romantic love, the idealization of another, is not something new; there are references to it throughout history. Recall from the section on the history of love that in Western culture love became idealized during the Middle Ages with the rise of courtly love. However, romantic love had never been viewed as a basis for marriage and did not begin to be linked with marriage until the 16th or 17th century (Evans, 1998), and even then it was uncommon. In colonial times, Americans agreed to marry more or less by arrangement, the main purpose of marriage being to have children (Rothman, 1984). Romantic love was not considered a good reason to enter into marriage until the 1800s.

In fact, in a study conducted in the early to mid-1960s, about one third of the U.S. men and three fourths of the women surveyed indicated that being "in love" was not a necessity for marriage (Kephart, 1967). By the middle 1980s, this had changed; all but about 15% of the men and women in one study said that romantic love was a necessary prerequisite for marriage (Simpson et al., 1986). The same is true today (Reis & Aron, 2008). The change in attitude, mostly by women, was attributed to better economic status— financial independence allowed people to make relationship decisions based on romance.

Anthropologists initially believed that the linkage of romantic love and marriage was a peculiar American phenomenon. As Linton (1936) put it, "Our present American culture is practically the only one which has attempted to …make…[emotional attachments]… the basis for marriage" (p. 175).

Anthropologists have found that rules about marriage are, in fact, influenced by economics and politics (Barry & Schlegel, 1984; Hsu, 1981). In industrialized countries, where importance is attached to individuals, monogamy is the standard. In simpler societies, where less importance is given to individuals and more to situations, *polygyny* (allowing a man to have more than one wife) is often the rule. A few societies even allow *polyandry* (woman with more than one husband) (Fisher, 1989; Frayser, 1985). In a study of 862 cultures, 83% permitted polygyny and only 16% were monogamous (Murdock, 1967). In some countries, over 40% of women are in polygynous marriages (Effah, 1999). However, while another study of 853 cultures found that 84% allowed polygyny, only about 10% of the men in those cultures actually had two or more wives (Fisher, 1989).

There are many differences among cultures in the relationship between a husband and a wife. In a great many cultures, marriages are arranged by parents, sometimes at birth. In contrast to the highly romantic beginnings of marriages in the United States, Japanese arranged marriages start off with very little love, but there is no difference in the amount of love within the two types of marriages after 10 years (due largely to the decrease in romantic love over time in American marriages; Blood, 1967). Marriages in India are arranged according to caste, age, and other factors. Many Islamic societies require that a young man marry his father's brother's daughter (first cousin), and husband–wife relations are generally without affection and are often very

hostile (Lindholm & Lindholm, 1980). Pacific Islanders and people in Southeast Asia are often required to marry their mother's brother's daughter. Some cultures require the man to capture a wife from an enemy village (Barnes, 1999), as in the case of the Gusii of Kenya, who rape their wives whenever they wish to have sex (Levine, 1974). Marriage by capture was common in the early Indo-European world (Dumézil, 1979). A man of the Marind Anim of New Guinea must first share his newlywed wife with all the other men of his clan before he is allowed to consummate the marriage (Money & Ehrhardt, 1972).

So, is romantic love as the basis for marriage restricted to Western culture? The answer is no. Lindholm (1998) cites several simple hunting and gathering societies (including the western Apache, !Kung, and the Hottentot) that link marriage with romance. Two other studies have similarly identified many non-Western cultures that rate romantic love highly when choosing a mate (De Munck & Korotayev, 1999; Levine et al., 1995). Do they have anything in common? Romantic love as a basis for marriage is generally found in cultures that do not have strong sanctions against female sexuality and that have a permissive attitude about premarital sex (De Munck & Korotayev, 1999). Love may be found in collective cultures, but as a basis for marriage, it is still found predominantly in individualistic cultures (cultures that place emphasis on individuals rather than the group) (Levine et al., 1995). As the influence of Western culture spreads, this will include more and more cultures in which love as the basis for marriage was once prohibited.

and found evidence of romantic love in 147 of them, including many that had strong rules against it (pp. 153–54). In 18 of the remaining 19 cultures they were unable to conclude whether romantic love existed. Romantic marriages may not be universal, but love is apparently "a very primitive, basic human emotion, as basic as fear, anger, or joy" (anthropologist Helen Fisher, quoted by Gray, 1993a)—one that escapes all the restrictions and barriers imposed by numerous cultures.

FIGURE 12–1 *Psyche and Cupid* by François Gérard conveys many people's idealistic view of romantic love.
Source: Gerard, Francois (1770–1837), "Psyche and Cupid" or "Psyche Receiving Cupid's First Kiss" 1797. Oil on canvas. 186 × 132 cm. INV 4739. Photo: Gérard Blot. Musee du Louvre/RMN Reunion des Musees Nationaux, France. Art Resource, NY.

Let us now focus on Western culture. Romantic love may not be a modern phenomenon, but what has changed in modern times is the way people in Western culture view the nature of romantic love. There are instances in antiquity in which romantic love and sexual desire were linked, such as the homoerotic love in classical Greece (Evans, 1998) or between patrician men and slaves in imperial Rome (Grimal, 1986). However, within the Christian church (perhaps the major influence in early Western culture), love came to be viewed as spiritual and sexuality was deemphasized (Singer, 1984, p. 340).

Romantic love as idealization of another really emerged in medieval times (beginning in the 12th century) when men returning from the Crusades transformed the cult of the Virgin Mary into *courtly love*. Here, courtiers expressed their undying love for a beloved (always a married woman), whom they worshiped from afar as the epitome of virtue (Lindholm, 1998). Sexual relations were never even considered, and this romantic love was not expressed within marriage. It was not until the 16th or 17th century that romantic love began to be

linked with marriage (Evans, 1998). Eventually, in Western culture, the erotic aspects have come to be regarded as equally, if not more, important than the idealization of another (see next section).

There is a relatively new field of science called *sociobiology* that not only claims that romantic love is universal, but also says that it is an evolutionary mechanism that keeps men with their mates so that they can offer the protection and provisions necessary to raise children (Gonzaga et al., 2008). However, this theory ignores the fact that in most cultures the beloved is not one's mate in marriage, nor the mother of the lover's children (see Lindholm, 1998).

We will study love in the remainder of this chapter from a Western perspective. However, keep in mind that in most cultures romantic love does not have the erotic aspects that it now has here, but that the aspect which is common in all cultures (yesterday and today) is idealization of another.

WHAT INITIALLY ATTRACTS US TO SOMEONE?

We touched on this subject in Box 10–A (How Do People Select a Mate?). Did it surprise you to read that men place a high value on physical attractiveness (Buss, 1989; Sangrador & Yela, 2000; Walster et al., 1966)? In fact, they prefer younger women with small waist-to-hip ratios (e.g., Furnham et al., 2006; Singh, 1993) and longer leg-to-body ratios (Swami et al., 2006). Although women may be interested in men who could be good providers (Buss, 1989), for them, too, physical attraction is usually the primary stimulus (see Jayson, 2009). Studies done at speed-dating events reveal that people initially pay much more attention to the physical characteristics of a potential date (Lenton & Francesconi, 2010). Generally speaking, women are attracted to men with angular faces with larger jaws and a muscular build (Jayson, 2009). In a study of online daters, 85% said that they would not contact someone unless they could see a photo of them first (Fiore et al., 2008). People tend to attribute more positive attributes to physically attractive people than to ordinary looking or unattractive people (Marcus & Miller, 2003; Sangrador & Yela, 2000). Interestingly, people also tend to seek out others who they perceive to be at least as equally attractive as themselves (Lee et al., 2008).

What about after one's first impression of another's physical attractiveness? Supportive of evolutionary theory (Box 10–A), female online daters weigh income heavily, whereas men continue to consider physical attractiveness to be most important (Hitsch et al., 2009). Nevertheless, similarity of interests is also very important. There is little evidence to support the old saying that "opposites attract" (Arrindell & Luteijn, 2000; Byrne et al., 1986).

Research with online daters (where users state their preferences) also support this—people look for others who have the same interests as their own (Fiore & Donath, 2004; see Conkle, 2010).

We often consider sight (vision) to be the foremost of the five senses in humans, but could our sense of smell affect how attracted we are to another? Look again at the section in Chapter 3 on pheromones. Recall, for example, the study that found men who smelled T-shirts that had been worn by ovulating women had higher testosterone levels than men who smelled T-shirts worn by nonovulating women (Miller & Maner, 2010). Men rate odors form ovulating women to be very pleasant (Singh & Bronstad, 2001).

Certain hormones may also be involved in attraction. In one study, men who were given oxytocin via a nasal spray were able to recognize sexually themed words better than other men (Unkelbach et al., 2008).

Finally, there is reciprocity—we tend to be attracted to and like people who show that they like us; no one likes rejection (Berscheid & Walster, 1978; Curtis & Miller, 1988). However, in a study of people participating in speed dating, it was found that both men and women are much better at predicting a man's interest in another person than they were at predicting a woman's interest (Place et al., 2009).

All of this may help explain initial attraction, but what determines whether our initial interest in someone leads to love or ends in friendship or just a passing acquaintance?

FRIENDSHIP VERSUS ROMANTIC LOVE

Studies show that the structure of love is very similar for various types of close relationships (Sternberg & Grajek, 1984), yet there are some important differences. Let us first ask what distinguishes love from friendship. Nearly 2,000 years ago, the Roman statesman and philosopher Seneca wrote, "Friendship always benefits; love sometimes injures." Is this true? Are love and friendship qualitatively different feelings, or is love just a more intense form of the emotion felt in friendship?

Studies by Keith Davis (1985) revealed several characteristics that are essential for **friendship:** (1) *enjoyment* of each other's company most of the time (although periods of temporary annoyance or anger may occur); (2) *acceptance of one another* as is; (3) a *mutual trust* that each will act in his or her friend's best interest; (4) a *respect for each other* (an assumption that each will use good judgment in making life choices); (5) *mutual assistance* of one another during times of need; (6) *confiding* in one another; (7) an *understanding* of each other's behavior; and

(8) *spontaneity* (the freedom to be oneself rather than playing a role). Generally speaking, men and women experience friendship in the same way (Bleske & Buss, 2000).

Davis found that people rated their "spouse/lover" and best friend nearly the same for all of these characteristics except for enjoyment, which more people attributed to their relationship with a lover than to the company of their best friend. What about close friends (rather than best friends)? People tended to rate spouses and lovers higher for enjoyment, respect, mutual assistance, and understanding. Still, close friends also generally fared well on these characteristics. Other researchers have also found considerable overlap in the characteristics that people desire for spouses/lovers and friends (Hendrick & Hendrick, 1993; Laner & Russell, 1998).

Are there some characteristics unique to spouses and lovers? Davis found that people generally rated romantic love relationships much higher (compared with friends) in *fascination* (a preoccupation with the other person, even when one should be doing other things), *exclusiveness* (not having the same relationship with another person), *sexual desire* (a desire for physical intimacy), and *giving the utmost* when the other is in need. These feelings can be extremely intense. The loved one is perceived as able (and often solely able) to satisfy needs, fulfill expectations, and provide rewards and pleasure.

Many of the characteristics listed to this point are disposition or personality traits. Recent studies find that most people also prefer higher levels of physical attractiveness and social status (and resources) in a lover or sexual partner than in a friend (Fletcher & Simpson, 2000; Sprecher & Regan, 2002).

Notice again that romantic love includes a high degree of sexual desire (see Regan, 1998). (However, recall from the section on history that sexual desire as a major component of romantic love is relatively new in Western culture.) That brings us to an interesting question: "What is the difference between the word *love* and the expression '*in love*'?" "The word love is bandied about more promiscuously than almost any other word in the English language," according to Murstein (1988, p. 13). The word love "implies an intense degree of pleasure and interest" ("I love this book.") (Levine, 2005). Nevertheless, Meyers and Berscheid (1997) found that a large majority perceives a difference between "love" and "being in love." When they had people place their social relationships into

---

Friendship ■ A relationship that includes (a) enjoyment of each other's company, (b) acceptance of one another, (c) mutual trust, (d) respect for one another, (e) mutual assistance when needed, (f) confiding in one another, (g) understanding, and (h) spontaneity.

categories, they found that people put far many more people in the "love" category than in the "in love" category, and that people placed in the "in love" category (but not the "love" category) were also included within a "sexual attraction/desire" category. Meyers and Berscheid found that almost all of their subjects knew what it meant if someone told them "I love you, but I'm not in love with you." To them, it meant "I like you, I care about you, I think you're a marvelous person with wonderful qualities and so forth, but I don't find you sexually desirable." Their findings agree with Davis' that the major differences between friendship (love) and romantic love (being "in love") are fascination, exclusiveness, and sexual desire (see also Regan, 2000).

Davis and others report that most lovers find that their mood depends more on reciprocation of their feelings in romantic relationships than it does

FIGURE 12–2 Compared with friendship, romantic love rates high in fascination (a preoccupation with the other person), exclusiveness, sexual desire, and giving the utmost when the other is in need. Most people also prefer higher levels of physical attractiveness and social status in a romantic/sexual partner than in a friend.

in friendships. Romantic relationships also rate much higher in ambivalence (mutually existing but conflicting feelings) than friendships. Thus, while romantic relationships are generally more rewarding than friendships, they are also more volatile and frustrating than friendships.

HOW DO I KNOW IF THIS IS REALLY LOVE?

In addition to a preoccupation with the loved person, it has been argued that romantic love involves physiological arousal and the cognitive interpretation of that as being caused by the other person (Berscheid & Walster, 1974). Consider, for example, the following hypothetical scenario:

> Susan was in her first year of college. She had gone out a few times, but too many weekend nights had been spent with girlfriends, and she generally felt lonely and bored. She was surprised when David, a handsome junior who had sat next to her in sociology class, called and asked her to go to a movie Friday night. They had a good time and studied together on Sunday. However, David didn't sit next to her in class on Tuesday, and Susan worried all that day and the next if he would call again. She could hardly contain herself when he called Wednesday evening and asked her to a big party at his fraternity.
>
> Susan and David spent a lot of time together during the next two weeks. She was no longer lonely or bored, and, in fact, her girlfriends let her know that they envied her. On the other hand, when she and David were apart, she worried if and when he would call, and her growing sexual attraction to David was keeping her aroused and agitated.

Is Susan in love? She has feelings of extreme happiness (sometimes elation), periods of anxiety and frustration, and sexual desire, and she finds herself thinking about David when she should be concentrating on other things. David fulfills needs and satisfies desires (sexual, physical, and ego). There is no question that she is better off than before. But is this really love, or just infatuation?

Romantic love almost always includes certain *physiological responses*, such as heavy breathing, a pounding heart and increased blood pressure, sweaty palms, and a dry mouth when we are close to or thinking about the loved one. Researchers have found that feelings of romantic love are associated with an increase in three brain chemicals called dopamine, norepinephrine, and phenylethylamine (the last of which is chemically similar to amphetamines) and a decrease in brain levels of serotonin (Liebowitz, 1983; Fisher et al., 2002). When people who are in romantic love think about their loved one, two areas of the brain that are very rich in dopamine (the ventral tegmental area and caudate nucleus) become very active (Aron et al., 2005). The same is true when people look at photos of lovers, but not with photos of friends (Bartels & Zeki, 2004). It should also be noted that the areas of the brain that become active during feelings of romantic love are different when one is feeling only sexual desire.

Falling in love, with the release of these chemicals, literally gives the person a natural high. (Some people are known to eat large amounts of chocolate, which is high in phenylethylamine, when suffering the heartache of a broken romance.)

The problem is, of course, that almost any kind of excitement or stress will cause a pounding heart and other physiological responses. A *cognitive component* is necessary before one can interpret these responses as a particular type of emotion (Hatfield & Rapson, 1993). To prove this, psychologists Stanley Schacter and Jerome Singer (1962) administered adrenalin, which causes increased heart rate and other signs of physiological arousal, to volunteer subjects who were told it was a vitamin shot. The subjects were then instructed to wait in another room with a fellow subject. This other subject, however, was really working for the researchers, and in half the cases acted very happy and in the other half very angry. The real subjects were experiencing strange physiological responses of arousal due to the adrenalin, but it was the environmental cues that determined how they interpreted them. The subjects with the happy person acted happy, while those with the angry person acted angry. When subjects were warned in advance of the physiological changes they would experience, they were not affected by the phony subject's behavior.

If Susan's friends are having similar experiences and say they are "in love," the chances are good that Susan, too, will interpret her newly aroused state as love. Under other circumstances, she might not.

Will Susan's feelings of love for David last? Initially, Susan certainly loves the way David makes her feel. But as many of you have discovered, that initial high usually does not last, at least not at the peak it first was. Just as with amphetamines, the body builds up resistance to phenylethylamine, so that it takes larger amounts to experience the same high. Some people—call them "love junkies" if you like—go from relationship to relationship, ending each one as the initial high (passion) begins to subside. If love is to last for Susan, she must come to love David for who he is, and not just for what he causes her to experience.

COMPANIONATE LOVE

Today, researchers recognize that there is a real difference between romantic love and what we call companionate love (Reis & Aron, 2008). **Companionate**

love has been defined as "the affection we feel for those with whom our lives are deeply entwined" (Walster & Walster, 1978). It is based on togetherness, trust, sharing, affection, and a concern for the welfare of the other (more so than passion). It is a more stable kind of love than romantic love, for few relationships can sustain the initial level of excitement and sexual passion (see Meyers, 2007).

> **Young love is a flame; very pretty, often very hot and fierce but still only light and flickering. The love of the older and disciplined heart is as coals, deep burning, unquenchable.** *(Henry Ward Beecher)*

Scientists have discovered that companionate love is associated with two neuropeptides, oxytocin and vasopressin (see Fisher et al., 2002). Oxytocin is the hormone released during breast-feeding, labor, and orgasm. In recent years, people have started referring to it as the "cuddle hormone" because it plays an important role in mother–child bonding and adult bonding and the feeling of love (Gonzaga et al., 2006; Lemonick, 2004; Young, 2009). Oxytocin levels rise when couples hug or hold hands, but they also rise when people are in a distressed relationship (Taylor et al., 2010).

We have already seen that most people attach different meanings to the terms *love* and *in love* (Meyers & Berscheid, 1997). Researchers equate the word *love* with companionate love, and the expression *in love* with passionate love (Berscheid & Walster, 1978; Hendrick & Hendrick, 1989). **Passionate love** is defined as "a state of intense longing for union with another.... A state of profound physiological arousal" (Hatfield, 1988, p. 193). In this sense, it is similar to what we have called romantic love (and similar also to what many call infatuation). The two kinds of love are usually described as a dichotomy. However, Meyers and Berscheid (1997) found that people can experience both simultaneously, and propose instead that the more accurate distinction is passionate/companionate love versus companionate love.

Passionate love is more sexualized than companionate love and tends to decline with time (Sprecher & Regan, 1998). Passionate love, however, does not always come first in a relationship, for some people do not consider romance to be their most important goal when establishing a relationship. Some people desire companionship more than anything else. Companionate love very often includes a good, satisfying sexual relationship as well. This is understandable in that a good overall relationship often

Companionate love ■ Love based on togetherness, trust, sharing, and affection rather than passion.

Passionate love ■ "A state of intense longing for union with another...A state of profound physiological arousal" (Hatfield, 1988).

FIGURE 12–3 The ideal of love as a desire for another person "to be" acknowledge that love can be felt for a lover, a parent, a child, or a friend of the opposite or the same sex.

leads to a healthy and good sexual relationship. Many people refer to this type of relationship as *realistic love* because it is not based on the fantasies and ideals of romantic love. The predictability (and avoidance of extreme highs and lows) of companionate love offers security, so that people may enjoy their lives outside of the relationship as well as in.

A drab, mundane form of companionship might be called **attachment** (Berscheid, 1982), where one's partner gives few positive rewards for remaining in the relationship aside from predictability. (A different use of the term "attachment" is given in a later section.) For most people, familiarity is comforting, and this can also be true even when all other aspects of a relationship are poor. Knowing what to expect may cause less anxiety for some than the thought of leaving and venturing into an unknown future. An extreme example of this is the devotion displayed by some battered wives toward abusive husbands on whom they are economically dependent. The fear of having to support themselves on their own may seem worse than the abuse. I will return to the subject of companionate love in the section on maintaining a relationship.

SEX WITHOUT LOVE

Is it possible to have a lifestyle of sex without love and still be happy? In the movie *Annie Hall*, Diane Keaton says to Woody Allen, "Sex without love is an empty experience." Woody responds, "Yes, but as empty experiences go, it's one of the best." Throughout history there have been many famous

---

Attachment ■ Two meanings: (a) a drab, mundane form of companionship where one's partner gives few positive rewards, other than predictability, for remaining in the relationship; (b) the emotional tie between a parent and child, or between two adults.

---

people who were noted for their sexual relations with hundreds, often thousands, of partners (e.g., Cleopatra, Empress Theodora, Catherine the Great, Sarah Bernhardt, King Solomon, King Ibn-Saud).

Recall from Chapter 10 that today about 60% of college students have engaged in *hooking up* (short-term emotionless sexual relationship) and that over 50% have had a *friends with benefits* relationship (sex with a friend without a romantic involvement) (e.g., Bisson & Levine, 2009; Puentes et al., 2008; McGinty et al., 2007; Lambert et al., 2003). However, men are much more likely than women to enjoy sex without emotional involvement. Even within "friends with benefits" relationships, women are much more likely to value friendship, whereas men are much more likely to just want the benefits (McGinty et al., 2007). In a study of people's private wishes (Ehrlichman & Eichenstein, 1992), many more men than women wished "to have sex with anyone I choose."

For most people in our culture, sex without love is a passing stage in relationships. Eventually a large majority of women, and a small majority of men, wish "to deeply love a person who deeply loves me" (Ehrlichman & Eichenstein, 1992). However, this does not mean that a person cannot enjoy a lifestyle of sex without love. Some people may simply prefer their independence to emotional involvement. And remember, the emphasis in the United States of sex within a loving relationship is a culturally learned value. In some other cultures, people put considerably more emphasis on sexual pleasure (and think that Americans' attitude of "love first" is peculiar) and encourage sexual relations with many partners (see Chapter 1).

LOVE WITHOUT SEX

Keith Davis (1985), you recall, included sexual desire as one of the characteristics that distinguished romantic love from friendship. Other researchers agree.

> What is love?...[I end by] confessing that, in the case of romantic love, I don't really know. If forced against a brick wall to face a firing squad who would shoot if not given the correct answer, I would whisper "It's about 90% sexual desire as yet not sated." *(Ellen Berscheid)*

However, you have already learned that in other cultures romantic love may not include sexual desire, and that sexual desire may be a relatively new component of romantic love, even in Western culture. Is it possible for people living in Western culture today to experience romantic love without feeling sexual desire? Most people do not think so (Regan, 1998). However, a recent review of historical and cross-cultural studies concluded that the processes that lead to affectional bonding and sexual desire evolved independently (Diamond,

2003, 2004). The origin of sexual desire, according to this explanation, is its role in sexual mating, whereas the origin of romantic love is the attachment between the infant and caregiver. If this is correct, then "one can fall in love without experiencing sexual desire" (Diamond, 2003). It also means that "individuals can fall in love with partners of either gender, regardless of sexual orientation."

PERSONAL REFLECTIONS

How important to you is loving and being loved? Do you believe that you could enjoy sex without love? Why or why not? Could you enjoy being in a romantic love relationship for an extended period of time if the relationship did not include sex? Why or why not?

Unconditional Love

So far, most of our discussion about love has centered on romantic love, which tends to be **conditional love**, or what Maslow (1968) called *deficiency love* (or D-love). We fall in love with someone and remain in love because he or she satisfies certain needs and fulfills desires, and because it is positively reinforcing to be with him or her. We tend to fall out of love when our expectations and needs are no longer met. Our feelings for the other person depend to some extent, perhaps to a large extent, on how he or she makes us feel and contributes to our happiness.

Distinguished from conditional love is **unconditional love** (what Maslow called *being love* or B-love), in which one's feelings do not depend on the loved one meeting certain expectations and desires (Fromm, 1956). Unconditional love is the type of love that many mothers feel for their children (Fromm believed that love is conditional for most fathers), that many grown-up children continue to feel for their parents, and that many people feel for other individuals of the same or opposite sex. How one feels about his or her romantic partner can also eventually transcend the ability of the partner to satisfy needs and fulfill expectations. This is perhaps most closely approximated by what is called companionate love and which is expressed so well in Saint Augustine's definition of love, "I want you to be."

PREREQUISITES FOR LOVE

Self-Acceptance

> If an individual is able to love productively, he loves himself, too; if he can love only others, he cannot love at all. *(Erich Fromm, 1956, p. 60)*

In order to love another, it is first necessary that one be able to love oneself. The first prerequisite for a loving

Conditional love ■ Feelings of love that depend on the loved one satisfying needs and fulfilling desires.

Unconditional love ■ Feelings of love that do not depend on the loved one meeting certain expectations or desires.

FIGURE 12–4 For a loving relationship to develop, each person must have good self-esteem and there must be an exchange of vulnerabilities.

relationship, therefore, is a *positive self-concept* (good **self-esteem**).

Why is a positive self-concept so important? The comedian Groucho Marx once said, "I don't want to belong to any club that would have me as a member." If you cannot accept and love yourself, it will be impossible for you to accept that someone else might love you. And, like the comedian, people who cannot accept themselves generally reject other people.

People who feel positive about themselves are confident and self-sufficient—they do not require continual external validation. A positive self-concept does not mean that someone is self-centered or believes that he or she is always correct, good, and moral and can do no wrong. To accept oneself is to accept one's shortcomings as well as one's strengths—that is, "to accept myself for what I am" (Coutts, 1973). *The manner in which one is raised is important for acquiring a positive self-concept.*

> "I think the reason I don't like myself is because of all the problems I had in the past...the absence of Mom and Dad, and when they were around so was abuse. I feel that since my parents couldn't accept me, why should I? I felt like a failure, the ugliest person alive, and basically trash. I had tried to kill myself."
>
> (from the author's files)

It is not unusual for children who have been neglected or abused to have negative self-concepts as adults and sometimes to be unable to be loving to others (in fact, abused children often become abusive parents). Having loving, caring parents during infancy and childhood teaches us not only that other people do nice things that make us feel good (and thus, that they are good), but that we are worthy of having someone else care about us. The trust that is gained by this experience generalizes to other people as we grow older (see the section on attachment theory).

PERSONAL REFLECTIONS

Do you have positive self-esteem? Why or why not? If your self-esteem is less than totally positive, what effects do you think this has on your ability to participate in a loving relationship?

Self-Disclosure

Self-acceptance and trust in ourselves give us the potential to trust and love others, but for love to really develop, there must be **self-disclosure** by both parties,

Self-esteem ■ The feeling one has about oneself.

Self-disclosure ■ Revealing one's thoughts, feelings, and emotions to another.

resulting in an exchange of vulnerabilities (Derlega et al., 1993; Rubin et al., 1980). You cannot really love a person whom you do not really know, and, of course, the same is true for other people. They cannot really love you until they get to know the real you. This is what distinguishes love from infatuation.

Letting others get to know the real you is not always easy. In fact, for some people, emotional intimacy may be more difficult than sexual intimacy. We initially try to look and act our best, but for another person to really get to know you requires that you reveal your needs, feelings, emotions, and values. A review of 205 studies of self-disclosure found a gender difference in disclosure—women disclose slightly more than men in relationships (Dindia & Allen, 1992).

All of us need the perceptive ability to avoid placing our trust in those who would abuse it, but for love to develop, we must occasionally take that chance or risk. Relationships develop best when two people self-disclose to one another at about the same time. If Joe reveals some of his true thoughts and feelings to Mary, for example, it is expected that she will reciprocate. Well-timed self-disclosure makes a person more likable (Collins & Miller, 1994; Vittengl & Holt, 2000). Emotional intimacy is achieved only after a couple has shared a reasonable level of self-disclosure (an exchange of vulnerabilities) and each has accepted his or her partner's state of awareness. At this point, they can be said to be interdependent.

THEORIES OF LOVE

Any textbook that includes the topic of love must—as an obligation, I suppose—present some coverage of the theories of love. But which ones? There are as many theories of love as there are definitions, maybe more (Reis & Aron, 2008). Moreover, the theorists cannot even agree on how to organize love. In his preface to a book containing articles by many theorists, Rubin (1988) states:

> **Many of the contributors to this volume have developed their own taxonomies of love. Each categorizing scheme differs from the next, and there are no ready translation rules from one chapter's formulation to another's. Just as partners with different views of love may find themselves talking past each other...I suspect that some of the contributors to this volume may find it difficult to relate to others' perspectives. (p. ix)**

Most theorists touch on only certain aspects of love, and few take the time to support their ideas and conclusions with empirical data. Popular books on love rarely support their claims with any evidence at all. The works of some of the great thinkers (Plato, Aristotle, Kant), on the other hand, treat love as an academic subject and are often lacking in sensitivity.

Experimental social psychologists are the newest group to offer theories of love. As examples of this approach to love, I have selected the works of three pioneers in the field: Cindy Hazen and Phillip Shaver, Robert Sternberg, and John Lee. Other texts may have chosen different theories, but these will give you a good idea of how social psychologists perceive this complex topic we call love.

ATTACHMENT THEORY OF LOVE

At present, it seems fair to conclude that human beings are fundamentally and pervasively motivated by a need to belong, that is, by a strong desire to form and maintain enduring interpersonal attachments.
(Roy Baumesiter & Mark Leary, 1995).

How secure and protected did you feel as a child? How do you think your feelings of security (or insecurity) have affected your adult relationships? Questions like these are at the basis of what is called the *attachment theory of love.* Let us examine it in more detail.

The theory developed from early studies that showed that the strength of the infant-caregiver (parent) attachment bond depends on the amount of security offered to the child (i.e., how accessible and responsive the parents are to the child's needs) (Ainsworth et al., 1978; Bowlby, 1969). In young children, separation from the caregiver often causes anxiety and fear, and the researchers looked at how children reacted to this experience. From these studies, Ainsworth et al. (1978) identified three styles of **attachment**: (1) *secure* (children who learn that parents are a source of security and trust); (2) *anxious-ambivalent* (children whose parents are inconsistent, which eventually leads to uncertainty and a variety of emotional reactions that may include actively seeking to be near the parent, ambivalence, and angry outbursts); and (3) *avoidant* (children develop negative attitudes of others because their parents neglect them or either understimulate them or overstimulate them).

Hazen and Shaver (1987) proposed that these attachment styles could be extended to adult romantic relationships. Not only were the frequencies of the different attachment styles in infancy similar to those found in adults, but adults' experiences in romantic relationships were related to their attachment style. In other words, the type of attachment style that one acquires in childhood (parent-child relations) becomes the attachment style one has within adult relations (Aspelmeier & Kerns, 2003; Collins et al., 2006).

Adults with a *secure* attachment style do not fear abandonment and find it easy to get close to others. They have positive views of themselves and others, are well liked by others, and strive for a balance of closeness and independence. Adults with an *anxious-ambivalent* attachment style generally have negative attitudes about themselves and are insecure in their relationships. They fear rejection and try desperately to get close to their partners, in the process giving up much of their independence. Anxious-ambivalent lovers tend to fall easily in love and are very intense in their emotions, but their efforts often scare their partners away. *Avoidants* have negative views of others and therefore have difficulties with feelings of intimacy and letting someone get close to them. They desire independence. Individuals with a positive view of others regard relationships to be rewarding, whereas individuals with a negative view of others regard relationships as unrewarding or unnecessary. Studies have shown that slightly more than half of all adults can be called secure, while about one fourth are avoidant and one fifth are anxious-ambivalent (Shaver et al., 1988). Insecure men tend to have an avoidant attachment style, whereas insecure women tend to have an anxious–ambivalent style, and according to one evolutionary psychologist, this has adaptive significance (Del Giudice, 2009; see also Ein-Dor et al., 2010).

Researchers later expanded the model to four attachment styles (Bartholomew & Horowitz, 1991): *secure, preoccupied* (similar to anxious-ambivalent), and two variations of the avoidant style. *Dismissives* have negative attitudes about others, but positive attitudes about themselves, whereas *fearful avoidants* have negative attitudes about both themselves and others. These attachment styles remain relatively stable over time, although there is a tendency for people to become more secure and dismissive and less preoccupied as they grow older (Zhang & Labouvie-Vief, 2004).

What is the evidence to support attachment styles as a legitimate model for love? Attachment style is related to the formation of stable relationships, marital adjustment, and positive patterns of interaction (Gallo & Smith, 2001; Mikulincer et al., 2002). Among seriously committed couples, there is a high proportion of secure individuals, while among uncommitted individuals there is a much higher proportion of people with other attachment styles (e.g., Kirkpatrick & Davis, 1994). The most common pairing is a secure-secure matching. This is not surprising, as people have more positive responses to secure people, and prefer them as romantic partners, compared to any other style (Chappell & Davis, 1998; Holmes & Johnson, 2009). When they were not paired with a secure partner, persons with an anxious-avoidant attachment style are most likely to be paired with an avoidant partner. They are also more likely than others to experience unreciprocated love (Aron et al., 1998).

These pairings are consistent with the finding that people with different attachment styles differ in

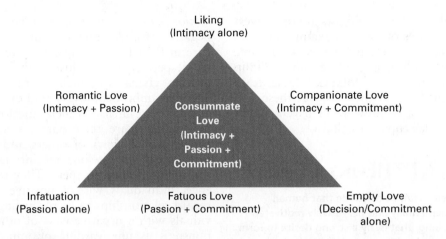

FIGURE 12–5 Sternberg's triangular model of love. All the different positive emotions that people can have for others are understood by the combinations of intimacy, passion, and decision/commitment.
Source: From *The Psychology of Love,* Editor: Michael Sternberg, Editor: Michael Barnes, © 1988. Reprinted by permission of Yale University Press.

their communication styles. People who are secure or preoccupied give more hugs and other physical comfort to their partners, and also show more involvement and positive responses during conversations (Guerrero, 1996; Kunce & Shaver, 1994). Dismissives and fearful avoidants are less fluent and tend to sit farther away from their partners. They are also much less likely to self-disclose to partners during conversation (Mikulincer & Nachshon, 1991). Avoidants are also more likely than others to experience little sexual satisfaction within a relationship (Butzer & Campbell, 2008).

Recently, a large international study of 62 cultural regions found that the secure romantic attachment style was the norm in 79% of the cultures, but that the preoccupied style was very common in East Asian cultures (Schmitt plus 128 authors, 2004). Obviously, there appears to be a most interesting relation between adult attachment style and the nature and quality of romantic relationships.

PERSONAL REFLECTIONS

What type of attachment style do you display in your romantic relations? Do you have negative or positive views of yourself? Of others? How has this affected the nature and quality of your romantic relations?

Intimacy ■ Those feelings in a relationship that promote closeness or bondedness and the experience of warmth.

Passion ■ The drive leading to physical attraction, sexual relations, and romance.

Decision/commitment ■ One of the three basic components in Sternberg's theory of love; the decision that one loves another person and the commitment to maintain the relationship.

ROBERT STERNBERG'S TRIANGULAR THEORY OF LOVE

Although most people rate their spouse or lover higher for some characteristics than they do their friends (Davis, 1985), this still does not tell us whether liking and loving are qualitatively different emotions or different regions along a single continuum of emotions. Robert Sternberg (1986, 1987) has proposed a *triangular theory of love* in which he takes a broader view of liking and loving. He suggests that all the different positive emotions that people can have for other individuals can be understood by the combination of three components. In his model, each component is viewed as the vertex of a triangle, as shown in Figure 12–5. The triangle should not be viewed as a geometric model, but rather as a useful metaphor for visualizing the way in which the three components are related.

The top vertex of the triangle is **intimacy**. Intimacy refers to those feelings in a relationship that promote closeness or bondedness and the experience of warmth. There are many signs of intimacy, including a desire to promote the welfare of the other, experiencing happiness with and having a high regard for the other, receiving and giving emotional support, having mutual understanding, and valuing the other person in your life (Sternberg & Grajek, 1984). The left-hand vertex represents the experience of **passion**, or those drives leading to physical attraction, sexual relations, and romance. The right-hand vertex is **decision/commitment**, which includes the decision to love another person and the commitment to maintain the relationship over time. Studies have verified that people's concepts of love are made up of these three components (Aron & Westbay, 1996).

Sternberg says that the different combinations of these three components result in different kinds of emotions. When all three components are absent, the result is *nonlove*. This characterizes most of our casual relationships, where there is no love or friendship in any meaningful way. If the intimacy component is expressed alone without passion or decision/commitment, it results in *liking*. The word *liking* is not used in a trivial manner to refer to casual acquaintances, but instead refers to the feelings of closeness, bondedness, and warmth in true friendships. When passion is felt in the absence of the other two components, the result is *infatuated love*, or what we call "love at first sight." A person feeling passion alone is obsessed with the other person as an ideal, rather than as the individual he or she is in reality. The decision and commitment to love another person without intimacy or passion is experienced as *empty love*. In our society, empty love often occurs at the end of stagnant long-term relationships, but in other cultures where marriages are arranged, it may be the first stage in a long-term relationship.

If you look at the triangle, you can see that there are four possible combinations of the components. If you add passionate arousal to liking (the intimacy component alone), the result is *romantic love*. It results from two people being drawn together both physically and emotionally. There is no commitment, and the lovers may even know that a permanent relationship is not possible, as in "summer love." This is the Romeo-and-Juliet type of love that poets, playwrights, and novelists are so fond of writing about.

The combination of intimacy and decision/commitment without passion leads to *companionate love*, a long-term committed friendship. Sternberg (1988) believes that most romantic love relationships that survive do so by eventually turning into companionate love relationships. There is a strong association between the secure attachment style, relationship satisfaction (previous section), and the combination of commitment and intimacy (Madey & Rogers, 2009).

When a commitment is made on the basis of passion without the experience of intimacy, the result is *fatuous love*. This leads to whirlwind romances, the type we often read about involving Hollywood stars. Without intimacy, there is a high risk that the relationship will end once the passion starts to fade (these romances are often over so quickly that there has been no chance for the intimacy component to develop).

Sternberg believes that complete love, what he calls *consummate love*, is found only in relationships that include all three components—passion, intimacy, and commitment. It is his belief that this is the type of love that most of us strive for in our romantic relationships. Thus, other types of relationships are viewed as lacking something (i.e., one or more of the three components).

MY IDEA OF LOVE IS NEVER HAVING TO YAMMER ON AND ON ABOUT MY IDEA OF LOVE. YOUR TURN.

© Nick Galifianakis

JOHN LEE'S "MANY COLORS OF LOVE"

The English language gives us only one word—*love*—to describe a number of interpersonal relationships. Words such as *liking*, *affection*, and *infatuation* are not considered to be synonymous with love. As a result, our different experiences of love tend to be measured as differences in quantity: "Tell me *how much* you love me" or "I love you more than I've ever loved anybody." In our search for a partner, we hope to find someone who loves us *as much* as we love them. When relationships do not work out, we often deny any experience of love (e.g., "After a while, I realized I really didn't love Suzy," or "Suzy really didn't love me"). It's as if our experiences of love are measured in black and white and shades of gray.

Sociologist John Lee (1974, 1976, 1988) believes that there is more than one type of partnering love, with none of them being singled out as "true love." Rather than black and white, Lee uses the analogy of colors to explain love. Different styles of love are portrayed by different colors. According to Lee, mutual love results from two styles or colors (not intensities) that make a good match.

Just as different colors result from blending red, yellow, and blue, the three primary pigment colors, Lee proposes that different styles of loving arise from blending three primary love-styles—eros, storge, and ludus. Let us look at each of these and their various combinations and then see what makes a good match.

The Primary Colors

Eros (named after the Greek mythological figure) is a highly idealized love based on physical beauty. According to Lee, every erotic lover has a specific ideal physical type that turns him or her on. Erotic lovers look for physical perfection, knowing it is rare, and when they find someone who embodies their ideal, they quickly feel a strong physical attraction and emotions they perceive as love. It is as if they have always known this person that they have just met—their romantic ideal. Thus, the erotic lover is inclined to feel "love at first sight" and wants to have an intimate relationship immediately. Erotic lovers are very affectionate and openly communicate with their idealized partners. However, they are usually quick to find flaws and shortcomings in their new partners, so that many of their relationships are quick to fizzle out because the partner cannot live up to their unrealistic ideal. Therefore, erotic love is generally very transient, and erotic lovers tend to fall in love very often. Erotic lovers desire to have an exclusive relationship with their partners, but they are not jealous and do not try to possess them.

Lee's eros is quite different from the eros of Plato's *Symposium*, which was totally good and wholesome. Lee's choice of terms here is perhaps unfortunate.

Ludus (from the Latin word for "play" and pronounced "loo'-dus") is a self-centered type of love. The ludic lover avoids commitment and treats love like a game, often viewing the chase as more pleasurable than the prize.

> "I'm a 23 year old male in your MWF Sex Class.... I first had intercourse at age 13.... As of this writing, I have had intercourse with 508 women. I have done it 1,823 times in the last 9½ years. My goal is 2,000 times by [date]. I've devoted a notebook strictly for recording names, dates, and places of sexual encounters.... I can say that I honestly love all women."
> (from the author's files)

Eros ■ A highly idealized type of romantic love that is based mainly on physical beauty. Erotic lovers look for physical perfection.

Ludus ■ A self-centered type of love. Ludic lovers avoid commitment and treat love as a game, often viewing the chase as more pleasurable than the prize.

Storge ■ An affectionate type of love that grows from friendship.

Pragma ■ A rational or practical type of love. Pragmatic lovers actively look for a "good match."

Ludus is similar to Sternberg's fatuous love. Ludic lovers have no romantic ideal and never see any one person often enough to become dependent on him or her, or vice versa. Sex is had for fun, not for expressing commitment, for ludic lovers are not very emotional and do not have feelings of falling in love. They avoid jealous partners who might spoil the fun and see nothing wrong with having more than one partner at the same time. Ludic lovers can be deceptive with their partners, like Don Juan, but many play the game honestly in order to avoid having feelings of guilt (and thus their partners know exactly what they are getting). This promiscuous type of love-style may seem empty to people with other love-styles, but most ludic lovers look back on their relationships with pleasure.

Storge (from the Greek, and pronounced stor'-gay) is an affectionate type of love that develops from friendship slowly over time. It is essentially the same as Sternberg's companionate love. The storgic lover does not have a physical ideal and does not go looking for love, but instead develops feelings of affection and commitment with a partner through experiencing activities that they both enjoy. Storgic lovers generally cannot recall a specific point in time when they fell in love. They are more practical than emotional, and their relationships lack the passionate emotional highs (but also avoid the dramatic downturns). In fact, storgic lovers would be embarrassed by having to say "I love you," or by excessive shows of emotion from their partners. They are more interested in talking about their shared interests than their mutual love. A true storgic lover would probably find this whole chapter very silly.

The Secondary Colors

How many different love-styles are there? You can get numerous colors by blending red, yellow, and blue, and the same is true for mixing the primary love-styles. Look at the color wheel in Figure 12–6. The apexes of the large triangle within the circle represent the three primary colors. Each pair can be combined by going either around the circle or along the edge of the triangle. When you combine two things, new properties may emerge and others may be lost. No one, for example, could have predicted the properties of water by looking at the properties of hydrogen and oxygen. Let us now look at a *few* of the numerous combinations that can result from mixing the primary love-styles (for other love-styles, see Lee, 1988).

Pragma (from the Greek, for "pragmatic") is a rational or practical style of loving resulting from combining ludus and storge. Pragmatic lovers have the manipulative confidence of ludic lovers and consciously look for a compatible mate. They are not looking for an exciting romance or affair, but instead (like the storgic lover) want love to grow out of friendship. However, unlike the storgic lover,

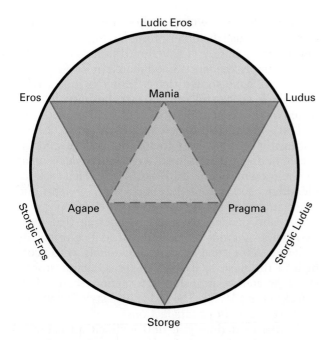

FIGURE 12–6 John Lee's color wheel of love-styles.

Source: From *The Colors of Love,* Revised Edition, by John Alan Lee. Copyright © 1976 by John Alan Lee.

the person with a pragmatic love-style has a shopping list of qualities he or she is looking for in a mate and consciously and carefully sorts candidates to see if they have all the desired qualities. If a suitable mate cannot be found at work or in the community, the pragmatic lover may join organizations (e.g., church, club) or even try computer dating services to find a compatible partner. Pragmatic lovers want their partners to reciprocate signs of thoughtfulness and commitment, but do not like excessive displays of emotion or jealousy. Sexual compatibility is not unimportant, but it is treated more as a technical skill that can be improved upon if need be rather than as the result of chemistry. A person with this love-style views herself or himself as "in love" and tends to remain loyal and faithful as long as the partner continues to be a good match.

Mania (from the Greek, meaning love that hits like a lightning bolt) is a love-style characterized by an intense, obsessive emotional dependency on the attention and affection of one's partner. People with manic love-styles are "in love with love" (the excitement of falling in love). This is "head over heels" love in which one is obsessed with the loved one (i.e., extreme preoccupation and acute longing for exclusivity). Mania is similar to Sternberg's (1987) infatuated love. The manic lover is intensely jealous and repeatedly needs to be assured of being loved. The feelings of mania are so intense that this kind of love can be like an addiction, with the manic lover often not even liking the partner, but at the same time unable to break off the relationship. As a result, manic lovers ride an emotional roller coaster:

extreme highs when the partner is showing them attention, and extreme lows when he or she is not.

This love-style results from mixing eros and ludus. The manic lover wants an intense, physically stimulating relationship, but usually chooses inappropriate partners and madly projects desired qualities onto them. Everyone but the manic lover can see that the partner does not really have those qualities. The manic lover attempts to manipulate the relationship (e.g., by pulling back and not calling the partner), but is too dependent on the partner's love to remain confidently detached like the ludic lover (guess who ends up breaking down and calling first?). Because the manic lover is unable to break off the relationship, it is usually the partner who does so, leaving the manic lover devastated. Although many people have had an experience of manic love, the true manic lover is apt to repeat the same type of relationship again and again.

Agape (from the Greek, and pronounced ah-gah'-pay) is a selfless, altruistic love-style that puts the interest of the loved person ahead of the lover's own interest, even if it means great sacrifice. It is similar to Maslow's (1968) "being love" and Sternberg's empty love. This is the style of loving proposed by Saint Augustine ("Love means: I want you to be") as a goal for all Christians. It is the result of combining eros and storge. Rather than yearning to find the perfect partner, the agapic lover becomes the devoted friend of those who need his or her love. Agapic lovers believe it is their duty to love, but the feelings are often not directed toward a specific person, but instead to all who need their love.

Lee believes that agape is the least common love-style, and he is probably correct. In fact, some have questioned whether humans even have the capacity to feel true agape, which is selfless (see Nygren's *Agape and Eros,* 1982, and Singer's trilogy *The Nature of Love,* 1984–1987). An example that is often given is found in Charles Dickens' novel *A Tale of Two Cities,* a love story that takes place during the French Revolution. The hero, Sidney Carton, is in love with Lucie Manette, who is in love with Charles Darnay. At the end of the story, Charles Darnay is sentenced to die by guillotine. Sidney's love for Lucie is so strong that he takes Darnay's place and is guillotined so that Lucie can be with the man she loves. But Sidney probably would not have done this if he had not felt passionately about her. He certainly would not have done it for anyone else. However, there is no passion or any other type of self-interest in agape. Humans may

Mania ■ A type of love characterized by an intense emotional dependency on the attention and affection of one's lover.

Agape ■ A type of romantic love that puts the interest of the loved person ahead of one's own, even if it means great sacrifice.

not be able to achieve agape, but they can strive to achieve a love-style that approaches it.

Finding a Good Match

Lee's theory has received support from the results of a large-scale study (Hendrick & Hendrick, 1986). Over 1,300 students were asked to agree or disagree with various statements about love. Their responses clustered into six different groups that closely fit the six categories just reviewed. There were some interesting gender and ethnic differences as well. Men tended to be more ludic than women, who tended to be more pragmatic, storgic, and manic (Hendrick & Hendrick, 2003). Asian Americans tended to be more pragmatic and storgic than other ethnic groups.

Did you recognize your love-style from the preceding list? There are tests you can take to determine your love-style preference (Hendrick & Hendrick, 1986, 2003), but Lee (1988) suggests that you just review your own experiences. When doing this, keep in mind that love-styles are not necessarily fixed. We are not born with a particular love-style that we are stuck with for life, but instead we can learn from our experiences and change our preferences. (We cannot learn from our experiences if we look at love as black and white and dismiss failed love as due simply to differences in intensity of feelings.) Thus, you may have experienced more than one of the preceding styles. It is not unusual, for example, for a person's first love-style to be mania, or for a person to experience mania for the first time in midlife after a storgic marriage has become dull and uninteresting (conversely, one may prefer a comfortable storgic relationship after experiencing mania).

Lee believes that the secret to finding mutual love is to find a good match; not in the amount of love each person gives, but in the style of loving. There are some obvious bad matches—a manic lover with a ludic lover, for example. The ludic lover's vanity will enjoy all the attention given by the manic lover, but the possessiveness and jealousy of the manic lover are not desired. Manic lovers thrive on problems, and the ludic lover is guaranteed to provide them. It is not uncommon, however, to find this pairing, and while not very happy and ultimately doomed, a manic-ludic relationship is always interesting.

With the exception of mania and ludus, *a good match generally results from two styles that are close on the chart* (see Figure 12–6). A pragmatic love-style and storgic love-style make a good match, for example. The further apart two love-styles are, the less likely it is that they would make a good match. The erotic or manic lover, for example, is likely to find the storgic love-style dull and regard it as friendship without passion and not love at all. The storgic lover will similarly accuse the behavior of the erotic or manic lover as not being love. A relationship between two people with these two different styles is probably doomed within a short time. In the end, each may accuse the other of not having really loved, but in reality both will have loved in his or her own way. It simply was not a good match in love-styles.

Studies have shown that whether or not a relationship is successful can, in fact, be partially predicted by the compatibility of Lee's love-styles (Davis & Latty-Mann, 1987; Hendrick et al., 1988, 2003). For example, it has been found that college students prefer dating partners who have love-styles similar to their own (Hahn & Blass, 1997; Hendrick & Hendrick, 2003). One exception noted by this and other studies is the attraction between people with mania and agape love-styles, suggesting that these two types may not be as different as Lee originally believed. As a general rule, individuals who score high in the positive love-styles (eros, agape, storge) show greater relationship satisfaction than others (Meeks et al., 1998). The ludus love-style is a strong negative predictor of satisfaction.

So the next time you find yourself attracted to someone, do not ask yourself how much this person loves you, but instead ask yourself how (in what style of love) he or she loves you and whether your colors make a good match. Lee (1988) warns us, however, not to define mutual love in terms of longevity. Two people may have a mutually satisfying relationship, but just because it ends because one of them has a change in love-style does not mean it was not wonderful while it lasted.

PERSONAL REFLECTIONS

How do you define love? Which of Lee's love-styles best describes you in your present or last relationship? Do you think that you are locked into this love-style for future relationships? Why or why not?

WHICH THEORY IS CORRECT?

At this point you may be very confused. Of the theories of love you have read about in this chapter, some have characterized love as a single dimension (Freud, 1933/1953; Tennov, 1979). Others have viewed love as resulting from two or more factors—Maslow's (1968) D-love and B-love; Hatfield's (1988) and Walster and Walster's (1978) passionate and companionate love; Sternberg's (1987) triangular theory. All of these focus on the structure of love. Still others focus on the processes of love—Lee's (1974, 1976, 1988) colors of love; Hazen and Shaver's (1987) attachment styles. Is any one of them correct? If so, does that mean the others are wrong?

Barnes and Sternberg (1997) proposed a *hierarchical model* to explain the structure of love, and say that the other theories appear to differ because they are looking at different levels of the hierarchy. At the top of the hierarchy is a single entity we call love. Underlying this are several related entities (the second level), which in turn are made up of even smaller entities (the third level). These entities can be broken down into even smaller features.

In a series of studies, Barnes and Sternberg identified eight clusters of features (the third level) that contribute to our feeling of love. The individual clusters were different, depending on how they collected the data, but included things such as sexuality, trust, sincerity, compatibility, fulfillment, mutual need, and intimacy. When they looked at how these clusters were related, two main clusters (the second level) emerged—a "hot" cluster, which some have called passionate love, and a "warm" cluster, which has been called companionate love. Eros and agape would also be a good comparison, as would Sternberg's passion and intimacy components in his triangular theory. Together, these two main clusters, in turn, form what we call love.

In summary, Barnes and Sternberg find evidence that the many structural theories only appear to be different because they are looking at different levels of the features that make up what we call love. On the other hand, perhaps we spend too much time analyzing what love is and why people love:

> There are, to be sure, reasons for love, but there is good reason for us philosophers to abstain from overanalyzing them and rendering overly rational an emotion whose charm consists at least in part in the illusion that it cannot be explained by reasons.
> *(Robert Solomon, 2002)*

JEALOUSY

Shakespeare, in *Othello*, described it as "the green-eyed monster which doth mock the meat it feeds on." He was referring, of course, to the emotion we call jealousy. How would you feel if your partner appeared to be forming an emotional attachment to a coworker and has been spending a great deal of time with him or her? How would you feel if your partner and another person appeared to be sexually interested in one another? These are situations that typically cause many people to feel jealous. **Jealousy** is an emotional state "that is aroused by a perceived threat to a valued relationship or position and motivates behavior aimed at countering the threat" (Daly et al., 1982; see Knox et al., 2007). The perceived threat can involve more than the actual loss of a partner; it can also include loss of face, loss of self-esteem, and loss of feeling special (Cano & O'Leary, 1997). There are both cognitive and emotional components to jealousy. As an emotion, it is hard to describe, but it usually involves anger, humiliation, fear, depression, and a sense of helplessness (Guerrero & Anderson, 1998).

At least 50% of people tend to be jealous (Pines & Aronson, 1983), but in only about 1% is it delusional or pathological (see Cano & O'Leary, 1997). Thus, some researchers look at jealousy as a dispositional (personality) variable. Some people become jealous if their partner has even casual interactions with other persons. What type of person is most likely to become jealous? Research has shown that people with low self-esteem who are personally unhappy with their lives (Knox et al., 2007; Pines & Aronson, 1983) and those who place great value on things like popularity, wealth, fame, and physical attractiveness are more likely than others to be jealous individuals (Salovey & Rodin, 1985).

However, cultural and situational factors also play a major role (Cano & O'Leary, 1997). Jealousy is most likely to occur in cultures that consider marriage as a means for guilt-free sex, security, and social recognition (Hupka, 1981). Distress to a partner's imagined sexual infidelity is also greater in cultures that have a permissive attitude about unmarried sexual relations. For example, American men and women show much more distress to a partner's imagined sexual infidelity than do Chinese men and women (Geary et al., 1995).

I SAW YOU TALKING TO <u>HER</u> AGAIN.

© Nick Galifianakis

Jealousy ■ An emotional state that is aroused by a perceived threat to a valued relationship or position.

Research shows that just as many women as men have feelings of jealousy (Bringle & Buunk, 1985). However, there are important gender differences. Considerable research has shown that men are much more likely to become jealous to the perception of a partner's sexual infidelity, whereas women are much more likely to experience jealousy as a result of a partner's emotional infidelity (e.g., Buss et al., 1992, 1996; Cann et al., 2001; Pietrzak et al., 2002; Sagarin et al., 2003; Schützwohl, 2008). This holds for Internet infidelity as well (Groothof et al., 2009). If this is true, South Carolina Governor Mark Sanford hurt his wife even more when he tried to justify his extramarital affair by referring to his mistress as his "soul mate" (Herbert, 2010).

Evolutionary psychologists argue that this difference between men and women is innate, resulting from men's need for certainty about paternity (after the energy spent in courting and mating, he wants to know that he is the father) and women's need for male investment in the children (Buss et al., 1992, 1996). Others question the evolutionary explanation and point out that the two types of infidelity, sexual and emotional, are not independent (DeSteno & Salovey, 1996; Harris, 2003). Men, for example, may be likely to think that if a partner is emotionally involved, she is also having sex. The differences in results might be explained by differences in attachment style (Levy & Kelly, 2010). People who are more jealous of sexual infidelity than emotional infidelity tend to have a dismissing avoidant attachment style, whereas people with secure attachment styles, including men, tend to be more jealous of emotional infidelity.

Men's and women's reactions to jealousy also tend to differ (Aylor & Dainton, 2001; White, 1981). Men are more likely to experience cognitive jealousy, whereas women are more likely to engage in communicative expression of their feelings. In addition, women tend to experience jealousy when feeling inadequate, and they tend to respond by making themselves more attractive to their partner. Men, on the other hand, tend to initially experience jealous feelings and then have feelings of inadequacy, and they tend to seek solace in outside relationships.

Paradoxically, while jealousy is an emotional reaction to a perceived threat to a relationship and self-esteem, the expression of jealousy is likely to further damage both (Cano & O'Leary, 1997). Withdrawing from or attacking one's partner, for example, may cause him or her to withdraw or attack, thus increasing the fear of loss, which, in turn, may increase or prolong the feeling of jealousy.

How, then, should you deal with occasional bouts of jealousy? Acknowledge your feelings to your partner and describe what caused them

(Anderson et al., 1995). If you choose to go to counseling (probably a good idea), go together—seek therapy as a couple (Cano & O'Leary, 1997). Conversely, never purposely try to make your partner jealous, as a few people do in order to get attention (Sheets et al., 1997; White, 1980). Establish mutual trust, while at the same time respecting your partner's need for some personal freedom. If you can do this, your chances are good of keeping that green-eyed monster at bay.

PERSONAL REFLECTIONS

Do you ever have feelings of jealousy? Are they so strong that they interfere with your relationship(s)? What are the conditions that usually cause you to become jealous? Does your partner ever try to make you jealous? What things might you do to control these feelings?

MAINTAINING A RELATIONSHIP

There is hardly any activity, any enterprise, which is started with such tremendous hopes and expectations and yet which fails so regularly as love. *(Erich Fromm, 1956)*

Let us return for a moment to our hypothetical example of Susan and David (see section entitled "How Do I Know if This Is Really Love?"). All four factors have played a role in encouraging these two people to begin a relationship. Susan—and David, let's suppose—have experienced physiological arousal in each other's presence and have interpreted their responses as "being in love." The relationship continues to develop if there is mutual self-disclosure, equity in what each wishes to gain from (and give to) the relationship, and finally, commitment. But will it last?

Relationships tend to last when partners idealize one another (Murray et al., 1996). Other studies show that personality characteristics are also important in determining whether or not a relationship lasts. People who are similar are not only attracted to one another, they are also more likely to stay together (Weber, 1998). However, even when a couple is well matched, they are going to have to learn to deal with change.

The divorce rate is so high not because people make foolish choices, but because they are drawn together for reasons that matter less as time goes on. *(Robert Sternberg, 1985)*

If there is anything that is unavoidable in life, it is change. Couples will be faced with a variety of new challenges in life, including parenthood, financial crises, career-related stress, and, inevitably, aging. Two people who believe themselves to be in complete harmony during the dating, passion, and romantic loving periods are often surprised to find themselves in disagreement on how to handle these matters. Many couples, for example, report the child-rearing years to be the most stressful and least satisfying in their marriages (Ahlborg et al., 2008; Hendrick & Hendrick, 1983). Fixed gender roles—or, conversely, changing gender roles—may contribute to this (see Chapter 8). Today, there are the added challenges of two-job families and job-related moves far away from family and friends.

The Decline of Passion

The challenges in life are not the only things that change. People also change over time. One of the things that normally occur in a relationship, leading to changes in how we interact with our partners, is **habituation**. Think of your favorite food. What makes it your favorite food? The taste and smell are no doubt important, but I am willing to bet that another factor is that you do not have it very often. If you were served your favorite food every day for a month, do you think it would remain your favorite? Would we look forward to Thanksgiving turkey if we ate turkey every week? It's doubtful. When organisms, including humans, are repeatedly exposed to a stimulus that is initially very positive, it becomes less positive over time. This is why popular weekly TV shows eventually go off the air and why hit songs eventually drop off the *Billboard* "Top 10" list. We grow tired of seeing and hearing them. The same is true of the ability of other people to stimulate us—socially, emotionally, intellectually, and alas, sexually. Of all the challenges that a couple face in a relationship, habituation is certainly one of the greatest ones (Byrne & Murnen, 1988).

The decline of passion is almost inevitable, for a large component of passion is novelty and fantasy. A new partner cannot continue to arouse strong emotions, and with the passage of time it takes greater and greater stimulation to cause the same response that once was brought about by a mere glance or touch. As the passion subsides and fantasy is replaced with reality, the result is often disappointment. In a study of 62 cultures, Fisher (1992) found that the divorce rate peaked around the fourth year of marriage (7 years if a couple has another child 2 or 3 years after the first). The reason most frequently given by couples in the process of divorce is that they had "fallen out of (romantic) love" and were bored (see Roberts, 1992).

Although passion will decline with time due to familiarity and habituation, there is no need for *intimacy* (those feelings and experiences that promote closeness and bondedness) to decline. The key to maintaining a relationship is replacing passion with those things that lead to companionate love. Some of the successful strategies couples use to maintain relationships include attending to one's partner (e.g., thinking about their partners, shared

activities), openness, a positive attitude, assuring one another, and working to establish a social network (Canary & Stafford, 1994). It is really important that each person acknowledge the other's positive experiences (Gable et al., 2006). Let us now use Susan and David as an example.

Growing Together/Growing Apart: Will Companionate Love Develop?

Intimate relationships frequently start on very positive notes but decline thereafter and yet relationships…are so important to our well being. *(Daniel Perlman, 2002)*

To maintain their relationship, Susan and David must simultaneously deal with the need for similarity in the relationship, the inevitable changes that occur (e.g., they will not always be in school together), and the natural process of habituation. Similarity, so important in establishing their relationship, can be maintained and habituation can be kept to a minimum by embarking on new activities together (Byrne & Murnen, 1988). For example, they may find it stimulating to engage in new sports and games together, share new hobbies, *try new sexual experiences together* (see Chapter 11), join dinner groups, and/or plan vacations together. One of the major predictors of marital success is the number of shared pleasurable activities (Ogden & Bradburn, 1968).

Couples in happy, long-lasting relationships frequently say that they regard their partner as their best friend. As stated by Schwartz (1994, p. 28), "The possibility of achieving a deep friendship with a spouse represents the most exciting goal of marriage." Couples who are unhappy in their relationships often report that their children are their only or their greatest source of satisfaction together (Luckey & Bain, 1970). Whether Susan and David develop intimacy and companionate love will depend, of course, on their commitment (the third component necessary in Sternberg's model for consummate love). Couples who successfully accomplish this grow together; those who do not grow apart.

Married lovers grow within love; they develop into better human beings. *(Erich Fromm, 1965)*

What is meant by growing together or growing apart? I will try to demonstrate this with the use of intersecting circles (Levinger, 1988). Each person in the relationship is represented by a circle; the degree of intimacy shared is shown by the amount of overlap. The amount of passion felt by one person for the other is represented by plus (+) signs within the circle at the periphery of the intersection.

Look now at Figure 12–7. At the beginning of Susan and David's relationship (two circles at top),

Habituation ■ Responding less positively to a stimulus with repeated exposure to it.

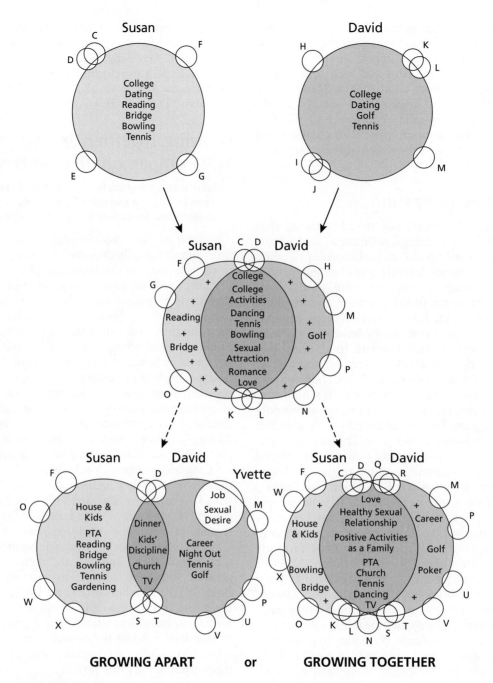

FIGURE 12–7 An example of growing apart or growing together.

both are going to college. Their interests are shown within the circles, and each has a different set of friends: C, D, E, F, and G for Susan, and H, I, J, K, L, and M for David. Susan and David met and began to date, you recall, while taking the same course. Because they have a great deal in common, they have a lot to talk about when they are together: their college courses; their good, bad, and peculiar professors; their campus activities and sporting events; and, of course, their career goals. Let us suppose that they both play tennis and that dancing is their favorite activity on dates. David even goes bowling with Susan, although he does not like it much. Over time they establish a

mutual set of friends, including other couples (C-D and K-L) and singles (N). They each still have their own sets of friends as well (each has lost contact with some, retained some, and gained some new ones, and each enjoys some activities not shared by the other—bridge and reading for Susan and golf for David). There is a great deal of passion felt by both Susan and David, and before long they tell one another that they are in love (decision). Dating is now more than just a good time, for there is a romantic component to being together. They realize that they share a great deal of each other's lives (i.e., there is a strong intimacy component, as shown by the amount of overlap in the circles in the middle), and neither can imagine life without the other. They make the commitment to have a lifelong relationship.

Let us now jump several years ahead and see what has happened to our imaginary couple. They no longer have the opportunity to spend most of the day together, for college is now just a distant memory. Instead, one of them is pursuing a career and spends 8 to 10 hours a day in an office (in today's world, it could be either Susan or David, but let us assume here that it is David), while the other is a full-time house-and-child caretaker. Yes, our imaginary couple now have children, and they only see each other briefly in the morning, in the evening before they go to sleep, and on the weekends (assuming that our career person does not work weekends as well). How they adjust to this big change will determine whether the relationship remains positive or turns negative.

Unfortunately, many couples **grow apart** over time. Let us assume, for example, that Susan now goes to bowling league, plays bridge and tennis with friends, and enjoys reading and gardening, all without David. David, on the other hand, plays golf and tennis with friends and enjoys an occasional night out with friends, all without Susan. They rarely go dancing anymore, and most of their time together is spent watching TV (with a minimal amount of conversation). Susan and David have children, but they do very little together as a family. David considers it Susan's duty to go to the PTA and drive the children to and from all their activities, even when he is home. Susan and David and their children eat dinner together (quickly) and go to church together, but most of Susan and David's conversations about their children involve school and discipline problems. Raising their children is treated more as a responsibility than as a blessing. Although Susan and David live together and have children, they actually share less now than when they were dating (e.g., there is less intimacy, indicated by less overlap in the circles at the lower left in Figure 12–7). There is no passion left, and very little affection (e.g., hugging, kissing, holding hands) is ever displayed between them. They have grown apart. This is not uncommon.

> "I am married, yet feel as if I do not have a husband. He goes hunting every weekend during hunting season, and goes fishing a lot too. Between his softball league and poker games at the club, most weeknights are taken as well. Most of my time is taken up by the kids' activities and what social life I have is spent with other wives. Most of the time I am too tired to make love when my husband is in the mood, which is not very often. A friend recently described our marriage as 'married singles.'"
> (from the author's files)

People generally grow apart very slowly, and by the time they realize it, they may have little left in common. At this point, some people may think that

"*When I fell in love with you, suddenly your eyes didn't seem close together. Now they seem close together again.*"

it is easier to form a new relationship than to work at their present one. For example, let us suppose that David spends a great deal of time with Yvette while at work (see Figure 12–7). They are together all day at least 5 days a week. They talk about the boss, fellow workers, job-related problems, and career goals. They even start telling each other about their personal problems at home. Add sexual attraction and feelings of passion, and David may conclude that he has as much in common with Yvette as he once had with Susan when they were in college together. David may decide to have an affair with Yvette, or leave Susan for Yvette. Unless David learns to work at keeping a relationship strong, however, this will just be a short-term solution, for over time David's passionate feelings for Yvette will subside as well and they, too, will grow apart.

Let us now look at another possible outcome for David and Susan. People change over time, but a couple who **grow together** substitute new common interests as old ones drop out (see Figure 12–7). In place of college, which once gave them both a great deal to talk about together, our couple view their children and family activities as something very positive. They go to movies as a family, have picnics together, go to the zoo together, and both are involved in Little League, the swimming team, the Boy Scouts and Girl Scouts, the PTA, and church and church social activities. Because they view their children's activities as positive experiences, our two adults have a great deal to talk about. They have substituted new shared

Growing apart ■ Having fewer common interests over time.
Growing together ■ Maintaining common interests over time.

activities for some of the ones they used to do together. They still find time (or *make time*) to play tennis on the weekends and go to movies, and they still enjoy dancing together as they did when they were dating. They also have a large number of mutual friends. It is not necessary for Susan and David to do everything together in order to be happy. In addition to being apart during weekdays, David still plays golf regularly and enjoys an occasional evening of poker with friends, while Susan has joined a bowling league (David refuses to bowl anymore) and plays bridge with friends. They are different from the way they were when they were dating, but the amount of shared interests is just as great as then. Their feelings of passion for one another have declined, of course (hearts don't beat faster, breathing doesn't get heavier, and palms don't sweat when they see each other), but their sexual interest in one another remains strong. They enjoy each other's bodies and seek variety in the way they stimulate one another. There has been no decline in intimacy. They have grown together.

PERSONAL REFLECTIONS

For those presently in a long-lasting relationship: Have the activities you share with your partner changed since you first began dating? Have new shared activities replaced old ones? Are you growing together or growing apart? If you feel that you are growing apart, what can you do to change this?

Coping with Breakups

Undo it, take it back, make every day the previous one until I am returned to the day before the one that made you gone. *(Rapoport, 1994, p. 24)*

We do not enter into a romantic relationship with expectations that it will end. Thus, breaking up is one of life's most painful experiences, but something that most of us have experienced. Many things commonly occur during the breakup process. Let us examine three of them (Weber, 1998; Weiss, 1975).

One thing that almost everyone engages in during a breakup is *obsessive review*, a "constant, absorbing, sometimes maddening preoccupation [of the other and the situation] that refuses to accept any conclusion" (Weiss, 1975, p. 79). We review, again and again, the relationship and the breakup, searching for reasons. "Why?" "What did I do that caused this?" This process can detract from all other endeavors, but can be useful if it helps prevent breakups in future relationships.

Breaking up almost always includes *emotional and social loneliness* as well. Emotionally, you feel isolated, missing your ex-partner and everything that he or she brought to your life. But you can also end up socially isolated as well. Friends you had in common with your ex-partner may have to pick sides, or, because they feel awkward, may avoid both of you. You may be left wondering who your friends are and where you fit in.

The third, common experience that people often have to deal with is that their *ex-partner is still*

FIGURE 12–8 Companionate love is a stable kind of love based on togetherness, trust, sharing, affection, and a concern for the welfare of the other.

around. If you are the one who was left, he or she is a constant reminder of the rejection (and possibly a reminder to others that you are rejectable). On the other hand, if you are the one who broke off the relationship, your ex may be telling everyone of how much you are to blame. Part of the process, then, is trying to "save face" (Weber, 1998).

To make matters worse, breaking up is usually a process, not limited to a clean break at a single point in time. When it is finally over, we want to believe that our ex-partner once felt as we did (do), that we will be remembered.

Psychologist Ann Weber (1998) has offered several suggestions to help the brokenhearted deal with their loss: (1) express your emotions (sorrow, anger) to someone who is a sympathetic listener, or write down your thoughts; (2) try to figure out what happened, and again, it may help to write it down; (3) do not idealize your ex, but instead focus on the real person, including his or her faults and shortcomings; (4) prepare to feel better (e.g., find what is funny or ironic in your experience) and expect to heal (think back on other physical or emotional injuries in your life and realize that you have always healed); (5) do not shut yourself off from others and let them know what you need from them at this time; and (6) take the perspective that your life is about to change and look at it as a new start. Do something new that you have always wanted to try—traveling, writing, entertainment, anything!

> **And so, we take our lessons to heart. We take this heart, this new heart and self, full of hope, humor, and irony, and we face the world—a new world with uncharted possibilities and dangers. Perhaps we try once again, explore a new love, although it will not be the same. Then again, the pain reminds us we do not want it to be exactly the same. We have some memories and fantasies to cherish, some sense of hard-won meaning, the moral of the story. Together these help to forge a sense of promise. Thus, silly to risk it, but crazy not to, we try again, and we take heart.** *(Weber, 1998, p. 304)*

Becoming More Intimate

For most couples, the passion component is generally greatest early in a relationship and then declines over time. Therefore, one of the most important things in maintaining a relationship is developing and maintaining intimacy. Sternberg (1986, 1988) defined intimacy as those feelings in a relationship that promote closeness or bondedness and the experience of warmth. Similarly, Elaine Hatfield (1984) defines it as "a process in which people attempt to get close to another; to explore similarities (and differences) in the way they think, feel, and behave."

True intimacy requires mutual understanding. It is easy to share our similarities and positive feelings, but what about our differences and negative feelings? In order to become really intimate with someone, you must share your differences as well. Hatfield (1988) has made several suggestions designed to teach couples to become more intimate. Let us briefly examine these.

1. Both individuals in a relationship need to *accept themselves as they are*. I have discussed this earlier in the chapter, but the need for self-acceptance bears repeating. *Your* best may not be *the* best, but it is all that anyone, including yourself, can ask of you. Learn to accept your ideas and feelings as legitimate.

2. Each individual in a relationship needs to *recognize his or her partner for what that person is*. As hard as we may be on ourselves, we are often harder on our partners because they are not everything we would want them to be, and we cannot understand why they will not change. Intimacy is not possible with an imaginary "perfect" partner. It can only occur when one recognizes one's mate for what he or she really is—weaknesses as well as strengths.

3. Each individual must *feel comfortable to express himself or herself*. People are often hesitant to express any doubts, irritation, or anger to their partners in a loving relationship. To do so requires that an individual be capable of independence, for independence and intimacy go hand in hand (Hatfield, 1988). An individual who is totally dependent on his or her mate is unlikely to express any anxieties or fears. It is important that we express positive feelings for our partners, for the ratio of positive to negative interactions is a key factor in maintaining a happy relationship (Byrne & Murnen, 1988; Gottman, 1993, 1994). However, we must also be able to express our anxieties, fears, and anger to our partners. If we cannot, then we are not really intimate.

PERSONAL REFLECTIONS

Do you reveal your true needs, feelings, emotions, and values to your partner? Why or why not? Do you think that your partner reveals his or her true needs, feelings, emotions, and values to you? Why or why not? Do you deal with your partner's reactions when he or she does not like you to express your true feelings, or do you back down and/or apologize? Why or why not?

4. Learn to *deal with your partner's reactions*. If you express your feelings to your partner, he or she may not like what you say. Your partner may become angry or feel very hurt, but you must learn not to automatically back down or apologize for expressing feelings.

Instead, keep calm and keep reminding yourself that your feelings are legitimate and that you are entitled to express them. In other words, keep trying. Only when both of you can express your own feelings and allow the other to do the same is there a chance for real intimacy.

The more intimate two people become, the greater the chance that the relationship will be maintained.

> **Love is an active power in man; a power which breaks through the walls which separate man from his fellow men.... In love the paradox occurs that two beings become one yet remain two.** *(Erich Fromm, 1956)*

STUDY GUIDE

KEY TERMS

agape 311
anxious-ambivalent 307
attachment 304
attachment theory of love 307
avoidant 307
companionate love 303
conditional love 305
consummate love 309
courtly love 300
decision/commitment 308
empty love 309
eros 310
fatuous love 309

friendship 301
growing apart 317
growing together 317
habituation 315
hierarchical model 312
infatuated love 309
"in love" 301
intimacy 308
jealousy 313
liking 309
love 297
ludus 310
mania 311

nonlove 309
passion 308
passionate love 303
polygyny 299
pragma 310
romantic love 298
secure 307
self-disclosure 306
self-esteem (self-acceptance) 306
storge 310
triangular theory of
  love 308
unconditional love 305

INTERACTIVE REVIEW

There have probably been as many definitions and descriptions of love as there have been poets, philosophers, and scientists who study love. For many years, anthropologists believed that romantic love, the (1) _____ of another, was a recent phenomenon and existed only in Western culture. However, evidence of romantic love has been found in nearly all cultures, although it is rarely accepted as a good reason for (2) _____. What is relatively new in Western culture is that our concept of romantic love includes the element of (3) _____.

Recent work has shown that although friendship and romantic love share many characteristics, romantic lovers differ from friends in terms of their (4) _____, (5) _____, (6) _____, and willingness to give the utmost when the other is in need. The feeling of romantic love initially includes physiological arousal, but a (7) _____ is required to interpret the responses as love. Feelings of passion almost always decrease with time, and long-term happy relationships are based more on together-

ness, trust, sharing, and affection, or what is called (8) _____ love.

The ability to love another person requires (9) _____ and (10) _____. Love can be (11) _____ and depend on another person's ability to satisfy our needs and desires, or it can be (12) _____ and not dependent on the loved one meeting certain expectations and desires. (13) _____ is an emotional state that is aroused by a perceived threat to a valued relationship. It is more common in people who have low (14) _____ and/or who are personally unhappy in their lives, or who put great value on things like (15) _____.

Hazen and Shaver have proposed that one's experiences in romantic relationships are related to his or her (16) _____ style. People with a (17) _____ style have positive views of themselves and others and find it easy to form relationships, whereas individuals with anxious-ambivalent or (18) _____ styles find it more difficult to form relations.

Robert Sternberg has suggested that liking, loving, and all the other positive emotions we feel for other individuals can be understood by the combination of three components: intimacy, passion, and decision/commitment. According to this triangular theory, (19) _____ is intimacy alone, without passion or commitment. (20) _____ is liking plus feelings of passion without commitment, while (21) _____ is intimacy and commitment without passion. (22) _____, which Sternberg believes to be true love, requires the presence of all three components together.

In contrast to Sternberg, John Lee does not believe that there is only one type of love that should be viewed as true love. He proposes that there are many styles of loving. (23) _____ is based on an ideal of physical perfection; (24) _____ grows from friendship; (25) _____ is rational and practical; (26) _____ involves intense emotional dependency; (27) _____ is self-centered; and (28) _____ puts the interest of the loved person first. According to Lee, the degree of happiness an individual feels in a loving relationship depends greatly on how well his or her love-style (29) _____ that of the loved one.

Relationships that last are generally more realistic than idealistic and based more on companionship and affection than on passion. In order to maintain a relationship, a couple must substitute new shared activities for old ones as their lives change, and they also must develop skills to achieve greater (30) _____, those feelings and experiences that promote closeness and bondedness.

SELF-TEST

A. TRUE OR FALSE

T	F	31. Romantic love is the basis for marriage in most cultures
T	F	32. In Western culture, romantic love is separate from sexual desire
T	F	33. In terms of attachment styles, the most common romantic pairing is a secure-secure matching
T	F	34. The least common attachment style is the avoidant style
T	F	35. People rate best friends and lovers similarly on characteristics such as acceptance, trust, respect, mutual assistance, and understanding
T	F	36. According to Lee, love-styles are fixed and repetitive
T	F	37. As a general rule, people are most attracted to opposites
T	F	38. The decision and commitment to love another person without intimacy or passion is experienced as empty love, according to Sternberg
T	F	39. One of the major predictors of marital success is the number of pleasurable activities the couple shares
T	F	40. The ludus love-style is a strong negative predictor of relationship satisfaction
T	F	41. Feelings of romantic love are associated with the release of amphetamine-like chemicals in the brain
T	F	42. Self-disclosure is always important in a relationship, but it is not necessary that both individuals self-disclose
T	F	43. Men and women are most likely to become jealous if they perceive a partner to be sexually unfaithful
T	F	44. Romantic love tends to be unconditional
T	F	45. Anthropologists have found that romantic love is an idealized notion that is found almost exclusively in industrialized cultures where emphasis is on the individual
T	F	46. In order for a couple to become more intimate, it is important for them to withhold their negative feelings about each other

B. MATCHING

_____ 47. agapic love

_____ 48. anxious-ambivalent attachment style

_____ 49. avoidant attachment style

_____ 50. companionate love

_____ 51. conditional love

_____ 52. consummate love

_____ 53. empty love

_____ 54. erotic love

_____ 55. fatuous love

_____ 56. infatuated love

_____ 57. ludic love

_____ 58. manic love

_____ 59. pragmatic love

_____ 60. romantic love

_____ 61. secure attachment style

_____ 62. storgic love

_____ 63. unconditional love

a. highly idealized love based on physical beauty; these type of lovers are inclined to feel "love at first sight," but it usually does not last long

b. a love based on the partner satisfying certain needs and desires; Maslow called it "deficiency love"

c. an affectionate type of love that develops from friendship slowly over time

d. the love that results when commitment is made on the basis of passion without the experience of intimacy; leads to whirlwind romances that usually end when the passion starts to fade

e. do not fear abandonment and find it easy to get close to others

f. a selfless love-style that puts the interest of the loved person ahead of the lover's own, even if it means great sacrifice

g. a love that does not depend on the loved one meeting certain expectations and desires; Maslow called it "being love"

h. commitment without intimacy or passion; often the first stage in arranged marriages

i. a self-centered love in which the lover avoids commitment and treats love like a game

j. have negative views of others and have difficulties with feelings of intimacy

k. a love characterized by passionate arousal and liking without commitment; the idealization of another

l. a love that results when passion is felt in the absence of intimacy and commitment, where the lover is obsessed with the other person as an ideal; similar to what Lee calls erotic love

m. love characterized by an intense emotional dependency on the attention and affection of the partner; "head over heels" love in which one is obsessed with the loved one

n. have negative attitudes about themselves, fear rejection, and desperately try to get close to their partners

o. a love found only in relationships that include intimacy, passion, and commitment

p. the combination of intimacy and commitment without passion; based on togetherness, trust, sharing, and affection

q. a rational or practical style of love; this type of lover consciously looks for a compatible mate (a "good match")

C. FILL IN THE BLANKS

64. Fatuous love in Sternberg's model most closely resembles _____ in Lee's theoretical model.
65. Companionate love in Sternberg's model most closely resembles _____ in Lee's theoretical model.
66. Infatuated love in Sternberg's model most closely resembles _____ in Lee's theoretical model.
67. Saint Augustine's idea of love ("I want you to be") is probably closest to _____ in Lee's theoretical model.
68. Companionate love is often referred to as _____ love because it is not based on the fantasies and ideals of romantic love.
69. Elaine Hatfield has suggested that couples can achieve greater intimacy by (a) _____, (b) _____, (c) _____, and (d) _____.
70. From culture to culture, and in different time periods, the concept of romantic love has one thing in common: the _____ of another.
71. _____ is defined as "a state of intense longing for union with another…a state of profound physiological arousal."
72. Barnes and Sternberg's hierarchical model says that love is composed of two main clusters of features, which they identify as _____ and _____.
73. Three things that commonly occur during breakups are _____, _____, and having to deal with the fact that your ex-partner is still around.
74. Many studies have found that the first thing that generally attracts us to another is _____.

SUGGESTED READINGS

Avery, C. S. (1989, May). How do you build intimacy in an age of divorce? *Psychology Today*.

Fisher, H. (2009). *Why him? Why her?* New York: Henry Holt & Co. Discusses personality types and brain chemicals in attraction and love.

Fromm, E. (1956). *The art of loving*. New York: Harper & Row. An oldie, but a classic.

Jankowiak, W. R. (2008). *Intimacies: Love and sex across cultures*. New York: Columbia University Press. An in-depth look at how different cultures treat love.

Lindholm, C. (1998). Love and structure. *Theory, Culture and Society*, 15, 243–263. The best short article on the history of love that I have seen.

Regan, P. C. (2000). Love relationships. In L. T. Szuchman and F. Muscarella (Eds.), *Psychological perspectives on human sexuality* (pp. 232–282). New York: John Wiley & Sons. Good discussion of the various theories of love.

Schnarch, D. M. (1998). *Passionate marriage: Love, sex, and intimacy in emotionally committed relationships*. New York: Henry Holt & Co. The most frequently recommended book by the Society for Sex Therapy and Research for "keeping relationships vital" (Kingsberg et al., 2002).

Slater, L. (2006). This thing called love. *National Geographic*, February. Explains why we cannot keep feelings of passion long term.

13 | Sexual Problems and Therapy

In the fantasy world of sex, nothing ever hurts, nothing rubs or chafes, nobody is anxious, no one is tired, there are no menstrual cramps, strange viruses, or pregnancy fears, nothing bad ever happens and everything fits perfectly; in the fantasy world of sex, erections function, orgasms are easy, desire surges, birth-control methods don't interfere with spontaneity, and bodies melt. In the real world, it doesn't always happen this way.

—Excerpt from *What Really Happens in Bed* by Steven Carter & Julia Sokol, 1989, M. Evans and Company, Inc.

When you have finished studying this chapter, you should be able to:

- Discuss the common sexual differences couples may encounter in their relationship.

- Describe some techniques commonly used in sexual therapy.

- Classify sexual problems as desire disorders, arousal disorders, orgasmic disorders, or sexual pain disorders.

- Describe the sexual problems that occur in men (hypoactive sexual desire, erectile disorder, premature ejaculation, orgasmic disorder, dyspareunia, benign coital cephalalgia, and priapism).

- Explain the sexual problems that occur in women (hypoactive sexual desire, sexual arousal disorder, orgasmic disorder, dyspareunia, and vaginismus).

- Discuss the controversy about including hypersexuality as a sexual disorder.

- Discuss the pros and cons of the "medicalization" of sexual disorders.

- Understand the importance of a couple's overall relationship to sexual problems.

- Talk to your partner about sexual differences and problems.

Several studies have found that half or more of all couples have had, or will eventually have, sexual problems at some time in their relationship. In their nationally representative survey, Laumann, Paik, and Rosen (1999) found that in just the previous year many Americans aged 18–59 had experienced sexual problems lasting several months. Nearly one third of the women reported a lack of interest in sex, nearly one fifth of men said they were impotent, and nearly 30% of men reported continual problems with premature ejaculation, to name just three examples. Very similar results were reported for a nationally representative sample of Australian men and women (Richters et al., 2003c). What does this mean? Laumann concluded that "everyone is at risk of sexual dysfunction, sooner or later. It's a myth that young, healthy people aren't going to have sexual problems" (quoted in Leland, 1999a, p. 47).

In this chapter you will learn about the types of sexual problems that men and women may experience. In some cases, individuals have sexual problems regardless of who their partner is. Within a relationship, however, sexual problems frequently arise because of other problems in the relationship, or simply because of individual differences—people are different in what they want and how often they want it. I will begin with a discussion of the types of differences that can lead to sexual problems within a relationship.

INDIVIDUAL DIFFERENCES AND RELATIONSHIP CONFLICTS

Different Expectations

Men and women often have different ideas about sex and love, and therefore often differ on why they have sex. Many women are looking for affection and are interested in what their partner thinks (the context in which sex occurs), while many men engage in sex for a physical experience (McNulty & Fisher, 2008). As a result, many men are goal-(orgasm) directed during sex, whereas many women are partner-directed (Basson, 2000, 2002c). Many men equate sex with intimacy. When asked to give six responses to the question "What things do you personally like best in a sexual partner?" for a survey in my course, most of the men listed specific anatomical characteristics (e.g., "nice ass," "big breasts," "sexy legs") or sexual behaviors (e.g., positions, oral sex, no inhibitions). Women, on the other hand, were less concerned about anatomy and much more concerned about being in a relationship in which they felt cared for, loved, and/or respected. The behaviors they desired were affectionate in nature (e.g., holding, hugging, caressing). Nearly every woman expressed the desire for her male partner to take his time. In fact, this was often expressed as a complaint—the male partners (who are goal-directed) were not taking their time (see Witting et al., 2008). These different expectations about a sexual relationship can lead to problems.

> "I got married at a very early age. Sex to me was usually just wifely duties because it was demanded. I used to make up excuses just so I didn't have to do it. Our marriage finally broke up."
>
> (from the author's files)

Dear Ann Landers:

Two years ago I found out that my wife of 27 years was having an affair with another man. She was driving 40 miles to a motel twice a week to meet him for "lunch."

When I learned what was going on, I asked her, "Why? It seemed to me you were getting more than enough sex at home."

Her reply was, "What I am getting at home is just that. SEX. And sex is no substitute for love."

Her answer made me stop and think. I had to admit she was right.

I am writing this letter to all you husbands out there who are making the same mistake. Ask yourselves this question, "Am I making love to my wife, or am I just having sex with her?"

Glad I Got Smart

Both men and women say that they would prefer about 18 minutes of foreplay. In actuality, it usually lasts about 11 to 13 minutes (Miller & Byers, 2004). Sexual intercourse usually lasts 3 to 13 minutes (Corty & Guardiani, 2008), with an average of about 7 to 8 minutes (Miller & Byers, 2008). Both men and woman, but particularly men, wish it would last several minutes longer.

Different Assumptions

Men and women often have different initial sexual experiences, which can lead to incorrect assumptions about the opposite sex. The first sexual experience to orgasm for most men is masturbation. Most men masturbate by moving a hand up and down the penis at a continually accelerating rate as they approach orgasm. Women are more variable in their masturbation techniques, but most prefer indirect stimulation of the clitoris. Only 20% or less of women masturbate by inserting a finger in the vagina (Hite, 1976; Kinsey et al., 1953). It takes women longer to masturbate to orgasm on the average than it does for men (Kinsey et al., 1953). Without any evidence to the contrary, it is logical for people to assume that what feels best for them must feel best for others as well. Men often assume that women greatly enjoy having their genitals vigorously stimulated (as by rapid thrusting of a finger in and out of the vagina) during foreplay, when in fact this may not be the case. Similarly, a woman might assume that her male partner prefers gentle indirect stimulation, when in fact this may not be the case.

Differences in Desire

One of the most common types of problems that a couple might encounter is a difference in the frequency with which sex is desired (Davies et al., 1999). In the 1970s movie *Annie Hall* there is a scene where a man, played by Woody Allen, and a woman, played by Diane Keaton, are shown talking to their respective therapists. Woody says that he and his girlfriend (Diane Keaton) hardly ever have sex, perhaps three times a week. Diane Keaton tells her therapist that they have sex all the time, maybe three times a week. Who has the problem? Is the woman played by Diane Keaton undersexed and to blame, or is the problem that Woody is oversexed? In a study that followed newlywed couples for 6 months, women's sexual satisfaction depended mainly on the context (how happy they were in the overall relationship), whereas men's sexual satisfaction depended mainly on the frequency of sex (McNulty & Fisher, 2008).

In many relationships, it does no good to point the finger and put the blame on one person or

FIGURE 13–1 Studies have shown that one half or more of all couples have had, or eventually will have, sexual problems at some time in their relationship.

the other. People are generally only oversexed or undersexed relative to their partners' desires. *It is the couple that has the problem.*

Sexual desire is not necessarily set at a fixed level. An individual's desire for sex often varies, depending on the circumstances. For example, stress and fatigue can greatly affect interest in sex. If your partner is showing less interest in sex than he or she once did, this may be due to other things that are happening in your partner's life. Our understanding of the other person's feelings would be greatly enhanced, of course, if we could only switch places for a little while:

"When I stayed home and my husband worked, I did not understand his seeming lack of desire. Not that he didn't enjoy it, but it could be placed low on a list of priorities. He would tell me about his problems at work, and I was really interested in making love then. I didn't want to hear how obnoxious, rude, or unintelligent his boss could be.

"I took all of these 'excuses' as a personal put-down. I would say, 'You're home now, forget what happened in the day.' Little did I realize then, he could not separate them.

"After a while, he started telling me that maybe he would be more interested if I didn't push him. Then I would get mad and say, 'You don't understand me and what I need.'

"This period was heightened by his decision to quit his job of 25 years. When he finally decided to do this, I said I would go out to work and became

a Kelly Girl. I really only wanted temporary work, but I'd go on short assignments of 2 or 3 weeks and stay 3 or 4 months. I never turned down an assignment and gave it my all. Now I am receiving tension, problems with bosses, and plain being physically and mentally tired.

"When I came home from work, I'd look for dinner, make remarks about the house, or want to know if he checked on the children's homework. He would be ready to be cuddly and kiss and I had a barrage of questions. I'd also start telling him about problems I had during the day. Finally, I told him, 'I can't believe I'm doing and saying the same things you did to me.'

"After a while it became a joke, and I'd say these things and we'd laugh about it. He then knew how it felt and so did I. Well, this same attitude spilled over to the bedroom. We now are more understanding of each other's feelings, because we know where they are coming from."

(from the author's files)

PERSONAL REFLECTIONS

What do you do when your partner desires sex and you are not in the mood? What would you expect your partner to do if you desired sex and he or she was not in the mood? Why? Have you ever pretended to be tired or feeling poorly in order to avoid sex with your partner? If so, why? Do you think that responses like these are the best way to communicate with your partner about sexual needs?

Differences in Preferred Behaviors

Differences in the type of sexual activities each person wants to engage in can also lead to problems. Suppose, for example, that person A (who can be either a man or a woman) wants to have sex only in the missionary position and is in a relationship with person B, who wants to have sexual intercourse in a variety of positions and locations.

> "My girlfriend and I are sexually active. I am tired of doing the same old missionary position. Whenever I mention a new position, she doesn't want to do it. I am so tired of the same old position I lose interest in sex. I don't want to even have sex sometimes."
>
> (from the author's files)

Who is to blame for the problem here? Is A inhibited, or is B abnormal? Once again, it is all relative. It does no good to point a finger. Suppose that instead of having a relationship with A, person B was in a relationship with person C, who wanted to try bondage and anal intercourse (which B does not want to try). Should person B now be viewed as inhibited?

In summary, there are many differences two people can have that can cause sexual problems. When this happens, it is far too common for one person to get upset and blame the other. It is generally best, however, that a couple view these types of problems as *their* problem, rather than as a particular individual's problem. This means working together to resolve it. Disclosing your preferences to your partner helps him or her understand and often leads to a better relationship (MacNeil & Byers, 2009). Within a relationship, sexual satisfaction is often associated with how well one understands his or her partner's sexual preferences (Purnine & Carey, 1997).

Relationship Conflict

Sexual relations, of course, are only part of a couple's overall relationship. As you learned in previous chapters, if a couple's overall relationship is good and positive, this generally carries over to sexual relations (Laumann et al., 2006). Conversely, if a couple is experiencing relationship problems, this generally will affect sexual relations as well. In this chapter you will see many references about how the overall quality of a relationship can affect sexual desire, arousal, and sexual satisfaction.

To work out sexual differences or relationship problems requires that a couple be able to talk about their differences, but most people do not know how to talk about sex comfortably. The addendum to this chapter provides you with some guidelines. When couples cannot work out individual differences or relationship problems by themselves, they may need the aid of a counselor.

Be sure that you pick one who is properly trained and certified. The names and addresses of certified marriage and family therapists in your area can be obtained by writing to the *American Association for Marriage and Family Therapy (AAMFT)*, 112 South Alfred Street, Alexandria, VA 22314. The Web address for this organization is www.aamft.org.

Not all sexual problems are the result of individual differences within a relationship. If a particular sexual behavior is causing an individual a great deal of stress and anxiety and possibly interfering with his or her ability to function in a relationship, then that person may be regarded (and probably regards himself or herself) as having a problem. In this case, the individual would probably benefit by seeing a sex therapist.

PERSONAL REFLECTIONS

Are you able to comfortably communicate your sexual values and needs to your sexual partner or your potential partner? If not, what barriers are preventing you from doing so? Do you create any barriers that may prevent your partner from comfortably communicating his or her sexual values and needs to you?

SEXUAL THERAPY

What is a sex therapist? What does he or she do? When you have a toothache you go to a dentist, and when you have a chest pain you go to a cardiologist. Just as physicians specialize in different kinds of medical problems, therapists often specialize as well. A sex therapist is someone who specializes in helping people with sexual problems. They do not do so by having sex with their clients, and, in fact, this is considered highly unethical. Like any other specialist, a sex therapist has had several years of training before beginning practice.

Sex therapy is a relatively new field. Until Masters and Johnson published their pioneering book *Human Sexual Inadequacy* in 1970, most people with sexual problems went to their family doctor, a urologist, or a psychoanalyst. Most doctors and therapists were not prepared to deal with such problems. Psychoanalysis generally involved long-term treatment (sometimes years) and attempted to "cure" the problem by resolving childhood conflicts, viewing the behavioral problem as merely a symptom of some other deeper conflict.

Masters and Johnson (1970) originally believed that most sexual problems were the result of faulty learning and could be undone in a relatively short period of time by using **cognitive-behavioral therapy.** This kind of therapy focuses on sexual behaviors and how we feel about them. It does not focus on past events. The problem behaviors *are* the problem, and if the behaviors can be changed, the client is "cured."

Sex therapy is still refining its techniques, and in the years since Masters and Johnson began their clinical practice it has become clear that **psychosexual therapy,** designed to give insight into the historical cause of clients' problems, is often more successful for some types of problems (e.g., low sexual desire or sexual aversion; Kaplan, 1983). In fact, a recent review concluded that "sex therapy, as it is practiced today, is [not] sufficiently different from other psychotherapies…" (Binik & Meana, 2009). Perhaps the biggest change in the treatment of sexual problems today has to do with the role of the medical field (see Rowland, 2007). We know now that not all sexual problems are due to faulty learning; many have an organic (medical) cause. Our understanding of the biology of sexual behavior has also greatly increased during the last 4 decades. In the **medical model,** physicians have increasingly begun treating sexual problems with medical techniques (medications, surgery). I will describe and critique medical approaches in the sections on specific sexual problems.

Sexual therapy programs generally have many things in common. Most follow what is called the **PLISSIT model.** PLISSIT is an acronym for *permission, limited information, specific suggestions, and intensive therapy*—the four levels of therapy. Each represents a successively deeper level of therapy. In the first level, the therapist "gives permission" for the client to feel and behave sexually. This is important, because many people and institutions (e.g., parents, some religions) cause people to suppress their sexuality while growing up. In the second level, the therapist gives information to the client (educates him or her about the sexual problem by providing information that relates to the problem). This is done in such a manner that the client continues to acquire a positive attitude about sexuality. At the specific suggestion (third) stage, the therapist gives the client exercises to do at home that will help with the specific problem. If the client is still experiencing problems after completing the specific suggestions, then intensive psychosexual therapy will be employed. Only about 10% of people who go to sex therapy require this last step.

Now, let us return to the importance of the overall relationship. Sex therapy is only going to work if a couple is in a committed relationship, does not have major nonsexual conflicts, has good communication skills, and is motivated to help each other with the sexual problem (and in the relationship as a whole). If any of these factors are missing, then **couples therapy** to improve communication and resolve conflicts will probably be necessary (Borelli-Kerner & Bernell, 1997).

If you ever think that you may need the help of a sex therapist, be sure to check the credentials of therapists first. In some places, almost anyone can advertise as a "counselor." The names and addresses of certified sex counselors and therapists in your area can be obtained by writing to the *American Association of Sexuality Educators, Counselors and Therapists (AASECT)*, P.O. Box 1960, Ashland, VA 23005 (www.aasect.org).

Many of you may not be able to afford a therapist. What about self-help therapies? Hundreds of them can be found on the amazon.com website (search for "sexual" and "self-help"). A recent review concluded that if you have a high level of motivation and good coping skills, self-help therapies can be successful (van Lankveld, 2009).

SEXUAL THERAPY TECHNIQUES

Medical History

Sexual problems are sometimes caused by physical or medical problems. Circulatory problems (e.g., arteriosclerosis), hormone abnormalities (e.g., low testosterone levels), or anything that causes damage to the central nervous system (e.g., diabetes, spinal cord injury) can cause a sexual problem. Alcohol and drugs often cause sexual impairment as well. One common cause of impotence in men, for example, is some prescription medications used to treat hypertension and heart disease. It is important, therefore, that a therapist take a complete *medical history* of the patient (and possibly refer the patient to a physician for a medical exam) before beginning therapy in order to rule out any physiological basis for the presenting problem. Behavioral therapy will do little good if the problem has an organic cause.

Sexual History

Nearly all sex therapists will take a complete *sexual history* of the client before treatment begins. These histories are very thorough, and the length of time devoted to a history will depend on how candid the client is about his or her past experiences. Some

---

Cognitive-behavioral therapy ■ Therapy that views problems as resulting from faulty learning and that focuses on specific sexual behaviors and how we feel about them. It does not focus on past events.

Psychosexual therapy ■ Therapy that attempts to provide insight into the historical cause of a client's problem.

Medical model ■ Attributing sexual problems to organic causes and treating them with medical techniques.

PLISSIT model ■ An acronym for the four levels of treatment in sexual therapy: permission, limited information, specific suggestions, and intensive therapy.

Couples therapy ■ Therapy that focuses on the overall relationship and communication skills between two people.

therapists prefer to work with couples because "There is no such thing as an uninvolved partner." A person's partner (or partners) is involved in the problem in some manner, and even when he or she is not the initial cause (e.g., in those cases where the problem existed before the relationship started), when one partner has a sexual problem, it is common for the other partner to develop one as well.

Self-Awareness and Masturbation

As you learned in Chapter 2, some people have never explored their own bodies. As a result, they lack **self-awareness** and are totally out of touch with their own physical responses. If you do not know what your body looks like and how it responds, it will be difficult to communicate your needs and feelings to a partner. Therapists are likely to tell those who are not in touch with their bodies to spend time examining themselves. Some therapists give their clients instructions on how to masturbate (Heiman & Meston, 1997; LoPiccolo & Stock, 1986). Isn't it interesting that what once was taboo is now sometimes used as a therapeutic technique?

Sensate Focus

Many people are goal- or performance-oriented during sexual relations. As a result, many people never really learn how to give or receive physical pleasure. Most therapists, therefore, instruct couples to use *nondemand mutual pleasuring techniques* when touching each other. They are instructed to go home, get undressed, and take turns touching each other without thinking about the goal of having intercourse or having an orgasm. Touching the breasts and genitals is forbidden at first, but all other areas of the body are to be explored (see Figure 13–2). The receiver is instructed to focus on the sensations produced by the giver and to provide feedback as to what feels good and what does not. The giver learns what makes his or her partner feel good while simultaneously learning the pleasure of touching. The couple learns to be sensual in a nondemanding situation.

Masters and Johnson, who created these **sensate focus exercises,** often had patients spend several days doing this nongenital-oriented touching. The purpose is to reduce anxiety and teach nonverbal communication skills (De Villers & Turgeon, 2005). Eventually, the couple is instructed to include breast and genital stimulation in their touching, but to avoid orgasm-oriented touching. A successful outcome for the treatment of sexual problems is often directly related to the amount of sensate focus that is completed during therapy.

Self-awareness ■ In sexual therapy, getting in touch with one's own physical responses.

Sensate focus exercises ■ Exercises designed to reduce anxiety and teach mutual pleasuring through nongenital touching in nondemanding situations.

FIGURE 13–2 Sensate focus is a nondemand mutual pleasuring technique in which a couple learns how to touch and be touched without worrying about performing or reaching a goal.

PERSONAL REFLECTIONS

Stop and reflect on the physical interactions you have with your partner(s). In most of your interactions, are you able to engage in extended nongenital touching and caressing of your partner, or are you usually in a hurry to achieve some immediate genital or breast touching? Is your partner able to caress your arms, legs, neck, and so on, without you quickly attempting to steer the behavior toward sexual play? Why or why not?

Specific Exercises

After the sensate focus exercises are successfully completed, therapists generally assign specific exercises to help with the problem for which the person came for treatment. These will be described as we discuss some of the most common types of problems. When the therapist allows sexual intercourse, it is almost always in a woman-on-top or side-by-side position, where neither partner is in total control. Therapists believe that these positions have much more erotic potential than the missionary position frequently used by many couples.

CLASSIFICATION OF SEXUAL DISORDERS

The World Health Organization's *International Classifications of Diseases-10 (ICD-10)* defines sexual problems as "the various ways in which an individual is unable to participate in a sexual relationship as he or she would wish" (WHO, 1992). The American Psychiatric Association's *Diagnostic and Statistical Manual of Mental Disorders (DSM-IV-TR)* defines sexual disorders as "disturbances in sexual desire and in the psychophysiological changes that characterize the sexual response cycle and cause marked distress and interpersonal difficulty." Notice that an important criterion in both classification systems is subjective distress—it is only a problem if the individual considers it to be a problem. Many people do not consider their sexual disorder to be distressing (Bancroft et al., 2003; Shifren et al., 2008).

Notice also that sexual disorders are classified, in large part, according to the sexual response cycle as first described by Masters and Johnson (1966, 1970) and Helen Kaplan (1979). The four major categories are desire disorders, arousal (excitement phase) disorders, orgasmic disorders, and sexual

---

Hypoactive sexual desire ■ A sexual problem characterized by a persisting and pervasive absence of sexual fantasies and desire. See **female hypoactive sexual desire**.

---

pain disorders. Be sure to review the sections on the Sexual Response Cycle in Chapter 4 before you read the following sections.

MALE SEXUAL PROBLEMS

Sexual Desire Disorders: Hypoactive Sexual Desire and Sexual Aversion

Today, many therapists believe that the most common problem of couples going into sex therapy is hypoactive sexual desire. In fact, Laumann et al.'s (1999) national survey found that about 16% of men under the age of 60 reported a lack of interest in sex in the previous year. A representative sample of Australian men found an even higher percentage (Richters et al., 2003c). About 28% of men aged 60–75 have little or no interest in sex (Laumann et al., 2009; Lindau et al., 2007; Waite et al., 2009). Some people have a self-identify as asexual (Prause & Graham, 2007). However, these estimates are probably high because the surveys did not use the *DSM-IV-TR* definition. Some therapists believe that from a clinical perspective, the numbers are much lower (Simons & Carey, 2001).

Before we proceed, let us first review what is meant by the term *sexual desire*. You were introduced to this term in Chapter 4. Recall that Helen Kaplan (1979) included it as the first phase of the sexual response cycle. Since then, researchers have attempted to show that desire is composed of three components (e.g., Levine, 2003): (1) sexual drive—the biological component; (2) sexual "wish"—the subjective, psychological component; and (3) sexual motivation—an individual's willingness to engage in sexual *behavior* with a person. A person may willingly engage in sex with a partner (e.g., because he or she wishes to please the partner), but have little subjective desire. Because of this, we will focus on the subjective aspect of desire.

So, how do we define **hypoactive sexual desire?** The *DSM-IV-TR* (American Psychiatric Association, 2000) defines a lack of interest in sex as a problem when there is *persistent or recurrent absence of sexual fantasies and sexual desire*. People with hypoactive (or inhibited) sexual desire show decreased frequencies of sexual arousal, self-initiated sexual activity, and sexual fantasy. The problem in diagnosing hypoactive sexual desire, of course, is defining what is meant by the normal frequency of sexual desire. *Hypoactive* is a relative term that must take into account the partner's frequency of desire and the level of desire of other people in the community.

Hypoactive sexual desire is more than just a lack of sexual activity, however. Therapist Helen Kaplan's studies (1979) suggest that on some level, inhibited persons suppress their desire because they do not want to feel sexual. Another therapist has called it "sexual anorexia nervosa." In its most extreme form, the avoidance of sex becomes phobic in nature and is called **sexual aversion** (Kaplan, 1987). The anticipation of any kind of sexual interaction (even conversation about sex) causes great anxiety, so persons with sexual aversion simply "turn it off" at a very early stage.

It is difficult for people who enjoy sex to imagine that others find it unpleasant. What could cause such a lack of interest in sex? *Primary hypoactive sexual desire* (people who have never had sexual feelings) is much more common in women than men (McCarthy & McDonald, 2009). *Secondary* or *acquired hypoactive sexual desire* is sometimes due to organic factors such as low testosterone levels (Sternbach, 1998) or antidepressant drugs (see Werneke et al., 2006). Testosterone replacement therapy is helpful for some of these men, but there are concerns about long-term health risks (Kolata, 2002). However, only a few men with hypoactive sexual desire have abnormally low testosterone levels (Wespes & Schulman, 2002), and thus most cases are believed to be due to psychological factors (Heiman, 2002). Some cases may be due to a past trauma, such as contracting a sexually transmitted infection:

> "When I was 15 I had sex with a prostitute. My friends encouraged me to do so. One week later I noticed two sores on my penis. I couldn't tell my parents, they would kill me. I couldn't sleep. I asked a friend for help. I remember how he looked at me. I felt rejected.... I was horrified.... His father was a doctor and he treated me. I remember the anxiety when he told me I had chancroid. I didn't know if it was curable.... Today, I'm afraid of having sex with anyone. I have not had relations with a woman in nearly 5 years."
> (from the author's files)

Hypoactive sexual desire is often associated with depression, anger at one's partner, severe stress (financial, work), or a sexually repressive upbringing (Donahey & Carroll, 1993; Hawton et al., 1991). For probably half or more of the couples who go into therapy for sexual desire problems, one partner or the other has a coexisting sexual problem (see Leiblum & Rosen, 1988). In some cases, hypoactive sexual desire may be a way of avoiding the sexual failure due to the other problem.

Hypoactive sexual desire is probably the most difficult sexual problem to treat (McCarthy & McDonald, 2009). Many therapists report only a 10% to 20% success rate with conventional sex therapy techniques. One of the problems is that hypoactive sexual desire is frequently found in couples for which there is great unhappiness in the overall relationship (McCarthy & McDonald, 2009). Today, most therapists begin with behavioral and cognitive techniques that are designed to increase pleasure and communication and decrease anxiety, but add couples therapy (to resolve relationship problems and rebuild intimacy) and individual psychosexual therapy (to help the person understand what it is that is causing anxieties about sex) (e.g., LoPiccolo & Friedman, 1988; McCarthy & McDonald, 2009).

Sexual Arousal Disorder: Erectile Disorder

The term **erectile disorder** (or *erectile dysfunction*) refers to a man's inability to get or maintain an erection. It refers to more than a total inability to get an erection; it includes any inability to get or maintain an erection adequate for "satisfactory sexual performance." This condition is sometimes called *impotence*, but this is an unfortunate term because it has negative connotations about a man's masculinity. Most therapists prefer the purely descriptive term (National Institutes of Health Consensus Statement, 1992). Erectile disorders can be *primary* (i.e., the man has always had problems) or *secondary* (i.e., the individual has not had erectile problems in the past); and *global* (i.e., the problem occurs in all situations) or *situational* (e.g., a man cannot get an erection with his partner, but can during masturbation).

How common are erectile problems? It is a rare man who will not experience an erectile problem at least once in his life. Any number of things can impair functioning, including fatigue, stress, alcohol, and drugs. A drink or two loosens our inhibitions, but most men are unaware that alcohol is also a central nervous system depressant, and it is quite common to experience erectile problems after drinking too much (which sometimes may be only a couple of drinks; Rosen 1991).

So should we say that all men have erectile problems? No. The American Psychiatric Association's *DSM-IV-TR's* diagnostic criteria are that the problem must be *persistent or recurrent and causes distress or interpersonal difficulty*. In national surveys, it has been found that about 10% of men aged 30 to 49, 24% of men aged 50 to 59, and 37% of men aged 60 to 75 had erectile problems lasting at least a few months during the previous year (Laumann et al., 1999, 2007, 2009; Lindau et al., 2007; Waite et al., 2009). (Although by the DSM-IV-TR definition, the numbers are probably smaller [see Dunn et al., 2002]). Thus, the National Institutes of Health estimate that 30 million American men have erectile problems.

Sexual aversion ■ An extreme form of hypoactive sexual desire in which an individual's avoidance of sex becomes phobic.

Erectile disorder ■ A sexual problem in which a man has persistent or recurrent difficulty getting and maintaining an erection.

What is responsible for the fact that so many men have an erectile disorder? Masters and Johnson once argued that as many as 80% of all cases are due to psychological factors, but physicians now estimate that the large majority of cases (perhaps 80%) have a physical basis (NIH Consensus Statement, 1992). Actually, there is an easy test that can often (but not always) determine whether the cause of a complete erectile disorder is physical or psychological. Men, you remember, get erections at night during REM sleep. If a man gets normal erections during REM sleep, then the problem is most likely psychological. If not, then it is physical (Koskimaki et al., 2008).

The biggest change in the treatment of erectile disorders in the past 10 years has been its *medicalization*—whereby erectile disorders are viewed as a medical problem resulting from organic causes that should be treated with medical solutions (drugs, devices, or surgery). We will focus on the medical approach first, then return to treatment for psychogenic disorders.

Circulatory problems (e.g., arteriosclerosis or sickle-cell anemia), neurological disorders (e.g., resulting from accidents or pelvic surgery), prostate surgery, low testosterone levels, and groin injuries often result in erectile disorders (Laumann et al., 2007). Men with erectile disorders sometimes have decreased penile sensitivity (Rowland, 1998). One fourth of all erectile problems are due to medications

prescribed for other conditions, particularly antidepressants and the beta-blocking medications used to treat blood pressure and heart disease (e.g., Rosen & Marin, 2003). Men who drink alcohol every day have nearly twice the rates of erectile disorders as other men (Laumann et al., 1999). Eighty percent of alcoholics are impaired. Smokers are 50% more likely than nonsmokers to suffer from erectile problems (Mannino et al., 1994). It is important, therefore, that a client with an erectile problem have a complete medical exam before treatment begins.

Some of the first medical treatments for erectile disorder included vacuum devices (that forced blood into the penis) and self-injection of drugs into the penis. Today, oral medications (pills) are commonly prescribed: Viagra (sildenafil), Cialis (tadalafil), and Levitra (vardenafil). They work by relaxing smooth muscles in the penis, thus allowing arteries to expand and blood to rush into the penis. The pills work directly on the penis (not the brain) and work only when a man is sexually stimulated. However, they can cause headaches, indigestion, and blurred vision (among other things). About 14% to 22% of men aged 45 and older have used these pills on at least one occasion (Jacoby, 2005; Lindau et al., 2007; Schick et al., 2010). Unfortunately, many young men are using these drugs recreationally (Musacchio et al., 2006).

For those men for whom medications and therapy do not work, such as those who have suffered permanent nerve or vascular damage, *penile implants* can be used. Tens of thousands of American men are presently using these implants, and although postsurgical levels of sexual satisfaction do not always match presurgical expectations, a large majority of the patients and their partners are satisfied with the results (Chiang et al., 2000).

The medical model for the treatment of erectile disorders has failed to address some important issues. For example, quite often it is not easy to attribute an erectile problem solely to organic or psychological factors (Ackerman & Carey, 1995; NIH Consensus Statement, 1992). If a man has a problem due to a physical cause (or a temporary problem due to medication), he can become so apprehensive that he becomes completely impaired. In addition, it is easier for many men to view themselves as having a medical problem that can be cured with a magic pill than it is to accept that they have psychological or sexual problems that may require seeing a sex therapist. There are probably psychological and/or relationship problems associated with all erectile problems, even those that are clearly caused by physical problems, and *most patients would probably benefit from a combination of medication and therapy* (see Ackerman & Carey, 1995; Aubin et al., 2009; Perelman, 2002; Rowland & Burnett, 2000). Let us now focus on traditional sexual therapy techniques.

FIGURE 13–3 Serious stressors, such as financial or job-related problems, can lead to erectile problems or a loss of interest in sex.

If the cause of an erectile problem is determined to be psychological, the success rate during therapy depends largely on whether it is primary or secondary. Men with primary (psychological) erectile disorders are often found to have had a strict religious upbringing in which sex was equated with sin and guilt (Masters & Johnson, 1970).

> "I was raised a _____ throughout my life.... I do remember in the seventh or ninth grade my father and I were talking about sex and he told me not to have sex until I was married or I would go to hell—I thought that for the longest time. Then when I discovered masturbation I felt terribly guilty, so I went to talk to a priest. He told me how wrong it was and gave me some prayers to say. From that time on I felt very guilty every time I did it.... I haven't had a full erection in 10 years (I'm 26)."
> (from the author's files)

An early traumatic experience might also result in long-term erectile problems:

> "At 16 years old...my best friend thought it was a shame I was still a virgin.... In a drunken stupor I was goaded into going downtown to pick up a hooker with my friend. The next day I walked tall and proud (although I felt no different), that is until I noticed a week later a greenish-yellow discharge on my underwear. A doctor diagnosed gonorrhea. I brought it up with my father, who became enraged, and to this day he still teases me about it. My brother laughed at me.... I did not date anyone for 3 years. Once I began, it took me 3 or 4 years to have sex.... I would get to the point of intercourse, then I would lose my erection."
> (from the author's files)

Men who were victims of adult–child sexual contact experience erectile problems three times more often than other men (Laumann et al., 1999). Therapists find that these primary disorders are much more difficult to treat than secondary disorders.

Situational erectile disorders are quite clearly psychological in origin:

> "My husband doesn't stay hard when we make love. Everything is OK at the start, but then he gets soft in a minute or two. He stays hard when I give him oral sex or masturbate him."
> (from the author's files)

If this man's erectile problem were caused by something physically wrong with him, he would be unable to maintain an erection with any type of sexual activity.

For men with a secondary erectile disorder due to psychological factors, the most common cause is performance anxiety (Bancroft et al., 2005). **Performance anxiety** is a fear of failure.

> "My girlfriend and I are sexually active. Since we first started having sex, I would have an orgasm but she wouldn't. She still hasn't had one, and we have had sex plenty of times. I feel that I am not doing my job as a man. I also feel embarrassed. It makes me feel I do not know much about sex. Lately...I have trouble getting an erection."
> (from the author's files)

Erectile problems are not uncommon during first intercourse (Santtila et al., 2009). Men who feel they are competing with a real or imagined suitor often put enormous pressure on themselves:

> Billy and Karen were in their mid-30s and had been married for 3 years. They both worked full-time; he as the manager of a small insurance office and she as a lab technician in a hospital. Their sexual relationship, which began while they were dating, had always been "wonderful." In their third year of marriage, Karen was promoted to a job selling hospital equipment. About 6 months later, Billy began to have erectile difficulties.

"Do those pills seem to be working, sweetie?"

Performance anxiety ■ A fear of failure during sexual relations that can lead to erectile disorder in men and inhibited orgasm in women.

When Billy and Karen started therapy, they still had no idea what was causing the problem. In actuality, Billy was threatened by Karen's impressive career advancement. Although he tried hard to be a liberated male, he was threatened by her increased income and status and the time she spent entertaining the various physicians and hospital administrators in her territory.

During sexual relations, Billy had begun to worry if Karen found him as appealing as she had when she was more "naive and unworldly." He also had the secret fear that Karen was having an affair, and although she wasn't, he had begun to compete with his own fantasy of Karen's other partner. As with many men, this was sufficient to produce Billy's initial difficulty in maintaining an erection. Once the difficulty began, Billy's anticipation of it happening made it begin to occur earlier in each subsequent sexual encounter.

(Case history courtesy of David Schnarch, PhD., Marriage & Family Health Center of Evergreen, Colorado.)

Another common cause is a life change. For example, the stress caused by unemployment frequently leads to erectile problems (Morokoff & Gilliland, 1993). Erectile problems are very common in men who are depressed (Seidman, 2002). According to Levine and Althof (1991), "Typically, the man does not fully appreciate his response to these life changes.... He avoids recognizing what

Spectatoring ▪ Observing and evaluating one's own sexual responses. This generally causes distraction, with subsequent erectile and/or orgasm problems.

these affect-laden events mean to him and only focuses on his loss of sexual confidence—that is, performance anxiety. He remains baffled by how he became dysfunctional."

Although an erectile problem in any of the previously mentioned situations is normal, many men are not aware of that and begin to worry about being "impotent." The next time they have sex, the anxiety caused by fear of failure can result in what is called **spectatoring**—observing and evaluating their own responses rather than experiencing sexual pleasures. Spectatoring is distracting, resulting in a loss of arousal, and it can lead to loss of an erection, which results in even greater anxiety the next time. The behavior becomes a vicious cycle, and what started as a normal response to fatigue, alcohol, drugs, or other factors can become a chronic psychological disorder.

What is the best therapy for a man with a psychologically caused erectile problem (performance anxiety)? In the Masters and Johnson model of sexual therapy, men with an erectile disorder are usually assigned sensate focus exercises. Many men are amazed to find that they are able to get a full erection during these initial sessions. The reason, of course, is that the touching in sensate focus exercises involves nondemand pleasuring—the man does not have to perform, but instead learns (or relearns) how to experience pleasure. When genital touching is allowed, the female partner is instructed to stop fondling the penis after the man gets an erection (see Figure 13–4). This is intended to teach the man that he does not have to use his erection immediately (many men with erection problems

FIGURE 13–4 A commonly used training technique for men.

rush their performance for fear that they will lose their erection). With this *"teasing" procedure*, the man's erection comes and goes, and thus he also learns that loss of erection does not mean that he has failed, for it will come back again. When intercourse is finally allowed, it is always in a woman-on-top or side-by-side position, and the woman is the one who inserts the penis into her vagina. Thus, the man is not put in a position of feeling that he has to perform.

The long-term success rate of behavior modification techniques (used alone) is often not good. As a result, today, many therapists are emphasizing the importance of the couple's dynamics and interpersonal issues in the cause and treatment of erectile problems. Many therapists worry that, when used alone, the medical solution of popping pills (e.g., Viagra) focuses on fixing the mechanics of erectile disorder, while ignoring the personal and relationship problems that may have caused it (Kleinplatz, 2004). The case history of Billy and Karen is a good example. Here, a combination of approaches—couples therapy that focuses on interpersonal issues and communication, behavior modification techniques, and pharmacological assistance—would be of great benefit (Ackerman & Carey, 1995; Aubin et al., 2009; Perelman, 2002; Rowland & Burnett, 2000).

PERSONAL REFLECTIONS

Have you ever experienced performance anxiety during sexual relations (e.g., anxiety about pleasing your partner, maintaining an erection, reaching orgasm)? If so, what do you think is the cause of the anxiety?

Orgasmic Disorders: Premature Ejaculation

"I have a problem with premature ejaculation. As soon as I start to have sex I ejaculate. I feel like the whole world is laughing at me.... All my other friends are having sex and doing it right."
(from the author's files)

When many people think of someone who prematurely ejaculates, they think of a man who reaches orgasm before intercourse even begins. Although this does sometimes happen, it is more often the case that a man ejaculates shortly after the couple begins intercourse. National surveys have found that about 30% of men experience premature ejaculation (Laumann et al., 1999, 2009; Lindau et al., 2007; Waite et al., 2009). This was across all age groups up through age 75 and makes it the most common male sexual problem. Others have con-

cluded that the figure is closer to 15% to 21% (Dunn et al., 2002; Rowland et al., 2004), but part of the problem is that there is no agreement about how premature ejaculation is defined (Barnes & Eardley, 2007). How, then, do we define **premature ejaculation?** The American Psychiatric Association's *DSM-IV-TR* (2000) says that its essential feature is "the persistent or recurrent onset of orgasm and ejaculation with minimal sexual stimulation before, on, or shortly after penetration and before the person wishes it," accompanied by *"marked distress or interpersonal difficulty."*

How long does a man have to continue in intercourse without being classified as a premature ejaculator? At various times in the past, premature ejaculation has been defined by a specified minimal number of thrusts, a minimal amount of time engaged in intercourse, or in terms of whether the female partner reaches orgasm at least 50% of the time (see Rowland et al., 2000). The problem with the first two types of definition is that they do not consider the partner. For example, while it is true that most men with premature ejaculation ejaculate within 2 minutes after beginning intercourse (compared with an average of 7.3 minutes for others) (Patrick et al., 2005), suppose that a man always reaches orgasm in only 1½ minutes after beginning intercourse, but that his female partner always reaches orgasm within that time period as well. Should he be considered as having a problem? The trouble with the last definition is that it depends exclusively on the partner's responses. What if the partner has difficulties reaching orgasm regardless of who her partner is? A man could continue intercourse until he's blue in the face and still be classified as a premature ejaculator. Most therapists choose to view premature ejaculation in terms of *absence of reasonable voluntary control* of ejaculation. By this definition, orgasm should not be a totally involuntary event, and a man should be able to have some control over when it occurs.

A man who is disturbed by his own inability to exert any control over when he ejaculates may develop low self-esteem and performance anxiety (Corretti & Baldi, 2007; Symonds et al., 2003). This, in turn, can lead to an erectile problem (and commonly does). Others may avoid dating new partners because of embarrassment or fear of rejection.

What causes some men to ejaculate too quickly? Traditionally, it was believed that in most cases premature ejaculation was due to psychological factors or relationship problems. However, studies indicate that there may be two different types of premature ejaculation: one caused by psychological factors and another caused by organic factors (Waldinger & Schweitzer, 2006). Some

Premature ejaculation ■ A recurrent and persistent absence of reasonable voluntary control of ejaculation.

types of injuries and illnesses have been known to cause premature ejaculation, as do some medications and withdrawal from some narcotics (see Metz et al., 1997). There is also growing evidence that some men have "neurological constitution" premature ejaculation—a physiological (and perhaps genetic) predisposition to ejaculate quickly (Metz & Pryor, 2000; Santtila et al., 2009). For example, hyperthyroidism is associated with premature ejaculation (Cihan et al., 2009). If premature ejaculation has an organic cause, pharmacological treatment may be best. There are several pharmacological agents that delay ejaculation, e.g., serotonin reuptake inhibitors (Shindel et al., 2008).

What about cognitive-behavioral therapy? The *squeeze technique* was developed by Masters and Johnson (1970) and is still regarded as the most effective treatment. After a couple has completed the sensate focus exercises described earlier, the woman is instructed to manually stimulate the man's penis until he gets close to orgasm. She then squeezes his penis firmly between her thumb and first and second fingers for 3 to 5 seconds and discontinues stimulation until he calms down. She repeats this three to four times before finally bringing him to orgasm. This teaches the man that he can delay ejaculation. When intercourse resumes, it is in a side-by-side or woman-on-top position (it generally takes longer to reach orgasm if you are not in total control).

Masters and Johnson (1970) reported success rates of 95%. However, long-term follow-up studies showed disappointing results. Most men who completed therapy successfully later regressed to pretreatment levels (Metz et al., 1997; Schover & Leiblum, 1994). Today, a wider variety of techniques are being used, depending on the diagnosed cause (Metz & Pryor, 2000). A recent review concluded that "the approach most likely to provide success is a combination of cognitive and sex therapy with a pharmacologic agent of proven efficacy that has an easy-to-follow regimen" (Barnes & Eardley, 2007; see also Shindel et al., 2008).

Male Orgasmic Disorder

This problem can be thought of as just the opposite of premature ejaculation. **Male orgasmic disorder** refers to a difficulty reaching orgasm and ejaculat-

ing in a woman's vagina, and it can be either *primary* or *secondary*. A review of many studies concluded that 1% to 3% of men suffered from this problem, but other studies indicate that perhaps as many as 7% to 9% of all men have this disorder on more than just an occasional basis (Laumann et al., 1999; Simons & Carey, 2001) and that it becomes more common after the age of 60 (Laumann et al., 2009; Waite et al., 2009). It is often referred to as **ejaculatory incompetence** if the man is totally unable to ejaculate in a woman's vagina. Although a few cases can be traced to organic causes (e.g., drugs, alcohol, or neurological disorders; see Munjack & Kanno, 1979), most of these men are able to reach orgasm either during masturbation or during manual or oral stimulation by the partner (Kaplan, 1979), indicating that the usual cause is psychological and not physical.

Masters and Johnson (1970) reported that primary orgasmic disorder was often associated with a strict religious upbringing, a fear of getting a woman pregnant, negativity and hostility toward the partner, and/or maternal dominance. Secondary problems are less common and are often associated with some kind of previous trauma. Apfelbaum (1989) found that men with orgasmic disorder focus too much on performance and pleasing their partners, and as a result are subjectively not as aroused (as they are during masturbation, for example).

Orgasmic disorder is often treated by what is called a *bridge maneuver*. The man is first taught to masturbate to orgasm while alone, and then in the presence of the partner. Once this is successfully completed, the partner manually stimulates the man to orgasm. When this is consistently successful, the female partner stimulates the man until he is very close to orgasm and then quickly inserts his penis into her vagina. The idea is that if this can be done several times, the man will overcome his fears of ejaculating inside her vagina. Apfelbaum additionally encourages men to be more assertive with partners in letting them know what they find to be arousing.

Sexual Pain Disorders

Painful intercourse is called **dyspareunia.** It usually, but not always, is caused by a physical problem. In men, the most common causes are a prostate, bladder, or urethral infection (Davis et al., 2009), or the foreskin of the penis being too tight (a condition called **phimosis**). In rare cases, fibrous tissue deposits around the corpora cavernosa of the penis cause curvature of the penis (known as *Peyronie's disease*) and pain during erection (Deveci et al., 2007).

If the physical factors responsible for dyspareunia are not quickly taken care of, dyspareunia can lead to other sexual problems. The anticipation of pain, for example, can become so great that it can lead to erectile problems or loss of sexual desire.

Male orgasmic disorder ■ A condition in which a man has difficulty reaching orgasm and ejaculating in a woman's vagina.

Ejaculatory incompetence ■ A condition in which a man is totally unable to ejaculate in a woman's vagina during sexual intercourse.

Dyspareunia ■ Recurrent or persistent genital pain during intercourse, usually resulting from organic factors (e.g., vaginal, prostate, or bladder infections).

Phimosis ■ A condition in uncircumcised men in which the foreskin of the penis is too tight, causing pain during erection.

The resultant psychological stress can also damage relationships. Remember, pain during intercourse is generally an indication that there is something physically wrong, so see a physician immediately before there are greater problems.

> **NOTE: The following two problems are generally not included as sexual pain disorders, but I have included them here because both, in fact, do involve pain.**

To many men, the idea of having a *long-lasting erection* might seem appealing. **Priapism** is a rare condition in which the penis remains erect for prolonged periods of time, sometimes days (Broderick et al., 2010). It results from damage to the valves regulating penile blood flow and can be caused by tumors, infection, chemical irritants (such as Spanish fly or some antidepressant drugs). It is not usually accompanied by a desire for sex. Priapism is often painful, not to mention inconvenient, and men with this condition would gladly trade it for a normal erection. Depending on the cause, treatment may include medications or surgery.

Some men (and a few women) get severe headaches that start just before, during, or slightly after orgasm (see Diamond & Maliszewski, 1992). This condition is called **benign coital cephalalgia** ("benign orgasmic/sex headache"; alternative spelling: *cephalgia*). This is not a new problem, and in fact was first reported by Hippocrates, the father of modern medicine, in the fifth century B.C.E. It has been estimated that as many as 250,000 Americans may presently suffer from this problem. Most are men who are middle-aged, mildly obese, and somewhat hypertensive. The severe headaches may last for minutes or hours and are most common in men who suffer from migraines. They are not related to type of sexual activity, and although physicians sometimes mistake the pains as the sign of an imminent stroke, they are usually not associated with any other serious disorder. The headaches are in the general category of "exertional headaches" and are generally caused by contraction of scalp muscles and increased blood flow to the head, neck, or upper body during intercourse. For reasons that are not understood, the headaches often disappear for weeks or months at a time and then suddenly reappear. Treatment may include the teaching of relaxation techniques, medication for high blood pressure, or anti-inflammatory drugs (taken one-half hour before sex).

FEMALE SEXUAL PROBLEMS

Classification of Sexual Disorders

Read again the section on classification of men's sexual disorders. Recall that the *DSM-IV-TR* and *ICD-10* classification systems are generally medical models. Many therapists believe that the *DSM-IV-TR* does not adequately describe women's sexual problems. As a result, a group of experts (hereafter referred to as the International Consensus Conference) met and recommended a new classification system (Basson et al., 2000). Some therapists believe that the new system did not go far enough—and, in fact, the definitions of women's sexual dysfunctions are still evolving (see Basson et al., 2003). The new classification system keeps the four major categories (desire, arousal, orgasmic, and sexual pain disorders), but uses new definitions for several disorders and places greater emphasis on the criterion of subjective experience and personal distress. For many women with sexual problems, it is not accompanied by personal distress (Palacios et al., 2009; Shifren et al., 2008). Greater importance is given to the relationship and to the contextual assessment of stimuli. Most importantly, the new attempts at classification shift the emphasis from function-centered (the medical model) to meaning-centered (Tiefer, 2001). This book will attempt to follow the new recommendations. Before you continue, review the section on women's sexual response cycle in Chapter 4.

Sexual Interest/Desire Disorders: Hypoactive Sexual Desire and Sexual Aversion

Recall that the *DSM-IV-TR* defines hypoactive sexual desire as a persistent or recurrent absence of sexual fantasies and sexual desire. The International Consensus Conference recommended that the definition of **female hypoactive sexual desire** be "the persistent or recurrent deficiency (or absence) of sexual fantasies/thoughts, and/or desire for or *receptivity to sexual activity*, which causes *personal distress*" (Basson et al., 2000). The term sexual "interest" is preferred by many because in women sexual arousal often precedes desire and thus "desire" is often not the reason for engaging in sex (Basson et al., 2003; see Chapter 4). **Sexual aversion disorder** is defined as "the persistent or recurrent phobic aversion to and avoidance of sexual contact with a sexual partner, which causes personal distress."

Priapism ■ A condition in which the penis remains erect for a prolonged period of time, sometimes days.

Benign coital cephalalgia ■ Severe headaches that start during or slightly after orgasm, usually in men.

Female hypoactive sexual desire ■ "The persistent or recurrent deficiency (or absence) of sexual fantasies/thoughts, and/or desire for or receptivity to sexual activity, which causes personal distress" (Basson et al., 2000).

Sexual aversion disorder ■ "The persistent or recurrent phobic aversion to and avoidance of sexual contact with a sexual partner, which causes personal distress" (Basson et al., 2000).

National surveys have found that about 27% to 33% of women in all age groups (up to age 59) had little or no interest in sex lasting a few months or more within the last year (Laumann et al., 1999; West et al., 2008). A nationally representative Australian survey found higher numbers (Richter et al., 2003c). For women aged 60 and older, as many as 40% to 52% have hypoactive sexual desire (Laumann et al., 2009; Waite et al., 2009; West et al., 2008).

Some of the causes of hypoactive sexual desire in women are the same as for men: extreme sexually restrictive upbringing, past traumas (such as rape or molestation; Campbell et al., 2006), some medications (such as antidepressant drugs), low testosterone levels, or a coexisting sexual problem (such as pain during intercourse). However, a major change in the definition for women is the addition of "receptivity to sexual activity"—and that brings us back to the importance of the overall relationship. Recall from Chapter 4 (desire phase in women's sexual response cycle) that for many women sexual desire depends less on innate biological urges than it does on a desire to enhance emotional closeness to the partner (Basson, 2000, 2002c; Byers, 2001; Haning et al., 2007; Peplau, 2003; Regan & Berscheid, 1999; Tiefer, 2000).

> "I find it much more pleasurable and rewarding to make love with my partner. We have times when we have sex but I enjoy making love much more. My partner caresses me and makes me feel more special and loved." (from the author's files)

> "My husband was drunk on our wedding night. He could hardly walk and practically tore my clothes off. I wanted to kiss and hug and feel like I was loved, but all he wanted was to screw. I wasn't ready and it hurt real bad. He made me do things I didn't want to do. Afterwards he threw up in the bathroom and passed out. I cried all night. Now I still don't want him to touch me." (from the author's files)

> "After I gave birth, he was in the hospital bed pushing me.... He was so forceful. He was so nasty. 'You are a cold fish!' he'd say.... I couldn't go in the bathroom. He'd have me by the sink. He was just constantly.... Just constantly."
> (from Clarke, 2006)

Which one of these women do you suppose has sexual desire for her partner?

Today, many therapists believe that problems in a relationship are one of the most important factors contributing to hypoactive sexual desire in women (Basson, 2001c; Byers, 2001; Leiblum et al., 2006; Metz & Epstein, 2002; Tiefer, 2001). For many women we cannot look at sexual desire in isolation, but instead must focus on the relational context of their sexuality: "Women's sexual inhibitions, avoidance, or distress can arise from betrayal, dislike, or fear of partner; partner's abuse or couple's unequal power; or from a sexual partner's negative patterns of communication" (Tiefer et al., 2002, p. 229). Women who are unhappy in their relationships, and as a result show little or no interest in sex, would typically be diagnosed with hypoactive sexual desire, when in fact "the dysfunction" is with the partner (Basson, 2001b). Under the new definition, it should only be regarded as a sexual problem if her lack of sexual desire was causing *her* personal distress. Many women, especially older women, with hypoactive sexual desire experience little or no personal distress about it (Hayes et al., 2007).

Not surprisingly, attempts to apply the medical model for treating low sexual interest/desire in women have generally failed. In 2004, Pfizer announced that it had stopped its research on using Viagra to treat female hypoactive desire and arousal disorder. Procter & Gamble has marketed a testosterone patch (Intrinsa) for women who have had their ovaries removed, but in 2005 the Food and Drug Administration refused to approve it for postmenopausal women. Testosterone may be helpful for women with very low testosterone levels (Davis et al., 2008; Schwenkhagen & Studd, 2009), but there are concerns about its safety (Shufelt & Braunstein, 2009). In fact, only a minority of women's sexual desire problems can be attributed to low testosterone levels. Studies continue to explore the effects of "treatments" like Zestra (a topical bocanical) and Ginkgo bilobo extract (from a Chinese tree) (Ferguson et al., 2010; Meston et al., 2008), but as of 2010 there were no drugs for the treatment of female desire/arousal/orgasmic disorders that were approved by the Food and Drug Administration.

In one study of women referred for hypoactive sexual desire, the major factors were insufficient emotional intimacy, depression, psychological factors (e.g., remembered painful intercourse, sexual abuse, or abusive relationships), and lack of appropriate sexual stimuli. As for sexual stimuli, "the most common needs expressed were those outside of the bedroom—an appropriate atmosphere, partner's consideration, respect, and warmth and physical affection..." (Basson, 2001c, p. 400).

Masters and Johnson's sexual therapy with its emphasis on sexual functioning has also been very unsuccessful in treating female hypoactive sexual desire disorder (Hawton et al., 1991; Kaplan, 1987). Instead, behavioral-cognitive techniques must be accompanied by couples therapy to resolve relationship problems and rebuild intimacy. According to two researchers, "Every sexual problem, to some extent, embodies an actual or anticipated unresolved relationship conflict that is sufficiently distressing to bring the individual or couple to therapy" (Metz & Epstein, 2002).

Sexual Arousal Disorder

The International Consensus Conference defined **female sexual arousal disorder** as "the persistent or recurrent inability to attain or maintain sufficient sexual excitement, causing personal distress, which may be expressed as a lack of subjective excitement, or genital (lubrication/swelling) or other somatic responses" (Basson et al., 2000). More recently, women's sexual arousal disorder has been divided into three distinct subcategories (Basson et al., 2003): physical/genital disorder, psychological (subjective) disorder, and a combination of the two.

If we focus only on physiological arousal (vaginal lubrication and other vasocongestive responses), different studies (which use different definitions and methodologies) report that 6% to 19% of women have sexual arousal disorder (see Simons & Carey, 2001). The percentage of postmenopausal women experiencing vaginal dryness is about 25% for 60-year-old women, and it increases with age (Dunn et al., 2002). For *some* postmenopausal women, low testosterone levels may be a contributing factor. However, recall from Chapter 4 that for women physiological arousal is poorly correlated with subjective arousal (Chivers et al., 2010). Recall also that most women do not separate desire from arousal (Basson, 2002c; Tiefer, 2000), and for many women their thoughts and emotions are more important in evaluating their own desire than feedback from the genitals. Thus, much of what was covered in the previous section applies here as well (Graham, 2010). Therapy must focus on psychological factors (e.g., depression, past abuse) and partner and relationship problems.

A few women suffer from **persistent sexual arousal syndrome.** In this condition, women have persistent genital arousal, but no feelings of sexual desire (Leiblum & Chivers, 2007). The women are otherwise normal. We do not know what causes this syndrome, but it is sometimes seen after withdrawal from some types of antidepressant medicines (Leiblum & Goldmeier, 2008).

Female Orgasmic Disorder

The vast majority of women who seek sexual therapy do so because of problems in reaching orgasm. The International Consensus Conference defines **female orgasmic disorder** as "the persistent or recurrent difficulty, delay in, or absence of attaining orgasm following sufficient sexual stimulation and arousal, which causes personal distress" (Basson et al., 2000). National surveys have found that about 27% of women aged 18 to 59 and about 40% of women aged 60 to 75 said that they had been unable to achieve orgasm for at least sev-

eral months of the previous year (Laumann et al., 1999, 2009; Lindau et al., 2007; Shifren et al., 2008; Waite et al., 2009). A review of many studies concluded that 20% of women at age 50 years "never or rarely achieve orgasm" (with higher rates for young women aged 18 to 24 years) (Dunn et al., 2002). These numbers are for orgasm induced by any means. One thing is for sure—a larger number of women have difficulty reaching orgasm during sexual intercourse as opposed to during masturbation or oral-genital sex (Fugl-Meyer et al., 2006).

Female orgasmic disorder can be *primary* or *absolute* (never having had an orgasm under any circumstances), *secondary* (having once been regularly orgasmic), or *situational.* Many women's orgasm problems are situational—they may have great difficulty reaching orgasm during intercourse, but no difficulty during masturbation. Secondary orgasmic disorder is often due to a deteriorating relationship (the context in which sex occurs has become negative).

The definition of female orgasmic disorder assumes that there was "sufficient sexual stimulation and arousal." Therefore, one of the first questions to ask, of course, is whether a woman with problems reaching orgasm during sexual intercourse is receiving sufficient stimulation from her partner. Has there been enough time and foreplay?

"My problem seems like one that some of my friends have—short foreplay. It takes me a long time to reach orgasm. When we take a long time and work up slowly to lovemaking, I have intense orgasms. It is wonderful for both of us. But this happens very rarely. Because 'John' works a 9-hour work day and usually comes home exhausted, our lovemaking is short and to the point. He's satisfied and I lay there feeling nothing because I faked an orgasm for him. Then, when I insist on continuing, I start to feel guilty for wasting his time."
(from the author's files)

Remember that in response to a survey question asked in my course ("What things do you personally like best in a sexual partner?"), well over half of the women who indicated that they were sexually experienced answered that they wanted

Female sexual arousal disorder ■ "The persistent or recurrent inability to attain or maintain sufficient sexual excitement, causing personal distress, which may be expressed as lack of subjective excitement, or genital (lubrication/swelling) or other somatic responses" (Basson et al., 2000).
Persistent sexual arousal syndrome ■ Persistent genital arousal without subjective feelings of desire.
Female orgasmic disorder ■ A persistent or recurrent delay in, or absence of, orgasm following a normal sexual excitement phase and which causes personal distress.

their partner (or partners) to take his time. Here are some examples:

> "Lover takes his time and is as concerned with fondling and foreplay as he is with intercourse."

> "Unhurried attitude toward sex and lovemaking in general."

> "Partner who likes to take time with foreplay and not rush into intercourse. A caring and sensitive person who is not out just to get a 'piece of ass.'"

Even if her partner takes his time, many women may still have difficulties reaching orgasm during intercourse. The key for many women is the degree of stimulation to the clitoris. Most women need clitoral stimulation to reach orgasm, with or without vaginal stimulation (Darling, Davidson, & Cox, 1991). During sexual intercourse, the penis only indirectly stimulates the clitoris by causing the clitoral hood to rub back and forth over the clitoral glans. Unfortunately, many men take the attitude that what feels good to the gander must also feel good to the goose—if it feels good to the man to have his penis in his partner's vagina, then it must also feel equally good to the woman. The stimulation provided by the vaginal walls to the penis during intercourse is similar to that experienced by men during masturbation, but the reverse is not true for women. The inner two thirds of the vagina have relatively few nerve endings. Most women who masturbate do so by stimulating their clitoris. Men should not feel inadequate if their female partners require manual stimulation of the clitoris during intercourse to reach orgasm.

> "Your class has also taught me how to talk to my boyfriend about sex. Stimulation of the clitoris manually has brought great joy to my sex life. I now even reach orgasm from it during sex."
> (from the author's files)

If a man cares for his partner, he will do (or let her do) whatever she says feels best, not what he believes ought to feel best. *Therapists agree that clitoral stimulation during intercourse is not cheating.*

Not all cases of female orgasm problems can be blamed on insufficient physical stimulation. Sex is more than just the physical rubbing together of tissues. A healthy, positive attitude about sex and pleasure is also very important. Interestingly, Laumann et al. (1999) found that the prevalence of orgasm problems among women decreased as their education level increased (see Table 13–1), and education is associated with more positive attitudes about sex. Many cases of primary orgasmic disorder are associated with negative attitudes about sex or feelings of guilt about sex (often due to a very strict religious upbringing, where sexual feelings are associated with sin rather than something positive) (Kelly et al., 1990; Masters & Johnson, 1970).

> "I grew up sexually in marriage. In those days no one discussed sex, and my husband and I both only knew bits and pieces. I understood it to be very natural for women not to have orgasms. Therefore, if I did, my

TABLE 13–1	*Approximate Percentage of Men and Women Who Have Experienced Sexual Problems Lasting Several Months During the Previous Year*						
	Lack interest in sex		Can't reach orgasm		Erectile disorder	Pain during sex	Premature ejaculation
Respondents	Women	Men	Women	Men	Men	Women	Men
Age							
18–29	32%	14%	26%	7%	7%	21%	30%
30–39	32	13	28	7	9	15	32
40–49	35	15	22	9	11	13	28
50–59	36	20	28	12	24	15	30
60–75	40	28	40	19	37	18	29
Education							
Less than high school	42	19	34	11	13	18	38
High-school graduate	33	12	29	7	9	17	35
College graduate	24	14	18	7	10	10	27

Source: Laumann et al., 1999, 2007, 2009; Lindau et al., 2007; Shifren et al., 2008; Waite et al., 2009

private Catholic girl school upbringing made me feel ashamed of my own natural desires and pleasures."

"I was told my whole life as a child and as an adolescent that because I was a woman, I was not supposed to feel sexual, or be sexual. My daddy told me that good women who wanted to be loved by a man did not feel sexual. A good man did not look for a woman who was sexual."
(from the author's files)

In addition, sex involves sweating, underarm and vaginal odors (and often vaginal noises), and facial grimaces that many women were taught are unfeminine. To fully enjoy sex and experience the pleasures of orgasm, one must "let go." Simply telling a young woman that sex is now okay is not going to change these attitudes overnight. It may take years to overcome inhibitions about sex.

"I was raised as good girls don't, and if you do you are used property. After getting married, the morals were supposed to change. I had great difficulty in the transition of why it is OK now, after marriage. I am now divorced. I wish I would have had your class prior to marriage. It would have made the transition a lot easier."
(from the author's files)

Some studies have found that married women who have masturbated to orgasm have more orgasms during intercourse than married women who have not masturbated to orgasm (Hurlbert & Whittaker, 1991). In fact, many therapists now include masturbation therapy as a first step in the treatment of inhibited female orgasm in order to make a woman more aware of her own body (LoPiccolo & Stock, 1986; Meston et al., 2004). The hope is that once a woman can reach orgasm during masturbation, she will be able to achieve it during sexual intercourse. However, increased knowledge of the clitoris often is associated with increased frequency of orgasm during masturbation but not during intercourse (Wade et al., 2005).

Performance anxiety can also contribute to orgasm problems. This can easily happen if a woman's partner expects or demands that she have an orgasm during sex. The subsequent spectatoring then makes the problem even worse.

"My husband and I have a really good sex life, but I don't reach climax every time. This doesn't bother me, but it really bothers him. I've started worrying about it so much that I'm now having fewer orgasms and starting to fake more."
(from the author's files)

Women (and their partners) should not expect to reach orgasm with every experience of sexual intercourse. This is an unrealistic expectation that can lead to unnecessary feelings of guilt (Davidson & Moore, 1994).

Recently, there have been attempts to "medicalize" women's orgasm problems, but these approaches have not been successful. Why not? Recall that women's sexual desire and pleasure depends to a large extent on the quality of the overall relationship (e.g., Costa & Brody, 2007). But before we consider that, let us first look at the behavior modification techniques used in traditional sex therapy.

What procedures are used in therapy to help a woman become more orgasmic? Most therapists begin with sensate focus exercises. These nondemand exercises teach the couple to take their time and learn what gives each maximum pleasure. After several days of this, the therapist will probably instruct the partner to manually explore the woman's genitals, usually while both are sitting in the position shown in Figure 13–5.

FIGURE 13–5 A commonly used training technique for women.

When the couple is finally told that they may resume sexual intercourse, they will almost always be told to use a position that allows the woman a great deal of control, such as woman-on-top. She will decide when intromission begins and initiate pelvic movements once they start. By this point in therapy, both she and her partner will be comfortable with manual stimulation of the clitoris during intercourse. Remember, *manual stimulation of the clitoris during intercourse is not cheating*. Contrary to advice given in a popular book (Eichel & Nobile, 1992), no particular technique of intercourse can guarantee orgasms (Kaplan, 1992). The couple will have to try different techniques. With some practice, for example, the woman might be able to reach orgasm without manual stimulation by rubbing her clitoris against her partner's pubic bone, or vice versa (in a "high-ride" position).

If at this point you are thinking that female orgasm problems have been treated rather mechanically, as if the solution is nothing more than finding the correct manner of physical stimulation, you are probably right. For many women, sexual satisfaction is closely related to how emotionally involved they are with their partners and how happy they are in their overall relationship (Basson, 2000; Byers, 2001; Costa & Brody, 2007; Haning et al., 2007; Peplau, 2003; Regan & Berscheid, 1999; Tiefer, 2000). These things are better predictors of a woman's sexual satisfaction than are frequency of sex and number of orgasms (McNulty & Fisher, 2008). Conversely, the better a woman regards her emotional relationship with her partner, the more likely she is to judge her sex life satisfying (Costa & Brody, 2007; Jacoby, 1999; Kingsberg, 2000).

In summary, for many women the therapy steps outlined in this section may do little good if the emotional aspects of their relationships are not satisfying. Thus, today, therapy for women's orgasm problems (during intercourse) usually includes a variety of techniques. These will probably include education about the body, self-exploration exercises, cognitive-behavioral therapy (with sensate focus), and couples therapy (Meston et al., 2004).

PERSONAL REFLECTIONS

Are you able to "let go" totally during sex (i.e., no anxieties about nudity, sweat, odors, noises, facial expressions, etc.)? If not, why not?

Sexual Pain Disorder

The International Consensus Conference listed three types of sexual pain disorders (Basson et al., 2000). *Dyspareunia* is "the recurrent or persistent genital pain associated with sexual intercourse." It is assumed that there is no problem with arousal and there is sufficient lubrication when intercourse begins. How common is dyspareunia in the general population? Estimates for women aged 20 to 59 vary between 9% and 15% (Danielsson et al., 2003; Laumann et al., 1999). The percentage is higher in older women (Laumann et al., 2009; Waite et al., 2009), but many of these are probably due to vaginal dryness. There is increasing support for considering dyspareunia "as pain disorders that interfere with sexuality rather than as sexual disorders characterized by pain" (Binik, 2005).

FIGURE 13–6 For any sexual problem, when the therapist allows the couple to resume sexual intercourse, it is almost always in the woman-on-top position. Women with orgasm problems are encouraged to touch their clitoris (or have their partners touch it) during intercourse.

"....It hurt that bad! I figured that it would go away after I got more experienced, but it only got worse. It felt so bad that I could never orgasm during sex ..."

(from the author's files)

Chronic vulval pain is called **vulvodynia** (Goldstein & Burroughs, 2008). One of the most common causes is inflammation of the vestibular bulbs (*vulvar vestibulitis*). This can sometimes be alleviated with medications or surgery. Dyspareunia in women can also be caused by endometriosis (growth of the endometrium outside the uterus), pelvic inflammatory disease, yeast and other vaginal infections, Bartholin's gland infections, and urinary tract infections. If a woman has repeatedly painful experiences during intercourse, it can lead to reduced emotional intimacy, a loss of sexual desire, shame, and guilt (Ayling & Ussher, 2008).

Vaginismus refers to recurrent or persistent pain experienced during attempted sexual intercourse (intromission). It is believed to be caused by *involuntary contractions* of the muscles that surround the outer third of the vagina, although recent studies suggest that it sometimes includes dyspareunia and fear of pain (Crowley et al., 2009; Reissing et al., 2004). In many cases vaginismus occurs at attempts to insert anything into the vagina (e.g., a finger or tampon). A pelvic examination may be impossible for women with this condition. To a man attempting intercourse, it feels like his penis is hitting a wall, and forceful attempts at penetration can be quite painful for the woman.

"I was glad to see this topic addressed in your textbook and to know that it actually had a name. I was a virgin until I was 20 and when I did attempt intercourse, I encountered severe pain. My boyfriend at the time tried to be understanding, but it ended up tearing us apart. No matter how often we tried, we could not get it right.... I saw my ob/gyn and she gave me three different-sized vaginal dilators. I used these with KY Jelly but this was extremely humiliating.... I was helped over my fear by a much older man who took his time and made me feel extremely relaxed."

(from the author's files)

About 2% of all women have vaginismus (Renshaw, 1990). The cause of vaginismus is usually *psychological* (Kaplan, 1974; Kleinplatz, 1998). It is normal for inexperienced women to have anxieties before intercourse that may result in some degree of involuntary muscle contraction, but the vast majority of women soon learn to relax (and even gain voluntary control over these muscles). Vaginismus is often associated with very negative views about sex, a religious restrictive upbringing (where sex is equated with sin), or hostility toward or fear of men (Crowley et al., 2009). Treatment usually consists of sensate focus relaxation exercises followed by *systematic desensitization by gradual dilation of the vagina* (with a set of dilators). The use of dilators in an atmosphere that is free of sexual demand, so that there is no performance anxiety, allows the woman to slowly overcome her anxieties about having an object in her vagina. The success rate approaches 100% (Jeng et al., 2006). Psychotherapy may have to be used as well in order to deal with past sexual trauma, guilt about sex, or relationship problems (Leiblum et al., 1989).

The International Consensus Conference included a new category of female sexual pain disorder—**noncoital sexual pain disorder.** This refers to recurrent or persistent genital pain caused by sexual stimulation other than intercourse (Basson et al., 2000). The pain can be experienced during sexual arousal or orgasm.

HYPERSEXUALITY: COMPULSION, ADDICTION, OR MYTH?

Lately, several celebrities have sought therapy for hypersexuality. This includes Tiger Woods, David Duchovny, and Jesse James. What is hypersexuality?

At the beginning of this chapter, you learned that two people in a relationship often differ in the frequency with which they desire sex, but that ordinarily neither one should be considered hyposexual or hypersexual. By how much would one's sexual desire have to differ from that of most other people before he or she would be considered extraordinary? This is a matter of subjective judgment, which (as usual) varies across different cultures and times. As you learned earlier, some people can be classified as having hypoactive sexual desire. Can we make the same distinction at the other extreme? Can people be classified as "hypersexual"? Because diminished sexual desire is classified as a disorder, it seems logical that individuals at the other extreme could be considered as having a disorder. However, many therapists say no, and in fact, the American Psychiatric Association's diagnostic manual *DSM-IV-TR* (2000) has no such category. On

---

Vaginismus ■ A recurrent or persistent sexual problem in women in which pain is experienced during attempted intercourse because of involuntary spasms in the muscles surrounding the outer third of the vagina.

Noncoital sexual pain disorder ■ Recurrent or persistent genital pain caused by sexual stimulation other than intercourse.

FIGURE 13–7 Tiger Woods with ex-wife Elin Nordegren (left) and Jesse James with ex-wife Sandra Bullock (right). Despite being married to beautiful and supportive wives, both men allegedly had numerous extramarital affairs and later sought therapy for hypersexuality.

the other hand, the World Health Organization's *International Classification of Diseases* (1992) does recognize excessive sexual drive. Let us explore this controversial issue further. Recently, some therapists have argued that hypersexual disorder does, in fact, exist and should be included in the next APA diagnostic manual (DSM-V)(Kafka, 2010; Kaplan & Krueger, 2010).

Terms like *nymphomania* and *satyriasis* have long been used to describe people with seemingly insatiable sexual appetites. However, therapists who favor a new classification for hypersexuality say that hypersexuality is more than just numbers. Patrick Carnes (1983, 1991) was the first to use the designation "*sexual addiction*." Many therapists objected to this term, saying that there was no evidence of physical addiction as in the case of alcohol or drugs. Goodman (1992) redefined sexual addiction as follows:

A disorder in which a behavior that can function both to produce pleasure and to provide escape from internal discomfort is employed in a pattern characterized by (1) recurrent failure to control the behavior, and (2) continuation of the behavior despite significant harmful consequences.

This definition includes aspects of both dependency ("behavior motivated by an attempt to achieve a pleasurable internal state") and compulsivity ("behavior motivated by an attempt to evade or avoid an unpleasurable/aversive internal state") and is similar to the definition in *DSM-IV-TR* for psychoactive substance addiction (Goodman, 1998). Carnes (1983) says that "the sex addict relies on sex for comfort from pain, nurturing, or relief from stress, etc., the way an alcoholic relies on alcohol or a drug addict relies on drugs" . . . and he or she "transforms sex into the primary relationship or need for which all else may be sacrificed including family, friends, values, health, safety, and work."

Opponents of the designation "sexual addiction" argue that it is based on a repressive morality that can be used against anyone engaged in non-monogamous sex (e.g., Coleman & Edwards, 1986; Keane, 2004). As Coleman and Edwards (1986) note, "This concept can potentially be used to oppress sexual minorities . . . because they do not conform to the moral values of the prevailing culture (or therapist)." These therapists prefer to regard people who show a lack of sexual control as having a *sexual compulsion*.

Note that there is some common ground: Both sides admit that it is possible to engage in sex compulsively. I will use the purely descriptive term "hypersexual" to describe such individuals.

A **hypersexual individual** is distinguished from other people by the compulsiveness with which he or she engages in sex (Miner et al., 2007). Hypersexuals engage in sex repeatedly and compulsively to reduce anxiety and distress, usually finding little or no emotional satisfaction. This can include compulsive masturbation, use of pornography, cybersex, telephone sex, and/or compulsive sex with consenting adults (see Kaplan & Krueger, 2010). It has been estimated that about 5% of the population are hypersexual (Coleman, 1992; Society for the Advancement of Sexual Health, 2010). Coleman (1991) and others choose to divide hypersexual (compulsive sexual) behavior into two types: paraphilic and nonparaphilic. I will discuss paraphilic behaviors in the next chapter; this section is devoted to nonparaphilic hypersexuality.

Hypersexual individuals feel driven to have sex, looking for something in sex that they can never find. They have excessive numbers of sexual partners and/or engage in excessive masturbation (Keane, 2004). If they fall in love and establish a relationship, they often cannot stop their promiscuous behavior. Hypersexuality interferes with the ability to carry out normal daily living and results in unhappiness, lack of fulfillment, and the inability to break a pattern of compulsive behavior. Here is an example:

Dear Ann Landers:

I am a 20-year-old woman with a problem that could destroy my life. I've been living with a 23-year-old man for 2 years and I love him very much, but I have an obsession to go to bed with other men. It seems that I just can't be satisfied with one.

My guy and I have a great relationship. He's a terrific lover but I am always looking for others. Some of my lovers are married men, others I've been involved with have been close friends of mine. I've slept with men I barely knew. This problem has been with me since I was 16.

I once had an affair with a married high school teacher. It became public and caused him to lose his job. I felt awful about it but it didn't stop me from going to bed with another teacher the following year...I think my guy knows I am sleeping around, but he says nothing because he doesn't want to lose me. Please tell me what to do. I don't want to behave like a tramp for the rest of my life.

Never Satisfied

(Ann Landers column: Never Satisfied. Esther P. Lederer Trust and Creators Syndicate, Inc. Reprinted with permission.)

We can make a good case that this individual might be hypersexual. Her sexual behavior has caused great harm to herself and others and causes her great distress, yet she is unable to change. The threat of possibly contracting a sexually transmitted infection, including HIV infection and AIDS, also does not stop hypersexual people.

Today, therapists are becoming increasingly aware of individuals whose use of the Internet for sexual arousal and gratification has become pathological:

"Mr. A was a 42-year old married man, an academic sociologist...he had increased his use of the Internet, spending several hours a day searching for particular pornographic images. He clearly articulated stress at the loss of control this behavior represented for him and also noted that he was spending more time on Internet downloads than he could afford. His behavior had also led to a marked decline in research productivity...When he masturbated to orgasm during the day (sometimes three or more times), he was often unable to achieve orgasm if he and his wife had sex that night."

(from Stein et al., 2001)

Would it surprise you to learn that "sex" is the most frequently searched topic on the Internet? Of course, use of the Internet for sex falls along a continuum (from curiosity to pathological) and for the vast majority its use falls in the range we call "normal." However, one large study of 9,177 adults who had used the Internet for sex found that nearly 3% spent 20 hours or more per week engaged in online sexual activities (Cooper et al., 1999). The greater the amount of time spent online pursuing sexual interests, the more likely it was that it negatively impacted their professions and personal relationships. The female partners of these heavy Internet sex users are generally devastated when they discover it, yet this, too, rarely stops the behavior (Bergner & Bridges, 2002). All of this has led some researchers to conclude that there is a new and growing problem: Internet sex addiction (e.g., Boies et al., 2004; Griffiths, 2001; Young, 2004).

Again, some argue that individuals cannot have nonchemical addictions, but the behavior certainly has all the components of other addictions (see Cooper et al., 2000; Griffiths, 2001). There is greater agreement that individuals who engage in heavy Internet sexual behavior (that interferes with their personal and professional lives), who cannot stop (except only temporarily), and who are in denial of the negative effects on their lives, are displaying another form of compulsive sexual behavior (hypersexuality). What distinguishes online

Hypersexuality ■ A term reserved for people who engage in sex compulsively, with little or no emotional satisfaction. Sometimes called sexual addiction.

Box 13–A Cross-Cultural Perspectives

Sex Therapy

The model of sex therapy presented in this chapter is based primarily on Western, middle-class values (Lavee, 1991). The two most important assumptions in the model are that people engage in sex primarily for (physical) pleasure, and that men and women can be viewed as equals. The model also assumes that men and women want to know about sex and that better communication makes for better sex. The highest levels of subjective sexual well-being are, in fact, found in cultures in which men and women have egalitarian roles (Laumann et al., 2006).

Not all cultures share these attitudes. Traditional American sex therapy would not be accepted in many Chinese cultures (So & Cheung, 2005). Recall from Box 4–A that in large parts of northern Africa and the Middle East (with primarily Islamic populations), sexual pleasure is reserved for the men, and women's pleasure is denied by clitoral

circumcision and genital mutilation. Many Latin countries are also male-dominant to the point of denying women's sexual feelings (Guerrero Pavich, 1986). In these cultures, a woman's difficulty in reaching orgasm is not considered important, and certainly no grounds for therapy. Even painful intercourse (dyspareunia, vaginismus) is considered unimportant unless it interferes with a woman's ability to engage in sex (Aziz & Gurgen, 2009). For women, the only purposes of sex are procreation and the pleasure of the husband. For men, premature ejaculation is not regarded as a problem. Men do regard difficulty in getting and maintaining an erection as a problem, and may seek therapy in order to engage in sexual intercourse (Osman & Al-Sawaf, 1995). However, both men and women reject the very idea of engaging in sensate focus exercises as a solution, for this is a mutual pleasuring technique (Lavee, 1991).

In sharp contrast to these attitudes (and our own) about sex are those held by many Hindu and Buddhist societies (Voigt, 1991). Tantric scriptures urge people to strive for the goal of transcendent unity and harmony, and sex is viewed as an opportunity for spiritual growth. While Western therapists emphasize the mutual physical pleasures of sex, Asian societies emphasize spiritual union. For example, in this chapter orgasm is presented as resulting from proper physical stimulation and effective technique. Those who follow Tantrism, on the other hand, "understand orgasm as a product of deep relaxation and a profound level of contact between partners" (Voigt, 1991). Western culture emphasizes doing, stimulation, activation, and outcome-focus, while Tantrism emphasizes being, stillness, meditation, and process-immersion. Good sex is not achieved by focusing on one or the other partner, but by focusing on the "between."

compulsive sexual behavior from other hypersexual behaviors, and what makes it so easy, is the Internet's accessibility, affordability, and anonymity (Cooper, 1998). Among Internet sexually compulsive individuals, men account for about 80% (men tend to target porn sites, whereas women tend to get involved in online relationships) and 50% are married or in committed relationships (Griffiths, 2001; Young et al., 2000).

Sexually compulsive individuals are frequently found to have been victims of childhood abuse or neglect (Griffiths, 2001; van der Kolk et al., 1996). Such children often have low self-esteem and feelings of inadequacy and unworthiness as adults. They are often very lonely, and their emotional pain causes them to engage in behaviors (e.g., alcohol, drugs, food, sex) that give them pleasure and help them evade their internal discomfort. Hypersexuals tend to engage in sex when they are depressed or anxious (Bancroft & Vukadinovic, 2004).

Therapy is often twofold: (1) treating the internal discomfort (perhaps initially with antidepressants or stabilizing drugs), and (2) helping the

individual find healthy, adaptive ways of dealing with his or her emotions and needs (Coleman, 1991). Those therapists favoring the addictive viewpoint probably will also teach cognitive-behavioral strategies to help the individual abstain from the addictive behavior (Goodman, 1992). Today, for people in a relationship these approaches are generally followed by couples therapy (Bird, 2006).

PERSONAL REFLECTIONS

Almost all people experience sexual disorders at some point in their lives. If you were in an ongoing relationship and were consistently experiencing a problem, would you go to a sex therapist? Why or why not? If your answer was "yes," how long would you wait before you decided to go? Most therapists believe that the earlier therapy is initiated, the better the chance for a cure.

ADDENDUM

Talking with Your Partner About Sexual Differences and Problems

Why do Americans find it easier to have sex than to talk about it?
(Peggy Clarke, 1996/1997)

Communication is the act of making information known, the exchange of thoughts or ideas (to paraphrase the *American Heritage Dictionary*). This part of the chapter deals with communication between two people who have made a commitment to a long-term relationship. It assumes that each person genuinely cares for the other and that there is trust and intimacy. As you have just learned, most couples experience sexual differences or problems in their relationship (Laumann et al., 1999, 2009; Waite et al., 2009). How they work those problems out—how they communicate with one another about their differences and problems—will affect their sexual adjustment. In cohabiting couples, sexual satisfaction is associated with understanding (particularly by men) their partner's sexual preferences (Purnine & Carey, 1997). "In many cases, sexual dysfunction problems cannot be addressed until communication improves" (Wincze & Carey, 1991, p. 110). Good communication also leads to a better relationship, and a better relationship generally leads to better sex (Cupach & Metts, 1991). It is generally the case that within happy marriages there is also good sexual satisfaction (Laumann et al., 2006).

Why Is It Difficult to Talk About Sex?

> "I have a tendency to be the only person in a relationship that realizes that the other person is not psychic. I tell the other person what I want but usually I can never get accurate feedback."
> (from the author's files)

Intercourse means "communication," but there are few topics that people have more difficulty talking about than sex. One of the major reasons for this is that most people have little experience talking about sex in an intelligent and mature manner. Surveys in my own course consistently indicate that fewer than one third of the students I teach every semester have ever had a serious discussion with their parents about sex. Very few ever had a course in sex education during junior high or high school. This means, of course, that most people's only experience with discussing sex is "dirty" stories and jokes, usually with individuals of the same gender. Adolescents often avoid talking to members of the opposite gender about sex because they fear that this will be interpreted as an invitation or come-on. Thus, men generally have some experience talking about sex with other men, and women with other women, but many adults have great difficulty talking to members of the opposite gender about sex (Athenstaedt et al., 2004).

Are there any gender differences that may contribute to communication difficulties in heterosexual relationships? In the popular book *Men Are from Mars, Women Are from Venus* (Gray, 1992), it is claimed that "not only do men and women communicate differently but they think, feel, perceive, react, respond, love, need, and appreciate differently. They almost seem to be from different planets, speaking different languages" (p. 5). Deborah Tannen's best-seller *You Just Don't Understand: Women and Men in Conversation* (1990) also portrays men and women as polarized in their conversation styles.

Research has shown that although there are gender differences in communication, the differences are not as large as popular books would have us believe (see Aries, 1998, for a review). For example, a review of 256 studies found that women self-disclose more than men, but that the difference is not that great. The authors concluded: "It's time to stop perpetuating the myth that there are large differences in men's and women's self-disclosure" (Dindia & Allen, 1992).

Nevertheless, there are some gender differences in communication styles. Starting early in childhood, men's communications are generally more concerned with self-assertion, dominance, and task completion, whereas women's communications are warmer, more collaborative, and other-oriented (Carli & Bukatko, 2000). Men also may be less likely to maintain eye contact during conversation, be less clear or neutral in their responses, and be more likely to withdraw (Klinetrob & Smith, 1996). During arguments, women are more likely to set the emotional tone. Many people believe that it is not masculine for a man to express his feelings and emotions (including during sex).

> "Recently I was involved in a relationship with a very 'sex-typed' guy.... Every time I would try to talk to him about how I felt about things or let him know how my emotional needs were going unfulfilled, he would change the subject or dismiss the whole discussion as being 'sissified.'"
> (from the author's files)

All people of both genders need to express their feelings and emotions and be able to communicate them. The image of a man as "strong and silent" robs him of a fundamental part of his humanity and robs his partner of a true companion.

Finally, power differences in a relationship can affect communication (Blanc, 2001; Quadagno et al., 1998). We are most likely to express an opinion, particularly a difference of opinion, to those persons we perceive as having equal status. In some relationships, there is a power imbalance; in heterosexual relationships, it is usually in favor of the man. Although the following suggestions for improving communication should be helpful to everyone, they will be most useful to individuals in an egalitarian relationship. (To resolve a major power imbalance in a relationship may require professional counseling.)

How Can My Partner and I Get Used to Talking About Sex?

One of the best ways to get used to talking with your partner about sex is to discuss together any sexuality-related topics in your daily newspaper. Hardly a day goes by when there is not at least one article (and there are often many) in the paper about sexuality—AIDS, birth control, fertility research, and, best of all, results of sex surveys. Show your partner some selected topic in this book and start off with a statement like "I didn't know this" or "This is really interesting."

Communication ■ The exchange of information, thoughts, ideas, or feelings.
Intercourse ■ The word means communication.

When you both become more comfortable talking about sex together, then you can more safely talk about your own sexual relationship. Often a good place to start is to talk about why it is difficult for you both to talk about sex. If, for example, your parents had a negative attitude about talking about sex, talk about that and how you would like to be different. Next you might talk about normal bodily functions related to sexuality and how they affect your sexual relationship. Try talking about menstruation, for example. Many people have learned (and thus can unlearn) negative attitudes about that (see Chapter 3). When you and your partner are comfortable enough to talk about sexual differences (in attitudes, preferred behaviors, etc.), you might want to discuss when and how to talk about such matters.

What If I Am Uncomfortable with the Language of Sex—What Words Should I Use?

Many of the commonly used words for our sexual anatomy and functions reflect the negativity about sex that is common in our culture. Words like *prick, cock, cunt, pussy, screw,* and *fuck* are common in conversations among men (Fischer, 1989), but many women (and men) might feel uncomfortable using such words with their partners, particularly if they wish to express positive emotions (Geer & Bellard, 1996). Medically correct terms such as *penis, vagina,* and *sexual intercourse* may not have any negative connotations, but are so unerotic that they, too, may seem inappropriate in conversations between two people in a deeply emotional relationship. Euphemisms such as "go to bed with," "sleeping with," and "making love" may seem more erotic to some and convey that there is a relationship, but they are often inappropriate as well. Do we always "make love" when we have sex? Some couples develop a private vocabulary for body parts that is used only in conversations between themselves.

It is not for me to tell you what words to use with your partner when talking about sex. However, it is important that you both be comfortable with a sexual vocabulary. Therefore, as part of the process of getting used to talking about sex, be sure to discuss this with your partner until you both agree on a vocabulary that is explicit and specific enough to convey your feelings and desires and that you also find nonoffensive (yet still erotic).

When (and Where) Should I Try to Talk to My Partner?

When is a good time to tell your partner that you prefer different behaviors, or wish to be touched or made love to in a different manner (or any other preference)? If you do it right after sex, you run the risk of making your comments sound like a report card or performance rating, and perhaps not a very good one at that. If you do it during sex, you might distract or frustrate your partner, and if you express your dissatisfaction before you start, that might cause performance anxiety.

Perhaps a neutral time would be best. Recall from the previous section that one of the general topics you and your partner might first discuss is when to talk about sexual differences. Whenever you do it, make sure you are not frustrated, angry, or highly emotional at the time. It is not so much when you

Positive reinforcement ■ A stimulus that follows a response and increases the probability of the response occurring again.

discuss your differences but *how* you go about it, and your concerns may not be well received if you begin in a negative emotional state.

Finally, if you have most of your sexual relations in the bedroom, never worry about or discuss your sexual problems while in bed. If you do this too often, the bed can become a stimulus for sexual tension and anxiety; that is, just being in bed can cause you to start worrying. Save the bed for pleasant experiences and pick a neutral site like the living room for worrying about problems.

How Should I Approach My Partner with Concerns About Our Sexual Relationship?

Because of their inexperience in talking about sex—particularly sexual problems—many people say nothing and allow a problem to continue, with the end result often being increasingly greater frustration and/or anger. When they finally do get around to saying something, many people begin with statements like these:

"I don't like it when you ..."

"You don't ..."

These types of statements accentuate the negative and are often met with defensive reactions and counter-accusations. This can quickly escalate into a full-scale argument.

There are few things that easily insult a person's ego as criticizing his or her sexual expression or interaction. Nearly everyone would like to believe that he or she is a good sexual partner. To try to solve your own frustrations by criticizing your partner, therefore, is asking for trouble. Sometimes people ask for feedback about sex and then get upset with the response. Some people, for example, ask questions like "How was it?" "Did you like it?" or "Wasn't that great?" after having sex. Sometimes they are really looking for a pat on the back or ego reinforcement rather than an honest answer, so this is really not a good time to express any negative reactions. Whenever possible, *accentuate the positive rather than the negative.* This is the most important advice that I can give you. Rather than beginning the conversation with "I don't like it when you...," try:

"I like it when you ..."

"It really feels good when you ..."

Your partner must do something that you like while having sex, so give him or her some **positive reinforcement.** Thousands of studies have shown that behaviors increase when they are reinforced, and praise is generally a powerful reinforcer for human beings.

PERSONAL REFLECTIONS

Suppose that you are unsure of your partner's sexual desires and preferences, and you are unsure whether he or she is totally aware of yours. How might you communicate with one another? Suppose your desires and preferences are not exactly the same?

What If I Think That My Partner Is to Blame— Can I Ever Complain?

If you have not expressed your concerns to your partner in a clear, specific manner (because you are uncomfortable talking about sex or for any other reason), do not lay the blame entirely on your partner. The problem has continued because you have allowed it to. Your partner cannot know what you want unless you tell him or her. It is wrong for you to think, or expect, that your partner should know what you want or how to please you. *You must take the responsibility for your own pleasure,* and you can do this only if you tell your partner of your needs and desires.

> "My husband and I are very open about our sexual ideas and feelings. When I don't like something he's doing I tell him and he does the same. We are at our sexual peak and communicating openly is very important."
> (from the author's files)

Although I emphasized the use of positive reinforcement in the previous section, that does not mean that you can never complain or express anger. However, when you are angry, learn to control your anger. Express it only after you have calmed down. Ask yourself what your motivation is for expressing complaints. Is it to hurt or ridicule your partner, or is it for constructive change? Couples with good relationships accept that there will be differences, and sometimes even conflict, but they resolve those differences and conflicts in constructive, not destructive, ways. If you criticize your partner, make sure you criticize his or her behavior, not his or her character. There is a big difference between saying

> "You are an uncaring person."

and saying

> "You don't show me often enough how much you care."

If you must criticize your partner's behavior, be sure to praise other aspects of his or her behavior as well.

How Should I Express My Needs and Desires?

Most communications experts suggest that individuals use **"I" language** when expressing desires to their partners. That means beginning sentences with "I," followed by an expression of *your* feelings, desires, or thoughts (see Simmons et al., 2005). There are some important advantages to this. By directly stating your feelings, you are taking the responsibility for your own well-being. In addition, "I" sentences avoid the blaming or accusatory tone common in statements that begin with "You." Statements such as "You don't like to hug me anymore" or "You don't love me" attack the other person's character and may well be met with a defensive response. The statement "I would like you to hug me more often" more directly expresses your feelings and desires and is less likely to elicit a defensive negative response.

Questions that begin with "Why" ("Why don't you... ?") are also often used to criticize a partner. Avoid those as well. Even sentences that begin with "We" can cause problems because they make assumptions about your partner's desires, moods, thoughts, or feelings. Do not talk for your partner.

When expressing your desires with "I" language, try to be as specific as possible. Vague statements such as "I want you to make love to me differently" will probably not be understood by your partner. On the other hand, he or she will easily understand statements such as:

> "I want you to kiss my breasts more gently when we make love."

> "I like it when you stroke my penis firmly."

> "I want to have sex with you on top."

How Can I Find Out About My Partner's Desires and Needs?

Yes, it is important that you know and understand your partner's sexual desires and needs, but as a preliminary step, be sure that you are aware of your own. Once you are certain, a good place to start is with **self-disclosure.** Studies show that the more sexual self-disclosure there is in a relationship, there is usually greater sexual and relationship satisfaction (Byers & Demmons, 1999; Derlega et al., 1993; MacNeil & Byers 2009).

> "Two years into the marriage our relationship took a downward spiral. Sex began to get boring and felt like just another chore. We finally began to talk openly about what we wanted from one another sexually. After much discussion, we are more attentive to each other's sexual needs. When I think back to our 'down' times I am sorry we didn't talk openly earlier. Sex is once again pleasurable."

> "My boyfriend and I of 2 years had never really talked about sex in a serious manner...we both felt really open that night so we played a game of 20 questions. The questions all had to deal with sexuality. For example, what we enjoyed, what he liked done to him, what I liked done to me, fantasies, etc. That one night opened the door for us to be able to talk about our sexual relationship in a serious manner. I felt more comfortable about what we were doing and why. It also brought us closer together as a couple. He told me after the conversation that night that he felt much closer to me than ever before."
> (All examples are from the author's files.)

Reveal to your partner (using "I" language) your thoughts, feelings, desires, and needs. This creates an environment of trust and understanding, and most people will self-disclose in return. Compare and discuss how each of you feels about different behaviors.

Of course, you can also ask your partner about his or her preferences, but try to avoid questions that can be answered with one word such as **yes-or-no questions.** Think about it. What opportunity does your partner have to express his or her feelings if you ask questions like these?

> "Did you like it?"

> "Do you like me to kiss your neck?"

> "Do you want to try different positions of intercourse?"

"I" language ■ Communicating your desires to another person by beginning sentences with "I," followed by your feelings, desires, or thoughts.

Self-disclosure ■ Revealing one's thoughts, feelings, and emotions to another.

Yes-or-no questions ■ Questions that call for a simple one-word "yes" or "no" response. These should be avoided when striving for communication.

FIGURE 13–8 When talking with your partner, disclose your own feelings and desires by using "I" language, accentuate the positive, and (like this couple) make eye contact.

Questions expressed this way ask for a one-word "yes" or "no" answer. Instead, ask questions that are **open-ended.** For example, the previous questions might be rephrased this way:

"What are the things I do during sex that you like best?"

"Where do you like me to kiss you when we make love?"

"How do you feel about trying different positions of intercourse?"

When questions are posed like this, they place no limitations on your partner's response. Your partner is free to divulge any and all feelings and beliefs that he or she considers important.

Keep in mind also that your partner may not feel comfortable expressing his or her feelings or desires, perhaps out of concern that you will react negatively. To overcome this obstacle, *give your partner permission* to talk about a particular topic. In other words, let him or her know it is okay to talk about something (for example, how you like to be touched), without you getting upset.

Is Listening Important? If So, How Can I Become a Better Listener?

Effective communication is what holds close relationships together and enables them to grow. However, many people forget that communication requires not just talking, but listening as well. This is as true for sexual relations as it is for any other behavior. How well do you listen?

We may hear with our ears, but *we show how attentive we are with body language*—body position (Do you face your partner

while he or she talks to you?), eye contact, facial expressions. Be supportive of your partner's attempts to communicate with you. In addition to positive body language, interact with him or her in a constructive manner. Make comments or **paraphrase** (reword) what your partner is saying so that you both are sure what the other is trying to say—not everyone conveys messages clearly. For example, suppose your partner tells you:

Other: "I think I would like sex better if you were more affectionate."

You: "You mean you want me to touch you more gently during sex."

Other: "No; the way you touch me is fine, but I want you to tell me how much you love me before we have sex."

By rewording your partner's first statement, it was clear to him or her that you did not understand, so your partner rephrased his or her wishes. Sometimes you may have to paraphrase your partner's message several times until you are certain that you have understood what he or she really means.

To improve your listening skills, try giving your partner a massage. Giving one another a massage strengthens relationships by promoting better communication (Comiskey, 1989). When starting the massage, it is normal to assume that what feels best to you will feel best to others as well. If you like your shoulders and neck massaged with a lot of pressure, for example, it is only natural that you will start off by attempting to please your partner in this manner. However, not everyone likes the same things you do. Your partner may prefer gentle massaging of the lower back. How will he or she communicate this to you? He or she may tell you, but it is important to realize that a person does not have to use words to communicate. When a massage really feels good, most people emit little noises like "ooh" and "aah." These responses should be just as effective as words in letting you know that what you are doing feels good. Listen to your partner's responses while you are massaging. If you listen well and care about your partner, you can modify your behavior and give a massage that pleases him or her instead of giving one that might please only you.

If you are a good enough listener to adjust a massage to please your partner, you can easily do the same while having sex. All of us want to believe we are (or will be) a good sexual partner, but to be one we must first be a good listener.

Open-ended questions ■ Questions asked in a manner that place no limitations on your partner's response.

Paraphrase ■ A rewording of the meaning expressed by someone else.

PERSONAL REFLECTIONS

Suppose that you are in a long-term monogamous relationship that includes sexual relations. Suppose also that your partner often does not take as much time during foreplay as you would like and does not spend much time holding and touching you afterwards. This often leaves you sexually unfulfilled and frustrated. How would you go about correcting this situation? Be as specific as possible.

Is It Possible to Communicate Nonverbally?

The answer, of course, is yes. Actually, I have already partially answered this question in my answer to the last question. Things like eye contact, facial expressions, and interpersonal distance (how close you stand or sit next to someone) all express messages. Single persons commonly use these types of messages to convey interest, or lack of interest, in another person. Silence can convey a message (e.g., anger, anxiety). Touch, in particular, is a very powerful means of *nonverbal communication*. As one person who studies communication and intimacy puts it, "If intimacy is proximity, then nothing comes closer than touch, the most intimate knowledge of another" (Thayer, 1986).

When two people are communicating verbally, it is important for there to be agreement between the verbal and nonverbal aspects of the communication. How do you suppose your partner would feel if, while telling him or her how much you care, you were inattentive, with little or no eye contact?

Dealing with Anger and Conflict: An Example

In the real world, couples are going to have moments of anger and conflict. No section on communication would be complete without some advice about how to deal with our own anger and that of our partner. In fact, one of the best predictors of long-term success in a relationship is the manner in which couples handle their disagreements (Notarius & Markman, 1993; Metz & Epstein, 2002). During a disagreement, couples can display three different patterns of communication: *mutual constructive communication, avoidance of communication,* or *demand/withdraw* (Christensen, 1988). The demand/withdraw pattern in which one partner criticizes or nags and the other avoids can be particularly damaging. It is associated with a high degree of relationship dissatisfaction (Caughlin, 2002; Metz & Epstein, 2002) and is frequently observed in distressed (e.g., divorcing) couples (Gottman & Levenson, 2000; Heavey et al., 1995). It is usually the person who initiates the conflict who assumes the role of demander (Papp et al., 2009).

> "My ex-girlfriend would get upset and demand to be left alone and would block me out if I tried to ask and understand what was bothering her. She pulled back into her shell for days and this behavior caused me stress because I did not know what was wrong, or if I could help. After several days she would open up but not discuss what it was that she had been upset about. She would just try and pick up where we left off like nothing happened. This occurred several times throughout our relationship. Notice I refer to her as my ex-girlfriend."
>
> (from the author's files)

In place of withdraw, or demand/withdraw, what can we do? The following metaphor is provided by Notarius, Lashley, and Sullivan (1997) to help couples deal better with their anger:

> We ask partners to imagine a scenario in which one person is in the kitchen cutting up some vegetables for dinner right after the partners have had a huge fight and are not talking to each other. The anger in the relationship is palpable. Just as one partner happens into the kitchen, the person cutting the vegetables slips and badly cuts a finger. There is blood spurting everywhere. At this point we ask both partners to state what would happen. With no exception to date, all couples report that there would be caretaking—every effort would be made to do whatever was necessary to take care of the wounded partner. In this scenario, there is a physical wound, and the wounded partner's body is taking care of alerting the other that attention is required. When one partner bleeds, the other takes care of him or her. If the other stood by and watched him or her bleed without providing care, this would be a powerful message indeed.

> Now we ask couples to consider a similar scenario in which a partner suffers a psychological wound that causes "internal bleeding." The hurt is not visible to the world, and therefore support will not be immediately forthcoming. Instead, the injured party must "emotionally bleed" in order to get support. The likelihood of getting support in this scenario will be directly related to the clarity of the "emotional bleeding." If the wounded person decides to bare his or her teeth as some wounded animals do, then this is likely to keep away a potential caretaker. If, on the other hand, the wounded person decides to show the wound plainly to another, to "bleed," then caretaking will most likely follow. Thus, the advice we offer to couples is for partners to "bleed" when they are psychologically hurt. We say, "Show your wounds to your partner, and just as if you were physically bleeding, more often than not you will receive the caretaking you desire."

> The primary difference between cutting oneself while slicing vegetables and suffering an emotional wound is that in the latter case, the other partner is usually held responsible for the injury. And in this case, the "emotional bleeding" that we encourage will be directed at the person blamed for the injury, who is also the potential caregiver. We find it useful to have the "bleeding" partner focus primarily on his or her own wound rather than on blaming the other for the injury. We remind couples that the goal is caretaking, and that at the moment anything that interferes with it will be self-destructive.
>
> *(Satisfaction in Close Relationships, by Notarius et al. Copyright 1997 by Guilford Publications, Inc. Reproduced with permission of Guilford Publications, Inc. in the format Textbook via Copyright Clearance Center.)*

Notice that in resolving their conflict and anger, the couple would employ several of the good communication tools that you have learned. These include "I" language, self-disclosure, listening, and attentiveness.

In any relationship, there will be both positive and negative interactions. John Gottman (1993, 1994) has found that *the ratio of these positive and negative emotional interactions is the best predictor of whether a relationship will survive.* If the ratio is at least five positive interactions to one negative interaction, the chances of a successful long-term relationship are very good. Gottman's group (1998) also found that couples are more likely to avoid negative interactions when addressing problems if: (1) the woman takes a "softened start-up approach" (caring, calm, and diplomatic rather than demanding or confrontational) and (2) the man accepts the woman's influence (instead of avoidance, withdrawal, and refusal to share power).

PERSONAL REFLECTIONS

What communication style do you use when you are angry with your partner? Is it the best style for clearly conveying your emotions to your partner?

What if We Cannot Agree?

No one person will always be able to satisfy all the needs and desires of another. That is true even in the best of relationships. People simply have differences of opinion and different preferences. When this happens, good communication can only lead to an understanding of those things that the two of you disagree about. It is often helpful to agree that you disagree. However, if either you or your partner is greatly bothered because your needs and desires are going unfulfilled, then it would be wise to seek professional counseling. In this chapter you can find the names and addresses of two organizations that will help you locate qualified professionals in your area.

STUDY GUIDE

KEY TERMS

benign coital cephalalgia 337	"I" language 349	priapism 337
cognitive-behavioral therapy 328	intercourse 347	primary sexual problem 331
	male orgasmic disorder 336	psychosexual therapy 328
communication 347	medical history 328	secondary sexual problem 331
couples therapy 328	medical model 328	
demand/withdraw 351	noncoital sexual pain disorder 343	self-awareness 329
dyspareunia 336		self-disclosure 349
ejaculatory incompetence 336	nonverbal communication 351	sensate focus exercises 329
erectile disorder 331	open-ended questions 350	sexual addiction 344
female hypoactive sexual desire 337	paraphrase 350	sexual aversion 331
	performance anxiety 333	sexual aversion disorder 337
female orgasmic disorder 339	persistent sexual arousal syndrome 339	sexual history 328
female sexual arousal disorder 339		situational sexual problem 331
	phimosis 336	
global sexual problem 331	PLISSIT model 328	spectatoring 334
hypersexuality 345	positive reinforcement 348	vaginismus 343
hypoactive sexual desire 330	premature ejaculation 335	yes-or-no questions 349

INTERACTIVE REVIEW

Studies have found that (1) _____ of all couples in the United States will eventually experience sexual problems. It is common for two people in a relationship to differ in their preferences for frequency and type of sex. This often results from different expectations and assumptions about sex. When this happens, it is best to consider the problem as the (2) _____ problem. If the problem persists and is causing stress and anxiety, it is advisable to seek professional help. Most sexual problems are treated with (3) _____, developed by Masters and Johnson; psychosexual therapy; or a combination of both. Sexual therapy programs generally have many things in common and follow the (4) _____ model, an acronym for permission, limited information, specific suggestions, and intensive therapy. Each represents a progressively deeper level of therapy. Most therapists will probably take a (5) _____ and (6) _____ history first. Some clients will need self-awareness exercises, but for most couples the first set of general exercises will be nondemand mutual pleasuring techniques called (7) _____. After completing these, the couple will then be assigned specific exercises. Many sexual problems are due to a failure to resolve conflicts in other aspects of the relationship, and thus sex therapy may also require (8) _____ therapy.

Many therapists believe that the most common problem of couples seeking therapy is (9) _____. This refers to a persistent and recurrent inhibition of sexual desire. In its most extreme form, the avoidance of sex becomes phobic in nature and is called (10) _____. This generally requires psychosexual therapy. At the other extreme, hypersexual individuals are distinguished by the (11) _____ with which they engage in sex. Painful intercourse, or (12) _____, can occur in either men or women and can have a variety of causes.

The most common sexual problem specific to men is probably (13) _____, which is usually defined as a recurrent and persistent absence of (14) _____. Probably the most psychologically devastating male problem is (15) _____, which can have organic and/or psychological causes. The most common psychological cause is (16) _____. Difficulty reaching orgasm and ejaculating in a woman's vagina is called (17) _____ and usually has a psychological cause. Some men suffer from benign coital cephalalgia, or (18) _____.

For many women, lack of sexual desire or subjective arousal is due to (19) _____. Some women experience involuntary contractions of the muscles surrounding the vaginal opening when they attempt intercourse, which results in pain. (20) _____, as it is called, usually has a psychological cause. The vast majority of women who go to sexual therapy do so because of problems (21) _____. This can be due to a variety of causes, including poor techniques by the partner, sexual repression during the woman's upbringing, and general relationship problems. When one member of a couple has a sexual problem, it is not unusual for the partner to develop a corresponding sexual difficulty.

Communication is the exchange of information. Because of our culture's negative attitudes, many people feel uncomfortable talking about sex, even with their sexual partners. (22) _____ and _____ differences in a relationship also contribute to this difficulty. You and your partner can get used to talking about sex together by discussing sexuality-related articles in newspapers, books, and magazines. One of the first things you must do is agree on a comfortable (23) _____ to use when talking about sex. When talking about sexual differences or problems, be sure to emphasize the (24) _____ rather than the (25) _____ things that your partner does. That does not mean that you can never complain, but when you do, focus on your partner's behavior rather than on his or her character.

Take responsibility for your own pleasure by expressing your feelings and desires to your partner in a clear, specific manner. Whenever possible, begin sentences with "I" rather than (26) _____. It is often easier to find out about your partner's sexual desires and needs if you first (27) _____. However, good communication is a two-way street; it requires that you also become a good (28) _____. In addition to communicating verbally, we also communicate nonverbally with (give four examples) (29) _____. Even with good communication skills, people will not always agree, but it is possible to agree that you disagree.

SELF-TEST

A. TRUE OR FALSE

[T] [F]   30. Women's physiological arousal (e.g., vaginal lubrication) is poorly correlated with subjective arousal.

[T] [F]   31. Bob wants to have sex twice a week but is in a relationship with Sue, who wants to have sex every day. In this example, it is clear that Sue is hypersexual.

[T] [F]   32. The most frequent sexual problem for women seeking sex therapy is difficulty reaching orgasm.

[T] [F]   33. Stimulation of the clitoris during intercourse should not be necessary, and a woman should be able to be orgasmic through intercourse alone.

[T] [F]   34. Performance anxiety can cause sexual problems in men, but not women.

[T] [F]   35. The American Psychiatric Association defines a premature ejaculator as any man who usually reaches orgasm within 2 minutes of beginning sexual intercourse.

[T] [F]   36. Most women who have difficulty reaching orgasm do not enjoy sex.

[T] [F]   37. In order to help their clients, most sex therapists require them to stop masturbating.

[T] [F]   38. Dyspareunia is usually caused by a physical problem.

[T] [F]   39. Many men with psychologically caused erectile problems get full erections during sensate focus exercises.

[T] [F]   40. Most women do not separate sexual desire from sexual arousal.

[T] [F]   41. Female orgasm problems are almost always the result of insufficient physical stimulation.

[T] [F]   42. Low sexual desire in women is usually due to low testosterone levels.

[T] [F]   43. Therapists are in agreement that hypersexuality is a form of addiction similar to alcoholism.

T	F	44. Erectile problems are inevitable as men grow older.
T	F	45. A majority of erectile problems have a physical basis.
T	F	46. Headaches during orgasm occur mainly in men.
T	F	47. The sex therapy model presented in this chapter is applicable to most peoples of the world.

B. MATCHING

For each of the sexual problems below, match which techniques therapists would be likely to use (in order) according to the text. Answers may be used more than once.

_____ 48. hypoactive sexual desire
_____ 49. hypersexuality
_____ 50. dyspareunia
_____ 51. psychological erectile problem
_____ 52. premature ejaculation
_____ 53. male orgasmic disorder
_____ 54. benign coital cephalalgia
_____ 55. vaginismus
_____ 56. female orgasmic disorder

a. sensate focus
b. psychosexual (or psycho-) therapy
c. couples therapy
d. bridge maneuver
e. use of dilators
f. resume woman-on-top position of intercourse
g. self-exploration and masturbation
h. tease technique
i. treatment of the internal discomfort (antidepressants or stabilizing drugs)
j. treatment of specific organic cause (usually has organic cause)
k. squeeze technique or stop-start technique
l. relaxation techniques or medication for high blood pressure

C. FILL IN THE BLANKS

57. Most women need stimulation of the _____ in order to reach orgasm, even during intercourse.
58. Most therapists believe that the _____ position has the most erotic potential for both people during intercourse.
59. When a person begins to observe and evaluate his or her own sexual responses during sex, that is called _____, and it can be a cause of sexual problems.
60. For most women, sexual desire depends on _____.
61. Sensate focus exercises are _____ techniques.
62. In men, painful intercourse can be caused by the foreskin of the penis being too tight, a condition called _____.
63. If a man is totally unable to ejaculate in a woman's vagina, this is called _____.
64. Probably the most difficult sexual problem to treat successfully is _____.
65. The word *intercourse* means _____.
66. When communicating with another, it is important that there be agreement between the _____ and _____ aspects of communication.
67. One of the best predictors of long-term success in a relationship is the manner in which couples handle _____.

SUGGESTED READINGS AND RESOURCES

Berman, J., & Berman, L. (2001). *For women only: A revolutionary guide to overcoming sexual dysfunction and reclaiming your sex life.* New York: Henry Holt. The title says it all.

Gottman, J. M., & Silver, N. (1999). *The seven principles for making marriage work.* New York: Crown Publishing. On the subject of couple communication, this was the most frequently recommended book by members of the Society for Sex Therapy and Research (Kingsberg et al., 2002).

Heiman, J., & LoPiccolo, J. (1992). *Becoming orgasmic: A sexual and personal growth program for women.* New York: Simon & Schuster. Highly recommended by members of the Society for Sex Therapy and Research.

Kaplan, H. S. (1995). *Sexual desire disorders: Dysfunctional regulation of sexual motivation.* New York: Brunner/Mazel. Extensive coverage of hypoactive sexual desire and hypersexuality from the therapist who pioneered work in desire disorders.

Kaschak, E., & Tiefer, L. (Eds.) (2002). *A new view of women's sexual problems*. Binghamton, NY: Haworth Press. Emphasizes the importance of relationships in women's sexual desire and problems.

Schnarch, D. M. (1998). *Passionate marriage: Love, sex, and intimacy in emotionally committed relationships*. New York: Holt. Schnarch's earlier work written for the public. On the subject of keeping relationships vital, the most frequently recommended book by members of the Society for Sex Therapy and Research.

Tannen, D. (1990). *You just don't understand: Women and men in conversation*. New York: William Morrow; Paperback: Ballantine (1991). How to talk to the other sex.

Watkins, P. L., & Clum, G. A. (2008). *Handbook of self-help therapies*. New York: Routledge.

Weeks, G., & Winters, J. (2002). What problem? *Psychology Today*. A brief, but excellent, introduction to hypoactive sexual desire.

Zilbergeld, B. (1999). *The new male sexuality*. New York: Bantam Books. A readable book about male sexuality

and overcoming problems. The most frequently recommended book on male sexuality by members of the Society for Sex Therapy and Research.

AAMFT (American Association for Marriage and Family Therapy)
112 South Alfred Street
Alexandria, VA 22314
(703) 838-9808
www.aamft.org

They will provide names and addresses of certified marriage and family therapists in your area.

AASECT (American Association of Sex Educators, Counselors and Therapists)
P.O. Box 1960
Ashland, VA 23005-1960
(804) 752-0026
www.aasect.org

They will provide names and addresses of certified sex counselors and therapists in your area.

14 Paraphilias and Sexual Variants

One fact about human behavior that is so obvious that it needs no research program to establish its truth is that humans judge some sexual practices to be undesirable and changeworthy.... The particulars surrounding these negative judgments made by mental health professionals about some sexual practices are, unfortunately, not so clear. For example, it is not clear on what grounds humans in general, or mental health professionals in particular, either do evaluate or should evaluate sexual practices. That is, should sexual practices be evaluated on the grounds of whether they harm others (if so, what kinds of harm, and how much harm, are necessary for the behavior to be regarded as a mental disorder?), or whether the sexual practices are unhealthy (utilizing this criterion is clearly problematic as it simply pushes the question to how properly healthy practices can be distinguished from unhealthy ones), or whether the behaviors deviate from a statistical norm, or whether the behaviors seem to be maladaptive in some evolutionary sense?

—D. Richard Laws & William O'Donohue, 1997

When you have finished studying this chapter, you should be able to:

- Describe the various ways one can define a behavior as being unconventional.

- Explain the difference between a sexual variant and a paraphilia.

- Define and discuss the courtship disorders: voyeurism, exhibitionism, telephone scatophilia, and frotteurism.

- Define pedophilia and discuss its relationship to the courtship disorders.

- Describe the paraphilias that focus on nonhuman objects for sexual arousal: fetishism, transvestism, urophilia, coprophilia, mysophilia, klismaphilia, and zoophilia.

- Discuss and explain sadomasochism.

- Discuss the various theories of how paraphilias develop and why nearly all paraphiliacs are men.

- Discuss the treatment (therapy) for individuals with a paraphilia.

There are enormous individual differences among people in every aspect of human behavior. It should be obvious from the many references to other cultures throughout this book that this includes sexual behavior as well. Variety in behavior is usually considered to be good. We enjoy wearing different clothing, eating different foods, listening to different kinds of music—and, as you learned in Chapter 11, most of us enjoy practicing a variety of sexual behaviors. In that chapter, we began to define normal versus abnormal behavior. Let us continue.

What determines whether a behavior is designated "normal" or "conventional" as opposed to "abnormal" or "unconventional"? You may be surprised that what is considered to be normal or conventional is not always easy to define. Most of us would probably agree that someone who ate beetles was abnormal, but this is common in some African cultures. Obviously, cultural factors must be considered (see Bhugra et al., 2010). Even within the same culture, what is believed to be normal today may not have been viewed as normal in the past, and may not be viewed as normal in the future. Here is an example. If a woman wears a string bikini on the beach today, she is considered normal. But if a woman living in 1900 (or maybe even 1950) had worn that outfit to a beach, she would have been arrested. On the other hand, if a woman wore a full-length swimsuit with bloomers to the beach today (the typical swimwear for American women in 1900), she might be considered sexually inhibited.

Even at the same point in time in the same culture, normal behavior might be a matter of where it is observed. If someone tried to sunbathe in the nude at the local public swimming pool, he or she would probably be arrested. If this same person were sunning himself or herself on certain beaches on the West or East Coast, on the other hand, he or she could walk in naked splendor along with a whole beach full of other naked people. When does such behavior start being normal—before getting to the beach, after getting to the beach, never, or always? Again, the point is that "normal" is not an absolute thing. It can be determined by many factors, including where you are and when you are there.

Researchers have attempted to define "normal" or "abnormal" in one of three ways. One way is called the *statistical approach*, in which a behavior is considered normal or conventional if a large number of people engage in it, and abnormal or unconventional if only a few people do it (Pomeroy, 1966). However, the fact that only a minority of

FIGURE 14–1 Walking on the beach naked might seem unusual and unacceptable to you, but if it is not done in front of unwilling observers, it is a sexual variant, not a paraphilia.

people have engaged in a behavior does not necessarily make that behavior bad or wrong, or the individuals disturbed or sick. Probably only a small minority of people in our culture, for example, have ever had sex outdoors (in private) at night under the stars, but most would agree that doing so would certainly not be a sign of mental illness. Because of the limitations of the statistical approach—defining normal and abnormal purely in terms of numbers—others have preferred a sociological or psychological approach.

The *sociological approach* also calls a behavior unconventional if it is not customary within a society. Customs vary, not only from culture to culture but also within subcultures. Followers of the sociological approach are concerned with the social conditions that give rise to abnormal behavior.

The *psychological approach* focuses on the psychological health of the individual and the impact that behaviors have on this health. A sexual activity is considered to be a problem behavior if it makes an individual feel distressed or guilty or causes him or her problems in functioning efficiently in ordinary social and occupational roles.

The behaviors that you will read about in this chapter are uncommon (the statistical approach), but we will focus primarily on the psychological approach. Let us now take a look at how the psychiatric/psychological profession has dealt with the subject of sexual abnormalities.

HISTORICAL PERSPECTIVE

By the middle of the 11th century, Christian Church leaders had begun to regard sexual intercourse in any other position except the missionary position as an unnatural act, a sin against nature (Brundage, 1984). Shortly afterwards, Thomas Aquinas declared in his *Summa theologiae* that there were four categories of unnatural acts: masturbation, bestiality, sodomy (which included homosexuality), and unnatural positions of intercourse (Murray, 1998).

In the Victorian era, sexual behaviors that were considered abnormal were referred to as "perversions" and later as "deviations." In fact, the first modern classification of sexual deviations was made in 1886 by Richard von Krafft-Ebing (*Psychopathia Sexualis*), whose work was based on the premise that people are genetically predisposed toward sexual deviation. Sigmund Freud believed that any type of sexual behavior that took precedence over heterosexual vaginal intercourse was an indication of impaired psychosexual development (see Parsons, 2000). A person's sexual behavior was considered deviant if it was not directed toward an appropriate object (a heterosexual partner) and/or the aim was not sexual intercourse. According to this view, masturbation and oral-genital sex were considered very disturbed. (This is another excellent example of how what is considered abnormal depends on the time and culture.)

Simon (1994) has made an interesting distinction between the terms *deviance* and *perversion*. According to him, *sexual deviance* is "the inappropriate or flawed performance of a conventionally understood sexual practice." He uses rape as an example; we rarely refer to it as a perversion. Rape would be considered a perversion only if committed on someone whose inclusion in the act went beyond what we consider to be normal. Simon emphasizes that as sexual practices change, so do our definitions of deviance (oral sex being a good example). *Perversion*, on the other hand, "can be thought of as a disease of sexual desire not only in the sense that it appears to violate the sexual practices of a time and place, but also because it constitutes a violation of common understandings that render current sexual practice plausible. The 'pervert' is disturbing because, at the level of folk psychology, we have difficulty understanding why someone 'might want to do something like that.'" Thus, according to Simon, deviance is a problem of control, while perversion is a problem of desire. Here, too, Simon emphasizes that our concept of perversion can change with time. Masturbation is a good example. So, too, is homosexuality. Until the mid-1970s, the American Psychiatric Association regarded homosexuality as an official mental illness, a perversion (see Chapter 9).

Today, the American Psychiatric Association's handbook *Diagnostic and Statistical Manual of Mental Disorders* (*DSM-IV-TR*, 2000) refers to psychosexual disorders of the type considered in this chapter as **paraphilias,** derived from the Greek *para* (meaning "besides," "beyond," or "amiss") and *philia* ("love"). Not all statistically or sociologically unusual behaviors are paraphilias. For an unusual behavior to be called a paraphilia, the distinguishing feature must be that engaging in or thinking (fantasizing) about the behavior is a preferred way of obtaining sexual arousal and gratification.[1] Other essential features of a paraphilia are that the sexual fantasies, urges, and behaviors are recurrent for a period of at least 6 months.

Paraphilias ■ General term for a group of sexual disorders in which repeatedly engaging in or fantasizing about unusual behaviors is a preferred way of obtaining sexual arousal and gratification.

Sexual variant ■ Unusual behaviors that are engaged in for variety and not as one's preferred manner of becoming sexually aroused.

---

[1] The full *DSM-IV-TR* definition of a paraphilia is "recurrent, intense sexually arousing fantasies, sexual urges, or behaviors generally involving 1) nonhuman objects, 2) the suffering of humiliation of oneself or one's partner, or 3) children or other nonconsenting persons that occur over a period of at least 6 months."

As you read this chapter, there will probably be one or more behaviors that you have either fantasized about or engaged in yourself on occasion. This does not mean you have a paraphilia. Again, it would be a paraphilia only if that was the *preferred* way in which you become sexually aroused. Other-wise, the behaviors are referred to as **sexual variants** (Stoller, 1977).

Some of the paraphilias covered in this chapter can result in physical harm to oneself (e.g., masochism) or physical or psychological harm to others (e.g., sadism, exhibitionism, voyeurism, pedophilia). Some can lead to arrest and prosecution. However, others would appear to be harmless—transvestism (cross-dressing) in the privacy of one's own home, for example. Some clinicians argue that harmless behaviors (this assumes that the behavior is engaged in without feelings of guilt, shame, or remorse) should not have a negative label. Others say that no paraphilia is harmless because, as the preferred source of sexual gratification, it deprives the individual of physically affectionate relations with others.

Multiple and Related Paraphilias

In 2008, a New Jersey policeman and his girlfriend were arrested for allegedly committing sexual assault on three young girls. During the investigation, video-tapes were found of the policeman having oral sex with five calves.

In the American Psychiatric Association's *DSM-III* published in 1980, paraphiliacs were believed to have a single sexual interest. However, it was difficult to study paraphilias because most sexual offenders do not wish to describe their "private" lives.

In order to learn more about sex offenders' behaviors, a study was conducted with outpatient offenders in which the participants were guaranteed immunity from prosecution for any crimes they described in the research interviews (Abel et al., 1987, 1988a). In this study, 62% admitted to having committed a previously concealed deviant sexual behavior. Over half reported that they had engaged in more than one type of the previously described behaviors, with the average being three to four types. Most had developed their sexual interests and fantasies by age 12 or 13, but were afraid to discuss their arousal patterns with their parents. Many studies subsequently found that individuals in treatment for one type of paraphilia often engage in other paraphilias (see Heil & Simons, 2008). In fact, some types of paraphilias tend to cluster together more often than others. This chapter attempts to organize clustered paraphilias in that manner.

Other paraphilias are related by their very nature. For example, for several paraphilias the focus of arousal is on nonhuman objects, and thus these paraphilias can be regarded as specific types of fetishes. Related paraphilias will also be considered together.

THE COURTSHIP DISORDERS

One group of paraphilias often seen together are known as *courtship disorders*—voyeurism, exhibitionism, frotteurism, and the obscene telephone caller (Abel et al., 1987, 1988a; Bradford et al., 1992; Freund et al., 1997). These are often referred to as nonviolent offenses (e.g., Krueger & Kaplan, 2000), but at least half of the men who engage in these paraphilias also meet the criteria for pedophilia (sexual arousal to young children), and a sizable minority have also engaged in rape (Abel et al., 1988a; Bradford et al., 1992; Freund & Seto, 1998).

Why are these paraphilias called **courtship disorders?** The term is short for "disorder of phasing of the courtship behavior" (Freund & Watson, 1990). Freund and colleagues say that humans normally go through a four-phase sequence when interacting sexually:

1. *Finding phase*—in this phase we locate and appraise a potential sexual partner.
2. *Affiliative phase*—in this phase we make verbal and nonverbal overtures (e.g., looking, smiling, talking) to the potential partner.
3. *Tactile phase*—here, physical contact (e.g., touching, hugging, petting) takes place.
4. *Copulatory phase*—sexual intercourse occurs.

According to Freund, what the courtship disorders have in common is that there is "extreme intensification or distortion of one of these four phases wherein the remaining phases are entirely omitted or retained in a vestigial way" (Freund et al., 1997). Individuals with these courtship disorders are almost always men, who have a "preference...for a virtually instant conversion of arousal into orgasm" (generally accomplished by masturbation). Let us now take a closer look at some of these behaviors.

Voyeurism

"Last month, I was sitting on my bed and I saw a shadow move across my window. I reluctantly peeked through the blinds and there was this man stroking his penis.... Last night I got a phone call from a neighbor telling me someone was looking in my window. I reported it. Apparently, they've been trying to catch this guy for a while. I'm very frightened right now."

(from the author's files)

What is a voyeur (from the French *voir*, meaning "to see")? Are men who like to look at naked women in magazines or at topless shows voyeurs? What about people who go to nudist colonies, or men who enjoy looking at women in string bikinis at the beach? What if a man sneaks a peek up a woman's skirt as she is sitting down, or, if he is innocently walking down the street, notices a woman undressing in her room and stops to watch? Although the word *voyeurism* is often used to describe such behavior, these are really just examples of normal variants.

To be a **voyeur** (a paraphiliac), one must *repeatedly* seek sexual arousal by observing people undressing or in the nude *without their consent or knowledge* (see Lavin, 2008). The voyeur is aroused

Courtship disorders ■ A group of paraphilias (voyeurism, exhibitionism, frotteurism, and telephone scatophilia) often seen together.

Voyeurism ■ Repeatedly seeking sexual arousal by observing nude individuals without their knowledge or consent.

FIGURE 14–2 Voyeurs repeatedly seek sexual arousal by secretly watching people undress.

by the risk of discovery, and thus is not interested in going to nudist colonies or other places where people know that they are being watched (Tollison & Adams, 1979). A similar paraphiliac behavior (but technically not voyeurism) is "an erotic *preference* for masturbating to pornographic videos or photographs when attractive sexual partners of the individual's preferred age and sex are readily available" (Freund et al., 1997). This does not include similar behavior when partners are not available.

Voyeurism is a disorder of the first phase, the *finding phase*, of the normal courtship sequence (Freund et al., 1997) and is often just one of several paraphiliac behaviors displayed by an individual (exhibitionism and pedophilia being the most common other ones) (Abel & Rouleau, 1990). The great majority of voyeurs are men, and thus the term *Peeping Tom* applies. The latter term comes from the story of Lady Godiva, who according to legend rode a horse through her town naked to protest taxes imposed by her husband. The people were ordered to stay inside and not look, but Tom the tailor could not resist.

Voyeurs have low self-esteem, feelings of inadequacy and insecurity, shyness and poor social skills, and a history of great difficulty in heterosexual relations (Kaplan & Krueger, 1997; Tollison & Adams, 1979).

> "I often 'do it' (masturbate) in my car while parked in areas where I can watch women. My social skills are poor, and I do not get on well with people easily."
> (from the author's files)

Voyeurs may masturbate while observing their victims, or they may masturbate later while fantasizing about the incident. The large majority of voyeurs are not dangerous, preferring to keep their distance, but there are exceptions (Kaplan & Krueger, 1997). If you are ever a victim, you should consider a voyeur to be potentially dangerous if either he tries to draw attention to the fact that he is watching or he attempts to approach you or enters your building.

Exhibitionism

> "One day at sunset, I was walking back to my car in the...parking lot. As I was opening my car door I glanced over at the car facing mine.... This man was almost in a backbend over his driver seat masturbating at full speed. For a moment I was stunned and shocked. I just got in my car and drove off."
> (from the author's files)

Exhibitionism (from the Latin *ex-*, meaning "out," and *habere*, meaning "to hold") is defined

as repeatedly exposing one's genitals to unsuspecting (unwilling) strangers in order to obtain sexual arousal and gratification (see Murphy & Page, 2008). It is considered to be a disorder (exaggeration) of the *affiliative phase* of courtship.

Many people, including many celebrities, have posed naked for magazines, and some even star in sexually explicit films or "topless-bottomless" stage shows. Some of you may have gone to a nudist colony, or engaged in "sexting" (posting online photos of yourself naked to a friend). However, none of these are examples of exhibitionism because they involve willing observers. (You will read more about sexting in Chapter 16.) Others of you may have "mooned" someone on occasion, or participated in "streaking," or engaged in flashing at events like New Orleans' Mardi Gras (called "playful deviance"; see Redmon, 2003). Although these acts often involve involuntary observers, they are also generally not considered exhibitionism, for another characteristic of exhibitionists is that they engage in the behavior *compulsively*—it is their *preferred* means of sexual arousal. In their study of outpatient sexual offenders, Abel et al. (1987, 1988a) found that for only 7% of exhibitionists this was their only paraphilia (see also Bradford et al., 1992). The other 93% had engaged in an average of 4.3 paraphilias. Again, the most common ones were voyeurism, telephone scatophilia, frotteurism—all courtship disorders—and pedophilia.

Most victims of exhibitionists, or "flashers," are women or children (Murphy & Page, 2008). Some studies have found that as many as 33% to 48% of women have been victims of exhibitionism on at least one occasion (Cox, 1988; Riordan, 1999). One fifth of the victims found the experience very distressing and another one fourth said that their attitude about men or sex had been affected. Most victims say that the experience resulted in their limiting the number of places or areas they would go to alone.

It is generally believed that almost all exhibitionists are men, but a recent study found that exhibitionistic behavior may be more common among women than previously thought (Långström & Seto, 2006). Most started exposing themselves in their midteens or 20s, and half or more either are or have been married (Murphy & Page, 2008). The large majority of these men are described as shy and/or personally immature, but otherwise without serious emotional or mental disorders. They typically have very low self-esteem, feel inadequate and insecure, fear rejection, and have problems forming close, intimate (including sexual) relations (Blair & Lanyon, 1981; Marshall et al., 1991). Although some rapists engaged in exhibitionism when younger, there is no clear evidence that exhibitionism

---

Exhibitionism ■ Exposing one's genitals compulsively in inappropriate settings in order to obtain sexual gratification.

usually leads to aggressive sex crimes (Krueger & Kaplan, 2000).

> Lance Rentzel was a star wide receiver for the Dallas Cowboys professional football team and had recently married one of the top young actresses in Hollywood. The Cowboys were headed to the Super Bowl in 1970, but on November 19, while in the middle of a slump, Lance exposed himself to a 10-year-old girl. The media soon discovered that he had been arrested for the same thing 4 years earlier while playing for the Minnesota Vikings—and in the midst of another personal slump. Lance Rentzel had always been a hero on the football field and felt that he had to be highly successful to please his family. In his autobiography and account of his exhibitionism, *When All the Laughter Died in Sorrow* (1972), he says that he felt pressure to prove his masculinity over and over again, and as part of this he avoided close, intimate relations with women and instead proved his masculinity to himself by sexual conquests. During times of stress, when he wasn't a "winner," Lance Rentzel resorted to exposing himself as a way to prove his masculinity.

Although most exhibitionists are of normal or above-normal intelligence, some cases of exhibitionism occur among people who are intellectually impaired, either since birth or as a result of a neurological disorder or age. In these cases, the cause is usually an inability to understand what society considers (or the individual previously considered) to be right as opposed to wrong (Zeiss et al., 1996).

Only about half of all exhibitionists have erections while exposing themselves, and they may or may not masturbate during the act (Langevin et al., 1979). But they usually do masturbate shortly afterwards, while fantasizing about the experience, and their erotic turn-on is directly related to the victim's reaction of shock, disgust, and fear (Blair &

Lanyon, 1981). Exhibitionists rarely attempt to molest their victims (American Psychiatric Association, *DSM-IV-TR*, 2000); thus, the best response (if you are ever a victim) is to give no facial or verbal reaction, leave the scene, and report the incident immediately. Interestingly, many exhibitionists compulsively expose themselves in the same location; perhaps the danger of being caught increases the arousal (Stoller, 1977). As a result, they are the most frequently caught paraphiliac offenders, comprising about one third of all arrests for sexual offense.

Obscene Phone Callers

> "The calls came three to four times a night. The caller would make obscene suggestions about his penis, oral sex, and bondage, and say that he was 'masturbating to the sound of my voice and the thought of my pussy.' Then he would start moaning. I was very shocked and disgusted."
> (from the author's files)

Many of you may have made an obscene telephone call as a prank during adolescence. Although inappropriate, this behavior is different from that of the paraphiliac phone caller who repeatedly makes obscene calls as a primary source of sexual arousal and gratification. **Telephone scatophilia** (from the Greek *skato*, meaning dung, and *logos*, meaning speech), or *scatologia*, is often considered a kind of verbal exhibitionism (Price et al., 2001a, 2001b) and, like exhibitionism, is a disorder of the *affiliative phase* of courtship (Freund et al., 1997). Telephone scatophilia should not be confused with telephone-sex dependence, because the latter involves mutual consent (see Kafka & Hennen, 1999). However, telephone sex (masturbation) would be considered a paraphilia when the behavior was preferred and sexual partners were available (Freund et al., 1997).

As with exhibitionists, the scatophiliac's arousal is proportionate to the victim's reaction of disgust, shock, and fear and to the sense of control it gives him. The scatophiliac often masturbates while making his calls. One difference between telephone scatophilia and exhibitionism is that many scatophiliacs want complete anonymity (Milner et al., 2008).

> In April, 1990, the president of American University resigned after police traced obscene phone calls to his office phone. His victims were women who had advertised home day-care services in the local newspaper. He had degrees from Ivy League schools and was a well-known civic activist who had appeared on television hundreds of times as a spokesman for higher education.
> (Gelman, 1990)

"NO THANKS, I'M TRYING TO QUIT."

Bob Dayton

Telephone scatophilia ■ A condition in which sexual arousal is achieved repeatedly by making obscene telephone calls.

What can explain behavior like this on the part of an intelligent (and in this case, prominent) individual? Like the exhibitionist, telephone scatophiliacs are greatly lacking in self-esteem (Price et al., 2001a). They feel inadequate and insecure and have difficulty maintaining normal sexual relations, much like exhibitionists. They compulsively use the telephone for sexual interactions when they need to boost their esteem (by inducing shock and fear in their victims)—it is safe, distant, and avoids intimacy. They can be anonymous, yet verbally interact with the victim and fantasize visually all at the same time. They masturbate either during or after the call.

It is uncommon for telephone scatophiliacs to be the only paraphilia displayed by an individual (Abel et al., 1988a; Bradford et al., 1992). Most have engaged in at least four other paraphilias (most commonly the other courtship disorders).

Surveys indicate that more than half of adult women have received an obscene telephone call, and that 6% to 14% of men admit to having made such calls, making it one of the most common sexual offenses (see Price et al., 2001a, b) (although for the large majority of these man it would not be a long-term, preferred means of arousal, and thus not a paraphilia). Many obscene callers know the names of the people they call, which can make the experience particularly frightening to the victim. It is rare, however, for scatophiliacs to molest (or even approach) their victims.

If you should ever be a victim, the best advice is to say nothing and hang up *immediately* (remember, the scatophiliac is aroused by your reactions; even slamming the phone down can give him reinforcement). If the calls persist, your telephone company will cooperate in helping the police trace calls. Ask your phone company about Call Trace, a technology that allows the phone company to instantly record the source of a call made to you. When the caller is identified, do not be surprised if he turns out to be someone you know or have met; that is often the case.

Frotteurism

"A year ago I went with a small group of friends from my high school to London. Well, we were on a very crowded tube [subway] and were packed in so tight that we could barely move. But the guy behind me was able to move. He kept rubbing up and down against me the whole ride. I just thought that someone kept pushing him against me. My friends told me that he

looked like he was 'getting off' by doing that. I never wore those pants again because I felt used and dirty."
(from the author's files)

Frotteurism (from the French *frottage*, meaning "rubbing") involves repeatedly rubbing one's genitals against other people in public while fully clothed (see Lussier & Piché, 2008). It is considered to be a disorder of the third phase, the *tactile phase*, of the normal courtship process (Freund et al., 1997). Most frotteurists exhibit other paraphilias as well, most notably voyeurism, exhibitionism, pedophilia, and telephone scatophilia (Abel et al., 1988a; Bradford et al., 1992). They are also likely to have engaged in a wide variety of nonsexual antisocial behaviors (Lussier & Piché, 2008).

In a study of college men, one third admitted to having rubbed up against a woman in a crowded place (Templeman & Stinnett, 1991). Of course, most of these men are not frotteurists because this is not their preferred means of arousal and the behavior may have occurred only once or twice. One study of nonincarcerated paraphiliacs found that the median number of acts of frottage was 29, but many frotteurists had committed the act several hundred times (Abel et al., 1987). Frotteurists seek out crowded buses or other places where bumping into strangers is less likely to cause them to be arrested.

PEDOPHILIA

He was a man loved by children. He played a clown at birthday parties, and little ones loved to see him coming into their homes. Then he was caught molesting a child at a party where he had been hired to entertain. Interviews were conducted with children at parties he had worked before. They revealed that he had used his job as a means to repeatedly engage in sexual behavior with children. He was a pedophile.
(summarized from news articles)

Pedophilia (from the Greek, meaning "love of children") is a condition in which an adult's sexual arousal and gratification depend primarily or exclusively on having sex with children. Although the legal age of consent differs from state to state (ranging from 14 to 18), sex researchers generally define a child as someone who is younger than 13 years old (Gebhard et al., 1965). Thus, we are discussing *sexual relations by an adult with prepubertal children* (see Seto, 2008). To be considered an example of pedophilia, the adult must be at least 16 years old and at least 5 years older than the child (American Psychiatric Association, *DSM-IV-TR*, 2000).

An isolated act of child molestation, although reprehensible, does not necessarily qualify as pedophilia. Remember, to be designated a pedophile, the molester must *repeatedly* seek sexual relations with children.

Frotteurism ■ A condition in which sexual arousal is achieved repeatedly by rubbing one's genitals against others in public places.

Pedophilia ■ A condition in which sexual arousal is achieved primarily and repeatedly through sexual activity with children who have not reached puberty.

Pedophilia is introduced here because it is frequently found to exist in individuals diagnosed with courtship disorders. Half or more of men diagnosed as voyeurs, exhibitionists, telephone scatophiliacs, or frotteurists also meet the criteria for pedophilia (Abel et al., 1988a; Bradford et al., 1992). In fact, in their theory of courtship disorders, Freund and colleagues include the "preferential rapist," defined as "a pathological, nonsadistic preference for committing rape" (Freund et al., 1997). This definition applies to the large majority of pedophiles (see Chapter 15).

This is the most serious of the paraphilias, each year resulting in many thousands of victims who suffer long-term emotional and psychological problems. We will cover this paraphilia in depth in Chapter 15.

FETISHISM, TRANSVESTISM, AND RELATED PARAPHILIAS

Fetishism

John's sisters began to complain that he was going through their dresser drawers. He denied it, but his mother found their panties under his pillow. This pattern continued, with John denying it each time their underwear was discovered under his pillow. In private, John would masturbate while playing with the female undergarments. His school work deteriorated and he was in repeated fights, resulting in his being sent to reform school at age 18. There, he continued to steal and masturbate with women's underwear.
(Case history courtesy of Dr. David Schnarch)

In anthropology, a *fetigo* (in Portuguese) is a carved wooden or stone object that is believed to have magical powers (usually by capturing or embodying a powerful spirit). The term **erotic fetishism** was coined by Alfred Binet (inventor of the first standardized intelligence test) in 1887. It generally refers to repeatedly achieving sexual arousal and gratification by handling or fantasizing about an inanimate object. A variation of fetishism, called *partialism*, is strong and recurrent sexual arousal to a specific part of the body that is not usually considered to be an erogenous zone. For men who have fetishism as their primary paraphilia, it is not uncommon for them to also have secondary paraphilias—most commonly pedophilia, masochism, and transvestism (Abel & Osborn, 1992).

Some of the more common fetishes involve women's undergarments (panties, bras, or stockings), shoes (usually high-heeled) or boots, parts of the body, and objects made of leather or rubber (Darcangelo, 2008). Fetishes involving hard objects such as boots, leather, or rubber objects are often associated with sadomasochistic practices and fantasies. Heterosexual male fetishists are aroused by the theme of "femininity" in their preferred object, while homosexual male fetishists are aroused by the theme of "masculinity" in the preferred objects (Weinberg et al., 1994).

Fetishists are almost exclusively men (Darcangelo, 2008). When their fetish involves clothing or shoes, these men greatly prefer articles that have been used and have an odor. A man with a panty fetish, for example, would become highly aroused by a used pair of panties that retained vaginal odor, but would probably not be very aroused by the same panties if they were clean.

> "I work at a department store. One night I was folding towels when a man came over and started asking silly questions like, 'How often do you put rugs on sale?' I noticed that while he was talking, he kept glancing at my feet. He asked me where I got my shoes and if the inside was soft. He also asked if they held an odor. Not thinking, I said 'no' and took off a shoe. By this time, he had knelt down, picked up the shoe, and smelled it several times. He then gave it back and immediately left the store."

> "I know a married man in his late 20s who has a fetish. He goes around asking women (the ones he has affairs with) for a pair of their dirty underwear."
> (All examples are from the author's files.)

Be sure to distinguish the difference between a paraphilia and a variant. Most heterosexual men are aroused by women's panties, and many men have purchased sheer, lacy lingerie items for their partners. Some of you may have even sniffed a pair of panties sometime in your lifetime. For the large majority of men, none of these are the end goal; they merely serve to enhance sexual activity with their partners, not to compete with them. The fetishist, on the other hand, is focused exclusively on the object (e.g., panties). The partner's personality or body cannot sustain arousal; her only role is to serve as a vehicle by which to enact the fantasy. In its most extreme form, the fetishist does not need or desire the partner at all.

Sexual arousal to specific objects or body parts has been explained in terms of a two-step learning process involving both classical and operant conditioning (see Darcangelo, 2008). Other explanations will be considered later. Consider, for example, heterosexual men's arousal by women's panties. Most men's first exposure to women's panties comes during early necking or petting experiences, at which time they are highly sexually aroused. A few associations of panties with this emotional state, and panties themselves elicit some degree of arousal. This is an example of classical conditioning. A demonstration

---

Fetishism ▪ A condition in which sexual arousal occurs repeatedly when using or fantasizing about an inanimate object.

FIGURE 14–3 Edward Hyde (left), governor of New York (1702–1709), chose to have his portrait painted while dressed in female clothing. A modern day transvestite is shown in the right photograph.

of this process was provided several years ago (Rachman, 1966). Under laboratory conditions, men were shown pictures of women's boots paired with pictures of nude women. After many pairings, pictures of the boots alone elicited sexual arousal (measured by penile blood volume). Men's sexual arousal can be classically conditioned to other objects as well (Lalumière & Quinsey, 1998).

Some clinicians have suggested that sexual arousal to an object could develop into a fetish by a person's repeatedly reinforcing the behavior by including the object in fantasies during masturbation. This is an example of operant conditioning. Many men with fetishes were first attracted to their desired objects at an early age, perhaps as a result of the objects' being associated with some of their first experiences of sexual arousal. The average age at which men first displayed paraphiliac interests is 16 years old (Abel & Rouleau, 1990).

How common is fetishism? We do not really know, but it is believed to be rare (Darcangelo, 2008). Fetishists rarely are arrested or seek therapy on their own. Cases in which fetishism is the primary problem are very uncommon (see Mason, 1997).

Transvestism

"He was an officer in the army (respected by his fellow officers and men), a devoted husband, and

Transvestism ■ A condition in which sexual arousal is achieved repeatedly by dressing as a member of the opposite sex.

Transvestic fetishism ■ Same meaning as transvestism.

a father. He also wore women's clothing at home, often passing as a female relative, and was known as 'aunt' to his child when he assumed his womanly role."
(cited in Hirschfeld, 1948, pp. 174–78)

Transvestism (from the Latin *trans*, meaning "across," and *vestia*, meaning "dress") refers to repeatedly dressing as a member of the opposite sex *in order to achieve sexual arousal and gratification*. In fact, many experience orgasm while cross-dressing (Docter & Prince, 1997). Most researchers regard transvestism as very similar to a clothing fetish (and thus it is often called **transvestic fetishism**), except that the clothing is worn rather than just held and looked at (see Wheeler et al., 2008). Transvestism frequently co-occurs with masochism, voyeurism, and exhibitionism (Långström & Zucker, 2005). Mention should also be made of a related paraphilia called *autogynephilia*, where a man is highly aroused by the fantasy of himself as a woman (Blanchard, 2005).

Cross-dressing is not considered an example of transvestism if it is done for fashion (as in the case of most women who dress in "men's" clothing), if the clothes are worn as a party costume or for an act (as with female impersonators, for example), or as part of transsexualism (in which case individuals cross-dress not for sexual arousal, but because they believe themselves to be members of the opposite sex). It is also common for young children aged 4 or 5 years (before they acquire the concept of gender constancy at age 6–7 years) to dress up as both mom and dad.

"SOMETIMES I THINK YOU MARRIED ME FOR MY CLOTHES!"

The large majority of transvestites are heterosexual men and most are married (Docter & Prince, 1997; Långström & Zucker, 2005). In fact, the definition of transvestism in the American Psychiatric Association's *DSM-IV-TR* (2000) focuses exclusively on heterosexual men. The majority of transvestites are college educated and in professional careers. About half are distressed by their transvestite activities, but half are not (Långström & Zucker, 2005).

A few men completely cross-dress as women and walk about in public for short periods of time, but most transvestites cross-dress secretly in the privacy of their own homes. Many wear only female undergarments under their male clothing during their cross-dressing. The transvestite may masturbate during a cross-dressing episode or during fantasies of cross-dressing, or may use the experience to become aroused enough to have sex with a partner. About one fourth of the wives of transvestites accept their husbands' behaviors, but most only tolerate it, and many are distressed and resent it, especially if they discovered it only after they were married (Brown, 1994; Docter & Prince, 1997).

How many transvestites are there in the United States? Enough so that there exists an entire transvestite subculture, with clubs, magazines, and newsletters (transvestites generally identify themselves in underground newspapers by the abbreviation TV). Researchers estimate the prevalence of transvestism to be about 1% to 3% of the adult male population (Bullough & Bullough, 1993; Långström & Zucker, 2005).

Why do some men dress in women's clothing? Transvestites are a very diverse group. Bullough (1991) says transvestism can be looked at "as an attempt for males to escape the narrow confines of the masculine role." Most transvestites started cross-dressing before or during puberty (Wheeler et al., 2008), but most research has found that transvestite men were not effeminate during childhood and did not display cross-gender behaviors as children (Zucker & Blanchard, 1997). Some clinicians believe that transvestism arises at an early age through association of opposite-sex clothing with sexual arousal (in the same manner that fetishes are acquired).

PERSONAL REFLECTIONS

Do you believe that it is okay for consenting adults to engage in any sexual behavior in private as long as it does not cause physical and/or emotional injury and does not interfere with normal social and occupational activities? Why or why not?

Related Fetish-Like Paraphilias

There are many less common paraphilias (see Milner et al., 2008 for an exhaustive list), but some of them have a common feature—*the focus of these paraphilias are nonhuman objects*. Thus, some authors consider them to be fetishes or fetish-like (e.g., Money, 1986; Stoller, 1986). Several involve sexual arousal by specific body discharges (urophilia, coprophilia, mysophilia, klismaphilia). Let us examine a few of these paraphilias.

> "I personally know someone that was a urophiliac. He used to talk to one of my friends. She told me that every time they were together, he used to ask if he could urinate on her belly."

> "My boyfriend likes to watch as I urinate. I even let him taste it one time."
> (All examples are from the author's files.)

Urophiliacs (from the Greek *ouron*, meaning "urine") are sexually aroused by the act of urination. They enjoy watching others urinate, and many are sexually aroused by urinating on their partner or having their partner urinate on them (often called "golden showers"). Some even drink urine. Urination is commonly included as part of sadomasochistic activities.

Coprophiliacs (from the Greek *kropos*, meaning "dung") are sexually aroused by excrement. They may play with or masturbate with feces. In some brothels around the world, coprophiliac patrons can pay to watch from under a glass as prostitutes defecate. Although you might think that urophilia and coprophilia are extremely rare, they are common enough that there is a market for videocassettes showing people engaged in these behaviors. Adolph Hitler was allegedly a coprophiliac (Rosenbaum, 1999).

Closely related to urophilia and coprophilia is **mysophilia** (from the Greek *mysos*, meaning "uncleanliness"), sexual arousal caused by filth. For example, there are documented cases of people who are sexually aroused by sweaty clothing or used menstrual products (e.g., tampons).

> "I know a man who has a very high position within a large company. His favorite thing sexually is to be given an enema containing Tabasco sauce. He would hold the fluid in and masturbate."
> (from the author's files)

Another paraphilia is **klismaphilia** (from the Greek *klisma*, meaning "enema"), obtaining sexual arousal by receiving an enema (Milner et al., 2008). Individuals who are aroused by this often have an interest in sadomasochistic activities as well. Many klismaphiliacs self-administer the enema, but many others give and/or receive enemas with a partner. Many use warm water, while others use alcoholic solutions or coffee. Unlike most other paraphiliac behaviors, many klismaphiliacs are women.

> "In my early teens my cousins and I penetrated a horse. I did it because of a dare. I've grown up now and have three children and a wife. Every now and

then I think about what I've done and it makes me want to throw up."

> "One night several years ago myself and a few acquaintances were sharing some college experiences. One of the group stated that to become a member of _____ he had to have sexual intercourse with a goat."
> (All examples are from the author's files.)

Bestiality is the act of having sexual contact with an animal. Only a few studies have attempted to estimate the prevalence of sexual contact with animals. Kinsey and his colleagues (1948, 1953) reported that about 8% of the men in his sample and over 3% of the women had had sexual contact with an animal on at least one occasion. Seventeen percent of boys raised on a farm admitted to such experiences. A more recent study confirms that a fair number of people have experienced sex with an animal on at least one occasion (Alvarez & Freinhar, 1991). The large majority of people who have engaged in bestiality did so only once or a few times, often during adolescence (Tollison & Adams, 1979). It might have happened as a dare, as an initiation stunt, or out of curiosity.

Bestiality becomes a paraphilia, called **zoophilia** (from the Greek *zoon*, meaning "animal"), only when it is the preferred means of sexual arousal. In a study of 114 male zoophiliacs, the large majority preferred dogs or equines (e.g., horses) as sexual partners. "The most common sexual behaviors they reported ever having engaged in were performing oral-genital sex (81%), having vaginal intercourse with a female animal (75%), masturbating the animal (68%), and receiving anal intercourse from a male animal (52%)" (Williams & Weinberg, 2003). The two most common reasons given by the men were "pleasurable sex" and the "animal's love was unconditional."

> "My relationship with animals is a loving one in which sex is an extension of that love as it is with humans, and I do not have sex with a horse unless it consents..."
> (cited in Williams & Weinberg, 2003)

Zoophilia is very rare and is usually a sign of severe psychological problems. Zoophiliacs are often withdrawn, have poor interpersonal skills, and frequently have other paraphilias (Milner et al., 2008).

SADOMASOCHISM

Sadism refers to the infliction of pain on another person for sexual arousal and gratification. The term is named after the Marquis de Sade (1740–1814), a French aristocrat and novelist who wrote stories, supposedly based on his own experiences, of beating and torturing women while being

---

Urophilia ■ Sexual arousal caused by urine or the act of urination.

Coprophilia ■ Sexual arousal caused by feces or the act of defecation.

Mysophilia ■ A condition in which sexual arousal is caused repeatedly by filth or filthy surroundings.

Klismaphilia ■ A condition in which sexual arousal is achieved repeatedly by being given an enema.

Bestiality ■ The act of having sexual contact with an animal.

Zoophilia ■ Using sexual contact with animals as the primary means of achieving sexual gratification.

Sadism ■ A condition in which individuals repeatedly and intentionally inflict pain on others in order to achieve sexual arousal.

sexually stimulated himself (his works include the novels *Justine* and *120 Days of Sodom*). **Masochism** refers to achieving sexual arousal by experiencing pain. It is named after Leopold von Sacher-Masoch (1835–1895), a practicing masochist who wrote novels (e.g., *Venus in Furs*) about people getting sexual pleasure by having pain inflicted on them. If the partner of a sadist participates willingly, as is usually the case, then he or she is, of course, a masochist, and the linkage of the two behaviors is indicated in the term **sadomasochism (S&M)**.

The terms *sadism* and *masochism* were coined by Richard von Krafft-Ebing, who also was one of the first to report clinical cases:

> There was a man who habitually attacked young girls on the street with a knife, wounding them in the upper arm. When arrested, he said that he did it because he would have an ejaculation at the moment he cut them.
> (cited in Krafft-Ebing, 1951, p. 223)

> A 28-year-old man would have a woman tie him up with straps he brought for that purpose. Then he would have the woman take whips (which he had also brought) and beat him on the soles of his feet, the calves, and backside until he ejaculated.
> (cited in Krafft-Ebing, 1951, p. 261)

How common are sadism and masochism? In their mildest forms, they are probably very common. Many people, for example, enjoy being bitten, slapped (e.g., on the buttocks), pinched, scratched, or pinned down during sex.

> "I consider myself to be a normal sexual person.... I love to be spanked." (woman)

> "I figured I could ask you if it's 'normal' if you like to be bitten during sex? My arousal does not depend exclusively on biting nor does my boyfriend have to bite me hard, I just love it."
> (All examples are from the author's files.)

Some people are sexually aroused by inflicting or experiencing pain that goes beyond love bites or spanking:

> "My best friend always talked about how he wanted to have anal sex with his girlfriend. All he really talked about was how he wanted to hear her let out a cry when he finally got to."
> (from the author's files)

Janus and Janus (1993) reported that 16% of the men and 12% of the women they surveyed agreed or strongly agreed that "pain and pleasure really go together in sex." However, only half as many felt that S&M was very normal or all right, indicating that many people do not regard their own behaviors as S&M. Where, then, do we draw the line as to what characterizes S&M?

To qualify as a paraphilia, sadomasochism must be the *preferred* means of sexual arousal. Until the 1980s, most of what was known about sadists and masochists was obtained from clinical case studies (such as Krafft-Ebing's) of individuals who had inflicted or experienced tremendous physical pain and harm. For example, two extreme types of sadists are "lust murderers" and sadistic rapists (see Yates et al., 2008). Lust murderers get sexual pleasure from killing, and they are frequently serial killers. Sadistic rapists use far more force to subdue their victims than is necessary, and are sexually aroused by this gratuitous violence. Examples of these types of rapists include Ted Bundy, Jeffrey Dahmer, and John Wayne Gacy. Although not common, some masochists consent to extreme physical pain and suffering (Hucker, 2008).

Sadomasochism was thus viewed as a psychological abnormality, practiced by people with severe personality disorders. In its extreme form, sadism is less common than masochism (Gebhard et al., 1965), and male sadists far outnumber female sadists (Hucker, 2008). Sadists who act out their aggressive impulses share many features with other sexual aggressors (Langevin et al., 1988). Some of these features include abuse of alcohol and drugs, poor socialization, frequent history of abuse as children, tendency toward committing nonsexual crimes as well as sexual crimes, and long histories of antisocial behavior. Sadists often engage in fetishism and transvestism as well (see Hucker, 2008).

Extreme sexual sadism is believed to be uncommon (Yates et al., 2008). In fact, only about 2% to 5% of sexual offenders are of this type. More recent studies in nonclinical settings reveal that the majority of people who participate in sadomasochism are consenting and differ substantially from individuals who have come to the attention of clinicians. Weinberg (1987) found that the distinctive feature in most sadomasochistic relations is not pain, but **domination** (or discipline) and **submission (D&S)**. The main features are pain (within well-defined limits), loss of control (e.g., bondage), and humiliation and/or embarrassment (Baumeister & Butler, 1997). Dominators ("master," "mistress," "tops") and submissives ("slaves," "bottoms") act out roles in highly structured scenarios (often involving *bondage*).

Masochism ■ A condition in which individuals obtain sexual pleasure primarily from having pain and/or humiliation inflicted on them.

Sadomasochism (S&M) ■ A term used to indicate the linkage of sadism with masochism.

Domination ■ Ruling over and controlling another individual. In sexual relations, it generally involves humiliation of the partner as well.

Submission ■ Obeying and yielding to another individual. In sexual relations, it generally involves being humiliated by the partner as well.

Another study found that in their structured role playing there are four qualitatively different sexual scripts: hypermasculinity (generally associated with men and with homosexual orientation), administration and receiving of pain, physical restriction, and psychological humiliation (generally associated with women and heterosexual men) (Alison et al., 2001). The role playing is usually done with a trusted partner (thus allowing them to explore dominance and submission safely), with both agreeing beforehand on the activities that follow.

> "My most favorite sexual activity is bondage. This is usually done with a partner with whom I have had sex enough times to develop a feeling of trust. I explain that I will tie her spread-eagle to the bed and do anything to her that I want. After doing so, communication is active and only things that bring pleasure are done. At no time is fear or physical abuse implied. There has never been a bad experience to me or my partner during these adventures."
>
> "The dominatrix (female dominator) commands me to clean a toilet, then 'rewards' me by allowing me to chew on one of her dirty socks."
>
> (All examples are from the author's files.)

The scenarios often include fetish-like clothing (e.g., leather garments, high-heeled shoes or boots) and gadgets (e.g., leashes, collars, whips, chains; see Figure 14–4), but pain-inducing behaviors are more symbolic than real.

Dominators and submissives generally are not interested in injury or extreme pain, and pain is erotically arousing only when it is part of the agreed-upon ritual. (Male homosexual S&M tends to be more violent than heterosexual S&M; Breslow et al., 1986.) Activities preferred by a majority of both men and women include spanking, master-slave relationships, oral sex, masturbation, bondage, humiliation, erotic lingerie, restraint, and anal sex (Breslow et al., 1985; Moser & Levitt, 1987; Sandnabba et al., 1999). People who participate in dominance and submission have a strong desire to control their environment, and the acting out of the highly structured D&S scenarios can become the preferred means of sexual arousal:

> "Growing up I had fantasies about having a partner that would enjoy being on the submissive end of S&M. Well I found one and...I never knew my tendencies for that could become so everyday. We both fed on that behavior."
>
> (from the author's files)

Most nonclinical D&S participants are men (2-to-1 ratio over women), heterosexual, and well educated (often with prominent jobs), and generally engage in ordinary consensual sex (Breslow et al., 1985; Moser & Levitt, 1987; Sandnabba et al., 1999). In their D&S activities, most have a strong preference for dominant or submissive roles, but many are able to switch between the two, and some change their preference over time (Sandnabba et al., 1999). Many female participants do so to please their male partners (Breslow et al., 1985). They, too, tend to be well educated, and while most prefer the submissive role, a sizable minority prefer the

FIGURE 14–4 Participants in S&M and D&S often wear leather garments and boots and use whips, chains, leashes, and collars in highly structured scenarios.

dominant role or have no preference (Ernulf & Innala, 1995; Levitt et al., 1994). Most people who engage in D&S are socially and emotionally well adjusted (Weinberg, 2006). Male (but not female) masochism often coexists with transvestism (Baumeister & Butler, 1997). Today, some therapists believe that masochism (submission) in particular "does not appear to be itself pathological or a symptom of deeper problems, nor does it generally involve wish for injury, punishment for sexual guilt, or self-destructive impulses" (Baumeister & Butler, 1997, p. 237).

Several explanations have been proposed to explain S&M (see Hucker, 2008; Yates et al., 2008). Psychoanalytic explanations of sadism often focus on unconscious anger directed at one's mother, while masochism is sometimes explained as sadism directed at oneself. Behavior therapists, on the other hand, contend that S&M results from early associations of pain or aggression with orgasm. One study found that 80% of male sadomasochists and 40% of women attributed their interest in S&M to childhood or adolescent experiences (Breslow et al., 1985). However, a recent study found that the most important aspect for people in S&M or D&S is power and control. This was true for both the dominators and submissives (Cross & Matheson, 2006).

OTHER PARAPHILIAS

You read about some "atypical" paraphilias in the section on fetishes. They were included in that section because they all had nonhuman objects as the focus of sexual arousal. However, there are other "paraphilias not otherwise specified" (this term replaced "atypical" in *DSM-IV*). The list is lengthy (see Milner et al., 2008) and only a few are included here.

Hypoxyphilia (also called *asphyxiophilia* or *autoerotic asphyxiation*) refers to individuals depriving themselves of oxygen when highly sexually aroused with the hope of intensifying their orgasm. This is often done with a rope, belt, or plastic bag.

> "A friend of mine was a bodyguard to a call girl. He went on a call with her once where the customer liked having plastic (plastic wrap) around his head while she squatted over his face naked. He said the sounds the man was making while he was gasping for breath made him sick to his stomach."
> (from the author's files)

Hypoxyphilia (from the Greek *hypo*, meaning "under," and *oxy*, for "oxygen") is often associated with (self) bondage. The behavior results in an estimated 500 to 1,000 deaths every year (Saunders, 1989). Fatal hypoxyphilia almost always occurs with men masturbating alone (Milner et al., 2008).

You may recall that actor David Carradine (who starred in *Kill Bill*) allegedly died in this manner.

Perhaps the most bizarre paraphilia is **necrophilia** (from the Greek *necros*, meaning "dead")—obtaining sexual arousal and gratification by having sex with dead bodies. Almost all known cases involve men, although a few cases of female necrophiliacs have been reported (Rosman & Resnick, 1989). Most experts consider these people to be severely emotionally disturbed or psychotic. Necrophiliacs often seek employment in mortuaries or morgues in order to have access to their "partners." Some necrophiliacs murder in order to obtain corpses, and thus can be regarded to be both sexual sadists and necrophiliacs (Milner et al., 2008).

A few of the other "paraphilias not otherwise specified" include *vampirism* (sexual arousal attained by extraction of blood), *narratophilia* (sexual arousal by using dirty language with a partner), *vomerophilia* (sexual arousal by focusing on the process of vomiting), and *stigmatophilia* (sexual arousal by a partner who is tattooed or scarred).

WHAT CAUSES PARAPHILIAS?

Truthfully, after decades of research we still have very little understanding of what causes people to become paraphiliacs (see Laws & O'Donohue, 2008). They come from all areas of society. In fact, many are well educated, married, and successful in their careers. Various explanations have at times included genetic predispositions, abnormal brain function, bad experiences during development, psychological traits, and social/learning processes. It is probably the case that the cause of paraphilias is multifactorial (Ward & Beech, 2008).

Freudian (psychoanalytic) *theorists* believe that paraphilias are the result of arrested psychosexual development, often due to a failure to resolve emotional conflicts. In this theory, paraphilias serve as defense mechanisms to reduce anxiety. Although Freudian theory has the advantage of being very flexible, the effectiveness of psychoanalysis as a therapy for paraphiliacs is very debatable, and is seldom used.

Learning theorists (behaviorists) attribute paraphilias to (usually early) learned associations. Conditioning of men's sexual responses to a specific stimulus has been demonstrated in the laboratory (Lalumière & Quinsey, 1998). Recall, too, the study by Rachman (1966) regarding acquisition of a "fetish" to boots. Some individual case studies also

Hypoxyphilia ■ Depriving oneself of oxygen during masturbation-induced orgasm.
Necrophilia ■ Sexual arousal by a dead body.

lend credence to learning theory explanations. A man's fetish for plaster casts, for example, was traced to an experience he had at age 11 after he broke his leg (Tollison & Adams, 1979). He got an erection as the nurse held his leg, and later masturbated while fantasizing about it. His repeated fantasy/masturbation episodes led to the fetish.

It is certainly the case that fantasy plays an important role in the developmental history of many paraphiliacs. About half of paraphiliacs recall having deviant sexual fantasies in their teens, well before acting out the behavior(s) (Abel et al., 1987; Marshall et al., 1991). Masturbation to orgasm gave positive reinforcement to the fantasized behaviors.

An interesting question still remains: Why are the large majority of paraphiliacs men? With the exception of masochism, and perhaps klismaphilia, female paraphiliacs are uncommon (Hunter & Mathews, 1997). (The prevalence of women involved in child molestation is greater than once believed [Logan, 2008]—you will read about this in the next chapter.) Many studies have shown that men have a higher sex drive than women (see Chapter 10), and testosterone levels certainly play a role (Barbaree & Blanchard, 2008), but this alone doesn't explain the prevalence of paraphilias in men.

Most paraphiliac men describe themselves as heterosexual, but they generally have poor social skills, low self-esteem, histories of childhood abuse or neglect (or were raised in families where sex was thought of as evil and normal erotic development was inhibited), and anger at women. As a result, paraphiliacs have difficulties with intimacy, especially when they attempt to have sexual relationships. These characteristics are very common in men with the courtship disorders (voyeurism, exhibitionism, telephone scatophilia, and frotteurism) and in some types of rapists (Freund et al., 1997).

Conventional sexual relationships are too complex and threatening for most paraphiliacs, who need to have a great deal of control in order to become sexually aroused. Think for a minute. What do a pair of panties, a dead body, an animal, a person being secretly watched, and a young child—all of them objects of paraphiliacs' fantasies—have in common? These objects are nonrejecting. Consider, for example, the following case history of necrophilia:

> "Two males worked with me at _____. There we worked in the morgue and they used to always want me to watch one morgue while they watched another. Well, one day I went to their morgue after hearing about a young Puerto Rican female body which had been delivered after she died of a drug overdose. There was one guy on top of her and the other was waiting his turn. After talking with them, I found out that they had done this many times before. They tried to get me to do it but I refused, saying

> they were crazy. They said, 'No, you're crazy because this is the best. We have them any way we want, how we want and do whatever we want to them without any back talk!'"
> (from the author's files)

Today, many researchers are recognizing the similarity between paraphilias and other obsessive-compulsive disorders (e.g., Bradford, 1999). Recall from Chapter 13 the cycle of events that drives the individual who is hypersexual (or the sex addict, as some prefer to call such people). The individual is first preoccupied with obsessive thoughts, which lead to ritualistic behaviors, causing further sexual excitement, which eventually leads to the sexual act. The act, however, produces despair; and in order to reduce the anxiety, the individual becomes preoccupied again (Carnes, 1983, 1991). In fact, there is a close association between hypersexuality and paraphiliac disorders (Kafka, 2008; Långström & Hanson, 2006). The fact that a great many paraphiliacs engage in their behaviors compulsively cannot be denied. Men with paraphilias engage in sexual activities much more often than most people (Kafka, 1997). This often includes compulsive masturbation, protracted promiscuity, and heavy use of pornography (Kafka & Hennen, 1999). As sexologist Eli Coleman explains it, the paraphiliac's behavior "may initially be driven by the sexual excitement....But the primary motivation is the reduction of stress and anxiety. There is usually a short-lived feeling of relief, followed by the recurrence of the anxiety" (quoted by Thompson, 1991; see also Coleman, 1991).

Research in recent years has suggested that men with paraphilias may have abnormal brain chemistry (Kafka, 1997), abnormal prenatal neurodevelopment (Rahman & Symeonides, 2008), and/or abnormal frontal-temporal lobe function (Joyal et al., 2007). Although a disturbance of brain neurotransmitters and function might explain an individual's overall sex drive, it "does not explain why individuals differ in the particular manifestation of sexual impulsivity" (i.e., why some individuals may become telephone scatophiliacs, whereas others become voyeurs). Nevertheless, as you will see, pharmacological interventions are playing an increasingly greater role in the treatment of paraphilias.

THERAPY

If we still do not understand the causes of paraphiliac behaviors, it should come as no surprise that we are still trying to find an effective therapy. In fact, two of the leading experts in the field have concluded that, "Research does not show that there are treatments that cause long-term change" and "Currently...there is little evidence that these therapies actually work" (Laws & O'Donohue, 1997, pp. 6–7).

To begin with, one of the biggest problems is that the large majority of paraphiliacs do not want to change. In one researcher's words:

> **Throughout the assessment and treatment process, the clinician should begin with the assumption that the client does not wish to give up the atypical sexual behavior and will do everything possible to conceal important information from the therapist and to resist change.** *(Paul Schewe, 1997)*

Others agree that paraphiliacs in therapy do "not fully and honestly report information" (Laws & O'Donohue, 1997).

Of the types of therapy that have been tried, cognitive-behavioral therapy has been the most effective (Laws & O'Donohue, 2008). However, the problem is that no type of therapy for *any* problem (not just paraphilias) has a high success rate unless the individual wants to change. This is one reason that therapy ordered by criminal courts is often unsuccessful; the individual does not come to therapy on his own. For many paraphiliacs, the urge to engage in the behavior is so strong that it never seriously occurs to them to give it up (Money, 1986). The recidivism rate (the rate at which treated individuals return to their behaviors) is very high (Feierman & Feierman, 2000; Laws & O'Donohue, 2008).

Today, paraphiliacs are increasingly being treated for hypersexual (compulsive) disorder (Kafka, 2008). For those paraphiliacs who are considered to be hypersexual (most) or those who engage in behaviors that cause harm to others (e.g., pedophilia, sadism), *medical approaches* to reduce the sex drive are commonly being used (Grubin, 2008). Reducing paraphiliacs' testosterone levels is one method. Earlier studies found that surgical castration greatly reduced both the sex drive and the recidivism rate (see Bradford, 1999). In place of surgical castration, therapists now use antiandrogen drugs (e.g., cyproterone acetate or medroxyprogesterone acetate) to reduce testosterone levels (Grubin, 2008). The most promising advance is in pharmacological treatment with drugs that regulate a brain chemical called serotonin (see Grubin, 2008). Serotonin inhibits many behaviors, including sexual behavior. These serotonergic antidepressant drugs (e.g., fluoxetine, sertraline) are also often used to treat obsessive-compulsive disorders, which again suggests a relationship between these two types of disorders.

It must be emphasized that these drugs are not cures. They "may reduce the strength of sexual urges, [but] they have no effect on the direction of the urge" (e.g., voyeurism, exhibitionism, etc.) (Grubin & Mason, 1997; see also Grubin, 2008). Instead, the drugs are used to curb the sexual urges while other therapies can be tried.

The present consensus was summarized by Laws and O'Donohue (1997) in the first edition of their book *Sexual Deviance*:

> **Because of our skepticism regarding changing our own orientations and the lack of evidence that paraphilic orientations are more modifiable, we believe that these problems are not "curable." That is, there is little evidence suggesting that a paraphilic orientation can be reliably and permanently replaced by a normal orientation. Rather, we believe that the assumptions associated with a relapse prevention model are the most tenable. The client may for his entire life have a paraphilic orientation, but the goals are to decrease the intensity of these interests and most importantly to learn skills to decrease the likelihood that he will act on this orientation. Thus, the goal of therapy is not a "cure," but rather the maintenance of abstinence from acting on the interest. (p. 7)**

Has there been any progress since then? In the 2008 second edition, they concluded:

> **We now have a 50-year history of…treatments, and it is entirely reasonable to ask: What have we got to show for it? The answer, sadly, is very little. (p. 13)**

PERSONAL REFLECTIONS

Do you engage in sexual practices that may be physically or psychologically harmful to yourself or others (e.g., exhibitionism, obscene telephone calls, voyeurism, sadomasochism, pedophilia)? If so, have you sought therapy to help with your behavior? If you have not sought therapy, why not?

STUDY GUIDE

KEY TERMS

bestiality 366
coprophilia 366
courtship disorders 359

domination 367
exhibitionism 360
fetishism 363

frotteurism 362
hypoxyphilia 369
klismaphilia 366

INTERACTIVE REVIEW

This chapter considers three different ways to define a behavior as unconventional or abnormal. The (1) _____ approach defines a behavior as normal if most people do it. Therefore, unconventional behaviors are those that are engaged in by relatively few people. The (2) _____ approach looks at various behaviors to determine if they are customary within a given society. The (3) _____ approach evaluates the behaviors with respect to whether they cause an individual to feel distressed or guilty, and/or cause the person problems in functioning efficiently in ordinary social and occupational roles. What is considered unconventional depends on the time and (4) _____ in which the behavior is displayed.

Paraphiliacs are individuals whose sexual arousal and gratification to unusual behaviors are (5) _____ over the usual and accepted sexual patterns for adults. Unusual behaviors that are used to enhance sexual activity with a partner, not to compete with him or her, are called (6) _____. It is not unusual for several paraphilias to coexist in the same individual. One group of paraphilias commonly seen together are called (7) _____, short for "disorder of phasing of the courtship behavior." The normal four-phase courtship sequence includes a finding phase, (8) _____ phase, (9) _____ phase, and a copulatory phase. (10) _____ have a disorder of the finding phase and prefer to seek sexual gratification by watching people undress without their knowledge or consent. Two disorders of the affiliative phase are (11) _____, achieving sexual gratification by exposing one's genitals compulsively in inappropriate settings, and (12) _____, repeatedly making obscene phone calls for sexual arousal. (13) _____ is a disorder of the tactile phase and refers to repeatedly achieving

sexual arousal by rubbing one's genitals against others in public places. These paraphilias are often associated with (14) _____, achieving sexual arousal by having sex with (15) _____ children.

(16) _____ refers to achieving sexual arousal when using or fantasizing about an inanimate object or a specific part of the body. (17) _____, also called transvestic (18) _____, refers to sexual arousal and gratification from dressing as a member of the opposite sex. Other fetish-like paraphilias that focus on nonhuman objects for sexual arousal include (19) _____ (sexual arousal by the act of urination), (20) _____ (arousal by feces), (21) _____ (arousal by filth), (22) _____ (arousal by being given an enema), and (23) _____ (arousal by sex with animals).

(24) _____ intentionally inflict pain and/or humiliation on others for sexual arousal and gratification, whereas (25) _____ obtain sexual pleasure from having pain and/or humiliation inflicted on them. Mainstream S&M is really (26) _____ and (27) _____, which usually involves acting out well-scripted scenarios. (28) _____ refers to sexual arousal by having sex with dead bodies.

The large majority of paraphiliacs are (29) _____. Most describe themselves as heterosexual, but have difficulty maintaining intimate (particularly erotic) relations. The paraphiliacs' behavior(s) allows them to have control over the objects of their sexual arousal. Therapy is generally unsuccessful in eliminating the paraphilia, often because the individual does not want to give it up. However, management of paraphiliacs is often possible by administering (30) _____ drugs that lower testosterone levels and reduce sexual desire.

SELF-TEST

A. TRUE OR FALSE

| T | F | 31. All abnormal behaviors are called paraphilias. |

| T | F | 32. Most men who buy scanty, frilly panties for their female partners have a panty fetish. |

| T | F | 33. Young children who occasionally dress up in clothing of the opposite sex usually grow up to be transvestites. |

| T | F | 34. Most transvestites are heterosexual men and married. |

| T | F | 35. Exhibitionists often behave as if they wish to be caught. |

| T | F | 36. Strippers and nudists are the most common examples of exhibitionists. |

| T | F | 37. The best way to react to an exhibitionist is to show disgust. |

| T | F | 38. Voyeurs often like to go to nudist colonies to observe naked bodies. |

| T | F | 39. A person may commit bestiality and not have a paraphilia. |

| T | F | 40. Sadomasochists act out highly structured scenarios in which pain-inducing behaviors are more symbolic than real. |

| T | F | 41. Many men involved in S&M prefer the submissive role and are well educated and successful. |

| T | F | 42. Most paraphiliacs have difficulties with intimacy. |

| T | F | 43. Most paraphiliacs wish to be cured. |

B. MATCHING

(Match the behavior with the name of the paraphilia that best fits it)

_____ 44. hypoxyphilia
_____ 45. autogynephilia
_____ 46. bestiality
_____ 47. coprophilia
_____ 48. exhibitionism
_____ 49. fetishism
_____ 50. frotteurism
_____ 51. klismaphilia
_____ 52. masochism
_____ 53. mysophilia
_____ 54. necrophilia
_____ 55. pedophilia
_____ 56. sadism
_____ 57. sexual variant
_____ 58. telephone scatophilia
_____ 59. transvestism
_____ 60. urophilia
_____ 61. voyeurism

a. Billy must seek crowded places in order to get away with this paraphilia.

b. Henry is trying to find employment in a morgue in order to act out his paraphiliac fantasies.

c. Joe has volunteered to serve as counselor at the elementary school's summer camp to have access to the objects of his sexual arousal.

d. John is highly aroused by watching his partner have a bowel movement.

e. Jim has sneaked out to the barn to find a four-footed sexual partner.

f. Allen repeatedly peeks in windows in order to become aroused.

g. Bert is hanging around the laundromat hoping to steal the object of his sexual desire from an unwashed basket of clothing.

h. Carl is crawling on his hands and knees and being pulled by a leash in order to get sexually aroused.

i. Stan asks his partner to urinate on him whenever they have sex.

j. Greg is wearing frilly panties and a bra underneath his suit and tie.

k. Walter is waiting in his car in the grocery parking lot to show his penis to the first woman who walks by.

l. Susan gets highly aroused whenever she ties her partner up and orders him to lick her feet.

m. Sam gets highly aroused when his wife wears a negligee or teddy.

n. David is describing his erect penis to a woman in his class he has called but does not know.

o. Lenny is becoming highly aroused by his partner's nasal mucus.

p. Paul has paid a prostitute to give him an enema.

q. Larry puts a plastic bag over his head when he is highly sexually aroused.

r. Bob has repeated fantasies about himself as a woman while masturbating.

s. Jerry's arousal and gratification depends almost exclusively on his partner's feet.

C. FILL IN THE BLANKS

62. Transvestism is most closely related to _____.

63. The most frequently caught paraphiliac offenders are _____.

64. Telephone scatophilia is most closely related to _____.

65. For pedophilia, sex researchers generally define a child as someone who is younger than _____.

66. Weinberg and others have found that the distinctive features in nonclinical sadomasochism are _____ and _____.

67. Urophilia, coprophilia, mysophilia, and klismaphilia involve sexual arousal by _____ and thus might be considered specific types of _____.

68. The objects of paraphiliacs' sexual arousal (e.g., a pair of used panties, a dead body, an animal, a young child) have in common that they are _____.

69. According to Simon, deviance is a problem of _____, while perversion is a problem of _____.

SUGGESTED READINGS

Clayton, J. (2004, January 19). Bondage unbound. *Time.* A look at D&S.

Garber, M. (1992). *Vested interests: Cross-dressing and cultural anxiety.* New York: Routledge. Interesting and provocative.

Laws, D. R., & O'Donohue, W. (Eds.). (2008). *Sexual deviance: Theory, assessment, and treatment* (2nd ed.). New York: Guilford Press. Several up-to-date articles on all the various paraphilias.

Money, J., & Lamacz, M. (1989). *Vandalized lovemaps.* New York: Prometheus. Excellent case histories.

Weinberg, T. S. (1995). *S&M: Studies in dominance and submission.* Amherst, NY: Prometheus.

Sexual Victimization
Rape, Coercion, Harassment, and Abuse of Children

Not only does [rape] harm the subordinated victim, those who care about her, and those whose fear of rape is increased by her rape, but it also injures society, which loses the full participation of those women who alter their behavior as a function of fear.

—Owen D. Jones, 1999

RAPE

Rape is "nonconsensual oral, anal, or vaginal penetration, obtained by force, by threat of bodily harm or when the victim is incapable of giving consent" (Koss, 1993) In biblical times, rape was viewed as a crime against a man's property rather than against a person (the woman). In fact, the word *rape* comes from the Latin *rapere*, meaning "to steal" or "carry off."

In the 1990s, the United States had a rape rate 3 times greater than that of Sweden or Denmark, 5 times greater than that of Canada, 7 times greater than that of France, 13 times higher than that of England, and 20 times higher than that of Japan or Israel (U.S. Senate Judiciary Committee, 1990; United Nations/Economic Commission, 1995; see Figure 15–1). Compared with men in other cultures, men in the United States obviously have difficulty in their relations with women. Why? Before we address this, let's first examine rape.

RAPE STATISTICS

According to the U.S. Justice Department (2010), forcible rape rates in the United States reached a peak in 1992 with 109,062 reported cases. Since then, the rape rate has been declining dramatically. There were 50 million more people living in the

When you have finished studying this chapter, you should be able to:

- Describe some characteristics of rapists and discuss why rape is common in some cultures and rare in others.
- Describe acquaintance rape, date rape, sexual coercion, marital rape, gang rape, and statutory rape.
- Evaluate the different explanations of rape.
- Identify several myths about rape and appreciate why they are not true.
- Describe post-rape posttraumatic stress disorder and other reactions to rape.
- Describe sexual harassment in the workplace and the classroom and ways to deal with it.
- Describe the different types of child molesters and the situations in which sexual abuse of children is most likely to occur.
- Understand the devastating long-term effects that can result from sexual abuse of children.

Rape ■ "Nonconsensual oral, anal, or vaginal penetration, obtained by force, by threat of bodily harm, or when the victim is incapable of giving consent" (Koss, 1993).

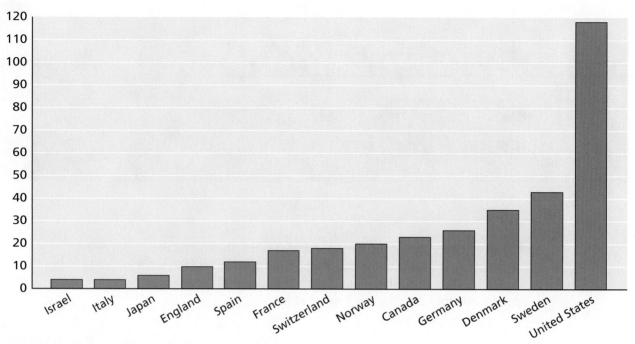

FIGURE 15–1 Rape rates per 100,000 women aged 15 to 59.

Source: United Nations/Economic Commission, 1995

United States in 2008 than in 1992, but the number of reported cases had fallen to 89,000 (with 22,584 arrests). It is believed that the use of DNA evidence to convict rapists has served as a deterrent (Leinwand, 2009). Still, everyone agrees that rape is possibly the most underreported crime, and that the U.S. rape rate continues to be much higher than in many other countries.

The statistics just presented are for a single year. Many studies have found that about 20% of American women have been victims of rape or attempted rape in their lifetimes (see Gannon & Ward, 2008). Over 10% of high school girls have been forced to have sexual intercourse when they did not want to (Eaton et al., 2010; Gavin et al., 2009).

Women between 12 and 34 years of age are the most frequently reported victims of rape (U.S. Department of Justice, 2010). However, the records show that anyone can be a victim of rape, including young children, men, and elderly women (Jones & Powell, 2006). For example, my grandmother was raped by a teenager when she was 85 years old:

By the age of 80, Hazel's failing health no longer allowed her to make the trip next door to her daughter's house to prepare the family dinner. She was hunched over due to osteoporosis, and her hands were so arthritic that she had to give up playing the organ at church. Her face was heavily wrinkled, and her hair was gray and thin.

When she was 85, a man in his late teens or early 20s broke into her room one night. He forced her to display herself, and he made her lean over his

knees while he spanked her. This went on for 2 or 3 hours. He beat her up, permanently damaged one of her eyes, and raped her.

A study by the National Victims Center, which included both reported and unreported rapes, found that nearly 62% of all victims were under the age of 18; 29.3% were under the age of 11. Karen Hanna of the National Victims Center says that young people are frequently the target of rape because "the youngest are the least likely to fight back and often don't realize they are victimized" (quoted in Sniffen, 1994).

Even infants can be the victims of rape:

Eight-month-old "Susan" was placed in the care of her mother's boyfriend, "Joe," for a few hours. Upon returning home, her mother found Susan hemorrhaging badly. The baby was rushed to the emergency room of a local hospital, where evidence of vaginal penetration was found. Susan had to have an immediate operation, in which all of her reproductive organs except the vagina were removed in order to stop the bleeding.

(summarized from news releases)

Women are much more likely to report a rape if they are raped by a stranger; thus, most men convicted of rape were strangers to their victims. However, *most rapes are committed by someone the victim knows.* The younger the rape victim, the more likely it is that the attacker is an acquaintance or relative (U.S. Department of Justice, 2005). Of rapes of girls under 12 years old, 96% were committed by a

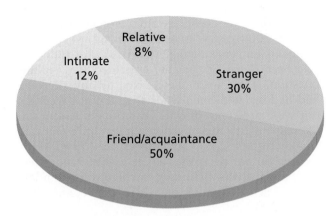

FIGURE 15–2 Relationship between rapists and their victims (U.S. Department of Justice, 2005).

family member or acquaintance; the figure is 70% for women 18 or older (see Figure 15–2).

Some Characteristics of Rapists

Most rapists are young men of low socioeconomic status. The large majority of rapists have no more history of psychiatric illness than men convicted of other crimes, nor are their IQs any lower (see Gannon & Ward, 2008).

There is no compelling evidence to show that rapists, in general, are either oversexed or deprived. Some studies have found higher than normal levels of testosterone in sex offenders, but this appears to be true only in the most aggressive of offenders (Studer et al., 2005). But, of course, not all men with high testosterone levels are rapists. Other studies have found that many rapists have sexual partners (wives or girlfriends) that they live with (Groth & Burgess, 1977).

Are rapists highly aroused by rape-related stimuli? Early studies suggested this might be so, finding that rapists became sexually aroused while listening to audiotapes of rape, whereas nonrape sex offenders did not (Abel et al., 1977; Barbaree et al., 1979). They also found that rapists were less aroused by listening to tapes of consenting sex than were nonrapists (Quinsey et al., 1984). While this is true for most rapists (Lalumière & Rice, 2007), it is particularly true for the subgroup of rapists that use a great amount of violence in their attacks (Lalumière & Quinsey, 1994; Marshall, 1992). In the real world, these men are likely to become aroused by watching violent pornography, especially while drinking (Davis et al., 2006).

What about the developmental history of rapists? A recent review found that adolescent sex offenders differed from adolescent non-sex offenders (Seto & Lalumière, 2010). Teenage sex offending is not "a simple manifestation of general antisocial tendencies."

Other studies show that two developmental factors differentiate rapists from other adult men: caregiver inconsistency (e.g., a distant or no relationship with parents) and sexual deviation and abuse in the family (Barbaree et al., 1998; Prentky et al., 1989). An unusually high number of sexual offenders were themselves physically and sexually abused as children (Dhawan & Marshall, 1996). Even if they were not abused themselves, the family environment in which they were raised often included a great deal of verbal or physical abuse by the father, directed at the mother. With this type of family history, a child may well come to view aggression toward women as normal.

Rapists may not have internal controls such as fear, guilt, or sympathy, or they may have learned to suppress them, in contrast to nonrapists. Many (but not all) had been drinking prior to the assault (Davis et al., 2008; Seto & Barbaree, 1995; see Noel et al., 2009), thus further releasing any inhibitions or internal controls.

Most rapists have distorted cognitive processes—distorted attitudes and beliefs about sex roles and female behavior, belief in rape myths (see later section), acceptance of violence toward women, and denial of responsibility (for reviews, see Polaschek et al., 1997; Ward et al., 1997). Men who force sex on women also have adversarial relationships with women in general and frequently have strong negative, hostile attitudes about women (Abbey, 2005; Murnen et al., 2002). One thing that is clear is that most rapists lack empathy—the ability to see things from the victim's perspective (Abbey, 2005; Barbaree et al., 1998; Marshall, 1996). Most are convinced that their victims wanted to have sex with them, or deserved to be raped (Blumenthal et al., 1999). As an example, psychiatrist Gene Abel, one of the foremost experts on rapists, related the story of a rapist (a patient) with a long arrest record for rape who said that he had never raped anyone. When asked how he knew when a woman wanted to have sex with him, Abel's patient responded that he knew a woman wanted sex if she spoke to him (cited in Gelman et al., 1990).

PERSONAL REFLECTIONS

Have you ever used sexual coercion to have sex with someone when she or he did not want to? This includes (but is not limited to) (a) purposely getting someone drunk to have sex; (b) physical coercion (e.g., persistent and relentless touching, holding, grabbing); and (c) verbal coercion (e.g., anger and/or threats to break up, other threats, putdowns). If so, why do you suppose you act like this? What effects might your behavior have on those you coerce?

Date Rape and Sexual Coercion

One way to classify rapes is by the relationship that exists between the rapist and victim. I will use the term **stranger rape** to refer to a rape committed by someone the victim does not know. But remember that most rapes are committed by someone the victim knows, and thus are often called **acquaintance rape.** Among college women who have been victims of rape, at least 90% knew the rapist (Fisher et al., 2000).

Acquaintance rape is called **date rape** if the rape occurs during a social encounter agreed to by the victim. The expression *date rape*, though purely descriptive in intent, has turned out to be unfortunate because many people believe that it is somehow different from rape by a stranger (see Krahé, 2000). Many people attribute more blame, and are less sympathetic, to victims of date rape than to victims of rape by a stranger (Bridges & McGrail, 1989; Cowan, 2000). *Rape by a date or an acquaintance is no less real than rape by a stranger*, and we should simply refer to it as rape. Here are two examples:

> "I met this guy in one of my college classes. We had four very fun dates. We would go to movies, dancing, parties, and he would always act like a perfect gentleman. On our fifth date, he had a little too much to drink. Our friends dropped us at his apartment because he did not want to drive. I knew I was there for the night. I was not worried because he had always treated me with such respect. But that was soon to change. He became very aggressive with me. He told me he wanted to have sex with me because he cared for me so much. I begged him to leave me alone. I tried to fight him off, but I was not strong enough.... I was raped."

> "Robby lived around the corner while I was growing up. I thought of him like a brother, so when I was 17 and he asked me if I was still a virgin, I was not embarrassed to tell him that I was. About a month later a bunch of us went out and after too much to drink, I passed out. I thought I was safe since I was with friends, but he made them leave and I woke up with his fat 270 pound body on top of me. It was horrible and I passed out again. There went 5½ years of friendship and trust."
>
> (All examples are from the author's files.)

How commonly are women forced into unwanted sexual activity during a mutually agreed-on social interaction? The answer depends, in part, on the wording of questions that women are asked (Fisher, 2009). Koss and Oros (1982) surveyed a group of university women and asked if they had ever been raped. Six percent answered "yes" to this question. They were then asked if any of them had had sex with men when they did not want to, but were pressured into it. Twenty-one percent answered "yes" to this question. Others have reported similar results (e.g., Laumann et al., 1994). Many women do not regard sexual assault as rape unless the assailant was a stranger or there were high levels of violence (Bondurant, 2001; Kahn et al., 2003; Krahé, 2000).

Only about 5% of such rapes are ever reported to the police, and nearly half of the victims have never told anyone (Koss et al., 1988). Victims of rape often blame themselves (see later section), and this is particularly true when the rape was committed by a date or a close acquaintance.

> "When I was 16 I was raped by four guys at a college frat party. In a way I still blame myself for being put in that position.... It was my fault for getting drunk. Especially at the age of 16. Guys take advantage of young 16-year-old girls."

> "Exactly 6 months ago today, I was 'date raped.' Though before taking your course, I blamed myself, now I see it was him and not me who was in the wrong. I actually felt responsible and as if I had provoked it."
>
> (All examples are from the author's files.)

Laumann and colleagues (1994) found that only 3% of the men in their national survey felt that they had ever forced a woman into having sex. However, Koss et al. (1987) found that 4.4% of the men in their large survey admitted to acts that are legally defined as rape, and another 3.3% admitted having attempted rape. One fourth admitted some form of sexual aggression. Another study found that 15% of a sample of college men admitted that they had forced intercourse on a date (Rapaport & Burkhart, 1984).

Most people have no difficulty defining sex without consent of the partner as rape if the act involved physical force, violence, or the use of a weapon. But what about physical coercion? What about getting a partner heavily intoxicated (to the point of offering little or no resistance, as in the "Robby" case history) in order to have sex? Since the early 1990s, there has been a big increase in the use of Rohypnol ("roofies"), gamma hydroxybutyrate (GHB), and other "date rape drugs" (odorless and tasteless but powerful tranquilizers) that were slipped into unknowing victims' drinks. Victims have no memory of any events that take place while under the drug's influence, including rape (Slaughter, 2000). (In response to this, the manufacturer of Rohypnol has changed the formula so that it now causes drinks to change color.)

Stranger rape ■ Rape committed by someone who is not known by the victim.

Acquaintance rape ■ A rape committed by someone who is known by the victim.

Date rape ■ A type of acquaintance rape, committed during a social encounter agreed to by the victim.

What about verbal coercion (e.g., verbal pressure, anger)? Close to 10% of women have engaged in unwanted sex because their partners insisted (Kaestle, 2009).

> "Many times my boyfriend forced me into having sex when I didn't want to. He thought that kissing always led to sex and when I said 'No,' he would become very angry."
>
> (from the author's files)

Koss and colleagues have been criticized for calling experiences like this rape (e.g., Gilbert, 1991) and fewer than half of the victims in Koss' studies viewed their own experiences as rape (Koss et al., 1987). Whether these behaviors are rape is not the real issue. The real issue is whether it is right to have sex with people against their will, and the answer to that is "No!"

I will refer to cases in which a person is forced into unwanted sexual activity through physical or verbal coercion as **sexual coercion**. About 20% of women have experienced sexual coercion (see de Visser et al., 2007). If we define sexual coercion as nonconsensual sex, how do we determine whether a situation was consensual? Men are much more likely than women to view a sexual interaction as consensual (Humphreys, 2007). The law uses the standard of how a *reasonable person* would have responded in the same situation (see Hubin & Haely, 1999). Some instances of coercive sex avoid the label "rape" only because the victims, fearing that they might be raped, "consent" to have sex. Victims of coercion experience negative psychological, sexual, and physical well-being (de Visser et al., 2007).

Studies have found that women, too, sometimes use sexual coercion with partners (see Anderson & Struckman-Johnson, 1998; Struckman-Johnson et al., 2003). A national survey found that 6% of young men felt that they had been forced to have sexual intercourse by a woman (Smith & Ford, 2010). At a West Coast university, 8.1% of the women surveyed admitted to such activity (Gwartney-Gibbs et al., 1987), while at Texas A&M University, 13.4% said that they had used verbal coercion and 6.5% said that they had used physical coercion to pressure a man into sex (Muehlenhard & Cook, 1988). In a series of studies, Muehlenhard (1998) found that nearly as many men as women had been the victims of sexual coercion. However, there is an important difference: The coercion used by men is often physical, whereas the coercion used by women is generally verbal (see also Larimer et al., 1999; Próspero & Fawson,

FIGURE 15–3 Rubens' *The Rape of the Daughters of Leucippus* (1617), although a great work of art, has been criticized for glorifying rape.

2010). Women with high status and/or hostile attitudes toward men, or who engage in sex compulsively, are most likely to use force or verbal coercion during sex with men (Hines, 2007; Schatzel-Murphy et al., 2009).

Many researchers believe that *some* unwanted sexual experiences with social partners are due to poor or misleading communication skills. Muehlenhard and her colleagues found that over one third of the college women surveyed admitted to having engaged in **token resistance**—saying "no" when they meant "yes"—during such encounters (Muehlenhard & Hollabaugh, 1989; Muehlenhard et al., 1996). Another form of ambiguous communication is **compliance**—agreeing to sexual intercourse when you do not really want to. About one third to one half of women report having engaged in compliance (Shotland & Hunter, 1995; Sprecher et al., 1994).

Sexual coercion ■ The act of forcing another person into unwanted sexual activity by physical or verbal coercion (restraint or constraint).

Token resistance [to sex] ■ Saying "no" to sex when one means "yes."

Compliance ■ Agreeing to sexual intercourse when you do not really want to engage in it.

Men who have had experiences with women who offer token resistance or who engage in compliance are likely to push ahead with another partner when she says "no." Some men may even use a negative answer as a rationale to force sex on a partner.

The use of alcohol further complicates interpersonal communication about sexual intentions (Abbey et al., 1998; Bernat et al., 1998). National surveys have found that about half of date rapists and their victims had been drinking before the attack (Ullman et al., 1999; see Noel et al., 2009).

Unfortunately, many people, including many women, believe that it is okay for a man to force a woman into unwanted sexual intercourse in some circumstances (Gibbs, 1991; Monroe et al., 1990), i.e., that men are *entitled* to sex (Ryan, 2004). These attitudes are learned early in life. For example, a survey was taken of 1,700 seventh to ninth graders (Kikuchi, 1988). Opinions about male behavior toward a woman on a date included the following:

- Twenty-nine percent of the boys and 20% of the girls said that a man has a right to force his date to have sexual intercourse if she has had sexual intercourse with other men.

- Twenty-two percent of the boys and 10% of the girls said that a man has the right to have sexual intercourse without the woman's consent if he had spent a lot of money on her.

- Forty-eight percent of the boys believed that it was okay for a man to force a date to have sexual intercourse if she let him touch her above the waist.

Marital rape ■ Rape of a wife by her husband.

Gang rape ■ Rape in which a victim is assaulted by more than one attacker.

It is best to make a firm decision about your sexual behavior for a social occasion before it begins (and before you start to drink alcohol), and then to communicate your sexual intentions clearly and verbally to your partner. This will prevent some unwanted sexual experiences. It will not, of course, stop someone who would use force to have sex, or who would take advantage of a defenseless (e.g., intoxicated) person. When this occurs, it is rape, and no less real than any other type of rape.

Rape in Marriage

> "In the fifth year of my marriage I was raped by my husband after a violent physical attack. He blamed me for the attack and also said it was my obligation to provide sex whenever he desired it.... My marriage ended quite bitterly. For the last 3½ years I was blaming myself for what happened."
> (from the author's files)

In the 17th century, a chief justice of England named Sir Matthew Hale wrote, "The husband cannot be guilty of rape committed by himself upon his lawful wife. For by their mutual consent and contract, the wife hath given herself up in this kind." This idea found its way into the American system of justice (which is based on British common law) and remained until the late 1900s. Today, all 50 states make **marital rape** a crime, but about half require that there be extraordinary violence before the rape is prosecuted.

About 10% to 14% of married women have been victims of marital rape (Martin et al., 2007). These rapes tend to be more physically violent than rapes by acquaintances (Finkelhor & Yllo, 1985; Stermac et al., 2001). Nearly half of all battered wives have been raped by their husbands (Martin et al., 2007). The male partners were often drinking heavily or taking drugs at the time of the abuse (Coker et al., 2000).

Gang Rape

Gang rape refers to cases in which a victim is assaulted by more than one attacker. On college campuses, many gang rapes are committed by fraternity members (with whom there is often an emphasis on heavy drinking and machismo; Sanday, 1990).

> "When I was 16, I was a very attractive and rebellious teenager. One Friday night my friends and I decided to go to a fraternity party. I did some drugs and I drank a lot of alcohol. I danced with a lot of guys and then a guy that I liked for some time asked me to dance. We danced for some time and he finally asked me to go to a little private party in the back room.

Box 15–A Cross-Cultural Perspectives

Rape

At the beginning of this chapter, you learned that the rape rate in the United States is much higher than in other Western countries (see Figure 15–1). Rape of women is common in many other societies throughout the world as well. For example, there is a warlike tribe in Africa called the Gusii in which it is the custom for men to obtain brides by stealing young women from neighboring tribes. On the wedding night, the Gusii warrior rapes his new bride as many times as possible to prove his manhood to others (Levine, 1959). Some tribes use rape to punish women (Chappell, 1976). In the Mangaian culture in the South Pacific, for example, women who violate the sanctity of male-only gathering areas are taken into the forest and gang raped (Marshall, 1971). In 2002, a village council in Pakistan ordered that a woman be gang raped because her brother was accused of having an affair with an older woman (Moreau & Hussain, 2005). In Islamic countries and many other areas of the world, victims of rape are regarded as "dishonored" and are cast out by their community (e.g., Zaman, 2005).

As you can also see from Figure 15–1, rape is not common in all cultures. In fact, anthropologist Peggy Sanday (1981) found over 40 societies that were free of rape. More recently, several other cultures have been found that are rape-free (see Watson-Franke, 2002). These cultures tend to be matrilineal, value the contributions of women, and in many cases raise boys not to be aggressive.

Rape-prone societies like the United States are usually patriarchal, promote and glorify male aggression, treat women as inferior and demean their nurturant roles (from which men remain aloof), view relationships between men and women as adversarial, and, to make matters worse, instill these attitudes in children early in their development.

A comparison of university students in the United States and Sweden found that U.S. women were three times as likely as Swedish women to be victims of physical sexual coercion (Lottes & Weinberg, 1996). Very few Swedish men had ever used physical force with a woman. The authors attributed the results to a difference in sex education in the two countries. In Sweden, boys and girls receive sex education in school beginning early in life, and this education emphasizes how to behave ethically. Few American children receive such guidance in school.

The fact that rape is almost nonexistent in some societies proves that it can be eliminated, but for that to happen here we will have to raise boys to have different values than in the past. What type of values will you teach your sons?

When we went into the room, I saw four of his friends standing around a bed. The guy I was with started to kiss me while his friends began removing my clothes. I tried resisting, but with five pairs of hands holding me, it didn't do much good. After they each had a turn, they just left me there and told me if I told anyone, that they would kill me."

(from the author's files)

In other instances, the victim may be chosen at random. A study by Amir (1971) found that 43% of the rape victims surveyed had been attacked by more than one assailant. Of the rapists studied, 71% had taken part in rapes with more than one assailant involved.

Gang rapes often have a dynamic of their own. Individuals acting alone may not be capable of sexual assault, but being a member of a group creates special circumstances (O'Sullivan, 1991). For a group member, individuality is lost. This also means that individual responsibility for things a person does can be evaded or diffused while committing a rape as a member of a group. Furthermore, taking part in gang rape may be a way of demonstrating loyalty to the group in the eyes of group members, and hesitant individuals may decide to take part in order not to be seen as cowards (Sanday, 1990). Gang rapes are usually more violent than rapes committed by individuals because each member of the group is challenged to outdo the other (Gidycz & Koss, 1990). They may even bait one another into hideously shocking acts.

Statutory Rape

Most states have laws involving the crime **statutory rape,** sometimes referred to as *carnal knowledge of a juvenile*. These laws make it illegal for an adult to have sexual intercourse with anyone under a certain age, even if that person has consented to have sex. The *legal age of consent* varies from state to state, ranging from 14 to 18. The idea behind these laws is that underage individuals are not capable of giving informed consent (i.e., they are not capable of fully understanding the meaning and consequences of sexual relations).

Statutory rape ■ Sexual intercourse by an adult with a (consenting) partner who is not yet of the legal "age of consent." Sometimes called "carnal knowledge of a juvenile."

The mentally handicapped are often protected by these laws as well. A landmark case was the Glen Ridge gang rape. In 1989, seven teenagers were arrested in Glen Ridge, New Jersey, for enticing a mentally impaired 17-year-old girl to have sex. In addition to intercourse, she was assaulted with a stick, a broom handle, and a miniature baseball bat. Although the victim allegedly agreed to have sex and had been sexually active since the age of 12, the defendants were convicted after the prosecution showed that she had an IQ of 64 and the social skills of an 8-year-old, and thus could not fully understand her actions. Thus, in some cases, a person can be found guilty of rape even if the victim was consenting.

Same-Sex Sexual Assault and Coercion

The FBI's Uniform Crime Report does not even acknowledge that same-sex sexual assault exists—yet it does. Many people assume that **male rape** occurs only in prison. The victims are usually gang raped by men who otherwise consider themselves heterosexual (Cotton & Groth, 1982). However, men are also raped by other men outside of prison. Laumann et al. (1994) reported that 1.9% of the men in their survey had had forced sex with a man. This includes college students (Scarce, 1997). About half of male victims were raped when they were a child, and many were gang raped, often by older boys they knew (King & Woollett, 1997).

> "I am a 24-year-old male. I am writing this because I feel it can help others in my situation. At 9 years of age, I was raped by three friends. They invited me in[to] their house to play 'strip poker.' I didn't know how to play, so I lost my shirt. Last, but not least, my underwear came off. At this point, the oldest, aged 16, told me to play with his penis. I refused and he punched me in the face. I started to cry and he hit me over and over. I still remember the look on his face. Well, anyway, they all took their penises and proceeded to rape me. I still have nightmares about it. I still remember the blood, the pain, and the shame. What happened to them? Nothing. I never told anyone until this year."
> (from the author's files)

Grown men are also victims of rape by other men:

> On a stopover in St. Louis, he decided to stroll from the bus station to the Mississippi River. He was standing by the waves looking out at the water when a man approached and asked if he wanted to smoke some marijuana. Senter accepted the offer.

> He followed the man, then suddenly found himself being pushed into an empty tractor-trailer rig.... "He had his arm on my shoulder and his hand on my belt," Senter said. "I tried to get away once. He slammed me up on the side of the truck and told me not to do that again."
>
> At first, Senter tried to protest. His attacker told him that if he kept quiet, it would be over sooner. So Senter bit down on his thumb to keep from crying out. He bit so hard his thumb was left without feeling for days afterward.
>
> Inwardly, though, his feelings exploded.
> (Read, 1993, p. E3.)

Several groups have published accounts of male rapes committed outside of prison (King & Woollett, 1997; Lipscomb et al., 1992; Mezey & King, 1989). Weapons were used in many of the assaults. Most of the rapists identified themselves as heterosexuals and so did the victims. One study found that there was nothing that distinguished the victims from other men and concluded that "all men are potential victims" (Lipscomb et al., 1992).

About 12% to 27% of gay men also report being raped by other gay men, generally within a dating relationship (Krahé et al., 2001; Waldner-Haugrud, 1999; see Davies, 2002, for a review).

Can a Man Be Raped by a Woman?

Many people have difficulty believing that a man could get an erection while feeling great fear or terror, but it does happen. Sarrel and Masters (1982) reported 11 instances in which men had been kidnapped by a woman or a group of women who then forced them (often with use of a weapon) to engage in sexual intercourse. Anderson reported that some college women admitted to having used physical force or a weapon to have sex with a man (see Anderson & Struckman-Johnson, 1998). Others have also reported cases where men were victims of female sexual assault (King & Woollett, 1997; Smith et al., 1988). These male victims of rape suffered long-term problems similar to those of female rape victims (see "Reactions to Rape") and generally felt guilt, or thought that something was wrong with them, because they were able to respond sexually under the circumstances (Masters, 1986; Sarrel & Masters, 1982).

Explanations of Rape

There have been many published theories about rape (see Gannon & Ward, 2008). Until recently, most were single-factor theories. Today, multifactorial theories are most prominent. The prevailing view is that there are many types of rapists and that violence and sexual desires are present to differing

Male rape ■ Rape in which the victim is a man.

degrees in different types of rape. Let us review some of the explanations of rape.

Psychodynamic Theories

These are among the first of the single-factor theories. Psychodynamic theories view sexually deviant behavior as psychopathology—a character disorder that is very resistant to change. In the 1970s, two such theories about rapists were proposed that have had a substantial impact. Both attempted to classify offenders by their motivation. The first theory, by Cohen et al. (1971), classified rapists according to whether their aim was aggression, sex, or sadism. I will focus on the second theory, by Groth, Burgess, and Holmstrom (1977). The two theories, however, have much in common.

Groth, Burgess, and Holmstrom describe three types of rapists. **Power rapists** commit premeditated attacks in order to overcome personal feelings of insecurity and inadequacy. The rape "is the means by which he [the rapist] reassures himself of his sexual adequacy and identity, of his strength and potency" (p. 1240). Rapes give power rapists a sense of mastery and control. These rapists seek to humiliate and degrade their victims through language and acts. Power rapists use whatever force is required to overcome the will of their victims, including threats and weapons. Although this sometimes can lead to injury, there is usually little physical harm to the victim beyond the act itself. The rape may last for an extended time. Groth (1979) estimated that 55% of all rapes are power rapes.

A second type commit what are called anger rapes. An **anger rapist** generally commits unplanned assaults in an attempt to express his hostility or anger about some wrong he feels has been done to him—by life or by his victim. His anger is often directed at women in general.

There are many examples of anger rape. The following letter illustrates a clear case of rape used to act out the rapist's hostility toward women:

Dear Ann Landers:

You have printed letters from bartenders, secretaries, lawyers, musicians, housewives, lovesick teenagers..., but I have never seen a letter from a rapist. This may be your first, if you have the guts to publish it.

I am 32 years old and started on this rotten road when I was 20. As of last week, I have raped 25 women, mostly in Oklahoma, Arizona, and California. I've never been caught. The system I use is virtually risk-free. I am highly intelligent—a college graduate from an Ivy League school.

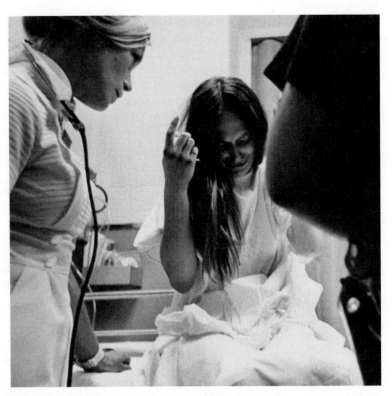

FIGURE 15–4 If you have ever been a victim of rape or child sexual molestation, just listening to a lecture about sexual abuse can bring back bad memories and upsetting emotions.

I am writing in the hope that you will print the letter and educate the public. They need to know why men rape. Perhaps if the reason were known, today's mothers of young children will do a better job and prevent another generation from growing up to be rapists who terrorize women of all ages. I hate what I am; but I know what caused me to be like this, and hope you will give my views as much coverage as possible.

I have read repeatedly in your column, "Rape is not an act of lust. It is an act of violence." You are so right. Actually, rape has very little to do with sex. It has a lot to do with the way a male relates to females. Almost always, if you put it all together it spells M-O-T-H-E-R.

I came from a well-to-do family and was raised by a domineering, overpowering mother (divorced). My miserable, cruel grandmother lived with us. Almost every day since I can remember, I was slapped, punched, kicked, beaten with a belt or a hairbrush. Once I suffered three broken ribs from being pushed down a flight of stairs. When I was taken to the doctor (Mom thought I might have a broken leg), I was instructed to say I fell off my bike.

Power rapists ■ Rapists who commit their attacks in order to overcome personal feelings of insecurity and inadequacy. Their rapes give them a sense of mastery and control.

Anger rapists ■ Rapists who commit their attacks out of hostility or anger directed at their victims or at women in general.

I have never had a girlfriend because I despise all women. I know I am sick in the head, but I have this uncontrollable urge to punish all females, and rape is the best way to get even....

No Name, No City, and No Fingerprints

(*Ann Landers* column: No name, no city, and no fingerprints. Esther P. Lederer Trust and Creators Syndicate, Inc. Reprinted by permission.)

Anger rapists often use more physical abuse than is necessary to commit the rape in an effort to punish their victims. The attack usually is of short duration. Groth estimated that 40% of all rapes are anger rapes.

Finally, there is the sadistic rape. **Sadistic rapists** are erotically aroused by physical force and derive pleasure from inflicting physical pain on their victims. They may not be sexually satisfied if the victim does not resist, and may torture or even murder their victims to satisfy themselves. The attacks usually are of extended duration. Groth estimated that only 5% of all rapes are sadistic rapes.

Groth et al. (1977) concluded that although rape involves a sexual act, first and foremost it is an act of violence. Rape is motivated by the need to dominate, humiliate, and exert power over women. According to Groth, "We look at rape as the sexual expression of aggression, rather than as the aggressive expression of sexuality" (quoted by Gelman et al., 1990).

Studies have provided some validity to classifying rapists in this manner (McCabe & Wauchope, 2005). Groth et al.'s (1977) classification was based on in-depth research of convicted rapists. But recall that most convicted rapists are stranger rapists and that stranger rapists commit a minority of all rapes. On the basis of what we now know about acquaintance (including date) rapes, some researchers have proposed a fourth type of rapist—the **opportunistic rapist** (Prentky et al., 1988). Here, the primary motivation is sex, but these men have strongly distorted attitudes and beliefs about sex roles and female behavior that negate normal social inhibitions. These men rape impulsively when there is an opportunity, as on a date. They use only enough force to commit the act, and their only anger is at the victim's resistance. Opportunistic rapists probably account for the majority of date rapes.

PERSONAL REFLECTIONS

Do you ever use sex to express power, dominance, control, or anger? If so, under what circumstances? Why do you use sex as an outlet for these desires and emotions?

Sadistic rapists ■ Rapists who are aroused by physical force and who derive pleasure by harming their victims.

Opportunistic rapists ■ Rapists motivated by a desire for sex who rape impulsively when there is an opportunity.

Feminist (Sexual Script) Theories

These, too, are among the early single-factor theories. Look again at the rape statistics at the very beginning of the chapter. Why is the incidence of rape so much higher in the United States than in many other countries? Studies have found that rape is most common in societies that glorify violence by men, particularly when the society is also sexually repressive (Baron et al., 1987; Sanday, 1981). These societies not only encourage boys to be aggressive (see Box 15-A), but have distinct gender roles for men and women, with men regarding women's roles as inferior. In our culture, the stereotypic gender role for male sexuality is "active, aggressive, thrusting and powerful," and for female sexuality it is "passive, powerless, submissive and receptive" (Moore, 1994). Feminist theory holds that the traditional sexual script "supports and condones male sexual coercion against women and that this sexual script remains the normative dating script in our society" (Byers, 1996). In this viewpoint, "rape is the logical and psychological extension of a dominant-submissive, competitive, sex-role stereotyped culture" (Burt, 1980, p. 229). One study concluded that "the socialization of the macho man, if it does not directly produce a rapist, appears to produce calloused sex attitudes toward women and rape and [the use of] forceful and exploitive tactics to gain sexual access to reluctant women" (Mosher & Anderson, 1986).

Throughout history, men of victorious armies have raped the women of defeated nations (see Gottschall, 2004). For example, when the Japanese army invaded China in 1937, the soldiers raped virtually every woman and girl in the wartime capital of Nanking. Feminist theory claims that this is done to demonstrate power—to destroy the national pride, the manhood, and the honor of the vanquished country (Brownmiller, 1993).

Social-Cognitive Theories

Social-cognitive explanations state that rapists have distorted offense-supportive schemas about what women believe and desire (Polaschek & Gannon, 2004; Polaschek & Ward, 2002). They tend to view women as sexual objects who are unknowable and deceptive. They also have a strong believe that men are entitled to sex (Ryan, 2004). In adition, recall that many rapists either were themselves abused as children or witnessed abuse within the family (Groth, 1979; Seghorn et al., 1987). Whatever type of family life a child experiences while growing up and accepts as "normal," it is likely that he or she will model the same behavior as an adult. One study found that rapists often interpret rejection as seduction and positive cues as hostility (Malamuth & Brown, 1994).

Evolutionary (Sociobiological) Theories

Evolutionary theories of rape assume that the inclination of men to rape has a genetic basis (Ellis,

1993; Shields & Shields, 1983; Thornhill & Thornhill, 1992). Basically, these theories state that by having sex with many partners, men maximize their reproductive potential, and that evolution has favored sexually aggressive men by their producing more offspring. This view has received considerable attention with the publication of a book by Thornhill and Palmer (2000) in which they claim that rape is about sex and propagation (not violence). Some say that this is the only explanation that explains large-scale wartime rape. Others have pointed out that evolutionary theory does not explain why men rape children, old women, and other men. Another criticism is that evolutionary theories generally ignore cultural and social learning influences (Gannon & Ward, 2008).

In a thoughtful review, Jones (1999) pointed out that evolutionary theory does not say that there is a gene responsible for directly heritable features specific to rape, but that rape is very possibly a byproduct of other behaviors that are adaptive for organisms. For example, "If eager pursuit of possible sex partners on average increases reproductive success, and if such pursuit occasionally results in nonconsensual sex...then rape behavior could be a byproduct of a psychology evolved by direct selection to pursue eagerly, and persist in obtaining, possible sex partners."

Comprehensive Theories

As you have seen, at various times the motivation for rape has been attributed to sex or to power. It is an ongoing debate fueled by politics as well as science. Today, more and more people are recognizing that *there are probably multiple paths to sexual aggression, motivated by both sex and power to different degrees.* Date rape, for example, is now often viewed as "the use of power to get sex" (Spitzberg, 1998).

Malamuth and colleagues were among the first to offer a comprehensive theory (Malamuth, 1986; Malamuth et al., 1993). They say that sexual aggression results from several converging factors: evolution (resulting in different mating strategies for men and women), motivation, elimination of the inhibitors (both internal and external) that normally prevent aggression, and opportunity. The social environment (including experiences during development such as parental violence and sexual abuse) then increases or decreases the probability that sexual aggression will proceed. Malamuth and colleagues provide six predictors for whether sexual aggression will proceed: sexual arousal, dominance as a motivation, hostile attitudes toward women, aggressive attitudes toward women, antisocial personality, and promiscuous experience. The more of these features that a man possesses, the more likely that he will use aggression to obtain sex. In the end, two interacting pathways result in

rape/sexual coercion: hypermasculinity with hostile attitudes and sexual promiscuity.

Marshall and Barbaree (1990) offered another integrated model that is very similar except that it gives greater importance to early developmental factors (e.g., abuse, family violence) that result in an inability to inhibit aggressive behavior. Both theories acknowledge the importance of situational cues and socially created inhibitors. How important are these factors? Recall the research that found that convicted rapists, but not nonrapists, were sexually aroused by listening to tapes of or viewing rape scenes (see the section on characteristics of rapists). Are there any situations in which normal men might also respond to rape scenes, becoming aroused as rapists do? Barbaree and Marshall (1991) found that many men could become aroused by rape scenes when they had been drinking—remember, most date rapes occur when the man or both people have been drinking (Ullman et al., 1999). Barbaree's team also found that normal men's reactions to rape scenes became more like those of rapists if a woman had made them angry just before testing (this was done purposely as part of the research). How might these men behave if they incorrectly believed that a woman had "led them on"? As Barbaree concluded, "With the right combination of factors, most men can be aroused by violent sex" (cited in Goleman, 1992).

More recently, Ward and Beech (2008) have proposed a theory of rape that integrates three causal factors: brain development (evolution and genetics), social and cultural environment, and personal circumstances, and "three core neuropsychological factors (i.e., the motivational/emotional, action selection/control, and perception/ memory systems)." Although these integrated theories differ in some respects, the important point is that there is growing agreement that there are multiple causes for rape (and thus single-factor theories are not adequate).

Rape Myths

By this point in the chapter, you have probably learned some facts about rapes and rapists that have challenged the beliefs you held before enrolling in the course. Mistaken beliefs about rape are so widespread that they are often referred to as **rape myths** (Burt, 1980; Chapleau et al., 2008). These myths serve the function of placing the blame on the victims. In general, men are more accepting of these myths than women (Johnson et al., 1997; Jones et al., 1998). This is particularly true of men who accept conservative gender-role stereotypes, and also for men who associate power with sex (Chapleau & Oswald, 2010). Let us examine some of these incorrect beliefs.

Rape myths ■ Widespread mistaken beliefs about rape.

© Jules Feiffer

Myth 1: Women who are raped usually provoked it by their dress and behavior

Recall that many people believe that date rape is okay if the woman engages in certain behaviors (Gibbs, 1991; Monroe et al., 1990; Kikuchi, 1988). Many adults, especially men, continue to hold these beliefs. One third to one half of all people believe that a woman was at least partially to blame for rape if she wore a short skirt or went braless, went to the man's home or room, or was drinking alcohol (Burt, 1980; Goodchilds & Zellman, 1984; Monroe et al., 1990). As a result, many rape victims blame themselves. Here is the response of a young woman who was gang raped at a party:

> "I still don't know exactly who to blame. I know that some of the blame goes to the guys who did it, but I do still feel that some of the blame should be placed on me because I was drinking."
>
> (from the author's files)

When rape cases go to trial, male jurors who believe in rape myths are less likely than others to vote for conviction (Gray, 2006; Schutte & Hosch, 1997). A jury in Ft. Lauderdale, Florida, acquitted a drifter on trial for rape because his victim was wearing a lace miniskirt at the time. The jury foreman was quoted as saying, "She asked for it." The man was a serial rapist who was later convicted of another rape.

Why is rape the only crime for which we have a tendency to blame the victims? Consider the following hypothetical scenario:

> Steve wore his finest Italian suit and shoes to the company's reception. He was particularly proud of his new Rolex watch and felt sure it would make an impression on the brunette in Accounting. At the party he had two or three drinks. Steve enjoyed a drink on these occasions because it made him feel more sociable, but he often found that he had had one more than he wanted because of peer pressure—others made him feel like an outcast if he didn't have a drink in his hand. He intermingled freely, and toward the end of the evening finally struck up a conversation with the woman in Accounting. They made plans to get together for lunch the next day, so by the time Steve left, around midnight, he was feeling really good.
>
> On the way home, Steve remembered he was out of bread and eggs, so he stopped at a convenience store, parking his BMW slightly off to the side. When he went to get back in his car, he was stopped by a man who said that he had a gun under his coat and that Steve had better give him his Rolex, wallet, and ring. Steve wanted to avoid injury and quickly handed over his valuables while pleading with the man not to hurt him. The man took the valuables and ran.
>
> Steve called the police immediately, hoping to catch the robber. But when the police arrived, rather than asking for a description of the robber, they started

to act suspicious about him. One asked why he was out so late. Didn't he know this was when most muggings take place? The other wanted to know how much he'd had to drink and made him take a Breathalyzer test. When Steve finally got to tell them what the robber took, they were not sympathetic, but instead made comments that insinuated that he had invited the robbery by dressing so well and wearing a Rolex in public.

When Steve got home, his two male roommates couldn't believe that he hadn't resisted. They would have put up a fight, they said; it would never have happened to them. Steve went to bed feeling ashamed and guilty. The next day he didn't mention it at the office.

You probably found this scenario ridiculous, and well you should. So, if you have ever thought that it is women's behavior that leads to their being raped, stop for a moment and reexamine your attitude.

Myths 2 and 3: Women subconsciously want to be raped; no woman can be raped if she truly does not want it

These two closely related ideas are also widely believed (Burt, 1980; Holcomb et al., 1991). Although many women have had submission fantasies (Leitenberg & Henning, 1995; Meuwissen & Over, 1991), this does not mean that they actually wish to be raped. Most of us have fantasized about things we would never do in real life; the difference between fantasy and reality is that we are in control of our fantasies. Real rape involves someone else taking away all of your control.

A common male phrase is "You can't thread a moving needle." However, most rapists are bigger and stronger than their victims, and many assaults involve more than one man. In our culture, most men are reinforced for their physical aggressiveness while growing up, while many women are reinforced for being passive. The end result is that most women would not even know how to fight back if they were attacked. Nearly a third of all rapists use some kind of weapon (Bureau of Justice Statistics). The use of force and threats can result in anyone being raped.

Myth 4: Women frequently make false accusations of rape

The false accusations of rape by a stripper against some members of the Duke University lacrosse team in 2006 reinforced many people's beliefs that women frequently lie about being raped. However, FBI statistics show that the percentage of reported rapes that are false is actually lower (2%) than for most other crimes. We do not automatically doubt people when they claim that they were the victim of some other type of crime. So

why do you suppose some people are so quick to doubt a woman's accusation of rape?

Reactions to Rape

In their initial reactions and long-term coping strategies, female victims of rape go through what has been called *rape trauma syndrome* (Burgess & Holmstrom, 1974). For most victims, it is probably better from a clinical and a legal aspect to consider it as a form of *posttraumatic stress disorder* (Boeschen et al., 1998; Foa & Riggs, 1995), now called **post-rape posttraumatic stress disorder.** First, there is an *acute phase*, which begins right after the rape and continues for several weeks. During this phase, the victim's body has to recover from the physical damage that may have been caused by the rape. About one-fourth of all rape victims suffer minor injuries, and about 4% are seriously injured (National Victims Center). In addition, the victim must begin to recover from the psychological damage that was done (Arata & Burkhart, 1996; Rynd, 1987). Some victims become very expressive about their feelings and may cry and experience severe depression, become angry or fearful, and/or experience great anxiety. Others may have what is called a controlled reaction, as if they were trying to deny that the rapist had affected them in any way. However, these victims must also work through a great deal of anguish and may become expressive later. Many rape victims experience dissociative symptoms (restricted affect, detachment from other people, concentration problems) (Foa & Riggs, 1995). Many victims believed rape myths prior to the rape, and as a result experience guilt and self-blame, which makes the depression even worse (Weiss, 2009). Because the trauma for many victims is long term, rape victims may well be referred to as *rape survivors*.

"The lectures on rape were traumatic for me because I could remember everything so vividly. But I stuck with the lecture so I could find out if it was my fault. Now I don't feel as dirty."
(from the author's files)

Next, the victim enters a *period of long-term reorganization*. In this stage, the rape victim attempts to regain control of her or his life (including taking steps to prevent rape from occurring again) and may move or change jobs. Each of us wants to

Post-rape posttraumatic stress disorder ■ A group of clinical symptoms displayed by many victims of rape; previously called *rape trauma syndrome*. It includes an acute phase (involving initial physical and psychological recovery from the attack) and long-term psychological reorganization (involving attempts to deal with the long-term effects of the attack and to prevent a future rape).

FIGURE 15–5 Most communities now offer rape crisis counseling.

believe that our world is a relatively safe, secure, and predictable place to live in and to feel that we have control over our lives and what happens to us. This belief allows us to reduce our fears and anxieties about the world we live in so that we can function efficiently and effectively in it. However, when a violent crime such as rape is committed, our belief system is shaken and our security is threatened. Rape victims often feel as if they no longer have any control over what is going to happen to them. Many of the reactions to rape are attempts by victims to reassert control over their lives.

Many victims lose their desire for sex and have trouble becoming sexually aroused (Burgess & Holmstrom, 1979; Gilbert & Cunningham, 1987). Reread the story of the teenage girl who was gang raped. Here is part of her long-term reaction:

> "I talked to other rape victims and I worked through my guilt and blame. I still have a lot of fears about sexual relationships and have not had a sexual relationship since I was raped."
> (from the author's files)

Other victims have long-term psychological problems or begin engaging in high-risk behaviors, including having multiple sexual partners (Howard & Wang, 2005; Ullman, 1996). With rape victims who initially suppress their feelings, it is not unusual for symptoms to emerge months or even years after the incident:

> "The first thing I went and did after your class today was run to my car and cry for a half hour. Fourteen years ago I was raped."
> (from the author's files)

Just like female victims, men who are the victims of rape suffer long-term problems (Mezey & King, 1989; Walker et al., 2005; Weiss, 2010). If the rapist was a man, the victims are also likely to have doubts about their sexual self-identity. Recovery is made more difficult because male victims are even less likely than female victims to tell anyone else, and thus are less likely to seek counseling.

The rates for child molestation, incest, and rape are high in our society, and thus, unfortunately, some victims of sexual abuse are later revictimized:

> "When growing up, I was raped by five males in my neighborhood.... The speaker and your lectures helped me to realize that it wasn't my fault.... Recently, I was raped again...and it was very traumatic to me. When I told a close friend of mine, she reacted as if I had done it. She just couldn't understand how it could happen to me twice, and to be honest, neither can I."
> (from the author's files)

A sizable minority of rape victims have been sexually assaulted before (Acierno et al., 1999; Cohen & Roth, 1987; Ellis et al., 1982; Turchik et al., 2009). Studies have found that some (but not all) people attribute greater blame to a repeat victim than to a first-time victim, regarding her as the type of person to get herself into rape situations (Schult & Schneider, 1991). Counseling to eliminate self-blame is very important for repeat victims.

Box 15–B **Sexuality and Health**

Sexual Victimization, Pregnancy, and STIs

Only one third or fewer of rape victims receive medical care after the attack (Resnick et al., 2000; Tjaden & Thoennes, 1998). In addition to the immediate physical trauma that may occur during rape, the victim of sexual abuse is also burdened with the fear of possible pregnancy and/or sexually transmitted infection. A national survey found that about 32,000 pregnancies a year result from the rape of women aged 18 and older (Holmes et al., 1996). Many more pregnancies occur from the rape of younger girls. Half of these pregnancies are terminated by abortion.

Other studies have found that teenage rape victims are 2½ times as likely as others to have sexually transmitted infections. Between 2% and 13% of female rape victims have gonorrhea,

while 2% to 17% have chlamydia and 1.5% to 20% have trichomoniasis (Beck-Sagué & Solomon, 1999; Glaser et al., 1991; Jenny et al., 1990; Teerapong et al., 2009).

STIs are very common, so not all of the infected victims in these studies had contracted the infections during rape. STIs that are found in the first 24 hours after the assault may represent preexisting conditions. Nevertheless, studies have verified that many rape victims do, in fact, acquire STIs at the time of the rape (Glaser et al., 1991; Jenny et al., 1990). In a review of child sexual abuse cases, 1% to 4.6% had gonorrhea, 0.4% to 11.1% had chlamydia, 2% to 33% had HPV, and many others had bacterial vaginosis (Beck-Sagué & Solomon, 1999). As a result, authorities are saying that all

rape victims should be treated with a variety of medications shortly after the rape (e.g., Glaser et al., 1991).

What about the possibility of becoming infected with HIV, the virus that causes AIDS, during a rape? The large majority of rape victims have fears about contracting HIV (Resnick, 2002). However, remember that it is difficult to spread HIV from person to person—and most AIDS experts believe that the chance of getting HIV during a rape is extremely low (Gostin et al., 1994).

To this point, we have considered only the immediate effects of rape. In the 30 years that follow childhood rape, victims are much more likely than others to have multiple sexually transmitted infections (Wilson & Widom, 2009).

Have you ever been the victim of rape or sexual coercion? If so, has it affected how you feel about yourself and your relationship with others? If it has affected you in any way (including leaving you with any sense of self-blame), have you ever sought counseling? If you have not sought counseling, why not?

Reactions of the Partner

A rape victim's partner and family must also deal with their reactions and emotions. It is important that a male partner put his feelings aside and direct his attention and emotions to the real victim. He should let her recover from the assault at her own pace and allow her to make her own decisions. After all, one of the biggest steps on the road to recovery is regaining control of one's own life.

Perhaps the most devastating thing that can happen to a rape victim *after* the attack is if her partner and/or family blames her because they believe in rape myths. This will make recovery all the more difficult (Davis et al., 1991).

"My girlfriend...about 1 year ago (3 years into the relationship) was walking alone on her college campus and was violently raped. I somehow held her

responsible for 'letting' this happen to her. Both her parents also blamed her. I know I treated her with a little less respect after this happened. Now I feel like a complete schmuck. I realize that she had no control over what happened. Fortunately, her therapist convinced her that it was not her fault."
(from the author's files)

If your partner is ever the victim of rape, do not ask questions such as "Why did you have to go there?" or "Why were you out so late?" or "What were you wearing?" Questions like these imply that the rape must have somehow been the victim's fault. Both the victim and the partner often find counseling very useful in learning how to cope with rape.

What Happens When a Rape Is Reported?

In most metropolitan areas, the police department has special units for dealing with rape victims. The investigation of the case will be carried out by a detective from a rape investigation unit. Most large cities now have *rape victim advocate programs* as well. These programs provide a specially trained counselor to be with the woman from the initial investigation through the prosecution. After the initial investigation, the victim is referred to a hospital for a medical exam.

The majority of rape victims do not seek medical care after being assaulted (Resnick et al., 2000; Tjaden & Thoennes, 1998). However, to maximize the chance of a successful prosecution, it is very important to get a medical exam as soon as possible after a rape. It is crucial not to wash, douche, or change clothing after being raped, as doing so may destroy vital evidence (such as semen in the vagina) needed by the police to catch the rapist and prove that the crime was committed. The use of DNA evidence has substantially increased successful prosecution of rapists (Leinwand, 2009). Some victims are initially reluctant to prosecute, but later change their minds. If a medical exam has taken place, this option is still available. Without such medical attention, a successful prosecution (or even an attempted prosecution) is less likely.

Preventing Rape

In general, there are three basic perspectives or approaches regarding the prevention of rape. *The first approach focuses on the rapist* and the use of legal deterrents to prevent rape. Malamuth (1981) found that many men indicated that they would commit rape if they were certain they would not get caught. An approach focusing on the rapist would call for more policemen on patrol, more lights in dark parking lots, tougher laws that are more rigorously enforced, more arrests, and longer prison sentences for rapists. However, this approach deals with the symptom only (rape behavior), and not the cause.

The second approach focuses on the potential victim. Part of this approach involves decreasing the chances that a woman will be the target of a rape. Women are often urged to avoid settings or people that might increase the likelihood of rape (e.g., avoiding dark alleys and not picking up hitchhikers). They are also taught to keep deadbolts on doors, to avoid advertising the fact that they might live alone, and so on. This approach also involves reacting to an attempted rape. Women are urged to learn at least a little bit about self-defense. Non-forceful resistance increases the chance of rape (Turchik et al., 2009), whereas women who resist significantly decrease the chance of being raped (Brecklin & Ullman, 2005; Marchbanks et al., 1990; Ullman & Knight, 1991). Studies have also found that resistance does not increase the rapists' level of violence (Ullman, 1998).

Verbal assertiveness can also help prevent an attack, especially if a woman is assertive when she is first approached. Brodsky (1976) reported that

being assertive and fighting back are most likely to be successful when the rapist initially is polite or hesitant, or precedes the attack with conversation.

A problem with this approach to rape prevention is that by placing the responsibility for preventing rape in the hands of the victim, women who are raped may feel that they have somehow failed and that the rape was their fault. This approach to prevent rape still does not deal with the underlying causes of rape.

A final approach is based on a *social systems perspective.* From this point of view, rape is caused by our society's belief that men should be sexually aggressive and dominant. The explanation of rape as resulting from sexual scripts fits this point of view (look again at the feminist theories of rape). In a society where violence has become both commonplace and acceptable (look at our TV and movie heroes), it should come as no surprise that men use violence as a means of subjugating women. From this perspective, rape can best be prevented by changing social attitudes about the way that men and women relate to each other. Sexual assault prevention programs on college campuses do, in fact, result in less belief in rape myths and rape-supportive attitudes (Breitenbecher, 2000).

PERSONAL REFLECTIONS

What do you think? Is a tougher law-and-order approach to rape needed? Should more women become prepared to deal with attempted rape? Is this enough? Will rape ever stop being a serious problem in our society? Why or why not?

SEXUAL HARASSMENT

A recent nationally representative survey found that 41% of women and 32% of men have experienced sexual harassment in the workplace at least once in their lifetime (Das, 2009). What is sexual harassment? In 1980, the Equal Employment Opportunity Commission (EEOC) established a legal definition of **sexual harassment** in the workplace:

Unwelcome sexual advances, requests for sexual favors, and other verbal or physical conduct of a sexual nature constitute unlawful sexual harassment when (a) submission to such conduct is made either explicitly or implicitly a term or condition of an individual's employment, (b) submission to or rejection of such conduct by an individual is used as the basis for employment decisions affecting such individual, or (c) such conduct has the purpose or effect of unreasonably interfering with an individual's work performance or creating an intimidating, hostile, or offensive working environment.

Sexual harassment ■ Unwelcome sexual advances that persist after the recipient has indicated that they are unwanted. See text for an expanded definition.

Behavior is considered harassment when it persists after the recipient has indicated that it is unwanted. In 1986, the U.S. Supreme Court expanded the definition by ruling that harassment based on sex, which creates a hostile or offensive work environment, is also illegal (*Meritor Savings Bank v. Vinson*, 1986). In other words, *a victim does not have to prove that sexual favors were demanded in exchange for job benefits.* A hostile or offensive work environment can include such things as nude calendars, lewd jokes, touching, and obsessive staring.

How do the courts decide whether there is a hostile work environment? In a 1991 decision (*Ellison v. Brady*), the Court established the *"reasonable woman" standard:* When examining the particular workplace, would a reasonable woman conclude that there was sexual harassment that resulted in a hostile work environment (see Gutek et al., 1999)? In 1998, the Court ruled that sexual harassment included same-sex harassment (e.g., a male employer and male employee) (*Oncale v. Sundowner Offshore Services, Inc.*). Charges of sexual harassment are usually prosecuted as civil suits (rather than criminal cases) under Title VII of the Civil Rights Act of 1964, which bans discrimination in employment based on sex.

Obviously, harassment can take many forms, some more serious than others. Gruber (1990) subdivided harassment of women into five types: pressure for dates/relationships (experienced by about 13% of women), sexual comments (28%), sexual posturing (24%), sexual touching (17%), and sexual assault (1%). Using these more restrictive terms, O'Hare and O'Donohue (1999) found that 12% of women in the work force had been pressured to cooperate sexually in order to be treated well. Here are two examples of sexual harassment in the workplace provided to me by students:

> "My boss started off saying nasty jokes. Then he began to relate the jokes to his own personal experiences. Next he started making comments about how big my breasts were or how my butt looked in jeans. At this time I got real scared."

> "I started working as a legal assistant at the second largest law firm in New Orleans. I was assigned to two young associates. One of the associates was 28, engaged to be married, and took interest in helping me learn how the trial process is handled. I began to notice little things that 'Rich' did that were making me feel uncomfortable. First, compliments or personal remarks about my looks. Then he would

make insinuations in front of others about how late we worked the night before, and how well we worked together. All of these were said in a manner that made me extremely uncomfortable.

> "The last straw was the touching, at first on the back as I was typing or reading, but later on the thighs and calves. I went to my superior and we met with the head of personnel and the director of our law department. I quit that day without pressing charges or causing a big fuss. Why? Because the department I worked in was the Labor Department. 'Rich' defended sexual harassment cases and won. He actually defended employees against sexual harassment—he knew better."

It is obvious from this last case history that "some men just don't get it." Many more men than women feel that the problem of sexual harassment has been greatly exaggerated, and many men believe

FIGURE 15–6 Many women regard this type of behavior by a male supervisor to be inappropriate and a form of sexual harassment. Do you suppose that this man would behave the same way with a male employee?

that women should not be so quickly offended when men show sexual interest in them (Dietz-Uhler & Murrell, 1992). Although men recognize certain overt behaviors as harassment (e.g., offering favors in return for sex), many men do not view less overt behaviors (e.g., sexual jokes and remarks) as harassment. Why? While women focus on the power relationship between them and the harasser, men attend to the sexual aspects of the situation, which they tend to define very broadly (Perry et al., 1998). Thus, men generally take the issue of sexual harassment less seriously than women. The U.S. Supreme Court's application of the "reasonable woman" standard in hostile environment cases is a clear indication that the courts realize that many men and women see the same behaviors differently.

Why is this a serious issue to women? Sexual harassment *usually occurs in a relationship where there is unequal power,* such as employer–employee or teacher–student relationships (MacKinnon, 1979). This makes the victims of harassment very vulnerable, especially if they are economically dependent on their jobs. Not surprisingly, victims of harassment display a wide variety of responses, from passivity or leaving the field, to confrontation and reporting the behavior (O'Donohue et al., 1998). Victims may feel that there is no recourse. Who do you complain to if it is the boss who is doing the harassing? If a woman refuses sexual advances or objects to an offensive work environment, she might be the target of retaliation (e.g., she may be passed over for raises and promotions, given poor ratings, or even fired). If she quits, she may be ineligible for unemployment compensation. Whether she is fired or she quits, she will be unable to ask for references from this employer because he will no doubt invent reasons for her termination having to do with poor performance. The end result is that victims of sexual harassment often have negative outcomes related to their jobs (e.g., job satisfaction, withdrawal), psychological health (e.g., depression and lower self-esteem), and physical health (Chan et al., 2008).

Some Causes of Sexual Harassment

There has been a long-running debate as to whether sexual harassment is due to sexual desire or attraction (e.g., Katz, 2004) or to gender-based power dynamics (e.g., Uggen & Blackstone, 2004). Today, most experts favor the power-based view. Research has shown that the more a man believes in traditional stereotypical roles for men and women, the more accepting he is of sexual harassment (Dietz-Uhler & Murrell, 1992). Sexual harassment is most common, for example, in blue-collar occupations in which women are underrepresented (Fitzgerald, 1993).

Even in social situations, the signals between men and women are often ambiguous and the possibility of misunderstanding is great. A man may misinterpret how a woman is dressed or behaving as interest in him. Some men, however, construe every smile or pleasantry as sexual interest. In our culture, men are also expected to be sexually aggressive, so if a man interprets a behavior as interest (correctly or incorrectly), he is likely to pursue it. Many men interpret initial resistance on the part of a woman as part of the "game," influenced perhaps by the fact that some women first say "no" even when they want to be pursued (Osman, 2007). When, then, does sexual interest become sexual harassment? When a woman has made it clear that sexual advances or comments are unwanted, then any persistence on the part of the man is clearly harassment.

Stalking and Unwanted Sexual Attention

There are several behaviors that, although they do not meet the legal definition, are commonly referred to as sexual harassment. Before we continue, let us examine these behaviors.

Nearly half of college co-eds are going to experience sexism (Ayres et al., 2009). A sizable minority of both girls and boys have experienced unwanted sexual jokes, slurs, rumors, and/or touching (Chiodo et al., 2009). Some of you have experienced what is called *obsessive relational intrusion*, defined as "repeated and unwanted pursuit and invasion of one's sense of physical or symbolic privacy by another person…who desires or presumes an intimate relationship," and may include **stalking** behavior (Spitzberg & Cupach, 2007). Today, this may involve online cyberstalking (Dressing et al., 2009).

A national survey found that 7% of women and 2% of men have been the victims of stalking (Basile et al., 2006). A review of stalking studies estimated the lifetime prevalence to be 12–16% for women and 4–7% for men (Dressing et al., 2006). The numbers are greater for young adults. For many victims, the stalker is someone they have known, and a good proportion of these are ex-partners (Björklund et al., 2010; Buhi et al., 2009; Purcell et al., 2009). Stalking generally lasts several months and frequently involves threats and violence. Only about half of victims ever seek help, and of those who do it is usually from friends, not the police (Buhi et al., 2009).

Sexual Harassment of College Students

Sexual harassment can occur in any setting in which there are power differences between people. College campuses are certainly an example of this. Studies

---

Stalking ■ Repeated pursuit of another individual who does not want a relationship.

have found that 30% or more of college women have been sexually harassed by an instructor (e.g., Dziech & Hawkins, 1998; Kalof et al., 2001). On college campuses, men also are often the target of sexual harassment (e.g., Shepela & Levesque, 1998).

Harassment can be direct (e.g., offering "an 'A' for a lay") or less obvious (e.g., hugs, insistence on seeing the student alone). As can happen in the workplace, an instructor can create an offensive environment for a student even if there are no direct propositions or threats:

> "It was during my second semester in college when I became the target of sexual harassment from my instructor. The ordeal started when he began to stare at me in class for long periods of time. I grew uncomfortable and more importantly, self-conscious. I couldn't figure out why he was staring at me. He then began to approach me and make small talk. In between 'Hello' and 'How are you?' he would squeeze in a compliment. Eventually his compliments became suggestive, and before long, he was making blatant sexual innuendoes to me in front of the class. He would say 'I can't concentrate on my lectures with you sitting in the front row looking like that,' or, 'You sure do make it hard (emphasis on hard) on a guy.'
>
> "Once, when I wore a skirt to class, he asked, 'Did you wear this for me?' as he fixed his eyes on my legs. On another occasion as I was picking up my school bag he tapped me on the shoulder and said, 'Don't bend over in those jeans like that.' Once he said he'd like to take me to lunch and have me for dessert.
>
> "I finally had enough and I began to sit in the back of the lecture hall. He would come to me after class and tell me he 'missed me in the front row.' That was when I quit going altogether. I had four friends in class who knew what was going on and they insisted after about two weeks of absences that I come back to class. They begged me to press charges against him.
>
> "The day I returned, my professor asked me where I'd been and told me that 'if I knew what he was thinking I could charge him with sexual harassment.' The next week I wore a tie to class and he touched my tie and commented, 'I'd like to tie you up.' A girl I didn't know approached me after class and offered herself as a witness if I wanted to file a formal complaint. I wanted to do just that. However, I was and still am very concerned about my grades; I was sure that if I charged him with this behavior he would have penalized me through my grade."
>
> (from the author's files)

It is *never* appropriate for an instructor to make sexual, or even romantic, overtures to a student presently enrolled in his or her class or under his or her supervision. As in the workplace, students who are the victims of sexual harassment may feel that there is no recourse, and the experience often results in negative emotional effects. The U.S. Supreme Court ruled that under Title IX of the Education Amendment of 1972, schools can be held liable for not taking action (*Franklin v. Gwinnett County Public Schools*, 1992; see also *Fitzgerald v. Barnstable School Committee*, 2009). Do you know if your campus has established a policy about sexual harassment?

How to Deal with Sexual Harassment

The number of sexual harassment cases reported to the EEOC doubled during the 1980s and more than doubled again in the 1990s. Still, only 5% of victims ever decide to take formal action.

Sexual harassment can often be prevented if the recipient is assertive at the first sign of inappropriate behavior. Unfortunately, some women are uneasy about being assertive for fear that they will appear "unfriendly" or "impolite." Keep in mind that you are not the one who has behaved improperly. Giving the harasser a firm "no" (or saying that you will not tolerate being talked to like that) is expressing your right to personal dignity.

If the harasser continues his or her behavior after you have delivered a clear message that it is not appreciated, then you will have to take other steps to deal with it. When the harassment is blatant, persistent, and highly offensive, as in the example of the university professor in the case history, strong measures are necessary. Talk to the harasser, or write a letter to him or her relaying the facts and again expressing clearly and firmly that the behavior must stop. Document all the episodes of harassment (dates, places) and list all witnesses. The very next time the behavior occurs, follow the grievance procedure of your company or school and report it. Those *companies and schools that have implemented grievance procedures will protect you against retaliation.* If you should be treated unjustly, report the problem to the EEOC or file a civil suit (remember, companies and schools can now be held liable for not taking action).

PERSONAL REFLECTIONS

Have you ever been the victim of sexual harassment by a supervisor, employer, or instructor? Did you report it? If not, why not? Are you familiar with your campus' procedures for dealing with sexual harassment? If you are not familiar with the procedures, where can you go to find out?

SEXUAL ABUSE OF CHILDREN

In 2002, a former priest was accused of sexually molesting over 150 children over 3 decades. In 1992, a former national "teacher of the year" was sentenced to a year in jail for molesting young boys at his cabin home. In 2000, an award-winning pediatrician had his license revoked after dozens of accusations of sexual abuse.

How common is sexual abuse of children? There is great variability in results among studies. The answer depends in large part on how one defines child sexual abuse (see next section). A recent thorough review of studies conducted in many countries found that in the United States most studies report between 10% and 20% of girls and under 10% of boys are victims of child sexual abuse (Pereda et al., 2009). Similar prevalence rates were found for Canada, Asia, and many European countries. South Africa had alarmingly high rates. Another review of many studies calculated the prevalence of severe child sexual abuse (involving at least genital touching) in the United States to be 16.8% for women and 7.9% for men (Putnam, 2003).

As these data show, nearly twice as many girls as boys are targeted as victims. A 1985 *Los Angeles Times* poll found that for about 15% of all victims, the abuse continues for more than a year. Other studies have found that at least 10% to 15% of victims are abused by more than one adult (Conte et al., 1986; Tufts New England Medical Center, 1984).

Laumann et al. (1994) found that sexual contact with children usually involved fondling the genitals, but that 10% of the girls and 30% of the boys who had been molested had been forced to perform oral sex. Fourteen percent of the girls had been forced into vaginal intercourse and 18% of the cases involving boys included anal intercourse.

There has been a decline in the number of substantiated (reported) child sexual abuse cases since the early 1990s. (Finkelhor & Jones, 2003; Jones et al., 2001). This may be due, in part, to more vigorous prosecution of offenders and increased public awareness.

What Is Child Sexual Abuse?

A review of many studies concluded that victims of child sexual abuse were, on average, only "slightly less well adjusted" than individuals who had not been abused, and even this was attributed to factors (e.g., family dysfunction) other than abuse (Rind et al., 1998). The authors found so little effect that they suggested that we quit calling the behavior child sexual abuse, and instead simply refer to it as "child–adult sex." Not surprisingly, the article was met with a storm of protest (see Garrison & Kobor, 2002) and many rebuttal articles (e.g., Dallam et al., 2001; Ondersma et al., 2001). Even the United

States Congress voted to condemn the article. However, a previous review study had also found that many sexually abused children had no long-term negative emotions (Kendall-Tackett et al., 1993), and a few studies had even reported that some victims recall their experiences as having been positive or pleasurable (e.g., Haugaard & Emery, 1989; Okami, 1991; Rind, 2001). The controversy continues today (see Rind & Tromovitch, 2007 vs. Najman et al., 2007).

One outcome of this controversy has been a reexamination of the term *child sexual abuse*. Haugaard (2000) points out that each word in this term has been defined and used differently by different groups. For example, what is a child? In some states the age of consent is 14, whereas in others it is 18. Similarly, some researchers define children as those younger than 18; others say 17, or 16. Within psychology and psychiatry, the term *"children" refers to prepubescent children (before age 13)*, and most professionals also stipulate that the abuse must be by someone at least 5 years older (*DSM-IV-TR*, 2000). The Laumann et al. (1994) survey used this definition.

What is sexual (behavior)? This can include everything from an unwanted sexual advance or being spoken to in a sexual manner, to an incident of indecent exposure (none of which involve physical contact), to inappropriate touching or acts of penetration (oral, vaginal, and anal). The behavior might be one isolated incident or long term. And abuse?

TABLE 15–1	*Relationship of Child Molesters to Their Victims, as Recalled by Adults Who Had Been Sexually Abused as Children (Aged 12 or Younger)*	
	Abused[a]	
Abuser	Women (17%)	Men (12%)
Stranger	7%	4%
Acquaintance		
Family friend	29%	40%
Older brother	9	4
Stepfather or mother's boyfriend	9	2
Father	7	1
Other relative	29	13
Teacher	3	4
Other	20	21

[a]Total percentages exceed 100% because some victims were abused by more than one person.

Source: From *The Social Organization of Sexuality* by Edward O. Laumann. Copyright © 1994 by the University of Chicago Press. Reprinted by permission of the University of Chicago Press.

There is no accepted definition here. Must there be physical or emotional harm, or merely violation of social norms?

Keep in mind that when we discuss adult–child sexual behavior, we must also consider the culture (see Nieto, 2004). As such, child sexual abuse can be considered a social concept. You read in Chapter 9 (see Box 9–A) that sexual relations between adults and children (generally pederasty) is the norm in some cultures and has been so at times in Western culture as well. There is no question, however, that it is not normal or acceptable in Western culture today where children are dependent on adults until late adolescence. The power difference between adults and children in Western culture makes sexual consent between them impossible (Schmidt, 2002).

The end result is that the term *child sexual abuse* has become a broad catch-all phrase that as a concept presently has little discriminative power. *Depending on how abusive behavior is defined, prevalence rates will be high or low. The effect of abuse will also depend on the type, or severity, of the abuse.* In the Rind et al. (1998) article, many of the studies they reviewed were of inappropriate touching of adolescents or unwanted sexual advances. One would expect that the effects would be less negative than for forced intercourse. In this chapter, I have attempted to indicate when studies are referring to "severe" forms of abuse.

Who Molests Children?

The stereotype of a child molester is often that of a dirty old man who hangs around playgrounds offering candy to young boys and girls and who snatches the children away when their parents are not present. However, this is usually not the case. Studies have found that in the large majority of molestation cases, the molester is an adult known to the victim, and often a relative (Laumann et al., 1994; see Table 15–1).

"When I was 12 years old I was sexually molested by my sister's boyfriend. My mother and sister earlier that day had a doctor's appointment and he had offered to keep an eye on me while they were gone....He dared me to do sexual things. If I refused he would then get forceful toward me and out of being scared I went along with it. He forced me to have oral sex on him."

"When I was little (ages 5–7), I was molested. My parents worked but let me stay with our elderly neighbors. The old man did this to me. He taught me how to kiss and touch his penis. He did this when his wife would either go to the store or leave out of the room. I hated it. What I can't understand is why: why me...."

(All examples are from the author's files.)

Researchers have attempted to classify molesters in many different ways. For example, Howells (1981), Lanyon (1986), and others distinguish between **preference molesters** (who have a primary sexual orientation toward children and are relatively uninterested in adult partners) and **situational molesters** (whose primary interest is toward adults and who consider their urges toward children, often done impulsively during stress, as abnormal). This classification has much in common with the one in the American Psychiatric Association's *DSM-IV-TR* (2000), which classifies molesters as pedophiles or nonpedophiles. You were introduced to the topic of pedophilia (from the Greek, meaning "love of children") in Chapter 14. A **pedophile** is a person for whom prepubescent children provide the "repeatedly preferred or exclusive method of achieving sexual excitement." (Sexual attraction to pubescent children is called *hebephilia* [Blanchard et al., 2009]). Thus, if a man were to commit an act of child molestation but was not repeatedly attracted to children, he would not be considered a pedophile (here the term *situational molester* is appropriate). Pedophilia is a distinct sexual orientation.

An older classification of incestuous molesters versus nonincestuous molesters, which assumed that the former limited their offenses to family members and were not a threat to the general community, is no longer regarded as a useful distinction. Both groups have similar sexual preference patterns (Abel et al., 1981; Barsetti et al., 1998), and nearly half of all incestuous fathers and stepfathers have sexually abused other children during the same period when they were abusing their own children (Abel et al., 1988b).

"I am a victim of child sexual abuse. I was 6 years old and my godmother's fiance was the predator.... He made me do everything from vaginal penetration to oral-genital sex.... Later it was found that he did this to four of his six children, myself, two of my cousins and six other children."
(from the author's files)

Pedophiles have been further classified according to their psychological characteristics (Cohen et al., 1969). The *personally immature pedophile* is the most common. He is attracted to children because he has never developed the social skills necessary to

Preference molesters (pedophiles) ■ Child molesters who have a primary sexual orientation to children and who are relatively uninterested in adult partners.

Situational molesters ■ Child molesters who have a primary sexual orientation to adults. They have sex with children impulsively and regard their behavior as abnormal.

Pedophilia ■ A condition in which sexual arousal is achieved primarily and repeatedly through sexual activity with children who have not reached puberty.

initiate and maintain a sexual relationship with an adult. Many child molesters are, in fact, severely lacking in social competence (Dreznick, 2003; Miner et al., 2010). A relationship with a child allows this individual to be in control, which he cannot achieve with an adult. Notice that the primary motivation here, control, is similar to the motivation in many rape cases. The *regressive pedophile*, on the other hand, is likely to engage in sexual relations in an impulsive manner, often with a child who is a stranger. These people describe their acts as the result of an uncontrollable urge. Unlike the personally immature pedophile, the regressive pedophile has a history of normal adult sexual relations. Regressive pedophiles begin turning to children as a result of developing feelings of sexual inadequacy, often due to stress. The problem is often complicated by alcohol abuse (Gebhard et al., 1965), which they often use as an excuse for their behavior. A third type, and fortunately the least common, is the *aggressive pedophile*. These people are not satisfied with just having sex with their young victims, but are aroused by inflicting physical injury. Here, too, notice that the primary motivation, sadistic acts, is similar to the motivation in one of the classifications of rape discussed earlier. In fact, these men can be called child rapists (Groth et al., 1982), and they often show a variety of other antisocial behaviors. Seven percent to 15% of all child molestation cases include physical harm to the victims (Conte, 1991).

Pedophiles typically have molested many children before they are caught, if they are caught at all. For example, in one study of male pedophiles who were undergoing treatment, nonincestuous offenders who targeted girls had averaged 20 victims each, and those targeting boys had averaged nearly 200 victims each (Abel et al., 1987). Child molestation committed by men who are not pedophiles is usually within a father–daughter (or stepfather–stepdaughter) relationship and generally involves only one child (Freund et al., 1991).

Only a small minority of male sex offenders target both boys and girls (Groth & Birnbaum, 1978). "Heterosexual" men account for 95% of the cases of sexual abuse of girls, and "homosexual" men account for most cases involving boys (Finkelhor & Russell, 1984). (The words *heterosexual* and *homosexual* were placed in quotes because most molesters of boys do not have homosexual attractions to adults; see Freund & Langevin, 1976.) The ratio of female to male victims is 2 to 1, but because male offenders who target boys generally have many more victims, the ratio of "heterosexual" pedophiles to "homosexual" pedophiles has been estimated to be approximately 11 to 1 (Freund & Watson, 1992).

What is the child molester like personally? As many as one third of pedophiles were themselves the victims of sexual abuse as children (see Jespersen et al., 2009; Putnam, 2003). Many are shy, passive, and unassertive (Langevin, 1983). Most are respectable and otherwise law-abiding citizens (Lanyon, 1986). Recent work has found that child molesters have distorted cognitions (i.e., they truly believe that the act has positive effects on the children) (Blumenthal et al., 1999; Bumby, 1996). However, for the most part there are no reliable personality characteristics correlated with pedophilia (Lanyon, 1986; Okami & Goldberg, 1992). In short, there is no single personality profile; child molesters are a very heterogeneous group.

One thing that is well established is that the deviant behavior often begins early in life. One study found that the median age for the first offense was 16 (Groth et al., 1982). Adolescents are responsible for about one third of child sexual abuse cases (Koch, 2010). Very young children (6 to 12 years old) who sexually abuse other children have often been sexually abused themselves and/or have come from highly chaotic families (De Angelis, 1996; Elkovitch et al., 2009).

Tragically, the true pedophile, in order to satisfy his sexual urges, often finds positions where he has access to children (teacher and "other" category in Table 15–1). Pedophiles have been found in positions as teachers, scout leaders, camp counselors, and even ministers or priests.

"I entered a monastery for boys.... As a novice, I was told to go to confession daily and the Father Superior would counsel me in both Christian education and my personal life. Confessions were very informal. The Father Superior heard them from 7:30 p.m. until midnight in his room.... One night he said, 'And do you know how they took oaths in the Old Testament? One would put his hand on the other man's genitals. But there was no sexual connotation intended.' I was a little puzzled and didn't ask any questions.

"About a week later I went to see one of the brothers for confession, but he told me that the Father Superior wanted to see me.... He said, 'Do you want to take an oath like in the Old Testament?' I was stunned and didn't really know what he meant. Finally he took my hand and placed it under his robe on his penis. I was shocked and pulled my hand away immediately, but he said, 'Don't be afraid, there is no sexual intent here. You are keeping a very ancient form of taking an oath.' As he was saying this he took my hand again and placed it on his penis. I wanted to pull back, but I was afraid he would go into another temper tantrum.... He didn't do anything else that night, but he talked to me about how much we had to be obedient children. He often stressed obedience— total obedience. (This was how he set us up. We must be totally obedient.)

"Then it happened. One night we were talking and he said, 'Do you want to kiss my penis?'—I was

FIGURE 15–7 Chris Hanson catches another online predator on NBC's "To Catch a Predator."

so naive. I didn't know what he was talking about. He said, 'Do you want me to kiss your penis? That's how much I love you.' I said no, but then he said, 'Don't you think I love you? There is no sexual intent. It is a pure act of platonic love.' Then he drew me closer to him, he opened my robe, unzipped my pants, put his hands into my underwear, brought my penis into the open and kissed it.

"It later turned into fellatio.... He taught me what he wanted done to him. He had orgasms every time that 'I went for confession.' I was instructed never to have orgasm. Never! 'That would not be good for me spiritually.'

"I have some very deep scars and am now receiving therapy."*

(from the author's files)

In today's technological world, pedophiles often use online chat rooms to find and seduce victims. The children are generally aware that the predator is an adult, and thus some researchers believe that this is an example of statutory rape (Wolak et al., 2008). The *Dateline NBC* television series "To Catch a Predator" with Chris Hanson has made Americans aware of just how pervasive the problem is. In city after city, Hanson's team uses adults to pose as very young adolescents who visit online chat rooms. The series has exposed hundreds of men who had sent sexually explicit messages (and often explicit photographs of themselves) and set up a meeting with someone they thought was a child (see Figure 15–7).

In 2006, the *New York Times* published the results of a 4-month study of pedophiles' online world (Eichenwald, 2006). In an elaborate online infrastructure, pedophiles exchanged their fantasies, details of their personal lives, and information about how to get near children (see Holt et al., 2010).

PERSONAL REFLECTIONS

Are you ever sexually aroused by children? If so, have you ever sought counseling? If you have not sought counseling, why not? Would it be better to seek counseling before you acted on an urge, or afterwards?

Female Perpetrators of Child Sexual Abuse

Just a few decades ago most experts believed that child sexual abuse by women was extremely rare. Today, experts realize that this is not true. As one researcher stated, "The traditional images of women as nonviolent and as protectors of vulnerable others, particularly children, are increasingly acknowledged as flawed and as constituting a barrier to the recognition of some women's harmful potential"

---

*Author's note: This young man later found out that many other boys had been victimized by the same man.

(Logan, 2008). In recent years, abuse by women has been brought to the nation's attention with the case of Mary Kay LeTourneau, a married (with children) Seattle teacher who gave birth to two children by one of her teenaged students. The United States has seen dozens of cases like this in recent years (e.g., Eversley, 2010). A recent study by the Department of Justice found that 12% of youths aged 13 to 21 who were in juvenile prisons were sexually abused while in custody, usually by female staff (Moore, 2010).

As with abuse by men, estimates of sexual abuse by women vary widely. In one of the first studies, women committed at least 5% of the sexual abuse involving girl victims and at least 20% of the abuse involving boy victims (Finkelhor & Russell, 1984). A recent review of victimization data concluded that 4% to 5% of sex offenses are committed by women (Cortoni & Hanson, 2005). However, victimization studies suggest that the prevalence of child sexual abuse by women is much higher (see Logan, 2008).

Who are these women? There is considerable heterogeneity, but the "typical" female offender is young (20s and 30s), has been a victim of prolonged sexual and/or physical abuse in her own childhood, is psychologically disturbed and has many problems in her present life, and has average to low intellectual ability (Grayston & DeLuca, 1999; Wijkman et al., 2010). They generally prefer young victims (Peter, 2009; Wijkman et al., 2010). Some female molesters act alone, but many have a male accomplice (Wijkman et al., 2010). Many are "passive" (supporting their male partner), but some are "active." Who are the victims? They are almost always known to their female molesters, often their own children (see Logan, 2008).

Child Pornography

"Directly after high school I worked at a photo developing store. One day while sorting some pictures I noticed that the first six shots were of boys that looked to be no older than 10 having fellatio and sodomy with each other. The last eight pictures introduced an older man of about 40 years old. I, of course, showed my manager and he called the police. When the man's wife came to pick up the pictures she was arrested. She was charged with passing pornographic material through our store. Her husband was given a heavier sentence—20 years. He was a prestigious teacher at an uptown school and a career pedophile. In that year alone he had molested 12 boys."

(from the author's files)

By the mid-1990s, over 15% of material downloaded from commercial bulletin boards was pedophilic material (Rimm, 1995). Today, it is probably even more common (Jenkins, 2001). The U.S. Supreme Court ruled unanimously in 1982 (*New York v. Ferber*) that publishers and distributors of child pornography can be prosecuted for child abuse without requiring the prosecutors to prove that the material is obscene, thus avoiding arguments about First Amendment rights. Adults who participate in child pornography in any capacity can be prosecuted. In 1990, the Supreme Court upheld an Ohio law that made it a crime even to possess pornography showing children under the age of 18. In 2008, the court ruled that it was a crime to advertise and promote child pornography online.

Could looking at child pornography cause someone to molest children? A study of men charged with a child pornography offense (a study in which blood flow in the penis was measured) found that these men were considerably more sexually aroused by children than by adults (Seto et al., 2006). In fact, child pornography offenders who are caught are highly likely to offend again, and this often includes a contact sexual offense against a child (Seto & Eke, 2005).

Effects of Abuse on the Children

Because of the strong social stigma against sexual relations between adults and children in our culture, it has traditionally been assumed that the effects on the child were always very negative and long lasting. However, recall the review that concluded that child sexual abuse generally was not associated with long-term psychological harm (Rind et al., 1998). The children in those studies must have had a different experience than the many others who report anxiety, fear, depression, panic disorder, high prevalence of suicidal behavior, sexual dysfunctions, and other (often long-term) negative reactions (see Maniglio, 2009; Putnam, 2003; and Wilson, 2010, for reviews).

What are we to conclude? Considerable research has now shown that, in fact, there is no single "post-sexual abuse syndrome" with a specific course or outcome (e.g., Beitchman et al., 1991, 1992). Instead, the effects of adult–child sexual relations represent a continuum of experiences. The results of many studies combined indicate that sexually abused children can be described as falling into one of four groups (Saywitz et al., 2000):

1. Children with no detectable problems (as many as one third may be included in this group) (see also Finkelhor & Berliner, 1995).
2. Children with a few symptoms (e.g., anxiety, low self-esteem) but not of a clinical nature.
3. Children with major psychiatric symptoms (e.g., depression).
4. Children with posttraumatic stress disorder and other major psychiatric disorders (at least half of abused children are included in these last two groups).

Among children with no initial symptoms, about 10% to 30% develop problems later (Finkelhor & Berliner, 1995; Gomes-Schwartz et al., 1990; Kendall-Tackett et al., 1993).

For many victims, not all of their problems can be attributed to the sexual abuse (Fassler et al., 2005; Friedrich, 1998; Kendall-Tackett et al., 1993; Saywitz et al., 2000). Many experience other severely stressful life events that existed even before the sexual abuse began (e.g., dysfunctional family, generally maltreated in all other ways).

Several factors contribute to the particular response of a child. Some children are more resilient than others, and in some cases the abuse was minor. *The greatest harm in terms of long-lasting negative effects is seen in cases where the abuse is frequent or long-lasting; where the abuse involves penetration, force, threats, or violence; where the abuser is the father or stepfather; and where there is little support from the mother* (Beitchman et al., 1992; Kendall-Tackett et al., 1993; Molnar et al., 2001; Najman et al., 2007; Rind & Tromovitch, 1997; Tyler, 2002). The most frequent symptoms include fears, poor self-esteem, inappropriate sexual behavior by children, and depression. Because childhood sexual abuse can impair emotional development, many victims later engage in increased sexual risk taking and/or display a variety of sexual problems. (Friedrich, 1993; Leonard & Follette, 2003; Najman et al., 2005; Paolucci et al., 2001; Senn et al., 2007; Stock et al., 1997; Tyler, 2002). Because of their psychological vulnerability, many victims of severe childhood abuse are revictimized again in childhood (Finkelhor et al., 2007) and/or later in life as adults (Noll et al., 2009).

About half of all child victims never inform their parents or another adult of the abuse (Paine & Hansen, 2002), and reactions that are perceived by the child as less than supportive can greatly add to the negativity of the experience (Jonzon & Lindblad, 2005). Consider, for example, the following two cases:

"At the age of 9, I was molested by a man right outside of my neighborhood. I told my mother what had happened. I was very hurt and scared, but instead of talking to me, my mother refused to talk about it and acted as if it was my fault. Years later I discovered the man had done the same thing to other children. By then it was too late, I was already emotionally scarred." (woman)

"I was about 8 years old when I was sexually abused by a friend of my father. I refused, but he beat me up and made me have sexual intercourse with him. Later the same night I told my father, but my father, instead of going to the police as I thought, beat me very harshly with a wood stick." (man)

(All examples are from the author's files.)

Like victims of rape, victims of child molestation have a tendency to blame themselves, especially if they were less than 10 years old and the abuse was by a family member (Barker-Collo, 2001). The self-blame is associated with more problems as adults.

"I was sexually abused for 9 years as a child by my older sister's husband. For years I believed it had happened because there was something wrong with me."
(from the author's files)

A review of many studies concluded that about two thirds of all victims of child sexual abuse show substantial recovery during the first 12 to 18 months (Kendall-Tackett et al., 1993). Even for these individuals, however, some symptoms, such as sexual preoccupation and aggressiveness, may worsen (Friedrich & Reams, 1987). From 10% to 24% of all abused female children not only fail to improve over time but actually get worse (see Kendall-Tackett et al., 1993). As adults, these women display problems

FIGURE 15–8 This self-portrait by a victim of sexual abuse shows the emotional suffering that is often experienced long after the crime.

(e.g., emotional distress, drug and alcohol abuse, suicide attempts) that are just as great as in women presently being abused (McCauley et al., 1997). Sexual dysfunctions are common among women who experienced childhood abuse involving penetration (see Mullen et al., 2000). Many adults who were sexually abused as children also have disturbances relating to body image and as a result have serious eating disorders (anorexia nervosa, bulimia) (van Gerko et al., 2005).

Recovered (False?) Memory Syndrome

"For the first time, when I was 17 a boyfriend reached out to touch me in a sexual manner. In that split second, I flashed back to when I was 9 and my uncle (by marriage) was molesting me. Until that moment I had no conscious memory of that event. I began to scream and cry and the poor guy didn't know what to do other than bring me home. "I recently found out that this man repeatedly molested all seven of my female cousins."

(from the author's files)

When childhood sexual abuse was not traumatic, many people go for years without thinking about it (McNally & Geraerts, 2009). But what about when the abuse was traumatic? One of the most bitter debates in the field of sexual abuse today is whether people can forget sexually traumatic past experiences and later remember them. On the one hand, there are therapists who believe that sexual abuse can be so traumatic that individuals, in order to cope, forget or suppress memories of the event, often for many years. Later, either spontaneously or while undergoing therapy, the individual remembers the past events. Many studies have documented that people can experience amnesia for nonsexual traumatic events (e.g., disasters, combat) (Arrigo & Pezdek, 1997). Many others have reported cases of sexual abuse victims who said that they also had experienced some degree of amnesia of the events for a period of time (e.g., Feldman-Summers & Pope, 1994; Gold et al., 1994; Herman, 1992; Wilsnack et al., 2002). These studies find that, on average, about 50% of all victims report some amnesia (see Kristiansen et al., 1996).

On the other hand, others claim that most "recovered" memories are, in fact, false memories created by overzealous therapists working with vulnerable people (e.g., Loftus, 1997a, 1997b; Ofshe & Watters, 1994). These claims are bolstered by lab studies demonstrating that people can "remember" events that never occurred (Brainerd & Reyna, 1998; Zaragoza et al., 2001). For example, many children can be led to falsely remember a serious animal attack that never actually occurred (Porter et al., 1999). Sexually abused women with posttraumatic stress disorder are especially likely to show this in the lab (Bremner et al., 2000). Accounts of abuse victims who have retracted their "memories" have been published (e.g., de Rivera, 1997).

Proponents of the theory of repressed memories cite evidence that few claims of amnesia are false (Hovdestad & Kristiansen, 1996). In one study, women with well-substantiated cases of childhood sexual abuse 20 years earlier were interviewed. Over one third did not recall the abuse (Williams, 1994).

Today, most people take a balanced view, accepting that in some cases memories of abuse are false, but that in other cases repressed memories are true.

INCEST

The term *incest* comes from a Latin word (*incestus*) meaning "impure." **Incest** refers to sexual activity between relatives who are too closely related to marry. It is illegal in all 50 states. One reason incest is illegal is that this type of mating has the highest probability of producing defective offspring (Thornhill, 1992). Until recently, many people thought that incest was rare, but it happens much more often than people might (or might want to) believe. Look again at Table 15–1. About 8.5% of women and 2.4% of men in Laumann et al.'s (1994) nationally representative survey said that they had been sexually abused by a family member before the age of 13. Only about 2% of adult–child incestuous relations ever get reported to authorities (Russell, 1984), and some victims do not understand that what happened to them was abuse (Kikuchi, 1988).

Although they have received little attention by researchers, **polyincestuous families** are not uncommon (Faller, 1991). In these families, there are both multiple abusers and multiple victims, both across generations and within the same generation. Victims often become abusers, and in many cases view the activity as acceptable, or even expected. It is common in polyincestuous families for women to participate as well (Faller, 1987; McCarty, 1986). In over half of such families, there are also abusers and victims from outside the family (Faller, 1991).

Much more is known about specific types of incest. After you have read about these, we will return to a discussion of family dynamics in incest.

Incest Between Siblings

Brother–sister incest, or in some cases *brother–brother incest*, is believed to be five times more

---

Incest ■ Sexual contact between two closely related persons.

Polyincestuous family ■ A family in which there are both multiple incestuous abusers and multiple victims, across generations and within the same generation.

common than parent–child incest (Cole, 1982; Gebhard et al., 1965). In families in which sibling sexual activity occurs, the families are frequently found to be dysfunctional, often including physical abuse and heavy use of alcohol (see Cyr et al., 2002).

> "I was a victim from age 4 until 13. My two brothers continually cornered me and forced me. My mother worked and was much too busy or tired to observe. She did not believe me when I tried to tell her. To this day, I still have problems sexually, emotionally, and mentally. My way of solving it was to move away (1200 miles away)."
>
> "When I was around 6, my oldest adoptive brother decided that he needed 'more fun.' Every week, about two or three times a week, he would pin me down, place a gag in my mouth, and rape me until he would say 'go shower, I'm done for now.'...One day Jimmy was careless and my parents came home early from work. My father banged my door down, threw him off me."
>
> (All examples are from the author's files.)

There is considerable debate among professionals about the long-term effects of sibling incest. Some believe that if the experience occurs between siblings of nearly the same age (less than a 4- to 5-year age difference), if there is no betrayal of trust, and if the children are not traumatized by adults in cases where their activity is discovered, then it is just "sex play" and "part of growing up" (Finkelhor, 1980; Steele & Alexander, 1981). However, as you can see from the previous case history, the effects can sometimes be quite negative. Some studies have found that the effects on victims of brother–sister incest are just as negative as father–daughter incest (Cyr et al., 2002). This is particularly so when the incest involves coercion, threats, force, or betrayal of trust (Canavan et al., 1992). Only about 12% of all people with childhood sibling incest experiences have ever told anyone, and "the pain of secrecy" adds to the negative experience (Finkelhor, 1980).

Parent–Child Incest

> "At the age of 5, I was the oldest of two children (my little sister was one year old). My mom would go to church and leave me in the care of my father. He would take out his penis and have me look at it and touch it, but I didn't know what was happening. It stopped for a while, but then he would try to put his tongue into my mouth. At the age of 8, after my mom had another baby, he would touch my vagina and lay on top of me (all 195 lbs.). At the age of 11, he got into my bed trying to take off my panties. I put up a fight but they were removed. He then took out his penis...I am a sophomore here at UNO, and

it still hurts. I try to get over the hating of my father, but I don't really care what he thinks about me." (woman)
>
> "My father began to molest me when I was 12—on the night after my mother's funeral. I am an only child and he explained that since my mother was gone I was going to have to function as the 'woman' of the house. At first I was only required to function as a woman in the evenings (and most mornings too), sharing his bed as my mother had. As I grew older additional chores were added such as cooking and cleaning. It was always explained that if I truly loved him I would never hesitate to do his bidding—oral and anal sex, giving him showers, dressing him, etc. Finally I managed to get the courage to leave my father.... Throughout my entire adult life I have never had a successful relationship. I'm not gay, but I don't know how a man should act. I only know how to function as the 'lady of the house.'" (man)
>
> "I was 12 years old...my dad would touch me a lot. That was the year I started to get my breasts. In the middle of the night I would be woken up by my dad feeling my breasts. I would act as though I was still sleeping. One day when my mom went to the store my dad made me go in his room so he could shave around my vagina. When doing this, he got naked ... he kept telling me that I needed to learn how to shave myself down there because guys don't like it hairy..."
>
> (All examples are from the author's files)

Of all the types of incest, parent–child incest probably evokes the greatest emotional response in people. After all, most people believe that it is the role of parents to nurture, provide for, and protect their children, not turn them into sexual objects for their own selfish needs.

> "I realize that it wasn't just what he did to me physically. At that moment I lost my father. He was no longer a person to love and protect me. I was there to satisfy him."
>
> (from Spiegel, 2000)

Adults who commit incest with their children come from all walks of life. Former Miss America Marilyn Van Derbur focused much attention on this issue when she revealed that she had been repeatedly assaulted sexually beginning at age 5 by her father, a millionaire businessman, socialite, and philanthropist— a pillar of the community (Figure 15–9).

Although parent–child incest accounts for only 10% of all incest cases (Finkelhor, 1979), nearly 80% of arrests involve *father (stepfather)–daughter incest*. Stepfathers are more likely to victimize their children than are biological fathers (Finkelhor, 1979), but both types of cases are common. Fathers who commit incest are generally shy and publicly devoted family men who appear to be quite average, but in their own

FIGURE 15–9 Former Miss America Marilyn Van Derbur later announced that her father (seen here congratulating her) had sexually abused her when she was a child.)

homes they are very domineering and authoritarian—"king of their castle" (Meiselman, 1978). In relations with their children, they are often overprotective, selfish, and jealous. Incestuous fathers, obviously, have the capacity to become sexually aroused by children (remember, nearly half of all incestuous fathers also molest other children; Abel et al., 1988b).

The role of the mother in father–child incest is critical, and her response, or lack of any, is often as traumatizing to the child as the molestation. Consider, for example, the responses of the following four victims:

> "My mother didn't believe me. Even at age 19, I still feel resentment for her for not protecting me and for not believing me. At the time she was totally dependent on him (stepfather) and the thought of losing him was unthinkable."

> "I thought every father did that to their daughter. I thought it was a part of growing up, especially because my mom knew about it."

> "I eventually told my mother and she told me that it was nothing, that he probably thought it was her and she didn't mention it again."

> "I grabbed onto her leg saying—screaming, crying—'Don't leave me please. I don't want to be here with him!' She said I had to behave and then left without

even looking at me. From this moment on I knew she was not going to listen to me, let alone protect me. This is why I am angry today."
>
> (All examples are from the author's files.)

Some mothers do call authorities when they become aware of the incest, but more than two thirds do not try to protect their daughters (Herman & Hirschman, 1977). Although some mothers of incest victims have normal personalities (Groff, 1987), many are emotionally distant from their children and dependent on their husbands. They fear abandonment more than living with the fact that their children are victims of incest (Finkelhor, 1984). Many were victims of child abuse themselves (Summit & Kryso, 1978), and continue to suffer physical abuse within the marriage (Truesdell et al., 1986).

In some cases, the mother is the abuser (Wijkman et al., 2010). *Mother–child* incest has generally been regarded as rare, but some believe that it may be underreported because surveys rarely ask specific questions about this type of incest (Lawson, 1993). Mother–son incest typically occurs in disrupted families where the mother seeks emotional support and physical closeness from her son rather than from other adults (Krug, 1989). However, recall from the previous section that daughters are as likely (or more likely) to be the victims as sons (Grayston & DeLuca, 1999). The mothers were generally the victims of sexual and/or physical abuse as children themselves.

Grandparents as incest perpetrators have also been found to be uncommon (e.g., Cupoli & Sewell, 1988; Kendall-Tackett & Simon, 1987), but may be on the increase because of the increased number of working parents leaving their children with the grandparents.

> "I only had to see him when we visited in the summer. He would get me downstairs in the cellar alone.... He would touch my vagina and I remember it hurting all of the time. He would sometimes take his penis out of his pants.... I never talked to anyone about it. One time I briefly talked to my sister about it at his funeral. She asked me why I did not seem sad.... She said it happened to her also."
>
> (from the author's files)

Effects of Incest on Children

In this section, I will focus on the effects of father–child incest, although much of what you learn will be true of victims of other types of incest as well. Father–child incest generally involves frequent, long-term abuse, and in many cases there is vaginal and/or anal penetration. Recall that these are precisely the factors that often cause the greatest long-term harm in child molestation cases (Beitchman et al., 1992; Kendall-Tackett et al., 1993). A lack of support from the mother also substantially affects the victim's outcome.

Another important factor that leads to long-term problems in victims of father–child incest is that many victims blame themselves (often with encouragement from the father; Barker-Collo, 2001). Thus, victims of incest are similar to rape victims in this respect. Consider, for example, the feelings of the following two victims:

> "I am 18 now and I believe that it was my fault. No matter how I look at it, I feel as though I could have prevented it."

> "[I] still question myself about if there was something I could have done to prevent it, or worse yet, if there was, somehow, something I did to cause it."
>
> (All examples are from the author's files.)

Victims can be very confused if they experienced any degree of physical pleasure during the abuse:

> "In my mind, I blamed me, not him. To make matters worse, somewhere along the way my 12-year-old adolescent body had my first orgasm. I hated it, hated myself, hated him.... I couldn't understand something I hated feeling good. Heavy, heavy guilt trip."
>
> (from the author's files)

Children who are victims of incest often suffer from posttraumatic stress disorder (Lindberg & Distad, 1985). However, as with other types of child molestation, there is no definite or typical "incest syndrome" (Haesevoets, 1997). As adults, victims may have feelings of anxiety, helplessness, and powerlessness. Many victims suffer from low self-esteem and poor self-image (Cole & Putnam, 1992).

> "I've always felt alone, disassociated. Even when I'm with friends I don't feel like a part of the group. In class, I've never felt like I belonged."

> "...But deep down I feel really disgusted about my body."
>
> (All examples are from the author's files.)

Some victims later develop eating disorders (Hall et al., 1989), while others suffer from major depressive episodes and alcohol or drug abuse.

> "By the time I was 13, I had found alcohol and drugs as a safe haven from the immense pain inside me. By the age of 17, I was a full-blown alcoholic experiencing blackouts."
>
> (from the author's files)

Victims of child incest may also suffer from a variety of sexual problems. Some abused children may even victimize other children in an attempt to work out the distressing events (Johnson, 1989). As adults, they may be unable to form close, trusting relationships because they expect to be betrayed, rejected, and further abused (Cole & Putnam, 1992). This can lead to avoidance of relationships, or, at the other extreme, promiscuity. Victims are also a likely target for revictimization.

> "I find I cannot have open relationships with guys. It is hard for me to trust anyone. For the one time I tried to open up to a guy, I ended up even more hurt. I am 20 years old and I cannot even kiss a guy, much less give a simple hug to someone."

> "My relationships with men have all been abusive, even to the point that I have been battered and raped on several occasions.... I choose men that are very similar to my Dad...mainly because that's all I know."
>
> (All examples are from the author's files.)

Men who have been victims of incestuous mothers generally experience more adjustment problems than do other sexually abused men (Kelly et al., 2002). They often experience such anxiety and disgust that they emotionally reject all women (Krug, 1989).

PERSONAL REFLECTIONS

Have you ever been the victim of child sexual abuse? If so, has it affected how you feel about yourself or your relationships with others? If it has affected you in any way (including leaving you with any sense of self-blame), have you ever sought counseling? If you have not sought counseling, why not?

Family Dynamics

Father–child or stepfather–stepchild incest (and in many cases, sibling incest) typically occurs in certain family contexts (Canavan et al., 1992; Finkelhor, 1978). We have considered some of their characteristics, but let us review them here.

Within the home there is an all-powerful, authoritarian man (who may appear shy but otherwise normal to others) who sets hard, fixed gender roles for everyone and establishes an isolated, rigid system with strong external boundaries that separates the family from the outside world. However, boundaries within the family become blurred, and all emotional needs are met within the family. Independent thoughts and feelings are considered destructive as the family becomes isolated and family members become overdependent on one another. Although marital problems are common, the

Box 15–C Cross-Cultural Perspectives

Incestuous Inbreeding–A Universal Taboo?

Incest has often been called the universal taboo, and there are many theories as to why it is supposedly banned throughout the world. One of the major theories came from Freud (1913), who believed that most people prefer close kin as mating partners:

> [It is] beyond the possibility of doubt that an incestuous love choice is in fact the first and regular one. . . . *(Freud, 1933/1953, pp. 220–221)*

But inbreeding can lead to serious genetic defects in offspring (Thornhill, 1992) and would eventually ruin a society if it were practiced widely. Freud believed it was for this reason that societies make rules against incest.

A second, much different theory was proposed by Edward Westermarck in 1891. He believed that close physical contact between two people during childhood naturally results in loss of sexual attraction. Findings of several anthropological studies have been used as support for this theory (e.g., McCabe, 1983; Pastner, 1986; Shepher, 1971; Wolf, 1970). However, Nancy Thornhill (1991) has proposed that incest rules are not aimed at close family members (because of the Westermarck effect), but instead are directed at more distant kin (cousins) and special kinds of adultery (e.g., a man and his father's wife).

Inbreeding between cousins, she says, "can concentrate wealth and power within families to the detriment of the powerful positions of (male) rulers in stratified societies."

Claude Lévi-Strauss (1969) offered yet a fourth explanation. His "alliance theory" says that the incest taboo exists not to prohibit marriage within the family, but is "a rule obliging the mother, sister, or daughter to be given to others." It ensures that women are exchanged between groups. According to Lévi-Strauss, "The incest taboo is where nature transcends itself. It brings about and is the advent of a new order."

There is no question that incestuous inbreeding is viewed very negatively in Western cultures. In the United States, marriage between first cousins is illegal in most states. Fewer than 0.5% of all marriages in North America and Western Europe are between first cousins. But what about elsewhere: Is inbreeding viewed with equal negativity in non-Western societies?

In times past in some cultures (e.g., Egyptian, Inca, Hawaiian), brothers and sisters married within royal families (Gregersen, 1982). For example, the Egyptian pharaoh Rameses II's wives included his younger sister and three of his daughters. Today, in areas that are primarily Muslim (northern Africa; western and southern Asia; Central Asian

republics of the former Soviet Union; and northern, eastern, and central India), one fourth to one half of all marriages are between persons who are second cousins or closer (see Bittles et al., 1991, for a review). Marriages between parallel first cousins (a man and his father's brother's daughter) are particularly preferred. Among the Hindus of southern India, between 20% and 45% of marriages are between close relatives, with the preferred unions being uncle–niece or cross-first cousins (a man and his mother's brother's daughter). One third to one half of all marriages in sub-Saharan Africa are believed to be between relatives, and the practice is also thought to be very common in China.

Are there sociological or economic factors that might predict the acceptance of incestuous inbreeding? Yes: In those areas of the world where it is practiced, it is most common among either poor, uneducated rural people, or very rich land-owning families (see Bittles et al., 1991).

In conclusion, mother–son incestuous inbreeding is unheard of in any culture, and with rare exceptions, all cultures similarly frown upon father–daughter and brother–sister relations. However, outside Western culture, marriage between first cousins or between uncles and nieces is widely practiced.

mother fails to protect her children, adding to their sense of abandonment and fear. Children who grow up in an environment like this may view it as normal and repeat the pattern when they become parents.

Preventing and Dealing with Child Sexual Abuse

The first thing to do to minimize the chance of your child becoming a victim of sexual abuse is to *educate yourself*. You should be able to talk openly and candidly about sexual matters, including sexual abuse, with your child. You should be aware of the

fact that young children who tell people about being molested are almost never making the stories up. Remember that most molesters are known to their victims, so do not doubt your child if he or she tells you that the molester is someone you know.

The next thing to do is to *educate your child*. As I have indicated in previous chapters, it is important that children know the correct names for the parts of their anatomy. Children should not be ashamed of their bodies, but they should also know which parts of their bodies are personal or private and should not be touched by other people. Discuss this with all family members present—incest is difficult in families in which there are no secrets. Finally, it is

FIGURE 15–10 Many people have been the victims of child sexual abuse. This includes actress Teri Hatcher (above) and talk-show hostess Oprah Winfrey.

crucial that your child know that he or she can communicate with you about sexual matters in general. If you are always open to discussion about sex, your child will be more likely to confide in you.

Know what to do if your child is molested or approached by a molester. Reassure him or her that talking to you about it was the right thing to do. Let your child know that being molested was not his or her fault and stress that it is the adult who was wrong. Do not confront the molester in front of your child, and let your child know that he or she will not be harmed by the molester. Finally, contact the police, even if you do not intend to press charges. By doing so, you may help them prevent further child abuse.

There are certain signs to look for that may indicate that a child has been a victim of sexual abuse. A victim may suddenly begin to have episodes of depression, crying, or other out-of-character changes in mood or personality. He or she may begin to want to be alone or become afraid to go to a certain place or see a certain person. A victim may suddenly start to have problems at school or with discipline. Remember, if abuse is occurring, a victim may be

unwilling or fearful to ask for help (abusers often threaten their victims). If you are a parent, do not write off these types of behaviors as a phase. Something serious might be hurting your child.

PROSECUTION OF SEXUAL OFFENDERS

Rape

In the past, almost half of all reported rapes were dismissed before trial. However, with increased education (of the public, police, and courts) there have been dramatic changes in the manner in which rape victims are treated by the courts. For example, the U.S. Supreme Court has upheld broad **rape-shield laws** that make prosecution easier and prevent the victim from feeling as if she (or he) is on trial. In 1991, the Court ruled that states can enact laws that bar an accused acquaintance rapist from introducing evidence that he and his victim had previously had consensual sex. In addition, a victim's past sexual history is no longer allowed to be introduced during trial. The Federal Rules of Evidence (numbers 413–415) do allow rapists' and child molesters' past sexual offenses to be introduced in court (Eads et al., 2000).

Previously, evidence of emission of semen had to be found before an assault could be called a rape. Today, many states no longer require evidence of ejaculation for rape to be charged. However, prosecution of rape is made easier when semen (in the vagina or on pubic hair or clothing) is found during the medical examination, especially now that there is DNA testing (Leinwand, 2009). As a result of these reforms, rape victims today are much more likely to report the crime than in the past (Clay-Warner & Burt, 2005).

Child Sexual Abuse

In a case that went before the U.S. Supreme Court, the Court stated, "Child abuse is one of the most difficult crimes to detect and prosecute, in large part because there often are no witnesses except the victim" (*Pennsylvania v. Ritchie*, 1987). One of the greatest difficulties was that the Sixth Amendment of the U.S. Constitution guarantees that in all criminal cases, the accused has the right to confront all witnesses against him. Face-to-face confrontations were often very traumatic for children, who, in addition, were no match for shrewd and manipulative defense lawyers. However, in 1990 the Supreme Court ruled that individuals being prosecuted for

---

Rape-shield laws ■ Laws that make the prosecution of rapists easier and that also prevent the victims from feeling as if they are on trial.

child abuse had no guaranteed right to face-to-face confrontations with their young accusers if the children would suffer emotional trauma as a result. The Court upheld state laws that allowed use of videotaped testimony and testimony by one-way closed-circuit television. Courts are also allowing minors to testify with the aid of anatomically correct dolls so that they can show what happened to them. In the case of young girls, genital trauma and tearing of the hymen can validate sexual abuse (Berkoff et al., 2008).

Conviction of Sex Offenders

As the extent of sexual abuse of children has become better known, the states and federal government have taken a tougher stand. Washington was the first state to pass a "*sexual predator law*" that allows the state to confine pedophiles and rapists in mental institutions beyond their prison terms if it can be shown that it is likely that they will commit similar crimes again. All 50 states have enacted similar laws. The U.S. Supreme Court upheld this law in a 1997 decision (*Kansas v. Hendricks*) involving a Kansas man who had sexually abused children his entire adult life. The court upheld the law again in a 2000 case and upheld a similar 2006 federal law in 2010. What about juvenile sex offenders, whose numbers are increasing every year? If they are not stopped early in their abusive careers, their behavior will only escalate. However, because of their age, should society focus on incarceration or therapy? (See Martin & Pruett, 1998, for a thoughtful review.)

There are about a quarter of a million convicted sex offenders on probation nationwide. A federal law passed in 1996 established a nationwide registry to keep track of sex offenders, and all states now require sex offender registration. The laws also require states to inform local communities whenever a sex offender moves into the neighborhood (see Scott & Gerbasi, 2003). "Megan's law," as it is called, resulted from the publicity that followed the rape and murder of 7-year-old Megan Kanka in 1994 by a convicted pedophile who was living across the street from the Kanka family. However, some experts worry that by preventing sex offenders from successfully reintegrating back into the community, these laws may do more harm than good (Bonnar-Kidd, 2010).

THERAPY

Therapy for Rapists

One of the biggest problems in treating men arrested for rape is their tendency to deny or minimize their offenses (Thakker et al., 2008). Recall that most rapists have distorted cognitive beliefs and attitudes

and that it is not uncommon for rapists to believe that their victims wanted to have sex (see the section on rape). Early programs focused on deviant sexual arousal, but programs today take a multifaceted approach. Successful outcome depends on tailoring the type of therapy to the particular deficits and needs of the individual rapist (Thakker et al., 2008).

Programs generally combine cognitive techniques with the traditional behavioral techniques (see Thakker et al., 2008), and many employ antiandrogen hormone treatment to reduce sex drive (Grossman et al., 1999; Marshall et al., 1993; Polaschek et al., 1997). Again, however, a big problem is that rapists are reluctant to engage in therapy, and even with those who do, the dropout rate is high (see Polaschek et al., 1997). Several studies in the 1990s found that the recidivisim rate (the percentage of offenders completing therapy who rape again) was about 20% in the first 5 years (Greenberg et al., 2000; Hanson, 2000; Prentky et al., 1997). A more recent review found the recidivism rate to be 14% within 5 years and 24% within 15 years (Harris & Hanson, 2004). This is high, but modern therapy programs do result in a modest reduction in recidivism (see Thakker et al., 2008).

Therapy for Child Molesters

For the nonpedophile incestuous molester, a family systems approach is often chosen as therapy. Here, therapy for each family member is combined with therapy for each pair of family members and is followed by therapy for all the family members together (Lanyon, 1986). Group therapy with other families is also often included. For positive change to occur, the father must accept responsibility for what he has done and the mother must also accept responsibility often for what she has not done. The child, on the other hand, must learn to believe that he or she is not responsible. The father must also give up his complete authoritarian rule, and each family member must learn to become more independent. Among rapists and child molesters, the recidivism rate is lowest for incestual child molesters (Greenberg et. al., 2000).

As for the nonpedophile (situational) molester, whose sexual attraction is primarily to adults, many experts believe that society is best served by seeing to it that he receives therapy. Most therapists use cognitive-behavioral approaches. For juvenile sex offenders in particular, treatment is often effective (Reitzel & Carbonell, 2006). The same is true for female child abusers (Sandler & Freeman, 2009).

The outcome of therapy for adult pedophiles is less certain. For these men, sexual orientation is primarily and repeatedly directed toward children, and they have little or no sexual interest in adults. As you have already learned, many of these men have victimized dozens, and in some cases hundreds, of children (Abel et al., 1987), yet they typically display considerable denial and defensiveness (Grossman et al., 1992). Some therapists consider pedophilia to be incurable but treatable (Cloud, 2002). The antiandrogen drugs cyproterone acetate and medroxyprogesterone acetate have proved effective in lowering sex drive, thus allowing clinicians to attempt therapy while the subject is not driven to commit his crimes (Bradford & Greenberg, 1997). As with rapists, a comprehensive cognitive/behavioral/social therapy approach is generally used today (Barbaree & Seto, 1997; Polaschek et al., 1997). However, the judicial system is full of examples of pedophiles who have been caught, been confined, and undergone therapy time and time again. One study found that 14% of child molesters had been rearrested 3 years after release from prison, 30% after 10 years, and nearly half after 20 years (Prentky et al., 1997; see also Hanson, 2000). These types are often referred to as career pedophiles or, more recently, as career sexual predators. Prentky argues that simply allowing offenders to complete their prison terms and return to the community is dangerous and that community notification laws such as Megan's law are shortsighted. Thus, the reason that state and federal laws now allow pedophiles to be confined in mental institutions after they have served their prison terms (see Conviction of Sex Offenders).

PERSONAL REFLECTIONS

As you have learned, several states have passed sexual predator laws that require that molesters identified as career predators be confined for life. Our society will no doubt continue to debate this sensitive issue, weighing the rights of offenders against the rights of victims and future victims, for many years to come. What do you think is best?

Therapy for Victims

For many victims, initial therapy may have to be geared to their posttraumatic stress (Mueser & Taylor, 1997). Abuse-focused cognitive-behavioral therapy has proven particularly effective in reducing the fear and distress experienced when recalling traumatic events (Cohen et al., 2000; Saywitz et al., 2000). Eventually, however, the victim must overcome any self-blame, and the involvement of the victim's partner and family can be very beneficial here (Cohen & Mannarino, 2000; Grosz et al., 2000).

For counseling, contact RAINN (Rape, Abuse, and Incest National Network) for information about the rape crisis center nearest you. Services include a 24-hour rape crisis line and programs for victims of adult and child sexual assault and incest as well as programs for families and friends of victims.

STUDY GUIDE

KEY TERMS

acquaintance rape 378
aggressive pedophile 396
anger rapists 383
compliance 379
date rape 378
gang rape 380
incest 400
male rape 382
marital rape 380
opportunistic rapists 384
pedophilia 395

personally immature
  pedophile 395
polyincestuous family 400
post-rape posttraumatic stress
  disorder 387
power rapists 383
preference molesters
  (pedophiles) 395
rape 375
rape myths 385
rape-shield laws 405

regressive pedophile 396
sadistic rapists 384
sexual coercion 379
sexual harassment 390
situational molesters 395
stalking 392
statutory rape 381
stranger rape 378
token resistance
  [to sex] 379

INTERACTIVE REVIEW

Historically, rape has been viewed as a violation of (1) _____ and victims were treated like "damaged goods." Even today, in the United States, many states will not prosecute a husband for

raping his wife unless there is extreme physical harm to the victim.

There are fewer than 100,000 reported cases of rape in the United States every year, but the actual number of rapes committed is many times greater. Most rapes are committed by (2) _____. Most victims are women between (3) _____ years of age, but anyone can be a victim of rape, including men. Rapists generally plan their crimes and seek victims who appear to be (4) _____.

Studies of convicted rapists reveal that most have (5) _____ IQs, have no more history of psychiatric illness than other criminals, are not oversexed, and have normal social skills. However, many were physically or sexually abused as children, or come from families in which they witnessed abuse of the mother by the father. Most rapists are (6) _____ men who repeat the crime and who lack internal controls and (7) _____.

Rape by a date or an acquaintance is no less real than rape by a stranger. Rape is rape. About 25% of all college women have been pressured into sex when they did not want to have it. About 7% to 15% of all men admit to using physical force in order to have sex on a date, while two-thirds admit to using (8) _____ to have sex. Women, too, often use coercion to have sex, but the coercion used by women is generally (9) _____, while that used by men is generally (10) _____. Many adolescents and young adults believe that a man has the right to force a date to have sexual intercourse under some circumstances. Poor communication skills regarding sexual intentions also contribute to unwanted sexual activities.

Many rapes involve more than one assailant, and these (11) _____ rapes are usually more violent than rapes committed by individuals. Marital rape, too, is often accompanied by severe beatings and physical abuse. Most states have laws that make it illegal for an adult to have sex with anyone under the age of consent; this crime is generally called (12) _____. The mentally handicapped are often protected by these laws as well.

There are several explanations for rape. Psychodynamic theories explain rape as resulting from psychopathology. Studies of convicted rapists have found that rapists can be divided into three types, according to their motivation: (13) _____, (14) _____, and (15) _____. For these men, rape is not a crime of passion; it is a crime of violence and aggression. On the basis of what we now know of date rapists, some researchers have proposed a fourth type of rapist, the (16) _____ rapist, who has distorted cognitive processes and for whom the primary motivation is sex. Recent studies have shown that cultural factors and social learning also help explain why rape occurs. Rape is almost nonexistent in some societies, but is common in countries like the United States that promote and glorify (17) _____, and where large numbers of people conform to conservative

stereotypic gender roles and men view relationships between the two sexes as (18) _____.

Many mistaken beliefs about rape are so widespread that they are called myths. This chapter considered four rape myths: (19) _____, (20) _____, (21) _____, and that women frequently make false accusations of rape. None of these myths are true, but people who believe them tend to blame the victim for being raped.

Rape victims experience short- and long-term reactions in what is called (22) _____. In the acute phase, a victim's reactions may be either expressive or (23) _____. In the period of (24) _____, the victim attempts to regain control of her or his life. Long-term sexual problems are not uncommon. The reactions of a victim's partner and family are important to the recovery process, and it is crucial that they do not attribute blame to the victim.

If you are ever raped, it is important to report the crime immediately and get a medical exam as soon as possible. Do not wash, douche, or change clothes until the exam is completed. Today, most police forces have specially trained units, including counselors, to work with rape victims, and the U.S. Supreme Court has approved broad (25) _____ laws to protect victims from feeling as if they are on trial during court proceedings.

There are three basic approaches to rape prevention. One focuses on the rapists and advocates the creation of safer physical environments and tougher laws and punishments. Another focuses on potential victims and suggests educating women to be less vulnerable to assault. The third, a (26) _____ perspective, advocates changing society's values and its attitudes toward how men and women interact with one another.

Unwelcome sexual advances, requests for sexual favors, and other unwanted verbal or physical conduct of a sexual nature in the workplace or classroom is called (27) _____. The Supreme Court has ruled that this also includes the creation of a hostile or offensive work environment, and that a victim does not have to prove that sexual favors were demanded in exchange for job benefits. Companies and schools can be held liable for not taking immediate and appropriate corrective action.

We now know that sexual abuse of children is more widespread than previously believed. Most victims are molested by (28) _____. We can divide child molesters into two classifications: the (29) _____ molester, or pedophile, whose primary sexual orientation is to children, and the (30) _____ molester, whose primary sexual orientation is to adults. Pedophiles have been further classified according to their psychological characteristics as either (31) _____,

(32) _____, or aggressive. Of pedophiles who have been caught, those who target girls average about 20 victims each, while those who target boys average nearly (33) _____ victims each. Heterosexual pedophiles outnumber homosexual pedophiles by 11 to 1. The effects of sexual abuse on children are often long-lasting, but there is no single "post–sexual abuse syndrome."

Sexual relations between relatives who are too closely related to marry is called incest. (34) _____ incest is five times more common than parent–child incest, although father–daughter and stepfather–stepdaughter incest account for 80% of all arrests. Incestuous fathers often appear to be shy and family-oriented publicly, but are dominating and authoritarian in their own homes. In these cases, the mothers are usually aware that the incest is going on. It is important for children who have been sexually abused to receive counseling and support from professionals and organizations familiar with sexual abuse.

SELF-TEST

A. TRUE OR FALSE

| T | F | 35. An adult woman cannot be raped if she truly does not want to be raped. |

| T | F | 36. Rape was originally considered to be a crime against a man's property. |

| T | F | 37. The percentage of reported rapes that are false is lower than for most other crimes. |

| T | F | 38. Anyone can be a victim of rape, including any man. |

| T | F | 39. If a woman willingly engages in necking or petting with a man, she cannot charge him with rape if he then forces her to have sexual intercourse. |

| T | F | 40. Most rapists prefer victims who are feisty and who will try to physically resist. |

| T | F | 41. Most rapists believe that their victims want to have sex with them or deserve to be raped. |

| T | F | 42. About 55% of all rapists are found to be psychotic. |

| T | F | 43. Date rape is not as real as rape by a stranger. |

| T | F | 44. Muehlenhard and colleagues found that over one third of all college women had said "no" to a date when they really meant "yes" (to having sex). |

| T | F | 45. A man cannot be convicted of rape if the woman agreed to have sexual intercourse. |

| T | F | 46. A man cannot be raped by a woman. |

| T | F | 47. Women who are raped usually have done something to provoke it. |

| T | F | 48. Many victims of rape do not show any emotional reactions afterwards. |

| T | F | 49. A man who tells sexual jokes, makes sexual references, and/or stares obsessively at a female coworker cannot be prosecuted for sexual harassment unless he demands sexual favors. |

| T | F | 50. About 80% of all child molesters are known by their victims. |

| T | F | 51. Pedophile is the term used by the American Psychiatric Association for all child molesters. |

| T | F | 52. In families with father–child incest, the large majority of mothers do not try to protect their children. |

| T | F | 53. Incestuous inbreeding (first cousins or closer in relation) is a universal taboo. |

| T | F | 54. Victims of sexual abuse tend to blame themselves. |

B. MATCHING

_____ 55. aggressive pedophile

_____ 56. anger rapist

_____ 57. opportunistic rapist

_____ 58. personally immature pedophile

_____ 59. power rapist

_____ 60. preference molester

_____ 61. regressive pedophile

a. Herbert feels insecure and inadequate. He commits rape to reassure himself of his sexual adequacy, strength, and potency.

b. Frank's sexual urges are primarily toward adults, but he has fondled a child and had the child touch his penis. He considers his behavior abnormal.

c. Jim tells crude sexual jokes and makes sexual references to his female employees.

_____ 62. sadistic rapist
_____ 63. sexual harasser
_____ 64. situational molester

d. Steve has sex with prepubescent boys and beats them before and afterwards.
e. Joe is sexually aroused and impulsively forces his date to have sex with him when they are alone.
f. Albert loves it when his rape victims try to resist and enjoys hurting them for a prolonged time.
g. David has never had a successful relationship with a woman and seeks out children, whom he can control, for sexual gratification.
h. Mike has no interest in adults as sexual partners. His sexual orientation is to children only.
i. Robert rapes because he despises all women, whom he blames for his lack of success.
j. Tom has always had sexual relations with adults, but work and marital problems have led him to drink, and when he feels sexually inadequate, he molests a child.

C. FILL IN THE BLANKS

65. People with mental disabilities are often protected against sexual abuse by the same laws that protect _____.
66. Give four examples of sexually coercive behavior: _____, _____, _____, and _____.
67. Give two characteristics of cultures that are "rape-free": _____ and _____.
68. In _____ rape, the individual responsibility for things a person does can be diffused or forgotten.
69. Psychodynamic theories of rape explain it as resulting from _____.
70. The majority of date rapes are probably committed by _____ rapists.
71. In the _____ of post-rape posttraumatic stress disorder, victims attempt to regain control of their lives.
72. Charges of sexual harassment are usually prosecuted as civil suits under Title VII of the _____ of 1964.
73. Sexual harassment usually occurs in a relationship where there is _____.
74. Research has shown that the more a man believes in _____, the more accepting he is of sexual harassment.

SUGGESTED READINGS AND RESOURCES

Parents: For an updated list of books and materials that are appropriate for children and adolescents, contact SIECUS at 212-819-9770. You can find them on the Web at www.siecus.org.

Anderson, P. B., & Struckman-Johnson, C. (Eds.). (1998). *Sexually aggressive women*. New York: Guilford Press.

Cloud, J. (2002, April 29). Pedophilia. *Time*.

Lalumière, M. L., et al. (2005). *The causes of rape: Understanding individual male propensity for sexual aggression*. Washington, DC: American Psychological Association. The title explains it all.

Maltz, W. (2001). *The sexual healing journey*. New York: HarperCollins. The most frequently recommended book by members of the Society for Sex Therapy and Research (Kingsberg et al., 2002).

Paludi, M. A. (Ed.). (1996). *Sexual harassment on college campuses: Abusing the ivory power*. Albany: State University of New York Press. Updated chapters by many leading scholars.

Parrot, A., and Bechofer, L. (Eds.). (1991). *Acquaintance rape: The hidden crime*. New York: John Wiley & Sons. Many scholarly articles.

Salter, A. (2003). *Predators: Pedophiles, rapists, & other sex offenders: Who they are, how they operate, and how we can protect ourselves and our children*. New York: Basic Books.

Sanday, P. R. (1990). *Fraternity gang rape*. New York: New York University Press. Analysis of a seldom-discussed type of sexual violence.

Tewksbury, R. (2007). Effects of sex assault on men. *International Journal of Men's Health*, Spring.

CHILDHELP National Child Abuse Hotline 1(800) 4-A-CHILD

www.childhelpusa.org

Provides information, crisis intervention, and referrals to local services if you wish to report abuse.

National sexual assault hotline: 1(800) 656-HOPE

Operated by RAINN (Rape, Abuse, and Incest National Network)

Contact them for the number and address of the rape crisis program nearest to you.

Selling Sex
Social and Legal Issues

16

> Morality is about right and wrong, and that's what laws attempt to put into legal form. Can you think of one law which doesn't declare one behavior right and its opposite wrong? The truth is, all laws legislate morality (even speed limits imply a moral right to safety on the roads). And everyone in politics—conservatives, libertarians and liberals—is trying to legislate morality. The only question is whose morality should be legislated?
>
> —From "Legislating Morality," by Frank Turek, July/August 1999, *New Man Magazine*

Sex is an important part of most people's lives. Sex provides physical pleasure, it can be given and received as an expression of love and affection, and it can make us feel more masculine or feminine. Sex is also a business—a really big business! The annual revenues in the United States for sexually explicit material are between $10 and $20 billion (Byassee, 2008). This is more than Americans spend to watch all professional sports. Hollywood makes about 400 mainstream films a year, but the porn industry makes 11,000—and Americans rent 800 million of these X-rated videos and DVDs every year (Paul, 2004). Prostitution revenues are over $52 billion a year worldwide (Altman, 2001).

There are laws that are designed to ban or regulate the commercial sex industry. As you might suspect, these laws are controversial, with many people objecting to attempts by others to regulate their private lives. Some of these laws were proposed and passed by politicians who were concerned about health-related issues (e.g., the spread of STIs), but some appear to be attempts by individuals to force the public to conform to their own moral standards. In this chapter, you will read about two topics for which there has been a long history of individuals attempting to regulate the sexual activity of others. I have purposely attempted not to show my own bias regarding these issues and have tried to take a neutral stand. My intent is to stimulate your own thinking by presenting both sides of an issue. You be the judge as to whether there should be laws regulating these activities.

When you have finished studying this chapter, you should be able to:

- Trace the history of sexually explicit material and the legal actions taken to control it.
- Discuss the uses of sexually explicit material.
- Compare and evaluate the effects of nonviolent and violent sexually explicit material.
- Understand how the Internet has affected the commercial sex industry.
- Define and explain the different types of prostitution.
- Describe the characteristics of prostitutes and their customers.
- Evaluate the pros and cons of prostitution from a legal as well as a moral point of view.

PORNOGRAPHY

Explicit drawings, paintings, and other representations of human genitals and sexual behavior are not new to modern society. Etchings of human sexual behaviors date as far back as prehistoric cave dwellings. In ancient Greece and Rome, phallic (from the Greek word *phallus*, meaning penis) worship was common. Monuments, statues, carvings, and pottery of the penis (generally greatly enlarged) have been found throughout the ruins of Greece, Rome, Pompeii, and pre-Columbian Mexico and Peru. Greek and Roman art commonly showed humans engaged in sexual intercourse, fellatio, and group sex. Temple carvings from 16th-century India graphically portray humans engaging in every imaginable variety of sexual behavior (see Figures 16–1 and 16–2). However, as you will soon learn, erotic material is not considered pornographic unless there is widespread opposition to it, and it is likely that within these ancient cultures erotic material was regarded positively.

The first known sex manual was the *Kama Sutra* from 5th-century India. It instructed people about a variety of sexual positions and behaviors. In Japan during the 1600s, *schunga* paintings showing different

FIGURE 16–1 Sexual themes in art have been common throughout history. Top left: pottery from ancient Peru. Top right: an example from the *Kama Sutra*, a sex manual from 5th-century (A.D.) India. Bottom: painting from 5th-century (B.C.E.) Greece.

Source: (bottom left) Polygnotos (5th BCE). Red Figure Vase, Side A: Erotic Scene, 5th BCE. Height: 0.415 m. Photo: Christian Larrieu. Musee du Louvre/RMN Reunion des Musees Nationaux, France. SCALA/Art Resource, NY.

FIGURE 16–2 Left: A phallic monument from 4th-century (B.C.E.) Greece. Right: Temple carvings from 16th-century India.

positions of intercourse were given by mothers to their daughters when they became engaged to marry. European sex manuals originated in 1527 with the publication of Giulio Romano's *Sedici Modi* (meaning "the ways"), which showed his drawings (engraved by Marcantonio Raimondi) of couples in different positions of intercourse. The Pope sentenced anyone who published the book to death.

Post-Renaissance European art frequently had erotic themes. Rembrandt's *The Four-Poster Bed* and François Boucher's *Hercules and Omphale* (see Figure 16–3) are classic early examples of this. Auguste Rodin celebrated the human body in his drawings and sculptures (e.g., *The Kiss*).

Erotic themes in European literature were common by the 1600s. However, the first true pornographic novel (in the sense that it was written with the purpose of arousing the reader) was John Cleland's *Fanny Hill* (originally titled *Memoirs of a Woman of Pleasure*) in 1748. Its publication marked the beginning of attempts to control sexually explicit literature.

Obviously, sexually explicit material is not new. What is new is how readily available it is. Sexually explicit material seems to be everywhere today: on TV, in the movies, in books and magazines, over the telephone, and on the Internet. Only in the last few decades has there been such an eruption in the quantity of this material that even those who do not seek it out have difficulty avoiding it.

How did all this happen? The United States for a long time was a very puritanical country. The first real erotic literature by an American was Walt Whitman's *Leaves of Grass*, written in 1855. However, the **Comstock law**, passed in 1873, made

the mailing of this or any other material considered obscene or lewd a felony. Moral crusader Anthony Comstock became a special agent of the U.S. Post Office and personally saw to it that the law named after him was enforced. Even information about birth control was not allowed to be mailed. Importation of James Joyce's novel *Ulysses* was banned when it was first published in 1922. The ban was lifted in 1933, but other novels, such as D. H. Lawrence's *Lady Chatterley's Lover* and Henry Miller's *Tropic of Cancer*, were banned in the United States and most other English-speaking countries until the late 1950s.

Censorship in movies was also very strict during this era. The movie industry was banned from filming erotica in 1935. Clark Gable's final words to Vivien Leigh (who played Scarlett O'Hara) in the movie *Gone with the Wind*—"Frankly, my dear, I don't give a damn!"—were shocking to many people.

The brief love scene on the beach (with bathing suits on) in the 1953 movie *From Here to Eternity* was considered scandalous. Because it came into people's living rooms, TV was censored even more heavily than movies during the 1950s and 1960s. Many people were outraged when Lucy first used the word "pregnant" on the *I Love Lucy* show. Rock and roll was opposed by many parents in the 1950s, not only for its "suggestive" words (e.g., "Whole Lot of Shakin' Going On," "Let Me Be Your Teddy Bear"), but also because of the performers' gyrations. Elvis Presley was shown only

Comstock law ■ A law passed in 1873 that made it a felony to mail any material regarded as obscence or lewd.

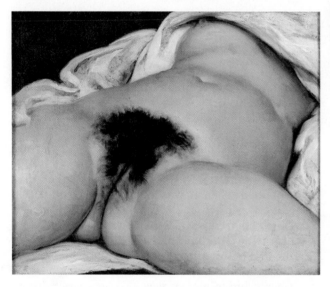

FIGURE 16–3 Art with erotic themes from post-Renaissance Western culture. Top left: Rembrandt's *The Four-Poster Bed* (1646). Top right: Boucher's *Hercules and Omphale* (1730s). Bottom left: Gustave Courbet's *The Origin of the World* (1866). Why are many paintings with sexually explicit themes considered great art when modern photos with the same theme are often regarded to be pornographic?

Source: (bottom left) Gustave Courbet (1819–1877), "The Origin of the World." 1866. Oil on canvas. 46 X 55 cm. RF 1995-10. Musee d'Orsay, Paris, France. Reunion des Musees Nationaus/Art Resource, NY.

from the waist up when he appeared on the *Ed Sullivan Show* in 1956.

What about sexually explicit magazines? In the 1950s and 1960s there was really only *Playboy* (on a large scale, anyway). Hugh Hefner spent $600 in 1953 to publish the first issue, which featured nude photos of Marilyn Monroe, and sold it on the street himself. He turned *Playboy* into a multimillion-dollar publishing empire. Hefner really did not have any competitors until the late 1960s and early 1970s, about the same time that movies and TV became more explicit.

Why the move toward more permissiveness in the middle and late 1960s? The story of Hugh Hefner's success pretty much tells the answer. It became obvious that despite efforts at censorship, there was a large demand for sexually oriented material. As a result, other magazines (e.g., *Penthouse, Hustler, Playgirl*) started to compete for a share of the market, and in an effort to outdo one another,

these magazines continually expanded the borders of sexual license. At the same time, Americans flocked to see erotic European movies, and their box office success led Hollywood to explore sexual boundaries as well.

So where are we in the 2000s? We can easily buy magazines that show hetero- or homosexual couples (or groups of people) having every imaginable kind of sex, using every position, having oral and anal sex, sex with violent themes, or sex with animals, and much more that is probably beyond your imagination. There is a booming $4.2 billion-a-year market in XXX-rated movies and video rentals. The total comes to $10–20 billion if you include porn networks, cable, Internet websites, motel movies, phone sex, and magazines (Byassee, 2008). The XXX-rated movie *Deep Throat* cost only $24,000 to make in the early 1970s, but it earned over $25 million in profits within 10 years (eventually earning $600 million). You no longer have to turn to X-rated material for full frontal nudity and torrid sex scenes. R-rated movies such as 1992's *Body of Evidence* with Madonna and Willem Dafoe or *Basic Instinct* with Sharon Stone were clearly designed to shock us. But with all the sexually explicit material available, it takes a lot to shock us today.

Do we want it? Well, apparently many Americans do. In fact, about 75% of men and 41% of women have intentionally looked at Internet porn (Albright, 2008). Nearly all college men and women have looked at an explicit magazine such as *Playboy* or *Playgirl* by the time they leave high school, and 85% to 90% have done so in junior high school (Bryant & Brown, 1989). In short, a majority of young Americans now accept sexually explicit content in the mass media and believe that adults should have the right to obtain it (Carroll et al., 2008). The large majority of men (and many women) believe that pornography has had a positive effect on their lives (Hald & Malamuth, 2008).

Here are some representative views of students enrolled in my own course. Men were generally positive about sexually explicit material:

> "I do feel as though *Spice*, *Playboy*, and porn videos should be available. Reason being my parents didn't have that talk to me about the birds and bees. I learned from the streets, friends, and porn videos."

> "I really don't have a problem with porn. There is a huge market for it and a ton of people enjoy it. The only problem is that the Internet has made it easy for kids to access it."

> "I think that there is nothing at all wrong with sexually explicit material. It serves a need in our society, as evidenced by its success. If people didn't want it, they wouldn't buy it, and the companies providing it would collapse and become bankrupt."

Women were more variable in their views:

> "I for one am bothered by sexually explicit material. Women are exploited while men are hardly shown. It bothers me to flip through the channels of the TV and see a naked woman bouncing across the screen."

> "Pornography? If it's not violent, I don't have a problem with it. I used to think it was gross, but I've viewed it with my fiancé and we were actually educated. We were both pretty inexperienced and we learned many positions that we would like to try out and never thought of before."

> "I personally think that sexually explicit magazines are degrading to women in that they reinforce feelings men have about women as mere sex objects, put on earth to please them."

> "I personally think that people should choose whether or not they view sexually explicit material. I think that

if people would stop treating sex like a taboo, then it wouldn't be such a big business ... the funny thing is that sex is something that we know we all do, but we like to pretend we don't or like to keep it secret from others."

PERSONAL REFLECTIONS

How would you respond if someone told you that this textbook was obscene and pornographic?

Uses of Sexually Explicit Material

Why do people look at, read, or listen to sexually explicit material? Bryant and Brown (1989) have identified four major reasons. Some people, they say, turn to sexually explicit material to learn about sex. In fact, teens and many college students use sexually explicit material (often on the Internet) as a source of sexual information (Hald & Malamuth, 2008):

> "My boyfriend was very misinformed about females when I first started dating him. He didn't know what they like/disliked or what a woman's anatomy should look like. He now has a more accurate view of things. He got his info from porno movies."
> (from the author' files)

A second reason is that it allows people to rehearse sexual behaviors, much as fantasy does. A third, related reason is that today many people consider fantasy and masturbation while looking at sexually explicit material to be a form of safe sex (e.g., safe from sexually transmitted infections).

Probably the foremost reason many people use sexually explicit material, however, is that they enjoy the sexual arousal it produces. Many people masturbate while using sexually explicit material. Many couples watch sexually explicit videos together to heighten their arousal, although in some cases this results in dissatisfaction with a partner's sexual attraction and performance (Albright, 2008). In short, most people regard sexually explicit material as a form of fantasy and use it to escape from the monotony of their daily routines.

Effects of Nonviolent Sexually Explicit Material

Evolutionary psychologists suggest that, in the past, the sight of a naked woman was a good indicator of a sexual opportunity for a man, resulting in arousal and sexual behavior, but that modern means of presenting visual sexual stimuli to men (on a screen or page) may be maladaptive (Confer et al., 2010). People would not be concerned, of course, if they did not believe that exposure to sexually explicit material has a negative effect on behavior.

In order to determine if this is true, President Lyndon Johnson in 1968 appointed an 18-member commission that spent 2 years collecting and studying evidence. The findings of the President's Commission on Obscenity and Pornography were released in 1970 and stimulated a decade of research (much of it originally funded by the commission). Here are some of the major conclusions from that era:

1. Looking at, reading, or listening to sexually explicit material (movies, pictures, books, tapes) produces *physiological* arousal in a majority of both men and women (e.g., Report of the Commission, 1970; Heiman, 1977; Henson et al., 1979; McConaghy, 1974). It was once believed that only men were aroused by sexually explicit material, but similar physiological responses were observed in both sexes. Many women may actively avoid sexually explicit material, but still respond to it physiologically when they see or hear it.

2. People are more aroused by looking at sexual behaviors they consider to be normal than they are by unconventional behaviors. Sexually explicit material does not seem to create desires that were not already there (Report of the Commission, 1970).

3. When exposed to sexually explicit material, some people show an increase in sexual behavior, a smaller proportion show a decrease, but the majority of people report no change in their behaviors. Increases (almost always expressed as masturbation or sexual intercourse with the usual partner) are short-lived and disappear within 48 hours (Report of the Commission, 1970).

4. Continued exposure to sexually explicit material leads to a marked decrease in interest (indifference, boredom) in the same materials (Report of the Commission, 1970; Lipton, 1983).

5. Contrary to many people's belief that sex offenders are generally obsessed with pornography, convicted sex offenders in prisons (e.g., rapists or child molesters) were often found to have had no greater exposure, and often less exposure, to sexually explicit materials (sex education as well as pornography) during adolescence than nonoffenders (Cook & Fosen, 1970; Goldstein, 1973; Report of the Commission, 1970; Walker, 1970; see also Nutter & Kearns, 1993).

6. Consistent with the previous findings, it was found that when Denmark legalized the sale of hard-core pornographic material to adults in the mid-1960s there was over a 30% drop in sex crimes in the first few years after legalization, suggesting that pornography served as an outlet for some people who might otherwise have committed sex crimes (Report of the Commission, 1970; Kutchinsky, 1973).

The commission concluded that there was no significant link between exposure of adults to sexually explicit materials and sex crimes or other deviant or harmful behavior. They recommended the repeal of obscenity and pornography laws and advocated the teaching of sex education in public schools:

> Failure to talk openly and directly about sex has several consequences. It overemphasizes sex, gives it a magical, non-natural quality, making it more attractive and fascinating. It diverts the expression of sexual interest out of more legitimate channels, into less legitimate channels.... The Commission believes that interest in sex is normal, healthy, good.

Richard Nixon was president when the commission's report was released in 1970. He dismissed it as "morally bankrupt" and rejected its findings.

Studies conducted after the release of the report generally supported the commission's conclusions. For example, studies that looked at the rate of sex crimes in states that had suspended prosecution of antipornography statutes have also concluded there is no link between exposure to sexually explicit material and sex offenses (Winick & Evans, 1996). However, the conclusion that women are aroused by sexually explicit material has been found to be in need of some qualification. Early studies focused on physiological arousal (e.g., vasocongestion of genitals), but subsequent studies have shown that physiological arousal is not necessarily accompanied by subjective feelings of arousal (Chivers et al., 2010). A review of many studies found that men report moderately greater arousal to sexual stimuli than do women and that the difference was greatest with very explicit material (Murnen & Stockton, 1997). Other studies have confirmed that most women's arousal to sexually explicit material is greater when the material is female-initiated/female-centered and romantic (recall from Chapter 4 that sexual arousal for most women depends on the context) as compared with male-initiated/male-centered and not romantic (Laan et al., 1994; Quackenbush et al., 1995; see Rupp & Wallen, 2008).

Effects of Violent and Degrading Sexually Explicit Material

Sexual themes that include high-level types of violence (e.g., choking, punching, kicking, bondage, torture, weapons) have never accounted for more than a very small proportion of sexually explicit films and magazines. In fact, by the 1990s explicit videos and magazines almost always showed women and men in egalitarian, consensual sexual roles (Barron & Kimmel, 2000; Bogaert, 2001; Ferguson & Hartley, 2009). Nevertheless, there is still a small percentage of explicit magazines and videos that show sexually violent material, or "gonzo" porn films in which the sexual behaviors engaged in obviously would be painful for the woman.

Does looking at *violent sexually explicit material* have negative effects on men? The President's Commission did not specifically examine this issue. In numerous studies designed to answer this question, volunteer subjects were shown films or heard tapes of (a) mutually consenting erotic behavior, (b) scenes of aggression toward women, or (c) scenes with both sexual explicitness and aggression. In many of the studies, violent sexually explicit material was found to cause arousal in male subjects (Malamuth & Donnerstein, 1984). In fact, they were often more aroused by violent sexually explicit scenes (e.g., of naked women bound and appearing distressed) than they were by scenes of women enjoying sex (Heilbrun & Seif, 1988; Malamuth, 1981). Men with lower IQs and those with rape-prone attitudes or high levels of aggressiveness are especially likely to be aroused by violent sexually explicit scenes (Bogaert et al., 1999; Davis & Bauserman, 1993; Linz, 1989; see Kingston et al., 2009). Arousal to violent pornography is even more likely under the influence of alcohol (Davis et al., 2006; Noel et al., 2009). Nevertheless, there is little evidence that looking at violent pornography leads to sex crimes (Ferguson & Hartley, 2009).

After watching violent sexually explicit films, many of the male subjects became less sympathetic

FIGURE 16–4 Explicit sexual material was once available only in XXX movie theaters or video stores, but today it is readily available on the Internet.

toward female rape victims, showed greater belief in rape myths (viewing rape victims as more responsible for their assaults), displayed increased hostility to women in the lab, and were more likely to indicate that they would commit rape themselves if they were certain that they would not get caught (see Linz, 1989, or Malamuth & Donnerstein, 1984, or Donnerstein et al., 1987, for reviews). Similar results were found when men looked at *degrading sexually explicit material* (i.e., *nonviolent* material showing women as sex objects where there is a clearly unequal balance of power) (Zillmann & Bryant, 1982). Unlike many men, women are not aroused by watching realistic rape scenes.

It must be noted that in these studies men had no choice of what they viewed. Bogaert (2001) allowed undergraduate male subjects to choose among 14 videos. Half (51%) chose not to watch any type of sexually explicit theme, 15% chose nonviolent erotic themes, 8% chose sexual novelty themes, and 7% chose common sexual acts. Only 4% of the men chose sexually violent videos and 3% chose child pornography. Most people today have a negative response to sexually explicit films that are violent or are degrading to women (Bauserman, 1998). Thus, outside the laboratory, probably only a small percentage of men would even seek out pornography with violence-against-women themes.

To explore whether there really is a causal relationship between violent pornography and sex crimes, Edwin Meese, then attorney general of the United States, appointed an 11-member commission on pornography in 1985. They released their conclusions in the spring of 1986, less than a year after they were formed (see Figure 16–5). Their conclusion: A "causal relationship" exists between sexually violent pornography and violence toward women. In contrast to the recommendations of the 1970 commission, they advocated stronger government enforcement of present obscenity laws and additional laws that would result in greater restrictions of sexually explicit material.

The 1986 commission funded no original research, but instead relied heavily on the findings of previously conducted laboratory experiments. However, the scientists who conducted that research accused the commission of drawing conclusions and making legal recommendations that did not follow from their data (see D'Amato, 2006). Behavioral scientists conducting work in this area were brought together in their own conference in 1986. They agreed with the 1970 commission's conclusion that exposure to nudity alone has no detrimental effects on adult behavior (see Linz et al., 1987). They suggested that the real

FIGURE 16–5 With the bare-breasted *Spirit of Justice* behind him, U.S. Attorney General Edwin Meese accepts the Report of the 1986 Commission on Pornography. Later, U.S. Attorney General John Ashcroft ordered that the statue be covered with drapes when he spoke. What is erotica to some people is pornography to others.

focus of concern should be depictions of violence toward women, regardless of whether it was in a sexually explicit context. Studies consistently found, for example, that viewing nonexplicit movies showing violence toward women results in many men becoming less sensitive toward rape victims (Linz, 1989). So what is the conclusion of the leading behavioral scientists in the field?

> **The most clear and present danger...is all violent material in our society, whether sexually explicit or not, that promotes violence against women.**
> *(Donnerstein & Linz, 1986)*

This type of potentially harmful material (violence toward women without sexual explicitness) is precisely the type of material that is common in R-rated movies and on TV today. In order to eliminate possible detrimental effects to society, we would have to suppress all materials showing violence toward women, not just sexually explicit material with violent themes. Scientists suggest that rather than imposing stricter laws, it might be easier to educate the public about the effects of viewing violence so that they can make better choices about which programs, movies, and books they choose to expose themselves and their children to.

PERSONAL REFLECTIONS

Are you ever physically aroused by looking at sexually explicit photos or movies? What is your emotional reaction to this material and any arousal it causes? Why? Have you ever learned anything from photos of naked persons or by watching R-rated or X-rated sex scenes? If you had the power to do it, would you ban this material or allow unrestricted distribution to adults? Why?

Internet Sex

In the past, the possible embarrassment of being recognized probably kept many adults from going to XXX stores to rent or buy videos and magazines. Today, thanks to the Internet, sexually explicit material is readily available in the privacy of your own home at the touch of a mouse. Moblie wireless devices now allow people to watch (and send) sexually explicit material from any location. This has resulted in what one researcher has called the "Triple A Engine"—accessibility, affordability, and anonymity (Cooper et al., 2000). Not only do companies like *Playboy* have websites (it averages 5 million hits a day), but anyone can start his or her own porn website. In fact, it has been estimated that there are now well over 4 million websites displaying sexually explicit material (Young, 2008). For a fee, subscribers can watch live masturbation, oral sex, and anything else. One third of all use of the Internet is connected to porn sites (Friess, 2003). In fact, over two thirds of all spending by Americans on the Internet is for sexually related materials.

Bulletin boards and chat rooms that cater to specific interests allow individuals to "talk" to each other and exchange sexual fantasies. Have a fetish? With the push of a few keys you can find many others with your same interest. The percentage of violent pornography on Internet sites is higher than for other media. This is particularly true for Internet newsgroups (Usenet), where close to half of the sexual scenes display high or extreme sexual violence, almost always with women as the victims (Barron & Kimmel, 2000). Software (CD-ROMs) offers explicit material and even allows for some interaction. One group of researchers concluded, "The influence of the Internet on sexuality is likely to be so significant that it will ultimately be recognized as the next 'sexual revolution'" (Cooper et al., 2000). Experts predict that within 20 years people will be able to wear a special body suit, walk into a booth, and have virtual reality sex of any kind with anyone of their choice (Chang, 2000). Yes, explicit sex is everywhere today, and you would have to be a hermit living without computers, radio, TV, and magazines to avoid it.

Who watches Internet porn? Recall that 75% of men and 41% of women have done so intentionally on at least one occasion (Albright, 2008). Over half of adolescents have visited a sexually explicit website (Braun-Courville & Rojas, 2009), including about two thirds of young teenage boys and one third of young teenage girls (Brown, 2009). Many teens who do not intentionally seek sexually explicit material on the Internet are exposed to it anyway (via pop-up ads or e-mails) (Wolak et al., 2007). Some teens (and adults) have sent photos of themselves nude to a boyfriend or girlfriend (a practice called "sexting"), only to have them then distributed widely on the Internet (*Contemporary Psychology*, 2009). An online survey found that about 22% of girls and 18% of boys aged 13 to 19 and about 30% of young men and women aged 20 to 26 have engaged in sexting (National Campaign to Prevent Teen and Unplanned Pregnancy, 2010).

Over 80% of Internet users who access porn websites are recreational users who average a little over 1 hour a month online (Paul, 2004). About 6% are compulsive users, averaging over 11 hours a week (Cooper et al., 1999). This is true even of many evangelicals (Martin, 2007). (See Chapter 13 on sexual addiction.) Similar to what was found for other forms of pornography, in those states that have had the greatest increase in Internet access there has been a decrease in rapes (D'Amato, 2006).

However, that is not to say that easy access to Internet porn has not had negative effects on teens. Those teens who seek Internet porn tend to view women as sex objects (Peter & Valkenburg, 2009a), retain stereotyped views of gender roles (Brown, 2009), have more permissive sexual attitudes and behaviors (Brown & L'Engle, 2009; Braun-Courville & Rojas, 2009; Kraus & Russell, 2008), and have lower sexual satisfaction (Peter & Valkenburg, 2009b). Women, in particular, are likely to have lowered body image as a result of watching (or their partner watching) porn (Albright, 2008). Heavy use of paraphiliac sexually explicit material can result in suppression of intimacy (Štulhofer et al., 2010).

Complete Legalization or Censorship?

What should we do about sexually explicit material? Should we remove all restrictions to the sale and distribution of hard-core material to adults (i.e., make it completely legal), or should we attempt to ban all such material? There are good arguments for both cases.

Recall that many studies have found evidence that when sexually explicit material is made readily available to people, there is often a reduction in sex crimes (D'Amato, 2006; Kutchinsky, 1973; Report of the Commission, 1970; Winick & Evans, 1996; see Ferguson & Hartley, 2009, for a review). In fact, many sex therapists believe that socially unacceptable sexual behaviors often result from attempts to severely repress sexuality. It is probably difficult for you to believe that material you find offensive and repugnant may actually do some good, but that is because you are normal and have no deviant tendencies.

On the other hand, we are really just in the first generation of Americans who have had easy access to sexually explicit material via the Internet since their early teens (or younger). The findings presented at the end of the previous section suggest that early and constant exposure can have some negative effects (e.g., Albright, 2008). There have been numerous attempts by citizens, school boards, and local governments to ban sexually oriented materials that they consider offensive. The producers or distributors of the materials, along with others, invariably protest on the grounds of First Amendment rights, and many cases have reached the U.S. Supreme Court. The First Amendment of our Constitution guarantees, among other things, that Congress "shall make no law...abridging the freedom of speech, or of the press." I suspect that the Founding Fathers never intended this to apply to explicit pictures of couples having anal sex, but the problem is deciding where to draw the line.

Guess which of the following magazines and books have been targets of censorship by some communities in recent years:

> *The American Heritage Dictionary*
> *The Bible*
> *Brave New World*
> *The Catcher in the Rye*
> *Cinderella*
> *Club* magazine
> *The Diary of Anne Frank*
> *Gorillas in the Mist*
> *The Grapes of Wrath*
> *Huckleberry Finn*
> *Hustler* magazine
> *Macbeth*
> *Penthouse* magazine
> *Playboy* magazine
> *Romeo and Juliet*
> *Sports Illustrated* (swimsuit issues)
> Stories about dinosaurs
> *The Wizard of Oz*

If you guessed all of them, you were correct. Yes, there are some people who believe that parts of the Bible are too explicit for others to read (for example, Song of Solomon 7: 1–8). The *American Heritage Dictionary* was banned in some places because it included "bad words." High school teachers in Erie, Pennsylvania, blacked out passages in *Gorillas in the Mist* (by naturalist Dian Fossey) describing the mating habits of apes. Not all of these materials were banned because they were sexually explicit, however. *Cinderella*, for example, was banned from public schools in a Tennessee community in 1986 because it mentioned witchcraft, and *Macbeth* was banned by the same community because it mentioned magic (this ban was overturned by a decision of the U.S. Supreme Court). Attempts to censor or ban sexually explicit material continue today.

With regard to sexually explicit material, the problem the Supreme Court has had to deal with (in cases appealed on First Amendment rights) is trying to distinguish between erotica and pornography. **Erotica** (from the Greek word *erotikos*, meaning "love poem") is any literature or art with a sexual theme, while **pornography** (from the Greek words *porne*, which means "prostitute," and *graphos*, meaning "depicting or writing about") is

© Jim Meddick/Dist. by united Feature syndicate, Inc.

literature or art with a sexual theme that is designed to cause arousal and that is considered to be obscene. The key, therefore, is how we define *obscene*. What is erotica to one person is pornography to another. The *Venus de Milo* may be regarded as a great work of art by most people (erotica), but to some it is just a statue of a nude woman (obscene and pornographic). Why are old paintings of nude persons having sex generally considered art, but modern photos of the same thing often considered pornographic? (See Figure 16–3.) Why are drawings of couples having sex considered educational if they appear in sexuality textbooks (such as those in Chapter 11 in this book), but pornographic if the same thing is found in magazines (see King & Lococo, 1990)?

After grappling with this issue for many years, in 1973 the Supreme Court supported a three-part definition of **obscenity** (*Miller v. California*) that had originally been rendered in 1956 (*Roth v. United States*). Material was considered obscene if (1) by contemporary community standards it depicts patently offensive sexual conduct; (2) it lacks "serious literary, artistic, political, or scientific value"; and (3) it appeals to prurient interest (lustful craving) in sex.

Even the Supreme Court justices recognized problems with this definition, however. For example, in the following year (*Jenkins v. Georgia*, 1974) the Court ruled that local communities do not have "unbridled discretion" to decide what is obscene. (A Georgia community had decided that the Hollywood movie *Carnal Knowledge* was obscene.)

Who determines what is patently offensive or which art or literature lacks serious value? Former Supreme Court Justice Potter Stewart admitted that he could not come up with a good definition of hard-core pornography, but said, "I know it

---

Erotica ■ Any literature or art that has a sexual theme. This is a morally neutral term.

Pornography ■ Literature or art with a sexual theme that is designed to cause arousal and excitement and is considered to be obscene.

Obscenity ■ In legal terminology, the classification of material that by contemporary community standards depicts patently offensive sexual conduct, lacks serious value, and appeals to prurient interests.

when I see it" (*Jacobelis v. Ohio*, 1965). We all see things differently, however. You know what you find to be obscene, but do you want someone else to make that decision for you?

Even if it should eventually be proven that explicit hard-core material reduces sex crimes, it nevertheless is true that many people find it highly offensive and degrading. Some people oppose it on the grounds that it causes men to view women as sex objects and leads to sex discrimination (e.g., Peter & Valkenburg, 2009a). There is evidence that the more men watch pornography, the more they categorize and "objectify women—seeing them as an assemblage of breasts, legs, and buttocks" (Paul, 2004; see also Peter & Valkenburg, 2009a). Catherine MacKinnon (1993, 1996) believes that pornography perpetuates sexual inequality, male dominance, and the dehumanization of women, and argues that the antidiscrimination provisions of the Fourteenth Amendment of the Constitution should take precedence over the First Amendment. However, other feminists worry that attempts to ban sexually explicit material on grounds of discrimination reinforce a double standard. "It reasserts that women are sexually different from men and in need of special protection. Yet special protection inadvertently reinforces the ways in which women are legally and socially said to be different from men" (Vance, 1988; see also A. M. Smith, 1993).

The Internet, with its easy accessibility to porn sites, bulletin boards, and chat rooms, has posed new problems for parents and others attempting to regulate sexually explicit material. In 1996, Congress passed the Communications Decency Act, which made it a crime to transmit sexually explicit images through the Internet. In a unanimous decision, the U.S. Supreme Court struck this down in 1997 (*Reno v. ACLU*), giving the Internet full protection under the First Amendment. A second attempt by Congress, the Child Online Protection Act, met a similar fate, as did a third attempt, the Children's Internet Protection Act. So what are parents to do? Some overzealous prosecutors have attempted to prosecute young teens for sexting by charging them with child pornography, but the courts have prevented this (see *Contemporary Psychology*, 2009).

A variety of Internet-blocking software (e.g., CyberPatrol, Cybersitter, Net Nanny, Net Shepherd, Surfwatch) is available that parents can use to block websites. The court concluded that this software is a "reasonably effective method by which parents can prevent their children from accessing material which the parents believe is inappropriate."

We are one of the few countries in the world whose people have freedom of expression. Most people are offended by at least some of the sexually explicit material that is published or filmed today, but many worry that allowing others to have the power to ban certain materials might eventually infringe on their own presently enjoyed freedom of expression. After all, there are those who would ban passages in the Bible. What do you think should be done?

PROSTITUTION AND OTHER SEX WORK

Sex as a business has found so many markets in recent years that the term **sex worker** is now preferred by many who exchange sexual activities for money. This includes (but is not limited to) people whose work is in nude dancing, commercial phone sex, erotic massage parlors, the porn industry and Internet sex, and of course, escort services and prostitution. You read about the porn industry and Internet sex sites in the previous sections.

There are over 2,500 "gentlemen's clubs" in the United States, with many earning well over $1 million a year. The "exotic dancing" of the performers has steadily become more personal since the 1970s, going from stage dancing to personal lap dancing, often with some degree of touching allowed. The U.S. Supreme Court has ruled that states may ban this type of activity (or restrict it to certain geographical locations) in order to protect "order and morality." Commercial phone sex is a booming $1 billion-a-year business. Charged by the minute, callers can talk about any fantasy to a person who has the gender and sexual orientation of choice. The phone sex services work through phone numbers beginning with 900. When the Federal Communications Commission banned "obscene communications for commercial purposes" within the domestic United States, the companies simply rerouted the calls through foreign markets.

Prostitution

Prostitution is often referred to as "the world's oldest profession." While this may or may not be true, the trade of sex for money or other favors has been around for as long as the recorded history of human beings (Parsons, 2005). In the ancient Hebrew culture, it was not a crime for a father to prostitute his daughter. Prostitution was very common in Roman society.

In the Bible, Jesus told Mary Magdalene to "go, and sin no more," but prostitution flourished in Europe during the Middle Ages, and the Church had a somewhat tolerant attitude about it. Saint Augustine believed that prostitution was necessary,

Sex worker ■ A person who exchanges sexual activity for money.

as did Saint Thomas Aquinas, who, although he considered prostitution a sordid evil, reasoned that just as a palace would become polluted without sewers, the world would become immersed in lust without prostitution (see Bullough & Bullough, 1997). Parisian prostitutes even adopted Mary Magdalene as their patron saint.

In Victorian times (mid-19th century to early 20th century), the upper class maintained a public attitude of purity and prudery, but prostitution was a common sexual outlet for husbands. The poverty and squalor of life in the lower class pushed many young women into prostitution, and it has been estimated that there were as many as 80,000 prostitutes in London at any one time. Prostitution was legalized and regulated by an act of the British Parliament in 1860.

In colonial America and the early years of the United States, Puritanism in the North and the availability of slaves in the South kept prostitution to a minimum. Immigration and industrialization, however, resulted in larger urban areas, and prostitution flourished in the latter half of the 19th century. Houses of prostitution (brothels) were commonplace, especially in the West, where men greatly outnumbered women. Ship captains imported thousands of women from the Orient and Central and South America to be forced into prostitution. San Francisco's population reached 25,000 in the early 1850s, and this included 3,000 prostitutes (Tannahill, 1980). Storyville, a 16-block district of legalized prostitution in New Orleans from 1897 to 1907, employed as many as 2,000 prostitutes at any one time (Warner, 1997).

Opposition to prostitution in the United States began to grow during the first part of the 20th century. Illinois became the first state to pass laws against prostitution in 1908. Federal laws passed at the start of World War I shut down many of the houses of prostitution that had existed near service bases (there were no cures for gonorrhea or syphilis at that time, and many men were being rejected for service because of infections).

Today, worldwide, prostitution is a $52 billion-a-year industry (Altman, 2001). How common is prostitution in the United States? At any one time, there are about 2 million, with 84,000 women working as full-time prostitutes (Potterat et al., 1990). This does not count the women who have sex in exchange for drugs at crack houses and other such places. Most prostitutes work part time or for a short time.

Prostitution ■ The exchange of sex for money. The feature that distinguishes a prostitute from other people who engage in illicit sexual intercourse is the indiscrimination with which she (or he) offers herself or himself to others for hire.

Streetwalker ■ A prostitute who solicits in public.

Definition and Types of Prostitution

We generally think of a prostitute as someone who exchanges sex for money. Your dictionary probably defines it this way. However, by this definition we would have to include people who allow someone to have sex with them for a job or career promotion, to gain a favor, or in return for a trip to Cancun or some other vacation spot. Some prostitutes bitterly complain that what they do is no different from what is done by a woman who remains married to and has sex with a man she does not care for just for the financial security. To get around these problems, legal definitions generally distinguish **prostitution** from other activities on the basis of the indiscriminate manner in which it occurs. The Oregon Supreme Court, for example, ruled that "The feature which distinguishes a prostitute from other women who engage in illicit intercourse is the indiscrimination with which she offers herself to men for hire."

Prostitution in the United States was transacted primarily in brothels until the turn of the 20th century, but the once common house of prostitution is now legal only in some counties in Nevada. Today, prostitution occurs in a variety of settings. Prostitutes can be divided generally into three types according to status. On the lowest tier are **streetwalkers**, who solicit in public. Street prostitutes account for about 10% to 20% of all prostitutes and nearly all of the arrests (Lucas, 2005). Almost all of these women become prostitutes for financial reasons (e.g., to escape poverty or to support a drug habit) and not because of pathological sexual needs. Most streetwalkers are protected by a pimp, who often takes a large share of the earnings (Williamson & Cluse-Tolar, 2002). The sexual activity generally takes place in a room in a cheap hotel or apartment where the manager is aware of what is occurring. The typical streetwalker has sex with four to five men a day, and

FIGURE 16–6 Streetwalkers solicit in public and are the lowest-paid type of prostitute. They typically have sex with four to five men a day.

the sexual activity usually involves giving oral-genital sex (Freund et al., 1989; Monto, 2001).

The **brothel prostitute** has been replaced by **B-girls,** who work in bars and hotels, generally with the approval of the ownership (which may take a cut of the profits or else benefit by the customers the prostitutes attract). Open solicitation, however, is generally frowned upon, so nonverbal messages are often used. The price is usually higher than for a streetwalker's services, and the sexual activity generally takes place in the customer's room.

"Candy" (her own fictitious name) is an attractive 33-year-old African-American B-girl. She solicits customers in New Orleans' French Quarter, in bars along Bourbon, Chartres, and Decatur Streets. Her minimum charge for sex is $50 for 15 minutes or $200 for a night. The vast majority of her customers are white men in town for conventions. She says that 75% of them are married. The sexual activity takes place either in the man's hotel room or in a neutral hotel. Whenever possible, however, she robs her customers rather than having sex with them. Candy says this is usually easy to do before they even get out of the bar. She rubs their genitals, and in their state of excitement they rarely notice that she is pickpocketing them with the other hand.

Candy has four children and is on welfare. After high school she worked as a housekeeper and at other minimum-wage jobs. When she was 27, a pimp showed her the expensive nightclubs around town and said that she, too, could enjoy this lifestyle. She turns all the money that she makes as a prostitute and thief over to him. In return, he gives her protection, buys her nice clothing and jewelry, and lets her drive a Cadillac Seville.

Candy doesn't think about the future. Although she sometimes makes $3,000 to $4,000 in one month, none of it has been saved for when the time comes that she cannot prostitute anymore. She just enjoys the lifestyle that the money will buy now.

(from the author's files)

More recently, sexual services have increasingly been offered through thinly disguised storefronts such as *massage parlors* (it should be noted, however, that some of these parlors are legitimate). Women who work in massage parlors are often called "hand whores" because toward the end of the massage (often given in the nude) they generally rub the thighs and groin area and let it be known that for a "tip" they will massage the genitals.

The highest-status prostitutes are the **call girls,** who generally have regular customers (Lucas, 2005). New customers are screened (recommendations from trusted sources are often required), and appointments are generally made by telephone. The call girl generally works out of her own apartment, but often offers herself as company for dinner and social occasions in addition to providing sexual services. The services do not come cheaply, however, with some of the most attractive call girls charging $2,000 per night or more. A more commercialized, and somewhat less expensive, variety of call girl prostitution today is offered through *escort services*, which advertise in newspapers. The Internet is changing how many higher-priced prostitutes solicit clients. In addition, potential customers often share information with one another on the Internet (Holt & Blevins, 2007).

Prostitution is not limited to women who cater to heterosexual men. Although not nearly as common as female prostitutes, men sometimes sell their bodies to women as well. These men, called **gigolos,** are the male counterparts of call girls and often work as part of an escort service (generally used by wealthy, older, single women). For example, the following account is from a 22-year-old student working as a male escort. He said that most of his female clients are 30 to 45 years old and 80% are single.

"Being a male escort is not all that people perceive it to be. In this day and age you have women that are successful, and in order for them to stay that way they must constantly work harder than any man they're in competition with. This causes women to be subjected to long hours of work and devotion to their jobs, leaving them with no time at all for a personal life. Every time they attempt to have a relationship, they end up neglecting either work or their partner. That is the point where I come in. I am the individual that can be there for them when they need someone either as a friend or a lover. One of the misconceptions of being a male escort is that they only have sex with their clients. That may be true for females, but in the male's case, out of ten women, only five of them only want sex. Three of them want to be held while watching a movie or listening to music. And as for the other two, they want someone who they can go to events with, someone who can carry on intellectual conversation and stand by their side as their showpiece."

Homosexual prostitution is more common than heterosexual prostitution in some large urban areas. Many are teenagers (Finkelhor & Ormrod, 2004). Male prostitutes, called **hustlers,** are similar to female streetwalkers in that they generally solicit their customers on the street. Many hustlers do not regard themselves as homosexual (Earls & David, 1989), because in America the male prostitute

Brothel prostitutes ■ Prostitutes who work in houses of prostitution.

B-girls ■ Prostitutes who work in bars and hotels, generally with the approval of the ownership.

Call girls ■ The highest-status prostitutes, who generally work out of their own apartments by appointment only.

Gigolo ■ A male prostitute who caters to women.

Hustler ■ A male prostitute who caters to men.

generally plays a passive role (i.e., the customers pay to give oral sex to the prostitute, and not vice versa).

Characteristics of Prostitutes

The primary reason given by persons engaging in prostitution is economics (Farley, 2004; Kempner, 2005; Rio, 1991). Most prostitutes come from poor families and have little education. However, even for call girls or prostitutes who are middle-class housewives working part time, the main attraction is still money—their income is higher than that of other women matched for age and education (Lucas, 2005).

The large majority of street and B-girl prostitutes are habitual users of addictive drugs such as heroin and crack cocaine (Dalla, 2002; Potterat et al., 1998; Simon et al., 1992). However, prostitution often precedes the use of drugs (Farley, 2004). Pimps often see to it that their prostitutes become addicted just so they will remain economically dependent. For the typical streetwalker or B-girl, prostitution does not turn out to be the gold mine it may have seemed at first, for most end up turning over most of their earnings to the pimp and are threatened with violence if they do not (Williamson & Cluse-Tolar, 2002).

Beyond the economic motives and aside from the frequent drug dependency is the fact that most prostitutes have very sad backgrounds. Many prostitutes—including the large majority of teenage prostitutes—were physically and sexually abused as children (Dalla, 2000; Farley et al., 2003, 2004; Nixon et al., 2002; Potterat et al., 1998; Rio, 1991). As a result, many grew up with severe self-esteem and self-identity problems, and generally are just less psychologically healthy than other people. With this kind of background, it is not surprising that most teenage prostitutes are runaway or throwaway (not wanted even if they return) children who, with no other job options, have turned their first trick by the time they are 15 (Dittmann, 2005; Nixon et al., 2002).

"Jean" looks like most other 15-year-old girls. In fact, when her hair is in a ponytail she is often mistaken for 13 or 14 years old. The men, most of whom are married with daughters as old as or older than she is, like her very young looks. They want to have sex with a "schoolgirl." Jean fulfills their fantasy by telling them that she is a sophomore at one of the local high schools. She charges them $30 to $50, depending on what they want (oral sex in their car is least expensive). Jean doesn't really go to school at all. She is a runaway. She ran away the last time at age 14 and found herself in New Orleans alone and hungry. That's when she met "Frank." He bought her a hamburger and offered her a place to stay. There were two other girls about her same age staying with Frank. He was particularly nice to Jean and bought her nice dresses. She felt wanted and cared for, and after a few days she and Frank had sex (her first time). He also introduced her to drugs. He told her that she was his special girl. Two weeks later he told her he needed money and asked her to go to bed with another man. The other girls told her it was easy. Jean was surprised to find out how easy it was, and within a short time she was having sex with up to six men a day. All she had to do was stand on a corner and within a short while older men would stop and talk to her.
(from the author's files)

A study of adult male street prostitutes found that nearly all had serious problems with feelings of personal inadequacy, loneliness and social alienation (most said they had no friends), mistrust of others, and depression (Simon et al., 1992). All were drug users and felt that they were locked into their deviate careers.

As bad as the developmental history of most prostitutes is, "on-the-job" conditions are often no better. A majority of street and B-girl prostitutes have been the victims of rape and assault (Monto, 2004). One study concluded, "Working as a streetwalker can be as traumatic as going to war" (Farley et al., 1998). Many prostitutes suffer from posttraumatic stress disorders (Chudakov et al., 2002; Farley et al., 1998), and the large majority wish that they could leave prostitution (Farley et al., 2003).

The Customer

Prostitution has continued to flourish for centuries despite laws, penalties, and the protests of outraged citizens. In order for it to flourish as it has, the demand for sexual services must be great.

Customers are called *johns*, *tricks*, or *scores* by prostitutes. In the national survey by Laumann et al. (1994), 17% of the men and 2% of the women over the age of 18 said that they had paid someone for sex. Other studies have found that between 10% and 23% of men have paid for sex at least once (Carael et al., 2006; Pitts et al., 2004), including 2% to 3% who have paid for sex with street prostitutes (Brewer et al., 2008). However, only a few men use prostitutes regularly (Monto, 2004). Customers of prostitutes tend to be older (average age—late 30s), employed full time, and often middle-class and unmarried or unhappily married (Monto, 2001, 2004; Monto & McRee, 2005; Pitts et al., 2004). The ethnicity of customers tends to reflect the locale of where the prostitution took place (Monto, 2004). Thus, in many respects, customers appear to be average men.

There are many reasons why men pay for sex (see Pitts et al., 2004; Monto, 2004). These include feelings of inadequacy with women (Busch et al., 2002), lack of a partner, the desire for a new partner or a novel sexual act, and the possibility of enjoying sex without the time or effort required of an emotional involvement (Pitts et al., 2004). Many men who use prostitutes feel that when they have paid for sex it entitles them to power and control (Busch et al.,

FIGURE 16–7 A prostitute prepares to work with her first clients of the day in Siliguri, West Bengal, India. Most of the girls are between the ages of 14 and 23. The younger the girl, the more money the client has to pay—as virginity is highly praised by clients.

2002). The majority of men who go to streetwalker prostitutes pay to have oral-genital sex performed on them (Leonard et al., 1989; Monto, 2001).

Men who pay to have sex with male prostitutes come from all walks of life (Morse et al., 1992). Most describe themselves as heterosexual or bisexual and are married. They are not part of the open gay community and they use prostitutes in order to conceal their same-sex activities. Despite their married status, very few use condoms, although the behaviors they engage in put them at risk for sexually transmitted infections.

Forced Prostitution and Sex Trafficking

Does prostitution really involve consenting adults? It is safe to say that customers are consenting (Monto, 2004), and this is probably also true for most high-priced call girls (Lucas, 2005), but what about the others? Recall that most street prostitutes and B-girls come from extreme poverty and a background of violence (and in many cases are throwaway children), and that they can find no other way to support themselves (Farley, 2004). Thus, in many respects this is "survival sex work." In many countries, 10% to 15% of street children have exchanged sex for money in order to survive (Marshall & Wood, 2009).

Many children and young adults are forced into prostitution. In World War II the Japanese army forced 200,000 foreign girls to work in brothels to serve the soldiers. But forced prostitution takes place in peace time as well. In many parts of the world, girls' families sell them into prostitution (Barry, 1995; Power et al., 2003). Internationally, many children and young women are trafficked to the sex industry from one country to another (Dinen, 2002). They are forced to have sex and are provided with just enough to survive. All the profits go to the traffickers and handlers (Skinner, 2010). The estimated number of victims is at least 1 million worldwide each year (Farr, 2004; Power et al., 2003; Willis & Levy, 2002) and this includes 50,000 trafficked into the United States each year (Monto, 2004). The total number of child prostitutes worldwide is well over 10 million, and sex tourism (going to foreign countries to have sex with young child prostitutes) is a big business (Farr, 2004). Sex trafficking totals $7 to $10 billion a year in earnings (Cwikel & Hoban, 2005). In 2000, Congress made it a crime to traffic humans within the United States, but the U.S. is one of only two countries that has refused to ratify United Nations resolutions about international trafficking.

Prostitution and the Law

Opponents of prostitution argue that it is often accompanied by drug addiction, a high risk of contracting sexually transmitted infections (see Box 16–A), and the possibility of assault and battery by the prostitute and her pimp. (What do you suppose the chances are of a victimized john filing charges?) The primary concern of many people, however, is the moral issue. They believe that prostitution is a sinful and degrading sexual activity, both for the individuals involved and for society as a whole.

Some people, on the other hand, argue that prostitution is a victimless crime that occurs between consenting adults (see Rio, 1991). Many researchers, feminists, and organized groups of prostitutes (e.g., COYOTE) have called for decriminalization or legalization of prostitution (Barry, 1995; Bullough & Bullough, 1997; Vanwesenbeeck, 2002). Prostitution is legal in some European countries (e.g., Germany, the Netherlands) and has been decriminalized in other countries (e.g., Australia, New Zealand). Proponents advocate the licensing and regulation of prostitutes, including regular required health checks for sexually transmitted infections. This is already done in Nevada's legalized houses of prostitution, where customers are required to use condoms (see Albert et al., 1998). Proponents say that if prostitution were legalized or decriminalized everywhere, pimps and organized crime would become less influential, and the taxes collected on prostitutes' fees could be used to fight more serious crimes. Decriminalization in New Zealand did not lead to an increase in the number of

Box 16–A Sexuality and Health

Prostitution and HIV/AIDS

You learned about the human immunodeficiency virus (HIV) and AIDS in Chapter 5. HIV infection, you recall, is the leading cause of death of Americans aged 25 to 44. Although once uncommon, heterosexual transmission is now the major cause of most new AIDS cases in women (Centers for Disease Control and Prevention, 2007b).

Because of their sexual relations with multiple partners, as well as the high percentage who use drugs intravenously, prostitutes are at high risk for contracting HIV and are high-risk sexual partners for those who use them. Worldwide, the greater the number of prostitutes in a country, the greater is the rate for HIV (Talbott, 2007). This is especially true in impoverished areas

where children engage in prostitution in order to survive (Marshall & Wood, 2009; see Marshall et al., 2010).

Fewer than 1% of all U.S. citizens are infected with HIV, but what about prostitutes? The risk of HIV infection is greatest for prostitutes working on the street (Pyett & Warr, 1997). Studies have found that 25% to 50% of female street prostitutes in many large U.S. cities may be infected with HIV (McKeganey, 1994; Steen & Dallabetta, 2003; Turner et al., 1989, Weiner, 1996). The same percentage is found among male prostitutes (Boles & Elifson, 1994; Elifson et al., 1989). Several of these studies found high rates of infection with hepatitis B and syphilis as well.

You might think that men engaging in high-risk sexual behavior, such as sex

with a prostitute, would use condoms. Regular use of condoms does substantially reduce the risk of getting HIV. In legalized brothels in Nevada, condom use is required. However, condom use by men in the U.S. general population is quite low (Catania et al., 1995), and this is also true of men who pay for sex with prostitutes (Leonard et al., 1989; Weiner, 1996). Condom use among children who have been trafficked as sex slaves is very low (Marshall & Wood, 2009).

What can we conclude? By their use of prostitutes, especially when condoms are not used, many men are putting themselves and *their noncommercial partners* at high risk for infection with HIV and other sexually transmitted infections.

---

prostitutes. On the other hand, opponents point to the experience in the Australian state of Victoria. After prostitution was legalized there, it led to a dramatic increase in the number of brothels (legal and illegal) "and a large-scale trafficking industry of girls and women into Victoria...to meet this new demand" (Sullivan & Jeffreys, 2002).

The United States seems to have very ambivalent attitudes about prostitution. It is illegal in some places and legal in others. Although illegal in most places, many only halfheartedly prosecute it. While all states prosecute the sellers (prostitutes), very few seriously go after the buyers (johns who patronize them). In Sweden, on the other hand, the law targets the customers. Prostitution is the only sexual offense for which more women than men are prosecuted; in the

United States, over 40,000 women a year are arrested for prostitution or commercialized vice (Norton-Hawk, 2001). Experts believe that prostitution will decrease only when law enforcement vigorously targets customers. As long as the demand is there, the supply of prostitution will always be there, and thus our society's present treatment of prostitution probably ensures that it will continue unabated.

PERSONAL REFLECTIONS

How do you feel about prostitution: Should it remain illegal, or should we attempt to legalize and regulate it? Why? If you feel it should be illegal, should the "clients" be prosecuted?

STUDY GUIDE

KEY TERMS

B-girls 423
brothel prostitutes 423
call girls 423
Comstock law 413
degrading sexually explicit
    material 417
erotica 420

gigolo 423
hustler 423
johns 424
nonviolent sexually explicit
    material 417
obscenity 420
pornography 420

prostitution 422
sex worker 421
streetwalker 422
violent sexually explicit
    material 417

INTERACTIVE REVIEW

The sale of sexually explicit material is a multibillion-dollar-a-year business. This could not have happened, of course, if there were not a large demand for such material. According to surveys, about (1) _____ of all Americans have seen an X-rated movie or video in the past year. One third of all use of the Internet is to access porn sites. The President's Commission of 1970 and subsequent researchers have generally concluded that exposure to nonviolent sexually explicit material has (2) _____ effect on individuals. Subsequent research has shown that many men are aroused by sexually explicit material depicting violence toward women. Exposure to sexually explicit material with violent themes often results in men becoming (3) _____ toward rape victims, having greater belief in (4) _____, displaying (5) _____ to women, and being more likely to say that they would (6) _____. However, behavioral scientists have concluded that it is the (7) _____ in this material, not the (8) _____, that is potentially harmful. Most people find some types of sexually explicit material offensive, but attempts to censor or ban this material raise questions about First Amendment rights. What is (9) _____ to

one person is pornography to another, and who is to decide where to draw the line?

Prostitution is illegal in all parts of the United States except for a few counties in (10) _____. In recent surveys, (11) _____% of the male respondents indicated that they had paid for sex on at least one occasion. Female prostitutes can be divided into three types according to status: (12) _____, who solicit in public; brothel prostitutes and (13) _____; and (14) _____, who generally work out of their own apartments. Male prostitutes who cater to homosexuals are called (15) _____. The primary reason most individuals engage in prostitution is (16) _____. Most prostitutes were sexually or physically abused as children. Most customers are (17) _____ and (18) _____. Opponents of prostitution argue that many children are forced into prostitution and that prostitution spreads sexually transmitted infections and is often associated with other crimes. Proponents of legalization argue that licensing and required health checks would reduce both STIs (including HIV infection) and the influence of organized crime.

SELF-TEST

A. TRUE OR FALSE

T F 19. Most people who become prostitutes do so because of abnormal sexual needs.

T F 20. When exposed to sexually explicit material, most people show an increase in sexual behavior.

T F 21. The 1970 President's Commission concluded that there was no significant link between exposure of adults to sexually explicit materials and sex crimes.

T F 22. Prostitution is the only sexual offense for which more women than men are prosecuted.

T F 23. Erotica and pornography are synonyms and are really the same thing.

T F 24. When Denmark legalized the sale of hard-core pornographic material to adults, there was a marked decrease in sex crimes afterward.

T F 25. People are most aroused by looking at sexually explicit material showing behaviors they regard as normal.

T F 26. HIV infection is uncommon among prostitutes, probably because most have their customers use condoms.

T F 27. Nearly all junior high school boys and girls have looked at a sexually explicit magazine.

T F 28. A majority of both men and women are physiologically aroused by sexually explicit material.

T F 29. There is substantial evidence that sex offenders have had more exposure to sexually explicit material than have nonoffenders.

T F 30. Exposure to violent sexually explicit material often results in men adopting attitudes that are more supportive of sexual violence against women.

T F 31. Saint Augustine and Saint Thomas Aquinas believed prostitution was necessary.

B. MATCHING

_____ 32. B-girl
_____ 33. brothel prostitute
_____ 34. call girl
_____ 35. gigolo
_____ 36. hustler
_____ 37. john
_____ 38. not a prostitute
_____ 39. pimp
_____ 40. streetwalker

a. Susan has sex for money at a legalized house in Nevada.
b. Joan has sex with her boss in the hope that it will get her a promotion.
c. Hank works out of an escort service and is paid by older women to have sex.
d. Stephanie works out of her own apartment, and her clients must make an appointment to have sex with her.
e. David takes 75% of the money earned by six women who do tricks on the west side of town.
f. Joe pays women to give him oral-genital sex.
g. Sam accepts money from men on the street who want to have sex with him.
h. Sally solicits for sex in a downtown bar.
i. Bonnie solicits men in public.

C. FILL IN THE BLANKS

41. The feature that distinguishes a prostitute from other women who engage in illicit sexual intercourse is the _____ with which she offers herself to men for hire.
42. A hustler is on the same status level as a female _____.
43. Pornography is distinguished from erotica in that it is literature or art with a sexual theme that is considered to be _____.
44. Recent evidence suggests that it is exposure to _____, rather than just sexual explicitness, that results in potentially harmful attitude and behavioral changes.
45. In *Miller v. California*, 1973, the Supreme Court ruled that material was obscene if (a) _____, (b) _____, and (c) _____.
46. The _____, passed in 1873, made the mailing of material considered to be obscene a felony.
47. Probably the foremost reason many people use sexually explicit material is that _____.
48. With regard to pornography, men and women rate themes in which there is _____ as the most degrading.
49. Some negative effects of frequent viewing of pornography on the Internet include _____.

SUGGESTED READINGS

Bullough, V., and Bullough, B. (1988). *Women and prostitution: A social history*. Buffalo, NY: Prometheus Books. A sociological, historical, and cross-cultural examination. Very comprehensive.

Cooper, A., Boies, S., Maheu., M., and Greenfield, D. (2000). Sexuality and the Internet: The next sexual revolution. In L. T. Szuchman and F. Muscarella (Eds.). *Psychological perspectives on human sexuality* (pp. 519–545). New York: John Wiley & Sons. Addresses the question of whether the Internet will be the start of the new sexual revolution.

Donnerstein, E. J., and Linz, D. G. (1986, December). The question of pornography. *Psychology Today*. Authors of pornography research challenge the conclusions of the attorney general's commission and say that we should be more concerned with violence in the media.

Ferguson, C. J., & Hartley, R.D. (2009). The pleasure is momentary...the expense damnable? The influence of pornography on rape and sexual assault. *Aggression and Violent Behavior, 14*, 323–329. An updated review of the relationship between pornography and sexual aggression.

Heins, M. (1993). *Sex, sin, and blasphemy : A guide to America's censorship wars*. New York: New Press. Takes the view that sexually explicit material should be protected as a First Amendment right (see MacKinnon for an alternative viewpoint).

Lane, F. (2006). *The decency wars: The campaign to cleanse American culture*. Amherst, NY: Prometheus Books. Examines the roles of politics and morality.

MacKinnon, C. (1993). *Only words*. Cambridge, MA: Harvard University Press. Takes the view that pornography should be banned as discriminatory against women under the Fourteenth Amendment (see Heins for an alternative viewpoint).

Skinner, E.B. (2008). *A crime so monstrous: Face-to-face with modern-day slavery*. New York: Free Press. Winner of the 2009 Dayton Literary Peace Prize.

ecpat.net

End Child Prostitution, Child Pornography and Trafficking of Children for Sexual Proposes (ECPAT). This is a global network of individuals attempting to stop child exploitation.

GLOSSARY

A

Abortion   Termination of pregnancy. Depending on how far the pregnancy has advanced, this can be done by taking a pill (RU 486); scraping the uterine lining (dilation and curettage); removing the uterine lining by suction (dilation and evacuation); or inducing labor (by injecting hypertonic saline or prostaglandins). (Ch. 6)

Accepting   Letting your child know that all questions are okay and will not be met with a negative attitude. (Ch. 10)

Acquaintance rape   A rape committed by someone who is known by the victim. (Ch. 15)

Acquired immunodeficiency syndrome (AIDS)   An often fatal infection caused by a virus (HIV) that destroys the immune system. It is spread by intimate sexual activity (the exchange of bodily fluids) or contaminated blood. (Ch. 5)

Adolescence   (ad″ ′l es′ ′ns) The time of life between puberty and adulthood. (Ch. 10)

Adrenal (ad- re′ nal) **glands**   Endocrine glands located near the kidneys that secrete steroid hormones and small amounts of gonadal hormones. (Ch. 3)

Adrenarche   (ad″ ren-ar′ ke) The maturation of the adrenal glands, usually between the ages of 6 and 8. (Ch. 10)

Adrenogenital (ah-dre″ no-jen′ y-tal) **syndrome (AGS)**   A condition in girls in which the adrenal glands excrete too much testosterone during fetal development, causing masculinization. This includes enlargement of the clitoris and labia, so that at birth the genitals are sometimes mistaken for those of a boy. Also called *congenital adrenal hyperplasia*. (Ch. 8)

Adultery   Sexual intercourse with someone other than one's husband or wife. (Ch. 10)

Afterbirth   The expulsion of the placenta from the uterus after a baby is born. (Ch. 7)

Agape   (ah′ gah pā″) A type of romantic love that puts the interest of the loved person ahead of one's own, even if it means great sacrifice. (Ch. 12)

Aggressive pedophile   A pedophile who is sexually aroused by inflicting physical injury on victims. (Ch. 15)

Alpha-fetoprotein (AFP) screening   A test conducted between the 16th and 18th week of pregnancy to detect abnormalities in neural development, including spina bifida. (Ch. 7)

Amebiasis (am″ e-bi′ ah-sis)   Dysentery caused by infestation of amoebae, one-celled organisms. (Ch. 5)

Amenorrhea (ah-men″ o-re′ ah)   The absence of menstruation for 6 months or longer. (Ch. 3)

Amniocentesis (am″ ne-o-sen-te′ sis)   A technique for detecting fetal problems, involving collection of amniotic fluid between the 14th and 18th weeks of pregnancy. (Ch. 7)

Amnion (am′ ne-on)   A thick-skinned sac filled with water that surrounds the fetus. (Ch. 7)

Anabolic (an″ ah-bol′ ik) **steroids**   Synthetic steroid hormones that combine the growth (anabolic) effects of adrenal steroids with the masculinizing effects of androgenic steroids. (Ch. 3)

Anal intercourse   Insertion of the penis into the anus and rectum of a sexual partner. (Ch. 11)

Anaphrodisiacs (an″ af-ro-dĭz′ e-aks)   Substances that suppress sexual functioning. (Ch. 4)

Androgen insensitivity syndrome   A condition in which the testicles secrete normal amounts of testosterone during male embryonic development, but the tissues do not respond to it. As a result, a clitoris, labia, and a short vagina develop, but the internal female structures do not develop because the testicles still secrete Mullerian duct–inhibitory substances. (Ch. 8)

Androgens (an′ dro-jens)   Hormones that possess masculinizing properties. (Ch. 2)

Androgyny (an-droj′ ĭ-ne)   The ability of an individual to display a variety of personality characteristics, both masculine and feminine, depending on whether a trait or behavior is appropriate in a given situation. It is often viewed as a positive characteristic that gives an individual greater adaptability. (Ch. 8)

Anger rapists   Rapists who commit their attacks out of hostility or anger directed at their victims or at women in general. (Ch. 15)

Anxious-ambivalent   A style of attachment in which individuals have negative attitudes about themselves and are therefore insecure in their relationships. (Ch. 12)

Aphrodisiacs (af″ ro-dĭz′ e-aks)   Substances that enhance sexual desire or performance. (Ch. 4)

Areola (ah-re′ o-lah)   The darkened ring surrounding the nipple of a breast. (Ch. 2)

Artificial insemination   A method of treating infertility caused by a low sperm count in men. Sperm are collected during several ejaculations and then inserted into the partner's vagina at the time of ovulation. (Ch. 7)

Ascetic (ah set′ ik) **philosophy**   A philosophy that originated among the ancient Greeks. It emphasizes that virtue comes from wisdom and that these qualities can be achieved only by avoiding strong passions. (Ch. 1)

Askable   Being perceived as receptive, a good listener, and accepting. (Ch. 10)

Asymptomatic   Showing no symptoms. (Ch. 5)

Asymptomatic HIV infection   A stage of HIV infection in which infected individuals show no visible symptoms. (Ch. 5)

Attachment   Two meanings: (a) a drab, mundane form of companionship where one's partner gives few positive rewards, other than predictability, for remaining in the relationship; (b) the emotional tie between a parent and child, or between two adults. (Ch. 12)

Attachment theory of love   The theory that the quality of the attachment between parents and child greatly affects the child's ability to form romantic relations as an adult. (Ch. 12)

Autoerotic asphyxiation   See *hypoxyphilia*.

Autoinoculation   The act of infecting oneself. (Ch. 5)

Avoidant   A style of attachment in which individuals have negative attitudes about others and have difficulty with feelings of intimacy and letting another person get close to them. (Ch. 12)

B

Bacteria   Small, single-celled organisms that lack a nuclear membrane, but have all the genetic material (RNA and DNA) to reproduce themselves. (Ch. 5)

Bacterial vaginosis (vaj″ ĭ-no′ sis)   A type of vaginitis caused by the interaction of several vaginal bacteria (particularly *Gardnerella vaginalis*). (Ch. 5)

Barrier (blockade) method   General term for contraceptive methods that block the passage of sperm. (Ch. 6)

Bartholin's (bar′ to-linz) **glands**   Glands located at the base of the labia minora in women that contribute a small amount of an alkaline fluid to their inner surfaces during sexual arousal. (Ch. 2)

Basal body temperature   The temperature of the body while resting. It rises slightly after ovulation. (Ch. 6)

Benign coital cephalalgia (sef′ ah-lal′ je-ah)   Severe headaches that start during or slightly after orgasm, usually in men. (Ch. 13)

Berdache (bar dash′)   See **two-spirit.**

Bestiality (bes-te-al′ ĭ-te)   The act of having sexual contact with an animal. (Ch. 14)

B-girls   Prostitutes who work in bars and hotels, generally with the approval of the ownership. (Ch. 16)

Billings method   A fertility awareness method of birth control in which changes in the consistency and quantity of cervical mucus are used to tell when ovulation has occurred. (Ch. 6)

Biological determinism   The belief that biological influences establish predetermined limits to the effects of cultural influences. (Ch. 8)

Bisexual   An individual with a sexual orientation toward both men and women. (Ch. 9)

Blastocyst (blas′ to-sist)   The fluid-filled sphere that reaches the uterus after fertilization and which was created by the transformation of the morula through continued, rapid cell division. (Ch. 7)

Blockade method   See **barrier (blockade) method.**

Bradley method   A method of prepared childbirth that emphasizes childbirth without medication; named after its founder, Robert Bradley. (Ch. 7)

Braxton-Hicks contractions   Uterine contractions experienced during the last trimester of pregnancy that are often incorrectly interpreted as the beginning of labor; also called *false labor.* (Ch. 7)

Breast-feeding   In reference to contraception, see **lactational amenorrhea method.** (Ch. 6)

Breasts   In women, glands that provide milk for infants; located at the front of the chest. (Ch. 2)

Breech birth   A birth in which the baby is born feet or buttocks first. (Ch. 7)

Brothel prostitutes   Prostitutes who work in houses of prostitution. (Ch. 16)

Bulb (of penis)   The expanded inner end of the spongy body of the penis. (Ch. 2)

Bulbocavernosus (bul″ bo-kav′ er-no′ sus) **muscle**   A ring of sphincter muscles that surrounds the vaginal opening in women or the root of the penis in men. (Ch. 2)

Bulbourethral (bul″ bo-u-re′ thral) **glands**   See **Cowper's glands.**

C

Calendar method   A fertility awareness method of birth control that attempts to determine a woman's fertile period by use of a mathematical formula. (Ch. 6)

Call girls   The highest-status prostitutes, who generally work out of their own apartments by appointment only. (Ch. 16)

Candidiasis (kan″ dĭ-di′ ah-sis)   See **moniliasis.**

Capacitation   A process that sperm undergo while traveling through the woman's reproductive tract in which their membranes become thin enough so that an enzyme necessary for softening the ovum's membrane can be released. (Ch. 7)

Carnal knowledge of a juvenile   See **statutory rape.**

Case study   An in-depth study of an individual. (Ch. 1)

Cephalalgia   See **benign coital cephalalgia.**

Cervical cap   A contraceptive device that fits over the cervix by suction, thus blocking the passage of sperm into the uterus. (Ch. 6)

Cervical mucus   The slimy secretion of mucous membranes located inside the cervix. (Ch. 6)

Cervicitis (ser″ vĭ-si′ tis)   Inflammation of the cervix. (Ch. 5)

Cervix (ser′ viks)   The narrow lower end of the uterus that projects into the vagina. (Ch. 2)

Cesarean (se-sa′ re-an) **section (C-section)**   The surgical removal of a fetus through the mother's abdomen. (Ch. 7)

Chancre (shang′ ker)   The painless sore that is the main symptom of the primary stage of syphilis. (Ch. 5)

Chancroid (shang′ kroid)   A sexually transmitted infection caused by the *Haemophilus ducreyi* bacterium, which is characterized by small, painful bumps. (Ch. 5)

Child molestation   Sexual contact between an adult and a child. (Ch. 15)

Chlamydia (klah-mid′ e-ah)   A sexually transmitted infection caused by the *Chlamydia trachomatis* bacterium, which lives on mucous membranes. (Ch. 5)

Chorion (ko′ re-on)   The fourth membrane of the trophoblast; it develops into the lining of the placenta. (Ch. 7)

Chorionic villus sampling   A technique used for detecting problems in a fetus during the 10th to 12th weeks of pregnancy. Hairlike projections (villi) of the chorion are collected and examined. (Ch. 7)

Chromosomes (kro′ mo-somz)   Rod-shaped structures containing the genetic material that determines a person's inherited characteristics. (Ch. 8)

Circumcision (ser″ kum-sizh′ un)   In men, the removal of all or part of the foreskin of the penis. In women, the removal of the clitoral hood. (Ch. 2)

Climacteric (kli-ma˘k′ ter-ik)   The changes that occur in women in the few years that precede and the first year that follows menopause. (Ch. 10)

Clitoral hood   The part of the labia minora that covers the clitoris in women. (Ch. 2)

Clitoridectomy (klĭ″ to-rĭ-dek′ to-me)   Removal of the clitoris, often accompanied by removal of the labia minora. In an extreme form, called *infibulation,* the labia majora are also removed, and the sides of the vulva are then sewn together. (Ch. 4)

Clitoris (klĭ′ to-ris)   A small, elongated erectile structure in women that develops from the same embryonic tissue as the penis. It has no known function other than to focus sexual sensations. (Ch. 2)

Coach   In the Lamaze birthing technique, an individual (usually the woman's partner) who works with the expectant mother during labor to help her use her training and provide support and encouragement. (Ch. 7)

Cognitive-behavioral therapy   Therapy that views problems as resulting from faulty learning and that focuses on specific sexual behaviors and how we feel about them. It does not focus on past events. (Ch. 13)

Cohabitation   Living together in an unmarried relationship. (Ch. 10)

Coitus (ko′ ĭ-tus)   Sexual intercourse. (Ch. 11)

Coitus interruptus   See **withdrawal.**

Colostrum (ko-los′ trum)   A thick, sticky liquid produced by a mother's breasts before milk starts to flow. (Ch. 7)

Combination pill   An oral contraceptive that contains both synthetic estrogen and synthetic progesterone. (Ch. 6)

Coming out   Disclosing to others one's homosexual orientation, from the expression "coming out of the closet." (Ch. 9)

Communication   The exchange of information, thoughts, ideas, or feelings. (Ch. 13)

Companionate love   Love based on togetherness, trust, sharing, and affection rather than passion. (Ch. 12)

Compliance   Agreeing to sexual intercourse when you do not really want to engage in it. (Ch. 15)

Comstock law   A law passed in 1873 that made it a felony to mail any material regarded as obscene or lewd. (Ch. 16)

Conception   The union of an egg and a sperm. (Ch. 7)

Conditional love   Feelings of love that depend on the loved one satisfying needs and fulfilling desires. (Ch. 12)

Condom   *For men,* a thin sheath made of latex rubber, lamb intestine, or polyurethane that fits over the penis. *For women,* a polyurethane intravaginal pouch held in place by two flexible rings. Condoms are effective as contraception and for prevention of sexually transmitted infections. (Ch. 6)

Congenital adrenal hyperplasia   See **adrenogenital syndrome.**

Consummate love   According to Sternberg, the complete love found in relationships that include passion, intimacy, and commitment. (Ch. 12)

Contraception   The prevention of conception. (Ch. 6)

Contraceptive sponge   A contraceptive device made of polyurethane sponge that contains enough spermicide to be effective for 24 hours after being inserted into the vagina. (Ch. 6)

Coprophilia (kop″ ro-fil′ e-ah)   Sexual arousal caused by feces or the act of defecation. (Ch. 14)

Copulation (kop″ u-la′ shun)   Sexual intercourse. (Ch. 11)

Corona (ko-ro′ nah)   The rounded border of the glans of the penis. (Ch. 2)

Corpora cavernosa (kor′ po-rah kav″ er-no′ sah)   The two cavernous bodies of the penis or clitoris that fill with blood during sexual arousal. (Ch. 2)

Corpus luteum (kor′ pus lew′ te-um)   The follicular cells that remain in the ovary after the follicle expels the ovum during ovulation. They begin to secrete progesterone in large quantities in the postovulatory stage. (Ch. 3)

Corpus spongiosum (kor′ pus spun″ je-o′ sum)   The spongy body of the penis that fills with blood during sexual arousal; the urethra passes through it. (Ch. 2)

Correlation   A mathematical measure of the degree of relationship between two variables. (Ch. 1)

Couples therapy   Therapy that focuses on the overall relationship and communication skills between two people. (Ch. 13)

Courtly love   In medieval times, when courtiers expressed their undying love for a woman who they worshipped from afar as the epitome of virtue. (Ch. 12)

Courtship disorders   A group of paraphilias (voyeurism, exhibitionism, frotteurism, and telephone scatophilia) often seen together. (Ch. 14)

Couvade (koo-vahd′) **syndrome**   The experiencing of pregnancy symptoms by male partners; sometimes called "sympathy pains." (Ch. 7)

Cowper's (kow′ perz) **glands**   Two pea-shaped structures located beneath the prostate gland in men that secrete a few drops of an alkaline fluid prior to orgasm. (Ch. 2)

Critical period   In relation to teratogens, the time during embryonic or fetal development during which a particular part of the body is most susceptible to damage. (Ch. 7)

Crowning   The appearance of the fetus' head at the vaginal opening during childbirth. (Ch. 7)

Crura (kroo′ rah)   The leglike ends of the cavernous bodies of the clitoris or penis that attach to the pubic bone. (Ch. 2)

Cryptorchidism (krip-tor′ kĭ-dizm)   A defect in which the testicles fail to descend into the scrotum. (Ch. 2)

Cunnilingus (kun″ ĭ-ling′ gus)   Oral stimulation of a woman's genitals. (Ch. 11)

Cystitis (sis-ti′ tis)   A bacterial infection of the bladder (often caused by the bacterium *Escherichia coli*). (Ch. 5)

D

Date rape   A type of acquaintance rape, committed during a social encounter agreed to by the victim. (Ch. 15)

Decision/commitment   One of the three basic components in Sternberg's theory of love; the decision that one loves another person and the commitment to maintain the relationship. (Ch. 12)

Degrading sexually explicit material   Nonviolent sexually explicit material that shows women as sex objects and where there is a clear unequal balance of power. (Ch. 16)

Delayed puberty   A condition in which the appearance of secondary sex characteristics and physical growth do not begin until well after they have begun in most children. (Ch. 10)

Demand/withdraw   A dysfunctional communication pattern often displayed during conflict, where one partner makes demands (criticizes or nags) and the other avoids. (Ch. 13)

Depo-Provera   Market name for medroxyprogesterone acetate, a chemical that when injected suppresses ovulation for 3 months. (Ch. 6)

Desensitization   See **systematic desensitization.**

Desire   A state that "is experienced as specific sensations which move the individual to seek out, or become receptive to, sexual experiences" (Kaplan, 1979). (Ch. 4)

Desire (women)   For many women, sexual desire is motivated less by biological urges than it is by relationship and intimacy needs. (Ch. 4)

Detumescence (de″ tu-mes′ ens)   Loss of erection. (Ch. 4)

DHT deficiency syndrome   A type of androgen insensitivity syndrome in which, because testosterone is not converted into dihydrotestosterone, boys' external genitals do not develop properly. Development occurs at puberty with the rise in testosterone. (Ch. 8)

Diaphragm A dome-shaped rubber cup with a flexible rim that fits over the cervix and thus acts as a contraceptive device by serving as a barrier to the passage of sperm into the uterus. (Ch. 6)

Dilation Becoming wider or larger. (Ch. 7)

Dilation and curettage (D & C) An abortion technique in which the cervix is dilated and the endometrium is removed by scraping it with an instrument called a curette. (Ch. 6)

Dilation and evacuation (D & E) An abortion technique in which the cervix is dilated and the endometrium is removed by suction. (Ch. 6)

Dilation and extraction (D & X) See **intact dilation and evacuation.**

Direct observation Observing and recording the activity of subjects as they conduct their activities. (Ch. 1)

Domination Ruling over and controlling another individual. In sexual relations, it generally involves humiliation of the partner as well. (Ch. 14)

Douching (doosh-ing) A feminine hygiene practice of rinsing out the vagina, usually with specifically prepared solutions. (Ch. 6)

Dualism The belief that body and soul are separate and antagonistic. (Ch. 1)

Dyke A slang term for a masculine lesbian. This is a stereotype that generally does not reflect how most lesbians look or behave. (Ch. 9)

Dysmenorrhea (dĭs″ men-o-re′ ah) Painful menstruation. (Ch. 3)

Dyspareunia (dĭs″ pah-roo′ ne-ah) Recurrent or persistent genital pain during intercourse, usually resulting from organic factors (e.g., vaginal, prostate, or bladder infections). (Ch. 13)

E

Eclampsia (e-klamp′ se-ah) An advanced case of toxemia of pregnancy, characterized by convulsions and coma. (Ch. 7)

Ectopic (ek-top′ ik) **pregnancy** The implantation of a fertilized egg outside of the endometrium of the uterus. (Ch. 7)

Effacement The thinning of the cervix during labor. (Ch. 7)

Effleurage (ef-loo-rahzh′) In the Lamaze birthing technique, a light self-massage of the abdomen that is used to counter the discomfort of labor contractions. (Ch. 7)

Ejaculation The expulsion of semen from the body. (Ch. 4)

Ejaculatory ducts One-inch-long paired tubes that pass through the prostate gland. The third part of the duct system that transports sperm out of a man's body. (Ch. 2)

Ejaculatory incompetence A condition in which a man is totally unable to ejaculate in a woman's vagina during sexual intercourse. (Ch. 13)

Embryo (em′ bre-o) The term given to the blastocyst after it has implanted. (Ch. 7)

Emergency contraception Methods that prevent contraception when used in the first few days *after* sexual intercourse. (Ch. 6)

Emerging adulthood A developmental stage of life; an extended period of being a single adult that occurs between adolescence and young adulthood. (Ch. 10)

Emission The first stage of an orgasm in men. Rhythmic muscular contractions in the vas deferens, prostate gland, and seminal vesicles force the sperm and prostate and seminal fluids into the ejaculatory ducts, thus forming semen. (Ch. 4)

Empty love According to Sternberg, the emotion felt when there is decision and commitment to love another person, but no intimacy or passion. (Ch. 12)

Endocrine system A network of ductless glands that secrete their chemical substances, called *hormones*, directly into the bloodstream, where they are carried to other parts of the body to exert their effects. (Ch. 3)

Endoderm The layer of the embryo that forms the internal organs of the fetus. (Ch. 7)

Endometriosis (en″ do-me′ tre-o′ sis) The growth of endometrial tissue outside of the uterus. (Ch. 3)

Endometrium (en″ do-me′ tre-um) The inner mucous membrane of the uterus where a fertilized egg implants. Its thickness varies with the phase of the menstrual cycle. (Ch. 2, 3)

Epididymis (ep″ ĭ-did′ ĭ-mis) The elongated cordlike structure on the back of a testicle. It is the first part of the duct system that transports sperm out of a man's body. (Ch. 2)

Episiotomy (e-piz″ e-ot′ o-me) A surgical procedure performed on women just before giving birth to reduce the risk of tearing the perineum. (Ch. 7)

Erectile disorder A sexual problem in which a man has persistent or recurrent difficulty getting and maintaining an erection. (Ch. 13)

Erection (of penis) The state of the penis during sexual arousal (i.e., hard and elongated) due to vasocongestion of tissues. (Ch. 4)

Eros A highly idealized type of romantic love that is based mainly on physical beauty. Erotic lovers look for physical perfection. (Ch. 12)

Erotica Any literature or art that has a sexual theme. This is a morally neutral term. (Ch. 16)

Essure A nonsurgical (transcervical) female sterilization technique in which the Fallopian tubes are blocked by micro-inserts. (Ch. 6)

Estrogen (es′ tro-jen) A hormone that is produced by the ovaries (and in very small amounts by the testicles and adrenal glands). (Ch. 3)

Estrous cycle The cycle of hormonal events that occurs in most nonhuman mammals. The females are sexually receptive ("in heat," or in estrus) to males only during ovulation. (Ch. 3)

Ethnocentric The attitude that the behaviors and customs of one's own ethnic group or culture are superior to others. (Ch. 1)

Evolutionary (sociobiological) theory In reference to sex differences in human behavior, states that the behavioral differences are due to the different reproductive pressures men and women faced over thousands of generations. (Ch. 8)

Excitement phase (men) The first phase of the sexual response cycle as proposed by Masters and Johnson. The first sign is vasocongestion of the penis, leading to erection. (Ch. 4)

Excitement (arousal) phase (women) The first phase of the sexual response cycle as proposed by Masters and Johnson. Arousability has been defined as "the capacity to become sexually aroused in response to situational cues" (Peplau, 2003). For many women, relationship and intimacy needs provide the situational cues. (Ch. 4)

Exhibitionism Exposing one's genitals compulsively in inappropriate settings in order to obtain sexual gratification. (Ch. 14)

Experiment A study in which an investigator attempts to establish a cause-and-effect relationship by manipulating a variable of interest (the independent variable) while keeping all other factors the same. (Ch. 1)

Expressive   A personality characteristic; a cognitive focus on "an affective concern for the welfare of others." (Ch. 8)

Expulsion   The second stage of an orgasm in men. Contractions in the urethra and muscles at the base of the penis force the semen from the penis (ejaculation). (Ch. 4)

F

Fallopian (fal-lo′ pe-an) **tubes**   The passageways that eggs follow on their way to the uterus. (Ch. 2)

False labor   A set of temporary contractions of the uterus that resemble the start of labor. (Ch. 7)

False memory syndrome   False memories of childhood sexual abuse, often inadvertently planted by therapists. (Ch. 15)

Fatuous love   According to Sternberg, the emotion felt when a commitment is made on the basis of passion without the experience of intimacy. (Ch. 12)

Fear–tension–pain cycle   According to prepared childbirth advocates, the cycle of events that women experience during labor when they are not properly educated about labor and childbirth. (Ch. 7)

Fecundity (fe kun′ deh te)   The ability of a couple to conceive within a certain period of time. (Ch. 7)

Fellatio (fe-la′ she-o)   Oral stimulation of a man's genitals. (Ch. 11)

Female condom   See **condom.**

Female hypoactive sexual desire   "The persistent or recurrent deficiency (or absence) of sexual fantasies/thoughts, and/or desire for or receptivity to sexual activity, which causes personal distress" (Basson et al., 2000). (Ch. 13)

Female orgasmic disorder   A persistent or recurrent delay in, or absence of, orgasm following a normal sexual excitement phase and which causes personal distress. (Ch. 13)

Female sexual arousal disorder   "The persistent or recurrent inability to attain or maintain sufficient sexual excitement, causing personal distress, which may be expressed as lack of subjective excitement, or genital (lubrication/swelling) or other somatic responses" (Basson et al., 2000). (Ch. 13)

FemCap   A barrier contraceptive that fits over the cervix and prevents the passage of sperm into the uterus. (Ch. 6)

Fertility awareness methods   Methods of birth control that attempt to prevent conception by having a couple abstain from sexual intercourse during the woman's ovulation. (Ch. 6)

Fertility drugs   Drugs that improve the chance of conception in women who are infertile owing to hormone deficiencies. The drugs either stimulate the pituitary gland to secrete FSH and LH or stimulate the ovaries directly. (Ch. 7)

Fertilization   Impregnation; the fusion of a sperm with an ovum. (Ch. 7)

Fetal alcohol syndrome (FAS)   A condition common to infants born to alcoholic mothers, involving physical and nervous system abnormalities. (Ch. 7)

Fetal surgery   A surgical operation on the fetus while it is still in the uterus. (Ch. 7)

Fetishism (fet′ ish-ĭ-zum)   A condition in which sexual arousal occurs repeatedly when using or fantasizing about an inanimate object. (Ch. 14)

Fetus   The term given to the embryo after the 8th week of pregnancy. (Ch. 7)

Fibrocystic (fi″ bro-sis′ tik) **disease**   A benign overgrowth of fibrous tissue in the breast. (Ch. 2)

Fimbria (fim′ bre-ah)   The fingerlike processes at the ovarian end of the Fallopian tubes. (Ch. 2)

Follicle (fol′ lĭ-k′l)   A sac in the ovary containing an ovum and surrounding follicular cells. (Ch. 3)

Follicle-stimulating hormone (FSH)   A gonadotropin hormone released by the pituitary gland that stimulates the development of a follicle in a woman's ovary and the production of sperm in a man's testicles. (Ch. 3)

Follicular (proliferative) phase   The preovulatory phase of the menstrual cycle, lasting from about day 5 to day 13 in a 28-day cycle. (Ch. 3)

Foreskin   The loose skin of the penis that folds over the glans and that is sometimes cut away in a procedure known as circumcision. (Ch. 2)

Friendship   A relationship that includes (a) enjoyment of each other's company, (b) acceptance of one another, (c) mutual trust, (d) respect for one another, (e) mutual assistance when needed, (f) confiding in one another, (g) understanding, and (h) spontaneity. (Ch. 12)

Frotteurism (fro-tur′ izm)   A condition in which sexual arousal is achieved repeatedly by rubbing one's genitals against others in public places. (Ch. 14)

Fundus (fun′ dus)   The broad end of the uterus. (Ch. 2)

G

Galactorrhea (gah-lak″ to-re′ ah)   The spontaneous flow of milk. (Ch. 2)

Gamete intrafallopian transfer (GIFT)   A procedure for treating female infertility in which sperm and eggs are gathered and placed directly into a Fallopian tube. (Ch. 7)

Gang rape   Rape in which a victim is assaulted by more than one attacker. (Ch. 15)

Gay   A term generally used to refer to male homosexuals, although in some places it is used to refer to homosexuals of either sex. (Ch. 9)

Gender   The social construction of femininity and masculinity. (Ch. 8)

Gender constancy   The knowledge that one's sex is constant and will not change. This knowledge is usually acquired by age 6 or 7. (Ch. 8)

Gender dysphoria (dis-fo′ re-ah)   The feeling of being trapped in a body of the opposite sex. (Ch. 8)

Gender identity   One's subjective sense of being a man (or boy) or a woman (or girl). This sense is usually acquired by the age of 3. (Ch. 8)

Gender identity disorder (GID)   A disorder with the criteria: (a) behaviors that indicate identification with the opposite gender, and (b) behaviors that indicate discomfort with one's own anatomy and gender roles. (Ch. 8)

Gender role   A set of culturally specific norms concerning the expected behaviors and attitudes of men and women. (Ch. 8)

Gender schemas   A set of ideas about gender roles that children create from their interactions with their environment. (Ch. 8)

Gender-role stereotypes Oversimplified, preconceived beliefs about the gender roles of men and women. (Ch. 8)

Genital herpes Herpes infection in the genital region. It can be caused by herpes simplex virus types 1 or 2. (Ch. 5)

Genital (venereal) warts Warts in the genital and anal regions caused by human papillomaviruses (mainly types 6 and 11). The warts are cauliflowerlike growths. (Ch. 5)

Genitalia (jen″ ĭ-ta′ leah) The external reproductive organs of the man or woman. (Ch. 2)

Gigolo (jig′ ah-lo) A male prostitute who caters to women. (Ch. 16)

Gland An organ or specialized group of cells that separates substances from the blood and secretes them for use by, or elimination from, the body. (Ch. 3)

Glans (glanz) The rounded end of the penis or clitoris. (Ch. 2)

Global moralities Values that are supposed to apply to all people under all circumstances. (Ch. 10)

Gonadarche (go″ nad-ar′ ke) The maturation of the ovaries and testicles. (Ch. 10)

Gonadotropin (gon″ ah-do-tro′ pin) A hormone that has a stimulating effect on the ovaries or testicles. (Ch. 3)

Gonadotropin-releasing hormone (GnRH) A hormone released by the hypothalamus in the brain that causes the pituitary gland to release the hormones FSH and LH. (Ch. 3)

Gonococcus (gon″ o-kok′ us) Common name for the bacterium that causes gonorrhea. (Ch. 5)

Gonorrhea (gon″ o-re′ ah) A sexually transmitted infection caused by the *Neisseria gonorrhoeae* bacterium (often referred to as "the gonococcus"), which lives on mucous membranes. (Ch. 5)

Graafian (graf′ e-an) **follicle** A mature follicle. (Ch. 7)

Grafenberg (graf′ en-burg) **(G) spot** A small, sensitive area on the front wall of the vagina found in about 10% of women. (Ch. 2, 4)

Granuloma inguinale (gran″ u-lo′ mah ing′ gwĭ-nah le) A rare (in the United States) sexually transmitted infection that is characterized by ulceration of tissue. (Ch. 5)

Growing apart Having fewer common interests over time. (Ch. 12)

Growing together Maintaining common interests over time. (Ch. 12)

G-spot See **Grafenberg (G) spot.**

Gumma (gum′ ah) A soft, gummy tumor that appears in late (tertiary) syphilis. (Ch. 5)

Gynecomastia (jin″ ĕ-ko-mas′ te-ah) Excessive development of the male breasts. (Ch. 10)

H

Habituation Responding less positively to a stimulus with repeated exposure to it. (Ch. 12)

HCG See **human chorionic gonadotropin (HCG).**

Hepatitis (hep″ ah-ti′ tis) **A, B, and C** Liver infections caused by viruses. Type A is spread by direct or indirect contact with contaminated feces. Type B is transmitted by infected blood or body fluids, with about 50% of the cases contracted during sex. Type C is spread mainly by contaminated blood, but may possibly be spread during sexual intercourse in some cases. (Ch. 5)

Hermaphrodite (her-maf′ ro-dīt″) A person with both male and female reproductive systems as a result of failure of the

primitive gonads to differentiate properly during embryonic development. (Ch. 8)

Herpes (her′ pez) Painful blisters usually found on the mouth (fever blisters; cold sores) or genitals that are caused by a virus (herpes simplex virus type 1 or 2). Genital herpes is almost always contracted by intimate sexual activity, but oral herpes may be spread by casual kissing. (Ch. 5)

Heterosexual An individual with a sexual orientation primarily to members of the opposite sex. (Ch. 9)

HIV See **human immunodeficiency virus (HIV).**

Homophobia An irrational fear of homosexual individuals and homosexuality. (Ch. 9)

Homosexual An individual with a sexual orientation primarily to members of the same sex. (Ch. 9)

Hooking up Sexual relations with a nonromantic partner (usually a friend). (Ch. 10)

Hormones Chemical substances that are secreted by ductless glands into the bloodstream. They are carried in the blood to other parts of the body, where they exert their effects on other glands or target organs. (Ch. 3)

Hot flashes A warm feeling over the upper body experienced by menopausal women as a result of increased levels of FSH and LH. (Ch. 10)

HPV See **human papillomaviruses (HPV).**

Human chorionic (ko″ re-on′ ik) **gonadotropin (HCG)** A hormone secreted by the chorion that stimulates the ovaries during pregnancy. (Ch. 3, 7)

Human immunodeficiency virus (HIV) A virus that kills CD4+ cells, eventually resulting in AIDS. (Ch. 5)

Human papillomaviruses (pap″ ĭ-lo′ mah) **(HPV)** Viruses that cause abnormal growths in epithelial cells. There are over 100 types. A few (types 6 and 11) cause genital warts, while others (types 16, 18, 31, 33, and 45) can lead to cancer of the cervix. (Ch. 5)

Hustler A male prostitute who caters to men. (Ch. 16)

Hymen (hi′ men) The thin membrane that partially covers the vaginal opening in many sexually inexperienced women. Its presence or absence, however, is really a poor indicator of prior sexual experience. (Ch. 2)

Hypersexuality A term reserved for people who engage in sex compulsively, with little or no emotional satisfaction. Sometimes called *sexual addiction*. (Ch. 13)

Hypoactive sexual desire A sexual problem characterized by a persisting and pervasive absence of sexual fantasies and desire. See **female hypoactive sexual desire.** (Ch. 13)

Hypothalamus (hi″ po-thal′ah-mus) A part of the brain that regulates the release of hormones from the pituitary gland. (Ch. 3)

Hypoxyphilia Depriving oneself of oxygen during masturbation-induced orgasm. (Ch. 14)

Hysterectomy (his″ tĕ-rek′ to-me) Surgical removal of the uterus. (Ch. 2)

I

Identification Two meanings: (1) The adoption of the sex roles of the same-sex parent by a child (Ch. 8), and (2) in advertising, to identify or relate to a product. (Ch. 1, 8)

"I" language Communicating your desires to another person by beginning sentences with "I," followed by your feelings, desires, or thoughts. (Ch. 13)

Imitation Following the behaviors of someone taken as one's model. (Ch. 8)

Immune system The bodily mechanisms involved in the production of antibodies in response to bacteria, viruses, and cancerous cells. (Ch. 5)

Implanon A hormone implant with a single progestin-releasing rod that is effective for 3 years. (Ch. 6)

Implantation The process by which the blastocyst attaches itself to the wall of the uterus. (Ch. 7)

Impotence A common term for erectile disorders in men, but generally not used by therapists because it has negative connotations about a man's masculinity. (Ch. 13)

Incest Sexual contact between two closely related persons. (Ch. 15)

Incontinence The inability to control one's bladder. (Ch. 4)

Infatuated love According to Sternberg, the emotion felt when there is passion in the absence of intimacy and commitment. (Ch. 12)

Infertility The inability of a couple to conceive. (Ch. 7)

Infibulation See **clitoridectomy.**

Inhibin (in-hib′ in) A hormone produced by the testicles and ovaries that inhibits release of follicle-stimulating hormone from the pituitary gland. (Ch. 3)

Inhibited ejaculation See **male orgasmic disorder.**

Inhibited female orgasm See **female orgasmic disorder.**

Instrumental A personality characteristic; a cognitive focus on "getting the job done." (Ch. 8)

Intact dilation and evacuation (intact D & E) An abortion procedure performed in very-late-term pregnancies in which the fetus' head is partially delivered and its brain is then removed by suction. Also called *dilation and extraction (D & X).* (Ch. 6)

Intercourse The word means communication. (Ch. 13)

Intersexual Individuals with a combination of male and female anatomical features, or in which chromosomal sex is inconsistent with anatomical sex. (Ch. 8)

Intimacy Those feelings in a relationship that promote closeness or bondedness and the experience of warmth. (Ch. 12)

Intracytoplasmic sperm injection (ICSI) A procedure used to treat men who have a low sperm count; injection of a single sperm directly into an egg. (Ch. 7)

Intrauterine device (IUD) A birth control device, usually made of plastic with either a copper or progesterone coating, that is placed in the uterus to prevent conception and implantation. (Ch. 6)

Introitus (in-tro′ ĭ-tus) The entrance to the vagina. (Ch. 2)

In vitro fertilization A process in which a mature ovum is surgically removed from a woman's ovary, placed in a medium with sperm until fertilization occurs, and then placed in the woman's uterus. This is usually done in women who cannot conceive because of blocked Fallopian tubes. (Ch. 7)

IUD See **intrauterine device (IUD).**

J

Jadelle A hormone implant with two progestin-releasing rods that is effective for 5 years. (Ch. 6)

Jealousy An emotional state that is aroused by a perceived threat to a valued relationship or position. (Ch. 12)

John A street term for a man who pays for sex with a prostitute; johns are also called *tricks* or *scores.* (Ch. 16)

K

Kaposi's sarcoma (kap′-o-sez sar-ko′mah) A cancer of the capillary system that often occurs in people with AIDS. (Ch. 5)

Kegel exercises Exercises that are designed to strengthen the pubococcygeus muscle that surrounds the bladder and vagina. (Ch. 2)

Klinefelter's syndrome A condition in men in which there is one or more extra X chromosomes. (Ch. 8)

Klismaphilia (kliz″ mah-fil′ e-ah) A condition in which sexual arousal is achieved repeatedly by being given an enema. (Ch. 14)

L

Labia majora (la′ be-ah ma-jo′ rah) Two elongated folds of skin extending from the mons to the perineum in women. Its outer surfaces become covered with pubic hair during puberty. (Ch. 2)

Labia minora (la′be-ah mi-no′rah) Two hairless elongated folds of skin located between the labia majora in women. They meet above the clitoris to form the clitoral hood. (Ch. 2)

Lactational amenorrhea method (breast-feeding) In reference to contraception, the sucking response by a baby on the mother's nipple inhibits release of follicle-stimulating hormone, thus preventing ovulation. (Ch. 6)

Lamaze method A method of prepared childbirth; named after its founder, Fernand Lamaze. (Ch. 7)

Lanugo (lah-nu′ go) Light hair that covers a newborn baby. (Ch. 7)

Laparoscopy (lap″ ah-ros′ko-pe) A technique that involves inserting a slender, tubelike instrument (laparoscope) into a woman's abdomen to examine (via fiberoptics) her reproductive organs or a fetus. The procedure is often used to perform female sterilizations. (Ch. 6, 7)

Leboyer method A method of prepared childbirth that advocates gentle birth; named after its founder, Frederick Leboyer. (Ch. 7)

Lesbian (lez′ be-an) A female homosexual. (Ch. 9)

Leydig (li′ dig), **interstitial cells of** The cells in the testicles that produce male hormones. (Ch. 2)

Lightening Rotation of the fetus prior to childbirth so that its head is downward, resulting in decreased pressure on the mother's abdomen. (Ch. 7)

Liking According to Sternberg, the emotion felt when there is intimacy without passion or commitment. (Ch. 12)

Love Many possible definitions, and, according to researchers, many different types. For example, see **agape, companionate love, eros, ludus, mania, pragma,** and **storge.** (Ch. 12)

Ludus A self-centered type of love. Ludic lovers avoid commitment and treat love as a game, often viewing the chase as more pleasurable than the prize. (Ch. 12)

Lumpectomy A surgical procedure in which only a breast tumor and a small bit of surrounding tissue are removed. (Ch. 2)

Luteal (lu′ te-al) **(secretory) phase** The postovulatory phase of the menstrual cycle, lasting from about day 15 to day 28 in a 28-day cycle. (Ch. 3)

Luteinizing (lu′ te-in″ i-zing) **hormone (LH)** A gonadotropin hormone released by the pituitary gland that triggers ovulation in women and stimulates the production of male hormones in men. (Ch. 3)

Lymphogranuloma venereum (lim″ fo-gran″ u-lo′ mah ve-ne′ reum) (**LGV**)   A sexually transmitted infection common in tropical countries that is caused by chlamydia. If left untreated, it causes swelling of the inguinal lymph nodes, penis, labia, or clitoris. (Ch. 5)

M

Male orgasmic disorder   A condition in which a man has difficulty reaching orgasm and ejaculating in a woman's vagina. (Ch. 13)

Male rape   Rape in which the victim is a man. (Ch. 15)

Mammary glands   Milk-producing glands of the breast. (Ch. 2)

Mammogram   Low-radiation X-rays used to detect breast tumors. (Ch. 2)

Mania   A type of love characterized by an intense emotional dependency on the attention and affection of one's lover. (Ch. 12)

Marital rape   Rape of a wife by her husband. (Ch. 15)

Masochism (mas′ o-kiz′m)   A condition in which individuals obtain sexual pleasure primarily from having pain and/or humiliation inflicted on them. (Ch. 14)

Mastectomy (mas-tek′ to-me)   Surgical removal of a breast. (Ch. 2)

Masturbation   Self-stimulation of one's genitals. (Ch. 11)

Medical abortion   Abortion induced by taking a pill (see **RU 486**). (Ch. 6)

Medical history   One of the first steps used by most sex therapists. A complete medical history or exam is important because many sexual problems have an organic basis. (Ch. 13)

Medical model   Attributing sexual problems to organic causes and treating them with medical techniques. (Ch. 13)

Menarche (me˘-nar′ ke)   The term for a girl's first menstrual period. (Ch. 3, 10)

Menopause (men′ o-pawz)   The term for a woman's last menstrual period. (Ch. 3, 10)

Menorrhagia   Heavy bleeding during menstruation. (Ch. 3)

Menstrual cycle   The monthly cycle of hormonal events in a woman that leads to ovulation and menstruation. (Ch. 3)

Menstrual taboos   Incorrect negative attitudes about menstruating women. (Ch. 3)

Menstruation (men″ stroo-a′ shun)   The monthly discharge of endometrial tissue, blood, and other secretions from the uterus that occurs when an egg is not fertilized. (Ch. 3)

Mesoderm   The layer of the embryo that forms the muscles, skeleton, and blood vessels. (Ch. 7)

Microbicide   A cream or gel that is applied intravaginally or intrarectally before sex in order to kill, block, or inactivate bacteria and viruses that cause sexually transmitted infections. (Ch. 6)

Microstructural theory   See **sociocultural theory**. (Ch. 8)

Midwife   See **nurse-midwife**.

Miscarriage   A spontaneous abortion. (Ch. 7)

Missionary position   A face-to-face position of sexual intercourse in which the woman lies on her back and the man lies on top with his legs between hers. It was called this because Christian missionaries instructed people that other positions were unnatural. (Ch. 1, 11)

Mittelschmerz (mit′ el-shma-rts)   Abdominal pain at the time of ovulation. (Ch. 3)

Molluscum contagiosum (mo-lus′ kum con-ta-gio′ sum)   A sexually transmitted virus with symptoms that look like small pimples filled with kernels of corn. (Ch. 5)

Moniliasis (mon-ĭ-lī′ ah-sis)   Sometimes called *candidiasis*. A type of vaginitis caused by the overgrowth of a microorganism (*Candida albicans*) that is normally found in the vagina. Moniliasis is a fungus or yeast infection and usually is a sexually related, rather than a sexually transmitted, infection. (Ch. 5)

Mons veneris (monz ven′ eris)   The soft layer of fatty tissue that overlays the pubic bone in women. It becomes covered with pubic hair during puberty. (Ch. 2)

Morning sickness   A symptom of early pregnancy involving nausea. (Ch. 7)

Morula (mor′ u-lah)   The collection of cells formed when the zygote begins rapid cell division. (Ch. 7)

Mullerian duct–inhibiting substance   A chemical secreted by the testicles during embryonic development that causes the Mullerian ducts to shrink and disappear. (Ch. 8)

Mullerian (mil-e′ re-an) **duct system**   A primitive duct system found in embryos, which, if allowed to develop, becomes the female reproductive system. (Ch. 8)

Multiple orgasms   Having two or more successive orgasms without falling below the plateau level of physiological arousal. (Ch. 4)

Mycoplasma genitalium   A bacterium responsible for many cases of nongonococcal urethritis. (Ch. 5)

Mysophilia (mi″ so-fil′ e-ah)   A condition in which sexual arousal is caused repeatedly by filth or filthy surroundings. (Ch. 14)

N

Necking   Erotic physical contact above the waist (kissing, touching breasts). (Ch. 10)

Necrophilia (nek″ ro-fil′ e-ah)   Sexual arousal to a dead body. (Ch. 14)

Nipple   The protuberance on the breast that in women contains the outlets for the milk ducts. It consists of smooth muscle fibers. (Ch. 2)

Nocturnal emission   An ejaculation that occurs during sleep in teenaged boys and men; a "wet dream." (Ch. 10)

Nocturnal orgasm   An orgasm that occurs during sleep (sometimes called "*wet dreams*" in men). (Ch. 10)

Noncoital sexual pain disorder   Recurrent or persistent genital pain caused by sexual stimulation other than intercourse. (Ch. 13)

Nongonococcal (nonspecific) urethritis (**NGU**)   Any inflammation of the urethra that is not caused by the *Neisseria gonorrhoeae* (gonococcus) bacterium. (Ch. 5)

Nonlove   According to Sternberg, the absence of all three components of love: intimacy, passion, and commitment. (Ch. 12)

Nonoxynol-9   The active chemical in most spermicides. (Ch. 6)

Nonverbal communication   Communicating with another person without using words (such as by eye contact, facial expressions, and touch). (Ch. 13)

Nurse-midwife   A registered nurse, trained in obstetrical techniques, who delivers babies, often at the expectant mother's home. (Ch. 7)

NuvaRing   A flexible ring containing the same hormones as the combination birth control pill that is inserted into the vagina and is effective for 3 weeks. (Ch. 6)

O

Obscenity In legal terminology, the classification of material that by contemporary community standards depicts patently offensive sexual conduct, lacks serious value, and appeals to prurient interests. (Ch. 16)

Observer bias The prejudicing of observations and conclusions by the observer's own belief system. (Ch. 1)

Open marriage A marital relationship in which the couple agrees that it is permissible to have sexual relations outside of the marriage. (Ch. 10)

Open-ended questions Questions asked in a manner that place no limitations on your partner's response. (Ch. 13)

Operant conditioning A type of learning in which an individual's behavior is modified by the consequences of the behavior. (Ch. 8)

Opportunistic diseases (infections) A variety of diseases that occur in individuals with a very weakened immune system, as in AIDS. (Ch. 5)

Opportunistic rapists Rapists motivated by a desire for sex who rape impulsively when there is an opportunity. (Ch. 15)

Oral contraceptive The birth control pill. (Ch. 6)

Oral herpes A herpes infection in or around the mouth. It can be caused by herpes simplex virus types 1 or 2. (Ch. 5)

Orchiectomy (or″ ke-ek′ to-me) Removal of one or both testicles. (Ch. 3)

Orgasm The brief but intense sensations (focused largely in the genitals but really a whole body response) experienced during sexual arousal. During orgasm, rhythmic muscular contractions occur in certain tissues in both the man and woman. The third phase of the sexual response cycle proposed by Masters and Johnson. (Ch. 4)

Orgasmic disorder See **male orgasmic disorder, female orgasmic disorder.**

Orgasmic platform The engorgement and consequent swelling of the outer third of the vagina during the plateau stage, causing the vaginal opening to narrow by 30% to 50%. (Ch. 4)

OrthoEvra A contraceptive patch (containing the same hormones as the combination birth control pill) that applies to the skin and is effective for 1 week. (Ch. 6)

Os The opening of the cervix. (Ch. 2)

Ovary (o′ vah-re) The female gonad in which ova are produced. (Ch. 2)

Ovulation (o″ vu-la′ shun) The expulsion of an egg from one of the ovaries. (Ch. 3)

Ovum An egg; the female reproductive cell (plural, ova). (Ch. 2, 7)

Oxytocin (ok″ se-to′ sin) A pituitary hormone associated with milk release, labor and orgasmic contractions, and erotic attraction and touch. (Ch. 3, 7)

P

Pap smear A test for cancer of the cervix in women; named for Dr. Papanicolaou, who developed it. (Ch. 2)

Paraphilias (par″ ah-fil′ e-ahs) General term for a group of sexual disorders in which repeatedly engaging in or fantasizing about unusual behaviors is a preferred way of obtaining sexual arousal and gratification. (Ch. 14)

Paraphrase A rewording of the meaning expressed by someone else. (Ch. 13)

Partialism Strong and recurrent sexual arousal to a specific part of the body. (Ch. 14)

Passion The drive leading to physical attraction, sexual relations, and romance. (Ch. 12)

Passionate love "A state of intense longing for union with another...A state of profound physiological arousal" (Hatfield, 1988). (Ch. 12)

Patch See **OrthoEvra.** (Ch. 6)

Pederasty (pehd′ ah ras″ te) A same-sex sexual behavior between adult men and boys. (Ch. 9)

Pedophilia (pe″ do-fil′ e-ah) A condition in which sexual arousal is achieved primarily and repeatedly through sexual activity with children who have not reached puberty. (Ch. 14, 15)

Peer pressure Expectations by one's peer group about how one is supposed to behave. (Ch. 10)

Pelvic exam A necessary part of women's health care to check for cervical and vaginal infections; it includes a Pap smear. (Ch. 2)

Pelvic inflammatory disease (PID) A bacterially caused inflammation of a woman's reproductive tract, particularly the Fallopian tubes, that can result in sterility. The most common (though not the only) cause is untreated gonorrhea and/or chlamydia. (Ch. 5)

Penis (pe′ nis) The male organ for sexual intercourse and the passageway for sperm and urine. (Ch. 2)

Perfect-use pregnancy rate For a particular birth control technique, the percentage of pregnancies during the first year of use by couples who use the technique properly and consistently. See also **typical-use pregnancy rate.** (Ch. 6)

Performance anxiety A fear of failure during sexual relations that can lead to erectile disorder in men and inhibited orgasm in women. (Ch. 13)

Perineum (per″ ĭ-ne′ um) Technically, the entire pelvic floor, but more commonly used to refer to the hairless bit of skin between the anus and either the vaginal opening (in women) or the scrotum (in men). (Ch. 2)

Persistent sexual arousal syndrome Persistent genital arousal without subjective feelings of desire. (Ch. 13)

Personally immature pedophile A pedophile who is attracted to children because he never developed the social skills necessary to initiate and maintain a sexual relationship with an adult. (Ch. 15)

Petting Noncoital sexual contact below the waist. (Ch. 10)

Pheromones (fer′ ah monz) Chemical substances secreted externally by animals that convey information to, and produce specific responses in, members of the same species. (Ch. 3)

Phimosis (fi-mo′ sis) A condition in uncircumcised men in which the foreskin of the penis is too tight, causing pain during erection. (Ch. 13)

PID See **pelvic inflammatory disease (PID).**

Pill See **oral contraceptive.**

Pinworms Small worms (*Enterobius vermicularis*) that live in the large intestine and are generally transmitted through nonsexual contact with the worms' eggs, but which can be transmitted sexually by manual or oral contact with the anus of an infected person. (Ch. 5)

Pituitary (pĭ-tu′ ĭ-tar″ e) **gland** A gland located at the base of the brain that secretes eight hormones, including follicle-stimulating hormone and luteinizing hormone. (Ch. 3)

Placenta (plah-sen′ tah)   An organ that serves as a connection or interface between the fetus' systems and those of the mother. (Ch. 7)

Placenta previa   A condition in which the placenta blocks the cervical opening. (Ch. 7)

Plateau   The second phase of the sexual response cycle proposed by Masters and Johnson. Physiologically, it represents a high state of arousal. (Ch. 4)

PLISSIT model   An acronym for the four levels of treatment in sexual therapy: permission, limited information, specific suggestions, and intensive therapy. (Ch. 13)

PMS   See **premenstrual syndrome (PMS)**.

Polyandry (pahl′ e an″ dre)   The practice of allowing women to have more than one husband at the same time. (Ch. 10, 12)

Polygamy (puh lig′ uh me)   The practice of allowing men or women to have more than one mate at the same time. (Ch. 10)

Polygyny (puh lij′ uh ne)   The practice of allowing men to have two or more wives at the same time. (Ch. 10, 12)

Polyincestuous family   A family in which there are both multiple incestuous abusers and multiple victims, across generations and within the same generation. (Ch. 15)

Population   The complete set of observations about which a researcher wishes to draw conclusions. (Ch. 1)

Pornography   Literature or art with a sexual theme that is designed to cause arousal and excitement and is considered to be obscene. (Ch. 16)

Positive reinforcement   A stimulus that follows a response and increases the probability of the response occurring again. (Ch. 13)

Postpartum blues   A mild, transient emotional letdown experienced by a majority of women after giving birth. (Ch. 7)

Postpartum depression   A deep depression experienced by about 10% of women in the first few months after giving birth. (Ch. 7)

Postpartum psychosis   A psychotic state experienced by about 1 in 1,000 women after giving birth. (Ch. 7)

Post-rape posttraumatic stress disorder   A group of clinical symptoms displayed by many victims of rape; previously called *rape trauma syndrome*. It includes an acute phase (involving initial physical and psychological recovery from the attack) and long-term psychological reorganization (involving attempts to deal with the long-term effects of the attack and to prevent a future rape). (Ch. 15)

Power rapists   Rapists who commit their attacks in order to overcome personal feelings of insecurity and inadequacy. Their rapes give them a sense of mastery and control. (Ch. 15)

Pragma   A rational or practical type of love. Pragmatic lovers actively look for a "good match." (Ch. 12)

Precocious puberty   A condition in which puberty begins before the age of 8 in girls and 9 in boys. (Ch. 10)

Preeclampsia (pre″ e-klamp′ se-ah)   The early stage of toxemia of pregnancy, characterized by high blood pressure, weight gain, and swollen joints. (Ch. 7)

Preference molesters (pedophiles)   Child molesters who have a primary sexual orientation to children and who are relatively uninterested in adult partners. (Ch. 15)

Premature ejaculation   A recurrent and persistent absence of reasonable voluntary control of ejaculation. (Ch. 13)

Premenstrual dysphoric disorder (PMDD)   A severe form of PMS that markedly interferes with social relations, work, or education. (Ch. 3)

Premenstrual syndrome (PMS)   A group of physical and/or emotional changes that many women experience in the last 3 to 14 days before the start of a menstrual period. (Ch. 3)

Prenatal examination   A health checkup by a physician during pregnancy. (Ch. 7)

Prepared childbirth   Courses or techniques that prepare women for labor and childbirth, with the goal of making it a positive experience. (Ch. 7)

Preterm infant   An infant born weighing less than 51/2 pounds and before week 37 of pregnancy. (Ch. 7)

Priapism (pri′ ah-piz′m)   A condition in which the penis remains erect for a prolonged period of time, sometimes days. (Ch. 13)

Primary follicle   An immature ovum enclosed by a single layer of cells. (Ch. 2, 7)

Primary HIV infection   The first few weeks of HIV infection, during which HIV reaches enormous levels in the blood and 50% to 75% of infected individuals experience flulike symptoms. (Ch. 5)

Primary sexual problem   A sexual problem that has existed throughout an individual's life. (Ch. 13)

Procreation   The act of producing offspring. (Ch. 1)

Progesterone (pro-jes′ te˘-ron)   A hormone that is produced in large amounts by the ovaries after ovulation. It prepares the endometrium of the uterus to nourish a fertilized egg. (Ch. 3)

Progestin (pro-jes′ tin)   A synthetic form of progesterone. (Ch. 6)

Progestin-only pill   An oral contraceptive that contains only progestins. (Ch. 6)

Prolactin (pro-lak′ tin)   A hormone released from the pituitary gland that stimulates milk production in the breasts. (Ch. 3, 7)

Proliferative phase   See **follicular (proliferative) phase**.

Prophylactic   See **condom**.

Prostaglandins (pros″ tah-glan′ dinz)   Chemical substances in the body that cause uterine contractions. (Ch. 3)

Prostate (pros′ ta–t) **gland**   A gland in men that surrounds the origins of the urethra and neck of the bladder and contributes many substances to the seminal fluid. (Ch. 2, 5)

Prostatitis (pros″ tah-ti′ tis)   Inflammation of the prostate gland. (Ch. 5)

Prostitution   The exchange of sex for money. The feature that distinguishes a prostitute from other people who engage in illicit sexual intercourse is the indiscrimination with which she (or he) offers herself or himself to others for hire. (Ch. 16)

Pseudohermaphroditism (su″ do-her-maf′ ro-di-tiz′m′)   A condition in which a person is born with ambiguous genitalia as a result of a hormonal abnormality. See also **adrenogenital syndrome** and **androgen insensitivity syndrome**. (Ch. 8)

Psychosexual therapy   Therapy that attempts to provide insight into the historical cause of a client's problem. (Ch. 13)

Puberty (pu′ ber-te)   The time in life when an individual first shows sexual attraction and becomes capable of reproduction. (Ch. 10)

Pubic (pu′ bik) **hair**   Hair that grows in the genital region starting at puberty; a secondary sex characteristic. (Ch. 2)

Pubic (pu′ bik) **lice**   An infestation of the parasite *Phthirus pubis*, which attach themselves to pubic hair and feed on blood. Also known as "crabs." (Ch. 5)

Pubococcygeus (pu″ bo-kok-sij′ e-us) **muscle** The major muscle in the pelvic region. In women, voluntary control over this muscle (to help prevent urinary incontinence or to enhance physical sensations during intercourse) is gained through Kegel exercises. (Ch. 2)

Q

Quickening The first time a pregnant woman experiences movement of the fetus, usually in the 5th month. (Ch. 7)

R

Random sample A sample in which observations are drawn so that all other possible samples of the same size have an equal chance of being selected. (Ch. 1)

Rape "Nonconsensual oral, anal, or vaginal penetration, obtained by force, by threat of bodily harm, or when the victim is incapable of giving consent" (Koss, 1993). (Ch. 15)

Rape myths Widespread mistaken beliefs about rape. (Ch. 15)

Rape-shield laws Laws that make the prosecution of rapists easier and that also prevent the victims from feeling as if they are on trial. (Ch. 15)

Rape trauma syndrome Older term for reactions of a rape victim. See **post-rape posttraumatic stress disorder.** (Ch. 15)

Refractory period In men, the period of time after an orgasm in which their physiological responses fall below the plateau level, thus making it impossible for them to have another orgasm (until the responses build back up to plateau). (Ch. 4)

Regressive pedophile A pedophile with a past history of normal adult sexual relations. (Ch. 15)

Resolution The fourth and final phase of the sexual response cycle proposed by Masters and Johnson. It refers to a return to the unaroused state. (Ch. 4)

Respiratory distress syndrome An illness common in premature infants; caused by insufficient levels of surfactin. (Ch. 7)

Retarded ejaculation See **male orgasmic disorder.**

Retrograde ejaculation An abnormal condition experienced by some men during orgasm in which the semen is forced into the bladder instead of out of the body. (Ch. 4)

Rh factor A protein in the blood of most individuals. If a mother does not have it and the fetus she carries does, she can develop antibodies against the Rh factor. This is called an *Rh incompatibility problem.* (Ch. 7)

Rhythm method See **fertility awareness methods.**

Romantic love The idealization of another; the combination of passion and liking (intimacy). (Ch. 12)

Root (of penis) The part of the penis consisting of the crura and the bulb. (Ch. 2)

RU 486 A pill that chemically induces an abortion by blocking progesterone. (Ch. 6)

S

Sadism (sad′ iz'm) A condition in which individuals repeatedly and intentionally inflict pain on others in order to achieve sexual arousal. (Ch. 14)

Sadistic rapists Rapists who are aroused by physical force and who derive pleasure by harming their victims. (Ch. 15)

Sadomasochism (S&M) A term used to indicate the linkage of sadism with masochism. (Ch. 14)

Safer sex Sexual behaviors involving a low risk of contracting a sexually transmitted infection. These include consistent use of condoms and/or abstaining from sex until one enters a long-term monogamous relationship. (Ch. 5)

Sample A subset of a population of subjects. (Ch. 1)

Scabies (ska′ bez) A contagious infestation of parasitic mites (*Sarcoptes scabiei*) that burrow under the skin to lay their eggs. (Ch. 5)

Schemas See **gender schemas.**

Scrotum (skro′ tum) The pouch beneath the penis that contains the testicles. (Ch. 2)

Secondary sex characteristics Bodily changes that occur during puberty and differentiate men and women. (Ch. 10)

Secondary sexual problem A sexual problem occurring in an individual who has not had the problem in past sexual relations. (Ch. 13)

Second stage of labor The stage of labor that begins when the cervix is fully dilated and the fetus begins moving through the birth canal. It ends with birth. (Ch. 7)

Secretory phase See **luteal (secretory) phase.**

Secure A style of attachment in which individuals do not fear abandonment and find it easy to get close to others. (Ch. 12)

Self-awareness In sexual therapy, getting in touch with one's own physical responses. (Ch. 13)

Self-disclosure Revealing one's thoughts, feelings, and emotions to another. (Ch. 12, 13)

Self-esteem The feeling one has about oneself. (Ch. 12)

Semen (se′ men) The fluid expelled from a man's penis during orgasm, consisting of sperm and fluids from the prostate gland and seminal vesicles. (Ch. 2, 4)

Seminal vesicles (sem″ ĭ-nal ves′ ĭ-k'lz) Two structures in a man that contribute many substances to the seminal fluid. (Ch. 2)

Seminiferous (se″ mĭ-nif′ er-us) **tubules** The tubules in the testicles that produce sperm. (Ch. 2)

Sensate focus exercises Exercises designed to reduce anxiety and teach mutual pleasuring through nongenital touching in nondemanding situations. (Ch. 13)

Sensuality The state of being sensual. It encompasses all of our senses and who we are as a total person. (Ch. 2)

Serial monogamy The practice of having a series of monogamous sexual relationships. (Ch. 5, 10)

Sertoli (ser-to′ le-) **cells** Cells in the testicles that produce the hormone inhibin. (Ch. 2, 3)

Sex ("had sex") Many people limit this term to vaginal intercourse. In this text, unless otherwise specified, it refers to "any mutually voluntary activity with another person that involves genital contact and sexual excitement even if intercourse or orgasm did not occur" (Laumann et al., 1994). (Ch. 1)

Sex roles Behaviors that are associated with being stereotypically masculine or feminine. (Ch. 8)

Sex-tension flush The rash that appears on the skin (due to vasocongestion) in 50% to 75% of all women and 25% of all men during the plateau phase of the sexual response cycle. (Ch. 4)

Sexual addiction See **hypersexuality.**

Sexual aversion disorder An extreme form of hypoactive sexual desire in which an individual's avoidance of sex becomes phobic. (Ch. 13)

Sexual coercion The act of forcing another person into unwanted sexual activity by physical or verbal coercion (restraint or constraint). (Ch. 15)

Sexual deviance "The inappropriate or flawed performance of a conventionally understood sexual practice" (Simon, 1994). (Ch. 14)

Sexual harassment Unwelcome sexual advances that persist after the recipient has indicated that they are unwanted. See text for an expanded definition. (Ch. 15)

Sexual identity development The process of disclosing one's homosexuality or bisexuality. (Ch. 9)

Sexuality All of the sexual attitudes, feelings, and behaviors associated with being human. The term does not refer specifically to a person's capacity for erotic response or to sexual acts, but rather to a dimension of one's personality. (Ch. 1, 4)

Sexual learning Knowledge about sex that is received (usually informally) from family, friends, the media, and society in general. (Ch. 10)

Sexually healthy person Someone who feels positively about his or her sexuality and who feels free to choose whether to try a variety of sexual behaviors. (Ch. 11)

Sexually related diseases Diseases of the reproductive system or genitals that are not contracted through sexual activity. Often involve overgrowths of bacteria, yeasts, viruses, or fungal organisms that are found naturally in sexual and reproductive organs. (Ch. 5)

Sexually transmitted infections (STIs) Infections that can be, but are not necessarily always, transmitted by sexual contact. (Ch. 5)

Sexual orientation A distinct preference for sexual partners of a particular sex in the presence of clear alternatives. (Ch. 9)

Sexual perversion A problem of sexual desire, "not only in the sense that it appears to violate the sexual practices of a time and place, but also because it constitutes a violation of common understandings that render current sexual practice plausible" (Simon, 1994). (Ch. 14)

Sexual prejudice Socially reinforced negative attitudes toward homosexuals, homosexual communities, and homosexual behaviors. (Ch. 9)

Sexual response cycle The physiological responses that occur during sexual arousal, which many therapists and researchers have arbitrarily divided into different phases. (Ch. 4)

Sexual revolution A period in U.S. history, beginning about 1960, of increased sexual permissiveness. (Ch. 1)

Sexual variant Unusual behaviors that are engaged in for variety and not as one's preferred manner of becoming sexually aroused. (Ch. 14)

Sex worker A person who exchanges sexual activity for money. (Ch. 16)

Shaft The long body of the penis or clitoris. (Ch. 2)

Shigellosis (she″ gel-lo′ sis) An infection that can be contracted during sexual activity by exposure to feces containing the *Shigella* bacterium. (Ch. 5)

Situational ethics Values or ethics that emphasize the proper thing to do in particular situations. (Ch. 10)

Situational molesters Child molesters who have a primary sexual orientation to adults. They have sex with children impulsively and regard their behavior as abnormal. (Ch. 15)

Situational sexual problem A sexual problem that occurs only in specific situations. (Ch. 13)

Skene's (skenz) **glands** Glands located in the urethras of some women that are thought to develop from the same embryonic tissue as the man's prostate, and that may be the source of a fluid emitted by some women during orgasm. (Ch. 4)

Smegma (smeg′ mah) The cheesy secretion of sebaceous glands that can cause the clitoris to stick to the clitoral hood or the foreskin of the penis to stick to the glans. (Ch. 2)

Socialization The process of internalizing society's beliefs; the manner in which a society shapes individual behaviors and expectations of behaviors. (Ch. 1, 8)

Socializing agent The social influences (e.g., parents, peers, the media) that shape behaviors. (Ch. 1)

Sociocultural (microstructural) theory States that the psychological differences between men and women are a social construction. (Ch. 8)

Sodomy (sod′ o-me) **laws** Laws that prohibit oral and/or anal sex. (Ch. 11)

Spectatoring Observing and evaluating one's own sexual responses. This generally causes distraction, with subsequent erectile and/or orgasm problems. (Ch. 13)

Sperm The germ cell of a man. (Ch. 2, 7)

Spermatic (sper-mat′ ik) **cord** The cord that suspends a testicle in the scrotum. (Ch. 2)

Spermicides Chemicals that kill sperm. In most products, the chemical is nonoxynol-9. (Ch. 6)

Stalking Repeated and unwanted pursuit and invasion of one's sense of physical or symbolic privacy by another person. (Ch. 12, 15)

Standard Days Method A fertility awareness method of birth control for women who typically have menstrual cycles of 26 to 32 days. (Ch. 6)

Start-up stage of labor The stage of labor that begins with uterine contractions pushing the fetus downward toward the cervix and ends when the cervix is fully dilated. (Ch. 7)

Statistically normal A range of behaviors or values that encompasses a large number of individuals. (Ch. 11)

Statutory rape Sexual intercourse by an adult with a (consenting) partner who is not yet of the legal "age of consent." Sometimes called "carnal knowledge of a juvenile." (Ch. 15)

Sterilization A general term for surgical techniques that render an individual infertile. (Ch. 6)

Storge (stor′ ga) An affectionate type of love that grows from friendship. (Ch. 12)

Straight A term used by homosexuals for a heterosexual. (Ch. 9)

Stranger rape Rape committed by someone who is not known by the victim. (Ch. 15)

Stratified random sample A sample in which subgroups are randomly selected in the same proportion as they exist in the population. Thus the sample is representative of the target population. (Ch. 1)

Streetwalker A prostitute who solicits in public. (Ch. 16)

Submission Obeying and yielding to another individual. In sexual relations, it generally involves being humiliated by the partner as well. (Ch. 14)

Surfactin A liquid that lets the lungs transmit oxygen from the atmosphere to the blood. (Ch. 7)

Surrogate mother A woman who carries a fetus to full term for another couple, agreeing to give the infant to the other couple after it is born. The infant generally represents a union of the sperm from the man and either his partner's ovum or the ovum of the surrogate mother. (Ch. 7)

Survey   A study of people's attitudes, opinions, or behaviors. Responses are usually obtained either in a face-to-face interview or on a paper-and-pencil questionnaire. (Ch. 1)

Swinging   A type of open marriage relationship in which a couple has extramarital relations together with other couples. (Ch. 10)

Symptomatic HIV infection   The early symptoms of HIV infection, which eventually lead to AIDS. (Ch. 5)

Sympto-thermal method   A combination of the basal body temperature and Billings fertility awareness methods. (Ch. 6)

Syphilis (sif′ ĭ-lis)   A sexually transmitted infection caused by the *Treponema pallidum* bacterium (spirochete), which can also pass directly through any cut or scrape into the bloodstream. (Ch. 5)

T

Telephone scatophilia (skat″ o-fil′e-ah)   A condition in which sexual arousal is achieved repeatedly by making obscene telephone calls. (Ch. 14)

Teratogens (teh rat′ o-jinz)   Substances that can harm an embryo or fetus. (Ch. 7)

Testicles (tes′ tĭ-k′ls)   The male gonads that produce sperm and male hormones. (Ch. 2)

Testicular torsion   An uncommon condition in which the spermatic cord twists and cuts off the blood supply to the testicles. (Ch. 2)

Testosterone (tes-tos′ te-ron)   A hormone that is produced by the testicles (and in very small amounts by the ovaries and adrenal glands). (Ch. 3)

Third stage of labor   Detachment and expulsion of the placenta from the uterus after childbirth. (Ch. 7)

Thrush   A yeast infection (candidiasis) of the mouth. (Ch. 5)

Token resistance [to sex]   Saying "no" to sex when one means "yes." (Ch. 15)

Toxemia of pregnancy   A disease of pregnancy characterized in its early stage (preeclampsia) by high blood pressure, weight gain, swollen joints, and protein in the urine. Unless it is corrected, it can lead to convulsions and coma. (Ch. 7)

Toxic shock syndrome (TSS)   A syndrome with symptoms of high fever, vomiting, diarrhea, and dizziness; caused by toxins produced by the *Staphylococcus aureus* bacterium. (Ch. 3)

Transgendered   An individual whose gender roles are opposite of those that society expects based on his or her anatomy. (Ch. 8)

Transition phase   The last part of the start-up stage of labor, during which the cervix dilates to 10 cm in order for the baby to be able to enter the birth canal. (Ch. 7)

Transsexual   An adult whose gender identity does not match his or her biological sex. (Ch. 8)

Transvestic fetishism   Same meaning as *transvestism*. (Ch. 14)

Transvestism   A condition in which sexual arousal is achieved repeatedly by dressing as a member of the opposite sex. (Ch. 14)

Triangular theory of love   Sternberg's theory of love, which says that all of our different positive emotions are the result of different combinations of intimacy, passion, and decision/commitment. (Ch. 12)

Trichomoniasis (trik″ o-mo-ni′ ah-sis)   A type of vaginitis caused by a one-celled protozoan that is usually transmitted during sexual intercourse. (Ch. 5)

Trimesters   Three-month periods of pregnancy (months 1–3, 4–6, and 7–9), so labeled for descriptive purposes. (Ch. 7)

Trophoblast (trof′ o-blast)   The outer four cell layers of the embryo. (Ch. 7)

Tubal sterilization   A female sterilization technique that originally referred only to the tying of the Fallopian tubes, but which is now often used as a general term for a variety of female sterilization techniques. (Ch. 6)

Tubal pregnancy   Implantation of a blastocyst in a Fallopian tube. (Ch. 7)

Turner's syndrome   A condition in which women have only one X chromosome; as a result, their ovaries never develop properly. (Ch. 8)

Two-spirit   In North American Indian tribes of past centuries, a person, usually a man, who assumed the dress, occupations, and behavior of the other sex in order to effect a change in gender status. The term now preferred by Native Americans and anthropologists over *berdache*. (Ch. 8)

Typical-use pregnancy rate   For a particular birth control technique, the percentage of pregnancies during the first year of use by all couples who use the technique, regardless of whether or not they use it properly or consistently. See also **perfect-use pregnancy rate**. (Ch. 6)

U

Ultrasound   A noninvasive technique for examining the internal organs of a fetus; it uses sound waves like a radar or sonar scan to create a picture. (Ch. 7)

Umbilical (um-bil′ i-kal) **cord**   The cord that connects an embryo or fetus to the mother's placenta. (Ch. 7)

Unconditional love   Feelings of love that do not depend on the loved one meeting certain expectations or desires. (Ch. 12)

Undifferentiated   Individuals who are low on both masculine and feminine traits. (Ch. 8)

Urethra (u-re′ thrah)   The passageway from the bladder to the exterior of the body. In men, it also serves as a passageway for semen during ejaculation. (Ch. 2)

Urophilia (u″ ro-fil′ e-ah)   Sexual arousal caused by urine or the act of urination. (Ch. 14)

Uterus (u′ ter-us)   The womb. The hollow, muscular organ in women where the fertilized egg normally implants. (Ch. 2)

V

Vagina (vah-ji′ nah)   The sheathlike canal in a woman that extends from the vulva to the cervix and that receives the penis during intercourse. (Ch. 2)

Vaginal lubrication   The first sign of sexual arousal in women; the result of the vaginal walls becoming engorged with blood. (Ch. 4)

Vaginismus (vaj″ ĭ-niz′ mus)   A recurrent or persistent sexual problem in women in which pain is experienced during attempted intercourse because of involuntary spasms in the muscles surrounding the outer third of the vagina. (Ch. 13)

Vas deferens (vas def′ er-enz)   The second part of the duct system that transports sperm out of a man's body. (Ch. 2)

Vasectomy (vah-sek′ to-me)   The male sterilization technique in which the vas deferens is tied off and cut, thus preventing passage of sperm through the reproductive tract. (Ch. 6)

Vasocongestive response (vasocongestion) (vas′ o kun-jes′ chun)   The engorgement (filling) of tissues with blood. (Ch. 4)

Venereal warts   See **genital warts.**

Vernix caseosa   A waxy bluish substance that covers a new-born baby. (Ch. 7)

Vestibular (ves-tĭb′ u-lar) **area**   A term used to refer to the area between the two labia minora. (Ch. 2)

Vestibular (ves-tĭb′ u-lar) **bulbs**   Structures surrounding the vaginal opening that fill with blood during sexual arousal, resulting in swelling of the tissues and a narrowing of the vaginal opening. (Ch. 2)

Victorian era   The period during the reign of Queen Victoria of England (1819–1901). With regard to sexuality, it was a time of great public prudery (the pleasurable aspects of sex were denied) and many incorrect medical beliefs. (Ch. 1)

Viral load   The amount of virus in the blood of an individual. (Ch. 5)

Virus   A protein shell around a nucleic acid core. Viruses have either RNA or DNA, but not both, and thus cannot reproduce themselves. They invade host cells that provide the material to manufacture new virus particles. (Ch. 5)

Volunteer bias   A bias in research results that is caused by differences between people who agree to participate and others who refuse. (Ch. 1)

Voyeurism (voi′ yer-iz′m)   Repeatedly seeking sexual arousal by observing nude individuals without their knowledge or consent. (Ch. 14)

Vulva (vul′ vah)   A term for the external female genitalia, including the mons veneris, labia majora, labia minora, clitoris, vaginal opening, and urethral opening. (Ch. 2)

W

Wet dream   See **nocturnal emission.**

Withdrawal (coitus interruptus)   Withdrawal of the man's penis from his partner's vagina before ejaculation in order to avoid conception. It is sometimes ineffective because fluids from the Cowper's glands may contain sperm. (Ch. 6)

Wolffian duct system   A primitive duct system found in embryos that, if allowed to develop, becomes the male reproductive system. (Ch. 8)

Y

Yes-or-no questions   Questions that call for a simple one-word "yes" or "no" response. These should be avoided when striving for communication. (Ch. 13)

Z

Zona pellucida (zo′ nah pel-lu′ cĭ-da)   The surface of an ovum. (Ch. 7)

Zoophilia (zo″ o-fil′ e-ah)   Using sexual contact with animals as the primary means of achieving sexual gratification. (Ch. 14)

Zygote (zi′ got)   The one-celled organism created from the fusion of a sperm and egg. (Ch. 7)

Zygote intrafallopian transfer (ZIFT)   A method of treating infertility caused by blocked Fallopian tubes. An ovum taken from the infertile woman is fertilized by sperm from her partner and then transferred to the unblocked portion of a Fallopian tube. (Ch. 7)

CREDITS

Chapter 1

Page 6: Erich Lessing/Art Resource, NY; **page 7 (top row, left to right):** Courtesy of Dr. Martha Ward, Department of Anthropology, University of New Orleans; © Jack Fields/CORBIS; Courtesy President & Fellows of Harvard College Peabody Museum, Harvard University 2000. Neg. no: N6059; **page 7 (center row, left to right):** Pakistan Images/Alamy; © Otto Lang/CORBIS; © Jonathan Blair/CORBIS; **page 7 (bottom row, left to right):** © Hulton-Deutsch Collection/CORBIS; © Kevin R. Morris/CORBIS; **page 11:** Photo Courtesy of Historic St. Augustine Preservation Board; **page 13 (left):** William P. Didusch Center for Urologic History; **page 15:** Courtesy of Gail King; **page 16 (left):** JGM, Pacific Coast News/Newscom; **page 16 (top right):** AP Images/Matt Sayles; **page 16 (bottom right):** AP Images/Awout David Phillip; **page 17 (left to right):** © Mitchell Gerber/CORBIS; AP Images/ Damian Dovarganes; **page 18:** Billy E. Barnes/PhotoEdit; **page 20:** © Mary Evans/The Image Works; **page 21 (left to right):** © Bettmann/CORBIS; © Topham/The Image Works; **page 22:** Art Shay/Getty Images; **page 23:** Bruce Powell

Chapter 2

Page 36 (left to right): Custom Medical Stock Photo; Daniel Sambraus/Photo Researchers, Inc.; Medicimage/Photolibrary; **page 39 (left to right):** © Steve Preznant/CORBIS; David J. Green-studio/Alamy; © Masterfile; **page 48 (left and right):** John Henderson/Alamy

Chapter 3

Page 66: Courtesy of Dr. Martha Ward, Department of Anthropology, University of New Orleans; **page 69:** Bruce King; **page 73:** Phil Velasquez/MCT/Landov

Chapter 4

Page 79 (left and right): Behavioral Technology, Inc.; **page 90:** Stephanie Welsh/Getty Images; **page 93:** Erich Lessing/ Art Resource, NY; **page 96 (left to right):** Rob Brimson/ Getty Images; © Belinda Images/SuperStock

Chapter 5

Page 103: Centers for Disease Control & Prevention; **page 104:** Centers for Disease Control & Prevention; **page 106 (top left):** Science Photo Library/Photo Researchers, Inc.; **(bottom left):** Centers for Disease Control & Prevention; **(top right):** Susan Lindsley/Centers for Disease Control & Prevention; **(bottom right):** © Lester V. Bergman/CORBIS; **page 107 (top and bottom):** Centers for Disease Control & Prevention; **page 109 (left to right):** Centers for Disease Control & Prevention; Dr. M. A. Ansary/Photo Researchers, Inc.; Drs. N. J. Flumara & Gavin Hart/Centers for Disease Control & Prevention; **page 110 (left and right):** Centers for Disease Control & Prevention; **page 112:** Garry Watson/ Photo Researchers, Inc.; **page 113 (left to right):** Dr. P. Marazzi/Photo Researchers, Inc.; Centers for Disease Control & Prevention; **page 115:** Chuck Nacke/Alamy; **page 117:** Biophoto Associates/Photo Researchers, Inc.; **page 123 (top and bottom):** Eye of Science/Photo Researchers, Inc.; **page 126 (left and right):** National Medical Slide Bank/ Custom Medical Stock Photo, Inc.; **page 128:** Black Star

Chapter 6

Page 138: © Bettmann/CORBIS; **page 144:** Photo provided by Cycle Technologies, Inc.; **page 147:** Bruce King; **page 149 (left to right):** Dorling Kindersley/Getty Images; Reproduced by the permission of the Cervical Barrier Advancement Society (CBAS) and Ibis Reproductive Health; **page 150:** Allendale Pharmaceuticals, Inc.; **page 151:** Saturn Stills/Photo Researchers, Inc.; **page 154:** Ian Miles - Flashpoint Pictures/ Alamy; **page 155 (left to right):** N Aubrier/Photolibrary; Gusto/Photo Researchers, Inc.

Chapter 7

Page 169: Eye of Science/Photo Researchers, Inc.; **page 170:** Lennart Nilsson/Scanpix; **page 171 (top left and bottom right):** Lennart Nilsson/Scanpix; **page 171 (top right and bottom left):** Lana B. Callahan; **page 172 (left and right):** Lennart Nilsson/Scanpix; **page 173:** Lennart Nilsson/Scanpix; **page 175:** Annie Liebovitz/Contact Press Images; **page 185 (top and bottom):** Michele Davidson/Pearson Education/PH College; **page 187:** Gladskikh Tatiana/Shutterstock; **page 191:** Mauro Fermariello/Photo Researchers, Inc.

Chapter 8

Page 200: ullstein bild/The Granger Collection; **page 201:** John Money, *Sex Errors of the Body and Related Syndromes: A Guide for Counseling Children, Adolescents and Their Families,* 1994, published by Paul H. Brooks Publishing Company, Baltimore, MD. Reprinted by permission of The Kinsey Institute for Research in sex, Gender, and Reproduction, Inc.; **page 202 (left to right):** National Library of Medicine; Howard W. Jones, Jr., M. D., Eastern Virginia Medical School; **page 204:** Reuters/Landov; **page 206:** Manny Millan/Getty Images; **page 208:** © fstop/Superstock; **page 211:** Guillermo Hung/Photolibrary; **page 214 (left):** The Advertising Archives; **page 214 (top right):** Luke Air Force Base; **page 214 (bottom right):** A. Ramey/PhotoEdit; **page 215:** Imagesource/Photolibrary; **page 216 (left to right):** National Anthropological Archives/Smithsonian Institution; Nick Cardillicchio; **page 218 (left to right):** Erich Lessing/Art Resource, NY; © Bettmann/CORBIS; Lucido Inc./Photolibrary

Chapter 9

Page 225: CORBIS/Photolibrary; **page 226:** Library of Congress; **page 228:** Library of Congress; **page 230:** Creatas Images/Thinkstock; **page 233:** Frances Roberts/Alamy;

Winslow Townson; **page 238:** AP Images/Winslow Townson; **page 239:** © Liz Mangelsdorf/San Francisco Chronicle/CORBIS

CHAPTER 10

Page 244: Maya Barnes/The Image Works; **page 246:** Michael Newman/PhotoEdit; **page 249 (left and right):** From Wilkins, Blizzard, and Midgeon, "The Diagnosis and Treatment of Endocrine Disorders in Childhood and Adolescence." 2-4-2008, Figures 6, 8 on pp. 253 and 255. Courtesy of Charles C. Thomas Publisher, Ltd., Springfield, IL.; **page 250:** John Powell Photographer/Alamy (posed by models); **page 253:** © Exactostock/Superstock; **page 255:** Siepmann Siepmann/Photolibrary; **page 256:** Creatas Images/Thinkstock; **page 259:** Asia Images Group Pte Ltd/Alamy; **page 261:** Stuart Pearce/Photolibrary; **page 265:** HBSS/Photolibrary; **page 267:** Angela Hampton Picture Library/Alamy; **page 270:** Susan Szasz/Photo Researchers, Inc.; **page 272:** Jack Hollingsworth/Thinkstock

Chapter 12

Page 300: Réunion des Musées Nationaux/Art Resource, NY; **page 302:** Flashon Studio/Shutterstock; **page 304:** Bill Aron/PhotoEdit; **page 305:** ONOKY– Photononstop/Alamy; **p. 318:** Fancy/Alamy

Chapter 13

Page 326: Explorer/Photo Researchers, Inc.; **page 332:** SuperStock; **page 344 (left to right):** Darren Carroll/Icon SMI/Newscom; Hubert Boes/dpa/Landov; **page 350:** AGE Fotostock America, Inc.

Chapter 14

Page 357: camera lucida lifestyle/Alamy; **page 359:** David Young-Wolff/PhotoEdit, Inc.; **page 364 (left to right):**

Collection of The New-York Historical Society, accession number 1952.80, negative number 4260; Bill Aron/Photo Researchers, Inc.; **page 368:** © Reuters/CORBIS

Chapter 15

Page 379: Erich Lessing/Art Resource, NY; **page 383:** Roberta Goldstein/Photo Researchers, Inc.; **page 388:** Dana White/PhotoEdit; **page 391:** Ryan McVay/Photolibrary; **page 397:** NBC Newswire/NBCU Photobank; **page 402:** AP Images; **page 405:** © Frank Trapper/CORBIS

Chapter 16

Page 412 (top left): © Werner Foreman/Topham/The Image Works; **page 412 (right):** The Granger Collection, NYC; **page 412 (bottom left):** Réunion des Musées Nationaux/Art Resource, NY; **page 413 (left to right):** Erich Lessing/Art Resource, NY; John P. Stevens/Ancient Art & Architecture Collection; **page 414 (top left):** The Pierpont Morgan Library/Art Resource, NY; **page 414 (right):** SuperStock; **page 414 (bottom left):** Réunion des Musées Nationaux/Art Resource, NY; **page 417:** Bill Aron/PhotoEdit; **page 418 (left to right):** Cynthia Johnson/Getty Images; AP Images/Joe Marquette; **page 422:** Michael Goldman/Photolibrary; **page 425:** Jonathan Alpeyrie/Getty Images

Illustrations by Sven Hennze

Figure 2–1, **page 34;** Figure 2–4, **page 39;** Figure 2–6, **page 40;** Figure 2–9, **page 47;** Figure 2–12, **page 52;** Figure 4–6, **page 85;** Figure 6–4, **page 146;** Figure 6–6, **page 148;** Figure 8–1, **page 199;** Figure 11–1, **page 286;** Figure 11–2, **page 286;** Figure 11–3, **page 287;** Figure 11–4, **page 287;** Figure 11–5, **page 289;** Figure 11–6, **page 289;** Figure 13–2, **page 329;** Figure 13–4, **page 334;** Figure 13–5, **page 341;** and Figure 13–6, **page 342.**

Chapter 1

1. their friends
2. the media (e.g., TV)
3. 85
4. sexuality
5. the biblical Hebrews
6. Christians
7. Saint Augustine
8. Queen Victoria
9. penicillin
10. the birth control pill and IUD
11. socialization
12. the media
13. identification
14. Europe
15. Sigmund Freud
16. Henry Havelock Ellis
17. Alfred Kinsey
18. Masters and Johnson
19. true
20. false
21. false
22. false
23. false
24. false
25. false
26. true
27. true
28. false
29. false
30. false
31. true
32. true
33. true
34. true
35. true
36. false
37. false
38. f
39. n
40. g
41. h
42. d
43. m
44. c
45. a
46. j
47. o
48. Inis Baeg
49. leisure time, mobility, birth control, antibiotics
50. each possible sample of that size
51. Plato
52. body, soul
53. spermatorrhea
54. "Any mutually voluntary activity with another person that involves genital contact … "
55. television

Chapter 2

1. vulva
2. mons veneris
3. labia majora
4. labia minora
5. clitoris
6. vaginal opening
7. urethral opening
8. mons veneris
9. outer surfaces of the labia majora
10. clitoris
11. penis
12. labia minora
13. vestibular area
14. hymen
15. eight
16. vagina
17. uterus
18. Fallopian tubes
19. ovaries
20. vagina
21. vagina
22. Grafenberg (G) spot
23. ovary
24. Fallopian tube
25. uterus
26. endometrium
27. cancer of the cervix
28. scrotum
29. testicles
30. corpora cavernosa
31. corpus spongiosum
32. glans
33. foreskin
34. circumcision
35. testicles
36. testosterone
37. epididymis
38. vas deferens
39. ejaculatory ducts
40. urethra
41. prostate gland
42. seminal vesicles
43. semen
44. Cowper's glands
45. testicles
46. prostate gland
47. true
48. true
49. true
50. false
51. false
52. true
53. false
54. false
55. false
56. true
57. false
58. false
59. false
60. false
61. false
62. b
63. e
64. c
65. a
66. f
67. l
68. h
69. i
70. j
71. k
72. d
73. g
74. m
75. n
76. prostate gland
77. labia majora
78. endometrium
79. blood
80. Cowper's glands
81. amount of fatty tissue
82. just after menstruation
83. ejaculatory ducts
84. seminal vesicles
85. after a warm bath or shower
86. Bartholin's glands
87. seminiferous tubules
88. clitoris
89. pubococcygeus (PC)
90. front
91. prolactin

Chapter 3

1. endocrine
2. testosterone
3. estrogen
4. progesterone
5. pituitary gland
6. 28
7. follicle-stimulating hormone (FSH)
8. follicle
9. follicular (or proliferative)
10. endometrium
11. FSH
12. luteinizing hormone (LH)
13. LH
14. ovulation
15. abdominal cavity
16. Fallopian tube
17. luteal (or secretory)
18. corpus luteum
19. endometrium
20. endometrium
21. menstruation
22. at least 8 days
23. estrous
24. estrus (ovulation)
25. taboos
26. sloughed off endometrial tissue
27. cervical mucus
28. blood
29. sperm production
30. luteinizing hormone
31. male hormones (e.g., testosterone)
32. high blood pressure; liver, prostate, and breast tumors; impaired reproductive function; masculinization in women; emotional or psychological problems
33. amenorrhea
34. 3 to 14
35. premenstrual syndrome (PMS)
36. with the start of menstruation
37. dysmenorrhea
38. prostaglandins
39. endometrial tissue grows outside the uterus
40. toxic shock syndrome
41. testosterone
42. estrogen
43. progesterone
44. testosterone
45. false
46. false
47. false
48. false (28 days is an average)
49. true
50. true

51. false (there is no strong evidence for this)
52. false
53. false
54. true
55. false
56. false
57. h
58. d
59. n
60. j
61. l
62. k
63. b
64. m
65. f
66. o
67. e
68. p
69. i
70. a
71. c
72. g
73. pituitary
74. pheromones
75. follicle
76. corpus luteum
77. human chorionic gonadotropin (HCG)
78. gonadotropin-releasing hormone (GnRH)
79. progesterone
80. testosterone
81. inhibin
82. oxytocin
83. 5, 1, ovulation

Chapter 4

1. Masters and Johnson
2. excitement
3. plateau
4. orgasm
5. resolution
6. sexual response cycle
7. Helen Kaplan
8. desire
9. vasocongestive
10. penile erection
11. vaginal lubrication
12. subjective arousal
13. plateau
14. orgasmic platform
15. pulls back against the pubic bone and disappears beneath the clitoral hood
16. 50% to 75
17. sex-tension flush
18. rhythmic muscular contractions
19. the brain
20. similar

21. emission
22. expulsion
23. ejaculation
24. refractory period
25. multiple orgasms
26. resolution
27. 50% to 75
28. clitoral
29. clitoral
30. vaginal
31. clitoris
32. front
33. Grafenberg (G) spot
34. emission of fluid
35. prostate gland
36. not important
37. aphrodisiacs
38. false
39. true
40. true
41. false (not necessarily)
42. true
43. false
44. true
45. false
46. false
47. true
48. true
49. true
50. false
51. true
52. false
53. true
54. false
55. true
56. false
57. d
58. b, g, j, k, l, n, s
59. a, c, f, i, q, r, t
60. e, p, u
61. h, m, o
62. b, c, g, i, k, q, t
63. vasocongestion
64. urethra
65. sex-tension flush
66. orgasmic platform
67. Grafenberg (G) spot
68. refractory period

Chapter 5

1. 2
2. bacteria
3. viruses
4. parasites
5. gonorrhea
6. chlamydia
7. syphilis
8. gonorrhea
9. chlamydia
10. pelvic inflammatory disease (PID)
11. syphilis

12. antibiotics
13. skin, skin
14. recurrent
15. liver
16. feces
17. blood and other body fluids
18. human papilloma
19. human immunodeficiency virus (HIV)
20. CD4+
21. immune
22. opportunistic
23. 10
24. intimate sexual activity
25. blood
26. casual contact
27. men and women
28. infestations of parasites
29. trichomoniasis
30. monilial
31. bacterial vaginosis
32. false
33. true
34. false
35. false
36. false
37. true
38. false
39. true
40. false
41. true
42. false
43. false
44. false
45. true
46. false
47. true
48. false
49. false
50. false
51. false
52. false
53. false
54. true
55. true
56. true
57. true
58. false
59. true
60. false
61. a
62. l
63. c
64. q
65. h
66. f
67. o
68. i
69. m
70. j
71. e

72. n
73. g
74. b
75. d
76. p
77. k
78. parasites
79. pelvic inflammatory disease
80. human papillomavirus infection
81. human immunodeficiency virus (HIV) infection
82. types of vaginitis
83. hepatitis
84. ectopic pregnancy, infertility
85. syphilis, human immunodeficiency virus, hepatitis
86. stress
87. mucous membranes
88. nongonococcal (or nonspecific) urethritis
89. yeast (moniliasis)
90. pinworms
91. chlamydia
92. CD4+ cells
93. during the first 60 days and late in the infection (AIDS)
94. HIV antibodies
95. gonorrhea, chlamydia, syphilis (the chancre is often internal), HPV infection, HIV infection
96. HPV infection, HIV infection, trichomoniasis
97. to always use condoms, to abstain from sex until you are in a long-term monogamous relationship
98. trichomoniasis
99. HPV infection

Chapter 6

1. over twice
2. half
3. abstaining from sex
4. calendar
5. basal body temperature
6. Billings
7. ovulation
8. lactational amenorrhea
9. spermicides
10. the diaphragm
11. the cervical cap
12. condoms
13. the contraceptive sponge

14. uterus or vagina
15. offer some protection against sexually transmitted infections
16. estrogen
17. progesterone
18. patch
19. NuvaRing
20. Depo-Provera
21. Implanon
22. 72
23. vas deferens
24. tubal ligation
25. laparoscopy
26. true
27. true
28. false
29. true
30. false
31. false
32. true
33. true
34. false
35. false
36. false
37. false
38. false
39. false
40. true
41. true
42. true
43. false
44. false
45. true
46. true
47. true
48. true
49. true
50. true
51. true
52. true
53. true
54. c
55. i
56. k
57. d
58. b, e
59. h
60. h
61. e
62. e
63. b, e, g
64. n
65. c, j, m
66. a, n
67. c, j, m
68. j
69. l
70. f
71. f
72. c, j, m
73. j

74. the Cowper's glands
75. he has had 12 to 16 ejaculations
76. 7, 20
77. rises slightly
78. clear and slippery
79. oil-based
80. who are not at high risk for STIs
81. male condom, female condom, contraceptive sponge
82. the male condom, the female condom, the diaphragm
83. using emergency contraception
84. 5 days
85. to abstain from sex

Chapter 7

1. 5
2. ovulation
3. 1
4. Fallopian tube
5. endometrium
6. ectopic
7. chlamydia and/or gonorrhea
8. human chorionic gonadotropin (HCG)
9. trimesters
10. embryo
11. 2
12. fetus
13. 7
14. quickening
15. 4th or 5th
16. teratogens
17. amniocentesis
18. fear-tension-pain
19. midwife
20. contractions
21. dilation
22. start-up
23. amniotic sac
24. transition phase
25. fully dilated
26. head
27. umbilical cord
28. placenta
29. cesarean (C-section)
30. proteins
31. postpartum blues or depression
32. 4 to 6
33. the sharing of child-care and housekeeping responsibilities
34. 10
35. 40
36. 40

37. 20
38. a low sperm count
39. artificial insemination
40. Fallopian tubes
41. ovulate
42. in vitro fertilization
43. false
44. true
45. false
46. true
47. false
48. false
49. false
50. false
51. true
52. false
53. false
54. true
55. false
56. false
57. false
58. false
59. c
60. d
61. h
62. b
63. g
64. f
65. a
66. e
67. c
68. morula, blastocyst
69. umbilical cord
70. preeclampsia
71. lightening
72. whether contractions are coming 10 minutes apart (or sooner) on a regular basis; whether contractions are at least 30 seconds long on a regular basis; whether cervix is dilated to at least 2 to 3 centimeters; whether cervix is at least 70% effaced
73. first
74. tubal
75. 25 to 35
76. blastocyst
77. the head
78. 24 hours
79. amnion
80. episiotomies, cesarean sections
81. 23 to 24 weeks
82. 6 months
83. at least 11 months

Chapter 8

1. gender identity
2. gender roles

3. XX
4. XY
5. Klinefelter's
6. Turner's
7. testosterone
8. girl
9. intersexuals
10. gender dysphoria
11. gender identity disorder (transsexuals)
12. Freudian
13. social learning
14. gender constancy
15. 6 or 7
16. evolutionary (sociobiological)
17. sociocultural
18. independent
19. androgyny
20. schemas
21. sexual desire
22. sociosexuality
23. false
24. true
25. true
26. true
27. true
28. false
29. true
30. true
31. true
32. true
33. true
34. false
35. false
36. true
37. true
38. f, g, n
39. e
40. i
41. p
42. q
43. b, j, l
44. b, d, j, l
45. c
46. f, g, o
47. a, l, j
48. m
49. k
50. h, j
51. gender constancy
52. 1800s (when the United States and other countries became industrialized)
53. sociocultural
54. identification
55. socialization
56. stereotypes
57. undifferentiated
58. phallic
59. androgynous

60. testosterone
61. transvestites; transsexuals
62. imitation
63. the social construction of masculinity and femininity
64. expressive
65. 2
66. gender schema
67. testosterone
68. two-spirit

Chapter 9

1. distinct preferences
2. 3.0% to 7
3. 1.5% to 4.5
4. 2, 3, or 4
5. gender identities
6. roles
7. Oedipus
8. social learning theory
9. Sambian
10. genetic
11. brains
12. hormones
13. interact
14. more
15. ancient Greeks
16. Romans
17. Thomas Aquinas
18. coming out
19. admitting to oneself that one has a homosexual orientation
20. sexual prejudice
21. true
22. false
23. false
24. false
25. false
26. false
27. false
28. true
29. true
30. true
31. false
32. false
33. false
34. false
35. false
36. false
37. false
38. true
39. false
40. false
41. a
42. b
43. e
44. d
45. b
46. e

47. c
48. a
49. e
50. d
51. b
52. adolescence
53. before or shortly after birth
54. predispose
55. admitting a homosexual orientation to oneself; getting to know other homosexuals; telling family and friends of one's sexual orientation; complete openness about one's homosexuality
56. Socrates, Leonardo da Vinci, Michaelangelo, Gertrude Stein, Walt Whitman

Chapter 10

1. 3 through 5
2. modesty (and inhibitions about exposing their bodies in public)
3. puberty
4. reproduction
5. hormone
6. self-identity
7. half
8. peer pressure
9. monogamy
10. lasting relationship
11. chastity
12. economic and physical protection
13. mid-20s to mid-30s
14. menopause
15. vaginal lubrication
16. testosterone
17. refractory
18. their sexual activity when they were younger
19. sexual learning
20. in early childhood (preschool years)
21. how you say it
22. scare tactics
23. askable
24. willingness to come to you when they have questions and problems
25. true
26. false
27. true
28. false
29. false
30. true
31. false

32. true
33. false
34. true
35. true
36. false
37. true
38. false
39. true
40. false
41. false
42. false
43. true
44. true
45. false
46. true
47. false
48. true
49. false (true for men only)
50. false
51. true
52. a
53. b
54. e (caused by b)
55. c
56. a
57. c
58. e
59. d
60. a
61. d
62. d
63. f, c (from DHEA)
64. lack of a partner
65. the climacteric
66. self-exploration
67. latency
68. secondary sex characteristics
69. emotional intimacy
70. test their virility
71. have multiple wives
72. emotional
73. opportunity, alienation
74. adrenarche, gonadarche

Chapter 11

1. range
2. Kinsey
3. 92
4. 62
5. romantic and emotional
6. man
7. missionary
8. fellatio
9. cunnilingus
10. White
11. Latinos
12. African Americans
13. sexually healthy
14. oral-genital
15. anal
16. false

17. true
18. false
19. false
20. true
21. false
22. true
23. false
24. true
25. false
26. true
27. true
28. true
29. true
30. rectal bacteria
31. the replacement fantasy
32. variety
33. ritualized
34. vaginal intercourse, watching one's partner undress
35. a sexually active lifestyle
36. face-to-face
37. woman-on-top
38. feels comfortable with his or her sexuality; feels free to choose whether or not he or she wishes to try a variety of sexual behaviors
39. White, higher

Chapter 12

1. idealization
2. marriage
3. sexual desire
4. fascination (preoccupation with the other person)
5. exclusiveness
6. sexual desire
7. cognitive component
8. companionate
9. a positive self-concept
10. self-disclosure
11. conditional
12. unconditional
13. jealousy
14. self-esteem
15. popularity, wealth, fame, and physical attractiveness
16. attachment
17. secure
18. avoidant
19. liking
20. romantic love
21. companionate love
22. consummate love
23. eros
24. storge
25. pragma

26. mania
27. ludus
28. agape
29. matches
30. intimacy
31. false
32. false
33. true
34. false
35. true
36. false
37. false
38. true
39. true
40. true
41. true
42. false
43. false (true for men only)
44. false
45. false
46. false
47. f
48. n
49. j
50. p
51. b
52. o
53. h
54. a
55. d
56. l
57. i
58. m
59. q
60. k
61. e
62. c
63. g
64. ludus
65. storge
66. mania
67. agape
68. realistic
69. (a) both individuals accepting themselves as they are, (b) each individual recognizing his or her partner for what they are, (c) each individual feeling comfortable to express himself or herself, (d) learning to deal with the partner's reactions
70. idealization
71. passionate love
72. passionate love, companionate love
73. obsessive review, emotional and social loneliness
74. physical attractiveness

Chapter 13

1. at least half
2. couple's
3. cognitive-behavioral therapy
4. PLISSIT
5. medical
6. sexual
7. sensate focus exercises
8. couples
9. hypoactive sexual desire
10. sexual aversion
11. compulsiveness
12. dyspareunia
13. premature ejaculation
14. reasonable voluntary control
15. erectile disorder
16. performance anxiety
17. orgasmic disorder
18. headaches after orgasm
19. relationship problems
20. vaginismus
21. reaching orgasm
22. stereotypic gender roles, power
23. vocabulary
24. positive
25. negative
26. "you"
27. self-disclose
28. listener
29. eye contact, facial expressions, interpersonal distance, touch
30. true
31. false
32. true
33. false (not necessarily)
34. false
35. false
36. false
37. false
38. true
39. true
40. true
41. false
42. false
43. false
44. false
45. true
46. true
47. false
48. c, a, b
49. i, b
50. j
51. c, a, h, f
52. a, k, f
53. g, d
54. l
55. a, e

56. c, g, a, f
57. clitoris
58. woman-on-top
59. spectatoring
60. a good relationship
61. nondemand mutual pleasuring
62. phimosis
63. ejaculatory incompetence
64. hypoactive sexual desire
65. communication
66. verbal, nonverbal
67. disagreements

Chapter 14

1. statistical
2. sociological
3. psychological
4. place
5. preferred
6. sexual variants
7. courtship disorders
8. affiliative
9. tactile
10. voyeurs
11. exhibitionism
12. telephone scatophilia
13. frotteurism
14. pedophilia
15. prepubertal
16. fetishism
17. transvestism
18. fetishism
19. urophilia
20. coprophilia
21. mysophilia
22. klismaphilia
23. zoophilia
24. sadists
25. masochists
26. dominance
27. submission
28. necrophilia
29. men
30. antiandrogen
31. false
32. false
33. false
34. true
35. true
36. false
37. false
38. false
39. true
40. true
41. true
42. true
43. false
44. q
45. r
46. e

47. d
48. k
49. g
50. a
51. p
52. h
53. o
54. b
55. c
56. l
57. m
58. n
59. j
60. i
61. f
62. fetishism
63. exhibitionists
64. exhibitionism
65. 13 years old
66. domination, submission
67. bodily discharges, fetishes
68. quiet, passive, and nonrejecting
69. control, desire

Chapter 15

1. property
2. someone the victim knows
3. 16 and 24
4. vulnerable
5. average
6. young
7. empathy
8. coercion
9. verbal
10. physical
11. gang
12. statutory rape
13. power
14. anger
15. sadism
16. opportunistic
17. violence by men
18. adversarial
19. that women who are raped usually provoke it by their dress and behavior
20. that women subconsciously want to be raped
21. no woman can be raped if she truly does not want it
22. post-rape posttraumatic stress disorder
23. controlled
24. long-term reorganization
25. rape-shield

26. social systems
27. sexual harassment
28. someone they know
29. preference
30. situational
31. personally immature
32. regressive
33. 200
34. brother–sister
35. false
36. true
37. true
38. true
39. false
40. false
41. true
42. false
43. false
44. true
45. false
46. false
47. false
48. true
49. false
50. true
51. false
52. true
53. false
54. true
55. d
56. i
57. e
58. g
59. a
60. h

61. j
62. f
63. c
64. b
65. juveniles (persons under the legal "age of consent")
66. getting a partner intoxicated in order to have sex, physical (relentless) pressure, verbal pressure (e.g., anger), emotional/psychological pressure (e.g., threatening to end the relationship)
67. boys are raised to be nurturant, not aggressive; boys are raised to view women as equals who share power and responsibility
68. gang
69. psychopathology (a character disorder)
70. opportunistic
71. period of long-term reorganization
72. Civil Rights Act
73. unequal power
74. traditional stereotypical gender roles

Chapter 16

1. one fourth
2. no harmful
3. less sympathetic
4. rape myths
5. increased hostility
6. commit rape themselves if they were certain they would not get caught
7. depictions of violence toward women
8. sexual explicitness
9. erotica
10. Nevada
11. 10% to 23
12. streetwalkers
13. B-girls
14. call girls
15. hustlers
16. economics (the need for money)
17. middle-class
18. married
19. false
20. false (not in the long term)
21. true
22. true
23. false
24. true
25. true
26. false
27. true
28. true
29. false
30. true
31. true

32. h
33. a
34. d
35. c
36. g
37. f
38. b
39. e
40. i
41. lack of discrimination
42. streetwalker
43. obscene
44. material portraying violence toward women
45. (a) by contemporary community standards it depicts patently offensive sexual conduct; (b) it lacks serious literary, artistic, political, or scientific value; and (c) it appeals to prurient interests
46. Comstock law
47. they enjoy the sexual arousal it produces
48. active subordination of women
49. view women as sex objects; retain stereotyped views of gender roles; more permissive sexual attitudes; lower sexual satisfaction

REFERENCES

A

AARONSON, I. A. (1994). Micropenis: Medical and surgical implications. *Journal of Urology, 152*, 4–14.

ABBEY, A. (2005). Lessons learned and unanswered questions about sexual assault perpetration. *Journal of Interpersonal Violence, 20*, 39–42.

ABBEY, A., MCAUSLAN, P., & ROSS, L. T. (1998). Sexual assault perpetration by college men: The role of alcohol, misperception of sexual intent, and sexual beliefs and experiences. *Journal of Social and Clinical Psychology, 17*, 167–195.

ABC News/Washington Post Poll/2010, April 22–25, Abortion and birth control. http://www.pollingreport.com/abortion2.htm

ABDALLA, R. H. D. (1982). *Sisters in affliction: Circumcision and infibulation of women in Africa.* London: Zed Press (Westport, CT: L. Hill).

ABEL, G. G., & OSBORN, C. (1992). The paraphilias: The extent and nature of sexually deviant and criminal behavior. *Psychiatric Clinics of North America, 15*, 675–686.

ABEL, G. G., & ROULEAU, J. L. (1990). The nature and extent of sexual assault. In W. L. Marshall, D. R. Laws, & H. E. Barbaree (Eds.), *Handbook of sexual assault* (pp. 9–20). New York: Plenum Press.

ABEL, G. G., et al. (1977). The components of rapists' sexual arousal. *Archives of General Psychiatry, 34*, 895–903.

ABEL, G. G., et al. (1981). Identifying dangerous child molesters. In R. B. Stuard (Ed.), *Violent behavior: Social learning approaches to prediction, management, and treatment* (pp. 116–137). New York: Brunner/Mazel.

ABEL, G. G., et al. (1987). Self-reported sex crimes of nonincarcerated paraphiliacs. *Journal of Interpersonal Violence, 1*, 3–25.

ABEL, G. G., et al. (1988a). Multiple paraphiliac diagnoses among sex offenders. *Bulletin of the American Academy of Psychiatry and the Law, 16*, 153–168.

ABEL, G. G., et al. (1988b). Predicting child molesters' response to treatment. *Annals of the New York Academy of Sciences, 528*, 223–234.

ACEIJAS, C., & RHODES, T. (2007). Global estimates of prevalence of HCV infection among injecting drug users. *International Journal of Drug Policy, 18*, 352–358.

ACIERNO, R., et al. (1999). Risk factors for rape, physical assault, and post-traumatic stress disorder in women: Examination of differential multivariate relationships. *Journal of Anxiety Disorders, 13*, 541–563.

ADAM, T., et al. (2010). Estimating the obstetric costs of female genital mutilation in six African countries. *Bulletin of the World Health Organization, 88*, 281–288.

ADDIEGO, F., et al. (1981). Female ejaculation: A case study. *Journal of Sex Research, 17*, 13–21.

ADDUCCI, C., & ROSS, L. (1991). Common urethral injuries in men. *Medical Aspects of Human Sexuality*, October, 32–44.

ADLERCREUTZ, H., et al. (1992). Dietary phytoestrogens and the menopause in Japan. *The Lancet, 339*, 1233.

ADZICK, N. S., et al. (1998). Successful fetal surgery for spina bifida. *The Lancet, 352*, 1675–1676.

AFIFI, W. A. (1999). Harming the ones we love: Relational attachment and perceived consequences as predictors of safe-sex behavior. *Journal of Sex Research, 36*, 198–206.

AGNEW, J. (1986). Hazards associated with anal erotic activity. *Archives of Sexual Behavior, 15*, 307–314.

AHIA, R. N. (1991). Compliance with safer-sex guidelines among adolescent males: Application of the health belief model and protection motivation theory. *Journal of Health Education, 22*, 49–52.

AHLBORG, T., DAHLÖF, L.-G., & HALLBERG, L. R.-M. (2005). Quality of the intimate and sexual relationship in first-time parents six months after delivery. *Journal of Sex Research, 42*, 167–174.

AHLBORG, T., et al. (2008). Sensual and sexual marital contentment in parents of small children—A follow-up study when the first child is four years old. *Journal of Sex Research, 45*, 295–304.

AHROLD, T. K., & MESTON, C. M. (2010). Ethnic differences in sexual attitudes of U.S. college students: Gender, acculturation, and religiosity factors. *Archives of Sexual Behavior, 39*, 190–202. Hillsdale, NJ: Lawrence Erlbaum.

ALANKO, K., et al. (2010). Common genetic effects of gender atypical behavior in childhood and sexual orientation in adulthood: A study of Finnish twins. *Archives of Sexual Behavior, 39*, 81–92.

AL-AZZAWI, F., & PALACIOS, S. (2009). Hormonal changes during menopause. *Maturitas, 63*, 135–137.

ALBERMAN, E. (1988). The epidemiology of repeated abortion. In R. W. Beard & F. Sharp (Eds.), *Early pregnancy loss: Mechanisms and treatment* (pp. 9–17). London: Royal College of Obstetricians and Gynaecologists.

ALBRIGHT, J. (2008). Sex in American online: An exploration of sex, marital status, and sexual identity in Internet sex seeking and its impacts. *Journal of Sex Research, 45*, 175–186.

ALEXANDER, C. J., SIPSKI, M. L., & FINDLEY, T. W. (1993). Sexual activities, desire, and satisfaction in males pre- and post-spinal cord injury. *Archives of Sexual Behavior, 22*, 217–228.

ALEXANDER, G. M., & HINES, M. (1994). Gender labels and play styles: Their relative contribution to children's selection of playmates. *Child Development, 65*, 869–879.

ALEXANDER, G. M., & SHERWIN, B. B. (1993). Sex steroids, sexual behavior, and selection attention for erotic stimuli in women using oral contraceptives. *Psychoneuroendocrinology, 18*, 91–102.

ALEXANDER, G. M., WILCOX, T., & WOODS, R. (2009). Sex differences in infants' visual interest in toys. *Archives of Sexual Behavior, 38*, 427–433.

ALEXANDER, G. M., et al. (1997). Androgen-behavior correlations in hypogonadal men and eugonadal men. *Hormones and Behavior, 31*, 110–119.

ALI, L., & KELLEY, R. (2008, April 17). The curious lives of surrogates. *Newsweek*, 45–51.

ALI, L., & MILLER, L. (2004, July 12). The secret lives of wives. *Newsweek*, 47–54.

ALISON, L., et al. (2001). Sadomasochistically oriented behavior: Diversity in practice and meaning. *Archives of Sexual Behavior, 30*, 1–12.

ALLEN, D. J., & OLESON, T. (1999). Shame and internalized homophobia in gay men. *Journal of Homosexuality, 37*, 33–43.

ALLEN, K. R., & GOLDBERG, A. E. (2009). Sexual activity during menstruation: A qualitative study. *Journal of Sex Research, 46*, 535–545.

ALLEN, L. S., & GORSKI, R. A. (1992). Sexual orientation and the size of the anterior commissure in the human brain. *Proceedings of the National Academy of Sciences of the U.S.A., 89*, 7199–7202.

ALLGEIER, E. R., & MURNEN, S. K. (1985, March). Perception of parents as sexual beings: Pocs and Godow revisited. *SIECUS Report, 4*, 11–12.

ALLSWORTH, J. E., RATNER, J. A., & PEIPERT, J. F. (2009). Trichomoniasis and other sexually transmitted infections: Results from the 2001–2004 National Health and Nutrition Examination Surveys. *Sexually Transmitted Diseases, 36*, 738–744.

ALMOND, P. (2009). Postnatal depression: A global public health perspective. *Perspectives in Public Health, 129*, 221–227.

ALTMAN, D. (2001). *Global sex.* Chicago: University of Chicago Press.

ALVAREZ, W. A., & FREINHAR, J. P. (1991). A prevalence study of bestiality zoophilia in psychiatric in-patients, medical in-patients, and psychiatric staff. *International Journal of Psychosomatics, 38*, 45–47.

ALZATE, H., & LONDONO, M. L. (1984). Vaginal erotic sensitivity. *Journal of Sex & Marital Therapy, 10*, 49–56.

AMBROGGIO, L., et al. (2009). Congenital anomalies and resource utilization in neonates infected with herpes simplex virus. *Sexually Transmitted Diseases, 36*, 680–685.

AMERICAN ACADEMY OF PEDIATRICS TASK FORCE ON CIRCUMCISION. (1999). Circumcision policy statement. *Pediatrics, 103*, 686–693.

AMERICAN CANCER SOCIETY. (2007). www.cancer.org

AMERICAN CANCER SOCIETY. (2010). American Cancer Society fact sheets. www.cancer.org

AMERICAN COLLEGE HEALTH ASSOCIATION. (2004). *Reference group executive summary of National College Health Assessment, Fall 2003.* Baltimore, MD: Author.

AMERICAN COLLEGE OF OBSTETRICIANS and GYNECOLOGISTS. (2009). Educational Pamphlet AP085.

AMERICAN MEDICAL ASSOCIATION (AMA). (1994). *Health care needs of gay men and lesbians in the U.S.* Policy paper adopted December 6. Chicago: Author.

AMERICAN PSYCHIATRIC ASSOCIATION. (2000). *Diagnostic and statistical manual of mental disorders (DSM-IV-TR)* (4th ed.). Washington, DC: Author.

AMERICAN PSYCHOLOGICAL ASSOCIATION. (2010). Sexual orientation and homosexuality. http://www.apahelpecenter.org/articles/article.php?id=31

AMERICAN PSYCHOLOGICAL ASSOCIATION, TASK FORCE ON THE SEXUALIZATION OF GIRLS. (2007). *Report of the APA Task Force on the Sexualization of Girls.* Washington, DC: American Psychological Association. Retrieved from www.apa.org/pi/wpo/sexualization.html

AMERICAN PSYCHOLOGIST. (2005, July/August). Resolution on sexual orientation, parents, and children. *American Psychologist*, 446.

AMERICAN SOCIETY FOR REPRODUCTIVE MEDICINE (2008). Patient fact sheet: Diagnostic testing for male factor infertility. Birmingham, AL; American Society for Reproductive Medicine.

AMES, T. R. H. (1991). Guidelines for providing sexuality-related services to severely and profoundly retarded individuals: The challenge for the nineteen-nineties. *Sexuality and Disability, 9,* 113–122.

AMIR, M. (1971). *Patterns in forcible rape.* Chicago: University of Chicago Press.

AMY, J.-J., & TRIPATHI, V. (2009). Contraception for women: An evidence based overview. *British Medical Journal, 339,* 563–568.

ANDERSON, P. A., et al. (1995). Romantic jealousy and relational satisfaction: A look at the impact of jealousy experience and expression. *Communication Reports, 8,* 77–85.

ANDERSON, P. B., & STRUCKMAN-JOHNSON, C. (1998). Sexually aggressive women—Current perspectives and controversies—Introduction. In P. B. Anderson & C. Struckman-Johnson (Eds.), *Sexually aggressive women* (pp. 1–8). New York: Guilford Press.

ANDERSON, R. A., BANCROFT, J., & WU, F. C. (1992). The effects of exogenous testosterone on sexuality and mood of normal men. *Journal of Clinical and Endocrinological Metabolism, 75,* 1503–1507.

ANDREWS, G., SKINNER, D., & ZUMA, K. (2006). Epidemiology of health and vulnerability among children orphaned and made vulnerable by HIV/AIDS in sub-Saharan Africa, *AIDS Care, 18,* 269–276.

ANGIER, N. (1991, September 1). The biology of what it means to be gay. *The New York Times,* sec. 4, p. 1.

ANGIER, N. (1992, May 20). A male menopause? Jury is still out. *The New York Times.*

ANGIER, N. (1999). *Woman: An intimate geography.* Boston: Houghton Mifflin.

APFELBAUM, B. (1989). Retarded ejaculation: A much misunderstood syndrome. In S. R. Leiblum & R. C. Rosen (Eds.), *Principles and practice of sex therapy: Update for the 1990s* (pp. 168–206). New York: Guilford Press.

AQUINAS, T. (1968). Temperance. In T. Gilby (Ed. and Trans.), *Summa Theologiae* (Vol. 43). New York: McGraw-Hill.

ARAL, S. O., & GORBACH, P. M. (2002). Sexually transmitted infections. In G. M. Wingood & R. J. DiClemente (Eds.), *Handbook of women's sexual and reproductive health* (pp. 255–279). New York: Kluwer Academic/Plenum Publishers.

ARATA, C. M., & BURKHART, B. R. (1996). Post-traumatic stress disorder among college student victims of acquaintance assault. *Journal of Psychology & Human Sexuality, 8,* 79–92.

ARIÈS, E. (1998). Gender differences in interaction: A re-examination. In D. J. Canary & K. Dindia (Eds.), *Sex differences and similarities in communication: Critical essays and empirical investigations of sex and gender in interaction* (pp. 65–81). Mahwah, NJ: Lawrence Erlbaum.

ARIES, P. (1962). *Centuries of childhood.* London: Cape.

ARMSTRONG, K., EISEN, A., & WEBER, B. (2000). Assessing the risk of breast cancer. *New England Journal of Medicine, 342,* 564–571.

ARNETT, J. J. (2000). Emerging adulthood: A theory of development from the late teens through the twenties. *American Psychologist, 55,* 469–480.

ARON, A., & WESTBAY, L. (1996). Dimensions of the prototype of love. *Journal of Personality and Social Psychology, 70,* 535–551.

ARON, A., et al. (2005). Reward, motivation, and emotion systems associated with early-stage intense romantic love. *Journal of Neurophysiology, 94,* 327–337.

ARONOVSKY, A., & FURNHAM, A. (2008). Gender portrayals in food commercials at different times of the day: A content analytic study. *Communications: The European Journal of Communication Research, 33,* 169–190.

ARRIGO, J. M., & PEZDEK, K. (1997). Lessons from the study of psychogenic amnesia. *Current Directions in Psychological Science, 6,* 148–152.

ARRINDELL, W. A., & LUTEIJN, F. (2000). Similarity between intimate partners for personality traits as related to individual levels of satisfaction with life. *Personality and Individual Differences, 28,* 629–637.

ASCH, R. H., et al. (1984). Pregnancy after translaparoscopic gamete intra-fallopian transfer [Letter]. *The Lancet, 2,* 1034–1035.

ASKEW, M. W. (1965). Courtly love: Neurosis as institution. *Psychoanalytic Review, 52,* 19–29.

ASPELMEIER, J., & KERNS, K. (2003). Love and school: Attachment/exploration dynamics in college. *Journal of Social and Personal Relationships, 20,* 5–30.

ASPY, C. B., et al. (2007). Parental communication and youth sexual behaviour. *Journal of Adolescence, 30,* 449–466.

ATANACKOVIC, G., WOLPIN, J., & KOREN, G. (2001). Determinants of the need for hospital care among women with nausea and vomiting of pregnancy. *Clinical and Investigative Medicine, 24(2),* 90–94.

ATHENSTAEDT, V., HAAS, E., & SCHWAB, S. (2004). Gender role self-concept and gender-typed communication behavior in mixed-sex and same-sex dyads. *Sex Roles, 50,* 37–52.

ATKINSON, M. J., & PETROZZINO, J. J. (2009). An evidence-based review of treatment-related determinants of patients' nonadherence to HIV medications. *AIDS Patient Care and STDs, 23,* 903–914.

ATTANÈ, I. (2000). La fécondité chinoise à l'aube du XXI siècle: Constats et incertitudes. *Population, 55,* 233–264.

ATTIA, S., et al. (2009). Sexual transmission of HIV according to viral load and antiretroviral therapy: Systematic review and meta-analysis. *AIDS, 23,* 1397–1404.

AUBIN, S., et al. (2009). Comparing Sildenafil alone vs. Sildenafil plus brief couple sex therapy on erectile dysfunction and couples' sexual and marital quality of life: A pilot study. *Journal of Sex & Marital Therapy, 35,* 122–143.

AUYEUNG, B., et al. (2009). Fetal testosterone predicts sexually differentiated childhood behavior in girls and boys. *Psychological Science, 20,* 144–148.

AVILA-SAAVEDRA, G. (2009). Nothing queer about queer television: Televised construction of gay masculinities. *Media, Culture & Society, 31,* 5–21.

AVIS, N. E., et al. (2001). Is there a menopausal syndrome? Menopausal status and symptoms across racial/ethnic groups. *Social Science and Medicine, 52,* 345–356.

AYLING, K., & USSHER, J. M. (2008). "If sex hurts, am I still a woman?" The subjective experience of vulvodynia in heterosexual women. *Archives of Sexual Behavior, 37,* 294–304.

AYLOR, B., & DAINTON, M. (2001). Antecedents in romantic jealousy experience, expression, and goals. *Western Journal of Communication, 65,* 370–391.

AYRES, M. M., FRIEDMAN, C. K., & LEAPER, C. (2009). Individual and situational factors related to young women's likelihood of confronting sexism in their everyday lives. *Sex Roles, 61,* 449–460.

AZIZ, Y., & GURGEN, F. (2009). Marital satisfaction, sexual problems, and the possible difficulties on sex therapy in traditional Islamic culture. *Journal of Sex and Marital Therapy, 35,* 68–75.

B

BAGATELL, C. J., et al. (1994). Metabolic and behavioral effects of high-dose exogenous testosterone in healthy men. *Journal of Clinical and Endocrinological Metabolism, 79,* 561–567.

BAGGALEY, R. F., WHITE, R. G., & BOILY, M.-C. (2008). Systematic review of orogenital HIV-1 transmission probabilities. *International Journal of Epidemiology, 37,* 1255–1265.

BAILEY, J. M. (2003). *The man who would be queen: The science of gender-bending and transsexualism.* Washington, DC: Joseph Henry Press.

BAILEY, J. M., DUNNE, M. P., & MARTIN, N. G. (2000). Genetic and environmental influences on sexual orientation and its correlates in an Australian twin sample. *Journal of Personality and Social Psychology, 78,* 524–536.

BAILEY, J. M., & PILLARD, R. C. (1991). A genetic study of male sexual orientation. *Archives of General Psychiatry, 48,* 1089–1096.

BAILEY, J. M., & ZUCKER, K. J. (1995). Childhood sex-typed behavior and sexual orientation: A conceptual analysis and quantitative review. *Developmental Psychology, 31,* 43–55.

BAILEY, J. M., et al. (1993). Heritable factors influence sexual orientation in women. *Archives of General Psychiatry, 50,* 217–223.

BAILEY, N. W., & ZUK, M. (2009). Same-sex sexual behavior and evolution. *Trends in Ecology & Evolution, 24,* 439–446.

BAILL, J. C., CULLINS, V. E., & PATI, S. (2003). Counseling issues in tubal sterilization. *American Family Physician, 67,* 1287–1294, 1301–1302.

BAIRD, D. D., et al. (1996). Vaginal douching and reduced fertility. *American Journal of Public Health, 86,* 844–850.

BAKER, B. (1990). Birth control. *Common Cause Magazine, 16(3),* 11–14.

BALLARD-REISCH, D., & ELTON, M. (1992). Gender orientation and the Bem Sex Role Inventory: A psychological construct revisited. *Sex Roles, 27,* 291–306.

BALSAM, K., et al. (2008). Three-year follow-up of same-sex couples who had civil unions in Vermont, same-sex couples not in civil unions, and heterosexual married couples. *Developmental Psychology, 44,* 102–116.

BANCROFT, J., LOFTUS, J., & LONG, J. (2003). Distress about sex: A national survey of women in heterosexual relationships. *Archives of Sexual Behavior, 32,* 193–209.

BANCROFT, J., & VUKADINOVIC, Z. (2004). Sexual addiction, sexual compulsivity, or what? Toward a theoretical model. *Journal of Sex Research, 41,* 225–234.

BANCROFT, J., et al. (2005). The relevance of the dual control model to male sexual dysfunction: The Kinsey Institute/BASRT collaborative project. *Sexual & Relationship Therapy, 20,* 13–30.

BANFIELD, S., & McCABE, M. P. (2001). Extra relationship involvement among women: Are they different from men? *Archives of Sexual Behavior, 30,* 119–142.

BARBACH, L. G. (1976). *For yourself: The fulfillment of female sexuality.* New York: Anchor/Doubleday.

BARBACH, L. G., (1980). *Women discover orgasm.* New York: Free Press.

BARBAREE, H. E., & BLANCHARD, R. (2008). Sexual deviance over the lifespan: Reductions in deviant sexual behavior in the aging sex offender. In D. R. Laws & W. T. O'Donohue (Eds.), *Sexual deviance: Theory, assessment, and treatment* (2nd ed., pp. 37–60). New York: Guilford Press.

BARBAREE, H. E., & MARSHALL, W. L. (1991). The role of male sexual arousal in rape: 6 models. *Journal of Consulting and Clinical Psychology, 59,* 621–630.

BARBAREE, H. E., MARSHALL, W. L., & LANTHEIR, R. (1979). Deviant sexual arousal in rapists. *Behavior Research and Therapy, 17,* 215–222.

BARBAREE, H. E., MARSHALL, W. L., & MCCORMICK, J. (1998). The development of deviant sexual behavior among adolescents and its implications for prevention and treatment. *Irish Journal of Psychology, 19,* 1–31.

BARBAREE, H. E., & SETO, M. C. (1997). Pedophilia: Assessment and treatment. In D. R. Laws & W. T. O'Donohue (Eds.), *Sexual deviance: Theory, assessment, and treatment* (pp. 175–193). New York: Guilford Press.

BARCUS, F. E. (1983). *Images of life on children's television: Sex roles, minorities, and families.* New York: Praeger.

BARDONI, B., et al. (1994). A dosage sensitive locus at chromosome XP21 is involved in male to female sex reversal. *Nature Genetics, 7,* 497–501.

BARGER, M. K. (2005). The history of nurse-midwifery/midwifery practice. *Journal of Midwifery & Women's Health, 50,* 87–90.

BARKER-COLLO, S. L. (2001). Adult reports of child and adult attributions of blame for childhood sexual abuse: Predicting adult adjustment and suicidal behaviors in adults. *Child Abuse & Neglect, 25,* 1329–1341.

BARNES, M. L., & STERNBERG, R. J. (1997). A hierarchical model of love and its prediction of satisfaction in close relationships. In R. J. Sternberg & M. Hojjat (Eds.), *Satisfaction in close relationships* (pp. 79–101). New York: Guilford Press.

BARNES, R. H. (1999). Marriage by capture. *Journal of the Royal Anthropology Institute, 5,* 57–73.

BARNES, T., & EARDLEY, I. (2007). Premature ejaculation: The scope of the problem. *Journal of Sex & Marital Therapy, 33,* 151–170.

BARNETT, R. C., & HYDE, J. S. (2001). Women, men, work, and family. An expansionist theory. *American Psychologist, 56,* 781–796.

BARNHART, K., FURMAN, I., & DEVOTO, L. (1995). Attitudes and practice of couples regarding sexual relations during the menses and spotting. *Contraception, 51,* 93–98.

BARNHART, K. T. (2009). Ectopic pregnancy. *New England Journal of Medicine, 362,* 379–387.

BARON, L., STRAUS, M., & JAFFEE, D. (1987). Legitimate violence, violent attitudes, and rape: A test of the cultural spillover theory. *Annals of the New York Academy of Sciences,* SR121, 1–23.

BAROUCH, D. H., & KORBER, B. (2010). HIV-1 vaccine development after STEP. *Annual Review of Medicine, 61,* 153–167.

BARRON, N., & KIMMEL, M. (2000). Sexual violence in three pornographic media: Towards a sociological explanation. *Journal of Sex Research, 37,* 1–8.

BARROW, G., & SMITH, T. (1992). *Aging, ageism, and society.* St. Paul, MN: West.

BARRY, H., III, & SCHLEGEL, A. (1984). Measurements of adolescent sexual behavior in the standard sample of societies. *Ethnology, 23,* 315–329.

BARRY, K. (1995). *The prostitution of sexuality: The global exploitation of women.* New York: New York University Press.

BARSETTI, I., et al. (1998). The differentiation of intrafamilial and extrafamilial heterosexual child molester. *Journal of Interpersonal Violence, 13,* 275–286.

BARSON, M. (1984, March). Penis size: A sexual or political issue? *Cosmopolitan,* 224–226.

BARTELS, A., & ZEKI, S. (2004). The neural correlates of maternal and romantic love. *Neuroimage, 21,* 1155–1166.

BARTHOLOMEW, K., & HOROWITZ, L. M. (1991). Attachment styles among young adults: A test of a four-category model. *Journal of Personality and Social Psychology, 61,* 226–244.

BARTON, M. B., HARRIS, R., & FLETCHER, S. W. (1999). Does this patient have breast cancer? The screening clinical breast examination: Should it be done? How? *Journal of the American Medical Association, 282,* 1270–1280.

BASILE, K. C., et al. (2006). Stalking in the United States: Recent national prevalence estimates. *American Journal of Preventive Medicine, 31,* 172–175.

BASOW, S. A., & JOHNSON, K. (2000). Predictors of homophobia in female college students. *Sex Roles, 42,* 391–404.

BASSON, R. (2000). The female sexual response: A different model. *Journal of Sex & Marital Therapy, 26,* 51–65.

BASSON, R. (2001a). Human sex-response cycles. *Journal of Sex & Marital Therapy, 27,* 33–43.

BASSON, R. (2001b). Are the complexities of women's sexual function reflected in the new consensus definitions of dysfunction? *Journal of Sex & Marital Therapy, 27,* 105–112.

BASSON, R. (2001c). Using a different model for female sexual response to address women's problematic low sexual desire. *Journal of Sex & Marital Therapy, 27,* 395–403.

BASSON, R. (2002a). A model of women's sexual arousal. *Journal of Sex & Marital Therapy, 28,* 1–10.

BASSON, R. (2002b). Women's sexual desire—disordered or misunderstood? *Journal of Sex & Marital Therapy, 28*(s), 17–28.

BASSON, R. (2002c). Are our definitions of women's desire, arousal and sexual pain disorders too broad and our definition of orgasmic disorder too narrow? *Journal of Sex & Marital Therapy, 28,* 289–300.

BASSON, R. (2009). Testosterone for low libido. *New England Journal of Medicine, 360,* 728.

BASSON, R., et al. (2000). Report of the International Consensus Development Conference on Female Sexual Dysfunction: Definitions and classifications. *The Journal of Urology, 163,* 888–893.

BASSON, R., et al. (2003). Definitions of women's sexual dysfunction reconsidered: Advocating expansion and revision. *Journal of Psychosomatic Obstetrics & Gynecology, 24,* 221–229.

BAUER, G. R., & JAIRAM, J. A. (2008). Are lesbians really women who have sex with women (WSW)? Methodological concerns in measuring sexual orientation in health research. *Women & Health, 48,* 383–408.

BAUMEISTER, R. F. (2000). Gender differences in erotic plasticity: The female sex drive as socially flexible and responsive. *Psychological Bulletin, 126,* 347–374.

BAUMEISTER, R. F., & BUTLER, J. L. (1997). Sexual masochism: Deviance without pathology. In D. R. Laws & W. T. O'Donohue (Eds.), *Sexual deviance: Theory, assessment, and treatment* (pp. 225–239). New York: Guilford Press.

BAUMEISTER, R. F., CATANESE, K. R., & VOHS, K. D. (2001). Is there a gender difference in strength of sex drive? *Personality and Social Psychology Review, 5,* 242–273.

BAUMEISTER, R. F., & LEARY, M. R. (1995). The need to belong: Desire for interpersonal attachments as a fundamental motivation. *Psychological Bulletin, 117,* 497–529.

BAUSERMAN, R. (1998). Egalitarian, sexist, and aggressive sexual materials: Attitude effects and viewer responses. *Journal of Sex Research, 35,* 244–253.

BAUSERMAN, R., & DAVIS, C. (1996). Perceptions of early sexual experiences and adult sexual adjustment. *Journal of Psychology & Human Sexuality, 8*(3), 37–59.

BAXTER, J., & WESTERN, M. (1998). Satisfaction with housework: Examining the paradox. *Sociology, 32,* 101–120.

BEAVER, K. M., et al. (2008). Anabolic-androgenic steroid use and involvement in violent behavior in a nationally representative sample of young adult males in the United States. *American Journal of Public Health, 98,* 2185–2187.

BECK-SAGUÉ, C. M., & SOLOMON, F. (1999). Sexually transmitted diseases in abused children and adolescent and adult victims of rape: Review of selected literature. *Clinical Infectious Diseases, 28,* S74–S83.

BECK, U. (1995). *Ecological enlightenment: Essays on the politics of the risk society.* Atlantic Highlands, NJ: Humanities Press.

BECKER, J., et al. (2008). *Sex differences in the brain: From genes to behavior.* New York: Oxford University Press.

BECKETT, M. K., et al. (2010). Timing of parent and child communication about sexuality relative to children's sexual behaviors. *Pediatrics, 125,* 34–42.

BEER, J., & HORN, J. M. (1999). The influence of rearing order on personality development within two adoption cohorts. *Journal of Personality, 68,* 789–819.

BEGLEY, S., & GLICK, D. (1994, March 21). The estrogen complex. *Newsweek,* 76–77.

BEITCHMAN, J. H., et al. (1991). A review of the short-term effects of child sexual abuse. *Child Abuse & Neglect, 15,* 537–556.

BEITCHMAN, J. H., et al. (1992). A review of the long-term effects of child sexual abuse. *Child Abuse & Neglect, 16,* 101–118.

BELCASTRO, P. (1985). Sexual behavior differences between African American and white students. *Journal of Sex Research, 21,* 55–67.

BELL, A. P., & WEINBERG, M. S. (1978). *Homosexualities.* New York: Simon & Schuster.

BELL, A. P., WEINBERG, M. S., & HAMMERSMITH, S. K. (1981). *Sexual preference: Its development in men and women.* Bloomington: Indiana University Press.

BELL, J. (2009). Why embarrassment inhibits the acquisition and use of condoms: A qualitative approach to understanding risky sexual behavior. *Journal of Adolescence, 32,* 379–391.

BELL, K. (2005). Genital cutting and Western discourses on sexuality. *Medical Anthropology Quarterly, 19,* 125–148.

BELL, R. (1998, April 12). Felony status of sex offense fought. *New Orleans Times-Picayune,* p. A1, A12.

BELZER, G. (1981). Orgasmic expulsions of women: A review and heuristic inquiry. *Journal of Sex Research, 17,* 1–12.

BEM, D. J. (1996). Exotic becomes erotic: A developmental theory of sexual orientation. *Psychological Review, 103,* 320–335.

BEM, S. L. (1974). The measurement of psychological androgyny. *Journal of*

Consulting and Clinical Psychology, 42, 155–162.

BEM, S. L. (1981). Gender schema theory: A cognitive account of sex typing. *Psychological Review*, 88, 354–364.

BEM, S. L. (1983). Gender schema theory and its implications for child development: Raising gender-aschematic children in a gender-schematic society. *Signs*, 8, 598–616.

BENTLER, P. M., & PEELER, W. H. (1979). Models of female orgasm. *Archives of Sexual Behavior*, 8, 405–424.

BERENBAUM, S. A., & SNYDER, E. (1995). Early hormonal influences on childhood sex-typed activity and playmate preferences: Implications for the development of sexual orientation. *Developmental Psychology*, 31, 31–42.

BERENSON, A. B. (1993). Appearance of the hymen at birth and one year of age: A longitudinal study. *Pediatrics*, 91, 820–825.

BERG, R. C. (2009). Barebacking: A review of the literature. *Archives of Sexual Behavior*, 38, 754–764.

BERGNER, R. M., & BRIDGES, A. J. (2002). The significance of heavy pornography involvement for romantic partners: Research and clinical implications. *Journal of Sex & Marital Therapy*, 28, 193–206.

BERKOFF, M. C., et al. (2008). Has this prepubertal girl been sexually abused? *Journal of the American Medical Association*, 300, 2779–2792.

BERLINER, D., et al. (1996). The functionality of the human vomeronasal organ (VNO): Evidence for steroid receptors. *Steroid Biochemistry & Molecular Biology*, 58, 259–265.

BERMANT, G., & DAVIDSON, J. M. (1974). *Biological bases of sexual behavior.* New York: Harper & Row.

BERNAT, J. A., CALHOUN, K. S., & STOLP, S. (1998). Sexually aggressive men's responses to a date rape analogue: Alcohol as a disinhibiting cue. *Journal of Sex Research*, 35, 341–348.

BERSAMIN, M. M., et al. (2005). Promising to wait: Virginity pledges and adolescent sexual behavior. *Journal of Adolescent Health*, 36, 428–436

BERSCHEID, E. (1982). Interpersonal attraction. In E. Aronson & G. Lindzey (Eds.), *Handbook of social psychology* (3rd ed.). Reading, MA: Addison-Wesley.

BERSCHEID, E., & WALSTER, E. (1974). A little bit about love. In T. L. Huston (Ed.), *Foundations of interpersonal attraction* (pp. 355–381). New York: Academic Press.

BERSCHEID, E., & WALSTER, E. (1978). *Interpersonal attraction* (2nd ed.). Reading, MA: Addison-Wesley.

BEST, K. (2002). The many meanings of menopause. *Network*, 22(1), 30–31.

BEYNE, Y. (1989). *Menarche to menopause: Reproductive lives of peasant women in two cultures.* Albany: State University of New York Press.

BEYNE, Y., & MARTIN, M. C. (2001). Menopausal experiences and bone density of Mayan women in Yucatan, Mexico. *American Journal of Human Biology*, 13, 505–511.

BHUGRA, D., POPELYUK, D., & MCMULLEN, I. (2010). Paraphilias across cultures: Contexts and controversies. *Journal of Sex Research*, 47, 242–256.

BIANCHI, S. M., & CASPER, L. M. (2000). American families. *Population Bulletin*, 55(4), 1–42.

BIBLARZ, T. J., & STACEY, J. (2010). How does the gender of parents matter? *Journal of Marriage and Family*, 72, 3–22.

BIEBER, I., et al. (1962). *Homosexuality: A psychoanalytic study.* New York: Basic Books.

BILLINGS, E. L., BILLINGS, J. J., & CATARINCH, M. (1974). *Atlas of the ovulation method.* Collegeville, MN: Liturgical Press.

BILLY, J. O. G., GRADY, W. R., & SILL, M. E. (2009). Sexual risk-taking among adult dating couples in the United States. *Perspectives on Sexual and Reproductive Health*, 41, 74–83.

BINDER, R. L. (1998). American Psychiatric Association resource document on controversies in child custody: Gay and lesbian parenting, transracial adoptions, joint versus sole custody, and custody gender issues. *Journal of the American Academy of Psychiatry and the Law*, 26, 267–276.

BINIK, Y. M. (2005). Should dyspareunia be retained as a sexual dysfunction in DSM-V? A painful classification decision. *Archives of Sexual Behavior*, 34, 11–21.

BINIK, Y., & MEANA, M. (2009). The future of sex therapy: Specialization or marginalization? *Archives of Sexual Behavior*, 38, 1016–1027.

BINOVA, S., & CRITELLI, J. (2009). The nature of women's rape fantasies: An analysis of prevalence, frequency, and contents. *Journal of Sex Research*, 46, 33–45.

BIRD, M. H. (2006). Sexual addiction and marriage and family therapy: Facilitating individual and relationship healing through couple therapy. *Journal of Marital and Family Therapy*, 32, 297–310.

BIRNS, B., & STERNGLANZ, S. H. (1983). Sex-role socialization: Looking back and looking ahead. In M. B. Liss (Ed.), *Social and cognitive skills: Sex roles and children's play.* New York: Academic Press.

BIRO, F. M., & DORN, L. D. (2005). Puberty and adolescent sexuality. *Pediatric Annals*, 34, 777–783.

BISSON, M. A., & LEVINE, T. R. (2009). Negotiating a friends with benefits relationship. *Archives of Sexual Behavior*, 38, 66–73.

BITTLES, A. H., et al. (1991). Reproductive behavior and health in consanguineous marriages. *Science*, 252, 789–794.

BJÖRKLUND, K., et al. (2010). The prevalence of stalking among Finnish university students. *Journal of Interpersonal Violence*, 25, 684–698.

BLACK, D., et al. (2000). Demographics of the gay and lesbian population in the United States: Evidence from available systematic data sources. *Demography*, 37, 139–154.

BLACKARD, J. T., et al. (2002). Human immunodeficiency virus superinfection and recombination: Current state of knowledge and potential clinical consequences. *Clinical Infectious Diseases*, 34, 1108–1114.

BLACKMAN, D. K., BENNETT, E. M., & MILLER, D. S. (1999). Trends in self-reported use of mammograms (1989–1997) and Papanicolaou tests (1991–1997)—Behavioral risk factor surveillance system. *Morbidity and Mortality Weekly Report*, 48, 1–22.

BLACKWOOD, E. (2000). Culture and women's sexualities. *Journal of Social Issues*, 56, 223–238.

BLAIR, C. D., & LANYON, R. I. (1981). Exhibitionism: Etiology and treatment. *Psychological Bulletin*, 89, 439–463.

BLAKEMORE, J. E. O., & CENTERS, R. E. (2005). Characteristics of boys' and girls' toys. *Sex Roles*, 53, 619–633.

BLANC, A. K. (2001). The effect of power in sexual relationships on sexual and reproductive health: An examination of the evidence. *Studies in Family Planning*, 32, 189–213.

BLANCHARD, R. (2001). Fraternal birth order and the maternal immune hypothesis of male homosexuality. *Hormones and Behavior*, 40, 105–114.

BLANCHARD, R. (2005). Early history of the concept of autogynephilia. *Archives of Sexual Behavior*, 34, 439–446.

BLANCHARD, R., & BOGAERT, A. F. (1996). Homosexuality in men and number of older brothers. *American Journal of Psychiatry*, 153, 27–31.

BLANCHARD, R., et al. (2009). Pedophilia, hebephilia, and the DSM-V. *Archives of Sexual Behavior*, 38, 335–350.

BLANCHARD-FIELDS, F., & SUHRER-ROUSSEL, L. (1992). Adaptive coping and social cognitive development of women. In E. E. Guice (Ed.), *Women and aging: Now and the future?* Westport, CT: Greenwood Press.

BLANK, H. (2007). *Virgin: The untouched history.* New York: Bloomsbury U.S.A.

BLEAKLEY, A., et al. (2008). It works both ways: The relationship between exposure to sexual content in the media and adolescent sexual behavior. *Media Psychology*, 11, 443–461.

BLEAKLEY, A., et al. (2009). How sources of sexual information relate to adolescents' beliefs about sex. *American Journal of Health Behavior*, 33, 37–48.

BLESKE, A. L., & BUSS, D. M. (2000). Can men and women be just friends? *Personal Relationships*, 7, 131–151.

BLOND, A. (2008). Impacts of exposure to images of ideal bodies on male body dissatisfaction: A review. *Body Image*, 5, 244–250.

BLOOD, R. O., JR. (1967). *Love match and arranged marriage.* New York: Free Press.

BLUME, J. (1970). *Are you there, God? It's me, Margaret.* Englewood Cliffs, NJ: Bradbury Press.

BLUMENTHAL, S., GUDJONSSON, G., & BURNS, J. (1999). Cognitive distortions and blame attribution in sex offenders against adults and children. *Child Abuse & Neglect*, 23, 129–143.

BLYTH, B., & DUCKETT, J. W. (1991). Gonadal differentiation: A review of physiological process and influencing factors based on recent experimental evidence. *Journal of Urology*, 145, 689–694.

BOCKTING, W., BENNER, A., & COLEMAN, E. (2009). Gay and bisexual identity development among female-to-male transsexuals in North America: Emergence of a transgender sexuality. *Archives of Sexual Behavior*, 38, 688–701.

BOESCHEN, L. E., SALES, B. D., & KOSS, M. P. (1998). Rape trauma experts in the courtroom. *Psychology, Public Policy, and Law*, 4, 414–432.

BOGAERT, A. F. (1996). Volunteer bias in human sexuality research: Evidence for both sexuality and personality differences in males. *Archives of Sexual Behavior*, 25, 125–140.

BOGAERT, A. F. (2000). Birth order and sexual orientation in a national probability sample. *Journal of Sex Research*, 37, 1–8.

BOGAERT, A. F. (2001). Personality, individual differences, and preferences for the sexual media. *Archives of Sexual Behavior*, 30, 29–53.

BOGAERT, A. F. (2005a). Sibling sex ratio and sexual orientation in men and women: New tests in two national probability samples. *Archives of Sexual Behavior*, 34, 111–116.

BOGAERT, A. F. (2005b). Gender role/identity and sibling sex ratio in homosexual men. *Journal of Sex & Marital Therapy*, 31, 217–227.

BOGAERT, A. F., & HERSHBERGER, S. (1999). The relationship between sexual orientation and penile size. *Archives of Sexual Behavior*, 28, 213–221.

BOGAERT, A. F., WOODARD, V., & HAFER, C. L. (1999). Intellectual ability and reactions to pornography. *Journal of Sex Research, 36,* 283–291.

BOGREN, L. (1991). Changes in sexuality in women and men during pregnancy. *Archives of Sexual Behavior, 20,* 35–46.

BOHLEN, J. G., HELD, J. P., & SANDERSON, M. (1980). The male orgasm: Pelvic contractions measured by anal probe. *Archives of Sexual Behavior, 9,* 503–521.

BOHLEN, J. G., et al. (1982). The female orgasm: Pelvic contractions. *Archives of Sexual Behavior, 11,* 367–386.

BOIES, S. C., KNUDSON, G., & YOUNG, J. (2004). The Internet, sex, and youths: Implications for sexual development. *Sexual Addiction & Compulsivity, 11,* 343–363.

BOLES, J., & ELIFSON, K. W. (1994). Sexual identity and HIV: The male prostitute. *Journal of Sex Research, 31,* 39–46.

BOLLING, D. R. (1988, November). Survey of women and heterosexual anal intercourse. Paper presented at the annual meeting of the Scientific Study of Sexuality, San Francisco.

BONDURANT, B. (2001). University women's acknowledgement of rape. *Violence Against Women, 7,* 294–314.

BONETTI, A., et al. (2007). Side effects of anabolic androgenic steroids abuse. *International Journal of Sports Medicine, 29,* 679–687.

BONGAARTS, J., & SINDING, S. (2008). A response to critics of family planning programs. *Perspectives on Sexual and Reproductive Health, 35(3),* 39–44.

BONNAR-KIDD, K. K. (2010). Sexual offender laws and prevention of sexual violence or recidivism. *American Journal of Public Health, 100,* 412–419.

BORELLI-KERNER, S., & BERNELL, B. (1997). Couple therapy of sexual disorders. In R. S. Charlton (Ed.), *Treating sexual disorders* (pp. 165–199). San Francisco: Jossey-Bass.

BOS, H., & VAN BALEN, F. (2008). Children in planned lesbian families: Stigmatization, psychological adjustment and protective factors. *Culture, Health and Sexuality, 10,* 221–336.

BOSTON WOMEN'S HEALTH BOOK COLLECTIVE. (1984). *The new our bodies, ourselves.* New York: Simon & Schuster.

BOSTON WOMEN'S HEALTH BOOK COLLECTIVE. (2005). *Our bodies, ourselves: A new edition for a new era.* New York: Simon & Schuster.

BOSTWICK, J. M., & MARTIN, K. A. (2007). A man's brain in an ambiguous body: A case of mistaken gender identity. *American Journal of Psychiatry, 164,* 1499–1505.

BOSWELL, J. (1980). *Christianity, social tolerance, and homosexuality: Gay people in Western Europe from the beginning of the Christian era to the fourteenth century.* Chicago: University of Chicago Press.

BOTH, S., & EVERAERD, W. (2002). Comment on "The female sexual response: A different model." *Journal of Sex & Marital Therapy, 28,* 11–15.

BOTROS, S., et al. (2006). Effect of parity on sexual function. *Obstetrics and Gynecology, 107,* 765–770.

BOUMAN, F. G. (1988). Sex reassignment surgery in male to female transsexuals. *Annals of Plastic Surgery, 21,* 526–531.

BOWDEN, F. J., & GARNETT, G. P. (2000). Trichomonas vaginalis epidemiology: Parameterising and analysing a model of treatment interventions. *Sexually Transmitted Infections, 76,* 248–256.

BOWLBY, J. (1969). *Attachment and loss: Vol. 1. Attachment.* New York: Basic Books.

BOWMAN, E. A. (2010). An explanation for the shape of the human penis. *Archives of Sexual Behavior, 39,* 216.

BOYLE, G. J., et al. (2002). Male circumcision: Pain, trauma and psychosexual sequelae. *Journal of Health Psychology, 7,* 329–343.

BRADFORD, J. (1997). Medical interventions in sexual deviance. In D. R. Laws & W. T. O'Donohue (Eds.), *Sexual deviance: Theory, assessment, and treatment* (pp. 449–464). New York: Guilford Press.

BRADFORD, J. M. W., BOULET, J., & PAWLAK, A. (1992). The paraphilias: A multiplicity of deviant behaviors. *Canadian Journal of Psychiatry, 37,* 104–107.

BRADLEY, R. A. (1981). *Husband coached childbirth.* New York: Harper & Row.

BRADLEY, S. J., & ZUCKER, K. J. (1997). Gender identity disorder: A review of the past 10 years. *Journal of the American Academy of Child and Adolescent Psychology, 36,* 872–880.

BRADSHAW, C., et al. (2006). Etiologies of nongonococcal urethritis: Bacteria, viruses, and the association with orogenital exposure. *Journal of Infectious Diseases, 193,* 333–345.

BRAINERD, C. J., & REYNA, V. F. (1998). When things that were never experienced are easier to "remember" than things that were. *Psychological Science, 9,* 484–489.

BRAMBATI, B., & TULVI, L. (2005). Chorionic villus sampling and amniocentesis. *Current Opinions in Obstetrics & Gynecology, 17,* 197–201.

BRAUN, M., & SCOTT, J. (2009). Gender-role egalitarianism—Is the trend reversal real? *International Journal of Public Opinion Research, 21,* 362–367.

BRAUN, M. F., & BRYAN, A. (2006). Female waist-to-hip and male waist-to-shoulder ratios as determinants of romantic partner desirability. *Journal of Social and Personal Relationships, 23,* 805–819.

BRAUN, V., & KITZINGER, C. (2001). "Snatch," "hole," or "honey-pot"? Semantic categories and the problem of nonspecificity in female genital slang. *Journal of Sex Research, 38,* 146–158.

BRAUN-COURVILLE, D. K., & ROJAS, M. (2009). Exposure to sexually explicit web sites and adolescent attitudes and behaviors, *Journal of Adolescent Health, 45,* 156–162.

BRECKLIN, L. R., & ULLMAN, S. E. (2005). Self-defense or assertiveness training and women's responses to sexual attacks. *Journal of Interpersonal Violence, 20,* 738–762.

BREEDLOVE, S. M. (1994). Sexual differentiation of the human nervous system. *Annual Review of Psychology, 45,* 389–418.

BREEDLOVE, S. M. (1997). Sex on the brain. *Nature, 389,* 801.

BREITENBECHER, K. H. (2000). Sexual assault on college campuses: Is an ounce of prevention enough? *Applied & Preventive Psychology, 9,* 23–52.

BREMNER, J. D., SHOBE, K. K., & KIHLSTROM, J. F. (2000). False memories in women with self-reported childhood sexual abuse: An empirical study. *Psychological Science, 11,* 333–337.

BRESLAU, K. (2002, June 3). The "sextasy" craze. *Newsweek,* 30.

BRESLOW, N., EVANS, L., & LANGLEY, J. (1985). On the prevalence and roles of females in the sadomasochistic subculture. *Archives of Sexual Behavior, 14,* 303–317.

BRESLOW, N., EVANS, L., & LANGLEY, J. (1986). Comparisons among heterosexual, bisexual, and homosexual sadomasochists. *Journal of Homosexuality, 13,* 83–107.

BRETSCHNEIDER, J. G., & MCCOY, N. L. (1988). Sexual interest and behavior in healthy 80- to 102-year-olds. *Archives of Sexual Behavior, 17,* 109–129.

BREWER, D., et al. (2008). Prevalence of male clients of street prostitute women in the United States. *Human Organization, 67,* 346–357.

BREWSTER, K. L., & PADAVIC, I. (2000). Change in gender-ideology, 1977–1996: The contributions of intracohort change and population turnover. *Journal of Marriage and Family, 62,* 477–487.

BREWSTER, K. L., & TILLMAN, K. H. (2008). Who's doing it? Patterns and predictors of youths' oral sexual experiences. *Journal of Adolescent Health, 42,* 73–80.

BREWSTER, K. L., et al. (1998). The changing impact of religion on the sexual and contraceptive behavior of adolescent women in the United States. *Journal of Marriage and Family, 60,* 493–504.

BRIDGES, A. (2006, July 13). Single pill cases burden of HIV "cocktail" therapy. *New Orleans Times-Picayune,* p. A15.

BRIDGES, J. S., & MCGRAIL, C. A. (1989). Attributions of responsibility for date and stranger rape. *Sex Roles, 21,* 273–286.

BRINGLE, R. G., & BUUNK, B. P. (1985). Jealousy and social behavior: A review of personal, relationship and situational determinants. In P. Shaver (Ed.), *Review of personality and social psychology* (Vol. 2, pp. 241–264). Beverly Hills, CA: Sage.

BRODERICK, G.A., et al. (2010). Priapism: Pathogenesis, epidemiology, and management. *Journal of Sexual Medicine, 7,* 476–500.

BRODSKY, S. L. (1976). Prevention of rape: Deterrence by the potential victim. In M. J. Walker & S. L. Brodsky (Eds.), *Sexual assault.* Lexington, MA: D. C. Heath.

BROOKS-GUNN, J., & PAIKOFF, R. (1997). Sexuality and developmental transitions during adolescence. In J. Schulenberg, J. L. Maggs, & K. Hurrelmann (Eds.), *Health risks and developmental transitions during adolescence* (pp. 190–219). New York: Cambridge University Press.

BROWN, D. (1990). The penis pin. In V. Sutlive (Ed.), *Female and male in Borneo: Contributions and challenges to gender studies* (pp. 435–454). Borneo: Borneo Research Council.

BROWN, G. R. (1994). Women in relationships with cross-dressing men: A descriptive study from a nonclinical setting. *Archives of Sexual Behavior, 23,* 515–530.

BROWN, J. D. (2002). Mass media influences on sexuality. *Journal of Sex Research, 39,* 42–45.

BROWN, J. D., CHILDERS, K. W., & WASZAK, C. S. (1990). Television and adolescent sexuality. *Journal of Adolescent Health Care, 11,* 62–70.

BROWN, J. D., HALPERN, C. T., & L'ENGLE, K. L. (2005). Mass media as a sexual super peer for early maturing girls. *Journal of Adolescent Health, 36,* 420–427.

BROWN, J. D. & L'ENGLE, K. L. (2009). X-rated. *Communication Research, 36,* 129–151.

BROWN, J. D., & NEWCOMER, S. F. (1991). Televison viewing and adolescents' sexual behavior. *Journal of Homosexuality, 21,* 77–91.

BROWN, S. L. (2002). Epidemiology of silicone-gel breast implants. *Epidemiology, 13(S),* S34–39.

BROWN, T. J., YEN-MOORE, A., & TYRING, S. K. (1999). An overview of sexually transmitted diseases. Pt. II. *Journal of the American Academy of Dermatology, 41,* 661–677.

BROWN, Z. A., et al. (1997). The acquisition of herpes simplex virus during pregnancy.

New England Journal of Medicine, 337, 509–515.

BROWNE, J., & MINICHIELLO, V. (1996). Condoms: Dilemmas of caring and autonomy in heterosexual safe sex practices. *Venereology, 9,* 24–33.

BROWNING, C. R., LEVENTHAL, T., & BROOKS-GUNN, J. (2005). Sexual initiation in early adolescence: The nexus of parental and community control. *American Sociological Review, 70,* 758–778.

BROWNMILLER, S. (1975). *Against our will: Men, women, and rape.* New York: Simon & Schuster.

BROWNMILLER, S. (1993, January 4). Making female bodies the battlefield. *Newsweek,* 37.

BRUCE, K. E., & WALKER, L. J. (2001). College students attitudes about AIDS: 1986 to 2000. *AIDS Education and Prevention, 13,* 428–437.

BRÜCKNER, H., & BEARMAN, P. (2005). After the promise: The STD consequences of adolescent virginity pledges. *Journal of Adolescent Health, 36,* 271–278.

BRUMBERG, J. J. (1997). *The body project.* New York: Random House.

BRUNDAGE, J. A. (1984). Let me count the ways: Canonists and theologians contemplate coital positions. *Journal of Medieval History, 10,* 81–93.

BRUNHAM, R. C., et al. (1988). Etiology and outcome of acute pelvic inflammatory disease. *Journal of Infectious Diseases, 158,* 510–517.

BRUNO, K. (2005, May). Sudden infertility. *Ladies' Home Journal, 190,* 192.

BRYANT, J., & BROWN, D. (1989). Uses of pornography. In Z. Dolf & B. Jennings (Eds.), *Pornography: Research advances and policy considerations.* Hillsdale, NJ: Lawrence Erlbaum.

BRYANT, J., & ROCKWELL, S. C. (1994). Effects of massive exposure to sexually oriented prime-time television programming on adolescents' moral judgment. In D. Zillman, J. Bryant, & A. C. Huston (Eds.), *Media, children, and the family: Social scientific, psychodynamic, and clinical perspectives* (pp. 183–195). Hillsdale, NJ: Lawrence Erlbaum.

BRYNER, C. (1989). Recurrent toxic shock syndrome. *American Family Physician, 39,* 157–164.

BUCHBINDER, S. P., et al. (1994). Long-term HIV-1 infection without immunologic progression. *AIDS, 8,* 1123–1128.

BUCK, G. M., et al. (1997). Life-style factors and female infertility. *Epidemiology, 8,* 435–441.

BUFFUM, J., et al. (1981). Drugs and sexual function. In H. Lief (Ed.), *Sexual problems in medical practice.* Monroe, WI: American Medical Association.

BUHI, E. R., CLAYTON, H., & SURRENCY, H. H. (2009). Stalking victimization among college women and subsequent help-seeking behaviors, *Journal of American College Health, 57,* 419–426.

BUKOWSKI, R., et al. (2009). Preconceptional folate supplementation and the risk of spontaneous preterm birth: A cohort study. *Plos Medicine,* 6,e1000061.

BULLIVANT, S. B., et al. (2004). Women's sexual experience during the menstrual cycle: Identification of the sexual phase by noninvasive measurement of luteinizing hormone. *Journal of Sex Research, 41,* 82–93.

BULLOUGH, B., & BULLOUGH, V. L. (1997). Female prostitution: Current research and changing interpretations. In R. Rosen, C. M. Davis, & H. J. Ruppel, Jr. (Eds.), *Annual review of sex research, 7* (Vol. VII, pp. 158–180). Allentown, PA: Society for the Scientific Study of Sexuality.

BULLOUGH, V. L. (1981). Age at menarche: A misunderstanding. *Science, 213,* 365–366.

BULLOUGH, V. L. (1991). Transvestism: A reexamination. *Journal of Psychology & Human Sexuality, 4,* 53–67.

BULLOUGH, V. L. (1998). Alfred Kinsey and the Kinsey Report: Historical overview and lasting contributions. *Journal of Sex Research, 35,* 127–131.

BULLOUGH, V. L., & BULLOUGH, B. (1993). *Cross dressing, sex, and gender.* Philadelphia: University of Pennsylvania Press.

BULUN, S.E. (2009). Endometriosis. *New England Journal of Medicine, 360,* 268–279.

BUMBY, K. M. (1996). Assessing the cognitive distortions of child molesters and rapists: Development and validation of the MOLEST and RAPE scales. *Sexual Abuse, 8,* 37–54.

BUMPASS, L., & LU, H.-H. (2000). Trends in cohabitation and implications for children's family contexts in the United States. *Population Studies, 54,* 29–41.

BUMPASS, L. L., THOMSON, E., & GODECKER, A. L. (2000). Women, men, and contraceptive sterilization. *Fertility and Sterility, 73,* 937–946.

BURGESS, A. W., & HOLMSTROM, L. L. (1974). Rape trauma syndrome. *American Journal of Psychiatry, 131,* 981–986.

BURGESS, A. W., & HOLMSTROM, L. L. (1979). Rape: Sexual disruption and recovery. *American Journal of Orthopsychiatry, 49,* 648–657.

BURT, M. R. (1980). Cultural myths and supports for rape. *Journal of Personality and Social Psychology, 38,* 217–230.

BURTON, R. (1963). The anatomy of melancholy. In A. M. Witherspoon & F. Warnke (Eds.), *Seventeenth-century prose and poetry* (pp. 132–133). New York: Harcourt Brace Jovanovich. (Original work published 1651.)

BUSCH, N. B., et al. (2002). Male customers of prostituted women. *Violence Against Women, 8,* 1093–1112.

BUSS, D. M. (1985). Human mate selection. *American Scientist, 73,* 47–51.

BUSS, D. M. (1989). Sex differences in human mate selection: Evolutionary hypotheses tested in 37 cultures. *Behavioral and Brain Sciences, 12,* 1–49.

BUSS, D. M. (1999). *Evolutionary psychology: The new science of the mind.* Boston: Allyn & Bacon.

BUSS, D. M., & BARNES, M. F. (1987). Preferences in human mate selection. *Journal of Personality and Social Psychology, 50,* 559–570.

BUSS, D. M., LARSEN, R. J., & WESTEN, D. (1996). Sex differences in jealousy: Not gone, not forgotten, and not explained by alternative hypotheses. *Psychological Science, 7,* 373–375.

BUSS, D. M., & SCHMITT, D. P. (1993). Sexual strategies theory: An evolutionary perspective on human mating. *Psychological Review, 100,* 204–232.

BUSS, D. M., & SHACKELFORD, T. K. (1997). From vigilance to violence: Mate retention tactics in married couples. *Journal of Personality and Social Psychology, 72,* 346–361.

BUSS, D. M., et al. (1992). Sex differences in jealousy: Evolution, physiology, and psychology. *Psychological Science, 3,* 251–255.

BUTLER, C. A. (1976). New data about female sexual response. *Journal of Sex & Marital Therapy, 2,* 40–46.

BUTLER, J. (1990). *Gender trouble: Feminism and the subversion of identity.* New York: Routledge.

BUTLER, J., et al. (1993). Supportive nurse-midwife care associated with a reduced incidence of cesarean section. *American Journal of Obstetrics & Gynecology, 168,* 1407–1413.

BUTZER, B., & CAMPBELL, L. (2008). Adult attachment, sexual satisfaction, and relationship satisfaction: A study of married couples. *Personal Relationships, 15,* 141–154.

BYASSEE, J. (2008). Not your father's pornography. *First Things: A Monthly Journal of Religion and Public Life, 179,* 15–19.

BYERS, E. S. (1996). How well does the traditional sexual script explain sexual coercion? Review of a program of research. *Journal of Psychology & Human Sexuality, 8,* 7–25.

BYERS, E. S. (2001). Evidence for the importance of relationship satisfaction for women's sexual functioning. In E. Kaschak & L. Tiefer (Eds.), *A new view of women's sexual problems* (pp. 23–26). Haworth Press.

BYERS, E. S., & DEMMONS, S. (1999). Sexual satisfaction and sexual self-disclosure within dating relationships. *Journal of Sex Research, 36,* 180–189.

BYERS, E. S., HENDERSON, J., & HOBSON, K. M. (2009). University students' definitions of sexual abstinence and having sex. *Archives of Sexual Behavior, 38,* 665–674.

BYERS, E. S., PURDON, C., & CLARK, D. A. (1998). Sexual intrusive thoughts of college students. *Journal of Sex Research, 35,* 359–369.

BYNE, W., & PARSONS, B. (1993). Human sexual orientation: The biologic theories reappraised. *Archives of General Psychiatry, 50,* 228–239.

BYRNE, D., CLORE, G., & SMEATON, G. (1986). The attraction hypothesis: Do similar attitudes affect anything? *Journal of Personality and Social Psychology, 51,* 1167–1170.

BYRNE, D., & MURNEN, S. K. (1988). Maintaining loving relationships. In R. J. Sternberg & M. L. Barnes (Eds.), *The psychology of love.* New Haven, CT: Yale University Press.

C

CABRERO, E., et al. (2010). Prevalence and impact of body physical changes in HIV patients treated with highly active antiretroviral therapy: Results from a study on patient and physician perceptions. *AIDS Patient Care and STDs, 24,* 5–13.

CALDERONE, M. S. (1983a). Childhood sexuality: Approaching the prevention of sexual disease. In G. Albee et al. (Eds.), *Promoting sexual responsibility and preventing sexual problems.* Hanover, NH: University Press of New England.

CALDERONE, M. S. (1983b). Fetal erection and its message to us. *SIECUS Report,* 11(5/6), 9–10.

CALDWELL, J. C., ORUBULOYE, I. O., & CALDWELL, P. (2000). Female genital mutilation: Conditions of decline. *Population Research and Policy Review, 19,* 233–254.

CALL, V., SPRECHER, S., & SCHWARTZ, P. (1995). The incidence and frequency of marital sex in a national sample. *Journal of Marriage and Family, 57,* 639–652.

CALLENDER, C., & KOCHEMS, L. (1987). The North American berdache. *Current Anthropology, 24,* 443–456.

CAMPBELL, R., et al. (2006). Gynecological health impact of sexual assault. *Research in Nursing and Health, 29,* 399–413.

CAMPSMITH, M. L., et al. (2010). Undiagnosed HIV prevalence among adults and adolescents in the United States at the end of 2006. *Journal of Acquired Immune Deficiency Syndromes, 53,* 619–624.

CANARY, D. J., & STAFFORD, L. (1994). Maintaining relationships through strategic and routine interaction. In D. J. Canary &

L. Stafford (Eds.), *Communication and relational maintenance* (pp. 3–22). San Diego: Academic Press.

CANAVAN, M. M., MEYER, W. J., III, & HIGGS, D. C. (1992). The female experience of sibling incest. *Journal of Marital and Family Therapy*, 18, 129–142.

CANCIAN, F. M. (1989). Love and the rise of capitalism. In B. J. Risman & P. Schwartz (Eds.), *Gender in intimate relationships: A microstructural approach*. Belmont, CA: Wadsworth.

CANN, A., MANGUM, J. L., & WELLS, M. (2001). Distress in response to relationship infidelity: The roles of gender and attitudes about relationships. *Journal of Sex Research*, 38, 185–190.

CANO, A., & O'LEARY, K. D. (1997). Romantic jealousy and affairs: Research and implications for couple therapy. *Journal of Sex & Marital Therapy*, 23, 249–275.

CANTARELLA, E. (1992). *Bisexuality in the ancient world*. New Haven, CT: Yale University Press.

CANTOR, J. M., et al. (2002). How many gay men owe their sexual orientation to fraternal birth order? *Archives of Sexual Behavior*, 31, 63–71.

CARAEL, M., et al. (2006). Clients of sex workers in different regions of the world: Hard to count. *Sexually Transmitted Infections*, 82(Suppl. 3), iii26–iii33.

CARLI, L. L., & BUKATKO, D. (2000). Gender, communication, and social influence: A developmental perspective. In T. Eckes & H. M. Trautner (Eds.), *The developmental social psychology of gender* (pp. 295–331). Mahwah, NJ: Lawrence Erlbaum.

CARLSEN, E., et al. (1992). Evidence for decreasing quality of semen during past 50 years. *British Medical Journal*, 305, 609–613.

CARLSON, A. E., et al. (2003). Catsperl required for evoked Ca^{2+} entry and control of flagellar function in sperm. *Proceedings of the National Academy of Sciences of the United States*, 100, 14864–14868.

CARNES, P. J. (1983). *Out of the shadows: Understanding sexual addiction*. Minneapolis: Compeare Publishers.

CARNES, P. J. (1991). *Don't call it love*. New York: Bantam Books.

CARPENTER, L. M., NATHANSON, C. A., & KIM, Y. J. (2006). Sex after 40? Gender, ageism, and sexual partnering in midlife. *Journal of Aging Studies*, 20, 93–106.

CARRIER, J. M. (1980). Homosexual behavior in cross-cultural perspective. In J. Marmor (Ed.), *Homosexual behavior* (pp. 100–122). New York: Basic Books.

CARROLL, J. S., et al. (2008). Generation XXX: Pornography acceptance and use among emerging adults. *Journal of Adolescent Research*, 23, 6–30.

CARTER, J. A., et al. (1999). Gender differences related to heterosexual condom use: The influence of negotiation styles. *Journal of Sex & Marital Therapy*, 25, 217–225.

CARTER, J. J., et al. (1996). The natural history of human papillomavirus type 16 capsid antibodies among a cohort of university women. *Journal of Infectious Diseases*, 174, 927–936.

CARTER, S., & SOKOL, J. (1989). *What really happens in bed: A demystification of sex*. New York: M. Evans.

CASTLEMAN, M. (1997, July/August). Recipes for lust. *Psychology Today*, 50–56.

CASTRO, K. G., et al. (1988). Transmission of HIV in Belle Glade, Florida: Lessons for other communities in the United States. *Science*, 239, 193–197.

CATANIA, J. A., et al. (1995). Risk factors for HIV and other sexually transmitted diseases and prevention practices among U.S. heterosexual adults: Changes from 1990 to 1992. *American Journal of Public Health*, 85, 1492–1499.

CATES, W. (2004). Reproductive tract infections. In R. A. Hatcher et al. (Eds.), *Contraceptive technology* (18th ed., pp. 191–220). New York: Ardent Media.

CATES, W. C. (2003). The "ABC to Z" approach. *Network*, 22(4), 3–4.

CATES, JR., W., & RAYMOND, E. G. (2008). Vaginal barriers and spermicides. In R. A. Hatcher et al. (Eds.), *Contraceptive technology* (19th ed., pp. 317–335). New York: Ardent Media.

CATOTTI, D. N., CLARKE, P., & CATOE, K. E. (1993). Herpes revisited: Still a cause of concern. *Sexually Transmitted Diseases*, 20, 77–80.

CATTERALL, R. D. (1974). *A short textbook of venereology*. Philadelphia: Lippincott.

CAUGHEY, A. B., et al. (2009). Systematic review: Elective induction of labor versus expectant management of pregnancy. *Annals of Internal Medicine*, 151, 252–263.

CAUGHLIN, J. P. (2002). The demand/withdraw pattern of communication as a predictor of marital satisfaction over time: Unresolved issues and future directions. *Human Communication Research*, 28, 49–85.

CAVAZOS-REHG, P. A., et al. (2009). Age of sexual debut among U.S. adolescents. *Contraception*, 80, 158–162.

CNN HEALTH LIBRARY. (2008). Penis-enlargement scams: You're more normal than you think. http://www.cnn.com/HEALTH/LIBRARY/MC/0026.html

CENTERS FOR DISEASE CONTROL AND PREVENTION. (2005). Teens and steroids. www.cdc.gov

CENTERS FOR DISEASE CONTROL and PREVENTION. (2007). 2005 assisted reproductive technology success rates: National summary and fertility clinic reports. Atlanta, GA: Author.

CENTERS FOR DISEASE CONTROL AND PREVENTION. (2007b). HIV/AIDS statistics and surveillance. www.cdc.gov

CENTERS FOR DISEASE CONTROL. (2009). HIV infection among injection-drug users—34 states, 2004–2007. *Morbidity and Mortality Weekly Report*, 58, 1291–1295.

CENTERS for DISEASE CONTROL and PREVENTION. (2010). *HIV/AIDS surveillance report*. http://www.cdc.gov/hiv/topics/surveillance/resources/reports/

CESARIO, S. K., & HUGHES, L. A. (2007). Precocious puberty: A comprehensive review of literature. *Journal of Obstetric, Gynecologic, & Neonatal Nursing*, 36, 263–274.

CHAN, D. K.-S., et al. (2008). Examining the job-related, psychological, and physical outcomes of workplace sexual harassment: A meta-analytic review. *Psychology of Women Quarterly*, 32, 362–376.

CHAN, W. S., et al. (2004). Risk of stroke in women exposed to low-dose oral contraceptives: A critical evaluation of the evidence. *Archives of Internal Medicine*, 164, 741–747.

CHANDRA, A., et al. (2008). Does watching sex on television predict teen pregnancy? Findings from a National Longitudinal survey of youth. *Pediatrics*, 122, 1047–1054.

CHANG, Y. (2000, January 1). Was it virtually good for you? *Newsweek*, 71.

CHAPLEAU, K. M., & OSWALD, D. L. (2010). Power, sex, and rape myth acceptance: Testing two models of rape proclivity. *Journal of Sex Research*, 47, 66–78.

CHAPLEAU, K. M., et al. (2008, May 1). Male rape myths: The role of gender, violence, and sexism. *Journal of Interpersonal Violence*, 23, 600–615.

CHAPPELL, D. (1976). Cross-cultural research on forcible rape. *International Journal of Criminology and Penology*, 4, 295–304.

CHAPPELL, K. D., & DAVIS, K. E. (1998). Attachment, partner choice, and perception of romantic partners: An experimental test of the attachment-security hypothesis. *Personal Relationships*, 5, 327–342.

CHARERS, M. L., et al. (2010). Agreement of self-reported and genital measures of sexual arousal in men and women: A meta-analysis. *Archives of Sexual Behavior*, 39, 5–56.

CHARLES, V. E., et al. (2008). Abortion and long-term mental health outcomes: A systematic review of the evidence. *Contraception*, 78, 433–514.

CHASELA, C. S., et al. (2010). Maternal or infant antiretroviral drugs to reduce HIV-1 transmission. *New England Journal of Medicine*, 362, 2271–2281.

CHAVARRO, J. E., WILLETT, W. C., & SKERRETT, P. F. (2008). *The fertility diet*. McGraw Hill.

CHEN, Z., et al. (1997). Human immunodeficiency virus type 2 (HIV-2) seroprevalence and characterization of a distinct HIV-2 genetic subtype 1133 from the natural range of simian immunodeficiency virus-infected sooty mangabeys. *Journal of Virology*, 71, 3953–3960.

CHIANG, H.-S., WU, C.-C., & WEN, T.-C. (2000). 10 years of experience with penile prosthesis implantation in Taiwanese patients. *Journal of Urology*, 163, 476–480.

CHIAPPA, J. A., & FORISH, J. J. (1976). *The VD book*. New York: Holt, Rinehart & Winston.

CHIGWEDERE, P., & ESSEX, M. (2010). AIDS denialism and public health practice. *AIDS and Behavior*, 14, 237–247.

CHILDBIRTH CONNECTION. (2007). www.childbirthconnection.org

CHIM, H., et al. (2002). The prevalence of menopausal symptoms in a community in Singapore. *Maturitas*, 41, 275–282.

CHIODO, D., et al. (2009). Impact of sexual harassment victimization by peers on subsequent adolescent victimization and adjustment: A longitudinal study. *Journal of Adolescent Health*, 45, 246–252.

CHIVERS, M. L., et al. (2010). Agreements of self-reported and genital measures of sexual arousal in men and women: A Meta-analysis. *Archives of Sexual Behavior*, 39 5–56.

CHLEBOWSKI, R. T., et al. (2009). Breast cancer after use of estrogen plus progestin in postmenopausal women. *New England Journal of Medicine*, 360, 573–587.

CHOI, K.-H., RICKMAN, R., & CATANIA, J. A. (1994). What heterosexual adults believe about condoms. *New England Journal of Medicine*, 331, 406–407.

CHRISLER, J. C., & CAPLAN, P. (2003). The strange case of Dr. Jekyll and Ms. Hyde: How PMS became a cultural phenomenon and a psychiatric disorder. In J. R. Heiman & C. M. Davis (Eds.), *Annual Review of Sex Research* (Vol. XIII, pp. 274–306). Allentown, PA: The Society for the Scientific Study of Sexuality.

CHRISLER, J. C., et al. (2006). The PMS illusion: Social cognition maintains social construction. *Sex Roles*, 54, 371–376.

CHRISTENSEN, A. (1988). Dysfunctional interaction patterns in couples. In P. Noller & M. A. Fitzpatrick (Eds.), *Perspectives on marital interaction* (pp. 31–52). Philadelphia: Multilingual Matters.

CHUDAKOV, B., et al. (2002). The motivation and mental health of sex workers. *Journal of Sex & Marital Therapy*, 28, 305–315.

CHUMLEA, W. C., et al. (2003). Age at menarche and racial comparisons in U.S. girls. *Pediatrics*, 111, 110–113.

CHUN, T. W., et al. (1999). Re-emergence of HIV after stopping therapy. *Nature*, 401, 874–875.

CIESIELSKI, C., TABIDZE, I., & BROWN, C. (2004). Transmission of primary and secondary syphilis by oral sex—Chicago, Illinois, 1998–2002. *Morbidity and Mortality Weekly Report*, 53, 966–968.

CIHAN, A., et al. (2009). The relationship between premature ejaculation and hyperthyroidism. *Journal of Urology*, 181, 1273–1280.

CLARK, L. R., JACKSON, M., & ALLEN-TAYLOR, L. (2002). Adolescent knowledge about sexually transmitted diseases. *Sexually Transmitted Diseases*, 29, 436–443.

CLARK, R. D., & HATFIELD, E. (1989). Gender differences in receptivity to sexual offers. *Journal of Psychology & Human Sexuality*, 2, 39–55.

CLARKE, L. H. (2006). Older women and sexuality: Experiences in marital relationships across the life course. *Canadian Journal on Aging*, 25, 129–140.

CLARKE, P. (1996/1997). Why do Americans find it easier to have sex than to talk about it? *STD News*, 4(2–3).

CLARNETTE, T., SUGITA, Y., & HUTSON, J. (1997). Genital anomalies in human and animal models reveal the mechanisms and hormones governing testicular descent. *British Journal of Urology*, 79, 99–112.

CLAWSON, C. L. & REESE-WEBER, M. (2003). The amount and timing of parent-adolescent sexual communication as predictors of late adolescent sexual risk-taking behaviors. *Journal of Sex Research*, 40, 256–265.

CLAY, R. A. (2006, September). Battling the self-blame of infertility. *Monitor on Psychology*, 44–45.

CLAYTON, A. H. (2008). Symptoms related to the menstrual cycle: Diagnosis, prevalence, and treatment. *Journal of Psychiatric Practices*, 14, 13–21.

CLAY-WARNER, J., & BURT, C. H. (2005). Rape reporting after reforms. *Violence Against Women*, 11, 150–176.

CLEAVER, E. (1968). *Soul on ice*. New York: Dell.

CLEMENTS, M. (1994, August 7). Sex in America today. *Parade*, 4–6.

CLIFFORD, D. B. (2000). Human immunodeficiency virus-associated dementia. *Archives of Neurology*, 57, 321–324.

CLOUD, J. (2010, August 9). The origin of cougar sex drives. *Time*, 49.

COCHRAN, S. D., & MAYS, V. M. (1990). Sex, lies, and HIV. *New England Journal of Medicine*, 322, 774–775.

COCHRAN, S. D., & MAYS, V. M. (2000). Relation between psychiatric syndromes and behaviorally defined sexual orientation in a sample of the U.S. population. *American Journal of Epidemiology*, 151, 516–523.

COCORES, J., DACKIS, C., & GOLD, M. (1986). Sexual dysfunction secondary to cocaine abuse. *Journal of Clinical Psychiatry*, 47, 384–385.

COHEN, A. (2000). Excess female mortality in India: The case of Himachal Pradesh. *American Journal of Public Health*, 90, 1369–1371.

COHEN J., et al. (2000). Trauma-focused cognitive-behavioral therapy for children and adolescents: An empirical update. *Journal of Interpersonal Violence*, 15, 1202–1223.

COHEN, J. A., & MANNARINO, A. P. (2000). Predictors of treatment outcome in sexually abused children. *Child Abuse & Neglect*, 24, 983–994.

COHEN, L. J., & ROTH, S. (1987). The psychological aftermath of rape: Long-term effects and individual differences in recovery. *Journal of Social and Clinical Psychology*, 5, 525–534.

COHEN, L. L., & SHOTLAND, R. L. (1996). Timing of first sexual intercourse in a relationship: Expectations, experiences, and perceptions of others. *Journal of Sex Research*, 33, 291–299.

COHEN, M. L., SEGHORN, T., & CALMAS, W. (1969). Sociometric study of the sex offender. *Journal of Abnormal Psychology*, 74, 249–255.

COHEN, M. L., et al. (1971). The psychology of rapists. *Seminars in Psychiatry*, 3, 307–327.

COHEN-KETTENIS, P. T., & GOOREN, L. J. G. (1999). Transsexualism: A review of etiology, diagnosis and treatment. *Journal of Psychosomatic Research*, 46, 315–333.

COHN, J. A. (1997). HIV infections—1. *British Medical Journal*, 314, 487–491.

COKER, A. L., et al. (2000). Frequency and correlates of intimate partner violence by type: Physical, sexual, and psychological battering. *American Journal of Public Health*, 90, 553–559.

COLAPINTO, J. (2000). *As nature made him: The boy who was raised as a girl*. New York: HarperCollins.

COLE, E. (1982). Sibling incest: The myth of benign sibling incest. *Women and Therapy*, 5, 79–89.

COLE, P. M., & PUTNAM, F. W. (1992). Effect of incest on self and social functioning: A developmental psychopathology perspective. *Journal of Consulting and Clinical Psychology*, 60, 174–184.

COLEMAN, E. (1991). Compulsive sexual behavior: New concepts and treatment. *Journal of Psychology & Human Sexuality*, 4(2), 37–52.

COLEMAN, E. (1992). Is your patient suffering from compulsive sexual behavior? *Psychiatric Annals*, 22, 320–325.

COLEMAN, E., & EDWARDS, B. (1986, July). Sexual compulsion vs. sexual addiction: The debate continues. *SIECUS Report*, pp. 7–10.

COLEMAN, L. M., & CATER, S. M. (2005). A qualitative study of the relationship between alcohol consumption and risky sex in adolescents. *Archives of Sexual Behavior*, 34, 649–661.

COLEY, R. L., & CHASE-LANSDALE, P. L. (1998). Adolescent pregnancy and childhood: Recent evidence and future directions. *American Psychologist*, 53, 152–166.

COLLABORATIVE GROUP ON HORMONAL FACTORS IN BREAST CANCER. (1996). Breast cancer and hormonal contraceptives: Collaborative reanalysis of individual data on 53,297 women with and 100,239 women without breast cancer from 54 epidemiological studies. *The Lancet*, 347, 1713–1727.

COLLABORATIVE GROUP ON HORMONAL FACTORS IN BREAST CANCER. (2002). Breast cancer and breastfeeding: Collaborative reanalysis of individual data from 47 epidemiological studies in 30 countries, including 50,302 women with breast cancer and 96,973 women without the disease. *The Lancet*, 360, 187–195.

COLLAER, M. L., & HINES, M. (1995). Human behavioral sex differences: A role for gonadal hormones during early development? *Psychological Bulletin*, 118, 55–107.

COLLIER, J, (2009). The rising proportion of repeat teenage pregnancies in young women presenting for termination of pregnancy from 1991 to 2007. *Contraception*, 79, 393–396.

COLLINS, N., et al. (2006). Working models of attachment and attribution processes in intimate relationships. *Personality and Social Psychology Bulletin*, 32, 201–219.

COLLINS, N. L., & MILLER, L. C. (1994). Self-disclosure and liking: A meta-analytic review. *Psychological Bulletin*, 116, 457–475.

COLLINS, R. L., et al. (2004). Watching sex on television predicts adolescent initiation of sexual behavior. *Pediatrics*, 114, e280–e289.

COMISKEY, K. M. (1989). Relationship workshops: How "good marriages" can be strengthened. *Contemporary Sexuality*, 1, 10.

COMMISSION ON OBSCENITY AND PORNOGRAPHY. (1970). *The report of the Commission on Obscenity and Pornography*. Washington, DC: U.S. Government Printing Office.

CONDRY, J., & CONDRY, S. (1977). Sex differences: A study of the eye of the beholder. *Child Development*, 47, 812–819.

CONFER, J. C., et al. (2010). Evolutionary psychology. Controversies, questions, prospects, and limitations. *American Psychologist*, 65, 110–126.

CONKLE, A. (2010). Scientific in sights from 21st century dating. *Psychological Sciences*, 28, 12–16.

CONNERY, J. (1977). *Abortion: The development of the Roman Catholic perspective*. Chicago: Loyola University Press.

CONSTANTINE, N. A. (2008). Converging evidence leaves policy behind: Sex education in the United States. *Journal of Adolescent Health*, 42, 324–326.

CONSTANTINOPLE, A. (1973). Masculinity-femininity: An exception to a famous dictum. *Psychological Bulletin*, 80, 389–407.

CONSUMER REPORTS. (1989, March). Can you rely on condoms? *Consumer Reports*, 135–141.

CONTE, J. R. (1991). The nature of sexual offenses against children. In C. R. Hollin & K. Howells (Eds.), *Clinical approaches to sex offenders and their victims* (pp. 11–34). New York: John Wiley & Sons.

CONTE, J. R., et al. (1986). Child sexual abuse and the family: A critical analysis. *Journal of Psychotherapy and the Family*, 2, 113–126.

CONTEMPORARY PSYCHOLOGY. (2009). Teen "sexting" attracts attention of prosecutors. *Contemporary Psychology*, 43(5), 8.

CONTRACEPTION (2010). Use of the Mirena™ LNG-IUS and Paragard™ CuT380A intrauterine devices in nulliparous women: Release date 15 December 2009 SFP Guideline 20092. *Contraception*, 81, 367–371.

COOK, R., & FOSEN, R. (1970). Pornography and the sex offender: Patterns of exposure and immediate arousal effects of pornographic stimuli. In *Technical Report of the Commission on Obscenity and Pornography* (Vol. 7). Washington, DC: U.S. Government Printing Office.

COOK, R. L., et al. (2001). Barriers to screening sexually active adolescent women for chlamydia: A survey of primary care physicians. *Journal of Adolescent Health*, 28, 204–210.

COOPER, A. (1998). Sexuality and the Internet: Surfing into the new millennium. *Cyberpsychology and Behavior*, 1, 181–187.

COOPER, A., McLOUGHLIN, I. P., & CAMPBELL, K. M. (2000). Sexuality in cyberspace: Update for the 21st Century. *Cyberpsychology & Behavior*, 3, 521–536.

COOPER, A., et al. (1999). Sexuality on the Internet: From sexual exploration to pathological expression. *Professional Psychology: Research and Practice*, 30, 154–164.

COOPER, A., et al. (2000). Sexuality and the Internet: The next sexual revolution. In L. T. Szuchman & F. Muscarella (Eds.), *Psychological perspectives on human sexuality* (pp. 519–545). New York: John Wiley & Sons.

CORBETT, A. M., et al. (2009). A little thing called love: Condom use in high-risk primary heterosexual relationships. *Perspectives on Sexual and Reproductive Health*, 41, 218–224.

CORBETT, E. L., et al. (2002). HIV-1/AIDS and the control of other infectious diseases in Africa. *The Lancet*, 359, 2177–2187.

COREY, L., et al. (2004). Once-daily Valacyclovir to reduce the risk of transmission of genital herpes. *New England Journal of Medicine*, 350, 11–20.

CORRETTI, G., & BALDI, I. (2007). The relationship between anxiety disorders and sexual dysfunction. *Psychiatric Times*, 24(9), 1–2.

CORTONI, F., & HANSON, R. (2005). *A review of recidivism rates of adult female sexual offenders.* Ottawa: Correctional Service of Canada.

CORTY, E. W., & GUARDIANI, J. M. (2008). Canadian and American sex therapists' perceptions of normal and abnormal ejaculatory latencies: How long should intercourse last? *Journal of Sexual Medicine*, 5, 1251–1256.

COSSEY, C. (1991). *My story.* London: Faber and Faber.

COSTA, R. M., & BRODY, S. (2007). Women's relationship quality is associated with specifically penile-vaginal intercourse orgasm and frequency. *Journal of Sex & Marital Therapy*, 33, 319–327.

COTT, N. F. (2002). Passionlessness: An interpretation of Victorian sexual ideology, 1790–1850. In K. Peiss (Ed.), *Major problems in the history of sexuality* (pp. 131–141). Boston: Houghton Mifflin Co.

COTTON, D., & GROTH, A. (1982). Innate rape: Prevention and intervention. *Journal of Prison and Jail Health*, 2, 45–57.

COUTINHO, E. M., & SEGAL, S. J. (1999). *Is menstruation obsolete?* New York: Oxford University Press.

COUTINHO, E. M., et al. (2000). Gossypol blood levels and inhibition of spermatogenesis in men taking gossypol as a contraceptive. *Contraception*, 61, 61–67.

COUTTS, R. L. (1973). *Love and intimacy: A psychological approach.* San Ramon, CA: Consensus.

COWAN, G. (2000). Beliefs about the causes of four types of rape. *Sex Roles*, 42, 807–823.

COX, B., et al. (2002). Vasectomy and risk of prostate cancer. *Journal of the American Medical Association*, 287, 3110–3115.

COX, D. J. (1988). Incidence and nature of male genital exposure behavior as reported by college women. *Journal of Sex Research*, 24, 227–234.

COXON, A. P. M., & MCMANUS, T. J. (2000). How many account for how much? Concentration of high-risk sexual behavior among gay men. *Journal of Sex Research*, 37, 1–7.

CRANDALL, C. (2002). Vaginal estrogen preparations: A review of safety and efficacy for vaginal atrophy. *Journal of Women's Health*, 11, 857–877.

CRAWFORD, P., & KAUFMANN, L. (2006). How safe is vaginal birth after cesarean section for the mother and fetus? *Journal of Family Practice*, 55, 149–151.

CREPAZ, N., et al. (2009). Prevalence of unprotected anal intercourse among HIV-diagnosed MSM in the United States: A meta-analysis. *AIDS*, 23, 1617–1619.

CRITCHELL, S. (2006, April 3). Parents' attitudes on sex influence kids. *New Orleans Times-Picayune*, p. C2.

CRITELLI, J. W., & BINOVA, J. M. (2008). Women's erotic rape fantasies: An evaluation of theory and research. *Journal of Sex Research*, 45, 57–70.

CROSBY, R. A., et al. (2000). Correlates of unprotected vaginal sex among African American female adolescents. *Archives Pediatric and Adolescent Medicines*, 154, 893–899.

CROSBY, R. A., et al. (2002). Condom use errors and problems among college men. *Sexually Transmitted Diseases*, 29, 552–557.

CROSBY, R. A., et al. (2010). Does it fit okay? Problems with condom use as a function of self-reported poor fit. *Sexually Transmitted Infections*, 86, 36–38.

CROSIGNANI, P. G., et al. (1999). Management of anovulatory infertility. *Human Reproduction*, 14 (Suppl. 1), 108–119.

CROSS, P. A., & MATHESON, K. (2006). Understanding sadomasochism: An empirical examination of four perspectives. *Journal of Homosexuality*, 50, 133–166.

CROWLEY, T., GOLDMEIER, D., & HILLER, J. (2009). Diagnosing and managing vaginismus. *British Medical Journal*, 339, 225–229.

CUMMING, D. C., CUMMING, C. E., & KIEREN, D. K. (1991). Menstrual mythology and sources of information about menstruation. *American Journal of Obstetrics and Gynecology*, 164, 472–476.

CUNNINGHAM, F. G., et al. (1997). *Williams obstetrics* (20th ed.). Norwalk, CT: Appleton & Lange.

CUPACH, W. R., & METTS, S. (1991). Sexuality and communication in close relationships. In K. McKinney & S. Sprecher (Eds.), *Sexuality in close relationships.* Hillsdale, NJ: Lawrence Erlbaum.

CUPOLI, J. M., & SEWELL, P. M. (1988). One thousand fifty-nine children with a chief complaint of sexual abuse. *Child Abuse & Neglect*, 12, 151–162.

CURTIN, S. C. (1999). Recent changes in birth attendant, place of birth, and the use of obstetric interventions, United States, 1989–1997. *Journal of Nurse-Midwifery*, 44, 349–354.

CURTIS, R., & MILLER, K. (1988). Believing another likes or dislikes you: Behavior making the beliefs come true. *Journal of Personality and Social Psychology*, 51, 284–290.

CUTLER, W. B., et al. (1985). Sexual behavior frequency and biphasic ovulatory-type menstrual cycles. *Physiology & Behavior*, 34, 805–810.

CUTLER, W. B., et al. (1986). Human axillary secretions influence women's menstrual cycles: The role of donor extract from men. *Hormones and Behavior*, 20, 463.

CUTLER, W. B., FRIEDMAN, E., & MCCOY, N. L. (1998). Pheromonal influences on sociosexual behavior in men. *Archives of Sexual Behavior*, 27, 1–13.

CWIKEL, J., & HOBAN, E. (2005). Contentious issues in research on trafficked women working in the sex industry: Study design, ethics, and methodology. *Journal of Sex Research*, 42, 306–317.

CYR, M., et al. (2002). Intrafamilial sexual abuse: Brother-sister incest does not differ from father-daughter and stepfather-step-daughter incest. *Child Abuse & Neglect*, 26, 957–973.

CNN HEALTH LIBRARY. (2008). Penis-enlargement scams: You're more normal than you think. http://www.cnn.com/HEALTH/LIBRARY/MC/0026.html

D

DALLA, R. L. (2000). Exposing the "pretty woman" myth: A qualitative examination of the lives of female streetwalking prostitutes. *Journal of Sex Research*, 37, 344–353.

DALLA, R. L. (2002). Night moves: A qualitative investigation of street-level sex work. *Psychology of Women Quarterly*, 26, 63–74.

DALLAM, S. J., et al. (2001). The effects of child sexual abuse: Comment on Rind, Tromovitch, and Bauserman (1998). *Psychological Bulletin*, 127, 715–733.

DALTON, K. (1960). Menstruation and accidents. *British Medical Journal*, 2, 1425–1426.

DALTON, K. (1964). *The premenstrual syndrome.* Springfield, IL: Charles C. Thomas.

DALTON, K. (1980). Cyclical criminal acts in premenstrual syndrome. *The Lancet*, 2, 1070–1071.

DALY, M., WILSON, M., & WEGHORST, S. J. (1982). Male sexual jealousy. *Ethology and Sociobiology*, 3, 11–27.

D'AMATO, A. (2006). *Porn up, rape down.* Chicago: Northwestern Law School.

DANIELSSON, J., et al. (2003). Prevalence and incidence of prolonged and severe dyspareunia in women: Results from a population study. *Scandinavian Journal of Public Health*, 31, 113–118.

DARCANGELO, S. (2008). Fetishism: Psychopathology and theory. In D. R. Laws & W. T. O'Donohue (Eds.), *Sexual deviance: Theory, assessment, and treatment* (pp. 108–118). New York: Guilford Press.

DARLING, C. A., DAVIDSON, J. K., & CONWAY-WELCH, C. (1990). Female ejaculation: Perceived origins, the Grafenberg spot/area, and sexual responsiveness. *Archives of Sexual Behavior*, 19, 29–47.

DARLING, C. A., DAVIDSON, J. K., & COX, R. P. (1991). Female sexual response and the timing of partner orgasm. *Journal of Sex & Marital Therapy*, 17, 3–21.

DARLING, C. A., DAVIDSON, J. K., & JENNINGS, D. A. (1991). The female sexual response revisited: Understanding the multiorgasmic experience in women. *Archives of Sexual Behavior*, 20, 527–540.

DA ROS, C., et al. (1994). Caucasian penis: What is the normal size? *Journal of Urology*, 151 (Suppl.), 323A, 381.

DAS, A. (2007). Masturbation in the United States. *Journal of Sex & Marital Therapy*, 33, 301–317.

DAS, A. (2009). Sexual harassment at work in the United States. *Archives of Sexual Behavior*, 38, 909–921.

DA SILVA LARA, L. A., et al. (2009). Sexuality during the climacteric period. *Maturitas*, 62, 127–133.

D'AUGELLI, A. R., HERSHBERGER, S. L., & PILKINGTON, N. W. (1998). Lesbian, gay, and bisexual youth and their families: Disclosure of sexual orientation and its consequences. *American Journal of Orthopsychiatry*, 68, 361–371.

DAVEY, R. T., et al. (1999). HIV-1 and T cell dynamics after interruption of highly active antiretroviral therapy (HAART) in patients with a history of sustained viral suppression. *Proceedings of the National Academy of Sciences USA*, 96, 15109–15114.

DAVID, H. P., DYTRYCH, Z., & MATEJCEK, Z. (2003). Born unwanted: Observations from the Prague study. *American Psychologist*, 58, 224–229.

DAVIDSON, J. K., & MOORE, N. B. (1994). Guilt and lack of orgasm during sexual intercourse: Myth versus reality among college women. *Journal of Sex Education and Therapy*, 20, 153–174.

DAVIDSON, J., & CHUTKA, D. (2008). Benign prostatic hyperplasia: Treat or wait? Questionnaire with "bother score" can help you decide. *Journal of Family Practice*, 57, 454–463.

DAVIES, S., KATZ, J., & JACKSON, J. L. (1999). Sexual desire discrepancies: Effects on sexual and relationship satisfaction in heterosexual dating couples. *Archives of Sexual Behavior, 28,* 553–567.

DAVIS, C., & BAUSERMAN, R. (1993). Exposure to sexually explicit materials: An attitude change perspective. *Annual Review of Sex Research, 4,* 121–209.

DAVIS, K. C., et al. (2006). Men's likelihood of sexual aggression: The influence of alcohol, sexual arousal, and violent pornography. *Aggressive Behavior, 32,* 581–589.

DAVIS, K. C., et al. (2008). The use of alcohol and condoms during sexual assault. *American Journal of Men's Health, 2,* 281–290.

DAVIS, K. E. (1985). Near and dear: Friendship and love compared. *Psychology Today,* February, 22–28.

DAVIS, K. E., & LATTY-MANN, H. (1987). Love styles and relationship quality: A contribution to validation. *Journal of Social and Personal Relationships, 4,* 409–428.

DAVIS, R. C., BRICKMAN, E., & BAKER, T. (1991). Supportive and unsupportive responses of others to rape victims: Effects on concurrent victim adjustment. *American Journal of Community Psychology, 19,* 443–451.

DAVIS, S., BINIK, Y., & CARRIER, S. (2009). Sexual dysfunction and pelvic pain in men: A male sexual pain disorder? *Journal of Sex and Marital Therapy, 35,* 182–205.

DAVIS, S., et al. (2008). Testosterone for low libido in postmenopausal women not taking estrogen. *New England Journal of Medicine, 359,* 2005–2017.

DAVIS, S. R., et al. (2008). Testosterone for low libido in postmenopausal women not taking estrogen. *New England Journal of Medicine, 359,* 2005–2017.

DE ANGELIS, T. (1996, October). Project explores sexual misconduct among children. *APA Monitor,* 43.

DE ANGELIS, T. (1997, November). Menopause symptoms may vary among ethnic groups. *APA Monitor,* 16–17.

DEANS, E. J., & GRIMES, D. A. (2009). Intrauterine devices for adolescents: A systematic review. *Contraception, 79,* 418–423.

DEAUX, K., & LEWIS, L. L. (1983). Components of gender role stereotypes. *Psychological Documents, 13,* 25.

DE BERRY, J. (2005, January 28). Rumors give AIDS a head start. *New Orleans Times-Picayune* p. B7.

DE CLERCQ, E., et al. (2007). Maternal outcomes associated with planned cesarean births compared with planned vaginal births. *Obstetrics and Gynecology, 109,* 669–677.

DEFOE, D. (1727). *Conjugal lewdness: Or, matrimonial whoredom.* London: T. Warner.

DE JUDICIBUS, M. A., & MCCABE, M. P. (2002). Psychological factors and the sexuality of pregnant and postpartum women. *Journal of Sex Research, 39,* 94–103.

DELAMATER, J. D., & SILL, M. (2005). Sexual desire in later life. *Journal of Sex Research, 42,* 138–149.

DELAMATER, J. (2007). Sexual behavior in later life. *Journal of Aging and Health, 19,* 921–945.

DELGIUDICE, M. (2009). Sex, attachment, and the development of reproductive strategies. *Behavioral and Brain Sciences, 32,* 1–67.

DEMING, W. (1995). *Paul on marriage and celibacy: The Hellenistic background of 1 Corinthians 7.* Cambridge: Cambridge University Press.

DE MUNCK, V. C., & KOROTAYEV, A. (1999). Sexual equality and romantic love: A reanalysis of Rosenblatt's study on the function of romantic love. *Cross-Cultural Research, 33,* 265–277.

DENNERSTEIN, L., DUDLEY, E., & BURGER, H. (1997). Well-being and the menopausal transition. *Journal of Psychosomatic Obstetrics and Gynecology, 18,* 95–101.

DENNERSTEIN, L., & LEHERT, P. (2004). Modeling mid-aged women's sexual functioning: A prospective, population-based study. *Journal of Sex & Marital Therapy, 30,* 173–183.

DENNY, D. (1997). Transgender: Some historical, cross-cultural, and contemporary models and methods of coping and treatment. In B. Bullough, V. L. Bullough, & J. Elias (Eds.), *Gender blending.* New York: Prometheus Books.

DENNY, D. (1998). Rachel and me: A commentary on gender: An ethnomethodological approach. *Feminism & Psychology, 10,* 62–65.

DE RIVERA, J. (1997). The construction of false memory syndrome: The experience of retractors. *Psychological Inquiry, 8,* 271–292.

DERLEGA, V. J., et al. (1993). *Self-disclosure.* Newbury Park, CA: Sage.

DE ROUGEMENT, D. (1969). *Love in the Western world.* New York: Fawcett.

DE SADE, D., MARQUIS. (1965). *Justine* (R. Seaver & A. Wainhouse, Trans.). New York: Grove Press. (Original work published 1791.)

DESIGNER BABIES. (1998, November 9). *Newsweek,* 61–62.

DESSENS, A. B., SLIJPER, F. M. E., & DROP, S. L. S. (2005). Gender dysphoria and gender change in chromosomal females with congenital adrenal hyperplasia. *Archives of Sexual Behavior, 34,* 389–397.

DESTENO, D. A., & SALOVEY, P. (1996). Evolutionary origins of sex differences in jealousy? Questioning the "fitness" of the model. *Psychological Science, 7,* 367–372.

DEUCHAR, N. (1995). Nausea and vomiting in pregnancy: A review of the problem with particular regard to psychological and social aspects. *British Journal of Obstetrics and Gynaecology, 102,* 6–8.

DEVECI, S., et al. (2007). Defining the clinical characteristics of Peyronie's disease in young men. *Journal of Sexual Medicine, 4,* 485–490.

DE VILLERS, L., & TURGEON, H. (2005). The uses and benefits of "sensate focus" exercises. *Contemporary Sexuality, 39,* i–vii.

DE VINCENZI, I., & EUROPEAN STUDY GROUP. (1994). A longitudinal study of human immunodeficiency virus transmission by heterosexual partners. *New England Journal of Medicine, 331,* 341–346.

DEVISSER, R. O., et al. (2007). The impact of sexual coercion on psychological, physical, and sexual well-being in a representative sample of Australian women. *Archives of Sexual Behavior, 36,* 676–686.

DEVISSER, R., & MCDONALD, D. (2007). Swings and roundabouts—Jealousy in heterosexual couples. *British Journal of Social Psychology, 46,* 459–476.

DHAWAN, S., & MARSHALL, W. L. (1996). Sexual abuse histories of sexual offenders. *Sexual Abuse: A Journal of Research and Treatment, 8,* 7–15.

DICLEMENTE, R. J., et al. (1990). College students' knowledge and attitudes about AIDS and changes in HIV-preventive behaviors. *AIDS Education and Prevention, 2,* 201–212.

DIFRANZA, J. R., & LEW, R. A. (1995). Effect of maternal cigarette smoking on pregnancy complications and sudden infant death syndrome. *Journal of Family Practice, 40,* 385–394.

DIAMANT, A. L., et al. (1999). Lesbians' sexual history with men: Implications for taking a sexual history. *Archives of Internal Medicine, 159,* 2730–2736.

DIAMOND, C., & BUSKIN, S. (1999). Continued risky behavior in HIV-infected youth.

American Journal of Public Health, 90, 115–118.

DIAMOND, L. M. (2003). What does sexual orientation orient? A biobehavioral model distinguishing romantic love and sexual desire. *Psychological Review, 110,* 173–192.

DIAMOND, L. M. (2004). Emerging perspectives on distinctions between romantic love and sexual desire. *Current Directions in Psychological Science, 13,* 116–119.

DIAMOND, L. M. (2005). A new view of lesbian subtypes: Stable versus fluid identity trajectories over an 8-year period. *Psychology of Women Quarterly, 29,* 119–128.

DIAMOND, L. M. (2007). A dynamical systems approach to the development and expression of female same-sex sexuality. *Perspectives on Psychological Science, 2,* 142–161.

DIAMOND, L. M. (2008). Female bisexuality from adolescence to adulthood: Results from a 10-year longitudinal study. *Developmental Psychology, 44,* 5–14.

DIAMOND, L. M., & SAVIN-WILLIAMS, R. C. (2000). Explaining diversity in the development of same-sex sexuality among young women. *Journal of Social Issues, 56,* 297–313.

DIAMOND, M. (1993). Homosexuality and bisexuality in different populations. *Archives of Sexual Behavior, 22,* 291–310.

DIAMOND, M. (1997). Sexual identity and sexual orientation in children with traumatized or ambiguous genitalia. *Journal of Sex Research, 34,* 199–211.

DIAMOND, M. (1998). Sex and gender: Same or different? *Feminism & Psychology, 10,* 46–54.

DIAMOND, M. (2004). Sex, gender, and identity over the years: A changing perspective. *Child and Adolescent Psychiatric Clinics of North America, 13,* 591–607.

DIAMOND, S., & MALISZEWSKI, M. (Eds.). (1992). *Sexual aspects of headaches.* Madison, CT: International University Press.

DICK-READ, G. (1972). *Childbirth without fear* (4th ed.). New York: Harper & Row. (First published 1932.)

DICKEY, R., & STEPHENS, J. (1995). Female-to-male transsexualism, heterosexual type: Two cases. *Archives of Sexual Behavior, 24,* 439–445.

DIETZ-UHLER, B., & MURRELL, A. (1992). College students perceptions of sexual harassment: Are gender differences decreasing? *Journal of College Student Development, 33,* 540–546.

DILLAWAY, H. E. (2005). Menopause is the "good old." Women's thoughts about reproductive aging. *Gender & Society, 19,* 398–417.

DINDIA, K., & ALLEN, M. (1992). Sex differences in self-disclosure: A meta-analysis. *Psychological Bulletin, 112,* 106–124.

DINEN, K. A. (2002). Migrant Thai women subjected to slavery-like abuses in Japan. *Violence Against Women, 8,* 1113–1139.

DITTMAN, R. W. (1998). Ambiguous genitalia, gender-identity problems, and sex reassignment. *Journal of Sex & Marital Therapy, 24,* 255–271.

DITTMANN, M. (2005). Getting prostitutes off the streets. *Monitor on Psychology, 35*(9), 71.

DOCTER, R. F., & PRINCE, V. (1997). Transvestism: A survey of 1032 cross-dressers. *Archives of Sexual Behavior, 26,* 589–605.

DODGE, B., et al. (2010). Sexual health among U.S. black and Hispanic women: A nationally representative sample. *Journal of Sexual Medicine, 7* (Suppl 5), 330–345.

DONAHEY, K. M., & CARROLL, R. A. (1983). Gender differences in factors associated with hypoactive sexual desire. *Journal of Sex & Marital Therapy, 19,* 25–40.

DONATI, S., et al. (2009). Menopause: Knowledge, attitude and practice among Italian women. *Maturitas, 63,* 246–252.

DONNERSTEIN, E., & LINZ, D. (1986, December). The question of pornography. *Psychology Today,* 56–59.

DONNERSTEIN, E., LINZ, D., & PENROD, S. (1987). *The question of pornography: Research findings and policy implications.* New York: Free Press.

DONOVAL, B., PASSARO, D., & KLAUSNER, J. (2006). The public health imperative for a neonatal herpes simplex virus infection surveillance system. *Sexually Transmitted Diseases, 33,* 170–174.

DORNADULA, G., et al. (1999). Residual HIV-1 RNA in blood plasma of patients taking suppressive highly active antiretroviral therapy. *Journal of the American Medical Association, 282,* 1627–1632.

DOSS, B., RHOADES, G., & SCOTT, S. (2009). The effect of the transition to parenthood on relationship quality: An 8-year prospective study. *Journal of Personality and Social Psychology, 96,* 601–619.

DOUGLAS, M. (1966). *Purity and danger: An analysis of concepts of pollution and taboo.* New York: Praeger.

DOUGLASS, W. C. (1988). *WHO murdered Africa?* [Circulated booklet.]

DOWNEY, J. I., & FRIEDMAN, R. C. (1998). Female homosexuality: Classical psychoanalytic theory reconsidered. *Journal of the American Psychoanalytic Association, 46,* 471–506.

DOYLE, J. (1985). *Sex and gender: The human experiment.* Dubuque, IA: W. C. Brown.

DOYLE, J., & PALUDI, M. (1991). *Sex and gender* (2nd ed.). Dubuque, IA: Brown and Benchmark.

DRAPER, E. S., et al. (1999). Prediction of survival for preterm births by weight and gestational age: Retrospective population based study. *British Medical Journal, 319,* 1093–1097.

DREGER, A. D. (2008). The controversy surrounding *The Man Who Would Be Queen*: A case history of the politics of science, identity, and sex in the Internet age. *Archives of Sexual Behavior, 37,* 366–421.

DRESSING, H., KUEHNER, C., & GASS, P. (2006). The epidemiology and characteristics of stalking. *Current Opinion in Psychiatry, 19,* 395–399.

DRESSING, H., et al. (2009). Cyberstalking. *Der Nervenarzt, 80,* 833–836.

DREZNICK, M. T. (2003). Heterosocial competence of rapists and child molesters: A meta-analysis. *Journal of Sex Research, 40,* 170–178.

DUBOIS-ARBER, F., et al. (1997). Increased condom use without other major changes in sexual behavior among the general population in Switzerland. *American Journal of Public Health, 87,* 558–566.

DUMEZIL, G. (1979). *Mariages Indo-Européens.* Paris: Payot.

DUNKLE, J. H., & FRANCIS, P. L. (1990). The role of facial masculinity/femininity in the attribution of homosexuality. *Sex Roles, 23,* 157–167.

DUNN, K. M., et al. (2002). Systematic review of sexual problems: Epidemiology and methodology. *Journal of Sex & Marital Therapy, 28,* 399–422.

DUNN, M. E., & CUTLER, N. (2000). Sexual issues in older adults. *AIDS Patient Care and STDs, 14,* 67–69.

DUNN, M. E., & TROST, J. E. (1989). Male multiple orgasms: A descriptive study. *Archives of Sexual Behavior, 18,* 377–387.

DURANT, L. E., & CAREY, M. P. (2000). Self-administered questionnaires versus face-to-face interviews in assessing sexual behavior in young women. *Archives of Sexual Behavior, 29,* 309–322.

DUSH, C. M. K., COHAN, C. L., & AMATO, P. R. (2003). The relationship between cohabitation and marital quality and stability: Change across cohorts? *Journal of Marriage and Family, 65,* 539–549.

DYKES, B. (2000). Problems in defining cross-cultural "kinds of homosexuality"—and a solution. *Journal of Homosexuality, 38,* 1–18.

DZIECH, B. W., & HAWKINS, M. W. (1998). *Sexual harassment in higher education: Reflections and new perspectives.* New York: Garland.

E

EADS, L. S., SHUMAN, D. W., & DELIPSEY, J. M. (2000). Getting it right: The trial of sexual assault and child molestation cases under Federal Rules of Evidence 413–415. *Behavioral Sciences and the Law, 18,* 169–216.

EAGLY, H. H., & WOOD, W. (1999). The origins of sex differences in human behavior: Evolved dispositions versus social roles. *American Psychologist, 54,* 408–423.

EARLS, C. M., & DAVID, H. (1989). A psychosocial study of male prostitution. *Archives of Sexual Behavior, 18,* 401–419.

EATON, D. K., et al. (2008). Youth risk behavior surveillance–United States, 2007. *Morbidity and Mortality Weekly Report, 57/55-4,* 1–131.

EATON, D. K., et al. (2010). Youth risk behavior surveillance—United States, 2009. *Morbidity and Mortality Weekly Report, 59*(SS-5), 1–142.

ECKER, N. (1994). Culture and sexual scripts out of Africa: A North American trainer's view of taboos, tradition, trouble and truth. *SIECUS Report, 22*(2), 16–21.

EDLIN, B., & CARDEN, M. (2006). Injection drug users: The overlooked core of the hepatitis C epidemic. *Clinical Infectious Diseases, 42,* 673–676.

EDWARDS, G. L., & BARBER, B. L. (2010). Women may underestimate their partners' desires to use condoms: Possible implications for behavior. *Journal of Sex Research, 47,* 59–65.

EDWARDS, W. M., & COLEMAN, E. (2004). Defining sexual health: A descriptive overview. *Archives of Sexual Behavior, 33,* 189–195.

EFFAH, K. B. (1999). A reformation of the polygyny-fertility hypothesis. *Journal of Comparative Family Studies, 30,* 381–408.

EHRHARDT, A. A. (1992). Trends in sexual behavior and the HIV pandemic. *American Journal of Public Health, 82,* 1459–1461.

EHRLICH, P. R., & EHRLICH, A. H. (1990). *The population explosion.* New York: Simon & Schuster.

EHRLICHMAN, H., & EICHENSTEIN, R. (1992). Private wishes: Gender similarities and differences. *Sex Roles, 26,* 399–422.

EICHEL, E. W., & NOBILE, P. (1992). *The perfect fit: How to achieve mutual fulfillment and monogamous passion through the new intercourse.* New York: Donald Fine.

EICHENWALD, K. (2006, August 21). On the web, pedophiles extend their reach. *The New York Times.*

EIN-DOR, T., et al. (2010). The attachment paradox: How can so many of us (the insecure ones) have no adaptive advantages? *Perspectives on Psychological Science, 5,* 123–141.

EINWALTER, L., et al. (2005). Gonnorrhea and chlamydia infection among women visiting family planning clinics: Racial variation in prevalence and predictors. *Perspectives on Sexual and Reproductive Health, 37,* 135–140.

EITZEN, D. S., & ZINN, M. B. (2000). *Social problems* (8th ed.). Boston: Allyn & Bacon.

ELIFSON, K. W., et al. (1989). Seroprevalence of human immunodeficiency virus among male prostitutes. *New England Journal of Medicine, 321,* 822–833.

ELKOVITCH, N., et al. (2009). Understanding child sexual behavior problems: A developmental psychopathology framework, *Clinical Psychology Review, 29,* 586–598.

ELLIOTT, L., & BRANTLEY, C. (1997). *Sex on campus.* New York: Random House.

ELLIS, E. M., ATKESON, B. M., & CALHOUN, K. S. (1982). An examination of differences between multiple and single incident victims of sexual assault. *Journal of Abnormal Psychology, 91,* 221–224.

ELLIS, H. (1918). *Studies in the psychology of sex, Vol. II. Sexual invention.* Philadelphia: Davis.

ELLIS, L. (1993). Rape as a biosocial phenomenon. In G. C. N. Hall et al. (Eds.), *Sexual aggression: Issues in etiology, assessment, and treatment* (pp. 17–41). Washington, DC: Taylor & Francis.

ELLIS, L., ROBB, B., & BURKE, D. (2005). Sexual orientation in United States and Canadian college students. *Archives of Sexual Behavior, 34,* 569–581.

ELLISON, C. (2000). *Women's sexualities.* Oakland, CA: New Harbinger.

ELSE-QUEST, N. M., HYDE, J. S., & DELAMATER, J. D. (2005). Context counts: Long-term sequelae of premarital intercourse or abstinence. *Journal of Sex Research, 42,* 102–112.

ENDELMAN, R. (1989). *Love and sex in twelve cultures.* New York: Psyche Press.

ENDICOTT, J. (2000). History, evolution, and diagnosis of premenstrual dysphoric disorder. *Journal of Clinical Psychiatry, 61*(Suppl. 12), 5–8.

ENERGY BULLETIN. (2009). Population—Oct 1. http://energybulletin.net/node/50270

EPSTEIN, E., & GUTTMAN, R. (1984). Mate selection in man: Evidence, theory, and outcome. *Social Biology, 31,* 243–278.

ERICKSEN, J. A. (2000, May/June). Sexual liberation's last frontier. *Society,* 21–25.

ERIKSON, E. (1968). *Identity: Youth and crisis.* New York: Norton.

ERNST, E., & PITTLER, M. (1998). Yohimbine for erectile dysfunction: A systematic review and meta-analysis of randomized clinical trials. *Journal of Urology, 159,* 433–436.

ERNULF, K. E., & INNALA, S. M. (1995). Sexual bondage: A review and unobtrusive investigation. *Archives of Sexual Behavior, 24,* 631–654.

ESCHENBACH, D. A. (1993). History and review of bacterial vaginosis. *American Journal of Obstetrics and Gynecology, 169,* 441–445.

ESKRIDGE JR., W. N. (1999). Hardwick and historiography. *University of Illinois Law Review, No. 2,* 631–702.

EUROPEAN COLLABORATIVE STUDY. (1992). Risk factors for mother-to-child transmission of HIV-1. *The Lancet, 339,* 1007–1012.

EUROPEAN COLLABORATIVE STUDY. (1994). Perinatal findings in children born to HIV-infected mothers. *British Journal of Obstetrics and Gynaecology, 101,* 136–141.

EVANS, M. (1998). "Falling in love with love is falling for make believe": Ideologies of romance in post-enlightenment culture. *Theory, Culture & Society, 15,* 265–275.

EVANS, M. I., & WAPNER, R. J. (2005). Invasive prenatal diagnostic procedures 2005. *Seminars in Perinatology, 29,* 215–218.

EVERSLEY, M. (2010, April 26). Teachers lose licences for misconduct. *USA Today,* 3A.

EX, C. T. G. M., & JANSSENS, J. M. A. M. (1998). Maternal influences on daughters' gender role attitudes. *Sex Roles, 38,* 171–186.

EYAL, K., & KELI, F. (2009). The portrayal of sexual intercourse on television: How, who, and with what consequence? *Mass Communication & Society*, 17, 143–169.

EYAL, K. et al. (2007). Sexual socialization messages on television programs most popular among teens. *Journal of Broadcasting & Electronic Media*, 51, 316–336.

F

FAGOT, B. I. (1995). Psychosocial and cognitive determinants of early gender-role development. In R. Rosen, C. M. Davis, & H. J. Ruppel, Jr. (Eds.), *Annual review of sex research* (Vol. VI, pp. 1–31). Mount Vernon, IA: Society for the Scientific Study of Sexuality.

FAIRLEY, C. K., et al. (2009). Rapid decline in presentations of genital warts after the implementation of a national quadrivalent human papillomavirus vaccination programme for young women. *Sexually Transmitted Infections*, 85, 499–502.

FALLER, K. C. (1987). Women who sexually abuse children. *Victims and Violence*, 2(4), 23–27.

FALLER, K. C. (1991). Polyincestuous families: An exploratory study. *Journal of Interpersonal Violence*, 6, 310–321.

FALOMIR-PICHASTOR, J. M., & MUGNY, G. (2009). "I'm not gay.... I'm a real man!": Heterosexual men's gender self-esteem and sexual prejudice. *Personality and Social Psychology Bulletin*, 35, 1233–1243.

FARLEY, M. (2004). *Prostitution, trafficking, and traumatic stress.* New York: Haworth.

FARLEY, M., et al. (1998). Prostitution in five countries: Violence and posttraumatic stress disorder. *Feminism & Psychology*, 8, 405–426.

FARLEY, M., et al. (2003). Prostitution and trafficking in nine countries: An update on violence and posttraumatic stress disorder. *Journal of Trauma Practice*, 2, 33–74.

FARR, K. (2004). *Sex trafficking: The global market in women and children.* New York: W. H. Freedman.

FASSLER, I. R., et al. (2005). Predicting long-term outcomes for women sexually abused in childhood: Contribution of abuse severity versus family environment. *Child Abuse & Neglect*, 29, 269–284.

FAUCI, A. S. (1999). The AIDS epidemic: Considerations for the 21st century. *New England Journal of Medicine*, 341, 1046–1050.

FAUSTO-STERLING, A. (1993). The five sexes: Why male and female are not enough. *The Sciences*, 33(3), 20–24.

FAUSTO-STERLING, A. (2000). *Sexing the body: Gender politics and the construction of sexuality.* New York: Basic Books.

FEIERMAN, J. R., & FEIERMAN, L. A. (2000). Paraphilias. In L. T. Szuchman & F. Muscarella (Eds.), *Psychological perspectives on human sexuality* (pp. 480–518). New York: John Wiley & Sons.

FELDMAN, S. S., & ROSENTHAL, D. A. (2000). The effect of communication characteristics on family members' perceptions of parents as sex educators. *Journal of Research on Adolescence*, 10, 119–150.

FELDMAN-SUMMERS, S., & POPE, K. S. (1994). The experience of "forgetting" childhood abuse: A national survey of psychologists. *Journal of Consulting and Clinical Psychology*, 62, 636–639.

FERGUSON, C. J., & HARTLEY, R. D. (2009). The pleasure is momentary... the expense damnable? The influence of pornography on rape and sexual assault. *Aggression and Violent Behavior*, 14, 323–329.

FERGUSSON, D. M., HOSMANE, B., & HEIMAN, J. R. (2010). Randomized, placebo-controlled, double-blind, parallel design trial of the efficacy and safety of Zestra® in women with mixed desire/interest/arousal/orgasm disorders. *Journal of Sex & Marital Therapy*, 36, 66–86.

FERGUSSON, D. M., BODEN, J. M., & HORWOOD, L. J. (2007). Abortion among young women and subsequent life outcomes. *Perspectives on Sexual and Reproductive Health*, 39, 6–12.

FETHERS, K. A., et al. (2009). Early sexual experiences and risk factors for bacterial vaginosis. *Journal of Infectious Diseases*, 200, 1662–1670.

FEY, M. C., & BEAL, M. W. (2004). Role of human papillomavirus testing in cervical cancer prevention. *Journal of Midwifery & Women's Health*, 49, 4–13.

FIELD, A., et al. (1999). Exposure to the mass media and weight concerns among girls. *Pediatrics*, 103, 361–365.

FIELDER, R. L., & CAREY, M. P. (2010). Prevalence and characteristics of sexual hookups among first-semester female college students. *Journal of Sex & Marital Therapy*, 36, 346–359.

FINE, M. (1988). Sexuality, schooling, and adolescent females: The missing discourse of desire. *Harvard Educational Review*, 58, 29–53.

FINER, L. B. (2007). Trends in premarital sex in the United States, 1954–2003. *Public Health Reports*, 122(1), 73–78.

FINER, L. B., et al. (2005). Reasons U.S. women have abortions: Quantitative and qualitative perspectives. *Perspectives an Sexual and Reproductive Health*, 37(3), 110–118.

FINKELHOR, D. (1978). Psychological, cultural and family factors in incest and family sexual abuse. *Journal of Marriage and Family Counseling*, 4, 41–49.

FINKELHOR, D. (1979). *Sexually victimized children.* New York: Free Press.

FINKELHOR, D. (1980). Sex among siblings: A survey on prevalence, variety, and effects. *Archives of Sexual Behavior*, 9, 171–194.

FINKELHOR, D. (1984). *Child sexual abuse: New theory and research.* New York: Free Press.

FINKELHOR, D., & BERLINER, L. (1995). Research on the treatment of sexually abused children: A review and recommendations. *Journal of the Academy of Child and Adolescent Psychology*, 34, 1408–1423.

FINKELHOR, D., & JONES, L. M. (2003). *Sexual abuse decline in the 1990s: Evidence for possible causes* (Bulletin). Washington, DC: Department of Justice, Office of Justice Programs, Office of Juvenile Justice Delinquency Prevention.

FINKELHOR, D., & ORMROD, R. (2004, June). Prostitution of juveniles: Patterns from NIBRS. *Juvenile Justice Bulletin*, 1–2.

FINKELHOR, D., ORMROD, R. K., & TURNER, H. A. (2007). Re-victimization patterns in a national longitudinal sample of children and youth. *Child Abuse & Neglect*, 31, 479–502.

FINKELHOR, D., & RUSSELL, D. (1984). The gender gap among perpetrators of child sexual abuse. In D. Russell (Ed.), *Sexual exploitation: Rape, child sexual abuse, and workplace harassment* (pp. 215–231). Beverly Hills, CA: Sage.

FINKELHOR, D., & YLLO, K. (1985). *License to rape: Sexual abuse of wives.* New York: Holt, Rinehart & Winston.

FIORE, A. T., & DONATH, J. S. (2004). Online personals: An overview. Paper presented at ACM Computer Human Interaction 2004.

FIORE, A. T., et al. (2008). Assessing attractiveness in online dating profiles. Paper presented at ACM Computer Human Interaction, 2008.

FISCHER, G. J. (1989). Sex words used by partners in a relationship. *Journal of Sex Education and Therapy*, 15(1), 50.

FISHER, B., et al. (1995). Reanalysis and results after 12 years of follow-up in a randomized clinical trial comparing total mastectomy and lumpectomy with or without irradiation in the treatment of breast cancer. *New England Journal of Medicine*, 333, 1456–1461.

FISHER, B. S., CULLEN, F. T., & TURNER, M. T. (2000). *The sexual victimization of college women.* Washington, DC: U.S. Department of Justice.

FISHER, B. S. (2009). The effects of survey question wording on rape estimates. *Violence Against Women*, 15, 133–147.

FISHER, H. E. (1989). Evolution of human sexual pairbonding. *American Journal of Physical Anthropology*, 78, 331–354.

FISHER, H. E., et al. (2002). Defining the brain systems of lust, romantic attraction, and attachment. *Archives of Sexual Behavior*, 31, 413–419.

FISHER, J. D., & FISHER, W. A. (1992). Changing AIDS-risk behavior. *Psychological Bulletin*, 11, 455–474.

FISHER, W., & GRAY, J. (1988). Erotophobia-erotophilia and sexual behavior during pregnancy and postpartum. *Journal of Sex Research*, 25, 379–396.

FISHER, W. A., BRANSCOMBE, N. R., & LEMERY, C. R. (1983). The bigger the better? Arousal and attributional responses to erotic stimuli that depict different size penises. *Journal of Sex Research*, 19, 337–396.

FITZ-GERALD, D. R., & FITZ-GERALD, M. (1998). A historical review of sexuality education and deafness: Where have we been this century? *Sexuality and Disability*, 16, 249–268.

FITZGERALD, L. F. (1993). Sexual harassment: Violence against women in the workplace. *American Psychologist*, 48, 1070–1076.

FLAMM, B. L., BERWICK, D. M., & KABCENELL, A. (1998). Reducing cesarean section rates safely: Lessons from a "breakthrough" collaborative. *Birth*, 25, 117–124.

FLAMM, S. L. (2003). Chronic hepatitis C virus infection. *Journal of the American Medical Association*, 289, 2413–2417.

FLETCHER, G. J. O., & KERR, P. S. G. (2010). Through the eyes of love: Reality and illusion in intimate relationships. *Psychological Bulletin*, 136, 627–658.

FLETCHER, G. J. O., & SIMPSON, J. A. (2000). Ideal standards in close relationships: Their structure and functions. *Current Directions in Psychological Science*, 9, 102–105.

FOA, E. B., & RIGGS, D. S. (1995). Posttraumatic stress disorder following assault: Theoretical considerations and empirical findings. *Current Directions in Psychological Science*, 4, 61–65.

FORBES, G. B., et al. (2003). The role of hostile and benevolent sexism in women's and men's perceptions of the menstruating woman. *Psychology of Women Quarterly*, 27, 58–63.

FORD, C. A., et al. (2005). Predicting adolescents' longitudinal risk for sexually transmitted infection. *Archives of Pediatrics and Adolescent Medicine*, 159, 657–664.

FORD, C. S., & BEACH, F. A. (1951). *Patterns of sexual behavior.* New York: Harper & Brothers.

FORD, W. C. L., et al. (2000). Increasing paternal age is associated with delayed conception in a large population of fertile couples: Evidence for declining fecundity in older men. *Human Reproduction*, 15, 1703–1708.

FORMAN, D., & MOLLER, H. (1994). Testicular cancer. *Cancer Surveillance*, 19–20, 323–341.

FORSTE, R., & HAAS, D. W. (2002). The transition of adolescent males to first intercourse: Anticipated or delayed? *Perspectives on Sexual and Reproductive Health, 34,* 184–190.

FORTENBERRY, J. D., et al. (2002). Condom use as a function of time in new and established adolescent sexual relationships. *American Journal of Public Health, 92,* 211–213.

FORTENBERRY, J. D. et al. (2010). Sexual behaviors and condom use at last vaginal intercourse: A national sample of adolescents ages 14 to 17 years. *Journal of Sexual Medicine,* 7 (Suppl 5), 305–314.

FRASER, L. (2002, December). The islands where boys grow up to be girls. *Marie Claire,* 72–80.

FRAYSER, S. (1985). *Varieties of sexual experience: An anthropological perspective on human sexuality.* New Haven, CT: Human Relations Area Files Press.

FRAYSER, S. (1994). Defining normal childhood sexuality: An anthropological approach. *Annual Review of Sex Research, 5,* 173–217.

FRAZIER, P. A. (1991). Self-blame as a mediator of postrape depressive symptoms. *Journal of Social and Clinical Psychology, 10,* 47–57.

FREDERICK, D. A., et al. (2007). Desiring the muscular ideal: Men's body satisfaction in the United States, Ukraine, and Ghana. *Psychology of Men & Masculinity, 8,* 103–117.

FREUD, S. (1905). Three essays on the theory of sexuality. *In Standard edition* (Vol. VII, pp. 125–245). London: Hogarth Press, 1953.

FREUD, S. (1913). *Totem and taboo.* New York: Vintage Books.

FREUD, S. (1924). The sexual life of man. In E. Jones (Trans.), *A general introduction to psychoanalysis* (pp. 312–328). New York: Washington Square Press.

FREUD, S. (1953). Contributions to the psychology of love: A special type of choice of objects made by men. In E. Jones (Ed.), *Collected papers* (Vol. 4, pp. 192–202). London: Hogarth Press. (Originally published 1933.)

FREUND, K., & LANGEVIN, R. (1976). Bisexuality in homosexual pedophilia. *Archives of Sexual Behavior, 5,* 415–423.

FREUND, K., & SETO, M. C. (1998). Preferential rape in the theory of courtship disorder. *Archives of Sexual Behavior, 27,* 433–443.

FREUND, K., SETO, M. C., & KUBAN, M. (1997). Frotteurism and the theory of courtship disorder. In D. R. Laws & W. T. O'Donohue (Eds.), *Sexual deviance: Theory, assessment, and treatment* (pp. 111–130). New York: Guilford Press.

FREUND, K., & WATSON, R. (1990). Mapping the boundaries of courtship disorder. *Journal of Sex Research, 27,* 589–606.

FREUND, K., & WATSON, R. J. (1992). The proportions of heterosexual and homosexual pedophiles among sex offenders against children: An exploratory study. *Journal of Sex & Marital Therapy, 18,* 34–43.

FREUND, K., WATSON, R., & DICKEY, R. (1991). Sex offenses against female children perpetrated by men who are not pedophiles. *Journal of Sex Research, 28,* 409–423.

FREUND, M., LEONARD, T. L., & LEE, N. (1989). Sexual behavior of resident street prostitutes with their clients in Camden, New Jersey. *Journal of Sex Research, 26,* 460–478.

FRIEDMAN, C. I., & KIM, M. H. (1985). Obesity and its effect on reproductive function. *Clinical Obstetrics and Gynecology, 28,* 645–663.

FRIEDMAN, R. (1947). *The story of scabies* (Vol. I). New York: Froben Press.

FRIEDRICH, W. N. (1993). Sexual victimization and sexual behavior in children: A review of recent literature. *Child Abuse & Neglect, 17,* 59–66.

FRIEDRICH, W. N. (1998). Behavioral manifestations of child sexual abuse. *Child Abuse & Neglect, 22,* 523–531.

FRIEDRICH, W. N., & REAMS, R. A. (1987). Course of psychological symptoms in sexually abused young children. *Psychotherapy, 24,* 160–170.

FRIEDRICH, W. N., et al. (1991). Normative sexual behavior in children. *Pediatrics, 88,* 456–464.

FRIESS, S. (2003, January 20). Hot and bothered. *Newsweek,* 13.

FRIESS, S. (2009, February 24). For some, shadow of regret cast over gender switch. *USA Today.*

FRIEZE, I. H. (2005). *Virginity lost: An intimate portrait of the first sexual experiences.* New York: New York University Press.

FROMM, E. (1956). *The art of loving.* New York: Harper & Row.

FROST, J. J., SINGH, S., & FINER, L. B. (2007). U.S. women's one-year contraceptive use patterns, 2004. *Perspectives on Sexual and Reproductive Health, 39,* 48–55.

FUGL-MEYER, K., et al. (2006). On orgasm, sexual techniques, and erotic perceptions in 18- to 74-year-old Swedish women. *Journal of Sexual Medicine, 3,* 56–68.

FURNHAM, A. (2009). Sex differences in mate selection preferences. *Personality and Individual Differences, 47,* 262–267.

FURNHAM, A., SWAMI, V., & SHAH, K. (2006). Body weight, waist-to-hip ratio, and breast size correlates of ratings of attractiveness and health. *Personality and Individual Differences, 41,* 443–454.

FURTADO, M. R., et al. (1999). Persistance of HIV-1 transcription in peripheral-blood mononuclear cells in patients receiving potent antiretroviral therapy. *New England Journal of Medicine, 340,* 1614–1622.

G

GABELNICK, H. L., SCHWARTZ, J., & DARROCH, J. E. (2008). Contraceptive research and development. In R. A. Hatcher et al. (Eds.), *Contraceptive technology* (19th ed., pp. 443–449). New York: Ardent Media.

GABLE, S., GONZAGA, G. C., & STRACHMAN, A. (2006). Will you be there for me when things go right? Supporting responses to positive event disclosures. *Journal of Personality and Social Psychology, 91,* 904–917.

GAGNON, J. H. (1977). *Human sexualities.* Glenview, IL: Scott, Foresman.

GAGNON, J. H. (1985). Attitudes and responses of parents to preadolescent masturbation. *Archives of Sexual Behavior, 14,* 451–466.

GALLAGHER, W. (1986, February). The etiology of orgasm. *Discover,* 51–59.

GALLAHAN, L. B. (2000). Research and conceptual approaches to the understanding of gender. In M. Biaggio & M. Hersen (Eds.), *Issues in the psychology of women* (pp. 33–52). New York: Kluwer Academic/Plenum Publishers.

GALLO, L. C., & SMITH, T. W. (2001). Attachment style in marriage: Adjustment and responses to interaction. *Journal of Social and Personal Relationships, 18,* 263–289.

GALLUP POLL. (2010, May 3–6). Abortion and birth control. http://www.pollingreport.com/abortion.htm

GANAHL, D. J., et al. (2003). A content analysis of prime time commercials: A contextual framework of gender representation. *Sex Roles, 49,* 545–551.

GANNON, C. L. (1998). The deaf community and sexuality education. *Sexuality and Disability, 16,* 283–293.

GANNON, T. A., & WARD, T. (2008). Rape: Psychopathology and theory. In D. R. Laws & W. T. O'Donohue (Eds.), *Sexual deviance: Theory, assessment, and treatment* (2nd ed., pp. 336–355). New York: Guilford Press.

GAO, F., et al. (1992). Human infection by genetically diverse SIVSM-related HIV-2 in West Africa. *Nature, 358,* 495–499.

GAO, F., et al. (1999). Origin of HIV-1 in the chimpanzee *Pan troglodytes troglodytes. Nature, 397,* 436–441.

GARNER, D. M. (1997, January/February). The 1997 body image survey results. *Psychology Today,* 30–36, 38–40, 42–44, 75, 76, 78, 84.

GARNER, D. M., et al. (1980). Cultural expectations of thinness in women. *Psychological Reports, 47,* 483–491.

GARNETS, L. D., & PEPLAU, L. A. (2000). Understanding women's sexualities and sexual orientation: An introduction. *Journal of Social Issues, 56,* 181–192.

GARNETS, L. D., & PEPLAU, L. A. (2001). A new paradigm for women's sexual orientation: Implications for therapy. *Women and Therapy, 24,* 111–121.

GARRISON, E. G., & KOBOR, P. C. (2002). Weathering a political storm: A contextual perspective on a psychological research controversy. *American Psychologist, 57,* 165–175.

GASCHEN, B., et al. (2002). Diversity considerations in HIV-1 vaccine selection. *Science, 296,* 2354–2360.

GATES, G. J., & SONENSTEIN, F. L. (2000). Heterosexual genital sexual activity among adolescent males: 1988 and 1995. *Family Planning Perspectives, 32,* 295–297, 304.

GAVIN, L., et al. (2009). Sexual and reproductive health of persons aged 10–24 years—United States, 2002–2007. *Morbidity and Mortality Weekly Report, 58*(SS06), 1–58.

GAZZOLA, L., et al. (2009). The absence of CD4⁺ T cell count recovery despite receipt of virologically suppressive highly active antiretroviral therapy: Clinical risk, immunological gaps, and therapeutic options. *Clinical Infectious Diseases, 48,* 328–337.

GEARY, D. C. (1998). *Male, female: The evolution of human sex differences.* Washington, DC: American Psychological Association.

GEARY, D. C. (1999). Evolution and developmental sex differences. *Current Directions in Psychological Science, 8,* 115–120.

GEARY, D. C., VIGIL, J., & BYRD-CRAVEN, J. (2004). Evolution of human mate choice. *Journal of Sex Research, 41,* 27–42.

GEARY, D. C., et al. (1995). Sexual jealousy as a facultative trait: Evidence from the pattern of sex differences in adults from China and the United States. *Ethology and Sociobiology, 16,* 355–383.

GEBHARD, P. H. (1985). Sexuality in cross-cultural perspective. In W. Masters, V. Johnson, & R. Kolodny (Eds.), *Human Sexuality* (2nd ed., pp. 620–637). Boston: Little, Brown.

GEBHARD, P. H., et al. (1965). *Sex offenders: An analysis of types.* New York: Harper & Row.

GEER, J. H., & BELLARD, H. S. (1996). Sexual content induced delays in unprimed lexical decisions: Gender and content effects. *Archives of Sexual Behavior, 25,* 379–395.

GEERTZ, C. (1960). *The religion of Java.* Chicago: University of Chicago Press.

GEISLER, W. M. (2010). Duration of untreated, uncomplicated *Chlamydia trachomatis* genital infection and factors associated with chlamydia resolution: A review of human studies. *Journal of Infectious Diseases, 201* (Suppl 2), S104–S113.

GELMAN, D. (1990, June 11). Was it illness or immorality? *Newsweek*, 55.

GELMAN, D., et al. (1990, July 23). The mind of a rapist. *Newsweek*, 46–52.

GEORGE, W. H., et al. (2009). Indirect effects of acute alcohol intoxication on sexual risk-taking: The roles of subjective and physiological sexual arousal. *Archives of Sexual Behavior*, 38, 498–513.

GERRESSU, M., et al. (2008). Prevalence of masturbation and associated factors in a British national probability survey. *Archives of Sexual Behavior*, 37, 266–278.

GIBBONS, J. L. (2000). Gender development in cross-cultural perspective. In T. Eckes & H. M. Trautner (Eds.), *The developmental social psychology of gender* (pp. 389–415). Mahwah, NJ: Lawrence Erlbaum.

GIBBS, N. (1991, June 3). When is it rape? *Time*, 50–51.

GIBBS, N. (2010, May 3). Love, sex, freedom and the paradox of the pill. *Time*, 40–47.

GIDYCZ, C. A., & KOSS, M. P. (1990). A comparison of group and individual sexual assault victims. *Psychology of Women Quarterly*, 14, 325–342.

GIFFORD, S. M. (1994). The change of life, the sorrow of life: Menopause, bad blood and cancer among Italian-Australian working class women. *Culture, Medicine, Psychiatry*, 18, 299–321.

GILBERT, B., & CUNNINGHAM, J. (1987). Women's post rape sexual functioning: Review and implications for counseling. *Journal of Counseling and Development*, 65, 71–73.

GILBERT, N. (1991). The phantom epidemic of sexual assault. *The Public Interest*, 103, 54–65.

GILBERT, W. M., NESBITT, T. S., & DANIELSEN, B. (1999). Childbearing beyond age 40: Pregnancy outcome in 24,032 cases. *Obstetrics & Gynecology*, 93, 9–14.

GILLMORE, M. R., et al. (1997). Repeat pregnancies among adolescent mothers. *Journal of Marriage and Family*, 59, 536–550.

GILLMORE, M. R., et al. (2002). Teen sexual behavior: Applicability of the theory of reasoned action. *Journal of Marriage and Family*, 64, 885–897.

GIULIANO, F., & RAMPIN, O. (2004). Neural control of erection. *Physiology & Behavior*, 83, 189–201.

GLADUE, B. A. (1988). Hormones in relationship to homosexual/bisexual/heterosexual gender orientation. In J. M. A. Sitesen (Ed.), *Handbook of sexology: Vol. 6. The pharmacology and endocrinology of sexual function*. Amsterdam: Elsevier.

GLADUE, B. A. (1994). The biopsychology of sexual orientation. *Current Directions in Psychological Science*, 3, 150–154.

GLASER, J. B., et al. (1991). Sexually transmitted diseases in postpubertal female rape victims. *Journal of Infectious Diseases*, 164, 726–730.

GLASER, S. (2006, August 14). Moms torn in heated debate over breast-feeding. *New Orleans Times-Picayune*, p. D3.

GLICK, L. (2005). *Marked in your flesh: Circumcision from ancient Judea to modern America*. Oxford, UK: Oxford University Press.

GLYNN, S. A., et al. (2000). Trends in incidence and prevalence of major transfusion-transmissible viral infections in U.S. blood donors, 1991 to 1996. *Journal of the American Medical Association*, 284, 229–235.

GOCHROS, H., GOCHROS, J. S., & FISHER, J. (Eds.). (1986). *Helping the sexually oppressed*. Englewood Cliffs, NJ: Prentice Hall.

GOERGE, R. M., & LEE, B. J. (1997). Abuse and neglect of the children. In R. A. Maynard (Ed.), *Kids having kids: Economic costs and social consequences of teen pregnancy* (pp. 205–230). Washington, DC: Urban Institute Press.

GOERGEN, D. (1975). *The sexual celibate*. New York: Seabury.

GOLD, S. N., HUGHES, D., & HOHNECKER, L. (1994). Degrees of repression of sexual abuse memories. *American Psychologist*, 49, 441–442.

GOLDBERG, A. B., & GRIMES, D. A. (2008). Injectable contraceptives. In R. A. Hatcher et al. (Eds.), *Contraceptive technology* (19th ed., pp. 157–179). New York: Ardent Media.

GOLDMAN, B., BUSH, P., & KLATZ, R. (1987). *Death in the locker room: Steroids, cocaine, and sport*. Tucson, AZ: Body Press.

GOLDSTEIN, A. T., & BURROWS, L. (2008). Vulvodynia. *Journal of Sexual Medicine*, 5, 5–15.

GOLDSTEIN, B. (1976). *Human sexuality*. New York: McGraw-Hill.

GOLDSTEIN, D. (1994). AIDS and women in Brazil: The emerging problem. *Social Science and Medicine*, 39, 919–929.

GOLDSTEIN, M. J. (1973). Exposure to erotic stimuli and sexual deviance. *Journal of Social Issues*, 29, 197–220.

GOLEMAN, D. (1990, July 10). Homophobia: Scientists find clues to its roots. *The New York Times*, C1, C11.

GOLEMAN, D. (1992). New studies map the mind of the rapist. *The New York Times*.

GOMES-SCHWARTZ, B., et al. (1990). The aftermath of child sexual abuse 18 months later. In B. Gomes-Schwartz et al. (Eds.), *Child sexual abuse* (pp. 132–152). Newbury Park, CA: Sage.

GONZAGA, G., et al. (2006). Romantic love and sexual desire in close relationships. *Emotion*, 6, 163–179.

GONZAGA, G., et al. (2008). Love, desire, and the suppression of thoughts of romantic alternatives. *Evolution and Human Behavior*, 29, 119–126.

GOODALL, J. (1971). *Tiwi wives*. Seattle: University of Washington Press.

GOODCHILDS, J., & ZELLMAN, G. (1984). Sexual signaling and sexual aggression in adolescent relationships. In N. Malamuth & E. Donnerstein (Eds.), *Pornography and sexual aggression*. Orlando, FL: Academic Press.

GOODMAN, A. (1992). Sexual addiction: Designation and treatment. *Journal of Sex & Marital Therapy*, 18, 304–314.

GOODMAN, A. (1998). *Sexual addiction: An integrated approach*. Madison, CT: International Universities Press.

GORDON, S. (1989). *Raising your child conservatively in a sexually permissive world*. New York: Fireside.

GORDON, S., & SNYDER, C. W. (1989). *Personal issues in human sexuality: A guidebook for better sexual health* (2nd ed.). Boston: Allyn & Bacon.

GORSKI, R., et al. (1978). Evidence for a morphological sex difference within the medial preoptic area of the rat brain. *Brain Research*, 148, 333–346.

GOSTIN, L. O., et al. (1994). HIV testing, counseling, and prophylaxis after sexual assault. *Journal of the American Medical Association*, 271, 1436–1444.

GOTTMAN, J. (1993). *What predicts divorce*. Hillsdale, NJ: Lawrence Erlbaum.

GOTTMAN, J. (1994). *Why marriages succeed or fail*. New York: Simon & Schuster.

GOTTMAN, J., et al. (1998). Predicting marital happiness and stability from newlywed interactions. *Journal of Marriage and Family*, 60, 5–22.

GOTTMAN, J. M., & LEVENSON, R. W. (2000). The timing of divorce: Predicting when a couple will divorce over a 14-year period. *Journal of Marriage and Family*, 62, 737–745.

GOTTMAN, J. M., et al. (2004). Correlates of gay and lesbian couples' relationship satisfaction and relationship dissolution. *Journal of Homosexuality*, 45, 23–43.

GOTTSCHALL, J. (2004). Explaining wartime rape. *Journal of Sex Research*, 41, 129–136.

GRABER, B. (Ed.). (1982). *Circumvaginal musculature and sexual function*. New York: Karger.

GRABER, J. A., & BROOKS-GUNN, J. (2002). Adolescent girls' sexual development. In G. M. Wingood & R. J. DiClemente (Eds.), *Handbook of women's sexual and reproductive health* (pp. 21–42). New York: Kluwer Academic/Plenum Publishers.

GRADY, W. R., BILLY, J. O. G., & KLEPINGER, D. H. (2002). Contraceptive method switching in the United States. *Perspectives on Sexual and Reproductive Health*, 34, 135–145.

GRAFENBERG, E. (1950). The role of the urethra in female orgasm. *International Journal of Sexology*, 3, 145–148.

GRAHAM, C. A. (2010). The DSM diagnostic criteria for female sexual arousal disorder. *Archives of Sexual Behavior*, 39, 240–255.

GRAHAM, C. A., et al. (2004). Turning on and turning off: A focus group study of the factors that affect women's sexual arousal. *Archives of Sexual Behavior*, 33, 527–538.

GRAHAM, I., & DAVIES, C. (2005). Episiotomy: The unkindest cut that persists. In C. Henderson & D. Bick (Eds.), *Perineal care: An international issue* (pp. 58–86). London: Quay Books.

GRAHAM, S. (1834). *A lecture to young men*. Providence, Rhode Island: Weeden and Corey.

GRANT, T., et al. (2009). Alcohol use before and during pregnancy in western Washington, 1989–2004. *American Journal of Obstetrics and Gynecology*, 200, 278–286.

GRAVHOLT, C. H., et al. (1996). Prenatal and postnatal prevalence of Turner's syndrome: A registry study. *British Medical Journal*, 312, 16–21.

GRAY, J. (1992). *Men are from Mars, women are from Venus: A practical guide to improving communication and getting what you want in your relationships*. New York: HarperCollins.

GRAY, J. M. (2006). Rape myth belief and prejudiced instructions: Effects on decisions of guilt in a case of date rape. *Legal and Criminological Psychology*, 11, 75–80.

GRAY, P. (1993a, February 15). What is love? *Time*, 46–49.

GRAY, P. (1993b, November 29). The assault on Freud. *Time*, 46–51.

GRAY, R. H., et al. (2009). The role of male circumcision in the prevention of human papillomavirus and HIV infection. *Journal of Infectious Diseases*, 199, 1–3.

GRAY, R. H., et al. (2010). Male circumcision decreases acquisition and increases clearance of high-risk human papillomavirus in HIV-negative men: A randomized trial in Raka, Uganda. *Journal of Infectious Diseases*, 201, 1455–1462.

GRAYSTON, A. D., & DELUCA, R. V. (1999). Female perpetrators of child sexual abuse: A review of the clinical and empirical literature. *Aggression and Violent Behavior*, 4, 93–106.

GREEN, R. (1987). *The "sissy boy syndrome" and the development of homosexuality*. New Haven, CT: Yale University Press.

GREEN, R. (2010). Transsexual legal rights in the United States and United Kingdom: Employment, medical treatment, and civil status. *Archives of Sexual Behavior, 39,* 153–160.

GREEN, R., & FLEMING, D. T. (1990). Transsexual surgery follow-up: Status in the 1990s. *Annual Review of Sex Research,* 1, 163–174.

GREENBERG, B., et al. (1993). Sex content in R-rated films viewed by adolescents. In B. S. Greenberg, J. D. Brown, & N. L. Buerkel-Rothfuss (Eds.), *Media, sex and the adolescent* (pp. 29–44). Cresskill, NJ: Hampton Press.

GREENBERG, D., et al. (2000). Recidivism of child molesters: A study of victim relationship with the perpetrator. *Child Abuse & Neglect,* 24, 1485–1494.

GREENBLATT, C. S. (1983). The salience of sexuality in the early years of marriage. *Journal of Marriage and Family,* 45, 289–299.

GREGERSEN, E. (1982). *Sexual practices.* New York: Franklin Watts.

GREGOR, T. (1985). *Anxious pleasures: The sexual lives of an Amazonian people.* Chicago: University of Chicago Press.

GRELLO, C. M., et al. (2003). Dating and sexual relationship trajectories and adolescent functioning. *Adolescent & Family Health,* 3, 103–112.

GRIFFITHS, M. (2001). Sex on the Internet: Observations and implications for Internet sex addiction. *Journal of Sex Research,* 38, 333–342.

GRIMAL, P. (1986). *Love in ancient Rome.* Norman: University of Oklahoma Press.

GRIMES, D. A. (2008). Intrauterine devices (IUDs). In R. A. Hatcher et al. (Eds.), *Contraceptive technology* (19th ed., pp. 117–156). New York: Ardent Media.

GRISARU-GRANOVSKY, S., et al. (2009). Effect of interpregnancy interval on adverse perinatal outcomes—A national study. *Contraception,* 80, 512–518.

GRISEZ, G. G. (1970). *Abortion: The myths, the realities, and the arguments.* New York: Corpus Books.

GROENENDIJK, L. F. (1997). Masturbation and neurasthenia: Freud and Stekel in debate on the harmful effects of autoerotism. *Journal of Psychology and Human Sexuality,* 91, 71–94.

GROFF, M. G. (1987). Characteristics of incest offenders' wives. *Journal of Sex Research,* 23, 91–96.

GROOTHOF, H. A. K., DIJKSTRA, P., & BARELDS, D. P. H. (2009). Sex differences in jealousy: The case of Internet infidelity. *Journal of Social and Personal Relationships,* 26, 1119–1129.

GROSSMAN, C. L. (2008, June 4). Most say gay marriage private choice. *USA Today,* 7D.

GROSSMAN, L. S., HAYWOOD, T. W., & WASYLIW, O. E. (1992). The evaluation of truthfulness in alleged sex offenders' self-reports: 16 PF and MMPI validity scales. *Journal of Personality Assessment,* 59, 264–275.

GROSSMAN, L. S., MARTIS, B., & FICHTNER, C. G. (1999). Are sex offenders treatable? A research overview. *Psychiatric Services,* 50, 349–361.

GROSZ, C. A., KEMPE, R. S., & KELLY, M. (2000). Extrafamilial sexual abuse: Treatment for child victims and their families. *Child Abuse & Neglect,* 24, 9–23.

GROTH, A. N. (1979). *Men who rape.* New York: Plenum Press.

GROTH, A. N., & BIRNBAUM, H. J. (1978). Adult sexual orientation and attraction to underage persons. *Archives of Sexual Behavior,* 7, 175–181.

GROTH, A. N., & BURGESS, A. W. (1977). Sexual dysfunction during rape. *New England Journal of Medicine,* 297, 764–766.

GROTH, A. N., BURGESS, A. W., & HOLMSTROM, L. (1977). Rape: Power, anger, and sexuality.

GROTH, A. N., HOBSON, W. F., & GARY, T. S. (1982). The child molester: Clinical observations. In J. Conte & D. A. Shore (Eds.), *Social work and child sexual abuse* (pp. 129–144). New York: Haworth Press.

GRUBER, J. E. (1990). Methodological problems and policy implications in sexual harassment research. *Population Research and Policy Review,* 9, 235–254.

GRUBIN, D. (2008). Medical models and interventions in sexual deviance. In D. R. Laws & W. T. O'Donohue (Eds.), *Sexual deviance: Theory, assessment, and treatment* (2nd ed., pp. 594–610). New York: Guilford Press.

GRUBIN, D., & MASON, D. (1997). Medical models of sexual deviances. In D. R. Laws & W. T. O'Donohue (Eds.), *Sexual deviance: Theory, assessment, and treatment* (pp. 434–448). New York: Guilford Press.

GRUENBAUM, E. (2006). Sexuality issues in the movement to abolish female genital cutting in Sudan. *Medical Anthropology Quarterly,* 20, 121.

GRULICH, A. E., et al. (2003). Sex in Australia: Homosexual experience and recent homosexual encounters. *Australian and New Zealand Journal of Public Health,* 27, 155–163.

GRULICH, A., CUNNINGHAM, P., & RAWLINSON, W. D. (2001). Human herpesvirus 8: A newly described sexually transmissible infection. *Venereology,* 14, 174–180.

GRUMBACH, M. M. (2002). The neuroendocrinology of human puberty revisited. *Hormone Research,* 57(Suppl 2), 2–14.

GRUNSEIT, A., et al. (1997). Sexuality education and young people's sexual behavior: A review of studies. *Journal of Adolescent Research,* 12, 421–453.

GUAY, A. (2001). Decreased testosterone in regularly menstruating women with decreased libido: A clinical observation. *Journal of Sex & Marital Therapy,* 27, 513–519.

GUERRERO, F., et al. (2010). "Ophthalmia venerea": A dreadful complication of fluoroquinolone-resistant Neisseria gonorrhoeae. *Sexually Transmitted Diseases,* 37, 340–341.

GUERRERO, L. K. (1996). Attachment-style differences in intimacy and involvement: A test of the four-category model. *Communication Monographs,* 63, 269–292.

GUERRERO, L. K. (1998). Attachment-style differences in the experience and expression of romantic jealousy. *Personal Relationships,* 5, 273–291.

GUERRERO PAVICH, E. (1986). A Chicano perspective on Mexican culture and sexuality. In L. Lister (Ed.), *Human sexuality, ethnoculture, and social work.* New York: Haworth Press.

GUITERMAN, A. (1992). Poem. In *Bartlett's familiar quotations* (15th ed.).

GURA, T. (1994, July 31). Mating study: Men seek variety, women security. *New Orleans Times-Picayune,* p. A7.

GURALNIK, J. M., BALFOUR, J. L., & VOLPATO, S. (2000). The ratio of older women to men: Historical perspectives and cross-national comparisons. *Aging Clinical and Experimental Research,* 12, 65–76.

GUTE, G., ESHBAUGH, E. M., & WIERSMA, J. (2008). Sex for you, but not for me: Discontinuity in undergraduate emerging adults' definitions of "having sex." *Journal of Sex Research,* 45, 329–337.

GUTEK, B. A., et al. (1999). The utility of the reasonable woman legal standard in hostile environment sexual harassment cases. *Psychology, Public Policy, and Law,* 5, 596–629.

GUTTMACHER INSTITUTE. (1999). *Survey on teen peer pressure.* www.teenpregnancy.org

GUTTMACHER INSTITUTE. (2007b). Induced abortion. *Facts in brief.* www.guttmacher.org

GUTTMACHER INSTITUTE. (2010). www.guttmacher.org

GUZICK, D. S., et al. (1999). Efficacy of superovulation and intrauterine insemination in the treatment of infertility. *New England Journal of Medicine,* 340, 177–183.

GUZZO, K. (2009). Marital intentions and the stability of first cohabitations. *Journal of Family Issues,* 30, 179–205.

H

HAAVIO-MANNILA, E., & KONTULA, O. (1997). Correlates of increased sexual satisfaction. *Archives of Sexual Behavior,* 26, 399–419.

HACKEL, L. S., & RUBLE, D. N. (1992). Changes in marital relationship after the first baby is born: Predicting the impact of expectancy disconfirmation. *Journal of Personality and Social Psychology,* 62, 944–957.

HAESEVOETS, Y.-H. (1997). L'enfant victime d'inceste: Symptomatologie spécifique ou aspécifique? (Essai de conceptualisation clinique). *Psychiatrie de l'enfant,* XL(1), 87–119.

HAFFNER, D. W., & CASSELMAN, M. (1996). Toy story: A look into the gender-stereotyped world of children's catalogs. *SIECUS Report,* 24(4), 20–21.

HAGE, J. J., BLOEM, J. J. A. M., & SULIMAN, H. M. (1993). Review of the literature on techniques for phalloplasty with emphasis on the applicability in female-to-male transsexuals. *Journal of Urology,* 150, 1093–1098.

HAGGERTY, C. L., et al. (2010). Risk of sequelae after *Chlamydia trachomatis* genital infection in women. *Journal of Infectious Diseases,* 201 (Suppl 2), S134–S155.

HAGLUND, B., et al. (1990). Cigarette smoking as a risk factor for sudden infant death syndrome: A population-based study. *American Journal of Public Health,* 80, 29–32.

HAHN, B. H., et al. (2000). AIDS as a zoonosis: Scientific and public health implications. *Science,* 287, 607–614.

HAHN, J., & BLASS, T. (1997). Dating partner preferences: A function of similarity of love styles. *Journal of Social Behavior and Personality,* 12, 595–610.

HALBREICH, U., et al. (2003). The prevalence, impairment, impact, and burden of premenstrual dysphoric disorder (PMS/PMDD). *Psychoneuroendocrinology,* 28, 1–23.

HALD, G. M., & MALAMUTH, N. M. (2008). Self-perceived effects of pornography consumption. *Archives of Sexual Behavior,* 37, 614–625.

HALL, G. S. (1904). *Adolescence: Its psychology and the relation to physiology, anthropology, sociology, sex, crime, religion and education* (Vols. 1–2). New York: Appleton.

HALL, R. C., et al. (1989). Sexual abuse in patients with anorexia nervosa and bulimia. *Psychosomatics,* 30, 73–79.

HALLER, J. S., & HALLER, R. M. (1977). *The physician and sexuality in Victorian America.* New York: Norton.

HALLSTROM, T., & SAMUELSSON, S. (1990). Changes in women's sexual desire in middle life: The longitudinal study of women in Gothenburg (Sweden). *Archives of Sexual Behavior,* 19, 259–267.

HALMAN, L. J., ABBEY, A., & ANDREWS, F. M. (1992). Attitudes about infertility interventions among fertile and infertile couples. *American Journal of Public Health,* 82, 191–194.

HALPERIN, D. (1998). HIV, STDs, anal sex and HIV prevention policy in a northeastern Brazilian city. *International Journal of STD and AIDS,* 9, 294–298.

HALPERN, C. T., UDRY, J. R., & SUCHINDRAN, C. (1998). Monthly measures of salivary testosterone predict sexual activity in adolescent males. *Archives of Sexual Behavior*, 27, 445–465.

HALPERN-FELSHER, B. L., et al. (2005). Adolescents and oral sex: Perceptions, attitudes, and behavior. *Journal of Adolescent Health*, 36, 109–110.

HAMMOND, P., et al. (2009). In vitro fertilization availability and utilization in the United States: A study of demographic social, and economic factors. *Sterility and Fertility*, 91, 1630–1635.

HANING, R. V., et al. (2007). Intimacy, orgasm likelihood, and conflict predict sexual satisfaction in heterosexual male and female respondents. *Journal of Sex & Marital Therapy*, 33, 93–113.

HANNAFORD, P. C., et al. (2010). Mortality among contraceptive pill users: Cohort evidence from Royal College of General Practitioners' Oral Contraception Study. *British Medical Journal*, 340, c927.

HANRAHAN, S. N. (1994). Historical review of menstrual toxic shock syndrome. *Women & Health*, 21, 141–165.

HANS, J. D., GILLEN, M., & AKANDE, K. (2010). Sex redefined: The reclassification of oral-genital contact. *Perspectives on Sexual and Reproductive Health*, 42, 74–78.

HANSON, R. K. (2000). Will they do it again? Predicting sex-offense recidivism. *Current Directions in Psychological Science*, 9, 106–109.

HARDEN, A., et al. (2009). Teenage pregnancy and social disadvantage: Systematic review integrating controlled trials and qualitative studies. *British Medical Journal*, 339, 64254.

HARDIE, E. A. (1997). PMS in the workplace: Dispelling the myth of cyclic dysfunction. *Journal of Occupational and Organizational Psychology*, 70, 97–102.

HARDING, R., & GOLOMBOK, S. E. (2002). Test-retest reliability of the measurement of penile dimensions in a sample of gay men. *Archives of Sexual Behavior*, 31, 351–357.

HARDING, S. (1986). *The science question in feminism*. Ithaca, NY: Cornell University Press.

HARGREAVES, S. (2007). 60% reduction in HIV risk with male circumcision, says WHO. *The Lancet*, 360, 313.

HARKLESS, L. E., & FLOWERS, B. J. (2005). Similarities and differences in relational boundaries among heterosexuals, gay men, and lesbians. *Psychology of Women Quarterly*, 29, 167–176.

HARLOW, H. F. (1959). Love in infant monkeys. *Scientific American*, 200(6), 68–74.

HARLOW, S. D., & EPHROSS, S. A. (1995). Epidemiology of menstruation and its relevance to women's health. *Epidemiologic Reviews*, 17, 265–286.

HARMER, P. A. (2010). Anabolic-androgenic steroid use among young male and female athletes: Is the game to blame? *British Journal of Sports Medicine*, 44, 26–31.

HARNISH, S. (1988, July). Congenital absence of the vagina: Clinical issues. *Medical Aspects of Human Sexuality*, 54–60.

HARPER, C. C., et al. (2008). Over-the-counter access to emergency contraception for teens. *Contraception*, 77, 230–233.

HARRIS, A. J. R., & HANSON, R. K. (2004). *Sex offender recidivism: A simple question* (User Report No. 2004-03). Ottawa: Department of the Solicitor General of Canada.

HARRIS, C. R. (2003). A review of sex differences in sexual jealousy, including self-report data, psychophysiological responses, interpersonal violence, and morbid jealousy.

Personality and Social Psychology Review, 7, 102–128.

HARRISON, M. R., et al. (1990). Successful repair in utero of a fetal diaphragmatic hernia after removal of herniated viscera from the left thorax. *New England Journal of Medicine*, 322, 1582–1584.

HASELTON, M. G., et al. (2007). Ovulatory shifts in human female ornamentation: Near ovulation, women dress to impress. *Hormones and Behavior*, 51, 40–45.

HASSELROT, K., et al. (2010). Orally exposed uninfected individuals have systemic anti-HIV responses associating with partners' viral load. *AIDS*, 24, 35–43.

HASSETT, J. (1978). Sex and smell. *Psychology Today*, 11, 40–42, 45.

HATCH, M., LEVIN, B., SHU, X-O., & SUSSER, M. (1998). Maternal leisure-time exercise and timely delivery. *American Journal of Public Health*, 88, 1528–1533.

HATCHER, R. A., et al. (2004). *Contraceptive technology* (18th ed.). New York: Ardent Media.

HATCHER, R. A., & NAMNOUM, A. B. (2008). The menstrual cycle. In R. A. Hatcher et al. (Eds.), *Contraceptive technology* (19th ed., pp. 7–17). New York: Ardent Media.

HATCHER, R. A., et al. (Eds.). (2008). *Contraceptive technology* (19th ed.). New York: Ardent Media.

HATFIELD, E. (1984). The dangers of intimacy. In V. Derlaga (Ed.), *Communication, intimacy, and close relationships* (pp. 207–220). New York: Academic Press.

HATFIELD, E. (1988). Passionate and companionate love. In R. J. Sternberg & M. L. Barnes (Eds.), *The psychology of love* (pp. 191–217). New Haven, CT: Yale University Press.

HATFIELD, E., & RAPSON, R. L. (1993). *Love, sex, and intimacy: Their psychology, biology, and history*. New York: HarperCollins.

HATHAWAY, S. R., & MCKINLEY, J. C. (1943). *The Minnesota Multiphasic Personality Inventory*. New York: Psychological Corporation.

HATOUM, I. J., & BELLE, D. (2004). Mags and abs: Media consumption and bodily concerns in men. *Sex Roles*, 51, 397–407.

HATZENBUEHLER, M.L. (2009). How does sexual minority stigma "get under the skin"? A psychological mediation framework. *Psychological Bulletin*, 135, 707–730.

HAUGAARD, J. J. (2000). The challenge of defining child sexual abuse. *American Psychologist*, 55, 1036–1039.

HAUGAARD, J. J., & EMERY, R. E. (1989). Methodological issues in child sexual abuse research. *Child Abuse & Neglect*, 13, 89–100.

HAWKESWORTH, M. (1997). Confounding gender. *Signs: Journal of Women in Culture and Society*, 22, 649–684.

HAWKINS, J. L., BEATY, B. R., & GIBBS, C. P. (1999). Update on anesthesia practices in the U.S. *Anesthesiology*, 91, A1060.

HAYES, R., et al. (2007). Relationship between hypoactive sexual desire disorder and aging. *Fertility and Sterility*, 87, 107–112.

HAZEN, C., & SHAVER, P. (1987). Love conceptualized as an attachment process. *Journal of Personality and Social Psychology*, 52, 511–524.

HEATH, D. (1984). An investigation into the origins of a copious vaginal discharge during intercourse—"enough to wet the bed"—that "is not urine." *Journal of Sex Research*, 20, 194–215.

HEAVEY, C. L., CHRISTENSEN, A., & MALAMUTH, N. M. (1995). The longitudinal impact of demand and withdrawal during marital conflict. *Journal of Consulting and Clinical Psychology*, 63, 797–801.

HECHT, F. M., et al. (2010). HIV RNA level in early infection is predicted by viral load in the transmission source, *AIDS*, 24, 941–945.

HEDRICKS, C. A. (1995). Female sexual activity across the human menstrual cycle. In R. Rosen, C. M. Davis, & H. J. Ruppel, Jr. (Eds.), *Annual review of sex research* (Vol. V, pp. 122–172). Allentown, PA: Society for the Scientific Study of Sexuality.

HEIDER, K. G. (1979). *Grand Valley Dani: Peaceful warriors*. New York: Holt, Rinehart & Winston.

HEIL, P., & SIMONS, D. (2008). Multiple paraphilias: Prevalence, etiology, assessment, and treatment. In D. R. Laws & W. T. O'Donohue (Eds.), *Sexual deviance: Theory, assessment, and treatment* (2nd ed., pp. 527–556). New York: Guilford Press.

HEILBRUN, A., & SEIF, D. (1988). Erotic value of female distress in sexually explicit photographs. *Journal of Sex Research*, 24, 47–57.

HEIMAN, J. (1977). A psychophysiological exploration of sexual arousal patterns in females and males. *Psychophysiology*, 14, 266–274.

HEIMAN, J. (2002). Sexual dysfunction: Overview of prevalence, etiological factors, and treatments. *Journal of Sex Research*, 39, 73–79.

HEIMAN, M. L., et al. (1998). A comparative survey of beliefs about "normal" childhood sexual behaviors. *Child Abuse & Neglect*, 22, 289–304.

HEIN, H. A., BURMEISTER, L. F., & PAPKE, K. R. (1990). The relationship of unwed status to infant mortality. *Obstetrics and Gynecology*, 76, 763–768.

HEISS, G., et al. (2008). Health risks and benefits 3 years after stopping randomized treatment with estrogen and progestin. *Journal of the American Medical Association*, 299, 1036–1045.

HELMREICH, R., SPENCE, J., & HOLAHAN, C. (1979). Psychological androgyny and sex role flexibility: A test of two hypotheses. *Journal of Personality and Social Psychology*, 37, 1631–1644.

HELWIG-LARSEN, M., & COLLINS, B. E. (1997). A social psychological perspective on the role of knowledge about AIDS in AIDS prevention. *Current Directions in Psychological Science*, 6, 23–26.

HENDERSON, D. J., BOYD, C. J., & WHITMARSH, J. (1995). Women and illicit drugs: Sexuality and crack cocaine. *Health Care for Women International*, 16, 113–124.

HENDERSON, K. D., et al. (2008). Incomplete pregnancy is not associated with breast cancer risk: The California Teachers Study. *Contraception*, 77, 391–396.

HENDERSON, R. (1990, November 22). Parents need right words, right time to tell kids about sex. *Los Angeles Times*, p. X1.

HENDRICK, C., & HENDRICK, S. (1983). *Liking, loving and relating*. Monterey, CA: Brooks/Cole.

HENDRICK, C., & HENDRICK, S. (1986). A theory and method of love. *Journal of Personality and Social Psychology*, 50, 392–402.

HENDRICK, C., & HENDRICK, S. S. (1989). Research on love: Does it measure up? *Journal of Personality and Social Psychology*, 56, 784–794.

HENDRICK, C., & HENDRICK, S. (2003). Romantic love: Measuring cupid's arrow. In S. Lopez and C. Snyder (Eds.), *Positive psychological assessment: A handbook of models and measures*. Washington, DC: American Psychological Association.

HENDRICK, C., HENDRICK, S., & ADLER, N. (1988). Romantic relationships: Love, satisfaction, and staying together. *Journal of*

Personality and Social Psychology, 54, 980–988.

HENDRICK, S. S., & HENDRICK, C. (1993). Lovers as friends. *Journal of Social and Personal Relationships, 10,* 459–466.

HENNESSEY, K. A., et al. (2000). AIDS onset at high CD4+ cell levels is associated with high HIV load. *AIDS Research and Human Retroviruses, 16,* 103–107.

HENSEL, D. J., et al. (2004). A daily diary analysis of vaginal bleeding and coitus among adolescent women. *Journal of Adolescent Health, 34,* 392–394.

HENSHAW, S. K. (1998a). Unintended pregnancy in the United States. *Family Planning Perspectives, 30,* 24–29, 46.

HENSHAW, S. K., SINGH, S., & HAAS, T. (1999). Recent trends in abortion rates worldwide. *International Family Planning Perspectives, 25,* 44–48.

HENSON, C., RUBIN, H. B., & HENSON, D. E. (1979). Women's sexual arousal concurrently assessed by three genital measures. *Archives of Sexual Behavior, 8,* 459–479.

HERBENICK, D., et al. (2010). Women's vibrator use in sexual partnerships: Results from a nationally representative survey in the United States. *Journal of Sex & Marital Therapy, 36,* 49–65.

HERBENICK D. et al. (2010a). Sexual behavior in the United States: Results from a national probability sample of men and women ages 14–94. *Journal of Sexual Medicine, 7* (Suppl 5), 225–265

HERBENICK D. et al. (2010b). Sexual behaviors, relationships, and perceived health status among adult women in the United States: Results from a national probability sample. *Journal of Sexual Medicine, 7* (Suppl 5), 277–290.

HERBENICK D. et al. (2010c). An event-level analysis of the sexual characteristics in composition among adults ages 18 to 59: Results from a national probability sample in the United States. *Journal of Sexual Medicine, 7* (Suppl 5), 346–361.

HERBERT, W. (2010). Revisiting the green monster. *APA Observer, 23,* 5.

HERDT, G. (1990). Mistaken gender: 5-Alpha reductase hermaphroditism and biological reductionism in sexual identity reconsidered. *American Anthropologist, 92,* 433–446.

HERDT, G. H. (1987). *The Sambia.* New York: Holt, Rinehart & Winston.

HERDT, G. H. (1993). Semen transactions in Sambia culture. In D. N. Suggs & A. W. Miracle (Eds.), *Culture and human sexuality* (pp. 298–327). Pacific Grove, CA: Brooks/Cole.

HERDT, G., & McCLINTOCK, M. (2000). The magical age of 10. *Archives of Sexual Behavior, 29,* 587–606.

HEREK, G. M. (1988). Heterosexuals' attitudes toward lesbian and gay men: Correlates and gender differences. *Journal of Sex Research, 25,* 451–477.

HEREK, G. M. (1989). Hate crimes against lesbian and gay men: Issues for research and policy. *American Psychologist, 44,* 948–955.

HEREK, G. M. (2000a). The psychology of sexual prejudice. *Current Directions in Psychological Science, 9,* 19–22.

HEREK, G. M. (2000b). Sexual prejudice and gender: Do heterosexuals' attitudes toward lesbians and gay men differ? *Journal of Social Issues, 56,* 251–266.

HEREK, G. M. (2002a). Gender gaps in public opinion about lesbians and gay men. *Public Opinion Quarterly, 66,* 40–66.

HEREK, G. M. (2002b). Heterosexuals' attitudes toward bisexual men and women in the United States. *Journal of Sex Research, 39,* 264–274.

HEREK, G. M., CAPITANIO, J. P., & WIDAMAN, K. F. (2002). HIV-related stigma and knowledge in the United States: Prevalence and trends, 1991–1999. *American Journal of Public Health, 92,* 371–377.

HEREK, G. M., WIDAMAN, K. F., & CAPITANIO, J. P. (2005). When sex equals AIDS: Symbolic stigma and heterosexual adults' inaccurate beliefs about sexual transmission of AIDS. *Social Problems, 52,* 15–37.

HERMAN, J., & HIRSCHMAN, L. (1977). Father-daughter incest. *Journal of Women in Culture and Society, 2,* 735–756.

HERMAN, J. L. (1992). *Trauma and recovery.* New York: Basic Books.

HERMAN-GIDDENS, M. E., et al. (1997). Secondary sexual characteristics and menses in young girls seen in office practice: A study from the pediatric research in office settings network. *Pediatrics, 99,* 505–512.

HERMAN-JEGLINSKA, A. GRABOWSKA, A., & DULKO, S. (2002). Masculinity, feminity, and transsexualism. *Archives of Sexual Behavior, 31,* 527–534.

HERRERO, R. (2009). Human papillomavirus (HPV) vaccines: Limited cross-protection against additional HPV types. *Journal of Infectious Diseases, 199,* 919–922.

HETEROSEXUAL AIDS: Setting the odds. (1988). *Science, 240,* 597.

HEWITT, C. (1998). Homosexual demography: Implications for the spread of AIDS. *Journal of Sex Research, 35,* 390–396.

HICKS, T. V., & LEITENBERG, H. (2001). Sexual fantasies about one's partner versus someone else: Gender differences in incidence and frequency. *Journal of Sex Research, 38,* 43–50.

HIGGINS, D. J. (2002). Gay men from heterosexual marriages: Attitudes, behaviors, childhood experiences, and reasons for marriage. *Journal of Homosexuality, 42(4),* 15–34.

HIGGINS, J. A., TANNER, A. E., & JANSSEN, E. (2009). Arousal loss related to safer sex and risk of pregnancy: Implications for women's and men's sexual health. *Perspectives on Sexual and Reproductive Health, 41,* 150–157.

HILLIER, L., HARRISON, L., & WARR, D. (1998). "When you carry condoms all the boys think you want it": Negotiating competing discourses about safe sex. *Journal of Adolescence, 21,* 15–29.

HINES, D. A. (2007). Predictors of sexual coercion against women and men: A multilevel, multinational study of university students. *Archives of Sexual Behavior, 36,* 403–422.

HINES, M. (2004). *Brain gender.* New York: Oxford University Press.

HINES, M. (2004). Psychosexual development in individuals who have female pseudohermaphroditism. *Child and Adolescent Psychiatric Clinics of North America, 13,* 641–656.

HINES, M., AHMED, F., & HUGHES, J. A. (2003). Psychological outcomes and gender-related development in complete androgen insensitivity syndrome. *Archives of Sexual Behavior, 32,* 93–101.

HIORT, O., & HOLTERHUS, P.-M. (2000). The molecular basis of male sexual differentiation. *European Journal of Endocrinology, 142,* 101–110.

HIRSCHEL, B., & OPRAVIL, M. (1999). The year in review: Antiretroviral treatment. *AIDS, 13*(Suppl. A), S177–S187.

HIRSCHFELD, M. (1948). *Sexual anomalies.* New York: Emerson.

HITE, S. (1976). *The Hite report.* New York: Macmillan.

HITSCH, G. J., HORTAÇSU, A., & ARIELY, D. (2010). Matching and sorting in online dating. *American Economic Review, 100,* 130–163.

HOCKEY, J., & JAMES, A. (1993). *Growing up and growing old.* London: Sage.

HODES, M. (Ed.). (1999). *Sex, love, race: Crossing boundaries in North American history.* New York: New York University Press.

HOFFERTH, S. L., REID, L., & MOTT, F. L. (2001). The effects of early childbearing on schooling over time. *Family Planning Perspectives, 33,* 259–267.

HOGAN, M. C., et al. (2010, April 12). Maternal mortality for 181 countries, 1980–2008: A systematic analysis of progress towards Millennium Development Goal 5. *The Lancet, 375,* 1609–1623.

HOGARTH, H., & INGHAM, R. (2009). Masturbation among young women and associations with sexual health: An exploratory study. *Journal of Sex Research, 46,* 558–567.

HOLCOMB, D. R., et al. (1991). Gender differences among college students. *College Student Journal, 25,* 434–439.

HOLMBERG, D., & BLAIR, K. L. (2009). Sexual desire, communication, satisfaction, and preferences of men and women in same-sex versus mixed-sex relationships. *Journal of Sex Research, 46,* 57–66.

HOLMBERG, L., et al. (2002). A randomized trial comparing radical prostatectomy with watchful waiting in early prostate cancer. *New England Journal of Medicine, 347,* 781–789.

HOLMES, B. M., & JOHNSON, K. R. (2009). Adult attachment and romantic partner preference: A review. *Journal of Social and Personal Relationships, 26,* 833–852.

HOLMES, M. M., et al. (1996). Rape-related pregnancy: Estimates and descriptive characteristics from a national sample of women. *American Journal of Obstetrics and Gynecology, 175,* 320–325.

HOLT, T. J., & BLEVINS, K. R. (2007). Examining sex work from the client's perspective: Assessing johns using on-line data. *Deviant Behavior, 28,* 333–354.

HOLT, T. J., et al. (2010). Considering the pedophile subculture online. *Sexual Abuse: A Journal of Research and Treatment, 22,* 3–24.

HONORÉ, G. M., HOLDEN, A. E. C., & SCHENKEN, R. S. (1999). Pathophysiology and management of proximal tubal blockage. *Fertility and Sterility, 71,* 785–795.

HOOKER, E. (1957). The adjustment of the male overt homosexual. *Journal of Projective Techniques, 21,* 18–31.

HOOKER, E. (1965). An empirical study of some relations between sexual patterns and gender identity in male homosexuals. In J. Money (Ed.), *Sex research: New developments.* New York: Henry Holt.

HOOKER, E. (1993). Reflections of a 40-year exploration: A scientific view on homosexuality. *American Psychologist, 48,* 1–4.

HOOTON, T. M. (2003). The current management strategies for community-acquired urinary tract infection. *Infectious Disease Clinics of North America, 17,* 303–332.

HOOVER, K. W., TAO, G., & KENT, C. K. (2010). Trends in the diagnosis and treatment of ectopic pregnancy in the United States. *Obstetrics & Gynecology, 115,* 495–502.

HORT, B. E., LEINBACH, M. D., & FAGOT, B. I. (1991). Is there coherence among the cognitive components of gender acquisition? *Sex Roles, 24,* 195–207.

HORWITZ, A. V., WHITE, H. R., & HOWELL-WHITE, S. (1996). Becoming married and mental health: A longitudinal study of a cohort of young adults. *Journal of Marriage and Family, 58,* 895–907.

HORWITZ, S. M., et al. (1991). Intergenerational transmission of school-age parenthood. *Family Planning Perspectives, 23,* 168–177.

HOSENFELD, C. B., et al. (2009). Repeat infection with chlamydia and gonorrhea among females: A systematic review of the literature. *Sexually Transmitted Diseases, 36,* 478–489.

HOVDESTAD, W. E., & KRISTIANSEN, C. M. (1996, Summer). A field study of "false memory syndrome": Construct validity and incidence. *Journal of Psychiatry & Law,* 299–338.

HOWELLS, K. (1981). Adult sexual interest in children: Considerations relevant to theories of etiology. In M. Cook & K. Howells (Eds.), *Adult sexual interest in children* (pp. 55–94). New York: Academic Press.

HOWES, M. (2010). Menstrual function, menstrual suppression, and the immunology of the human female reproductive tract. *Perspectives in Biology and Medicine, 53*(1), 16–30.

HOYERT, D. L, DANEL, I., & TULLY, P. (2000). Maternal mortality, United States and Canada, 1982–1987. *Birth, 27,* 4–11.

HSU, F. (1983). Eros, affect and pao. In F. Hsu (Ed.), *Rugged individualism reconsidered.* Knoxville: University of Tennessee Press.

HSU, F. L. K. (1981). *Americans and Chinese: Passage to difference* (3rd ed.). Honolulu: University Press of Hawaii.

HUBACHER, D. (2002). The checkered history and bright future of intrauterine contraception in the United States. *Perspectives on Sexual and Reproductive Health, 34*(2), 98–103.

HUBACHER, D., et al. (2009). Menstrual pattern changes from levonorgestrel subdermal implants and DMPA: Systematic review and evidence-based comparisons. *Contraception, 80,* 113–118.

HUBIN, D. C, & HAELY, K. (1999). Rape and the reasonable man. *Law and Philosophy, 18,* 113–139.

HUCKER, S. J. (2008). Sexual masochism: Psychopathology and theory. In D. R. Laws & W. T. O'Donohue (Eds.), *Sexual deviance: Theory, assessment, and treatment* (2nd ed., pp. 250–263). New York: Guilford Press.

HUDSON, B., PEPPERELL, R., & WOOD, C. (1987). The problem of infertility. In R. Pepperell, B. Hudson, & C. Wood (Eds.), *The infertile couple.* Edinburgh: Churchill-Livingstone.

HUDSON, T., & KOCHAN, L. (2005, August/September). Vaginitis: Two common causes, bacterial vaginosis and atrophic vaginitis. *Townsend Letter for Doctors and Patients,* 116–119.

HUHNER, M. (1916). *Disorders of the sexual function.* Philadelphia: Davis.

HULL, T. H., & BUDIHARSANA, M. (2001). Male circumcision and penis enhancement in Southeast Asia: Matters of pain and pleasure. *Reproductive Health Matters, 9*(18), 60–67.

HUMPHREYS, T. (2007). Perceptions of sexual consent: The impact of relationship history and gender. *Journal of Sex Research, 44,* 307–315.

HUNT, M. (1959). *The natural history of love.* New York: Knopf.

HUNT, M. (1974). *Sexual behavior in the 1970s.* Chicago: Playboy Press.

HUNT, P. W. (2009). Natural control of HIV-1 replication and long-term nonprogression: Overlapping but distinct phenotypes. *Journal of Infectious Diseases, 200,* 1636–1638.

HUNTER, J. A., & MATHEWS, R. (1997). Sexual deviance in females. In D. R. Laws & W. T. O'Donohue (Eds.), *Sexual deviance: Theory, assessment, and treatment* (pp. 465–480). New York: Guilford Press.

HUPKA, R. B. (1981, August). Cultural determinants of jealousy. *Alternative Life Styles, 4.*

HUPPERT, J. (2006, May). New detection methods for trichomoniasis may help curb more serious STIs. *Patient Care,* 32–36.

HURLBERT, D. F., & WHITTAKER, K. E. (1991). The role of masturbation in marital and sexual satisfaction: A comparative study of female masturbators and nonmasturbators. *Journal of Sex Education and Therapy, 17,* 272–282.

HUSTON, A. C. (1983). Sex-typing. In E. M. Hetherington (Ed.), *Handbook of child psychology: Vol. 4. Socialization, personality, and social development* (pp. 387–468). New York: John Wiley & Sons.

HUSTON, A. C., WARTELLA, E., & DONNERSTEIN, E. (1998). *Measuring the effects of sexual content in the media: A report to the Kaiser Family Foundation.* Menlo Park, CA: Kaiser Family Foundation.

HVILSOM, G. B., et al. (2009). Local complications after cosmetic breast augmentation: Results from the Danish Registry for Plastic Surgery of the Breast. *Plastic and Reconstructive Surgery, 124,* 919–925.

HYDE, J. S., & PRICE, M. (2007). Paper presented at the annual meeting of the Society for the Scientific Study of Sexuality, Indianapolis, IN.

HYDE, J. S., et al. (1996). Sexuality during pregnancy and the year postpartum. *Journal of Sex Research, 33,* 143–151.

HYLAN, T. R., SUNDELL, K., & JUDGE, R. (1999). The impact of premenstrual symptomatology on functioning and treatment-seeking behavior: Experience from the United States, United Kingdom, and France. *Journal of Women's Health & Gender-Based Medicine, 8,* 1043–1052.

HYNIE, M., et al. (1998). Relational sexual scripts and women's condom use: The importance of internalized norms. *Journal of Sex Research, 35,* 370–380.

I

IMBER, M. (1994). Toward a theory of educational origins: The genesis of sex education. *Educational Theory, 34,* 275–286.

IMPERATO-McGINLEY, J., et al. (1979). Androgens and the evolution of male-gender identity among male pseudohermaphrodites with 5-reductase deficiency. *New England Journal of Medicine, 300,* 1233–1237.

INSTITUTE OF MEDICINE. (1990). *Nutrition during pregnancy.* Washington, DC: National Academy of Sciences, Subcommittee on Nutritional Status and Weight Gain during Pregnancy.

INSTITUTE OF MEDICINE. (1991). *Nutrition during lactation.* Washington, DC: National Academy Press.

INTERNATIONAL PERINATAL HIV GROUP. (1999). The mode of delivery and the risk of vertical transmission of human immunodeficiency virus, type 1. *New England Journal of Medicine, 340,* 977–987.

IPPOLITO, G., et al. (1999). Occupational human immunodeficiency virus infection in health care workers: Worldwide cases through September 1997. *Clinical Infectious Diseases, 28,* 365–383.

ISAY, R. A. (1998). Heterosexually married homosexual men: Clinical and developmental issues. *American Journal of Orthopsychiatry, 68,* 424–432.

IYASU, S., et al. (1993). The epidemiology of placenta previa in the United States, 1979 through 1987. *American Journal of Obstetrics and Gynecology, 168,* 1424–1429.

INTERSEXUAL SOCIETY OF NORTH AMERICA (2010). www.isna.org

J

JACCARD, J., DITTUS, J., & GORDON, V. V. (2000). Parent-teen communication about premarital sex: Factors associated with the extent of communication. *Journal of Adolescent Research, 15,* 187–208.

JACOB, K. A. (1981). The Mosher report. *American Heritage, 32*(4), 56–64.

JACOBS, S.-H., & THOMAS, W. (1994). Native American two-spirits. *Anthropology Newsletter, 35*(8), 7.

JACOBY, S. (1999, September/October). Great sex: What's age got to do with it? *Modern Maturity,* 40–45, 91.

JACOBY, S. (2005, July/August). Sex in America. *AARP The Magazine,* 62–68, 98–99.

JAINI, R., et al. (2010, May). An autoimmune-mediated strategy for prophylactic breast cancer vaccination. *Nature Medicine,* doi:10,1038.

JAMES, A., et al. (1998). *Theorizing childhood.* Cambridge, UK: Polity.

JAMISON, P. L., & GEBHARD, P. H. (1988). Penis size increase between flaccid and erect states: An analysis of the Kinsey data. *Journal of Sex Research, 24,* 177–183.

JANKOWIAK, W. R., & FISCHER, E. F. (1992). A cross-cultural perspective on romantic love. *Ethnology, 31,* 149–155.

JANSSEN, D. F. (2007). First stirrings: Cultural notes on orgasm, ejaculation, and wet dreams. *Journal of Sex Research, 44,* 122–134.

JANSSEN, E., et al. (2008). Factors that influence sexual arousal in men: A focus group study. *Archives of Sexual Behavior, 37,* 252–265.

JANSSEN, P. A., HENDERSON, A. D., & VEDAM, S. (2009a). The experience of planned home birth: Views of the first 500 women. *Birth, 36,* 297–304.

JANSSEN, P. A., et al. (2009b). Outcomes of planned home birth with registered midwife versus planned hospital birth with midwife or physician. *Canadian Medical Association Journal, 181,* 377–383.

JANUS, S. S., & JANUS, C. L. (1993). *The Janus report on sexual behavior.* New York: John Wiley & Sons.

JAYSON, S. (2008, July 29). Living together isn't just "playing house." *USA Today,* 6D.

JAYSON, S. (2009, February 11). Science asks: What's the attraction? *USA Today,* D1–D2.

JAYSON, S. (2009, May 12). Obama budget shifts money from abstinence-only sex education. *USA Today,* 4D.

JAYSON, S. (2010, January 26). The truth about sex: Teen boys lie about it. *USA Today,* 5D.

JEFFRIES, IV., W. L. (2009). A comparative analysis of homosexual behaviors, sex role preferences, and anal sex proclivities in Latino and non-Latino men. *Archives of Sexual Behavior, 38,* 765–778.

JENG, C.-J., et al. (2006). Management and outcome of primary vaginismus. *Journal of Sex & Marital Therapy, 32,* 379–387.

JENKINS, P. (2001). *Beyond tolerance: Child pornography on the Internet.* New York: New York University Press.

JENKS, R. J. (1998). Swinging: A review of the literature. *Archives of Sexual Behavior, 27,* 507–521.

JENNINGS, V. H., & AREVALO, M. (2008). Fertility awareness-based methods. In R. A. Hatcher et al. (Eds.), *Contraceptive technology* (19th ed., pp. 343–360). New York: Ardent Media.

JENNY, C., et al. (1990). Sexually transmitted diseases in victims of rape. *New England Journal of Medicine, 322,* 713–716.

JENSEN, A., et al. (2009). Use of fertility drugs and risk of ovarian cancer: Danish population based cohort study. *British Medical Journal, 338,* b249.

JENSEN, J. T., et al. (2008). Effects of switching from oral to transdermal or transvaginal contraception on markers of thrombosis. *Contraception, 78,* 451–458.

JESPERSEN, A. F., LALUMIÈRE, M. L., & SETO, M. C. (2009). Sexual abuse history among adult sex offenders and non-sex offenders:

A meta-analysis. *Child Abuse & Neglect,* 33, 179–192.

JOENSEN, U., et al. (2009). Do perfluoroalkyl compounds impair human semen quality? *Environmental Health Perspectives,* 117, 923–927.

JOESOEF, M. R., SCHMID, G. P., & HILLIER, S. L. (1999). Bacterial vaginosis: Review of treatment options and potential clinical indications for therapy. *Clinical Infectious Diseases,* 28 (Suppl. 1), S57–S65.

JOFFE, G. P., et al. (1992). Multiple partners and partner choice as risk factors for sexually transmitted disease among female college students. *Sexually Transmitted Diseases,* 19, 272–278.

JOHANSSON, J. E., et al. (2004). Natural history of early, localized prostate cancer. *Journal of the American Medical Association,* 291, 2720–2726.

JOHN, G. C., & KREISS, J. (1996). Mother-to-child transmission of human immunodeficiency virus type 1. *Epidemiologic Reviews,* 18, 149–157.

JOHNSON, B. E., KUCK, D. L., & SCHANDER, P. R. (1997). Rape myth acceptance and sociodemographic characteristics: A multidimensional analysis. *Sex Roles,* 36, 693–707.

JOHNSTON, R., & COLLINS, C. (2010). Can we treat our way out of HIV? *AIDS Research and Human Retroviruses,* 26, 1–4.

JOHNSON, T. C. (1989). Female child perpetrators: Children who molest other children. *Child Abuse & Neglect,* 13, 571–585.

JOHNSTON-ROBLEDO, J., et al. (2003). To bleed or not to bleed: Young women's attitudes toward menstrual suppression. *Women & Health,* 38, 59–75.

JOHNSTON-ROBLEDO, I., et al. (2007). Reproductive shame: Self-objectification and young women's attitudes toward their reproductive functioning. *Women & Health,* 46, 25–39.

JONES, H., & POWELL, J. L. (2006). Old age, vulnerability, and sexual violence: Implications for knowledge and practice. *International Nursing Review,* 53, 211–216.

JONES, H. E., & JOHNSON, R. E. (2001). Pregnancy and substance abuse. *Current Opinion in Psychiatry,* 14, 187–193.

JONES, L. M., FINKELHOR, D., & KOPIEC, K. (2001). Why is sexual abuse declining? A survey of state child protection administrators. *Child Abuse & Neglect,* 25, 1139–1158.

JONES, M. E., RUSSELL, R. L., & BRYANT, F. B. (1998). The structure of rape attitudes for men and women: A three-factor model. *Journal of Research in Personality,* 32, 331–350.

JONES, O. D. (1999). Sex, culture, and the biology of rape: Toward explanation and prevention. *California Law Review,* 87, 827–941.

JONKER-POOL, G., et al. (2001). Sexual functioning after treatment for testicular cancer—review and meta-analysis of 36 empirical studies between 1975–2000. *Archives of Sexual Behavior,* 30, 55–74.

JONZON, G., & LINDBLAD, F. (2005). Adult female victims of child sexual abuse. *Journal of Interpersonal Violence,* 20, 651–666.

JORDAN, B., & WELLS, E.S. (2009). A 21st-century Trojan horse: The "abortion harms women" anti-choice argument disguises a harmful movement. *Contraception,* 79, 161–164.

JOSEPH, C. (1996). Compassionate accountability: An embodied consideration of female genital mutilation. *Journal of Psychohistory,* 24, 2–17.

JOYAL, C. C., BLACK, D. N., & DASSYLVA, B. (2007). The neuropsychology and neurology of sexual deviance: A review and pilot study. *Sex Abuse,* 19, 155–173.

K

KAESTLE, C. E. (2009). Sexual insistence and disliked sexual activities in young adulthood: Differences by gender and relationship characteristics. *Perspectives on Sexual and Reproductive Health,* 41, 33–39.

KAESTLE, C. E., & HALPERN, C. T. (2007). What's love got to do with it? Sexual behaviors of opposite-sex couples through emerging adulthood. *Perspectives on Sexual and Reproductive Health,* 39, 134–140.

KAFKA, M. P. (1997). A monoamine hypothesis for the pathophysiology of paraphilic disorders. *Archives of Sexual Behavior,* 26, 343–358.

KAFKA, M. P., & HENNEN, J. (1999). The paraphilia-related disorders: An empirical investigation of nonparaphilic hypersexuality disorders in outpatient males. *Journal of Sex & Marital Therapy,* 25, 305–319.

KAFKA, M. P. (2008). Neurobiological processes and comorbidity in sexual deviance. In D. R. Laws & W. T. O'Donohue (Eds.), *Sexual deviance: Theory, assessment, and treatment* (2nd ed., pp. 571–593). New York: Guilford Press.

KAFKA, M. P. (2010). Hypersexual disorder: A proposed diagnosis for DSM-V. *Archives of Sexual Behavior,* 39, 377–400.

KAGAN-KRIEGER, S. (1998). Women with Turner syndrome: A maturational and developmental perspective. *Journal of Adult Development,* 5, 125–135.

KAHN, A. S., et al. (2003). Calling it rape: Differences in experiences of women who do or do not label their sexual assault as rape. *Psychology of Women Quarterly,* 27, 233–242.

KAHN, J. A. (2005). Vaccination as a prevention strategy for human papillomavirus–related diseases. *Journal of Adolescent Health,* 37, S10–S16.

KAISER FAMILY FOUNDATION. (2001). *Sex on TV: Content and context.* Menlo Park, CA: Author.

KAISER FAMILY FOUNDATION. (2005). Number of sexual scenes on TV nearly double since 1998. www.kff.org

KALB, C. (2004, January 26). Brave new babies. *Newsweek,* 44–52.

KALB, C. (2006, February 20). Marriage: Act II. *Newsweek,* 62–63.

KALB, C., & MURR, A. (2006, May 15). Batting a black epidemic, *Newsweek,* 42–48.

KALICHMAN, S. C. (2004). Traditional beliefs about the cause of AIDS and AIDS-related stigma in South Africa. *AIDS Care,* 16, 573–581.

KALLMAN, F. J. (1952). Comparative twin study on the genetic aspects of male homosexuality. *Journal of Nervous and Mental Disease,* 115, 283–298.

KALOF, L., et al. (2001). The influence of race and gender on student self-reports of sexual harassment by college professors. *Gender & Society,* 15, 282–302.

KANDEL, D. B. (1990). Early onset of adolescent sexual behavior and drug involvement. *Journal of Marriage and Family,* 52, 783–798.

KANE, E. W. (2006). "No way my boys are going to be like that!" Parents' responses to children's gender nonconformity. *Gender & Society,* 20, 149–176.

KANE, M. A. (1995). Global programme for control of hepatitis B infection. *Vaccine,* 13(Suppl. 1), S47–S49.

KAPLAN, H. S. (1974). *The new sex therapy.* New York: Brunner/Mazel.

KAPLAN, H. S. (1979). *Disorders of desire.* New York: Brunner/Mazel.

KAPLAN, H. S. (1983). *The evaluation of sexual disorders: Psychological and medical aspects.* New York: Brunner/Mazel.

KAPLAN, H. S. (1987). *Sexual aversion, sexual phobias, and panic disorders.* New York: Brunner/Mazel.

KAPLAN, H. S. (1992). Does the CAT technique enhance female orgasm? *journal of sex & marital therapy,* 18, 285–291.

KAPLAN, H. S., & OWETT, T. (1993). The female androgen deficiency syndrome. *Journal of Sex & Marital Therapy,* 19, 3–24.

KAPLAN, L. (1996). Sexual and institutional issues when one spouse resides in the community and the other lives in a nursing home. *Sexuality and Disability,* 14, 281–293.

KAPLAN, M. S., & KRUEGER, R. B. (1997). Voyeurism: Psychopathology and theory. In D. R. Laws & W. T. O'Donohue (Eds.), *Sexual deviance: Theory, assessment, and treatment* (pp. 297–310). New York: Guilford Press.

KAPLAN, M. S., & KRUEGER, R. B. (2010). Diagnosis, assessment, and treatment of hypersexuality. *Journal of Sex Research,* 47, 181–198.

KAPLAN, S. S., & MOUNZER, K. C. (2008). Antiretroviral therapy in HIV-infected patients with multidrug-resistant virus: Applying the guidelines to practice. *AIDS Patient Care and STDs,* 22, 931–940.

KARLSON, P., & LUSCHER, M. (1959). Pheromones: A new term for a class of biologically active substances. *Nature,* 183, 55–56.

KARMEL, M. (1959). *Thank you Dr. Lamaze.* Philadelphia: Lippincott.

KATLAMA, C., & DICKINSON, G. M. (1993). Update on opportunistic infections. *AIDS,* 7, S185–S194.

KATZ, J. (1976). *Gay American history: Lesbian and gay men in the U.S.A.* New York: Crowell.

KATZ, M. G., & VOLLENHOVEN, B. (2000). The reproductive endocrine consequences of anorexia nervosa. *British Journal of Obstetrics and Gynaecology,* 107, 707–713.

KATZ, M. J. (2004). Reconsidering attraction in sexual harassment. *Indiana Law Journal,* 79, 101–176.

KAUFERT, P. A., & LOCK, M. (1997). Medicalization of women's third age. *Journal of Psychosomatic Obstetrics and Gynecology,* 18, 81–86.

KEANE, H. (2004). Disorders of desire: Addiction and problems of intimacy. *Journal of Medical Humanities,* 25, 189–197.

KEELE, B. F., et al. (2006). Chimpanzee reservoirs of pandemic and nonpandemic HIV-1. *Science,* 313, 523–526.

KEGEL, A. (1952). Sexual functions of the pubococcygeus muscle. *Western Journal of Surgery, Obstetrics, and Gynecology,* 60, 521–524.

KELLETT, J. M. (2000). Older adult sexuality. In L. T. Szuchman and F. Muscarella (Eds.), *Psychological perspectives on human sexuality* (pp. 355–379). New York: Wiley.

KELLOGG, J. H. (1887). *Plain facts for old and young: Embracing the natural history and hygiene of organic life.* Burlington, IA: I. F. Segner.

KELLY, J. A., & WORELL, J. (1977). New formulations of sex roles and androgyny: A critical review. *Journal of Consulting and Clinical Psychology,* 45, 1101–1115.

KELLY, M. A., & MCGEE, M. (1999). Report from a study tour: Teen sexuality education in the Netherlands, France, and Germany. *SIECUS Report,* 27(2), 11–14.

KELLY, M. P., STRASSBERG, D. S., & KIRCHER, J. R. (1990). Attitudinal and experiential correlates of anorgasmia. *Archives of Sexual Behavior,* 19, 165–177.

KELLY, R. J., et al. (2002). Effects of mother-son incest and positive perceptions of sexual abuse experiences on the psychosocial adjustment of clinic-referred men. *Child Abuse & Neglect, 26,* 425–441.

KELLY, S. J., OSTROWSKI, N. L., & WILSON, M. A. (1999). Gender differences in brain and behavior: Hormonal and neural bases. *Pharmacology Biochemistry & Behavior, 64,* 655–664.

KEMPNER, M. (2005). Sex workers: A glimpse into public health perspectives. *SIECUS Report, 33,* 2.

KENDALL-TACKETT, K. A., & SIMON, A. F. (1987). Perpetrators and their acts: Data from 365 adults molested as children. *Child Abuse & Neglect, 11,* 237–245.

KENDALL-TACKETT, K. A., WILLIAMS, L. M., & FINKELHOR, D. (1993). Impact of sexual abuse on children: A review and synthesis of recent empirical studies. *Psychological Bulletin, 113,* 164–180.

KENDLER, K. S., et al. (2000). Sexual orientation in a U.S. national sample of twin and nontwin sibling pairs. *American Journal of Psychiatry, 157,* 1843–1846.

KENDRICK, D. T., & KEEFE, R. C. (1992). Age preferences in mates reflect sex differences in reproductive strategies. *Behavioral and Brain Sciences, 15,* 75–133.

KENNEDY, K. I., & TRUSSELL, J. (2008). Postpartum contraception and lactation. In R. A. Hatcher et al. (Eds.), *Contraceptive technology* (19th ed., pp. 403–431). New York: Ardent Media.

KEPHART, W. M. (1967). Some correlates of romantic love. *Journal of Marriage and Family, 29,* 470–474.

KERRIGAN, C. (1999, October). Paper presented at the annual meeting of the American Society of Plastic and Reconstructive Surgeons, New Orleans, LA.

KESSLER, S. J., & MCKENNA, W. (1978). *Gender: An ethnomethodological approach.* New York: John Wiley & Sons.

KETCHANDJI, M., et al. (2008). Cause of death in older men after the diagnosis of prostate cancer. *Journal of The American Geriatrics Society, 57,* 24–30.

KHOSHNOOD, B., WALL, S., & LEE, K. S. (2005). Risk of low birth weight associated with advanced maternal age among four ethnic groups in the United States. *Maternal and Child Health Journal, 9,* 3–9.

KIKUCHI, J. J. (1988). Rhode Island develops successful intervention program for adolescents. *NCASA News,* Fall, 26.

KIMMEL, M. S. (1989). From separate spheres to sexual equality: Men's responses to feminism at the turn of the century. In B. J. Risman & P. Schwartz (Eds.), *Gender in intimate relationships: A microstructural approach.* Belmont, CA: Wadsworth.

KING, B. M. (2010). Opinion: A call for proper usage of "gender" and "sex" in biomedical publications. *American Journal of Physiology, 298,* R1701–R1702.

KING, B. M., & LOCOCO, G. C. (1990). Effects of sexually explicit textbook drawings on enrollment and family communication. *Journal of Sex Education and Therapy, 16,* 38–53.

KING, B. M., & LORUSSO, J. (1997). Discussions in the home about sex: Different recollections by parents and children. *Journal of Sex & Marital Therapy, 23,* 52–60.

KING, B. M., ROSOPA, P. J., & MINIUM, E. W. (2011). *Statistical Reasoning in the Behavioral Sciences* (6th ed.). New York: John Wiley.

KING, J. (2007). Contraception and lactation. *Journal of Midwifery & Women's Health, 52,* 614–620.

KING, M., & WOOLLETT, E. (1997). Sexually assaulted males: 115 men consulting a

counseling service. *Archives of Sexual Behavior, 26,* 579–588.

KING, V., & SCOTT, M. E. (2005). A comparison of cohabiting relationships among older and younger adults. *Journal of Marriage and Family, 67,* 271–285.

KINGSBERG, S. A. (2000). The psychological impact of aging on sexuality and relationships. *Journal of Women's Health & Gender-Based Medicine, 9,* S33–S38.

KINGSBERG, S. A., ALTHOF, S. E., & LEIBLUM, S. (2002). Books helpful to patients with sexual and marital problems. *Journal of Sex & Marital Therapy, 28,* 219–228.

KINGSTON, D. A., et al. (2009). The importance of individual differences in pornography use: Theoretical perspectives and implications for treating sexual offenders. *Journal of Sex Research, 46,* 216–232.

KINNISH, K. K., STRASSBERG, D. S., & TURNER, C. W. (2005). Sex differences in the flexibility of sexual orientation: A multidimensional retrospective assessment. *Archives of Sexual Behavior, 34,* 173–183.

KINSEY, A. C., POMEROY, W., & MARTIN, C. (1948). *Sexual behavior in the human male.* Philadelphia: Saunders.

KINSEY, A. C., et al. (1953). *Sexual behavior in the human female.* Philadelphia: Saunders.

KIRCHICK, J. (2008, November 12). Where's the outrage? *USA Today,* 11A.

KIRK, M., & MADSEN, H. (1989). *How America will conquer its fear and hatred of homosexuals in the '90s.* New York: Doubleday.

KIRKPATRICK, L. A., & DAVIS, K. E. (1994). Attachment style, gender, and relationship stability: A longitudinal analysis. *Journal of Personality and Social Psychology, 66,* 502–512.

KISTLER, M. E., & LEE, M. J. (2010). Does exposure to sexual hip-hop music videos influence the sexual attitudes of college students? *Mass Communication & Society, 13,* 67–86.

KITAHATA, M. M., et al. (2009). Effect of early versus deferred antiretroviral therapy for HIV on survival. *New England Journal of Medicine, 360,* 1815–1826.

KITAZAWA, K. (1994). Sexuality issues in Japan: A view from the front on HIV/AIDS and sexuality education. *SIECUS Report, 22*(2), 7–11.

KITE, M. E., & WHITLEY, JR., B. E. (1996). Sex differences in attitudes toward homosexual persons, behaviors and civil rights: A meta-analysis. *Personality and Social Psychology Bulletin, 22,* 336–352.

KITZINGER, C., & WILKINSON, S. (1995). Transitions from heterosexuality to lesbianism: The discursive production of lesbian identities. *Developmental Psychology, 31,* 95–104.

KLEBANOFF, M. A., et al. (2010). Personal hygienic behaviors and bacterial vaginosis. *Sexually Transmitted Diseases, 37,* 94–99.

KLEIN, J., et al. (1993). Adolescents' risky behavior and mass media use. *Pediatrics, 92,* 24–31.

KLEINPLATZ, P. J. (2004). Beyond sexual mechanics and hydraulics: Humanizing the discourse surrounding erectile dysfunction. *Journal of Humanistic Psychology, 44,* 215–242.

KLEPINGER, D. H., et al. (1993). Perception of AIDS risk and severity and their association with risk-related behavior among U.S. men. *Family Planning Perspectives, 25,* 74–82.

KLINETROB, N. A., & SMITH, D. A. (1996). Demand-withdraw communication in marital interaction: Tests of interspousal contingency and gender role hypotheses. *Journal of Marriage and Family, 58,* 945–957.

KLUSMANN, D. (2002). Sexual motivation and the duration of partnership. *Archives of Sexual Behavior, 31,* 275–287.

KNAFO, A., IERVOLINO, A. C., & PLOMIN, R. (2005). Masculine girls and feminine boys: Genetic and environmental contributions. *Journal of Personality and Social Psychology, 88,* 400–412.

KNOX, D., BREED, R., & ZUSMAN, M. (2007). College men and jealousy. *College Student Journal, 41,* 435–444.

KNUDSON-MARTIN, C., & SILVERSTEIN, R. (2009). Suffering in silence: A qualitative meta-data analysis of postpartum depression. *Journal of Marital and Family Therapy, 35,* 145–158.

KOCH, W. (2010, January 4). Many sex offenders are kids themselves. *USA Today,* 3A.

KOH, A. S., & ROSS, L. K. (2006). Mental health issues: A comparison of lesbian, bisexual, and heterosexual women. *Journal of Homosexuality, 51,* 33–57.

KOHLBERG, L. (1966). A cognitive-developmental analysis of children's sex-role concepts and attitudes. In E. E. Maccoby (Ed.), *The development of sex differences* (pp. 82–173). Stanford, CA: Stanford University Press.

KOHLBERG, L., & ULLIAN, D. Z. (1974). Stages in the development of psychosexual concepts and attitudes. In R. C. Friedman, R. M. Richart, & R. L. Van de Wiele (Eds.), *Sex differences in behavior* (pp. 209–222). New York: John Wiley & Sons.

KOHLER, P. K., et al. (2008). Abstinence-only and comprehensive sex education and the initiation of sexual activity and teen pregnancy. *Journal of Adolescent Health, 42,* 344–351.

KOLATA, G. (2002, August 29). The testosterone trap. New Orleans *Times-Picayune* (reprinted from the *The New York Times*), E1, E2, E4.

KOLLIN, G., et al. (2006). Testicular growth from birth to two years of age, and the effect of orchidopexy at age nine months: A randomized control study. *Acta Paediatrica, 95,* 318–324.

KOLODNY, R. C., MASTERS, W. H., & JOHNSON, V. E. (1979). *Textbook of sexual medicine.* Boston: Little, Brown.

KOLODNY, R. C., et al. (1974). Depression of plasma testosterone levels after chronic intensive marijuana use. *New England Journal of Medicine, 290,* 872–874.

KONTULA, O., & HAAVIO-MANNILA, E. (2009). The impact of aging on human sexual activity and sexual desire. *Journal of Sex Research, 46,* 46–56.

KORBER, B., et al. (2000). Timing the ancestor of the HIV-1 pandemic strains. *Science, 288,* 1789–1796.

KOSKIMAKI, J., et al. (2008). Regular intercourse protects against erectile dysfunction: Tampere aging male urologic study. *American Journal of Medicine, 121,* 592–596.

KOSS, C. A., DUNNE, E. F., & WARNER, L. (2009). A systematic review of epidemiologic studies assessing condom use and risk of syphilis. *Sexually Transmitted Diseases, 36,* 401–405.

KOSS, M. P. (1993). Rape: Scope, impact, interventions, and public policy responses. *American Psychologist, 48,* 1062–1069.

KOSS, M. P., GIDYCZ, C. A., & WISNIEWSKI, N. (1987). The scope of rape: Incidence and prevalence of sexual aggression and victimization in a national sample of higher education students. *Journal of Consulting and Clinical Psychology, 55,* 162–170.

KOSS, M. P., & OROS, C. J. (1982). Sexual experiences survey: A research instrument investigating sexual aggression and victimization. *Journal of Consulting and Clinical Psychology, 50,* 455–457.

KOSS, M. P., et al. (1988). Stranger and acquaintance rape: Are there differences in the victim's experience? *Psychology of Women Quarterly, 12,* 1–23.

KOSS, M. P., et al. (1988). Stranger and acquaintance rape: Are there differences in the victim's experience. *Psychology of Women Quarterly, 13,* 1–33.

KOWAL, D. (2008). Coitus interruptus (withdrawal). In R. A. Hatcher et al. (Eds.), *Contraceptive technology* (19th ed., pp. 337–342). New York: Ardent Media.

KOZINETZ, C. A. (2001). Epidemiology of HIV/AIDS in developing countries: The children. *AIDS Patient Care and STDs, 15,* 181–184.

KRAFFT-EBING, R. VON. (1951). *Aberrations of sexual life.* New York: Staples Press.

KRAFFT-EBING, R. VON. (1978; originally 1886). *Psychopathia sexualis.* New York: Stein & Day.

KRAHÉ, B., SCHEINBERGER-OLWIG, R., & SCHÜTZE, S. (2001). Risk factors of sexual aggression and victimization among homosexual men. *Journal of Applied Social Psychology, 31,* 1385–1408.

KRAHÉ, B., et al. (2000). The prevalence of sexual aggression and victimization among homosexual men. *Journal of Sex Research, 37,* 142–150.

KRAUS, S., & RUSSELL, B. (2008). Early sexual experiences: The role of Internet access and sexually explicit material. *Cyberpsychology & Behavior, 11,* 162–168.

KREAGER, D. A., & STAFF, J. (2009). The sexual double standard and adolescent peer acceptance. *Social Psychology Quarterly, 72,* 143–164.

KREIMER, A. R., et al. (2010). Oral human papillomavirus in healthy individuals: A systematic review of the literature. *Sexually Transmitted Diseases, 37,* 386–391.

KRIEGER, J. N. (2000). Consider diagnosis and treatment of trichomoniasis in men. *Sexually Transmitted Diseases, 27,* 241–242.

KRIEGER, N., CHEN, J. T., & WATERMAN, P. D. (2010). Decline in U.S. breast cancer rates after the women's health initiative: Socioeconomic and racial/ethnic differentials. *American Journal of Public Health,* 100(Suppl 1), S132–S139.

KRISTIANSEN, C. M., FELTON, K. A., & HOVDESTAD, W. E. (1996). Recovered memories of child abuse: Fact, fantasy or fancy? *Women & Therapy, 19,* 47–59.

KRONENBERG, F. (1994). Hot flashes. In R. A. Lobo (Ed.), *Treatment of the postmenopausal woman: Basic and clinical aspects* (pp. 97–117). New York: Raven Press.

KRUEGER, R. B., & KAPLAN, M. S. (2000). The nonviolent serial offender: Exhibitionism, frotteurism, and telephone scatologia. In L. B. Schlesinger (Ed.), *Serial offenders: Current thought, recent findings* (pp. 103–118). CRC Press.

KRUG, R. S. (1989). Adult male report of childhood sexual abuse by mothers: Case descriptions and long-term consequences. *Child Abuse & Neglect, 13,* 111–119.

KU, L., et al. (1998). Understanding changes in sexual activity among young metropolitan men: 1979–1995. *Family Planning Perspectives, 30,* 256–262.

KUEHN, B. (2005). Syphilis rates rise among men: Trends for other STDs mixed. *Journal of the American Medical Association, 294,* 3072–3073.

KUHN, D., NASH, S., & BRUCKEN, L. (1978). Sex role concepts of two- and three-year olds. *Child Development, 49,* 445–451.

KULIN, H. E. (1996). Extensive personal experience: Delayed puberty. *Journal of Clinical Endocrinology and Metabolism, 81,* 3460–3464.

KUNCE, L. J., & SHAVER, P. R. (1994). An attachment-theoretical approach to caregiving in romantic relationships. In K. Bartholomew & D. Perlman (Eds.), *Advances in personal relationships: Vol. 5 Attachment process in adulthood* (pp. 205–237). Bristol, PA: Kingsley.

KUNKEL, D., COPE, K. M., & BIELY, E. (1999). Sexual messages on television: Comparing findings from three studies. *Journal of Sex Research, 36,* 230–236.

KUSSELING, F. S., et al. (1996). Understanding why heterosexual adults do not practice safer sex: A comparison of two samples. *AIDS Education and Prevention, 8,* 247–257.

KUTCHINSKY, B. (1973). The effect of easy availability of pornography on the incidence of sex crimes. *Journal of Social Issues, 29,* 163–182.

KYMAN, W. (1998). Into the 21st century: Renewing the campaign for school-based sexuality education. *Journal of Sex & Marital Therapy, 24,* 131–137.

L

LAAN, E., et al. (1994). Women's sexual and emotional responses to male- and female-produced erotica. *Archives of Sexual Behavior, 23,* 153–169.

LABOUVIE-VIEF, G. (1990). Modes of knowledge and the organization of development. In M. L. Commons et al. (Eds.), *Adult development models and methods in the study of adolescents and adult thought.* New York: Praeger.

LADAS, A. K., WHIPPLE, B., & PERRY, J. D. (1982). *The G spot and other recent discoveries about human sexuality.* New York: Holt, Rinehart & Winston.

LALUMIÈRE, M. L., & QUINSEY, V. L. (1994). The discriminability of rapists from non-sex offenders using phallometric measures: A meta-analysis. *Criminal Justice and Behavior, 21,* 150–175.

LALUMIÈRE, M. L., & QUINSEY, V. L. (1998). Pavlovian conditioning of sexual interests in human males. *Archives of Sexual Behavior, 27,* 241–252.

LALUMIÈRE, M. L., & RICE, M. E. (2007). The validity of phallometric assessment with rapists: Comments on Looman & Marshall (2005). *Sex Abuse, 19,* 61–68.

LAMAZE, F. (1970). *Painless childbirth.* Chicago: Regnery. (Originally published 1956.)

LAMBERT, T., KAHN, A., & APPLE, K. (2003). Pluralistic ignorance and hooking up. *Journal of Sex Research, 40,* 129–133.

LANDESMAN, S. H., et al. (1996). Obstetrical factors and the transmission of human immunodeficiency virus type 1 from mother to child. *New England Journal of Medicine, 334,* 1617–1623.

LANER, M. R. (2000). "Sex" versus "gender": A renewed plea. *Sociological Inquiry, 70,* 462–474.

LANER, M. R., & RUSSELL, J. N. (1998). Desired characteristics of spouses and best friends: Do they differ by sex and/or gender? *Sociological Inquiry, 68,* 186–202.

LANGENBERG, A. G. M., et al. (1999). A prospective study of new infections with herpes simplex virus type 1 and type 2. *New England Journal of Medicine, 341,* 1432–1438.

LANGEVIN, R. (1983). *Sexual strands.* Hillsdale, NJ: Lawrence Erlbaum.

LANGEVIN, R., et al. (1979). Experimental studies of the etiology of genital exhibitionism. *Archives of Sexual Behavior, 8,* 307–332.

LANGEVIN, R., et al. (1988). Sexual sadism: Brain, blood, and behavior. *Annals of the New York Academy of Sciences, 528,* 163–171.

LANGFELDT, T. (1981). Sexual development in children. In M. Cook & K. Howells (Eds.), *Adult sexual interest in children.* London: Academic Press.

LANGLOIS, J. H., & DOWNS, A. C. (1980). Mothers, fathers, and peers as socialization agents of sex-typed play behaviors in young children. *Child Development, 51,* 1237–1247.

LANGMYHR, G. J. (1976). Varieties of coital positions: Advantages and disadvantages. *Medical Aspects of Human Sexuality,* June, 128–139.

LÅNGSTRÖM, N., & HANSON, R. K. (2006). High rates of sexual behavior in the general population: Correlates of predictors. *Archives of sexual behavior, 35,* 37–95.

LÅNGSTRÖM, N., & SETO, M. C. (2006). Exhibitionistic and voyeuristic behavior in a Swedish national population survey. *Archives of Sexual Behavior, 35,* 427–435.

LÅNGSTRÖM, N., & ZUCKER, K. J. (2005). Transvestic fetishism in the general population: Prevalence and correlates. *Journal of sex & Marital Therapy, 31,* 87–95.

LÅNGSTRÖM, N., et al. (2010). Genetic and environmental effects on same-sex sexual behavior: A population study of twins in Sweden. *Archives of Sexual Behavior, 39,* 75–80.

LANYON, R. I. (1986). Theory and treatment in child molestation. *Journal of Consulting and Clinical Psychology, 54,* 176–182.

LARIMER, M. E., et al. (1999). Male and female recipients of unwanted sexual contact in a college student sample: Prevalence rates, alcohol abuse, and depression symptoms. *Sex Roles, 40,* 295–308.

LARIMORE, W. (1995). Family-centered birthing: History, philosophy, and need. *Family Medicine, 27,* 132–137.

LARSON, M. S. (2001). Interactions, activities and gender in children's television commercials: A content analysis. *Journal of Broadcasting & Electronic Media, 45,* 41–56.

LARSON, N. C. (2006). Becoming "one of the girls." The transition to lesbian in midlife. *Affilia: Journal of Women and Social Work, 21,* 296–305.

LARSSON, I., & SVEDIN, C.-G. (2002a). Teachers' and parents' report on 3- to 6-year-old children's sexual behavior—a comparison. *Child Abuse & Neglect, 26,* 247–266.

LARSSON, I., & SVEDIN, C.-G. (2002b). Sexual experiences in childhood: Young adults' recollections. *Archives of Sexual Behavior, 31,* 263–273.

LAUMANN, E. O., MASI, C. M., & ZUCKERMAN, E. W. (1997). Circumcision in the United States: Prevalence, prophylactic effects, and sexual practice. *Journal of the American Medical Association, 277,* 1052–1057.

LAUMANN, E. O., PAIK, A., & ROSEN, R. C. (1999). Sexual dysfunction in the United States: Prevalence and predictors. *Journal of the American Medical Association, 281,* 537–544.

LAUMANN, E. O., & WAITE, L. J. (2008). Sexual dysfunction among older adults: Prevalence and risk factors from a nationally representative U.S. probability sample of men and women 57–85 years of age. *Journal of Sexual Medicine, 5,* 2300–2311.

LAUMANN, E. O., et al. (1994). *The social organization of sexuality: Sexual practices in the United States.* Chicago: University of Chicago Press.

LAUMANN, E. O., et al. (2006). A cross-national study of subjective sexual well-being among older women and men: Findings from the Global Study of Sexual Attitudes and Behaviors. *Archives of Sexual Behaviors, 35,* 145–161.

LAUMANN, E. O., et al. (2007). Prevalence and correlates of erectile dysfunction by race and ethnicity among men aged 40 or older in the United States: From the male attitudes regarding sexual health survey. *Journal of Sexual Medicine, 4,* 57–65.

LAUMANN, E. O., et al. (2009). A population-based survey of sexual activity, sexual problems and associated help-seeking behavior patterns in mature adults in the United States of America. *International Journal of Impotence Research, 21,* 171–178.

LAVEE, Y. (1991). Western and non-Western human sexuality: Implications for clinical practice. *Journal of Sex & Marital Therapy, 17,* 203–213.

LAVIN, M. (2008). Voyeurism: Psychopathology and theory. In D. R. Laws & W. T. O'Donohue (Eds.), *Sexual deviance: Theory, assessment, and treatment* (2nd ed. pp. 305–319). New York: Guilford Press.

LAWS, D. R., & O'DONOHUE, W. (1997). Fundamental issues in sexual deviance. In D. R. Laws & W. T. O'Donohue (Eds.), *Sexual deviance: Theory, assessment, and treatment* (pp. 1–21). New York: Guilford Press.

LAWS, D. R., & O'DONOHUE, W. T. (EDS.) (2008). *Sexual deviance: Theory, assessment, and treatment* (2nd ed.). New York: Guilford Press.

LAWSON, C. (1993). Mother-son sexual abuse: Rare or underreported? A critique of the research. *Child Abuse & Neglect, 17,* 261–269.

LAZAR, P. (1996). Maturation folliculaire, conceptions gémellaires dizygotes et âge maternal. *Comptes Rendus Académie des Sciences,* Paris, 319, 1139–1144.

LEBOYER, F. (1975). *Birth without violence.* New York: Knopf.

LEE, J. (2009). Bodies at menarche: Stories of shame, concealment, and sexual maturation. *Sex Roles, 60,* 615–627.

LEE, J. A. (1974, October 8). The styles of loving. *Psychology Today,* 43–50.

LEE, J. A. (1976). *The colors of love.* Englewood Cliffs, NJ: Prentice Hall.

LEE, J. A. (1988). Love-styles. In R. J. Sternberg & M. L. Barnes (Eds.), *The psychology of love* (pp. 38–67). New Haven, CT: Yale University Press.

LEE, L., et al. (2008). If I'm not hot, are you hot or not? Physical-attractiveness evaluations and dating preferences as a function of one's own attractiveness. *Psychological Science, 19,* 669–677.

LEFKOWITZ, E. S., et al. (2000). How Latino American and European American adolescents discuss conflicts, sexuality, and AIDS with their mothers. *Developmental Psychology, 36,* 315–325.

LEFKOWITZ, E. S., et al. (2004). Religiosity, sexual behaviors, and sexual attitudes during emerging adulthood. *Journal of Sex Research, 41,* 150–159.

LEIBLUM, S. R., PERVIN, L., & CAMPBELL, E. H. (1989). The treatment of vaginismus: Success and failure. In S. R. Leiblum & R. C. Rosen (Eds.), *Principles and practice of sex therapy: Update for the 1990s* (pp. 113–138). New York: Guilford Press.

LEIBLUM, S., & GOLDMEIER, D. (2008). Persistent genital arousal disorder in women: Case reports of association with anti-depressant usage and withdrawal. *Journal of Sex & Marital Therapy, 34,* 150–159.

LEIBLUM, S., et al. (2006). Hypoactive sexual desire disorder in postmenopausal women: U.S. results from the Women's International Study of Health and Sexuality. *Menopause, 13,* 46–56.

LEIBLUM, S. R., & CHIVERS, M. L. (2007). Normal and persistent genital arousal in women: New perspectives. *Journal of Sex & Marital Therapy, 33,* 357–373.

LEIGH, B. (1989). Reasons for having and avoiding sex: Gender, sexual orientation, and relationship to sexual behavior. *Journal of Sex Research, 26,* 199–208.

LEIGHTON, B. L., & HALPERN, S. H. (2002). The effects of epidural analgesia on labor, maternal, and neonatal outcomes: A systematic review. *American Journal of Obstetrics and Gynecology, 186,* S69–S77.

LEINWAND, D. (2009, October 7). DNA is behind decline in rape reports. *USA Today,* A1.

LEIT, R. A., POPE, H. G., & GRAY, J. J. (2001). Cultural expectations of muscularity in men: The evolution of playgirl centerfolds. *International Journal of Eating Disorders, 29,* 90–93.

LEITENBERG, H., DETZER, M. J., & SREBNIK, D. (1993). Gender differences in masturbation and the relation of masturbation experience in preadolescence and/or early adolescence to sexual behavior and sexual adjustment in young adulthood. *Archives of Sexual Behavior, 22,* 87–98.

LEITENBERG, H., & HENNING, K. (1995). Sexual fantasy. *Psychological Bulletin, 117,* 469–496.

LEITENBERG, H., & SALTZMAN, H. (2000). A statewide survey of age at first intercourse for adolescent females and age of their male partners: Relation to other risk behaviors and statutory rape implications. *Archives of Sexual Behavior, 29,* 203–215.

LELAND, J. (1995, July 17). Bisexuality. *Newsweek,* 44–50.

LELAND, J. (1999, February 22). Bad news in the bedroom. *Newsweek,* 47.

LEMONICK, M. D. (2004, January 19). The chemistry of desire. *Time.*

LENTON, A. P., & FRANCESCONI, M. (2010). How humans cognitively manage an abundance of mate options. *Psychological Science, 21,* 528–533.

LEONARD, L. M., & FOLLETTE, V. M. (2003). Sexual functioning in women reporting a history of child sexual abuse: Review of the empirical literature and clinical implications. In J. R. Heiman & C. M. Davis (Eds.), *Annual review of sex research* (vol. VIII). Allentown, PA: Society for the Scientific Study of Sexuality.

LEONARD, T. L., FREUND, M., & PLATT, J. J. (1989). Behavior of clients of prostitutes. *American Journal of Public Health, 79,* 903.

LERMAN, H. (1986). *A mote in Freud's eye: From psychoanalysis to the psychology of women.* New York: Springer.

LESERMAN, J., et al. (2000). Impact of stressful life events, depression, social support, coping, and cortisol on progression to AIDS. *American Journal of Psychiatry, 157,* 1221–1228.

LESSEY, B. A. (2000). Medical management of endometriosis and infertility. *Fertility and Sterility, 73,* 1089–1096.

LETOURNEAU, N. L., STEWART, M. J., & BARNFATHER, A. K. (2004). Adolescent mothers: Support needs, resources, and support-education interventions. *Journal of Adolescent Health, 35,* 509–525.

LEVAY, S. (1991). A difference in hypothalamic structure between heterosexual and homosexual men. *Science, 253,* 1034–1037.

LEVER, J., et al. (1992). Behavior patterns and sexual identity of bisexual males. *Journal of Sex Research, 29,* 141–167.

LÉVI-STRAUSS, C. (1969). *The elementary structures of kinship.* Boston: Beacon Press.

LEVIN, R. (2002). The physiology of sexual arousal in the human female: A recreational and procreational synthesis. *Archives of Sexual Behavior, 31,* 405–411.

LEVIN, R. J., & WAGNER, G. (1985). Orgasm in women in the laboratory—Quantitative studies on duration, intensity, latency, and vaginal blood flow. *Archives of Sexual Behavior, 11,* 367–386.

LEVINE, P. B., et al. (1999). Roe v. Wade and American fertility. *American Journal of Public Health, 89,* 199–203.

LEVINE, R. A. (1959). Gusii sex offenses: A study in social control. *American Anthropologist, 61,* 965–990.

LEVINE, R. A. (1974). Gusii sex offenses: A study in social control. In N. N. Wagner (Ed.), *Perspectives on human sexuality* (pp. 308–352). New York: Behavioral Publishers.

LEVINE, S. B. (2002). Reexploring the concept of sexual desire. *Journal of Sex & Marital Therapy, 28,* 39–51.

LEVINE, S. B. (2003). The nature of sexual desire: A clinician's perspective. *Archives of Sexual Behavior, 32,* 279–285.

LEVINE, S. B. (2005). What is love anyway? *Journal of Sex & Marital Therapy, 31,* 143–151.

LEVINE, S. B., & ALTHOF, S. E. (1991). The pathogenesis of psychogenic erectile dysfunction. *Journal of Sex Education and Therapy, 17,* 251–266.

LEVINGER, G. (1988). Can we picture "love"? In R. J. Sternberg & M. L. Barnes (Eds.), *The psychology of love* (pp. 139–158). New Haven, CT: Yale University Press.

LEVITT, E. E., MOSER, C., & JAMISON, K. V. (1994). The prevalence and some attributes of females in the sadomasochistic subculture: A second report. *Archives of Sexual Behavior, 23,* 465–473.

LEVY, K. N., & KELLY, K. M. (2010). Sex differences in jealousy: A contribution from attachment theory. *Psychological Sciences, 21,* 168–173.

LEWIS, L. N., et al. (2010). Implanon as a contraceptive choice for teenage mothers: A comparison of contraceptive choices, acceptability and repeat pregnancy. *Contraception, 81,* 421–426.

LI, C. I., et al. (2008). Timing of menarche and first full-term birth in relation to breast cancer risk. *Journal of Epidemiology, 167,* 230–239.

LIANG, K., et al. (2009). A case series of 104 women infected with HIV-1 via blood transfusion postnatally: High rate of HIV-1 transmission to infants through breast feeding. *Journal of Infectious Diseases, 200,* 682–686.

LICHTENSTEIN, P., et al. (2000). Environmental and heritable factors in the causation of cancer: Analyses of cohorts of twins from Sweden, Denmark, and Finland. *New England Journal of Medicine, 343,* 78–85.

LIDDON, N., et al. (2010). Acceptability of human papillomavirus vaccine for males: A review of the literature. *Journal of Adolescent Health, 46,* 113–123.

LIDSTER, C., & HORSBURGH, M. (1994). Masturbation—Beyond myth and taboo. *Nursing Forum, 29*(3), 18–26.

LIEBOWITZ, M. (1983). *The chemistry of love.* Boston: Little, Brown.

LIMA, V. D., et al. (2009). Association between HIV-1 RNA level and CD4 cell count among untreated HIV-infected individuals. *American Journal of Public Health, 99*(S1), S193–S196.

LINDAU, S. T., et al. (2007). A study of sexuality and health among older adults in the United States. *New England Journal of Medicine, 357,* 762–774.

LINDAU, S. T., & GAVRILOVA, N. (2010). Sex, health, and years of sexually active life gained due to good health: Evidence from two U.S. population based cross sectional surveys of ageing. *British Medical Journal*, 340, c810–c820.

LINDAU, S. T., et al. (2007). A study of sexuality and health among older adults in the United States. *New England Journal of Medicine*, 357, 762–774.

LINDBÄCK, S., et al. (2000a). Viral dynamics in primary HIV-1 infection. *AIDS*, 14, 2283–2291.

LINDBÄCK, S., et al. (2000b). Diagnosis of primary HIV-1 infection and duration of follow-up after HIV exposure. *AIDS*, 14, 2333–2339.

LINDBERG, F. H., & DISTAD, L. J. (1985). Post-traumatic stress disorders in women who experienced childhood incest. *Child Abuse & Neglect*, 9, 329–334.

LINDBERG, L. D., et al. (1997). Age differences between minors who give birth and their adult partners. *Family Planning Perspectives*, 29, 61–66.

LINDBERG, L. D., JONES, R., & SANTELLI, J. S. (2008). Noncoital sexual activities among adolescents. *Journal of Adolescent Health*, 43, 231–238.

LINDEGREN, M. L., et al. (1999). Trends in perinatal transmission of HIV/AIDS in the United States. *Journal of the American Medical Association*, 282, 531–538.

LINDHOLM, C. (1998). Love and structure. *Theory, Culture & Society*, 15, 243–263.

LINDHOLM, C., & LINDHOLM, C. (1980). Life behind the veil. *Science Digest* Special, Summer.

LINTON, R. (1936). *The study of man.* New York: Appleton-Century.

LINZ, D. (1989). Exposure to sexually explicit materials and attitudes toward rape: A comparison of study results. *Journal of Sex Research*, 26, 50–84.

LINZ, D., DONNERSTEIN, E., & PENROD, S. (1987). The findings and recommendations of the Attorney General's Commission on Pornography: Do the psychological "facts" fit the political fury? *American Psychologist*, 42, 946–953.

LIPPA, R. A. (2001). Gender-related traits in transsexuals and nontranssexuals. *Archives of Sexual Behavior*, 30, 603–614.

LIPPA, R. A. (2008). Sex differences and sexual orientation differences in personality: Findings from the BBC Internet Study. *Archives of Sexual Behavior*, 37, 173–187.

LIPPA, R. A. (2009). Sex differences in sex drive, sociosexuality, and height across 53 nations: Testing evolutionary and social structural theories. *Archives of Sexual Behavior*, 38, 631–651.

LIPS, H. (1992). *Sex and gender.* Mountain View, CA: Mayfield.

LIPSCOMB, G. H., et al. (1992). Male victims of sexual assault. *Journal of the American Medical Association*, 267, 3064–3066.

LIPTON, M. A. (1983). The problem of pornography. In W. E. Fann et al. (Eds.), *Phenomenology and treatment of psychosexual disorders* (pp. 113–134). New York: Spectrum.

LIU, P. Y., et al. (2008). Determinants of the rate and extent of spermatogamic suppression during hormonal male contraception: An integrated analysis. *Journal of Clinical Endocrinology & Metabolism*, 93, 1774–1783.

LIU, S., et al. (2007). Maternal mortality and severe morbidity associated with low-risk planned cesarean delivery versus planned vaginal delivery at term. *Canadian Medical Association Journal*, 676, 455–460.

LOCK, M. (1994). Menopause in cultural context. *Experimental Gerontology*, 29, 307–317.

LOCKE, K. A. (2004). The Bible on homosexuality: Exploring its meaning and authority. *Journal of Homosexuality*, 48, 125–156.

LOFTUS, E. F. (1997a). Creating false memories. *Scientific American*, 277, 70–75.

LOFTUS, E. F. (1997b). Memory for a past that never was. *Current Directions in Psychological Science*, 6, 60–65.

LOGAN, C. (2008). Sexual deviance in females: Psychopathology and theory. In D. R. Laws & W. T. O'Donohue (Eds.), *Sexual deviance: Theory, assessment, and treatment* (2nd ed., pp. 486–507). New York: Guilford Press.

LØKKEGAARD, E., et al. (2008). Hormone therapy and risk of myocardial infarction: A national register study. *European Heart Journal*, 29, 2660–2668.

LONDISH, G. J., & MURRAY, J. M. (2008). Significant reduction in HIV prevalence according to male circumcision intervention in sub-Saharan Africa. *International Journal of Epidemiology*, 37, 1246–1253.

LONDON, S. (2006). Consistent condom use reduces the risk of type 2 herpes virus. *Perspectives on Sexual and Reproductive Health*, 38, 54–55.

LONGMAN, P. (2009, March 24). Headed toward extinction? *USA Today*, 11A.

LOPICCOLO, J., & FRIEDMAN, J. (1988). Broad-spectrum treatment of low sexual desire: Integration of cognitive, behavioral, and systemic therapy. In S. R. Leiblum & R. C. Rosen (Eds.), *Sexual desire disorders*. New York: Guilford Press.

LOPICCOLO, J., & STOCK, W. (1986). Treatment of sexual dysfunction. *Journal of Consulting and Clinical Psychology*, 54, 158–167.

LOTHIAN, J., & DeVRIES, C. (2005). *The official Lamaze guide: Giving birth with confidence.* Amazon.

LOTTES, I. L. (2002). Sexual health policies in other industrialized countries: Are there lessons for the United States? *Journal of Sex Research*, 39, 79–83.

LOTTES, I. L., & WEINBERG, M. S. (1996). Sexual coercion among university students: A comparison of the United States and Sweden. *Journal of Sex Research*, 34, 67–76.

LOU, J.-H., & CHEN, S.-H. (2009). Relationships among sexual knowledge, sexual attitudes, and safe sex behaviour among adolescents: A structural equation model. *International Journal of Nursing Studies*, 46, 1595–1603.

LOUDERBACK, L. A., & WHITLEY, JR., B. E. (1997). Perceived erotic value of homosexuality and sex-role attitudes as mediators of sex differences in heterosexual college students' attitudes toward lesbians and gay men. *Journal of Sex Research*, 34, 175–182.

LOWIE, R. H. (1931). Sex and marriage. In J. F. McDermott (Ed.), *The sex problem in modern society* (pp. 146–160). New York: Modern Library.

LU, L., et al. (2008). The changing face of HIV in China. *Nature*, 455, 609–611.

LU-YAO, G. L., et al. (2009). Outcomes of localized prostate cancer following conservative management. *Journal of the American Medical Association*, 302, 1202–1209.

LUCAS, A. M. (2005). The work of sex work: Elite prostitutes' vocational orientations and experiences. *Deviant Behavior*, 26, 513–546.

LUCKEY, E. B., & BAIN, J. K. (1970). Children: A factor in marital satisfaction. *Journal of Marriage and Family*, 32, 43–44.

LUDWIG, D. S., & CURRIE, J. (2010, August 5). The association between pregnancy weight gain and birth weight: A within-family comparison. *The Lancet.* Early online publication.

LUEPTOW, L. B., GAROVICH-SZABO, L., & LUEPTOW, M. B. (2001). Social change and the persistence of sex typing: 1974–1997. *Social Forces*, 80, 1–35.

LUGER, A. (1993). The origin of syphilis. *Sexually Transmitted Diseases*, 20, 110–117.

LUKE, B., et al. (1994). The changing pattern of multiple births in the United States: Maternal and infant characteristics, 1973 and 1990. *Obstetrics and Gynecology*, 84, 101–106.

LUMIA, A. R., & McGINNIS, M. Y. (2010). Impact of anabolic steroids on adolescent males. *Physiology & Behavior*, 100, 199–204.

LURIE, N. O. (1953). Winnebago berdache. *American Anthropologist*, 55, 708–712.

LUSSIER, P., & PICHÉ, L. (2008). Frotteurism: Psychopathology and theory. In D. R. Laws & W. T. O'Donohue (Eds.), *Sexual deviance: Theory, assessment, and treatment* (2nd ed., pp. 131–149). New York: Guilford Press.

LUTFEY, K. E., et al. (2009). Prevalence and correlates of sexual activity and function in women: Results from the Boston Area Community Health (BACH) Survey. *Archives of Sexual Behavior*, 38, 514–527.

LYNCH, H. T., & LYNCH, J. F. (1992). Hereditary ovarian carcinoma. *Hematology/Oncology Clinics of North America*, 6, 783–811.

M

MacDONALD, A. P. (1981). Bisexuality: Some comments on research and theory. *Journal of Homosexuality*, 6, 21–35.

MacDONALD, A. P. (1982). Research on sexual orientation: A bridge which touches both shores but doesn't meet in the middle. *Journal of Sex Education and Therapy*, 8, 9–13.

MacKINNON, C. (1993). *Only words.* Cambridge, MA: Harvard University Press.

MacKINNON, C. (1996). *Just words.* Cambridge, MA: Harvard University Press.

MacKINNON, C. A. (1979). *Sexual harassment of working women.* New Haven, CT: Yale University Press.

MacNEIL, S., & BYERS, E. S. (2009). Role of sexual disclosure in the sexual satisfaction of long-term heterosexual couples. *Journal of Sex Research*, 46, 3–14.

MACKEY, S. (2009). Menstrual change during the menopause transition: Do women find it problematic? *Maturitas*, 64, 114–118.

MACRAE, C. N., et al. (2002). Person perception across the menstrual cycle: Hormonal influences on social-cognitive functioning. *Psychological Science*, 13, 532–536.

MADDOCK, J. W., et al. (1983). *Human sexuality and the family.* New York: Haworth Press.

MADEY, S. F., & RODGERS, L. (2009). The effect of attachment and Sternberg's triangular theory of love on relationship satisfaction. *Individual Differences Research*, 7, 76–84.

MADON, S. (1997). What do people believe about gay males? A study of stereotype content and strength. *Sex Roles*, 37, 663–685.

MAH, K., & BINIK, Y. M. (2001). The nature of human orgasm: A critical review of major trends. *Clinical Psychology Review*, 21, 823–856.

MAH, K., & BINIK, Y. M. (2002). Do all orgasms feel alike? Evaluating a two-dimensional model of the orgasm experience across gender and sexual context. *Journal of Sex Research*, 39, 104–113.

MAH, K., & BINIK, Y. M. (2005). Are orgasms in the mind or the body? Psychosocial versus physiological correlates of orgasmic pleasure and satisfaction. *Journal of Sex & Marital Therapy*, 31, 187–200.

MAHESHWARI, A., HAMILTON, M., & BHATTACHARYA, S. (2008). Effect of female age on the diagnostic categories of infertility. *Human Reproduction*, 23, 538–542.

MAJOR, B., et al. (2009). Abortion and mental health. *American Psychologist*, 64, 863–890.

MALAMUTH, N. (1981). Rape proclivity among males. *Journal of Social Issues*, 37, 138–157.

MALAMUTH, N. (1986). Predictors of naturalistic sexual aggression. *Journal of Personality and Social Psychology*, 50, 953–962.

MALAMUTH, N. M., & BROWN, L. M. (1994). Sexually aggressive men's perceptions of women's communications: Testing three explanations. *Journal of Personality and Social Psychology*, 67, 699–712.

MALAMUTH, N. M. & DONNERSTEIN, E. (Eds.). (1984). *Pornography and sexual aggression.* New York: Academic Press.

MALAMUTH, N. M., HEAVEY, C. L., & LINZ, D. (1993). Predicting men's antisocial behavior against women: The interaction model of sexual aggression. In G. C. N. Hall, R. Hirschman, J. R. Graham, & M. S. Zaragoza (Eds.), *Sexual aggression: Issues in etiology, assessment and treatment* (pp. 63–97). Washington, DC: Taylor & Francis.

MALIZIA, B. A., HACKER, M. R., & PENZIAS, A. S. (2009). Cumulative live-birth rates after in vitro fertilization. *New England Journal of Medicine*, 360, 236–243.

MANDOKI, M. W., et al. (1991). A review of Klinefelter's syndrome in children and adolescents. *Journal of the American Academy of Child and Adolescence Psychiatry*, 30, 167–172.

MANHART, L. E., et al. (2007). *Mycoplasma genitalium* among young adults in the United States: An emerging sexually transmitted infection. *American Journal of Public Health*, 97, 1118–1125.

MANIGLIO, R. (2009). The impact of child sexual abuse on health: A systematic review of reviews. *Clinical Psychology Review*, 29, 647–657.

MANNING, W. D., GIORDANO, P. C., & LONGMORE, M. A. (2006). Hooking up: The relationship contexts of "nonrelationship" sex. *Journal of Adolescent Research*, 21, 459–483.

MANNING, W. D., LONGMORE, M. A., & GIORDANO, P. C. (2000). The relationship context of contraceptive use at first intercourse. *Family Planning Perspectives*, 32, 104–110.

MANNING, W. D., LONGMORE, M. A., & GIORDANO, P. C. (2005). Adolescents' involvement in non-romantic sexual activity. *Social Science Quarterly*, 34, 384–407.

MANNING, W. D., et al. (2009). Relationship dynamics and consistency of condom use among adolescents. *Perspectives on Sexual and Reproductive Health*, 41, 181–190.

MANNINO, D. M., KLEVENS, R. M., & FLANDERS, W. D. (1994). Cigarette smoking: An independent risk factor for impotence? *American Journal of Epidemiology*, 140, 1003–1008.

MANSON, J. E., et al. (2003). Estrogen plus progestin and the risk of coronary heart disease. *New England Journal of Medicine*, 349, 523–534.

MANSON, J. E., et al. (2007). Estrogen therapy and coronary-artery calcification. *New England Journal of Medicine*, 356, 2591–2602.

MARCH of DIMES. (2010). Prematurity/index: http://www.marchofdimes.com/prematurity/index_map.asp

MARCHANT, S., et al. (1999). A survey of women's experiences of vaginal loss from 24 hours to three months after childbirth (the BLIPP study). *Midwifery*, 15, 72–81.

MARCHBANKS, P. A., KUNG-JONG, L., & MERCY, J. A. (1990). Risk of injury from resisting rape. *American Journal of Epidemiology*, 132, 540–549.

MARCUS, D., & MILLER, R. (2003). Sex differences in judgements of physical attractiveness: A social relations analysis. *Personality and Social Psychology Bulletin*, 29, 325–335.

MARMOR, J. (1980). Clinical aspects of male homosexuality. In J. Marmor (Ed.), *Homosexual behavior: A modern reappraisal* (pp. 267–279). New York: Basic Books.

MARRA, C., et al. (2009). Patients with genital warts have a decreased quality of life. *Sexually Transmitted Diseases*, 36, 258–260.

MARRAZZO, J. M., GUEST, F., & CATES, JR., W. (2008). Reproductive tract infections, including HIV and other sexually transmitted infections. In R. A. Hatcher et al. (Eds.), *Contraceptive technology* (19th ed., pp. 499–557). New York: Ardent Media.

MARSHALL, B. D. L., & WOOD, E. (2009). Sex work and sex exchange among street children: An urgent need for a global response. *Journal of Adolescent Health*, 44, 201–202.

MARSHALL, B. D. L., et al. (2010). Survival sex work and increased HIV risk among sexual minority street-involved youth. *Journal of Acquired Immune Deficiency Syndromes*, 53, 661–664.

MARSHALL, D. S. (1971). Sexual behavior on Mangaia. In D. S. Marshall & R. C. Suggs (Eds.), *Human sexual behavior* (pp. 103–162). New York: Basic Books.

MARSHALL, W. L. (1992). Pornography and sex offenders. In D. Zillman & J. Bryant (Eds.), *Pornography: Recent research, interpretation, and policy considerations* (pp. 185–214). Hillsdale, NJ: Lawrence Erlbaum.

MARSHALL, W. L. (1996). Assessment, treatment, and theorizing about sex offenders. *Criminal Justice and Behavior*, 23, 162–199.

MARSHALL, W. L., & BARBAREE, H. E. (1990). An integrated theory of the etiology of sexual offending. In W. L. Marshall, D. R. Laws, & H. E. Barbaree (Eds.), *Handbook of sexual assault: Issues, theories, and treatment of the offender* (pp. 257–275). New York: Plenum Press.

MARSHALL, W. L., & ECCLES, A. (1991). Issues in clinical practice with sex offenders. *Journal of Interpersonal Violence*, 6, 68–93.

MARSHALL, W. L., ECCLES, A., & BARBAREE, H. (1991). The treatment of exhibitionists: A focus on sexual deviance versus cognitive and relationship features. *Behavior Research and Therapy*, 29, 129–135.

MARSHALL, W. L., ECCLES, A., & BARBAREE, H. E. (1993). A three-tiered approach to the rehabilitation of incarcerated sex offenders. *Behavioral Sciences and the Law*, 11, 441–455.

MARSIGLIO, W. (1993). Attitudes toward homosexual activity and gays as friends: A national survey of heterosexual 15- to 19-year-old males. *Journal of Sex Research*, 30, 12–17.

MARSTON, C., & CLELAND, J. (2003). Relationships between contraception and abortion: A review of the evidence. *International Family Planning Perspectives*, 29, 6–13.

MARTIN, A. (2007, June 7). Survey finds evangelicals' addiction to internet porn on the rise. www.onenewsnow.com/2007/06/survey

MARTIN, C. L., & RUBLE, D. (2004). Children's search for gender cues. *Current Directions in Psychological Science*, 13, 67–70.

MARTIN, C. L., & RUBLE, D. N. (2010). Patterns of gender development. *Annual Review of Psychology*, 61, 353–381.

MARTIN, E. F., & PRUETT, M. K. (1998). The juvenile sex offender and the juvenile justice system. *American Criminal Law Review*, 35, 279–332.

MARTIN, E. K., TAFT, C. T., & RESICK, P. A. (2007). A review of marital rape. *Aggression and Violent Behavior*, 12, 329–347.

MARTIN, J. (1999, June-July). Nipple piercing: Is it compatible with breastfeeding? *LEAVEN*, 35, 64–65.

MARTIN, J., et al. (2009). Births: Final data for 2006. *National Vital Statistics Report*, 57, 1–120.

MARTINDALE, C. C. (1957). A sketch of the life and character of St. Augustine. In M. C. D'Arcy et al. (Eds.), *St. Augustine* (pp. 79–101). New York: Meridian Books. (First published in 1930.)

MARTINEZ, G., et al. (2006). Fertility, contraception, and fatherhood: Data on men and women from Cycle 6 (2002) of the National Survey of Family Growth. *Vital and Health Statistics*, 23, 26.

MARTINO, S. C., et al. (2008). Virginity pledges among the willing: Delays in first intercourse and consistency of condom use. *Journal of Adolescent Health*, 43, 341–348.

MARTINO, S. C., et al. (2009). It's better on TV: Does television set teenagers up for regret following sexual initiation? *Perspectives on Sexual and Reproductive Health*, 41, 92–100.

MASLOW, A. H. (1968). *Toward a psychology of being* (2nd ed.). Princeton, NJ: Van Nostrand.

MASON, F. L. (1997). Fetishism: Psychopathology and theory. In D. R. Laws & W. T. O'Donohue (Eds.), *Sexual deviance: Theory, assessment, and treatment* (pp. 75–91). New York: Guilford Press.

MASTERS, W. H. (1986). Sexual dysfunction as an aftermath of sexual assault of men by women. *Journal of Sex & Marital Therapy*, 12, 35–45.

MASTERS, W. H., & JOHNSON, V. E. (1966). *Human sexual response.* Boston: Little, Brown.

MASTERS, W. H., & JOHNSON, V. E. (1970). *Human sexual inadequacy.* Boston: Little, Brown.

MASTERS, W. H., & JOHNSON, V. E. (1979). *Homosexuality in perspective.* Boston: Little, Brown.

MATHEMATICA POLICY RESEARCH. (2007). www.mathematicampr.com/publications/PDFs/impactabstinence.pdf

MATHUR, R., & BRAUNSTEIN, G. D. (1997). Gynecomastia: Pathomechanisms and treatment strategies. *Hormone Research*, 48, 95–102.

MAULDON, J., & DELBANCO, S. (1997). Public perceptions about unplanned pregnancy. *Family Planning Perspectives*, 29, 25–29, 40.

MAYNARD, E., et al. (2009). Women's experiences with anal sex: Motivations and implications for STD prevention. *Perspectives on Sexual and Reproductive Health*, 41, 142–149.

MAYRAND, M. H., et al. (2007). Human papillomavirus DNA versus Papanicolaou screening tests for cervical cancer. *New England Journal of Medicine*, 357, 1579–1588.

MAZUR, A., & BOOTH, A. (1998). Testosterone and dominance in men. *Behavioral and Brain Sciences*, 21, 353–397.

MAZUR, T. (2005). Gender dysphoria and gender change in androgen insensitivity or micropenis. *Archives of Sexual Behavior*, 34, 411–421.

McBride, K. R., & Fortenberry, J. D. (2010). Heterosexual anal sexuality and anal sex behaviors: A review. *Journal of Sex Research*, 47, 123–136.

McCabe, M. P., & Cummins, R. A. (1998). Sexuality and quality of life among young people. *Adolescence*, 33, 761–770.

McCabe, M. P., Taleporos, G., & Dip, G. (2003). Sexual esteem, sexual satisfaction, and sexual behavior among people with physical disability. *Archives of Sexual Behavior*, 32, 359–369.

McCabe, M. P., & Wauchope, M. (2005). Behavioral characteristics of men accused of rape: Evidence for different types of rapists. *Archives of Sexual Behavior*, 34, 241–253.

McCabe, S. (1983). FBD marriage: Further support for the Westermarck hypothesis of the incest taboo? *American Anthropologist*, 85, 50–69.

McCarthy, B., & McDonald, D. (2009). Assessment, treatment, and relapse prevention: Male hypoactive sexual desire disorder. *Journal of Sex and Marital Therapy*, 35, 58–67.

McCarty, L. (1986). Mother-child incest: Characteristics of the offender. *Child Welfare*, 6, 447–458.

McCauley, J., et al. (1997). Clinical characteristics of women with a history of childhood abuse: Unhealed wounds. *Journal of the American Medical Association*, 277, 1362–1368.

McClintock, M. (1971). Menstrual synchrony and suppression. *Nature*, 229, 244–245.

McClintock, M. K. (1999). Whither menstrual synchrony? In R. C. Rosen, C. M. Davis, & H. J. Ruppel, Jr. (Eds.), *Annual Review of Sex Research* (Vol. IX, pp. 77–95). Allentown, PA: Society for the Scientific Study of Sexuality.

McConaghy, N. (1974). Penile volume responses to moving and still pictures of male and female nudes. *Archives of Sexual Behavior*, 3, 566–570.

McCoy, N. L., & Pitino, L. (2002). Pheromonal influences on sociosexual behavior in young women. *Physiology & Behavior*, 75, 367–375.

McFadden, D. (2008). What do sex twins, spotted hyenas, ADHD, and sexual orientation have in common? *Perspectives on Psychological Sciences*, 3, 309–324.

McGee, E. A., & Hsueh, A. J. W. (2000). Initial and cyclic recruitment of ovarian follicles. *Endocrine Reviews*, 21, 200–214.

McGinn, D. (2004, October 4). Mating behavior 101. *Newsweek*, 44–45.

McGinty, K., Knox, D., & Zusman, M. (2007). Friends with benefits: Women want "friends" men want "benefits." *College Student Journal*, 41, 1128–1131.

McHale, S. M., & Crouter, A. C. (1992). You can't always get what you want: Incongruence between sex-role attitudes and family work roles and its implications for marriage. *Journal of Marriage and Family*, 54, 537–547.

McKain, T. L. (1996). Acknowledging mixed-sex people. *Journal of Sex & Marital Therapy*, 22, 265–274.

McKay, A. (1997). Accommodating ideological pluralism in sexuality education. *Journal of Moral Education*, 26, 285–300.

McKay, A. (2005). Sexuality and substance abuse: The impact of tobacco, alcohol, and selected recreational drugs on sexual function. *Canadian Journal of Human Sexuality*, 14, 47–56.

McKeganey, N. P. (1994). Prostitution and HIV: What do we know and where might research be targeted in the future? *AIDS*, 8, 1215–1226.

McKirnan, D. J., et al. (1995). Bisexually active men: Social characteristics and sexual behavior. *Journal of Sex Research*, 32, 65–76.

McLeod, J. D., & Knight, S. (2010). The association of socioemotional problems with early sexual initiation. *Perspectives on Sexual and Reproductive Health*, 42, 93–101.

McNally, R. J., & Geraerts, E. (2009). A new solution to the recovered memory debate. *Perspectives on Psychological Science*, 4, 126–134.

McNulty, J. K., & Fisher, T. D. (2008). Gender differences in response to sexual expectancies and changes in sexual frequency: A short-term longitudinal study of sexual satisfaction in newly married couples. *Archives of Sexual Behaviors*, 37, 229–240.

Medlar, T. (1998). The sexuality education program of the Massachusetts statewide head injury program. *Sexuality and Disability*, 16, 11–19.

Meeks, B. S., Hendrick, S. S., & Hendrick, C. (1998). Communication, love and relationship satisfaction. *Journal of Social and Personal Relationships*, 15, 755–773.

Mehren, E. (1991, June 2). What we really think about adultery. *Los Angeles Times*, pp. E1, E8.

Meinking, T. L., & Taplin, D. (1996). Infestations: Pediculosis. In P. Elsner & A. Eichmann (Eds.), *Sexually transmitted diseases: Advances in diagnosis and treatment* (pp. 157–163). Basel: Karger.

Meinking, T. L., et al. (1995). The treatment of scabies with ivermectin. *New England Journal of Medicine*, 333, 26–30.

Meiselman, K. (1978). *Incest: A psychological study of causes and effects with treatment recommendations*. San Francisco: Jossey-Bass.

Melendy, M. R. (1903). *Perfect womanhood: For maidens-wives-mothers*. Philadelphia: K. T. Boland.

Mellors, J. W., et al. (1996). Prognosis in HIV-1 infection predicted by the quantity of virus in plasma. *Science*, 272, 1167–1170.

Meltzer, D. (2005). Complications of body piercing. *American Family Physician*, 72, 2029.

Mercer, C. H., et al. (2007). Women who report having sex with women: British national probability data on prevalence, sexual behaviors, and health outcomes. *American Journal of Public Health*, 97, 1126–1133.

Meriggiola, M. C., Costantino, A., & Cerpolini, S. (2002). Recent advances in hormonal male contraception. *Contraception*, 65, 269–272.

Messenger, J. (1971). Sex and repression in an Irish folk community. In D. Marshall & R. Suggs (Eds.), *Human sexual behavior* (pp. 3–37). New York: Basic Books.

Meston, C. M., & Ahrold, T. (2010). Ethnic, gender, and acculturation influences on sexual behaviors. *Archives of Sexual Behavior*, 39, 179–189.

Meston, C. M., & Buss, D. M. (2007). Why humans have sex. *Archives of Sexual Behavior*, 36, 477–507.

Meston, C. M., Rellini, A. H., & Telch, M. J. (2008). Short- and long-term effects of ginkgo biloba extract on sexual dysfunction in women. *Archives of Sexual Behavior*, 37, 530–547.

Meston, C. M., et al. (2004). Disorders of orgasm in women. *Journal of Sexual Medicine*, 1, 66–68.

Metts, S., & Fitzpatrick, M. A. (1992). Thinking about safer sex: The risky business of "Know your partner" advice. In T. Edgar, M. A. Fitzpatrick, & V. S. Freimuth (Eds.), *AIDS: A communication perspective*. Hillsdale, NJ: Lawrence Erlbaum.

Metz, M. E., & Epstein, N. (2002). Assessing the role of relationship conflict in sexual dysfunction. *Journal of Sex & Marital Therapy*, 28, 139–164.

Metz, M. E., & Pryor, J. L. (2000). Premature ejaculation: A psychophysiological approach for assessment and management. *Journal of Sex & Marital Therapy*, 26, 293–320.

Meuwissen, I., & Over, R. (1991). Multidimensionality of the content of female sexual fantasy. *Behavior Research and Therapy*, 29, 179–189.

Meyer, I. H. (2003). Prejudice, social stress, and mental health in lesbian, gay, and bisexual populations: Conceptual issues and research evidence. *Psychological Bulletin*, 129, 674–697.

Meyer-Bahlburg, H. F. L. (2005). Gender identity outcome in female-raised 46, XY persons with penile agenesis, cloacal exstrophy of the bladder, or penile ablation. *Archives of Sexual Behavior*, 34, 423–438.

Meyerowitz, B. E., et al. (1999). Sexuality following breast cancer. *Journal of Sex & Marital Therapy*, 25, 237–250.

Meyers, D. (2005). Screening for gonorrhea. *American Family Physician*, 72, 1799–1802.

Meyers, L. (2007, February). The eternal question: Does love last? *Monitor on Psychology*, 44–45.

Meyers, S. A., & Berscheid, E. (1997). The language of love: The difference a preposition makes. *Personality and Social Psychology Bulletin*, 23, 347–362.

Mezey, G., & King, M. (1989). The effects of sexual assault on men: A survey of 22 victims. *Psychological Medicine*, 19, 205–209.

Michael, R., et al. (1994). *Sex in America: A definitive survey*. Boston: Little, Brown.

Migueles, S. A., & Connors, M. (2010). Long-term nonprogressive disease among untreated HIV-infected individuals. *Journal of the American Medical Association*, 304, 194–201.

Mikulincer, M., & Nachshon, O. (1991). Attachment styles and patterns of self-disclosure. *Journal of Personality and Social Psychology*, 61, 321–331.

Mikulincer, M., et al. (2002). Attachment security in couple relationships: A systematic model and its implications for family dynamics. *Family Process*, 41, 407–436.

Miller, B. C. (2002). Family influences on adolescent sexual and contraceptive behavior. *Journal of Sex Research*, 39, 22–26.

Miller, B. C., et al. (1998). Pubertal development, parental communication, and sexual values in relation to adolescent sexual behaviors. *Journal of Early Adolescence*, 18, 27–52.

Miller, K. S., et al. (1998a). Family communication about sex: What are parents saying and are their adolescents listening? *Family Planning Perspectives*, 30, 218–222, 235.

Miller, K. S., et al. (1998b). Patterns of condom use among adolescents: The impact of mother-adolescent communication. *American Journal of Public Health*, 88, 1542–1544.

Miller, L. C., Putcha-Bhagavatula, A., & Pedersen, W. C. (2002). Men's and women's mating preferences: Distinct evolutionary mechanisms? *Current Directions in Psychological Science*, 11, 88–93.

Miller, L. J. (2002). Postpartum depression. *Journal of the American Medical Association*, 287, 762–765.

MILLER, S. A., & BYERS, E. S., (2004). Actual and desired duration of foreplay and intercourse: Discordance and misperceptions within heterosexual couples. *Journal of Sex Research, 41,* 301–309.

MILLER, S. L., & MANER, J. K. (2010). Scent of a woman: Men's testosterone responses to olfactory ovulation cues. *Psychological Science, 21,* 276–283.

MILLIGAN, M. S., & NEUFELDT, A. H. (2001). The myth of asexuality: A survey of social and empirical evidence. *Sexuality and Disability, 19,* 91–109.

MILLION WOMEN STUDY COLLABORATORS. (2003). Breast cancer and hormone-replacement therapy in the Million Women Study. *The Lancet, 362,* 419–427.

MILLNER, C. (2002, August). South Africa's shame. *Essence,* 114–117.

MILNER, J. S., DOPKE, C. A., & CROUCH, J. L. (2008). Paraphilia not otherwise specified. In D. R. Laws & W. T. O'Donohue (Eds.), *Sexual deviance: Theory, assessment, and treatment* (2nd ed., pp. 384–418). New York: Guilford Press.

MINER, M. H., et al. (2007). The compulsive sexual behavior inventory: Psychometric properties. *Archives of Sexual Behavior, 36,* 579–587.

MINER, M. H., et al. (2010). Understanding sexual perpetration against children: Effects of attachment style, interpersonal involvement, and hypersexuality. *Sexual Abuse: A Journal of Research and Treatment, 22,* 58–77.

MIRKIN, G., & HOFFMAN, M. (1978). *The sportsmedicine book.* Boston: Little, Brown.

MISHAIL, A., et al. (2009). Impact of a second semen analysis on a treatment decision making in the infertile man with varicocele. *Sterility and Fertility, 91,* 1809–1811.

MOENCH, T. R., CHIPATO, T., & PADIAN, N. S. (2001). Preventing disease by protecting the cervix: The unexplored promise of internal vaginal barrier devices. *AIDS, 15,* 1595–1602.

MOFENSON, L. M., et al. (1999). Risk factors for perinatal transmission of human immunodeficiency virus type 1 in women treated with zidovudine. *New England Journal of Medicine, 341,* 385–393.

MOIN, V., DUVDEVANY, I., & MAZOR, D. (2009). Sexual identity, body image and life satisfaction among women with and without physical disability. *Sexuality and Disability, 27,* 83–95.

MOLLER, L. C., HYMEL, S., & RUBIN, K. H. (1992). Sex typing in play and popularity in middle childhood. *Sex Roles, 26,* 331–335.

MOLNAR, B. E., BUKA, S. L., & KESSLER, R. C. (2001). Child sexual abuse and subsequent psychopathology: Results from the National Comorbidity Survey. *American Journal of Public Health, 91,* 753–760.

MONAGHAN, L. F. (2002). Vocabularies of motive for illicit use among bodybuilders. *Social Science & Medicine, 55,* 695–708.

MONEY, J. (1970). Clitoral size and erotic sensation. *Medical Aspects of Human Sexuality, 4,* 95.

MONEY, J. (1975). Ablatio penis: Normal male infant sex-reassigned as a girl. *Archives of Sexual Behavior, 4,* 65–72.

MONEY, J. (1986). *Lovemaps: Clinical concepts of sexualerotic health and pathology, paraphilia, and gender transposition in childhood, adolescence, and maturity.* New York: Irvington.

MONEY, J., & EHRHARDT, A. E. (1972). *Man & woman, boy & girl.* Baltimore: Johns Hopkins University Press.

MONTO, M. A. (2001). Prostitution and fellatio. *Journal of Sex Research, 38,* 140–145.

MONTO, M. A. (2004). Female prostitution, customers, and violence. *Violence Against Women, 10,* 160–188.

MONTO, M. A., & MCREE, N. (2005). A comparison of the male customers of female street prostitutes with national samples of men. *International Journal of Offender Therapy and Comparative Criminology, 49,* 505–529.

MOORE, H. (1994). In P. Harvey & P. Gow. (Eds.), *Sex and violence: Issues in representation and experience.* New York: Routledge.

MOORE, K. (1993). *The developing human: Clinically oriented embryology* (5th ed.). Philadelphia: Saunders.

MOORE, M.T. (2010, January 8). "Shocking" abuse in juvenile prisons. *USA Today,* 3A.

MOORE, N. B., & DAVIDSON, J. K. (1997). Guilt about first intercourse: An antecedent of sexual dissatisfaction among college women. *Journal of Sex & Marital Therapy, 23,* 29–46.

MORAN, J. P. (2000). *Teaching sex: The shaping of adolescence in the Twentieth Century.* Cambridge, MA: Harvard University Press.

MØRCH, L. S., et al. (2009). Hormone therapy and ovarian cancer. *Journal of the American Medical Association, 302,* 298–305.

MOREAU, R., & HUSSAIN, Z. (2005, March 28), "I decided to fight back." *Newsweek,* 36.

MORGAN, D., et al. (2002). Progression to symptomatic disease in people infected with HIV-1 in rural Uganda: Prospective cohort study. *British Medical Journal, 324,* 193–197.

MORLEY, J. E. (2001). Andropause: Is it time for the geriatrician to treat it? *Journal of Gerontology, 56A,* M263–M265.

MOROKOFF, P. J., & GILLILLAND, R. (1993). Stress, sexual functioning, and marital satisfaction. *Journal of Sex Research, 30,* 43–53.

MORSE, E. V., et al. (1992). Sexual behavior patterns of customers of male street prostitutes. *Archives of Sexual Behavior, 21,* 347–357.

MORTENSEN, E. L., et al. (2002). The association between duration of breastfeeding and adult intelligence. *Journal of the American Medical Association, 287,* 2365–2371.

MOSER, C., & LEVITT, E. (1987). An exploratory-descriptive study of a sadomasochistically oriented sample. *Journal of Sex Research, 23,* 322–337.

MOSHER, D., & ANDERSON, R. (1986). Macho personality, sexual aggression, and reactions to guided imagery of realistic rape. *Journal of Research in Personality, 20,* 77–94.

MOSHER, W. D., & PRATT W. F. (1991). Fecundity and infertility in the United States: Incidence and trends. *Fertility and Sterility, 56,* 192–193.

MOSKOWITZ, D. A., RIEGER, G., & ROLOFF, M. E. (2010). Heterosexual attitudes toward same-sex marriage. *Journal of Homosexuality, 57,* 325–336.

MOSTAD, S. B., & KREISS, J. K. (1996). Shedding of HIV-1 in the genital tract. *AIDS, 10,* 1305–1315.

MOYER, A. (1997). Psychosocial outcomes of breast-conserving surgery versus mastectomy: A meta-analytic review. *Health Psychology, 16,* 284–298.

MUEHLENHARD, C. L. (1998). The importance and danger of studying sexually aggressive women. In P. B. Anderson & C. Struckman-Johnson (Eds.), *Sexually aggressive women* (pp. 19–48). New York: Guilford Press.

MUEHLENHARD, C. L., & COOK, S. W. (1988). Men's self-reports of unwanted sexual activity. *Journal of Sex Research, 24,* 58–72.

MUEHLENHARD, C. L., & HOLLABAUGH, L. (1989). Do women sometimes say no when they mean yes? The prevalence and correlates of women's token resistance to sex. *Journal of Personality and Social Psychology, 54,* 872–879.

MUEHLENHARD, C. L., ANDREWS, S. L., & BEAL, G. K. (1996). Beyond "just saying no": Dealing with men's unwanted sexual advances in heterosexual dating contexts. *Journal of Psychology and Human Sexuality, 8,* 141–168.

MUELLER, K. E., & POWERS, W. G. (1990). Parent-child sexual discussion: Perceived communicator style and subsequent behavior. *Adolescence, 25,* 469–482.

MUESER, K. T., & TAYLOR, K. L. (1997). A cognitive-behavioral approach. In M. Harris & C. L. Landis (Eds.), *Sexual abuse in the lives of women diagnosed with serious mental illness* (pp. 67–90). Amsterdam: Harwood Academic Publishers.

MULLEN, P. E., KING, N. J., & TONGE, B. J. (2000). Child sexual abuse: An overview. *Behaviour Change, 17,* 2–14.

MUNJACK, D. J., & KANNO, P. H. (1979). Retarded ejaculation: A review. *Archives of Sexual Behavior, 8,* 139–150.

MUNOZ, A., & XU, J. (1996). Models for the incubation of AIDS and variations according to age and period. *Statistics in Medicine, 15,* 2459–2473.

MURDOCK, G. P. (1967). *Ethnographic atlas.* Pittsburgh: University of Pittsburgh Press.

MURNEN, S. K. (2000). Gender and the use of sexually degrading language. *Psychology of Women Quarterly, 24,* 319–327.

MURNEN, S. K., & STOCKTON, M. (1997). Gender and self-reported sexual arousal in response to sexual stimuli: A meta-analytic review. *Sex Roles, 37,* 135–153.

MURNEN, S. K., WRIGHT, C., & KALUZNY, G. (2002). If "boys will be boys," then girls will be victims? A meta-analytic review of the research that relates masculine ideology to sexual aggression. *Sex Roles, 46,* 359–375.

MURPHY, J. J., & BOGGESS, S. (1998). Increased condom use among teenage males, 1988–1995: The role of attitudes. *Family Planning Perspectives, 30,* 276–280, 303.

MURPHY, T. F. (1992). Redirecting sexual orientation: Techniques and justifications. *Journal of Sex Research, 29,* 501–523.

MURPHY, W. D., & PAGE, J. J. (2008). Exhibitionism: Psychopathology and theory. In D. R. Laws & W. T. O'Donohue (Eds.), *Sexual deviance: Theory, assessment, and treatment* (2nd ed., pp. 61–75). New York: Guilford Press.

MURRAY, J. (1995). Thinking about gender. The diversity of medieval perspectives. In J. Carpenter & S.-B. MacLean (Eds.), *Power of the weak. Women in the Middle Ages* (pp. 1–26). Chicago: University of Illinois.

MURRAY, J. (1998). Men's bodies, men's minds: Seminal emissions and sexual anxiety in the-Middle Ages. In J. R. Heiman & C. M. Davis (Eds.), *Annual review of sex research* (Vol. VIII, pp. 1–26). Allentown, PA: Society for the Scientific Study of Sexuality.

MURRAY, S. (1992). *Oceanic homosexualities.* New York: Garland.

MURRAY, S. L., HOLMES, J. G., & GRIFFIN, D. W. (1996). The self-fulfilling nature of positive illusions in romantic relationships: Love is not blind, but prescient. *Journal of Personality and Social Psychology, 71,* 1155–1180.

MURSTEIN, B. I. (1988). A taxonomy of love. In R. J. Sternberg & M. L. Barnes (Eds.), *The psychology of love* (pp. 13–37). New Haven, CT: Yale University Press.

MUSACCHIO, N. S., HARTRICH, M., & GAROFALO, R. (2006). Erectile dysfunction and Viagra use: What's up with college-age males? *Journal of Adolescent Health*, 39, 452–454.

MUSTANSKI, B. S., CHIVERS, M. L., & BAILEY, J. M. (2007). A critical review of recent biological research on human sexual orientation. In J. R. Heiman & C. M. Davis (Eds.), *Annual Review of Sex Research*, (Vol. XIII, pp. 89–140). Allentown, PA: The Society for the Scientific Study of Sexuality.

MYERS, G., MACINNES, K., & KORBER, B. (1992). The emergence of simian/human immunodeficiency viruses. *AIDS Research and Human Retroviruses*, 8, 373–386.

N

NAJMAN, J. M., DUNNE, M. P., & BOYLE, F. M. (2007). Childhood sexual abuse and adult sexual dysfunction: Response to commentary by Rind and Tromovitch (2007). *Archives of Sexual Behavior*, 36, 107–109.

NAJMAN, J. M., et al. (2005). Sexual abuse in childhood and sexual dysfunction in adulthood: An Australian population-based study. *Archives of Sexual Behavior*, 34, 517–526.

NAJMAN, J. M., et al. (2007). Sexual abuse in childhood and physical and mental health in adulthood: An Australian population study. *Archives of Sexual Behavior*, 36, 666–675.

NANDA, K. (2008). Contraceptive patch and vaginal contraceptive ring. In R. A. Hatcher et al. (Eds.), *Contraceptive technology* (19th ed., pp. 271–295). New York: Ardent Media.

NAPPI, R. E., & LACHOWSKY, M. (2009). Menopause and sexuality: Prevalence of symptoms and impact on quality of life. *Maturitas*, 63, 138–141.

NAROD, S., et al. (2002). Oral contraceptives and the risk of breast cancer in BR CA 1 and BR CA 2 mutation carriers. *Journal of the National Cancer Institute*, 94, 1773–1779.

NATIONAL CAMPAIGN TO PREVENT TEEN PREGNANCY. (1997). *Whatever happened to childhood? The problem of teen pregnancy in the United States.* Washington, DC: NCPTP.

NATIONAL CAMPAIGN to PREVENT TEEN and UNPLANNED PREGNANCY. (2010). http://www.thenationalcampaign.org/sextech/PDF/SexTech_summary.pdf

NATIONAL CENTER FOR HEALTH STATISTICS. (2005, 2006, 2007, 2008). www.cdc.gov/nchs

NATIONAL INSTITUTES OF HEALTH (NIH). (1992). *Impotence.* NIH Consensus Statement, 10(4), 1–33.

NATIONAL INSTITUTES OF HEALTH. (1997) Consensus Development Conference Statement, February, 11–13.

NAY, R., & GORMAN, D. (1999). Sexuality in aged care. In R. Nay & S. Garratt (Eds.), *Nursing older people: Issues and innovations* (pp. 193–211). Sydney, Australia: MacLennan & Petty.

NELSON, A. L. (2008). Combined oral contraceptives. In R. A. Hatcher et al. (Eds.), *Contraceptive technology* (19th ed., pp. 193–270). New York: Ardent Media.

NELSON, A. L., & BALDWIN, S. (2008). Menstrual disorders and related concerns. In R. A. Hatcher et al. (Eds.), *Contraceptive technology* (19th ed., pp. 451–498). New York: Ardent Media.

NELSON, A. L., & STEWART, F. H. (2008). Menopause and perimenopausal health. In R. A. Hatcher et al. (Eds.), *Contraceptive technology* (19th ed., pp. 699–745). New York: Ardent Media.

NELSON, H. D., et al. (2002). Post-menopausal hormone replacement therapy. Scientific review. *Journal of the American Medical Association*, 288, 872–881.

NELSON, L. J., et al. (2007). "If you want me to treat you like an adult, start acting like one!" Comparing the criteria that emerging adults and their parents have for adulthood. *Journal of Family Psychology*, 21, 665–674.

NELSON, W., et al. (2009). Adherence to cervical cancer screening guidelines for U.S. women aged 25–64: Data from the 2005 Health Information National Trends Survey (HINTS). *Journal of Women's Health*, 18, 1759–1768.

NESS, R. B., et al. (1993). Number of pregnancies and the subsequent risk of cardiovascular disease. *New England Journal of Medicine*, 328, 1528–1533.

NEWSWEEK. (1989). Pregnancy + alcohol = problems. July 31, 57–59.

NEWSWEEK. (2006, May 15). AIDS at 25.

NIELSON, J., & WOHLERT, M. (1991). Chromosome abnormalities found among 34,910 newborn children: Results from a 13-year incidence study in Arhus, Denmark. *Human Genetics*, 87, 81–83.

NIETO, J. A. (2004). Children and adolescents as sexual beings: Cross-cultural perspectives. *Child and Adolescent Psychiatric Clinics of North America*, 13, 461–477.

NIXON, K., et al. (2002). The everyday occurrence: Violence in the lives of girls exploited through prostitution. *Violence Against Women*, 8, 1016–1043.

NOAR, S. M., CARLYLE, K., & COLE, C. (2006). Why communication is crucial: Meta-analysis of the relationship between safer sexual communication and condom use. *Journal of Health Communication*, 11, 365–390.

NOAR, S. M., MOROKOFF, P. J., & HARLOW, L. L. (2002). Condom negotiation in heterosexual active men and women: Development and validation of a condom influence strategy questionnaire. *Psychology and Health*, 17, 711–735.

NOEL, J. E., et al. (2009). The effects of alcohol and cue salience on young men's acceptance of sexual aggression. *Addictive Behaviors*, 34, 386–394.

NOLL, N. E., et al. (2009). Sexual and physical revictimization among victims of severe childhood sexual abuse. *Child Abuse & Neglect*, 33, 412–420.

NONOYAMA, M., et al. (2005). Influences of sex-related information for STD prevention. *Journal of Adolescent Health*, 36, 442–445.

NOONAN, D., & SPRINGEN, K. (2001, August 13). When dad is a donor. *Newsweek*, 46.

NORDENTOFT, M., et al. (1996). Intrauterine growth retardation and premature delivery: The influence of maternal smoking and psychosocial factors. *American Journal of Public Health*, 86, 347–354.

NORTON-HAWK, M. A. (2001). The counterproductivity of incarcerating female street prostitutes. *Deviant Behavior: An Interdisciplinary Journal*, 22, 403–417.

NORWITZ, E. R., ROBINSON, J. N., & CHALLIS, J. R. G. (1999). The control of labor. *New England Journal of Medicine*, 341, 660–666.

NOSEK, M. A., et al. (1997). *National study of women with physical disabilities: Final report.* Houston, TX: Center for Research on Women with Disabilities.

NOTARIUS, C. I., & MARKMAN, H. J. (1993). *Love can work it out: Making sense of marital conflict.* New York: Putnam's.

NOTARIUS, C. I., LASHLEY, S. L., & SULLIVAN, D. J. (1997). Angry at your partner? Think again. In R. J. Sternberg & M. Hojjat (Eds.), *Satisfaction in close relationships* (pp. 219–248). New York: Guilford Press.

NUGTEREN, H. M., et al. (2010a). 18-year experience in the management of men with a complaint of a small penis. *Journal of Sex & Marital Therapy*, 36, 109–117.

NUGTEREN, H. M., et al. (2010b). Penile enlargement: From medication to surgery. *Journal of Sex & Marital Therapy*, 36, 118–123.

NUTTER, D. E., & KEARNS, M. E. (1993). Patterns of exposure to sexually explicit material among sex offenders, child molesters, and controls. *Journal of Sex & Marital Therapy*, 19, 77–85.

NYGREN, A. (1982). *Agape and eros.* Chicago: University of Chicago Press.

NYITRAY, A. G., et al. (2010). Prevalence of and risk factors for anal human papillomavirus infection in men who have sex with women: A cross-national study. *Journal of Infectious Diseases*, 201, 1498–1508.

O

O'BRIEN, M., & HUSTON, A. C. (1985). Development of sex-typed play behavior in toddlers. *Developmental Psychology*, 21, 866–871.

O'BRIEN, M. E., et al. (2003). Prevalence and correlates of HIV serostatus disclosure. *Sexually Transmitted Diseases*, 30, 731–735.

O'BRIEN, W. A., et al. (1996). Changes in plasma HIV-1 RNA and CD4+ lymphocyte counts and the risk of progression to AIDS. *New England Journal of Medicine*, 334, 426–431.

O'CONNELL, H. E., & DELANCEY, D. O. (2005). Clitoral anatomy in nulliparous, healthy, premenopausal volunteers using enhanced magnetic resonance imaging. *Journal of Urology*, 173, 2060–2063.

ODDEN, T., & FICK, D. (1998). Identifying and managing exercise-induced amenorrhea. *Journal of the American Academy of Physician Assistants*, 11, 59–80.

ODENDAAL, H. J., et al. (2009). Combined effects of cigarette smoking and alcohol consumption on perinatal outcome. *Gynecologic and Obstetric Investigation*, 67, 1–8.

O'DONOHUE, W., DOWNS, K., & YEATER, E. A. (1998). Sexual harassment: A review of the literature. *Aggression and Violent Behavior*, 3, 111–128.

OFSHE, R., & WATTERS, E. (1994). *Making monsters.* New York: Scribner's.

OGDEN, S. R., & BRADBURN, N. M. (1968). Dimensions of marriage happiness. *American Journal of Sociology*, 73, 715–731.

OGLE, S., GLASIER, A., & RILEY, S. C. (2008). Communication between parents and their children about sexual health. *Contraception*, 77, 283–288.

O'HARE, E. H., & O'DONOHUE, W. (1999). Sexual harassment: Identifying risk factors. *Archives of Sexual Behavior*, 27, 561–580.

OINONEN, K. A., & MAZMANIAN, D. (2002). To what extent do oral contraceptives influence mood and affect? *Journal of Affective Disorders*, 70, 229–240.

OKAMI, P. (1991). Self-reports of "positive" childhood and adolescent sexual contacts with older persons: An exploratory study. *Archives of Sexual Behavior*, 20, 437–457.

OKAMI, P., & GOLDBERG, A. (1992). Personality correlates of pedophilia: Are they reliable indicators? *Journal of Sex Research*, 29, 297–328.

OKAZAKI, S. (2002). Influences of culture on Asian Americans' sexuality. *Journal of Sex Research*, 39, 34–41.

OLIVER, M. B., & HYDE, J. S. (1993). Gender differences in sexuality: A meta-analysis. *Psychological Bulletin*, 114, 29–51.

OLIWENSTEIN, L. (2005). On fertile ground. *Psychology Today*, 38, 62–66.

OLSSON, S.-E., & MÖLLER, A. R. (2003). On the incidence and sex ratio of transsexualism in Sweden, 1972–2002. *Archives of Sexual Behavior*, 32, 381–386.

ONAMI, S., et al. (2010). Male breast cancer: An update in diagnosis, treatment and molecular profiling. *Maturitas*, 65, 308–314.

ONCALE, R. M., & KING, B. M. (2001). Comparison of men's and women's attempts to dissuade sexual partners from the couple using condoms. *Archives of Sexual Behavior*, 30, 379–391.

ONDERSMA, S. J., et al. (2001). Sex with children is abuse: Comment on Rind, Tromovitch, and Bauserman (1998). *Psychological Bulletin*, 127, 707–714.

O'RAND, M. G., et al. (2004). Reversible immunocontraception in male monkeys immunized with eppin. *Science*, 306, 1189–1190.

ORGEBIN-CRIST, M.-C. (1998). The epididymis across 24 centuries. *Journal of Reproduction and Fertility*, 53(Suppl.), 285–292.

OSMAN, A., & AL-SAWAF, M. (1995). Cross-cultural aspects of sexual anxieties and the associated dysfunction. *Journal of Sex Education and Therapy*, 21, 174–181.

OSMAN, S. L. (2007). Predicting perceptions of sexual harassment based on type of resistance and belief in token resistance. *Journal of Sex Research*, 44, 340–346.

OSTRANDER, N. (2009). Sexual pursuits of pleasure among men and women with spinal cord injuries. *Sexuality and Disability*, 27, 11–19.

O'SULLIVAN, C. S. (1991). Acquaintance gang rape on campus. In A. Parrot & L. Bechhofer (Eds.), *Acquaintance rape: The hidden crime*. New York: John Wiley & Sons.

OSWALT, S. B., CAMERON, K. A., & KOOB, J. J. (2005). Sexual regret in college students. *Archives of Sexual Behavior*, 34, 663–669.

OTT, M. A., et al. (2002). The trade-off between hormonal contraceptives and condoms among adolescents. *Perspectives on Sexual and Reproductive Health*, 34, 6–14.

OTT, M. A., et al. (2006). Greater expectations: Adolescents' positive motivations for sex. *Perspectives on Sexual and Reproductive Health*, 38, 84–89.

OTT, M. A. et al. (2008). The influence of hormonal contraception on mood and sexual interest among adolescents. *Archives of Sexual Behavior*, 37, 605–613.

OWEN, J. J., et al. (2010). "Hooking up" among college students: Demographic and psychosocial correlates. *Archives of Sexual Behavior*, 39, 653–663.

OWEN, L. (1993). *Her blood is gold*. San Francisco: HarperCollins.

ÖZKAN, S., & ARICI, A. (2009). Advances in treatment options of endometriosis. *Gynecologic and Obstetric Investigation*, 67, 81–91.

P

PAIK, A. (2010). The contexts of sexual involvement and concurrent sexual partnerships. *Perspectives on Sexual and Reproductive Health*, 42, 33–42.

PAINE, M. L., & HANSEN, D. J. (2002). Factors influencing children to self-disclose sexual abuse. *Clinical Psychology Review*, 22, 271–295.

PAINTER, K. (2009, July 20). Prisoners of their periods. *USA Today*, 4D.

PAINTER, K. (2010, August 2). Hot flashes: An 'enigma.' The marker of menopause still not fully understood. *USA Today*, 5D.

PALACIOS, S., CASTAÑO, R., & GRAZZIOTIN, A. (2009). Epidemiology of female sexual dysfunction. *Maturitas*, 63, 119–123.

PALEFSKY, J. M. (2010). Human papillomavirus-related disease in men: Not just a women's disease. *Journal of Adolescent Health*, 46 (Suppl 4), S12–S19.

PALMER, L. D. (1999, December 12). Hermaphrodite activists urge-medical reforms. *New Orleans Times-Picayune*, pp. A28–A30. Newhouse News Service nationally released article.

PANCHAUD, C., et al. (2000). Sexually transmitted diseases among adolescents in developed countries. *Family Planning Perspectives*, 32, 24–32, 45.

PAOLUCCI, E. O., GENUIS, M. L., & VIOLATO, C. (2001). A meta-analysis of the published research on the effects of child sexual abuse. *Journal of Psychology*, 135, 17–36.

PAPP, I. M., KOUROS, C. D., & CUMMINGS, G. M. (2009). Demand-withdraw patterns in marital conflict in the home. *Personal Relationships*, 16, 285–300.

PARDUN, C. J., & MCKEE, K. B. (1995). Strange bedfellows: Images of religion and sexuality on MTV. *Youth and Society*, 26, 438–449.

PARK, A. (2010, January 25). The man who would beat AIDS. *Time*, 44–47.

PARROTT, D. J. (2009). Aggression toward gay men as gender role enforcement: Effects of male role norms, sexual prejudice, and masculine gender role stress. *Journal of Personality*, 77, 1137–1166.

PARSONS, J. T. (2005). Researching the world's oldest profession: Introduction. *Journal of Psychology and Human Sexuality*, 17, 1–3.

PARSONS, M. (2000). Sexuality and perversion a hundred years on: Discovering what Freud discovered. *International Journal of Psychoanalysis*, 81, 37–51.

PASTERSKI, V., et al. (2007). Increased aggression and activity level in 3- to 11-year-old girls with congenital adrenal hyperplasia (CAH). *Hormones and Behavior*, 52, 368–374.

PASTNER, C. M. (1986). The Westermarck hypothesis and first cousin marriage: The cultural modification of negative imprinting. *Journal of Anthropological Research*, 24, 573–586.

PATRICK, D. L., et al. (2005). Premature ejaculation: An observational study of men and their partners. *Journal of Sexual Medicine*, 2, 358–367.

PATTATUCCI, A. M. L., & HAMER, D. H. (1995). Development and familiarity of sexual orientation in females. *Behavior Genetics*, 25, 407–420.

PATTERSON, C. J. (2006). Children of lesbian and gay parents. *Current Directions in Psychological Science*, 15, 241–244.

PATTERSON, C. J. (2009). Children of lesbian and gay prevents: Psychology, law, and policy. *American Psychologist*, 8, 727–736.

PATTON, G. C., & VINER, R. (2007). Pubertal transitions in health. *The Lancet*, 369, 1130–1139.

PATTON, M. (1986). Twentieth-century attitudes toward masturbation. *Journal of Religion and Health*, 25, 291–302.

PAUL, M., & STEWART, F. H. (2008). Abortion. In R. A. Hatcher et al. (Eds.), *Contraceptive technology* (19th ed., pp. 637–672). New York: Ardent Media.

PAUL, P. (2004, January 19). The porn factor. *Time*.

PAULOZZI, L. J., ERICKSON, J. D., & JACKSON, R. J. (1997). Hypospadias trends in two U.S. surveillance systems. *Pediatrics*, 100, 831–834.

PAULSON, J. F., & BAZEMORE, S. D. (2010). Prenatal and postpartum depression in fathers and its association with maternal depression. *Journal of the American Medical Association*, 303, 1961–1969.

PAULY, I. B. (1985). Gender identity disorder. In M. Farber (Ed.), *Human sexuality: Psychosexual effects of disease* (pp. 295–316). New York: Macmillan.

PAZ-BAILEY, G., et al. (2005). The effect of correct and consistent condom use on chlamydial and gonococcal infection among urban adolescents. *Archives of Pediatric and Adolescent Medicine*, 159, 536–542.

PEARLSTEIN, T., et al. (2009). Postpartum depression. *American Journal of Obstetrics & Gynecology*, 200, 357–364.

PEELE, S. (1988). Fools for love: The romantic ideal, psychological theory, and addictive love. In R. J. Sternberg & M. L. Barnes (Eds.), *The psychology of love* (pp. 159–188). New Haven, CT: Yale University Press.

PELLETIER, L., & HAROLD, E. (1988). The relationship of age, sex guilt, and sexual experience with female sexual fantasies. *Journal of Sex Research*, 24, 250–256.

PENLAND, L. (1981). Sex education in 1900, 1940, and 1980: A historical sketch. *Journal of School Health*, 51, 305–309.

PENTON-VOAK, I. S., et al. (1999). Menstrual cycle alters face preference. *Nature*, 399, 741–742.

PEPLAU, L. A. (1988). Research on homosexual couples. In J. De Cecco (Ed.), *Gay relationships*. New York: Haworth Press.

PEPLAU, L. A. (2003). Human sexuality: How do men and women differ? *Current Directions in Psychological Science*, 12, 37–40.

PEPLAU, L. A., & FINGERHUT, A. W. (2007). The close relationships of lesbians and gay men. *Annual Review of Psychology*, 58, 10.1–10.20.

PEREDA, N., et al. (2009). The international epidemiology of child sexual abuse: A continuation of Finkelhor (1994). *Child Abuse & Neglect*, 33, 331–342.

PERELMAN, M. A. (2002). FSD partner issues: Expanding sex therapy with sildenafil. *Journal of Sex & Marital Therapy*, 28(s), 195–204.

PERELSON, A. S., et al. (1996). HIV-1 dynamics in vivo: Virion clearance rate, infected cell life-span, and viral generation time. *Science*, 271, 1582–1586.

PERLMAN, D. (2002). Maintaining and enhancing relationships: Concluding commentary. In J. M. Harvey and A. E. Wenzel (Eds.), *Close romantic relationships: Maintenance and enhancement*. Mahwah, NJ: Lawrence Erlbaum.

PERRY, E. L., SCHMIDTKE, J. M., & KULIK, C. T. (1998). Propensity to sexually harass: An exploration of gender differences. *Sex Roles*, 38, 443–460.

PERRY, J. D., & WHIPPLE, B. (1981). Pelvic muscle strength of female ejaculators: Evidence in support of a new theory of orgasm. *Journal of Sex Research*, 17, 22–39.

PERSKY, H., et al. (1982). The relation of plasma androgen levels to sexual behavior and attitudes of women. *Psychosomatic Medicine*, 44, 305–319.

PETER, J., & VALKENBURG, P. M. (2009a). Adolescents' exposure to sexually explicit material and notions of women as sex objects: Assessing causality and underlying processes. *Journal of Communication*, 59, 407–433.

PETER, J., & VALKENBURG, P. M. (2009b). Adolescents' exposure to sexually explicit Internet material and sexual satisfaction: A longitudinal study. *Human Communication Research*, 35, 171–194.

PETER, T. (2009). Exploring taboos. *Journal of Interpersonal Violence*, 24, 1111–1128.

PETERSEN, J. L., & HYDE, J. S. (2010). A meta-analytic review of research on gender differences in sexuality, 1993–2007. *Psychological Bulletin*, 136, 21–38.

PETERSON, H. B., et al. (2000). The risk of menstrual abnormalities after tubal sterilization. *New England Journal of Medicine*, 343, 1681–1687.

PETERSON, J. L., MOORE, K. A., & FURSTENBERG, F. F. (1991). Television viewing and early initiation of sexual intercourse: Is there a link? *Journal of Homosexuality, 21*, 93–119.

PETRI, JR., W. A., & SINGH, V. (1999). Diagnosis and management of amebiasis. *Clinical Infectious Diseases, 29*, 1117–1125.

PHAM, P. A. (2009). Antiretroviral adherence and pharmacokinetics: Review of their roles in sustained virologic suppression. *AIDS Patient Care and STDs, 23*, 803–807.

PHILLIPS, G., & OVER, R. (1995). Differences between heterosexual, bisexual, and lesbian women in recalled childhood experiences. *Archives of Sexual Behavior, 24*, 1–10.

PIETRZAK, R. H., et al. (2002). Sex differences in human jealousy: A coordinated study of forced choice, continuous rating-scale and physiological responses on the same subjects. *Evolution and Human Behavior, 23*, 83–94.

PIMENTEL, D. (1998). Too many people for food resources and the environment. *Politics and the Life Sciences, 16*, 217–219.

PINES, A., & ARONSON, E. (1983). Antecedents, correlates, and consequences of sexual jealousy. *Journal of Personality, 51*, 108–136.

PIOT, P., et al. (2009). AIDS: Lessons learnt and myths dispelled. *The Lancet, 374*, 260–263.

PIPKIN, F. B. (2001). Risk factors for preeclampsia. *New England Journal of Medicine, 344*, 925–926.

PITTS JR., L. (2001, August 3). Give girls credit for delaying motherhood. *New Orleans Times-Picayune*, p. B7.

PITTS, M. K., et al. (2004). Who pays for sex and why? An analysis of social and motivational factors associated with male clients of sex workers. *Archives of Sexual Behavior, 33*, 353–358.

PLACE, S. S., et al. (2009). The ability to judge the romantic interest of others. *Psychological Sciences, 20*, 22–26.

PLANT, T. M., et al. (1993). The follicle stimulating hormone–inhibin feedback loop in male primates. *Human Reproduction, 8*(Suppl. 2), 41–44.

PLECK, J. H. (1976). The male sex role: Definitions, problems and sources of change. *Journal of Social Issues, 32*(3), 155–164.

PLÖDERL, M., KRALOVEC, K., & FARTACEK, R. (2010). The relation between sexual orientation and suicide attempts in Austria. *Archives of Sexual Behavior, 39*, 1403–1414.

PLUMMER, D. C. (2001). The quest for modern manhood: Masculine stereotypes, peer culture and the social significance of homophobia. *Journal of Adolescence, 24*, 15–23.

POCS, O., & GODOW, A. G. (1977). Can students view parents as sexual beings? *Family Coordinator, 26*, 31–36.

POIRIER, J. C., & FRANKOVIC, J. (1996). Celibacy and charism in 1 Corinthians 7:5–7. *Harvard Theological Review, 89*, 1–19.

POLAND, R. L. (1990). The question of routine neonatal circumcision. *New England Journal of Medicine, 322*, 1312–1315.

POLASCHEK, D. L. L., & GANNON, T. A. (2004). The implicit theories of rapists: What convicted offenders tell us. *Sexual Abuse: A Journal of Research and Treatment, 16*, 299–315.

POLASCHEK, D. L. L., & WARD, T. (2002). The implicit theories of potential rapists: What our questionnaires tell us. *Aggression and Violent Behavior, 7*, 385–406.

POLASCHEK, D. L. L., WARD, T., & HUDSON, S. M. (1997). Rape and rapists: Theory and treatment. *Clinical Psychology Review, 17*, 117–144.

POLICAR, M. S. (2008). Female genital tract cancer screening. In R. A. Hatcher et al.

(Eds.), *Contraceptive technology* (19th ed., pp. 559–590). New York: Ardent Media.

POLLACK, A. E., THOMAS, L. J., & BARONE, M. A. (2008). Female and male sterilization. In R. A. Hatcher et al. (Eds.), *Contraceptive technology* (19th ed., pp. 361–401). New York: Ardent Media.

POMEROY, W. B. (1966). Normal vs. abnormal sex. *Sexology, 32*, 436–439.

POPE, H. G., et al. (1999). Evolving ideals of male body image as seen through action toys. *International Journal of Eating Disorders, 26*, 65–72.

POPE, JR., H. G., & KATZ, D. L. (1988). Affective and psychotic symptoms associated with anabolic steroid use. *American Journal of Psychiatry, 145*, 487–490.

POPE, J. (2004, August 5). Special delivery. *New Orleans Times-Picayune*, p. A1, A4.

PORTER, S., YUILLE, J. C., & LEHMAN, D. R. (1999). The nature of real, implanted, and fabricated childhood emotion events: Implications for the recovered memory debate. *Law and Human Behavior, 23*, 517–537.

POTTER, J., et al. (2009). Premenstrual syndrome prevalence and fluctuation over time: Results from a French population-based survey. *Journal of Women's Health, 18*, 31–39.

POTTERAT, J. J., et al. (1990). Estimating the prevalence and career longevity of prostitute women. *Journal of Sex Research, 27*, 233–243.

POTTERAT, J. J., et al. (1998). Pathways to prostitution: The chronology of sexual and drug abuse milestones. *Journal of Sex Research, 35*, 333–340.

POTTS, M. (2000, January). The unmet need for family planning. *Scientific American*, 88–93.

POWER, C., RADCLIFFE, L., & MACGREGOR, K. (2003, November 17). Preying on children. *Newsweek International, 34*–35.

POWLISHTA, K., SERBIN, L., & MOLLER, L. (1993). The stability of individual differences in gender typing: Implication for understanding gender segregation. *Sex Roles, 29*, 723–737.

PRÓSPERO, M., & FAWSON, P. (2010). Sexual coercion and mental health symptoms among heterosexual men: The pressure to say "yes." *American Journal of Men's Health, 4*, 98–103.

PRAUSE, N., & GRAHAM, C. A. (2007). Asexuality: Classification and characterization. *Archives of Sexual Behavior, 36*, 341–356.

PRENDERGAST, S., DUNNE, G. A., & TELFORD, D. (2002). A story of "difference," a different story: Young homeless lesbian, gay and bisexual people. *International Journal of Sociology and Social Policy, 21*, 64–91.

PRENTKY, R. A., KNIGHT, R. A., & ROSENBERG, R. (1988). Validation analysis on a taxonomic system for rapists: Disconfirmation and reconceptualization. *Annals of the New York Academy of Sciences, 528*, 21–40.

PRENTKY, R. A., et al. (1989). Developmental antecedents of sexual aggression. *Development and Psychopathology, 1*, 153–169.

PRENTKY, R. A., et al. (1997). Recidivism rates among child molesters and rapists: A methodological analysis. *Law and Human Behavior, 21*, 635–659.

PRETI, G., et al. (1986). Human axillary secretions influence women's menstrual cycles: The role of donor extract of females. *Hormones and Behavior, 20*, 474–482.

PRICE, M., et al. (2001a). Telephone scatologia: Comorbidity and theories of etiology. *Psychiatric Annals, 31*, 226–232.

PRICE, M., et al. (2001b). Redefining telephone scatologia: Treatment and classification. *Psychiatric Annals, 31*, 282–289.

PRICE, S. (2008). Women and reproductive loss: Client-worker dialogues designed to

break the silence. *Social Work, 53*, 367–375.

PROFET, M. (1993). Menstruation as a defense against pathogens transported by sperm. *Quarterly Review of Biology, 68*, 335–381.

PUENTES, J., KNOX, D., & ZUSMAN, M. (2008). Participants in "friends with benefits" relationships. *College Student Journal, 42*, 176–180.

PURCELL, R., et al. (2009). Stalking among juveniles. *British Journal of Psychiatry, 194*, 451–455.

PURINE, D. M., & CAREY, M. P. (1997). Interpersonal communication and sexual adjustment: The roles of understanding and agreement. *Journal of Consulting and Clinical Psychology, 65*, 1017–1025.

PUTNAM, F. W. (2003). Ten-year research update review: Child sexual abuse. *Journal of the American Academy of Child and Adolescent Psychiatry, 42*, 269–278.

PYETT, P. M., & WARR, D. J. (1997). Vulnerability on the streets: Female sex workers and HIV risk. *AIDS Care, 9*, 539–547.

Q

QUADAGNO, D., et al. (1998). Ethnic differences in sexual decisions and sexual behavior. *Archives of Sexual Behavior, 27*, 57–75.

QUAKENBUSH, D. M., STRASSBERG, D. S., & Turner, C. W. (1995). Gender effects of romantic themes in erotica. *Archives of Sexual Behavior, 24*, 21–35.

QUINN, T. C., et al. (2000). Viral load and heterosexual transmission of human immunodeficiency virus type 1. *New England Journal of Medicine, 342*, 921–929.

QUINSEY, V., CHAPLIN, T., & UPFOLD, D. (1984). Sexual arousal to nonsexual violence and sadomasochistic themes among rapists and non-sex-offenders. *Journal of Consulting and Clinical Psychology, 52*, 651–657.

R

RABOCH, J., & RABOCH, J. (1992). Infrequent orgasms in women. *Journal of Sex & Marital Therapy, 18*, 114–120.

RACHMAN, S. (1966). Sexual fetishism: An experimental analogue. *Psychological Record, 16*, 293–296.

RAFFAELLI, M., BOGENSCHNEIDER, L., & FLOOD, M. F. (1998). Parent-teen communication about sexual topics. *Journal of Family Issues, 19*, 315–333.

RAHMAN, Q., COCKBURN, A., & GOVIER, E. (2008). A comparative analysis of functional cerebral asymmetry in lesbian women, heterosexual women, and heterosexual men. *Archives of Sexual Behavior, 37*, 566–571.

RAHMAN, Q., & SYMEONIDES, D. J. (2008). Neurodevelopmental correlates of paraphilic sexual interests. *Archives of Sexual Behavior, 37*, 166–172.

RAHMAN, Q., & WILSON, G. D. (2003). Born gay? The psychobiology of human sexual orientation. *Personality and Individual Differences, 34*, 1337–1382.

RAISLER, J., ALEXANDER, C., & O'CAMPO, P. (1999). Breast-feeding and infant illness: A dose-response relationship? *American Journal of Public Health, 89*, 25–30.

RAKO, S., & FRIEBELY, J. (2004). Pheromonal influences on sociosexual behavior in postmenopausal women. *Journal of Sex Research, 41*, 372–380.

RANDOLPH, M. E., et al. (2007). Sexual pleasure and condom use. *Archives of Sexual Behavior, 36*, 844–848.

RANGARAJAN, A., & GLEASON, P. (1998). Young unwed fathers of AFDC children: Do they provide support? *Demography*, 35, 175–186.

RAPAPORT, K., & BURKHART, B. R. (1984). Personality and attitudinal characteristics of sexually coercive college males. *Journal of Abnormal Psychology*, 93, 216–221.

RAPKIN, A. J., & WINER, S. A. (2008). The pharmacologic management of premenstrual dysphoric disorder. *Expert Opinions in Pharmacotherapy*, 9, 429–445.

RAPOPORT, N. (1994). *A woman's book of grieving*. New York: William Morrow.

RAPP, S. R., et al. (2003). Effect of estrogen plus progestin on global cognitive function in postmenopausal women. *Journal of the American Medical Association*, 289, 2663–2672.

RASBERRY, C. N., & GOODSEN, P. (2009). Predictors of secondary abstinence in U.S. college undergraduates. *Archives of Sexual Behavior*, 38, 74–86.

RAUBE, K., & MERRELL, K. (1999). Maternal minimum-stay legislation: Cost and policy implications. *American Journal of Public Health*, 89, 922–923.

RAYMOND, E. G. (2008a). Progestin-only pills. In R. A. Hatcher et al. (Eds.), *Contraceptive technology* (19th ed., pp. 181–191). New York: Ardent Media.

RAYMOND, E. G. (2008b). Contraceptive implants. In R. A. Hatcher et al. (Eds.), *Contraceptive technology* (19th ed., pp. 145–156). New York: Ardent Media.

READ, K. (1993, April 27). Male rape: One of the last taboo topics. *New Orleans Times-Picayune*, p. E1, E3.

REBAR, R. (2004). Assisted reproductive technology in the United States. *New England Journal of Medicine*, 350, 1603–1604.

REDMON, D. (2003). Playful deviance as an urban leisure activity: Secret selves, self-validation, and entertaining performances. *Deviant Behavior*, 24, 27–51.

REECE, M., et al. (2010a). Condom use rates in a national probability sample of males and females ages 14 to 94 in the United States. *Journal of Sexual Medicine*, 7 (Suppl 5), 266–276.

REECE, M., et al. (2010b). Sexual behaviors, relationships, and perceived health among adult men in the United States: Results from a national probability sample. *Journal of Sexual Medicine*, 7 (Suppl 5), 291–304.

REECE, M., et al. (2010c). Background and considerations on the National Survey of Sexual Health and Behavior (NSSHB) from the investigators. *Journal of Sexual Medicine*, 7 (Suppl 5), 243–245.

REGAN, P. (2000). The role of sexual desire and sexual activity in dating relationships. *Social Behavior and Personality*, 28, 51–59.

REGAN, P., & ATKINS, L. (2006). Sex differences and similarities in frequency and intensity of sexual desire. *Social Behavior and Personality*, 34, 95–102.

REGAN, P. C. (1998). Of lust and love: Beliefs about the role of sexual desire in romantic relationships. *Personal Relationships*, 5, 139–157.

REGAN, P. C., & BERSCHEID, E. (1997). Gender differences in characteristics desired in a potential sexual and marriage partner. *Journal of Psychology & Human Sexuality*, 9, 25–37.

REGAN, P. C., & BERSCHEID, E. (1999). *Lust: What we know about human sexual desire*. Thousand Oaks, CA: Sage.

REGAN, P. C., et al. (2003). Pregnancy and changes in female sexual desire: A review. *Social Behavior and Personality*, 31, 603–612.

REICHERT, T. (2003). Sex in advertising research: A review of content, effects, and functions of sexual information on consumer advertising.

In J. R. Heiman & C. M. Davis (Eds.), *Annual Review of Sex Research* (Vol. XIII, pp. 241–273). Allentown, PA: The Society for the Scientific Study of Sexuality.

REINHOLTZ, R. K., & MUEHLENHARD, C. L. (1995). Genital perceptions and sexual activity in a college population. *Journal of Sex Research*, 32, 155–165.

REINISCH, J. M. (1990). *The Kinsey Institute new report on sex*. New York: St. Martin's.

REIS, H. T., & ARON, A. (2008). Love: What is it, why does it matter, and how does it operate? *Perspectives on Psychological Science*, 3, 80–86.

REISS, I. L., & LEIK, R. K. (1989). Evaluating strategies to avoid AIDS: Number of partners versus use of condoms. *Journal of Sex Research*, 4, 411–433.

REISS, M. J. (1995). Conflicting philosophies of school sex education. *Journal of Moral Education*, 24, 371–382.

REISSING, E. D., et al. (2004). Vaginal spasm, pain, and behavior: An empirical investigation of the diagnosis of vaginismus. *Archives of Sexual Behavior*, 33, 5–17.

REITZEL, L. R., & CARBONELL, J. L. (2006). The effectiveness of sexual offender treatment for juveniles as measured by recidivism: A meta-analysis. *Sex Abuse*, 18, 401–421.

REMPEL, J. K., & BAUMGARTNER, B. (2003). The relationship between attitudes towards menstruation and sexual attitudes, desires, and behavior in women. *Archives of Sexual Behavior*, 32, 155–163.

RENAUD, C. A., & BYERS, E. S. (2001). Positive and negative sexual cognitions: Subjective experience and relationships to sexual adjustment. *Journal of Sex Research*, 38, 252–262.

RENSHAW, D. (1990). Short-term therapy for sexual dysfunction: Brief counseling to manage vaginismus. *Clinical Practice in Sexuality*, 6(5), 23–29.

RENTZEL, L. (1972). *When all the laughter died in sorrow*. New York: Saturday Review Press.

REPORT OF THE COMMISSION ON OBSCENITY AND PORNOGRAPHY. (1970). New York: Bantam Books.

RESNICK, H. (2002). Rape-related HIV risk concerns among recent rape victims. *Journal of Interpersonal Violence*, 17, 746–759.

RESNICK, H. S., et al. (2000). Predictors of post-rape medical care in a national sample of women. *American Journal of Preventive Medicine*, 19, 214–219.

RESNICK, M., et al. (1997). Protecting adolescents from harm: Findings from the National Longitudinal Study on Adolescent Health. *Journal of the American Medical Association*, 278, 823–832.

RESNIK, R. (2006). Can a 29% cesarean delivery rate possibly be justified? *Obstetrics & Gynecology*, 107, 752–753.

RHOADES, G., STANLEY, S., & MARKMAN, H. (2009). Couples' reasons for cohabitation. *Journal of Family Issues*, 30, 233–258.

RICE, P. A., & SCHACHTER, J. (1991). Pathogenesis of pelvic inflammatory disease. *Journal of the American Medical Association*, 266, 2587–2593.

RICHARDS, E., et al. (1997). Women with complete spinal cord injury: A phenomenological study of sexuality and relationship experiences. *Sexuality and Disability*, 15, 271–283.

RICHARDS, R., & AMES, J. (1983). *Second serve*. New York: Stein & Day.

RICHMAN, K. M., & RICKMAN, L. S. (1993). The potential for transmission of human immunodeficiency virus through human bites. *Journal of Acquired Immune Deficiency Syndromes*, 6, 402–406.

RICHTERS, J., GEROFI, J., & DONOVAN, B. (1995). Are condoms the right size(s)? A method

for self-measurement of the erect penis. *Venereology*, 8, 77–81.

RICHTERS, J., et al. (2003a). Sex in Australia: Autoerotic, esoteric, and other sexual practices engaged in by a representative sample of adults, *Australian and New Zealand Journal of Public Health*, 27, 180–190.

RICHTERS, J., et al. (2003b). Sex in Australia: Contraceptive practices among a representative sample of women. *Australian and New Zealand Journal of Public Health*, 27, 210–216.

RICHTERS, J., et al. (2003c). Sexual difficulties in a representative sample of adults. *Australian and New Zealand Journal of Public Health*, 27, 164–170.

RICHTERS, J., et al. (2006). Sexual practices at last heterosexual encounter and occurrence of orgasm in a national survey. *Journal of Sex Research*, 43, 217–226.

RICHTERS, J. M. A. (1997). Menopause in different cultures. *Journal of Psychosomatic Obstetrics and Gynecology*, 18, 73–80.

RICKERT, V. I., et al. (2002). Is lack of sexual assertiveness among adolescent and young adult women a cause for concern? *Perspectives on Sexual and Reproductive Health*, 34(4), 178–183.

RIMM, M. (1995). Marketing pornography on the information superhighway: A survey of 917, 410 images. *Georgetown Law Review*, 83, 1849–1925.

RIND, B. (1998). Biased use of cross-cultural and historical perspectives on male homosexuality in human sexuality textbooks. *Journal of Sex Research*, 35, 397–407.

RIND, B. (2001). Gay and bisexual adolescent boys' sexual experiences with men: An empirical examination of psychological correlates in a nonclinical sample. *Archives of Sexual Behavior*, 30, 345–368.

RIND, B., & TROMOVITCH, P. (1997). A meta-analytic review of findings from national samples on psychological correlates of child sexual abuse. *Journal of Sex Research*, 34, 237–255.

RIND, B., & TROMOVITCH, P. (2007). National samples, sexual abuse in childhood, and adjustment in adulthood: A commentary on Najman, Dunne, Purdie, Boyle, and Coxeter (2005). *Archives of Sexual Behavior*, 36, 101–106.

RIND, B., TROMOVITCH, P., & BAUSERMAN, R. (1998). A meta-analytic examination of assumed properties of child sexual abuse using college samples. *Psychological Bulletin*, 124, 22–53.

RIO, L. (1991). Psychological and sociological research and the decriminalization or legalization of prostitution. *Archives of Sexual Behavior*, 20, 205–217.

RIORDAN, S. (1999). Indecent exposure: The impact upon the victim's fear of sexual crime. *Journal of Forensic Psychiatry*, 10, 309–316.

RIVKIN-FISH, M. (1999). Sexuality education in Russia: Defining pleasure and danger for a fledgling democratic society. *Social Science & Mechanics*, 49, 801–814.

ROAN, S. (1993, July 12). Are we teaching too little, too late? *Los Angeles Times*, p. E1, E4.

ROBB-NICHOLSON, C., & SCHATZ, C. (2004, May 10). The mystery of cystitis. *Newsweek*, 77.

ROBBINS, M., & JENSEN, G. (1978). Multiple orgasm in males. *Journal of Sex Research*, 14, 21–26.

ROBERTS, D. (2000). Media and youth: Access, exposure, and privatization. *Journal of Adolescent Health*, 27, 8–14.

ROBERTS, J. M., et al. (2010). Vitamins C and E to prevent complications of pregnancy-associated hypertension. *New England Journal of Medicine*, 362, 1282–1291.

ROBERTS, T.-A., et al. (2002). "Feminine protection": The effects of menstruation on attitudes towards women. *Psychology of Women Quarterly, 26,* 131–139.

ROBERTS, T. W. (1992). Sexual attraction and romantic love: Forgotten variables in marital therapy. *Journal of Marital and Family Therapy, 18,* 357–364.

ROBERTSON, D., et al. (2000). HIV-1 nomenclature proposal. *Science, 288,* 55–56.

ROBINSON, A. J., & RIDGWAY, G. L. (1994). Sexually transmitted diseases in children: Non viral including bacterial vaginosis, *Gardnerella vaginalis,* mycoplasmas, *Trichomonas vaginalis, Candida albicans,* scabies and pubic lice. *Genitourinary Medicine, 70,* 208–214.

ROBINSON, T. N., et al. (2001). Effects of reducing television viewing on children's requests for toys: A randomized controlled trial. *Journal of Developmental and Behavioral Pediatrics, 22,* 185–187.

RÖDER, S., BREWER, G., & FINK, B. (2009). Menstrual cycle shifts in women's self-perception and motivation: A daily report method. *Personality and Individual Differences, 47,* 616–619.

RODRIGUEZ, I. (2004). Pheromone receptors in mammals. *Hormones & Behavior, 46,* 219–230.

ROGERS, D. E. (1992). Report card on our national response to the AIDS epidemic—some A's, too many D's. *American Journal of Public Health, 82,* 522–524.

ROHLINGER, D. A. (2002). Eroticizing men: Cultural influences on advertising and male objectification. *Sex Roles, 46,* 61–74.

ROISMAN, G., et al. (2008). Adult romantic relationships as contexts of human development: A multimethod comparison of same-sex couples with opposite-sex dating, engaged, and married dyads. *Developmental Psychology, 44,* 91–101.

ROMIEU, I., BERLIN, J. A., & COLDITZ, G. (1990). Oral contraceptives and breast cancer: Review and meta-analysis. *Cancer, 66,* 2253–2263.

ROSARIO, M., et al. (2009). The coming-out process of young lesbian and bisexual women: Are there butch/femme differences in sexual identity development? *Archives of Sexual Behavior, 38,* 34–49.

ROSE, M. K., & SOARES, H. H. (1993). Sexual adaptations of the frail elderly: A realistic approach. *Journal of Gerontological Social Work, 19,* 167–178.

ROSELLI, C. E., RESKO, J. A., & STORMSHAK, F. (2002). Hormonal influences on sexual partner preference in rams. *Archives of Sexual Behavior, 31,* 43–49.

ROSEN, R. C. (1991). Alcohol and drug effects on sexual response: Human experimental and clinical studies. In J. Bancroft, C. M. Davis, & N. J. Ruppel, Jr. (Eds.), *Annual review of sex research* (Vol. II, pp. 119–179). Allentown, PA: Society for the Scientific Study of Sexuality.

ROSEN, R. C., & MARIN, H. (2003). Prevalence of antidepressant-associated erectile dysfunction. *Journal of Clinical Psychiatry, 64* (Suppl. 10), 5–10.

ROSENBAUM, J. E. (2006). Reborn a virgin: Adolescents' retracting of virginity pledges and sexual histories. *American Journal of Public Health, 96,* 1098–1103.

ROSENBAUM, J. E. (2009). Patient teenagers? A comparison of the sexual behavior of virginity pledgers and matched non-pledgers. *Pediatrics, 123,* e110–e120.

ROSENBAUM, R. (1999). *Explaining Hitler: The search for the origins of his evil.* New York: HarperCollins.

ROSENBERG, D. (2007, May 21). (Rethinking) gender, *Newsweek,* 50–57.

ROSENBERG, H. M., et al. (1996). Birth and deaths: United States, 1995. *Monthly Vital Statistics Report, 45*(3, Suppl. 2).

ROSENFELD, I. (2005, March 6). Good news—A better treatment for breast cancer. *Parade,* 10–11.

ROSENTHAL, D. A., & FELDMAN, S. S. (1999). The importance of importance: Adolescents' perceptions of parental communication about sexuality. *Journal of Adolescence, 22,* 835–851.

ROSMAN, J. P., & RESNICK, P. J. (1989). Sexual attraction to corpses: A psychiatric review of necrophilia. *Bulletin of the American Academy of Psychiatry and the Law, 17,* 153–163.

ROSS, J. A. (1989). Contraception: Short-term vs. long-term failure rates. *Family Planning Perspectives, 21,* 275–277.

ROSTOSKY, S. S., REGNERUS, M. D., & WRIGHT, M. L. C. (2003). Coital debut: The role of religiosity and sex attitudes in the Add Health survey. *Journal of Sex Research, 40,* 358–367.

ROTHMAN, E. K. (1984). *Hands and hearts: A history of courtship in America.* New York: Basic Books.

ROTHMAN, K. J., et al. (1995). Teratogenicity of high vitamin A intake. *New England Journal of Medicine, 333,* 1369–1373.

ROWLAND, D. L. (1998). Penile sensitivity in men: A composite of recent findings. *Urology, 52,* 1101–1105.

ROWLAND, D. L. (2007). Will medical solutions to sexual problems make sexological care and science obsolete? *Journal of Sex & Marital Therapy, 33,* 385–397.

ROWLAND, D. L., & BURNETT, A. L. (2000). Pharmacotherapy in the treatment of male sexual dysfunction. *Journal of Sex Research, 37,* 226–243.

ROWLAND, D. L., COOPER, S. E., & SCHNEIDER, M. (2000). Defining premature ejaculation for experimental and clinical investigations. *Archives of Sexual Behavior, 30,* 235–253.

ROWLAND, D. L., KALLAN, K., & SLOB, A. (1997). Yohimbine, erectile capacity, and sexual response in men. *Archives of Sexual Behavior, 26,* 49–62.

ROWLAND, D. L., et al. (1987). Endocrine, psychological and genital response to sexual arousal in men. *Psychoneuroendocrinology, 12,* 149–158.

ROWLAND, D., et al. (2004). Self-reported premature ejaculation and aspects of sexual functioning and satisfaction. *Journal of Sexual Medicine, 1,* 225–232.

ROZEMA, H. J. (1986). Defensive communication climate as a barrier to sex education in the home. *Family Relations, 35,* 531–537.

ROZENBERG, S., et al. (1994). Osteoporosis prevention with sex hormone replacement therapy. *International Journal of Fertility, 39,* 262–271.

RUBIN, A. M., & ADAMS, J. R. (1986). Outcomes of sexually open marriages. *Journal of Sex Research, 22,* 311–319.

RUBIN, R. (2007, November 1). Popular, successful Pap test faces challenge. *USA Today,* p. 11D.

RUBIN, Z. (1988). Preface. In R. J. Sternberg & M. L. Barnes (Eds.), *The psychology of love* (pp. vii–xii). New Haven, CT: Yale University Press.

RUBIN, Z., et al. (1980). Self-disclosure in dating couples: Sex roles and the ethic of openness. *Journal of Marriage and Family, 42,* 305.

RUDLINGER, R., & NORVAL, M. (1996). Human papillomavirus infections. In P. Elsner & A. Eichmann (Eds.), *Sexually transmitted diseases. Advances in diagnosis and treatment* (pp. 67–76) Basel: Karger.

RUPP, H. A., & WALLEN, K. (2008). Sex differences in response to visual sexual stimuli: A review. *Archives of Sexual Behavior, 37,* 206–218.

RUSSELL, D. E. H. (Ed.). (1984). *Sexual exploitation: Rape, child sexual abuse and workplace harassment.* Beverly Hills, CA: Sage.

RUSSELL, D. E. H. (1990). *Rape in marriage* (rev. ed.). Bloomington: Indiana University Press.

RUST, P. C. R. (2000). Bisexuality: A contemporary paradox for women. *Journal of Social Issues, 56,* 205–221.

RUST, P. C. R. (2003). Bisexuality: The state of the union. In J. R. Heiman & C. M. Davis (Eds.), *Annual review of sex research,* (Vol. XIII, pp. 180–240). Allentown, PA: The Society for the Scientific Study of Sexuality.

RUTHERFORD, G. W., et al. (1990). Course of HIV-1 infection in a cohort of homosexual and bisexual men: An 11 year follow up study. *British Medical Journal, 301,* 1183–1188.

RYAN, G. (2000). Childhood sexuality: A decade of study. Pt. I. Research and curriculum development. *Child Abuse & Neglect, 24,* 33–48.

RYAN, K. M. (2004). Further evidence for a cognitive component of rape. *Aggression and Violent Behavior, 9,* 579–604.

RYND, N. (1987). Incidence of psychosomatic symptoms in rape victims. *Journal of Sex Research, 24,* 155–161.

S

SADKER, M., & SADKER, D. (1994). *Failing at fairness: How America's schools cheat girls.* New York: Scribner's.

SAGARIN, B. J., et al. (2003). Sex differences (and similarities) in jealousy. The moderating influence of infidelity experience and sexual orientation of the infidelity. *Evolution and Human Behavior, 24,* 17–23.

SAKELLARIOU, D. (2006). If not the disability, then what? Barriers to reclaiming sexuality following spinal cord injury. *Sexuality and Disability, 24,* 101–111.

SALEM, R. (2006, February). New attention to the IUD. *Population Reports,* Series B, No. 7., 47–56. John's Hopkins Bloomberg School of Public Health. The INFO Project.

SALOVEY, P., & RODIN, J. (1985). The heart of jealousy. *Psychology Today,* September, 22–29.

SANCHEZ, D. T., & KIEFER, A. K. (2007). Body concerns in and out of the bedroom: Implications for sexual pleasure and problems. *Archives of Sexual Behavior, 36,* 808–820.

SANDA, M. G., et al. (2008). Quality of life and satisfaction with outcome among prostate-cancer survivors. *New England Journal of Medicine, 358,* 1250–1261.

SANDAY, P. (1981). The socio-cultural context of rape: A cross-cultural study. *Journal of Social Issues, 37,* 5–27.

SANDAY, P. (1990). *Fraternity gang rape: Sex, brotherhood and privilege on campus.* New York: New York University Press.

SANDBERG, D. E., & MEYER-BAHLBURG, H. F. L. (1994). Variability in middle childhood play behavior: Effects of gender, age, and family background. *Archives of Sexual Behavior, 23,* 645–663.

SANDERS, S. A., et al. (2010). Condom use during most recent vaginal intercourse event among a probability sample of adults in the United States. *Journal of Sexual Medicine, 7* (Suppl 5), 362–373.

SANDERS, S. A., & REINISCH, J. M. (1999). Would you say you "had sex" if… ? *Journal of the American Medical Association, 281,* 275–277.

SANDFORT, T. G. M. (2005). Sexual orientation and gender: Stereotypes and beyond. *Archives of Sexual Behavior, 34,* 595–611.

SANDFORT, T. G. M., DE GRAAF, R., & BIJL, R. (2003). Same-sex sexuality and quality of life: Findings from the Netherlands Mental Health Survey and Incidence Survey. *Archives of Sexual Behavior*, 32, 15–22.

SANDLER, J. C., & FREEMAN, N. J. (2009). Female sex offender recidivism: A large-scale empirical analysis. *Sexual Abuse: A Journal of Research and Treatment*, 21, 455–473.

SANDNABBA, N. K., SANTTILA, P., & NORDLING, N. (1999). Sexual behavior and social adaptation among sadomasochistically-oriented males. *Journal of Sex Research*, 36, 273–282.

SANDNABBA, N. K., et al. (2003). Age and gender specific sexual behaviors in children. *Child Abuse & Neglect*, 27, 579–605.

SANGRADOR, J. L., & YELA, C. (2000). "What is beautiful is loved": Physical attractiveness in love relationships in a representative sample. *Social Behavior and Personality*, 28, 207–218.

SANTTILA, P., SANDNABBA, N. K., & JERN, P. (2009). Prevalence and determinants of male sexual dysfunction during first intercourse. *Journal of Sex & Marital Therapy*, 35, 86–105.

SARREL, P., & MASTERS, W. (1982). Sexual molestation of men by women. *Archives of Sexual Behavior*, 11(1), 117–131.

SAUNDERS, E. J. (1989). Life-threatening autoerotic behavior: A challenge for sex educators and therapists. *Journal of Sex Education and Therapy*, 15(2), 77–81.

SAVIC, I., BERGLUND, H., & LINDSTROM, P. (2005). Brain responses to putative pheromones in homosexual men. *Proceedings of the National Academy of Sciences*, 102, 7356–7361.

SAVIN-WILLIAMS, R. C., & REAM, G. L. (2007). Prevalence and stability of sexual orientation components during adolescence and young adulthood. *Archives of Sexual Behavior*, 36, 385–394.

SAX, L. (2002). How common is intersex? A response to Anne Fausto-Sterling. *Journal of Sex Research*, 39, 174–178.

SAX, P. E., & GATHE, J. C. (2005). Beyond efficacy: The impact of combination antiretroviral therapy on quality of life. *AIDS Patient Care and STDs*, 19, 19–32.

SAYWITZ, K. J., et al. (2000). Treatment for sexually abused children and adolescents. *American Psychologist*, 55, 1040–1049.

SCANLON, T. F. (2005). The dispersion of pederasty and the athletic revolution in sixth-century B.C. Greece. *Journal of Homosexuality*, 49(3/4), 63–85.

SCARCE, M. (1997). Same-sex rape of male college students. *Journal of American College of Health*, 45, 171–173.

SCHACHTER, M., & SHOHAM, Z. (1994). Amenorrhea during the reproductive years—Is it safe? *Fertility and Sterility*, 62, 1–16.

SCHACTER, S., & SINGER, J. (1962). Cognitive, social and physiological determinants of emotional state. *Psychological Review*, 69, 379–399.

SCHAFFIR, J. (2006). Hormonal contraceptives and sexual desire: A critical review. *Journal of Sex & Marital Therapy*, 32, 305–314.

SCHATZEL-MURPHY, E.A., et al. (2009). Sexual coercion in men and women: Similar behaviors, different predictors. *Archives of Sexual Behavior*, 38, 974–986.

SCHEWE, P. A. (1997). Paraphilia not otherwise specified: Assessment and treatment. In D. R. Laws & W. T. O'Donohue (Eds.), *Sexual deviance: Theory, assessment, and treatment* (pp. 424–433). New York: Guilford Press.

SCHICK, V., et al. (2010). Sexual behaviors, condom use, and sexual health of Americans over 50: Implications for sexual health promotion for older adults. *Journal of Sexual Medicine*, 7 (Suppl 5), 330–345.

SCHLEGEL, A., & BARRY III, H. (1980). The evolutionary significance of adolescent initiation ceremonies. *American Ethnologist*, 7, 696–715.

SCHLEGEL, W. S. (1962). Die konstitutionbiologischen grundlagen der homosexualitat. *Zeitschrift fuer Menschliche Vererbungs und Konstitutionslehre*, 36, 341–364.

SCHMID, G. P., et al. (2009). The unexplored story of HIV and ageing. *Bulletin of the World Health Organization*, 87, 162–163.

SCHMIDT, G. (2002). Reply: Is there nothing special about adult-child sex? *Archives of Sexual Behavior*, 31, 509–510.

SCHMITT, D. P., PLUS 128 AUTHORS. (2004). Patterns and universals of adult romantic attachment across 62 cultural regions. Are models of self and of other pancultural constructs? *Journal of Cross-Cultural Psychology*, 35, 367–402.

SCHMITT, D. P., et al. (2003). Universal sex differences in the desire for sexual variety: Tests from 52 nations, 6 continents, and 13 islands. *Journal of Personality and Social Psychology*, 85, 85–104.

SCHOOLER, D., et al. (2005). Cycles of shame: Menstrual shame, body shame, and sexual decision-making. *Journal of Sex Research*, 42, 324–334.

SCHULT, D. G., & SCHNEIDER, L. J. (1991). The role of provocativeness, rape history, and observer sex in attributions of blame in sexual assault. *Journal of Interpersonal Violence*, 6, 94–101.

SCHUTTE, J. W., & HOSCH, H. M. (1997). Gender differences in sexual assault verdicts: A meta-analysis. *Journal of Social Behavior and Personality*, 12, 759–772.

SCHÜTZWOHL, A. (2008). The intentional object of romantic jealousy. *Evolution and Human Behavior*, 29, 92–99.

SCHWARCZ, S., et al. (2007). Prevalence of HIV infection and predictors of high-transmission sexual risk behaviors among men who have sex with men. *American Journal of Public Health*, 97, 1067–1075.

SCHWARTZ, G. (1973). Devices to prevent masturbation. *Medical Aspects of Human Sexuality*, May, 141–153.

SCHWARTZ, G., et al. (2010). Biodemographic and physical correlates of sexual orientation in men. *Archives of Sexual Behavior*, 39, 93–109.

SCHWARTZ, P. (1994). *Peer marriage*. New York: Free Press.

SCHWEBKE, J. R. (2009). Bacterial vaginosis: Are we coming full circle? *Journal of Infectious Diseases*, 200, 1633–1635.

SCHWENKHAGEN, A., & STUDD, J. (2009). Role of testosterone in the treatment of hypoactive sexual desire disorder. *Maturitas*, 63, 152–159.

SCOTT, C. L., & GERBASI, J. B. (2003). Sex offender registration and community notification challenges: The Supreme Court continues its trend. *The Journal of the American Academy of Psychiatry and the Law*, 31, 494–501.

SCOTT, J. E. (1986). An updated longitudinal content analysis of sex references in mass circulation magazines. *Journal of Sex Research*, 22, 385–392.

SCOTTI, J. R., et al. (1996). College student attitudes concerning the sexuality of persons with mental retardation: Development of the perceptions of sexuality scale. *Sexuality and Disability*, 14, 249–263.

SEAL, A. (1996). Women, STDs and safe sex: A review of the evidence. *Venereology*, 9, 48–53.

SEAMAN, B. (1972). *Free and female*. New York: Coward, McGann & Geoghegan.

SEDGH, G., et al. (2007). Legal abortion worldwide: Incidence and recent trends. *Perspectives on Sexual and Reproductive Health*, 39, 216–225.

SEGHORN, T. K., PRENTKY, R. A., & BOUCHER, R. J. (1987). Childhood sexual abuse in the lives of sexually aggressive offenders. *Journal of the American Academy of Child and Adolescent Psychiatry*, 26, 262–267.

SEIDMAN, S. N. (2002). Exploring the relationship between depression and erectile dysfunction in aging men. *Journal of Clinical Psychiatry*, 63 (Suppl. 5), 5–12.

SEIDMAN, S. N., MOSHER, W. D., & ARAL, S. O. (1992). Women with multiple sexual partners: United States, 1988. *American Journal of Public Health*, 82, 1388–1394.

SEIDMAN, S. N., & RIEDER, R. O. (1994). A review of sexual behavior in the United States. *American Journal of Psychiatry*, 151, 330–341.

SENN, T. E., et al. (2007). Characteristics of sexual abuse in childhood and adolescence influence sexual risk behavior in adulthood. *Archives of Sexual Behavior*, 36, 637–645.

SEROVICH, J. M., & MOSACK, K. E. (2003). Reasons for HIV disclosure or nondisclosure to casual sexual partners. *AIDS Education and Prevention*, 15, 70–80.

SETO, M. C. (2008). Pedophilia. In D. R. Laws & W. T. O'Donohue (Eds.), *Sexual deviance: Theory, assessment, and treatment* (2nd ed., pp. 164–182). New York: Guilford Press.

SETO, M. C., & BARBAREE, H. E. (1995). The role of alcohol in sexual aggression. *Clinical Psychology Review*, 15, 545–566.

SETO, M. C., & LALUMIÈRE, M. L. (2010). What is so special about male adolescent sexual offending? A review and test of explanations through meta-analysis. *Psychological Bulletin*, 136, 526–575.

SETO, M. C., CANTOR, J. M., & BLANCHARD, R. (2006). Child pornography offenses are a valid diagnostic indicator of pedophilia. *Journal of Abnormal Psychology*, 115, 610–615.

SETO, M. C., & EKE, A. W. (2005). The criminal histories and later offending of child pornography offenders. *Sexual Abuse: A Journal of Research and Treatment*, 17, 201–210.

SHAH, K., & MONTOYA, C. (2007). Do testosterone injections increase libido for elderly hypogonadal patients? *Family Practice*, 56, 301–303.

SHAPIRO, L. (1990, May 28). Guns and dolls. *Newsweek*, 54–65.

SHARP, P. M., & HAHN, B. H. (2008). Prehistory of HIV-1. *Nature*, 455, 605–606.

SHAUGHNESSY, M. F., & SHAKESBY, P. (1992). Adolescent sexual and emotional intimacy. *Adolescence*, 27, 475–480.

SHAVER, P., HAZEN, C., & BRADSHAW, D. (1988). Love as attachment. In R. J. Sternberg & M. L. Barnes (Eds.), *The psychology of love* (pp. 68–99). New Haven, CT: Yale University Press.

SHAW, J. (1994). Aging and sexual potential. *Journal of Sex Education and Therapy*, 20, 134–139.

SHEARS, K. H. (2002a). Increasing contraception reduces abortion. *Network*, 21(4), 28–33.

SHEARS, K. H. (2002b). Abstinence: An option for adolescents. *Network*, 22(1), 4–7.

SHEERAN, R., ABRAHAM, C., & ORBELL, S. (1999). Psychosocial correlates of heterosexual condom use: A meta-analysis. *Psychological Bulletin*, 125, 90–132.

SHEETS, V., FREDENDALL, L., & CLAYPOOL, H. (1997). Jealousy evocation, partner reassurance, and relationship stability: An exploration of the potential benefits of jealousy. *Evolution and Human Behavior*, 18, 387–402.

SHENKIN, S. D., STARR, J. M., & DEARY, I. J. (2004). Birth weight and cognitive ability in childhood: A systematic review. *Psychological Bulletin*, 130, 989–1013.

SHEPELA, S. T., & LEVESQUE, L. L. (1998). Poisoned waters: Sexual harassment and the college climate. *Sex Roles*, 38, 589–611.

SHEPHER, J. (1971). Mate selection among second generation kibbutz adolescents and adults: Incest avoidance and negative imprinting. *Archives of Sexual Behavior*, 1, 293–307.

SHERWIN, B. B. (1988). A comparative analysis of the role of androgens in human male and female sexual behavior: Behavior specificity, critical thresholds and sensitivity. *Psychobiology*, 16, 416–425.

SHERWIN, B. B. (2002). Estrogen and cognitive aging in women. *Trends in Pharmacological Sciences*, 23, 527–534.

SHIELDS, W. M., & SHIELDS, L. M. (1983). Forcible rape: An evolutionary perspective. *Ethology and Sociobiology*, 4, 115–136.

SHINDEL, A., NELSON, C., & BRANDES, S. (2008). Urologist practice patterns in the management of premature ejaculation: A nationwide survey. *Journal of Sexual Medicine, 5*, 199–205.

SHORT, S. E., LINMAO, M., & WENTAO, Y. (2000). Birth planning and sterilization in China. *Population Studies*, 54, 279–291.

SHOTLAND, R. L., & HUNTER, B. A. (1995). Women's "token resistant" and compliant sexual behaviors are related to uncertain sexual intentions and rape. *Personality and Social Psychology Bulletin*, 21, 226–236.

SHTARKSHALL, R. A., SANTELLI, J. S., & HIRSCH, J. S. (2007). Sex education and sexual socialization: Roles for educators and parents. *Perspectives on Sexual and Reproductive Health, 39*, 116–118.

SHUFELT, C., & BRAUNSTEIN, G. D. (2009). Safety of testosterone use in women. *Maturitas*, 63, 63–66.

SHUGARS, D. C., et al. (1999). Endogenous salivary inhibitors of human immunodeficiency virus. *Archives of Oral Biology*, 44, 445–453.

SIEBERS, A. E., et al. (2009). Comparison of liquid-based cytology with conventional cytology for detection of cervical cancer precursors: A randomized controlled trial. *Journal of the American Medical Association*, 302, 1757–1764.

SIECUS NATIONAL GUIDELINES TASK FORCE. (1996). *Guidelines for comprehensive sexuality education* (2nd ed.). New York: Author.

SIECUS. (1992, August/September). Sexuality education and the schools: Issues and answers. *SIECUS Report* (Fact Sheet No. 3), 13–14.

SIECUS. (1994). Teens talk about sex: Adolescent sexuality in the 90s. A survey of high school students. *SIECUS Report*, 22(5), 16–17.

SIEVING, R. E., et al. (2006). Friends' influence on adolescents' first sexual intercourse. *Perspectives on Sexual and Reproductive Health*, 38, 13–19.

SIGAL, J. J., et al. (2003). Unwanted infants: Psychological and physical consequences of inadequate orphanage care 50 years later. *American Journal of Orthopsychiatry*, 73, 3–12.

SILVERMAN, B. G., & GROSS, T. P. (1997). Use and effectiveness of condoms during anal intercourse. *Sexually Transmitted Diseases*, 24, 11–17.

SILVERMAN, E. K. (2004). Anthropology and circumcision. *Annual Review of Anthropology*, 33, 419–445.

SIMMONS, M., & MONTAGUE, D. (2008). Penile prosthesis implantation: Past, present and future. *International Journal of Impotence Research*, 30, 437–444.

SIMMONS, R. A., GORDON, P. C., & CHAMBLESS, D. L. (2005). Pronouns in marital interaction. What do "You" and "I" say about marital health? *Psychological Science*, 16, 932–936.

SIMON, P. M., et al. (1992). Psychological characteristics of a sample of male street prostitutes. *Archives of Sexual Behavior*, 21, 33–44.

SIMON, W. (1994). Deviance as history: The future of perversion. *Archives of Sexual Behavior*, 23, 1–20.

SIMONS, J. S., & CAREY, M. P. (2001). Prevalence of sexual dysfunctions: Results from a decade of research. *Archives of Sexual Behavior*, 30, 177–219.

SIMONS, L. G. (2009). The effect of religion on risky sexual behavior among college students. *Deviant Behavior*, 30, 467–485.

SIMPSON, J. A., CAMPBELL, B., & BERSCHEID, E. (1986). The association between romantic love and marriage: Kephart (1967) twice revisited. *Personality and Social Psychology Bulletin*, 12, 363–372.

SINGER, I. (1984–1987). *The nature of love* (Vols. 1–3). Chicago: University of Chicago Press.

SINGER, I. (1984). *The nature of love, Vol. 1: Plato to Luther*. Chicago: University of Chicago Press.

SINGER, L. T., et al. (2002). Cognitive and motor outcomes of cocaine-exposed infants. *Journal of the American Medical Association*, 287, 1952–1960.

SINGH, D. (1993). Body shape and women's attractiveness: The critical role of waist-to-hip ratio. *Human Nature*, 4, 297–321.

SINGH, D., & BRONSTAD, P. M. (2001). Female body odour is a potential cue to ovulation. *Proceedings of the Royal Society of London B*, 268, 797–801.

SINGH, G. K., & YU, S. M. (1995). Infant mortality in the United States: Trends, differentials, and projections, 1950 through 2010. *American Journal of Public Health*, 85, 957–964.

SINGH, R., & McCLOSKEY, J. (2001). Syphilis in pregnancy. *Venereology*, 14, 121–131.

SINGH, S., & DARROCH, J. E. (2000). Adolescent pregnancy and childbearing: Levels and trends in developed countries. *Family Planning Perspectives*, 32, 14–23.

SINGH, S., et al. (2000). Gender differences in the timing of first intercourse: Data from 14 countries. *International Family Planning Perspectives*, 26, 21–28, 43.

SINGH, S., et al. (2001). Socioeconomic disadvantage and adolescent women's sexual and reproductive behavior: The case of five developed countries. *Family Planning Perspectives*, 33, 251–258, 289.

SINICCO, A., et al. (1993). Risk of developing AIDS after primary acute HIV-1 infection. *Journal of Acquired Immune Deficiency Syndromes*, 6, 575–581.

SIPSKI, M. L., ALEXANDER, C. J., & ROSEN, R. C. (1999). Sexual response in women with spinal cord injuries: Implications for our understanding of the able bodied. *Journal of Sex & Marital Therapy*, 25, 11–22.

SKINNER, E. B. (2010, January 18). The new slave trade. *Time*, 54–57.

SLAUGHTER, L. (2000). Involvement of drugs in sexual assault. *Journal of Reproductive Medicine*, 45, 425–430.

SLEEK, S. (1998, September). Chinese psychiatrists debate meaning of sex orientation. *APA Monitor*, 33.

SMALL, C., et al. (2006). Menstrual cycle characteristics: Associations with fertility and spontaneous abortion. *Epidemiology*, 17, 52–60.

SMITH, A. M. (1993). "What is pornography?": An analysis of the policy statement of the campaign against pornography and censorship. *Feminist Review*, 43, 71–87.

SMITH, A. M. A., ROSENTHAL, D. A., & REICHLER, H. (1996). High schoolers' masturbatory practices: Their relationship to sexual intercourse and personal characteristics. *Psychological Reports*, 76, 499–509.

SMITH, A. M. A., et al. (1998). Does penis size influence condom slippage and breakage? *International Journal of STD and AIDS, 9*, 444–447.

SMITH, A. M. A., et al. (2003). Sex in Australia: Sexual identity, sexual attraction, and sexual experience among a representative sample of adults. *Australian and New Zealand Journal of Public Health*, 27, 138–145.

SMITH, G. (2001). Heterosexual and homosexual anal intercourse: an international perspective. *Venereology*, 14, 28–37.

SMITH, G., KIPPAX, S., & CHAPPLE, M. (1998). Secrecy, disclosure, and closet dynamics. *Journal of Homosexuality*, 35, 53–73.

SMITH, J., PLAAT, F., & FISK, N. M. (2008). The natural caesarean: A woman-centred technique. *British Journal of Gynecology*, 115, 1037–1042.

SMITH, J. D., & OAKLEY, D. (2005). Why do women miss oral contraceptive pills? An analysis of women's self-described reasons for missed pills. *Journal of Midwifery & Women's Health*, 50, 380–385.

SMITH, J. S., et al. (2002). Herpes simplex virus-2 as a human papillomavirus cofactor in the etiology of invasive cervical cancer. *Journal of the National Cancer Institute*, 94, 1604–1613.

SMITH, L. (1993, January 6). Saying no to birth control. *Los Angeles Times*, pp. A1, A12.

SMITH, L. H., & FORD, J. (2010). History of forced sex and recent sexual risk indicators among young adult males. *Perspectives on Sexual and Reproductive Health*, 42, 87–92.

SMITH, R., PINE, C., & HAWLEY, M. (1988). Social cognitions about adult male victims of female sexual assault. *Journal of Sex Research*, 24, 101–112.

SMITH, R. A., & SASLOW, D. (2002). Breast cancer. In G. M. Wingood & R. J. DiClemente (Eds.), *Handbook of women's sexual and reproductive health* (pp. 345–365). New York: Kluwer Academic/Plenum Publishers.

SMITH, S. J., AXELTON, A. M., & SAUCIER, D. A. (2009). The effects of contact on sexual prejudice: A meta-analysis. *Sex Roles*, 61, 178–191.

SMITH, T. W. (1999). The JAMA controversy and the meaning of sex. *Public Opinion Quarterly*, 63, 385–400.

SMYTHERS, R. (1894). *Instruction and advice for the young bride*. New York: Spiritual Guidance Press.

SNEGROFF, S. (2000). No sexuality education is sexuality education. *Family Planning Perspectives*, 32, 257–258.

SNIFFEN, M. J. (1994, June 23). Study: Most rape victims young. *New Orleans Times-Picayune*, p. A9.

SO, H. W., & CHEUNG, F. M. (2005). Review of Chinese sex attitudes & applicability of sex therapy for Chinese couples with sexual dysfunction. *Journal of Sex Research*, 42, 93–102.

SOBLE, A. (2009). A history of erotic philosophy. *Journal of Sex Research*, 46, 104–120.

SOLOMON, R. C. (2002). Reasons for love. *Journal for the Theory of Social Behavior*, 32, 1–28.

SOMERS, C. L., & SURMANN, A. T. (2005). Sources and timing of sex education: Relations with American adolescent sexual attitudes and behavior. *Educational Review*, 57, 37–54.

Song, Y. B., et al. (2009). Innervation of vagina: Microdissection and immunohisto-chemical study. *Journal of Sex & Marital Therapy*, 35, 144–153.

Sowers, M. F. R. (2000). The menopause transition and the aging process: A population perspective. *Aging Clinical and Experimental Research*, 12, 85–92.

Sparling, J. (1997). Penile erections: Shape, angle, and length. *Journal of Sex & Marital Therapy*, 23, 195–207.

Spear, L. P. (2000). Neurobehavioral changes in adolescence. *Current Directions in Psychological Science*, 9, 111–114.

Spector, I., & Carey, M. (1990). Incidence and prevalence of the sexual dysfunctions: A critical review of the empirical literature. *Archives of Sexual Behavior*, 19, 389–408.

Spence, J. T., & Hahn, E. D. (1997). The Attitude Toward Women Scale and attitude change in college students. *Psychology of Women Quarterly*, 21, 17–34.

Spence, J. T., & Helmreich, R. L. (1972). Who likes competent women? Competence, sex-role congruence of interests, and attitudes towards women as determinants of interpersonal attraction. *Journal of Applied and Social Psychology*, 2, 197–213.

Spence, J. T., & Helmreich, R. L. (1978). *Masculinity & femininity: Their psychological dimensions, correlates, and antecedents.* Austin: University of Texas Press.

Spence, J. T., Helmreich, R. L., & Stapp, J. (1974). The personal attributes questionnaire: A measure of sex role stereotypes and masculinity-femininity. *JSAS Catalog of Selected Documents in Psychology*, 4, 43.

Spencer, A. L., Bonnema, R., & McNamara, M. C. (2009). Helping women choose appropriate hormonal contraception: Update on risks, benefits, and indications. *American Journal of Medicine*, 122, 497–506.

Speroff, L., & Fritz, M. (2005). *Clinical gynecologic endocrinology and infertility* (7th ed.). Philadelphia: Lippincott Williams and Wilkins.

Spiegel, D. (2000, May/June). Suffer the children: Long-term effects of sexual abuse. *Society*, 18–20.

Spinola, S. M., Bauer, M. E., & Munson, Jr., R. S. (2002). Immunopathogenesis of Haemophilus ducreyi infection (chancroid). *Infection and Immunity*, 70, 1667–1676.

Spitz, R. A. (1945). Hospitalism: An inquiry into the genesis of psychiatric conditioning in early childhood. In D. Fenschel & A. Freud (Eds.), *Psychoanalytic studies of the child* (Vol. 1). New York: International Universities Press.

Spitz, R. A. (1946). Hospitalism: A follow-up report. In D. Fenschel, P. Greenacre, & A. Freud (Eds.), *Psychoanalytic studies of the child* (Vol. 2, pp. 113–117). New York: International Universities Press.

Spitzberg, B. H. (1998). Sexual coercion in courtship relations. In B. H. Spitzberg & W. R. Cupach (Eds.), *The dark side of close relationships* (pp. 179–232). Mahwah, NJ: Lawrence Erlbaum.

Spitzberg, B. H., & Cupach, W. R. (2007). The state of the art of stalking: Taking stock of the emerging literature. *Aggression and Violent Behavior*, 12, 64–86.

Sprecher, S., Harris, G., & Meyers, A. (2008). Perceptions of sources of sex education and targets of sex communication: Sociodemographic and cohort effects. *Journal of Sex Research*, 45, 17–26.

Sprecher, S., & Regan, P. C. (1998). Passionate and companionate love in courting and young married couples. *Sociological Inquiry*, 68, 163–185.

Sprecher, S., & Regan, P. C. (2002). Liking some things (in some people) more than others: Partner preferences in romantic relationships and friendships. *Journal of Social and Personal Relationships*, 19, 463–481.

Sprecher, S., Barbee, A., & Schwartz, P. (1995). "Was it good for you, too?": Gender differences in first sexual intercourse experiences. *Journal of Sex Research*, 32, 3–15.

Sprecher, S., et al. (1994). Token resistance to sexual intercourse and consent to unwanted sexual intercourse: College students' dating experiences in 3 countries. *Journal of Sex Research*, 31, 125–132.

Springen, K. (2003, January 13). New year, new breasts? *Newsweek*, 65–66.

Springen, K. (2005, February 7). The miscarriage maze. *Newsweek*, 63–64.

Spruance, S. L., et al. (1997). Penciclovir cream for the treatment of herpes simplex labialis. *Journal of the American Medical Association*, 277, 1374–1379.

Stall, S. (1897). *What a young man ought to know.* Philadelphia: Virginia Publishing Co.

Stanberry, L. R., et al. (2002). Glycoprotein-D-adjuvant vaccine to prevent genital herpes. *New England Journal of Medicine*, 347, 1652–1661.

Stanton, H. (1922). *Sex: Avoided subjects discussed in plain English.* New York: Social Mentor.

Stapleton, A., et al. (1990). Postcoital antimicrobial prophylaxis for recurrent urinary tract infection. *Journal of the American Medical Association*, 264, 703–706.

Steele, B. F., & Alexander, H. (1981). Long-term effects of sexual abuse in childhood. In P. B. Mzazek & C. H. Kempe (Eds.), *Sexually abused children and their families* (pp. 223–233). New York: Pergamon.

Steele, J. R. (1999). Teenage sexuality and media practice: Factoring in the influences of family, friends, and school. *Journal of Sex Research*, 36, 331–341.

Steen, R., & Dallabetta, G. (2003). Sexually transmitted infection control with sex workers: Regular screening and presumptive treatment augments efforts to reduce risk and vulnerability. *Reproductive Health Matters*, 11, 74–90.

Stein, D. J., et al. (2001). Hypersexual disorder and preoccupation with Internet pornography. *American Journal of Psychiatry*, 158, 1590–1594.

Stein, R. (2007, May 23). FDA approves pill that eliminates menstrual periods. *New Orleans Times-Picayune*, p. A9.

Steinem, G. (1983). *Outrageous acts and everyday rebellions.* New York: Holt, Rinehart & Winston.

Steiner, M. (2000). Premenstrual syndrome and premenstrual dysphoric disorder: Guidelines for management. *Journal of Psychiatry & Neuroscience*, 25, 459–468.

Stephens, E. (2009). Coining spermatorrhoea: Medicine and male body fluids, 1836–1866. *Sexualities*, 12, 467–485.

Stephenson, P., et al. (1992). Commentary: The public health consequences of restricted induced abortion—Lessons from Romania. *American Journal of Public Health*, 82, 1328–1331.

Stermac, L., Del Bove, G., & Addison, M. (2001). Violence, injury, and presentation patterns in spousal sexual assaults. *Violence Against Women*, 7, 1218–1233.

Sternbach, H. (1998). Age-associated testosterone decline in men: Clinical issues for psychology. *American Journal of Psychiatry*, 155, 1310–1318.

Sternberg, R. J. (1986). A triangular theory of love. *Psychological Review*, 93, 119–135.

Sternberg, R. J. (1987). Liking vs. loving: A comparative evaluation of theories. *Psychological Bulletin*, 102, 331–345.

Sternberg, R. J. (1988). Triangulating love. In R. J. Sternberg & M. L. Barnes (Eds.), *The psychology of love* (pp. 119–138). New Haven, CT: Yale University Press.

Sternberg, R. J., & Grajek, S. (1984). The nature of love. *Journal of Personality and Social Psychology*, 47, 312–329.

Sternberg, S. (2009, September 25–27). Pair of HIV vaccines show promise. *USA Today*, 1A.

Stewart, F., & Gabelnick, H. L. (2004). Contraceptive research and development. In R. A. Hatcher et al. (Eds.), *Contraceptive technology* (18th ed., pp. 601–616). New York: Ardent Media.

Stewart, F., Trussell, J., & Van Look, P. F. A. (2008). Emergency contraception. In R. A. Hatcher et al. (Eds.), *Contraceptive technology* (19th ed., pp. 87–116). New York: Ardent Media.

Stock, J. L., et al. (1997). Adolescent pregnancy and sexual risk-taking among sexually abused girls. *Family Planning Perspectives*, 29, 200–203 & 207.

Stokes, J., et al. (1996). Female partners of bisexual men: What they don't know might hurt them. *Psychology of Women Quarterly*, 20, 267–284.

Stoller, R. J. (1986). *Perversion: The erotic form of hatred.* London: Maresfield Library.

Stone, K. M., et al. (1989). National surveillance for neonatal herpes simplex virus infections. *Sexually Transmitted Diseases*, 16, 152–160.

Strassberg, D. S., & Lowe, K. (1995). Volunteer bias in sexuality research. *Archives of Sexual Behavior*, 24, 369–382.

Streicher, H. W. (1974). The girls in the cartoons. *Journal of Communication*, 24, 125–129.

Stroman, D. (2003). *The disability rights movement.* Lanham, MD: University Press of America.

Strong, E. K. (1936). Interests of men and women. *Journal of Social Psychology*, 7, 49–67.

Strong, S. M., Singh, D., & Randall, P. K. (2000). Childhood gender nonconformity and body dissatisfaction in gay and heterosexual men. *Sex Roles*, 43, 427–439.

Strouse, J., & Fabes, R. A. (1985). Formal versus informal sources of sex education: Competing forces in the sexual socialization of adolescents. *Adolescence*, 20, 251–263.

Struckman-Johnson, C., Struckman-Johnson, D., & Anderson, P. B. (2003). Tactics of sexual coercion: When men and women won't take no for an answer. *Journal of Sex Research*, 40, 76–86.

Studd, J., & Schwenkhagen, A. (2009). The historical response to female sexuality. *Maturitas*, 63, 103–111.

Studer, L. H., Aylwin, A. S., & Reddon, J. R. (2005). Testosterone, sexual offense recidivism, and treatment effect among adult male sex offenders. *Sexual Abuse: A Journal of Research and Treatment*, 17, 171–181.

Stulhofer, A. (2006). How (un)important is penis size for women with heterosexual experience? *Archives of Sexual Behavior*, 35, 5–6.

Stulhofer, A., Busko, V., & Landripet, I. (2010). Pornography, sexual socialization, and satisfaction among young men. *Archives of Sexual Behavior*, 39, 168–178.

Sulik, K. K., Johnson, M. C., & Webb, M. A. (1981). Fetal alcohol syndrome:

Embryogenesis in a mouse model. *Science*, 214, 936–938.

SULLIVAN, M. L., & JEFFREYS, S. (2002). Legalization: The Australian experience. *Violence Against Women*, 8, 1140–1148.

SUMMIT, R., & KRYSO, J. (1978). Sexual abuse of children: A clinical spectrum. *American Journal of Orthopsychiatry*, 48, 237–251.

SUN, S. S., et al. (2005). Is sexual maturity occurring earlier among U.S. children? *Journal of Adolescent Health*, 37, 345–355.

SUTTIE, I. D. (1952). *The origins of love and hate*. New York: Julian Press.

SWAAB, D. F., GOOREN, L. J. G., & HOFMAN, M. A. (1992). The human hypothalamus in relation to gender and sexual orientation. *Progress in Brain Research*, 93, 205–219.

SWAAB, D. F., & HOFMAN, M. A. (1990). An enlarged suprachiasmatic nucleus in homosexual men. *Brain Research*, 537, 141–148.

SWAMI, V., EINON, D., & FURNHAM, A. (2006). The leg-to-body ratio as a human aesthetic criterion. *Body Image*, 3, 317–323.

SWAMY, G. K., et al. (2008). Association of preterm birth with long-term survival, reproduction, and next generation preterm birth. *Journal of the American Medical Association*, 299, 1429–1436.

SYMONDS, T., et al. (2003). How does premature ejaculation impact a man's life? *Journal of Sex & Marital Therapy*, 29, 361–370.

SZABO, L. (2010). Early puberty for girls is raising health concerns. *USA Today*, August 9.

T

TACH, L., & HALPERN-MEEKIN, S. (2009). How does premarital cohabitation affect trajectories of marital quality? *Journal of Marriage and Family*, 71, 298–317.

TALBOTT, J. (2007). Size matters: The number of prostitutes and the global HIV/AIDS pandemic. *PLOS One*, 6, e 543.

TANFER, K., & SCHOORL, J. J. (1992). Premarital sexual careers and partner change. *Archives of Sexual Behavior*, 21, 45–68.

TANNAHILL, R. (1980). *Sex in history*. New York: Stein & Day.

TANNE, J. H. (2009). HIV prevalence in U.S. capital is at epidemic level. *British Medical Journal*, 338, 61205.

TANNEN, D. (1990). *You just don't understand: Women and men in conversation*. New York: William Morrow.

TARIN, J. J., & GOMEZ-PIQUER, V. (2002). Do women have a hidden heat period? *Human Reproduction*, 17, 2243–2248.

TARIS, T. W., & SEMIN, G. R. (1997a). Gender as a narrative of the effects of the love motive and relational context on sexual experience. *Archives of Sexual Behavior*, 26, 159–180.

TARIS, T. W., & SEMIN, G. R. (1997b). Passing on the faith: How mother-child communication influences transmission of moral values. *Journal of Moral Education*, 26, 211–221.

TATE, F. B., LONGO, D. A., & IMHOF, H. V. (2002). Safer-sex education: Evaluating effectiveness with test scores. *AIDS Patient Care and STDs*, 16, 197–199.

TAYLOR, D., et al. (1997). Risk factors for adult paternity in births to adolescents. *Obstetrics and Gynecology*, 89, 199–205.

TAYLOR, S. E., SAPHIRE-BERNSTEIN, S., & SEEMAN, T. E. (2010). Are plasma oxytocin in women and plasma vasopressin in men biomarkers of distressed pair-bond relationships? *Psychological Science*, 21, 3–7.

TAYWADITEP, K. J. (2001). Marginalization among the marginalized: Gay men's anti-effeminacy attitudes. *Journal of Homosexuality*, 42, 1–28.

TEACHMAN, J. (2003). Premarital sex, premarital cohabitation, and the risk of subsequent marital dissolution among women. *Journal of Marriage and Family*, 65, 444–455.

TEASDALE, B., & BRADLEY-ENGEN, M. S. (2010). Adolescent same-sex attraction and mental health: The role of stress and support. *Journal of Homosexuality*, 57, 287–309.

TEERAPONG, S., et al. (2009). Physical health consequences of sexual assault victims. *Journal of the Medical Association of Thailand*, 92, 885–890.

TEICHMANN, A., et al. (2009). Continuous, daily levonorgestrel/ethinyl estradiol vs. 21-day, cyclic levonorgestrel/ethinyl estradiol: Efficacy, safety and bleeding in a randomized, open-label trial, *Contraception*, 80, 504–511.

TEMPLEMAN, T. L., & STINNETT, R. D. (1991). Patterns of sexual arousal and history in a "normal" sample of young men. *Archives of Sexual Behavior*, 20, 137–150.

TERMAN, L., & MILES, C. C. (1936). *Sex and personality*. New York: McGraw-Hill.

TEW, M. (1990). *Safer childbirth? A critical history of maternity care*. London: Chapman & Hall.

THAKKER, J., et al. (2008). Rape: Assessment and treatment. In D. R. Laws and W. T. O'Donohue (Eds.), *Sexual deviance: Theory, assessment, and treatment* (2nd ed., pp. 356–383). New York: Guilford Press.

THAKUR, M., et al. (2009). A comparative study on aphrodisiac activity of some ayurvedic herbs in male albino rats. *Archives of Sexual Behavior*, 38, 1009–1015.

THAYER, L. (1986). *On communication*. Norwood, NJ: Ablex.

THE LANCET. (2009). Sexual and reproductive health and climate change. *The Lancet* (editorial), 374, 949.

THEIM, R. (1994, August 6). Gay parents' custody rights debated by lawyers. *New Orleans Times-Picayune*, p. A7.

THOMAS, J. (2010). New method is as effective as levonorgestrel after unprotected intercourse. *Perspectives on Sexual and Reproductive Health*, 42, 134–135.

THOMPSON, B. J. (2009). Hepatitis C virus: The growing challenge. *British Medical Bulletin*, 89, 153–167.

THOMPSON, H. B. (1903). *The mental traits of sex*. Chicago: University of Chicago Press.

THOMPSON, L. (1991). Paraphilia spans extremes of sexual disorders. *The Washington Post*.

THOMPSON, M. A., et al. (2010). Antiretroviral treatment of adult HIV infection. *Journal of the American Medical Association*, 304, 321–333.

THOMPSON, S. (1990). Putting a big thing into a little hole: Teenage girls' accounts of sexual initiation. *Journal of Sex Research*, 27, 341–361.

THOMPSON, T. L., & ZERBINOS, E. (1997). Television cartoons: Do children notice it's a boy's world? *Sex Roles*, 37, 415–432.

THORNHILL, N. W. (1991). An evolutionary analysis of rules regulating human inbreeding and marriage. *Behavioral and Brain Sciences*, 14, 247–293.

THORNHILL, N. W. (1992). Human inbreeding. In N. W. Thornhill (Ed.), *The natural history of inbreeding and outbreeding: Theoretical and empirical perspectives*. Chicago: University of Chicago Press.

THORNHILL, R., & GRAMMER, K. (1999). The body and face of woman: One ornament that signals quality? *Evolution and Human Behavior*, 20, 105–120.

THORNHILL, R., & PALMER, C. T. (2000). *A natural history of rape: Biological bases of sexual coercion*. Cambridge, MA: MIT Press.

THORNHILL, R., & THORNHILL, N. W. (1992). The evolutionary psychology of men's coercive sexuality. *Behavioral and Brain Sciences*, 15, 363–421.

TIEFER, L. (1991). Historical, scientific, clinical and feminist criticisms of "The human sexual response" model. In J. Bancroft, C. M. Davis, & H. J. Ruppel, Jr. (Eds.), *Annual review of sex research* (Vol. II, pp. 1–23). Allentown, PA: Society for the Scientific Study of Sexuality.

TIEFER, L. (2000). Sexology and the pharmaceutical industry: The threat of co-optation. *Journal of Sex Research*, 37, 273–283.

TIEFER, L. (2001). A new view of women's sexual problems: Why new? Why now? *Journal of Sex Research*, 38, 89–96.

TIEFER, L., HALL, M., & TAVRIS, C. (2002). Beyond dysfunction: A new view of women's sexual problems. *Journal of Sex & Marital Therapy*, 28(S), 225–232.

TIEZZI, L., et al. (1997). Pregnancy prevention among urban adolescents younger than 15: Results of the 'In Your Face' program. *Family Planning Perspectives*, 29, 176–186, 197.

TIME ESSAY. (1966, January 21). The homosexual in America. *Time*, 40–41.

TIME (2010, August 2). Short of a vaccine, new hope for an anti-HIV gel. *Time*, p. 15.

TOBIAN, A. A. R., et al. (2009). Male circumcision for the prevention of HSV-2 and HPV infections and syphilis. *New England Journal of Medicine*, 360, 1298–1309.

TOLLISON, C. D., & ADAMS, H. E. (1979). *Sexual disorders: Treatment, theory, and research*. New York: Gardner Press.

TORASSA, U. (2000, May 27). Maternal choice caesareans. *New Orleans Times-Picayune*, p. E1, E4.

TOUBIA, N. (1988). Women and health in Sudan. In N. Toubia (Ed.), *Women of the Arab world* (pp. 98–109). London: Zed Books.

TOUBIA, N. (1994). Female circumcision as a public health issue. *New England Journal of Medicine*, 331, 712–716.

TRAVIS, J. (2001). Sperm protein may lead to male pill. *Science News*, 160, 228.

TREISMAN, G. J., & KAPLIN, A. I. (2002). Neurologic and psychiatric complications of antiretroviral agents. *AIDS*, 16, 1201–1215.

TRELOAR, A. E., et al. (1967). Variation of the human menstrual cycle through reproductive life. *International Journal of Fertility*, 12, 77–126.

TRONO, D., et al. (2010). HIV persistence and the prospect of long-term drug-free remissions for HIV-infected individuals. *Science*, 329, 174–180.

TRUDEL, G. (2002). Sexuality and marital life: Results of a survey. *Journal of Sex & Marital Therapy*, 28, 229–249.

TRUDGILL, E. (1976). *Madonnas and Magdalens: The origins and development of Victorian sexual attitudes*. New York: Holmes & Meier.

TRUESDELL, D., MCNEIL, J., & DESCHNER, J. (1986). Incidence of wife abuse in incestuous families. *Social Work*, 31, 138–140.

TRUSSELL, J. (2008). Contraceptive efficacy. In R. A. Hatcher et al. (Eds.), *Contraceptive Technology* (19th ed., pp. 747–826). New York: Ardent Media.

TSAI, C. S., SHEPHERD, B. E., & VERMUND, S. H. (2009). Does douching increase risk for sexually transmitted infections? A prospective study in high-risk adolescents. *American Journal of Obstetrics & Gynecology*, 200, 38.e1–38.e8.

TSITSIKA, A., et al. (2009). Adolescent pornographic Internet site use: A multivariate regression analysis of the predictive factors

486 *References*

of use and psychosocial implications. *Cyberpsychology & Behavior, 12,* 545–549.

TUFTS NEW ENGLAND MEDICAL CENTER. (1984). *Sexually exploited children: Services and research project.* Boston: Author.

TUITEN, A., et al. (2000). Time course of effects of testosterone administration on sexual arousal in women. *Archives of General Psychiatry, 57,* 149–153.

TURCHIK, J. A., et al. (2009). Prediction of sexual assault experiences in college women based on rape scripts: A prospective analysis. *Journal of Consulting and Clinical Psychology, 77,* 361–366.

TUREK, F. (1999, July/August). Legislating morality. *New Man Magazine,* 50–55.

TURLEY, J. (2010, April 26). The scarlet letter lives on. *USA Today,* 9A.

TURNBULL, D., et al. (1996). Randomized, controlled trial of efficacy of midwife-managed care. *The Lancet, 348,* 213–218.

TURNER, C. F., MILLER, H. G., & MOSES, L. E. (Eds.). (1989). *AIDS: Sexual behavior and intravenous drug use.* Washington, DC: National Academy Press.

TURNER, C. F., et al. (2002). Untreated gonococcal and chlamydial infection in a probability sample of adults. *Journal of the American Medical Association, 287,* 726–733.

TWENGE, J. M. (1997a). Attitudes toward women, 1970–1995. *Psychology of Women Quarterly, 21,* 35–51.

TWENGE, J. M. (1997b). Changes in masculine and feminine traits over time: A meta-analysis. *Sex Roles, 36,* 305–325.

TYLER, K. A. (2002). Social and emotional outcomes of childhood sexual abuse: A review of recent research. *Aggression and Violent Behavior, 7,* 567–589.

TYRE, P., & MCGINN, D. (2003, May 12). She works, he doesn't. *Newsweek,* 44–52.

U

UDRY, J. R. (2000). Biological limits of gender construction. *American Sociological Review, 65,* 443–457.

UGGEN, C., & BLACKSTONE, A. (2004). Sexual harassment as a gendered expression of power. *American Sociological Review, 69,* 64–92.

ULLMAN, S. E. (1996). Social relations, coping strategies, and self-blame attributions in adjustment to sexual assault. *Psychology of Women Quarterly, 20,* 505–536.

ULLMAN, S. E. (1998). Does offender violence escalate when rape victims fight back? *Journal of Interpersonal Violence, 13,* 179–192.

ULLMAN, S. E., KARABATSOS, G., & KOSS, M. P. (1999). Alcohol and sexual aggression in a national sample of college men. *Psychology of Women Quarterly, 23,* 673–689.

ULLMAN, S. E., & KNIGHT, R. A. (1991). A multivariate model for predicting rape and physical injury outcomes during sexual assaults. *Journal of Consulting and Clinical Psychology, 59,* 724–731.

ULLRICH, H. E. (1992). Menstrual taboos among Havik Brahmin women: A study of ritual change. *Sex Roles, 26,* 19–40.

UNITED KINGDOM TESTICULAR CANCER SOCIETY STUDY GROUP. (1994). Aetiology of testicular cancer: Association with congenital abnormalities, age at puberty, infertility, and exercise. *British Medical Journal, 308,* 1393–1399.

UNITED NATIONS. (2007). *Demographic Yearbook 2006.* Department of Economic and Social Affairs. New York: Author.

UNITED NATIONS/ECONOMIC COMMISSION FOR EUROPE. (1995). *Trends in Europe and North America: The statistical yearbook of the Economic Commission for Europe.* Author.

UNITED NATIONS POPULATION DIVISION. (2001). *World contraceptive use 2001.* New York: United Nations.

U.S. ATTORNEY GENERAL'S COMMISSION ON PORNOGRAPHY. (1986). *Final Report of the Attorney General's Commission on Pornography.* Washington, DC: U.S. Justice Department.

U.S. DEPARTMENT OF JUSTICE. (1996). *Hate crime statistics. Uniform Crime Reports.* Washington, DC: Federal Bureau of Investigation.

U.S. DEPARTMENT OF JUSTICE. (2005). *Criminal victimization in the United States, 2003 statistical tables.* Washington, DC: Bureau of Justice Statistics.

U.S. DEPARTMENT OF JUSTICE (2010). Federal Bureau of Investigation Uniform Crime Reports. Crime in the United States–2008. U.S. Department of Justice.

U.S. GENERAL ACCOUNTING OFFICE. (1990). *Drug exposed infants: A generation at risk.* Publication GAO/HRD-90-138. Washington, DC: Author.

U.S. PREVENTIVE SERVICES TASK FORCE. (2009). Screening for breast cancer: U.S. Preventive Services Task Force recommendation statement. *Annals of Internal Medicine, 151,* 716–726.

UNKELBACH, C., GUASTELLA, A. J., & FORGAS, J. P. (2008). Oxytocin selectively facilitates recognition of positive sex and relationship words. *Psychological Science, 19,* 1092–1094.

UPCHURCH, D. M., et al. (1998). Gender and ethnic differences in the timing of first sexual intercourse. *Family Planning Perspectives, 30,* 121–127.

URMAN, B., & YAKIN, K. (2006). Ovulatory disorders and infertility. *Journal of Reproductive Medicine, 51,* 267–282.

URSUS. (2004). Query: Pubic hair. *Canadian Medical Association Journal, 171,* 1569.

USKUL, A. K. (2004). Women's menarche stories from a multicultural sample. *Social Science & Medicine, 59,* 667–679.

UTIAN, W. (1997). Women's experience and attitudes toward menopause. Paper presented at the annual meeting of the North American Menopause Society, Boston.

UTZ-BILLING, I., & KENTENICH, H. (2008). Female genital mutilation: An injury, physical and mental harm. *Journal of Psychosomatic Obstetrics & Gyneocology, 29,* 225–229.

V

VALENTICH, M., & GRIPTON, J. (1989). Teaching children about AIDS. *Journal of Sex Education and Therapy, 15*(2), 92.

VAN BEIJSTERVELDT, C. E. M., HUDZIAK, J. J., & BOOMSMA, D. I. (2006). Genetic and environmental influences on cross-gender behavior and relation to behavioral problems: A study of Dutch twins at ages 7 and 10 years. *Archives of Sexual Behavior, 35,* 647–658.

VANCE, C. S. (1988). Ordinances restricting pornography could damage women. In R. T. Francoeur (Ed.), *Taking sides: Clashing views on controversial issues in human sexuality.* Guilford, CT: Dushkin.

VANCE, E. B., & WAGNER, N. N. (1976). Written descriptions of orgasm: A study of sex differences. *Archives of Sexual Behavior, 5,* 87–98.

VAN DEN HEUVEL, M. W., et al. (2005). Comparison of ethinylestradiol pharmacokinetics in three hormonal contraceptive formulations: The vaginal ring, the transdermal patch, and an oral contraceptive. *Contraception, 72,* 168–174.

VAN DER GRAAF, Y., et al. (2002). Human papillomavirus and the long-term risk of cervical neoplasia. *American Journal of Epidemiology, 156,* 158–164.

VAN DER KOLK, B., et al. (1996). Dissociation, somatization, and affect dysregulation: The complexity of adaptation to trauma. *American Journal of Psychiatry, 153,* 83–93.

VAN DER LOEFF, M. F. S., & AABY, P. (1999). Towards a better understanding of the epidemiology of HIV-2. *AIDS, 13*(Suppl. A), S69–S84.

VAN GERKO, K., et al. (2005). Reported childhood sexual abuse and eating-disordered cognitions and behaviors. *Child Abuse & Neglect, 29,* 375–382.

VAN HALL, E. V. (1997). The menopausal misnomer. *Journal of Psychosomatic Obstetrics and Gynecology, 18,* 59–62.

VAN LANKVELD, J. (2009). Self-help therapies for sexual dysfunction. *Journal of Sex Research, 46,* 143–155.

VAN OSS MARIN, B., & GOMEZ, C. (1994). Latinos, HIV disease, and culture: Strategies for HIV prevention. In P. Cohen, M. Sande, & P. Volberding (Eds.), *The AIDS knowledge base* (pp. 10.8-1–10.8-13). New York: Little, Brown.

VANWESENBEECK, I. (2002). Another decade of social scientific work on sex work: A review of research, 1990–2000. *Annual Review of Sex Research, 12,* 242–289.

VAN WYK, P. (1984). Psychosocial development of heterosexual, bisexual, and homosexual behavior. *Archives of Sexual Behavior, 13,* 505–544.

VENIEGAS, R. C., & CONLEY, T. D. (2000). Biological research on women's sexual orientations: Evaluating the evidence. *Journal of Social Issues, 56,* 267–282.

VENTURA, S. J., et al. (1997). Report of final natality statistics, 1995. National Center for Health Statistics. *Monthly Vital Statistics Report, 45*(11).

VILAIN, E. (2001). Genetics of sexual development. *Annual Review of Sex Research, 11,* 1–25.

VIRGIN, H. W., & WALKER, B. D. (2010). Immunology and the elusive AIDS vaccine. *Nature, 464,* 224–u.

VISNESS, C. M., & KENNEDY, K. I. (1997). The frequency of coitus during breastfeeding. *Birth, 24,* 253–257.

VITTENGL, J. R., & HOLT, C. S. (2000). Getting acquainted: The relationship of self-disclosure and social attraction to positive affect. *Journal of Social and Personal Relationships, 17,* 53–66.

VLAJINAC, H. D., et al. (1997). Effect of caffeine intake during pregnancy on birth weight. *American Journal of Epidemiology, 145,* 335–338.

VOELLER, B. (1991). AIDS and heterosexual anal intercourse. *Archives of Sexual Behavior, 201,* 233–269.

VOIGHT, D. Q. (1984). A tankard of sporting taboos. In R. B. Brown (Ed.), *Forbidden fruits: Taboos and tabooism in culture.* Bowling Green, OH: Bowling Green University Popular Press.

VOIGT, H. (1991). Enriching the sexual experience of couples: The Asian traditions and sexual counseling. *Journal of Sex & Marital Therapy, 17,* 214–219.

VON SYDOW, K. (1999). Sexuality during pregnancy and after childbirth: A metacontent analysis of 59 studies. *Journal of Psychosomatic Research, 47,* 27–49.

VONK, R., & ASHMORE, R. D. (2003). Thinking about gender types: Cognitive organization of female and male types. *British Journal of Social Psychology, 42,* 257–280.

W

WADE, L. D., KREMER, E. C., & BROWN, J. (2005). The incidental orgasm: The presence of clitoral knowledge and the absence of orgasm for women. *Women & Health*, 42, 117–138.

WAINBERG, M. A., & CLOTET, B. (2007). Immunologic response to protease inhibitor-based highly active antiretroviral therapy: A review. *AIDS Patient Cave and STDs*, 21, 609–620.

WAITE, L. J., et al. (2009). Sexuality: Measures of partnerships, practices, attitudes, and problems in the National Social Life, Health, and Aging Study. *Journal of Gerontology: Social Sciences*, 64B(S1), i56–i66.

WAITE, L. J., et al. (2009). Sexuality: Measures of partnerships, practices, attitudes, and problems in the National Social Life, Health, and Aging study. *Journal of Gerontology: Social Services*, 64B(S1), i56–i66.

WALBOOMERS, J. M., et al. (1999). Human papillomavirus is a necessary cause of invasive cervical cancer worldwide. *Journal of Pathology*, 189, 12–19.

WALDENSTRÖM, U. (1996). Modern maternity care: Does safety have to take the meaning out of birth? *Midwifery*, 12, 165–173.

WALDENSTRÖM, U., & NILSSON, C.-A. (1997). A randomized controlled study of birth center care versus standard maternity care: Effects on women's health. *Birth*, 24, 17–26.

WALDENSTRÖM, U., et al. (2004). A negative birth experience: Prevalence and risk factors in a national sample. *Birth*, 31, 17–27.

WALDINGER, M., & SCHWEITZER, D. (2006). Changing paradigms from a historical DSM-III and DSM-IV view toward an evidence-based definition of premature ejaculation. Part II. Proposals for DSM-V and ICD-11. *Journal of Sexual Medicine*, 3, 693–705.

WALDNER-HAUGRUD, L. K. (1999). Sexual coercion in lesbian and gay relationships; A review and critique. *Aggression and Violent Behavior*, 4, 139–149.

WALKER, A., & HUMPHRIES, C. (2007, September 27). Starting the good life in the womb. *Newsweek*, 56–58.

WALKER, B. L., & HARRINGTON, D. (2002). Effects of staff training on staff knowledge and attitudes about sexuality. *Educational Gerontology*, 28, 639–654.

WALKER, C. E. (1970). Erotic stimuli and the aggressive sexual offender. In *Technical Report of the Commission on Obscenity and Pornography* (Vol. 7, pp. 91–147). Washington, DC: U.S. Government Printing Office.

WALKER, J., ARCHER, J., & DAVIES, M. (2005). Effects of rape on men: A descriptive analysis. *Archives of Sexual Behavior*, 34, 69–80.

WALL, G. (2007). How involved is involved fathering? *Gender & Society*, 21, 508–527.

WALLIEN, M. S. C., & COHEN-KETTENIS, P. T. (2008). Psychosexual outcomes of gender-dysphonic children. *Journal of the American Academy of Child & Adolescent Psychiatry*, 47, 1413–1423.

WALLING, A. (2005). Prevention and diagnosis of fetal alcohol syndrome. *American Family Physician*, 73, 18–37.

WALSH-CHILDERS, K., GOTTHOFFER, A., & LEPRE, C. R. (2002). From "Just the Facts" to "Downright Salacious": Teen's and women's magazines coverage of sex and sexual health. In J. D. Brown, J. R. Steele, & K. Walsh-Childers (Eds.), *Sexual teens, sexual media* (pp. 153–172), Mahwah, NJ: Lawrence Erlbaum.

WALSTER, E., & WALSTER, G. W. (1978). *A new look at love*. Reading: MA: Addison-Wesley.

WALSTER, E., et al. (1966). Importance of physical attractiveness in dating behavior. *Journal of Personality and Social Psychology*, 4, 508–516.

WALTERS, S. T., FOY, B. D., & CASTRO, R. J. (2002). The agony of ecstasy: Responding to growing MDMA use among college students. *Journal of American College Health*, 51, 139–141.

WANG, A., RANA, S., & KARUMANCHI, S. A. (2009). Preeclampsia: The role of angiogenic factors in its pathogenesis. *Physiology*, 24, 147–158.

WARD, L. M. (2002). Does television exposure affect emerging adults' attitudes and assumptions about sexual relationships? Correlational and experimental confirmation. *Journal of Youth and Adolescence*, 31, 1–15.

WARD, L. M., & FRIEDMAN, K. (2006). Using TV as a guide: Associations between television viewing and adolescents. Sexual attitudes and behavior. *Journal of Research on Adolescence*, 16, 133–156.

WARD, M. C. (1989). *Nest in the wind: Adventures in anthropology on a tropical island*. Prospect Heights, IL: Waveland Press.

WARD, T., & BEECH, A. (2006). An integrated theory of sexual offending. *Aggression and Violent Behavior*, 11, 44–63.

WARD, T., & BEECH, A. R. (2008). An integrated theory of sexual offending. In D. R. Laws & W. T. O'Donohue (Eds.), *Sexual deviance: Theory, assessment, and treatment* (2nd ed., pp. 21–36). New York, Guilford Press.

WARNER, C. (1997, September 29). Storied history. *New Orleans Times-Picayune*, p. A1, A6–A7.

WARNER, L., & STEINER, M. J. (2008). Male condoms. In R. A. Hatcher et al. (Eds.), *Contraceptive technology* (19th ed., pp. 297–316). New York: Ardent Media.

WASSON, J. H., et al. (1995). A comparison of transurethral with watchful waiting for moderate symptoms of benign prostatic hyperplasia. *New England Journal of Medicine*, 332, 1995.

WATSON-FRANKE, M.-B. (2002). A world in which women move freely without fear of men. An anthropological perspective on rape. *Women's Studies International Forum*, 25, 599–606.

WAYLEN, A. E., et al. (2010). Romantic and sexual behavior in young adolescents: Repeated surveys in a population-based cohort. *Journal of Early Adolescence*, 30, 432–443.

WEAVER, A. D., & BYERS, E. S. (2006). The relationships among body image, body mass index, exercise, and sexual functioning in heterosexual women. *Psychology of Women Quarterly*, 30, 333–339.

WEBER, A. L. (1998). Losing, leaving, and letting go: Coping with nonmarital breakups. In B. H. Spitzberg & W. R. Cupach (Eds.), *The dark side of close relationships* (pp. 267–306). Mahwah, NJ: Lawrence Erlbaum.

WEBER, M. (1993). Images in clinical medicine: Pinworms. *New England Journal of Medicine*, 328, 927.

WEEKS, J. D., & KOZAK, L. J. (2001). Trends in the use of episiotomy in the United States: 1980–1998. *Birth*, 28, 152–160.

WEINBERG, M., & WILLIAMS, C. (1988). African American sexuality: A test of two theories. *Journal of Sex Research*, 25, 197–218.

WEINBERG, M. S., WILLIAMS, C. J., & CALHAN, C. (1994). Homosexual foot fetishism. *Archives of Sexual Behavior*, 23, 611–626.

WEINBERG, T. (1987). Sadomasochism in the United States: A review of recent sociological literature. *Journal of Sex Research*, 23, 50–69.

WEINBERG, T. S. (2006). Sadomasochism and the social sciences: A review of the sociological and social psychological literature. *Journal of Homosexuality*, 50, 17–40.

WEINER, A. (1996). Understanding the social needs of streetwalking prostitutes. *Journal of the National Association of Social Workers*, 41, 97–105.

WEINSTOCK, H., et al. (1994). Chlamydia trachomatis infections. *Infectious Disease Clinics of North America*, 8, 797–819.

WEIS, D. L. (1983). Affective reactions of women to their initial experience of coitus. *Journal of Sex Research*, 19, 209–237.

WEIS, D. L. (1985). The experience of pain during women's first sexual intercourse: Cultural mythology about female sexual initiation. *Archives of Sexual Behavior*, 14, 421–428.

WEISS, K. G. (2009). "Boys will be boys" and other gendered accounts. *Violence Against Women*, 15, 810–834.

WEISS, K. G. (2010). Male sexual victimization. *Men and Masculinities*, 12, 275–298.

WEISS, M., et al. (2004). Length of stay after vaginal birth: Sociodemographic and readiness-for-discharge factors. *Birth*, 31, 93–101.

WEISS, R. A., & HEENEY, J. L. (2009). An ill wind for wild chimps? *Nature*, 460, 470–471.

WEISS, R. S. (1975). *Marital separation*. New York: Basic Books.

WELLER, A., & WELLER, L. (1993). Menstrual synchrony between mothers and daughters and between roommates. *Physiology & Behavior*, 53, 943–949.

WELLER, A., & WELLER, L. (1997). Menstrual synchrony under optimal conditions: Bedouin families. *Journal of Comparative Physiology*, 111, 143–151.

WELLER, L., et al. (1999). Menstrual synchrony in a sample of working women. *Psychoneuroendocrinology*, 24, 449–459.

WERNEKE, U., NORTHEY, S., & BHUGRA, D. (2006). Antidepressants and sexual dysfunction. *Acta Psychiatrica Scandinavica*, 114, 384–397.

WESPES, E., & SCHULMAN, C. C. (2002). Male andropause: Myth, reality and treatment. *International Journal of Impotence Research*, 14 (supp.1. 1), 593–598.

WESSELLS, H., LUE, T. F., & MCANINCH, J. W. (1996). Penile length in the flaccid and erect states: Guidelines for penile augmentation. *Journal of Urology*, 156, 995–997.

WEST, R. (1982). *St. Augustine*. Chicago: Thomas More Press. (Originally published in 1933.)

WEST, S., et al. (2008). Prevalence of low sexual desire and hypoactive sexual desire disorder in a nationally representative sample of U.S. women. *Archives of Internal Medicine*, 168, 1441–1449.

WESTERMARCK, E. A. (1891). *The history of human marriage*. New York: Macmillan.

WESTHOFF, C., PICARDO, L., & MORROW, E. (2003). Quality of life following early medical or surgical abortion. *Contraception*, 67, 41–47.

WHALEN, R. (1977). Brain mechanisms controlling sexual behavior. In F. A. Beach (Ed.), *Human sexuality in four perspectives*. Baltimore: Johns Hopkins University Press.

WHEELER, J., NEWRING, K. A. B., & DRAPER, C. (2008). Transvestic fetishism: Psychopathology and theory. In D. R. Laws & W. T. O'Donohue (Eds.), *Sexual deviance: Theory, assessment, and treatment* (2nd ed., pp. 272–284). New York: Guilford Press.

WHEN to START CONSORTIUM. (2009). Timing of initiation of antiretroviral therapy in

AIDS-free HIV-1-infected patients: A collaborative analysis of 18 HIV cohort studies. *The Lancet,* 373, 1352–1363.

WHIPPLE, B., & KOMISARUK, B. R. (1999). Beyond the G spot: Recent research on female sexuality. *Psychiatric Annals,* 29, 34–37.

WHIPPLE, B., OGDEN, G., & KOMISARUK, B. R. (1992). Physiological correlates of imagery-induced orgasm in women. *Archives of Sexual Behavior,* 21, 121–133.

WHITAKER, D. J., et al. (1999). Teenage partners' communication about sexual risk and condom use: The importance of parent-teenager discussions. *Family Planning Perspectives,* 31, 117–121.

WHITAM, F. L. (1983). Culturally invariable properties of male homosexuality: Tentative conclusions from cross-cultural research. *Archives of Sexual Behavior,* 12, 207–226.

WHITAM, F. L., DIAMOND, M., & MARTIN, J. (1993). Homosexual orientation in twins: A report on 61 pairs and three triplet sets. *Archives of Sexual Behavior,* 22, 187–205.

WHITAM, F. L., & MATHY, R. M. (1986). *Male homosexuality in four societies: Brazil, Guatemala, the Philippines, and the United States.* New York: Praeger.

WHITBECK, L. B., CONGER, R. D., & SIMONS, R. L. (1993). Minor deviant behaviors and adolescent sexual activity. *Youth and Society,* 25, 24–37.

WHITE, G. L. (1980). Inducing jealousy: A power perspective. *Personality and Sexual Psychology Bulletin,* 6, 222–227.

WHITE, G. L. (1981). Relative involvement, inadequacy, and jealousy: A test of a causal model. *Alternative Lifestyles,* 4, 291–309.

WHITEHURST, R. N. (1972). Extramarital sex: Alienation or extension of normal behavior. In J. N. Edwards (Ed.), *Sex and society.* Chicago: Rand McNally.

WHITLEY, JR., B. E. (1998). False consensus on sexual behavior among college women: Comparison of four theoretical explanations. *Journal of Sex Research,* 35, 206–214.

WIDMAN, L., et al. (2006). Sexual communication and contraceptive use in adolescent dating couples. *Journal of Adolescent Health,* 39, 893–899.

WIDMER, E. D., TREAS, J., & NEWCOMB, R. (1998). Attitudes toward nonmarital sex in 24 countries. *Journal of Sex Research,* 35, 349–358.

WIEDERMAN, M. W. (1997a). Extramarital sex: Prevalence and correlates in a national survey. *Journal of Sex Research,* 34, 167–174.

WIEDERMAN, M. W. (1997b). The truth must be in here somewhere: Examining the gender discrepancy in self-reported lifetime number of sex partners. *Journal of Sex Research,* 34, 375–386.

WIEDERMAN, M. W., & HURST, S. R. (1998). Body size, physical attractiveness and body image among young adult women: Relationships to sexual experience and sexual esteem. *Journal of Sex Research,* 35, 272–281.

WIEDERMAN, M. W., & KENDALL, E. (1999). Evolution, sex, and jealousy: Investigation with a sample from Sweden. *Evolution and Human Behavior,* 20, 121–128.

WIELANDT, H., & KNUDSEN, L. B. (1997). Birth control: Some experiences from Denmark. *Contraception,* 55, 301–306.

WIESENFELD, H. C., et al. (2005). Knowledge about sexually transmitted diseases in women among primary care physicians. *Sexually Transmitted Diseases,* 32, 649–653.

WIEST, W. (1977). Semantic differential profiles of orgasm and other experiences among men and women. *Sex Roles,* 3, 399–403.

WIJKMAN, M., BIJLEVELD, C., & HENDRIKS, J. (2010). Women don't do such things! Characteristics of female sex offenders and offender types. *Sexual Abuse: A Journal of Research and Treatment,* 22, 135–156.

WILCOX, A., DUNSON, D., & BAIRD, D. (2000). The timing of the "fertile window" in the menstrual cycle: Day-specific estimates from a prospective study. *British Medical Journal,* 321, 1259–1262.

WILCOX, A. J., BAIRD, D. D., & WEINBERG, C. R. (1999). Time of implantation of the conceptus and loss of pregnancy. *New England Journal of Medicine,* 340, 1796–1799.

WILCOX, A. J., WEINBERG, C. R., & BAIRD, D. D. (1995). Timing of sexual intercourse in relation to ovulation: Effects on the probability of conception, survival of the pregnancy, and sex of the baby. *New England Journal of Medicine,* 333, 1517–1521.

WILCOX, A. J., et al. (1988). Incidence of early loss of pregnancy. *New England Journal of Medicine,* 319, 189–194.

WILCOX, A. J., et al. (2004). On the frequency of intercourse around ovulation: Evidence for biological influences. *Human Reproduction,* 19, 1539–1543.

WILDSMITH, E., GUZZO, K. B., & HAYFORD, S. R. (2010). Repeat unintended, unwanted and seriously mistimed childbearing in the United States. *Perspectives on Sexual and Reproductive Health,* 42, 14–22.

WILHELM, D., PALMER, S., & KOOPMAN, P. (2007). Sex determination and gonadal development in mammals. *Physiological Reviews,* 87, 1–27.

WILLFORD, J., LEECH, S., & DAY, N. (2006). Moderate prenatal alcohol exposure and cognitive status of children at age 10. *Alcoholism: Clinical and Experimental Research,* 30, 1051–1059.

WILLIAMS, C. J., & WEINBERG, M. S. (2003). Zoophilia in men: A study of sexual interest in animals. *Archives of Sexual Behavior,* 37, 523–535.

WILLIAMS, J. E., & BEST, D. L. (1990). *Measuring sex stereotypes: A multinational study.* Newbury Park, CA: Sage.

WILLIAMS, L., & SOBIESZCZYK, T. (1997). Attitudes surrounding the continuation of female circumcision in the Sudan: Passing the tradition to the next generation. *Journal of Marriage and Family,* 59, 966–981.

WILLIAMS, L. M. (1994). Recall of childhood trauma: A prospective study of women's memories of child sexual abuse. *Journal of Consulting and Clinical Psychology,* 62, 1167–1176.

WILLIAMS, N., CHELL, J., & KAPILA, L. (1993). Why are children referred for circumcision? *British Medical Journal,* 306, 28.

WILLIAMSON, C., & CLUSE-TOLAR, T. (2002). Pimp-controlled prostitution. *Violence Against Women,* 8, 1074–1092.

WILLIAMSON, D. M., et al. (2008). Current research in preterm birth. *Journal of Women's Health,* 17, 1545–1549.

WILLIS, B. M., & LEVY, B. S. (2002). Child prostitution: Global health burden, research needs, and interventions. *The Lancet,* 359, 1417–1421.

WILSNACK, S. C., et al. (2002). Self-reports of forgetting and remembering childhood sexual abuse in a nationally representative sample of U.S. women. *Child Abuse & Neglect,* 26, 139–147.

WILSON, C. (2005). Recurrent vulvovaginitis candidiasis: An overview of traditional and alternative therapies. *Advanced Nurse Practitioner,* 13, 24–29.

WILSON, C. M., et al. (2010). Epidemiology of HIV infection and risk in adolescents and youth. *Journal of Acquired Immune Deficiency Syndrome,* 54 (Suppl 1), S5–S6.

WILSON, D. R. (2010). Health consequences of childhood sexual abuse. *Perspectives in Psychiatric Care,* 46, 56–64.

WILSON, E. K., et al. (2010). Parents' perspectives on talking to preteenage children about sex. *Perspectives on Sexual and Reproductive Health,* 42, 56–63.

WILSON, H. W., & WIDOM, C. S. (2009). Sexually transmitted diseases among adults who had been abused and neglected as children: A 30-year prospective study. *American Journal of Public Health,* 99(S1), S197–S203.

WILSON, H. W., & WIDOM, C. S. (2010). Does physical abuse, sexual abuse, or neglect in childhood increase the likelihood of same-sex sexual relationships and cohabitation? A prospective 30-year follow-up. *Archives of Sexual Behavior,* 39, 63–74.

WILSON, R. A. (1966). *Feminine forever.* London: W. H. Allen.

WINER, R. L., et al. (2006). Condom use and the risk of genital human papillomavirus infection in young women. *New England Journal of Medicine,* 354, 2645–2654.

WINGOOD, G. M., & DICLEMENTE, R. J. (1998). Gender-related correlates and predictors of consistent condom use among young adult African-American women: A prospective analysis. *International Journal of STD & AIDS,* 9, 139–145.

WINICK, C., & EVANS, J. T. (1996). The relationship between nonenforcement of state pornography laws and rates of sex crimes arrests. *Archives of Sexual Behavior,* 25, 439–453.

WITELSON, S. F., et al. (2008). Corpus callosum anatomy in right-handed homosexual and heterosexual men. *Archives of Sexual Behavior,* 37, 857–863.

WITT, S. D. (1996). Traditional or androgynous: An analysis to determine gender role orientation of basal readers. *Child Study Journal,* 26, 303–318.

WITTE, S. S., et al. (2010, March). Lack of awareness of partner STD risk among heterosexual couples. *Perspectives on Sexual and Reproductive Health,* 42, 49–55.

WITTING, K., SANTTILA, P., & VARJONEN, M. (2008). Female sexual dysfunction, sexual distress, and compatibility with partner. *Journal of Sexual Medicine,* 5, 2587–2599.

WOLAK, J., MITCHELL, K., & FINKELHOR, D. (2007). Unwanted and wanted exposure to online pornography in a national sample of youth Internet users. *Pediatrics,* 119, 247–258.

WOLAK, J., et al. (2008). Online "predators" and their victims. *American Psychologist,* 63, 111–128.

WOLF, A. P. (1970). Childhood association and sexual attraction: A further test of the Westermarck hypothesis. *American Anthropologist,* 72, 503–515.

WOLFE, P. S. (1997). The influence of personal values on issues of sexuality and disability. *Sexuality and Disability,* 15, 69–90.

WOLFF, C. (1971). *Love between women.* New York: Harper & Row.

WOOD, W., & EAGLY, A. H. (2002). A cross-cultural analysis of the behavior of women and men: Implications for the origins of sex differences. *Psychological Bulletin,* 128, 699–727.

WORLD HEALTH ORGANIZATION. (1984). Mental health and female sterilization: Report of a WHO collaborative prospective study. *Journal of Biosocial Sciences,* 16, 1–21.

WORLD HEALTH ORGANIZATION. (1985). Mental health and female sterilization: A follow-up. *Journal of Biosocial Sciences,* 17, 1–18.

WORLD HEALTH ORGANIZATION. (1992). *ICD-10: International statistical classification of diseases and related health problems.* World Health Organization: Geneva.

WORLD HEALTH ORGANIZATION. (2008). Eliminating female genital mutilation: An interagency statement. Geneva: Author.

WORLD HEALTH ORGANIZATION. (2009). Maternal mortality in 2005: Estimates developed by WHO, UNICEF, UNFPA and the World Bank. General: World Health Organization.

WORLD HEALTH ORGANIZATION. (2009). Viral cancers. http://www.who.int/vaccine_research/diseases/viral_cancers/en/print.html

WREN, B. G. (2009). The benefits of oestrogen following menopause: Why hormone replacement therapy should be offered to postmenopausal women. *Medical Journal of Australia, 190,* 321–325.

WRIGHT, A. L. (1983). A cross-cultural comparison of menopause symptoms. *Medical Anthropology, 7,* 20–36.

WYNN, L. L., FOSTER, A. M., & TRUSSELL, J. (2009). Can I get pregnant from oral sex? Sexual health misconceptions in e-mails to a reproductive health website. *Contraception, 79,* 91–97.

X

XU, F., et al. (2006). Trends in herpes simplex virus type 1 and type 2 seroprevalence in the U.S. *Journal of the American Medical Association, 296,* 964–973.

XU, F., et al. (2007). Prevalence of circumcision and herpes simplex virus type 2 infection in men in the United States: The National Health and Nutrition Examination Survey (NHANES), 1999–2004. *Sexually Transmitted Diseases, 34,* 479–484.

Y

YANG, Z., & GAYDOS, L. M. (2010). Reasons for and challenges of recent increases in teen birth rates: A study of family planning service policies and demographic changes at the state level. *Journal of Adolescent Health, 46,* 517–524.

YATES, P. M., HUCKER, S. J., & KINGSTON, D. A. (2008). Sexual sadism: Psychopathology and theory. In D. R. Laws & W. T. O'Donohue (Eds.), *Sexual deviance:*

Theory, assessment, and treatment (2nd ed., pp. 213–230), New York: Guilford Press.

YOUNG, A. (2008). The state is still in the bedroom of the nation: The control and regulation of sexuality in Canadian criminal law. *Canadian Journal of Human Sexuality, 17,* 203–218.

YOUNG, A. (2010, April 26). States seek new ways to restrict abortions, *USA Today,* 1A.

YOUNG, K. S. (2004). Internet addiction. *American Behavioral Scientist, 48,* 402–415.

YOUNG, K. S., et al. (2000). Online infidelity: A new dimension in couple relationships with implications for evaluation and treatment. In A. Cooper (Ed.), *Cybersex: The dark side of the force* (pp. 59–74). Philadelphia: Brunner Routledge.

YOUNG, L. (2009). Being human: Love—Neuroscience reveals all. *Nature, 457,* 148–149.

Z

ZAMAN, A. (2005, May 24). Where girls marry rapists for honor. *Los Angeles Times,* p. A9.

ZAMBONI, B. D., CRAWFORD, I., & WILLIAMS, P. G. (2000). Examining communication and assertiveness as predictors of condom use: Implications for HIV prevention. *AIDS Education and Prevention, 12,* 492–504.

ZANJANI, E. D., & ANDERSON, W. F. (1999). Prospects for in utero human gene therapy. *Science, 285,* 2084–2088.

ZARAGOZA, M. S., et al. (2001). Interviewing witnesses: Forced confabulation and confirmatory feedback increase false memories. *Psychological Science, 12,* 473–477.

ZAVIACIC, M., & ABLIN, R. (2000). The female prostate and prostate-specific antigen. *Histology and Histopathology, 15,* 131–142.

ZAVIACIC, M., et al. (1988a). Female urethral expulsions evoked by local digital stimulation of the G-spot: Differences in the response patterns. *Journal of Sex Research, 24,* 311–318.

ZAVIACIC, M., et al. (1988b). Concentrations of fructose in female ejaculate and urine: A comparative biochemical study. *Journal of Sex Research, 24,* 319–325.

ZEISS, A. M., DAVIES, H. D., & TINKLENBERG, J. R. (1996). An observational study of sexual behavior in demented male patients. *Journal of Gerontology: Medical Sciences, 51A,* M325–M329.

ZEVIN, D. (1992, August). The pleasure people. *US,* 32–36.

ZHANG, F., & LABOUVIE-VIEF, G. (2004). Stability and fluctuation in adult attachment style over a 6-year period. *Attachment & Human Development, 6,* 419–437.

ZHANG, J., THOMAS, A. G., & LEYBOVICH, E. (1997). Vaginal douching and adverse health effects: A meta-analysis. *American Journal of Public Health, 87,* 1207–1211.

ZHANG, Y., MILLER, L. E., & HARRISON, K. (2008). The relationship between exposure to sexual music videos and young adults' sexual attitudes, *Journal of Broadcasting & Electronic Media. 52,* 368–386.

ZHOU, J., et al. (1995). A sex difference in the human brain and its relation to transsexuality. *Nature, 378,* 68–70.

ZHOU, Q., O'BRIEN, B., & RELYEA, J. (1999). Severity of nausea and vomiting during pregnancy: What does it predict? *Birth, 26,* 108–114.

ZHU, B.-P., et al. (1999). Effect of the interval between pregnancies on perinatal outcomes. *New England Journal of Medicine, 340,* 589–594.

ZHU, T. F., et al. (1998). An African HIV-1 sequence from 1959 and implications for the origin of the epidemic. *Nature, 391,* 594–597.

ZILBERGELD, B. (1978). *Male sexuality: A guide to sexual fulfillment.* Boston: Little, Brown.

ZILLMANN, D., & BRYANT, J. (1982). Pornography, sexual callousness, and the trivialization of rape. *Journal of Communication,* Autumn, 10–21.

ZILLMANN, D. (2000). Influence of unrestrained access to erotica on adolescents' and young adults' dispositions toward sexuality. *Journal of Adolescent Health, 27,* 41–44.

ZUCKER, K. J., & BLANCHARD, R. (1997). Transvestic fetishism: Psychopathology and theory. In D. R. Laws & W. T. O'Donohue (Eds.), *Sexual deviance: Theory, assessment, and treatment* (pp. 253–279). New York: Guilford Press.

ZULE, W. A., et al. (2009). Effects of a Hepatitis C virus educational intervention or a motivational intervention on alcohol use, injection drug use, and sexual risk behaviors among injection drug users. *American Journal of Public Health, 99* (Suppl 1), S180–S186.

INDEX

A

Abortion, 160–162
  dilation and curettage (D&C), 161
  dilation and evacuation (D&E), 161
  future of, 161–162
  health risks of, 160–161
  induced labor, 161
  medical (nonsurgical), 161
  Roe v. Wade, 162
  RU 486, 161
  spontaneous (miscarriage), 178–179
  statistics, 160
Abstaining from sex, 28–29,
    142, 254
Acquaintance rape, 378–380
Acquired immunodeficiency syndrome
    (AIDS), 114–123, 157, 389
  in Africa, 120
  and birth control, 157
  and condoms, 128–129, 157
  infected populations, 118–120
  opportunistic infections, 116
  origins of, 116–117
  progression of HIV, 115–116
  and prostitution, 426
  public reactions to, 122–123
  and rape, 389
  symptoms of, 115–116
  teaching children about, 270–271
  testing for, 121
  transmission of, 117–118
  treatment for, 121–122
  vaccine, 122
  See also Human immunodeficiency
    virus (HIV); Sexually transmitted
    infections (STIs)
Addictions, sexual, 343–346
Adolescence, 249–254
  defined, 249
  masturbation, 250
  necking and petting, 250
  peer pressure, 254
  sexual development in, 250–254
  sexual intercourse, 252–254
  teenage pregnancy, 135–137
Adrenal glands, 59, 246
Adrenarche, 246
Adrenogenital syndrome (AGS), 201
Adultery, 257–258, 292
  cross–cultural perspectives, 292
  and Judaism, 9
  See also Extramarital sex
Afterbirth, 185
Agape love–style, 311
Ageism, 260–261

Aggressive pedophiles, 396
AGS, *See* Adrenogenital syndrome (AGS)
AIDS, *See* Acquired immunodeficiency
    syndrome (AIDS)
Alcohol:
  and erectile disorder, 331–332
  fetal alcohol syndrome (FAS),
    174–176
  and rape, 377–378
  and sexual coercion, 378
  and sexual response, 94
Alpha-Fetoprotein (AFP) screening, 178
Amebiasis, 124
Amenorrhea, 68
Amniocentesis, 178
Amnion, 169
Amniotic sac, breaking of, 184
Anabolic steroids, 73–74
Anal intercourse, 290–291
  and AIDS, 118, 291
  ethnic differences in, 281–282
Anal stimulation, 281–282, 290–291
Anaphrodisiacs, 94
Anatomy:
  female:
    external, 34–41
    internal, 42–46
  male:
    external, 46–50
    internal, 50–53
Androgen insensitivity syndrome, 201
Androgens, 50, 73
Androgyny, 209–219
Anesthetics, and childbirth, 182–183
Anger and conflict, 351
Anger rapists, 383
Ano-genital warts, 113
Anxious–ambivalent lovers, 307
Aphrodisiacs/anaphrodisiacs, 93–95
  alcohol, 94
  amphetamines, 94
  cocaine, 94
  "Ecstasy," 94
  marijuana, 94
  pheromones, 94
  Spanish fly, 94
  yohimbine, 94
Areola, 38
Artificial insemination, 190
Ascetic philosophy, 10
Assisted reproductive technology, 192
Asymptomatic HIV infection, 116
Attachment, 304, 307–308
Attachment theory of love, 307–308
Autoerotic asphyxiation, 369
Avoidant lovers, 307

B

Bacteria, 101
Bacterial vaginosis, 127
Bag of water, *See* Amniotic sac
Barrier methods of birth control, 145–150
  cervical cap, 149–150
  contraceptive sponge, 150
  diaphragm, 148–149
  female condoms, 147–148
  FemCap, 149–150
  future technology, 159
  male condoms, 145–147
Bartholin's glands, 36, 343
Basal body temperature method,
    143–144
Being love (B–love), 305
Bem Sex Role Inventory, 209–210
Benign coital cephalalgia, 337
Benign prostatic hyperplasia, 53
Bestiality, 366
B-girls, 423
Billings method, of fertility
    awareness, 144
Biological determinism, 208
Birth control methods, 139–163
  abortion, 160–162
  abstinence, 142
  barrier methods, 145–150
    cervical cap, 149–150
    contraceptive sponge, 150
    diaphragm, 148–149
    female condoms, 147–148
    FemCap, 149–150
    male condoms, 145–147
  birth control pills, 151–154
  breast–feeding, 142
  effectiveness rates, 139–141
  emergency, 155–156
  fertility awareness, 143–144
    basal body temperature method,
      143–144
    Billings method, 144
    calendar method, 143
    standard days method, 143
    symptom–thermal method, 144
  future technology, 159
  hormonal methods, 151–155
    Implanon, 154
    Jadelle, 155
    Norplant, 154
    Nuva Ring, 155
    oral contraception (The Pill),
      151–154
    OrthoEvra patch, 155
    the "Shot," 154

comprehensive theories, 385
cross–cultural perspectives on, 381
date rape, 378–380
defined, 375
evolutionary theories, 384–385
explanations of, 382–385
feminist theories, 384
gang rape, 380–381
historical perspective, 375
male rape, 382
marital rape, 380
opportunistic rapists, 384
post–rape posttraumatic stress
    disorder, 387–388
power rapists, 383
and pregnancy, 389
preventing, 390–391
prosecution of, 405–406
psychodynamic theories of, 383
rape myths, 385–387
rape–shield laws, 405
rape victim advocacy
    programs, 389
reactions of partners, 389
reactions of victims, 387–388
reporting, 389–390
sadistic rapists, 384
same–sex assault, 382
self-defense, 390
sexual coercion, 378–380
and sexually transmitted
    infections, 389
social cognitive theories of, 384
social systems perspective of, 390
statistics, 375–377
statutory rape, 381–382
stranger rape, 378
therapy for rapists, 406
therapy for victims, 407
Rape myths, 385–387
Rape–shield laws, 405
Rape victim advocacy programs, 389
Realistic love, 304
"Recovered memory" of child sexual
    abuse, 400
Recurrent miscarriages, 179
Refractory period, 83, 91, 265
Regressive pedophiles, 396
Relationships:
    communication, 347–352
    conflicts, 327, 351
    coping with breakups, 318–319
    and jealousy, 313–314
    homosexual, 236–237
    and love, 297–320
    maintaining, 314–318
        decline of passion, 315
        growing together/growing apart,
            315–318
        and intimacy, 308, 315, 319–320
    romantic, 298–300, 309

Religion and sex:
    Judaism, 9–10, 65
    rape, 375
    socializing agent, 14
    St. Augustine, 11, 217, 284, 298,
        311, 421
    St. Paul, 10, 284
    St. Thomas Aquinas, 231, 279, 284,
        357, 422
REM sleep, 248, 332
Representative sample, 23
Reproductive anatomy, 33–53
    female, 34–46
    male, 46–53
Resolution phase of sexual response:
    in women, 87
    in men, 83
Respiratory distress syndrome, 187
Retrograde ejaculation, 83
Rh factor, 177
Rh incompatibility, 177
Rhogam, 178
Rhythm method of birth control,
    See Fertility awareness
Richards, Renee, 206
Roe v. Wade, 162
Romans, 10
Romantic love, 298–300, 309
    cross–cultural perpectives, 299
    friendship vs., 301–302
    history, 298–300
    physiological responses, 302
RU 486, 161
Rubbers, *See* Condoms

S

S&M, *See* Sadomasochism
Sadistic rapists, 384
Sadists, defined, 366
Sadomasochism, 366–369
    bondage, 367
    domination, 367–369
    submission, 367–369
    See also Masochism; Paraphilias
Safer sex:
    and condoms, 128–129, 157
    defined, 129
    and monogamy, 129
    practicing, 128–130
        impediments to, 128–129
St. Augustine, 11, 217, 284, 298,
    311, 421
St. Paul, 10, 284
St. Thomas Aquinas, 231, 279, 284,
    357, 422
Sample, 23–24
Satyriasis, 344
Scabies, 124
Science and sex, 20–22
    Ellis, Henry Havelock, 21
    Freud, Sigmund, 20–21

Kinsey, Alfred C., 21–22
Laumann, Edward O., 22
Masters and Johnson, 22
Scientific methodology, 23–26
    case studies, 26
    correlation, 25
    direct observations, 25–26
    experimental research, 26
    random sampling, 23
    samples, 23–24
    surveys, 23–24
Scrotum, 49–50, 82
Secondary infertility, 189
Secondary sex characteristics, 246
Second stage, labor, 184
Secure lovers, 307
Self-disclosure, 306, 349
Self-esteem, 249–250, 306
Self-examination:
    breast cancer, 40–41
    testicular cancer, 52
Semen, 50, 83
    loss of, and Victorian era, 12, 279
Seminal vesicles, 51
Seminiferous tubules, 50
Sensate focus exercises, 329
Sensuality, 54
Serial monogamy, 129, 256
Serotonin, 69
Sertoli Cells, 50, 71
Sex ("had sex"), definition, 24–25
Sex education, 2–3, 26–29
    history of, 26–27
Sexless love, 304
Sex reassignment surgery, 206
Sex role classifications, 209
Sex–tension flush, 82, 86
Sexual abuse, *See* Sexual victimization
Sexual addiction, 343–346
Sexual anatomy, *See* Reproductive
    anatomy
Sexual attractiveness, 5–7, 53–54
    cross–cultural comparisons, 5–7
Sexual aversion, 331, 337
Sexual behaviors/attitudes:
    in adolescence, 250–253
    in adults, 255–268, 277–294
    anal stimulation, 281–282, 290–291
    coital positions and locations, 284–288
    cross–cultural comparisons, 5–9,
        281–282, 285, 293
    in early childhood, 244–245
    in the elderly, 266–268
    in emerging adulthood, 255–256
    extramarital sex, 257–259
    and homosexuals, 236
    in infancy, 243–244
    in initial school years, 245–246
    masturbation, 244–245, 250, 267,
        278–282
    mate selection, cross–cultural perspec-
        tives on, 251–252

Student Notes

Student Notes

Student Notes

Student Notes